The SAGE Handbook of
Social Media Research Methods

SAGE was founded in 1965 by Sara Miller McCune to support the dissemination of usable knowledge by publishing innovative and high-quality research and teaching content. Today, we publish over 900 journals, including those of more than 400 learned societies, more than 800 new books per year, and a growing range of library products including archives, data, case studies, reports, and video. SAGE remains majority-owned by our founder, and after Sara's lifetime will become owned by a charitable trust that secures our continued independence.

Los Angeles | London | New Delhi | Singapore | Washington DC | Melbourne

The SAGE Handbook of Social Media Research Methods

Edited by
Luke Sloan and
Anabel Quan-Haase

Los Angeles | London | New Delhi
Singapore | Washington DC | Melbourne

SAGE Publications Ltd
1 Oliver's Yard
55 City Road
London EC1Y 1SP

SAGE Publications Inc.
2455 Teller Road
Thousand Oaks, California 91320

SAGE Publications India Pvt Ltd
B1/I1 Mohan Cooperative Industrial Area
Mathura Road
New Delhi 110044

SAGE Publications Asia-Pacific Pte Ltd
3 Church Street
#10-04 Samsung Hub
Singapore 049483

Editor: Mila Steele
Assistant Editor: Matthew Oldfield
Production Editor: Sushant Nailwal
Copyeditor: Cenveo Publisher Services
Proofreader: Cenveo Publisher Services
Indexer: Cenveo Publisher Services
Marketing Manager: Sally Ransom
Cover design: Wendy Scott
Typeset by Cenveo Publisher Services
Printed in the UK

At SAGE we take sustainability seriously. Most of our products are printed in the UK using FSC papers and boards. When we print overseas we ensure sustainable papers are used as measured by the PREPS grading system. We undertake an annual audit to monitor our sustainability.

Introduction, Conclusion and editorial arrangement © Luke Sloan and Anabel Quan-Haase 2017

Chapter 2 © Lori McCay-Peet and Anabel Quan-Haase 2017
Chapter 3 © Rob Kitchin 2017
Chapter 4 © Anabel Quan-Haase and Lori McCay-Peet 2017
Chapter 5 © Kelsey Beninger 2017
Chapter 6 © Shuzhe Yang, Anabel Quan-Haase, Andrew D. Nevin and Yimin Chen 2017
Chapter 7 © Luke Sloan 2017
Chapter 8 © Philipp Mayr and Katrin Weller 2017
Chapter 9 © David M. Brown, Adriana Soto-Corominas, Juan Luis Suárez and Javier de la Rosa 2017
Chapter 10 © Dietmar Janetzko 2017
Chapter 11 © Alex Voss, Ilia Lvov and Sara Day Thomson 2017
Chapter 12 © Janet Salmons 2017
Chapter 13 © Guillaume Latzko-Toth, Claudine Bonneau and Mélanie Millette 2017
Chapter 14 © Martin Hand 2017
Chapter 15 © Diane Rasmussen Pennington 2017
Chapter 16 © Bonnie Stewart 2017
Chapter 17 © Alexandra Georgakopoulou 2017
Chapter 18 © Olga Buchel and Diane Rasmussen Pennington 2017
Chapter 19 © Shadi Ghajar-Khosravi and Mark Chignell 2017
Chapter 20 © Niels Buus Lassen, Lisbeth La Cour and Ravi Vatrapu 2017
Chapter 21 © Victoria L. Rubin 2017
Chapter 22 © Nadav Hochman 2017
Chapter 23 © Frauke Zeller 2017
Chapter 24 © Jack Jamieson and Jeffrey Boase 2017
Chapter 25 © Bernhard Klein and Ulf-Dietrich Reips 2017
Chapter 26 © Jeffrey Morgan 2017
Chapter 27 © Ulf-Dietrich Reips and Pablo Garaizar 2017
Chapter 28 © Simon Hegelich 2017
Chapter 29 © Kalina Bontcheva 2017
Chapter 30 © Anatoliy Gruzd, Philip Mai and Andrea Kampen 2017
Chapter 31 © Daniel Angus 2017
Chapter 32 © Mike Thelwall 2017
Chapter 33 © Dhiraj Murthy 2017
Chapter 34 © Linnea Laestadius 2017
Chapter 35 © Xiao Hu, Chen Qiao and King-wa Fu 2017
Chapter 36 © Matthew J. Williams and Martin Chorley 2017
Chapter 37 © Jessica Vitak 2017
Chapter 38 © Anatoliy Gruzd and Ben O'Bright 2017
Chapter 39 © Luke Sloan and Anabel Quan-Haase 2017

Apart from any fair dealing for the purposes of research or private study, or criticism or review, as permitted under the Copyright, Designs and Patents Act, 1988, this publication may be reproduced, stored or transmitted in any form, or by any means, only with the prior permission in writing of the publishers, or in the case of reprographic reproduction, in accordance with the terms of licences issued by the Copyright Licensing Agency. Enquiries concerning reproduction outside those terms should be sent to the publishers.

Library of Congress Control Number: 2016940832

British Library Cataloguing in Publication data

A catalogue record for this book is available from the British Library

ISBN 978-1-4739-1632-6

Contents

List of Figures	ix
List of Tables	xv
Notes on the Editors and Contributors	xvii
Acknowledgements	xxviii

1 Introduction to the Handbook of Social Media Research Methods: Goals, Challenges and Innovations 1
   Anabel Quan-Haase and Luke Sloan

PART I CONCEPTUALISING & DESIGNING SOCIAL MEDIA RESEARCH 11

2 What is Social Media and What Questions Can Social Media Research Help Us Answer? 13
   Lori McCay-Peet and Anabel Quan-Haase

3 Big Data – Hype or Revolution? 27
   Rob Kitchin

4 Building Interdisciplinary Social Media Research Teams: Motivations, Challenges, and Policy Frameworks 40
   Anabel Quan-Haase and Lori McCay-Peet

5 Social Media Users' Views on the Ethics of Social Media Research 57
   Kelsey Beninger

6 The Role of Online Reputation Management, Trolling, and Personality Traits in the Crafting of the Virtual Self on Social Media 74
   Shuzhe Yang, Anabel Quan-Haase, Andrew D. Nevin and Yimin Chen

7 Social Science 'Lite'? Deriving Demographic Proxies from Twitter 90
   Luke Sloan

PART II COLLECTION & STORAGE 105

8 Think Before You Collect: Setting Up a Data Collection Approach for Social Media Studies 107
   Philipp Mayr and Katrin Weller

9 Overview – The Social Media Data Processing Pipeline 125
   David M. Brown, Adriana Soto-Corominas, Juan Luis Suárez and Javier de la Rosa

10	The Role of APIs in Data Sampling from Social Media *Dietmar Janetzko*	146
11	Data Storage, Curation and Preservation *Alex Voss, Ilia Lvov and Sara Day Thomson*	161
12	Using Social Media in Data Collection: Designing Studies with the Qualitative E-Research Framework *Janet Salmons*	177

PART III QUALITATIVE APPROACHES TO SOCIAL MEDIA DATA — **197**

13	Small Data, Thick Data: Thickening Strategies for Trace-based Social Media Research *Guillaume Latzko-Toth, Claudine Bonneau and Mélanie Millette*	199
14	Visuality in Social Media: Researching Images, Circulations and Practices *Martin Hand*	215
15	Coding of Non-Text Data *Diane Rasmussen Pennington*	232
16	Twitter as Method: Using Twitter as a Tool to Conduct Research *Bonnie Stewart*	251
17	Small Stories Research: A Narrative Paradigm for the Analysis of Social Media *Alexandra Georgakopoulou*	266

PART IV QUANTITATIVE APPROACHES TO SOCIAL MEDIA DATA — **283**

18	Geospatial Analysis *Olga Buchel and Diane Rasmussen Pennington*	285
19	Pragmatics of Network Centrality *Shadi Ghajar-Khosravi and Mark Chignell*	309
20	Predictive Analytics with Social Media Data *Niels Buus Lassen, Lisbeth la Cour and Ravi Vatrapu*	328
21	Deception Detection and Rumor Debunking for Social Media *Victoria L. Rubin*	342

PART V DIVERSE APPROACHES TO SOCIAL MEDIA DATA — **365**

22	From Site-specificity to Hyper-locality: Performances of Place in Social Media *Nadav Hochman*	367

23	Analyzing Social Media Data and Other Data Sources: A Methodological Overview *Frauke Zeller*	386
24	Listening to Social Rhythms: Exploring Logged Interactional Data Through Sonification *Jack Jamieson and Jeffrey Boase*	405
25	Innovative Social Location-aware Services for Mobile Phones *Bernhard Klein and Ulf-Dietrich Reips*	421

PART VI   RESEARCH AND ANALYTICAL TOOLS — 439

26	COSMOS: The Collaborative On-line Social Media Observatory *Jeffrey Morgan*	441
27	Social Lab: An 'Open Source Facebook' *Ulf-Dietrich Reips and Pablo Garaizar*	475
28	R for Social Media Analysis *Simon Hegelich*	486
29	GATE: An Open-source NLP Toolkit for Mining Social Media *Kalina Bontcheva*	499
30	A How-to for Using Netlytic to Collect and Analyze Social Media Data: A Case Study of the Use of Twitter During the 2014 Euromaidan Revolution in Ukraine *Anatoliy Gruzd, Philip Mai and Andrea Kampen*	513
31	Theme Detection in Social Media *Daniel Angus*	530
32	Sentiment Analysis *Mike Thelwall*	545

PART VII   SOCIAL MEDIA PLATFORMS — 557

33	The Ontology of Tweets: Mixed-Method Approaches to the Study of Twitter *Dhiraj Murthy*	559
34	Instagram *Linnea Laestadius*	573
35	Weibo *Xiao Hu, Chen Qiao and King-wa Fu*	593

36	Foursquare *Matthew J. Williams and Martin Chorley*	610
37	Facebook as a Research Tool in the Social and Computer Sciences *Jessica Vitak*	627
38	Big Data and Political Science: The Case of VKontakte and the 2014 Euromaidan Revolution in Ukraine *Anatoliy Gruzd and Ben O'Bright*	645
39	A Retrospective on State of the Art Social Media Research Methods: Ethical Decisions, Big-small Data Rivalries and the Spectre of the 6Vs *Luke Sloan and Anabel Quan-Haase*	662

Index   673

List of Figures

2.1	A model of social media engagement in context	22
7.1	The geographic distribution of geocoded tweets in the UK and Ireland from a sample of 13 million	93
7.2	Comparison of age profile of UK Twitter users against the 2011 Census	96
7.3	Comparison of NS-SEC breakdown for Twitter users and the 2011 Census	101
8.1	Schematic of the technical architecture of SODATO	118
8.2	Schematic of the technical architecture of a Twitter TweetObserver	119
9.1	Basic Twitter entities and their attributes	128
9.2	A simple conceptual model of the Twitterverse	129
9.3	The final conceptual model of the Twitterverse	130
9.4	SylvaDB's type creation form	131
9.5	SylvaDB's property graph schema creation interface	132
9.6	The Twitterverse conceptual model mapped to a property graph schema with SylvaDB	133
9.7	OpenRefine's custom facet creation tool	137
10.1	Major access control schemes in social media	150
10.2	Basic HTTP authentication (RFC 2617)	151
10.3	Authorization flow of OAuth 1.0a (RFC 5849)	152
10.4	Authorization flow of via OAuth 2.0 (RFC 6749)	153
10.5	Twitter's public APIs and endpoints	154
11.1	The Digital Curation Centre's Data Curation Model	164
12.1	The Qualitative E-Research Framework	180
12.2	Ethical issues in Qualitative E-Research Design	186
12.3	Level of structure	187
15.1	The author's 'happy' dog	235
15.2	Glencoe, Scotland	241
18.1	Geospatial Analysis pipeline	289
18.2	A visualization of three different methods for measuring flu prevalence in the US	291
18.3	Example of a map as a retrieval tool	293
18.4	Health data over time as a linear plot graph and as a cyclic spiral	294
18.5	Distribution of counts of images linked to different locations	295
18.6	Classification control	295
18.7	Map showing Craigslist market territories	297
18.8	Standard Deviational Ellipse	298
18.9	Real time tweet map	299
18.10	Sample GeoTime story snapshot	300
18.11	Network topology represented on a map	301
19.1	An example ego network surrounding the ego node. Alter nodes or neighbors are in dark grey and the rest of the network outside of the ego network is shaded in light grey	314

19.2	List of variables for the structural analysis of social networks	319
19.3	Network topology variables before and after the factor analysis	320
19.4	The three clusters with their members labelled by their names	321
19.5	Three samples of networks from Cluster 2 and Cluster 3. The first row presents the visualized graphs of the six networks. The second row presents their clustering coefficient distribution histogram. The third row presents the scatter plots of Page Rank centrality vs. Eigenvector centrality	323
20.1	Predictive model of iPhone sales from Twitter data	337
20.2	Predictive model of H&M revenues from Facebook data	338
21.1	Summary of Zhou et al's (2004) Linguistic Features for Deception Detection. Twenty seven linguistic-based features, amenable to automation, were grouped into nine linguistic constructs: quantity, complexity, uncertainty, nonimmediacy, expressivity, diversity, informality, specificity, and affect. All the linguistic features are defined in terms of their measurable dependent variables	347
21.2	Conceptualization of the Components of Big Data Veracity. Veracity – as the 4th V in addition to Volume, Velocity and Variety – portrayed across three primary orthogonal dimensions in the conceptual space – objectivity, truthfulness, credibility. The dimensions intersect in the center and the nebula represents a certain degree of variability within the phenomena that together constitute the big data veracity. Secondary dimensions of lesser concern in textual data are presented in dotted lines. The tree main components of veracity index are normalized to the (0,1) interval with 1 indicating maximum objectivity, truthfulness and credibility, and 0, otherwise. Then, the big data veracity index is calculated as an average of the three, assuming that each of the dimensions equally contributes to veracity establishment. The three primary dimensions reduce 'noise' and potential errors in subsequent inferences from the textual big data due to minimization of bias, intentional misinformation, and implausibility	350
21.3	Verification feature for rumor debunking on Twitter (Liu et al., 2015). The six proposed categories of verification features largely based on insights from journalists	352
21.4	Rumor busting features for Sina Weibo Microblogs (Yang, 2012). Grouped into five broad types (content-based, client-based, account-based, propagation-based, and location-based), rumor detection features were extracted on Sina Weibo, the Chinese leading micro-blogging platform, for the binary classification purposes (rumor or not). Each predictive feature is described in terms of its implementation	353
21.5	Examples of clickbait via Twitter (Chen, Conroy and Rubin, 2015 presentation). Two examples of clickbaits or online content that primarily aims to attract attention and encourage visitors to click on a link to a particular web page. The claims made in headlines of clickbaits and the associated imagery are often outrageous and/or misleading, as the reader finds out from reading the full message	357
21.6	Dashboard-Style Interface of the BotOrNot System (Davis et al., 2015). The system evaluates the extent to which a Twitter account exhibits similarity to the known characteristics of social bots	359
22.1	31 Instagram photos taken by Banksy documenting his month long artistic residency in the streets of New York City during October 2013. The photos	

	are sorted by their upload date from 1–31 October 2013 (left to right, top to bottom)	368
22.2	Elmgreen & Dragset (2014) The 'Named Series'. Each frame consists of the color layer of a wall from a number of prominent art institutions' white cube exhibition spaces (i.e. Centre Pompidou, Guggenheim, Tate Liverpool and others). The removed layers are mounted on canvas and framed in a black waxed oak frame. Photo by Anders Sune Berg (Installation view as part of the exhibition Biography, Astrup Fearnley Museum, Oslo)	371
22.3	Robert Smithson (1970) Spiral Jetty. Sculpture. Rozel Point, Great Salt Lake, Utah	372
22.4	The nomadic is turn into native: A comparison of Instagram photos taken at Tate Modern, London (left) and the Museum of Modern Art (MoMA), NYC. Each radial visualization contains 10,000 photos actively tagged to the location of the museum by its users. The photos are sorted by saturation mean and brightness mean	374
22.5	Instagram photos of 7 of Banksy's artworks used in our case study (selected from the larger set of photos for each artwork). Top: original photo posted by Banksy. Bottom: a montage of 4 photos taken by other users	375
22.6	Montage visualization of all photos from each cluster sorted by time from no.1–7 (top to bottom). Each cluster includes the following number of photos: Cluster 1: 575 photos. Cluster 2: 704 photos. Cluster 3: 783 photos. Cluster 4: 638 photos. Cluster 5: 267 photos. Cluster 6: 1,142 photos. Cluster 7: 449 photos	376
22.7	Number of photos annotated with the hashtags #banksy and #banksyny (a total of 28,419 photos) for each day from October 1st to November 20th 2013	377
22.8	A temporal plot of each cluster organized by time (X) and volume (Y)	377
22.9	A global spread of all geo-tagged images with the tags #banksyny or #banksy. 16,164 images are in NYC, and 2,571 images are outside of NYC area	378
22.10	A map of locations of all photos from our 7 clusters (Only NYC area is shown)	378
22.11	Radial visualization of 16,164 Instagram photos geo-tagged to NYC area between October 1st and November 20th, 2013. The photos are organized by location (perimeter) and upload date and time (angle)	379
22.12	A matrix image plot visualization of 6 clusters. In each cluster, (X) – brightness mean, (Y) hue mean. A black square represents the original photo of an artwork posted to Instagram by Banksy himself. Top row from the left: cluster 1, cluster 2, cluster 3. Bottom row from the left: cluster 4, cluster 6 and cluster 7	380
22.13	Visualization of cluster 2 (left) and cluster 1 (middle), sorted by hue mean (X) and date (Y). Right panel shows a close up of cluster 1. The visualization is rotated 90 degrees	381
23.1	The extended empirical research process in social media research	390
23.2	Extract from word frequencies calculation on Greenpeace Corpus, June 2012	399
23.3	Auto coding dialogue window in Atlas.ti	400
24.1	Screenshot of E-Rhythms Data Sonifier	414
25.1	MUGGES Application interfaces – a) muggesNote, b) muggesNote photo view, c) muggesJournal, d) muggesTrail	424
25.2	Mugglet Creation Wizard	425
25.3	Study design overview	426

25.4	a) Personal phone features b) Monthly spending on personal phone	428
25.5	a) Home locations b) Daily travel distance	429
25.6	Technical infrastructure	429
25.7	Comparison of first and long-term impression	431
25.8	Creation and editing hotspots in Bilbao. The circle size corresponds with the number of similar events in the same location	433
25.9	a) Applied mugglet templates b) Observed mashup size	433
25.10	a) Measured provision duration b) Reasons to stop provision	434
25.11	Community size of correlated mugglets	435
25.12	a) Applied search techniques and b) preferred search topics	435
26.1	COSMOS aims to help social scientists move towards the top-right corner of the spectrum of data and research-question-definition needs	443
26.2	The COSMOS software application is a tool that fits into broader social-scientific workflows	444
26.3	The COSMOS user interface is composed of three main areas: the Data Set Library (1) the Data View Library (2) and the Workspace (3) Users build visualizations by dragging and dropping data sets and data views onto the Workspace, as shown by the arrows	445
26.4	COSMOS users engage in an iterative workflow of querying, visualizing and refining data to explore their research questions	447
26.5	The COSMOS Start New Twitter Collection dialog enables users to collect tweets from the one percent Twitter stream by either randomly sampling tweets or by filtering tweets using keywords, hashtags and user accounts	450
26.6	The COSMOS collection snapshot controls enable users to monitor the progress of an ongoing Twitter collection without stopping the collection. Automated snapshots enable users to set up an event monitoring system	451
26.7	The COSMOS query dialog enables users to query Twitter data sets by content, demographics, sentiment, time and geography	452
26.8	The COSMOS Choose Sampling Method dialog enables COSMOS to handle large data sets with user-defined data sampling strategies	454
26.9	The COSMOS temporal filtering controls enable users to filter data sets by time and replay events like a data movie	455
26.10	COSMOS provides a consistent method of creating selection data sets. Users select data in a data view – here data is selected by clicking a segment in the pie chart data view (1) – and dragging from the data-selection control (2) onto the Data Set Library. The selection is added as a new data set under the data set from which it was taken (3)	456
26.11	The COSMOS Export Data dialog supports the use of other software by providing extensive facilities for exporting data in a wide variety of commonly used formats including CSV, Microsoft Excel and JSON	456
26.12	A combination of multiple-coordinated visualizations enables users to understand data sets more deeply than they could with any single visualization. Here, the map, word cloud and frequency data views combine to help users understand a data set concerning the 2013 bombing of the Boston Marathon	459
26.13	The table data view presents a data set as a multi-column table. Binding the font size and the foreground and background colours of each row enables the table to visualize data	459

26.14	The text data view presents a plain-text view of a single data column. Here, a text data view supports the map data view by enabling users to click on a map marker that represents a geocoded tweet to reveal the text of the tweet	460
26.15	The word cloud data view sizes the words in a text column based on their frequency across all the rows in the table	461
26.16	The frequency analysis data view provides interactive frequency views at three levels of temporal granularity: days, hours and minutes	461
26.17	The network analysis data view presents a social network graph created from retweets or mentions. The network is laid out automatically with a force-directed layout algorithm	462
26.18	The map data view plots geocoded data as markers on a map provided by OpenStreetMap	463
26.19	The shapefile data view plots geocoded data as markers on shapefiles of the UK and its constituent territories: England, Wales, Scotland, Northern Ireland and the London boroughs	464
26.20	The polygons in the shapefile data view are shaded by 2011 UK Census data retrieved from the Office of National Statistics via the ONS API	465
26.21	The pie chart data view segments data into two columns: one column provides the data that sizes the angles of each segment; the other column provides the labels for the segments	466
26.22	The line chart data view plots the values in the numeric data columns against the temporal values in the timestamp column	467
26.23	COSMOS data view plugin developers have three opportunities to integrate new data views into the COSMOS application framework: when users drag a data set onto the new data view (1); when users select data in another data view (2); and when users select data in the new data view (3)	468
26.24	The COSMOS high-performance computing prototype uses the MongoDB database and Hadoop's distributed Map/Reduce algorithm to investigate how COSMOS can scale to meet the challenges of big data	470
27.1	Analysis of searches for the terms 'Web 2.0' and 'social media' over time in Google Trends	476
27.2	Main display of Social Lab	478
27.3	Simple social bot for Social Lab	479
27.4	Setting up triggers and routines for a social bot in Social Lab's backend application	480
27.5	Three slightly different social bots to gather participants for an online promotion	481
27.6	Messages can be deployed by researchers or social bots or to provoke user actions	482
28.1	Diagnostic plots	494
28.2	Tweets in California	496
28.3	Spacial distribution of hashtags	497
29.1	The GATE developer interface	501
29.2	The TwitIE information extraction pipeline	502
29.3	Classication interface: sense disambiguation example	506
29.4	Sequential selection interface: named entity recognition example	507
29.5	Mimir dynamic co-occurrence matrix	508
30.1	Frequently used words in the three datasets (after removing 'stopwords')	519

30.2	Frequently used word in the three datasets displayed over time (after removing 'stopwords')	520
30.3	Name vs chain ties derived from sample Tweets	522
30.4	Communication networks showing who replies to whom on Twitter (chain network)	523
30.5	'Communities' automatically detected by netlytic in the 'english' dataset	524
30.6	Viewing direct connections of a selected node (marked as #2)	525
30.7	Top ten most connected users based on in-degree centrality	526
31.1	The Leximancer graphical user interface	535
31.2	Leximancer concept map. The map highlights the theme groups using the large coloured circles, and the individual nodes represent the concepts. Node proximity implies conceptual relatedness	536
31.3	This figure highlights the interactive nature of Leximancer and how an analyst can select a concept to interrogate and reveal the raw data that aligns with that concept	539
31.4	This figure highlights the nature of the evidence terms that invoke a specific concept. The term weightings can be seen here as they relate to the concept 'citizenship'	540
31.5	The Streamgraph reveals the prominence of themes on Twitter over time	541
31.6	The Gephi plot reveals networks of conceptual overlap between Tweeters, and can be useful in locating groups of topically aligned Tweeters	542
33.1	Theory building	564
33.2	Data collection and relationship model	566
33.3	Continuous open coding Twitter data model applied to #accidentalracist	566
33.4	Operationalization of Twitter coding model	567
35.1	Screenshot of Weibo interface	594
35.2	Screenshot of Weibo search	595
35.3	Workflow of applying the Open API for Weibo data collection	596
35.4	Data flow of a Sina Weibo crawler	597
35.5	Screenshot of the online Weibo data crawler	598
35.6	Fragment of a coding scheme and results	599
35.7	A chinese text string on Weibo (translated as 'AlphaGo defeated Lee Se-dol, but artificial intelligence has not conquered human being')	600
35.8	Segmented words and part-of-speech tagging (by the ICTCLAS tool)	600
35.9	The process of a classification task with three classifiers	601
35.10	Weibo topic dynamics with identified significant points (reprinted from Fan et al., 2014)	602
35.11	User network constructed with co-mentioned relations on keywords	603
36.1	A conceptual overview of Foursquare	612
36.2	The Foursquare mobile app interface (2016)	614
36.3	The Swarm mobile app interface (2016)	614
38.1	Country-to-Country networks	650

List of Tables

2.1	Selection of social media definitions from the research literature organised by themes	16
2.2	Types of social media	18
3.1	Comparing small and big data	28
8.1	Selected attributes of tweets available in JSON format	120
10.1	Use of Facebook's graph API via R	154
10.2	Access levels of Twitter's streaming endpoint	156
10.3	Use of Twitter's REST API via twitter	157
10.4	Use of Twitter's streaming API via streamR	158
11.1	Data management and curation guidance	163
12.1	Selecting research types, communication features and social media sites	182
12.2	Characteristics of qualitative exemplars	192
15.1	Overview of research methods for non-text social media data	235
19.1	A summary of generic measures for 62 social networks	318
19.2	Means of clusters in homogenous subsets are displayed. Cluster 1 & 2 make one homogenous subset together for the ClsCff.PgRk and ClsCff.EigV variables	322
20.1	Categorization of research publications on predictive analytics with social media data	334
20.2	Overview of dataset	337
21.1	Deception research disciplines and associated data type examples. Various contemporary disciplines that study deception for the purpose of its detection are listed with corresponding typical data types that have been studied in the recent past. The data type distinctions are made based on the mode of obtaining data and the predominant discourse variety in the data type. Both columns are non-exhaustive	349
21.2	Blog credibility assessment factors with additional details added from the associated presentation	355
23.1	Methods overview	392
23.2	Social media monitoring and analytics in commercial market analysis	394
23.3	Case study corpus overview	397
24.1	Mean and median response times among sonified sample	416
24.2	Hypotheses generated through sonification compared to results of statistical analysis	423
25.1	Comparison of analysis tools	432
25.2	Questionnaire items with underlying dimensions and indicators	524
30.1	Case study datasets	537
30.2	Definitions of common network-level SNA measures	538
31.1	Thematic overview of the Twitter corpus. All examples provided here originally contained the #qanda hashtag which has been omitted for brevity	619
33.1	Three sample cancer related Twitter topic clusters	569

38.1	Study dataset description	649
38.2	Top ranked countries based on the number of group members	649
38.3	Top ranked countries based on the degree centrality	651
38.4	Immigration receptor states	652

Notes on the Editors and Contributors

THE EDITORS

Luke Sloan is a Senior Lecturer in Quantitative Methods and Deputy Director of the Social Data Science Lab (http://socialdatalab.net/) at the School of Social Sciences, Cardiff University, UK. Luke has worked on a range of projects investigating the use of Twitter data for understanding social phenomena covering topics such as election prediction, tracking (mis) information propagation during food scares and 'crime-sensing'. His research focuses on the development of demographic proxies for Twitter data to further understand who uses the platform and increase the utility of such data for the social sciences. He sits as an expert member on the Social Media Analytics Review and Information Group (SMARIG) which brings together academics and government agencies. Luke's most recent work is focused on exploring the possibility gaining informed consent for linking Twitter content to survey data.

Anabel Quan-Haase is an Associate Professor and holds a joint appointment at the Faculty of Information and Media Studies and the Department of Sociology, the University of Western Ontario. She is the director of the SocioDigital Lab and her research interests focus on how people integrate social media into their everyday lives and work settings. Her particular focus is on user engagement and the role of social context in how individuals use and make sense of messages and interactions on social media. Dr Quan-Haase is the author of *Technology and Society* (2015, 2nd ed. with Oxford University Press) and *Information Brokering in the High-Tech Industry* (2009 with Lambert). She is the past president of the Canadian Association for Information Science and a Council Member of the CITAMS section of the American Sociological Association.

THE CONTRIBUTORS

Daniel Angus is a Lecturer in Computational Social Science at The University of Queensland, and leads the Discursis computational speech and language analysis project funded by the Australian Research Council's Centre of Excellence for the Dynamics of Language. His research focuses on the development of information visualization and analysis methods for communication data, with a specific focus on conversation data.

Kelsey Beninger is a Associate Director in the Qualitative Research team at the independent social research agency, TNS-BMRB, based in London, England. Previously with NatCen Social Research, her research interests include the ethical implications of social media and online research on researcher practice and participants. Kelsey is also a contributing member to the network of methodological innovation, New Social Media, New Social Science.

Jeffrey Boase is an Associate Professor in the Institute of Communication, Culture, Information and Technology and the Faculty of Information at the University of Toronto. His research focuses on the relationship between communication technology and personal networks. He is particularly interested in how emerging technologies such as smartphones and social media platforms may enable or hinder the transfer of information and support within personal networks. In recent years he has incorporated digital trace data (so-called 'Big Data') into his project designs, merging it with more traditional survey and interview data.

Claudine Bonneau is Associate Professor in the Department of Management and Technology at Université du Québec à Montréal (UQAM), where she is a member of the Laboratory on Computer-Mediated Communication (LabCMO) and teaches in graduate and undergraduate programs in Information Technology. Her current work focuses on social media uses and online collaboration practices at work. She is also interested in methodological issues related to qualitative research and online ethnography. Besides her contributions to edited books, her work has been published in the *International Journal of Project Management* (2014), *tic&société* (2013) and other French-language publications.

Kalina Bontcheva (University of Sheffield) is leading a research team of nine RAs and five PhD students, working on five projects on Information Extraction for social media, including an EPSRC career acceleration fellowship (EP/I004327/1) and the SoBigData and OpenMinTeD H2020 eInfrastructure projects. Her research lies at the intersection of Natural Language Processing (NLP), web science, and computational social media analysis. Prof. Bontcheva is also one of the leading researchers and developers behind the world leading GATE infrastructure. GATE has had over 44,000 downloads in 2014 alone, nine annual summer schools for researchers and companies, and over 3,800 citations of the eight key GATE papers on Google Scholar. GATE is used in many products and services, including: *Financial Times*, the BBC, Fizzback (now NICE); the UK National Archives; the Press Association; Nesta, the British Library, Text Mining Solutions, and Ontotext.

David M. Brown is a PhD candidate in the Department of Modern Languages and Literatures at Western University. He received his BA from the University of Oregon, where he graduated Summa Cum Laude. His dissertation focuses on data-driven approaches to understanding book history in the Spanish Empire. As an RA at the CulturePlex Lab, he is part of the core data analytics team, specializing in network analysis, software development, and graph databases. He is also an active Python programming language community developer, and maintains several projects designed to interact with graph database servers.

Olga Buchel is an interdisciplinary researcher specializing in geovisualization, information visualization, visual analytics, and geographic information retrieval. She holds a PhD in Library and Information Science from Western University. In the past she has worked at the Alexandria Digital Library in Santa Barbara, CA, the forerunner of Google Maps. Olga's most recent publications are about geospatial analysis of user interactions with Flickr image collections, and the role of interactive exploratory visualizations in research and knowledge discovery in public health and international business. She has presented her research at a number of international conferences, including GEOMED, iConference,

Annual Meetings of the Association for Information Science and Technology, visualization workshop at the American Academy of Management, workshop on Provenance of Sensemaking at IEEE VIS, and other conferences. She currently works with Big Data at SiTechnologyGroup, Inc., where she develops health applications and visualizations from clinical health records.

Yimin Chen is a PhD candidate in the Faculty of Information and Media Studies at the University of Western Ontario and holds an MLIS from the same institution. Driven by a long-standing fascination with the internet and its cultures, Yimin's PhD work revolves around understanding how internet trolling is defined, portrayed, and discussed in print and online. His other research interests include news and journalism, deception detection, information literacy, and humour.

Mark Chignell is a Professor of Mechanical and Industrial Engineering, and a Professor in the Faculty of Information, at the University of Toronto, where he has been on the faculty since 1990. Prior to that, he was an Assistant Professor in Industrial and Systems Engineering at the University of Southern California from 1984 to 1990. He has a PhD in Psychology (specializing in mathematical psychology) from the University of Canterbury (New Zealand, 1981), and an MS in Industrial and Systems Engineering (Ohio State, 1984). In addition to being Director of the Interactive Media Lab, he is President of Vocalage Inc., a University of Toronto spinoff company and a visiting scientist at both the IBM Centre for Advanced Studies and Keio University in Japan. He is currently the director of the Knowledge Media Design Institute, and BUL Chair in Human-Computer Interaction, at the University of Toronto.

Martin J. Chorley is a Lecturer at the School of Computer Science & Informatics at Cardiff University. He completed an MSc in High End Computing at Edinburgh University in 2007 and received a PhD degree in computer science from Cardiff University in 2012. His research interests include mobile and social computing, and computational journalism.

Ian Colville is Professor of Organization and Management Studies at the University of Bath, UK. His research interests lie theoretically in the areas of organizing and sensemaking combined with an abiding concern with their relevance to practice. Most recently he has been studying organizing and sensemaking in complex and fast moving contexts, e.g. Counter Terrorism and Environmental Flooding, which perforce require a process perspective. His work is published in journals such as *Accounting, Organization and Society, Public Administration, Human Relations, Management Learning, Organization Studies* and *Organization*. He is on the editorial board of *Organization Studies* and *Human Relations*.

Sara Day Thomson works for the Digital Preservation Coalition (dpconline.org) where she researches new methods and technologies to support member organisations in ensuring long-term access to their digital data. She has also helped coordinate community-building and sustainability for the EU-funded project TIMBUS, which aligns digital preservation with business continuity solutions. More recently, she has conducted a 15-month study into preserving forms of Big Data in collaboration with the UK Data Service. She is the author of 'Preserving Social Media', a DPC Technology Watch report that articulates the challenges of capturing and preserving user-generated content on web-based platforms. Her main interests include the preservation of web and social media content, community uptake of new methods and tools, and practical case studies for implementing digital preservation.

Javier de la Rosa is a Postdoctoral fellow at the CulturePlex Lab, where he also works as Tech Lead and Chief Developer. He holds a PhD in Hispanic Studies by the University of Western Ontario (Canada), and both MSc in Artificial Intelligence and BSc in Computer Engineering by the University of Seville (Spain). As a humanist and computer scientist, he combines his knowledge in machine learning and data science with humanistic inquiries, focusing his research on topics such as graph and network theory, computer vision, digital art history, sentiment analysis, and authorship attribution. Javier also has experience in the industry, where he worked for over five years writing open source software, and doing web development and research.

King-wa Fu is an Associate Professor at the Journalism and Media Studies Centre (JMSC), The University of Hong Kong. His research interest includes political participation and media use, computational media studies, mental health/suicide and the media, health communication, and young people's Internet use. He has a PhD from the JMSC, a MA in Social Sciences and an MPhil in Engineering from the Hong Kong University of Science and Technology. He obtained an undergraduate degree in Engineering from HKU. He was a journalist at the *Hong Kong Economic Journal*.

Pablo Garaizar is a Lecturer and Researcher at the University of Deusto, Bilbao, Spain. He holds a PhD in Computer Engineering and a BSc in Psychology. As a lecturer, he is specialized in GNU/Linux, Computer Networks, Web Development and Computer Security. As a researcher, he explores new ways of using Information and Communication Technologies to enhance Learning. He is also actively involved in research projects regarding associative learning processes, biases in education, and Internet-based research.

Alexandra Georgakopoulou is Professor of Discourse Analysis & Sociolinguistics, King's College London. Drawing on sociocultural linguistic and interactional perspectives, she has researched the role of everyday life stories (both face-to-face and on new/social media) in the (re)formation of social relations. She has specifically investigated the links of narrative communication practices with youth and gender identities in the context of late modernity. She has (co)-authored nine books which include *Analyzing narrative: Discourse and sociolinguistic perspectives* (with Anna De Fina, 2012, Cambridge University Press) and she has (co)-edited several Special Issues and edited volumes, including *The Handbook of Narrative Analysis* (with Anna De Fina, 2015, Wiley-Blackwell) and *The Routledge Handbook of Language & Digital Communication* (with Tereza Spilioti, 2016).

Shadi Ghajar-Khosravi is currently an NSERC visiting fellow at the Socio-Cognitive Systems section of DRDC-Toronto (Defence Research and Development Canada in Toronto). She has a PhD in Mechanical and Industrial Engineering (human factors) from the University of Toronto, and an MISt from the Faculty of Information at the University of Toronto. She was an HCTP fellow from 2011 to 2013 and an IBM CAS research assistant from 2011 to 2012. Her research interests include social network analysis, information systems design and analysis, and the user-centered design and evaluation of user interfaces.

Anatoliy Gruzd is a Canada Research Chair in Social Media Data Stewardship, Associate Professor and Director of the Social Media Lab in the Ted Rogers School of Management at Ryerson University (Toronto, Canada). He is also a co-editor of a multidisciplinary journal on *Big Data & Society*. Dr Gruzd's research initiatives explore how the advent of social media and the growing availability of social big data are changing the ways in which people communicate, collaborate and disseminate information and how these changes impact the social, economic and political norms and structures of modern society.

Martin Hand is an Associate Professor of Sociology at Queen's University, Canada. He is the author of *Ubiquitous Photography* (Polity, 2012), *Making Digital Cultures* (Ashgate, 2008), co-author of *The Design of Everyday Life* (Berg, 2007) and co-editor of *Big Data? Qualitative Approaches to Digital Research* (Emerald, 2014). His current research interests are in the range of temporal expectations and experiences emerging with increased use of smartphone and wearable technologies.

Simon Hegelich is Professor for Political Data Science at the Technical University of Munich, Bavarian School of Public Policy. He is focused in his research on the connection between political science and data science. Simon Hegelich is interested in the political dimension of the ongoing digital revolution as well as in implementing new methods in political science like machine learning, data mining, computer vision and simulations. He has published – amongst others – in Policy Studies Journal, Swiss Political Science Review and European Policy Analysis. He is writing about political data science on his blog https://politicaldatascience.blogspot.de.

Xiao Hu is an Assistant Professor in the Division of Information and Technology Studies in the Faculty of Education of the University of Hong Kong. Her research interests include applied data/text mining, information retrieval, and social media for learning. Dr Hu holds a PhD degree in Library and Information Science and a Master's degree in Computer Science, both from the University of Illinois at Urbana-Champaign. She also holds a Master's degree in Electronic Engineering from Beijing University of Posts and Telecommunications, China and a Bachelor's degree in Electronics and Information Systems from Wuhan University, China.

Jack Jamieson is a PhD student at the University of Toronto's Faculty of Information. His research examines how emerging communication technologies affect and are affected by cultural and social activities. In particular, his work examines the influence of social, cultural, and political values on web development technologies. Other interests include user-generated mobile literature and exploratory analysis using data sonification.

Dietmar Janetzko studied Psychology, Philosophy and Computer Science and holds a PhD both in psychology and education. He is a Professor of business computing and business process management at Cologne Business School in Germany. His research interests focus on statistics, data mining, and quantitative analysis of data sourced from the Internet and social media.

Andrea Kampen is a Research Collaborator with the Ryerson University Social Media Lab and the Manager of Conference Publications of the International Conference on Social Media & Society. She has graduated from the School of Information Management with a Masters in Library and Information Management degree from Dalhousie University, Canada. Through her work with the Social Media Lab, Andrea has developed expertise in social media analysis and how to use various analytical tools like Netlytic to study what people are sharing and how they are interacting with information online.

Bernhard Klein received his diploma degree in Computer Science from the Technical University of Munich and a doctoral degree at the University of Vienna in Economic and

Social Sciences. During his PhD studies at the University of Vienna he was a research assistant and lecturer for the Distributed and Multimedia Systems research group. In 2009, he transferred during a research collaboration with the University of Deusto to Spain, where he led as a postdoctoral researcher several European projects in the area of smart homes and smart cities. In February 2014, he moved to the Singapore-ETH Centre (ETH Zuerich), where he was responsible for the Value Lab Asia and headed research projects for urban modeling, simulation and visualization. Since September 2015 he has worked as a project coordinator for the Big Data – Informed Urban Design project. His research interests include big data analytics, ambient intelligence, complex systems and multi-scale simulation.

Rob Kitchin is Professor and ERC Advanced Investigator at the National University of Ireland Maynooth. He is principal investigator of the Programmable City project, the Dublin Dashboard, the All-Island Research Observatory, and the Digital Repository of Ireland, and the author of Code/Space: Software and Everyday Life (MIT Press, 2011) and The Data Revolution (Sage, 2014). He was the 2013 recipient of the Royal Irish Academy's Gold Medal for the Social Sciences.

Tetsuro Kobayashi (PhD, University of Tokyo) is an Associate Professor of Department of Media & Communication at City University of Hong Kong. His research focuses on political communication and mobile communication in East Asian countries.

Lisbeth la Cour is a Professor of Time Series Analysis at the Department of Economics, Copenhagen Business School. Her current research topics are in the fields of big social data analytics, FDI spill-over on productivity in European firms, educational economics, statistical analysis of public procurement data in the EU and time series analysis of economic historical data. In her research in big social media data analytics she focuses on the use of predictive modeling and tries to look deeper into the basic time series properties of social media data and their preprocessing. Also, she works on specification and evaluation of the predictive models in relation to economic and financial outcomes of firms. Prof. la Cour holds a Doctor of Philosophy (PhD) in Economics from University of Copenhagen and a Master of Science in Economics (MSc) also from University of Copenhagen.

Linnea I. Laestadius is an Assistant Professor of Public Health Policy and Administration at the Joseph J. Zilber School of Public Health at the University of Wisconsin-Milwaukee. She holds a PhD from the Johns Hopkins Bloomberg School of Public Health and a Master of Public Policy from George Washington University. Her research focuses on the intersections of public health, society, and technology. She is particularly interested in the drivers and effects of health-related posting behaviors on visual social media platforms, as well as the ethics and public health implications of corporate solicitation and use of user-generated content.

Niels Buus Lassen is PhD Fellow at the Department of IT Management of the Copenhagen Business School, and researcher at the Computational Social Science Laboratory (http://cssl.cbs.dk). His main research interests are predictive modelling with social media data. He has built predictive models of sales for iPhone, H&M, Nike and others, based on Twitter and Facebook data, and a predictive model for Net Promoter Score based on Facebook feelings. He holds a MSc in Economics and BSc in Economics/Mathematics from Copenhagen Business School, and an MBA from Edinburgh Business School.

Guillaume Latzko-Toth is Associate Professor in the Department of Information and Communication at Université Laval (Quebec City, Canada) and codirector of the Laboratory on Computer-Mediated Communication (LabCMO, www.labcmo.ca). Rooted in a Science and Technology Studies (STS) perspective, his research and publications address the role of users in the development of digital media, the transformations of publics and publicness, and methodological and ethical issues related to Internet research. Besides several contributions to edited books, his work appeared in the *Journal of Community Informatics* (2006), the *Bulletin of Science, Technology and Society* (2010), and the *Canadian Journal of Communication* (2014).

Ilia Lvov is a PhD student in the School of Computer Science at the University of St Andrews working under supervision of Dr Voss. He studies the issues that are brought into social research by new forms of data and new research methods. Through collaboration with academics, journalists and NPOs, Ilia has participated in a number of research projects studying social media data.

Philip Mai MA, JD, is the Manager of Academic Communications at Ryerson University in Toronto, a member of the Office of Communications, Government and Community Engagement, the Office of the Provost and Vice President Academic. He is also the Research and Communications Manager at the Ryerson Social Media Lab and a co-founder of the International Conference on Social Media & Society. In his work, Philip focuses on knowledge mobilization, information diffusion and social media analytics with the aim to connect people, knowledge and ideas.

Philipp Mayr is a postdoctoral researcher and team lead at the GESIS department Knowledge Technologies for the Social Sciences. He was the computer science project head in the PEP-TF project mentioned in the abstract (see Kaczmirek et al., 2014) and responsible for the technical collection infrastructure. Philipp Mayr has published in the areas Informetrics, Information Retrieval and Digital Libraries.

Lori McCay-Peet is an Assistant Professor in the School of Information Management (SIM) in the Faculty of Management at Dalhousie University. She has an interdisciplinary PhD (Management and Computer Science), a Master of Library and Information Studies (MLIS), and a BA (History). Dr McCay-Peet's research focuses on people's perceptions and uses of digital information environments such as social media and digital libraries, particularly in the context of knowledge work. She has published and presented her research in several information science and computer science publications and venues including the *Journal of the Association of Information Science and Technology*, *Information Research*, *Information Processing and Management*, and the SIGCHI Conference on Human Factors in Computing Systems.

Mélanie Millette is Assistant Professor of Social Media at Université du Québec à Montréal (UQAM), and a member of the Laboratory on Computer-Mediated Communication (LabCMO). Her work concerns social, political, and cultural aspects of social media uses, more specifically how citizens mobilize online platforms to achieve political participation. She won a SSHRC-Armand-Bombardier grant and a Trudeau Foundation scholarship for her thesis research which examines media visibility options offered by online channels such as Twitter for francophone minorities in Canada. She has co-edited a book on social media (*Médias sociaux*, PUQ, 2012, in French). She has recently co-authored a chapter in *Hashtag Publics* (N. Rambukkana (ed.), 2015, Peter Lang). Her additional research interests include methodology, digital, and feminist methods. Her work has been published in many French-language publications.

Jeffrey Morgan is a user interface and data visualization designer and developer as well as a data scientist specializing in social media. His research interests include human–computer interaction and the design of highly-interactive information retrieval and visualization systems.

Dhiraj Murthy is an Associate Professor in the School of Journalism and the Department of Sociology at University of Texas at Austin. His research explores social media, digital research methods, race/ethnicity, qualitative/mixed methods, big data quantitative analysis, and virtual organizations. Dr Murthy has authored over 40 articles, book chapters, and papers and the book Twitter: social communication in the Twitter Age, the first on the medium (2013, Polity Press). He was funded by the National Science Foundation's Office of CyberInfrastructure for pioneering work on social networking technologies in virtual organization breeding grounds. Dr Murthy's work also uniquely explores the potential role of social technologies in diversity and community inclusion.

Andrew D. Nevin is a PhD student in the department of Sociology at the University of Toronto. He holds a Bachelor of Arts in Criminology and a Masters of Arts in Sociology from the University of Western Ontario. Andrew's current research addresses topics of online deviance and how the internet may facilitate shifts in identity and personality expression in ways that support misconduct in digital environments. His additional research interests include cyber-bullying, digital piracy, hacktivism, social networks and online communities, internet culture, and digital inequality.

Diane Rasmussen Pennington is a Lecturer in Information Science in the Department of Computer and Information Sciences at the University of Strathclyde in Glasgow, Scotland, where she is a member of the iLab and the Digital Health and Wellness research groups. She is also the Social Media Manager of the Association for Information Science & Technology (ASIS&T). Dr Rasmussen Pennington has taught classes on research methods, social media, knowledge organisation, and a range of information technology topics. Her diverse research areas encompass non-text information indexing and retrieval, Emotional Information Retrieval (EmIR), user behaviours on social media, and online health information preferences. She is the editor of *Indexing and Retrieval of Non-Text Information* (2012) and *Social Media for Academics: A Practical Guide* (2012). She is currently editing a book series entitled *Computing for Information Professionals*.

Chen Qiao is currently a PhD student in the Division of Information & Technology Studies in the University of Hong Kong. He is interested in natural language processing (NLP) and machine learning (especially probabilistic graphical models), and is trying to apply and adapt these techniques to research questions in the education domain. Before joining the PhD program, he was a software engineer at the NLP group of a company in Shanghai. Mr. Qiao obtained a Bachelor of Arts degree in Russian Language & Literature, and a Master of Science degree in Educational Technology from East China Normal University, China. He also has experience in developing Web projects and Augmented Reality applications for classrooms, and is interested in viewing social phenomena through the lens of complexity theory.

Ulf-Dietrich Reips is the Full Professor for Research Methods, Assessment & iScience at the University of Konstanz and was recently offered to become the director of the Leibniz Institute for Psychology Information (http://zpid.de). He received his PhD in 1996 from the University of Tübingen. His research focuses on Internet-based research methodologies, the psychology of the Internet, measurement, development, the cognition of causality, personality, privacy, Social Media, crowdsourcing, and Big Data. In 1994, he founded the Web Experimental Psychology Lab, the first laboratory for conducting real experiments on the World Wide Web. Ulf was a founder of the German Society for Online Research and was elected the first non-North American president of the Society for Computers in Psychology. He is the founding editor of the free open access journal *International Journal of Internet Science* (http://ijis.net). Ulf and his team develop and provide free Web tools for researchers, teachers, students, and the public. They received numerous awards for their Web applications (available from the iScience Server at http://iscience.eu/) and methodological work serving the research community.

Victoria L. Rubin is an Associate Professor at the Faculty of Information and Media Studies and the Director of the Language and Information Technologies Research Lab (LiT.RL) at the University of Western Ontario. She specializes in information retrieval and natural language processing techniques that enable analyses of texts to identify, extract, and organize structured knowledge. She studies complex human information behaviors that are, at least partly, expressed through language such as deception, uncertainty, credibility, and emotions. Her research on Deception Detection has been published in recent core workshops on the topic and prominent information science conferences, as well as the *Journal of the Association for Information Science and Technology*. Her 2015–2018 project entitled *Digital Deception Detection: Identifying Deliberate Misinformation in Online News* is funded by the Government of Canada Social Sciences and Humanities Research Council (SSHRC) Insight Grant. For further information, see http://victoriarubin.fims.uwo.ca/.

Janet Salmons is an independent researcher and consultant through Vision2Lead. She is the author of five books about online research; the most recent are *Doing Qualitative Research Online* (2016) and *Qualitative Online Interviews* (2015). Dr Salmons is a frequent presenter for conferences and webinars, and currently serves as the Chair for the Academy of Management Ethics Education Committee. Dr Salmons serves on the PhD faculty in Educational Technology at Walden University. She previously served on the graduate faculty of the Capella University School of Business, where was honored with the Harold Abel Distinguished Faculty Award for 2011–2012 and the Steven Shank Recognition for Teaching in 2012, 2013, 2014 and 2015. Dr Salmons lives and works in Boulder, Colorado.

Adriana Soto-Corominas is a PhD student of Hispanic Linguistics at Western University (Canada). She received her BA from Universitat Autònoma de Barcelona (Spain) and her specialization in Linguistics from University of California Los Angeles (USA). Her current research focuses on language acquisition and bilingualism. She has been part of the CulturePlex Lab at Western University since early-2015, where she is currently investigating loanwords and neologisms in Spanish.

Bonnie Stewart is an education researcher and practitioner fascinated by who we are when we're online. Coordinator of Adult Teaching and Professional Learning at the University of Prince Edward Island, where she completed her PhD in Educational Studies, Bonnie leads digital strategy and professional learning initiatives. Her research focuses primarily on digital literacies, networked scholarship, and the intersections of knowledge and technologies. A networked educator who began working in online education in the 1990s, Bonnie was involved with Massive Open Online Course (MOOC) research in its early Canadian incarnations. Bonnie has published in *Salon.com*, *The Guardian UK*, and *Inside Higher Ed* in addition to a variety of peer-reviewed venues, and he does her best thinking aloud on Twitter as @bonstewart.

Juan Luis Suárez is the Director of the CulturePlex Lab at Western University, Canada. He holds an e-MBA (IE Business School), a PhD in Hispanic Studies (McGill) and a PhD in Philosophy (Salamanca). His current research focuses on cultural analytics, big data, cultural networks, and digital humanities. His publications include over 60 articles and chapters, and four authored books.

Mike Thelwall leads the Statistical Cybermetrics Research Group at the University of Wolverhampton in the UK Midlands. He has developed free software and methods for systematically gathering and analysing web and social web data. His sentiment analysis program SentiStrength is sold commercially and given away free for research, with thousands of downloads and hundreds of citations. SentiStrength has also been used for social media driven art installations, such as on the London Eye during the 2012 Olympic Games and on the Empire State Building during the 2014 Super Bowl final. Mike sits on four editorial boards, has co-authored hundreds of refereed journal articles and has written three books.

Ravi Vatrapu is the Director of the Centre for Business Data Analytics (http://bda.cbs.dk), Professor of Human Computer Interaction at the Department of IT Management, Copenhagen Business School; and Professor of Applied Computing at the Westerdals Oslo School of Arts Communication and Technology. His current research focus is on big social data analytics. Based on the enactive approach to the philosophy of mind and phenomenological approach to sociology and the mathematics of classical, fuzzy and rough set theories, his current research program seeks to design, develop and evaluate a new holistic approach to computational social science, Social Set Analytics (SSA). SSA consists of novel formal models, predictive methods and visual analytics tools for big social data. Prof. Vatrapu holds a Doctor of Philosophy (PhD) degree in Communication and Information Sciences from the University of Hawaii at Manoa, a Master of Science (MSc) in Computer Science and Applications from Virginia Tech, and a Bachelor of Technology in Computer Science and Systems Engineering from Andhra University.

Jessica Vitak (PhD, Michigan State University) is an Assistant Professor in the College of Information Studies and an Affiliate Professor in the Department of Communication at the University of Maryland. Her research seeks to span social and computational sciences regarding how people interact with new communication technologies – and the social consequences of technology use. Specifically, her research evaluates ICT users' mental models around privacy and disclosure in digital spaces by focusing on unpacking the privacy negotiation processes uses engage in on social media platforms and the perceived and actual social consequences of information disclosure, including benefits like social support and harms like harassment. More information is available at http://jessicavitak.com.

Timothy Vogus is an Associate Professor of Management at the Vanderbilt University Owen Graduate School of Management. He studies how organizations create and sustain highly reliable, nearly error-free performance. His focus has primarily been on the role that the processes of mindful organizing – a set of behaviors focused on detecting and correcting errors and unexpected events – play in generating high reliability and the roles that safety culture and reliability-enhancing work practices play in supporting it. He typically studies this in health care organizations, but has also investigated child welfare agencies, offshore oil rigs, social entrepreneurial ventures, and software firms. His research has been published in health policy (e.g., Health Services Research, Medical Care), industrial relations (ILR Review), and management (e.g., Academy of Management Review)

Alex Voss is a Lecturer in Software Engineering in the School of Computer Science at the University of St Andrews. He works at the intersection of computer science and the social sciences, with an interest in how people make sense of the social world and the implications for the design of information and communication technologies. His work on social media involves academic as well as practical uses of social media data.

Katrin Weller is an information scientist and postdoctoral researcher at GESIS – Leibniz Institute for the Social Sciences, department Computational Social Science. She is co-editor of *Twitter and Society* (2014). Her research interests include interdisciplinary methods in social media studies, altmetrics and web science.

Matthew J. Williams received the BSc degree in computer science from Cardiff University, UK in 2008. He received the PhD in computer science degree from the same institution in 2013. He is currently a Postdoctoral Research Fellow at the University of Exeter and an Associate Research Fellow at the University of Birmingham. His research interests include computational social science, spatio-temporal complex systems, and human mobility patterns.

Shuzhe Yang is a research and teaching assistant working at the Chair of Mobile Business and Multilateral Security in the Institute for Business Informatics at the Goethe University Frankfurt, Germany. He received his PhD degree in Information Systems and Master of Science degree in Information Management and Finance from the same university. Shuzhe's research interests include personal online reputation management, privacy on social media, online self-tracking, information retrieval and information system design and architectures. Within these topics, his particular focus is on people's behaviour on and outside social media platforms and the factors that influence people's motivation formation.

Frauke Zeller is Assistant Professor in the School of Professional Communication, at Ryerson University in Toronto, Canada. Her research interests are in digital communication analysis methods, human–computer interaction and human–robot interaction.

Acknowledgements

We would like to thank the team at SAGE for their incredible support throughout this project including Katie Metzler, Mila Steele, Judi Burger and Matthew Oldfield. We are also very grateful to Gareth Morrell and Kandy Woodfield for their expert advice. We started this Handbook by asking colleagues across the globe for their ideas and contributions and we would like to thank them all for their enthusiasm and participation. We would also like to thank all the anonymous reviewers for their insights and expert feedback, this project would not have come to fruition without their commitment to excellence.

Finally, thank you to Sarah (for the patience and for keeping me on task) and to Tilly (for not understanding patience and providing the perfect distraction).

Luke Sloan

And thank you to Bruce for his support and love and to Max + Daniella for inspiring me every day.

Anabel Quan-Haase

Introduction to the Handbook of Social Media Research Methods: Goals, Challenges and Innovations

Anabel Quan-Haase and Luke Sloan

This introductory chapter provides an overview of the most pressing methodological issues and challenges social media scholars need to address. Social media is pervasive in people's daily lives and provides new platforms for socialization, public debate, and information exchange which in turn generates data that is potentially of great interest to social scientists. This has created a growing need for the development of methodologically sound, transparent and replicable techniques to capture, collate and analyze these new forms of data. This chapter starts with an introduction to *The SAGE Handbook of Social Media Research Methods* by presenting its goals, key features and merits. It then provides a succinct definition of social media and presents an overview of key characteristics of social media data frequently discussed in the literature. These characteristics present new challenges to scholars, as they necessitate novel approaches to data collection, analysis and interpretation. We highlight the

issues that derive from the data (using the 6 Vs) and direct readers to the chapters in this edition which provide solutions. The chapter concludes that the academic community has risen to the challenge of developing methodologically innovative approaches, techniques and tools that are specifically tailored to address the uniqueness of social media research – the challenge now is to disseminate this information to the wider social science community. It is our sincere hope that this edition contributes to this ambitious goal.

INTRODUCTION

It is indeed thrilling to write the introduction to this comprehensive, timely, and cutting-edge Handbook. Since we started working on this Handbook, several exciting developments have occurred in the field of social media scholarship. Firstly, a new journal *Social Media + Society* was launched in April 2015 dedicated solely to the publication of original work in the field. This is in addition to numerous other journals that have social media as a key focus of scholarship such as *Big Data and Society, Social Media and Society, Information, Communication & Society, New Media and Society* and the *Journal of Computer-Mediated Communication*. Secondly, the relevance of social media in everyday life continues to grow and this relevance is further increased by the move by citizens toward adopting mobile devices (e.g., smartphones, phablets, and tablets) that provide flexible, on-the-go capabilities to access information from social media apps, as well as to contribute text, images, commentary and opinion. Finally, new data collection, data analysis and data visualization tools as well as web and mobile applications continue to be developed and existing ones are constantly updated and refined. These represent a new toolkit for scholars to embark on social media projects that allow for the integration of multiple data sources on a large scale. Hence, *The SAGE Handbook of Social Media Research Methods* represents an important step towards sharing the novel methodologies, tools and techniques specifically geared toward taking full advantage of the unique characteristics of social media data.

The amount, scale and scope of social media data have created a need for methodological innovations that are uniquely suited to examine social media data. This is not only restricted to big data analysis of a quantitative vein, which has perhaps received the most media and scholarly attention, but also to new approaches in qualitative methodology (Salmons, Chapter 12, this volume), from small stories in narrative analysis (Georgakopoulou, Chapter 17, this volume), to close reading (Stewart, Chapter 16, this volume), to thick data description (Latzko-Toth, Bonneau and Millete, Chapter 13, this volume), to methodologies that examine non-verbal data such as images, representations and sound (Rasmussen Pennington, Chapter 15, this volume). Furthermore, the linking of data at different scales is a major challenge in social media data requiring approaches that are qualitatively different from existing methods, often combining image, text and interactions across time and contexts. Perhaps we can assert that we are observing what Kuhn (1970) described as 'anomalies' which lead toward new paradigms in science, after all, as we will discuss in more detail below, social media scholarship does require novel approaches and new ways of looking at social phenomena. As a result it also requires scholars to develop new skills in order to harvest, analyze and most importantly, interpret research findings and place them in context.

The SAGE Handbook of Social Media Research Methods is the first book to cover not only the entire research process in social media scholarship from question formulation to data analysis to the interpretation of research findings, but also to include designated chapters on how data collection, analysis, presentation and interpretation takes place on specific social media platforms such as Twitter (Murthy, Chapter 33, this volume), Facebook (Vitak, Chapter 37, this volume), Weibo (Hu, Qiao and Fu, Chapter 35, this volume), VKontakte (Gruzd and O'Bright, Chapter 38, this volume) and Instagram (Laestadius, Chapter 38, this volume). It provides a step-by-step guide to overcoming the challenges inherent in the nature of research projects that deal with 'big and broad data' and the need to add context to this data to help with result interpretation. To help those interested in acquiring the skills needed to complete a social media project, the chapters provide examples and case studies of a wide range of approaches to illustrate how to implement these with real data. The chapters are detailed and allow scholars who are unfamiliar with specific approaches or techniques to quickly grasp the strengths, limitations and key considerations. The aim of the Handbook is for scholars to have a reference volume that will allow them to apply and tailor the various methodologies to their own research questions. The Handbook will be the single most comprehensive resource for any scholar or graduate student embarking on a social media project.

Four key highlights of the Handbook include:

1. Exploring the foundations for social media research including the development of interdisciplinary teams (McCay-Peet & Quan-Haase, Chapter 2, this volume), ethical considerations (Beninger, Chapter 5, this volume) and the wider impact of 'big data' on the social sciences (Kitchin, Chapter 3, this volume).
2. Demonstrating how both established and new qualitative and quantitative methods can be applied to social media data (Hand, Chapter 14, this volume).
3. Navigating what tools are available to help researchers with social media data collection, analysis, and representation (e.g., visual, sound, video and textual) and how they can be used (Rasmussen Pennington, Chapter 15, this volume; Vitak, Chapter 37, this volume; Zeller, Chapter 23, this volume).
4. Evaluating the characteristics and applications of different social media platforms for academic research purposes (Gruzd and O'Bright, Chapter 38, this volume; Laestadius, Chapter 34, this volume; Vitak, Chapter 37, this volume; Hu, Qiao & Fu, Chapter 35, this volume).

This introductory chapter seeks to place the volume in the wider context of the big data revolution through further defining what social media is and what it means to develop a 'social media methodology'. We then move on to explore what makes social media research so different to traditional social scientific endeavour in terms of the generic non-platform specific characteristics of the data. Having identified the difficulties and frustrations of using social media data, we conclude with how the contributions in this book have established an accessible foundation for social scientific enquiry in this area.

SOCIAL MEDIA FOR SOCIAL RESEARCH?

While some scholars have studied social phenomena on social media as a separate sphere from 'real life', we argue that these applications need to be viewed as integrated into and as an integral part of society at large. It is myopic to think that social media data emerge in a vacuum. Interactions and engagement on social media are often directly linked, or even result from, events taking place outside of it. Moreover, they are produced within a specific historical, social, political, and economic context. Thus, social media scholarship needs to take this context into account in any study of social media. This perspective is critical as it directly influences a study's research design and interpretation of findings. Often additional information, in the form of maps, historical events, newspaper articles, demographic information or political upheavals, need to be included to provide additional context that can aid in the interpretation of research findings.

Following the interest in the role social media played in the 2011 London Riots, the 2012 Barak Obama presidential campaign, the 2014 Ukraine political crises, the recent announcement in the UK of a multimillion pound government-funded data science institute, and the increasing disenfranchisement of social science data at the expense of privately owned transactional datasets (Savage and Burrows 2007, Hong and Nadler 2012), the social science community has become increasingly interested in non-traditional approaches to research design and data collection. The massive and unprecedented generation of 'big and broad data' necessitates the development of novel and innovative approaches to make sense of the social world through social media data, which in itself is often de-contextualized and 'data light' with regards to the demographic staples of social scientific analysis (Sloan et al. 2013, 2015; Sloan, Chapter 7, this volume). Social media data also presents challenges with data preparation not seen to this scale in past data sets. The identification and handling of outliers is not new to scholars. In purely quantitative approaches, outliers are often eliminated as they introduce undesired 'noise' and can bias analytical findings, for example, in multivariate regression analysis. Qualitative data has handled outliers very differently, focusing on anomalies in data sets and integrating them in the interpretation of findings (Bradley, 1993). Social media data confronts several new types of noise and it remains unclear as yet as to how to integrate them into the analysis and interpretation of findings (Yang, Chen, Nevin and Quan-Haase, Chapter 6). For instance, misinformation can either be deceitful or accidental, depending on the individual's motivation (Rubin, Chapter 21, this volume). Either way, scholars need to be aware of these extraneous factors and handle data analysis and interpretation accordingly. This Handbook provides an overview of the cutting-edge developments in this field that establish how to tackle these problems and overcome unique challenges, thus enabling more researchers to study the digital world through developments in methodology at the nexus of the social and computer sciences and digital humanities.

DEFINING SOCIAL MEDIA

The global proliferation of social media is unprecedented both in growth of take-up and content production.[1] Duggan, M. (2015) shows that in 2015, as much as 72% of American online adults used Facebook, 31% Pinterest, 28% Instagram, 25% LinkedIn, and 23% Twitter. Most young people are constantly updating their Facebook status, retweeting messages and uploading pictures to Instagram. Zephoria reports that as of June 2015, Facebook had 1.49 billion monthly active users: every 60 seconds these users provide 293,000 status updates, post 510 comments, and upload 136,000 photos (Zephoria, 2015). The amount of data generated and stored every minute is unprecedented. In short, social media usage has become a daily practice for many. For scholars, this revolution in communication provides both opportunities and challenges. The sheer amount of digitized user-generated content is a potentially rich source of information about the social world including interactions, attitudes, opinions and virtual reactions to real-world events. Yet the computational and analytical challenges are significant – how to process the vast amount of data, how to filter noise, how to democratize access to social media data for the wider social science community, how to understand online behaviour, and how to apply traditional social scientific concepts of sampling and inference, and coding and interpretation to understand the relationship between online communities and the wider population.

One key challenge is providing a definition for what social media is. Chapter 2, co-authored by McCay-Peet and Quan-Haase (this volume), provides a review of how scholars have approached this conceptual challenge and discusses what key elements are constant across various definitions. Creighton et al. (2013) get at the heart of the problem by stating that social media is closely linked to digital technology in general, making it difficult to articulate where the boundaries lie between various applications, tools and sites. This results from the heavy emphasis on social features in many applications, be it mobile, Internet-based or other platforms. Moreover, most web sites provide capabilities to seamlessly interact with social media further blurring the boundaries. It is also increasingly difficult to distinguish social media from digital technology in general (Creighton et al. 2013) because of the social elements that are now embedded in everything from smartphone applications to wearable technologies.

What distinguishes social media from traditional media such as print and radio and from other new media such as web sites and podcasts? Hogan and Quan-Haase (2010) suggest that a definition of social media needs to specifically focus on what is unique about the applications and tools that are included and Bruns (2015) points out that the uniqueness of social media is its focus on connecting: 'All media are social, but only a particular subset of all media are fundamentally defined by their sociality, and thus distinguished (for example) from the mainstream media of print, radio, and television' (2015: 1). For the purpose of *The SAGE Handbook of Social Media Research Methods* we propose to include applications that have the following three characteristics:

1 Have the capability to support user-generated content in forms such as images, text, videos and statuses (such as geolocation check ins) (Blackshaw 2006, Gruzd et al. 2012, Kaplan and Haenlein 2010, Xiang and Gretzel 2010).
2 Provide a means for users to connect with one another (through follows or likes on Twitter, friendship connections on Facebook, or checking in with Foursquare) (Correa, Hinsley, and de Zúñiga 2010).
3 Support various means for members to engage with one another in the form of collaboration, community building, participation, sharing, linking and other means (Bruns 2015, Otieno and Matoke 2014)

Once these three elements come together, a medium can be described as falling under the rubric of social media.

THE METHODOLOGICAL CHALLENGES WE MUST RESPOND TO

Using social media data for social scientific analysis requires a reorientation of how we think about data and its relationship with the social world. The data exists and proliferates whether it is observed or not, it is not created solely for the purpose of research – in this sense its role in academic work could be labelled as incidental, yet that cannot detract from its importance in recording and shedding light on a whole range of social phenomena including attitudes, intentions, identity, networks, opinions, locations and representations. Of course, the incidental nature of the data is not entirely new to the social sciences (observational studies and ethnography as examples), but social media data inherently creates specific challenges that we must tackle head on. The challenges are not discipline-specific and can most poetically be presented as the 6 Vs: volume, variety, velocity, veracity, virtue and value (Williams et al. 2016).

Volume refers to the sheer amount of data being produced on social media platforms. BIS (2013) estimates that around 90% of the world's data was created in two years prior to 2013 and Twitter reports the creation of 500 million tweets a day (Twitter, 2015) with around 15 million Twitter users in the UK alone (Rose, 2014). Collecting and storing this data raises significant challenges (Mayr and Weller, Chapter 8, this volume; Voss, Lvov and Thomson, Chapter 11, this volume) and sorting the useful data from the noise can take time and skill.

Variety is related to the multimodal nature of the data including text (Angus, Chapter 31, this volume; Georgakopoulou, Chapter 17, this volume; Thelwall, Chapter 32, this volume), images (Hand, Chapter 14, this volume; Laestadius, Chapter 34, this volume), videos, geospatial check ins (Buchel & Rasmussen Pennington, Chapter 18, this volume; Williams and Chorley, Chapter 36, this volume; Reips and Garaizar, Chapter 27, this volume) and audio. Also relevant is the ability of social media platforms to often facilitate multiple data types. This means that the 'big data' problem is not an issue solely for quantitative studies and the chapters in this edition demonstrate the huge potential for analysis of many data types using social media including mixed methods studies (Hochman, Chapter 22, this volume).

Velocity refers to both the speed at which social media data is generated and how quickly users respond to real world events. The speed of data generation poses some very particular problems for data collection that need computational solutions rather than manual recording, such as the use of Application Program Interfaces (APIs) (Brown, et al., Chapter 9, this volume; Hegelich, Chapter 28, this volume). This is a particular problem for the social science community because of the paucity of computing and coding knowledge amongst researchers and in response we have covered the topic in this book from several angles. The speed of response to events creates a different set of problems around researchers reacting quickly enough to commence data collection when an event occurs and understanding the role of fine-grained temporality with 'locomotive' data (Jamieson and Boase, Chapter 24, this volume).

Veracity is primarily concerned with the accuracy, reliability and quality of the data. Social media data are often lacking important information that we would normally collect as standard in social research, most notably the demographic characteristics of the respondent and/or content producer. The development of demographic proxies (Sloan, Chapter 7, this volume) is key to understanding who is represented on social media, thus enabling further conversations around sampling and populations. Concerns around how (and if) social media data reflects real world events can be addressed through data linkage and augmentation with existing curated and administrative data sources (Zeller, Chapter 23, this volume), although we must still deal with the question of how the self is presented and to what extent the online identity of a user is crafted (Yang, Quan-Haase, Nevin and Chen, Chapter 6, this volume).

Virtue means ethics. Current ethical guidelines for social research are not fit for purpose when applied to social media data and much work has been done internationally to coordinate a response from the social science community on what such an ethical framework may look like (the 'New Social Media, New Social Science' #NSMNSS scholarly network has been particularly active in this area and practical guidelines are starting to emerge (see Townsend and Wallace 2016) which provide pragmatic advice to researchers). To complicate matters further, general ethical principles such as participant anonymity are at odds with the legal terms and conditions of data use for some platforms. Twitter will not allow tweets to be presented without usernames). This, in turn, has implications for protecting participants from harm when presenting data that may be incendiary (such as tweets containing hate speech). A starting point for the development of an ethical framework for social media is to understand how participants feel about their data being used for research (Beninger, Chapter 5, this volume).

Value is an assessment of how social media data increases our understanding of the social world by opening hitherto unavailable avenues of research and/or augmenting existing work through access to new data (McCay-Peet and Quan-Haase, Chapter 2, this volume). Certainly there are questions to be asked about how new 'big data' really is and what role theory can play within the data deluge (Kitchin, Chapter 3, this volume), but perhaps an unexpected outcome of the challenge this data has thrown at us has been an increase in interdisciplinary work across the social and computing sciences as well as the humanities from which all sides have benefitted (Quan-Haase and McCay-Peet, Chapter 4, this volume).

In response to these challenges a range of tools have been identified or developed that account for the complex characteristics of social media data. Popular and free analytical packages such as 'R' enable users to collect

Twitter data (Janetzko, Chapter 10, this volume) and analyze it in a variety of ways, whilst other tools provide more bespoke functionality in the areas of Natural Language Processing (NLP) and language analysis (Bontecheva, Chapter 29, this volume; Rubin, Chapter 21, this volume; Thelwall, Chapter 32, this volume) and social network analysis (Ghajar-Khosravi and Chignell, Chapter 19, this volume; Gruzd, Mai and Kampen, Chapter 30, this volume). Importantly, the development of graphical interface platforms, such as COSMOS, have democratized access by lowering the level of technical knowledge required to ascertain, process, filter and explore social media data (Morgan, Chapter 26, this volume).

CONCLUSION

The introductory chapter highlights and discusses many of the challenges encountered in studies of social media ranging from practical decisions that influence the research design (i.e., timeline of data collection, what hashtags to follow and what tools to use to collect data) to more philosophical questions around the ethical treatment of human subjects. These challenges also emerge from the complexity of social media data and we discussed the 6 Vs as a means of summarizing the key characteristics (volume, variety, velocity, veracity, virtue and value) that any social media project needs to come to terms with and the tools that facilitate working with this data. The contributions to this Handbook demonstrate that the academic community has responded with gusto to these challenges with over 40 experts from around the world from a plethora of disciplines and a variety of methodological viewpoints coming together in one place for the first time. The Handbook covers not only the entire research process for social media research, from question formulation to the interpretation of research findings, but it also presents numerous examples and case studies of various approaches to showcase how to implement various techniques with real data. The chapters provide methodological detail and allow scholars who are unfamiliar with the domain to quickly grasp the strengths, limitations and key considerations of this type of data with the aim of:

- Encouraging skill development: An easy to follow, step-by-step approach encourages scholars to immerse themselves in new techniques and thereby widen their methodological toolkit.
- Showcasing tool use: Many of the chapters rely on tools developed specifically for either the collection, analysis or visualization of social media data. Both pros and cons of various tools are discussed and the possibilities for analysis presented via case studies and examples.
- Covering of the entire research process: Scholars are encouraged to think about the entire research process from study design to interpretations of data. This provides a uniquely holistic perspective of social media research.
- Promoting ethical considerations: The chapters highlight how the person, the self, cannot be separated from the data trace in particular types of studies. This necessitates novel approaches to research ethics and the treatment of both big data and small data.
- Demonstrating data harvesting and cleaning practices and techniques: Social media data has particular characteristics and these need to be taken into account when harvesting data either for large quantitative analysis or analysis at a small scale. Also misinformation, deception and trolling practices can influence data interpretation and need to be considered seriously as part of the data set.
- Highlighting multi-method and multi-data approaches: The use of multiple methods of data collection, analysis, visualization and interpretation are critical for developing distinct understandings of social media practice and social phenomena. Triangulating data and also analyzing social media data in conjunction with other data sources can provide a fuller picture of social phenomena.

To tackle the challenges of social media research we must embrace an interdisciplinary approach (Quan-Haase and McCay-Peet, Chapter 4, this volume), drawing on methodological traditions from across and outside of the social sciences, computer sciences and humanities. It is our sincere hope that this edition widens the pool of researchers who feel confident and competent when working with social media data and that the methodological discussions spread and grow because, as Bob Dylan almost said, these methods they are a changin'.

NOTE

1 As McCay-Peet and Quan-Haase (Chapter 2, this volume) report between 2009 and 2014 there are almost twice as many references in Scholar's Portal (http://www.scholarsportal.info) in peer-reviewed articles to the term 'social media' in comparison to 'social networking sites (SNSs)'. In recent years, usage of both terms has increased exponentially, the trend suggests that social media is more 'social media' than 'social networking site (SNS)'.

REFERENCES

BIS (2013). Seizing the data opportunity: A strategy for UK data capability. London: Department of Business, Innovation and Skills.

Blackshaw, P. (2006). 'The consumer-controlled surveillance culture', ClickZ. Retrieved October 15, 2015 from http://www.clickz.com/clickz/column/1706163/the-consumer-controlled-surveillance-culture

Bradley, J. (1993). 'Methodological issues and practices in qualitative research', *The Library Quarterly: Information, Community, Policy*, 63(4): 431–449.

Bruns, A. (2015). 'Making sense of society through social media', *Social Media + Society*, 1(1): 1–2.

Correa, T., Hinsley, A. W., and de Zúñiga, H. G. (2010). 'Who interacts on the Web? The intersection of users' personality and social media use', *Computers in Human Behavior*, 26(2): 247–253.

Creighton, J. L., Foster, J. W., Klingsmith, L., and Withey, D. K. (2013). 'I just look it up: Undergraduate student perception of social media use in their academic success', *Journal of Social Media in Society*, 2(2): 26–46.

Duggan, M. (2015). Mobile messaging and social media 2015 | Pew Research Center. Retrieved September 6, 2016, from http://www.pewinternet.org/2015/08/19/mobile-messaging-and-social-media-2015/

Gruzd, A., Staves, K., and Wilk, A. (2012). 'Connected scholars: Examining the role of social media in research practices of faculty using the UTAUT model', *Computers in Human Behavior*, 28(6): 2340–2350.

Hogan, B., and Quan-Haase, A. (2010). 'Persistence and change in social media', *Bulletin of Science, Technology & Society*, 30(5): 309–315.

Hong, S., and Nadler, D. (2012). 'Which candidates do the public discuss online in an election campaign? The use of social media by 2012 presidential candidates and its impact on candidate salience', *Government Information Quarterly*, 29(4): 455–461. http://doi.org/10.1016/j.giq.2012.06.004

Kaplan, A. M., and Haenlein, M. (2010). 'Users of the world, unite! The challenges and opportunities of social media', *Business Horizons*, 53(1): 59–68.

Kuhn, T. S. (1970). *The structure of scientific revolutions*. Chicago, IL: University of Chicago Press.

Otieno, D. O., and Matoke, V. B. (2014). 'Social media as tool for conducting academic research', *International Journal of Advanced Research in Computer Science and Software Engineering*, 4(1): 962–967.

Rose, K. (2014). 'The UK Social Media Landscape for 2014', Available at: http://www.rosemcgrory.co.uk/2014/01/06/uk-social-media-statistics for 2014/

Savage, M., and Burrows, R. (2007). 'The coming crisis of empirical sociology', *Sociology*, 41(5): 885–899. http://doi.org/10.1177/0038038507080443

Sloan, L., Morgan, J., Burnap, P., and Williams, M. (2015). 'Who tweets? Deriving the demographic characteristics of age, occupation and social class from Twitter user meta-data', *Plos One*, 10(3), article number: e0115545 (10.1371/journal.pone.0115545).

Sloan, L., Morgan, J., Housley, W., Williams, M., Edwards, A., Burnap, P., and Rana, O. (2013). 'Knowing the Tweeters: Deriving sociologically relevant demographics from Twitter', *Sociological Research Online*, 18(3), article number: 7. (10.5153/sro.3001).

Townsend, L., and Wallace, C. (2016). 'Social Media Research: A Guide to Ethics'. Available at: http://www.dotrural.ac.uk/socialmediaresearchethics.pdf

Twitter (2015). 'Twitter Usage/Company Facts', Available from: https://about.twitter.com/company.

Williams, M., Burnap, P., and Sloan, L. (2016). doi: 10.1093/bjc/azw031 'Crime sensing with Big Data: The affordances and limitations of using open source communications to estimate crime patterns', *British Journal of Criminology - Special Issue*.

Xiang, Z., and Gretzel, U. (2010). 'Role of social media in online travel information search', *Tourism Management*, 31(2): 179–188.

Zephoria. (2015). 'The Top 20 valuable Facebook statistics – Updated October 2015', Retrieved 9 November 2015, from https://zephoria.com/top-15-valuable-facebook-statistics/

PART I
Conceptualising & Designing Social Media Research

What is Social Media and What Questions Can Social Media Research Help Us Answer?

Lori McCay-Peet and Anabel Quan-Haase

This chapter critically engages with the plurality of meanings given to the term social media, ranging from mainstream blogging platforms to niche communication tools. A brief historical overview is first presented of how the term has evolved, showing that in academia it has only gained widespread popularity since the mid-2000s. The chapter then discusses various categorization frameworks available in the literature to examine what applications and platforms are commonly considered a part of the social media spectrum. The chapter ends with a discussion of what kinds of research questions social media scholarship can help answer. We show how social media raises novel methodological and ethical issues linked to its use as a tool for research to aid in data collection, the dissemination of online surveys, and the recruitment of participants. Further, we identify two types of research questions central to social media scholarship: a) those relating to social media use itself, and b) those that inform our understanding of social phenomena. Finally, we propose a framework of social media engagement to explore key domains of analysis and to show the significance of each for providing a holistic understanding of social media adoption, use, and social implications.

INTRODUCTION

In the past ten years, social media has become an integral part of everyday life with large economic, political, and societal implications. While the influence of traditional media dwindles, social media platforms 'have been taken up around the globe at an unprecedented speed, revealing the extraordinary nature of the social media phenomenon. For this reason alone, it is imperative to analyze the phenomenon of social media' (boyd, 2015: 2). Because the term social media has multiple meanings, its definition has become highly contested and it is not always clear what tools, platforms, and social phenomena count as social media, though its integration into the daily lives of many is indisputable. A 2015 report from the Pew Research Center shows 70 per cent of Facebook users logged into the site at least once a day, and as many as 45 per cent logged into the site numerous times throughout the day (Duggan, Ellison, Lampe, Lehnhart, and Madden, 2015). The same report shows that 52 per cent of online adults adopted two or more social media sites. Because of its proliferation in society as well as its unique technological affordances, social media provides new avenues for researchers across multiple disciplines, including health sciences, sociology, and political science, to collect rich, vast, and networked data, recruit diverse groups of participants and perform complex analyses. Despite the plurality of voices on these sites, scholarly work has consistently shown that social media only provides a narrow view of our social world, as not all social groups are equally represented (Haight, Quan-Haase, and Corbett, 2014). Moreover, there continue to be segments of the population and parts of the world that are absent from the internet altogether (Girish, Williams, and Yates, 2014). Hence, it is important to realize that social media adoption, usage, and its social implications are dynamic social processes that occur within existing patterns of inequality: some social groups are simply being left out of the social media conversation.

Often social media scholarship is associated with big data because of the 3Vs – volume, velocity, and variety – that may be culled from sites such as Twitter, Instagram, and Facebook (Kitchin, 2014). Data derived from user-generated content, such as posts, 'likes', and connections signalled through 'friends' and 'follows', have become central to many areas of study, including politics (Rainie et al., 2012), healthcare (Reavley and Pilkington, 2014), and business (Gopaldas, 2014). The analysis of such massive amounts of data is unprecedented and brings with it many challenges, including ethical considerations, hardware constraints, and the development of software for data collection and analysis. However, social media scholarship is not limited to big-scale analysis and examination can take place at a small scale through qualitative approaches, despite being characterized by large volume. Scholars have also called for the integration of big data analysis and small-scale approaches in mixed methods designs (Quan-Haase, Martin, and McCay-Peet, 2015; Murthy and Bowman, 2014; Zeller, Chapter 23, this volume).

In this chapter, we first examine how prior research has defined and conceptualized social media. We then propose a definition of social media and briefly discuss how various types of social media, such as social networking sites (SNSs), microblogs, and social news sites, fit within the concept. We then turn to the research relating to social media, focusing on questions about social media as well as research that uses social media data to answer social science research questions. As Jürgens wrote, 'In recent years, social media have matured in terms of design and in terms of adoption rates – to become a platform for rich expression and exchange for a highly diverse user base, attracting intense scholarly interest' (2012: 186). In light of this recent surge, we further explore what types of questions social media research can answer and the advantages and challenges of social media scholarship.

WHAT IS SOCIAL MEDIA?

Despite the proliferation of research on social media in recent years, there are relatively few formal definitions. The lack of definitions is potentially due to the difficulty in defining the term, as it is relatively nascent and still evolving (Ellison and boyd, 2013). Papacharissi goes so far as to argue that a definition of social media can only be dynamic and context specific.

Our understanding of social media is temporally, spatially, and technologically sensitive – informed but not restricted by the definitions, practices, and materialities of a single time period or locale. How we have defined social media in societies has changed, and will continue to change. (2015: 1)

The term social media is also conceptually related to other terms including SNSs and online social networks (OSNs). Several sites were launched around 2003 and included rapidly growing sites such as MySpace, Friendster, and Facebook (boyd and Ellison, 2007). As a result, the terms SNS and OSN saw a rapid growth in usage across journals, monographs, and media releases in various domains, including computer science, communication, and sociology. A search of Scholar's Portal[1] reveals there were almost twice as many references in peer-reviewed papers using the term 'social networking site (SNS)' versus 'social media' between 2003 and 2008, though usage of both terms increased exponentially in the years to follow. However, between 2009 and 2014 the trend reversed with more than twice as many papers including the term 'social media' than 'social networking site (SNS)'. Two reasons may explain this shift. First, social media is a broader term that includes, for example, blogging, which is not specifically geared toward building social connections, but rather toward the broadcasting of information. Second, the term social media is associated with platforms such as Twitter, Instagram, Pinterest, and Snapchat, while the term SNS is specifically associated with the use of sites such as Facebook, MySpace, and hi5. The academic literature continues to make use of both terms, but SNSs and OSNs are considered to be types of social media.

Often scholarship tends to focus on specific proprietary platforms, that is, it examines platforms such as Twitter, Facebook, or Pinterest. But what brings social media scholarship together are the many commonalities shared across platforms (e.g., features for sharing and evaluating content, means for connecting with a social network, search and save functions), making it relevant to discuss social media both in general as well as at the platform level. In particular, identifying how users engage with features that are similar across platforms seems relevant for developing theories that have applicability across platforms.

Part of the difficulty in defining the term is figuring out what makes social media distinguishable from other media (Hogan and Quan-Haase, 2010). Bruns directly compares social media with traditional media to highlight what is unique: 'All media are social, but only a particular subset of all media are fundamentally defined by their *sociality*, and thus distinguished, for example, from the mainstream media of print, radio, and television' (2015: 1, emphasis added). Certainly social media tends to support sociality, but different platforms emphasize the social to different extents. For example, Kwak et al. (2010) found that Twitter was used primarily as an information network, rather than a social network. At the same time it is also increasingly difficult to distinguish social media from digital technology in general (Creighton et al., 2013) because of the social elements that are now embedded in everything from smartphone applications to wearable technologies. Despite a lack of formal definitions, those that do exist generally agree on its key elements. Based on an analysis of a selection of definitions available in the academic literature, we identified three main themes: (a) what activities social media enables, (b) how it enables these activities, and (c) the content it contains. Table 2.1 provides an overview of key definitions and analyses of each of these themes.

Based on our analysis of a selection of definitions from the literature (see Table 2.1), we conclude that there exists relative consensus as to the meaning of social media. While some definitions stop short of specifying the type of content available, those that do specify content all

Table 2.1 Selection of social media definitions from the research literature organised by themes

Definitions of social media	Themes		
	What social media enables	How social media does it	Content of social media
Social media 'provides a mechanism for the audience to connect, communicate, and interact with each other and their mutual friends through instant messaging or social networking sites' (Correa, Hinsley, and de Zúñiga, 2010: 247–248)	Mechanism for connecting, communicating, and interacting with others	Instant messaging sites; social networking sites	
'Any website or web-based service that includes web 2.0 characteristics and contains some aspect of user generated content.' Web 2.0 'was used to describe an emerging way of using the internet, with more participatory and collaborative surfing of the web as well as the creation and modification of online content by internet surfers' (Gruzd et al., 2012: 2341)	Enables the creation and modification of online content	Websites or web-based services	User-generated content
'Social Media is a group of Internet-based applications that build on the ideological and technological foundations of Web 2.0, and that allow the creation and exchange of User Generated Content' (Kaplan and Haenlein, 2010: 61)	Allows for the creation and exchange of content	Group of internet-based applications that build on the ideological and technological foundations of Web 2.0	User-generated content
'Social media is a form of computer-mediated communication' (McIntyre, 2014: 6)	Communication	Computer-mediated	
'Social media, derived from the social software movement, are a collection of Internet websites, services, and practices that support collaboration, community building, participation, and sharing' (Otieno and Matoke, 2014: 962)	Support collaboration, community building, participation, and sharing	Internet websites, services, and practices	
'"Social Media" can be generally understood as Internet-based applications that carry consumer-generated content which encompasses "media impressions created by consumers, typically informed by relevant experience, and archived or shared online for easy access by other impressionable consumers" (Blackshaw, 2006)' (Xiang and Gretzel, 2010: 180)	Carry content	Internet-based applications that carry content, archived or shared online for easy access by other consumers	Consumer-generated content; media impressions created by consumers informed by relevant experience

agree that it is user- or consumer-generated (Gruzd et al., 2012; Kaplan and Haenlein, 2010; Xiang and Gretzel, 2010). All definitions in Table 2.1 indicate what social media does; namely, it allows individuals, communities, and organizations to interact with one another by providing a service that enables them to communicate and collaborate and to create, modify, and share content. The definitions in Table 2.1 also concur that interactions occur through computer-mediated, web-based services.

Thus, it can be stated based on the definitions listed in Table 2.1 that:

> Social media are web-based services that allow individuals, communities, and organizations to collaborate, connect, interact, and build community by enabling them to create, co-create, modifies, share, and engage with user-generated content that is easily accessible.

The proposed definition of social media is broad and has the potential to include numerous technologies with social elements at their core. Gruzd et al. argue that social media 'includes a wide variety of technologies from video/teleconferencing tools such as Skype and online media repositories such as Flickr, to microblogging tools like Twitter and social networking sites like Facebook and Academia.edu' (2012: 2341). Though much of the social media research literature makes no attempt at a formal definition, a definition is often implied by the websites or applications selected for investigation.

Frequently Facebook and Twitter are the platforms examined in social media research, though other platforms such as Pinterest, YouTube, Yelp, Weibo, and LinkedIn are similarly explored under the umbrella of social media (see the recent issues of the new journal *Social Media + Society* at http://sms.sagepub.com). There are two reasons why scholars have tended to give preference to Facebook and Twitter over other sites. First, Facebook is by far the most widely adopted SNS in North America and was one of the first to gather a large and loyal user base. Pew data from 2014 show that 71 per cent of Americans have adopted Facebook, while only 28 per cent use Pinterest and Instagram (Duggan et al., 2015). Second, while Twitter is not as widely used as Facebook among the general population, it has had a transformative effect on how information and news diffuse throughout society. The mainstream media, including daily newspapers, broadcasting channels, and weekly magazines, often make reference to Twitter activity in news stories; as a result, Twitter has become an important part of public discourse, despite not being widely adopted by the general population; indeed in 2014 only 23 per cent of Americans used it (Duggan et al., 2015). We feel the time is ripe for more in-depth analysis and greater attention to sites like Vine, Instagram, and Snapchat, which emphasize non-text forms of media. For example, current innovations under development provide much-needed tools to not only study images and their surrounding discourse, but also the interlink of image, text, and content producer (see e.g., Martin, Chapter 14, this volume; Rasmussen Pennington, Chapter 15, this volume; Warfield et al., 2015).

There have been several attempts to categorize social media and identify what technologies can be considered social media. Arora (2012), for example, developed a metaphor-based typology to help identify boundaries among social media spaces; she organized them into five cultural dimensions:

1 utilitarian-driven,
2 aesthetic-driven,
3 context-driven,
4 play-driven, and
5 value-driven.

More common are categorizations of social media by technology type for the purposes of marketing or research. Grahl (2013), for example, identified six types of social media applications:

1 social networking,
2 bookmarking,
3 social news,
4 media sharing,
5 microblogging, and
6 blogs and forums.

Grahl's (2013) typology serves as a means to explain to clients and users how each type may be leveraged for specific marketing purposes and goals. To examine the use of social media in the research work flow of scholars, Nicholas and Rowlands (2011) surveyed over 2,000 researchers. Based on their analysis, they identified similar types of social media as Grahl

(2013), though did not explicitly identify social news as a specific type of social media, and identified three additional types of social media relevant to scholars and professionals:

1 collaborative authoring,
2 conferencing, and
3 scheduling and meeting tools.

Based on previous literature, Table 2.2 outlines ten main types of social media (Grahl, 2013; Nicholas and Rowlands, 2011) and includes examples and definitions of each.

This typology (Table 2.2) will help authors indicate what type of social media and platform they are examining and thereby help other scholars more quickly search for relevant literature as well as to identify commonalities and differences across types of social media. Through such approaches we will be able to build a more systematic body of knowledge.

Table 2.2 Types of social media

Type of social media	Examples	Definitions
Social networking sites	Facebook, LinkedIn	'Web-based services that allow individuals to (1) construct a public or semi-public profile within a bounded system, (2) articulate a list of other users with whom they share a connection, and (3) view and traverse their list of connections and those made by others within the system' (boyd and Ellison, 2007: 211)
Bookmarking	Delicious, StumbleUpon	'Provide a mix of both direct (intentional) navigational advice as well as indirect (inferred) advice based on collective public behavior. By definition – these social bookmarking systems provide "social filtering" on resources from the web and intranet. The act of bookmarking indicates to others that one is interested in a given resource. At the same time, tags provide semantic information about the way the resource can be viewed' (Millen, Yang, Whittaker, and Feinberg, 2007: 22)
Microblogging	Twitter, Tumblr	'Services that focus on short updates that are pushed out to anyone subscribed to receive the updates' (Grahl, 2013: n.p.)
Blogs and forums	LiveJournal, Wordpress	'Online forums allow members to hold conversations by posting messages. Blog comments are similar except they are attached to blogs and usually the discussion centers around the topic of the blog post' (Grahl, 2013: n.p.)
Media sharing	YouTube, Flickr, Pinterest	'Services that allow you to upload and share various media such as pictures and video. Most services have additional social features such as profiles, commenting, etc.' (Grahl, 2013: n.p.)
Social news	Digg, Reddit	'Services that allow people to post various news items or links to outside articles and then allows it's users to "vote" on the items. The voting is the core social aspect as the items that get the most votes are displayed the most prominently. The community decides which news items get seen by more people' (Grahl, 2013: n.p.)
Collaborative authoring	Wikipedia, Google Docs	Web-based services that enable users to create content and allow anyone with access to modify, edit, or review that content (Archambault et al., 2013)
Web conferencing	Skype, GoToMeeting, Zoho Meeting	'Web conferencing may be used as an umbrella term for various types of online collaborative services including web seminars ("webinars"), webcasts, and peer-level web meetings' (Web conferencing, n.d.)
Geo-location based sites	Foursquare, Yik-Yak, Tinder	Services that allow its users to connect and exchange messages based on their location
Scheduling and meeting	Doodle, Google Calendar, Microsoft Outlook	Web-based services that enable group-based event decisions (Reinecke et al., 2013)

WHAT QUESTIONS CAN SOCIAL MEDIA RESEARCH ANSWER?

What makes the study of social media relevant to many disciplines is the availability of vast amounts of varied data. Social media produces what has been referred to as big data and is characterized by high velocity, large volume, diverse variety, exhaustivity in scope, fine-grained resolution, relational in nature, and flexibility in its approach (Kitchin, 2014). This creates new challenges for scholars, while also presenting great opportunity – this has given rise to several questions.

First, social media research has prompted questions that force researchers to look inward to grapple with its inherent challenges.

1   **Methodological questions**: Novel methodological questions emerge from the collection, analysis, and visualization of social media data. Some of these questions are platform-specific while others are applicable to all kinds of social media. To some extent social media allows easy and convenient access to large quantities of data, on the other hand, it can be costly or even impossible to obtain a specific data set. Melissa Terras (2012) for instance lamented on a blog post entitled 'What Price a Hashtag? The cost of #digitalhumanities', how it would cost her around US$25,000 to purchase from Gnip the historical set containing the hashtag #digitalhumanities. In other words, data is readily available if scholars can pay the price.
2   **Ethical questions**: Data collection, aggregation, and reporting of social media data has raised numerous ethical questions relating to issues such as personal privacy, accuracy, and accountability with which researchers and practitioners are only beginning to grapple. While social media data is often publicly available, there are still many ethical considerations that should give researchers reason to pause. Consent is often at the center of debates, as not all users of social media sites are comfortable with (or aware of) the use of their data for analysis (Beninger et al., 2014). Ethical considerations do not exclusively apply to scraping big data, but are also of relevance in small-scale studies relying on few cases. As Quan-Haase and McCay-Peet argue this 'may actually be an even greater concern for small-scale qualitative researchers, where it is easier to identify single users' (Chapter 4, this volume: 44). Hence, scholars need to address a wide range of research questions around data stewardship and what ethical guidelines need to be set up to both help scholars gain new insights, while protecting the right of users to data privacy. These kinds of discussions become increasingly relevant with new legislation being introduced in various countries. For example, the European Union has passed a new law that allows individuals to better control personal data on the web, which has been discussed under the right to be forgotten. Unfolding legal challenges open up new research questions for scholars relating to the biases of the data collected for analysis as well as the legality of storing data that users may want deleted.
3   **Questions of scale**: Scale is one of the greatest challenges to be overcome by social media scholars. Social media data allow for the examination of a different phenomenon or issue from different angles. A study can rely on either large data sets that aggregate terabytes of information or, through small-scale studies, examine the local behaviour of a few users. While both approaches are relevant and valid, they provide qualitatively different insights into a single phenomenon. So, how do we integrate findings from such disparate means of gaining knowledge? New theoretical and methodological assumptions are needed to link and integrate distinct data sets and findings.

Second, social media data provide opportunities for scholars to address new types of questions and shed light on existing research problems from a different angle.

1   **Questions relating to social media use itself**: Social media scholarship can provide answers to new questions that arise from individuals', organizations', and governments' interaction and engagement on these information and social spaces. Social media activity is the focus of research in this case (e.g., how people discuss issues relating to personal health on Facebook, topological features of Twitter networks, and social media usage patterns). For example, social

media research is important from the perspective of workplaces, schools, and universities. These organizations and institutions need to understand social media in order to develop appropriate policies to support or, in some cases, control its use. Citation counts are a traditional measure of research impact which informs the academic reward system, however universities need to understand whether and how social media can be used as a new way to measure research impact (Holmberg and Thelwall, 2014). Institutions of higher education are also exploring how social media spaces for students may be integrated into college and university experiences to improve student outcomes (e.g., DeAndrea, Ellison, Larose, Steinfield, and Fiore, 2012). Research is also needed to help inform public school policy, to address, for example, social media use by American teachers whose First Amendment rights may be threatened by limits placed on what they can and cannot do on social media (Papandrea, 2012).

2 **Questions that inform our understanding of social phenomena:** A second stream of social media research is the use of social media as a tool or method for academic research, for examining research questions and understanding complex problems otherwise examined through other, more traditional, methods (Otieno and Matoke, 2014). This second type of social media research significantly broadens the base of scholars doing 'social media research', by bringing in scholars from disciplines that do not explicitly study social media, but whose research could benefit from the characteristics of social media that make it conducive to the study of a variety of phenomena: its potential as a recruitment platform, its reach into a particular demographic, and the behaviours, attitudes, and perceptions that are readily observable and extractable via social media. Social phenomena such as involvement in social movements, giving, and political participation and consuming can be examined through an analysis of social media data. Yuan et al. (2014), for example, note the value of recruitment via social media when barriers such as stigma and mistrust exist. Yuan et al. recruited 1,221 HIV-positive participants for their survey via Facebook, Twitter, and other internet resources and concluded it was a 'feasible and efficient tool' (2014; n.p.).

Early scholarly work from 2003 to 2008 investigating social media tended to examine a single platform, its affordances, uses, and social implications. For instance, Gross and Acquisti (2005) looked at how users were engaging on Facebook, what information they shared on the platform, and the implications for their privacy. Thus, a large body of scholarship has addressed specific questions surrounding the development of various platforms, how users engage on these platforms, and the social implications of their engagement. Despite the quick proliferation of research addressing questions linked to social media, three issues were often insufficiently taken into account.

1 **Social media use as toolkit:** Much work tended to look at specific platforms and their affordances as if these were utilized in isolation, rather than examining how individuals employed various platforms in tandem. Quan-Haase and Young (2010) suggested that scholars think of social media use as a kind of toolkit, where different platforms fulfilled different uses and gratifications. This would help explain why users often adopt multiple social media platforms. Pew, for instance, shows that multi-platform use is becoming fairly common with 52 per cent of online American adults adopting two or more social media sites, which represents a significant increase from 2013 data, where 42 per cent of internet users adopted more than one platform (Duggan et al., 2015). Further, Quan-Haase and Young argued that more work needed to be done on comparing platforms, as this would add to our understanding of why individuals prefer one social media site over another, and why and how they integrate different platforms on the basis of the gratifications they fulfill.

2 **Online-offline gap:** Examining social media often gives the impression that it is a universe unto itself that exists in isolation from other spheres of life. This kind of perspective is myopic, however, and disregards how social media and the phenomena that emerge within it are closely interlinked to other spheres of life. Perhaps most importantly, social media usage is closely interwoven with everyday life's rhythms and patterns. In a study of digital humanities scholars

(Quan-Haase, Martin and McCay-Peet, 2015), the scholars integrated their use of Twitter into their work practices, tweeting and interacting with content in between meetings and during downtime. Moreover, the social contexts in which interactions and behaviours are occurring need to be taken into account, as these help explain topological features of networks of interaction and connection. Without taking cultural, political, and historical contexts into account, important aspects of social media use and its social implications may be missed. The framework discussed below will specifically elaborate on this link between social contexts and social media engagement. This link also became evident in the analysis of social media usage during the Arab Spring, where social media played a critical role. Despite the importance of social media during the Arab Spring of Tunisia and Egypt, many analysts showed that social media was utilized as a means to organize and mobilize citizens, spread news, and engage with the political landscape, *in tandem with* and *in addition to* informal, face-to-face networks on the ground. Rather than the digital sphere being separate from the offline sphere, the two work in relation to one another (Wellman et al., 2001). Hence social media needs to be studied as an expansion of daily life, a means to amplify social phenomena, and a catalyst for social phenomena in order to understand the larger ramifications of social media in society and points of intersection.

3 **Discipline orientation**: Early social media research drew from a variety of approaches and tended to be less grounded in any one discipline. This has changed, though. Scholars within specific disciplines have come on board and are now utilizing social media data to answer issue-specific questions, which are often closely linked to their disciplines of origins. This is an important development in three ways. First, it frames questions within a set of theoretical approaches and discourses. Second, this is allowing for methods around social media to develop and fit with the unique requirements of a set of questions. Finally, it also suggests that social media research is becoming mainstream and its data more acceptable as a viable means of gaining insight into phenomena.

To further expand on the types of questions that social media can answer, we adapt McCay-Peet and Quan-Haase's (2016) framework of social media engagement to explore key domains of analysis. The authors identified six elements of social media engagement, which may be examined through any number of disciplinary, theoretical, and methodological perspectives and traditions: (1) presentation of self, (2) action and participation, (3) uses and gratifications, (4) positive experiences, (5) usage and activity counts, and (6) social context. We have augmented this model and added a seventh element – (7) platform characteristics (see Figure 2.1). Platform characteristics are critical for understanding how users create, share, interact with, and mobilize content as well as for understanding how community is created and maintained in different platforms. For example, Twitter allows individuals to follow a person, institution or account, without reciprocation. That is, Twitter supports one-way flows of information. By contrast, Facebook only allows linkages between users when both parties agree to the connection: two users are equally connected to one another. This difference in how features work across platforms has important implications for the flow of information, the formation of gatekeepers, and the topology of networks. Hence, understanding how features relate to social phenomena provides further insight into the affordances of these platforms for social behaviour. Each of the seven elements are briefly described below and we illustrate how they can be studied in relation to one another.

1 *Presentation of self, reputation management, and privacy*: Identity is crafted through the development of a personal profile or virtual self over time on social media. An example of a research question designed to address the presentation of self aspect of social media is: 'Are university student Facebook users more concerned about social privacy or institutional privacy?' (Young and Quan-Haase, 2013: 483).

2 *Action and participation*: Social media enables users to perform a variety of activities such as viewing, posting, or sharing content,

collaboration, and discussion. Veletsianos, for example, posed the following research question which aims to understand the nature of scholarly participation in social media: 'What kinds of activities do scholars engage with on the Twitter network?' (2012: 339).

3   *Uses and gratifications*: Social media users have different motivations for adoption and use including, for example, the exchange of information and the social benefits derived from its use. To understand why people use social recommendations (e.g., 'likes'), Kim asks, for example, 'What are online user motives for using social recommendation systems?' (2014: 186).

4   *Positive and negative experiences*: Aspects of social media that compel people to use it such as positive emotions, serendipity, and flow. One research question that reflects this visceral element of social media engagement is related to deep involvement and flow: 'What are the factors affecting users to be deeply involved in social media?' (Chan and Ma, 2014: 17). Equally, negative experiences such as spam, fraud, and cyberbullying may lower user engagement with social media and these experiences have led to a wealth of research questions as well.

5   *Usage and activity counts*: Usage and activity counts refer to the data associated with users' actions and participation within a particular social media site, which may be presented in realtime in raw or aggregate form to users. Research in this area may examine, for example, the impact of the counts provided by social media sites such as Twitter and Facebook on users. Westerman, Spence, and Van Der Heide asked, 'How does the ratio of followers to follows impact perceived credibility?' (2012: 201).

6   *Social context*: Social context refers to the social, political, economic, work, and personal phenomena or characteristics that underlie a users' social networks within social media sites, including the size and nature of these local and global networks (e.g., a small, close-knit peer group; a large, diffuse network of social activists). Social media research may, for example, attempt to understand the implications of social context to the use of social media by asking, 'Does (national) culture determine how we schedule events online?' (Reinecke et al., 2013: 45). Other social media research is interested in who is using social media to help understand the social context, asking questions such as, 'Are Twitter users a representative sample of society?' (Mislove et al., 2011: 554). Furthermore, social movements provide a unique context from which to examine social media and how it serves as a tool for engagement, mobilization, and coordination (Castells, 2014; Poell, 2013).

7   *Platform characteristics*: Factors relating to features of specific platforms may influence engagement – for example, features that enable users to share information or communicate directly with one another. Smock et al. (2011) developed a number of research questions in their study on the uses and gratifications of Facebook, specifically relating to feature use. One of these research questions was, 'Are the motivations that predict general Facebook use different from the motivations that predict use of specific Facebook features?' (Smock et al., 2011: 2324).

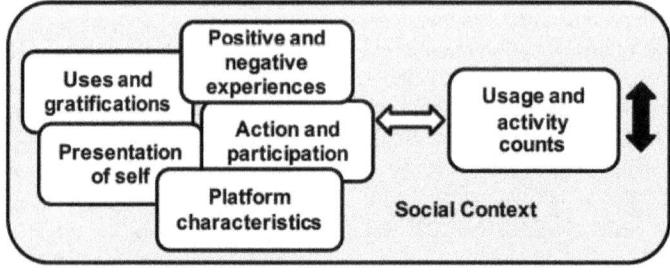

Figure 2.1   A model of social media engagement in context (adapted from McCay-Peet and Quan-Haase, 2016, p. 201)

Responses to the research questions outlined above inform our understanding of the reach of social media, how and why people engage with social media and to what effect, as well as our understanding of society. For example, Reinecke et al. (2013) examined the use of Doodle, a web-based scheduling tool, to understand cultural differences in time-perception and group decisionmaking. They found through an analysis of 1.5 million Doodle date and time polls from 211 countries that the process of scheduling is shaped by cultural norms and values. Studies such as these have the potential to not only expand our understanding of social media use, but more broadly our understanding of collectivist and individualistic societies.

In terms of the disciplines that have examined social media-related questions, we can identify marketing, communications, politics, computer science and human–computer interaction specifically, economics, health, business, and education. There are, however, many more. Often interdisciplinary research teams come together to tackle complex questions around social phenomena as they take place on social media (see Quan-Haase and McCay-Peet, Chapter 4, this volume).

CONCLUSION

This chapter presents and contrasts various definitions of social media. Based on an analysis of these definitions, we found some consensus among scholars. Drawing on key elements of existing definitions, we propose a broad definition:

> Social media are web-based services that allow individuals, communities, and organizations to collaborate, connect, interact, and build a community by enabling them to create, co-create, modify, share, and engage with user-generated content that is easily accessible.

Given the growing pervasiveness and impact of social media on a broad range of social phenomena including politics, presentation of self, social interaction, social movements, and scholarship itself, it has become both a fruitful area of research as well as a promising tool for data collection. If current efforts are any indication, there will be a growth in the development of new social media research methods and their assessment which will help integrate social media research methods and knowledge into existing frameworks (Bruns, 2015). There has already been a proliferation in social media research with niche journals emerging that either cover social media phenomena themselves or the methodological challenges associated with social media research, such as the journals *Social Media + Society, Social Media and Society,* and *Big Data and Society.* However, we would also argue that given the growth of social media scholarship more critical research is needed to understand the biases inherent in using social media methodologies and to develop best practices concerning social media research, with the aim of both supporting researchers and protecting social media users. Of particular importance is the need to determine best practices around ethical considerations. For instance, can scholars make use of social media data without the consent of authors of user-generated content? If they make use of the data, should this be done only in aggregate form? What repercussions, for example, imprisonment, stigma, ridicule, and harm to reputation can participants suffer from scholars making tweets and blog text searchable, even if anonymized? There is much work to be done not only around the social phenomena under investigation on social media platforms, but also concerning how scholars are procuring, storing, interpreting, and making use of social media data.

ACKNOWLEDGEMENTS

We would like to thank two anonymous reviewers for their useful comments and

Chandell Gosse for her feedback on an earlier draft. This research is funded by a SSHRC Insight Grant No. R3603A13.

NOTE

1 Scholar's Portal is a digital repository, which provides access to the electronic resources of 21 university libraries in Ontario, Canada, including more than '40 million scholarly articles drawn from journals covering every academic discipline' (Ontario Council of University Libraries, n.p.).

REFERENCES

Archambault, P. M., van de Belt, T. H., Grajales, F. J., Faber, M. J., Kuziemsky, C. E., Gagnon, S., Turgeon, A. F., Aubin, K., Gold, I., Poitras, J., Eysenbach, G., Kremer, J. A. M., and Légaré, F. (2013). 'Wikis and collaborative writing applications in health care: A scoping review', *Journal of Medical Internet Research*, 15(10): e210.

Arora, P. (2012). 'Typology of Web 2.0 spheres: Understanding the cultural dimensions of social media spaces', *Current Sociology*, 60(5): 599–618.

Beninger, K., Fry, A., Jago, N., Lepps, H., Nass, L., and Silvester, H. (2014). Research using social media: Users' views [Report]. London, UK: NatCentre Social Research. http://natcen.ac.uk/our-research/research/research-using-social-media-users-views/

Blackshaw, P. (2006, 10 January *The consumer-controlled surveillance culture*. ClickZ. Retrieved 15 October 2015 from http://www.clickz.com/clickz/column/1706163/the-consumer-controlled-surveillance-culture

boyd, d. (2015). 'Social media: A phenomenon to be analyzed', *Social Media + Society*, 1(1): 1–2.

boyd, d. and Ellison, N. B. (2007). 'Social network sites: definition, history, and scholarship', *Journal of Computer-Mediated Communication*, 13: 210–230.

Bruns, A. (2015). 'Making sense of society through social media', *Social Media + Society*, 1(1): 1–2.

Castells, M. (2014). *Networks of outrage and hope: Social movements in the Internet age* (2nd ed.). Cambridge, UK: Polity Press.

Chan, W. W. L. and Ma, W. W. K. (2014). 'The influence of playfulness and subject involvement on focused attention when using social media', *Journal of Communication and Education*, 1(1): 16–27.

Correa, T., Hinsley, A. W., and de Zúñiga, H. G. (2010). 'Who interacts on the Web? The intersection of users' personality and social media use', *Computers in Human Behavior*, 26(2): 247–253.

Creighton, J. L., Foster, J. W., Klingsmith, L., and Withey, D. K. (2013). 'I just look it up: Undergraduate student perception of social media use in their academic success', *Journal of Social Media in Society*, 2(2): 26–46.

DeAndrea, D. C., Ellison, N. B., Larose, R., Steinfield, C., and Fiore, A. (2012). 'Serious social media: On the use of social media for improving students' adjustment to college', *Internet and Higher Education*, 15(1): 15–23.

Duggan, M., Ellison, N. B., Lampe, C., Lehnhart, A., and Madden, M. (2015). *Social media update 2014*. Pew Research Centre. Retrieved September 21, 2015 from http://www.pewinternet.org/2015/01/09/social-media-update-2014/

Ellison, N. B. and boyd, d. (2013). 'Sociality through social network sites', in William H. Dutton (ed.), *The Oxford Handbook of Internet Studies* (pp. 151–172). Oxford, UK: Oxford University Press.

Girish, J., Williams, C. B., and Yates, D. J. (2014). 'Predictors of on-line services and e-participation: A cross-national comparison', *Government Information Quarterly*, 31(4): 526–533.

Gopaldas, A. (2014). 'Marketplace sentiments', *Journal of Consumer Research*, 41(4): 995–1014.

Grahl, T. (2013). 'The 6 types of social media', http://timgrahl.com/the-6-types-of-social-media/ (accessed 26 July 2016)

Gross, R. and Acquisti, A. (2005). 'Information revelation and privacy in online social networks'. In *Proceedings of the 2005 ACM Workshop on Privacy in the Electronic Society*, November 7, 2005. Alexandria, VA: ACM Press.

Gruzd, A., Staves, K., and Wilk, A. (2012). 'Connected scholars: Examining the role of social media in research practices of faculty using the UTAUT model', *Computers in Human Behavior*, 28(6): 2340–2350.

Haight, M., Quan-Haase, A., and Corbett, B. (2014). 'Revisiting the digital divide in Canada: The impact of demographic factors on access to the internet, level of online activity, and social networking site usage', *Information, Communication, & Society*, 17(4): 503–519.

Hogan, B. and Quan-Haase, A. (2010). 'Persistence and Change in Social Media', *Bulletin of Science, Technology & Society*, 30(5): 309–315.

Holmberg, K. and Thelwall, M. (2014). Disciplinary differences in Twitter scholarly communication. *Scientometrics*, 101(2), 1027–1042.

Jürgens, P. (2012). 'Communities of communication: Making sense of the "social" in social media', *Journal of Technology in Human Services*, 30(3–4): 186–203.

Kaplan, A. M. and Haenlein, M. (2010). 'Users of the world, unite! The challenges and opportunities of Social Media', *Business Horizons*, 53(1): 59–68.

Kim, J. W. (2014). 'Scan and click: The uses and gratifications of social recommendation systems', *Computers in Human Behavior*, 33: 184–191.

Kitchin, R. (2014). 'Big Data, new epistemologies and paradigm shifts', *Big Data & Society*, 1(1): 1–12.

Kwak, H., Lee, C., Park, H., and Moon, S. (2010). 'What is Twitter, a social network or a news media?' In *Proceedings of the 19th international conference on World Wide Web – WWW '10* (pp. 591–600). New York, New York, USA. ACM Press.

McCay-Peet, L. and Quan-Haase, A. (2016). 'A model of social media engagement: User profiles, gratifications and experiences' in Heather L. O'Brien and Luke Sloan (eds.), *Why Engagement Matters: Cross-disciplinary Perspectives and Innovations on User Engagement with Digital Media* (pp. 199–217). New York: Springer-Verlag.

McIntyre, K. (2014). 'The evolution of social media from 1969 to 2013: A change in competition and a trend toward complementary, niche sites', *The Journal of Social Media in Society*, 3(2): 5–25.

Millen, D. R., Yang, M., Whittaker, S., and Feinberg, J. (2007). 'Social bookmarking and exploratory search', in L. J. Bannon, I. Wagner, C. Gutwin, R. H. R. Harper, and K. Schmidt (eds.), *ECSCW'07: Proceedings of the 10th European Conference on Computer-Supported Cooperative Work, 24–28 September 2007, Limerick, Ireland* (pp. 21–40). London: Springer.

Mislove, A., Lehmann, S., Ahn, Y.-Y., Onnela, J.-P., and Rosenquist, J. N. (2011). 'Understanding the Demographics of Twitter Users', in *Proceedings of the Fifth International AAAI Conference on Weblogs and Social Media*, AAI Organization.(pp. 554–557). http://www.aaai.org/ocs/index.php/ICWSM/ICWSM11/paper/viewFile/2816/3234 (accessed 26 July 2016)

Murthy, D. and Bowman, S. A. (2014). 'Big Data solutions on a small scale: Evaluating accessible high-performance computing for social research', *Big Data & Society*, 1(2): 1–12.

Nicholas, D. and Rowlands, I. (2011). 'Social media use in the research workflow', *Information Services and Use*, 31(1–2): 61–83.

Ontario Council of University Libraries (2014). 'Journals'. (http://ocul.on.ca/node/2115) (accessed 26 July 2016)

Otieno, D. O. and Matoke, V. B. (2014). 'Social media as tool for conducting academic research', *International Journal of Advanced Research in Computer Science and Software Engineering*, 4(1): 962–967.

Papacharissi, Z. (2015). 'We have always been social', *Social Media + Society*, 1(1): 1–2.

Papandrea, M. (2012). 'Social media, public school teachers, and the First Amendment', *North Carolina Law Review*, 90: 1587 1642.

Poell, T. (2013). 'Social media and the transformation of activist communication: Exploring the social media ecology of the 2010 Toronto G20 protests'. *Information, Communication & Society*, 17(6): 716–731. http://doi.org/10.1080/1369118X.2013.812674

Quan-Haase, A., Martin, K., and McCay-Peet, L. (2015). 'Networks of digital humanities scholars: The informational and social uses and gratifications of Twitter'. *Big Data & Society*, January-June: 1–12. http://bds.sagepub.com/content/2/1/2053951715589417

Quan-Haase, A. and Young, A. L. (2010). 'Uses and gratifications of social media: A comparison of Facebook and instant messaging'. *Bulletin of Science, Technology and Society*, 30(5): 350–361.

Rainie, L., Smith, A., Lehman Schlozman, K., Brady, H., and Verba, S. (2012). 'Social media and political engagement'. *Pew Research*, Washington, DC.

Reavley, N. J. and Pilkington, P. D. (2014). 'Use of Twitter to monitor attitudes toward depression and schizophrenia: An exploratory study', *PeerJ*, 2: e647.

Reinecke, K., Nguyen, M., and Bernstein, A. (2013). 'Doodle around the world: Online scheduling behavior reflects cultural differences in time perception and group decision-making', In *Proceedings of CSCW*, '13: 45–54, ACM, New York, NY.

Smock, A. D., Ellison, N. B., Lampe, C., and Wohn, D. Y. (2011). 'Facebook as a toolkit: A uses and gratification approach to unbundling feature use'. *Computers in Human Behavior*, 27(6): 2322–2329.

Terras, M. (2012). *Adventures in digital humanities and digital culture heritage: Plus some musings on academia* [Blog]. Retrieved from http://melissaterras.blogspot.ca/2012/04/is-blogging-and-tweeting-about-research.html (accessed 26 July 2016)

Veletsianos, G. (2012). 'Higher education scholars' participation and practices on Twitter', *Journal of Computer Assisted Learning*, 28(4): 336–349.

Warfield, K., Abidin, C., Andreallo, F., Murtell, J., Cambre, C., Miguel, C., Whitington-Wash, F., and Duguay, S. (2015). *Selfies: Inter-faces and 'me'-diated bodies, Social Media and Society*, Toronto, ON, July 27–28.

Web conferencing. (n.d.). Wikipedia. http://en.wikipedia.org/wiki/Web_conferencing (accessed 26 July 2016)

Wellman, B., Quan-Haase, A., Witte, J., and Hampton, K. (2001). 'Does the Internet increase, decrease, or supplement social capital? Social networks, participation, and community commitment', *American Behavioral Scientist*, 45(3): 437–456.

Westerman, D., Spence, P. R., and Van Der Heide, B. (2012). 'A social network as information: The effect of system generated reports of connectedness on credibility on Twitter', *Computers in Human Behavior*, 28(1): 199–206.

Xiang, Z. and Gretzel, U. (2010). 'Role of social media in online travel information search', *Tourism Management*, 31(2): 179–188.

Young, A. L. and Quan-Haase, A. (2013). 'Privacy protection strategies on Facebook', *Information, Communication & Society*, 16(4): 479–500.

Yuan, P., Bare, M. G., Johnson, M. O., and Saberi, P. (2014). 'Using online social media for recruitment of human immunodeficiency virus-positive participants: A cross-sectional survey', *Journal of Medical Internet Research*, 16(5): e117.

Big Data – Hype or Revolution?

Rob Kitchin

INTRODUCTION

The etymology of 'big data' can be traced to the mid-1990s, first used to refer to the handling and analysis of massive datasets (Diebold, 2012). Laney (2001) refined the definition to refer to data characterized by the now standard 3Vs, with big data being:

- huge in *volume*, consisting of terrabytes or petabytes of data;
- high in *velocity*, being created in or near real-time;
- diverse in *variety* in type, being structured and unstructured in nature.

More recently, these characteristics have been refined further to include:

- *exhaustive* in scope, striving to capture entire populations or systems (n=all);
- fine-grained in *resolution*, aiming to be as detailed as possible, and uniquely *indexical* in identification;
- *relational* in nature, containing common fields that enable the conjoining of different data sets;
- *flexible*, holding the traits of extensionality (can add new fields easily) and scalability (can expand in size rapidly) (boyd and Crawford, 2012; Dodge and Kitchin, 2005; Marz and Warren, 2012; Mayer-Schonberger and Cukier, 2013).

Data holding all or most of these qualities have existed in a number of domains, such as remote sensing, weather forecasting, and financial markets, for some time. By the turn of the new millennium they were starting to become more common given the development and convergence of new technological developments such as ubiquitous computing, widespread internetworking, Web 2.0. and the creation of social media, No-SQL database designs and cloud storage solutions, and data analytics designed to cope with data abundance (Kitchin, 2014a). From 2008 onward the term started to gain traction, quickly rising up a hype cycle aided by a strong boosterist discourse that contended big data was set to revolutionize how business is conducted and governance enacted. Not long after, the term drifted into common academic use accompanied by an argument that big data would transform how research would be conducted.

This chapter examines the latter contention and the extent to which big data and its associated data analytics represent a genuine revolution with respect to how we make sense of the world or whether it has been over-hyped and is merely a new inclusion amongst a suite of options in the academy's research armoury. The chapter starts by detailing how big data differs from traditional datasets used by social scientists. It then examines the argument that it is leading to the creation of new research paradigms across disciplines, what have been termed data-driven science, computational social science and digital humanities. In particular, it focuses on the extent to which social media data, in combination with other big social data, offers the possibility for a different kind of social science.

BIG DATA AND NEW DATA ANALYTICS

There is some scepticism within the literature as to the extent to which big data is anything new. Critics, usually focusing on the characteristic of volume, suggest that we have long possessed very large datasets that have been challenging to process and analyze. In part this is a reaction to the term 'big' which tends to emphasize the volume aspect of the 3Vs. However, it is the total sum of the characteristics noted above, especially the qualities of velocity and exhaustivity (see Kitchin and McArdle, 2016, for an examination of the ontological characteristics of 26 datasets drawn from seven domains: mobile communication; websites; social media/crowdsouring; sensors; cameras/lasers; transaction process generated data; and administrative), that make the nature of big data differ from traditional data, or what might be termed 'small data' (see Table 3.1). The distinction is apparent if

Table 3.1 Comparing small and big data

Characteristic	Small data	Big data
Volume	Limited to large	Very large
Exhaustivity	Samples	Entire populations
Resolution and indexicality	Coarse & weak to tight & strong	Tight & strong
Relationality	Weak to strong	Strong
Velocity	Slow, freeze-framed	Fast
Variety	Limited to wide	Wide
Flexible and scalable	Low to middling	High

Source: Kitchin (2014a: 28)

one compares a national census with a social media site such as Facebook.

While a national census has a large volume and attempts to be exhaustive (it seeks to sample all people resident in a country), it has very weak velocity (carried out once every ten years in most countries), weak variety (restricted to generally 30–40 highly structured questions), and no flexibility or scalability (once the census is initiated there is no opportunity to alter the questions or format). Moreover, while the raw data has high resolution and indexicality (individuals and households) it is released to researchers in an aggregated form. Other small data datasets are typically produced using a tightly controlled method using sampling techniques that limit their scope (non-exhaustive), temporality and size in order to produce high quality, representative data and make the process manageable and less costly. In contrast, Facebook has over a billion registered users globally and in 2014 was processing 10 billion messages (and associated comments and links), 4.5 billion 'Like' actions, and 350 million photo uploads *per day* (Marr, 2014). All that content and associated metadata is linked indexically to all individual users and through friending and tagging they are interlinked between users. Moreover, Facebook is a dynamic environment with the company constantly tweaking its platform and experimenting with different versions of its algorithms.

While the census is producing voluminous 'small data', Facebook is producing data that are qualitatively different in nature. In fact, Facebook is producing a data deluge – a constantly flowing torrent of rich, highly informative information about people, their lives, and what is happening in different societies in places around the world. The same is true of Twitter, Whatsapp, Snapchat, Foursquare and other social media platforms. When we compare Facebook to the data produced in most social science studies through surveys, political polls, interviews, or focus groups – where the number of respondents might be in the order of 10s or 100s and rarely exceeds 1000, the data are generated at a single point in time (usually over a couple of weeks or months), and are limited in variety – the difference becomes more stark. As detailed below, however, it should be noted that while the data produced within Facebook or Twitter is exhaustive, the data made available to researchers external to those companies might be sampled (though the sample generally consists of tens of thousands of records).

This kind of qualitative difference in the nature of data is happening across domains – health, education, work, consumption, finance, policing, public administration, science, etc. – in which new socio-technical systems are producing data through algorithmicallycontrolled and automated cameras, sensors, scanners, digital devices such as smart phones, clickstreams, and networked interactions such as online transactions (e.g., shopping) and communication (e.g., social media) (Kitchin, 2014a). For example, if we consider the developing areas of urban informatics a wealth of urban big data are being generated, much of it at the level of the individual: digital CCTV footage with facial/clothes recognition, automatic number plate recognition, sensor networks that track mobile phone unique signatures, and travel passes such as the London Oyster card (Kitchin, 2016). Other kinds of real-time data include the locations of buses and trains, how many bikes/spaces are in bike stands, road speeds on different segments, the number of spaces in car parks, general CCTV footage, air traffic, air quality, pollution readings, water levels, sound levels, current weather – all of which are increasingly becoming open in nature and underpin a diverse apps economy (e.g., see the Dublin Dashboard – http://www.dublindashboard.ie). To this we can add geo-referenced social media data (such as Twitter or Foursquare), crowdsourced data such OpenStreetMap, and live citizen city reporting (e.g., 311 services in the US and websites such as fixyourstreet.ie), and citizen science data such as personal weather stations.

These data are systematic and continuous in operation and coverage, verifiable and replicable, timely and traceable over time, and relatively easy to visualize and to compare across locales through graphs/maps (though they are not straightforward to plug into modelling, profiling and simulations). They offer the potential to shift from 'data-scarce to data-rich analysis, static snapshots to dynamic unfoldings, coarse aggregations to high resolution, and relatively simple hypotheses and models to more complex, sophisticated theories' (Kitchin, 2013: 263). How we come to know and understand cities, and how we can govern and operate their various systems, then is being transformed through access to big data streams (Batty, 2013; Townsend, 2013; Kitchin, 2014b; Kitchin et al., 2015). These big data also raise a whole series of ethical questions with respect to their use in dataveillance (surveillance through data records), social sorting (differential treatment to services), anticipatory governance (predictive profiling), control creep (data generated for one purpose being used for another) and the extent to which their systems make the city hackable, brittle and buggy (Townsend, 2013; Kitchin, 2014b, 2016).

Importantly, the development of the data deluge has been accompanied by the creation of new analytical methods suited to trying to extract insights from massive datasets using machine learning techniques, wherein the power of computational algorithms are used to process and analyze data. Again, there has been much hype concerning these new data analytics for three reasons. First, until recently, data analysis techniques were designed to extract insights from scarce, static, clean and poorly relational datasets, that were scientifically sampled and adhere to strict assumptions (such as independence, stationarity, and normality), whereas new data analytics can cope with a deluge of variable quality data (Miller, 2010). Second, whereas data was traditionally generated with a specific question in mind, new data analytics can repurpose data, detect and mine patterns, and identify potential questions that the data might answer (Kelling et al., 2009; Prensky, 2009). In other words, the hypotheses can be generated from the data. Third, an ensemble approach can be adopted in which, rather than selecting a single approach to analyze a phenomena, hundreds of different algorithms can be applied to a dataset to determine the best explanatory model (Franks, 2012; Siegel, 2013). These new analytical techniques have been in development since the start of computing but have become a significant area of recent research investment in order to increase the big data toolkit in four main areas: data mining and pattern recognition; data visualization and visual analytics; statistical analysis; and prediction, simulation, and optimization (National Science Foundation, 2012; Kitchin, 2014a). For many, big data and new data analytics will inevitably challenge dominant paradigms across the academy, ushering in new epistemologies in all disciplines and it is to this issue the chapter now turns.

A DATA REVOLUTION?

In Thomas Kuhn's (1962) well-known explanation as to how science periodically transforms from one dominant paradigm (an accepted way of interrogating the world and synthesizing knowledge) to another, an established body of knowledge is challenged and destabilized by a new set of ideas, eventually reaching a tipping point wherein the latter replaces the former. An example would be the shift from creationism to evolution, or Newtonian laws of physics to Einstein's theories of relativity. In Kuhn's account, a paradigm shift occurs because the dominant mode of science cannot account for particular phenomena or answer key questions. In contrast, Jim Gray (Hey et al., 2009) proposed that the transitions between paradigms can also be founded on advances in data production and the development of new analytical methods. Underpinning this view is the observation that '[r]evolutions in science have often been preceded by revolutions in measurement' (Sinan Aral, cited in Cukier, 2010). Gray thus proposed that science was entering a fourth paradigm (exploratory science) based on the growing availability of big data and new analytics (his first paradigm was 'experimental science' that operated pre-Renaissance, the second was 'theoretical science' operating pre-computers, and the third was 'computational science' operating pre-big data) (Hey et al., 2009).

The idea of academic paradigms has been subject to much critique, not least because within some disciplines there is little evidence of paradigms operating (notably some social sciences) and the idea tends to produce overly linear stories about how disciplines evolve, smoothing over the messy, contested and plural ways in which they unfold in practice. Nevertheless, the idea has utility here for considering whether the creation of big data has initiated a revolution in how academic research is being conducted. In particular, I explore three developments: (a) the notion that big data gives rise to the end of theory enabling a new form empiricism in which data can speak for themselves; (b) the creation of data-driven rather than knowledge-driven science; and (c) the formation of the digital humanities and computational social sciences.

The End of Theory?

For Chris Anderson (2008), big data, new data analytics and ensemble approaches signalled a new era of knowledge production characterized by 'the end of theory'. He argued that 'the data deluge makes the scientific method obsolete', with the patterns and relationships contained within big data inherently producing meaningful and insightful knowledge about phenomena. He continued:

> There is now a better way. Petabytes allow us to say: 'Correlation is enough.' ... We can analyze the data without hypotheses about what it might show. We can throw the numbers into the biggest computing clusters the world has ever seen and let statistical algorithms find patterns where science cannot. ... Correlation supersedes causation, and science can advance even without coherent models, unified theories, or really any mechanistic explanation at all. There's no reason to cling to our old ways.

Similarly, Prensky (2009) contends: 'scientists no longer have to make educated guesses, construct hypotheses and models, and test them with data-based experiments and examples. Instead, they can mine the complete set of data for patterns that reveal effects, producing scientific conclusions *without* further experimentation.' Dyche (2012) thus states that 'mining big data reveals relationships and patterns that we didn't even know to look for'. Dyche's example is a retail chain which analyzed 12 years' worth of purchase transactions for possible unnoticed relationships between products. Discovering correlations between certain items in shoppers' baskets led to new product placements and a 16 percent increase in revenue in the first month's trial. There was no hypothesis that Product A was often bought with Product H that was then tested. The data were simply queried to discover what relationships existed that might have previously been unnoticed. Similarly, Amazon's recommendation system produces suggestions for other items a shopper might be interested in without knowing anything about the culture and conventions of books and reading; it simply identifies patterns of purchasing across customers in order to determine if Person A likes Book X are they also likely to like Book Y given their own and others' consumption patterns?

There are a powerful and attractive set of ideas at work in this empiricist epistemology that run counter to the deductive approach that is hegemonic within modern science: big data can capture a whole of a domain and provide full resolution; there is no need for *a priori* theory, models or hypotheses; through the application of agnostic data analytics the data can speak for themselves free of human bias or framing, and that any patterns and relationships within big data are inherently meaningful and truthful; meaning transcends context or domain-specific knowledge, thus can be interpreted by anyone who can decode a statistic or data visualization. These work together to suggest that a new mode of science is being created, one in which the *modus operandi* is purely inductive in nature. Whilst this empiricist epistemology is attractive, it is based on fallacious thinking with respect to the four ideas that underpin its formulation. First, big data are not exhaustive being both a representation and a sample, shaped by the technology and platform used, the data ontology employed, the regulatory environment, and are subject to sampling bias (Crawford, 2013; Kitchin, 2013). Second, big data do not arise from nowhere, free from the 'the regulating force of philosophy' (Berry, 2011: 8). Contra, systems are designed to capture certain kinds of data and the analytics and algorithms used are based on scientific reasoning and have been refined through scientific testing. Third, just as data are not generated free from theory, neither can they simply speak for themselves free of human bias or framing. Making sense of data is always cast through a particular lens that frames how they are interpreted. Further, patterns found within a data set are not inherently meaningful and correlations between variables within a data set can be random in nature and have little or no casual association. Fourth, whilst data can be interpreted free of context and domain-specific expertise, such an epistemological interpretation is likely to be anemic or unhelpful as it lacks embedding in wider debates and knowledge.

Data-driven Science

In contrast, data-driven science seeks to hold to the tenets of the scientific method, but is more open to using a hybrid combination of abductive, inductive and deductive approaches to advance the understanding of a phenomenon. It differs from the traditional, experimental deductive design in that it seeks to generate hypotheses and insights 'born from the data' rather than 'born from the theory' (Kelling et al., 2009: 613). In other words, it seeks to incorporate a mode of induction into the research design, though explanation through induction is not the intended end-point (as with empiricist approaches). Instead, it forms a new mode of hypothesis generation before a deductive approach is employed. Nor does the process of induction arise from nowhere, but is situated and contextualized within a highly evolved theoretical domain. As such, the epistemological strategy adopted within data-driven science is to use guide knowledge discovery techniques to identify potential questions (hypotheses) worthy of further examination and testing. The process is guided in the sense that existing theory is used to direct the process of knowledge discovery, rather than simply hoping to identify all relationships within a dataset and assuming they are meaningful in some way. Any relationships revealed within the data do not then arise from nowhere, nor do they simply speak for themselves. The process of induction – of insights emerging from the data – is contextually framed. And those insights are not the end-point of an investigation, arranged and reasoned into a theory. Rather, the insights provide the basis for the formulation of hypotheses and the deductive testing of their validity. In other words, data-driven science is a reconfigured version of the traditional scientific method, providing a new way in which to build theory. Nonetheless, the epistemological change is significant.

Rather than empiricism and the end of theory, it is argued by some that data-driven science will become the new paradigm of scientific method in an age of big data because the epistemology favoured is suited to extracting additional, valuable insights that traditional 'knowledge-driven science' would fail to generate (Kelling et al., 2009; Miller, 2010; Loukides, 2010). Knowledge-driven science, using a straight deductive approach, has particular utility in understanding and explaining the world under the conditions of scarce data and weak computation. Continuing to use such an approach, however, when technological and methodological advances mean that it is possible to undertake much richer analysis of data and to identify and tackle questions in new and exciting ways, makes little sense. Moreover, the advocates of data-driven science argue that it is much more suited to exploring, extracting value and making sense of massive, interconnected data sets; fostering interdisciplinary research that conjoins domain expertise (as it is less limited by the starting theoretical frame); and will lead to more holistic and extensive models and theories of entire complex systems rather than elements of them (Kelling et al., 2009).

Computational Social Sciences and Digital Humanities

Whilst the epistemologies of big data empiricism and data-driven science seems set to transform the approach to research taken in the natural, life, physical and engineering sciences, its trajectory in the humanities and social sciences is less certain. These areas of scholarship are highly diverse in their philosophical underpinnings, with only some scholars employing the epistemology common in the sciences. For scholars in the social sciences who employ quantitative approaches big data offers a significant opportunity to develop more sophisticated, wider-scale, finer-grained models of human life.

Moreover, the variety, exhaustivity, resolution, and relationality of data, plus the growing power of computation and new data analytics, address some of the critiques of such scholarship to date, especially those of reductionism and universalism, by providing more sensitive and nuanced analysis that can take account of context and contingency, and can be used to refine and extend theoretical understandings of the social and spatial world (Lazer *et al.*, 2009; Batty *et al.*, 2012; Kitchin, 2013). Further, given the extensiveness of data (e.g., all social media posts of a society, all movements within a city) it is possible to test the veracity of such theory across a variety of settings and situations.

For post-positivist scholars, big data offers both opportunities and challenges. The opportunities are a proliferation, digitization and interlinking of a diverse set of analogue and unstructured data, much of it new (e.g., social media) and many of which have heretofore been difficult to access (e.g., millions of books, documents, newspapers, photographs, art works, material objects, etc.) from across history that have been rendered into digital form over the past couple of decades by a range of organizations (Cohen, 2008); and the provision of new tools of data curation, management and analysis that can handle massive numbers of data objects. Consequently, rather than concentrating on a handful of novels or photographs, or a couple of artists and their work, it becomes possible to search and connect across a large number of related works; rather than focus on a handful of websites or chat rooms or videos or online newspapers, it becomes possible to examine hundreds of thousands of such media (Manovich, 2011). These opportunities are most widely being examined through the emerging field of digital humanities.

Initially, the digital humanities consisted of the curation and analysis of data that are born digital and the digitization and archiving projects that sought to render analogue texts and material objects into digital forms that could be organized and searched and be subjected to basic forms of overarching, automated or guided analysis such as summary visualizations of content (Schnapp and Presner, 2009). Subsequently, its advocates have been divided into two camps. Those that believe new digital humanities techniques – counting, graphing, mapping and distant reading – will bring methodological rigour and objectivity to disciplines that heretofore been unsystematic and random in their focus and approach (Moretti, 2005; Ramsay, 2010). And those that argue the new techniques complement and augment existing humanities methods and facilitate traditional forms of interpretation and theory building, enabling studies of much wider scope and to answer questions that would all but impossible without computation (Berry, 2011; Manovich, 2011).

The digital humanities has not been universally welcomed with detractors contending that using computers as 'reading machines' (Ramsay, 2010) to undertake 'distant reading' (Moretti, 2005) runs counter to and undermines traditional methods of close reading. Marche (2012) contends that cultural artefacts, such as literature, cannot be treated as mere data. A piece of writing is not simply an order of letters and words, it is contextual and conveys meaning and has qualities that are ineffable. Algorithms are very poor at capturing and deciphering meaning or context. For many, the digital humanities is fostering weak, surface analysis, rather than deep, penetrating insight. It is overly reductionist and crude in its techniques, sacrificing complexity, specificity, context, depth and critique for scale, breadth, automation, descriptive patterns and the impression that interpretation does not require deep contextual knowledge.

The same kinds of argument can be levelled at computational social science. For example, a map of the language of tweets in a city might reveal patterns of geographic concentration of different ethnic communities (Rogers, 2013), but the important questions are who constitutes such concentrations, why do they exist, what were the processes of formation and reproduction, and what are their social and economic consequences? It is one thing to identify patterns; it is another to explain them. This requires social theory and deep contextual knowledge. As such, the pattern is not the end point, but rather a starting point for additional analysis, which almost certainly is going to require other data sets. As with earlier critiques of quantitative and positivist social sciences, computational social sciences is taken to task by post-positivists as being mechanistic, atomizing, and parochial, reducing diverse individuals and complex, multidimensional social structures to mere data points (Wyly, 2014).

There is a potentially fruitful middle ground to this debate that adopts and extends the epistemologies employed in critical GIS and radical statistics. These approaches employ quantitative techniques, inferential statistics, modelling and simulation whilst being mindful and open with respect to their epistemological shortcomings, drawing on critical social theory to frame how the research is conducted, how sense is made of the findings, and the knowledge employed. Here, there is recognition that there is an inherent politics pervading the datasets analysed, the research conducted, and the interpretations made (Haraway, 1991). As such, it is acknowledged: that the researcher possesses a certain positionality (with respect to their knowledge, experience, beliefs, aspirations, etc.); that the research is situated (within disciplinary debates, the funding landscape, wider societal politics, etc.); the data are reflective of the technique used to generate them and hold certain characteristics (relating to sampling and ontological frames, data cleanliness, completeness, consistency, veracity and fidelity); and the methods of analysis utilized produce particular effects with respect to the results produced and interpretations made. Such an epistemology also does not foreclose complementing situated computational social science with small data studies that provide additional and amplifying insights (Crampton et al., 2012). In other words, it is possible to think of new epistemologies that do not dismiss or reject big data analytics, but rather employ the methodological approach of data-driven science within a different epistemological framing that enables social scientists to draw valuable insights from big data.

THE LIMITS OF SOCIAL MEDIA BIG DATA

The discussion so far has argued that there is something qualitatively different about big data from small data and that it opens up new epistemological possibilities, some of which have more value than others. In general terms, it has been intimated that big data does represent a revolution in measurement that will inevitably lead to a revolution in how academic research is conducted; that big data studies will replace small data ones. However, this is unlikely to be the case for a number of reasons.

Whilst small data may be limited in volume and velocity, they have a long history of development across science, state agencies, non-governmental organizations and business, with established methodologies and modes of analysis, and a record of producing meaningful answers. Small data studies can be much more finely tailored to answer specific research questions and to explore in detail and in-depth the varied, contextual, rational and irrational ways in which people interact and make sense of the world, and how processes work. Small data can focus on specific cases and tell individual, nuanced and contextual stories.

Big data is often being repurposed to try and answer questions for which it was never designed. For example, geotagged Twitter data have not been produced to provide answers with respect to the geographical concentration of language groups in a city and the processes driving such spatial autocorrelation.

We should perhaps not be surprised then that it only provides a surface snapshot, albeit an interesting snapshot, rather than deep penetrating insights into the geographies of race, language, agglomeration and segregation in particular locales. Moreover, big data might seek to be exhaustive, but as with all data they are both a representation and a sample. What data are captured is shaped by: the field of view/sampling frame (where data capture devices are deployed and what their settings/parameters are; who uses a space or media, e.g., who belongs to Facebook); the technology and platform used (different surveys, sensors, lens, textual prompts, layout, etc. all produce variances and biases in what data are generated); the context in which data are generated (unfolding events mean data are always situated with respect to circumstance); the data ontology employed (how the data are calibrated and classified); and the regulatory environment with respect to privacy, data protection and security (Kitchin, 2013, 2014a). Further, big data generally capture what is easy to ensnare – data that are openly expressed (what is typed, swiped, scanned, sensed, etc.; people's actions and behaviours; the movement of things) – as well as data that are the 'exhaust', a by-product, of the primary task/output.

Small data studies then mine gold from working a narrow seam, whereas big data studies seek to extract nuggets through open-pit mining, scooping up and sieving huge tracts of land. These two approaches of narrow versus open mining have consequences with respect to data quality, fidelity and lineage. Given the limited sample sizes of small data, data quality – how clean (error and gap free), objective (bias free) and consistent (few discrepancies) the data are; veracity – the authenticity of the data and the extent to which they accurately (precision) and faithfully (fidelity, reliability) represent what they are meant to; and lineage – documentation that establishes provenance and fit for use; are of paramount importance (Lauriault, 2012). In contrast, it has been argued by some that big data studies do not need the same standards of data quality, veracity and lineage because the exhaustive nature of the dataset removes sampling biases and more than compensates for any errors or gaps or inconsistencies in the data or weakness in fidelity (Mayer-Schonberger and Cukier, 2013). The argument for such a view is that 'with less error from sampling we can accept more measurement error' (p. 13) and 'tolerate inexactitude' (p. 16).

Nonetheless, the warning 'garbage in, garbage out' still holds. The data can be biased due to the demographic being sampled (e.g., not everybody uses Twitter) or the data might be gamed or faked through false accounts or hacking (e.g., there are hundreds of thousands of fake Twitter accounts seeking to influence trending and direct clickstream trails) (Bollier, 2010; Crampton et al., 2012). Moreover, the technology being used and their working parameters can affect the nature of the data. For example, which posts on social media are most read or shared are strongly affected by ranking algorithms not simply interest (Baym, 2013). Similarly, APIs structure what data are extracted, for example, in Twitter only capturing specific hashtags associated with an event rather than all relevant tweets (Bruns, 2013), with González-Bailón et al. (2012) finding that different methods of accessing Twitter data – search APIs versus streaming APIs – produced quite different sets of results. As a consequence, there is no guarantee that two teams of researchers attempting to gather the same data at the same time will end up with identical datasets (Bruns, 2013). Further, the choice of metadata and variables that are being generated and which ones are being ignored paint a particular picture (Graham, 2012). With respect to fidelity there are question marks as to the extent to which social media posts really represent peoples' views and the faith that should be placed in them. Manovich (2011: 6) warns that '[p]eoples' posts, tweets, uploaded photographs, comments, and other types of online participation are not transparent windows into their selves; instead, they are often carefully curated and systematically managed'.

There are also issues of access to both small and big data. Small data produced by academia, public institutions, non-governmental organizations and private entities can be restricted in access, limited in use to defined personnel, or available for a fee or under license. Increasingly, however, public institution and academic data are becoming more open. Big data are, with a few exceptions such as satellite imagery and national security and policing, mainly produced by the private sector. Access is usually restricted behind pay walls and proprietary licensing, limited to ensure competitive advantage and to leverage income through their sale or licensing (CIPPIC, 2006). Indeed, it is somewhat of a paradox that only a handful of entities are drowning in the data deluge (boyd and Crawford, 2012) and companies such as mobile phone operators, app developers, social media providers, financial institutions, retail chains, and surveillance and security firms are under no obligation to share freely the data they collect through their operations. In some cases, a limited amount of the data might be made available to researchers or the public through Application Programming Interfaces (APIs). For example, Twitter allows a few companies to access its firehose (stream of data) for a fee for commercial purposes (and have the latitude to dictate terms with respect to what can be done with such data), but with a handful of exceptions researchers are restricted to a 'gardenhose' (c. 10 percent of public tweets), a 'spritzer' (c. 1 percent of public tweets), or to different subsets of content ('white-listed' accounts), with private and protected tweets excluded in all cases (boyd and Crawford, 2012). The worry is that the insights that privately owned and commercially sold big data can provide will be limited to a privileged set of academic researchers whose findings cannot be replicated or validated (Lazer et al., 2009).

Given the relative strengths and limitations of big and small data it is fair to say that small data studies will continue to be an important element of the research landscape, despite the benefits that might accrue from using big data such as social media data. However, it should be noted that small data studies will increasingly come under pressure to utilize the new archiving technologies, being scaled-up within digital data infrastructures in order that they are preserved for future generations, become accessible to re-use and combination with other small and big data, and more value and insight can be extracted from them through the application of big data analytics.

CONCLUSION

There is little doubt that much of the rhetoric concerning big data is hyped and is boosterist, especially that produced by companies seeking to push new big data products, or research centres seeking to capture grant income. At the same time, there is no doubt that big data are qualitatively different to traditional small data and it does offer the potential to change how business is conducted, societies are governed, and academic research conducted. Big data and new data analytics do offer the possibility of reframing the epistemology of science, social science and humanities (though it will not lead to the 'end of theory'), and such a reframing is already actively taking place across disciplines. Nonetheless, small data studies will continue to be valuable because they have a tried and tested track record of producing insights by working a narrow seam and due to the various shortcomings of big data. As such, one can argue that there is a revolution underway, and that it will have profound effects, but that it will not lead to full-scale regime change. With respect to social media data then, its analysis will no doubt have a strong and positive impact on sociological and geographical research, providing a very rich, extensive, longitudinal set of data and studies, but these are most likely to complementary to a plethora of other studies.

ACKNOWLEDGEMENTS

The research for this chapter was funded by a European Research Council Advanced Investigator Award (ERC-2012-AdG-323636-SOFTCITY). The chapter draws heavily on a previously published paper – Kitchin, R. (2014) Big data, new epistemologies and paradigm shifts. *Big Data and Society* 1 (April-June): 1–12 – and also Chapter 2 of Kitchin, R. (2014) *The Data Revolution: Big Data, Open Data, Data Infrastructures and Their Consequences*. SAGE, London.

REFERENCES

Anderson, C. (2008) The End of Theory: The Data Deluge Makes the Scientific Method Obsolete. *Wired*, 23rd June, http://www.wired.com/science/discoveries/magazine/16-07/pb_theory (last accessed 12 October 2012).

Batty, M. (2013) *The New Science of Cities*. MIT Press: Cambridge, MA.

Batty, M., Axhausen, K.W., Giannotti, F., Pozdnoukhov, A., Bazzani, A., Wachowicz, M., Ouzounis, G. and Portugali, Y. (2012) Smart cities of the future. *European Physical Journal Special Topics* 214: 481–518.

Baym, N.K. (2013) Data not seen: The uses and shortcomings of social media metrics. *First Monday* 18(10), http://firstmonday.org/ojs/index.php/fm/article/view/4873/3752 (last accessed 3 January 2014).

Berry, D. (2011) The computational turn: Thinking about the digital humanities. *Culture Machine* 12, http://www.culturemachine.net/index.php/cm/article/view/440/470 (last accessed 3 December 2012).

Bollier, D. (2010) *The Promise and Peril of Big Data*. The Aspen Institute. http://www.aspeninstitute.org/sites/default/files/content/docs/pubs/The_Promise_and_Peril_of_Big_Data.pdf (last accessed 1 October 2012).

boyd, D. and Crawford, K. (2012) Critical questions for big data. *Information, Communication and Society* 15(5): 662–679.

Bruns, A. (2013) Faster than the speed of print: Reconciling 'big data' social media analysis and academic scholarship. *First Monday* 18(10), http://firstmonday.org/ojs/index.php/fm/article/view/4879/3756 (last accessed 3 January 2014).

CIPPIC (2006) *On the Data Trail: How detailed information about you gets into the hands of organizations with whom you have no relationship. A Report on the Canadian Data Brokerage Industry*. The Canadian Internet Policy and Public Interest Clinic, Ottawa. http://www.cippic.ca/uploads/May1-06/DatabrokerReport.pdf (last accessed 17 January 2014).

Cohen, D. (2008) Contribution to: The Promise of Digital History (roundtable discussion), *Journal of American History* 95(2): 452–491.

Crampton, J., Graham, M., Poorthuis, A., Shelton, T., Stephens, M., Wilson, M.W. and Zook, M. (2012) *Beyond the Geotag? Deconstructing 'Big Data' and leveraging the Potential of the Geoweb*. http://www.uky.edu/~tmute2/geography_methods/readingPDFs/2012-Beyond-the-Geotag-2012.10.01.pdf (last accessed 21 February 2013).

Crawford, K. (2013) The hidden biases of big data. *Harvard Business Review Blog*. April 1st. http://blogs.hbr.org/2013/04/the-hidden-biases-in-big-data/ (last accessed 18 September 2013).

Cukier, K. (2010) Data, data everywhere. *The Economist*, February 25th. http://www.economist.com/node/15557443 (last accessed 12 November 2012).

Diebold, F. (2012) *A personal perspective on the origin(s) and development of 'big data': The phenomenon, the term, and the discipline*. http://www.ssc.upenn.edu/~fdiebold/papers/paper112/Diebold_Big_Data.pdf (last accessed 5 February 2013).

Dodge, M. and Kitchin, R. (2005) Codes of life: Identification codes and the machine-readable world. *Environment and Planning D: Society and Space* 23(6): 851–881.

Dyche, J. (2012) Big Data 'Eurekas!' Don't Just Happen. *Harvard Business Review Blog*, 20th

November. http://blogs.hbr.org/cs/2012/11/eureka_doesnt_just_happen.html (last accessed 23 November 2012).

Franks, B. (2012) *Taming the Big Data Tidal Wave: Finding Opportunities in Huge Data Streams with Advanced Analytics*. Wiley: Hoboken, NJ.

González-Bailón, S., Wang, N., Rivero, A., Borge-Holtoefer, J. and Moreno, Y. (2012) Assessing the Bias in Communication Networks Sampled from Twitter. Working Paper. http://arxiv.org/abs/1212.1684 (last accessed 17 January 2014).

Graham, M. (2012) Big data and the end of theory? *The Guardian*, 9th March. http://www.guardian.co.uk/news/datablog/2012/mar/09/big-data-theory (last accessed 12 November 2012).

Haraway, D. (1991) *Simians, Cyborgs and Women: The Reinvention of Nature*. Routledge: New York.

Hey, T., Tansley, S. and Tolle, K. (2009) Jim Grey on eScience: A transformed scientific method, in Hey, T., Tansley, S. and Tolle, K. (eds) *The Fourth Paradigm: Data-Intensive Scientific Discovery*. Microsoft Research; Redmond, Washington. xvii-xxxi.

Kelling, S., Hochachka, W., Fink, D., Riedewald, M., Caruana, R., Ballard, G. and Hooker, G. (2009) Data-intensive Science: A New Paradigm for Biodiversity Studies. *BioScience* 59(7): 613–620.

Kitchin, R. (2013) Big data and human geography: Opportunities, challenges and risks. *Dialogues in Human Geography* 79(1): 1–14.

Kitchin, R. (2014a) *The Data Revolution: Big Data, Open Data, Data Infrastructures and Their Consequences*. SAGE: London.

Kitchin, R. (2014b) The real-time city? Big data and smart urbanism. *Geojournal* 3(3): 262–267.

Kitchin, R. (2016) *Getting smarter about smart cities: Improving data privacy and data security*. Data Protection Unit, Department of the Taoiseach, Dublin, Ireland.

Kitchin, R. and McArdle, G. (2016) What makes big data, big data? Exploring the ontological characteristics of 26 datasets. *Big Data & Society* 3: 1–10.

Kitchin, R., Lauriault, T. and McArdle, G. (2015) Knowing and governing cities through urban indicators, city benchmarking and real-time dashboards. *Regional Studies, Regional Science* 2: 1–28.

Kuhn, T. (1962) *The Structure of Scientific Revolutions*. University of Chicago Press, Chicago.

Laney, D. (2001) 3D Data Management: Controlling Data Volume, Velocity and Variety. *Meta Group*. http://blogs.gartner.com/doug-laney/files/2012/01/ad949–3D-Data-Management-Controlling-Data-Volume-Velocity-and-Variety.pdf (last accessed 16 January 2013).

Lauriault, T.P. (2012) *Data, Infrastructures and Geographical Imaginations: Mapping Data Access Discourses in Canada*. PhD Thesis, Carleton University, Ottawa.

Lazer, D., Pentland, A., Adamic, L., Aral, S., Barabási, A-L., Brewer, D., Christakis, N., Contractor, N., Fowler, J., Gutmann, M., Jebara, T., King, G., Macy, M., Roy, D. and Van Alstyne, M. (2009) Computational Social Science. *Science* 323: 721–733.

Loukides, M. (2010) What is data science? *O'Reilly Radar*, 2nd June 2010, http://radar.oreilly.com/2010/06/what-is-data-science.html (last accessed 28 January 2013).

Manovich, L. (2011) *Trending: The Promises and the Challenges of Big Social Data*. http://www.manovich.net/DOCS/Manovich_trending_paper.pdf (last accessed 9th November 2012).

Marche, S. (2012) Literature is not Data: Against Digital Humanities. *Los Angeles Review of Books*, 28 October 2012, http://lareviewofbooks.org/article.php?id=1040&fulltext=1 (last accessed 4 April 2013).

Marr, B. (2014) Big Data: The 5 Vs Everyone Must Know. Mar 6, https://www.linkedin.com/pulse/20140306073407–64875646-big-data-the-5-vs-everyone-must-know (last accessed 4th September 2015)

Marz, N. and Warren, J. (2012) *Big Data. Principles and Best Practices of Scalable Realtime Data Systems*. MEAP edition. Manning, Shelter Island, New York.

Mayer-Schonberger, V. and Cukier, K. (2013) *Big Data: A Revolution that will Change How We Live, Work and Think*. John Murray: London.

Miller, H.J. (2010) The data avalanche is here. Shouldn't we be digging? *Journal of Regional Science* 50(1): 181–201.

Moretti, F. (2005) *Graphs, Maps, Trees: Abstract Models for a Literary History.* Verso, London.

National Science Foundation (2012) *Core Techniques and Technologies for Advancing Big Data Science & Engineering (BIGDATA).* Programme solicitation NSF 12–499, http://www.nsf.gov/pubs/2012/nsf12499/nsf12499.pdf (last accessed 25 February 2013).

Prensky, M. (2009) H. sapiens digital: From digital immigrants and digital natives to digital wisdom. *Innovate* 5(3), http://www.innovate-online.info/index.php?view=article&id=705 (last accessed 12 October 2012).

Ramsay, S. (2010) *Reading Machines: Towards an Algorithmic Criticism.* University of Illinois Press: Champaign, IL.

Rogers, S. (2013) Twitter's languages of New York mapped. *The Guardian*, 21st February 2013 http://www.guardian.co.uk/news/datablog/interactive/2013/feb/21/twitter-languages-new-york-mapped (last accessed 3 April 2013).

Schnapp, J. and Presner, P. (2009) *Digital Humanities Manifesto 2.0.* http://www.humanitiesblast.com/manifesto/Manifesto_V2.pdf (last accessed 13 March 2013).

Siegel, E. (2013) *Predictive Analytics.* Wiley: Hoboken, NJ.

Townsend, A. (2013) *Smart Cities: Big Data, Civic Hackers, and the Quest for a New Utopia.* W.W. Norton & Co: New York.

Wyly, E. (2014) Automated (post)positivism. *Urban Geography* 35(5): 669–690.

Building Interdisciplinary Social Media Research Teams: Motivations, Challenges, and Policy Frameworks

Anabel Quan-Haase and Lori McCay-Peet

Interdisciplinary research (IDR) has become integral to the evolving field of social media research. But, what drives interdisciplinary approaches in social media research? Is it the methodological challenges of understanding multilevel social phenomena that lead to the formation of teams that integrate concepts, frameworks, and methodologies from various disciplines? In the context of social media research, this chapter describes what interdisciplinary teams are, motivations for their development, challenges faced, and the policies that currently help and hinder their success. Prior research demonstrates the importance of interdisciplinarity for creativity and innovation as well as the difficulties associated with achieving coherence when teams consist of members with diverse disciplinary backgrounds, who are located in different institutions or geographical locations. This leads us to conclude that some diversity is necessary, but too much diversity can get in the way of achieving successful research outcomes. We propose ways in which the social media research community can strengthen the outcomes of IDR teams and work satisfaction through community discussions on the composition, practices, and outcomes of IDR teams and the development of social media IDR toolkits.

INTRODUCTION

Social media are generally defined as 'web sites and applications which enable users to create and share content or to participate in social networking' (Merriam Webster, n.d.). Social media research entails the study of various platforms that host user-generated content, the data created by users on these sites–including profiles, updates, posts, and comments—and the patterns and networks that emerge from interactions among users. As a result of the diversity of research problems that can be examined, it is an area of research best tackled by scholars from a variety of different disciplines (Kane, Alavi, Labianca, and Borgatti, 2014) who can draw on diverse methods, theoretical lenses, and interpretative frameworks (Aragón, Laniado, Neff, Ruiz de Querol, Kaltenbrunner, Ullod, Kappler, and Volkovich, 2012).

The literature on IDR teams that focuses on social media research questions is sparse (exceptions include, Aragón et al., 2012; Stieglitz, Dang-Xuan, Bruns, and Neuberger, 2014). While much academic writing has addressed what interdisciplinarity means (Huutoniemi, Klein, Bruun, and Hukkinen, 2010), how it is implemented (Quan-Haase, Suarez, and Brown, 2014; Balakrischnan, Kiesler, Cummings, and Zadeh, 2011), its benefits and challenges (Siemens, 2009), and the role of policy (Cummings and Kiesler, 2007), few studies explicitly focus on teams investigating social media-related research problems. Rather, research has examined academics' use of social media in the context of work (Gruzd, Staves, and Wilk, 2012; Rasmussen Neal, 2012), their integration of specific platforms for research purposes (Holmberg and Thelwall, 2014; Quan-Haase, Martin, and McCay-Peet, 2015), and their personal experiences with reaching other scholars and the public through their social media engagement (Ross, Terras, Warwick, and Welsh, 2011; Clavel, Fox, Leo, Quan-Haase, Saitta, and LaDale, 2015). We begin this chapter by defining what interdisciplinary research teams are in the context of social media scholarship. We then explore some of the motivations for the development of IDR teams and the challenges that accompany this particular type of teamwork. Our discussion ends with an overview of current policy initiatives and how these affect the building of IDR teams.

INTERDISCIPLINARY RESEARCH TEAMS DEFINED

Since the 1960s, interdisciplinary research (IDR) has become a very attractive, yet challenging, research approach (Huutoniemi et al., 2010): it has the potential to address research questions and problems, but does not align with a single academic discipline (Stember, 1991). IDR is difficult to define, operationalize, and evaluate and 'best understood not as one thing but as a variety of different ways of bridging and confronting the prevailing disciplinary approaches' (Huutoniemi et al., 2010: 80). IDR does not necessarily call for a team approach. Rather, it may be practiced by a single scholar who draws on theoretical and/or methodological approaches from two or more disciplines or fields to address a research problem or question that does not fit within the confines of a traditional discipline. For example, an interdisciplinary doctoral project conducted at the University of Oslo by Niamh Ní Bhroin (University of Oslo, 2014) titled 'Social Media and Minority Language Users' draws on both social sciences and humanities research methods to examine the meanings minority language users give to the term *social media*. IDR has also been used to refer to collaborations between researchers and industry, non-profit, and government partners who come together with the aim of developing new products or processes. An example of this kind of collaboration is the interdisciplinary team of researchers from the Museum of Anthropology (MOA), the Musqueam Indian Band, and Simon Fraser University in Canada, who worked together to develop an interactive tabletop exhibit designed to encourage dialogue among visitors to the Museum of Anthropology (MOA) (Luckow, 2015). Most commonly IDR is associated with the efforts of a team of researchers from disparate disciplines, working toward a shared goal. Conole, Scanlon,

Mundin, and Farrow, in their discussion of IDR research in the field of technology enhanced learning, described interdisciplinarity as a way in which 'researchers from two or more disciplines bring their approaches and adapt them to form a solution to a new problem' (2010: 6). Our discussion of IDR shows that numerous approaches exist to embark on this kind of work, varying in scope, scale, and mode of integration.

IDR is often used as an umbrella term for a variety of forms of research that cross disciplinary boundaries. Each type of research, however, has its own processes, goals, and outcomes (Huutoniemi et al., 2010; Stember, 1991). Stember (1991) proposed a research typology, which ranged from *intradisciplinary*, or within disciplinary research, to *transdisciplinary*, the most holistic approach to research, which seeks to unify disparate disciplinary perspectives into a new discipline. Between intradisciplinary and transdisciplinary lie a wide range of research approaches. *Cross-disciplinary* research occurs when a researcher views a discipline from an alternative discipline's perspective. *Multidisciplinary* research requires researchers from multiple disciplines working independently to provide multiple perspectives on a research problem, while *interdisciplinary* research seeks to integrate multiple disciplines in order to best solve a single research problem.

We use the term interdisciplinary in its broadest form, referring to 'all collaboration across epistemological boundaries' (Huutoniemi et al., 2010: 83) or 'a mode of research that transgresses traditional disciplinary boundaries' (Siedlok and Hibbert, 2014: 197). One definition of IDR that captures this broad perspective on interdisciplinarity is provided by the National Science Foundation (NSF) on its web site:

> a mode of research by teams or individuals that integrates information, data, techniques, tools, perspectives, concepts, and/or theories from two or more disciplines or bodies of specialized knowledge to advance fundamental understanding or to solve problems whose solutions are beyond the scope of a single discipline or area of research practice. (National Science Foundation, 2014: n.p.)

The NSF stresses that integration *can* occur across disciplines in a wide range of areas, including the use of tools and techniques, which is of particular relevance to discussions of IDR in social media scholarship, as illustrated in our discussion on motivations for IDR social media teams. The take away message then is that different groups interpret the meaning of interdisciplinarity in different ways, and for some it is simply working in teams while for others it consists of a deeper level of integration in terms of mixing philosophical standpoints such that the starting point for the research is an interdisciplinary theoretical framework (e.g., Love and Cooper, 2015).

MOTIVATIONS FOR BUILDING IDR SOCIAL MEDIA TEAMS

Much effort has gone into the creation of boundary spanning teams that are large, diverse, and geographically dispersed as a means to foster innovation and creativity, and to solve complex problems (Balakrishnan et al., 2011; Quan-Haase et al., 2014). This movement toward interdisciplinarity is also visible in social media research, which has attracted a diverse set of scholars from a wide range of disciplines. Social media IDR focuses on integrating very specific kinds of expertise: there is a need to integrate technical expertise more common in computer science and engineering with domain-specific knowledge about social phenomena existent in the social sciences and humanities. Analysis cannot be limited to looking at and visualizing patterns, rather approaches need to be developed that give justice to what is essentially social data and interpret the data in light of social processes.

Through a systematic review of the IDR literature, Siedlok and Hibbert (2014) identified three main 'drivers' of IDR, which shed light on why social media researchers may be drawn to this kind of collaborative endeavour:

1. *Complexity*: the assumption that complex problems require complex solutions through IDR approaches.
2. *Motivational factors*: the combination of personal and professional reasons for undertaking IDR (e.g., intellectual curiosity and career opportunities).
3. *Creative potential*: the idea that IDR will lead to innovative and new approaches and solutions, that can also benefit 'native disciplines'.

All three of these factors apply to what motivates social media IDR teams to form and will be discussed next in more detail.

Complexity

Social media research problems tend to be complex. As various studies have demonstrated, there is an 'emerging need to continuously collect, monitor, analyze, summarize, and visualize relevant information from social interactions and user-generated content in various domains' (Stieglitz et al., 2014: 90). Each of these activities requires an understanding of the intricacies of how social media platforms work and their technical specifications. What further complicates the study of social media data is that these data tend to be networked in nature, making it difficult to determine what data to collect and where to draw boundaries. Also, social media data are dynamic and can be investigated at various levels of analysis ranging from characteristics of individuals, to network topological features, to changes occurring over time.

Previous studies suggest that social media scholarship is best addressed in IDR teams because social media research requires the integration of technical expertise with knowledge of social phenomena. Kane et al. (2014) have described this unique requirement of social media scholarship in terms of two challenges:

1. *the technological challenge*: understanding which platforms count as social media, and where the boundaries need to be drawn between these sites and
2. *the behavioral challenge*: investigating what users of these sites do, why they do this, and what it actually means.

Hence, a genuine curiosity for providing answers to research questions that require a seamless integration of the technological and behavioural domains drive the building of IDR teams. While Kane et al. (2014) originally define the technological challenge as identifying social media platforms, it is important to realize that many other technological challenges are present in a social media project. These also include such tasks as scraping data, data preparation for analysis, and data manipulation. Social theory can drive the formulation of important research questions and hypotheses, instead of relying on *data fishing* (Anderson, 2008). But technical expertise alone does not provide a good understanding of social phenomena, only through the application of pertinent social theory can scholars make sense of patterns in data – this is the behavioural challenge.

Teams can be particularly relevant. When 'off the shelf' tools are unavailable for answering a specific research question, it is then imperative to have team members who are able to develop a sound approach to acquire the needed data. One participant in Balakrishnan et al.'s study on research team integration, for example, reported that 'a lot of the code in my group has been written with a computer scientist and an astronomer working side-by, literally, sitting side-by-side at a single keyboard' (2011: 523). There are regular requests for information via the Association of Internet Researchers list serv (AIR-L), for example, on how to collect and analyze specific types of social media data from particular groups of people. While there are an increasing number of tools available to social media researchers, developing an interdisciplinary social media team that is able to tackle the intricacies of the group's research problem by creating the right tools for the job is advantageous. Moreover, tools such as Topsy (http://topsy.com) provide researchers with a way to search and analyse social media data, but having team members with the knowledge and understanding of the technological limitations of specific data collection and analysis techniques is critical.

While the technological and behavioral challenges are key drivers in the building of IDR teams, a third key factor is the ethical challenge. Much recent writing has called for careful consideration of the ethical underpinnings in collecting and storing massive amounts of user-generated content, even if technically possible. Beninger et al. (2014) report that not all users of social media sites are comfortable with (or aware of) their data being utilized for analysis without their prior consent. boyd and Crawford (2012) also draw attention to problems inherent in the collection of big data without sufficient consideration of the ethical dimensions. While small-scale studies do not harvest massive amounts of data, they may equally encounter ethical concerns with the use of data from participants without prior consent (Sloan and Quan-Haase, Chapter 39, this volume). This may actually be an even greater concern for small-scale qualitative researchers, where it is easier to identify single users. As a result it becomes increasingly important to engage in critical discourses around how data from social media are gathered and used in scholarly research. To properly assess and take into account the ethical dimensions of any social media project, it is important to include team members who have this kind of expertise.

Motivational Factors

Individual-level motivational factors for joining social media IDR teams include a genuine curiosity to discover how a research problem can be tackled from different perspectives. Networking with colleagues in other disciplines can have many benefits including the sharing of ideas, consulting about technical aspects of the problem, discussing appropriate theoretical approaches, and disseminating research findings (Quan-Haase et al., 2014). The premise of conducting research activities in social media IDR teams is to fall nothing short of fully integrating research activities, thus it goes 'beyond post facto reporting back by networking across sectors throughout the entire research process' (Sprain, Endres, and Petersen, 2010: 443). This entails engaging as a team in a wide range of activities including research design, data collection, analysis, interpretation, and the write-up and dissemination of findings. In some social media IDR teams, this networking is not limited to scholars but often includes trans-sectoral ties with stakeholders and policy makers who are interested in a specific research problem (Quan-Haase et al., 2014; Sprain et al., 2010).

Hand-in-hand with personal motivations for IDR research are the career opportunities that can include, for example, the establishment of large clusters of interdisciplinary scholars with the goal of increasing the exchange of information, collaborative writing and publishing, as well as the possibilities for networking with experts across domains. Becoming a member of large research clusters can be beneficial in applying for grants, as funding agencies encourage, and often also require, an IDR component in their call for proposals (Siedlok and Hibbert, 2014). This suggests that the move towards IDR teams is not only an organic development, but is also a result of pressures from funding organizations and their views of how innovation, new insights, and complex research problems are best tackled. These funding pressures will be discussed in more detail in the section on policy to follow.

Creative Potential

The third driver for IDR is the creative potential resulting from combining diverse domains of knowledge and skill sets. Social media IDR has seen creativity emerge in three areas. First, innovative approaches have resulted from combining quantitative and qualitative scholarship to provide a more complete picture of social phenomena (Aragón et al., 2012). Second, a wide range of tools have been developed geared toward specific aspects of data management. The Collaborative Online Social Media Observatory (COSMOS) is a prime example of a software platform 'that reduces the technical and methodological barriers to accessing and analysing social media and other forms of open digital data' (COSMOS, n.d.; Morgan, Chapter 26, this volume) and is under development by an IDR team that crosses disciplines and institutions. But more importantly, social media IDR has generated new insights that are qualitatively different from those generated within a single discipline, through the application of theories, methodologies, and epistemologies that integrate the strengths of varied disciplinary approaches.

CHALLENGES

There are numerous motivations for building IDR teams in the context of social media research as discussed above. At the same time, it is important to realize that these projects also face a number of challenges that may lead to failure. While successful social media research gets published and discussed, little is known about those projects that falter. A series of workshops organized in 2015 by Katrin Weller and Luca Rossi entitled *#Fail – the Workshop Series* aim to 'collect cases in which approaches for social media studies did not work out as expected' (#Fail!, 2015: n.p.). This workshop series, described in more detail at https://failworkshops.wordpress.com, will provide important insights into the challenges experienced by IDR teams and social media research teams in general and help with the development of best practices for their future implementation.

Next we discuss eight central challenges that IDR presents in general and in the context of social media research specifically.

1. Technological: The more complex the problem under investigation, requiring the collection, for example, of very specific types of data from a subset of social media data, the more difficult it may be to overcome some of the technological challenges associated with social media data collection. While some social media research may rely on methods such as surveys and interviews to collect data (e.g., Quan-Haase et al., 2015), a significant portion of social media research relies on data scraped directly from social media sites; for example, Twitter network analysis (Kwak, Lee, Park, and Moon, 2010) or content analysis of tweets (Bogers and Björneborn, 2013). What data can be scraped is dependent on the technological nature, affordances, and limitations of the social media site (e.g., privacy settings, data accessibility). For example, users can generally provide as little or as much information about themselves as they wish to create and establish a profile and they can choose to make some or all of the information they do share with a social media site private. Questions relating to the representativeness of any data collected from social media sites have been raised as a result of the lack of information about users. Though efforts are underway to automatically identify characteristics such as age, gender, and occupation of social media users (Sloan et al., 2015), social media researchers often cannot collect the data needed to ensure representativeness or even describe the sample population.

Representativeness is an issue for non-IDR teams such as computer scientists examining an entire social media population (e.g., all Twitter data within a particular time frame), as representativeness is in part a function of technology. Results may be skewed by data missing due to privacy settings. Holes in the data are potentially a serious issue for IDR teams who are tackling complex problems relating to a subset of the population of a social media site or a particular social phenomenon. Bogers and Björneborn (2013) note that, at the time of their research, Twitter limited the total number of public tweets that could be accessed using the API to 1%. The unknown number of missing private messages together with the 99% of missing public tweets, however, did not present a significant methodological issue for Bogers and Björneborn (2013). This was because of their specific interest in the use of the word serendipity in tweets and the unlikelihood the 1% of tweets would be biased for or against tweets with #serendipity in them. But the potential for bias exists. For example, Abdesslem, Parris and Henderson (2012) point out the difficulty of investigating attitudes toward privacy using data collected from Facebook, as the data from a portion of Facebook users who keep their profiles private are missing from their dataset by default, leading to potentially significant biases in results.

2. Data collection, management, and sharing: Related to technological issues are the challenges of collecting, managing, and sharing data and the software necessary to store, build, analyze, and visualize data sets across multiple departments or institutions in IDR collaborations. Social media IDR teams must be aware of the policies and ethics around the collection and sharing of social media users' information that may differ from institution to institution, and the laws that may differ from country to country (Simeone, Guiliano, Kooper, and Bajcsy, 2011). Wilkinson and Thelwall (2011) point out that there are three main ethical issues in the social sciences that extend, however imperfectly, to social media research: informed consent, privacy, and anonymity (see Beninger, Chapter 5, this volume). User expectations in the context of social media research relating to all three issues vary based on, for example, the social media site used for research and the sensitivity of the data collected and for what purpose (Beninger, Fry, Jago, Lepps, Nass, and Silvester, 2014). Through focus groups and in-depth interviews with 34 participants, Beninger et al. (2014) found that some social media users believe that if posts are published in papers emanating from the research, informed consent may be necessary. In particular, they advocate for informed consent when the post is sensitive in nature, to confirm that the user's opinion has not changed and to allow users to understand the purpose of the research and its quality. Because of the relative novelty of social media research, ethics policies will continue to change as researchers push the boundaries and users push back, making it imperative for social media IDR researchers to be aware of differences in ethics policies that may exist across institutions as policies change based on deeper understanding of the types of user expectations Beninger et al. (2014) found.

3. Dissemination/Publication: The pressure to publish in academia is intense. For large IDR projects with many different researchers making significant intellectual and practical contributions, deciding authorship on publications requires the development of team policies regarding acknowledgements and authorship credit (Simeone et al., 2011). Beyond issues of authorship within teams, there are multiple challenges relating to the dissemination of IDR team findings and products that have the potential to dissuade researchers from IDR, make institutional recognition for IDR difficult, or prevent IDR projects from reaching outcomes that could be valuable to the larger research community. Social media IDR teams need to be aware of challenges relating to discipline, quality, transferability, and peer review, to help mitigate or overcome them. We discuss each of these challenges next.

a. Disciplinary and institutional differences: Different disciplines and institutions may place different values on research products. This is particularly pertinent for social media IDR teams that may not only be publishing their findings, but also developing the research tools that enable data analysis and subsequent publication. For example, while scholars in the humanities are increasingly not only using but developing digital tools for their research, these activities are not always identified in tenure and promotion policies (Siemens, 2013). It may be challenging for IDR teams to work together in software development when members may not be equally recognized for their work by their respective departments or institutions.

b. Perception of quality: It is difficult to assess the quality of IDR outputs when disciplines have different criteria (Borrego and Newswander, 2010). As such, some IDR detractors perceive it as less rigorous and superficial with more trivial outcomes (see Siedlok and Hibbert, 2014). Overall in the literature there is little to no evidence suggesting that IDR is of lesser quality compared to disciplinary research. It is also important to consider that IDR is an emerging work structure that needs time to develop best practices and as a result needs to be allowed room for trial and error. Also, relevant markers of quality (validity and reliability) need to be developed to ensure they are relevant to evaluating IDR research outcomes. Publishing IDR is thus challenging (Aragón et al., 2012); journals often favour disciplinary research (Siedlok and Hibbert, 2014) and disciplinary journals are generally more highly cited and prestigious than interdisciplinary ones (Conole et al., 2010). When IDR is conducted across institutions, where to publish becomes further complicated by differences in institution's perspectives on the best journals in which to publish (Cummings and Kiesler, 2007).

c. Transferability: One outcome of IDR teams can be the creation of tools for the collection, analysis, and visualization of social media data. Despite their innovativeness, these tools may be widely used beyond the project, unlike that enjoyed by tools such as Gephi and Netlytic, because of their specificity. While some propose the development of more generic tools that could be used by researchers and industry (Aragón et al., 2012), one of the challenges may be the lack of funding to sustain tool development and provide support to users that goes beyond the life of a project (Balakrishnan et al., 2011).

d. Peer review: Traditionally, peer-review is discipline-specific, but to evaluate IDR, the peer-review process needs to be both flexible and expert enough to assess research that crosses disciplinary boundaries (Conole et al., 2010; Bammer, 2012). For example, in practice, due to the nature of IDR, referees are often not peers and are unfamiliar with components of the research, leading either to overly harsh criticisms (Bammer, 2012) or a lack of criticism. Consideration for the data collection tools and techniques produced by IDR teams is also needed. How are these tools best evaluated? TaPoR (http://www.tapor.ca/), a portal for research tools for textual study, has links to over 20 tools for social media analyses. But what kind of peer-review system is in place for tools developed for use by social media IDR teams?

4. Financial: Though funding for interdisciplinary research exists, securing sufficient funds to manage and support large teams is a challenge, particularly when multiple institutions are involved that have different institutional structures and policies (Cummings and Kiesler, 2007). IDR projects often need infrastructure support (e.g., labs) and 'glue money' (Bammer, 2012) that will provide teams with the necessary funds to meet in person (see section 5 on 'language, culture, and communication') to overcome further financial burdens relating to the geographical distance between IDR team members due to the cost of travel for face-to-face meetings (Cummings and Kiesler, 2007).

5. Language, culture, and communication: Borrego and Newswander (2010) note that language is one of the more commonly cited challenges to interdisciplinary research, underlining the importance of establishing common ground, for example, in the form of terminology within IDR teams during the team-building process. Though concepts are often studied across numerous disciplines, each develops its own vocabulary, making communication among scholars on interdisciplinary teams difficult (Chuk, Hoetzlein, Kim, and Panko, 2011; Conole et al., 2010). Because IDR teams are often separated by distance, the opportunity to establish common ground through face-to-face communication can be rare, leading to a reliance on synchronous and asynchronous communication and collaboration technologies (Quan-Haase, 2012). However, even with technologies that afford communication, colocation is preferable for optimal conditions for collaboration and interdisciplinary work (Cummings and Kiesler, 2007; Wellman, Dimitrova, Hayat, Mo, and Smale, 2014). Cummings and Kiesler (2007) suggest that providing training for researchers on how to manage interdisciplinary and multi-university projects may mitigate the problems associated with the complexity of collaboration. For example, knowledge transfer activities – such as co-authorship, workshops, brainstorming, and student exchanges – were good predictors of short-term outcomes for multi-university collaborations including knowledge transfer, tools, training, outreach, collaboration, and opportunities for new lines of research (Cummings and Kiesler, 2007).

While the use of communication technology and, training opportunities for in-person team interactions can assist in overcoming language and communication barriers and challenges, Balakrishnan et al. (2011) found in their research on team integration that misunderstandings and conflict may not be all bad. Instead, they can yield unexpected ideas, help to view a concept from new perspectives, and question established beliefs. This finding suggests that initial problems stemming from different disciplinary cultures and language can benefit the project if teams take the opportunity to critically examine their 'preconceived notions of the world' (Eco, 1998: 54) in order to see something from a new angle.

6. Theory and method: IDR social media teams bring a variety of theories and methods to the table, which are not always easily understood by fellow team members. Any study drawing on social media data is burdened with a myriad of decisions concerning how the data will be collected, what parsing, scraping, and standardization techniques will be employed, and how the analysis will proceed. For example, qualitative approaches to research are often foreign to those researchers trained in quantitative methodology and vice versa. When a sociologist working in an interdisciplinary social media research team voiced concern that the team collect data from at least a couple of hundred social media users, a computer scientist commented, 'Either we study the whole network of 10 million users, or it doesn't make sense to study it at all!' (Aragón et al., 2012: 1). This conversation suggests that regardless of whether scholars come from a humanities, social science, or computer science background, they need to make decisions that will affect the kinds of results they will obtain and ultimately the insights they can produce.

Stieglitz et al. (2014) also identified variations in perspectives and objectives as a major challenge for social media teams. They contrast the objectives of computer scientists to develop 'algorithms and tools for analyzing, mining and predicting changes in the structures and processes of social networks' (2014: 91) with those of social scientists who seek to investigate the effects of social media adoption and use on social phenomena such as activism, political participation, and voter turnout. Another key difference in perspective is that computer scientists aim to develop new methods to harvest social media data effectively, while social science, business, and humanities researchers see social media as 'a sensor network and a laboratory for natural experimentation, providing valuable indicators and helping to test hypotheses about social interactions as well as their economic, political and societal implications' (Stieglitz et al., 2014: 91). This necessitates close collaboration to be able to articulate shared goals and methodologies.

7. *Education*: Borrego and Newswander (2010) note that despite the proliferation of interdisciplinarity, there has been very little graduate student training provided to help ensure scholars and scientists are sufficiently prepared to successfully implement IDR. Borrego and Newswander (2010) found that graduate students in interdisciplinary programs were not being trained in how to establish common ground with researchers from other disciplines, a skill highly transferable to work in IDR teams. For work in social media IDR teams, being able to establish common ground is essential, as team members may either be more familiar with large-scale quantitative approaches or with small-scale studies aimed at modelling or theorizing social phenomena. Balakrishnan et al. (2011) show that frequently meeting to examine intermediate results of the project can help increase awareness of various disciplines' cultures and knowledge domains. For all involved in social media IDR (including junior and senior academics and graduate students) then, it is important to be closely involved in discussions around intermediate project results to obtain that understanding and be able to use it to guide the collaboration. We discuss graduate education further in the section to follow on policy.

8. *Leveraging knowledge and skills*: Reflecting on their challenges as an IDR team conducting social media research, Aragón et al. (2012) note, 'we are constantly grappling with the challenge of how to leverage the unique array of methodological approaches and theoretical perspectives that our team members bring to the table in order to produce cutting edge research' (Aragón et al., 2012: n.p.). For Aragón et al.'s (2012) team this goes beyond what they refer to as 'siloed research communities, rarely interacting with one another' a to develop 'integrated approaches, which incorporate methods and results from both types of research [quantitative and qualitative]'. In this way, the team leverages different types of expertise from each team member.

INSTITUTIONAL POLICIES AND PROCEDURES TO ENCOURAGE SOCIAL MEDIA IDR

This section discusses existing problems that may impede the development of good IDR policy, how policy may be hampering IDR, and shortfalls of education policy relative to IDR, which all have direct implications for social media IDR. Policies designed to encourage IDR are evident in universities and national and international research funding agencies and programs. A good example of how at the university-level IDR policy is reflected in funding initiatives can be seen at the University of Aberdeen's Principal's Interdisciplinary Fund awards grants which 'support activities which lead to the development of high quality research proposals that are clearly interdisciplinary' (University of Aberdeen, 2015: n.p.). On the national level, one of the objectives of the Social Sciences and Humanities Research Council of Canada's (SSHRC) Insight Grant competition is to 'build knowledge and understanding from disciplinary, interdisciplinary and/or cross-sector perspectives through support for the best researchers' (SSHRC, 2016: n.p.). These university level and national initiatives are not specifically aimed at social media IDR, but are supportive of the types of collaboration that underlie social media research. The Digging into Data Challenge, an international research funding initiative, is designed 'to foster interdisciplinary collaboration among researchers in the humanities, social sciences, computer sciences, library, archive, information sciences, and other fields, around questions of text and data analysis' (Digging into Data Challenge, 2014: n.p.). Again, international funding initiatives do not directly target social media IDR, but could support such projects. There are also national funding programs in place that promote IDR by connecting researchers with end users (e.g., ARC Linkage Projects in Australia; Mitacs in Canada). The Australian Research Council's (ARC) Linkage Projects scheme is one example and states that it:

> ...provides funding to Eligible Organizations to support research and development (R&D) projects which are collaborative between higher education researchers and other parts of the national innovation system, which are undertaken to acquire new knowledge, and which involve risk or innovation. (Australian Research Council, 2013: n.p.)

One social media IDR project that was recently funded by ARC is entitled 'Social networks, belonging and active citizenship among migrant youth in Australia' (#LP0989182). The project involved researchers from two universities as well as the Australian Red Cross and the Centre for Multicultural Youth (Deakin University, 2014), and integrated sociology, political theory, and cultural studies perspectives (F. Mansouri and Z. Skrbis, personal communication, February 17, 2015).

Despite what appears to be support for IDR at many levels and in various countries through funding earmarked for IDR (or at least open to it), there is disagreement over whether there is enough support for IDR and whether policies designed to foster IDR are sufficiently informed to truly facilitate it in practice (Bammer, 2012; Siedlok and Hibbert, 2014).

IMPEDIMENTS TO THE DEVELOPMENT OF GOOD IDR INSTITUTIONAL POLICY

There exists a range of parameters and activities that change the dynamics of IDR teams and require consideration when it comes to developing meaningful policy. This is evident, for example, in the scope and scale of the IDR work.

Scope: The disciplines combined in social media IDR may be close together (e.g., history and literature) or farther apart (e.g., linguistics and biology), i.e., the scope of IDR can be 'narrow' or 'broad' in nature (Klein, 2014). Social media research often necessitates the synergizing of diverse sets of technical skills combined with methodological innovations and knowledge of social phenomena, thus lending itself to IDR research broad in scope. For example, the data collection and analysis process can be cumbersome and skills that enable the scraping, cleaning, and manipulating of large sets of data are more in line with those of computer scientists than social science or humanities scholars. But the data alone cannot provide answers, as the analysis and interpretation of data often needs to be informed by theoretical understandings of human behavior. An example of broad social media IDR is the NSF project undertaken by Ming-Hsiang Tsou (Principal Investigator) which examines 'Spatiotemporal modelling of human dynamics across social media and social networks' (award #1416509) and comprises a disciplinary mix of geography, linguistics, computer science, social science, and communication (National Science Foundation, 2014). The question we must ask is, what policies best support narrow versus broad social media IDR? Do we need different policies to encourage and support diverse kinds of social media IDR teams?

Scale: The scale of social media IDR may range considerably in terms of time period, geography, and expected goals. A local team may come together for a one-to-two-year period and with a clear, manageable goal. An example of a small-scale project is the team of researchers from MOA, the Musqueam Indian Band, and Simon Fraser University, mentioned earlier in this chapter, who pooled the knowledge and expertise of multiple stakeholders and disciplines to develop an interactive tabletop exhibit (Luckow, 2015).

Alternatively, the scale of a project may be much larger, involving an international team, comprising multiple universities and involving multiple stakeholders, like the previously mentioned ARC-funded project which involved two universities and two community stakeholders with multiple goals (Deakin University, 2014). Similarly, we should find ourselves asking, what kinds of funding policies are needed to support small- versus large-scale research? At what scale do social media IDR teams work best?

The combinations of scope and scale of IDR illustrate the complexity of developing policies to support social media IDR and highlight the need for more research on IDR. Because of a lack of understanding of successful IDR research, team composition and practices, 'policy to support and encourage interdisciplinary research currently involves "muddling through"' (Bammer, 2012: 4). To remedy this, Bammer (2012) and others suggest IDR research needs clearer demarcations among the different types of IDR, standardized reporting processes in order to assess IDR projects and make recommendations for future projects, and the development of *IDR toolkits* to help guide teams through the research process without having to continuously reinvent the wheel. Toolkits specifically designed for social media IDR would be a valuable resource for teams, making them aware of and guiding them through some of the complexities of social media research that crosses traditional disciplinary boundaries

HOW POLICY HAMPERS IDR

While policy intent may be to encourage interdisciplinarity and collaboration across institutions (Cummings and Kiesler, 2007), policy does not appear to be sufficiently fostering and supporting of the unique funding needs, research processes, team members and outcomes of IDR. We briefly discuss three ways in which policies may currently be hampering IDR.

1. Surface level interdisciplinarity: Because IDR is desirable or even required by some funding agencies and programs, it can have the effect of encouraging the hasty development of superficial collaborations among researchers in order to 'tick the right boxes' (Siedlok and Hibbert, 2014: 203). This also applies to social media IDR, as collaborations between computer scientists and social scientists could be developed without a clear understanding of what each discipline would contribute and how the diverse knowledge domains may work in tandem. Stember (1991) argues that once funding for an IDR project has been secured, proposed IDR research may devolve into purely separate disciplinary research strands that are not fully integrated. As a result of policy, therefore, complex projects with multiple PIs from more than one institution are created (Balakrishnan et al., 2011) while only 'surface level' collaboration may ensue (Conole et al., 2010: 5). Too much diversity can have a negative impact on the integration and outcomes of IDR teams (Balakrishnan et al., 2011; Cummings and Kiesler, 2007); likewise, 'having fewer PIs can help focus tasks and also make opportunities for cross-fertilization easier to plan' (Balakrishnan et al., 2011: 531). In social media IDR, ensuring clear roles exist among team members may help ensure a team's success.

2. Time: The length of time social media IDR takes is also an important consideration relative to institutional and funding policies. Continuous funding can pose a problem for those projects whose outcomes are in the form of innovative processes, tools, or products. As funding agency priorities change the likelihood of securing funding beyond the projects initial stages decreases (Balakrishnan et al., 2011). Tool development for the gathering, analysis, and visualization of social media data is laborious, challenging, and unpredictable. The time from initiation of the IDR project to the dissemination of research often extends past periods of research funding and there is often little support within university departments for research that is both time consuming and risky (Balakrishnan et al., 2011), dissuading researchers from conducting IDR (van Rijnsoever and Hessels, 2011).

3. *Recognition*: Current measures of academic success in universities do not favour social media IDR. Researchers in academic institutions are evaluated on the strength of their publication record, which may have the effect of punishing IDR researchers who publish in interdisciplinary venues, which have less impact and prestige than disciplinary publications (Conole et al., 2010). Similarly, graduate students involved in IDR teams must also keep their end-goal in mind. Despite the funding that may be available, the difficulty of publishing in top disciplinary journals and thus landing a job in academia may dissuade them from conducting IDR research (Balakrishnan et al., 2011). With regard to technology enhanced learning (TEL) research, Conole et al. note that while its success (not unlike social media research) hinges on interdisciplinarity, the TEL community must play its part in fostering IDR practices, 'and there is a need for changes at policy level too, to recognize and reward this type of research' (2010: 5).

GRADUATE EDUCATION POLICY

As with IDR research in general, there are also gaps in our understanding of graduate student participation in social media IDR teams that is preventing the development of good policy in higher education. Graduate students could benefit greatly from appropriate policy frameworks because they are often an integral part of IDR teams and they stand to gain valuable, transferable skills for the workplace including the development of critical thinking skills, an awareness of and ability to communicate with researchers from various disciplines, an understanding of group dynamics within a complex project, and the ability to give and receive feedback (Borrego and Newswander, 2010). One key challenge that graduate student training faces is the lack of experience of supervisors, course leaders, and personnel in setting up IDR teams and helping them exchange and integrate expertise across domains. With a lack of experienced instructors, these kinds of skills cannot be passed on to trainees.

Policy with respect to IDR has the potential to have a significant impact on student learning and outcomes through the funding available to hire students to work on social media IDR teams. Despite the growing interest in preparing graduate students for collaboration in IDR teams, little is known about 'learning outcomes, methods, or benchmarks for assessing interdisciplinary graduate programs and associated student learning, particularly in science and engineering' (Borrego and Newswander, 2010: 61–62). Bammer noted there are 'few helpful answers about how best to educate future interdisciplinary researchers' (2012: 4) and this also applies to the social media context. The skills and knowledge to be gained from involvement in social media IDR are easily transferrable to industry – skills such as social media analytics and knowledge of how and why people engage with social media. Graduate students could potentially find jobs outside of academia based on their involvement, regardless of whether they are located more on the computer science or social science side of the spectrum.

Borrego and Newswander (2010) analyzed interdisciplinary proposals that were funded by the *Integrative Graduate Education and Research Traineeship (IGERT) program*, which is one of the most well-regarded funding programs for the NSF's Division of Graduate Education (DGE). DGE's mandate is to foster cultural change in graduate education and to develop collaborative models that transcend traditional disciplinary boundaries. Their study's findings show that a majority of interdisciplinary projects identified awareness or some understanding of another discipline as their primary learning outcome. Still other projects viewed a solid grounding in one discipline as central to interdisciplinary work because this would allow graduate students to bring that knowledge to bear on problems from other disciplines. Only a few of the funded projects provided more detail in terms of the learning involved, outlining three core areas that aligned with past literature (Boix Mansilla and Dawes Duraisingh, 2007):

1. To appreciate and comprehend methods used in other disciplines;
2. To understand and value other disciplines as they relate to their focus discipline, and
3. To critically reflect on methodological limitations within their own as well as other disciplines.

Relative to the inclusion of graduate students in IDR teams, it could be expected that students would not only obtain a general awareness of studies conducted in other disciplines, but would more deeply become involved in critical examinations of their methodologies, theoretical perspectives and biases. For social media IDR projects, the integration of technical skills and knowledge about social phenomena could constitute a central learning outcome. This kind of critical engagement with the technical aspects of social media scholarship would lead to deep learning as graduate students would need to have a good grasp of data collection methods, data analysis approaches, and data interpretation in both quantitative and qualitative traditions. It is this kind of involvement with the data, their collection, analysis, visual representation, and interpretation that characterizes in part the learning outcomes of graduate students who participate in IDR teams that tackle research problems in social media research.

CONCLUSION

What should interdisciplinarity look like in social media research? Three conclusions can be drawn with regards to the building of social media IDR teams. First, little is known about the composition of IDR social media teams in terms of their disciplinary orientation and the technical skills and knowledge team members contribute. Existing gaps in our knowledge of social media IDR teamwork prevents the implementation of programs for graduate students, the development of appropriate policy, and the implementation of IDR teams based on best practice. The social media research community would make a significant contribution to our understanding of IDR by sharing experiences of their IDR teamwork with the larger community. Community discussion could begin with online discussion groups and workshops and panels at conferences and extend to publications with a social media and interdisciplinary focus. The #Fail! (2015) workshop series addressing how social media researchers can learn from each other's mistakes is a great example of how this kind of gained experience can be shared and made available online. To get the research on IDR to those teams and administrators in the trenches, toolkits grounded in case studies could be developed to provide guidelines. Toolkits could address, for example, best practices for integrating team members from the social sciences and computer sciences, how to build understanding and trust and foster communication, and develop learning outcomes for graduate students that could be adapted across other disciplines.

Second, we have proposed a framework for IDR in social media, expanding on Kane et al.'s (2014) work, which integrates three core areas:

1. *the technological challenge*: understanding the technical intricacies of various platforms in order to harvest, analyze, interpret, and visualize quantitative and qualitative data;
2. *the behavioral challenge*: investigating what users of these sites do and why through the application of appropriate social theory; and
3. *the ethical challenge*: consideration of the ethical and epistemological debates around the collection, analysis, and use of data from users.

The need for interdisciplinarity in social media research is most salient when we consider the technological challenges of social media research, best approached through the computer sciences, and the behavioural challenge, best approached through the social sciences (Kane et al., 2014). Scholars engaged in social media IDR can bring to the table three core areas of understanding, ranging from the technical aspects of data collection, analysis, and visualization, to the theories underlying social phenomena, to the ethical aspects of engaging with user-generated content.

Finally, there are many challenges that impede IDR including, for example, effectively leveraging the skills and knowledge of diverse team members and overcoming language, culture, and communication barriers. In some cases these challenges can be overcome through creativity, but it is clear that IDR teams need a broad base of support (e.g., institutions, funding agencies) for these teams to succeed.

ACKNOWLEDGEMENTS

We would like to thank two anonymous reviewers for their useful comments. This research is funded by a SSHRC Insight Grant No. R3603A13.

REFERENCES

#Fail! (2015). *#Fail! The workshop series. Things that didn't work out in social media research – and what we can learn from them* [Online]. Retrieved from https://failworkshops.wordpress.com/

Abdesslem, F.B., Parris, I., and Henderson, T. (2012). Reliable online social network data collection. In *Computational Social Networks: Mining and Visualization* (pp. 183–210). London: Springer-Verlag. doi:10.1007/978-1-4471-4054-2

Anderson, C. (2008). The end of theory: The data deluge makes the scientific method obsolete. *Wired*. Available from: http://archive.wired.com/science/discoveries/magazine/16-07/pb_theory (accessed 3 August 2015).

Aragón, P., Laniado, D., Neff, J.G., Ruiz de Querol, R., Kaltenbrunner, A., Ullod, C., Kappler, K., and Volkovich, Y. (2012). Bridging the gap: A reflection on an interdisciplinary approach to social media research. In *21st International World Wide Web Conference (www2012)* (pp. 1–6).

Australian Research Council (ARC) (2013). *Linkage projects* [Online]. Retrieved from http://www.arc.gov.au/linkage-projects (accessed 26 July 2016)

Balakrishnan, A.D., Kiesler, S., Cummings, J.N., and Zadeh, R. (2011). Research team integration: What it is and why it matters. *Proceedings of the ACM 2011 Conference on Computer Supported Cooperative Work - CSCW '11*, 523–532. doi:10.1145/1958824.1958905

Bammer, G. (2012). *Strengthening interdisciplinary research: What it is, what it does, how it does it and how it is supported* (pp. 1–29). Australian Council of Learned Academies. Retrieved from http://www.acola.org.au/PDF/Strengthening%20Interdisciplinary%20Research.pdf (accessed 26 July 2016)

Beninger, K., Fry, A., Jago, N., Lepps, H., Nass, L., and Silvester, H. (2014). *Research using social media: Users' views*. London, UK: NatCen Social Research. Retrieved from http://www.natcen.ac.uk/our-research/research/research-using-social-media-users-views/ (accessed 26 July 2016)

Bogers, T., and Björneborn, L. (2013). Meaningful Coincidences in everyday life shared on Twitter. In *iConference 2013 Proceedings* (pp. 196–208). doi:10.9776/13175

Boix Mansilla, V., and Dawes Duraisingh, E. (2007). Targeted assessment of students' interdisciplinary work: An empirically grounded framework proposed. *Journal of Higher Education*, 78(2): 215–237.

Borrego, M., and Newswander, L. K. (2010). Definitions of interdisciplinary research: Toward graduate-level interdisciplinary learning outcomes. *The Review of Higher Education*, 34(1): 61–84. doi:10.1353/rhe.2010.0006 boyd, d., and Crawford, K. (2012). Critical questions for big data: Provocations for a cultural, technological, and scholarly phenomenon. *Information Communication & Society*, 15(5): 662–679.

Chuk, E., Hoetzlein, R., Kim, D., and Panko, J. (2011). Creating socially networked knowledge through interdisciplinary collaboration. *Arts and Humanities in Higher Education*, 11: 93–108. doi:10.1177/1474022211426906

Clavel, P., Fox, K., Leo, C., Quan-Haase, A., Saitta, D., and LaDale, W. (2015). Blogging the city: Research, collaboration, and engagement in urban e-planning. Critical notes from a conference. *International Journal of E-Planning Research (IJEPR)*, 4(1). doi: 10.4018/ijepr.2015010104.

Conole, G., Scanlon, E., Mundin, P., and Farrow, R. (2010). *Interdisciplinary research: Findings from the technology enhanced learning research programme* [Report], (pp. 1–184). UK: Institute of Educational Technology. Retrieved from http://www.tlrp.org (accessed 26 July 2016)

COSMOS (n.d.). *What is COSMOS?* [Online]. Retrieved from http://www.cs.cf.ac.uk/cosmos/ (accessed 26 July 2016)

Cummings, J. N., and Kiesler, S. (2007). Coordination costs and project outcomes in multi-university collaborations. *Research Policy*, 36: 1620–1634.

Deakin University (2014). *Australia-India Interdisciplinary Research Network* [Online]. Retrieved from http://www.deakin.edu.au/arts-ed/centre-for-citizenship-and-globalisation/research/research-networks/australia-india-interdisciplinary-research-network (accessed 26 July 2016)

Digging into Data Challenge (2014). *Digging into data phase 2 projects: Summary and reports* [Online]. Retrieved from http://did3.jiscinvolve.org/wp/2014/11/10/did2-summary-and-reports/ (accessed 26 July 2016)

Eco, U. (1998). *Serendipities: Language & Lunacy*. New York: Columbia University Press.

Gruzd, A., Staves, K., and Wilk, A. (2012). Connected scholars: Examining the role of social media in research practices of faculty using the UTAUT model. *Computers in Human Behavior*, 28(6): 2340–2350. doi:10.1016/j.chb.2012.07.004

Holmberg, K., and Thelwall, M. (2014). Disciplinary differences in Twitter scholarly communication. *Scientometrics*, 101(2): 1027–1042. doi:10.1007/s11192-014-1229-3

Huutoniemi, K., Klein, J. T., Bruun, H., and Hukkinen, J. (2010). Analyzing interdisciplinarity: Typology and indicators. *Research Policy*, 39(1): 79–88.

Kane, G.C., Alavi, M., Labianca, G., and Borgatti, S.P. (2014). Whats's different about social media networks? A framework and research agenda. *MIS Quarterly*, 38(1): 275–304.

Klein, J. T. (2014). *Interdisciplinary digital humanities: Boundary work in an emerging field*. Ann Arbor, MI: University of Michigan Press. doi: http://dx.doi.org/10.3998/dh.12869322.0001.001

Kwak, H., Lee, C., Park, H., and Moon, S. (2010). What is Twitter, a social network or a news media? In *Proceedings of the 19th international conference on World Wide Web - WWW '10*, pp. 591. New York: ACM Press.

Love, J. and Cooper, A.C.G. (2015). From social and technical to socio-technical: Designing integrated research on domestic energy use. *Journal of Indoor and Built Environment*, 24 (7): 986–998. doi: 10.1177/1420326X15601722

Luckow, D. (2015). *Museum of Anthropology exhibit features SFU SIAT team's design and technology* [Online]. *Simon Fraser University*. Retrieved from http://www.sfu.ca/sfunews/stories/2015/museum-of-anthropology-exhibit-incorporates-sfu-siat-teams-desig.html (accessed 26 July 2016)

Merriam-Webster online (n.d.). Social media. Retrieved from http://www.merriam-webster.com/dictionary/socialmedia (accessed 26 July 2016)

National Science Foundation (2014). IBSS: Spatiotemporal modeling of human dynamics across social media and social networks. Retrieved from http://www.nsf.gov/awardsearch/showAward?AWD_ID=1416509 (accessed 26 July 2016)

Quan-Haase, A. (2012). Research and teaching in real-time: 24/7 collaborative networks. In D. Rasmussen Neal (Ed.), *Social media for academics* (pp. 39-58). Sawston, UK: Chandos.

Quan-Haase, A., Martin, K., and McCay-Peet, L. (2015). Networks of digital humanities scholars: The informational and social uses and gratifications of Twitter. *Big Data &*

Society. Retrieved from http://bds.sagepub.com/content/2/1/2053951715589417

Quan-Haase, A., Suarez, J.L., and Brown, D.M. (2014). Collaborating, connecting, and clustering in the humanities: A case study of networked scholarship in an interdisciplinary, dispersed team. *American Behavioral Scientist*. doi:10.1177/0002764214556806

Rasmussen Neal, D. (2012). *Social media for academics*. Sawston, UK: Chandos.

Ross, C., Terras, M., Warwick, C., and Welsh, A. (2011). Enabled backchannel: conference Twitter use by digital humanists. *Journal of Documentation*, 67(2): 214–237. doi:10.1108/00220411111109449

Siedlok, F., and Hibbert, P. (2014). The organization of interdisciplinary research: Modes, drivers and barriers. *International Journal of Management Reviews*, 16(2): 194–210.

Siemens, L. (2009). 'It's a team if you use "reply all"': An exploration of research teams in digital humanities environments. *Literary and Linguistic Computing*, 24(2): 225–233.

Siemens, L. (2013). Developing Academic Capacity in Digital Humanities: Thoughts from the Canadian Community. *Digital Humanities Quartely*, 7(1). Retrieved from http://digitalhumanities.org:8081/dhq/vol/7/1/000114/000114.html (accessed 26 July 2016)

Simeone, M., Guiliano, J., Kooper, R., and Bajcsy, P. (2011). Digging into data using new collaborative infrastructures supporting humanities-based computer science research. *First Monday*, 16(5): URL: http://firstmonday.org/ojs/index.php/fm/article/view/3372/2950

Sloan, L., Morgan, J., Burnap, P. and Williams, M. (2015. Who tweets? Deriving the demographic characteristics of age, occupation and social class from Twitter user meta-data. *PLoS ONE*, 10(3), doi: 10.1371/journal.pone.0115545

Sprain, L., Endres, D. and Petersen, T. R. (2010). Research as a transdisciplinary networked process: A metaphor for difference-making research. *Communication Monographs*, 77(4): 441–444.

SSHRC (Social Sciences and Humanities Research Council of Canada) (2016). *Insight Grants* [Online]. http://www.sshrc-crsh.gc.ca/funding-financement/programs-programmes/insight_grants-subventions_savoir-eng.aspx (accessed 8 September 2016)

Stember, M. (1991). Advancing the social sciences through the interdisciplinary enterprise. *The Social Science Journal*, 28(1): 1–14.

Stieglitz, S., Dang-Xuan, L., Bruns, A., and Neuberger, C. (2014). Social media analytics: An interdisciplinary approach and its implications for information systems. *Business and Information Systems Engineering*, 6(2): 89–96.

University of Aberdeen (2015). *Principal's Interdisciplinary Fund* [Online]. Retrieved from http://www.abdn.ac.uk/staffnet/research/principals-interdisciplinary-fund-1661.php (accessed 26 July 2016)

University of Oslo (2014). Research projects: *Social media and minority language users* [Online]. Retrieved from http://www.hf.uio.no/imk/english/research/center/media-innovations/research/ (accessed 26 July 2016)

van Rijnsoever, F. J., and Hessels, L. K. (2011). Factors associated with disciplinary and interdisciplinary research collaboration. *Research Policy*, 40(3): 463–472. doi:10.1016/j.respol.2010.11.001

Wellman, B., Dimitrova, D., Hayat, Z., Mo, G. Y., and Smale, L. (2014). Networking scholars in a networked organization. In Brass, D.J., Labianca, G. J., Mehra, A., Halgin, D., & Borgatti, S. (eds.) Contemporary Perspectives on Organizational Social Networks (pp. 135–159). Howard House, UK: Emerald.

Wilkinson, D., and Thelwall, M. (2011). Researching personal information on the public web: Methods and ethics. *Social Science Computer Review*, 29(4): 387–401. doi:10.1177/08944393103789798

Social Media Users' Views on the Ethics of Social Media Research

Kelsey Beninger

Just because it is accessible doesn't mean using it is ethical.

(boyd, 2010)

INTRODUCTION

The nature of information captured on different social networking sites like Facebook, Twitter, LinkedIn and Instagram offer rich, naturally occurring data and present endless opportunities for research. For many researchers, practitioners and social media enthusiasts, social networking sites are a treasure trove of potential for recruitment, communication, observation and 'scraping'. But what about the millions of individuals who use these sites – what do they think about their posts, 'likes' and statuses being used for research purposes? In the rush to access this new, rich source of data, often what is missing from the conversation are the views of users. What do they understand about how their information is used and shared on the internet? What do users think about their information being used by researchers in online and social media research?

This chapter explores the complex realm of online and social media research ethics through the lens of media users. After summarising what the literature says about the key ethical considerations in online and social media research, this chapter provides an overview of an exploratory qualitative study capturing user views of the ethics of social media research.

Specifically, the findings are presented in relation to participants' views of research using social media in relation to core ethical principles of consent, anonymity and avoiding undue harm are discussed. The chapter concludes with considerations for researchers undertaking online and social media research, including practical suggestions for acknowledging ethical considerations in online research to consider where reasonable and appropriate.

AN OVERVIEW OF ETHICAL CONSIDERATIONS IN ONLINE RESEARCH

There is a wide degree of consensus about what ethical research involves, at least at the level of abstract principles (Webster, Lewis and Brown, 2013). These principles relate to: obtaining informed consent and maintaining anonymity and confidentiality.

Obtaining informed consent from participants requires individuals to understand the purpose of the research, what taking part will involve and how the data will be used (GSR, 2006; MRS, 2012, ESRC, 2012). Ensuring individuals have had this opportunity when conducting research online is much less clear-cut compared to traditional research methods. Questions have been raised about whether consent is required for all types of online research, or whether there are exceptions. One view expressed by researchers is that information shared on public social media platforms without password or membership restrictions can be used for research without the need for informed consent (see e.g., Thelwall, 2010; ESOMAR, 2011). In this school of thought, informed consent becomes necessary to obtain when data is collected from private or closed online platforms or websites. The other perspective amongst researchers is that effort should always be made to secure informed consent from individuals whose information is being used. The subject remains contentious amongst social media researchers and views change depending on the topic, website, and sample population one is working with. Regardless of the stance an individual takes on informed consent, obtaining it from individuals can in practice be very difficult.

Existing ethical guidelines express that researchers should ensure no one knows who has said what in a report (i.e. anonymity) and that participant information should be securely stored and shared (i.e. confidentiality) (GSR, 2006; MRS, 2012; ESRC, 2012). However, in online research the risks of not upholding confidentially are greater as a researcher has less control than an offline research to protect data (British Psychological Society, 2013). There is a permanent record of any information that is posted (Roberts, 2012), and direct quotations from participants can be traced back to the original source (BPS, 2007) through search engines like Google. In this case, anonymity cannot be protected. This is related to the issue of copyright. For example, in an attempt to anonymise participant data, researchers may exclude the participant's name, however some users may feel that they should be given credit for their information being used (Roberts, 2012; Liu, 2010; Barratt and Lenton, 2010). It is clear that thinking is not optional when it comes to applying ethical frameworks to changing online environments.

Ethical issues are inevitable and abundant throughout the social research lifecycle, from research design, to sampling and recruiting, collecting or generating data, analysing data, and reporting results. While it is appealing to think in relation to a rigid set of rules for regulating what ethical considerations to make throughout a study would be ideal and useful, doing research ethically is not about finding a set of rules to follow, nor is it about completing a checklist. Rather, researchers need to work through a set of context-specific decisions on a case-by-case basis and be guided by core ethical principles.

It has been argued that the existence of an 'ethical pluralism' means there is a spectrum of legitimate choices for a researcher to consider when researching online (Buchanan, 2011). Online data can present additional risk: for example, studies that publish direct text quotes from a social media website may directly identify participants. Entering a direct quote from a platform into a Google search engine can lead to a specific Web link, such as a link to that person's LinkedIn profile, and thus identify the participant (Moreno et al, 2013).

An exciting, and daunting, aspect of social media research is its ability to transcend boundaries – social, geographical, methodological. Researchers need to think about the type of data their research design anticipates using because data must satisfy the host country's legal and ethical requirements; data must satisfy the policy of institutions' research ethic committees (REC) and satisfy the professional standards the research is associated with (Jenkins, 2014).

Of particular relevance to researchers beginning studies across Europe is knowing where the data is to be stored because there are different data protection laws in European countries outside the EU (Cannataci, 2014). The ethical situation is more complex with any international research, and social media research is no exception, but the responsibilities you have as a researcher with respect to ethics are the same.

Ethical concepts are not just regulatory hurdles to be jumped through at the beginning stages of research, but concepts that ground ethical inquiry (Markham and Buchanan, 2012). Multiple judgements are possible, and ambiguity and uncertainty are part of the process. Research needs to be supported by an inductive and flexible approach to ethical thinking; what principles need to be considered in the context of your study and how can you think about these to ensure the actions you decide to take support an ethical study.

2014 researchers at NatCen Social Research[1] sought to answer this question by undertaking exploratory qualitative research with social media users in London (Beninger et al, 2014).

Thirty-four people took part in four focus groups and depth interviews. Participants were all users of social media with varying levels of use. Individuals were characterised as low, medium and high users depending on the frequency of their social media use. Low users did not use social media websites, or used them once a week or less; medium users used websites from twice a week up to once a day; high users used social media websites at least twice a week. The diversity of the sample was also monitored in relation to a number of characteristics including: age, gender, ethnicity, and use of a variety of social media platforms for different purposes. Topic guides and vignettes were used to structure and focus the discussions.

The remainder of this chapter describes the findings of this research, outlining the views of these social media users, from how they engage and interact with information online and their awareness and understanding of issues inherent in social media, to their views on social media research more specifically. The views we captured were frought with ethical considerations and reveal lessons that researchers and practitioners could apply in their research design, recruitment, collecting or generating of data, and reporting of results.

CAPTURING THE ETHICAL VIEWS OF SOCIAL MEDIA USERS

The existing literature provides a helpful starting point for thinking about how ethical principles should be applied to online and social media research. The literature on ethics is, however, typically written from the perspective of the researcher and the views of research participants and the general public are all too often missing from the debate. In

THE ONLINE BEHAVIOUR OF SOCIAL MEDIA USERS

Understanding how users' view and share information is necessary for understanding their views on the ethics of social media research. Unsurprisingly, users of social media use a range of social media and other websites, and use these in different ways, from creating and sharing content to observing content that others share online (think actively posting to Facebook versus browsing your friends' posts). The online behaviour users described engaging in included what platforms people used, for what purpose, how they engaged with content online, and how often. These behaviours varied widely and in some cases depended on one another, with behaviours motivating or reinforcing others. For example, platform type depended on intended purpose of use, which in turn influenced amount of time spent using the platform. The growing variety in sites available to access means users engage with different sites for different reasons, such as social, leisure and professional.

Specific sites, such as Facebook, were reportedly used for more than one purpose, though this did not always correspond with the intended purpose of the site. This reveals the many ways individuals adapted social media platforms for their unique needs and interests. The ways users engage with platforms are ever changing as the social media platforms are evolving to meet the changing needs of its user base.

Participants engaged with online content in a number of ways closely related to the type of platform they used and the purpose they used it for. These types of engagement saw users fall into three distinct but overlapping roles: creators, sharers and observers. These are summarised below.

'Creators' post original content on platforms such as discussion forums and Twitter. This includes text, videos and images. Participants, for example, talked about using YouTube to share examples of work in applying theatrical makeup, and Facebook and Twitter to promote their band. Within the 'creator' group there were individuals who shared their own content, but did not spend considerable time engaging with content posted by other social media users.

'Sharers' re-tweet, share or forward content posted by others. This was done by 'commenting' on a blog post, photo or video uploaded by another user. For example, a user working in the health and nutrition field described sharing with Twitter followers' information on what they should and should not eat, and warning against drinking and driving.

'Observers' read and view content on social media and other sites but tend not to pass on this information, like sharers, or contribute their perspectives through new content, like creators. For example, they may read blogs and tweets and view photos and videos but did not interact with the content or other users.

The three categories of social media user are not mutually exclusive. Participants described different contexts and scenarios where an individual can take on all of these roles when using different platforms. Individuals may also move between groups over time. For example, as someone becomes more experienced and familiar with a platform they may start to post original content and share content posted by others. One participant described using Facebook increasingly to share content after spending time getting used to the platform design. The reverse is also true. Individuals may moderate their behaviour over time due to concerns about how the information they share may be used by others.

CONCERNS AND BARRIERS TO BEING INFORMED ABOUT RISKS INHERENT IN SOCIAL MEDIA

The range of sources of information participants described helped them to understand and be aware of issues inherent in social media. Participants emphasised two prominent characteristics of social media: a sense that it is nearly entirely public and the difficulty of permanently deleting information. These two characteristics related to three key concerns participants had about using social media, including their ability to maintain their privacy online; protecting their reputation and identity of themselves, friends and family; and ensuring safety online.

The fact that information is widely accessible and public is most commonly described as a benefit of social media, yet participants also raised this as a concern. Users explained how easy it was to find profiles of people and for companies to use information online for commercial purposes like marketing. This made participants feel a loss of control when information, including their personal details, can be so readily available and out to a use for which it was not intended. Participants discussed how other users, such as Facebook friends, could pass on their information without their knowledge or even having an account. For example, someone on Facebook can tag you in a photo posted without your knowledge and that can be passed to the friends of the person who posted, and so on.

The public nature of social media platforms and their content was also problematic for participants because it raises the issue of data ownership. Participants' understanding of who owns content on social media sites and who can use it varied. Participants raised the distinction between legal and moral ownership. One view was that the platform owns all data on the site and so can use your content as it wants, using it in advertising campaigns or selling it to third parties. Another view was that people have a moral obligation to be responsible with content online and that the author of the content has a moral ownership of it. This difference in views of data ownership, and the lack of understanding about which interpretation is legally correct, caused concern amongst participants as they worried what this means for the information they have put on social media sites.

A similar distinction was raised by Ginnis, Evans, Bartlett and Barker (2015); in social media research ethics there is a distinction between legal considerations, regulatory considerations and responsibilities to research subjects. However, the underlying ethical principles of each perspective are similar.

The second concern expressed by participants was the difficulty of permanently deleting content online. Awareness and understanding of cookies varied and resulted in confusion about the personal information retained by websites and browsers.

The view that content is easily copied and shared by others online, greatly extending the content's shelf-life and reach, prompted the worry about the ability to delete content. This is because you cannot know the reach of your content or be able to trace all the possible places it appears. For example, one participant used a pseudonym for a Facebook account because of his profession in education to avoid students and colleagues having access to his personal life. When he accidently uploaded a profile photo that he felt was inappropriate he immediately '*scrubbed the whole thing, just actually wiped out the Facebook account.*' As he put it, '*I couldn't think of any other way of dealing with that profile picture because as far as I was concerned, it was gonna always be there somewhere... but I felt confident it was resolved*' (Male, aged 61+, high user).

Other than immediate concerns of the difficulty to delete content, participants shared stories they heard about others in which career prospects were damaged by something online from their past. More generally, the view was held that young people in particular '*get carried away with themselves when they are writing [on social media platforms]*'. In this case young people were perceived to '*pour their heart out*' and then '*once it is on there, to try and get rid of it, it's too late or it's too hard*' (Male, aged 61+, high user).

These concerns are compounded by considerable barriers for users to be informed about social media – how it can and should be used, and how this impacts on their identities and personal information. Users expect simple and immediate encounters with their social media platforms and some find it difficult to stay up-to-date with dense and frequently evolving terms and conditions.

Most users neither read nor understand these complex conditions and are also unlikely to consider themselves as subjects of research, which makes upholding informed consent and disclosure a challenge.

Social media regulated by a country's laws may differ from the users' country of residence and users struggle to negotiate this variation. While social media is 'geographically boundless' there are influential national or local considerations.

STRATEGIES FOR MANAGING ONLINE RISKS

As a result of these concerns and barriers for users to be informed about social media, users developed strategies for managing online risks. These strategies included restricting content shared and adjusting privacy settings. This all has an implication on studies using data from social media platforms. Now more than ever, users of social media are becoming aware of inherent risks of sharing their information online. The added challenge of this to researchers seeking to undertake social media research is the growing scepticism and apprehension of users to share their information and to agree to researchers to undertake research.

We've explored the different ways users engage with content online and the extent to which they are aware and understand inherent risks associated with the characteristics of social media. Next we discuss how these users view research online and using social media data.

USER VIEWS OF THE VALUE OF SOCIAL MEDIA RESEARCH

Understanding how users view online and social media research is useful for understanding how online and social media research can gain public acceptance much the same as more traditional methods are accepted. This understanding also has an added benefit; if we know how to encourage greater acceptance in this form of research maybe we can inspire more people to participate in it.

To capture these views we simulated scenarios by using vignettes. The topics explored were difficult to explain to participants who may not be familiar with social media or the terminology used. For example, using software to mass download tweets or a researcher using self-help online forums to research sensitive subjects and using that information to inform a study. Many of the topics covered also required participants to think hypothetically so it was decided to use vignettes to illustrate key points and stimulate discussion (see Appendix B in Beninger et al, 2014).

Users' feelings about research using social media fell into three categories: scepticism, acceptance and ambivalence. Views were closely related to a participant's knowledge and awareness of social media websites and how their information could be used for research. Views also varied greatly depending on the research context. Users' feelings were influenced by scenarios where they or others were actively rather than passively involved in social media research; Netnography requires participants to interact with a researcher, whereas the role of the participant is passive when tweets are mined alongside millions of others. Let's look at these three views in turn.

Scepticism

Scepticism about social media research was expressed and found to be related to uncertainty about the validity of data compared to traditional methods and the lack of transparency of the 'online world'. Those expressing scepticism about research using social media felt unsure and confused about how researchers would use social media posts and why this would be more beneficial than traditional face-to-face methods. The view that face-to-face research is superior highlights the general public's lack of understanding of the value of social media research. For users to participate in social media research they first need to know what personal information is held online, what people like researchers are doing with their data and why this research might be valuable.

Participants were also concerned about the lack of transparency associated with the 'online world'. Lack of transparency was due to the fact that people can hide their identity online, have their views overrepresented by sharing their views strongly and frequently and that anyone can misrepresent views online by taking them out of context. Concerns around transparency manifested themselves in two ways: the legitimacy of research agency, and transparency of the research purpose.

Concern was expressed about a research agency potentially using information in a way participants had not intended it to be used or to support a cause they did not agree with. This was more strongly represented by participants thinking about the passive use of their online information (e.g., through data mining). Participant's felt that there was a particular risk of this happening given that what people post online is often lacking context. The inability of users to confirm 'who they're dealing with' – whether the research agency was legitimate – made them hesitant about participating in online research and worry about the possible uses of their information if they did participate.

This concern over agency legitimacy was compounded by a lack of knowledge of how researchers were governed, or what rules or guidelines they were bound by when working online. These sceptical users wondered whether an 'ethical code of practice' existed and, if so, what it included. For example, participants were keen to know whether there were rules about the type and amount of information researchers could access online. It was felt that even if an 'ethical code' did exist there were concerns over who had created it, and whose interests they had at heart.

Those participants who thought of actively participating in online research (e.g., through an online forum or focus group) were less concerned by the legitimacy of researchers or how they were governed. This was because they interact with the researcher rather than being a passive bystander to the research.

Users also had concerns about the research purpose and were particularly worried about not being aware of this before they became involved/took part. There were concerns that findings would be used to defend or promote something that had not been explicitly explained at the outset or that certainly was not in their mind when they posted their data. It is for this reason that some participants were happy for researchers to use a verbatim quote however felt that '*if it actually involves taking your comments and interpreting it, then it's a very different thing*' (Male, 26–35, high user). It is the interpretation element, and the possibility for distorting the context in which something was said, and thus the meaning intended, that made participants have reservations.

Participants also discussed the audience of the research, for example, for commercial or academic and not-for profit use. The distinction between the uses of data for commercial or a social good made by participants determined whether research was considered of a 'good quality'. Research being conducted by a not-for-profit organisation, rather than for 'commercial' reasons, was preferred for two reasons. Participants preferred not-for-profit research uses because this was felt to be more '*productive*', more '*ethical*' and '*not exploitative*'. Not-for-profit uses of research were also preferred because participants did not like to think of their social media posts being used to generate a profit for others. It was acknowledged, however, that while it is not 'a good thing' for researchers to 'make money' from social media posts, it is already happening and *'we're way down the line now, it is way too far down to stop'* (Male, aged 26–35, medium user). This view held that if researchers did want to make money from social media posts and other information then *'you have a right to be informed'* (Male, aged 26–35, medium user).

Acceptance

An alternative view of research using social media was acceptance of the method. Participants holding this view discussed the value of its methodological approach and the benefits it may have to society. Accepting views were also expressed by those users who 'self-regulated' online. These participants only posted online what they were happy for others to access, and therefore accepted that researchers may take/use their information and were comfortable with this.

Firstly, it was recognised that the data collection methods used in online research could be beneficial when trying to analyse and understand broad social trends. Participants felt that using large amounts of data would mitigate the effect of spurious information or extreme views and would therefore be useful for analysis. It was felt that this could make the research accurate.

Research using social media was also seen as valuable by participants as it was felt to avoid bias inherent in having to answer questions in the presence of others, such as in a survey. This ties in strongly with the idea that for some more personal/private subjects, people are more likely to be open and honest online. Users believed this made social media research valuable.

Secondly, participants were also accepting of being included in research using their social media information if it was for 'social benefit'. This was particularly the case if the research was about something the participant deemed important, for example, if its findings helped to improve public services or raise awareness about an important social issue, such as domestic violence.

Some, but not all, participants who accepted social media research saw value in more commercial purposes, such as market or for-profit. The reason for this related to the recurring view that once you post publicly on a social media website, you waive your right to ownership. One user outlined this viewpoint about social media by saying, *'If you've written on it and you know that it's open, every single person in the whole world has that if they want to…and it doesn't really matter [who the researcher is]'* (Female, aged 18–25, high user).

Thirdly, acceptance of social media research stemmed from participant's belief that users should take personal responsibility for what they post on social media websites. Due to regulating their own online behaviour, these participants did not see any issues with researchers taking data and using it for analysis. Participants extended this view to others and felt that it was the user's fault if something was taken that they did not want published.

It is important to recognise that although this point indicates acceptance of research using social media it also sheds light on the fact that many people severely limit what they say/post online.

Ambivalence

The final view on social media research can be described as ambivalent, with users having no feelings towards research using social media. This was because participants felt they could do little to stop it happening. Participants worried about 'Big Brother' culture and saw the use of social media data (whether ethically or unethically) as inevitable.

It was accepted that having your information taken was *'just part and parcel of it, that's what happens when you put stuff on the Internet'*. The expression of neither concern nor acceptance was because users felt, whatever their view, it would not be listened to.

In discussing general views on research using social media, users in this study spontaneously raised the underlying issues that core research ethics principles represent. These principles include informed consent, anonymity and undue harm. These ethical concepts have been applied to what users in the study said, enabling the research to locate the findings in the wider context of debates and research ethics.

USER VIEWS OF THE ETHICS OF SOCIAL MEDIA RESEARCH

If a research project is to be deemed ethical, researchers must gain informed consent (in most instances); anonymity must be ensured and undue harm to participants avoided (ESRC, 2012). These are core research ethics principles that were echoed by the users of social media in our study. The factors which make it especially important for researchers to gain consent or promise anonymity in research from the perspective of user are discussed. These included the content of the post; the social media website being used; the intention the user had when posting and the nature of the research.

Informed Consent

Participants expressed a range of views about the extent to which researchers should seek informed consent when observing how people interact in social media or when collecting posts made on social media sites. The two main views were that consent is unnecessary and, on the other hand, that it should be sought by a researcher. Participants who did not think consent needed to be gained believed this because *'there is no such thing as privacy online'*, and by posting content you automatically consent to its wider use. In contrast, users who believed consent should always be sought said so for two reasons; common courtesy and the 'intellectual property' rights of users. These two views are discussed in more detail below.

The view that no online space is truly private was expressed by participants who felt that gaining informed consent was unnecessary. This was because users of social media can choose what to share online and utilise privacy settings if they want to restrict a researcher's access to their information.

It was thought that by posting information online, you automatically surrender your right to ownership and imply consent for the material you generate to be used by others. Users should know that *'if you put the data up there, expect it to be trawled through'* (Male, aged 34, medium user) and that *'anybody could be logged in, listening, watching, stealing'* (Male, aged 26–35, medium user).

The reasons given by those supporting the alternative view; that researchers should seek consent to use information obtained online, were varied. Gaining consent to use another's words or imagery was seen as part of common decency. Consent should not solely be obtained to ensure good ethical practice but rather because *'In reality you wouldn't dream of doing something or stepping on somebody's toes without having to ask permission first of all anyway, would you?'* (Male, aged 36–49, high user).

There was also a belief that users are the intellectual property owners of content they post to social media websites. Not to gain consent *'would be like hacking'* (Female, aged 45, medium user) and therefore viewed as an illegal practice. It was believed researchers should treat the posts in line with copyright laws because *'…They've got no right to take that…because even though it is on a public site, if your name's underneath surely you own what you've said?'* (Male, aged 26–35, low user),

Despite the belief that researchers have a legal and moral obligation to gain permission before using online content from social media websites, it was not thought to happen currently, and would not in the future. Users' inability to trust researchers to seek consent was captured in the view that *'you couldn't know who you're dealing with'* online. Participants felt there was no tangible evidence that researchers could provide to reassure them. Given these viewpoints, it is important that researchers do seek informed consent to allay such suspicions and concerns.

Despite the view that researchers should ask permission before using content from social media websites, the impracticalities of obtaining consent were recognised by participants. It was acknowledged that a researcher who had 'scraped' a large number of tweets (by using legal software) would find it hard if not impossible to contact all the users.

Those participants who wanted consent to be gained, did not think the logistical burdens of doing so were a justification for not seeking permission. However, suggestions about how to contact numerous Twitter users, for example, were not discussed.

Anonymity

Anonymity for some participants meant not having their name, or username, used in any research outputs alongside any content they posted online. There were two reasons expressed for why anonymity should be upheld: to avoid judgement from others and to prevent reputational risk. To make the situation more complicated, the terms and conditions of some platforms, like Twitter, contradict this view of upholding anonymity. Twitters' terms state that the verbatim tweet and the username of the person who tweeted it must appear if a researcher wants to use the information.

For participants who disagreed with the need for anonymity, the reason was they felt it was the responsibility of a social media user to not post any content that they would not want to have associated within another context or alongside other content. It is up to the user to manage their identity when online. There was also a view that some responsibility should fall on social media website owners to educate users about the potential risks of sharing content online.

The view that *'it's absolutely fine for [researchers] to take anything that you've posted as long as they don't give your name'* (Female, aged 50–60, high user) illustrates the importance some users put on protecting anonymity. Participants expressed concern about having their name or username published by a researcher alongside one of their posts because it could put them at risk of judgement or ridicule.

Risks to reputation were another reason raised by advocates of anonymity. Individuals with responsibility for potentially vulnerable or impressionable individuals were concerned that their professional reputation could be compromised if they were quoted next to something they had said that was then taken out of context. A school teacher and a health professional were among those who expressed this view. Similarly, participants using social media as part of their professional communications envisaged possible risks on their careers.

The opposing view, that researchers do not need to provide anonymity, was also expressed. The reason was similar as that given for why gaining consent is unnecessary: that it is the responsibility of the user. One participant explained that you *'can always be anonymous if you want to be'* (Male, aged 26–35, medium user). It was believed, for example, that a user could protect their identity by using a username unrelated to their real name.

It was thought that researchers could also 'do away with' anonymity because it was not their responsibility but that of social media website owners. Website owners should make it clearer to their customers how accessible their posts are. The user could then make an informed decision about what and where to post. Discussed at this point were the terms and conditions that social media websites present to new users. Our participants acknowledged that the accessibility of posts to 'third parties', which researchers were considered to be, is probably explained in the 'small print'. However, it was believed that terms and conditions are too long and that most people 'can't be bothered' to sift through them. As such, we suggest social media website owners or hosts should take on some of the responsibility of informing users about privacy by shortening terms and conditions.

The importance of 'proper' referencing of the author of an online post used by researchers was also discussed. By referencing participants meant the type of content researchers should cite when attributing content they include in their studies. For example, the platform the content was taken from and the online username of the author of the content. However, including a 'handle' or the online username in a reference was perceived to be problematic because it can make a person traceable online. Researchers will need to find a way to balance the opposing needs for anonymity and acknowledgment of their sources. This is tricky because mentioning that a quote is from Twitter, for example, does not ensure that the user remains anonymous. Even if their Twitter handle is not given, typing the text of a tweet into an online search engine can lead straight to the user's profile (Dawson, 2014).

The potential ethical implications of referencing participants are only part of the challenge; It is hardly feasible to reference every user of a million tweets harvested from Twitter as part of a big data study. Even on a small-scale study, spot-checking the traceability of content taken from online platforms is a substantial task. The human, time and financial cost make referencing a difficult activity to undertake for many types of studies.

Avoiding Undue Harm

The third ethical principle relevant to participants was about ensuring social media website users are not put at risk in the research context and that they are not caused harm that could be avoided. Participants were wary about how they could be sure of what researchers were saying, and how difficult it would be online to decide if they were even 'legitimate' researchers, such as those working for an 'accredited firm' that is registered by the Market Research Society or Social Research Association.

Closely related to anonymity as discussed above, participants felt that being identifiable in research could lead to unsolicited attention online and, more seriously, 'abuse'. This might be from people they knew, or from organisations that could 'exploit' them. For others it meant use by the police or courts, for purposes of prosecution.

FACTORS INFLUENCING USERS' VIEWS OF ETHICS

Elements of the research context influenced users' views and expectations of informed consent and anonymity. The ethical rationale for gaining informed consent is that the participant understands exactly what their participation will entail and how their data will be used. This also has a practical benefit, building trust between the researcher and the participant. Similarly, the principle of anonymity is often sought to protect the identity of the participant and encourage more open and honest discussion. In our group discussions, we used real and hypothetical examples of how researchers could use social media websites (in the form of vignettes). The vignettes focused participants thinking of examples of scenarios wrought with ethical considerations, allowing the research team to gain a more nuanced understanding of the variation in research contexts that influence users' views of ethics. Participants mentioned a range of factors which made it particularly important for researchers to gain consent or promise anonymity. These factors, listed below, are described in detail in the remainder of the chapter.

- Mode and content of the posts;
- Social media website being used;
- The expectations the user had when posting;
- The nature of the research.

Mode and Content of the Posts

The content of social media posts was an important consideration for users when discussing the necessity of anonymity. Format was viewed in two ways: as written forms (tweets, or forum posts) and as visual media (photos, or video). Participants who actively 'self-regulated' when they were online did not think researchers needed to gain consent and this held true whatever the type and content of the post. Alternatively, other users felt that the format of post and the content would dictate whether a researcher should gain consent.

Written Content

One view was that researchers should ask to use any written content posted by users to social media websites. This would especially be the case if the researcher intended to include the username with the written content. A different, less feasible, view was that the researcher did not need to ask for consent to use tweets, so long as they were sure the tweet was an accurate representation of the users' views. However, it was not mentioned how a researcher might verify what is or is not an accurate representation of what a user thinks.

Photos

Users were more concerned about researchers accessing and using photos than for written content because '*if you write something, anybody could've written it, whereas with your picture they know it's you*' (Female, aged 18–25, high user). Due to the user – or their friends and family – being identifiable from photos, the participants were keen to claim ownership of images. The interplay between being identifiable and ownership meant they were more concerned about their photos being used in research without consent, compared to written content like a tweet or a status update.

A different view was that you give up your right to ownership the minute you post a photo on a social media website. This is because most social media websites, like Facebook, allow you to save another's photo by right clicking on the image. Researchers therefore have as much right as anyone to obtain photos and do not need to ask for consent.

Additionally, participants queried what rights users have over a photo which features them but which had been posted by someone else – would a third party need their permission to use it? This remained unresolved in the discussions.

Sensitivity of Content

Participants also explained that the sensitivity of the content was important for researchers to consider when deciding whether to seek consent and uphold anonymity. Users thought that if something posted to a social media website was particularly sensitive or personal, then informed consent should be gained by the researcher.

It is often difficult to determine what is sensitive; everyone will have a different interpretation of this. 'Mundane' or 'generic' content was excluded from this expectation. For example, tweets about the London Olympic Games were not considered sensitive. Another example was attitudes about bottle versus breastfeeding, which we probed about when discussing Vignette 2 (See Appendix B in Beninger et al, 2014). Viewpoints about this topic were not considered to be sensitive or personal either.

However, if the topic of a tweet '*goes down a little bit deeper*' (Female, aged 50–60, low user) in that it has a 'sexual, political or religious' focus, then it was felt that the researcher would need to ask permission to use it. Irrespective of the sensitivity of a post, the way in which the post was used mattered for users depending on whether they envisioned themselves as active participants compared to passive participants in online research. Participants actively involved in an online study, who have had interactions with the researcher and an understanding of how and why findings will be used were more likely to think that the researcher should not be barred completely from using the material, only that they should take the necessary steps to uphold the ethical principles of research, such as ensuring the participants' anonymity.

Type of Platform

The type of social media website was another factor that influenced whether our participants thought consent definitely needed to be gained by a researcher, or could just be assumed. Social media websites with a fun, social purpose were viewed differently from websites with a professional aim.

The difference is based on how personal the information that is usually posted to the two sites and links to the section above about sensitive content. Websites with a social purpose contain much more 'personal' content, whereas content posted to 'professional' sites like LinkedIn is less so. In light of this, participants thought that it would be acceptable for researchers to access the latter without gaining consent because the nature of the information on professional sites like LinkedIn is less sensitive.

User Expectations

Whether a researcher needed to gain consent to use social media posts was also influenced by user expectations. If a user intended for their post to be widely accessible or public (e.g., on Twitter or LinkedIn where profiles tend to be open to a very wide potential audience), then there was a view that a researcher would not necessarily need to gain consent to use it. This is because the user, by posting publicly online, implies that they are surrendering ownership. Participants acknowledged that this view assumed Twitter or LinkedIn users understood the openness and accessibility of the platform, which may not be the case.

An alternative view was that users did not want something published by researchers if they had not meant it to be public in the first place or it was posted for a different purpose. This would include a Facebook status where the user's profile was limited to friends and 'friends-of-friends'. The intention for a post was felt to be more important than the site from which a researcher took it.

For researchers, this means that no matter how open or public a site is considered to be, the user's expectation about how the post should be used is what should be considered at the recruitment stage. While checking users' expectations of how their information is used is ideal, in practice this would be difficult. The time and effort needed to do this is significant and researchers need to weigh up the pros and cons of this activity if considering assessing users' expectations.

Nature of the Research

The nature of the research in question also affected participant's views on research ethics. Use of social media website posts by researchers was affected by the affiliation of the researcher and the purpose of the research. What these features mean for researchers needing to gain informed consent and afford anonymity is subject of the next two sections.

Researcher Affiliation

The type of organisation or company that the research was affiliated with, such as charitable or commercial, influenced whether or not participants viewed research to be of 'good quality'. There was no mention of government or a comparison between government and non-government in the discussions.

Instead, a distinction was made between not-for-profit and commercial organisations. Research being conducted by a not-for-profit organisation or academic institution, rather than for 'commercial' reasons, was preferred for two reasons.

Participants who preferred not-for-profit researchers to commercial organisations did so because the former were felt to be more 'productive', more 'ethical' and 'not exploitative'. The focus here for participants was on the perceived social good not-for-profit or academic organisations can provide through their research. It was felt there was more value to this type of research because it looked to make a difference rather than being primarily motivated by financial gain.

The second reason not-for-profit researchers were preferred is because participants did not like to think of their social media posts being used to generate a profit for others. There was a perception, however, that while it is not 'a good thing' for researchers to 'make money' from social media posts, it is already happening and *'we're way down the line now, it is way too far down to stop'* (Male, aged 26–49, medium user).

Not all of the participants were concerned about the affiliation of the researcher. The reason for this related to the recurring view that once you post publicly on a social media website, you waive your right to ownership. One user outlined this viewpoint about social media by saying, *'If you've written on it and you know that it's open, every single person in the whole world has that if they want to...and it doesn't really matter [who the researcher is]'* (Female, aged 18–25, high user).

Other users were unaware of the differences between not-for-profit and commercial researchers or did not care about the distinction. As such, they had little to say about how researcher affiliation might influence their desire to agree to informed consent.

Research Purpose

Although concern about the affiliation of the researcher was not widespread, the concern about the 'purpose' of the research was. The research purpose had a bearing on whether participants wanted to be informed about their social media posts being used in research. Participants expressed worry about their posts being used to 'drive an agenda' they would not have agreed to if the researcher had asked them.

Using social media content to 'drive a [commercial] agenda' was seen differently from research offering a social benefit. By commercial agenda, participants were primarily referring to the use of social media information for market research purposes. Participants felt the use of their content for financial gain that they did not benefit from was morally problematic.

For our participants, research for a 'good reason' meant a study that had some social benefit. For example, research aimed at providing more knowledge about a particular social issue such as domestic violence would be of social benefit particularly if it were to improve support for victims. Research for a good purpose could also include research 'genuinely used to try and improve our services'; services in this instance being public transport or customer service provision.

In discussions around the vignette about domestic violence (see Appendix B in Beninger et al, 2014) the potential benefit to society of using online content to understand the experience of abuse, was felt to outweigh the risk to the user who shared that information.

While there is variation in views, it is clear from what our participants told us that researchers well in advance of beginning their work and throughout their study should explore these principles. Many of the views of social media users are not captured in research ethics forms or applications to conduct research, nor flushed out in emerging guidance on conducting research online. Assumptions should not be made about what is and what is not right because users' views vary dramatically.

CONCLUSION

This chapter explored the views and experiences of a qualitative sample of the general public to better understand what they think constitute 'good' ethical practice in online and social media research. It began with a summary of existing literature on ethical considerations in online and social media research then introduced how some users engage and interact with and understand information online. We then moved from users' views and behaviours about social media generally to explore initial impressions of online and social media research. Lastly, users views on the underlying issues that core research ethics principles – informed consent, anonymity and undue harm – represent were discussed. The value of this research lies in its ability to shed light on a previously underrepresented group in the field of social media research: the user.

The research presented here muddies the water, making the application of traditional ethical principles more challenging and vulnerable to the dynamic progress of social media platforms and functions. The quickly evolving landscape and the complexities of online and social media research means it is more important than ever for online researchers to speak loud and proud about what design and methodology led to their outputs. Case studies capturing where ethical considerations in online and social media research could have been improved may support this body of knowledge and encourage the move towards developing a toolkit of conceptual and practical approaches to upholding ethical practice in research (e.g. Zimmer, 2010). In order for the field of online and social media research to retain the good will of participants and gain credibility from the sceptics it's important that researchers are brave and acknowledge the strengths and limitations of their research designs and though processes from which they are drawn.

Ethical considerations in research have been and will continue to be a balancing act. We need to balance the concerns of our participants with our desire to research and understand social behaviour. Online and social media research has the potential for unearthing new understandings and adding unique insight to existing knowledge about social phenomenon, but the ethical implications require on-going scrutiny. As with any research study, ethical considerations should become an integral part of research design and conduct, a crucial component of high quality research. So rather than being viewed as part of the set-set up stage of research and perceived as an obstacle to overcome, we should consider ethics as part of each research decision made to improve the validity and credibility of our work. Careful consideration of how and when to apply guidelines and principles to the quickly evolving online platforms will help practitioners and researchers to better deliver robust research. For this to happen in a nascent research field, researchers may need collaborative and supportive guidance rather than rigid, inflexible guidelines.

Three key practical suggestions for improving research practice have been drawn from this research and researchers may want to consider the proportionality of these suggestions against the context of their research.

To ethically recruit participants to online and social media research take steps to appear legitimate, accommodate different user types and be transparent in your purpose and aims. To achieve this consider explicitly stating the security and privacy terms in recruitment materials of the platform the research will involve and explain where you got a participants contact details (i.e. Searched Facebook for public profiles). Another option may be to include a link to your company or institutions webpage or examples of previous work.

To uphold protection and trust of participants, improve the representativeness of findings and understand the privacy risks of the platform used in a study. An example of how to do this in practice is to take time to consider the openness of a platform you are using and whether steps can be taken to gain trust of users (i.e. if a closed chatroom consider introducing yourself and state your research purposes and ask participants to opt into your research). You may also wish to acknowledge the different ways users engage online – create, share and observe – and how your data may include a very specific view or type of user in your outputs.

To protect the identity of participants, maintain their trust in the value of the research and contribute to the progression of the field by being open and honest in reporting you can take several steps. You can take responsible steps to inform the user of your intention to use their information through mass tweets, direct tweets, private messaging or email. As with all rigorous research, you should acknowledge the limitations of the representativeness and validity of your findings and explicitly state the platform used (i.e. Facebook rather than generally saying social media) when reporting research findings.

NOTE

1   A special thanks to my co-authors of the report Alexandra Fry, Natalie Jago, Hayley Lepps, Laura Nass and Hannah Silvester, and to Gareth Morrell for his invaluable mentoring.

REFERENCES

Barratt, M.J. and Lenton, S. (2010). Beyond recruitment? Participatory online research with people who use drugs. *International Journal of Internet Research Ethics*, 3(12), 69–86.

Beninger, K., Fry, A., Jago, N., Lepps, H., Nass, L., and Silvester, H. (2014). Research using social media; Users' Views. NatCen Social Research.

boyd, d. (2010, April). *Privacy and Publicity in the Context of Big Data*. 2010. Raleigh, North Carolina.

Buchanan, E. (2011). Internet Research Ethics. In *The Handbook of Internet Studies*. London: Wiley-Blackwell. Edited by Consalvo, M., Ess, C. p. 93.

British Psychological Society (2007). Report of the working Party on Conducting Research on the Internet: Guidelines for ethical practice in psychological research online. Leicester: The British Psychological Society.

British Psychological Society (2013). 'Ethics Guidelines for Internet-mediated Research'. INF206/1.2013. Leicester: Author. Available from: www.bps.org.uk/publications/policy-and- guidelines/research-guidelines-policy-documents/research-guidelines-poli [Accessed 3 March 2015]

Cannataci, J. (2014, April). *Data protection and the use of personal data from the internet.* Paper presented at Research Ethics into the Digital Age. Sheffield: Sheffield University.

Dawson, P. (2014). Our anonymous online research participants are not always anonymous. Is this a problem? *British Journal of Educational Technology*, 45(3), 428–437.

ESOMAR (2011). ESOMAR guideline on social media research. Retrieved from https://www.esomar.org/uploads/public/knowledge-and-standards/codes-and-guidelines/ESOMAR-Guideline-on-Social-Media-Research.pdf [Accessed 18 March 2015]

ESRC (Economic and Social Research Council) (2012). *ESRC Framework for Research Ethics*. Swindon: Economic and Social Research Council.

Ginnis, S., Evans, H., Bartlett, J., and Barker, I. (2015). Unlocking the value of social media: Work package 3 Ethics. *Wisdom of the crowd*. Retrieved from https://www.ipsos-mori.com/researchareas/digitalresearch/sociallistening/wisdomofthecrowd/publications.aspx [Accessed 18 March 2015]

GSR (Government Social Research Unit) (2006). *GSR Professional Guidance: Ethical Assurance for Social Research in Government*. London: HM Treasury.

Jenkins, R. (2014, April). *Ethical challenges of international research.* Paper presented at Research Ethics into the Digital Age. Sheffield: Sheffield University.

Liu, S. B. (2010). The Emerging Ethics of Studying Social Media Use with a Heritage Twist. 'Revisiting Research Ethics in the Facebook Era: Challenges in Emerging CSCW Research'. *Workshop at ACM Conference on Computer-Supported Cooperative Work (CSCW 2010)*, Savannah, GA.

Markham, A., and Buchanan, E. (2012). *Ethical Decision-Making and Internet Research: Recommendations from the AoIR Ethics Working Committee*. Retrieved from http://aoir.org/reports/ethics2.pdf

Moreno, M., Goniu, N., Moreno, P., and Diekema, D. (2013). Ethics of Social Media Research: Common Concerns and Practical Considerations. *Cyber Psychology Behaviour and Social Networking*, 16(9), 708–713.

MRS (Market Research Society) (2012). *MRS Guidelines for Online Research*. London: MRS Evidence Matters.

Roberts, L. (2012). Ethical Issues in Conducting Qualitative Research in Online Communities, published on the NSMNSS blog, available at: http://nsmnss.blogspot.co.uk/2012/07/ethical-issues-in-conducting.html [Accessed 20.03.15]

Thelwall, M. (2010). Researching the public web 12 July. *eResearch Ethics*. [Online]. [Accessed 25 January 2015]. Available from: http://eresearch-ethics.org/position/researching-the-public-web/

Webster, S., Lewis, J., and Brown, A. (2013). Ethical Considerations in Qualitative Research. In *Qualitative Research Practice: A guide for Social Science Students and Researchers*. (pp 77–107). London: Sage Publications.

Zimmer, M. (2010). But the data is already public: On the ethics of research in Facebook. *Ethics & Information Technology*, 12(4), pp 313–325.

The Role of Online Reputation Management, Trolling, and Personality Traits in the Crafting of the Virtual Self on Social Media

Shuzhe Yang, Anabel Quan-Haase, Andrew D. Nevin and Yimin Chen

This chapter investigates how users craft a virtual self to engage with their networks on social media. An important consideration in social media research methodology is the extent to which users' accounts, including their profile and engagement, reflect elements of the self. To inform and expand data-driven approaches – both quantitative and qualitative – we examine three central aspects of digital engagement that are often ignored in social media scholarship, but directly impact data analysis and interpretation. First, we examine online reputation management, which describes the tendency for individuals to curate a desired self-image through selective presentation of personal data. Then, we look at shifts in personality traits and the role of e-personality in influencing online self-presentation and interaction on social media. Finally, we investigate trolling, which is a deliberate form of misleading, provoking, and making fun of others online. Using these three themes, we conclude that social media scholars need to carefully consider the context in which profiles are created and interactions take place in terms of platform-specific social norms and domain-specific knowledge. The real meaning of data is not always readily apparent, and its decoding may require further theorizing around social behaviour and its underlying motives.

INTRODUCTION

Much research has investigated how people craft a virtual self (Krämer and Winter, 2008; Rui and Stefanone, 2013), how the virtual self is both different from and an extension of the offline self (Amichai-Hamburger et al., 2002; Emanuel et al., 2014), and what strategies and processes underlie reputation management online (Tennie et al., 2010; Yang, 2016). These research questions have been of particular relevance to scholars of social media because the first step in social media participation and engagement is the creation of a profile (boyd and Ellison, 2007; McCay-Peet and Quan-Haase, 2016). Sundén (2003) recognized the deliberate nature of online self-presentation and introduced the notion of *writing oneself into being*, which highlights the agency involved in creating a virtual self through posting text, uploading images, and engaging with one's social network via likes, retweets, and favourites. What remains less clear is how the virtual self links to the offline self (Marwick et al., 2010; Palfrey and Gasser, 2008). For Turkle (1984) the virtual self is a second self, one that is more playful and allows for an escape from everyday life. By contrast, Hogan (2010) links self-presentation to data curation and argues that self-presentation is a careful crafting of the self for the purpose of reputation management and identity creation online. Hence, the virtual self is an extension of the offline self (Palfrey and Gasser, 2008), which sometimes presents facets of the offline self, those that are perceived as accepted and valued within specific digital sub-cultures. Scholars have consistently shown that the virtual self on social media does not fully overlap with the real self, but neither is it unrelated as Turkle had suggested (Amichai–Hamburger, 2005; Donath, 1999).

Shakespeare said that: 'All the world's a stage, and all the men and women merely players' (As you Like it, Act 2, Scene 7). Social media is yet another stage for performativity, but one where play is limited because our real-world connections to friends and family tend to serve as a means of data verification, thus keeping the virtual self close to the real self (Zhao, Grasmuck and Martin, 2008). Hogan and Quan-Haase (2010) have stressed this: the integration of the virtual self with the offline self has become increasingly pronounced as social media becomes integrated into the rhythms of everyday life. But, how close is the virtual self to the real self? Which facet(s) of the real self does the virtual self represent? Can we trust information representing the self on social media via profile information, likes, images, and social connections?

The purpose of this chapter is to show how processes of self-presentation influence methodological considerations and decisions in the study of social media phenomena both in large-scale quantitative analysis and in qualitative work. Scholars of social media need to grapple with questions of self-presentation because virtual selves are not always true representations of the self; they are often performances influenced by many factors including reputation management, social context, platform features, data curation, motivations, and also social and community norms. A user profile can either present a person in a more positive light through reputation management (Eisenegger and Imhof, 2008), or can contain purposefully deceitful information for the purposes of trolling (Buckels et al., 2014; Coleman, 2012). We analyze the prominent literature in three central areas and discuss the implications for deciding what methodologies to use in different contexts, as well as the challenges existent in these approaches. First, we explore how users engage in online reputation management in order to control their self-presentation, present themselves in a better light, and enhance trust during interactions with strangers (Eisenegger and Imhof, 2008; Farmer and Glass, 2010). Second, we examine how personality affects the crafting of the self in terms of shifts in trait expression on the Internet compared to offline (Nevin, 2015). Third, we investigate trolling, which is a deliberate form of misleading, provoking, and making fun of others (Coleman, 2012). Finally, we discuss several approaches and strategies for handling profile data and examining interactions on social media with an eye toward self-idealization, deception, and trolling. Through this review, we aim to discuss how discrepancies between the virtual and offline self arise, how these differences can be interpreted, what approaches exist for detecting differences, and how these differences can be taken into account in data collection, analysis, interpretation, and visualization.

ONLINE REPUTATION MANAGEMENT

A person's online reputation is the 'set of beliefs, perceptions, and evaluations a community forms about one of its members' (Anderson and Shirako, 2008: 320) and includes any activity on social media for the purpose of reputation building, maintenance, and enhancing (Burkhardt, 2008). People engage in online reputation management, employing a wide range of strategies to present themselves in the best light possible. As users create complex profiles on social media platforms the question arises as to how much of the digital representation is an idealized version of the self.

Previous studies have identified different strategies in self-presentation online and offline (Emanuel et al., 2014). Offline reputation management occurs more spontaneously and in the moment, whereas online reputation management is a more conscious, premeditated, and goal-driven type of engagement, in which information is edited, filtered, and modified (Stanculescu, 2011). For example, previous studies have shown that teens 'select photos based on the images' attractiveness' (Kapidzic and Herring, 2015: 971) before uploading them to social media platforms. Spontaneity in offline reputation management leads to disclosure of substantially more personal information than in online situations (Emanuel et al., 2014). This suggests that social media profiles are carefully curated and present a self that is edited, remixed, and framed.

Personal online reputation management strategies are platform and context dependent. On professional social media platforms, such as LinkedIn, individuals share different kinds of information than on private social media platforms because of the different social norms at play as well as different goals and motivations (e.g., new job opportunities or making professional connections) underlying their use (Mehdizadeh, 2010; Yang, 2015). Platform-specific features also influence people's online reputation management efforts. Facebook, for example, offers individual privacy settings, which facilitate the creation of partial identities and enhance control over what information is revealed and to whom (Deuker, 2014). This allows for different self-presentations to different social circles (Marwick and boyd, 2011). The importance of context becomes clear when we look at the example of inside jokes; in the offline context, inside jokes are told in specific social situations or social circles in which others are expected to understand the joke. The reputation of the joke teller increases because (inside) jokes signal social intelligence (Wierzbicki and Young, 1978). But such jokes are difficult to identify in data gathered from social media platforms because the researcher is often unaware of the context in which the joke was told. The intention and effect of the inside joke could be misinterpreted during data analysis, leading a researcher to mistakenly infer a negative reputation for the joke teller and deduct discrepancies between selves that don't actually exist. Therefore, evaluating a social media profile without taking platform-specific online reputation management strategies and communicative context into account can result in a limited or inaccurate view of who the person is. These considerations are critical for gaining a nuanced understanding of an individual's online self-presentation (Emanuel et al., 2014).

Evidence showing that personality traits influence how individuals present themselves online largely comes from research looking at the impact of anonymity on communication on the Internet. Introverts are more likely to use anonymous social media platforms, whereas extraverts prefer real name social media platforms as an extension of their offline selves (Amichai-Hamburger et al., 2002). Accordingly, analyzing introverts on real name social media platforms (e.g., Facebook) may lead to an incomplete view of a person's real self, as they share less information on such platforms. Researchers need to consider and include an introvert's activities on anonymous social media platforms (e.g., ello.co) in order to gain more data about that individual. Understanding the complex interaction between personality traits and personal goals is imperative for understanding what kinds of personal information is shared on various social media and why.

Another critical factor influencing the crafting of the virtual self is time, which is crucial on e-commerce platforms (Klewes and Wreschniok, 2009). On social media it is possible to trace back how individuals' reputation management motives, strategies, and/or goals evolve over time (Kim and Ahmad, 2013; Leary and Allen, 2011). A good example is the type of online reputation system in place on shopping platforms such as eBay or Amazon. These platforms store all published reviews since registration and provide an overall reputation score over a long period of time (Resnick et al., 2000). Thereby, the changes in a person's reputation on these platforms can be tracked.

When individuals create their social media profiles, they sometimes intentionally provide information that is false, incomplete, or misleading – such as sexual orientation, religion, and relationship status – in order to protect their privacy (boyd and Ellison, 2007; Dwyer et al., 2007; Gross and Acquisti, 2005). The reasons for providing false information are often trust concerns (e.g., misuse by other members of the social media platform). Others also publish false (e.g., social group affiliation) or fake information (e.g., fake photos for accusation of crime) about a person as a means of defamation or simply as a joke (Smith and Kidder, 2010). The inclusion of any inaccurate or false information in a study can result in reaching the wrong conclusions about a person's real self (Broadhurst and Kell, 2007).

Taking discrepancies between the offline and virtual self into account can reveal new research opportunities and provide new insights, as discrepancies can uncover gaps between one's current and desired online reputation. For instance, individuals often craft idealized profiles on professional social media platforms which differ from their real selves (van Dijck, 2013). By analyzing the variability across platforms, there is a chance to identify information individuals have hidden in order to protect themselves and information individuals have curated to enhance their professional reputations. The detection and measurement of gaps between various presentations of self is often crucial and time-consuming because scholars have to code data manually and cannot rely on software. Contextual anomalies can be detected by comparing a researcher's interpretation of an individual's reputation with the opinions of others (e.g., through sentiment analysis). Alternatively, collected data could be scrutinized and analyzed in order to identify sarcasm, irony, inside jokes, and/or cultural differences. Such analysis can provide insights into individuals' personal development over time, their creation of new identities, how social circles are organized, how individuals manage their online reputation differently in their social circles/roles, and how culture influences online reputation management. By reviewing these activities over time, it is possible to identify preferred strategies, the success of those strategies, and shifts in an individual's goals. Ultimately, gaps between the offline and virtual self can be a source for new research opportunities in personal online reputation management. For example, an idealized self-presentation of an employee's abilities and skills may result in disappointment when hired. Hence, researcher could investigate employer's expectations based on the virtual self and compared these to that employee's actual performance. The findings could provide insights into whether the creation of an idealized self is a worthwhile professional strategy.

Available social media data consisting of profiles, images, texts, and interactions such as retweets and likes are the constituents of a person's online self. This online self does not necessarily reflect the entire self, rather, such information often reflects a carefully curated and manipulated self to conform to platform-specific social norms and expectations, one that showcases a person's *idealized* self. The next section investigates in more detail how personality traits can affect the crafting of the self and how personality can be differently expressed between online and offline contexts in ways that can reflect tendencies toward increased deception on the Internet.

E-PERSONALITY AND SELF-PRESENTATION

Research on personality has stressed that personality traits are rather stable and consistent across social situations, characterizing an individual and his/her behaviours, dispositions, attitudes, cognitions, and emotions (McCrae and Costa, 1994). Even though personality traits are considered fairly stable over time, certain contexts can lead to shifts in personality expression (Allport, 1937; Kenrick et al., 1990; Mischel, 1973, 1977). This section suggests that social media is potentially one such context in which personality expression can change and, accordingly, influence the presentation of self online, which is something that should be taken into consideration by researchers. Personality traits often influence the presentation style, disclosure risk, and type of information that individuals tend to post on social media (Lee et al., 2014; Marcus et al., 2006; Michikyan et al., 2014), which can differ from intentional data curation and the meticulous reputation management that was discussed in the previous section. As such, this creates an additional layer of complexity when researchers are trying to interpret and understand the data available on social media.

While some scholars argue that anonymity on the Internet may allow for the emergence of latent personality traits that are usually constrained due to the social pressures of the material world (Amichai–Hamburger, 2005; Suler, 2004), others have proposed that there may be a multiplicity of online personalities that do not overlap with those in the offline realm (Turkle, 1984, 1995). The latter perspective is reflective of a theoretical framework of context-dependent personality expression, which suggests that situational cues and environmental factors can elicit changes in personality expression in different social contexts (Allport, 1937; Kenrick et al., 1990; Mischel, 1973, 1977). Research in this area has investigated the differences in online and offline personality – the former being encapsulated through the term *e-personality* (Aboujaoude, 2011). Studies examining e-personality have found reduced shyness (Stritzke et al., 2004) and increased psychopathic expression (Nevin, 2015) on the Internet. Scholars have tested this framework in the online context by using self-report data and methodologies that control for personality trait differences between online and offline environments (Blumer and Doering, 2012; Nevin, 2015; Stritzke et al., 2004). One common quantitative technique involves the use of similar scale measures that distinguish between online and offline situations by adding variations of the clause 'when on the Internet' in order to promote item consistency for contextual comparisons of the scores (Blumer and Doering, 2012; Nevin, 2015; Stritzke et al., 2004).

Various types of digital environments can differently impact the continuity between the virtual and offline self in terms of personality expression. When individuals know much of their judging audience from outside the Internet – as is often the case on social media platforms like Facebook where individuals largely connect with their circle of friends and family – there is a sense of accountability to express traits that align across social contexts. In these digital spaces there are *anchored relationships* (Zhao et al., 2008) that exist beyond the online world that serve to check the information posted on social media for personality and identity consistency with the offline self. On platforms with anchored relationships, expressing divergent e-personalities is more noticeable and incites confusion from peers or reinforces the impression that the individual is unpredictable, or even erratic and dishonest, across social contexts. As such, most individuals tend to exhibit traits from their actual offline personalities in their social media profiles (Back et al., 2010). However, adding elements of anonymity and pseudonymity in online communities, such as 4chan or Reddit, may reduce the sense of accountability, increasing the potential for misrepresentation or decreasing the desire for sincere and genuine self-disclosure (Bernstein et al., 2011; Galanxhi and Nah, 2007; Lapidot-Lefler and Barak, 2012). The difference in the types of interpersonal interactions and identity cues that differ between online platforms should be considered by scholars when interpreting data about the self on various social media platforms, with more critical scrutiny given to anonymous digital environments that lack internal checks and balances for ensuring self-congruence.

Digital interaction has been shown in some cases to influence the expression of personality traits in a positive direction. Stritzke et al. (2004) have suggested that some people can become more outgoing online when compared to how they typically express their shy personalities in offline interactions. They found that after previously dividing their study participants into shy and non-shy groups based on their responses to an offline inventory, both groups scored similarly on measures of rejection sensitivity, self-disclosure, and initiating relationships when completing a subsequent inventory that emphasized online interactions. On the other hand, social media may also bring about shifts toward the expression of negative traits, that is, *dark* e-personalities that are 'less restrained, a little bit on the dark side, and decidedly sexier' (Aboujaoude, 2011: 20), which can manifest in antisocial online behaviours. Nevin (2015) accordingly tested the discrepancy between online and offline expressions of dark personality – conceptualized in terms of psychopathy – using self-report survey data that specifically controlled for social context. For reference, psychopathy is a personality profile characterized by traits such as a lack of empathy or remorse, impulsiveness, manipulativeness, superficial charm, and a grandiose sense of self, as well as other antisocial indicators (Hare, 1991). This exploratory study found that individuals in the sample (especially males) expressed higher levels of *cyber-psychopathy* compared to offline psychopathy scores, suggesting that some Internet users slide toward expressions of subclinical psychopathic personality when online (Nevin, 2015). Cyber-psychopathy was also associated with increases in the participants' reported endorsements of deception and trolling practices, which are largely implicated in online misrepresentation (Nevin, 2015).

Heightened narcissism on the Internet is another important expression of dark e-personality that can impact the interpretation of data from social media. Narcissism, characterized by self-centeredness and vanity, is part of the Dark Triad of personality (Paulhus and Williams, 2002) and has become normalized online through self-promotional behaviours and *selfies* on social media platforms (Fox and Rooney, 2015). It has been suggested that such attention-seeking behaviours are reflective of a need to 'gain validation for inflated self-views' (Marshall et al., 2015: 36). As such, researchers need to consider that narcissistic e-personality may serve to reduce the objectivity of social media data by presenting misrepresented and idealized versions of self. Previous studies have found that narcissism can be observed on Facebook through high frequencies of status updates (Carpenter, 2012), as well as when the subjects of these posts are more focused on achievements, including boasts about diet and exercise (Marshall et al., 2015).

Linguistic methodologies such as text analyses and sentiment analyses can be used in text-based environments like social media to measure how personality traits are linked to online content (Boochever, 2012; Garcia and Sikström, 2014; Sumner et al., 2012). These methodologies are important considering that dark e-personality traits can now be identified via text analysis and can help with the interpretation of data by testing for the likelihood of misrepresentation. For example, some researchers have found that online posts that have many negative words, high levels of profanity, traces of anger, and unclear grammar can indicate psychopathy in social media platforms such as Facebook and Twitter (Boochever, 2012; Garcia and Sikström, 2014; Sumner et al., 2012). There are several different strategies that can be used to perform this type of text analysis. Sumner et al. (2012) have used machine learning algorithms to identify psychopathic personality traits from written content on social media by determining cases that have high or low scores on each trait of interest. They also statistically measured linguistic variables such as word length, tense, verb use, as well as semantic content in terms of emotions and topical themes to report correlations with personality variables. Boochever (2012) has taken a different approach by combining linguistic analyses with self-report personality measures to determine the linguistic indicators of psychopathy. She relied on a text analysis program called *Linguistic Inquiry and Word Count* (LIWC) (Pennebaker et al., 2007), which quantifies and categorizes linguistic units in a post in order to report the percentage of words that fall under each category. LIWC specifically focuses on 'linguistic dimensions, psychological constructs, personal concern categories, and paralinguistic dimensions' (Hancock et al., 2012: 15). Using such techniques can allow researchers to analyze previous posts or comment histories to test for dark e-personality traits (such as psychopathy or narcissism) that may underlie either deliberate or unintentional misrepresentation online. This method may serve as an initial check in order to flag cases that are high in dark e-personality expression, which might skew the data that are mined from social media profiles.

Overall, personality discrepancies between offline and online environments, as well as the inclination toward dark e-personality expression, may compromise the objectivity of the data on social media. As such, several approaches were discussed above, and other approaches in this book (Chapter 21, Rubin, this volume), can aid scholars in analyzing and interpreting rich and contextualized social media data. Such methods can sensitize scholars to discrepancies in personality across platforms and social contexts (Chapter 2 McCay-Peet and Quan-Haase, this volume). While some techniques show promise for assessing the likelihood of deception or misrepresentation, the conclusions drawn from social media data should always consider the limitations of potentially biased data resulting from shifts in personality expression on the Internet.

BIG DATA AND TROLLING

Big Data analytics have been heralded as revolutionary because they are data driven (Lohr, 2012). Some researchers and commentators have even gone so far as to proclaim that Big Data signals 'the end of theory' altogether (Anderson, 2008). With big enough data sets, the argument goes, 'knowledge discovery software tools find the patterns and tell the analyst what–and where–they are' (Dyche, 2012). Anderson (2008) has explained how inferences are drawn in this new paradigm, where '[c]orrelation supersedes causation, and science can advance even without coherent models, unified theories, or really any mechanistic explanation at all' (Anderson, 2008); or in other words, if only the humans and their often erratic behaviour would get out of the way, the data would be able to speak clearly for itself without the need to have theory as an interpreter.

There are many researchers, however, who dismiss this belief that data 'transcends context or domain-specific knowledge' (Kitchin, 2014: 4) as 'Big Data hubris' (Bruns, 2013; Lawson et al., 2015; Lazer et al., 2014: 1203). Indeed, an uncritical trust in the truthfulness of Big Data can be particularly myopic and even harmful in the realm of social media research. 'On the Internet', according to an adage almost as old as the Internet itself, 'no one knows you're a dog'.[1] Unfortunately, people tend to lie online (Caspi and Gorsky, 2006), and in some circles, deception may even be the norm rather than the exception (Knuttila, 2011). This poses a problem for Big Data analytics, which tends not to dwell on questions of truthfulness (Lukoianova and Rubin, 2014), such as what if the text does not mean what it says? What if, contrary to expectations, communicators are not engaging with each other frankly and in good faith?

Anyone who has spent time reading or writing messages on social media has likely encountered a troll: a person 'whose real intention(s) is/are to cause disruption and/or to trigger or exacerbate conflict for the purposes of their own amusement' (Hardaker, 2010: 237). This disruption can take many forms, including impersonation, pointless argumentation, off-topic or offensive messages, harassment, and pranking, and is often marked by 'a set of unifying linguistic and behavioural practices' (Phillips, 2015: 17) – i.e., memes. Despite general negativity towards trolls and their activities, the trolling subculture has largely been responsible for popularizing many of the Internet's most creative and enduring memes (Bernstein et al., 2011). For this reason, trolling is the most recognizable and widespread form of casual deception on the Internet and is likely to show up in any large social media dataset.

Trolling has traditionally been considered 'a game about identity deception' (Donath, 1999: 45), but it is a game that is often played with an audience in mind: other trolls. For example, in response to a user asking for computer help on a message forum, a troll might suggest deleting the System32 file, which is essential for Windows to run.[2] This action invites two opposite interpretations: to a naïve user, this is a hostile act of deception which may result in costly damages. For those who recognize the System32 meme, the initial trolling message can trigger a cascade of sarcastic banter as users who understand the joke offer encouragement and further misleading advice.[3] Among trolls, this type of transgressive, antagonistic humour at another's expense is known as *lulz*, a corruption of *laugh out loud* (Stoehrel and Lindgren, 2014). For social media research, recognizing these memetic signals (*lulz*) is the key to identifying and accurately interpreting trolling behaviour.

One of the core beliefs of many Internet trolls is the idea that 'nothing should be taken seriously' (Phillips, 2015: 26), which motivates them to mock, criticize, or denigrate Internet users who express strong opinions online. As such, trolls are drawn to social issues such as feminism, racism, and religion – issues that are often championed loudly by youthful proponents (Tatarchevskiy, 2011) across a wide variety of social media platforms. Twitter, for example, is home to many parody accounts poking fun at public[4] and religious figures.[5] Tumblr, which is known for its numerous gender-queer communities (Read, 2012), is often the target of trolls mocking those communities.[6] On Facebook, trolling might take place as a response to perceived insincere *slacktivism*, such as in the case of the Kony 2012 campaign (Collier, 2012).

While it may be tempting to dismiss trolling as random hostility or simply junk data, proper contextualization can reveal much about social relationships and norms online. In many ways, trolling can be interpreted as an extension of the Internet exceptionalism celebrated by early advocates like Rheingold (1993) and Barlow (1996). Trolls see the Internet as their home turf, and have even invented their own rules of netiquette.[7] Like the early hackers from whom they trace ancestry, trolls celebrate 'creative appropriation'; in their view, 'technologies were *made* to be played with' (Phillips, 2015: 131, emphasis in original). From this perspective, trolling is more a form of protest than an act of senseless aggression: 'trolls work to remind the *masses* that have lapped onto the shores of the Internet that there is still a class of geeks who, as their name suggests, will cause Internet grief' (Coleman, 2012: 109–110). From this perspective, it represents the 'tensions between dominant and subordinate groups' (Hebdige, 1979: 2) played out all across cyberspace.

Trolling messages are an important aspect to include in the data analysis. 'Trolls operate as agents of chaos on the Internet' (Buckels et al., 2014: 97) and can be crude, funny, obscene, and even criminal, but trolling is also the performance of an online, countercultural response to the encroachment of offline, mainstream sensibilities on the Internet (Hogan and Quan-Haase, 2010). At first glance, trolling may look like little more than hate speech and online abuse, but deeper readings reveal it to be 'a form of action that seeks to trick the person being trolled into revealing a hidden reality' (McDonald, 2015: 973). Through their antics, trolls poke and prod their targets into exposing the secret hypocrisies and antipathies that lie behind the mask of everyday politeness. In doing so, 'lulzy activity [transgressive jokes and pranks] defies boundaries but also re-erects them' and can be read as 'a form of cultural differentiation' (Coleman, 2014: 32).

What does trolling mean for social media analytics? In day-to-day life, people tend to exhibit a truth-bias; that is, they generally believe what they hear and read and information is taken at face value without much questioning of dominant discourses, unless they have reasons to suspect deception (Levine et al., 1999). In computer-mediated communication, physical and non-linguistic cues which might arouse suspicion or scepticism are often not present, making this effect even more pronounced and exploitable (Burgoon et al., 2010). While there is currently little data available on the extent and prevalence of online trolling, surveys have shown that 40 per cent of American adult Internet users have personally been the target of online harassment (Drake, 2015) and 73 per cent have witnessed it happening to other people (Duggan, 2014). It seems reasonable to infer from these statistics that trolls exert a very noticeable influence upon online communications and interactions and represent a population of Internet users who are much more likely than normal to be antagonistic, ironic, or deceptive. To interpret data from these sources only superficially is to miss the hidden layers of meaning that they encode. Researchers cannot simply assume that what is said is the same as what is meant; context and domain-specific knowledge is imperative in order to tease out the nuances of digital data on social media.

DATA MINING AND CONTEXTUALIZING THE VIRTUAL SELF

Most users are amused when they look back in their timeline or news feed and read over earlier posts and status updates. Some are even shocked to realize that they posted a picture of themselves in a compromising situation or made a comment that they now feel does not really reflect who they are. For example, a Canadian running as a candidate for parliamentary office experienced the detrimental effects of her earlier Twitter posts, which she had made public as a teenager (17 years of age, CBC, 2015). While we tend to think of the virtual self as a somewhat stable representation of a person and his/her true self, there is no clear link between data, traces, and footprints as found in social media and the offline self. Moreover, as individuals – particularly teenagers – mature, comments, posts, and behaviours that may reflect the frivolous nature of youth, may no longer reflect who they are as adults. Therefore, it is important for scholars embarking on a social media research project to take into account the following four suggestions.

Topic-dependency: The first step is to conduct a rigorous and systematic literature review of the research field of interest (vom Brocke et al., 2009), as a comprehensive literature review allows researchers to benefit from past experiences and best practices. This may be particularly relevant to identify developmentally-related changes to the self and changes related to context. For instance, existing publications provide insights into differences in online reputation management strategies on private and professional social media platforms (Yang, 2015). On professional social media platforms people are more likely to create an idealized profile (van Dijck, 2013) and update their profile information more often (Yang, 2015). A researcher can foresee and anticipate that data collection and analysis solely based on one social media platform may include discrepancies and lead to a distorted interpretation of a person's virtual self.

Data triangulation: Instead of relying on data collected from a single social media platform, data triangulation can be used to create a more comprehensive profile of a person. For example, sharing economy platforms, such as Airbnb, are a good source for verifiable demographic information on a person. Social media platforms that do not encourage people to use their real names (e.g., ello.co) are also a good source of data – even if very different in nature – for learning about expressions of dark e-personality traits and trolling behaviours that are less likely to surface on other public sites. On these platforms people often use nicknames and are at least partially anonymous to strangers. Anonymity encourages individuals to express their opinions more freely because they are less likely to encounter reprisal, such as social isolation (Reader, 2012). Alternative email addresses are unique identifiers that can also be used to link an anonymous profile to an individual's real identity. Mobile phone numbers are even more effective, as a mobile device usually has a one-to-one relation to its user (Feldmann, 2005). Although phone numbers are often not revealed in current platforms, a profile on a social media platform that is no longer in use may offer such information. Some people offered more personal information on their first social media platform such as MySpace.com, Last.fm, or Classmates.com, as they were not aware of privacy issues at the time of creation of those profiles. Information from obsolete profiles could also provide more unique identifiers such as nicknames, which could be used to identify a person on other social media platforms. Previous studies have demonstrated that an individual could be uniquely identified by a set of attributes. For example, Sweeney (2000) demonstrated that 87 per cent of the American population can be uniquely identified based on zip code, date of birth, and gender. Using these approaches, a researcher is able to create a comprehensive profile of a person based on information from several social media platforms, which contextualizes and enriches our understanding of self-presentation practices. Ethical considerations with regard to the use of such data are critical though, as consent from users may be important prior to data collection.

Digital traces as starting points. Recent methodological innovations suggest using digital traces as a starting point for analysis and either verifying or thickening data through other sources such as interviews (Dubois and Ford, 2015). A digital trace includes all user-related data from social media platforms such as user-generated content (e.g., pictures, videos, and tweets) and metadata like author or timestamp (Chapter 13 Latzko-Toth et al., this volume). Quantitative approaches are often used in trace-based social media research studies. However, the understanding of such massive amounts of data can be challenging, as it is nearly impossible to put all data into the right context (boyd and Crawford, 2012; McCay-Peet and Quan-Haase, 2016). As discussed in this chapter, the context of information is essential for data analysis. To address this issue, a researcher can use data 'thickening', which means to collect a few in-depth data instead of collecting many data (Chapter 13, Latzko-Toth et al., this volume). An example of data thickening is to combine in-depth interviews with content analysis. In such an approach, the researcher can go through an interviewee's social media activity log together with the interviewee and thereby gain important contextual information about the activities (e.g., Why was a content shared? Was the content shared to a specific event? How was the shared content perceived? Was there a target audience?). Such a research strategy can reveal aspects that quantitative or traditional qualitative approaches cannot. At the same time, it not only highlights the 'contrast between what participants reported and their actual practices as recorded in the logs (e.g., sharing/liking patterns and social network composition)' (Chapter 13, Latzko-Toth et al., this volume, p XX), but also puts the virtual self into the appropriate context.

Infer reputation management strategies and personality traits based on data traces: Individuals manage their virtual selves on various platforms differently based on their goals, social roles, and personality traits. By collecting social media data such as status updates (Marshall, Lefringhausen, and Ferenczi, 2015) one can make inferences about a person's personality traits and then use the personality traits to better understand how people express themselves online. In a study by Amichai-Hamburger et al. (2002), it was found that the depth of self-disclosure (e.g., personal preferences, experiences, or emotions) in status updates on non-anonymous social media platforms was a marker for introversion. This can then help to further contextualize a user's interaction patterns and self-presentation on various social media platforms.

CONCLUSION

Social context (anonymity, anchored relationships) and platform type (open vs. close network) influence reputation management, self-presentation strategies, the expression of e-personality, including dark e-personality traits, and the likelihood of trolling. Different contexts necessitate different data collection techniques and approaches for making sense of the data because social norms, values, and customs will vary (McCay-Peet and Quan-Haase, 2016). Social context may be cultural, work, or personal in nature – for example, a small, close-knit peer group, or a large, diffuse network of international social activists. Users who engage in platforms geared toward the development of professional connections, like LinkedIn or Academia.edu, have different biases than anonymous social media platforms such as 4chan. Social media platforms as a result of their distinct social affordances elicit different patterns of self-presentation, sharing of information, and engagement. Understanding these variations is important for making methodological decisions.

Scholars tend to disregard digital traces, footprints, and representations that deviate from the *real self* instead of contextualizing these and establishing counter-narratives that help explain users' underlying motivations for different means of self-presentation. However, exploiting this information could provide novel insights into how users of social media are crafting the self over time and the underlying social processes. Many social media methodologies tend to rely on cross-sectional data, but a person's behaviour over time may also provide important inferences about stability of the self and its development. We conclude that treating data from these sources naïvely yields potential interpretation errors and discarding them as outliers might remove important counter-narratives. *Data don't lie, but people lie with data*, and data can also be misinterpreted; in the age of Big Data, context and domain-specific knowledge may be more important than ever to make sure that messages are not lost in social media.

NOTES

1. https://upload.wikimedia.org/wikipedia/en/f/f8/Internet_dog.jpg
2. http://knowyourmeme.com/memes/delete-system32
3. http://i0.kym-cdn.com/photos/images/original/000/077/443/untitled.JPG
4. https://twitter.com/TOMayorFrod
5. https://twitter.com/Jesus_M_Christ
6. http://knowyourmeme.com/memes/i-sexually-identify-as-an-attack-helicopter
7. http://knowyourmeme.com/memes/rules-of-the-internet

REFERENCES

Aboujaoude E (2011) *Virtually You: The Dangerous Powers of the E-Personality*. New York, New York, USA: W. W. Norton & Company.

Allport GW (1937) *Personality: A Psychological Interpretation. American Journal of Sociology*, New York, New York, USA: H. Holt and Company.

Amichai–Hamburger Y (2005) Personality and the Internet. In: Amichai–Hamburger Y (ed.), *The social net: Human behavior in cyberspace*, New York, New York, USA: Oxford University Press.

Amichai-Hamburger Y, Wainapel G and Fox S (2002) 'On the Internet no one knows I'm an introvert': Extroversion, neuroticism, and internet interaction. *CyberPsychology & Behavior* 5(2): 125–128.

Anderson C (2008) The End of Theory: The Data Deluge Makes the Scientific Method Obsolete. *Wired*. Available from: http://archive.wired.com/science/discoveries/magazine/16-07/pb_theory (accessed 3 August 2015).

Anderson C and Shirako A (2008) Are individuals' reputations related to their history of behavior? *Journal of Personality and Social Psychology* 94(2): 320–333. Available from: http://www.ncbi.nlm.nih.gov/pubmed/18211180 (accessed 8 February 2013).

Back MD, Stopfer JM, Vazire S, Gaddis S, Schmukle SC, Egloff B and Gosling SD (2010) Facebook Profiles Reflect Actual Personality, Not Self-Idealization. *Psychological Science* 21(3): 372–374.

Barlow JP (1996) A Declaration of the Independence of Cyberspace. *Electronic Frontier Foundation*. Available from: https://projects.eff.org/~barlow/Declaration-Final.html (accessed 3 August 2015).

Bernstein MS, Monroy-Hernandez A, Harry D, André P, Panovich K and Vargas G (2011) 4chan and/b/: An Analysis of Anonymity and Ephemerality in a Large Online Community. In: *Proceedings of the Fifth International AAAI Conference on Weblogs and Social Media*, pp. 50–57.

Blumer T and Doering N (2012) Are we the same online? The expression of the five factor personality traits on the computer and the Internet. *Cyberpsychology: Journal of Psychosocial Research on Cyberspace* 6(3).

Boochever R (2012) Psychopaths Online: Modeling Psychopathy in Social Media Discourse. Cornell University.

boyd d and Ellison NB (2007) Social network sites: Definition, history, and scholarship. *Journal of Computer-Mediated Communication* 13(1): 210–230.

boyd d and Crawford K (2012) Critical questions for Big Data: Provocations for a cultural, technological, and scholarly phenomenon. *Information, Communication & Society* 15(5): 662–679.

Broadhurst DI and Kell DB (2007) Statistical strategies for avoiding false discoveries in metabolomics and related experiments. *Metabolomics* 2(4): 171–196.

Bruns A (2013) Faster than the speed of print: Reconciling 'big data' social media analysis and academic scholarship. *First Monday* 18(10).

Buckels EE, Trapnell PD and Paulhus DL (2014) Trolls just want to have fun. *Personality and Individual Differences* 67: 97–102.

Burgoon JK, Chen F and Twitchell DP (2010) Deception and its detection under synchronous and asynchronous computer-mediated communication. *Group Decision and Negotiation* 19(4): 345–366.

Burkhardt R (2008) *Reputation Management in Small and Medium-Sized Enterprises. Analysis and Evaluation of the Use of Reputation Management: A Survey of Small and Medium-Sized Enterprises in Germany*. 1st ed. Diplomica Verlag.

Carpenter CJ (2012) Narcissism on Facebook: Self-promotional and anti-social behavior. *Personality and Individual Differences* 52(4): 482–486.

Caspi A and Gorsky P (2006) Online Deception: Prevalence, Motivation, and Emotion. *CyberPsychology & Behavior* 9(1): 54–59.

CBC (2015) Liberal Ala Buzreba apologizes, steps downs after offensive tweets found. *CBC News*. Available from: http://www.cbc.ca/news/politics/canada-election-2015-ala-buzreba-tweets-1.3195193 (accessed 7 April 2016).

Coleman G (2012) Phreaks, Hackers, and Trolls and the Politics of Transgression and Spectacle. In: Mandiberg M (ed.), *The Social Media Reader*, New York, New York, USA: New York: NYU Press. Available from:

Coleman G (2014) *Hacker, Hoaxer, Whistleblower, Spy: The Many Faces of Anonymous*. 1st ed. London: Verso.

Collier K (2012) Trolling new Kony slacktivists with Carl Weathers. *The Daily Dot*. Available from: http://www.dailydot.com/culture/kony-trolling-carl-weathers-facebook/ (accessed 27 November 2015).

Deuker AS (2014) *Understanding the use of privacy controls on social networking sites: a grounded theory to support selective sharing with contacts*. Goethe University, Frankfurt am Main, Germany.

Donath JS (1999) Identity and Deception in the Virtual Community. In: Smith MA and Kollock P (eds), *Communities in Cyberspace*, New York, New York, USA: Routledge, pp. 1–28.

Drake B (2015) The darkest side of online harassment: Menacing behavior. *Pew Research Center*. Available from: http://www.pewresearch.org/fact-tank/2015/06/01/the-darkest-side-of-online-harassment-menacing-behavior (accessed 11 December 2015).

Dubois E and Ford H (2015) Trace Interviews: An Actor-Centered Approach. *International Journal of Communication* 9: 2067–2091. Available from: http://ijoc.org/index.php/ijoc/article/view/3378.

Duggan M (2014) Online Harassment. *Pew Research Center*. Available from: http://www.pewinternet.org/2014/10/22/online-harassment/ (accessed 11 December 2015).

Dwyer C, Hiltz SR and Passerini K (2007) Trust and privacy concerns within social networking sites: A comparison of Facebook and MySpace. In: *Proceedings of the Thirteenth Americas Conference on Information Systems, Keystone, Colorado*, pp. 339–350.

Dyche J (2012) Big Data 'Eurekas!' Don't Just Happen. *Harvard Business Review Blog*, 20 November.

Eisenegger M and Imhof K (2008) The True, the Good and the Beautiful: Reputation Management in the Media Society. In: Zerfass A, van Ruler B, and Sriramesh K (eds), *Public Relations Research*, Wiesbaden: VS Verlag für Sozialwissenschaften, pp. 125–146.

Emanuel L, Neil GJ, Bevan C, Fraser DS, Stevenage SV, Whitty MT and Jamison-Powell S (2014) Who am I? Representing the self offline and in different online contexts. *Computers in Human Behavior*, Elsevier Ltd 41: 146–152.

Farmer R and Glass B (2010) *Building Web Reputation Systems*. 1st ed. Treseler ME (ed.), Sebastopol, CA, USA: O'Reilly Media Inc.

Feldmann V (2005) *Leveraging Mobile Media*. Information Age Economy, Heidelberg: Physica-Verlag.

Fox J and Rooney MC (2015) The Dark Triad and trait self-objectification as predictors of men's use and self-presentation behaviors on social networking sites. *Personality and Individual Differences* 76 (April 2015): 161–165.

Galanxhi H and Nah FF-H (2007) Deception in cyberspace: A comparison of text-only vs. avatar-supported medium. *International Journal of Human-Computer Studies* 65(9): 770–783.

Garcia D and Sikström S (2014) The dark side of Facebook: Semantic representations of status updates predict the Dark Triad of personality. *Personality and Individual Differences* 67 (September 2014): 92–96.

Gross R and Acquisti A (2005) Information revelation and privacy in online social networks. In: *Proceedings of the 2005 ACM workshop on Privacy in the electronic society – WPES '05*, New York, New York, USA: ACM Press, p. 71.

Hancock J, Woodworth MT, Morrow R and McGillivray H and Boochever R (2012) Assessing credibility through text: A preliminary analysis for identifying psychopathy. Proceedings of the Rapid Screening Technologies, Deception Detection and Credibility Assessment. In: *Symposium of the 45th Hawaii International Conference on System Sciences*, IEEE.

Hardaker C (2010) Trolling in asynchronous computer-mediated communication: From user discussions to academic definitions. *Journal of Politeness Research. Language, Behaviour, Culture* 6(2).

Hare RD (1991) The Hare Psychopathy Checklist-Revised. Toronto, ON. Multi-Health Systems.

Hebdige D (1979) *Subculture: The Meaning of Style*. 1st ed. London: Routledge.

Hogan B (2010) The Presentation of self in the age of social media: Distinguishing performances and exhibitions online. *Bulletin of Science, Technology & Society* 30(6): 377–386.

Hogan B and Quan-Haase A (2010) Persistence and Change in Social Media. *Bulletin of Science, Technology & Society* 30(5): 309–315.

Kapidzic S and Herring SC (2015) Race, gender, and self-presentation in teen profile photographs. *New Media & Society* 17(6): 958–976.

Kenrick DT, McCreath HE, Govern J, King R and Bordin J (1990) Person-environment intersections: Everyday settings and common trait dimensions. *Journal of Personality and Social Psychology* 58(4): 685–698.

Kim YA and Ahmad MA (2013) Trust, distrust and lack of confidence of users in online social media-sharing communities. *Knowledge-Based Systems* 37: 438–450.

Kitchin R (2014) Big data, new epistemologies and paradigm shifts. *Big Data & Society* 1(1): 1–12. Available from: http://bds.sagepub.com/content/1/1/2053951714528481.

Klewes J and Wreschniok R (eds) (2009) *Reputation Capital: Building and Maintaining Trust in the 21st Century*. Berlin, Heidelberg: Springer Berlin Heidelberg.

Knuttila L (2011) User unknown: 4chan, anonymity and contingency. *First Monday* 16(10).

Krämer NC and Winter S (2008) Impression Management 2.0: The Relationship of Self-Esteem, Extraversion, Self-Efficacy, and Self-Presentation Within Social Networking Sites. *Journal of Media Psychology: Theories, Methods, and Applications* 20(3): 106–116.

Lapidot-Lefler N and Barak A (2012) Effects of anonymity, invisibility, and lack of eye-contact on toxic online disinhibition. *Computers in Human Behavior* 28(2): 434–443.

Lawson S, Sanders K and Smith L (2015) Commodification of the Information Profession: A Critique of Higher Education Under Neoliberalism. *Journal of Librarianship and Scholarly Communication* 3(1): eP1182.

Lazer D, Kennedy R, King G and Vespignani A (2014) The Parable of Google flu: Traps in Big Data analysis. *Science* 343(6176): 1203–1205.

Leary MR and Allen AB (2011) Personality and persona: personality processes in self-presentation. *Journal of Personality and Social Psychology* 79(6): 1191–1218.

Lee E, Ahn J and Kim YJ (2014) Personality traits and self-presentation at Facebook. *Personality and Individual Differences* 69: 162–167.

Levine TR, Park HS and McCornack SA (1999) Accuracy in detecting truths and lies: Documenting the 'veracity effect'. *Communication Monographs* 66(2): 125–144.

Lohr S (2012) The Age of Big Data. *New York Times*. Available from: http://www.nytimes.com/2012/02/12/sunday-review/big-datas-impact-in-the-world.html (accessed 3 August 2015).

Lukoianova T and Rubin VL (2014) Veracity roadmap: Is Big Data objective, truthful and credible? *Advances in Classification Research Online* 24(1).

Marcus B, Machilek F and Schütz A (2006) Personality in cyberspace: personal web sites as media for personality expressions and impressions. *Journal of Personality and Social Psychology* 90(6): 1014–1031.

Marshall TC, Lefringhausen K and Ferenczi N (2015) The Big Five, self-esteem, and narcissism as predictors of the topics people write about in Facebook status updates. *Personality and Individual Differences* 85: 35–40.

Marwick AE and boyd d (2011) I tweet honestly, I tweet passionately: Twitter users, context collapse, and the imagined audience. *New Media & Society* 13(1): 114–133.

Marwick AE, Diaz DM and Palfrey J (2010) Youth, Privacy, and Reputation Literature Review. *Social Science Research*, Berkman Center Research Publication, The Berkman Center for Internet & Society at Harvard University 7641(10): 1–82.

McCay-Peet L and Quan-Haase A (2016) User engagement in social media studies. In: O'Brien H and Lalmas M (eds), *Why Engagement Matters: Cross-Disciplinary Perspectives and Innovations on User Engagement with Digital Media*, Berlin, Germany: Springer.

McCrae RR and Costa PT (1994) The stability of personality: Observations and evaluations. *Current Directions in Psychological Science* 3(6): 173–175.

McDonald K (2015) From Indymedia to Anonymous: rethinking action and identity in digital cultures. *Information, Communication & Society* 18(8): 968–982.

Mehdizadeh S (2010) Self-presentation 2.0: narcissism and self-esteem on Facebook. *Cyberpsychology, behavior and social networking* 13(4): 357–64.

Michikyan M, Subrahmanyam K and Dennis J (2014) Can you tell who I am? Neuroticism, extraversion, and online self-presentation among young adults. *Computers in Human Behavior*, Elsevier Ltd 33: 179–183.

Mischel W (1973) Toward a cognitive social learning reconceptualization of personality. *Psychological review* 80(4): 252–283.

Mischel W (1977) The interaction of person and situation. In: Magnusson D and Endler N (eds), *Personality at the crossroads: Current issues in interactional psychology*, Hillsdale, New Jersey, USA: Lawrence Erlbaum Associates.

Nevin AD (2015) Cyber-psychopathy: Examining the relationship between dark e-personality and online misconduct. The University of Western Ontario. Available from: http://ir.lib.uwo.ca/etd/2926/.

Palfrey J and Gasser U (2008) *Born Digital: Understanding the First Generation of Digital Natives*. 1st ed. New York, New York, USA: Basic Books.

Paulhus DL and Williams KM (2002) The Dark Triad of personality: Narcissism, machiavellianism, and psychopathy. *Journal of Research in Personality* 36(6): 556–563.

Pennebaker JW, Booth RJ and Francis ME (2007) Linguistic Inquiry and Word Count (LIWC). Available from: http://www.liwc.net/.

Phillips W (2015) *This Is Why We Can't Have Nice Things: Mapping the Relationship between Online Trolling and Mainstream Culture*. 1st ed. *Massachusetts Institute of Technology Press*, Cambridge: Massachusetts Institute of Technology Press. Available from: https://mitpress.mit.edu/books/why-we-cant-have-nice-things (accessed 3 August 2015).

Read M (2012) From Otherkin to Transethnicity: Your Field Guide to the Weird World of Tumblr Identity Politics. *Gawker*. Available from: http://gawker.com/5940947/from-otherkin-to-transethnicity-your-field-guide-to-the-weird-world-of-tumblr-identity-politics (accessed 3 August 2015).

Reader B (2012) Free Press vs. Free Speech? The rhetoric of 'civility' in regard to anonymous online comments. *Journalism & Mass Communication Quarterly* 89(3): 495–513.

Resnick P, Kuwabara K, Zeckhauser R and Friedman E (2000) Reputation systems. *Communications of the ACM* 43(12): 45–48.

Rheingold H (1993) *The Virtual Community: Homesteading on the Electronic Frontier*. Reading, MA: MIT Press.

Rui JR and Stefanone MA (2013) Strategic image management online. *Information, Communication & Society* (July 2013): 1–20.

Smith WP and Kidder DL (2010) You've been tagged! (Then again, maybe not): Employers and Facebook. *Business Horizons* 53(5): 491–499.

Stanculescu E (2011) Online Self–Presentation from the Cyberpsychology Perspective. In: *7th International Scientific Conference eLearning and Software for Education*, Bucharest.

Stoehrel RF and Lindgren S (2014) For the Lulz: anonymous, aesthetics and affect. *tripleC: Communication, Capitalism & Critique* 12(1): 238–264.

Stritzke WGK, Nguyen A and Durkin K (2004) Shyness and Computer-mediated communication: A self-presentational theory perspective. *Media Psychology* 6(1): 1–22.

Suler J (2004) The online disinhibition effect. *CyberPsychology & Behavior* 7(3): 321–326.

Sumner C, Byers A, Boochever R and Park GJ (2012) Predicting Dark Triad Personality Traits from Twitter Usage and a Linguistic Analysis of Tweets. In: *2012 11th International Conference on Machine Learning and Applications*, IEEE, pp. 386–393.

Sundén J (2003) *Material Virtualities: Approaching Online Textual Embodiment. Order A Journal On The Theory Of Ordered Sets And Its Applications*, Linköping studies in arts and science, 0282-9800; 257, Peter Lang.

Sweeney L (2000) *Uniqueness of Simple Demographics in the U.S. Population, LIDAP-WP4. Forthcoming book entitled, The Identifiability of Data.*, Carnegie Mellon University, Laboratory for International Data Privacy.

Tatarchevskiy T (2011) The 'popular' culture of internet activism. *New Media & Society* 13(2): 297–313.

Tennie C, Frith U and Frith CD (2010) Reputation management in the age of the world-wide web. *Trends in cognitive sciences* 14(11): 482–8.

Turkle S (1984) *The Second Self: Computers and the Human Spirit*. 1st ed. New York, New York, USA: Simon & Schuster, Inc.

Turkle S (1995) *Life on the Screen: Identity in the Age of the Internet*. 2nd ed. Simon & Schuster.

van Dijck J (2013) 'You have one identity': performing the self on Facebook and LinkedIn. *Media, Culture & Society* 35(2): 199–215.

vom Brocke J, Simons A, Niehaves B, Riemer K, Plattfaut R and Cleven A (2009) Reconstructing the giant: on the importance of rigour in documenting the literature search process. In: Newell S, Whitley EA, Pouloudi N, et al. (eds), *17th European Conference on Information Systems*, Hampton Press, pp. 1–13.

Wierzbicki M and Young RD (1978) The relation of intelligence and task difficulty to appreciation of humor. *The Journal of General Psychology* 99(1): 25–32.

Yang S (2015) Understanding Personal Online Reputation Management: A Grounded Theory Study. In: *Proceedings of the 19th Pacific Asia Conference on Information Systems (PACIS 2015)*, Singapore.

Yang S (2016) Understanding the Pain: Examining Individuals' Online Reputation Management Behaviour and its Obstacles – A Grounded Theory. In: *The 49th Hawaii International Conference on System Sciences (HICSS)*, Kauai, Hawaii, USA: IEEE.

Zhao S, Grasmuck S and Martin J (2008) Identity construction on Facebook: Digital empowerment in anchored relationships. *Computers in Human Behavior* 24(5): 1816–1836.

Social Science 'Lite'? Deriving Demographic Proxies from Twitter

Luke Sloan

On the face of it, Twitter provides a social scientific goldmine of rich, voluminous data on reactions, attitudes, intentions and networks – yet the absence of explicit demographic data prevents researchers from being able to capitalise on this valuable source for two key reasons: we do not know who is represented on Twitter; and we do not know who is saying what. This chapter looks in detail at the cutting edge work recently and currently underway to understand the demographic characteristics of Twitter users through signatures identified within tweets and the metadata associated with Twitter activity. This chapter critically reviews methods for extracting or estimating location, age, gender, language, occupation and class and discuss techniques for testing the accuracy of these derived characteristics. We argue that by augmenting Twitter data with demographic proxies, we substantially increase the utility of the data for the wider social science community and enable new avenues of research to be explored.

INTRODUCTION

At its core, social science is interested in the differences and inequalities between groups broadly defined through common demographic characteristics. Traditional modes of social research collect data both on the phenomena of interest and the characteristics of a case be it a respondent on a survey, a member of a focus group or even an institution. We take for granted our ability to ask the relevant questions to ensure that the researcher collects demographic data on sex, ethnicity, nationality, socio-economic group, and religiosity and so on. However, the recent exponential increase in transactional and naturally occurring data (i.e. data not elicited through social research) has raised new methodological questions about *what can be known* and *how we can know it*. Twenty-first century social science must seek to understand what these new sources of data mean and how they can be robustly used, but a perennial criticism of naturally occurring data from social media sources such as Twitter is that these important background variables, which are the bread and butter of social science research, are generally absent (Gayo-Avello 2012). Without this information we cannot make group comparisons and, just as importantly, we have no measure of the representativeness of the data. Yet just because demographic information is not elicited does not mean that it cannot be estimated by proxy, and if we can reliably identify the background characteristics of Twitter users then we unlock a rich vein of information on attitudes and reactions *which are independent of researcher interference*.

Following from this, there are two rationales for the development of demographic proxies for Twitter users. The first is to address a fundamental question that has yet to be sufficiently answered: who tweets? There are studies using traditional survey methods (see IPSOS MediaCT 2014, Duggan and Brenner 2013) that identify who in the survey sample is using Twitter, but because the Twitter population is unknown we do not know if certain groups are accurately represented. Certainly the idea that Twitter provides a voice for the disenfranchised (Edwards et al. 2013) would suggest that some subsets of the Twitter population may well be people who typically do not respond to surveys. If we know who tweets (and, importantly, who does not) and we know where someone is tweeting from, then we can start to unravel the relationship between virtual activity on Twitter and real-world events such as elections, crime, and commuter travel patterns to name but a few. There are private sector companies that claim to be able to derive demographic characteristics of Twitter users, but this information is market sensitive and the methodologies are often neither public nor transparent. In contrast, all of the approaches discussed in this chapter are open for replication with clear, rigorous and replicable processes that can thus be scrutinised and improved upon by others.

The second reason has already been hinted at above – that understanding how group membership impacts upon an individual is one of the key areas of concerns for social scientists. As society moves even further into the virtual sphere we want to know if real-world demographic differences manifest in the virtual world and, if they do, is the effect the same? For example, does gender impact upon behaviour on Twitter? Do male and female users interact in the same type of online networks? Are inequalities in class, age, language and gender propagated online or is Twitter an emancipatory platform that levels the playing field? Certainly some studies have demonstrated that the use of social networking sites in general differ based on gender, education and age (Haight, Quan-Haase and Corbett 2014).

These are big questions that are shaping what social science looks like in the virtual world and before they can be answered, it is necessary to reconceptualise demographic characteristics in relation to Twitter and then explore how they can be extracted, estimated, measured and evaluated. This chapter outlines the cutting-edge research in this area around geography and location, age, gender, language, occupation and class. We review previous work to identify some of the features and characteristics of other social media platforms and discuss how the idiosyncrasies of Twitter demand adaptations or completely new approaches for deriving demographic information. Importantly, this chapter is careful not to overstate the accuracy of methods for deriving demographic characteristics and the critical observations that arise will hopefully encourage others to takes these ideas one step further. The issue of accuracy is addressed again towards the end in the context of future work that will evaluate the reliability and validity of some of the techniques for generating derived demographic characteristics.

GEOGRAPHY AND LOCATION

Geography is possibly the most useful demographic characteristic that can be extracted from Twitter, but it is also the most conceptually complex (see Chapter 18, Bushel and Pennington, this volume for a detailed discussion on analytics of geospatial social media data). There are four *signatures* of geography that can be ascertained – geocoding, explicit profile reference, explicit tweet reference, proximal reference – and all have different meanings. They form a 'hierarchy of utility' from the specific (geocoding) to the general (proximal) that can be considered analogous to the hierarchy of data types in quantitative research where interval is the most useful and the most informative, followed by ordinal and finally nominal.

IOn Twitter, geography precision matters – and there is nothing more precise than knowing the latitude and longitude coordinates of where a user was when they posted a tweet. This data is so granular that it is possible to place a tweeter outside of a particular shop in the high street at the time of tweeting. Tweets that contain this data are *geocoded* and users may choose to have this enabled or disabled on their account. Because the default mode is disabled, the reality is that many users do not generate geocoded tweets – only around 0.85% of Twitter traffic contains this information (Sloan et al. 2013). Figure 7.1 plots geocoded tweets captured during July 2012 through the 1% Twitter API and we can clearly see clusters of tweets in areas of high population density – a useful reminder that even a small proportion of tweets is a large number of data points in absolute terms. Note that the data points apparently in the middle of the sea are likely to be people tweeting from boats or planes.

Geocoded data is particularly useful because it provides a common geographic key that links Twitter data to other social and administrative datasets. Point long/lat data can be used to locate a user within existing geographies from output areas (OAs) and statistical wards used in Census outputs (CAS Wards) to parliamentary constituencies and policing neighbourhoods. This allows us to understand the *context* of the area in which a tweet was made and challenges the notion that social media platforms such as Twitter are 'data-light' (Gayo-Avello 2012). This data linkage adds value to both traditional sources of social data and social media as one augments the other (Edwards et al. 2013) allowing us to ask new questions such as: Do people use fearful language on Twitter when walking through a high crime area? How much support is there on Twitter for a political party within a particular constituency? Does the language profile of an area on Twitter reflect Census data on main language?

Published examples of the value added through augmentation include Gerber's (2014) investigation of the association between 25 crime types in a major US city using kernel density estimate (KDE) and statistical topic modelling tailored for use on Twitter and Malleson and Andresen's (2014) use of Twitter traffic volume to understand crime risk. This cutting edge research embraces Twitter data as another lens through which to study and investigate social phenomena. Indeed, the author of this chapter was part of a project looking at the association between reported crime in London, contextual area data from the 2011 Census and mentions of crime and disorder terms on Twitter (Williams, Burnap and Sloan 2016). The geographical granularity required to investigate these associations can only be achieved with geocoded data.

That is not to say that such data is without its problems (beyond the small proportion of total Twitter traffic that it consists of). Graham et al. hypothesise that 'the division between geocoding and non-geocoding users is almost certainly biased by factors such as

Figure 7.1 The geographic distribution of geocoded tweets in the UK and Ireland from a sample of 13 million

Source: Sloan et al. 2013.

social-economic status, location, education' (2014: 570), thus questioning whether this rich but small subset of data is representative of the wider Twitter population. Recent work has demonstrated that there are small (but significant) differences in enabling geoservices and using geocoding based on age, gender and class and there are even bigger discrepancies when looking at language of tweet and language of interface (Sloan and Morgan 2015).

Stepping down a rung of the hierarchy of utility, when geocoded data isn't available then we can turn to location information that can be garnered from user profiles. It is not unusual for tweeters to complete the location field of their profile description and with a little data-cleaning and common sense it is possible to automate the extraction of this data in a useable format. Using Yahoo! PlaceFinder (2012), Sloan et al. 2013 demonstrated on a subsample of data that it is possible to use profile data to identify the country of 52% of users, the state for 43% (understood to be England, Scotland, Wales and Northern Ireland in the UK and prefectures in Japan), the county for 36% and the city for 40%. Yahoo! PlaceFinder will identify the lowest geographical reference it can (such as a city) and then place it within a hierarchy such as: Cardiff, Wales, UK. Surprisingly the study found postcode level data for 10% of users, which would be enough to locate tweeters within the granular geographies usually used only with geocoded data.

There is, however, a catch. What is a user telling us when they write a location in their profile description? Is it where they live? Where they're born? Where they used to live? Where they work? The problem is that regardless of how many hierarchical geographical levels we can identify we don't know what this location *means* to the user or how they *relate* to it. Conceptually, identifying with a particular location is a very different thing to *being* in a location when a tweet is sent. Geocoded data always tells the truth and requires no manual update – it will always exactly identify your location, but someone who lives in Cardiff might regularly commute to Bristol or even London. They may even be tweeting from abroad whilst their profile places them in Manchester. Even if the researcher is to make the (very generous) assumption that the city in a user profile is where the user is, it is not a very useful geographical unit to work from. It may be possible to place tweeters within local authorities but that assumes that people understand and accurately realise where the boundaries between two areas is located. Arguably the information might be of more use in smaller cities than larger ones (e.g. Truro vs London), so in areas of low population density where administrative geographical units are larger (such as parliamentary constituencies) there may be more value to this data. The final point to make has already been hinted at but is worth highlighting – the location might be a lie. There may be an element of purposeful or even unintentional deception as UK geography can be complex (see Yang, Quan-Haase, Nevin & Chen, Chapter 6, this volume for a discussion around deception). For example, Salford is within Greater Manchester but it is not part of the City of Manchester.

Alternative geographical references can be found in tweets themselves. Explicit mentions of places can be easy to identify such as major landmarks, sporting events or concert venues. Other contexts in which clear geographical references might manifest in a tweet include everything from 'My train just passed through Reading Station' to 'Really wish I was at home in Edinburgh right now'. To make any sense of this data it is necessary to take into account the context of the geographical reference and it requires complex and deeper analysis (Sloan et al. 2013). Despite the difficulties, Cheng et al. (2010) built a probabilistic model to estimate the city in which a user lives and managed to do so through mining for geographical references in the archives of Twitter users. Their approach placed 51% of Twitter users within a 100-mile radius of their actual location. Considering the complexity of the task and the high amount of noise in the data this is an impressive achievement.

The final category of geographical data is not really explicitly spatial but might nevertheless be of use as the interface between natural language processing and geo-spatial analysis develops. Proximal references manifest in tweets in the format of 'just down the road' or 'a few streets away' and they are only of use if the reference point can be deduced (i.e. which street are you referring to?). It is also important to distinguish between whether the user is positioning themselves through a proximal term such as 'I'm just round the corner from the station' or an event which they are commenting on such as 'That burglary was just down the street from me'. Additional challenges to identifying geography in tweets include generating lexicons for slang and developing our understanding of how individuals recognise geographical boundaries.

AGE

The ability to extract age data from social media sources is very much dependent on the platform of interest. Schwartz et al. (2013) have demonstrated the link between word usage and age on Facebook profiles. Rather than specifying an *a priori* list of words that is theoretically associated with particular age groups, they advocate for an open vocabulary approach in which the terms that differentiate age groups are not pre-defined. For a platform such as Facebook for which the age is known, it is possible to collate and analyse posts that users have made, measure word frequencies and produce lists of words that are typically associated with particular age groups. In the blogosphere, Argamon et al. (2006) identified latent language concepts through factor analysis that explained the co-occurrence of certain words, resulting in the identification of latent factors such as 'poetic'. The frequency of latent factor occurrence can then be related to age groups (and, as discussed later, gender).

Whilst both of these approaches would then allow a predictive model to be specified based on either vocabulary on Facebook or latent language concepts in blogs, neither method is suitable for identifying age on Twitter for three reasons. The first is that Twitter metadata does not contain any explicit information on age, so building predictive models that associate particular content and/or behaviours with an age group is fruitless – the dependent variable is missing. Secondly, whilst vocabulary lists or latent language concepts might work well on Facebook posts (potentially in excess of 5,000 characters) and blogs (as long as you like), they are unlikely to be portable to a 140 character micro-blogging platform. Finally, the prevalence of retweets on Twitter means that substantial amounts of content are *not authored by the user*, thus the content of many tweets is not an accurate reflection of an individual's vocabulary.

With all this in mind, it is necessary to think more creatively about how age can be identified on Twitter. In particular, it is necessary to consider what parts of a Twitter profile might contain useful information on age that is genuine original data generated by the user. Sloan et al. (2015) offer a solution through the interrogation of the profile description field, which can be accessed via the Twitter API. The premise is a simple one: sometimes people write their age in their Twitter profiles, thus the question is not whether the data exists but how it can be identified and extracted. Using pattern matching, it is possible to identify *signatures* of age such as: a two digit integer followed by 'years', 'yrs', 'years old' or 'yrs old'; a two digit integer preceded by 'age', 'aged', 'I'm' or 'I am'; a four digit integer preceded by 'born' or 'born in' (with year or birthday an actual age can be calculated). It is also necessary to account for false positives such as 'I've worked at X for 24 years', 'I've spent 16 years as an X' or 'I have a 4 year old daughter'. To avoid making type one errors, an addition set of rules is used to exclude cases where: a two digit integer is preceded by 'for' or 'spent'; where 'years' is followed by 'as', 'working' or 'in'; where any of the positive identification rules are followed by 'son' or 'daughter'. A more detailed discussion of the challenges can be found in the original paper and it is worth noting that this analysis is limited to English language tweets which account for around 40.35% of Twitter content (Sloan et al. 2013).

Applying these apparently simple rules and checking via expert human validation, Sloan et al. (2015) identified age data in the description field of 1,470 users in a database of 32,032 cases (0.37%). Figure 7.2 shows the results of this process and compares the distribution of age according to Twitter against Census 2011 data on the age profile of the UK population. The fact that young people are much more populous on social media has been indicated by previous studies (see Duggan and Brenner 2013), but all estimates of age on Twitter have so far relied on surveys which ask whether respondents use the platform, meaning that estimates are a function of sampling and other limitations of survey methods. This is the first example of age estimates on Twitter which relies solely on explicit user generated references to age.

That is not to say that the method is error free. Although there is no *a priori* case why, for example, older users wouldn't wish to give their age online, it is not inconceivable that professing age is of more importance to younger users, or more common practice for particular age groups, social networks or users from particular countries, subcultures or backgrounds. Yet it is interesting to note that even if this provides an underestimate of older users on Twitter, the 1.1% between 51 and 60 years would account for around 165,000 users in the UK and 2,981,000 users worldwide (Sloan et al. 2015) if scaled up to a conservative estimate of the entire Twitter population of 271,000,000 monthly active users (Twitter 2014).

Further work in this area is likely to progress along the same lines as Swartz et al.

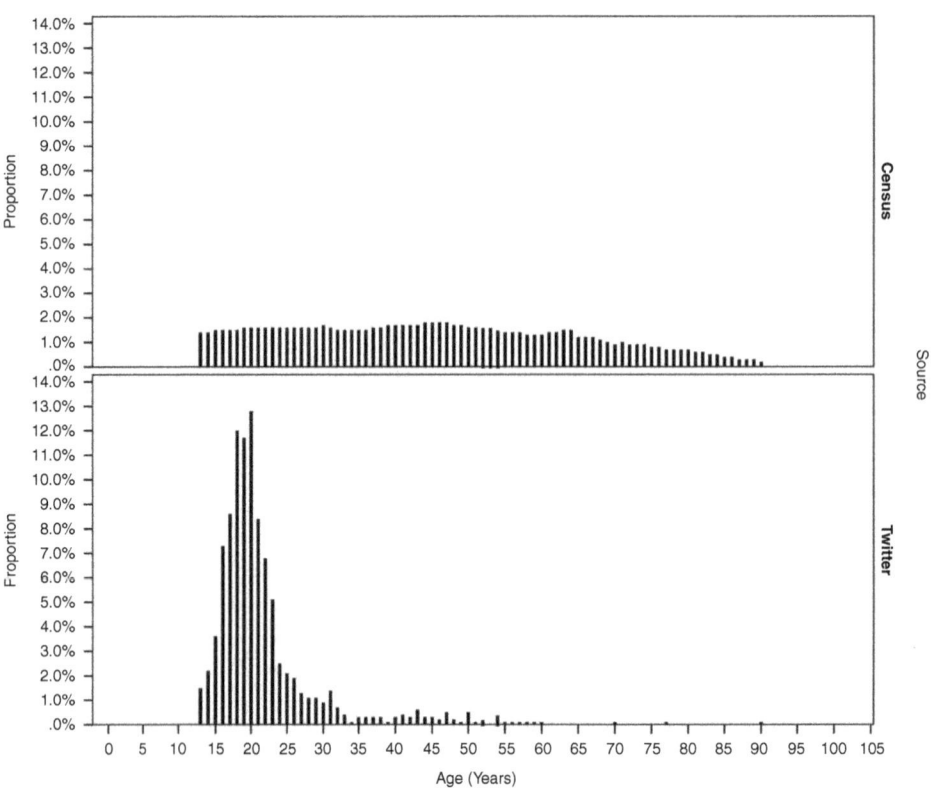

Figure 7.2 Comparison of age profile of UK Twitter users against the 2011 Census

Source: Sloan et al. 2015.

(2013) and Argamon et al. (2006) as the process defined above offers us a *baseline* measure of age, and when the dependent variable is know we can build predictive models of age based on other independent factors. It would be possible to look at vocabulary usage by age on Twitter if retweets were filtered out. It may also be interesting to look at hashtag and emoticon use as a predictor of age groups. Before this work can begin in earnest, the number of known user ages needs to increase to accommodate robust and defensible statistical models and this will only happen over time as either new users come online and supply *signature* age data that can be automatically identified or if a new and expanded set of rules is devised (and proven to work) which can classify more cases.

GENDER

To identify the gender of Twitter users we can follow a similar logic to identifying age. We know that some users include their first name within their Twitter handle and this information can be extracted through pattern matching and used to place them into one of four categories: male; female; unisex; or unclassifiable. Mislove et al. (2011) first demonstrated this using a database of 3,034 male and 3,643 female names from the US Social Security Administration (USSA) database. The limitation of this approach is that it captures the 1,000 most popular names given to girls and boys each year in the US and, despite the ethnic diversity of the US population, Anglicised names dominate the list as other groups are within the minority (Sloan et al. 2013). The alternative approach advocated by Sloan et al. (2013) is to use the 40,000 Namen (40N) database (Michael 2007). 40N contains over 44,000 names from 54 countries around the world, whether they are male (17,740 names), female (16,921 names) or unisex (9,907) and it can recognise abbreviations and classify the gender of shortened names (e.g. knowing that 'Matt' may be short for 'Matthew' which is a male name).

Before the 40N database can be utilised it is necessary to embark upon a thorough and rigorous process of data cleaning and preparation. Whilst identifying a first name from a username may be a simple task for the human eye (that most outstanding example of a pattern recogniser), it is not so simple for a machine that is reliant on following rules and procedures. The automation of such processes is the only viable way to mass-process big data and much time and care needs to be invested in specifying the rules and parameters of pattern matching. For gender on Twitter, cross-referencing every username with the 40N database is a computationally demanding task in terms of processing which can be aided and simplified by removing problematic characters. It is also possible to increase successful identification through character replacement (e.g. replacing '_' with a space) and making use of other *signatures* such as capitalisation (see Sloan et al. 2013 for a detailed discussion of rules and processes).

Using 40N, Sloan et al. (2013) demonstrate that around 48% of first names derived from Twitter usernames in a sample of over 13 million could be identified as male, female or unisex leaving 52% unclassified. The high number of unclassified cases may be seen as reassuring as it indicates a willingness to accept a reduction in classification rather than allowing type 1 errors. It is always preferable to treat uncertain cases with scepticism and to maintain a high level of certainty for positive classifications. However, there is still a degree of uncertainty as to whether the correct allocation has been made which is not related to the accuracy of 40N or the data preparation process, rather it arises from the potential for individuals to embark upon identity play in the virtual world (Yang, et al., Chapter 6, this volume). There is some evidence that females in particular may choose to mask their gender whilst interacting online (Jaffe et al. 1999), although this study was conducted before the advent of Twitter. Certainly more recent studies (such as Huffajer and Calvert 2005) suggest that virtual representations tend to reflect reality. Perhaps the most compelling evidence in support for the accuracy of this method for assigning gender to Twitter users is the close parity with Census 2011 data. When applying the 40N database to a subset of the 13 million tweets that could positively be identified as originating from the UK, the male to female split was 48.8% and 51.2% respectively – close to the proportion of males (49.1%) and females (50.9%) as recorded in the UK population by the 2011 Census. If one gender were to disproportionately engage in identity play (i.e. choose a first name associated with a different gender) then we would not expect the Census and Twitter results to be so closely aligned, thus it is reasonable to tentatively observe that gender swapping on Twitter is either proportionally practiced by both male and female users (although it seems unlikely for such parity to occur between individuals making this decision in both genders) or that it is very unusual. Consider that the sheer number of users on Twitter means that 'very unusual' can still mean many people at the same time as being a tiny *proportion* of the population of interest.

As with age, once the dependent variable is identified with a reasonable degree of certainty it is possible to start building predictive models that build upon the work of other scholars. Schwartz et al. (2013) and Argamon et al. (2006) also looked at the influence of gender on language, whilst an even earlier study had already identified how people use gender-preferential patterns of language in emails which trained individuals can use to identify the gender of the content producer (Thomson and Murachver 2001). Once features that are relevant to classifying gender have been identified it is possible to use machine-learning techniques to automate the process of identification (Cheng et al. 2011). As discussed above, the idiosyncrasies of the Twitter platform (e.g. retweets and character limits) mean that existing methods of gender detection need to be heavily adapted before being applied, but there is no reason in principle why similar approaches couldn't be successful.

LANGUAGE

Language has a complex relationship with group membership as it can be tied up with notions of nationality and people often speak multiple languages. The complexity of the multi-faceted nature of language is ameliorated in the social sciences often by asking respondents to specify their main language (this is the approach that the Census 2011 used, with an additional question on Welsh language for Wales-domiciled respondents). It is important to note that this does not differentiate between spoken and written language, neither does it account for the possibility of people consuming and producing content in different languages.

Why does this matter for Twitter? Essentially there are two simple ways to derive language information – the language of the user interface and the language of the tweet. More complex methods involve increasing the amount of data available for language identification through taking into account: the language of users who are mentioned, language of hyperlinks, language of tags and the language of an original post in a conversation (Carter et al. 2013 use such a variety of sources and build a model using these factors as priors). This section will concentrate on profile and tweet language as these are the most accessible.

The language of the Twitter interface is a reasonably stable measure and tends to be specified when a user sets up an account for the first time. It may be reasonable to assume that this is an indicator of language preference and that a user would choose the interface language in which they are most proficient (Sloan et al. 2013). However, this is not fixed and it is not inconceivable that users switch between language interfaces. If a researcher has multiple records for an individual user that have been collected over time, and collecting on the 1% API (see Burnap et al. 2013a) over a year makes this a statistical likelihood, then what is one to make of a change in user interface language? Which language is the *primary* language in which a user is categorised? Does it even make sense to specify a *primary* language and should we build in capacity for multilingualism?

The second method of categorising language is through analysis of tweet content and is more resource intensive, requiring substantial computational processing power to conduct in real-time. Using the Language Detection Library for Java (LDLJ 2012) each tweet can be analysed and allocated to one of 53 recognisable languages based on the presence of particular letter patterns. Using this approach, Sloan et al. (2013) found that around 40% of all Twitter content is produced in the English language, not withstanding some important observations around the efficacy of language detection algorithms on only 140 characters (Graham et al. 2014). Note that we are referring to the *proportion* of Twitter content in a given language, not the proportion of users who are English speakers. Although the profile language of a user can change there is only ever one user record, whilst a user can produce as many tweets as they like which may well be in different languages. Indeed, in a sample of 113 million tweets Sloan et al. (2013) found that around 33% (37,649,491) were in a language different to that of the user interface. How should a researcher categorise a multilingual user? For some users, does it even make conceptual sense to talk about a single language? Certainly great care should be taken to discuss the methodological decisions made for language identification in a clear and transparent manner (see Graham et al. 2014 for a well nuanced discussion on the efficacy of a range of tools).

Language detection of tweets is a computationally demanding process, but the investment pays off when applying other tools for analysis that are also resource hungry. Sentiment analysis, for example, is a useful technique for identifying the emotional content of a tweet (Dodds and Danforth 2010, Thelwall et al. 2010) but it is generally limited to the English language and is process intensive. Efficiency can thus be gained by identifying the tweet language and only passing on English content for analysis of sentiment, whereas using profile language as a proxy for tweet language would result in too many misclassifications and force the sentiment tool to process irrelevant data.

OCCUPATION AND CLASS

Social class is one of the cornerstones of social scientific analysis and comparisons between class groups are used to investigate differences in a wide range of areas including educational attainment, social mobility and life expectancy. From the perspective of Twitter use, it is important to estimate the class of individuals both to illuminate which class groups are disproportionately under or over represented and to enable researchers to map traditional sociological concepts onto the virtual world (for a Canadian example see Haight, Quan-Haase and Corbett 2014). Do real-world inequalities manifest in the virtual? Are individuals from the higher class groups better networked online? Alternatively does Twitter provide a mechanism for users from the lower class groups typically associated with having lower social capital to connect and network? Is it a voice for groups that are normally excluded from public debate?

The work conducted so far on social class for Twitter users is very much focused on British notions of classification, although the fact that it links occupations to the standard socio-economic groups (NS-SEC) means that international comparisons can be made (Erikson and Goldthorpe 1992). Certainly the method for extracting and inferring class from occupations is transferable and could be applied in other national contexts.

The key to the problem is in identifying the occupation of a Twitter user in much the same manner in which age can be identified. Sloan et al. (2015) outline a process for pattern matching occupational labels in Twitter profiles with SOC2010 codes – a list of occupational titles provided by the UK Office for National Statistics that gives every occupation a four digit number (in this case) which can then be located within an NS-SEC group using a look-up table. In principle this process appears simple but in reality it is fraught with difficulties and dangers. First, it is not unusual for a tweeter to list multiple occupations in their profile and it is often not clear which one should take precedent. Second, there is a certain class of terms that can be both occupations and hobbies such as 'painter', 'photographer' and 'gardener'. The third, problem that an occupation such as 'gardener' could also mean a 'landscape gardener', which would result in a different NS-SEC categorisation. Fourth, is the issue of false positives which arise due to changes in vocabulary over time and the historic nature of the SOC2010 list of occupations ('page' is an occupation but normally refers to a 'web page' when used in a profile description). There is also the perennial problem of deception on behalf of the user based on social desirability when creating a virtual identity (see Turkle 1995, Markham 1998 and Williams 2006), although there is some evidence that identity play is somewhat short-lived where prolonged interactions are taking place (Bechar-Israeli 1995) and that the public (and professional) nature of social media inherently reduces the tendency for identity play (Leonardi et al. 2014).

This final problem of deception must always be remembered and reflected upon when developing any demographic proxy, but Sloan et al. (2015) propose mechanisms for ameliorating the other issues including: choosing the first pattern-matched SOC2010 reference on the basis that it is the most important occupation to the user; the need to reflect on the presence of 'creative' occupations as potential hobbies (and to expect an over-inflation of these roles which will in turn over-estimate the membership for certain NS-SEC groups); choosing by default the longest occupational term so that occupations such as 'landscape gardener' are not classified as just 'gardener'; and the need for bespoke rules associated with particular terms that are common and known to generate false positives. This latter point is likely where occupation and class detection can incrementally improve over time with the addition of bespoke rules. A very good example is that a 'Doctor Who fan' is not necessarily a 'doctor'. Human validation also plays an important role in this process to check that the automated classification algorithm is accurate. For this study a three-way expert cross-validation was conducted, with three of the authors looking at that same subset of identified occupations and a calculation of inter-rater agreement via Krippendorff's Alpha. Sloan et al. (2015) demonstrate that occupational data could be identified in 8.1% of the sample of 32,032 cases although three-way expert agreement was only attained on 57.8% of these cases (which still amounts to a projected verified occupational for 18,638 UK Twitter users).

Figure 7.3 provides a summary of the findings, comparing the proportions of Twitter users from each class group according to three-way agreement, the subset of data selected for expert coding, the whole dataset of 32,032 cases and the 2011 Census. Interpretation should be tempered by the substantial error rate identified by the human validation, although the error between three-way agreement and automated detection is notably lower for NS-SEC 1 and 3 which is an artefact of the unambiguous job titles in these groups (e.g. 'doctor' and 'solicitor' for group 1, 'teacher' and 'nurse' for group 3). Perhaps the most interesting observation is the disproportionate number of tweeters in group 2 compared to Census 2011 data. NS-SEC 2 includes job titles such as 'artist', 'singer', 'coach' and 'dancer' which can all

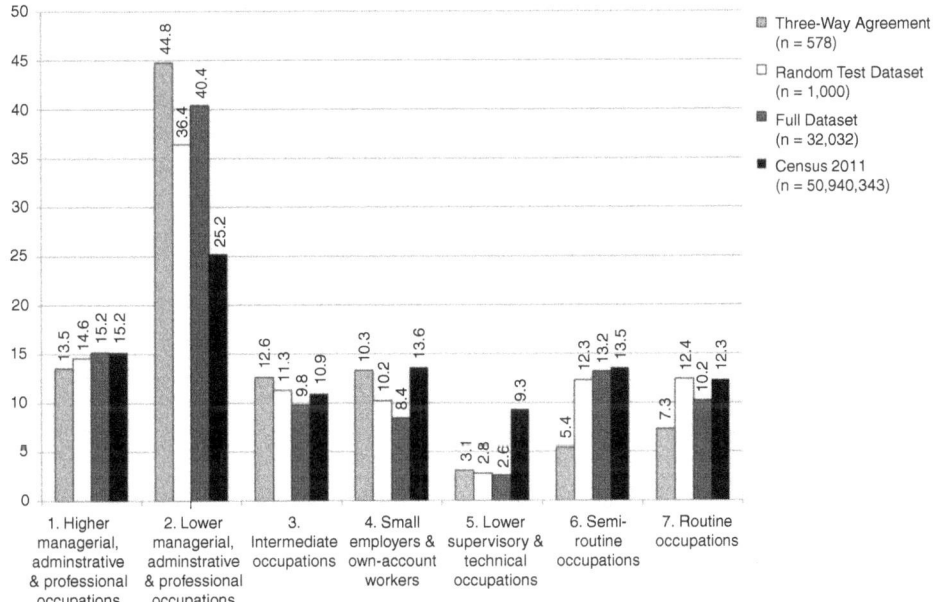

Figure 7.3 Comparison of NS-SEC breakdown for Twitter users and the 2011 Census
Source: Sloan et al. 2015.

be conflated with hobbies rather than occupations and this might explain the high number. An alternative explanation is that people with these occupations are genuinely over-represented on Twitter, perhaps because the creative arts and personal services ('coach') use Twitter to advertise their businesses and/or products (Sloan et al. 2015). There is current research into methods for validating class and other demographic proxies which may tell us which of these explanations is correct and these are discussed below.

Of course, occupation is only one method for identifying class groups. Recent work by Savage et al. (2013) advocate alternative measures focused around economic, social and cultural capital. Certainly there has been work on social capital in Facebook networks (Valenzuela et al. 2009) and understanding whose opinions carry the most weight for the purposes of understanding information propagation in Twitter networks is of great interest to social science.

VALIDATION OF DEMOGRAPHIC PROXIES – FUTURE WORK

Much of the discussion above has been qualified by the fact that the true demographic characteristics of Twitter users are not known and that we are reliant on using *signatures* to develop proxies (apart from geocoding), but there are methods through which accuracy can be tested. One way forward is to ask for Twitter handles on major social surveys so that the demographic characteristics of users are known, this 'gold-standard' data can then be cross-referenced with what we have inferred from Twitter behaviour and metadata. Such a project was undertaken as part of the NatCen Social Research British Social Attitudes Survey 2015 and will enable us to verify the accuracy of demographic proxies by providing a baseline of accurate information.

Other methods are less rigorous as they introduce human error and do not exclude deception, but they can still be used to triangulate demographic proxies with other methods. Crowdsourcing proxy validation through human intelligence tasks (HITs) using CrowdFlower, Amazon Mechanical Turk or an expert panel (Ackland 2013, Burnap et al. 2013b) allows a researcher to present the demographic proxy they have identified and ask other people if they agree. An example would be to present someone with a profile description, the occupation you have derived from it and then ask if this looks correct to the respondent. Multiple respondents can be shown the same records to increase reliability and measure certainty, following a similar logic to the expert validation used by Sloan et al. (2015) for testing an occupation detection algorithm.

Perhaps the most obvious way of testing accuracy is to ask Twitter users themselves what their gender/occupation/age etc. is, but unless this process could be automated then it is likely unpractical. It could also encourage identity play as users may react negatively to the revelation that so much can be inferred from the apparently innocuous metadata they provide.

A final method for validating proxies relies on the assumption that demographic differences do make a difference to online behaviour. Taking gender as an example, if an algorithm is accurately identifying male and female tweeters we may logically conclude that we would be able to observe differences between the two groups. The counter-factual of this is that, if the algorithm isn't discriminating between two real groups (and that categorisation is at least partly random), then the lack of group homogeneity would result in no differences manifesting in the Twittersphere. Burnap et al. (2012) demonstrate differences in sentiment during the London 2012 Olympics after classifying gender – suggesting that the detection algorithm is valid.

CONCLUSION

The augmentation of Twitter data with demographic proxies can enable social scientists to investigate new areas of research. Geography can be used to link social media data with other sources (such as crime rates and Census data) and the identification of other demographic characteristics enables us to study how (or if) group differences manifest online. However, whilst Twitter is not as 'data-light' as some researchers have argued, that does not mean that establishing demographic characteristic is a simple and clear-cut matter. There is still much testing and verification to be done to check both that the information gathered from metadata is accurate (i.e. people are telling the truth) and it is essential that automated processes are continually monitored, checked and improved. There are also important conceptual issues to address around what we mean by language (the difference between interface and tweets) and what some of the less granular geographical references in profiles and tweets are telling us. Having said that, these are just the first steps and there are ways in which techniques can be tested which in turn will lead to improvements in categorisation. There is also evidence that differences can be observed in sentiment and online behaviour based on gender, indicating a reasonable level of validity in the measure. As the accuracy of demographic proxies increases, so does the value of Twitter for social scientific analysis.

REFERENCES

Ackland, R. (2013) *Web Social Science: Concepts, Data and Tools for Social Scientists in the Digital Age*. London: SAGE.

Argamon, S., Koppel, M., Fine, J. and Shimoni, A. R. (2006) Gender, genre, and writing style in formal written texts. Text, 23(3): p. 321–346.

Bechar-Israeli, H. (1995) FROM <Bonehead> TO <cLoNehEAd>: NICKNAMES, PLAY, AND IDENTITY ON INTERNET RELAY CHAT. *Journal of Computer-Mediated Communication 1:0*. DOI:10.1111/j.1083-6101.1995.tb00325

Burnap, P., Housley, W., Morgan, J., Sloan, L., Williams, M., Avis, N., Edwards, A., Rana, O. and

Williams, M. (2012) Working Paper 153: Social media analysis, Twitter and the London Olympics 2012, *Cardiff School of Social Sciences Working Paper Series*, Cardiff University Press: Cardiff. Available at: http://www.cardiff.ac.uk/socsi/resources/Working%20Paper%20153%20-%20Burnap%20et%20al.%20(2013)%20Social%20Media%20Analysis,%20Twitter%20and%20the%20London%20Olympics%202012%20-%20A%20Research%20Note.pdf (accessed 20 February 2015).

Burnap, P., Rana, O. and Avis, N. (2013a) 'Making sense of self reported socially significant data using computational methods', in Housley, W., Edwards, A., Williams, M. and Williams, M. (Eds.), Special Issue, Computational Social Science: Research, Design and Methods, *International Journal of Social Research Methods*, 16(3): p. 215–230.

Burnap, P., Rana, O., Avis, N., Williams, M., Housley, W., Edwards, A. and Morgan, J. (2013b) Detecting tension in online communities with computational Twitter analysis, *Technological Forecasting and Social Change*. DOI:10.1016/j.techfore.2013.04.013

Carter, S., Weerkamp, W. and Tsagkias, M. (2013) Microblog language identification: overcoming the limitations of short, unedited and idiomatic text, *Language Resources and Evaluation*, 47(1): p. 195–215.

Cheng, N., Chandramouli, R. and Subbalakshmi, K. P. (2011) Author gender identification from text, *Digital Investigation*, 8(1): p. 78–88.

Cheng, Z., Caverlee, J. and Lee, K. (2010) You are where you tweet: a content-based approach to geo locating twitter users, *Proceedings of the 19th ACM International Conference on Information and Knowledge Management (CIKM '10)*, New York, NY, USA. Available at: http://dl.acm.org/citation.cfm?id=1871535

Dodds, P. S. and Danforth, C. M. (2010) Measuring the happiness of large-scale written expression: songs, blogs, and presidents. *Journal of Happiness Studies*, 11(4): p. 441–456.

Duggan, M. and Brenner, J. (2013) The Demographics of Social Media Users – 2012. *Pew Research Centre Report*. Available: http://pewinternet.org/Reports/2013/Social-media-users.aspx (accessed 11 August 2014).

Edwards, A., Housley, W., Williams, M., Sloan, L. and Williams, M. (2013) Digital social research, social media and the sociological imagination: Surrogacy, augmentation and re-orientation. *International Journal of Social Research Methodology*, 16(3): p. 245–260. DOI:10.1080/13645579.2013.774185

Erikson, R. and Goldthorpe, J. (1992) *The Constant Flux*. Oxford: Clarendon.

Gayo-Avello, D. (2012) *I Wanted to Predict Elections with Twitter and all I got was this Lousy Paper: A Balanced Survey on Election Prediction using Twitter Data*. Department of Computer Science, University of Oviedo (Spain). Arxiv: http://arxiv.org/pdf/1204.6441.pdf (accessed 20 February 2015).

Gerber, M. S. (2014) Predicting crime using Twitter and Kernel Density Estimation. *Decision Support Systems*, 61: p. 115–125.

Graham, M., Hale, S. A. and Gaffney, D. (2014) Where in the World are You? Geolocation and Language Identification in Twitter. *Professional Geographer*, 66(4): p. 568–578.

Haight, M., Quan-Haase, A. and Corbett, B. (2014) Digital divide in Canada: Demographic trends in internet access, digital skills and social networking. *Information, Communication & Society*, 17(4): p. 503–519. DOI: 10.1080/1369118X.2014.891633

Huffaker, D. A. and Calvert, S. L. (2005) Gender, identity and language use in teenage blogs. *Journal of Computer-Mediated Communication*, 10(2) article 1. http://jcmc.indiana.edu/vol10/issue2/huffaker.html

Ipsos MediaCT (2014) *Tech Tracker – Quarterly Release: Q3 2014*. Available at: https://www.ipsos-mori.com/Assets/Docs/Publications/IpsosMediaCT_Techtracker_Q3_2014.pdf (accessed 15 October 2014).

Jaffe, J. M., Lee, Y. E., Huang, L. and Oshagan, H. (1999) Gender identification, interdependence and pseudonyms in CMC: Language patterns in an electronic conference. *The Information Society*, 15: p. 221–234.

LDLJ (Language Detection Library for Java) (2012) http://code.google.com/p/language-detection/ (accessed October 2012).

Leonardi, P., Huysman, M. and Steinfield, C. (2014) Enterprise Social media: Definition, history, and prospects for the study of social technologies in organizations. Special Issue: Social Media and Communication in the

Workplace. *Journal of Computer-Mediated Communication*, 19(1) p. 1–19.

Malleson, N. and Andresen, M. (2014) 'The impact of using social media data in crime rate calculations: Shifting hot spots and changing spatial patterns', *Cartography and Geographic Information Science*. Available at: http://nickmalleson.co.uk/wp-content/uploads/2014/05/CaGIS-AAM.pdf (accessed 20 February 2015).

Markham, A. (1998) Life Online: Researching Real Experience in Virtual Space. California: Sage.

Michael, J. (2007) *40000 Namen, Anredebestimmung anhand des Vornamens*, http://www.heise.de/ct/ftp/07/17/182/ (in German) (accessed 15 October 2012).

Mislove, A., Lehmann, S., Ahn, Y.-Y., Onnela, J. P. and Rosenquist, J. N. (2011) Understanding the demographics of Twitter users. *Proceedings of the Fifth International AAAI Conference on Weblogs and Social Media*.

Savage, M., Devine, F., Cunningham, N., Taylor, M., Li, Y., Hjellbrekke, J., Le Roux, B., Friedman, S. and Miles, A. (2013) A new model of social class: Findings from the BBC's great British class survey experiment. *Sociology*, 47(2): p. 219–250.

Schwartz, H.A., Eichstaedt, J. C., Kern, M. L., Dziurzynski, L., Ramones, S. M., Agrawal, M., Shah, A., Kosinski, M., Stillwell, D., Seligman, M. and Ungar, L. (2013) Personality, Gender, and age in the language of social media: The open-vocabulary approach. *PLOS ONE*, 8(9): e73791. DOI:10.1371/journal.pone.0073791

Sloan, L., Morgan, J., Burnap, P. and Williams, M. (2015) Who Tweets? Deriving the Demographic characteristics of age, occupation and social class from Twitter user meta-data. *PLOS ONE*, 10(3): e0115545. DOI: 10.1371/journal.pone.0115545.

Sloan, L. and Morgan, J. (2015) Who Tweets with Their Location? Understanding the relationship between demographic characteristics and the use of geoservices and geotagging on Twitter. *PLOS ONE*, 10(11): e0142209. DOI:10.1371/journal.pone.0142209.

Sloan, L., Morgan, J., Housley, W., Williams, M., Edwards, A., Burnap, P. and Rana, O. (2013) Knowing the Tweeters: Deriving sociologically relevant demographics from Twitter. *Sociological Research Online*, 18(3): DOI:10.5153/sro.3001

Thelwall, M., Buckley, K., Paltoglou, G., Cai, D. and Kappas, A. (2010) Sentiment strength detection in short informal text. *Journal of the American Society for Information Science*, 61(12): 2544-2558.

Thomson, R. and Murachver, T. (2001) Predicting gender from electronic discourse. *British Journal of Social Psychology*, 40: p. 2193–2208.

Turkle, S. (1995) *Life on Screen: Identity in the Age of the Internet*. London: Weidenfield and Nicolson.

Twitter (2014) Company information page. Available: https://about.twitter.com/company (accessed 11 August 2014).

Valenzuela, S., Park, N. and Kee, K. F. (2009) Is there social capital in a social network site?: Facebook use and college students' life satisfaction, trust, and participation. *Journal of Computer-Mediated Communication*, 14(4): 875-901.

Williams, M. (2006) *Virtually Criminal: Crime, Deviance and Regulation Online*. London: Routledge.

Williams, M., Burnap, P. and Sloan, L. (2016). Crime Sensing with Big Data: The affordances and limitations of using Open Source communications to estimate crime patterns. *British Journal of Criminology*, DOI: 10.1093/bjc/azw031

Yahoo! PlaceFinder, http://developer.yahoo.com/geo/placefinder/ (accessed October 2012).

PART II
Collection & Storage

Think Before You Collect: Setting Up a Data Collection Approach for Social Media Studies

Philipp Mayr and Katrin Weller[1]

This chapter discusses important challenges of designing the data collection setup for social media studies. It outlines how it is necessary to carefully think about which data to collect and to use, and to recognize the effects that a specific data collection approach may have on the types of analyses that can be carried out and the results that can be expected in a study. We will highlight important questions one should ask before setting up a data collection framework and relate them to the different options for accessing social media data. The chapter will mainly be illustrated with examples from studying Twitter and Facebook. A case study studying political communication around the 2013 elections in Germany should serve as a practical application scenario. In this case study several social media datasets were constructed based on different collection approaches, using data from Facebook and Twitter.

INTRODUCTION

Social media research so far is not a defined discipline. Researchers across various disciplines are interested in social media platforms and their users. Researchers with different background may focus on different research questions – and they may have their own definitions about what counts as social media research (and even about what counts as social media). To some degree this is an advantage at the current stage of studying social media, as it leaves much room for exploring approaches to address novel research questions which helps in making it an exciting topic for researchers in several fields (Kinder-Kurlanda & Weller, 2014). But this diversity also brings along a lack of standardization of approaches and thus often a lack of comparability at the current state of social media research. The present chapter will focus on the challenges that arise in designing the setup for the collection of social media data. In this context, we do not look at approaches that mainly use surveys, interviews or experiments for studying social media users and their behavior in social media environments – examples of such approaches would be Marwick and boyd (2011) who interviewed Twitter users to learn about their behavior, or Junco et al. (2011) who created an experimental setting for studying Twitter use in academic learning. In contrast to this, we focus on research that is based on datasets directly collected from social media platforms.

In general, data collected from social media could be textual content or multimedia content, user profile pages or network data, or tracked activities such as likes, shares, upvotes (see Chapter 2 in this volume for an overview on data). It could be data from blogs or from platforms like Facebook, Twitter, YouTube, reddit, Wikipedia, and many more. For some platforms, data can be obtained via an application programming interface (API) or via third party tools that readily provide access using the API; sometimes data has to be crawled from the website and sometimes it can be purchased through official resellers (e.g. GNIP[2] and Datasift[3]). Other researchers have come up with their own solutions to obtain social media data in a less structured format: Some researchers manually copy-and-paste selected text passages from social media platforms into excel sheets or other databases in order to create a corpus that matches their research purpose. And yet others are interested in the look of profile pages and images and may, for example, take screenshots to archive them as their specific data collection approach. In some cases, already existing datasets may be reused in secondary studies, although this is still rather rare – also because data sharing may be prohibited or restricted by a social media platform's terms of services (Weller & Kinder-Kurlanda, 2015). Often, the chosen approach for data collection is also influenced by external factors, such as the technical limitations of a social media platform or of the data collection tool (Borra & Rieder, 2014). It might just not be possible to get the 'ideal' dataset due to legal or technical restrictions and researchers do not have a choice but to work with a substitute. This does not necessarily have to be a problem and may still lead to relevant results. But researchers have to be very clear about potential limitations of their collection approach and should outline the consequences this may have for the obtained results (e.g. in terms of representativeness of their data). Knowing the boundaries of what is possible in terms of data collection is important, but it is critical not to stop thinking about its implications and to reflect on the potential biases that may arise out of it. For example, many researchers use hashtags as a convenient way to collect datasets from Twitter and this may also in some cases be the only feasible way to collect data, for example, for an acute event. However, this may systematically exclude specific user types from the dataset, for example, users less familiar with hashtag conversation or users who use a different set of hashtags or hashtags in different languages – or complete strains of follow-up conversations as users may no longer use the hashtag within replies to original tweets. Lorentzen and Nolin (2015) remind us in more detail of the limitations arising from hashtag based data collection approaches.

Even when operating within some narrow limits of availability there are still choices to make: it is necessary to carefully think about which data to collect and to use; and it is important to recognize the effects that a data collection approach may have on the types of analyses that can be carried out and the results that can be expected in a study. This includes selecting the most appropriate social media channels, selecting the timeframe for data collection, constantly checking upon newly created user accounts or relevant hashtags, thinking about keywords that relate to different language communities, monitoring and documenting server outages or other technical problems. This chapter should help raise awareness of challenges around study design and data collection. For this purpose, we will highlight the most important questions one should ask before setting up a data collection framework and relate them to the different options for accessing social media data. Throughout the chapter, a specific case study will be used in order to illustrate the process of study design. The case study comes from the area of political communication in social media environments. Political communication is a frequent topic in social media research and studies that use data from Twitter for studying elections are particularly popular (Jungherr, 2016; Weller, 2014). Most of them analyze communication structures or user networks during specific cases of (national) elections (e.g. Elmer, 2013; Larsson & Moe, 2012; Towner, 2013), some also aim at predicting election outcomes (e.g. Soler et al., 2012; Tumasjan et al., 2011) – which in turn has led to some critical reflections on study design and methods (e.g. Jungherr et al., 2012; Metaxas et al., 2011) and general skepticism towards election predictions based on social media data. However, there is a potential of using social media data to monitor how people discuss political topics prior to elections and in general, how politicians interact with one another and with the public or how traditional media and social media focus on similar or different topics during elections. Research in this field includes studying politicians' interaction networks (e.g. Lietz et al., 2014), comparisons of different countries (e.g. Larsson and Moe, 2014) or close analysis of the social media campaigns of single presidential candidates (e.g. Christensen, 2013).

Even a very specific topic such as political communication during an election period can be studied in a variety of ways. Weller (2014) shows how studies on Twitter and elections vary in terms of research questions, collection period, size of the collected data set and tools for data collection. Dataset sizes can range from just single selected tweets to billions of them, from less than ten single users to networks of 200,000 user accounts (Weller, 2014).

A Practical Example: Social Media and Elections

We will now take a closer look at the challenges for collecting data in such cases of studying political communication through social media. We use a case study which was conducted at GESIS - Leibniz Institute for the Social Sciences (in cooperation with the Copenhagen Business School) and focused on political communication around the federal election that was held in September 2013 in Germany (see Kaczmirek et al., 2014 for a more detailed description of the case study). In this case study several social media datasets were constructed using data from Facebook and Twitter (a subset of the Twitter dataset has also been archived for reuse, see Kaczmirek and Mayr, 2015).

The project goal was to examine various aspects of communication structures in online media and to investigate how such data can add new insights in comparison to existing data from surveys and (traditional) media analyses (Kaczmirek et al., 2014). The project was tied to the broader framework of the German Longitudinal Election Study (GLES[4]), a long term research project that examines the German federal elections in 2009, 2013, and 2017 with the aim of tracking the German electoral process over an extended period of time (Schmitt-Beck et al., 2010). Data used in the GLES project includes surveys, media content analyses, and interviews with election candidates. The overall aim was to supplement the GLES candidate study – which is based on interviews – with new information about the candidates retrieved from social media sources. Another idea was to complement the traditional media corpus analysis of GLES (were different traditional mass media channels are analyzed) with an analysis of important topics as discussed in social media. As we will see below, we decided to do this based on data from Twitter and Facebook. We will use this exemplary case to illustrate some more general strategies for social media studies.

STRATEGIES FOR DATA COLLECTION

The first steps in setting up a social media study will usually be to formulate a research question and to then decide upon the most suitable data that will allow answering this question. It has been criticized that a lot of 'big data' studies are data driven, i.e. starting with a given dataset rather than with a research question or theory – and critical reflections are emerging on how such data-driven approaches affect knowledge production (e.g. Schroeder, 2014).

Starting with a given dataset and building the research questions around it, can make a lot of sense in some cases. This exploratory design may be useful for mapping out the properties of a specific social media platform and is thus applied in cases where one first needs to understand the overall usage scenario or the user behavior within a specific platform (as done by e.g. Cha et al., 2007 for YouTube; Weninger et al., 2013 and Singer et al., 2014 for Reddit). But in most cases, it is indeed recommended to start with the specific research question and then to think about the ideal dataset that would be needed to answer it. In the next steps, one may have to lower the expectations: the ideal dataset may not be possible due to, for example, technical, legal, or ethical limitations. For example, the ideal dataset for some research question might be all tweets ever sent on Twitter from locations in Germany. Unfortunately, it is not possible to collect tweet searches retrospectively via the public Twitter APIs[5], and even if one can afford buying such a large dataset from the official Twitter data reseller GNIP there still is the fact that only very few tweets are geo-coded, so that it is not easily feasible to identify tweets sent from Germany. In such cases, one has to find a way to approach the best possible dataset and acknowledge some drawbacks and limitations. Over time, the research community is learning which kind of data can be crawled from specific social media platforms, and which not, and is exchanging best practices and lessons learned (though it has to be kept in mind that as social media platforms and their APIs may change, all this expertise has to constantly evolve, too). Still, it is important to always envision the ideal dataset and then reduce it to the best one given the current limitations. If researchers simply work with the same kind of data which has been used before and proved to be easily accessible, there is a risk that they miss opportunities for creating better data collection approaches. For example, working with a Twitter dataset collected for a specific hashtag has become common practice, so that some researchers might forget to think about whether different synonymous keywords would have been more appropriate entry points for data collection.

Thinking about the ideal dataset should of course also include asking whether social media will really provide the best possible data source – or whether other data (e.g. experiments, survey data, content from traditional mass media) would be more appropriate. In the following we will introduce a set of questions that are critical to any data collection approach in social media research. The initial question should be:

1. Which social media platforms would be the most relevant for my research question? (Single platform vs. multi-platform approach)

When this is decided, the next step will be to prepare data collection from the selected platform(s), while asking the following questions:

2. What are my main criteria for selecting data from this platform? (Basic approaches for collecting data from social media)
3. How much data do I need? (Big vs. small data)
4. What is (unproportionally) excluded if I collect data this way? (Collection bias)

We will now take a closer look at these questions and the possible strategies for data collection related to them.

Single Platform and Multi-platform Studies

Many current social media studies focus on a single social media platform, with Twitter and Facebook being most prominent (Weller, 2015). For research that aims at gaining a deep understanding of a specific platform, this single platform approach is self-evident and appropriate: in order to, for example, fully understand how Twitter users make use of retweets (e.g. boyd et al., 2010) or hashtags it is most crucial to collect data from Twitter. But even in these cases, a comparison with other platforms would be desirable in order to prove whether the observed phenomena are unique to Twitter or in line with results from other contexts. Quan-Haase and Young (2010) demonstrate the value of comparisons across platforms in social media research.

While some research focuses on understanding a specific platform, other studies look into selected phenomena such as political activism (e.g. Faris, 2013; Thorson et al., 2013), disaster response (e.g. Bruns & Burgess, 2014; Vieweg et al., 2010), scholarly communication (Haustein et al., 2014) or journalism (e.g. Papacharissi, 2009). Often these cases are narrowed down to how a specific platform was used in a specific situation, like Twitter during the London Riots, Facebook during the presidential election, Flickr for interacting with street art, and YouTube for e-learning. All these examples would promise interesting insights. But in the long run, we also need more approaches that consider the role of different platforms within the broader landscape of traditional and new media formats, i.e. how different social media platforms are either interrelated or complement each other – as illustrated by Quan-Haase and Young who also argue for different needs being met by different platforms (Quan-Haase & Young, 2010). A lot of topics may not be discussed in isolation on just one platform. URLs may be included to explicitly link between different platforms: tweets may include links to Facebook, Facebook posts may reference YouTube videos, Wikipedia articles may reference blog posts etc. Memes (Zappavigna, 2012) may spread from one social media platform to the other. For many topics, the full picture will only become visible by including data from more than one social media platform. On the other hand, social media users may purposefully choose one platform over the other for different needs (Quan-Haase & Young, 2010). This means that different platforms may be used for different kinds of communication, and that some platforms may be more suitable for studying specific topics than others.

In our use case (studying online communication during the German federal election 2013) we also had to think about which social media platforms we wanted to study. We started by considering the social media platforms which are the most popular in Germany. As we wanted to collect data about election candidates, we focused on the platforms that were most broadly used by this group of people: Facebook and Twitter. For the purpose of collecting data about politicians' communication patterns we thus planned to include both of these platforms. Because of its greater ability to connect different forms of publics (Schmidt, 2014) and because of the feasibility to discuss topics spontaneously based on hashtags, Twitter was selected as a suitable platform to look for discussions around the electoral campaigns (which might be compared to contents of mass media coverage). After this was decided, we had to move on to clarify the exact setup for data collection.

Basic Approaches to Collect Data from Social Media

There are a number of ways that data can be composed and collected. First of all, for every study one has to decide upon the timeframe for collecting data. The selected timeframe may heavily influence the results, as, for example, demonstrated by Jungherr et al. (2012) for the case of election prediction, where different data collection periods lead to different predictions about election outcomes. Time is a fundamental dimension that needs to be considered in all data collection approaches, for example, should data be collected for single hours or maybe for months or even years? The timeframe then needs to be considered in combination with the basic strategies that can underlie data collection setups. The most common criteria for data collection are:

Based on user accounts. Given the case that we know a complete group of users, it might be desirable to collect data for all persons or instances in that group. This could be all soccer clubs within a country (Bruns et al., 2014), all Dow 30 companies, or – as in our example – all candidates running for a specific election. It is extremely helpful if a list of all individuals belonging to a group exists already, as this is the closest you can get to a full sample in social media research. If you can identify, for example, all members of parliament who are on Twitter, you have the ideal starting point for comparing them. However, identifying all members of a group is not always trivial, and in some cases – as we will see below – the outlines of the group may be fuzzy and decisions will have to be made about who to include or not. In many cases, it will not be possible to identify everyone belonging to a specific group, for example all people in a country who are eligible to vote. Cases in which we can assemble a full sample will thus most likely refer to some sort of elite users, rather than broad groups of people.

In our case study, it was possible to identify more than 2,000 candidates running for the German elections and to check if they had a Twitter or Facebook profile (more details below).

Based on topics and keywords. A very frequent approach is to collect social media content based on topics, for example, for a specific event (like elections or sports events) or a general topics that are being discussed by a group of people (like same sex marriage). Especially on Twitter, topical discussions are often labeled with specific hashtags, but other platforms also enable the users to apply content-descriptive metadata like tags or keywords. These may be used as a criterion for searching and collecting social media data. In other cases, the full texts of social media contents (tweets, Facebook posts, blog posts, comments etc.) can be used for collecting all cases that include a specific word. However, in many cases it is difficult to achieve 'completeness' in data collection when using text-based collection approaches. People may use different vocabulary to refer to the same topic, or the topic may not clearly be mentioned in very short posts at all. For example, on Twitter, some people may use one or more designated hashtags when commenting on a current event (e.g. #WorldCup2014 for the FIFA World Cup in 2014), others may use different hashtags (e.g. #Brazil2014, or also for example hashtags in different languages), or some may mention the event without using any hashtag and some may comment on the event even without saying its name.

When setting up a data collection approach based on keywords or other full text searches, it is important to document the choice of search terms and to consider potential alternatives. In some cases, it may be possible to collect entire threads of discussions even if only one single comment included a word that matched a query, which can lead to a more complete data collection approach.

In our case study, data was collected by utilizing a series of keywords (in addition to the collection approach based on users). We will describe this in more detail below.

Based on metadata. In some cases, data is collected based on some other structural criteria, which we call metadata in this context. This should reflect anything that is neither based on a person's or account's name nor on any content features based on semantics (keywords, hashtags). Examples for metadata that can be used for data collection include, but are not limited to, geo-locations (e.g. all status updates published in a specific country), timeframes (e.g. all status updates posted on a Sunday), language (e.g. all status updates in languages other than English), or format (e.g. only retweets, only status updates that include a URL or an image, all YouTube vides longer than 3 hours). Their availability depends on the selected social media platform and their data access policies.

Random sample. Finally, it may be possible and useful to collect a random sample of data from social media platforms. This is particularly useful for studies that want to investigate general characteristics of a social media platform (and not focus on a specific topic or user group). Some APIs may directly offer access to a random set of contents.

When collecting data based on one of the previous approaches, the resulting dataset may also be too large for some types of analysis (e.g. based on software limitations) or for some data infrastructures and may thus require some post-collection sampling.

Big Data or Small Data?

Big data has become a buzzword in different contexts and is also often used to refer to social media studies. Indeed, with the growing number of social media users, the rate at which content is being shared also increases. There are several examples of studies that have collected data from large numbers of social media users, for example, Kwak et al. (2010) and their network of more than 40 million Twitter users. And yet there is no shared definition about what counts as 'big' in a social media research context (see Schroeder, 2014 for an approach). People may probably quite easily agree that a given dataset of, for example, 10 user profile pages constitutes an example for 'small' data, but if these are heavy users of a certain platform who accumulate millions of status updates the perspective may change (see Chapter 13 on thick data, this volume). It is certainly more common to refer to the number of units for analysis (user accounts, nodes in a network, content units such as tweets or Facebook posts, actions such as likes or views) than to the size of the storage needed for handling the data (e.g. in gigabyte or terabyte). Still, questions of data storage and processing infrastructure have to be carefully considered when dealing with social media data.

There now are a couple of critical reflections on big data research and its drawbacks, focusing, for example, on representativeness, ethical issues and the role of APIs as black boxes. boyd and Crawford (2012) collected 'six provocations' for big data researchers to remind them of research ethics as well as the potential lack of objectivity. Ethical challenges of working with user data without explicit consent and with limited possibilities for anonymization are being discussed for specific case studies, for example, by Zimmer (2010). Bruns (2013) adds arguments about the lack of documentation of collection methods resulting in lack of replicability of many studies. Tinati et al. (2014) discuss the changing nature of social media platforms and the effects this has on data collection and analysis. Lazer et al. (2014) demonstrate how other changes, namely in user behavior, can also lead to problems with big data analyses. All this has practical implications for the data collection setup. And as little general guidelines exist, it is upon the individual researcher to figure out for him/herself how much data will be needed for answering a specific research question.

In addition to big data and small data, several other phrases have been used to refer to social media data and to highlight the specific qualities instead of the quantity, for example, 'compromised data' (Langlois et al., 2015). In many cases, the essential question is not about the actual size of a dataset – in the end it comes back to how the dataset has been composed, or what criteria were applied in order to collect it.

Dealing with Collection Biases

Many approaches to data collection induce a specific bias to the dataset (see Chapter 39 for a more detailed discussion of biases). Ruths and Pfeffer (2014) also discuss a variety of sources for bias in social media research, and Bruns and Stieglitz (2014) do so for the case of Twitter in particular.

Some common sources for biases are:

Biased social media populations. In many cases little is known about the exact population of a social media platform, for example, in terms of gender, age, location, or other factors such as political orientation, education etc. In most cases we can assume that social media platforms are not representative of a general population (e.g. of a specific country). Unless the relation is known, it is rarely possible to make statements beyond the platform users. Also, different social media platforms address different user populations and may not easily be compared.

Access restrictions. Most platform providers somehow restrict the access to their users' data. Often these restrictions are not completely transparent. For example, Morstatter et al. (2013) question whether the data provided through the Twitter API are representative of Twitter in total.

Sampling biases. The different approaches to data collection described above may also induce certain biases. For example, collecting tweets based on geo-codes only includes tweets by users who have deliberately chosen to share their geo-location, a sub-group which may not be representative of all Twitter users.

CASE STUDY FOR DATA COLLECTION[6]

In the following we will outline a case study which has been undertaken in 2013. More details of this study can be found in the working paper Kaczmirek et al. (2014).

We have briefly provided single examples drawn from the case study in the previous sections. Now we will give a more comprehensive account about how the working group approached data collection to illustrate some of the practical challenges we encountered – especially highlighting those challenges occurring before the actual data collection would begin.

The goal of Kaczmirek et al. (2014) was to collect social media communication which is closely related to the last German Bundestag elections on September 22nd, 2013. The corpus should enable the team to study both the election candidates and their behavior in social media environments (in contrast to other media channels) and different topics that were debated by social media users during the pre-election period.

> To this end we constructed different data sets which we refer to as the "Facebook corpus of candidates" (a corpus which shows how politicians communicate and represent on Facebook), the "Twitter corpus of candidates" (a corpus which shows how politicians communicate and represent on Twitter), the "Twitter corpus of media agents" (a corpus which shows how media agents and journalists communicate and represent on Twitter), the "Twitter hashtag corpus of basic political topics", the "Twitter hashtag corpus of media topics", and the "Twitter hashtag corpus of the Snowden affair". The first corpus includes data collected from the Facebook walls of candidates for the German Bundestag. For the other corpora we collected Twitter data. The last corpora contain tweets identified by a list of hashtags which was constructed following a topical approach (Kaczmirek et al., 2014, p. 9).

This topical approach was intended to compare different media channels for example, with the study of political topics in classical media in GLES.

> Technically, we collected tweets sent from account names of our lists (see below), tweets in which those names were mentioned (i.e., which included the @-prefix) and tweets which matched our hashtag lists (i.e., which included the #-prefix) (Kaczmirek et al., 2014, p. 9).

First Preparations for Data Collection: Setting Up a List of Candidates for the German Bundestag

For the goal of studying social media communication by election candidates, Kaczmirek et al. (2014) had to start by setting up the list of relevant persons and their social media accounts. This means that in this case, it was suitable to work with a person-based approach for data collection.

Principally, it would have been possible to use this approach for all candidates running for the 2013 election. However, some additional manual effort was needed to set up the list of candidates, as by the time the data collection from Twitter had to begin in real time the official lists of candidates had not been published yet.

> Although an official list of Bundestag candidates is published by the Bundeswahlleiter (federal returning officer) six weeks before the elections, we decided to investigate the candidate names ourselves. We did this in order to be able to start data collection of social media data simultaneously to the start of the GLES media content analysis in June 2013 and in order to collect data sufficiently in advance before the election would take place (Kaczmirek et al., 2014, p. 9)

(this means that in this case the decision about how long the data collection period should be was based on the desire to be able to match the data with another available dataset in a given collection period).

The working group thus wanted to construct a list of names of the relevant candidates which could be used as the starting point for the search of the social media accounts for both candidate corpora. 'Relevance was defined as the reasonable likelihood of becoming a member of the Bundestag. We refer to this list as the list of candidates although the complete number of overall candidates was higher. The data was collected in a two stage process.

In the first stage, the names of the Bundestag candidates and details of their candidature (list or direct candidature; constituency) were searched on the webpages of the party state associations (six parties × 16 state associations). If the candidates were not announced online, the names were requested via email or telephone call at their press and campaign offices. Since the direct candidates are elected separately in every constituency and since the party congresses, where the list candidates are elected take place at different times, our list of candidate names was continuously extended.

In the second stage, the Facebook and Twitter accounts of the candidates were identified based on the list of candidates. In addition to the internal Facebook and Twitter search function, the list of social media accounts of current members of parliament on the website pluragraph.de was useful. Furthermore, several of the politicians' or parties' websites linked to their social media accounts.

We applied the following criteria to verify that the accounts were related to the target person: (1) Is a reference to the party, for example, a party logo visible? Are Facebook friends and Twitter followers members of this party? (2) Do the candidate's personal or party website link to the profile? (3) Can the candidate be recognized via image or constituency (for direct candidates)? Where available, the verified badge in Twitter was used to select the correct account of a candidate in cases of multiple available accounts.

If the candidate had an account which he or she used for private purposes in addition to his professional account[7], only the professional account was included in our list. During our search for the accounts, this problem occurred primarily with Facebook accounts. Since a list of candidates of the 2009 Bundestag election was already available from the 2009 GLES candidate study, we also searched Facebook accounts for these candidates' (Kaczmirek et al., 2014, p. 9–10).

In the end the working group identified a list of persons who would run for the election (n=2,346). On Facebook the working group was able to collect information from 1,408 Facebook walls. On Twitter the working group followed a set of 1,009 candidates (and added 76 other agents, for example, journalists, for our additional research goals).

Kaczmirek et al. (2014) have used an approach based on a list of user accounts as described of one of the possible options for data collection outline above. So far the working group has seen that even for a defined group of persons realizing this approach may require considerable effort and has to be done manually. The main challenge is in identifying the actual accounts and verifying that they are correct and official. Sharing archived lists of identified user accounts (as done by Kaczmirek & Mayr, 2015 and recently for another case by Stier, 2016) thus is of value for other researchers who might be interested in the same set of accounts and reduces manual effort.

In a next step, we describe which other approaches in addition to the list of candidates was used for data collection in our context.

Defining Different Entities as Lists: e.g. Gatekeepers, Information Hubs and Hashtags

> Since Twitter is a fast medium which takes up and redistributes new information quickly, it is likely that conventional media also use Twitter as a data source. We assume that conventional media select information from Twitter and refine and redistribute the topics over the more conventional media (Kaczmirek et al., 2014, p. 10).

The 'Twitter corpus of media agents' was intended to reflect this. 'We refer to the individuals who would follow such an information gathering approach as "gatekeepers" and searched for them among journalists and editors.

In a first step, we identified journalists and editors working in internal political divisions of national daily newspapers and magazines and searched their Twitter accounts. The leading principle in selecting the media sources was whether they were included in the print media content analysis of GLES. The result of this first step is a list of all Twitter gatekeepers of conventional media.

In a second step, we retrieved all accounts that the gatekeepers followed. The assumption behind this approach is that the gatekeepers themselves track what we call "information authorities". The information authorities push topics into Twitter and it is likely that they play a central role in shaping the agenda on Twitter. In order to be counted in the list of information authorities we introduced the criterion that at least 25 percent of the gatekeepers have to follow the account. The list is extended by accounts which are followed by at least 25 percent of the journalists or 25 percent of the editors.

These data may prove useful to supplement research related to both the social media content analysis (…). Furthermore, the communication, bonds and agenda-setting among gatekeepers and information authorities themselves can be the target of research. The gatekeepers and information authorities constitute the source (…) for the Twitter corpus of media agents.' (Kaczmirek et al., 2014, p. 10).

> In defining (…) the Twitter hashtag corpora, we took an alternative approach which was not restricted to communication around specific Bundestag candidates or journalists. To gain information about the political communication of the population on Twitter, we used thematic hashtags. Here, we defined three procedures which serve to generate three lists of relevant hashtags. (Kaczmirek et al., 2014, p. 11).

The working group divided the hashtag corpora into 'basic political topics and keywords', 'media content' and a case study 'NSA/Snowden'.

The list 'basic political topics and keywords' 'is comprised of the common hashtags (abbreviations) of parties in the Bundestag (…) or of parties which are known to communicate substantially via social media (e.g. the party 'Piraten'). The list is complemented with the names of the party top candidates as hashtags (e.g. #merkel). A collection of hashtags for the parliamentary elections in general (e.g. #wahl2013 [#election2013]) completes the list. These hashtags comprise different conjunctions and abbreviations of election, Bundestag, and the year 2013' (Kaczmirek et al., 2014, p. 11 and appendix).

The list 'media content' 'is based on the coding scheme of the media content analysis of GLES (GLES, 2009). Wherever reasonable, one or more hashtags were generated for each code in the coding scheme (e.g. the coding scheme used "Landtagswahl" and the corresponding examples for the hashtags included #landtagswahl, #landtagswahl2013, #landtagswahl13, #ltw). The main challenge in setting up this list was that not all issues could be transformed into meaningful hashtags because topics would become too broad and produce more noise in the data than valuable content. This list is therefore subject to a higher selectivity and less objective than the first list.' (Kaczmirek et al., 2014, p. 11).

The Lack of Flexibility in the Fixed List Approach

With the election the party AfD (Alternative for Germany) made an important leap forward. In the initial concept we had not foreseen these events. Therefore, communication about and from AfD candidates is not initially included' (Kaczmirek et al., 2014, p. 12) in the candidate corpus from Twitter 'but 15 AfD candidates were added on the 27th of November 2013 to the Twitter data gathering procedure. While it is possible to collect tweets from these accounts back to the start of our data collection efforts, this is not possible for @-messages to these users or tweets including their names as a hashtag. Unfortunately, we are unable to add the Twitter communication for the other corpora because monitoring could only be implemented in real-time making it impossible to capture past events. (Kaczmirek et al., 2014, p. 12). The only option to include the missing data would be to buy them from official resellers.

Because Facebook posts are more persistent we were able to include data of the candidates of the party AfD. The Facebook walls of AfD candidates (...) were re-fetched and are part of the corpus definition. (Kaczmirek et al., 2014, p. 12).

Reusing Lists to Automatically Crawl Data

Collecting Data from Facebook

For the first candidate corpus, 'the Facebook data were collected and analyzed using the purpose-built software application Social Data Analytics Tool' (SODATO[8], see Figure 8.1 below, Hussain & Vatrapu, 2014). 'This tool allows examining public interactions on the Facebook walls of Bundestag candidates by extracting several conceptual core types of information: Breadth of engagement (on how many Facebook walls do individuals participate); depth of engagement (how frequently do individuals participate); specific analytical issues such as modes of address (measured use of first person, second person, and third person pronouns); the expression of emotion (positive, negative, and neutral sentiment); the use of resources such as webpages and YouTube videos; verbosity; and extent of participation. In the case of modes of address and expression of emotion, one can also examine how they evolve over time.' (Kaczmirek et al., 2014, p. 13).

'To fetch the relevant social graph and social text data from the Facebook walls, we used SODATO. SODATO uses and relies on Facebook's open source API named Graph API. SODATO is a combination of web as well as Windows based console applications that run in batches to fetch social data and prepare social data for analysis. The web part of the tool is developed using HTML, JavaScript, Microsoft ASP.NET and C#. Console applications are developed using C#. Microsoft SQL Server is used for data storage and data pre-processing for social graph analytics and social text analytics.' (Kaczmirek et al., 2014, p. 14). Figure 8.1 illustrates the technical architecture of SODATO.

Collecting Data from Twitter

'In the following we describe the technical aspects of creating the Twitter corpora. The Twitter monitoring builds upon previous work by Thamm & Bleier (2013).

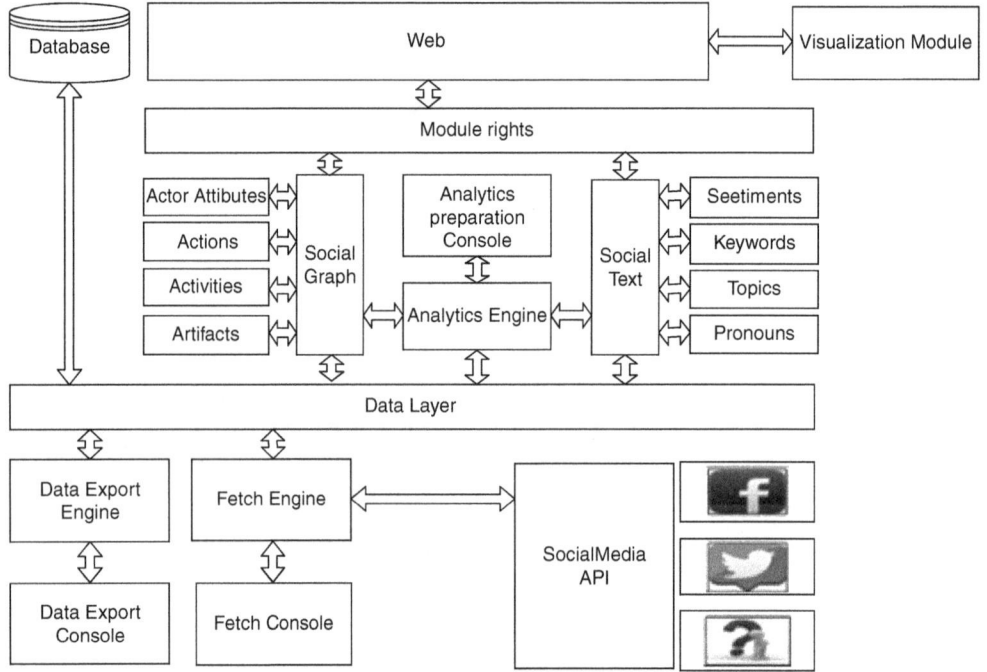

Figure 8.1 Schematic of the technical architecture of SODATO
Source: Hussain & Vatrapu, 2014.

As outlined above Twitter data is used to build different corpora. (…) Applying the list of candidate names which have an active professional Twitter account in the 2013 elections we used the Twitter streaming API[9] to receive messages directly from these candidates as well as the retweets of and replies to their messages. (…) For that purpose we developed a software component called TweetObserver that is instantly reading the stream from Twitter resulting from our query in a stable manner' (Kaczmirek et al., 2014, p.17) (see Figure 8.2).

'The software needs to register as a Twitter application in order to continuously receive update events for the requested items from the Twitter service. For each account the search query includes the account ID and the name, so that the application is geared towards receiving tweets from a certain account as well as any mentioning of its name. The software was implemented in Java and relied on the Twitter library twitter4j[10]. The software is connected to a MongoDB in which we store the data in JSON format. In the following we describe the data structure of the tweets in the Twitterdata set.' (Kaczmirek et al., 2014, p. 17).

As it is unclear if the TweetObserver software is always able to receive all tweets from the requested accounts the working group introduced a simple quality proofing mechanism. To assess the completeness another component called ObserverTester was introduced that controls the TO by automatically creating tweets at defined intervals matching its search criteria. Since all generated tweets need to be stored by the first program, the completeness is estimated as the difference between the created and the stored tweets (see Figure 8.2). $TO_{1…n}$ are instances of the program that observes different twitter accounts.

In table 1 the data structure of the tweets in the Twitter data set is explained. The collected

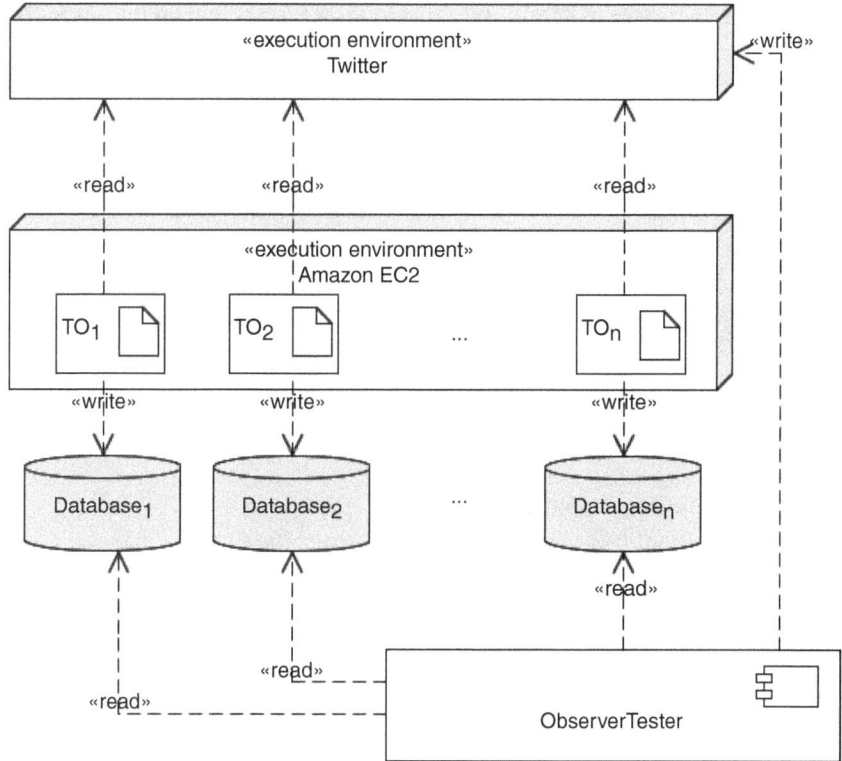

Figure 8.2 Schematic of the technical architecture of a Twitter TweetObserver

tweets are in JSON format and contain at least the attributes presented in Table 8.1.

CONCLUSION

A lot of the decisions that need to be made when setting up the data collection for a social media study rely on the considerations of the individual researcher and his/her team. So far, there are often no or very few guidelines that can help in this process. Social media research is still on its way towards establishing methodological standards or best practices.

In the exemplary case study we have seen that before the automatic crawling and collecting of social media data can begin, a lot of underlying research is necessary. Before data can be collected, different preparations may be necessary, such as strategic decisions about the period of data collection and the search criteria for collecting data. We have shown how this can be approached this for different types of datasets, a data collection approach based on lists of user accounts or based on topics and corresponding hashtags. The different types of collected data sets allow for dealing with different research questions.

Due to restrictions in the Twitter API it is not possible to collect some types of data retrospectively. In the presented case study this meant, that in one case it was not possible to fully react to some unforeseen event (the unexpected growth of a new political party in Germany, which was not anticipated when setting up the data collection approach). Other projects will have to face different challenges based on technical restrictions.

A dimension we have only touched upon very briefly in this chapter, but which also

Table 8.1 Selected attributes of tweets available in JSON format (adapted from Kaczmirek et al., 2014)

Attribute	Description	Example
_id	tweet ID	446226137539444736
userid	numeric user ID	630340041
screenName	alpha numeric user ID	lkaczmirek
createdAt	date of tweet	2014-03-19T11:08:00Z
tweettext	text of this tweet	@gesis_org is offering #CSES data, providing electoral data from around the world: https://t.co/phtZgGcIjs
hashtags	internal collection of hashtags with the following attributes:	
• start	• index of the start-character (the position in the tweet text as a number, the first letter equals index zero)	• 23
• end	• index of the end-character (the position in the string as a number)	• 28
• text	• the tag itself	• cses
mentions	internal collection of user mentions with the following attributes:	
• start	• index of the start-character (the position in the string as a number)	• 0
• end	• index of the end-character (the position in the string as a number)	• 10
• id	• user ID of the mentioned user	• 145554242
• screenName	• screen name of the mentioned user (account name)	• gesis_org
• name	• name of the mentioned user	• GESIS

plays a huge role in practice, are the legal and ethical challenges for working with social media datasets (both are increasingly being discussed in the research community). In this presented case, legal restrictions and ethical considerations mainly played their most crucial role after data collection, namely when it came to approaches for sharing the collected datasets. We wanted to make as much as possible of our datasets available for reuse.

In the end, the following data was shared (see the dataset published as Kaczmirek & Mayr, 2015): (1) A list of all candidates that were considered in the project, their key attributes and if available the identification of their Twitter and Facebook accounts. (2) A list of Tweet-IDs which can be used to retrieve the original tweets of the candidates which they posted between June and December 2013. It includes the Tweet-ID and an ID identifying the candidate. According to the Twitter terms of services[11] it was not possible to publish the full Twitter data (tweets plus metadata in its original format). During discussions at the GESIS data archive it was furthermore decided that the Twitter data may contain potentially sensitive information such as political opinion and maybe even information on voting behavior. It was decided to limit the shared dataset to data from actual election candidates, and for privacy reasons tweets from the general Twitter population are currently excluded.

Even publishing a small subset of a collected social media dataset still is an achievement; in most cases social media datasets are currently not being shared at all. Together with a white paper about the underlying data collection approach (Kaczmirek et al., 2014) a shared dataset constitutes a first step towards more detailed documentation for social media research projects. Both, documentation and data archiving, certainly need to be extended for social media research in general in the future, in order to make decisions behind data collection understandable and data collection approaches reproducible.

ACKNOWLEDGEMENTS

We thank our colleagues who were part of the working group for the project 'PEP-TF: Social Media Monitoring of the Campaigns for the 2013 German Bundestag Elections on Facebook and Twitter', which was the basis for the case study presented in this chapter. The project was initiated at GESIS – Leibniz Institute for the Social Sciences. The project goals and the conceptualization of the data were developed by GESIS, who also undertook data collection on Twitter. The project partner at the Copenhagen Business School, Computational Social Science Laboratory (CSSL), Department of IT Management used their Social Data Analytics Tool (SODATO) to conduct data collection on Facebook. The project was led by Lars Kaczmirek (for social science dimensions) and Philipp Mayr (for computer science dimensions). Thanks to Manuela Blumenberg and Tobias Gummer, who developed the project goals under the supervision of Lars Kaczmirek. Alexander Wenz helped in researching the politicians and their accounts. Together, they constructed the source information for data collection. Arnim Bleier and Mark Thamm contributed the technical realization of collecting Twitter data with TweetObserver. Kaveh Manshaei helped with resolving the shortened URL in the Twitter dataset into the original URL. Ravi Vatrapu was the supervisor in Copenhagen. Abid Hussein conducted the data collection on Facebook and developed the necessary tools under the supervision of Ravi Vatrapu.

The software SODATO was developed by our project partners at the Copenhagen Business School, Computational Social Science Laboratory (CSSL), Department of IT Management. We thank Ravi Vatrapu and Abid Hussein of CSSL for their collaboration and support. Katrin Weller, Katharina Kinder-Kurlanda and Wolfgang Zenk-Möltgen developed that framework for archiving first subsets of the collected Twitter data, Thomas Ebel and colleagues at the GESIS data archive furthermore supported the practical archiving process. Finally, we thank Christof Wolf as the scientific advisor of the project. The project started in March 2013.

NOTES

1. Authors have been listed alphabetically. Katrin Weller has provided the general discussion on data collection approaches (sections 'Introduction' and 'Strategies for data collection'). Philipp Mayr has contributed the particular case study (section 'Case study for data collection'). The section 'Case study for data collection' is a slightly extended version of sections in the working paper (see Kaczmirek et al. 2014).
2. GNIP: https://gnip.com/ (retrieved October 10, 2015)
3. Datasift: http://datasift.com/ (retrieved October 10, 2015)
4. http://www.gesis.org/en/elections-home/gles/
5. API is short for Application Programming Interface. For Twitter's APIs see Twitter's website on technical information (Twitter, no date a and b) and Gaffney & Puschmann (2014).
6. The section 'Case study for data collection' is a slightly extended version of sections in a previous working paper (see Kaczmirek et al., 2014). In this section we will quote major parts directly from the working paper.
7. We could only identify accounts that were publicly available. We did not search for accounts for which the account holder had decided to make it a 'private' account in the sense that it is not shared with the public.
8. http://cssl.cbs.dk/software/sodato/
9. https://dev.twitter.com/streaming/overview
10. http://twitter4j.org
11. https://twitter.com/tos

REFERENCES

Borra E and Rieder B (2014) Programmed method: developing a toolset for capturing and analyzing tweets. *Aslib Journal of Information Management* 66(3): 262–278.

boyd d and Crawford K (2012) Critical questions for Big Data: Provocations for a cultural, technological, and scholarly phenomenon. *Information, Communication & Society* 15(5): 662–679.

boyd d, Golder S and Lotan G (2010) Tweet, Tweet, Retweet: Conversational Aspects of Retweeting on Twitter. In: *43rd Hawaii International Conference on System Sciences (HICSS)*, IEEE, pp. 1–10. Available from: http://ieeexplore.ieee.org/lpdocs/epic03/wrapper.htm?arnumber=5428313 (accessed 5 March 2016).

Bruns A (2013) Faster than the speed of print: Reconciling 'big data' social media analysis and academic scholarship. *First Monday* 18(10). Available at: http://journals.uic.edu/ojs/index.php/fm/article/view/4879 (accessed 5 March 2016).

Bruns A and Burgess J (2014) Crisis communication in natural disasters: The Queensland Floods and Christchurch Earthquakes. In: Weller K, Bruns A, Burgess J, Mahrt M and Puschmann C, *Twitter and Society*. New York: Peter Lang, pp. 373–384.

Bruns A and Stieglitz S (2014) Twitter data: What do they represent? *it - Information Technology* 56(5): 240–245.

Bruns A, Weller K and Harrington S (2014) Twitter and Sports: Football Fandom in Emerging and Established Markets. In: Weller K, Bruns A, Burgess J, Mahrt M and Puschmann C, *Twitter and Society*. New York: Peter Lang, pp. 263–280.

Cha M, Kwak H, Rodriguez P, Ahn W-W and Moon S. (2007) I tube, you tube, everybody tubes: analyzing the world's largest user generated content video system. In: *Proceedings of the 7th ACM SIGCOMM conference on Internet measurement*. New York: ACM Press, pp. 1–14. Available at: http://portal.acm.org/citation.cfm?doid=1298306.1298309 (accessed 5 March 2016).

Christensen C (2013) Wave-riding and hashtag-jumping: Twitter, minority 'third parties' and the 2012 US elections. *Information, Communication & Society* 16(5): 646–666.

Elmer G (2013) Live research: Twittering an election debate. *New Media & Society* 15(1): 18–30.

Faris DM (2013) *Dissent and revolution in a digital age: social media, blogging and activism in Egypt*. London: I.B. Tauris.

Gaffney D and Puschmann C (2014) Data collection on Twitter. In: Weller K, Bruns A, Burgess J, Mahrt M and Puschmann C, *Twitter and Society*. New York: Peter Lang, pp. 55–68.

GLES. (2009). Wahlkampf-Medieninhaltsanalyse, Printmedien, ZA5307, Methodenbericht

Haustein S, Larivière V, Thelwall M, Amyot D and Peters I (2014) Tweets vs. Mendeley readers: How do these two social media metrics differ? *it - Information Technology* 56(5): 207–215.

Hussain A and Vatrapu R (2014) Social Data Analytics Tool: Design, Development and Demonstrative Case Studies. In: *Proceedings of IEEE 18th International Enterprise Distributed Object Computing Conference (EDOC 2014)*, Ulm, Germany, pp. 414–417.

Junco R, Heiberger G and Loken E (2011) The effect of Twitter on college student engagement and grades: Twitter and student engagement. *Journal of Computer Assisted Learning* 27(2): 119–132.

Jungherr A (2016) Twitter use in election campaigns: A systematic literature review. *Journal of Information Technology & Politics* 30(1): 72–91.

Jungherr A, Jurgens P and Schoen H (2012) Why the Pirate Party Won the German Election of 2009 or The Trouble With Predictions: A Response to Tumasjan A, Sprenger TO, Sander PG and Welpe IM. 'Predicting Elections With Twitter: What 140 Characters Reveal About Political Sentiment'. *Social Science Computer Review* 30(2): 229–234.

Kaczmirek L and Mayr P (2015) *German Bundestag Elections 2013: Twitter usage by electoral candidates*. Cologne: GESIS Data Archive. Available at: http://dx.doi.org/10.4232/1.12319 (accessed 5 August 2016).

Kaczmirek L, Mayr P, Vatrapu R, et al. (2014) Social Media Monitoring of the Campaigns for the 2013 German Bundestag Elections on Facebook and Twitter. *GESIS working papers*. Available at: http://www.gesis.org/fileadmin/upload/forschung/publikationen/gesis_reihen/

gesis_arbeitsberichte/WorkingPapers_2014-31.pdf. (accessed 5 August 2016).

Kinder-Kurlanda K and Weller K (2014) 'I always feel it must be great to be a hacker!': The role of interdisciplinary work in social media research. In: *Proceedings of the 2014 ACM Conference on Web Science*. New York: ACM Press, pp. 91–98.

Kwak H, Lee C, Park H and Moon S (2010) What is Twitter, a social network or a news media? In: *Proceedings of the 19th International Conference on World Wide Web*. New York: ACM Press, pp. 591–600.

Langlois G, Redden J and Elmer G (eds) (2015) *Compromised Data: From Social Media to Big Data*. New York; London: Bloomsbury Academic.

Larsson AO and Moe H (2012) Studying political microblogging: Twitter users in the 2010 Swedish election campaign. *New Media & Society* 14(5): 729–747.

Larsson AO and Moe H (2014) Twitter in politics and elections: Insights from Scandinavia. In: Weller K, Bruns A, Burgess J, Mahrt M and Puschmann C, *Twitter and Society*. New York: Peter Lang, pp. 319–330.

Lazer D, Kennedy R, King G and Vespignani A (2014) The Parable of Google Flu: Traps in Big Data Analysis. *Science* 343(6176): 1203–1205.

Lietz H, Wagner C, Bleier, A and Strohmaier M (2014) When politicians talk: assessing online conversational practices of political parties on Twitter. In: *Proceedings of the Eighth International AAAI Conference on Weblogs and Social Media (ICWSM2014)*. Ann Arbor, MI: AAAI Press. Available at: http://www.aaai.org/ocs/index.php/ICWSM/ICWSM14/paper/view/8069/8129 (accessed 5 March 2016).

Lorentzen DG and Nolin J (2015) Approaching Completeness: Capturing a Hashtagged Twitter Conversation and Its Follow-On Conversation. *Social Science Computer Review*. Published online ahead of print September 29, 2015. DOI: 10.1177/0894439315607018.

Marwick AE and boyd d (2011) I tweet honestly, I tweet passionately: Twitter users, context collapse, and the imagined audience. *New Media & Society* 13(1): 114–133.

Metaxas PT, Mustafaraj E and Gayo-Avello D (2011) How (not) to predict elections. In: *IEEE Third International Conference on Privacy, Security, Risk and Trust (PASSAT) and 2011 IEEE Third Inernational Conference on Social Computing (SocialCom)*. IEEE, pp. 165–171.

Morstatter F, Pfeffer J, Liu H and Carley KM (2013) Is the Sample Good Enough? Comparing Data from Twitter's Streaming API with Twitter's Firehose. In: *Proceedings of the Seventh International AAAI Conference on Weblogs and Social Media*, pp. 400-408. Available at: https://www.aaai.org/ocs/index.php/ICWSM/ICWSM13/paper/view/6071/6379 (accessed 5 August 2016).

Papacharissi Z (ed.) (2009) *Journalism and Citizenship: New Agendas in Communication*. New York: Routledge.

Quan-Haase A and Young AL (2010) Uses and gratifications of social media: A comparison of Facebook and instant messaging. *Bulletin of Science, Technology & Society* 30(5): 350–361.

Ruths D and Pfeffer J (2014) Social media for large studies of behavior. *Science* 346(6213): 1063–1064.

Schmidt J-H (2014) Twitter and the rise of personal publics. In: Weller K, Bruns A, Burgess J, Mahrt M and Puschmann C, Twitter and Society. New York: Peter Lang, pp. 3–14.

Schmitt-Beck R, Rattinger H, Roßteutscher S and Weßel B (2010) Die deutsche Wahlforschung und die German Longitudinal Election Study (GLES). In: Faulbaum F and Wolf C (eds), *Gesellschaftliche Entwicklungen im Spiegel der empirischen Sozialforschung*. Wiesbaden: VS Verlag für Sozialwissenschaften, pp. 141–172.

Schroeder R (2014) Big Data and the brave new world of social media research. Big Data & Society 1(2). Available at: http://bds.sagepub.com/lookup/doi/10.1177/2053951714563194 (accessed 1 March 2016).

Singer P, Flöck F, Meinhart C, Zeitfogel E. and Strohmaier M (2014) Evolution of Reddit: From the front page of the Internet to a self-referential community? In: *Proceedings of Web-Science Track at the 23rd International World Wide Web Conference*, pp. 517–522. Available at: http://dl.acm.org/citation.cfm?id=2567948.2576943&coll=DL&dl=GUIDE&CFID=710640694&CFTOKEN=75476029 (accessed 6 September 2015).

Soler JM, Cuartero F and Roblizo M (2012) Twitter as a tool for predicting elections results. In: *International Conference on Advances in*

Social Networks Analysis and Mining (ASONAM). IEEE, pp. 1194–1200. Available at: http://ieeexplore.ieee.org/lpdocs/epic03/wrapper.htm?arnumber=6425594 (accessed 10 October 2015).

Stier S (2016) Elite actors in the U.S. political Twittersphere. *Datorium*. Cologne: GESIS Data Archive. Available at: http://dx.doi.org/10.7802/1178 (accessed 5 March 2016).

Thamm M and Bleier A (2013) When politicians tweet: A study on the members of the German federal diet. In: *ACM Web Science Conference 2013*. Available at: http://arxiv.org/abs/1305.1734 (accessed 5 March 2016).

Thorson K, Driscoll K, Ekdale B, Edgerlyd S, Thompsone L. G, Schrockf A, Swartzg L, Vragah E. K, and Wellsi C (2013) YouTube, Twitter and the occupy movement: Connecting content and circulation practices. *Information, Communication & Society* 16(3): 421–451.

Tinati R, Halford S, Carr L and Pope C (2014) Big Data: Methodological Challenges and Approaches for Sociological Analysis. *Sociology* 48(4): 663–681.

Towner TL (2013) All political participation is socially networked? New media and the 2012 election. *Social Science Computer Review* 31(5): 527–541.

Tumasjan, A, Sprenger, TO, Sandner, PG, and Welpe, IM (2011) Election Forecasts With Twitter: How 140 Characters Reflect the Political Landscape. *Social Science Computer Review* 29(4): 402–418.

Twitter (2014) *REST APIs*. Available at: https://dev.twitter.com/rest/public (accessed 5 March, 2016).

Twitter (2014) *The Streaming APIs*. Available at: https://dev.twitter.com/streaming/overview (accessed 5 March, 2016).

Vieweg S, Hughes AL, Starbird K and Palen L (2010) Microblogging during two natural hazards events. In: *CHI 2010 – We are HCI: Conference Proceedings and Extended Abstracts of the 28th Annual CHI Conference on Human Factors in Computing Systems*. New York: ACM, pp. 1079–1088.

Weller K (2014) Twitter und Wahlen: Zwischen 140 Zeichen und Milliarden von Tweets. In: Reichert R (ed), *Big Data: Analysen zum digitalen Wandel von Wissen, Macht und Ökonomie*. Bielefeld: transcript, pp. 239–257.

Weller K (2015) Accepting the challenges of social media research. *Online Information Review* 39(3): 281–289.

Weller K and Kinder-Kurlanda KE (2015) Uncovering the challenges in collection, sharing and documentation: The hidden data of social media research. In: *Standards and Practices in Large-Scale Social Media Research: Papers from the 2015 ICWSM Workshop. Proceedings Ninth International AAAI Conference on Web and Social Media*. Ann Arbor, MI: AAAI Press, pp. 28–37. Available at: http://www.aaai.org/ocs/index.php/ICWSM/ICWSM15/paper/viewFile/10657/10552 (accessed 5 March 2016).

Weninger T, Zhu XA and Han J (2013) An exploration of discussion threads in social news sites: A case study of the Reddit community. In: *Proceedings of the 2013 IEEE/ACM International Conference on Advances in Social Networks Analysis and Mining*. New York: ACM Press, pp. 579–583. Available at: http://dl.acm.org/citation.cfm?doid=2492517.2492646 (accessed 1 September 2015).

Zappavigna M (2012) *The Discourse of Twitter and Social Media*. London; New York: Continuum International Publishing Group.

Zimmer M (2010) 'But the Data Is Already Public': On the Ethics of Research in Facebook. *Ethics and Information Technology* 12(4): 313–325.

Overview – The Social Media Data Processing Pipeline

David M. Brown, Adriana Soto-Corominas,
Juan Luis Suárez and Javier de la Rosa

This chapter provides a broad introduction to the modelling, cleaning, and transformation techniques that must be applied to social media data before it can be imported into storage and analysis software. While each of the above topics in itself encompasses a wide range of issues, they are also inextricably related in that each relies in some way upon the others. In order to discuss these processes as a group, we employ the term data processing to describe the preparatory phase between data collection and data analysis. The sections that follow demonstrate how data processing can be broken down into a pipeline of three phases:

- In the first phase, **modelling,** the data is manually evaluated for structure and meaning by identifying entities, their attributes, and how they are related. This information is then mapped to a data model, a schematic that will determine the requirements for cleaning and transformation. Also, the data model is often translated to a database schema in order to prepare for data import into a database management system.
- In the next phase, **cleaning**, the data is analyzed for possible sources of inconsistencies that could interfere with analysis. Inconsistent entries are then either removed, or resolved using one of a variety of statistical techniques. Furthermore, improperly formatted fields can be managed during the cleaning phase.
- Finally, in the **transformation** stage, the data is read from a data source using either programmatic techniques, or software designed for data manipulation. It is then parsed in order to extract and structure the information required by the data model. Finally, the data is output in a format that is compatible with the import system of the chosen storage or analysis software.

Each of these phases will be presented as a separate section that provides an overview of relevant concepts, as well as examples that put them into practice using state of the art tools and techniques. Due to the typically linked nature of social media data – think Twitter, Facebook, LinkedIn – this chapter focuses on preparing data for social network style analysis, which seeks to understand social structure and behavior by modelling reality as a collection of nodes (things) connected to one another through their interactions, or relationships (McCulloh, Armstrong, and Johnson, 2013). In the context of social media, network analysis seeks to understand how individuals interact within loosely connected information networks through the exchange of digital artifacts, such as Facebook posts and tweets on Twitter (Rainie and Wellman, 2012). All of the provided examples are based on Twitter, and were tested using a subset of the Paris Attacks Twitter Dataset, which consists of approximately 40,000 tweets formatted as JSON records collected by the CulturePlex Laboratory in a twenty-four hour period following the terrorist attacks in Paris, France on November 13, 2015. The subset was selected to include only geolocated tweets, which contain latitude/longitude information that identifies the geographic origin of the tweet (Sloan and Morgan, 2015).

SOCIAL MEDIA DATA MODELLING – FROM DOMAIN TO DATABASE

Data modelling is a broad topic that encompasses a variety of techniques and concepts. Generally speaking, data modelling attempts to recognize and define the structure and meaning contained within data in order to create a model, which is often represented as a schematic diagram. In essence, a data model is a calculated abstraction of a real world domain that is specifically designed to meet certain storage and analysis needs (Elmasri and Navathe, 2010; Robinson, Webber, and Eifrem, 2015). It guides the rest of the data processing procedures in that it determines the structure of the required output, and is typically mapped to a database system, thus defining how data will be stored and accessed. Traditionally, data is modelled at three levels:

- The *conceptual model*, sometimes referred to as a whiteboard model, describes the semantics of the data set. It provides a conceptual map that highlights the main entity types present in the data and how they are related to one another. This model will also be referred to as a domain model, because its goal is to represent the sphere of activity or knowledge associated with the data.
- The *logical model* is based on the conceptual model, but is created in anticipation of mapping the model to a database system. This model takes into account concepts such as access paths in order to increase efficiency in data storage, retrieval, and analysis; however, the logical model is generally considered to be independent of any particular technology.
- The *physical model* determines how data will physically be stored on a computer relative to the specifics of the database system being used. This model takes into account internal storage structures, such as data types, storage space requirements, indexing, etc.

While each of these levels is important for a complete discussion of data modelling, both logical and physical modelling can become very complex topics, especially when the modelling process targets relational databases. In light of this complexity, this chapter focuses primarily on the property graph model utilized by graph databases, which are designed and optimized to work with highly connected data. Furthermore, property graph style modelling provides a great introduction to data modelling because the physical and logical models are often very similar to the conceptual model. This allows the user to model complex problems in a very 'human' way, eschewing complex procedures such as de-/normalization. To demonstrate this, the following subsections introduce conceptual modelling, and illustrate how a simple model of the 'Twitterverse' can easily be mapped to a graph database management system using the property graph model.

The Conceptual Model

The conceptual data model describes a data set by identifying and mapping the main concepts of the domain associated with the data. These concepts are often referred to as *entities*, which represent general categories, or types of data present within the domain of the data set. In turn, entities are typically associated with one another through one or more types of *relationships*, which represent interactions or associations between entities. Furthermore, entities and relationships can have attributes, which describe the characteristics of entity and relationship classes. The concept model is usually expressed as a simple chart resembling a flow chart, or concept map that highlights possible entities, their attributes, and how they are related. The conceptual model is typically the first step in data modelling and database implementation, and is crucial for high-level communication of both architectural specifications and analytical procedures.

In order to create a conceptual model, we first identify the entities present within the data set. An entity can be defined as a reference to 'a thing in the real world with an independent existence' (Elmasri and Navathe, 2010: 203). This thing could be something tangible, like a building, person, or automobile, or something intangible, like a song, a scientific theory, or political party. A good general rule when looking for entities is that they are typically things named with nouns. Using the example of Twitter, both *users* and *tweets* could be identified as examples of entities within the data set. Each of these entities would then be assigned attributes: users have attributes such as username and location, tweets have time and text, etc. After identifying the relevant entities within the data set, the task becomes determining how they are associated to one another by relationships.

Relationships are generally not things, but instead represent the type of associations found between entities. We can define a relationship type as a 'set of associations – or a relationship set – among entities' (Elmasri and Navathe, 2010: 209). These associations define the semantics of the data model in that they illustrate the logical connection between entity types. As opposed to entities, relationships are usually identified using verbs. Again looking at Twitter, an example of a possible relationship would be *tweets*, as in *user tweets tweet*. In this example, *tweets* specifies a possible relationship between *user* and *tweet* entities, but it is important to recognize that there can be more than one type of relationship between two entity types. For example, a *user* could also *favorite* a *tweet*, thus creating a new possible relationship: *user favorites tweet*.

Example: Modelling Activities in Twitter

To further illustrate the idea and practice of conceptual modelling, this example creates a conceptual model using the Paris Attacks Twitter dataset mentioned above. The process of conceptual modelling often begins with a simple description of the domain to provide a contextual framework through which data can be interpreted. The following is a high-level description of the Twitter domain that provides a starting point for the conceptual modelling process.

- In the Twitter, users can follow, or be followed by, other users.
- Tweet activity is driven by users. Users are responsible for creating Tweets, the fundamental unit of information exchange. Users have a variety of associated personal data, including their username and other optional information, such as language or geolocation.
- Tweets contain the text produced by users. They have a variety of metadata associated with their production, including location and time stamp. Furthermore, they contain semantic information that is relative to other tweets and users, such as hashtags, user references, and retweets.

While the above description is admittedly a simplified version of the activites associated with Twitter, ignoring details like attached images and videos, favorites, and personal messages, it is sufficient for our purpose in that it provides the basis for understanding the domain. From the above description we can determine that the activity in Twitter is driven by two primary entities: the *tweet* and the *user*. Furthermore, each of these entities will have certain characteristics of interest, including tweet's text, date, and location, as well as the screen name associated with the user that created it.

To begin the modelling process, we map these two entities and their attributes to a simple model drawn with the Dia drawing program (Dia, 1998) (Figure 9.1).

Next, we must determine how they relate to one another. In many ways, this can often be the most challenging part of data modelling, as relationships are not always obvious. Fortunately, Twitter generally has very concrete and well defined relationships based on user interactions. A quick review of the above summary reveals the following possible relationships:

- *Users follow users.* Each user has a list of associated users who they follow.
- *Users tweet tweets.* Each tweet can be directly associated with the user who created it.
- *Tweet references user.* Optionally, a tweet can contain a direct reference to another user.
- *Tweet responds to tweet.* Optionally, a tweet can be a response to another tweet.
- *Tweet retweets tweet.* Optionally, a tweet can encapsulate a previous tweet, making it a retweet.

Adding these relationships to our data model, we begin to see a more complete image of the Twitter domain that encompasses a wide variety of the semantic possibilities represented (Figure 9.2).

However, before continuing it is important to compare the domain model to the actual dataset at hand to determine if there are any missing elements, or perhaps spurious information not included in the data set.

Looking through the fields of a JSON formatted tweet provided by the Twitter Application Programming Interface (API) – a service that allows users to collect up to one percent of total tweet traffic in real time based on filtering parameter – more on APIs in Janetzkos' chapter (this volume) – we see that a wide variety of metadata about the tweet is provided, including:

- Unique ids for both tweets and users
- Geolocation information for tweets when available
- Timestamps for each tweet
- A list of entities associated with each tweet

Looking more closely at the entity lists, we see that Twitter's data model considers hashtags to be entities, not just part of the tweet's text. This raises the question of whether or not our model should represent hashtags as a unique entity type. While the answer to this question depends entirely on

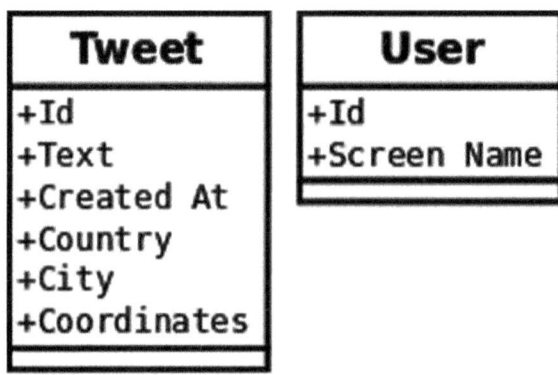

Figure 9.1 Basic Twitter entities and their attributes

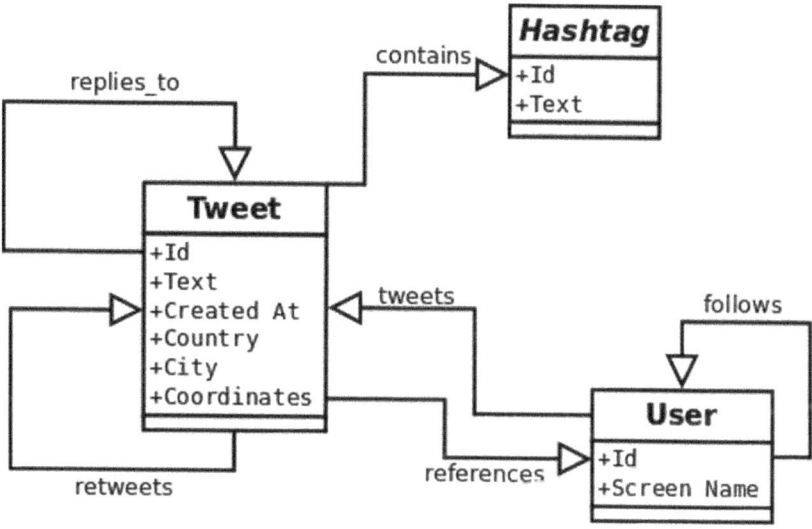

Figure 9.2 A simple conceptual model of the Twitterverse

analytic goals, it is easy to see how modelling hashtags as entities could be useful. Hashtags serve as an easy way to group tweets by thematic content without having to perform complex natural language processing (NLP) techniques such as topic modelling. Furthermore, they are user defined topic keywords, and therefore benefit from human judgment that is able to detect thematic nuances often overlooked by computers. In the case that they are not needed during analysis, hashtag entities and their relationships can simply be ignored.

Furthermore, we notice that there is no data that relates to one user following, or being followed by, another. As it turns out, Twitter's streaming API (Twitter Streaming APIs, 2010) only produces metadata relating specifically to tweets. In order to receive information about users, including follower information, one must issue specific queries to Twitter's REST API.

Therefore, the above conceptual model must be modified to reflect the semantics of the data at hand (Figure 9.3). While the original Twitter domain model that includes *user follows user* relationships is an accurate representation of activities on Twitter, it does not reflect the characteristics of the dataset. Furthermore, while hashtags were not considered in the original domain model, their presence in the data set prompted their inclusion in the data model. These sort of modifications are quite common, and this demonstrates the importance of performing multiple iterations during the modelling process.

The Property Graph Model

After the domain and dataset have been analyzed and modelled, the resulting conceptual model must be adapted to fit a database system. This is typically accomplished through an iterative process that incorporates both the logical and physical models. In this case, we will use the property graph model to create a design suitable for a graph database such as Neo4j (Neo4j, 2007) or Titan:db (Titan Distributed Graph Database, 2015). While a property graph model combines elements from both the logical and physical model, at its core it is very similar to a conceptual model in that it uses only three primitives that can be easily mapped to the three

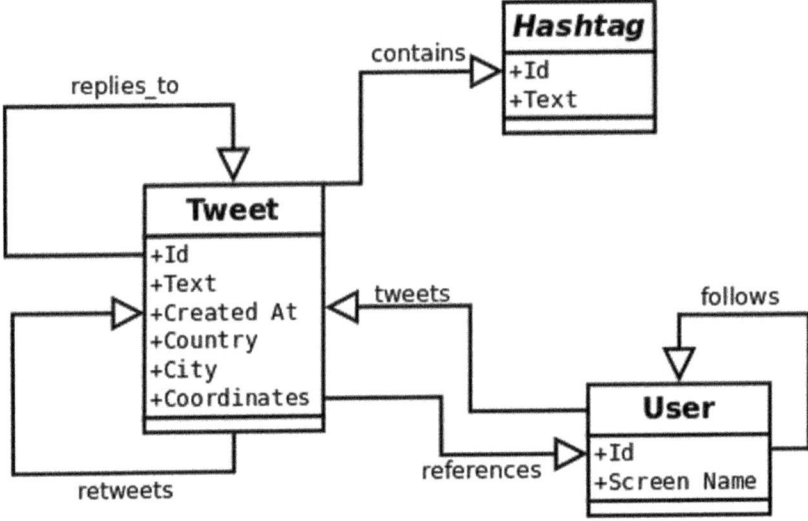

Figure 9.3 The final conceptual model of the Twitterverse

primitives used by a conceptual model (Robinson, Webber, and Eifrem, 2015):

- Properties are elements used to describe other elements. They consist of a key-value pair in which the key is a string, and the value can contain complex data types. Properties correspond to the conceptual model's attributes.
- Nodes (vertices) are elements that contain properties. Nodes typically have a type, often referred to as a label, which refers to a set of nodes that share predetermined properties. Nodes correspond to the conceptual model's entities.
- Relationships represent associations between nodes; they define the structure of the graph. Relationships often have a type, or label, that determines the semantics of a possible relationship between two node types. In a property graph, all relationships are directed in that they have a start node and an end node, which further specifies the semantics of the relationship between two nodes. Relationships can also contain properties. They correspond to the conceptual model's relationships.

In many cases, the conceptual model and property graph are identical in everything except the language used to describe them; however, the requirements of the graph database system in which the data will be stored must be taken into account. While schemaless databases like Neo4j do not require any sort of model definition prior to use, some graph database management systems, such as Titan:db, encourage the definition of a property graph style data model (schema) that includes the specification of the datatype of each property. Indeed, most database systems that implement the property graph model have some level of optional model definition designed to improve the performance or usability of the database. To illustrate this, the following section demonstrates flexible property graph style schema definition and data modelling with the SylvaDB (cite) graph database management system.

Example: Mapping Our Case-study of Twitter to a Property Graph with SylvaDB

To illustrate the process of mapping a conceptual model to a property graph, this section provides an example that utilizes SylvaDB's flexible schema creation tool to create a property graph model. SylvaDB is open source software that is free to use, and provides a wide variety of options for building queries, running network statistics, and visualizing the database. SylvaDB is unique in the sense that it provides a browser-based graphical user interface (GUI) that allows users to model, analyze, and visualize data stored in a graph database without writing code. While other database management systems such as Linkurious (Linkurious, 2013) provide GUIs for analysis and visualization, and Titan:db provides a specialized domain specific programming language for creating data models, no other commonly available system provides all of these capabilities in one software package.

To begin, simply go to www.sylvadb.com and create a free account. From the dashboard, click on the 'New Graph' button and give your graph a name. We will use the name 'Twitterverse'. You will be redirected back to the dashboard, but you should now see your graph listed on the left hand side of the screen in the 'Graphs' column. Click on your newly created graph, and you will see a notification telling you that your schema is empty. To remedy this, we will create a new schema based on our property graph model of the Twitterverse. Click on the 'Schema' button in the upper right hand corner of the screen. This will take you to the schema builder interface, where you have two options 'Import Schema' or 'New Type'. In SylvaDB, node's label corresponds to a *type*, and clicking on the 'New Type' button will redirect you to a type creation form. As you can see, SylvaDB provides you with several default fields. Under the 'Type' heading there are 'Name' and 'Description' fields, and under the 'Properties' heading, there are 'Key' and 'Description' fields. Starting with the 'Tweet' entity, we can enter the name of the *type* 'Tweet', and a short description. The description is optional, but it can help other users better understand your schema. In this case we will simply enter 'A user's tweet as provided by the Twitter API'.

After type creation, we must create the properties associated with this type. One of the most important attributes associated with a tweet is the date and time when it was published. Therefore, we will add the 'date' as the first property. To do this we simply type 'date' under the heading 'Key' in the properties list (Figure 9.4).

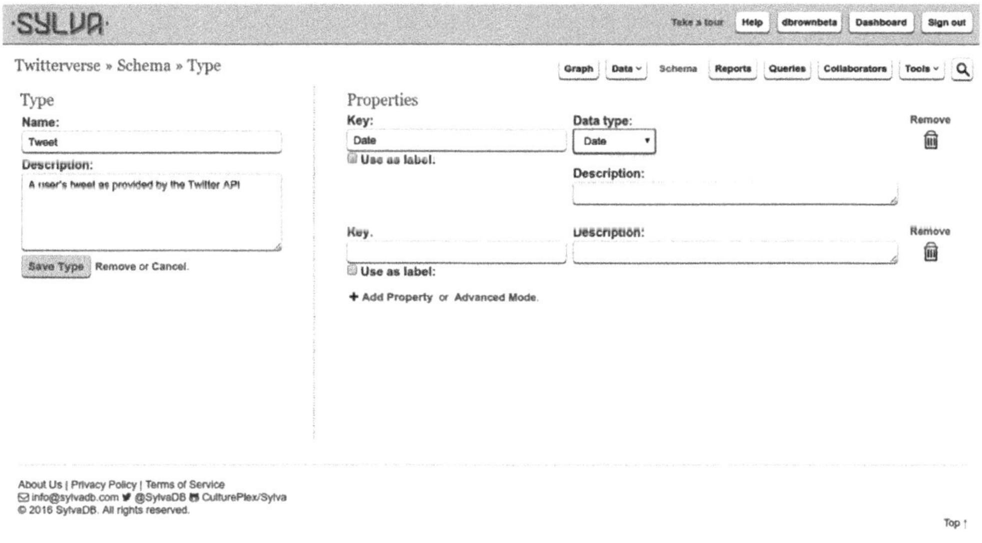

Figure 9.4 SylvaDB's type creation form

We have the option of entering a description for this property, but as date seems self-explanatory, we will leave this field blank. If we were to continue without doing anything else, the database would expect to receive a string, or a group of characters, in the date field. However, in order to leverage more advanced functionality for writing queries and performing analysis – date comparisons, advanced filtering, time series visualizations – we can instead choose to store the date in a specialized date format. To do so, we simply click on the link that says 'Advanced Mode', which expands the form field to provide a dropdown select menu that includes a wide variety of data types. Then, we simply select 'date', and SylvaDB will expect that all input for this field will be properly formatted as a date, and store it accordingly. We can continue this process, adding the other properties included in the original data model. When we have finished adding all of the attributes, we can simply click on the 'Save Type' button and the entity type will be added to the schema. In case we made an error or forgot a property, we can always go back to the *type* form and edit the information, even after there is already data in the database.

After all of the entities described in the data model have been entered as types in the SylvaDB schema builder, you should see something similar to Figure 9.5.

This means the schema is almost complete; however, it is still missing one crucial step. To finish the model, the user must define the allowed *relationships* between the different entities. Similar to defining a *type*, a *relationship* is defined by filling out a form. To access this form, a user can click the 'New Allowed Relationship' button on the schema page, or the 'new incoming' or 'outgoing allowed relationship' links that appear under the *types*.

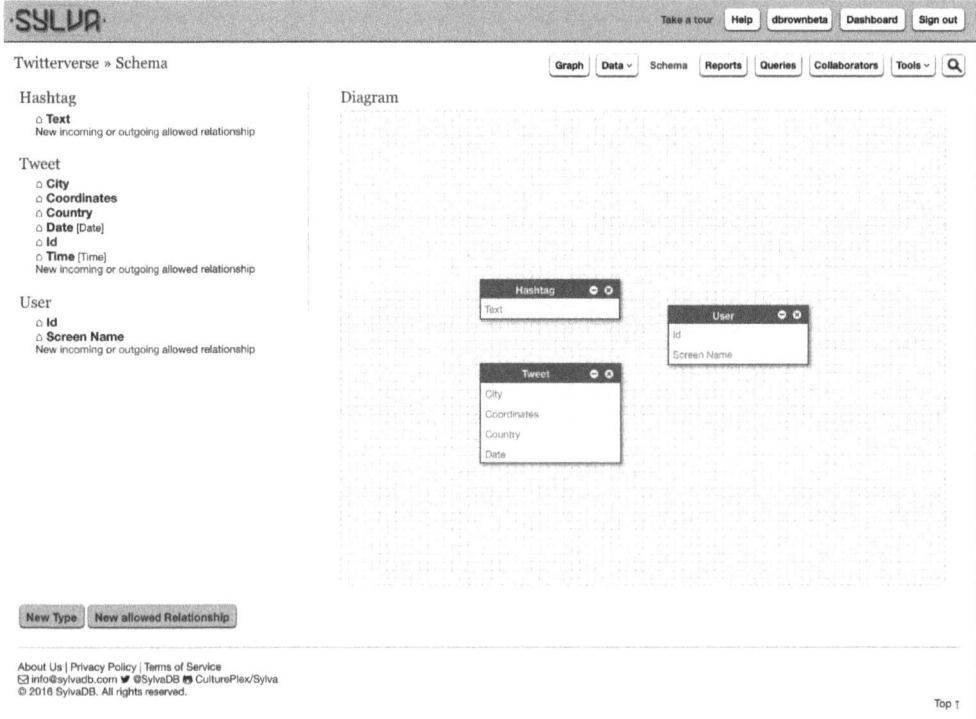

Figure 9.5 SylvaDB's property graph schema creation interface

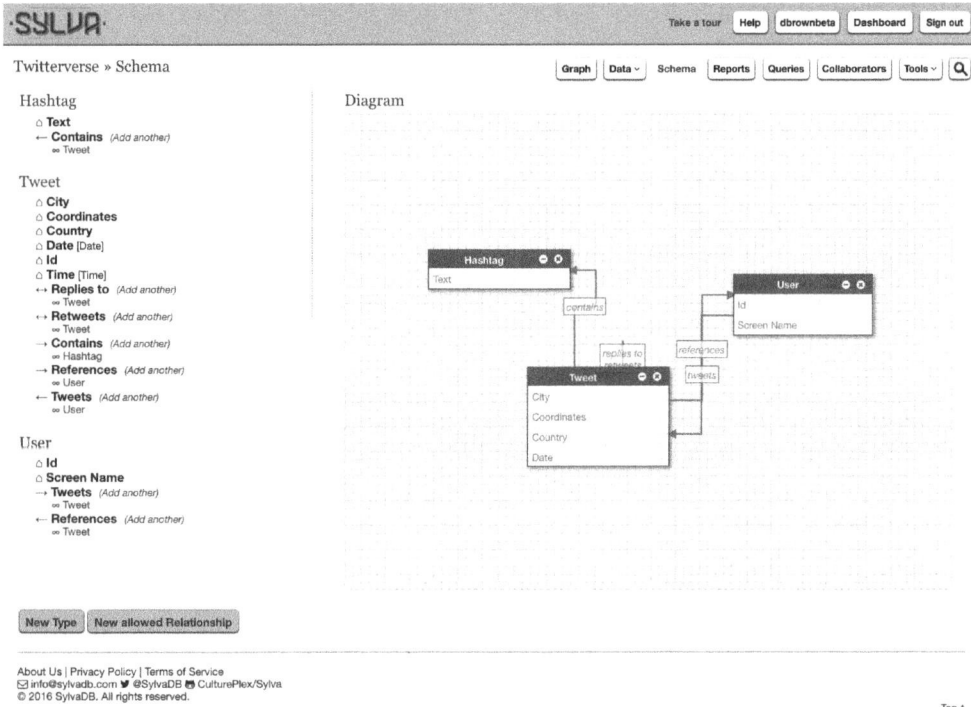

Figure 9.6   The Twitterverse conceptual model mapped to a property graph schema with SylvaDB

We then simply select the source node type using the drop down menu under the field 'Source', define the label of the relationship in the 'Name' field, and select the 'Target' node type. For example, we can select the source type 'Tweet', enter 'retweets' in the 'Name' field, and again select 'Tweet' as the 'Target' field. Properties can be added to relationships in the same manner that they are added to nodes, using the simple form fields to define keys and data types. This process can be repeated for all of the possible relationships defined in the conceptual model. After all relationships have been entered, we will see something similar to Figure 9.6. Now SylvaDB is ready to receive the Tweet data, which can be imported in a variety of formats including CSV and GEXF (a version of XML designed specifically for graph data), or entered manually.

CLEANING DATA – STANDARDIZING API DATA

After data has been modelled, but before it is parsed and formatted for use with analysis and storage software, it must be cleaned. Cleaning requires that data be inspected to determine if there are any inconsistencies, or errors that will be problematic later during analysis. There are many possible sources of errors in data, which can occur at the instance level, meaning that just one data entry is corrupt, or at the system/schema level, which can affect an entire data set (Rahm and Do, 2000). Typically, cleaning focuses more on instance level errors, as schema redesign or system modification are only possible through post collection data transformations. Due to the fact social media data is usually aggregated and stored in validated database fields, it is less prone to instance-level errors than hand-curated data; however, this is not always the case, as it is common to analyze fields that contain user generated text, which is prone to instance level errors such as typos, inconsistent spelling, etc. While spelling and vocabulary issues can often be attributed to dialectal variation or cultural factors, and in that sense do not qualify as dirty data, they can be problematic during analysis. Therefore, it is the task of the researcher to consider the implications of this type of variation as it relates to their specific research goals. Furthermore, instance level errors can appear as anomalies in otherwise clean datasets when certain aspects of schema validation or record creation fail, resulting in random, improperly formatted data. Regardless of the source of error, cleaning is fundamentally an ad hoc process that varies based on the source and quality of the data. Despite this, there are certain issues that appear repeatedly when dealing with data. The following sections outline some of these common problems and their solutions.

Missing Data

Missing data is one of the most common problems encountered when cleaning data. Missing data can occur at the instance level, or due to lack of (or overly permissive) validation within the social media application database schema. There are a wide variety of approaches to dealing with missing data that all depend on the type of data and the researcher's goals. In many cases, data with missing fields is simply deleted or ignored, which is particularly effective with very large datasets that contain few entries with missing data. However, this technique can introduce bias and affect the representativeness of the sample, particularly if the discarded cases differ systematically from the rest of the data (Schafer, 1999). To avoid this, many statisticians use a process called imputation, which uses a variety of techniques to replace the missing data. Imputation techniques often employ advanced statistical procedures or machine learning to replace missing values and account for the imputation during analysis. While these techniques go beyond the scope of this chapter, there is a wide variety of literature discussing imputation, as well as other approaches to handle missing data (Allison, 2001; Rubin, 2004; Schafer and Graham, 2002).

Data Entry Errors

Simple content generation (data entry) errors such as typos and inconsistent spelling are a common problem in all types of data. This sort of problem occurs almost exclusively at the instance level due to individual user error. Data entry errors can be very difficult to identify, particularly in large datasets that are impossible to inspect manually. They are often discovered during the analysis phase, and require the researcher to backtrack and perform another iteration of processing to reconcile the error. The most common approach to dealing with this sort of error is to use a process called fuzzy string matching (Chaudhuri, Ganjam, Ganti, and Motwani, 2003). This technique involves calculating a distance between two strings that indicates the similarity of two entries. When multiple entries are very similar, the researcher can either manually inspect the entries to determine if they indeed refer to the same instance, or determine a maximum difference that is acceptable to programmatically resolve similar entries.

Duplicate Data

Duplicate records can occur in all kinds of datasets. While they are most common at the instance level in hand curated datasets, they can also appear in social media data – particularly data that has already undergone parsing or transformation. For example, when parsing tweet data, you may find that the ids of retweeted tweets appear hundreds or even thousands of times. While this case can be dealt with during parsing, other cases are not so straightforward. Duplicates can be difficult to diagnose, as many duplicate entries are not recognized due to typos or missing data. Therefore, the first step in resolving duplicates often relates to the above technique of cleaning up data entry errors. After typos and spelling errors have been resolved, previously unrecognized duplicates are often visible within the dataset. However, missing data and other errors can continue to be problematic. After initial field cleaning, there are a variety of procedures used to compare the similarity of attributes across data entries to identify possible duplicates. Then, based on a minimum similarity measures determined by the researcher, highly similar entries can be merged. Many duplicate-removal techniques, also known as deduplication techniques, are also based upon advanced statistical procedures, fuzzy string matching, and machine learning (Gemmell, Rubinstein, and Chandra, 2011).

Inconsistent Units/Formats

Inconsistent use of units can also occur, especially in when combining data from a variety of sources. It is oftentimes quite difficult to identify this problem, as numeric values without specified units do not provide many clues. Resolving this sort of issue is highly dependent on the nature of the data, and common approaches are not easily delineated. For example, a wide sample of climate data from different countries may contain temperature information in both Fahrenheit and Celsius. In this case, the researcher could take into account the geographic location where the data was produced compared to the unit being used or the range of possible temperatures. This sort of error can also relate to formats, as sometimes applications store metadata such as datetimes – as specific data type that allows date and time to be precisely represented – using a format that is not compatible with other software. Schema level formatting problems are often addressed during the transformation stage; however, here we view it as part of the cleaning process because improperly formatted data are often the source of errors during data import and analysis.

These problems, whether created through data entry errors, or due to lack of constraints in the system responsible for aggregating the data, represent a small subset of possible sources of dirty data. In the end, it is the task of the researcher to determine what types of dirty data can affect their analysis based on their own goals and needs, and apply the appropriate solutions for the data at hand. Therefore, moving forward in this chapter the scope of this discussion will be narrowed to address social media data, and even further to address possible problems with generic Twitter data.

Social Media Data – Is it Dirty?

Social media data is often quite clean because it is typically produced, aggregated, and stored in high quality infrastructure based on well designed models. Indeed, social media sites like Facebook and Twitter enjoy state-of-the-art infrastructure, which translates to high standards of data quality. These standards are reflected in the data produced by their APIs, which tends to be perfectly formatted and complete; however, even complete and consistent API data can suffer from the above problems. For example, Twitter does not require geolocation data, and therefore it is common that only a small portion of API records contain coordinate data (Sloan and Morgan, 2015) . Although in this case non-geolocated tweets are allowed by Twitter's data model, and are therefore not technically dirty data, during a geographic analysis of tweets they could be considered as such. Furthermore, sometimes social media APIs produce 'dud' records: improperly formatted, partial, or otherwise impossible to parse; it is common to discover tweet records that do not contain text or user information, which can cause errors to be thrown in the parsing process. Finally, user generated text is often the most important aspect of social media data and is used for a variety of analytic tasks, many of which employ natural language processing techniques (Bifet and Frank, 2010; Kireyev, Palen and Anderson,

2009; Ronen, et al., 2014). Sometimes, in order to perform these tasks, text fields must be cleaned before they can be processed effectively. To demonstrate this, the following example employs the Twitter Paris Attacks dataset to illustrate user generated text cleaning in order to comply with later analysis requirements.

Example: Producing a Clean Tweet Field for Natural Language Processing

To illustrate field level cleaning of social media data, this example cleans the text contained within the Paris Attack tweets in order to produce a new field, *clean text*, that facilitates the application of natural language processing tasks commonly used with Twitter data such as language identification, topic modelling, and sentiment analysis. To better understand this process, as well as why it is necessary, consider the text field of the following tweet:

RT @MailOnline: 'General Curfew' ordered by French government for first time since WWII https://t.co/rk8MxzH7RT #Paris

As a human, it is relatively simple to decipher the components of this tweet:

- The RT flag identifies that this is a retweet.
- The @ symbol shows the original user that posted this tweet. Alternatively, this indicates a reference to another user as a recipient of the tweet's message.
- The # indicates a hashtag, which may or may not be part of a phrase. In this case, the word *Paris* is not included in the phrase.
- Finally, there is a link to another website, represented as a url.

After recognizing these components included with the text of the tweet, one can easily see that this tweet is written in English and that its message refers to the current situation in Paris. However, asking a computer to identify this is not as straightforward. Words beginning with characters such as # @ are not necessarily recognized as English, and URLs seem to just be strings of arbitrary characters. Furthermore, usernames are not necessarily real words, nor are they necessarily written in the same language as the rest of the tweet. Therefore, this sort of extra content in the text field can confound an algorithm designed to work with natural language. In order to make it easier for the computer to process tweet text, we can remove these sources of confusion to facilitate more accurate computer based text processing:

- The RT flag can be removed because it does not affect the content of the tweet. Instead, it indicates the endorsement of the content of a Tweet and the implied interaction between twitter users and content.
- The @ symbol, as well as the username can also be removed due to the fact that they are typically not directly related to the content of the tweet. They are, in some cases, used conversationally as proper nouns, and therefore may be included in a clean text field depending on the goals of the researcher.
- Dealing with hashtags can be a little trickier in the sense that they can be part of a phrase, or can be added to the tweet arbitrarily to indicate the content of the tweet. Due to the fact that they are generally real words and are often relevant to the content of the tweet, we will simply remove the #, while retaining the actual word used for the hashtag.
- Finally, urls will be removed as they are not natural language as such, and in that sense are not relevant to the language or sentiment associated with the tweet.

The produced *clean text* field will be considerably more readable for a computer. While this process can never be perfect when performed at a massive level, it will result in much better results than processing the raw tweet.

There are a variety of open source and commodity software packages that can be used to perform the above changes, including the commonly used Microsoft Office Excel and Libre Office Calculate, as well more specialized tools such as OpenRefine (OpenRefine, 2011). In this example, we will use the OpenRefine, which provides a wide range of functionality for cleaning and transforming large datasets. After downloading and starting OpenRefine as specified by the documentation for your operating system, we can create a new project simply by selecting the file containing the tweet data. OpenRefine will then request that we configure parsing options, and we can simply select the field that we are interested in working with: 'text'. OpenRefine then converts the field into what looks like a spreadsheet column, and we can continue by clicking 'Create Project' in the upper right hand portion of the browser. We can then create a custom text facet – the construct used by OpenRefine to perform operations on columns of text – for the column by clicking 'Text' > 'Facet' > 'Custom Text Facet' (Figure 9.7).

OpenRefine allows the user to write custom facets using a proprietary scripting language, General Refine Expression Language (GREL), Jython, or Clojure. In this example, we will use GREL, but any of these languages would work equally well. To clean this field, we will use a series of replace methods, which allow the user to search for substrings using regular expressions and replace them as needed. For more information about regular expressions, please refer to the OpenRefine documentation. To remove the unwanted elements from the tweets, we can use a series of four chained replace methods:

1 The first method, replace("#", " "), searches the the string for the "#" character. In the case that it finds this character, it is replaced with '""', an empty string, thereby removing it.
2 The second method, replace(/RT\s/, " "), looks for the characters "RT", followed by a mandatory space (designated by the symbol "\s"). In the case that it finds this sequence of characters, they are replaced by '""', an empty string.
3 The third method, replace(/http\S*/, " "), looks for the sequence "http", followed by any non-space character, designated by "\S". Furthermore, the non-space characters can be repeated, designated by the "*". This specifies that any string beginning with "http" followed by any characters up until a space should be replaced with '""', an empty string.
4 Finally, using a similar regular expression to the one used in step 3, the fourth replace looks for any string starting with "@", again followed by any sequence of non-space

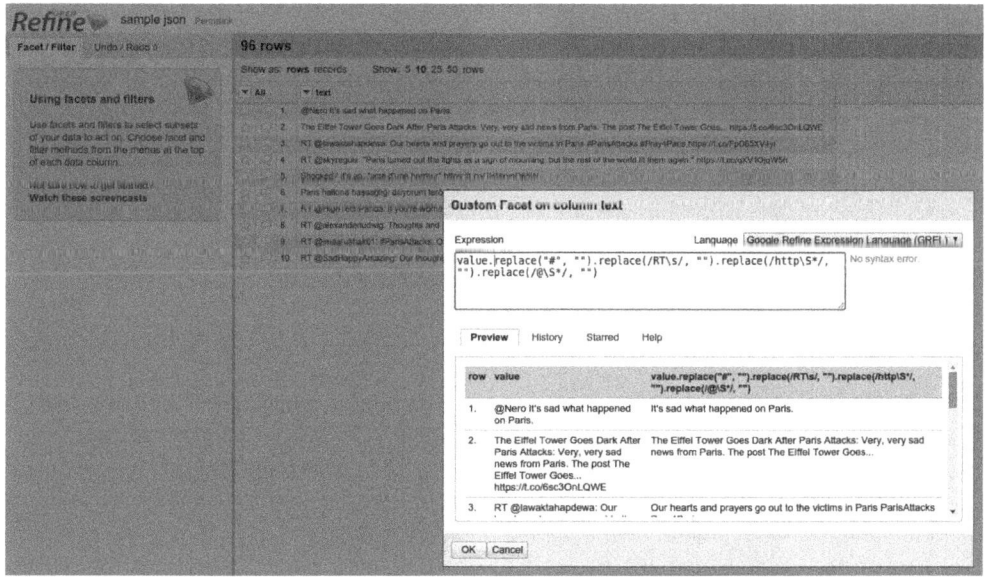

Figure 9.7 OpenRefine's custom facet creation tool

characters. If found, this string is replaced with an empty string.

Chaining together the four replace methods with the appropriate regular expressions results in the following expression:

    value.replace("#", "").replace(/RT\s/, "").replace(/http\S*/, "").replace(/@\S*/, "")

The unwanted characters have been removed from the tweet text and can be exported in one of many formats and used however necessary.

DATA TRANSFORMATION

After the dataset is modelled and cleaned, it is ready for the final stage of data processing: transformation. While the term *data transformation* can encompass a wide range of procedures, in the context of this chapter it refers to receiving input data and formatting it in a way that complies with a data model and can be imported into storage and analysis software. Essentially, the process consists of taking an input, often stored as formatted plain text, parsing the input by extracting the relevant information, and outputting the information in a specified format by writing to files or a database management system. There is a wide variety of software that can be used for this kind of task, ranging from browser based tools like OpenRefine to Python libraries such as Numpy (2006) and Pandas (2008) that feature powerful abstractions – arrays, matrices, hashmaps – for manipulating data.

The Transformation Pipeline: Techniques and Considerations

There are many approaches to creating this kind of processing pipeline that depend on the computing power available for processing, size of the dataset, and the required output; however, the transformation pipeline can be broken down into the three phases mentioned above: reading input data, parsing and transformation, and writing to an output. While each of these steps require ad hoc procedures, again there are general concerns that are relevant for all data sets. Here we broadly outline these concerns as well as potential approaches to a variety of situations.

Reading the Data: Sources and Approaches

To begin the processing pipeline, one must first consider the source and initial format of the dataset. Broadly, there are three possibilities:

- The data has not yet been acquired and it will be read directly from an API. This means that the data is still being stored by the social media application in which it was created. Typically, this kind of data is accessed programmatically and either written to an intermediate format like text files, or read dynamically from the API and processed 'on the fly'. This means that it will not be stored in any intermediate format and will be parsed, transformed, and written to output as it is produced by the API.
- The data has already been harvested from the API and is stored in flat text files. Most commonly, this data will be stored in JSON or CSV format, which can be read, parsed, and output using a wide variety of software, including all major programming languages.
- The data has already been harvested from the API, but was loaded into a database management system. Similar to data coming directly from a social media application API, relevant data will need to be read from the database and either processed on the fly, or stored in an intermediate format such as a flat text file.

Depending on the source of the data, the first step in the transformation pipeline will be accomplished in one of a variety of fashions. The following sections address possible solutions for reading input data; however, it is important to recognize that there is generally not one right way to accomplish this task. Instead, there are numerous valid approaches to this procedure that depend on the preference of the researcher.

Reading Data from an API

Typically, data is harvested from an API using one of many programmatic techniques. Each API will feature a specific architecture and protocol that provide a means to access the data it contains. Most commonly, social media site APIs use REST, an architectural style that typically uses the HTTP protocol (Massé, 2011). This is convenient because it provides a standard way to access data; although each social media site will have a unique way of providing the application data, the means for accessing is similar to other sites that use REST. This makes it easy for users to access data without having to learn specialized protocols, or use overly specialized tools.

REST resources are typically accessed using programmatic techniques. Popular programming languages like Python or Java provide a wide variety of built-in or third party software designed to facilitate the use of HTTP for accessing services like REST APIs. Generally, a researcher will write a small program specifically tailored to the target API that has been designed to harvest the data of interest. This program will then either pass the data to another program to finish the processing pipeline, or write the data to an intermediate format like flat text files. Even though writing data to an intermediate format adds an extra step to the processing pipeline, it is common to separate data collection from data processing. Furthermore, performing collection separately minimizes the moving parts involved with the pipeline; if there is a problem during the parsing or output phase, it will not affect data collection, thereby simplifying the process by compartmentalizing it.

Reading Data from Text Files

Reading data from text files is often considerably simpler than reading from an API. In many cases, it is as easy as choosing an application that is able to read the text file format. For example, there are a wide variety of desktop/browser applications that read files stored in CSV format, like Microsoft Excel, SPSS statistical software, and OpenRefine. However, depending on the operation that will be performed upon the data, these programs can be limited due to their lack of flexibility – they only provide specific hard coded procedures. Some software, such as OpenRefine, provide a balance in that they have a point and click user interface, but they also support limited scripting operations that allow the user to implement custom functionality.

In the case that the researcher needs complete flexibility (or they are comfortable with computer programming), flat text files can also be read programmatically using a wide variety of freely available programming languages. In this case, files are read and referenced by variables. Then the researcher can implement any procedure, or manipulation of the data without being limited by out-of-the-box functionality. The examples presented later in this chapter demonstrate this using the Python programming language to read and manipulate flat files.

Reading Data from a Database

In many ways, reading data from a database is similar to reading data from a web API: usually programmatic techniques are employed and relevant data is often transferred to flat files as an intermediate step before parsing and transforming the data. However, unlike a REST API, databases do not necessarily have similar architectural styles or protocols for data access. For example, some databases provide REST endpoints similar to an internet application API, others use websockets for duplex style communication between the database server and client program, and many use specialized TCP based protocols. Despite this inconsistency, most major programming languages have third party libraries that can be used to access popular databases without delving into the specifics of the database communication protocol. In this case, the researcher must choose an appropriate library from their favorite programming language, familiarize themselves with the library, and write a normally small program to access the desired data.

Beside this type of client-server communication, many databases provide a command line interface (CLI) that allows the user to manipulate and retrieve data. Typically, a database will employ a domain specific language (DSL), or small programming language that has been custom designed to perform only the operations possible with a particular database. Fortunately, many databases share a DSL that allows a user familiar with the DSL to use a variety of database software. For example, structured query language (SQL) is a DSL used by most relational databases such as MySQL, PostgreSQL, and Oracle RDBMS (Date and Darwen, 1997).

Finally, some database management systems provide a graphical interface that allows users to access data without doing any programming. While this scenario is less common, it is important in that it provides a way for researchers without the time or means to learn computer programing access to powerful data manipulation techniques. SylvaDB, seen in a previous example, is a good representative of this kind of system. Other examples of GUI based database management systems include commonly known tools such as Microsoft Access and MySQL workbench.

Practical Considerations: Size of Data Set vs. Computational Resources

Regardless of where the input data is stored, before determining how data will be parsed it is important to consider the size of the dataset and how this will affect the parsing process. Fundamentally, there are two scenarios: 1) the dataset is small and can fit in a computer's memory (RAM); 2) the dataset is too large and cannot be loaded into memory in its entirety. Of course, whether a dataset is considered to be large depends directly on the computational resources available for processing. Therefore, it is important to understand both the size of the dataset and the amount of RAM available for processing, as well as how much extra RAM will be required for running any necessary software, or performing transformations in memory. The latter is especially important, as it is tempting to think that 4 gigabytes of data can be processed with 4 gigabytes of RAM. In reality, this is not the case, because many operations require copying data, at least temporarily, hence requiring more memory. That said, in the case that the data is too big to load into memory there are still many options that allow the researcher to handle big datasets with relatively limited computational resources.

Approaching this problem programmatically, it is common for data to be parsed on the fly. Most programming languages allow files to be opened without loading their entire contents into memory. Then, the file can be read line by line, only loading a minimal chunk of data into memory, which is parsed and written to some sort of output. Furthermore, there are data processing tools, such as OpenRefine, that use internal programmatic constructs to be memory efficient. This allows the user to perform complex operations on large data sets with a relatively small amount of RAM without writing code. However, while on the fly programmatic parsing can be performed on enormous datasets and is only limited by hard disk space and time, most browser based or GUI style software has either fixed or practical limits. For example, OpenRefine has no fixed limits, but begins to suffer performance losses on CSV files containing more than 100,000 rows of data, both due to the time complexity of the algorithms it employs and RAM limitation of typical computers. Therefore, larger datasets are typically dealt with programmatically using a scripting language such as Python.

Parsing

Regardless of the size of the dataset, social media data generally requires some degree of parsing and transformation before it can be stored and analyzed. Parsing involves dividing the data into manageable or semantically cohesive chunks, extracting relevant information, and outputting it in a specific format. In general, parsing techniques are tightly coupled to the format and semantics of the data. Due to the extremely ad hoc nature of parsing, it is more effective to present an example of the parsing process instead of simply describing it. The following section provides a concrete example of how data is parsed using the Paris Attacks Dataset and the Python programming language.

Example: Parsing a List of Tweets with Python

Parsing a list of tweets is a process that can be accomplished using any major programming language (R, Java, Perl, etc.). This example employs one of the most versatile and widespread open source programming languages: Python. To begin, we identify that the input data is stored as a list of JSON serialized tweets in flat text files. Furthermore, we assume that the computer used has plenty of RAM to store the contents of the dataset in memory; however, in this example we do not load the whole dataset. Instead, we parse the tweets on the fly, storing relevant information in data structures that will later be written to files using the TSV format. TSV, like CSV, is similar to an Excel spreadsheet in that it stores data in tabular format with rows and columns. However, instead of using commas like a CSV, it separates entries within a row using the tab character, which is more space efficient and tends to import more smoothly into certain data management systems. The target output of this process is four TSV files:

1. The first file will be a list of users and related metadata. This list can be thought of as a list of user nodes that will be mapped to a property graph model and stored in a graph database.
2. The second file will be a list of tweets and related metadata. This list represents tweet nodes that comprise the second node type of the property graph model, which will also be stored in a graph database.
3. The third file will be a list of hashtags. This is the third node type in the property graph model, representing the final node type in the graph database.
4. The fourth file will be an edge list containing edges of four types: *user tweets tweet, tweet retweets tweet, tweet replies to tweet*, and *tweet contains hashtag*. This list represents the relationships included in the property graph model, and will be used to structure the information stored in the graph database.

Using Python, we can create these four files using the built in csv module. Furthermore, we will load the json module, which will be used later to parse the JSON formatted tweets.

```
import csv
import json
tweetfile = open("tweets.tsv", "wb")
tweet_writer = csv.writer(tweetfile, delimiter="\t")
userfile = open("users.tsv", "wb")
user_writer = csv.writer(userfile, delimiter="\t")
hashtagfile = open("hashtag.tsv", "wb")
hashtag_writer = csv.writer(hashtagfile, delimiter="\t")
edgefile = open("edges.tsv", "wb")
edge_writer = csv.writer(edgefile, delimiter="\t")
```

Using the csv module writer object, we can write data to csv files. To begin this process, we can create headers for each file. These headers specify the contents of each column in the TSV files that have been created.

```
tweet_header = ["tid", "lang", "text", "created_at", "country", "city", "coordinates"]
tweet_writer.writerow(tweet_header)
user_header = ["uid", "screen_name"]
user_writer.writerow(user_header)
hashtag_header = ["hid", "text"]
hashtag_writer.writerow(hashtag_header)
edge_header = ["source_id", "target_id", "type"]
edge_writer.writerow(edge_header)
```

These headers can serve as a guide during the parsing process, as they determine what data needs to be extracted from the tweet. Notice that the edge header also includes the column header 'type', which will allow us to distinguish between different relationship types. After inspecting the contents of a tweet record, we also notice that there are possibly two tweets contained within each record: if the tweet is a retweet, it also includes the metadata of the original tweet. In order to avoid code duplication, we will write a simple function that extracts data from the original tweet record that can also be used on the embedded retweet record.

```
def parse_tweet(tweet):
    tweet = json.loads(tweet)
    tid = tweet["id"]
    lang = tweet["lang"]
    text = tweet["text"]
    created_at = tweet["created_at"]
    place = tweet.get("place", {})
    country = place.get("country", "")
    city = place.get("full_name", "")
    coordinates = place.get("bounding_box", {}).get("coordinates", "")
    user_mentions = tweet.get("entities", {}).get("user_mentions", [])
    hashtags = tweet.get("entities", {}).get("hashtags", [])
    uid = tweet["user"]["id"]
    screen_name = tweet["user"]["screen_name"]
    replies_to = tweet["in_reply_to_status_id"]
    retweeted_status = tweet.get("retweeted_status", "")
    return (
        tid, lang, text, created_at, place, country, city, coordinates, user_mentions,
        hashtags, uid, screen_name, replies_to, retweeted_status)
```

We will then open the tweet file, iterate over all of the tweets in the file, call this function on each tweet, and store the results as a row in a Python dictionary containing all of the tweet data. If the tweet was a retweet, we will store the retweet data in the same dictionary.

User and hashtag data are stored in separate dictionaries, as they will be written to a different output file. Finally, any edges (user tweets, user mentions, in reply to, retweets, contains) will be written directly to the edge file.

```
tweet_dict = {}
user_dict = {}
hashtag_dict = {}
hashtag_id = 0
with open("paris_tweets.json", "rb") as f:
    for tweet in f:
        results = parse_tweet(tweet)
        # basic tweet data
        tid = results[0]
        if tid not in tweet_dict:
            row = [results[1], results[2], results[3], results[4],
                results[5], results[6], results[7]]
            tweet_dict[tid] = row
        user_id = results[10]
        if user_id not in user_dict:
            user_dict[user_id] = rt_results[11]
        edge_writer.writerow([user_id, tid, "TWEETS"])
        # user mention data
        user_mentions = results[8]
        for user_mention in user_mentions:
            uid = user_mention["id"]
            screen_name = user_mention["screen_name"]
            if uid not in user_dict:
                user_dict[uid] = screen_name
            edge_writer.writerow([tid, uid, "MENTIONS"])
        # hashtag data
        for hashtag in results[9]:
            hashtag = hashtag["text"].lower()
            if hashtag not in hashtag_dict:
                hid = "h{}".format(hashtag_id)
                hashtag_dict[hashtag] = hid
                edgewriter.writerow([tid, hid, "CONTAINS"])
                hashtag_id += 1
        # replies to data
        replies_to = results[12]
        if replies_to:
            edge_writer.writerow([tid, replies_to, "REPLIES_TO"])
            if replies_to not in tweet_dict:
                tweet_dict[replies_to] = ["", "", "", "", "", "", ""]
```

```
# retweet data
if results[-1]:
    rt_results = parse_tweet(results[-1])
    rt_tid = rt_results[0]
    if rt_tid not in tweet_dict:
        rt_row = [rt_results[1], rt_results[2], rt_results[3], rt_results[4],
        rt_results[5], rt_results[6], rt_results[7]]
        tweet_dict[rt_tid] = rt_row
    user_id = rt_results[10]
    if user_id not in user_dict:
        user_dict[user_id] = rt_results[11]
    edge_writer.writerow([results[0], rt_tid, "RETWEETS"])
    edge_writer.writerow([user_id, rt_tid, "TWEETS"])
```

Finally, we write the contents of the tweet, user, and hashtag dictionaries to TSV files, and then close the original input files.

```
for k, v in tweet_dict.items():
    row = [k] + v
    tweet_writer.writerow(row)
for k, v in user_dict.items():
    user_writer.writerow([k, v])
for k, v in hashtag_dict.items():
    hashtag_writer.writerow([v, k])
tweetfile.close()
userfile.close()
hashtagfile.close()
edgefile.close()
```

Now the list of tweets has been parsed into three separate TSV files that will be easy to load into most graph database systems and analysis software. To quickly demonstrate this, the next example loads the produced files into the Neo4j graph database using the Neo4j bulk loader CLI (Neo4j-import, 2015).

Bulk Loading TSV Files into Neo4j

Provided that data has already been formatted as a series of node lists and edge lists, we can use the Neo4j bulk import tool. However, there are certain changes that must be made to the TSV files produced in the previous example in order to prepare the data for import. Thankfully, only the headers need to be changed; can be done using the Python Pandas package. We will read the files one by one and reassign certain column header names so they comply with Neo4j's specifications. Specifically, all nodes require a unique id column denoted by the: ID postfix as well as a column for label, denoted as: LABEL. Edges require a column with: START_ID, which is the source of the relationship,: END_ID, which is the target of the relationship, as well as: TYPE.

```
import pandas as pd
tweets = pd.read_csv("tweets.tsv", sep="\t")
tweets.columns = ["tid:ID", "lang", "text", "created_at", "country", "city", "coordinates"]
tweets[":LABEL"] = "tweet"
tweets.to_csv("neo4j_tweets.tsv", sep="\t")
users = pd.read_csv("users.tsv", sep="\t")
users.columns = ["uid:ID", "screen_name"]
users[":LABEL"] = "user"
tweets.to_csv("neo4j_users.csv", sep="\t")
hashtags = pd.read_csv("hashtags.tsv", sep="\t")
hashtags.columns = ["hid:ID", "text"]
hashtags[":LABEL"] = "hashtag"
hashtags.to_csv("neo4j_hashtags.tsv", sep="\t")
edges = pd.read_csv("edges.csv", sep="\t")
edges.columns = [":START_ID", ":END_ID", ":TYPE"]
edges.to_csv("neo4j_edges", sep="\t")
```

After preparing the data set, one must install and unpack Neo4j, navigate to the root directory (something like neo4j-community-2.3.1/), and use the command line import tool to load the data. With the command line tool, we have to specify the destination directory where the data will be stored (by default/data/graph.db), each node list that will be imported, the edge list that will be imported, and the delimiter used for the files.

```
./bin/neo4j-import –into/neo4j-community-2.3.1/
data/graph.db –nodes neo4j_users.tsv –nodes
neo4j_tweets.tsv –nodes neo4j_hashtags.tsv –
relationships neo4j_edges.tsv –multiline-
fields=true –delimiter TAB
```

This command can be broken down as follows:

- The main command, "./bin/neo4j-import", runs the import executable included in the Neo4j database distribution.
- The –into argument specifies the destination directory for the processed output. This is where the data is stored and accessed by Neo4j. With Neo4j's default configuration, this directory should be "data/graph.db".
- The –nodes arguments are used to specify the names of the files that contain the data that will be imported to create nodes.
- The –relationships arguments are used to specify the names of the files that contain the data that will be imported to created relationships.
- The –multiline-field argument determines whether or not the input fields can contain newline characters ("\n"). Since tweet text can contain newlines, if this argument is not specified as true, the import will throw errors.
- Finally, the –delimiter argument specifies the character used to separate the entries in the input files. This argument value defaults to a comma, but because we are using TSV files, we indicate that this value should be a tab "\t".

After running this command and waiting for the data to be imported, we can start the Neo4j server, and begin writing queries using Neo4j's expressive graph query language: Cypher (Cypher Query Language, 2012).

CONCLUSION

As we have seen, processing social media data requires a wide variety of techniques and a broad range of skills. Fortunately, there are a wide range of tools, both programmatic and GUI based, that are specifically designed to work with this kind of data. As social media becomes even more prevalent, the number of individuals seeking to leverage the wealth of data provided by users will surely grow. As more and more researchers – in both academia and industry – dedicate themselves to studying this data and producing actionable information, the range and quality of techniques and tooling will increase. While no individual can be expected to master all of the software dedicated to this sort of data processing, this chapter demonstrates that despite the typically one-off nature of data processing, there are certain commonalities that span the range of possible data sets. Regardless of how big or small a dataset may be, whether it be rife with errors, or sparkling clean, to achieve satisfactory results all data must be modelled, assessed for cleanliness and field formatting, and parsed into a format that is compatible with target storage and analysis software. We hope that after reading this chapter you will feel more comfortable taking charge of your data to produce the best results possible.

REFERENCES

Allison, Paul D. (2001). *Missing Data* (Vol. 136). Thousand Oaks, CA: Sage.

Bifet, Albert and Frank, Eibe. (2010). 'Sentiment knowledge discovery in twitter streaming data', *Discovery Science*: 1–15. Berlin: Springer.

Chaudhuri, Surajit, Ganjam, Kris, Ganti, Venkatesh and Motwani, Rajeev. (2003). 'Robust and efficient fuzzy match for online data cleaning', *Proceedings of the 2003 ACM SIGMOD International Conference on Management of Data*, 313–324.

Cypher Query Language. (2012). Retrieved from http://neo4j.com/docs/stable/cypher-query-lang.html

Date, Chris J. and Darwen, Hugh. (1997). *A Guide To Sql Standard* (Vol. 3). Reading: Addison-Wesley.

Dia [computer software]. (1998). Retrieved from https://sourceforge.net/projects/dia-installer/

Elmasri, Ramez and Navathe, Shamkant. (2010). *Fundamentals of Database Systems* (6th ed.). Boston: Addison-Wesley Publishing Company.

Kireyev, Kirill, Palen, Leysia and Anderson, Kenneth. (2009). 'Applications of topics models to analysis of disaster-related twitter data', *NIPS*

Workshop on Applications for Topic Models: Text and Beyond (Vol. 1). Canada: Whistler.

Gemmell, Jim, Rubinstein, Benjamin, and Chandra, Ashok. (2011). Improving entity resolution with global constraints. *arXiv preprint arXiv:1108.6016*.

Linkurious [Computer software]. (2013). Retrieved from http://linkurio.us/

Massé, Mark. (2011). *REST API design rulebook*. Sebastopol, CA: O'Reilly Media, Inc.

McCulloh, Ian, Armstrong, Helen, and Johnson, Anthony. (2013). *Social network analysis with applications*. John Wiley & Sons.

Neo4j [Computer software]. (2007). Retrieved from http://neo4j.com/

Neo4j-import- [Computer software]. (2015). Retrieved from http://neo4j.com/docs/stable/import-tool.html

Numpy [Computer software]. (2006). Retrieved from http://www.numpy.org/

OpenRefine [Computer software]. (2011). Retrieved from http://openrefine.org/documentation.html

Pandas [Computer software]. (2008). Retrieved from http://pandas.pydata.org/

Rahm, Erhard, and Do, Hong Hai. (2000). 'Data cleaning: Problems and current approaches', *IEEE Data Eng. Bull.* 23.4: 3–13.

Rainie, Lee and Wellman, Barry. (2012). *Networked: The new social operating system*. Cambridge, MA: MIT Press.

Robinson, Ian, Webber, Jim and Eifrem, Emil. (2015). *Graph Databases: New Opportunities for Connected Data*. Sebastopol, CA: O'Reilly Media, Inc.

Ronen, Shahar, Gonçalves, Bruno, Hu, Kevin Z., Vespignani, Alessandro, Pinker, Steven, and Hidalgo, César A. (2014). 'Links that speak: The global language network and its association with global fame', *Proceedings of the National Academy of Sciences*, 111(52): E5616-E5622.

Rubin, Donald B. (2004). *Multiple imputation for nonresponse in surveys* (Vol. 81). John Wiley & Sons.

Schafer, Joseph L. (1999). 'Multiple imputation: a primer'. *Statistical Methods in Medical Research*, 8(1): 3–15.

Schafer, Joseph L. and Graham, John W. (2002). 'Missing data: our view of the state of the art', *Psychological Methods*, 7(2): 147.

Sloan, Luke and Morgan, Jeffrey. (2015). 'Who Tweets with Their Location? Understanding the relationship between demographic characteristics and the use of geoservices and geotagging on Twitter'. *PloS one*, *10*(11), p.e0142209.

Titan Distributed Graph Database [Computer software]. (2015). Retrieved from http://thinkaurelius.github.io/titan/

Twitter Streaming APIs. (2010). Retrieved from https://dev.twitter.com/streaming/overview

The Role of APIs in Data Sampling from Social Media

Dietmar Janetzko

Social media means different things to different people. For hundreds of millions, social media have become essential channels of communication. For a growing number of scientists from many academic disciplines, but also for many more applied researchers, social media have turned into a significant source of data. Parts of this data can be sourced in large volumes via the Web APIs (application programming interfaces) and web scraping – though the latter is often sued. While classical methodological discussions on the quality of data from social media are in full swing, the conceptual basics of data collection by way of APIs are usually not addressed. The same is true for various limitations of APIs like, for example, rate limits and privacy issues. Still, both the conceptual side and the limits of APIs are essential to collect and appropriately use and interpret social data. This chapter introduces into APIs for collecting data from social media. It looks into more general concepts of APIs like authentication and authorization via OAuth (Open Authorization), discusses limitations of APIs and presents examples how the APIs of Twitter and Facebook are deployed via R the statistical programming language R (see Chapter 28 of Simon Hegelich) to collect social data.

DATA ACCESS VIA APPLICATION PROGRAMMING INTERFACES (APIS)

Since the beginnings of the social sciences in the 19th century, the toolbox of methods used to study social phenomena has grown extensively. Alongside more traditional methods, like observation or interview, social scientists use increasingly computer-based methods, for example, online questionnaires. APIs are recent newcomers, about to find their way into the toolbox of social science methods. Their unique potential is to pave the way for studying psychological, social, economic and political phenomena via social networks. How do APIs achieve this?

Until recently, the concept of an API was relatively unknown outside the world of programming. The widespread use of social media and the possibility to source social data via APIs have contributed to their growing recognition. APIs are often described as 'glue' that sticks together different computer systems. Unlike glue, however, APIs are highly dynamic. They make different computer systems on the WWW and elsewhere interoperable. For example, if a company that generates weather reports wants to project its reports onto maps, it might consider deploying a commercial API of Google maps. If the company manages to secure an agreement with Alphabet Inc. (previously known as Google Inc.), then the API provider (Alphabet Inc.) will grant access to its API. In this case, the map generation functions can be controlled by the company that has been allowed to do so.

APIs are also essential in the corporate strategy of online firms. Without APIs, data monetization and the growing business with data would hardly be possible. Seen from the viewpoint of accessibility, there are basically two types of APIs: restricted and public APIs. APIs employed in commercial or security settings are called restricted simply because API access is granted only under special conditions. A number of firms offer in addition or exclusively freely accessible public APIs. Public APIs provided by social media firms are increasingly used by researchers to collect data for scientific studies. Deployment of public APIs and the use of data sourced is strictly regulated by policies of the API provider. They should be considered and followed by everybody who collects and uses social data.

This chapter looks into the use of APIs for data collection from social media. The typical use case of this deployment is a scientist who wants to collect data from social media like Facebook or Twitter. The technical and methodological issues around the API deployment for social data sampling are addressed in the four parts of this chapter. Firstly, the chapter explains the major concepts behind APIs. This involves an introduction into the technical language of APIs via a glossary of concepts. Understanding the concepts of this glossary is necessary to make sense of descriptions of API usage and of course to actually use APIs. The reader will notice that despite the differences on the surface between APIs of various social media there is a common core which will be carved out in this part. Collecting social data via APIs is only possible if the data collection programs are authorized to do so. By implication, this means that to understand social data collection via APIs social scientists need to be aware of access control on the web. This is the reason why the second part of this chapter presents and discusses concepts of access control like authentication and authorization and gives an outline of OAuth (Open Authentication), which is a widely used family of standards in this area. The third and fourth part of this chapter look into the open APIs of Facebook and Twitter, respectively. The freely accessible parts of their API ecosystems are described, for each of them a commented R example is provided, and they are evaluated against criteria that matter in data collection, for example, representativeness.

API Glossary

Getting to grips with APIs can be challenging. Some of the terms that describe how APIs work are technically demanding. Often, different expressions are used to refer to the same concept, and sloppy use of API-related concepts is not uncommon. An additional hurdle to understanding APIs is the large number of fully or partially outdated documentations and discussions that exist on the web. Next is a glossary of terms on API deployment set up to address these terminological hurdles. Concepts introduced here will be used to address the APIs of Facebook and Twitter in the remaining parts of this chapter.

API protocol. Also known as web service protocols or API types, API protocols are collections of rules that determine the technical communication between the API consumer (client) and the API provider. SOAP (Simple Object Access Protocol) and REST (Representational State Transfer) are two major API protocols. While SOAP is more complex and in use for quite a while, REST is a more simple API protocol that works well together with HTTP and that is organized around resources, for example, data. Most social media APIs ('social APIs') and Internet applications in general make use of REST. This is the reason why the focus in this chapter is on RESTful APIs.

API Endpoints or Methods. Endpoints are paths that refer to RESTful resources or methods used to fine-tune an API request. Usually, one social media API offers several endpoints. For instance, Facebook's graph API provides specific endpoints for specific data types, for example, an endpoint for photos, a different endpoint for comments etc.

Endpoints follow the syntax of the API protocol used, e.g., REST endpoints. If different APIs (e.g., Twitter's streaming and REST API) are provided, then each of them typically facilitate different endpoints or methods. Technical changes or changes of policy usually affect APIs. Often in these cases new endpoints are provided, while others are not technically supported any more, or they have changed from open to restricted. Note that it is not uncommon that the terms 'API' and 'endpoint' are used interchangeably.

Resource of Request URL. RESTful APIs leverage HTTP techniques. This becomes evident in a call of a request URL. Typically, this URL cannot be launched from an unauthenticated or unauthorized client, for example, a normal browser. But embedded into an app or program and successfully authenticated, it provides access to the resource requested. The specific resource URL of a social media API depends mainly on its name, its version number and the HTTP request method (e.g., GET, POST). Other parameters and corresponding values may be transmitted by adding them to the base URL in the query string or by transmitting them in the body of the request. If GET is used to initiate the resource request, the syntax of the resource URL of a social media API can often be described as a concatenation of the following components: an API URL path, an optional user-identifier (required, e.g., for Facebook and LinkedIn), an endpoint specification, which may include a format specification, and an optional query string. This can be more compactly described as follows

<Resource URL>:: = <API URL path> [user-identifier] <Endpoint>[query-string]

An instance of this scheme is the request URL that invokes Twitter's streaming API with sample endpoint/statuses/sample.json

https://stream.twitter.com/1.1/statuses/sample.json

Keys or Tokens. Keys or tokens used in connection with an API are long strings of numbers and letters leveraged to gain access to protected resources, for example data. They need to be protected carefully to avoid any misuse. In contrast to full access credentials (name, password) tokens facilitate only limited access. Often, there is a security-motivated back and forth of different keys in order to obtain the access token and access key (collectively called access token). These are the credentials that enable the client to access the protected resource.

API Access Language and API Kits. To access and control a social media API a programming language like, for example, Java, Python or R, a command line program like, for example, Curl or both is required. An API kit is a suite of software development tools for certain programming languages and platforms, for example, Android or iOS, which supports API deployment.

API Response Format. The API protocol determines the format of the request and the response. While SOAP deploys mainly XML (Extensible Markup Language), REST supports both JSON-formatted information (JavaScript Object Notation) and XML. Typically, social media APIs use JSON as a relatively simple export format. This is why data collected through a social media API has to be parsed to translate it from JSON to plain text.

Rate Limiting. API providers usually set limits to the use of public APIs. A general rule to reduce the risk of running into rate limits is that multiple API requests should not be launched in a small time window but be spread out in time. Access levels and associated rate limits of Twitter's streaming endpoint are presented in Table 10.1.

App. APIs are usually accessed from the web, mobile or desktop applications (apps). Together with a server and a user, an app forms a triangle, which is the typical setting of API usage. A necessary first step for any API deployment is the registration and creation of an app. On their developer sites, all major social media companies offer guidance on how this is accomplished. Upon registration, two keys, the consumer key and secret also known as API or app client key and secret, are created and issued. These keys are client credentials. They identify the app and are used in the deployment of the API. In contrast to other keys they usually do not expire.

API Explorer or Console. An API explorer is a system that can be used to study an API. It makes all options transparent an API offers, and it supports launching a dry-run of an API. While an API explorer checks the correctness of the syntax of the resource URL it does not execute it. A major supplier of API explorer software is Apigee Corp., the software of which is deployed, for example, by Facebook and Twitter for their API consoles.

Access control in APIs. Authentication and authorization are two forms of access control between entities, for example, computers or smartphones, in computer or mobile networks. Authentication means that entity A 'proves' to entity B that it is in fact A. Authorization proceeds by entity A giving consent to entity B to access on her behalf resource C. Often deployed in combination, authentication and authorization are leveraged to control who is entitled to access what kind of protected resources like, for example, social data, photos or addresses, and at which rate (amount or volume). The following section will address the topic of access control in more detail.

ACCESS CONTROL IN SOCIAL MEDIA

Facilitating data access to authorized persons or systems and blocking it otherwise is imperative on the Web and elsewhere. There are several basic methods available to control access to web pages and resources on the WWW, i.e., in HTTP services. Next to basic authentication via name and password, the open protocol framework OAuth (Open Authorization) is currently the most popular of these methods.

Though the focus in this chapter is on social media data it should be mentioned that OAuth is not only deployed by Twitter, Facebook, LinkedIn and other social media. OAuth is the de facto standard for authorization and authentication in connection with 3rd party use of resources on the WWW, it is widely used in mobile applications and to orchestrate data access via APIs. The Facebook 'like' button, social login mechanisms offered by Google+, Facebook or Twitter to log into a third-party web site or login with PayPal are examples of the almost ubiquitous deployment of OAuth. Knowing the basics of how authentication via OAuth works is essential for understanding data sampling in social media.

OAuth exists in different versions. Before OAuth became the de facto standard for access control on the Internet, various proprietary solutions like, for example, Google's

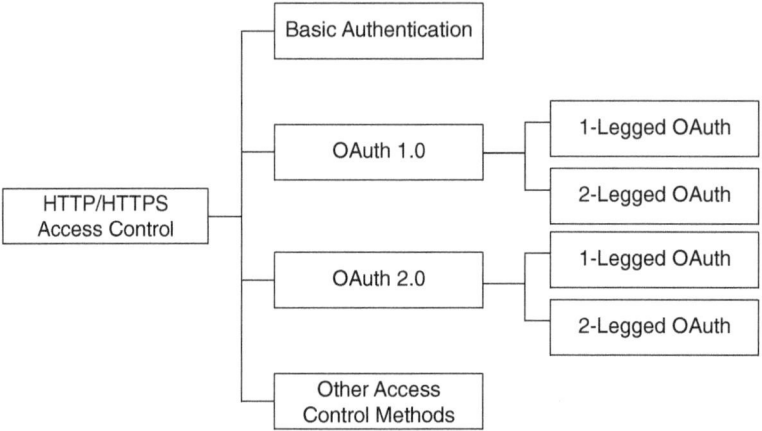

Figure 10.1 Major access control schemes in social media

AuthSub were explored. The very first version of OAuth, OAuth 1.0 (2007), has largely been given up in favour of its successor specifications OAuth 1.0a (RFC 5849, 2010)[1] or OAuth 2.0 (RFC 6749, 2012). Most social media and many other companies and services make use of OAuth 2.0. However, different social media companies may harness different versions of OAuth. For instance, Twitter leverages mainly OAuth 1.0a, but for some use cases OAuth 2.0 is also taken, while Facebook deploys exclusively OAuth 2.0. All authentication methods mentioned are to be understood as frameworks rather than single mechanisms. For instance, within OAuth there are multiple forms of authentication, and further OAuth may or may not work in connection with other authentication methods, for example, OpenID. In what follows, a basic outline of the major authentication and authorization schemes used in social media is given (see Figure 10.1).

Basic Authentication (RFC 2617)

Basic client-server authentication also known as Basic Auth or password authentication is the most popular HTTP/HTTPS access control method (see Figure 10.2). Organized around the roles of *client* and *server*, basic authentication is suitable for many situations that involve simple access control, for example, when a user wants to log into her email or social media account. Gaining access to Web resources via this dyadic authentication method requires provision of full-access credentials, i.e., name and password. This raises a number of security issues. For instance, with every login to the server, the client application needs to transmit full-access credentials. This is a security risk unless name and password are encrypted or HTTPS is used (LeBlanc, 2011). This is the reason, why basic authentication has rarely been used or its deployment has been stopped when third party systems (apps) are involved.

OAuth 1.0a (RFC 5849)

It has been mentioned earlier that in many situations the use of full-access credentials is risky. This is particularly true if the dyadic setting of basic authentication is extended to a triadic or even more complex setting that involves authentication/authorization across different systems. A triadic setting is one of the characteristics of distributed web services, and it applies to data collection from social media as well. OAuth has been designed to

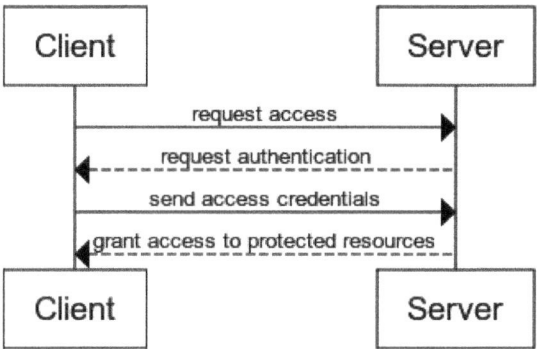

Figure 10.2 Basic HTTP authentication (RFC 2617)

orchestrate technical communication in distributed scenarios like these. Here, it offers two essential features that facilitate authentication and authorization: Firstly, OAuth makes use of limited-access credentials (access tokens) instead of full access credentials (name/password). Secondly, limited-access credentials allow the resource owner to authorize an app to access her account, which in OAuth lingo is called *delegated access*. The flow of OAuth 1.0a individuates three roles: resource owner, client and server. In this triadic setting, the resource owner is a person (user), system or corporation or any other 'entity capable of granting access to a protected resource' (IETF, 2012). Though this definition is gleaned from the specification of OAuth 2.0 it also applies to OAuth 1.0. The client is an application (app), also called consumer, which when authorized by the resource owner, interacts with the server. The server is an HTTP server of a service provider that hosts the protected resources (e.g., data, photos, contact addresses) of the resource owner which the client intends to access. The classical example that illustrates this setting is a web user (resource owner) who grants an app of a printing service (client) access to her private photos stored at a photo sharing service (server). In order for this and similar examples to work, the resource owner must authorize a client system to access the server which implies that the client authenticates to the server. If basic authentication was used in this example, the resource owner would have to reveal her full-access credentials (anti-pattern). OAuth offers a more secure alternative.

Figure 10.3 presents the abstract protocol flow of OAuth 1.0a. It illustrates a negotiation process (handshake) that starts with the client's submission of API key and secret. If successful, it ends with the server sending an access token and secret to the client. The latter two keys are instrumental in accessing protected resources, for example, social media data.

When setting up an API via a Web site of a social media company the back and forth illustrated in Figure 10.3 is reduced to a few mouse clicks and form-filling steps. OAuth 1.0a makes use of a digital signature and suggests three optional algorithms to generate it (HMAC-SHA1, RSA-SHA1, PLAINTEXT). In this way, each client request is signed so that the server can verify its authenticity to prevent unauthorized access.

So far, the full scheme of OAuth 1.a has been described as illustrated in Figure 10.3. In Twitter, this version of OAuth is the most common type of authentication, and it is called 3-legged OAuth or application-user authentication. In 3-legged OAuth, the user's consent to a third party request is required. Using a normal web browser, many users

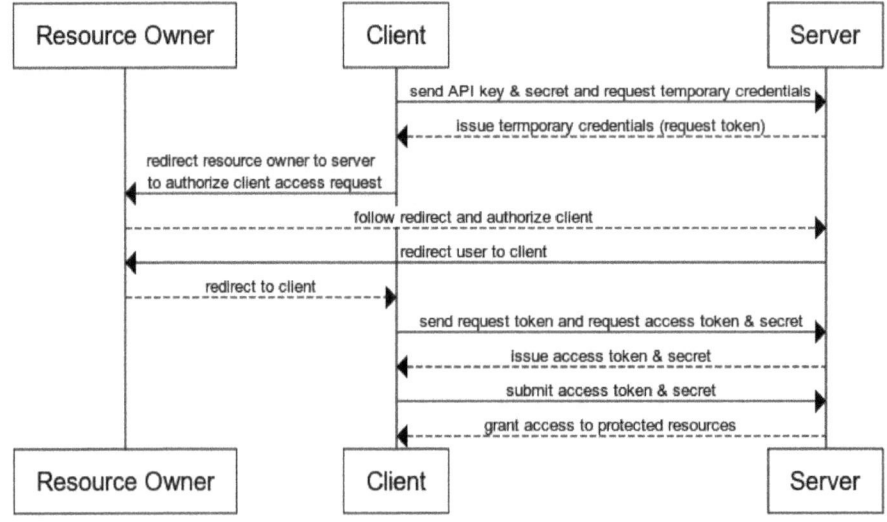

Figure 10.3 Authorization flow of OAuth 1.0a (RFC 5849). The API (consumer) key and secret authenticate the client and are usually issued when a client (app) is registered with a service provider, e.g., Twitter

have probably come across this version of app authorization. It proceeds by redirecting the user to Twitter where she authorizes the app with a mouse click (website redirect authorization). Alternatively or in addition, authorization may also proceed by taking the user to a site where a PIN number is displayed which is to be integrated into the API set up process (PIN-based authorization). An example of 3-legged authentication is the deployment of the Twitter's streaming API. The full triadic scheme of 3-legged authentication can be reduced again to a dyadic one also known as 2-legged authentication. This would then involve just client (app) and server quite similar to the basic authentication scheme. 2-legged authentication requires only a consumer key and a consumer secret which is then equivalent to username and password.[3]

OAuth 2.0 (RFC 6749,6750,6819)

OAuth 2.0 is the most recent version of the OAuth framework. Like OAuth 1.0a, OAuth 2.0 has been designed for a delegated access scenario. However, both versions of OAuth differ in the technical way delegated access is accomplished. A comprehensive comparison of both specifications is beyond the scope of this chapter. But to carve out the basics of OAuth 2.0 (see Figure 10.4) some commonalities and differences between both specifications will be briefly mentioned.

The roles considered (resource owner, client, server) don't differ much between OAuth 1.0a and OAuth 2.0. Similar to its predecessor, OAuth 2.0 distinguishes between resource owner and client. With regard to the server, however, a distinction is made between an authorization server and a resource server. OAuth 1.0a is often considered to be overly complex when it comes to implementing it. This was the main motivation for developing a successor version. OAuth 2.0 simplifies many aspects of the authorization flow ranging from an elimination of the request token to the removal of a signature as security relies on HTTPs. However, OAuth 2.0 has been sharply criticized mainly because of security risks (Hammer, 2012).

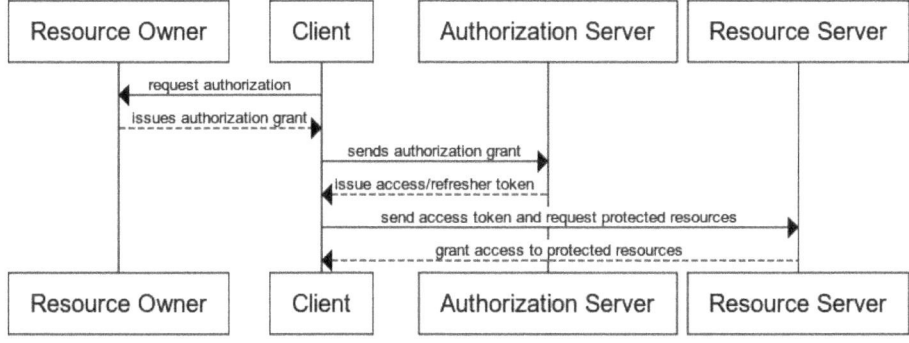

Figure 10.4 Authorization flow of via OAuth 2.0 (RFC 6749)

ACCESSING FACEBOOK DATA VIA PUBLIC APIS

The organization of Facebook data can be described as a network composed of nodes, edges and fields. Nodes are basically 'things' such as a user, a photo or a page. Edges are the connections between nodes like, for example, a photo on a page or comments on a photo. Fields are information about those nodes, such as the birthday of a user or the name of a page (Facebook, Inc, 2015). Facebook refers to this network as social graph.[4] The graph API is the public API of Facebook[5] that enables an app to read from and to write to the social graph. In contrast to the complex API landscape of Twitter, but in line with other social media, for example, LinkedIn, API-based data sampling from Facebook proceeds from just one API – the graph API. There is a close correspondence between the social graph and the graph API in that for each node of the social graph there is an endpoint available that facilitates in principle to read from and to write to it. In reality, however, any read–write access to the social graph is conditional to privacy settings and rate limits.

Next is a brief introduction of the graph API along the lines of some of the categories introduced in the preceding sections and with regard to its deployment in data collection. The graph API is still a RESTful API, data-exchange is organized via OAuth 2.0, and it typically returns JSON-formatted results. Facebook provides a large number of endpoints that facilitate read and write access to the social graph.[6] For instance, using the graph API for search can be achieved with its search endpoint. An example of the syntax used by the resource URL of the graph API for the search endpoint can be stated as

https://graph.facebook.com/user-id/search

Accessing the Public API of Facebook via R

In this chapter, accessing APIs is illustrated by using R. List 10.1 presents R example code to access the graph API of Facebook. The code uses the R package Rfacebook (Barberá and Piccirilli, 2015). It is simple and commented so that anybody with a basic understanding of R should have no problem using it.

Limits of the Open API of Facebook

The graph API is public, but subject to limitations. The two most important kinds of them are rate limits and privacy regulations.

List 10.1 Use of Facebook's graph API via R

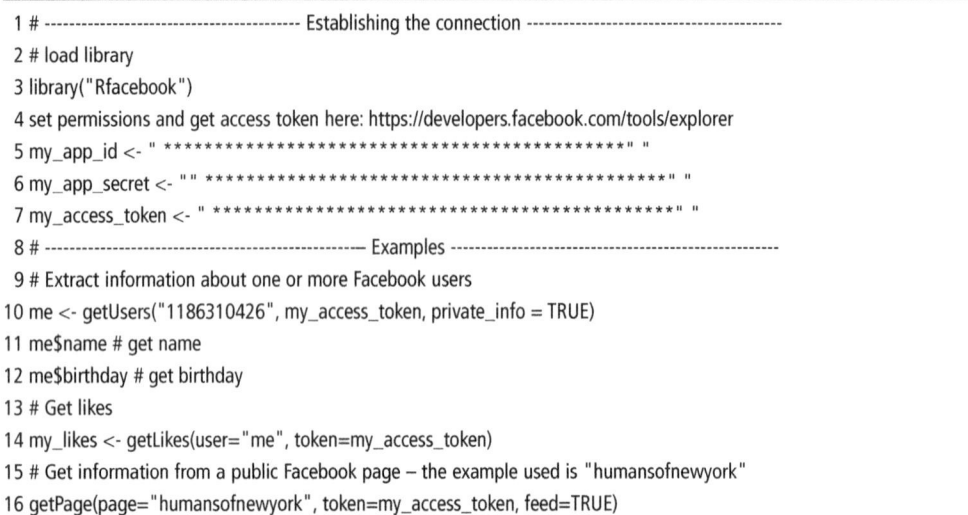

Data Collection and Rate Limits. Facebook has put a complex cascaded system of rate limits the specific details of which, i.e., the actual rate limits, are not clear, however (Russell, 2013). Its basic idea is that exceeding API deployment on whatever level (access token, app token, API, IP) will temporarily stop the graph API from working. The cascaded system of the graph API rate limits can be described in more general terms as follows:

- *User level rate limiting* refers to limits per access token.
- *App level rate limiting* is throttling that relates to counts of the App ID being used.
- *API level rate limiting* is connected with the maximum number of API calls per second as such. A rule of thumb, applicable here, is that 1 API request per second should be acceptable.
- *IP level rate limiting* means that the number of requests per IP must not exceed a set number.

If an app exceeds its rate limit, it will throw a rate limit error. This will enforce a waiting time of several hours before API calls can be initiated again.

Data Collection and Privacy. Facebook is a social network that encourages its users to reveal a lot of private information. To secure its own grasp on social data, but also to pacify Facebook users and privacy organizations Facebook has introduced a complex and changing set of privacy rules that cannot be discussed here at full length. Clearly, private data has to be respected, but seen from the vantage point of external data collection, privacy rules are major hurdles. They often lead to self-selection biases or simply non-accessibility of data.

Evaluation of Facebook's Open API

Social media are semi-structured multidimensional networks. In case of Facebook, this network – the social graph – is particularly complex and huge. Sampling from this social graph may focus on nodes, edges or fields. What possibilities are there to draw samples from Facebook's social graph (e.g., its users), in particular random samples? By definition, computer-based sampling in social media involves a one-to-many relationship between some sort of sampling device, for example, an API, and many objects of interest beyond the social graph of one user. Typically, the authorized graph API

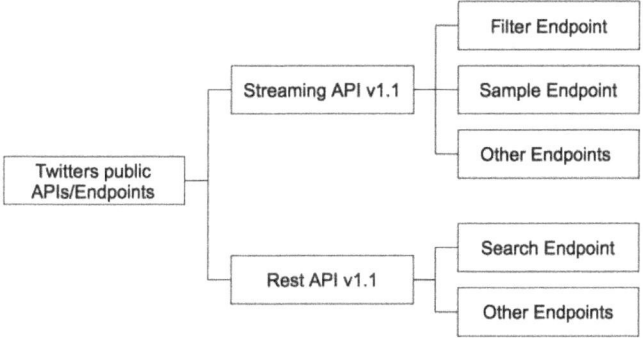

Figure 10.5 Twitter's public APIs and endpoints

can only be used for one-to-one or one-to-many relationships *within* the social graph of just one user.

Thus, if a researcher uses her Facebook account, she can only collect data via the graph API or otherwise on her her friends. This may be interesting for single-case studies or examinations of subpopulations organized around one Facebook account, for example, fans of a particular football club. But mainly due to privacy restrictions in combination with limitation of the API endpoints, there is no obvious way to extend extend data collection *beyond* a user's social graph. In other words, due to privacy restrictions in Facebook it is not possible to access the data of friends of friends let alone their friends (Stackoverflow, 2015). By implication, this means that the complete social graph cannot be accessed via the graph API. The search endpoint cannot be used for sampling either as its deployment is possible only if appropriate access tokensare provided.[7] In fact, many studies on Facebook admit that their findings should be considered with caution as they are not based on a random sample (e.g., Stutzman et al., 2013). This is the reason why many published studies do not harness the graph API but instead use crawler and scraping techniques in combination with complex graph sampling algorithms to obtain a representative sample of Facebook users (Gjok et al., 2011). But despite the authors' assertion that crawling allows researchers to generate a representative sample there are still question marks over such a claim, as the privacy restrictions mentioned above still apply.

ACCESS OPTIONS FOR TWITTER DATA

Twitter facilitates computer-based access to Twitter-data via APIs. Over the years, Twitter has built up, modified and renewed a complex system of APIs that is organized around two families of APIs: the REST API and the streaming API. Both APIs are still subject to ongoing changes. They include the introduction of new or updated versions, the terms of usage, data access limits and technical features of APIs, for example, geotagging and the focus on JSON (JavaScript Object Notation) as the unique output format. A more recent modification is the removal of the 140 character limit for tweets (Twitter, Inc, 2015b). Understanding Twitter's system of APIs is not trivial as publications on Twitter's APIs sometimes reflect an outdated state of affairs before June 11, 2013, (i.e., the day when the REST API v1.1. effectively superseded the REST API v1.0.) Around the same time, the previous version of the streaming API was also replaced by v1.1. Clearly, the modifications of Twitter's APIs and associated changes of rules and regulations of data access do not exclusively reflect technological progress. They have to be understood as essential instruments of Twitter's corporate strategy. Like most other APIs, Twitter's APIs are controlled by endpoints (methods), and both the streaming API and the REST API support specific endpoints. In what follows, the focus is on public APIs and endpoints.

Twitter's Public APIs and Endpoints

Figure 10.5 provides an overview of Twitter's public and freely accessible APIs and endpoints. They offer only a down-sampled access to the overall stream of tweets[8] called *firehose* and they are subject to rate limits.[9]

Streaming APIs

'The Streaming APIs give developers low latency access to Twitter's global stream of Tweet data' (Twitter, Inc, 2015e). This is achieved by establishing a persistent connection between client and server with different access levels individuating different endpoints of the streaming API (see Table 10.1). The persistent connection is a feature that sets Twitter's streaming APIs apart from Twitter's REST API which is based on a stateless architectural style. Supported only by application-user authentication (3-legged), the streaming API facilitates a near real-time push-type of delivery of Tweet data from defined streaming endpoints to the client. Examples of streaming endpoints are filter and sample (both public) and firehose (restricted).

Filter Endpoint The filter endpoint is used to obtain a stream of tweets that match one or more keywords that work as filter predicates.

Table 10.1 Access levels of Twitter's streaming endpoint

	Firehose	Gardenhose (b)	Spritzer
Data Volume	~100 %	~10 %	~1 %

[a] Free gardenhose-level of access is no longer provided by Twitter. Similar access options can be purchased from resellers of Twitter data, e.g., the Decahose of Gnip.

Both the GET and POST methods can be used, but the latter is to be preferred in case the query string gets too long as a result of many filter predicates. The filter endpoint of the streaming API facilitates applications like, for example, a sidebar on websites that presents Tweets that comply with some pre-defined criteria.

Sample Endpoint According to Twitter, the sample stream deployed in a streaming API is generated by randomly downsampling the firehose to 1%. The promise of a random sample from the firehose along with its free access are major reasons why the streaming API is often used by empirical researchers. Typically, repeated requests or requests made by different clients will result in the same down-sampled fraction of the firehose. A study by Morstatter et al. (2014) indicates that the sample endpoint provides a random sample of the firehose. Completely relying on external information and using only timestamps and IDs of tweets (Kergl et al., 2014) presented a reconstruction of the approach Twitter follows when drawing random samples of tweets.

REST API

The REST API provide programmatic access to read and write Twitter data (Twitter, Inc 2015c). It facilitates a pull-type of delivery of Tweet data from defined endpoints related to timelines, tweets and search to the client.

Search Endpoint 'The Twitter Search API is part of Twitter's v1.1 REST API' (Twitter, Inc, 2015d). In other words, when the REST API v1.1 is used to retrieve tweets it is called search API though strictly speaking it is the search endpoint of the REST API v1.1. Via a broad offering of query operators, for example, for hashtags, persons, text, a specific search among tweets is made possible. Designed to retrieve previous tweets the search endpoint of the REST API is limited in several respects.

- Only tweets of the recent past (last seven days to last 24 hours) can be retrieved.
- Due to its focus on relevance (and not completeness) not all tweets will be indexed or made available.

- The search API does not necessarily provide the same results as Twitters Web search.

Accessing the Public APIs of Twitter via R

In R, there is a number of packages available to access data from Twitter and even more to analyse the data returned. Two important packages that provide various functions to link to the Twitter APIs and to request data are *twitteR* for the REST API and *streamR* for the streaming API. Listings 10.2 and 10.3 describe how these packages are used to source data from Twitter's public APIs. Prior to using either of these APIs, a new or an existing Twitter account needs to be opened and a Twitter API has to be created via https://apps.twitter.com. List 10.2 illustrates the use of the Rest API via the R-package twitteR. Establishing the connection to the REST API works by *direct authentication*, i.e., all credential issued before (API key, API secret, access key, access token) are directly used by the server to authenticate the client, i.e., the R program. List 10.3 shows how the streaming API is deployed by using the R package streamR. In this case, a *PIN-based authorization* is used. This proceeds by entering lines 1–19 of list 10.3. The user should then be directed to a browser window. Here, she needs to authorize the app via a mouse click. A 7-digit PIN is displayed which has to be copied and pasted back into R as indicated ('Record the PIN given to you and provide it here'). Only when the connection is established, run the two examples initiated by the remaining lines of list 10.3.

Limits of the Open APIs of Twitter

Rate limits apply to many public APIs and endpoints and certainly to those of Twitter.

List 10.2 Use of Twitter's REST API via twitteR

```
1  # ---------------------------------------- Establishing the connection ----------------------------------------
2  # load libraries
3  library("ROAuth")
4  library("RCurl")
5  library("twitteR")
6  # Define components required to set OAuth credentials
7  requestURL <- "https://api.twitter.com/oauth/request_token"
8  accessURL <- "http://api.twitter.com/oauth/access_token"
9  authURL <- "http://api.twitter.com/oauth/authorize"
10 # API Key & Secret (also known as consumer key & secret) are client credentials
11 api_key <- " ******************************************" "
12 api_secret <- " ******************************************" "
13 # Access Token & Access Secret are Token Credentials
14 access_token <- " ******************************************" "
15 access_token_secret <- " ******************************************" "
16 # OAuth authentication handshake (required for each R session)
17 twitteR::setup_twitter_oauth(ap
   i_key,api_secret,access_token,access_token_secret)
18 # ---------------------------------------- Examples ----------------------------------------
19 # Search Tweets with hashtag Obama and return them as a list
20 Obama_Tweets <- twitteR::searchTwitter("#obama",n=450)
21 # Sending a Tweet via R using
22 twitteR::tweet("Ignore – This is a test Tweet")
```

List 10.3 Use of Twitter's streaming API via streamR

```
1  # ---------------------------------------- Establishing the connection ----------------------------------------
2  # load libraries
3  library("ROAuth")
4  library("RCurl")
5  library("streamR")
6  # Set a SSL certificate for secure communication
7  options(RCurlOptions = list(cainfo = system.file("CurlSSL","cacert.pem",package = "RCurl")))
8  api_key <- " *********************************************** "
9  api_secret <- " ******************************************* " "
10 access_token <- " ******************************************* " "
11 access_token_secret <- " *********************************************** " "
12 my_oauth <- OAuthFactory$ new(consumerKey=api_key,consumerSecret=api_secret,
13 reques tURL='https://api.twitter.com/oauth/request_token'
14 acces sURL='https://api.twitter.com/oauth/access_token',
15 authURL='https://api.twitter.com/oauth/authorize')
16 # Bundle information required for authentication via OAuth
17 # Start the authorisation. This will call a browser and show a
18 # 7-digit Pin number. Copy this Pin, switch to R and enter it
19 my_oauth$handshake(cainfo = system.file("CurlSSL", "cacert.pem", package = "RCurl"))
20 # -------------------------------------------------- Examples --------------------------------------------------
21 # For 6000 seconds capture Tweets that mention "Euro" and "Dollar" and write them to the file tweetsEUR-USD.json
22 streamR::filterStream("tweetsEUR-USD.json", track=c("Euro", "Dollar"), language="en", timeout = 6000, oauth=my_oauth )
23 # For 6000 seconds capture a random sample of Tweets and write them to the file tweets_sample.json
24 str eamR::sampleStream(file.name="tweets_sample.json", timeout=6000, oauth=my_oauth )
```

Depending on the type of API and endpoint, API throttling manifests itself in different ways. In a nutshell, the rate limits of the REST API are mainly organized by time-frames while the streaming API is mainly subject to a volume-based limit.

Data Collection and Rate Limits of the REST API. When using the REST API, the maximum number of request is defined by time windows of 15 minutes. In this interval, the maximum number of search requests possible is usually 15, but in cases of searches the maximum is 180 (Twitter, Inc, 2015a).

Data Collection and Rate Limits of the Streaming API. Data collection via the sampling endpoint is limited to about 1% of tweets randomly sampled from the firehose. When deploying the filter endpoint the number of tweets returned is limited both by the number of tweets that match the keyword(s) chosen and by the 1% rate limit. If for instance, one or several keywords are deployed that are rarely used in tweets, then ideally all of them should be returned. Otherwise, the return of tweets is capped (Twitter, Inc, 2014).

Rate limits can be overcome by whitelisted apps. These are apps that were or are fully or partially exempt from rate limits so that large amount of data could be requested from the REST API. In February 2011, Twitter stopped granting whitelisting requests. Existing whitelisted apps are still operational, however.

Data Collection and Privacy. Compared to other networks, users of Twitter reveal considerably less private data as part of usual activities on the social network. Their main activity is sending tweets, which is meant to be a public message and thus publicly available. This means if rate limits are overcome, for example, by whitelisted apps, the social graph of

Twitter is accessible (Gabielkov et al., 2014). This contrasts with other social media, in particular Facebook, where a similar endeavour is not possible due to privacy restrictions.

Evaluation of Twitter's Open APIs

Several years ago, Tim Berners-Lee (2010) used the metaphor of a *walled garden* to express his concern about social media sites which turn into information silos that can be accessed from within but not from outside. With regard to Facebook this metaphor makes some sense. But it is too soft. Even by using a Facebook account ('within') not all data is accessible via API or otherwise. In this sense, Facebook is a huge walled garden, which is additionally divided into strictly separated allotments, i.e., friends networks. Twitter, by contrast, is not really a walled garden. As of Summer 2015, at least, tweets can be accessed from outside via Google. Moreover, by using a Twitter account most of the more recent tweets can be reached via Twitter's open APIs provided rate limits are kept. Twitter is, however, closed as far as historical tweets are concerned, but there are other companies or organizations that can make historical tweets available.

Early on, Twitter's open APIs and the social data made accessible via them, have attracted a lot of attention among social scientists. To a large extent this interest has been fueled by the assumption that social data from Twitter are representative of the overall population, for example, of the USA. When sourcing data from Twitter researchers can choose among various API and endpoints to suit their research interests. They can secure large samples and have to deal with only some hurdles, in particular rate limits, that can be bypassed. But the social data sampled from Twitter is not representative of any population that exists outside the world of Twitter. A study by (Morstatter et al., 2013) has shown that tweets sourced via the open sample API are representative of the Twitter's firehose.

Social scientists have to come to terms with these findings. The holy grail of a representative sample is out of reach, and given the increase of bots and other fraudulent activities on social media this is not likely to change. While for some the scientific value of non-representative sample is dubious, there are others, for example, researchers using qualitative methods, who do not necessarily share these concerns. But even in the quantitative camp, scientists start developing new methods to work with non-representative sample that can unlock the potential of social data (Zagheni et al., 2014; Wang et al., 2014).

NOTES

1 RFC (request for comments) refers to specifications of the Internet Engineering Task Force that usually become widely accepted standards.
2 If general features of OAuth are described in this chapter, OAuth is referred to without RFC number.
3 3-legged authentication is also known as application-user authentication, and 2-legged authentication is often called application-only authentication.
4 While the notion of social graph when applied to other networks usually designates the relationship between persons, Facebook uses the term to refer to all nodes, for example, persons, events, photos etc.
5 The focus here is on public APIs. Hence, the restricted APIs of Facebook (e.g., Public Feed API, Keyword Insights API) and other data-related business activities of Facebook or other social-media company are outside the scope of this chapter.
6 Until August 7 2016, the Facebook query language will furnish an alternative to the Graph API for accessing data.
7 A sample of public posts is available via the Topic Feed API, which is a restricted API mechanism, however.
8 Usually, Twitter refers to tweets as *statuses*.
9 The firehose is made available via the restricted endpoint (method) of the streaming API.

REFERENCES

Barberá, P. and Piccirilli, M. (2015). *Rfacebook: Access to Facebook API via R*. R package version 0.5. https://cran.r-project.org/web/packages/Rfacebook/Rfacebook.pdf

Berners-Lee, T. (2010). Long live the web: A call for continued open standards and neutrality. *Scientific American*, 72(2): 149–159.

Gabielkov, M., Rao, A., and Legout, A. (2014). Studying social networks at scale: Macroscopic anatomy of the twitter social graph. In *The 2014 ACM international conference on measurement and modeling of computer systems*, pages 277–288. ACM.

Gjok, M., Kurant, M., Butts, C. T., and Markopoulou, A. (2011). A walk in Facebook: Uniform sampling of users in online social networks. *arXiv*. https://arxiv.org/pdf/0906.0060.pdf

Hammer, E. (2012). *OAuth 2.0 and the road to hell*. http://hueniverse.com/2012/07/26/oauth-2-0-and-the-road-to-hell/.

IETF (Internet Engineering Task Force) (2012). The OAuth 2.0 authorization framework. *Internet Engineering Task Force*. http://tools.ietf.org/html/rfc6749.

Kergl, Dennis, Robert Roedler, and Sebastian Seeber. (2014). On the endogenesis of Twitter's Spritzer and Gardenhose sample streams. *Advances in Social Networks Analysis and Mining (ASONAM)*, 2014 IEEE/ACM International Conference on. IEEE.

LeBlanc, J. (2011). *Programming Social Applications: Building Viral Experiences with OpenSocial, OAuth, OpenID, and Distributed Web Frameworks*. Sebastopol, CA: O'Reilly.

Madlberger, L. and Almansour, A. (2014). Predictions based on twitter – a critical view on the research process. In *International Conference on Data and Software Engineering (ICODSE)*, pages 1–6. IEEE.

Mane, S., Mopuru, S., Mehra, K., and Srivastava, J. (2005). *Network size estimation in a peer-to-peer network*. Technical Report TR 05–030, University of Minnesota, MN.

Morstatter, F., Pfeffer, J., and Liu, H. (2014). When is it biased?: Assessing the representativeness of Twitter's streaming API. In *Proceedings of the companion publication of the 23rd international conference on world wide web companion*, pages 555–556. International World Wide Web Conferences Steering Committee.

Morstatter, F., Pfeffer, J., Liu, H., and Carley, K. (2013). Is the sample good enough? Comparing data from Twitter's streaming API with Twitter's firehose. In *International AAAI Conference on Weblogs and Social Media*.

Russell, M. A. (2013). *Mining the Social Web: Data Mining Facebook, Twitter, LinkedIn, Google+, GitHub, and More (2nd ed.)*. Sebastopol, CA: O'Reilly Media, Inc.

Stackoverflow (2015). *Getting friends of friends in FB graph API*. http://stackoverflow.com/questions/3818588/getting-friends-of-friends-in-fb-graph-api.

Stutzman, F., Gross, R., and Acquisti, A. (2013). Silent listeners: The evolution of privacy and disclosure on Facebook. *Journal of Privacy and Confidentiality*, 4(2):7–41.

Twitter, Inc (2014). *Streaming API volume?* https://twittercommunity.com/t/streaming-api-volume/7544.

Twitter, Inc (2015a). *Rate limits: Chart*. https://dev.twitter.com/rest/public/rate-limits.

Twitter, Inc (2015b). *Removing the 140 character limit from direct messages*. https://twittercommunity.com/t/removing-the-140-character-limit-from-direct-messages/41348.

Twitter, Inc (2015c). *The rest API*. https://dev.twitter.com/rest/public.

Twitter, Inc (2015d). *The search API*. https://dev.twitter.com/rest/public/search.

Twitter, Inc (2015e). *The streaming API*. https://dev.twitter.com/streaming/overview.

Wang, W., Rothschild, D., Goel, S., and Gelman, A. (2014). Forecasting elections with nonrepresentative polls. *International Journal of Forecasting*. 31(3), 980–991.

Zagheni, E., Weber, I., Ziderman, A., and Zimmermann, K. (2014). Demographic research with non-representative internet data. *International Journal of Manpower*, 36(1), 13–25.

Data Storage, Curation and Preservation

Alex Voss, Ilia Lvov and Sara Day Thomson

While data are increasingly ubiquitous and seemingly cheap, datasets of high quality and relevance are often hard to come by. The value of existing research data is recognised by many funding and regulatory organisations at both national and international levels, and data management plans are often required for grant applications. At the same time, digital research data are incredibly fragile. They are at risk of becoming inaccessible to the wider scientific community or even to their original producers and of being eventually discarded. Inspired by the Data Curation Centre's Data Curation Model (Higgins 2012), in this chapter we consider different stages of the social media data lifecycle. We discuss the data curation issues arising at each of those stages, critically evaluate the choices available to the researchers and where possible provide best practice advice.

INTRODUCTION

Data are increasingly ubiquitous and seemingly abundant and cheap – in terms of the volumes we all access, communicate and store on personal devices every day. However, datasets that are of known provenance and quality, and that are available to serve a specific purpose are often hard to come by. Recognising the value of existing research data, OECD countries have endorsed a set of Principles and Guidelines for Access to Research Data from Public Funding (OECD 2007): 'Research data, in digital form, are increasingly being used in research endeavours beyond the original project for which they are gathered, in other research fields and in industry ... Scientific databases are rapidly becoming a crucial part of the infrastructure of the global science system' (OECD 2007: 9).

Based on the OECD recommendation, member countries, their national funding organisations as well as international funders are implementing 'a variety of laws, policies and practices concerning access to research data' (OECD 2007: 10). Researchers applying for funding are now often required to submit data management plans that specify how they intend to acquire, manage, preserve and (if possible) share research data. Funding organisations usually mandate that data be shared unless there are specific ethical, legal or commercial reasons not to do so (e.g., Research Councils UK 2015; Australian Government 2007; National Institutes of Health 2003; National Science Foundation 2014; European Commission 2016).

At the same time, research data are incredibly fragile. Not only can entire datasets be lost through misfortune – the failure of a hard drive or the destruction of paper records by fire – but they can be accidentally discarded, for example, to make space for the deluge of incoming data. In addition, data need to remain searchable, accessible and in a form that can be rendered into appropriate formats. The loss of important information about the datasets can also make it impossible to turn stored data into information. As Higgins (2012) points out, the ease with which digital data are modified creates an additional set of problems, especially since digital data may be transformed over time as new storage devices and rendering technologies are introduced.

In short, it is wise to assume that *data are at risk* and that, therefore, they need to be carefully *curated* and *preserved* to remain discoverable, accessible and of value to potential users. Merely 'preserving the bitstream' is not sufficient (Higgins 2012). Heidorn (2008: 284) defines *data curation* as 'the management and appraisal of data over the life cycle of scientific interest'. Rusbridge et al. (2005: 32) further expand this definition: '[curation embraces] stewardship that adds value through the provision of context and linkage: placing emphasis on publishing data in ways that ease re-use and promoting accountability and integration'.

Arguably, data that are not (yet) shared with others require the same stewardship as datasets deposited into public archives. These unshared data may be required for accountability and transparency and they may be reused by those who created them, either for new substantive research or for the ongoing development and refinement of research methods. Finally, researchers should not rule out the possibility of sharing data in the future, even if this seems unlikely at the time of acquisition. Therefore, anyone who acquires data should curate these as a matter of good practice.

If data are not curated, they become 'dark data' (Heidorn 2008) that are inaccessible to the wider scientific community or even to their original producers and are likely to be eventually discarded. Heidorn (2008) argues that while large-scale scientific collaborations tend to produce relatively well-curated datasets – because these immediately have users other than their creators – most research projects fall into the 'long tail' of smaller projects that do not have the resources or the same immediately obvious need for data curation. Heidorn (2008) argues that it is important to extend good data curation practice to these projects as the value of data often far exceeds the cost of generating them.

A number of organisations provide generic guidance (see Table 11.1), consisting of checklists of issues to address on the one hand and best practice advice on the other. One noteworthy offering is DMPOnline (https://dmponline.dcc.ac.uk), a web-based system that provides guidance on writing a data management plan with respect to the requirements of different funding organisation, allowing the generation of specifically targeted data management plans. That being said, more often than not, current guidelines either avoid the issue of social media data or emphasise challenges over possible solutions (Weller and Kinder-Kurlanda 2015). An

Table 11.1 Data management and curation guidance

Document	Organisation	Reference
Checklist for a Data Management Plan	Digital Curation Centre	DCC 2013
Managing and Sharing Data	UK Data Archive	UKDA 2011
Best Practice Guidelines for Researchers: Managing Research Data and Primary Materials	Griffith University	Searle 2014
Guidelines on Data Management in Horizon 2020	European Commission, Directorate-General for Research & Innovation	European Commission 2016
Research Data Management in Practice	Australian National Data Service	ANDS 2013
Guidance on best practice in the management of research data.	Research Councils UK	Research Councils UK 2015a.
Personal Digital Archiving	Digital Preservation Coalition	Redwine 2015
Preserving Social Media	Digital Preservation Coalition	Thomson 2016

exception is Thomson's (2016) recent report on Preserving Social Media, on which this chapter builds.

DATA MANAGEMENT PLAN

Considering what to do with data generated by or acquired for a project should be a part of planning the project, even if this is not mandated by a funding organisation or the institution hosting the research. Addressing issues of data curation only after the start of a projects risks making curation costly because work needs to be partly re-done, leaving the project without resources for effective data curation, allowing confusion about roles and responsibilities, neglecting curation because other work is more pressing and ultimately losing valuable data. In this section, we outline the general features of data management plans before moving on to discussing curation and storage of social media data.

As a starting point, we take the Data Curation Model developed by the UK's Data Curation Centre (Higgins 2012), which gives an overview of the *phases* of data curation. After this we will discuss the *issues* involved that need to be addressed.

The model (Figure 11.1) depicts the ideal situation, where data curation is considered at the concept stage when a project (or any other research undertaking) is being planned. What follows is the creation or acquisition of data, their appraisal and selection (are they of sufficient value and are all the conditions met for them to be preserved and curated?), ingestion (making them part of a formal collection), preservation actions (e.g., quality assurance, transformation into suitable data formats where necessary, generation of any missing metadata), storage (preservation of the bit-stream), access, use and reuse (the ultimate purpose of all this) and transformation (creating new artefacts such as versions in different formats or subsets of the whole). After re-appraisal, data might potentially be disposed of. In the long run, data may occasionally need to be migrated in response to hardware- or software obsolescence or to fit new organisational arrangements. You can find more information about the Data Curation Model on the Digital Curation Centre's website (www.dcc.ac.uk). We now turn to an overview of the issues involved in data curation, which we describe briefly before discussing them in depth in the remainder of this chapter:

- Data Selection and Acquisition: research questions and design will determine the scope of the research data, which can be acquired in a number of different ways that often have an impact on the rest of the data curation lifecycle.

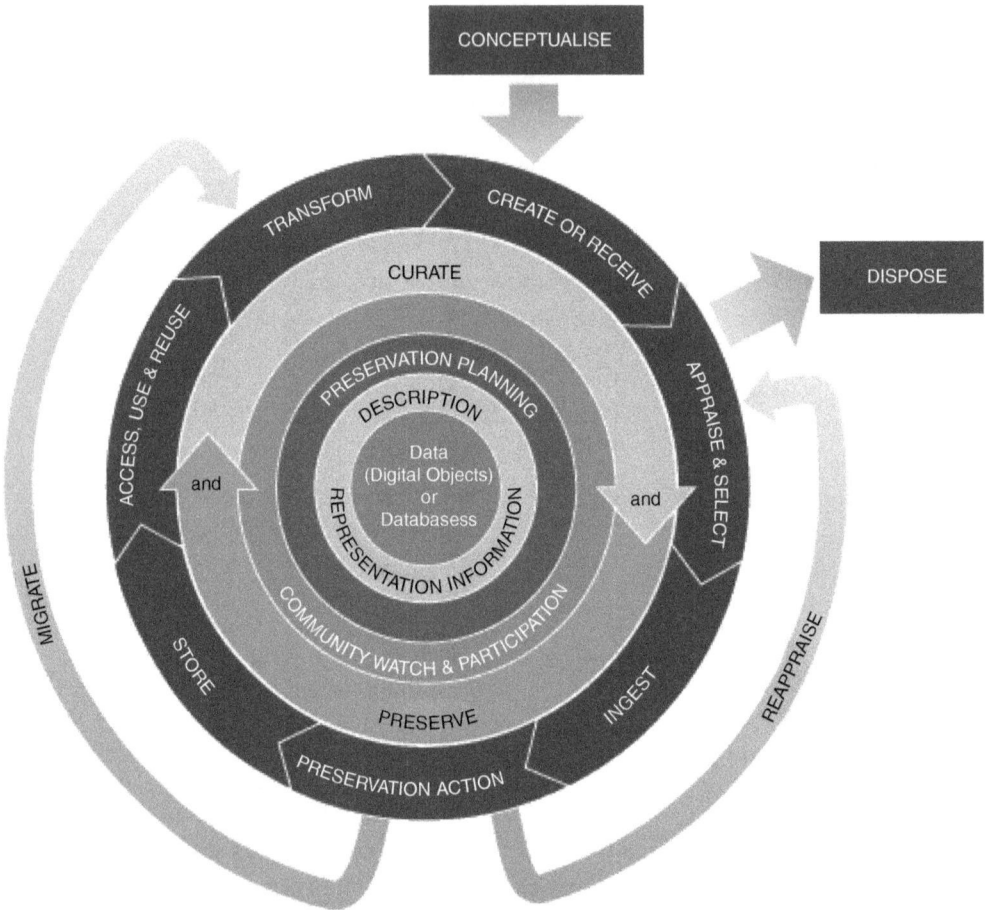

Figure 11.1 The Digital Curation Centre's Data Curation Model (Digital Curation Centre, University of Edinburgh, http://www.dcc.ac.uk/resources/curation-lifecycle-model, licensed under Creative Commons Attribution 4.0 International, http://creativecommons.org/licenses/by/4.0/)

- Metadata: with each dataset, additional structured information needs to be recorded that facilitates its identification, retrieval and subsequent use. This information is usually recorded in the form of additional structured and machine-processable data called 'metadata'.
- Documentation: human-readable documentation of the research process such as the procedures developed for data management needs to be archived alongside research data to document their provenance.
- Ethics and Legal Compliance: intellectual property laws as well as the rights of individuals to data about them constrain researchers' use of data.
- Storage and Backup: while preservation of the bitstream is not sufficient, it is essential. Data need to be stored in ways that facilitate active use, disaster recovery and archiving.
- Data Sharing: while sharing of most social media data is restricted by vendor licenses and legal and ethical constraints, it does pay to consider if a project has generated data that can be shared and to publish identifiers of records used as well as metadata and documentation.
- Responsibility and Resources: the best intentions come to nothing if resources are not available and responsibilities are not assigned.

In the following sections we will discuss these issues in more depth.

DATA ACQUISITION AND SELECTION

First, we discuss how to acquire social media data in a way that facilitates their storage, aids navigation through them and that tracks their provenance.

Research Design

Before *obtaining and ingesting* data and accompanying metadata (see Chapter 8, this volume, by Mayr and Weller; Chapter 9, this volume, by Brown, et al.), a researcher should consider their research questions and research design to identify a suitable source of data and define the criteria for data acquisition (De Vaus 2001). This important first step in data curation establishes provenance records by documenting the logic behind the data acquisition decisions. It also reinforces thinking about the usual issues involved in social media analysis, such as the representativeness of social media populations (Chapter 7, this volume, by Luke Sloan) or the veracity of social media data (Chapter 6, this volume, by Yang, Quan-Haase, Nevin, and Chen).

In social media studies the research design has implications for the choice of data acquisition modes. If a study requires no data on past events, it may be possible to set up a real-time data collection. For small studies, it may be possible to rely on APIs for retrospective data collection and on data scraping. For larger studies, especially those involving past events, the only option may be to obtain data from a data reseller or archive. The following sections outline how each of those data acquisition modes may affect data curation.

Data Acquisition Using APIs

Various social media platforms offer APIs that facilitate collecting data in real-time (e.g., Twitter Streaming API) and historically (e.g., Twitter REST API, Facebook Graph API).

A researcher using these has to construct a suitable query to the API. Such queries give the most direct account to what data are collected, so keeping records of them is essential.

It is important to bear in mind that most publicly available APIs limit access to the data. APIs for historical data collection usually place restrictions on the number of calls per time unit and on the number of data items returned per call. The Twitter Streaming API for real-time data collection puts a cap on the collection criteria as well as on how many data items are returned. It sends rate-limit messages if some tweets are omitted. The limitations to data access should be documented; where applicable, metadata such as the rate-limit messages should be kept.

As social media platforms constantly update their APIs, the version of the API needs to be recorded and its documentation archived along with the data.

Manual and Automatic Web Scraping

Data can be manually scraped from social media in numerous ways. Those include saving web pages, making screenshots of mobile applications or even copying and pasting the entries of interest. Automatic web scraping involves collecting data from the same channels using computer programs.

Whether done manually or automatically, it is important to document how the scraped data are retrieved, for example, which search function is used with what inputs. It is also important to record any other aspects of the scraping process such as the web browser and other tools, the operating system or the instructions to the person performing the scraping.

Manual data collection, of course, is prone to human mistakes (e.g., unintentionally skipping social media entries) while any errors in automated scraping processes are more likely to be systematic. Finally, while collecting data manually, a researcher may miss out the features of social media data that are not rendered by their website or applications. A possible quality assurance measure is to have a third-person check a well-defined sample of the collected data.

It is important to note that manual data collection is labour-intensive. While it may be appropriate for narrowly focused, qualitative studies, it can hardly be used for any 'big data'-style social media research.

Acquiring Data from External Organisations

In some cases, the only feasible option to obtain social media data is to acquire them from external organisations.

First, data can be purchased from an authorised data reseller such as GNIP, DataSift or Dialogfeed (to name three examples) that usually provide access to data from a number of social media systems and offer a platform for querying and retrieving these data. The costs for using these services often consist of a monthly or annual subscription, charges for data processing and a license fee paid to the social media vendor per data item (cf. Thomson 2016). Given the costs involved, a researcher would be well advised to conduct preliminary research to scope their requests. For example, they might first acquire some data from publicly available sources based on broad collection criteria, analyse these data to formulate precise retrieval criteria that can be used to purchase the final dataset. This will not only help to avoid unnecessary expenditures but will also provide a clear specification of what the resulting purchased dataset contains.

Alternatively, a researcher may want to use analytical platforms such as Sysomos MAP or Social Bakers (to name two). Instead of providing access to raw social media data, such platforms allow researchers to monitor social media using a set of pre-defined analytical tools, as well as to digest the data by collecting samples of them (Dennis et al. 2015). Unfortunately, such systems are not only often prohibitively expensive, their providers also often do not disclose the details of their methodologies (Procter et al. 2015).

Finally, a researcher may retrieve the data from archiving organisations. We are aware of only one effort to systematically collect and archive social media data for public use: the Internet Archive (n.d.) gathers the 1% sample of the Twitter Stream. There are fewer systematic archives of social media data as well. For example, the European Archive has snapshots of various official Facebook pages of the UK Parliament made at different points in time (Internet Memory Foundation n.d.). Finding relevant data this way is a non-trivial task.

Selecting Social Media Data

The practice of archiving social media data requires methods to account for their linked, interactive nature. In *Web-Archiving*, Pennock (2013: 13) argues: 'Twitter, for example, is not just about tweets, but about the conversation. To archive a single tweet, therefore, is to archive only one side of the conversation. How do you establish the boundaries for a coherent Twitter collection?'. Selecting the data that are relevant to a study is a crucial first step and involves a definition of what data items to select by specifying either their individual identifying characteristics or relationships – such as being a reply to a previous post.

The conversational nature of social media, particularly of social networking sites, makes it difficult to identify the boundaries of a collection and to establish selection criteria. Social media interactions extend across multiple user accounts and often evolve into related conversations or events without a clear delineation of when one conversation ends and another begins. Identifying all the important entities (persons, places, institutions, event names, etc.) also poses difficulties, as users do not always use uniform hashtags or keywords and communicate in natural language that introduces variations in terminology and even spelling errors (Risse *et al.* 2014: 212–213).

Establishing boundaries around a topic, major event or location provides a general scope for defining a collection. Limiting collection to a single platform or a small number of platforms may also make its scope more manageable. Even within these constraints, however, ensuring a complete collection is non-trivial.

Selection criteria that work well technically such as hashtags may well be ambiguous as the same hashtag may be used in different contexts (Procter *et al.* 2015). Dealing with the inclusion of false positives then becomes an important step in data cleaning. It is also important to scope collection criteria narrowly from the outset where there is a danger that a collection is rate-limited – or where data are purchased. However, there is no guarantee that any set of identifying criteria matches all of the data intended for selection as related hashtags may easily be missed or as some relevant tweets may not contain a hashtag at all. These challenges are further complicated by the difficulty of distinguishing bots from real users, potentially polluting harvests with false data.

Links that are embedded are often shortened and so the original URLs may need to be retrieved during acquisition as this may become impossible in the future. Whether or not the content that these URLs point to needs to be harvested is another question the researchers will need to consider. The ARCOMEM project offers a strategy for combining the capture of social media through an API alongside the capture of linked web URLs through the integration of harvesting tools (Risse *et al.* 2014: 215).

Further problems may arise from vendors' terms and conditions. For example, Twitter's Developer Policy forbids the preservation of deleted tweets – thus an important part of a conversation may be missing from a harvest resulting in an incomplete record in the archive. Even if an institution or researcher harvests data from the Twitter Streaming API or acquires them from a vendor fast enough to capture content before they can be deleted (unlikely in most cases), the deleted content could compromise the institution's compliance with Twitter's policies (plural). Twitter does not offer any guidance as to how deleted tweets might be identified. The Streaming API does provide delete messages but full compliance would mean running data collections ad infinitum and expunging deleted tweets from the archive.

The challenge of acquiring, using and preserving social media data lies in capturing enough content to provide meaning but also finding practical solutions to managing such large, diverse, and interlinked material.

METADATA AND DOCUMENTATION

A properly curated dataset should be supported by appropriate metadata and documentation. Metadata are *structured* data about a dataset that records aspects such as the provenance, ownership and licenses, ethical approval for a data collection or what research has made use of a dataset (ANDS n.d.; National Information Standards Organization 2004; UKDA 2011). Metadata for research datasets are usually generated as a by-product of the research and data management process. Generation of metadata can be both manual and automatic but metadata are usually stored in a machine-readable format such as JSON or XML following a standard schema to facilitate automated processing and to eliminate possible ambiguities (National Information Standards Organization

2004). Metadata are typically seen as being secondary to the dataset they annotate, but this is a misconception as without metadata, a dataset may be impossible to discover, assess and use.

In contrast to machine-readable metadata, supporting documentation is aimed at a human reader, is written in natural language and therefore not easy to process automatically. Documentation may include a statement of purpose for the acquired dataset, a list of data acquisition criteria, a description of the methods used to acquire and clean data, a codebook for the variables and values in the dataset as well as any guidance on possible further work with the dataset (UKDA 2011; Searle 2014).

Creating documentation usually requires effort from a researcher. However, such effort will pay off both during the research project and afterwards as it provides important information about the data produced. This is particularly important if research teams are interdisciplinary – as is often the case in social media research.

ETHICS AND LEGAL COMPLIANCE

Social media data present a particular challenge for curation and preservation because of their nature as user-generated content. Individual platforms' terms and conditions restrict how these data can be accessed, manipulated, or shared (Thomson 2016). These terms and conditions, particularly through user agreements and developer policies, often dictate how these data can be curated or archived (Weller and Kinder-Kurlanda 2015). However, beyond the requirements imposed by platforms, social media data remains subject to a number of other legal and ethical restrictions. This sections aims to describe both the issues of intellectual property rights and the more complex ethical concerns involved in curating social media data.

Intellectual Property Rights

Platform terms and conditions often pre-empt copyright infringement issues because they restrict acts of copying and distributing data captured through an API. The harvesting and processing of data does not necessarily involve copying or re-distributing protected material. However, individual posts on social media may contain content that enjoys copyright protection. If a researcher wants to publish reproductions of individual posts that contain images or other copyright-protected content, they may need permission. For instance, in the *Morel* v. *Agence France-Press* case, US courts ruled that photographs posted on social media sites are protected by copyright (North Carolina State Universities Libraries n.d.). Based on this decision, a Twitter dataset may contain proprietary images, but analytics performed on that dataset does not necessarily involve copying or sharing those images.

When curating research data, researchers or their institution need to preserve social media datasets. Copyright law in the UK and other countries prohibit the copying of certain digital material without a license, even for preservation purposes (Hoeren *et al.* 2013). However, many platform terms and conditions give permission to make copies as long as the researcher does not share them. For example, Twitter's user agreement stipulates that Twitter owns the right to share all data published publically by its users and the Twitter Developer Agreement & Policy governing the API does not limit the number of copies kept by the researcher (Twitter 2016). The issue of copyright infringement in this scenario does not present a significant risk. When researchers publish analyses of large aggregates of user data (as opposed to individual user accounts or posts), there is less (or no) risk of copyright infringement. Therefore, archiving and preserving large aggregates of user data from social media APIs poses very little risk of infringing copyright.

Ethics

Abiding by platform terms and conditions does not automatically answer ethical questions raised by curating and preserving social media data for reuse in research, as social media content is created by private individuals (Chapter 5, this volume, by Beninger, this volume; Chapter 39, this volume, by Sloan and Quan-Haase). The research data management sector has produced mature standards and guidelines for the ethical treatment of digital content containing personal and sensitive data. Data protection laws exist in many countries that define data subject rights and the responsibilities of data controllers and -processors (cf. Thomson 2016). Most immediately relevant to researchers will be their institutional ethics review boards, which govern the use of personal information in research and consider the wider legal and regulatory context. Researchers using social media data need to assess whether their work requires formal approval within their institution.

Social media data present new questions of ethics for curation and preservation. For instance, although most content on social media is publically available on the web, users may not be aware of how their data are used. Though users are the authors of the content, many platforms own the right to transfer and sell that content without alerting them. This brings into question whether or not ticking a box when signing up for a social media account constitutes an acceptable indication of consent (Cate and Mayer-Schönberger 2012). Any institution which holds curated social media data, however, may inadvertently pose risks to private individuals. They may also undermine individuals' rights not to have data about them held by a third party for longer than the period in which the data are relevant or of public interest. Puschmann and Burgess (2014: 52) articulate the ethical issue of user awareness and control quite clearly when they describe the shift of data ownership to commercial platforms and data resellers through access mechanisms like APIs and prohibitive developer policies:

> It follows that only corporate and government actors – who possess both the intellectual and financial resources to succeed in this race – can afford to participate, and that the emerging data market will be shaped to their interests. End users (both private individuals and non-profit institutions) are without a place in it, except in the role of passive producers of data.

This ownership framework exists around more social media platforms than just Twitter. Facebook, Google, LinkedIn, and most other platforms claim data ownership through their terms of service. This framework results in a system where end users have little control over what happens to their data once they are published. Platform ownership of data underlies the ecosystem that makes large amounts of user data available for commercial companies (Puschmann and Burgess 2014) as well as for research, journalism, heritage collections, government records, and other non-commercial use. Users are unlikely to know their data is being used for particular research or included in curated collections of social media data. Because of this lack of awareness, some researchers have identified a conflict of interest in using user data or in disclosing direct quotations from user-generated content (Weller and Kinder-Kurlanda 2015).

Research institutions have a different relationship with social media users than commercial companies do, as they rely on the trust and assent of the community as well as public funding. Social media research that supports the public good has an obligation to carry out these duties without doing harm to the communities it studies. In Europe, the obligation to avoid doing harm to individuals when saving their data over long periods of time is reflected in the principle of the right to be forgotten as established through the implementation of Article 12 of Directive 95/46/EC in multiple nations' case law (Mantelero 2013: 232).

On the other hand, with access to social media data, researchers are enabled to perform analyses that have the potential to greatly benefit society. Institutions who archive social media, therefore, must take measures to engender trust with that community. As the OECD Global Science Forum reported in February 2013, 'the challenge is to ensure that technology is used in ways that encourage the spread of best practice access arrangements, while ensuring that legal safeguards are adhered to and that the risk of inadvertent disclosure of identities is minimised' (OECD 2013: 8).

Just as researchers are obliged to minimise the risks of harming individuals, they also carry a responsibility to wider society. As social media increasingly become an information infrastructure (Schroeder 2014), research based on social media data can have significant repercussions. For example, research that has clear policy implications but does not consider and correct for bias inherent in many social media data sources risks adverse effects in society. It thereby may damage the trust upon which our ability to preserve and reuse data is built.

STORAGE AND BACKUP

Storage and backup refer to the preservation of the bitstream that represents the data on a storage medium such as a hard drive or flash disk (or optical disks for archiving purposes). At the time of writing, hard drives with up to 10 terabytes of storage space are on the market for a few hundred US dollars. However, the price of raw capacity is only one component of the cost of preservation.

For most applications measures are needed to ensure data are protected against drive failure, human error or other events such as natural disasters by storing multiple independent copies of any dataset. This increases not only the costs of media required but crucially also the administrative overhead. With large datasets, efficient data retrieval becomes important. Such datasets may need to be stored in distributed filesystems so they can be processed in parallel using clusters of computers. It is therefore important to distinguish between storage *for processing, for disaster recovery* and *for archiving*.

Data Organisation

A key decision to take is how to organise the data on storage media and how to facilitate efficient retrieval. Social media data can be stored in simple flat files, flat files plus indices that facilitate querying, relational database management systems or any of a range of 'NoSQL' database management systems. Each solution leads to a specific trade-off between the desirable characteristics of *space efficiency, speed, dependability and convenience*.

Storing social media data in *flat files* is the simplest thing to do but still does raise a number of issues such as how to encode the data, how to break up larger collections into multiple files to allow for selective processing and incremental backup and archival. A commonly used format is the JavaScript Object Notation or JSON (ECMA International 2013) – a lightweight format that is widely supported by the APIs of social media vendors. Storing data in the format they are originally received in – at last for archival purposes – minimises potential questions of provenance and integrity. Social media data often come in the form of a sequence of records represented as JSON objects. Since newline characters have to be encoded as a two-letter escape sequence in JSON, it is possible to store such data as one record per line in a flat text file. The 'JSON object per line' format is very common in social media research as it is easily archived and can be processed using minimal overhead. It is also compatible with the way that big data technologies such as Hadoop (http://hadoop.apache.org) or Spark (http://spark.apache.org) work.

While flat files are useful for processing of all the data, some analyses are better facilitated if an *index* into the data exists. This allows efficient querying and retrieval of subsets of the dataset. Lucene and Solr (http://lucene.apache.org/) are popular tools used for indexing large data files that can be used to quickly identify social media data that match certain criteria. Creating an index takes some time but is a one-off process that pays back every time a dataset is queried. When doing capacity planning, storage space for storing the index information needs to be taken into account.

As an alternative to a flat file with an index, *relational database management systems (RDBMS)* may be used. The problem here is that the data structures in social media data are often complex and to be fully reflected in a relation database would require a complex schema – and consequently significant skills in working with relational data. So, a compromise is often struck where only a part of the original data is mapped into the database (a copy of the full data may still be stored in the database as a 'large object'). This approach is taken, for example, in the COSMOS workbench that is described in Morgan (Chapter 26, this volume). To gain the most from using an RDMS, indices need to be created that facilitate rapid access, so these need to be accounted for in capacity planning just as the indices mentioned above. Another important aspect to consider is how well the RDBMS scales to larger data sizes. This is very much dependent on the particular product used and on the hardware it is running on – as well as on the use of an appropriate schema and indices.

Alternative database management systems that do not use the relational model have become popular and collectively known as *NoSQL databases* (Sadalage and Fowler 2013, Harrison 2015). By making different trade-offs than relational database management systems, they often scale much better across multiple computers in a cluster and so are popular with people working with very large data. For capacity planning, the size of indices needs again to be taken into consideration. Making an appropriate choice of a NoSQL system, installing it and fitting it to the specific data and research aims at hand is a complex topic and since the systems differ in many respects it is impossible to give general guidance.

Whatever choice is made for storing the data for processing, we advise to store any data acquired in a flat-file format for archiving purposes. Similarly, associated metadata should be stored in flat files, alongside the datasets. It is a common mistake to use filenames as the only place to store metadata. Not only is what can be encoded in the filename very limited, but the metadata also become difficult to use in automated processing and to exchange with others. In the absence of standards for metadata on social media data, using the JSON format seems appropriate (although XML has been used traditionally).

Capacity Planning

We have already commented on the impact that indexing has on the storage requirements for a given dataset. In addition, capacity planning needs to consider the need for redundant storage and the need to store extracts of datasets or copies that are required for some operations, not least for format conversions. Ultimately, datasets will be processed and results generated. Intermediate results that need to be stored when processing steps are time-consuming or costly. Therefore, the capacity required will be a *multiple of the size of the raw data*.

An estimation of the size of each dataset itself depends on many factors such as the data provided by the social media vendor, whether it is the full data or a sample, the scope of data acquisition (such as its timespan) and other factors besides these. Err on the side of caution and *over-provide*.

Data Compression

Social media data often contain repeating information and are stored in human-readable data formats such as JSON. As a result, the raw data can be *compressed* well using tools such as zip, gzip or bzip2. The compression factors achievable are quite satisfying but users need to keep in mind that data need to be uncompressed before they can be used, and there are marked differences in performance between different compression algorithms and tools. For example, the Twitter 1% sample for May 2014 from the Internet Archive (n.d.) comes in a 45GB archive file containing individually compressed files. The compression algorithm used is bzip2, which is patent-free and achieves good compression levels, so it is popular for data archival. Unfortunately, it takes 148 minutes to decompress this dataset for processing on a 3.4GHz Intel Core i7–6700. Different compression levels or the use of a different compression algorithm can help. Using gzip, the same dataset compresses to 60GB but is decompressed in only 33 minutes on the same machine. However, this is still a significant overhead when analysing the same data repeatedly. Clearly, there is a trade-off between space efficiency and processing times but if data are repeatedly analysed then it is preferable to store uncompressed data, even if this means investing in more storage capacity (the uncompressed dataset takes up 416GB). Archive copies can be compressed, as this will make them cheaper to store and faster to transfer.

Backup, Archiving and Ensuring Data Integrity

The procedures used for backing up data will depend on how the data are stored. Backup procedures for databases differ from backing up flat files and are vendor-specific. Therefore, in the following, we will assume that the data are stored in flat files.

The aim of a backup is to provide a current snapshot of the data to facilitate disaster recovery. Backup copies are made on a regular basis and used to restore files that have been destroyed. These copies are often overwritten with updated data on a regular basis, so older versions of files are lost. In contrast, an archive is designed to provide long-term preservation of data, often using write-once media such as suitable optical disks. Any version of the data entered into the archive will be retrievable from it.

It is important to note that backups and archives serve different purposes and complement each other. Most organisations provide some level of support for data storage and routine backups. Increasingly, organisations also provide archival services, for example, in the form of an institutional data repository. We advise to explore these options before attempting a do-it-yourself solution.

Storage media are not perfect and sometimes data files can become corrupted. Similarly, corruption can occur in transit between two computers over a network. Therefore, it is desirable to be able to verify the integrity of data (UKDA 2011). For this purpose, a hash function can be used, with the dataset as an input, that generates a hash value that can be stored alongside the dataset to check its integrity. It is sufficiently unlikely that an accidentally modified version of the dataset would generate the same hash value. If re-calculating the hash value yields a different result then the dataset has been corrupted. Tools that generate a hash value are readily available on Unix-style operating systems such as Linux or Mac-OS (md5sum, shasum) as well as Windows (certUtil).

DATA SHARING

While sharing of *most* social media data is restricted by vendor licenses as well as legal and ethical considerations, it does pay to consider if a project has generated data that can be shared such as annotations or if at least the identifiers of records may be made available for transparency and accountability.

Metadata should always be made available and it is likely that doing so will increasingly be demanded as a precondition for publication. While the limits on data sharing may mean that it is not possible to reproduce a given study, replicating it with new data may well be possible and desirable (cf. Peng 2011). If the aim of studying social media is to derive insights into the stable societal phenomena then it should be possible to replicate findings, even using different methods and different data.

Finally, it is too easy to assume that commercial interests preclude the possibility of data being made available in suitable form for researchers to use. For example, under its WebScope (Yahoo n.d.) programme, Yahoo makes available anonymised data from its discussion forums and data about searches on the Yahoo search engine. Twitter has offered data for ingestion into archives for long-term preservation and has shown a willingness to consider research uses (Thomson 2016).

While the steps taken to date are promising, it remains to be seen to what extent social media researchers will benefit in the long term and beyond a select few institutions. We would encourage social media vendors to come up with licenses for the data they control to enable research into social media. This would remove some of the uncertainty that many social media researchers face and help unlock the societal benefits their work can generate.

RESPONSIBILITIES AND RESOURCES

The data curation plan specifies how a research team intends to manage its social media data. In order to make sure that those intentions translate into practice, the team must identify the required resources and distribute the data curation responsibilities among its members.

Distributing Responsibilities

The previous sections of this chapter touched on various aspects of the 'lifecycle of data management' (Higgins 2012). Each results in at least one responsibility in regard to data curation. In addition to that, the overall supervision of the data curation process forms a responsibility on its own. This includes verification and (if necessary) modification of the data management plan.

Each responsibility needs to be mapped to a team member. In larger projects it might be important to distinguish between who is responsible for the completion of a data curation task, who is held accountable for the outcome, who may need to be consulted and who should be kept informed (Jacka and Keller 2015). While several team members may collectively work on a single data curation task, only one team member should be held accountable for its completion. The data curation model helps to ensure that tasks have clear borders and no overlaps, so that responsibilities are individual rather than collective and that data curation does not 'fall through the cracks'.

Resourcing Data Curation

The process of data curation requires both physical and human resources (DCC 2013). The physical resources include the software and the hardware for data collection, documentation, storage, preservation, and sharing. They may also include contracts, licensing agreements, permissions of ethical committees, and other documentation that guarantees ethical and legal use of data.

The human resources include the expertise required for effective use of the physical resources. Since the physical resources are so varied, so is the required expertise. This is yet another reason why it is beneficial to do social media research in interdisciplinary teams that include experts with technical- and social science backgrounds.

As the resources for data curation are likely to be scarce, research teams should consider what kind of external support they might get. While this varies from country to country, there is a worldwide trend to assist researchers in their data curation activities:

> The responsibility for data management lies primarily with researchers, but institutions and organisations can provide a supporting framework of guidance, tools and infrastructure and support staff can help with many facets of data management. Establishing the roles and responsibilities of all parties involved is key to successful data management and sharing. (UKDA 2011: 1)

An increasingly prominent role in resourcing data curation is played by the libraries and information services (Corral 2012). As Lewis (2010: 145) argues, the traditional activities of the libraries naturally extend to managing research data, as such data are 'an integral part of the global research knowledge base'. This is reflected in the agenda of the International Federation of Library Associations (plural) which puts assistance in sharing and curating data as part of its support to the open access movement (IFLA 2011).

CONCLUSION

In this chapter we have covered the process of data storage, curation and preservation, based on existing generic guidance and aiming to distil more specific guidance for social media researchers. Anecdotal evidence suggests that the practices of managing social media data are very much evolving, that there is much uncertainty especially about data sharing and legal and ethical considerations. Also, because work with social media data is done in projects that differ widely and are conducted by researchers from different disciplines and different levels of background knowledge about handling digital data, it is difficult to provide generic guidance that will satisfy everyone's needs.

We are also aware that the best intentions are sometimes frustrated by circumstances. Much data is essentially kept in a personal archive, controlled by and accessible to only a single researcher and therefore even more at risk than better curated datasets owned and managed collectively.

Our concern it to raise the level of education on matters of data storage, curation and preservation and we hope this chapter provides readers with an overview of the issues they face but also with enough pointers to solutions and further guidance.

REFERENCES

ANDS (Australian National Data Service) (2013) Research Data Management in Practice. Available at: http://ands.org.au/__data/assets/pdf_file/0009/394056/research-data-management-in-practice.pdf (accessed 14.04.2016)

ANDS (n.d.) Metadata: Working level. Australian National Data Service. URL http://ands.org.au/guides/metadata-working

Australian Government, National Health and Medical Research Council (Australia), Australian Research Council, Universities Australia (2007) Australian code for the responsible conduct of research revision of the Joint NHMRC/AVCC statement and guidelines on research practice. National Health and Medical Research Council, Canberra. Available at: https://www.nhmrc.gov.au/guidelines-publications/r39 (accessed 13.04.2016)

Cate, F. and Mayer-Schönberger, V. (2012) Notice and Consent in a World of Big Data, Microsoft Global Privacy Summit Summary Report and Outcomes. Available at: http://download.microsoft.com/download/9/8/F/98FE20D2-FAE7-43C7-B569-C363F45C8B24/Microsoft%20Global%20Privacy%20Summit%20Report.pdf

Corral, S. (2012) Roles and responsibilities: Libraries, librarians and data, in: Pryor, G. (Ed.), *Managing Research Data*. Facet Publishing: London.

DCC (Digital Curation Centre) (2013) Checklist for a Data Management Plan, v4.0. Edinburgh Digital Curation Centre. Available at: http:/www.dcc.ac.uk/resources/data-management-plans

DCC (n.d.) DMPOnline. Available at: https://dmponline.dcc.ac.uk (accessed 02.03.2016)

De Vaus, D.A. (2001) *Research design in social research*. SAGE, London; Thousand Oaks, Calif.

Dennis, J., O'Loughlin, B., Gillespie, M. (2015) Tweeting the Olympics: Towards a methodological framework for Big Data analysis of audience engagement during global media events. Participations: *Journal of Audience & Reception Studies* 12, 438–469.

ECMA International (2013) The JSON Data Interchange Format. 1st Edition. Available at: http://www.ecma-international.org/publications/files/ECMA-ST/ECMA-404.pdf

European Commission (2016). Directorate-General for Research & Innovation. Guidelines on Data Management in Horizon 2020. Available at: http://ec.europa.eu/research/participants/data/ref/h2020/grants_manual/hi/oa_pilot/h2020-hi-oa-data-mgt_en.pdf (accessed 14.04.2016)

Harrison, G. (2015) *Next generation databases: NoSQL, NewSQL, and Big Data*. Apress (IOUG): New York.

Heidorn, P.B. (2008) Shedding Light on the Dark Data in the Long Tail of Science. *Library Trends* 57, 280–299. doi:10.1353/lib.0.0036

Higgins, S. (2012) The lifecycle of data management. In: Pryor, G. (Ed.) *Managing research data*. Facet Publishing: London, pp. 17–45.

Hoeren, T., Kolany-Raiser, B., Yankova, S., Hecheltjen, M., Hobel, K. (2013) *Legal aspects of dgital preservation*. Cheltenham: Edward Elgar Publishing Ltd.

IFLA (International Federation of Library Associations) (2011) IFLA Statement on open access: clarifying IFLA's position and strategy. IFLA. http://www.ifla.org/files/assets/hq/news/documents/ifla-statement-on-open-access.pdf (accessed 14/04/16).

Internet Archive (n.d.) Archive Team: The Twitter Stream Grab. Internet Archive. https://archive.org/details/twitterstream (accessed 20/04/16)

Internet Memory Foundation (n.d.) UK Parliament Web Archive. European Archive. http://collection.europarchive.org/ukparliament/ (accessed 28/04/16)

Jacka, J.M., Keller, P.J. (2015) Spaghetti Maps and RACI Matrices, in: *Business Process Mapping Workbook*. John Wiley & Sons, Inc., Hoboken, NJ, USA, pp. 223–253.

Lewis, M. (2010) Libraries and the management of research data, in: McKnight, S. (Ed.), *Envisioning future academic library services: initiatives, ideas and challenges*. Facet Publishing, London.

Mantelero, A. (2013) The EU Proposal for a General Data Protection Regulation and the roots of the 'right to be forgotten', *Computer Law & Security Review*, 29:3, 229–235. doi:10.1016/j.clsr.2013.03.010

National Information Standards Organization (2004) Understanding metadata. NISO Press, Bethesda, MD.

National Institutes of Health (2003) NIH Data Sharing Policy and Implementation Guidance. Available at: http://grants.nih.gov/grants/policy/data_sharing/data_sharing_guidance.htm (accessed 14.04.2016)

National Science Foundation (2014) Proposal Preparation Instructions. US NSF. http://www.nsf.gov/pubs/policydocs/pappguide/nsf15001/gpg_2.jsp (accessed 4.20.16)

North Carolina State Universities (NCSU) Libraries (n.d.) Social Media Archives Toolkit, Available at: https://www.lib.ncsu.edu/social-media-archives-toolkit (accessed 02.05.2016)

OECD (Organisation for Economic Co-operation and Development) (2013) New Data for Understanding the Human Condition, OECD Global Science Forum Report. Available at: http://www.oecd.org/sti/sci-tech/new-data-for-understanding-the-human-condition.pdf

OECD (2007) Principles and Guidelines for Access to Research Data from Public Funding. OECD Publishing.

Peng, R.D. (2011) Reproducible Research in Computational Science. *Science* 334, 1226–1227. doi:10.1126/science.1213847

Pennock, M. (2013) Web-Archiving. Digital Preservation Coalition Technology Watch Report 13–01 doi:10.7207/twr13–01

Procter, R., Voss, A., and Lvov, I. (2015) Audience research and social media data: Opportunities and challenges. Participations: *Journal of Audience & Reception Studies* 12, 470–493.

Pryor, G. (Ed.) (2012) *Managing research data*. Facet Publishing: London.

Puschmann, C. and Burgess, J. (2014) The politics of Twitter data, In: K. Weller et al. (Eds),

Twitter and Society, Peter Lang Publishing: New York.

Redwine, G. (2015) Personal Digital Archiving. DPC TechWatch Report 15–01. Digital Preservation Coalition. doi:10.7207/twr15–01

Research Councils UK (2015) RCUK Common Principles on Data Policy. Available at: http://www.rcuk.ac.uk/research/datapolicy/ (accessed 02.05.2016)

Research Councils UK (2015a) Guidance on best practice in the management of research data. Available at: http://www.rcuk.ac.uk/documents/documents/rcukcommonprinciplesondatapolicy-pdf/ (accessed 11.04.2016)

Risse, T., Peters, W., Senellart, P., and Maynard, D. (2014) Documenting Contemporary society by preserving relevant information from Twitter. In Weller, K., et al. (Eds), *Twitter and Society*, Peter Lang Publishing: New York.

Rusbridge, C., Buneman, P., Burnhill, P., Giaretta, D., Ross, S., Lyon, L., and Atkinson, M. (2005) The Digital Curation Centre: A Vision for Digital Curation. IEEE International Symposium on Mass Storage Systems and Technology, 31–41. doi:10.1109/LGDI.2005.1612461

Sadalage, P.J. and Fowler, M. (2013) *NoSQL distilled: A brief guide to the emerging world of polyglot persistence*. Addison-Wesley: Upper Saddle River, NJ.

Schroeder, R. (2014) Big Data and the brave new world of social media research. Big Data & Society, doi:10.1177/2053951714563194

Searle, S. (2014) Best practice guidelines for researchers: Managing research data and primary materials. Griffith University. Available at: https://www.griffith.edu.au/__data/assets/pdf_file/0009/528993/Best_Practice_Guidelines.pdf (accessed 14.04.2016)

Thomson, S.D. (2016) Preserving Social Media. DPC TechWatch Report 16–01. Digital Preservation Coalition. doi:10.7207/twr16–01

Twitter (2016) Twitter Developer Agreement & Policy. Available at: https://dev.twitter.com/overview/terms/agreement-and-policy (accessed 10.07.2016)

UKDA (UK Data Archive) (2011) *Managing and sharing data: Best practice for researchers*. Third edition. Available at: http://www.data-archive.ac.uk/media/2894/managingsharing.pdf (accessed 11.04.2016)

Weller, K. and Kinder-Kurlanda, K. (2015) Uncovering the Challenges in Collection, Sharing and Documentation: the Hidden Data of Social Media Research? Standards and Practices in Large-Scale Social Media Research: Papers from the 2015 ICWSM Workshop. Available at: http://www.aaai.org/ocs/index.php/ICWSM/ICWSM15/paper/viewFile/10657/10552

Yahoo (n.d.) Webscope Datasets. http://webscope.sandbox.yahoo.com (accessed 01.05.2016)

Using Social Media in Data Collection: Designing Studies with the Qualitative E-Research Framework

Janet Salmons

Social media sites provide users with opportunities to post content, common to each other, and share each other's ideas. Users can create groups and networks, united by common interests. These features provide qualitative researchers with opportunities to observe users' interactions, or to communicate directly with participants. Emerging approaches designed to conduct such research must take into account the inherent complexities and ethical dilemmas associated with online interactions. The *Qualitative E-Research Framework* (Salmons, 2015, 2016) provides a holistic system researchers can use to consider interrelated elements and develop coherent research designs.

INTRODUCTION

This chapter discusses uses of communication and interactive features found in social media for collection of data for qualitative studies. Many researchers have found the abundance of material posted in social media by institutions, businesses, governmental and nongovernmental bodies, and individual users valuable for building an understanding diverse perspectives and experiences. However, there are times when it is important to dig more deeply and ask questions. Qualitative methods allow us to examine existing data, but at the same time, consider ways we might reach out to individuals or groups to learn more about their lived experiences. The *Qualitative E-Research Framework* provides ways to evaluate the appropriate methods to use and a holistic approach for exploring the inter-related aspects of research design in studies that use data collected online (Salmons, 2015, 2016).

Different roles are needed by e-researchers who collect existing online materials or *extant* data, who *elicit* data by questioning or observing participants, or who generate data by creating arts-based experiences, games or other *enacted* research events. As selected exemplars from the literature show, researchers use a wide range of Information and Communications Technologies (ICTs) available in social media sites including text or video chat, discussion forums, archived written, visual or multimedia materials to assemble rich collections of data.

QUALITATIVE E-RESEARCH AND SOCIAL MEDIA

Each individual experiences life in a unique way. Each finds significance in life events by interpreting and reinterpreting meaning through lenses of memory and identity, culture, and prior knowledge. Researchers who want to understand the complexities of human drama often choose qualitative methods. Before considering how these methods can be employed with social media, it is useful to step back and look at defining characteristics of qualitative approaches.

Some qualitative researchers conduct indepth interviews to gain entrée into another's inner reflections and thoughts, feelings, perceptions and responses to the external world (Kvale & Brinkman, 2014; Rubin & Rubin, 2012). Others conduct observations to learn more about participants by viewing their expressions and interactions, or to learn about the organizational, cultural or social context (Angrosino, 2007; Pink, 2013). Researchers read writings generated by people whose experience they want to understand, or view images or media that depict some aspect of their lives (Banks & Zeitlyn, 2015; Heath, Hindmarsh, & Luff, 2010; Kuckartz, 2014; Schreier, 2012). This definition provides a succinct description:

Successful qualitative researchers draw on the best of human qualities when interacting with participants. They demonstrate empathy and respect and they inspire trust. Interview researchers use thoughtful questioning, sensitive probing, and reflective listening. When individuals respond and share their stories, observant researchers make note of nonverbal signals and listen to verbal expressions. Researchers using observation methods, either as participants or external observers, traditionally go into the field where they can watch the ways people act and interact in their own environments. Implications of physical setting and the demeanour of the researcher are carefully considered.

In our contemporary world we question the assumption that individuals must sit in the same room to have a meaningful dialogue, or that observers be in the same physical space as the activities that interest them. Many areas of life, including carrying out personal and social conversations, shopping, working, and other activities previously reliant on physical proximity, are now conducted via the Internet. What does this mean for qualitative researchers? Online researchers (or *e-researchers* in short) can use adapt and re-invent qualitative approaches to study patterns of activity or behaviours exhibited in the online world, or they can use online communications to ask questions about any area of the lived experience. In other words, an e-researcher could observe how professional networking occurs in an online community, or communicate online with a participant located in another part of the world, to ask about how she networks professionally in her local community. In this chapter, the following short definition suffices to encompass a wide range of possibilities:

Qualitative research is an umbrella term used to describe ways of studying perceptions, experiences or behaviours through participants' verbal or visual expressions, actions or writings. (Salmons, 2016, p. 3)

Qualitative e-research is an umbrella term used to describe methodological traditions for using Information and Communication Technologies [including social media] to study perceptions, experiences or behaviours through participants' verbal or visual expressions, actions or writings. (Salmons, 2016, p. 6)

The diversity of ICTs now widely available for use on computers and mobile devices opens up many new ways to interact with individuals or groups and to gain insights into the research problem. While almost any kind of ICT can be used to purposely engage with research participant(s) or observe their online activities, social media (as defined elsewhere in this book) attributes are particularly beneficial to the qualitative researcher. These online platforms or applications allow for one-to-one, one-to-many, or many-to-many interactions between users who can create, archive and retrieve user-generated content (Salmons, 2014). In social media, the user is producer; communication is interactive and networked with fluid roles between those who generate and receive content (Bechmann & Lomborg, 2013).

Each commercial social media site offers its own mix of communication features and constraints. Some encompass a wide range of written, visual, verbal, and/or multimedia choices. Others are more focused or limited. For example, Twitter primarily offers text-based communications, but images, graphics or links to media can be embedded. In contrast, Pinterest or YouTube are visually oriented, but text comments can be added. These sites allow for varying levels of privacy: in some it is possible for individuals or small groups to have their own conversations, in others all posts are accessible to all users. Each of these considerations must be reviewed when deciding what to use and how, for research purposes.

Given the fluid nature of the businesses that host social media, and the fact that different services may be popular in different parts of the world, for the purpose of this chapter brand names will be avoided. Instead, we will focus on the ways social media features can be used for qualitative data collection. By understanding how all available alternatives work, researchers can make informed choices that best fit the research questions.

RETHINKING QUALITATIVE RESEARCH DESIGN FOR THE DIGITAL AGE

What kind of data is needed to answer the researcher questions and fulfil the study's purpose? This simple question belies the complexity of online research design. While e-researchers must address concerns common to any study, there is a further need to factor in the influences of technology for the ways we communicate with participants from the recruitment stage, through informing them and verifying consent, collecting data, and carrying out member checking (See Beninger, Chapter 5, this volume). At this time a widely accepted set of design specifications or criteria does not currently exist for these emerging research approaches. Where to begin? What questions should be asked? The *Qualitative E-Research Framework* shown in Figure 12.1 (Salmons, 2012, 2015, 2016) offers a conceptual system of key questions about inter-related facets of online qualitative research. This model was originally developed to explain dimensions of online interview research, but has been expanded to encompass any online qualitative approach. It is displayed as a circular system because examining design decisions in isolation is inadequate. An holistic approach as presented in this model reminds us to look at all the pieces of the research design puzzle before moving forward. It is beyond the scope of this chapter to examine each of these dimensions in-depth, but by thinking through some key questions and then seeing how they play out in published studies, you may find new ways of thinking about your own research designs.

The process begins by *Aligning Purpose and Design*. While this may indeed be the first step, the *Qualitative E-Research Framework* suggests that once the other categories have been examined it may be necessary to circle back to the beginning and make sure all pieces of the design fit together, that is, the design is iterative in nature.

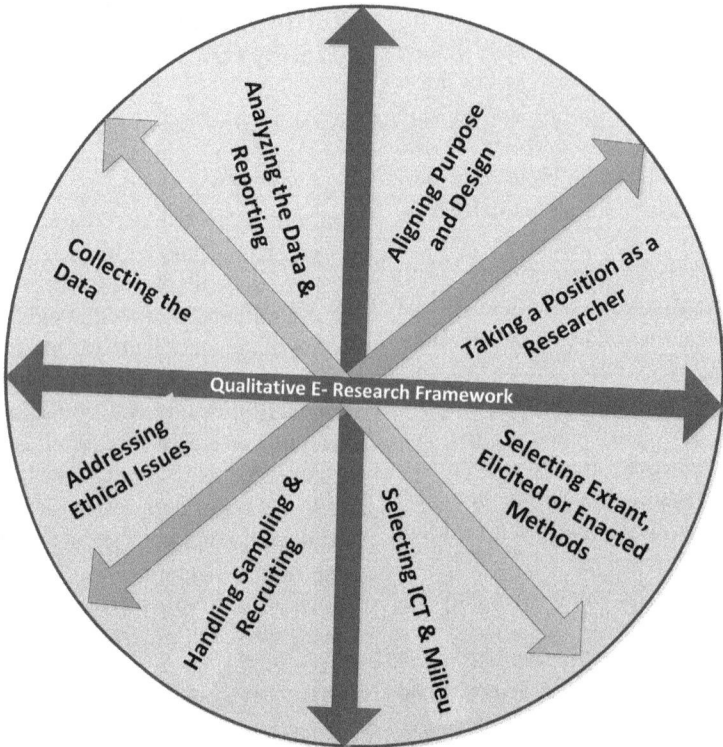

Figure 12.1 The Qualitative E-Research Framework

Aligning Purpose and Design

Key Questions:

- Are theories and epistemologies, methodologies and methods appropriate for the study and clearly aligned?
- How will qualitative data collected online relate to theories? Does the researcher want to explore, prove, or generate theory?

Any study is strengthened by coherent discussion of research purpose, theories, methodologies, and methods. By exploring these elements of the research design we can understand how the intended use of online data collection methods aligns with the overall purpose and theoretical framework of the study. Importantly, this exploration helps us decide whether we want to develop existing theories or generate new theory. The rationale for using electronic methods needs to be comprehensive and precise. It shows how selected theories and epistemologies are appropriate to the methodology, and that online methods will allow you to answer the research question.

Taking a Position as a Researcher

Key Questions:

- Does the researcher clearly delineate an insider or outsider position? Does the researcher explain implications related to that position, including any conflicts of interest or risks of researcher bias?

Positionality is essential to understand and explain as part of the design of a study to be conducted in or with social media. What is the researcher's connection or relationship to the social media site or community, to the phenomenon or participants being investigated? Is the researcher motivated by scholarly interests or by a gap identified in the literature? Or by personal interests?

The distinction between *insider* versus *outsider* perspectives is not unique to online research. Any researcher may choose to look at a research problem from an *emic* position to examine issues revealed from within the case or from an *etic* position to look at issues drawn from outside the case (Stake, 1995). VanDeVen contrasts the outside researcher as a 'detached, impartial onlooker who gathers data' with the inside researcher who is a 'participant immersed in the actions and experiences within the system being studied' (VanDeVen, 2007, pp. 269–270). VanDeVen (2007) describes the value found in complementarity of knowledge gained from research that uses the insider perspective to provide a concrete grounding in the research problem in a particular context or situation together with research from an outside perspective that uses empirical evidence to build a broader understanding of the scope of the problem.

By its nature, social media engages people. Individuals are connected formally and informally to social and professional networks, so researchers may have various degrees of relationship to the phenomenon or participants. Researchers may take advantage of these connections to gain access to a private milieu or to engage known members without an arduous recruitment process. While such access is invaluable, researchers need to balance the positive aspect of connections with the negative aspect of a prejudiced view based on familiarity with the members and features of the social media. The researcher needs to exercise caution in situations where such familiarity means research settings or participants are inadvertently excluded because the researcher stuck with what was already known. In qualitative studies the researcher is the instrument of data collection so being forthright is critical about any potential biases or conflicts of interest. By clarifying the purpose of the study and the position of the researcher, we have the basis to consider how the methods for data collection align with other elements of the research design.

Selecting Extant, Elicited or Enacted Methods

Key Questions:

- Does the researcher offer a compelling rationale for using one or more methods of data collected online to achieve the research purpose?

With a clear picture of the overarching contours of the study, next we look at why and how to select and justify data collection methods for the study by first looking at conventional qualitative approaches, then exploring ways studies can be conducted using social media.

Qualitative data collection methods are typically differentiated into three broad types:

Interviews: In one-to- one or group interviews the researcher poses questions or suggests themes for conversation with research participants. Research participants respond to questions and any follow-up prompts.

Observations: Researchers observe individuals, or group interactions, and makes note of activities or behaviours that relate to the topic of the inquiry. Research observations can take place in a controlled or laboratory setting; alternatively naturalistic observations can occur anywhere. Depending on the type of observation the researcher may or may not engage with those being observed.

Document or archival analysis: Historical or contemporary documents, media, and records of all kinds are analyzed in this type of qualitative research. The term *documents* may also refer to diaries, narratives, journals and other written or visual materials.

These types take new forms online to take advantage of the characteristics of the Internet generally and social media particularly. The Typology of Online Qualitative Methods, summarized in Table 12.1 (Salmons, 2016) describes new way to categorize qualitative data collection methods based on a differentiation according to the degree of direct interaction the researcher has with the data and with participants. Reconfiguring the approaches described above, three types are:

Extant: Collection of posts of text, images, media or other user-generated content. Extant material was created independent of any intervention, influence or prompts by the researcher. In this type of study the researcher has no direct contact with the users. Researchers gathering such data adapt qualitative methods such as unobtrusive observation, document analysis, archival research, narrative research or discourse analysis.

Elicited: By contrast, the researcher may evoke participants' responses to questions or other prompts. When eliciting data the researcher has a direct interaction with participants who consent to participate. The researcher can influence the direction or level of specificity and can probe for additional information in ways not possible with extant data. Researchers can elicit written, visual or multimedia responses from participants. Researchers adapt methods such as participant observation, interviews, focus groups or questionnaires.

Enacted: The term *enacted* refers to an online activity that engages researcher and consenting participants in the generation of data with highly collaborative, creative, and generative research approaches. Researchers adapt methods such as vignettes, role plays, simulations, arts-based research or games.

Selecting ICT & Milieu

Key Questions:

- How will researchers and participants communicate?
- Will any interactions with participants take place synchronously, asynchronously or with a mix of time-response communications?
- Are choices for social media site and communication features accessible to research participants?

Table 12.1 Selecting research types, communication features and social media sites

Typology of qualitative online methods		Data collected online from	Researcher and participant
Extant	Studies using existing materials developed without the researcher's influence	• Review of posts, discussions and archives including written materials, reports, drawings, graphics or other images, photographs and/or recorded audio or audio-visual media • Unobtrusive observation of communities or events on social media sites	No direct contact with Individual participants
Elicited	Studies using data elicited from participants in response to the researcher's questions	• Interviews (1-1 or group) conducted using video or text chat or messaging features • Participant observation of communities or events on social media sites	Interaction between researcher and one or more consenting participants
Enacted	Studies using data generated with participants during the study	• Vignette, scenario or problem-centered interviews conducted using video or text chat or messaging features on social media sites • Creative interactions using drawing or graphic applications • Activities using games	Collaboration involving researcher one or more consenting participants

Researchers may choose a social media site for the setting of the study for a variety of reasons, including the researcher's own preferences. Some researchers are looking for specific communications features to observe or to use in exchanges with participants. Timing and degree of immediacy possible between question and response are additional considerations.

Consider the types of communication social media sites facilitate, including:

- Text-based communication in writing.
- Posts or exchanges of visual images or media.
- Videoconference or video chat that uses visual and verbal exchange, usually with a webcam.
- Games that allow for text, verbal and visual exchange.
- Voting or signaling likes or dislikes, approval or disapproval of others' posts.

One distinction between these types relates to the timing of question and response. Online, asynchronous communication entails two types of displacement: time and space. Synchronous communication entails one type of displacement: space (Bampton & Cowton, 2002). Synchronous modes bring people one step closer together, but many people find that the reflective pause between message and response in asynchronous communications leads to deeper consideration of the matter at hand (LaBanca, 2011). Synchronous and asynchronous modes are generally available on social media sites. The culture of the particular social media site may lean more towards synchronous chats or quick successions of posts presented in a chronological stream, or a slower, more asynchronous pace of posts and responses on a discussion board. In any of these sites registered members can go back and review materials posted in the past to read them – or to make comments and bring them back into the current conversation. Social media sites aim to keep their members in a regular visitation schedule by pushing messages through email or text alerts when something is posted in an area where the member is subscribed.

Extant data collection can occur synchronously or asynchronously. The researcher could, for example, observe a synchronous streamed online event. The live event could be recorded or and viewed in the social media archive. Posts and archives of discussions from any era can be downloaded for analysis.

Elicitation of participant responses can also occur synchronously or asynchronously. For example, an interview may be conducted using a synchronous text or video exchange, or with asynchronous posts and responses in a private area of the social media site. Polling functions can be used to collect data asynchronously.

Researchers who want to generate data through collaborative events, simulations or games can construct such opportunities within social media settings.

Handling Sampling and Recruiting

Key Questions:

- How will the researcher assess whether the target population has access to the social media site and communication features as well as the capability and willingness to use the selected ICTs as a research participant?
- How can the researcher locate credible research participants? How will the researcher verify the identity and age (or other relevant criteria) of research participants recruited online?

Researchers using elicitation or enacted techniques rely on participants to provide data.

Nowhere are researchers' choices more critical than in determining how they will identify and select the individuals who will contribute relevant thoughts and experiences as research participants. Qualitative researchers use what is broadly defined as purposive or purposeful sampling when selecting participants, meaning the sample is intentionally selected according to the purpose of the study (Miles, Huberman, & Saldana, 2014).

Established qualitative sampling procedures can be adapted to organize the process, however, new approaches are needed when researchers use social media sites to locate and recruit participants. The online researcher can customize purposive sampling depending on the nature of the study, the selected social media site, and the target study population. Criterion sampling allows the researcher to specify the characteristics that serve as the basis for selection of research participants – important when participants must be able to access and use specific social media for the study. Sampling criteria should reference the social media site's access and/or the specific ICT being used. Will participants need webcams, headsets or microphones? Do they need to access a social media site differently than they typically do, such as logging into a private forum? Criteria may also specify the level of experience with the social media site or phenomena under investigation.

Reliable options for locating credible research participants online are: nomination and sample frames. The first relies on verification of identity by another person who knows the potential participant; the second relies on verification by membership in a group, organization, or reliable administrative list. Moderators or hosts of discussion groups, can assist the researcher in identifying people who meet the sampling criteria, and recommending that they participate in the study.

The term *sample frame* refers to a preselected list or grouping of people who meet the main inclusion criteria. The list may already exist, or the researcher may construct it from scratch to fit the specific study.

Existing Sample Frames. Existing frames usually consist of records previously constructed for administrative purposes. They could include membership lists for organizations or associations or lists of students or program participants.

Constructed Sample Frames. Where an existing frame or list is not available, researchers may have to create their own. In some cases, researchers can construct a frame from partially adequate or incomplete existing frames. Another way to construct a frame is by working through organizations that provide services to or represent a population of potential participants.

Once the researcher has a list of potential participants, online recruitment can be carried out. In a social media setting it might seem that simply posting a recruiting message would generate interest, however, this is rarely effective. First, check whether permissions are needed to post recruitment messages to specific groups. Next, consider the culture of the site, group or community. How do people communicate in this group – formally or informally? What ICTs are used? How similar are the ICTs commonly being used in the site to those you want to use in the data collection? For example, if you want to use web cams, or interactive graphical games, are those tools members on the site would commonly use? Again, where a moderator is present, he or she may be able to make an introduction or suggest the best way to get the message to encourage members to participate. Establishing a credible presence as a researcher can be helpful for recruitment – as well as for earning trust needed for ethical interactions with participants.

By understanding the sampling and recruiting plans, we can learn more about the individuals who will contribute data and determine whether choices made by the researcher best serve the purpose of the study.

Addressing Ethical Issues

Key Questions:

- Does the researcher need permission to access online profiles and/or observe posts and online interactions for studying extant data?
- Has the researcher informed participants and verified their consent to voluntarily participate when elicitation or enacted methods are used?
- Has the researcher taken appropriate steps to protect human subjects, and where appropriate, their avatars or online representations?

Ethical issues abound in any online research. In the case of online research in social media, there are some particular factors to address (see Beninger, Chapter 5, this volume). A fundamental factor is the presence and role of human participants. LeCompte defines human participants as 'a living individual whom a researcher obtains data about through interaction with that individual or with private information that identifies that person' (LeCompte, 2008, p. 805). For our purposes the human participant is the person on the other side of the monitor, the 'user' with a mobile device who is typing on the keyboard, chatting on a video call or uploading images or files. The human may be represented or expressed online by diverse avatars, pseudonyms or screen names. While some kinds of research with extant data that contains no personally identifiable information can be conducted without informed consent, any study using elicitation or enacted methods will require that participants are informed and voluntarily consent to participate.

Informed consent in online research should include as much (or more!) attention to the *informed* aspect as the *consent* aspect of the agreement. Prior to the study, communication with those recruited for the study could include the following. Use the suggestions that best fit the social media site, and the study purpose:

Introduce yourself as a credible researcher, and explain your motivation for conducting the research. Depending on the social media and the nature of the study, you may want to create a friendly social presence. Focus on the benefits associated with robust results from the study – rather than the benefits to you, such as completion of your degree or your professional reputation.

Consider creating a research page, site or blog to introduce yourself, your study and any associated institution or project. Alternatively, record a short media piece to introduce yourself and convey that you are a scholar, not someone trying to obtain personal data from participants for questionable reasons. Avoid use of academic or scientific jargon.

Let potential participants know what you need to achieve the purpose of the study.

Generate interest in study participation by showing the contribution it will make – in plain, not academic, terms.

Reassure potential participants about protection of data and anonymity, etc. Be clear about how data will be used, and where reports or articles will be published.

Clearly spell out specific expectations about time, technology access or other requirements

Informing participants does not end when they sign an agreement. Continuing to inform them during the study could include providing them with:

> Reminders about follow-up interviews, observations or member checking.

Any reminders or questions about use of images or media from user-generated materials or from recordings of interviews or events.

Information about any changes in the study that vary from those in the original consent agreement.

Signals for emergent directions such as new questions to discuss in follow-up interviews or observations.

Reiteration for use of data in publications or presentations.

Questions to ask about potential ethical risks in an e-interview study include the following:

> Does the research involve observation or intrusion in situations where the subjects have a reasonable expectation of privacy? Would reasonable people be offended by such an intrusion? Can the research be redesigned to avoid the intrusion?

Will the investigator(s) be collecting sensitive information about individuals? If so, have they made adequate provisions for protecting the confidentiality of the data through coding, destruction of identifying information, limiting access to the data, or

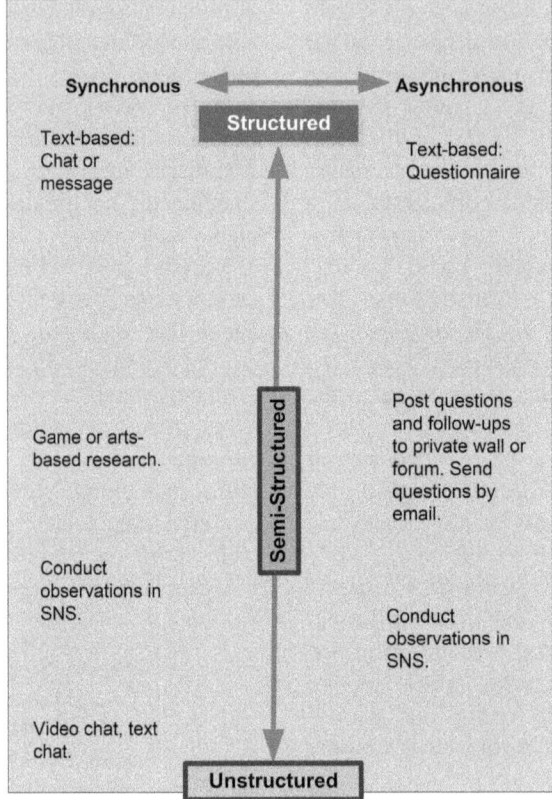

Figure 12.2 Ethical issues in Qualitative E-Research Design

whatever methods that may be appropriate to the study?

Are the investigator's disclosures to subjects about confidentiality adequate? Should documentation of consent be waived to protect confidentiality?

Is it clear to the participant that there is no penalty for withdrawing from the research?

Are safeguards in place to protect confidentiality of the participant at all stages of the study, including publication?

Can the researcher protect the data and ensure that it is not used for purposes other than those the participant consented to in the agreement? Is the researcher using communication features that allow any interview exchanges to be downloaded and deleted from the server?

Collecting the Data

Key Questions:

- Is the researcher experienced with all features of the selected technology, as needed to access conversations or archives, download media or images, or interact with participants?
- Has the researcher conducted practice interviews and/or practice observations?
- Does the researcher have a plan for conducting the interview with either prepared questions or an interview guide?
- Will the researcher use the same or different communication features to interact with participants in each of the four interview stages: (1) opening, (2) questioning and guiding, (3) closing, and (4) following up?

- Does the researcher have a plan for conducting any observations with either prepared checklists, objectives or an observation guide?
- Does the researcher have a contingency plan in case there are technical difficulties?

Once designs and plans are complete the researcher must actually be able to carry out the research, with all of the messy realities intrinsic to any communication. Does the researcher have the preparation, skills and abilities needed to scrape extant data from a site, carry out interviews, collaborative arts-based or creative research, and/or any related observations? Can the researcher bring together purpose and process when faced with the individual research participant or group of participants? What will the researcher do if the interview or observation does not proceed as planned, or if there are technical problems? These are some of the questions researchers need to address in order to collect data and answer the research questions.

Any researcher must decide whether a structured, unstructured, or semi-structured technique best achieves the purpose of the study. While this question is generally associated with interview research, the same principles apply to observations. In either case, a more structured approach allows for greater consistency between one data collection event and another and a more unstructured approach allows for more responsiveness and flexibility. Semi-structured approaches may include a mix of consistent and spur-of-the-moment questions, prompts, and/or observation priorities. There is no right or wrong approach – it is the researcher's determination in the context of the study's purpose, the kind of online setting, and characteristics of the participants.

As noted, social media sites variously allow for text-based, visual or multi-media exchanges. Some online communications, such as a video call or chat, are more natural and allow for the spontaneity associated with unstructured interview approaches. Other

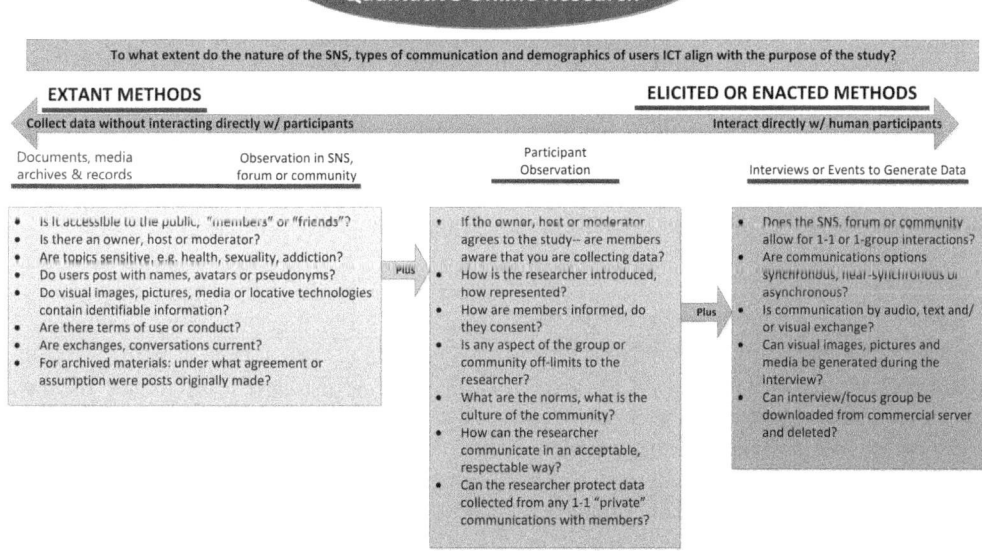

Figure 12.3 Level of structure

Source: Salmons, 2015.

communications technologies require more forethought prior to an interview, observation or other research event. The researcher may need to set up a private discussion chat, organize a game, or make sure the participant has accepted the invitation to connect in a meeting area. These are more suited to semi- or structured approaches.

Structured interviews can be conducted with almost any ICT since answers may be yes/no or simple statements. Semi-structured and unstructured interviews, however, require more careful thought because in some kinds of ICTs pausing to craft and type questions may disrupt the flow of the interview. This means an e-interview researcher must consider aligning their interview structure and questioning style with the choice of technology used to interact with participants, data type and online research setting – as well as alignment with the purpose of the study and the participants' communication preferences.

Structured interviews usually consist of the same questions posed in the same sequence to all participants (Salmons, 2015). They may include closed-ended or limited-response questions or open-ended questions designed to elicit short narrative answers. Interview respondents do not have the option to redirect questions or embroider on responses. To prepare for structured interviews, the researcher determines the exact wording of all questions in advance. Because the role of the interviewer is meant to be as neutral as possible, the researcher may recruit and train others to implement the interview.

Similarly, in a structured observation the researcher may have a checklist to guide consistent observations across all participants in the study (Salmons, 2015). The researcher may look for and make note of the same features in the setting for each interview. The researcher may make note of same kinds of non-verbal cues during the interview or the same kinds of online posts, records or activities for each participant.

Questions researchers using structured approaches need to ask include (Salmons, 2015):

Interviews

- Are questions and response items clearly stated?
- What communication features will allow the researcher to either read verbatim the questions and response options, or to cut and paste prepared questions into a text chat box for a written exchange?
- What will make it easy for participants to see or hear the questions and quickly respond?
- Is there a reason to conduct it synchronously (given the need to coordinate schedules to do so) or can you securely post the questions in a secure forum that allows for asynchronous responses?

Observations

- Will the same ICT be used for the interviews and for observations? If the observations will occur on a different social media site, has that been agreed upon with the participant?
- How will data be saved? Will the researcher record the observations or take notes in real time during the observation?

Semi-structured interviews balance the pre-planned questions of a structured approach with the spontaneity and flexibility of the unstructured interview (Salmons, 2015). The researcher prepares questions and/or discussion topics in advance and devises follow-up questions and prompts during the interview. In semi-structured observations the researcher identifies objectives or guidelines for the main characteristics, types of responses or other features central to the study. During the observation, other relevant evidence can be collected.

Questions researchers using semi-structured approaches need to ask include (Salmons, 2015):

Semi-structured Interviews

What ICT features of the social media site allow the researcher to deliver main questions so that participants can easily see or hear them? What features allow for timely delivery of follow-up and probing questions?

To what extent are synchronous spoken or written exchanges used for all or some of the interview? Are researcher and participant frequent text-chat communicators who are able to think and type quickly enough to make a less-structured interview work smoothly? Or might researchers find that trying to think of questions or follow-ups, and type them, is too slow a process.

If a game or other interactive event is used, will time be needed to navigate to different settings or to show various features that could create a gap between question and response? Would this type of interview be best conducted as a synchronous or asynchronous interview?

Semi-structured Observations

Will the same social media site be used for all observations?

To what extent will observations be consistent from one participant to the next?

What kinds of posts, records or activities will the researcher observe to learn about each participant? Or will the researcher follow-up particular responses by looking for related posts and materials?

Unstructured interviews are used to collect data through what is essentially a conversation between the researcher and participant (Salmons, 2015).

Unstructured Interviews

What social media features allows the researcher to achieve natural dialogue, such as video chats, so the conversation can easily flow and change course?

If you want to conduct an asynchronous, unstructured interview, how will you retain focus on the research purpose between communications?

Unstructured Observations

Will the same social media site be used for all participants?

Will the researcher develop unique observation protocols for each participant? Based on each interview? What will guide such observations?

Observation online can happen in two ways, *unobtrusive* or *participant*.

Unobtrusive observation, sometimes called *external* **observation**, allows researchers to collect data without asking questions, making posts or otherwise involving themselves in interactions with the online community, group, social media or social networking site. The researcher does not announce his or her presence or role.

A researcher might use unobtrusive observation to learn more about the population, phenomena or social media settings by observing ways of interacting or topics of discussion. Such observation can be done without collecting personally identifiable information. This type of observation may help in the selection of a site or group for further study – with extant, elicited or enacted methods.

In a study using elicitation or enacted methods with consenting participants the researcher may want to learn more about the individual by reading posts and/or interactions on social media. Permission to use data collected this way may be requested in the consent negotiations.

Participant observation occurs when the researcher collects data that includes researchers' own involvement. The researcher might, for example, post comments, prompts or questions to forums, boards or walls in SNSs where they are observing one or more participants.

SOCIAL MEDIA AND THE QUALITATIVE E-RESEARCH DESIGN: EXAMPLES FROM THE LITERATURE

Principles from the Qualitative E-Research Design can be understood by dissecting scholarly research. Six studies using social media demonstrate a variety of design approaches using extant data, data elicited in interviews, participant observation or focus groups, or enacted data generated through games or other experiences. Commercial social media sites in these exemplars included Twitter, Facebook, Pinterest, and YouTube. A privately run social network, and social comment areas on news sites were also studied in these innovative inquiries.

Studies using Extant Data Found on Social Media Sites

The article, 'The Care.Data Consensus? A Qualitative Analysis of Opinions Expressed on Twitter' (Hays & Daker-White, 2015) described a study of individuals' tweets. The aim of the study described in this article was to 'identify and describe the range of opinions expressedabout the care.data project on Twitter for the period during which the delay to this project was announced, analyzing the data in such a way as to provide insight into the strengths and flaws of the project' (p. 2). The researchers searched for tweets with the # CareData, which they captured using the data analysis software tool NVivo$^{tm.}$ They determined that they could capture a continuous stream of tweets by downloading them at the same time each day. Tweets were analyzed using automated NVivo features such as word counts, then, with a grounded theory analysis approach: 'the tweets were read in sequential order, line by line, and coded in iterative fashion according to an evolving list of themes' (p. 3).

The second exemplar of a study using extant data is 'Is she a pawn, prodigy or person with a message? Public responses to a child's political speech' (Raby & Raddon, 2015). The purpose of the study is an exploration of the implications for political participation of children based on the events surrounding the well-publicized speech made by a 12-year-old girl and posted on YouTube. Data included comments made to the YouTube video, as well as comments about the video posted to online news, comment sites.

Researchers Raby and Raddon (2015) collected a total of 600 comments. They captured the first 150 comments made to each of two major news stories posted on the Huffington Post and CBC, respectively. They also:

> identified the three postings of the video on YouTube that had the highest view counts. Each posted video had received between 100,000 and 650,000 views and a combined total of 2,214 comments at the time of our analysis. For each YouTube video we selected the first 50 comments and another 50 that appeared ten days later, after the video had presumably reached a wider online audience. (p. 170)

Victoria Grant, the girl whose YouTube video generated so much controversy, did not post any comments in a public discussion.

Since these sites require no registration or login to view comments, researchers treated the data as public information, and did not obtain informed consent. When quoting, users' synonyms were named, based on the researcher's premise that 'online pseudonyms already afford users a chosen degree of anonymity and their inclusion in research is appropriate given that the comments are in the public domain' (p. 170).

Qualitative content analysis methods were used to code and interpret the data, resulting in four themes. While the researchers recognized the limitation of this study, given that links to YouTube videos are often shared between people within existing social networks and so neither readership nor viewership is random or representative (p. 170), they believed that the findings provided a unique view on the diversity of opinion on the conceptualization of childhood and the roles of children in public life (p. 183).

Studies using Data Elicited from Participants on Social Media Sites

The next exemplar is, 'Wedding dresses and wanted criminals: Pinterest.com as an infrastructure for repository building' (Zarro, Hall, & Forte, 2013). The purpose of the study was an exploration of digital collecting and social curating as exemplified by behaviours on Pinterest. Zarro et al. (2013) wanted to 'understand activity on the site by investigating how diverse Pinterest users make sense of their activities and form connections in an interest-based social network' (p. 650). This phenomenological study uses both extant data and data elicited from participants. By combining participant observation and interviewing methods, Zarro et al. (2013) could drown their analysis in 'accounts of users themselves as well as in their observable actions and the collections they've assembled' (p. 650).

The researchers began by classifying Pinterest boards as either personal (used for hobbies, leisure, life or home events), or professional (used to network about their activities) and by selecting active accounts of both types (p. 652). Using contact information on the site, they sent messages to selected account owners, requesting the opportunity to interview them. Of 32 invited Pinterest owners, nine were interviewed.

The participant observation component of the study entailed looking at public activity on the Pinterest site generally, as well as content that was generated by participants specifically. Zarro et al. (2013) said that, 'inspecting user-contributed pins and pinboards enriched our understanding of activities taking place on the site, while inspecting the stated desires of the site operators provided insight into their goals and the types of activities they seek to support' (p. 652). Based on their analysis, the researchers generated four categories of interest, as well as discussion of the researcher's theorization of the social media site.

The second exemplar of an elicited approach is found in the article 'Online Facebook Focus Group Research of Hard-to-Reach Participants' (Lijadi & van Schalkwyk, 2015). Lijadi and van Schalkwyk (2015) described a study of adults whose childhood included multiple cultural perspectives. The researchers began by observing discussion groups in Facebook on topics related to the study; observations provided the basis for selecting groups where the research information and recruitment messages could be posted (p. 3). After reviewing the information, interested individuals sent private messages to the researchers and researchers followed up with a consent form, a biographic questionnaire, and an invitation to accept a 'friend' request (p. 4).

The focus group was run by having the facilitator poses questions and the participants post replies to the initial question as well as to others' comments (Lijadi & van Schalkwyk, 2015). 'Housekeeping' rules laid out guidelines for participation in the group, including suggested response time to the discussion (p. 5). One of the researchers served as the facilitator for all focus group. This role included monitoring the groups and following up with members who were missing; private messaging features were used to communicate with participants as needed throughout the monitoring process (p. 5). The facilitator also looked for off-topic responses, or responses that indicated a need for greater clarity in the question.

A third exemplar, 'On the creative edge: Exploring motivations for creating non-suicidal self-injury content online' illustrates the fact that while commercially owned social media sites are best known, sometimes private social networking opportunities are needed when the subject of discussion is highly sensitive (Seko, Kidd, Wiljer, & McKenzie, 2015). Seko et al. (2015) chose Self-Injury.net's SafeHaven community to study Non-Suicidal Self-Injury (NSSI) by adolescents (p. 3). This interactive social network community allows members to display and comment on user generated textual and visual materials. To access this delicate and confidential discussion, Seko et al. (2015) worked closely with the site moderator, including biweekly online chat sessions, and feedback on materials to be posted and all stages of the study. Researchers

Table 12.2 Characteristics of qualitative exemplars

	Purpose and design	Positions and roles of researchers	Extant, elicited or enacted method	Social media platform and ICT features
The Care.Data Consensus? A Qualitative Analysis of Opinions Expressed on Twitter (Hays & Daker-White, 2015)	This exploratory study used grounded theory approach to analyze the data obtained from Twitter	Researchers took an emic position, since they are patient safety researchers	Extant data generated by users without prompts or questions from the researchers	Participants voluntarily tweeted to #care data to express their responses to current events. Researchers used NVivo data analysis software to capture and analyze selected tweets
Is she a pawn, prodigy or person with a message? Public responses to a child's political speech (Raby & Raddon, 2015)	This discourse analysis study analyzed comments posted publicly online	Researchers took an etic position in the study	Extant data generated by users without prompts or questions from the researchers	Researchers studied the comments from YouTube and the two different news sources
Wedding dresses and wanted criminals: Pinterest.com as an infrastructure for repository building (Zarro et al., 2013)	This phenomenological study was designed to 'define and explain phenomena on Pinterest using the perceptions of the people who are directly involved in creating these phenomena' using principles outlined by Schutz and Seidman (Schutz, 1967; Seidman, 2006)	Researchers took an etic position in the study	Data elicited through interviews, complimented extant data collected participant observation with consenting participants	Messaging features in Pinterest used to communicate with participants; Pinterest boards and internal search capabilities used for observation
Online Facebook Focus Group Research of Hard-to-Reach Participants (Lijadi & van Schalkwyk, 2015)	This discovery-oriented qualitative study with interpretative phenomenological analysis	Researchers took an emic position in regard to the social media meleiu in that they were familiar with the platform. Researchers took an etic position in regard to the subject matter of the study	After an initial unobtrusive observation stage, elicitation methods were used with questions and prompts posted by the researchers. Participants consented to be in the study	Asynchronous focus group in Facebook. ICT features used included private messaging and threaded discussion in a private group

(Continued)

Table 12.2 (Continued)

On the creative edge: Exploring motivations for creating non-suicidal self-injury content online (Seko et al., 2015)	This exploratory study used Saldana's methods (Saldana, 2013) of thematic content analysis of interview responses	Researchers took an etic position	Researchers used unobtrusive observation of the community to gain background for the study. Data were elicited through interviews with consenting participants	1-1 interviews were conducted synchronously using text chat and asynchronously using email
Exploring Twitter as a game platform; Strategies and opportunities for microblogging-based games (Hicks et al., 2015)	This mixed methods research included a qualitative case study. Data were analyzed using inductive thematic analysis	Researchers had to take an emic position and immerse themselves in the game to understand players' steps and strategies. In conduct of the study, researchers took an etic position	Qualitative data were generated through game play, followed by interviews about their experiences. This interactive, multistage process fits the definition of an enacted approach	'[T]he game leverages Twitter connectivity along with collaborative content creation to enable interaction between players' (Hicks et al., 2015, p. 5). Authors did not explain what ICT was used for online interviews
Exploring playful experiences in social network games (Paavilainen et al., 2015)	This study used a qualitative experiment method to explore users experience of games played in Facebook	Researchers had to take an emic position to learn and categorize the games, in order to select those suitable for the study. In conduct of the study, researchers took an etic position	Qualitative data were generated through game play, followed by completion of the PLEX framework instrument. This interactive, multistage process fits the definition of an enacted approach	The study focused on two features of social games: the utilization of the social network service for play purposes and the free-to-play revenue model (Hicks et al., 2015, p. 2)

were able to observe the information posted on the Self-Injury.net site by the moderator, in addition to user-generated content on the Safe Haven community.

Recruitment for prospective interviewees included several important steps, including posting a moderator-approved notice in the community, with links to information about the study and an online consent form. Study participants were asked to meet a set of criteria, including a minimum age of 16 years.

As a part of the consent process, participants were asked to select the preferred online communication medium.

Semi-structured interviews were conducted using synchronous emails and synchronous text chats, based on participants' preferences. Questions and prompts were prepared in advance of the interview, and open-ended questions invited participants to add whatever descriptions or experiences they chose to share (p. 4). Anonymity was insured by removing any identifiable information, and assigning a numerical code to each participant.

After using a content analysis process to analyze the data, member-checking interviews were conducted with some of the participants to solicit their views on the findings. These follow up interviews were also conducted via email and text chat.

Studies using Data Generated on Social Media with Participants using Enacted Methods

Researchers who want to interact with participants in ways other than questioning and prompting techniques used in online interviews, look for generative ways to use technology. One way Internet users interact is through multiplayer games. While many games operate on their own platforms, commercial social media sites are increasingly incorporating games into their activities. The exemplars in this section describe studies using Twitter and Facebook, respectively.

'Exploring Twitter as a game platform; Strategies and Opportunities for Microblogging-Based Games' (Hicks, Gerling, Kirman, Linehan, & Dickinson, 2015) is a mixed methods case study of the game *Hashtag Dungeon*. This game uses Twitter as a means of creating, storing, and promoting game content (p. 1). The researchers did not play the game with participants, but in order to design the study, they needed to play the game and familiarize themselves with details about how it worked.

The first quantitative stage of the study used questionnaires and game metrics to understand how users play the game. For our purposes, we will focus on the second, qualitative part of the research.

Hicks et al. (2015) were interested in two research questions around Twitter integration and *Hashtag Dungeon* in the qualitative study: (1) asking how participants experienced the game with respect to Twitter connectivity, and (2) how participants perceived and managed social media integration (p. 5). While Twitter users can read content without holding an account, and inclusion criterion for this study was ownership of an account. After promoting the study on social media to recruit participants and obtaining informed consent, a link to a free download of the game was sent by email. Participants were assigned two tasks: 'Task 1 was to play through a Dungeon of their choice to familiarize themselves with the game. Task 2 was to design a new room for a dungeon and Tweet it out' (p. 5). After participants completed these tasks, researchers conducted structured interviews, with follow-up questions. Researchers analyzed the interview responses using an inductive thematic analysis.

'Exploring playful experiences in social network games' looked at how 110 participants played 23 different games in Facebook (Paavilainen, Koskinen, Korhonen, & Alha, 2015). The purpose of the study was to understand the experience of social games from the perspectives of those who play them. As with the Hicks et al. (2015) study, the researchers familiarized themselves with the games, but did not play with participants during data collection for the study. The process for recruiting participants was not explained in the article, however, researchers describe the value of having players with varying exposure to social games, which provided a balanced sample (Hicks et al., 2015, p. 3).

Participants were asked to use an existing Playful Experiences (PLEX) framework devised by Paavilainen, et al. in 2009. Paavilainen et al. (2015) conducted six experiments running where the participants played Facebook social games. Each experiment included a list of 2 to 5 games selected by the researchers. Each participant chose one game from the list to play; 4 to 6 participants played each of the games. Afterwards, participants provided narrative descriptions to report on 3 of the 22 categories spelled out in the PLEX framework. In the data analysis process, researchers looked at the 330 descriptions, to first identify the frequencies of all reported PLEX categories, then analyze the narrative descriptions (p. 3).

Metasynthesis

The studies selected as exemplars represent diverse research in diverse disciplines, and they used a wide variety of methods. Since the articles were intended to inform readers primarily about the studies' findings, not all elements of the *Qualitative E-Research Framework* are fully discussed. However, within this small sample we see the exploratory nature of online research.

None of these studies represents a truly emic position by researchers, yet all of them had to immerse themselves in the social media site, and learn its features in order to design the study. The studies using extant data displayed care in protecting personal information about the users whose posts were collected as data. The remaining studies that described recruitment used the features of the social media site to reach participants, sometimes with cooperation of a moderator or owner of a group. The articles that mentioned informed consent describes using an online form. They also described using the informed consent negotiation to provide background about the study as well as any instructions and expectations for participation.

The studies that used interviews or focus groups devised at least some of the questions prior to the research event, allowing the researchers to balance confidence based in a prepared direction for the interview with flexibility to respond to participants. Private messaging features within the social media sites, or email, were used for 1-1 communication with participants. Details were not provided in these articles about how exactly they carried out the interviews. Researchers using observational techniques did not describe whether or not they used guidelines to structure and prioritize the types of behaviours or activities to record. More details on the research process could enrich our understanding of these emerging methods.

CONCLUSION

Each choice the online researcher makes influences other aspects of the research design, as well as the findings. The *Qualitative E-Research Framework* can be used as a tool to analyze such choices at the design stages and make the most use of the opportunity to collect data from social networking sites. The format of Table 12.2 can be adapted for your own use, so you can dissect and learn from other published articles using qualitative methods and social media in empirical research.

REFERENCES

Angrosino, M. (2007). *Doing ethnographic and observational research*. London: SAGE Publications.

Bampton, R., & Cowton, C. J. (2002). The E-Interview. *Forum: Qualitative Social Research, 3*(2).

Banks, M., & Zeitlyn, D. (2015). *Visual methods in social research* (2nd ed.). Thousand Oaks: SAGE Publications.

Bechmann, A., & Lomborg, S. (2013). Mapping actor roles in social media: Different perspectives on value creation in theories of user participation. *New Media & Society, 15*(5), 765–781. doi: 10.1177/1461444812462853

Hays, R., & Daker-White, G. (2015). The care. data consensus? A qualitative analysis of opinions expressed on Twitter. *BMC Public Health, 15*(1), 1–13. doi: 10.1186/s12889-015-2180-9

Heath, C., Hindmarsh, J., & Luff, P. (2010). *Video in qualitative research: Analysing social interaction in everyday life*. Thousand Oaks: SAGE Publications.

Hicks, K., Gerling, K., Kirman, B., Linehan, C., & Dickinson, P. (2015). *Exploring Twitter as a game platform; Strategies and opportunities for microblogging-based games*. Paper presented at the CHI PLAY 2015, London.

Kuckartz, U. (2014). *Qualitative text analysis: A guide to methods, practice & using software*. Thousand Oaks: SAGE Publications.

Kvale, S., & Brinkman, S. (2014). *InterViews: Learning the craft of qualitative research interviewing* (Third ed.). Thousand Oaks: SAGE Publications.

LaBanca, F. (2011). Online dynamic asynchronous audit strategy for reflexivity in the qualitative paradigm. *The Qualitative Report, 16*(4), 1160–1171. doi: 10.1080/13645570802156196

LeCompte, M. (2008). Secondary participants. In L. M. Given (Ed.), *The SAGE Encyclopedia of Qualitative Research Methods*. Thousand Oaks, CA: SAGE Publications, Inc.

Lijadi, A. A., & van Schalkwyk, G. J. (2015). Online Facebook focus group research of hard-to-reach participants. *International Journal of Qualitative Methods, 14*(5), 1–9. doi: 10.1177/1609406915621383

Miles, M., Huberman, A. M., & Saldana, J. (2014). *Qualitative data analysis: A methods sourcebook* (Third ed.). Thousand Oaks: SAGE.

Paavilainen, J., Korhonen, H., Saarenpää, H., & Holopainen, J. (2009). *Player perception of context information utilization in pervasive mobile games*. Paper presented at the DiGRA '09 - Proceedings of the 2009 DiGRA International Conference: Breaking New Ground: Innovation in Games, Play, Practice and Theory, Brunel University.

Paavilainen, J., Koskinen, E., Korhonen, H., & Alha, K. (2015). *Exploring playful experiences in social network games*. Paper presented at the DiGRA 2015: Diversity of play: Games – Cultures – Identities, Lüneburg.

Pink, S. (2013). *Doing visual ethnography* (Third ed.). London: SAGE Publications.

Raby, R., & Raddon, M.-B. (2015). Is she a pawn, prodigy or person with a message? Public responses to a child's political speech. *Canadian Journal of Sociology, 40*(2), 163–187.

Rubin, H. J., & Rubin, I. S. (2012). *Qualitative interviewing: The art of hearing data* (Third ed.). Thousand Oaks: SAGE Publications.

Saldana, J. (2013). *Coding manual for qualitative researchers* (Second ed.). Thousand Oaks: SAGE Publications.

Salmons, J. (Ed.), (2012). *Cases in online interview research*. Thousand Oaks: SAGE Publications.

Salmons, J. (2014). Online research ethics: Questions researchers ask, answers guidelines provide. In K. Woodfield (Ed.), *Social media in social research: Blogs on blurring the boundaries*. London: NatCen Social Research.

Salmons, J. (2015). *Qualitative online interviews*. Thousand Oaks: SAGE Publications.

Salmons, J. (2016). *Doing qualitative research online*. London: SAGE Publications.

Schreier, M. (2012). *Qualitative content analysis in practice*. London: SAGE Publications.

Schutz, A. (1967). *The phenomenology of the social world*. Evanston: Northwestern University Press.

Seidman, I. (2006). *Interviewing as qualitative research: A guide for researchers in education and the social sciences* (Third ed.). New York: Teachers College Press.

Seko, Y., Kidd, S. A., Wiljer, D., & McKenzie, K. J. (2015). On the creative edge: Exploring motivations for creating non-suicidal self-injury content online. *Qualitative Health Research*. doi: 10.1177/1049732315570134

Stake, R. E. (1995). *The art of case study research*. Thousand Oaks: SAGE Publications.

VanDeVen, A. H. (2007). *Engaged scholarship*. Oxford: Oxford University Press.

Zarro, M., Hall, C., & Forte, A. (2013). *Wedding dresses and wanted criminals: Pinterest.com as an infrastructure for repository building*. Paper presented at the Seventh International AAAI Conference on Weblogs and Social Media.

PART III

Qualitative Approaches to Social Media Data

Small Data, Thick Data: Thickening Strategies for Trace-based Social Media Research

Guillaume Latzko-Toth, Claudine Bonneau and Mélanie Millette

The algorithmic processing of very large sets of 'traces' of user activities collected by digital platforms – so-called 'Big Data' – exerts a strong appeal on social media researchers. In the context of a computational turn in social sciences and humanities, is qualitative research based on small samples and corpuses ('small data') still relevant? It is argued that the unique value of such research lies in data *thickness*. This is achieved through a process we call thickening. Drawing on recent case studies in social media research we have conducted, we propose and illustrate three strategies to thicken trace data: trace interview, manual data collection and agile long-term online observation.

INTRODUCTION[1]

For about four decades, social sciences scholars have more or less agreed on what quantitative and qualitative methods could and could not do (Morgan, 2007). As an example, qualitative methods are considered more efficient to capture intentions, subjectivities and experiences, as well as historically situated phenomena and their processes (Denzin and Lincoln, 1994; Jensen, 2002). With these strengths, qualitative methods have been often mobilized to study traditional and new media uses and meanings.

Recently, the tacit division of labor between qualitative and quantitative methodologies to study media was challenged by a 'computational turn' in social sciences (Berry, 2011). With access to unprecedented computing resources and powerful algorithms, quantitative researchers can now overcome some of the limitations of the past and tackle the analysis of the massive datasets generated by digital media uses.

The problem with the very expression 'Big Data' is that it tends to direct attention to the sole size of the dataset, as if the scale of a sample was the ultimate indicator of how reliable the conclusion drawn from its analysis might be. While the volume of data is not the only dimension in Big Data research designs, some of their advocates clearly express an empiricist (and positivist) confidence in the fact that data abundance provides a direct access to 'social reality' (Anderson, 2008; Kitchin, 2014; Manovich, 2012). Beyond a rhetorical critique of the underlying assumptions of what makes quantity an indicator of research quality and insightfulness, we would like to point out, as Christine Borgman does, that

> distinguishing between big and little data is problematic due to the many ways in which something might be big. [...] Data are big or little in terms of what can be done with them, what insight they can reveal, and the scale of analysis required relative to the phenomenon of interest [...]. (2015: 6)

There is a convergence of interests between industry agenda and Big Data science to achieve mass modelization of audiences, clusters of users among platforms, consumption tendencies, and so on.[2] Qualitative approaches using small datasets have to reassess their capabilities and complementarity with quantitative approaches when studying online objects and digital uses. What is lost if we drop 'small data' research? And how do we pursue small data collection and analysis in a meaningful and productive way for today's science?

When it comes to studying social media, researchers need strategies to keep the size of the data manageable whilst gathering 'enough' information to draw rigorous findings. Even when dealing with a small number of cases or sources – i.e. 30 Facebook users – the amount of digital data that can be collected may quickly become overwhelming. Between 'likes' (Facebook), 'tweets' (Twitter), 'pins' (Pinterest), and 'snaps' (Snapchat), user interactions with and through social media platforms produce a huge amount of *digital traces*. Howison et al. define 'digital trace data' as 'records of activity [...] undertaken through an online information system [...;] recorded evidence that something has occurred in the past' (2011: 769). This definition stresses the recording of online events as a central aspect of trace data, but overlooks user-generated *contents* which also constitute 'traces' (Bowker, 2007) but of a specific kind. In this case, the content production (writing a tweet, posting a picture) *is* the activity, and the content itself is a trace of this activity, along with related metadata (e.g. author, timestamp, etc.). Therefore, digital traces comprise all user-related data that can be available on social media platforms. Traditional ethnographic approaches provide insights based on a limited number of observations or declarative accounts of practices relying on participants' memory – and honesty. As noted by Howison et al. (2011), the promise of digital trace data is to grant researchers 'direct' access to users' *real* practices by capturing and analyzing traces of their online activity. However, as noted by some critiques, interpreting and making sense of these loads of data can be very challenging (Kitchin, 2014), especially considering the importance of context in the study of media practices (boyd and Crawford, 2012; Quan-Haase et al., 2015). Quantity tends to stand for quality in massive trace-based social media research, drawing attention away from serious questions regarding representativeness and validity (Brooker et al., 2015; Freelon, 2014; Tufekci, 2014). On the other hand, the proliferation of digital traces is a serious challenge to their qualitative analysis using manual methods. Systematic collection of social media traces can easily build up a mass of textual and visual data, making it difficult and very time-consuming for the researcher to describe and interpret exhaustively.

A solution is to reduce the *breadth* of data (the number of data points) while enhancing their *depth* (i.e. 'thickness' of each datapoint). We call this process 'thickening' the data. Before providing a more rigorous definition of what we call data thickness, let us use an ecological science metaphor to illustrate what we mean by this trade-off of breadth for thickness, and why it may be fruitful. If each datapoint were a core sample drilled into the milieu under study, drilling deeper means that we get a more complete grasp of the complex interactions that can occur between different layers of the ground under observation. Assuming that multiplying the drillings will not significantly increase insights beyond a certain number of them – what is called 'saturation' in qualitative research (Bowen, 2008), then the lack of territorial representativeness that numerous ground samples would offer may be compensated by the deeper insights obtained from drilling deeper at fewer places.

In this chapter, we argue that qualitative methods to study uses of social media can gain from thickening data collected in social media. We explain this approach in the following section while situating it among other methodologies. The third section proposes strategies to achieve trace data thickening when conducting qualitative research on social media uses. The fourth section illustrates these strategies by presenting an overview of three case studies conducted by the authors. In the last section, we summarize the benefits of thickening strategies for qualitative inquiry and underline their complementarity with other approaches to social media research.

WHAT IS 'THICK' DATA?

The term 'thick data' seems to have emerged in the literature around the 1990s, probably as the ideas of cultural anthropologist Clifford Geertz were gaining influence within the field of ethnography and other qualitative research methods. 'Thick data' are associated with ethnographical work that produces detailed and dense descriptions of the cultural practices under study (Geertz, 1973). In an introduction to the case study approach, Robert Stake refers to Geertz when pointing out that 'case study data have been called "thick data", not necessarily stacked high, but "thick like spaghetti", highly interconnected' (Stake, 1985: 279). A decade later, Madeleine Leininger observes that 'in ethnography […], one often refers to "thick" or "in-depth" data' and that 'in grounded theory, the term may be "dense" data, which has a similar meaning to thick data' (Leininger, 1994: 104). We might add that the term resonates with another one: 'rich data', used by Howard Becker (1970) to refer to dense, highly textured and contextualized sociological data. In their reflections on the validity of qualitative research, Onwuegbuzie and Leech note that 'an important way of providing credibility of findings is by collecting rich and thick data, which correspond to data that are detailed and complete enough to maximize ability to find meaning' (2007: 244).

More recently, Tricia Wang has used the term 'thick data' – with 'a nod to Clifford Geertz' (Wang, 2013, 2016) – in her critique of the unbounded enthusiasm for Big Data research. In her perspective, the term encapsulates the enduring relevance of qualitative, ethnographic approaches in an 'Era of Big Data' (Wang, 2016: online). 'Thick data', she contends, 'is the opposite of Big Data'; 'It's the sticky stuff that's difficult to quantify' – 'emotions, stories', worldviews – that get stripped through the processes of 'normalizing, standardizing, defining [and] clustering' that make massive datasets analyzable by computers (Wang, 2016: online). As Wang puts it, thick data may be small in terms of sample size, but it offers 'an incredible depth of meanings and stories'.

Our thick data approach to social media research relates to virtual ethnography and netnography (Hine, 2000, 2015; Kozinets, 2010). These approaches typically include a broad spectrum of methods inspired by the fundamental principle that methods should co-evolve with their objects of study and continuously adapt to their fields. These methods produce large sets of qualitative data in different forms: field notes, interview transcripts, and a deep understanding of the culture under study, its language, rituals, and symbols.

By putting forth the notion of *thick* data, we want to articulate an alternative to Big Data approaches, at different levels. The first difference can be expressed in terms of scale, by turning to 'small data'. By small data we mean a dataset composed of a relatively small collection of datapoints or cases, so that their analysis can be performed single-handedly via human coding and with little algorithmic assistance, in contrast to Big Data strategies where computational support is required. Of course, just like 'big' in 'Big Data', a 'small N' is a fuzzy notion that may mean different things depending on the nature of datapoints. For instance, over a hundred participants, a corpus of semi-structured interviews is generally deemed large, while a hundred of 140-character messages will be considered a small sample. Smallness therefore needs to be appreciated in relation to the idea of manageability, which itself implicitly refers to the amount of human work, and time, needed to achieve the analysis. It is also influenced by accepted standards of statistical representativeness in positivist epistemologies. For instance, if a social network site has a population of hundreds of million users, a sample of a few hundreds of them will generally be considered too small to be considered statistically relevant.[3] In sum, small data is *too small* to be representative in a statistical sense, and *small enough* to be processed by a small team of human analysts in order to produce an exhaustive representation of a situated phenomenon.

Another way thick data differs from Big Data is by the research questions it affords. Where Big Data is relevant to investigate connections among users, clusters, and large-scale trends, thick data aims to capture the specificity of these uses, their motives and what they mean for the subjects. As Alice Marwick puts it:

> Identifying large-scale patterns can be useful, but it can also overlook *how* people do things with Twitter, *why* they do them, and how they *understand* them. Quantitative studies often determine connections and networks, and interpret them 'objectively' *ex post facto*, based on statistics and numbers. Instead, qualitative research seeks to understand meaning-making, placing technology use into specific social contexts, places, and times. (2013: 119, author's emphasis)

Just like any data, 'big' and 'thick' data are constructed: each form of data enables certain types of analysis, and limits others (Gitelman and Jackson, 2013). *Thickening* data refers to one aspect of this construction process, which is supplementing data with richly textured information or, in other words, *adding layers of thickness* to them. One could see thick data as onion-structured. It is 'coated' with several layers of rich metadata – in the literal sense of *data on data*. Like in our example of the ground made of superposed layers of matter, each layer has its individuality, but it interacts with surrounding layers, forming an organic whole. Instead of points, thick data are whole little structured worlds. Added at different times through the research process, multiple layers – of description, historical and social context, cultural meaning... – contribute to data thickness, but each layer is itself 'thick' in that it is textured in complex ways and does not easily lend itself to separation into discrete, computable elements. Hence the notion of stickiness and the comparison with spaghetti evoked above.

The process of 'thickening' data is in line with the interpretive/constructivist paradigm of qualitative inquiry, which recognizes that a social phenomenon can only be understood 1) in context; 2) through fine-grained accounts; 3) in light of the meaning attributed by actors to their own actions (Geertz, 1973; Lincoln and Guba, 1985; Schütz, 1967). Drawing on this idea we suggest a simple three-layer model of data thickening.[4] When undertaking a qualitative social media research based on a small dataset, the *first layer* consists of contextual information. The researcher seeks to understand the circumstances in which the online practice emerged as well as the technical affordances and cultural conventions shaping it (Hine, 2015). A *second layer* is added by enriching it with 'thick descriptions' of the practices under study. Such descriptions can be produced through an active engagement with the field of inquiry and the data itself. As any 'social products', the digital practices under study cannot be understood independently form the multiple perspectives of the actors and meaning-making processes (boyd and Crawford, 2012). Therefore, the researcher should add a *third layer* capturing users' experiences and the meaning they attribute to them. The content of this layer is produced through direct interactions with the subjects whose practices are the object of study, in an effort to make explicit their understanding of what they do online and the value they attach to it.[5]

Within these three main layers – contextualization, description, signification, sub-layers can be distinguished in order to meet specific research objectives. They can also lead to different data collection points and analysis methods. As an example, a researcher focusing on the presentation of the self could enrich the second layer by adding details about the visual organization of online profiles, or by providing a semiotic analysis of users' pictures (Hand, this volume). If a corpus of online publications constitutes the main dataset, collecting comments upon them and analyzing them may contribute to thicken the third layer by uncovering other social meanings attributed to these publications.

As the reader may have noted, we do not consider data as neutral or ready-made entities. We should be aware of the frames that, as situated scholars, we use to construct data (Markham, 2013). To put it another way, data are not just sitting there waiting to be gathered and consumed by researchers (Gitelman and Jackson, 2013), nor are they self-explanatory. Rather, data 'should be cooked with care' (Bowker, 2005: 183–184), that is, trimmed, prepared and dressed before they can be useful and enlightening. With such a prospect in mind, thickening data can be seen as a particular form of 'data cookery' besides others (formatting, labelling, standardization…). But this way of cooking data takes special care to respect the highly situated nature of qualitative data, by coating it with as much as possible of the field from which it originates, in its many dimensions.

HOW TO THICKEN TRACE DATA?

Rather than a general method, we propose three main strategies to thicken trace data when conducting qualitative social media research. These strategies are adaptable, may be mixed, and can be used when conducting studies on various platforms like blogs, wikis, Twitter, or Facebook, and for different uses on this kind of digital environment. They are not limitative and we expect that researchers will propose many other ways to thicken their trace data in the same methodological spirit that we intend to outline here.

The first strategy is the trace interview. Trace interviews are interviews in which users reflect on their own digital traces, therefore providing a metadiscourse about them. In a sense, they are a form of co-analysis of trace data by the researcher and the subject whose traces are examined. They come in different forms and shapes. For instance, Dubois and Ford (2015) have used a two-step protocol, where the participant's trace data is first captured and quantitatively processed in order to generate visualizations which are then presented to the interviewee for them to comment on. This hybrid approach is interesting in that it is an integration of Big Data tools within a qualitative research design. However, with this method, traces are for the most part not directly discussed with the participant. Visualizations may be difficult to interpret by interviewees and they steer attention to specific aspects while overlooking others; however, they are useful to 'kick off' the interview (Dubois and Ford, 2015). A variant is the use of a 'dashboard' presenting statistics of a user's social media account (e.g. Twitonomy). A different approach consists of examining a selection of actual traces with the interviewee. It requires a carefully reasoned selection method in order to prevent the interview from being excessively lengthy. The next section will present an instantiation of this approach.

The second strategy is based on a manual collection of digital traces, particularly messages, images, and other kinds of content posted by social media users. This approach is particularly fruitful when the boundaries of the 'field' are fuzzy, fluid and situated. Researchers can face this situation when their study is not circumscribed to a well-defined community, or if data search criteria cannot be predefined around a specific sociodemographic profile, subject matter, or event. In such cases it is impossible to use text mining functionalities to reach a moving target that cannot be delineated in advance. These challenges call for a flexible approach by which a corpus is built through serendipity and bricolage. As an additional benefit, manual data collection encourages exploration and fosters greater familiarity with the traces in their 'native' format, as they are envisioned by social media users. The second case study will show how this approach can be effective in thickening data.

The third strategy draws from ethnographic principles[6] and is based on long-term observation of the online phenomenon, jointly with an agility in following users from one platform to another (from Twitter to blogs, from blogs to Facebook, etc.). Ethnographers would stay on the field for a long period of time in order to collect a vast amount of data about the language, culture, rituals, symbols and values of the community. This third strategy would inform researchers about users' point of view, and immersion with them over months or even years would significantly contribute to this understanding. The agility component becomes an important aspect if the researcher wants to be able to follow users online. They quite often communicate in a transplatform fashion (Millette, 2013), tweeting about a blogpost they made, commenting on Facebook about news they read elsewhere. Agility implies an ability to move quickly and to be flexible in following users as they jump from platform to platform, so that a researcher focusing on Twitter may end up gathering data in blogs and Instagram, in addition to the main research site. This is in line with the principles of 'connective ethnography' (Hine, 2007). We will see in the third case study how this ethnographic influence can be translated into a thickening data strategy when studying an online group of users.

CASE STUDIES

The authors of this chapter have experimented with qualitative methods to develop innovative strategies to study social media uses. Each case study illustrates one of the thickening strategies that were applied on a small-N study in recent research.

Case 1: A Commented Visit of Facebook Users' Activity Logs

The first case combines in-depth interviews with content analysis, using a special type of trace interview based on the interviewers' active exploration of the participant's traces of activity on social media. The aim of the study was to better understand the part played by social media in the circulation of information around a major public issue, namely the massive student protests that soared in 2012 in Quebec in response to the provincial government's decision to steeply increase tuition fees. Conducted by Gallant, Latzko-Toth and Pastinelli (2015), the study sought to understand to what extent young adults had used Facebook to get informed, to have conversations, and to form their opinions on the student strike and related issues.

Since the study started over a year after the events took place, the research team had to devise a way to observe Facebook uses in an asynchronous way. The first step was to construct a sample of 30 young adults (aged 18–25 at the beginning of the crisis), providing an equal representation of key demographic characteristics (sex, region, student and non-student status, political orientation). While the typical face-to-face interview could provide background information on participants' media usage as well as insights on their experiences with social media during the events, it was not expected to yield a sufficiently faithful and detailed account of their actual daily practices. This is why researchers complemented a conventional semi-structured interview with an analysis of participants' digital traces as part of a trace interview protocol.

Rather than using a computer script requiring participants to provide their Facebook account log on information, the researchers took advantage of the 'activity log' feature of the platform, which keeps track of every single action of the user. The activity log is accessible to the user only, but instead of capturing these 'traces of activity' in bulk, the research team opted for a *data exploration* approach. It consists in a 'commented visit' of the activity log with the user around preselected dates.[7] Research assistants conducted the interviews and the exploration of the traces.[8] Sitting next to the participant, they would open the participant's Facebook activity log and systematically 'visit' items appearing under the specified dates. By clicking on the hyperlink appearing on the brief description of each activity, the interviewer could open the actual content – a 'status', a user-generated picture, or a media content – and see who liked it, who commented on it, etc. Often, the mere view of the trace prompted a comment, sometimes an emotional reaction, and the interviewee would tell a story related to the context of production or posting of the content (depending on its nature), or about the relationship with other users.

It was decided to limit the exploration to a set of predefined periods of two to three days each, the same for all participants. Some dates corresponded to key events and turns in the social and political crisis, while others (e.g. before and after the crisis) served as reference points allowing to check whether practices were stable or had evolved through the one-year time-span covered by the study. Guidelines were provided to interviewers in case they would find no traces or if traces were too abundant at the specified dates. If no activity was found at the specified date, the investigator would jump to the first 'active' day. If there was too much activity, the interviewer would sample it, guided by input from the user – with a focus on items that appeared most significant. This 'commented visit' was video-recorded using a dynamic screen capture software. The program used (Camtasia) produces a high-resolution video file and captures ambient sound as well. This allowed researchers to perform a *post hoc* content analysis of the digital traces – about 3,700 were captured on the screenshots – informed by the participants' oral comments about the contents shown on the screen.

This collection method showed two advantages. First, it effectively *reduced* the amount of traces collected, making the dataset 'human-codable', while maximizing the signal/noise ratio. Second, it enlightened captured traces with insights that only the user who generated them could provide Why was a content shared or 'liked'? Who were the people appearing in it or commenting on it? What kind of relationships existed between them? Why was it humorous? This was particularly helpful to answer some research questions, notably whether sharing or 'liking' content was reflecting political views of participants, or if they would engage in political discussions with strangers through Facebook.

In short, the 'commented visit' approach is a data collection and thickening strategy involving a selective exploration and capture of social media traces in their original setting, and in presence of the person who produced them. The concomitant dialogue between the interviewer and the participant about the traces is what constitutes the material which will thicken the data with layers of context, description and meaning. Overall, collecting digital traces *in context* and with interpretive inputs from the subjects proved very insightful. It revealed aspects not covered by the conventional part of the interview and highlighted a contrast between what participants *reported* and their *actual practices* as recorded in the logs (e.g. sharing/liking patterns, and social network composition).

Case 2: Construction of the Field Site through a Manual Data Collection Approach

This case is based on an ongoing research project focusing on an emergent online practice referred to as 'working out loud' (Bonneau and Sergi, 2015; Sergi and Bonneau, 2015), which can be described as a process of continuously narrating the work during the course of its realization. When 'working out loud', workers talk about how they go about their tasks at hand and share their results as they are being produced, instead of waiting until a final deliverable is ready to publish to a broader audience. What is unusual about this narration of work is that it takes place on social media, in a very public fashion.

While most researchers interested in microblogging practices at work have focused on enterprise social networking sites (SNSs) aimed at an internal audience (DiMicco et al., 2008; Zhang et al., 2010), the researchers investigate working out loud by starting directly from Twitter, rather than stemming from the context of a particular organization.

Their objective was to reflect on what these tweets accomplish, for the persons who do work out loud on Twitter and to document, empirically, the variety of forms that it can take. The researchers posited that the working out loud phenomenon is a practice (Nicolini, 2012) marked by diversity in its manifestations. In other words, that it can be practiced in many ways, producing a variety of effects. This plurality can be explained by the fact that working out loud is mainly informal, and does not correspond to any organizational requirement. Furthermore, working out loud can be practiced by any worker, employee or professional, in virtually any field of activity and in a wide range of settings, from temporary self-employment in a one-person business to being a permanent employee in a transnational firm. The only condition necessary to be working out loud, in the sense that we explore here, is to be using Twitter to convey, in the form of tweets, comments, observations and material related to the daily experience and processes of work. In this context, data collection cannot be circumscribed to specific organizations where it is encouraged by the employer, nor limited *a priori* to one professional community where working out loud would already be quite common.

Such open-endedness poses methodological challenges. While most social studies of Twitter practices focus on individuals and/or collectives sharing an interest (like the French-speaking minorities in the following case study) or auto-organized around an event (such as the student strike described in the previous case), the content of the working out loud related tweets is as diverse as work practices themselves. This means that text mining functionalities cannot be used to collect data, simply because it is impossible to predefine search queries using semantic or narrative patterns, nor specific keywords or hashtags. This is why a manual data collection strategy inspired by online ethnography was adopted (Hine, 2015) to build the corpus through serendipity and bricolage. On an operational level, the researchers' Twitter accounts were used to immerse in the setting of the practice. The initial tweets were identified by following users who were already part of the researchers' network (mainly scholars, journalists and knowledge workers) and by selecting tweets that corresponded to the definition of working out loud, that is: any tweet narrating the work as it is being done, spontaneously published by any worker or professional that can take the form of observation, description, questioning, reflection or exclamation. The tweet can be directed (or not) to other people and can include pictures, videos and/or links to external web pages or online documents (Sergi and Bonneau, 2015).

This definition is the main element that guided the researchers through the construction of the field. It is voluntarily inclusive to take account of a wide spectrum of work-related tweets, but at the same time, it excludes tweets consisting of content curation (e.g. selecting and sharing existing content, even if it is work-related) and promotion of finalized realization (for instance, journalists or scholars referring to their latest publications).

In order to collect WOL tweets in other professional areas, the researchers also performed queries on Twitter's internal search engine based on intuitions made by asking themselves: 'Who would share their work and what would they say to do it?' Using a snowball sampling approach, new users were found through their discussions and retweets. This data collection has been initiated in February 2014 and is still in progress. So far, a preliminary corpus of 200 public tweets in English and French has been collected and analyzed. All the tweets collected were documented in a log file, along with their date of publication, URL, user's professional status (if publicly available) and details about how we found them. The recording of the tweet's URL allows the researchers to retrieve them again a month later in order to capture discussions that followed their original publication. The log file also includes field notes, where researchers' impressions were recorded, along with provisional thoughts about what these observations may mean and ideas about what to look at next (Hine, 2015). The researchers relied on these metadata to build detailed accounts of each trace collected (2nd layer: description).

This method allows for the discovery of unpredictable events along the way. For instance, the researchers found that dedicated hashtags were adopted by some professionals (e.g. #showyourwork, #shareyourwork, #WOL, #WOLWeek) following the unexpected publication of books and articles on the topic of working out loud. The practice also started to get coverage from professional blogs and mainstream media, which drew the researchers' attention to users in unexpected domains, such as farming. The researchers documented these new practices and monitored the corresponding hashtags closely, while not limiting their selection to tweets found through those means. By examining the users' profile and their previous tweets, the researchers were able to include new contexts in which different types of working out loud practices unfold (1st layer: contextualization). Even if Twitter users do not need to pre-define their recipients, other users who are interested by the same topic can respond. The examination of such responses allowed the researchers to witness the potential of working out loud practices for creating new relationships, sharing knowledge and developing collaborations.

The thematic codification of the tweets allowed the identification of six distinct forms of practices reflected their nature and outcomes (see Sergi and Bonneau, 2015). In a following phase, trace interviews will be conducted (similar to those described in the first case) with users that were part of the initial corpus. This will add thickness to the data by discussing these digital practices retrospectively with the subjects and will provide a space for interpretations to be checked (3rd layer: significations).

In sum, such manual data collection strategy has proven beneficial to enhance the depth of trace data, by allowing the researchers to document their context of production, to identify new areas of interest and to make sense of the emerging patterns.

Case 3: Long-term Observation and Transplatform Agility

In this last case study, Millette (2015) analyzed a social minority's political uses and strategies of visibility involving social media. Users were selected among a geographically scattered group of social media users in Canada: francophone minorities located in various areas throughout the country. These minorities are distinct from the majority of English-speaking citizens in terms of culture and language, and also in terms of size, demographic profile, historical and symbolic heritage. The research focused on French-speaking *minorities* living outside Quebec; because Quebec is the only officially French-speaking province, francophones constitute the majority there, and were thus excluded. French–Canadians outside Quebec represent a bit less than a million people. Because of their varying demographic realities and social media adoption, and of a lack of recent data on social media uses in French–Canadian minorities, the researcher had to start with preliminary questions: who are the French–Canadian users? Which platforms do they use? Why and how do they use these? What do they talk about? Ultimately, this research sought to provide a better understanding of the potential of social media uses for citizenship and political visibility in an English-dominant media environment.

Four months of online observation on different platforms online (namely Facebook, Twitter, and a dozen of blogs and forums) as well as preliminary interviews with community leaders from grassroots organizations led the researcher to identify Twitter as the main locus of French–Canadian political uses online. While Twitter was selected as the main research field, the researcher decided to keep observing other platforms, mainly Facebook, and two online webzines. This decision was based on the preliminary observation that some of the communications overflowed Twitter to be pursued elsewhere, in a very embedded and organic way (e.g. through an URL in a tweet, linking to a detailed blogpost written by the author of the tweet). In order to constitute the first layer of data thickness (contextualization), an agile observation of online uses was needed.

The online observation spanned over more than 2.5 years. In the meantime, to get a more systematic sense of the activities in the francophone Twittersphere (i.e. what was being discussed, and in which terms, by whom, and from what locations), the researcher performed data mining from Twitter, targeting selected words, accounts, and hashtags. This technique was inspired by Big Data strategies, but because of the scattered nature of the minorities, the sample collected was small compared with the massive amounts of tweets usually gathered through data mining. A total of 8,764 tweets were collected over four months of digging. The researcher manually coded these tweets and identified key actors she wanted to get in touch with. This led to the last phase of data collection, where she travelled to nine different cities to conduct in-depth semi-structured interviews with 25 users.

To stay abreast of developments in the French–Canadian twittersphere, the researcher maintained an online involvement on an almost daily basis for the whole duration of the research (2.5 years). As an example, she made a private list of Twitter users she would consult every morning, paying attention to emerging or persisting political topics, new hashtags, and even new users being vocal about French–Canadian politics. Agility to extend observation from Twitter to other platforms was important to gather a detailed view on what was going on. This exercise would sometimes be as easy as to follow a hyperlink included in a tweet, or it could involve looking up a username in Google in order to identify his or her other online presences, comments on blogs or forums, and so on.

Cumulating different data collection methods contributed to the scientific validity of this research. Long-term commitment and agility in following users outside the main research site was key to develop a deep understanding of social media uses by French–Canadian minorities. For instance, this strategy allowed the researcher to witness fluctuations in the use of hashtags and the emergence of new ones (Rocheleau and Millette, 2015). She saw heavy users in Alberta and Ontario asking their peers from other provinces to develop their own hashtags in order to structure the online communication better. As #frcan got established as the main tag (meta-hashtag) to identify countrywide French–Canadian issues, provinces' specific hashtags emerged for more local topics, such as #skfr (for French Saskatchewan), #cbfr (for French British-Columbia), and so on. She also followed all the online conversations and comments about a new federal program for French minorities called 'Roadmap for Canada's Official Languages 2013–2018'. This program was heavily discussed online under the hashtag #ollo (for official languages – *langues officielles*). Finally, she observed the rise and decline of a group of young franco-activists called *TaGueule!* (Millette, 2014). This group, whose name means 'shut up' in French, was very active on Twitter and Facebook, yet its main online presence was a well-fed webzine where the users were posting strong, often ironic statements addressing French–Canadian identity, cultural and political challenges. All those activities, although not directly related to the core of the research, contributed to thicken the data by educating the researcher about both the context and the meaning of the social media uses under study.

In this case study, the thickening process took shape in a subtle way, through long-term engagement alongside with agile, fluid observation: both aspects were instrumental in 'cooking' data, coding them, and interpreting them. Through the agile transplatform observation of users on their blogs, Facebook pages, webzine posts, and tweets, the researcher developed a fine-grained understanding of their activities, news, local issues, etc. It highly contributed to thicken the second layer of data, where the researcher could describe various contextual dimensions of the French–Canadian uses. The interviews fed the thickening of their semantic dimension, thus contributing to thickening the third layer by capturing the meaning attached to the tweeting practices. Above all, the long-term observation was crucial, because being familiar with certain past events and debates increased the researcher's capacities in two ways. First, she used this knowledge of the field when coding the tweets and interviews to grasp ironic strategies, cynicism, and aspirations, which could have been missed otherwise. Second, it contributed to her legitimacy when she interacted with users. Consequently, participants engaged more genuinely during the interviews, revealing a lot about their values, political beliefs, and motivations. In the end, long-term observation contributed to thickening the data of every layers: both contextualization, description, and signification gained from this strategy.

Another important aspect of this research is the researchers' decision to *manually code* the traces in order to leverage the richness of the content and the format of collected messages. It does not represent a thickening strategy *per se*, but it was a coherent decision regarding all the time invested into getting to know the field. It was also the best way to capitalize on the agile observation of the online French–Canadian transplatform uses to shed light on the Twitter ones. Consequently, manual coding contributed to thicken both layers 2 and 3 (context and meaning), as it was informed by the researcher's knowledge gathered along the data collection process.

Inspired by netnography and qualitative research canons, this third thickening strategy based on long-term and agile observation may not be sophisticated in terms of technology or devices, but it does require a dedicated work routine to be maintained for a long period of time. As demonstrated with this case study, when conducted rigorously, such strategy does generate thicker data. By virtue of its low-key aspect, this strategy can be easily adapted to many different research agendas and settings, and it should be considered by young researchers and researchers who have little technological resources as an effective way to make sense social media qualitative research.

CONCLUSION

Several thoughtful critiques of Big Data methodologies have been articulated in the field of social media research, pointing toward their pitfalls and limitations (see boyd and Crawford, 2012; Ekbia et al., 2015; Tufekci, 2014). Beyond the mere affirmation that small data research conducted by a single or a handful of human analysts is not *obsolete* in an era where the assistance of computers and digital infrastructures has opened unprecedented opportunities for massive data analysis, the aim of this chapter was to offer concrete qualitative research strategies to make small datasets 'thick' and therefore insightful.

We outlined a layer-oriented approach to thickening trace data, where we distinguished between three 'layers of thickness': description, contextualization, and significations. We then proceeded to describe three thickening strategies and how they contributed to the three layers. It should be noted that each strategy was developed for a specific research project. We think that they are adaptable to other projects, but it is important to see them first and foremost as examples of the many ways by which qualitative researchers can creatively develop their own thickening strategies for small datasets. These strategies can also be combined, as they can complete each other in contributing to thicken the three layers in different respects. Adding multiple layers of information to trace data using different thickening approaches helps achieving a form of 'triangulation' increasing trustworthiness of researchers' analyses and conclusions (Erlandson et al., 1993; Guba, 1981).

The commented visit of user traces is more than a data collection method. To some extent, like other types of trace interviews, it constitutes a form of co-analysis of data between researchers and participants (Dubois and Ford, 2015: 2073). Besides contributing to thicken the traces with insights from the participants themselves, it comes with an *ethical* benefit. Contrary to bulk capture of personal digital traces, the selective, progressive, and joint exploration of these traces made participants fully aware of what they shared with researchers, therefore increasing trust and making the notion of 'informed consent' more meaningful. A participant may have even decided not to 'expand' a trace of activity to show the actual content, or specifically ask that a trace should be removed from the dataset while it is shown to the investigator. In practice, it didn't happen. Instead of being reluctant to letting researchers navigate into their Facebook account, participants enjoyed the commented visit of their activity log, thereby confirming that this approach is not perceived as more intrusive than a typical interview.

In the second case, what would seem at first like a last resort solution (e.g 'going manual') was used as an opportunity to gather valuable informations. The act of manually collecting and analyzing a modest corpus of tweets produced contextual insights that would have been difficult to interpret at the large scale of Big Data research projects. While an automated data collection would have forced the researchers to circumscribe their corpus around specific criteria (e.g. keywords, hashtags, user profiles, professional domain, timeframe, geography, etc.), the manual process allowed them to consider tweets that did not seem work-related at first. Such manual processing constitutes a relevant method for 'mapping unknown territory' and 'reveal[ing] the unexpected', a typical affordance of thick data (Wang, 2013). It may also lead to formulating research intuitions that could hardly emerge through a quantitative analysis of a large dataset – for instance, the role that Twitter can play in workers' daily lives.

In the third case, it would have been impossible to acknowledge hashtags strategies, ironic messages, and on-going issues of French minorities by quantitative methods. Because of their small number, French–Canadian minorities can easily fall off the charts and global patterns. Furthermore, qualitative methods were necessary to grasp these users' point of view that is embodied in ways that can hardly be captured by quantitative approaches (Marwick, 2013) – like rhetorical tropes, humour and satire, things that are quite common in Twitter and very grounded in culture. More fundamentally, the third thickening strategy (long-term, agile observation) contributed to each of the three layers of information around collected traces, thereby enhancing the researchers' capacity to make sense of the data and to produce trustworthy analyses based on them.

While each of the three strategies has its own unique characteristics, one can identify three common features that might be used as guidelines when it comes to figuring out a trace data thickening strategy: 1) *Contextuality* – traces are examined in context, and more specifically, in their original setting. In cases 1 and 2 (and also, in part, in case 3), social media contents are seen as users see them, as opposed to data that would be extracted in bulk from an application programming interface (API). This allows for a 'naturalistic' observation of digital traces, providing information that might be lost in the decontextualization of traces resulting from the extraction process – for example, spatial organization of content, proximity with other contents, and so on. 2) *Temporality* – A slow collection process (cases 1 and 2) and long-time engagement with the field (case 3) foster immersion *with* and *in* data, which are key in developing a fine-grained understanding and insightful interpretations of them. Slowness seems an important factor in thickening data. In that regard, thick data approaches are in line with the principles of 'slow science'.[9] 3) *Flexibility* in sample construction. While it is most stressed in case 3, this flexibility in picking relevant data is also present in the first two strategies. In case 2, selection criteria are not set in advance, but rather continuously revised (for instance, by including newly discovered hashtags). In case 1, dates used to pick activity traces are flexible in case no activity is found at these dates. And interviewers have some latitude in selecting traces when they are too plentiful. Together, preserved contextuality, extended time, and flexibility contribute to increase the relevance, diversity and density of information elements aggregated around traces that constitute the primary data.

Data thickening is essentially a relational process: it happens when connections are made with other data sources. Consequently, it is not unidirectionally oriented. In the process of thickening trace data, the thickening occurs not only on the side of digital traces, but it also happens with other qualitative data collected along the way. For instance, in cases 1 and 3, interview data was as much 'thickened' by their references to participants' traces as the traces where thickened by insights stemming from the interviews. Thus, thickening methods should be seen as research strategies whose scope crosses the boundaries between 'small' and 'big' datasets, and between 'trace data' and data of other origins.

Our intent in this chapter was not to contend that small samples are always the best choice in social media research. Small data projects cannot lead to the kind of robust, generalizable results that some large-scale, quantitative studies may yield. Nor should thickening strategies be conceived of as a 'cure' to the inherent limitations of 'small data' methodologies. Instead, we think that data thickening strategies can be highly beneficial to Big Data research designs too, which argues for increased collaboration between the two types of research (Ford, 2014; Lewis et al., 2013); for instance, in-depth interviews can help shed light on trends and findings based on Big Data studies (Quan-Haase et al., 2015). These benefits can be highlighted by imagining what would have been lost without them. Life stories, actual experiences and motivations, to name a few, cannot be uncovered by online behavioral data traces or metrics alone. These strategies can also be used to assess what is missing from the data traces. For instance, user activities that do *not* leave any trace – like the mere view and reading of a content on a Facebook or Twitter news feed.

NOTES

1. This chapter stems from a panel presented at the 5th Social Media and Society conference held in Toronto in July 2015. The authors are grateful to organizers and participants for providing them with this unique opportunity to exchange with other social media researchers on this topic. They would like to thank the two anonymous reviewers, whose comments and suggestions were helpful in clarifying our ideas and pushing them further. First author also thanks Madeleine Pastinelli and Nicole Gallant for fruitful discussions that helped outline the ideas that inspired both the panel and the core arguments of this chapter. Second author also thanks Viviane Sergi for her essential contribution to the development and refinement of the strategy presented in the second case study.
2. For instance, the Computing Research Association, which gathers both academic and entities, advocates for an increase of the budget of the National Science Foundation (NSF) in order for it to fund research initiatives in Big Data science, based on the joint benefits expected for 'commerce, science and society' (Bryant et al., 2008). See also Bollier (2010: 20–22).
3. Anyhow, the ultimate goal of researches based on small samples is not to produce generalizable results, but rather to understand complex human issues.
4. We are aware that this model can be complexified and refined. More layers can be considered and they may be ordered differently. Our point here is not to offer a definitive, exhaustive model, but rather to insist on the process of adding 'layers of thickness' to data.
5. This echoes 'member checking' procedures by which researchers validate their interpretations of data with participants (Lincoln and Guba, 1985).
6. See, for instance, Lincoln and Guba's (1985) proposed techniques of 'prolonged engagement' and 'persistent observation' to achieve trustworthiness in qualitative research. On flexibility in defining boundaries of the field, see Green (1999) and Wittel (2000).
7. At the time, Facebook activity log navigation interface allowed a quick jump to a specific month, which was no longer the case at the time this chapter was written.
8. They were trained to follow a precise protocol, which was tested through interview simulations using the team's Facebook accounts. These pre-tests were debriefed with the researchers, which allowed to refine and standardize the exploration technique.
9. The Slow Science Academy has released a 'Slow Science Manifesto' (2010): http://slow-science.org/

REFERENCES

Anderson, C. (2008) 'The end of theory: The data deluge makes the scientific method obsolete', *Wired*, 23 June 2008. (http://www.wired.com/science/discoveries/magazine/16–07/pb_theory)

Becker, H. S. (1970) *Sociological Work: Method and Substance*. New Brunswick, NJ: Transaction Books.

Berry, D. M. (2011) 'The computational turn: Thinking about the digital humanities', *Culture Machine*, 12. (http://www.culturemachine.net/index.php/cm/article/view/440/470)

Bollier, D. (2010) *The Promise and Peril of Big Data*. The Aspen Institute. (http://www.aspeninstitute.org/sites/default/files/content/docs/pubs/The_Promise_and_Peril_of_Big_Data.pdf)

Bonneau, C. and Sergi, V. (2015) 'Travailler à haute voix sur Twitter: raconter son travail pour l'organiser', in *Actes du colloque international Org&Co* (pp. 131–141).

Borgman, C. L. (2015) *Big Data, Little Data, No Data – Scholarship in the Networked World*. Cambridge, MA: MIT Press.

Bowen, G. A. (2008) 'Naturalistic inquiry and the saturation concept: A research note', *Qualitative Research*, 8(1): 137–152.

Bowker, G. C. (2007) 'The Past and the Internet', in J. Karaganis (Ed.), *Structures of Participation in Digital Culture* (pp. 20–36). New York: Social Science Research Council.

Bowker, G. C. (2005) *Memory Practices in the Sciences*. Cambridge, MA: MIT Press.

boyd, d. and Crawford, K. (2012) 'Critical questions for Big Data: Provocations for a cultural, technological and scholarly phenomenon', *Information, Communication & Society*, *15*(5): 662–679.

Brooker, P., Barnett, J., Cribbin, T. and Sharma, S. (2015) 'Have we even solved the first "Big Data challenge?" Practical issues concerning data collection and visual representation for social media analytics', in Snee, H., Hine, C., Morey, Y., Roberts, S., & Watson, H. (eds.), *Digital Methods for Social Science: An Interdisciplinary Guide to Research Innovation* (pp. 34–50). Basingstoke, UK: Palgrave Macmillan.

Bryant, R. E., Katz, R. H. and Lazowska, E. D. (2008) 'Big-Data Computing: Creating revolutionary breakthroughs in commerce, science, and society'. A white Paper prepared for the Computing Community Consortium committee of the Computing Research Association. (http://cra.org/ccc/resources/ccc-led-whitepapers)

Denzin, N. K. and Lincoln, Y. S. (1994) *The Handbook of Qualitative Research*. Thousand Oaks, CA: Sage.

DiMicco, J., Millen, D. R., Geyer, W., Dugan, C., Brownholtz, B. and Muller, M. (2008) 'Motivations for Social Networking at Work', in *CSCW 08: Proceedings of the 2008 ACM Conference on Computer-Supported Cooperative Work* (pp. 711–720).

Dubois, E. and Ford, H. (2015) 'Trace interviews: An actor-centered approach', *International Journal of Communication*, *9*(25). 2067–2091.

Ekbia, H., Mattioli, M., Kouper, I., Arave, G., Ghazinejad, A., Bowman, T., Suri, V. R., Tsou, A., Weingart, S. and Sugimoto, C. R. (2015) 'Big Data, Bigger Dilemmas: A Critical Review', *Journal of the Association for Information Science and Technology*, *66*(8): 1523–1545.

Erlandson, D. A., Harris, E. L., Skipper, B. L. and Allen, S. D. (1993) *Doing Naturalistic Inquiry: A Guide to Methods*. London: Sage.

Ford, H. (2014) 'Big Data and Small: Collaborations between Ethnographers and Data Scientists', *Big Data & Society*, *1*(2): 1–3.

Freelon, D. (2014) 'On the Interpretation of Digital Trace Data in Communication and Social Computing Research', *Journal of Broadcasting & Electronic Media*, *58*(1): 59–75.

Gallant, N., Latzko-Toth, G. and Pastinelli, M. (2015) 'Circulation de l'information sur les médias sociaux pendant la grève étudiante de 2012 au Québec'. Research report, Québec: Centre d'études sur les médias. (http://www.cem.ulaval.ca/pdf/Circulation Information.pdf)

Geertz, C. (1973) *Interpretation of Cultures: Selected essays*. New York: Basic Books.

Gitelman, L. and Jackson, V. (2013) 'Introduction', in Gitelman, L. (ed.) *"Raw Data" is an Oxymoron* (pp.1–14). Cambridge, MA: MIT Press.

Green, N. (1999) 'Disrupting the field: Virtual reality technologies and "multisited" ethnographic methods', *American Behavioral Scientist*, *43*(3): 409–421.

Guba, E. G. (1981) 'Criteria for assessing the trustworthiness of naturalistic inquiries', *ECTJ*, *29*(2): 75–91.

Hine, C. (2015) *Ethnography for the Internet: Embedded, Embodied and Everyday*. London: Bloomsbury Publishing.

Hine, C. (2007) 'Connective ethnography for the exploration of e-Science', *Journal of Computer-Mediated Communication*, *12*(2): 618–634.

Hine, C. (2000) *Virtual Ethnography*. Thousand Oaks, CA: Sage Publications.

Howison, J., Wiggins, A. and Crowston, K. (2011) 'Validity issues in the use of social network analysis with digital trace data', *Journal of the Association for Information Systems*, *12*(12). 767–797. (http://aisel.aisnet.org/cgi/viewcontent.cgi?article=1594&context=jais)

Jensen, K. B. (2002) *Handbook of Media and Communications Research: Qualitative and Quantitative Research Methodologies*. London: Routledge.

Kitchin, R. (2014) 'Big Data, new epistemologies and paradigm shifts', *Big Data & Society*, *1*(1): 1–12.

Kozinets, R.V. (2010) *Netnography: Doing Ethnographic Research Online*. London: Sage.

Leininger, M. (1994) 'Evaluation criteria and critique of qualitative research studies', in Morse, J. M. (ed.), *Critical Issues in Qualitative*

Research Methods (pp. 95–115), Thousand Oaks, CA: Sage.

Lewis, S. C., Zamith, R. and Hermida, A. (2013) 'Content analysis in an era of Big Data: A hybrid approach to computational and manual methods', *Journal of Broadcasting & Electronic Media*, 57(1): 34–52.

Lincoln, Y. S. and Guba, E. G. (1985) *Naturalistic Inquiry*. Newbury Park, CA: Sage Publications.

Manovich, L. (2012) 'Trending: The promises and challenges of big social data', in Gold, M. K. (ed.), *Debates in the Digital Humanities* (pp. 460–475), Minneapolis: University of Minnesota Press.

Markham, A. N. (2013) 'Undermining "data": A critical examination of a core term in scientific inquiry', *First Monday*, 18(10). (http://firstmonday.org/article/view/4868/3749)

Marwick, A. (2013) 'Ethnographic and Qualitative Research on Twitter', in Weller, K., Bruns, A., Puschmann, C., Burgess, J. and Mahrt, M. (eds), *Twitter and Society* (pp. 109–122), New York: Peter Lang.

Millette, M. (2015) 'L'usage des médias sociaux dans les luttes pour la visibilité: le cas des minorités francophones au Canada anglais'. PhD dissertation, Université du Québec à Montréal, Montreal (Quebec, Canada).

Millette, M. (2014) 'Contre-public et médias sociaux: le cas du collectif francophone TaGueule! au Canada anglais', in Proulx, S., Garcia, J. L. and Heaton, L. (eds.), *La contribution dans l'univers numérique. Pratiques participatives à l'ère du capitalisme informationnel* (pp. 91–102), Quebec City: Presses de l'Université du Québec.

Millette, M. (2013) 'Pratiques transplateformes et convergence dans les usages des médias sociaux', *Communication et organisation*, (43): 47–58. (http://doi.org/10.4000/communicationorganisation.4116)

Morgan, D. L. (2007) 'Paradigms lost and pragmatism regained: Methodological implications of combining qualitative and quantitative methods', *Journal of Mixed Methods Research*, 1(1): 48–76.

Nicolini, D. (2012) *Practice Theory, Work, and Organization: An Introduction*. Oxford: Oxford University Press.

Onwuegbuzie, A. J. and Leech, N. L. (2007) 'Validity and Qualitative Research: An Oxymoron?', *Quality & Quantity*, 41(2): 233–249.

Quan-Haase, A., Martin, K. and McCay-Peet, L. (2015) 'Networks of digital humanities scholars: The informational and social uses and gratifications of Twitter', *Big Data & Society*, 2(1): 1–12.

Rocheleau, S. and Millette, M. (2015) 'Metahashtag and Tag Co-occurrence: From organization to politics in the French Canadian twittersphere', in Rambukkana, N. (ed.), *Hashtag Publics: The Power and Politics of Discursive Networks* (pp. 243–254), New York: Peter Lang.

Schütz, A. (1967) *The Phenomenology of the Social World*. Evanston, IL: Northwestern University Press.

Sergi, V. and Bonneau, C. (2015) 'When talk is text: The performativity of working out loud on Twitter', in *31st EGOS Colloquium, Subtheme 16: Organization as communication: The performative power of talk*.

Stake, R. (1985) 'Case study', in Nisbet, J., Megarry, J. and Nisbet, S. (eds.), *World Yearbook of Education 1985: Research, Policy and Practice* (pp. 277–285), London: Kogan Page [Republished by Routledge in 2006].

Tufekci, Z. (2014) 'Big Questions for Social Media Big Data: Representativeness, Validity and Other Methodological Pitfalls', in *ICWSM 14: Proceedings of the 8th International AAAI Conference on Weblogs and Social Media*.

Wang, T. (2016, January 20) 'Why Big Data Needs Thick Data', *Ethnography Matters* (Medium channel) (https://medium.com/ethnography-matters/why-big-data-needs-thick-data-b4b3e75e3d7#.y9plmare1)

Wang, T. (2013, May 13) 'Big Data needs Thick Data', *Ethnography Matters* (blog) (http://ethnographymatters.net/2013/05/13/big-data-needs-thick-data)

Wittel, A. (2000) 'Ethnography on the Move: From Field to Net to Internet', *Forum: Qualitative Social Research*, 1(1). (http://nbn-resolving.de/urn:nbn:de:0114-fqs0001213)

Zhang, J., Qu, Y., Cody, J. and Wu, Y. (2010) 'A case study of micro-blogging in the enterprise: use, value, and related issues', in *Proceedings of the 28th international conference on Human factors in computing systems* (pp. 123–132). Atlanta, Georgia, USA: ACM.

Visuality in Social Media: Researching Images, Circulations and Practices

Martin Hand

This chapter identifies key issues in social media research related to broader concerns in visual culture. Visuality in social media is conceptualized as comprising three broad elements, each of which requires methodological negotiation. First, *images* in social media take many forms, and need careful consideration of established approaches in visual culture studies while acknowledging the specific qualities of social media. Second, the *circulation* of visual data in social media destabilizes research objects in ways that challenge visual analyses of textual meaning. Third, while the visualization of social *practices* through social media appears to offer unprecedented access to social life, the detail of such practices often remain obscure if we focus solely on images, however many. Social media researchers need to ask how visual objects are generated and used, and how people make sense of the visual in using social media. Pulling these dimensions apart and then together is difficult. This is the current predicament of visual studies of social media. The example of selfies is used to illustrate these points. Several approaches being used to address these issues are identified, highlighting some continuities of method in social media research, while pointing to some novelties in social media that offer challenges.

INTRODUCTION

Social media have become a significant part of contemporary visual culture (Duggan et al., 2015). In the global north, we now encounter many kinds of visual data for much of our daily lives, such that our interaction with the world is visually shaped. One reason for this is the rapid expansion and proliferation of visual technologies (television, photography, film, web, etc.) that construct particular ways of seeing the world (Rose, 2012, 2014). Social media such as Facebook, Twitter, Instagram, Pinterest,

Snapchat, Vine and others arguably extend and intensify, but also alter, many forms of visuality in ways that directly question existing methods of interpretation. Social media are now fully integrated into social life such that they multiply mediate social life (Hand, 2014a; Marres, 2012). They enable novel ways of organizing sociality while at the same time making social interaction available for established and emerging modes of analysis, most clearly in terms of the *visibility* of social media interactions. A key challenge for visual studies researchers is whether and how to extend existing methodologies to social media forms. Similarly, for non-visual researchers in media and communications, a central question now is how to apply existing methods to the increasingly visual phenomena encountered in and through social media.

There has been relatively little qualitative research in this field. Initial responses to these challenges are taking several directions, focusing on rather different aspects of visual social media. First, there have been studies seeking to understand user behavior (rather than visual content) within explicitly visual social media platforms such as Instagram, identifying key motivations for using these sites among distinct populations using survey methods (e.g. Sheldon and Bryant, 2016). Second, analyses of large data sets comprised of social media data and metadata have traced temporal and spatial patterns of events made visible. This has included the use of Google Street View, sentiment analysis of Twitter data, mapping geo-tagged photos in Flickr, Foursquare check-in data, and so on (Hochman and Schwartz, 2012; Kisilevich et al., 2010; San Pedro and Siersdorfer, 2009). In line with the premise that it is the *volume* of images requiring analysis, many studies here have been quantitative in orientation, seeking to develop algorithms for understanding complex patterns within thousands of images or using the ubiquity of user-generated images in Instagram to visualize the spatiotemporal dynamics of urban events (e.g. the Phototrails.net project). As part of the burgeoning digital humanities and 'big data analytics', these large-scale methodological innovations are often initially descriptive, but provide pertinent avenues for more specific qualitatively orientated research (Bruns and Burgess, 2012; Burgess and Green, 2009). It is not that new modes of quantitative research enabled through 'big' data visualizations replace qualitative data and analysis, but might complement one another or be recombined in interesting and productive ways.

Third, for others, the use of a range of qualitative methods such as in-depth interviewing, discourse and content analysis, has proved particularly useful in *contextualizing* a range of social media data (see boyd and Crawford, 2012; Miller, 2011) and these have the potential for researching the visual specifically.

There are three clear methodological issues regarding images in social media. First, the sheer volume of images present in social media platforms and the increasing rate of upload confront the qualitatively oriented researcher with novel problems of scope, scale and selection. It could be said that the numbers of 'found' images mean we have to abandon any idea of analyzing *individual* ones. Secondly, the production, distribution or 'circulation' of these images through different devices and platforms makes it very difficult to treat them as simply analogous to print images. Third, the alterable and malleable nature of these images raises difficult questions about establishing the contexts of interpretation, leading to the potential obscuring of the social practices of which the images are part.

All of this suggests complex dynamic relationships between the visual, social media, and practice that require careful methodological consideration. On the one hand, this presents new opportunities for drawing upon visual data to enrich our understanding of social media, and on the other hand, it illuminates some key problems in analyzing social media data in general. I suggest these issues are further complicated if we expand our understanding of social media:

- As 'visual phenomena' in their own right
- As the 'means of circulation' for visual objects of all kinds
- As the 'means of visualizing' culture and social life
- As sites for new 'visual practices'
- As diverse contexts for the interpretation of the visual
- As visual modes of participation
- As modes of participatory research.

If we adopt this broad view of visuality in social media there is much scope for 'thickening' our accounts (Latzko-Toth, Bonneau and Millette, Chapter 13, this volume). Such visual overload would seem to offer unprecedented access to social life, given that people often share images of what they are doing, and substantial amounts of this visual data are accessible by researchers. Much of this data is also connected with locational and temporal data (see Klein and Reips, Chapter 25, this volume). There is a seductive pitfall, however, of treating visual phenomena as simply transparent or naturalistic rather than mediated and *ambivalent*, as direct evidence rather than a partial account or construction. Visual phenomena are 'never transparent windows on the world. They interpret the world; they display it in very particular ways; they represent it' (Rose, 2012: 2). This recognition applies to individual and institutional practices of image making and sharing, but also to how particular 'ways of seeing' are socially and historically specific. A lack of recognition of this is evident in some attempts to visualize social media data using new data tools, where the visual form this takes is not subject to critical methodological reflection; for example, in the use of visualization tools for the structuring and analysis of social media data (e.g. *Truthy* for visualizing social media memes, http://truthy.indiana.edu/).

By contrast, in visual culture studies the central question of concern is commonly establishing *meaning*. This is not always treated as something to be gleaned solely from the image itself, but from the inter-textual dimensions of specific images and the social practices of which they are a part, becoming meaningful in viewing and circulation (see Sturken and Cartwright, 2010; Van House, 2011). Intertextuality refers to how the meanings of an image (or text) derive from that image but also from the meanings of other images and texts that might be closely related (a photograph within a particular newspaper text) or in broader cultural practices (a photograph being placed in a family album). Such meanings are made when people look at images, and allow them to be shared in particular ways (e.g. as a gift). The inter-textual visuality of social media allows us to examine broader issues of method, from access, scope and scale to indexicality, authenticity and ethics. These issues will be discussed in more detail later in the chapter.

VISUAL CULTURE AND SOCIAL MEDIA: ISSUES AND APPROACHES

Many of the problems faced by social media researchers – how to assess meaning, how to develop critique, how to identify continuity and discontinuity – are paralleled with those interpreting visual culture (Banks, 2008; Heywood and Sandywell, 2012; Jencks, 1995). In this section, I want to identify what might be novel in social media such that methodological innovation is required.

The scale and distribution dynamics of social media complicate issues of identifying the original and subsequent sources of visual data, which in turn makes it difficult to establish meaning. With this in mind, a useful orientation is Rose's (2012: 19) articulation of the three 'sites' where the meanings of images are made:

1. the site of production, including the technologies, genre conventions, and socioeconomic conditions shaping that production
2. the site of the image itself, including its meanings, its composition, and the effects it is thought to have, and

3 the site of 'being seen' by audiences, including how it is being interpreted and by whom, the range of viewing options, and the ways it is circulated and displayed.

Rose (2012) argues that each of these sites has three *modalities*: technological, compositional, and social. Multimodal research seeks to interpret the visual across these dimensions, but also recognizes that communication is rarely confined to the visual. For example, in interpreting an image embedded within a Tweet, a researcher would seek to analyze the production, composition, and audiencing of the image, but also the textual, visual and classification (#) dimensions of the Tweet. The relative emphasis placed on each of these modalities (e.g. technical, economic or cultural determinism) depends on the theoretical perspective and argument framing the analysis. In referring to this model of 'sites', we can identify ways in which social media might present methodological challenges. I will limit this discussion to images here, rather than video and other visual forms, although there are many similarities at a general level.

Analyzing Images in Social Media

Qualitative research that seeks to identify and interpret the meaning of specific images or sequences of images tends to adopt one or several techniques. First, content analysis – a methodologically explicit way of analyzing texts or images involving quantitative and qualitative procedures (Bell, 2011; Krippendorff, 1980; Mitchell, 2011) – has been a significant technique across disciplines. Qualitative content analysis tends to look for 'latent content' in images that is primarily symbolic, or has underlying meanings that can be systematically coded for (e.g. gender in advertising images). Social researchers usually distinguish between readily available or 'found' visual data (advertising, publically accessible photos, etc.) and visual data produced by the researcher or research subjects within the context of the research. In this latter case, researchers might produce screen capture, stills or video of the activities being researched, or ask research participants to make visual accounts of their practices.

Selection and Classification

In either of these processes, a daunting problem for the social media researcher is how to identify and select images for analysis. There is nothing new about this problem, but social media enables access to billions of images that are at the same time difficult to classify. Even if the researcher limits their scope to taking screen shots of a social media gaming event, these might run into the thousands (see Boellstorff et al., 2012). For qualitative researchers, the identification, selection and organization of visual materials always involve negotiating complex issues of sample, representation, authenticity and 'exhaustiveness'. For example, if we wanted to identify the dominant visual representations of social difference (e.g. race) during a particular event (e.g. protest) across a social media platform (e.g. Twitter), images could be selected through hashtags and coded accordingly. Given the aforementioned issues of scale, researchers have to constrain their analyzes to very discrete geo-temporal frames – tweets within a specific month, linked to a particular location, for example. Often, this will also require the use of the platform's own codes and classifications (e.g. in Flickr, YouTube, Twitter) that then requires researchers to have a robust knowledge of how those classifications will shape their analysis (see Rogers, 2013). A key example of this is the difficulties surrounding hashtag classifications. Researchers seeking to identify the 'right' hashtag to follow an event (e.g. a political demonstration) might select to follow the organizers' classification, or identify emerging hashtags throughout the event. These will be different ways of classifying the boundaries, nature, content and duration of any event, and thus involve crucial negotiations with issues of power and authenticity. Similar issues arise in any classification such as 'trending', or categories such as 'most popular' or 'most viewed' in platforms such as Twitter or Netflix.

Another immediate issue for the researcher is to acknowledge the multiple sources of visual data in social media. Social media can make the source of the still or moving image unclear. Images might be corporately or institutionally produced and regulated, or they might be user-generated, and the distinction between these might be unclear and may change (e.g. images reclassified in Pinterest). Perhaps more significantly, there are platform specific dynamics of making things visible and invisible, of classifying images differently. For users in a site like Flickr, uploaded images can be classified (tagged) and reclassified according to any number of subjective criteria from the ground up (a folksonomy), rather than in a top-down institutional framework. One of the difficulties for the researcher here is the role of largely invisible algorithmic processing in ordering images and thereby constructing a *narrative*. Photographic images are partly made meaningful in relation to sequence (think here of the care in making family albums), and so knowing how and why that sequence has been organized is essential for establishing meaning and making any kind of selection of 'found' images.

A related set of methodological approaches might be semiotics and discourse analysis, focusing on the broader sign systems of which specific images are part (Penn, 2000). As Rose (2012) has discussed, these approaches are not limited to understanding the image itself, but also how it is interpreted by audiences in specific social contexts. Briefly, a semiological approach to images attempts to take them apart and develop a critical analysis of how their meanings are generated. The meaning(s) of any particular image are related to broader systems of meaning (ideology) operating in a society (e.g. Alper, 2014; Ibrahim, 2015). Such systems might be dominant ideological forms of gender, ethnicity and class, examining how specific images (e.g. an advertisement) *construct* social difference in these ways. As advertising and branding have become elements within almost all social media, semiotics can provide resources for 'decoding' these images, and also for looking at how people make use of 'semiotic resources' in participatory social media practices (e.g. visual tropes in Pinterest). Recent research into the popularity of politicians' selfies on Twitter (Farci and Orefice, 2015), and how specific elements in consumer's photos generate 'word-of-mouth' marketing in social media (Farace et al., 2015) have employed combinations of visual and social semiotics, alongside content analysis to 'decode' sequences of images. The visual tropes associated with advertising and marketing are part of a general vernacular in contemporary social media, especially Instagram, making the issues of 'inter-textuality' particularly significant. This has been central to discourse analyses of visual materials, which focus on the sites of images themselves in relation to a broader discursive framing. For example, we might approach the making and sharing of selfies as part of broader discourses of the 'disciplined' female body, the 'makeover', projected 'happiness', or as discursive 'technologies of the self' (Hall, 2015). This would be another way of interpreting the meaning of these images. There are some emerging efforts to automate such analyses, through algorithmic APIs like Immaga.com. Like cultural analytics, these processes aim to categorize images on a large scale, identifying 'context' through matching tags, colour extraction and basic visual characteristics, garnered toward companies understanding of how their brand might be visually managed.

What is a Digital Image?

There is a bewildering array of images in social media, from the banal to the iconic, the corporate to the activist. In tandem with challenges of scale and source, social media researchers have to think about what a visual object in social media actually *is*. There is a basic distinction we can make between those approaches that view images in 'realist' or 'constructionist' terms. In realist terms, images in social media (e.g. photos in an Instagram account) are approached in terms of whether their content accurately corresponds to what it *represents*, allowing the researcher to potentially access and analyze the social world represented (in terms of self-representation, say). In constructionist terms, those images would be approached as partial constructions of a social world (of gender norms, say). These approaches construct different ontologies of the image: on the one hand, the image is an *evidential document* of something else (communities, identities, events), where on the other hand, the image is more like an inter-textual site of discursive *relationships*. Both approaches may treat images as representational or pictorial forms, meaning that images are taken to represent *something*, regardless of whether this is thought to 'mirror' or 'construct' that object.

There is an extensive literature on debates about the question of how differently produced images might have specific qualities and effects. Briefly, analogue and digital images are produced differently, and can be altered and distributed in different ways. To what extent this alters the ways in which they are viewed and interpreted is a matter of considerable debate (see Lister, 2013). In terms of photography, Barthes (1977) showed how the analogue image could have 'indexical' qualities – that it has a 'being thereness' because of the imprint of light – but the notion that this was 'natural' is itself a historically and cultural specific way of thinking about visuality. In mobile cellphone and smartphone photography, often immediately streamed in social media, it would be easy to assume that reality has simply been 'captured' in this way, and can be interpreted on that basis. But it is not only that there will be multiple interpretations of images by different viewers (the sites of the audience), but also that the architecture of social media platforms shapes the possible and *preferred* meanings of images just like any other mode of classification (i.e. in the album, gallery, archive, or database).

Digital images uploaded to social media have several characteristics that make their interpretation arguably more complex than the printed photograph. As Murray (2013: 174) argues, platforms such as Flickr encourage 'transience' rather than permanence. This is significant for the relationship between self-presentation and photography, where 'there is an accepted temporariness to the sense of a public-presented self' (Murray, 2013: 176). This does not mean that self-presentation in social media has *no* coherence or autobiographical narrative, but rather that such narratives embrace the speed and immediacy of social media and need to be understood in that light. In methodological terms, this temporariness encourages 'presentism', as images need to be contextualized within the 'feed' or webpage 'in the moment'. Archivists, for example, are finding this problem continually as they try to transform digital visual objects into 'documents' (Hand, 2008). The same problem arises for the qualitative researcher, simply trying to make sense of single images in a dynamic stream. It is arguable that a methodological focus on single images may miss important dynamics of visual social media, especially regarding *fluid* inter-textual meanings.

As Lister has argued, all still photography was intertextual anyhow; the photographic image has always been inserted within other contexts that have given it meaning, it is never 'met in isolation' (1995: 12). Anthropologists have long recognized this, where the materiality of photographs has been the outcome of how they are *used* rather than how they have been *made* (Edwards and Hart, 2006). What is now the case, however, is the sheer difficulty of identifying and capturing *stable* moments of intertextuality, as images move into different contexts both across platforms and mobile devices, and are meshed with other media forms and locational and temporal data, or simply 'layered' on top of one another. Many social media applications have recently developed their image uploading and sharing capacities, transforming themselves into primarily image-based media (e.g. Twitter, Facebook, Tumblr). In this sense, for some, images are explicitly communicative rather than commemorative (van Dijck, 2007), meaning that we have to conceptualize them differently as meaningful 'texts'. For example, in their significant work on the 'networked image' Rubenstein and Sluis (2008) argued that the significance of the 'stream' now outweighs that of the single image. The multiple ways in which images can be organized and reorganized in different sequences is quite different to the linear narrative of the album:

> Within this flow of images the value of a single photograph is being diminished and replaced by the notion of a stream of data in which both images and their significances are in a state of flux. Disassociated from its origins, identified only by semantic tags and placed in a pool with other images that share similar metadata, the snapshot's resonance is dependent on the interface which mediates our encounter with it (Rubenstein and Sluis, 2008: 22).

It is also worth commenting here on our assumptions about human agency and image making. An important question with methodological implications is whether images have been produced 'intentionally' by subjects (i.e. Instagram selfies) or 'automatically' (i.e. video surveillance, face recognition), with the latter becoming more prevalent. The recent concept of the 'algorithmic image' (Rubenstein and Sluis, 2013) has been employed to understand how images in social media never reach a 'fixed state' because they can always be altered or circulated in the future. This is highly significant for how researchers identify and analyze images, and the claims they can make about their representative or 'indexical' character as their context changes through distribution. For example, the algorithmic image is not an image 'of something' and cannot be used in that sense, but can of course tell us something about the *dynamics of algorithmic classification* in social media. Put in simpler terms, many social media images may have the same compositional form, especially in advertising, but the nature of their mobility and therefore their viewing are likely to be very different. Similarly, digital images are subject to different forms of 'decay', from distribution in databases that are no longer readable, to almost immediate disappearance from one day to the next in applications such as Snapchat. This dynamic of 'persistence' and 'potential' is especially important for interpretations of visual memory in social media (see Hand, 2014b).

As a consequence, social media researchers have to think about what specific images 'do' socially over time and space and how this might be accessed and assessed given the multiplying audiences. In addition, the dynamics of social media are such that the question of 'what people do' *with* images becomes paramount to understanding compositional and interpretive issues. In other words, the 'meaning' and 'doing' aspect of images being researched will partly be an outcome of everyday practices, and cannot be assumed by appealing to the history of a prior medium (photography, film, print, and so on).

Analyzing Visual Traces and Circulations

As discussed above in reference to streams, a key component of visual social media is mobility. This means several things. First, the ways in which visual objects circulate through platforms, databases and devices. Second, how these processes are not simply user-directed, but involve algorithmic processes that are often obscured from view (e.g. the underlying structures of 'feeds'). Third, the sites of production, image and viewing can also involve mobilities in terms of people and devices being 'on the move' (see Frith, 2015). All of these are involved in the production of 'visual digital traces' that are difficult to capture for analysis. Why is this? In terms of the images themselves many have argued that visual objects produced and stored in digital formats are ephemeral: sometimes fluid, often re-workable and less 'durable' than print equivalents (Bowker, 2005; Garde-Hansen, 2009; Hoskins, 2012; Murray, 2008; van Dijck, 2007, 2011, 2015). Much of this fluidity is the result of continual algorithmic classification and reordering discussed in recent scholarship on sociotechnical agency (Gillespie, 2013; Schwarz, 2014). This has been well documented in relation to digital images: how images and the contexts of their interpretation are subject to continual reconfiguration in networked environments such as Flickr, Facebook and Pinterest, unlike in the photo album or shoebox (Lister, 2013; van Dijck, 2007).

The issue of context is central here. It is a common statement that, say, tweets are often 'taken out of context', but there is an important point here about how, methodologically, to know what the context of an image actually is. The dynamic combinations of people, devices, and platforms that form the sites of image production and consumption are not always easily identifiable simultaneously. In other words, there is a distinctive challenge in being able to identify the 'sites' of a social media image in relatively stable terms. For example, an object as simple as a tagged Facebook photo is being redistributed across these sites, and is subject to ongoing sociotechnical re-composition and re-audiencing. In social media, it is often the circulation of an image that is the primary focus rather than its composition – how many times is an image retweeted, shared, liked, deleted. With iconic images – some of those in the ongoing Syrian refugee crisis for example – it is the multiplication of sites of viewing through social media that appears to ascribe affective power to the image. Furthermore, we are almost always dealing with multiple cultural forms – graphics, moving images, sounds, shapes, spaces, and texts mashed together and re-formed through metadata 'tagging' in social media and microblogging.

As such, a key problem with visual objects in social media is determining their context. There are quantitative methods for mapping 'traces' of 'likes' and other tags, but in qualitative terms the circulation of the 'same' image through different material contexts (e.g. phone, platform, screen, feed) shaped by algorithmic processes presents intractable problems of identifying multiplying audiences, sites of interpretation, and therefore the 'ways of looking' crucial to understanding meaning (Hartley, 2012). One approach is to focus on the vast numbers of visual objects but try to map patterns in what is being made visible and share in a geographically limited space through specific applications such as Instagram (Hochman and Manovich, 2013). Another is to try and understand the contexts of interpretation among users – how visual objects are being made, viewed and shared, but also how such objects are 'performative' in particular settings (Pink et al., 2015). I will concentrate on this latter, qualitative set of methods – particularly in-depth interviewing which may or may not be part of a larger ethnography – showing how they attempt to address key problems of content and context.

Practices of Image Making and Sharing

As visual technologies have become embedded in a range of other consumer-level technologies (e.g. phones), visual communication has become part of the infrastructure of everyday sociality. Qualitative interpretive researchers are faced with more visual data, but more significantly with the embedding of visual data within multiple uses and diverse practices that are not necessarily 'photographic'. Indeed, the general *uses* of social media are primarily visual in that they occur via screens; visual mediation via social media on portable screens has increased exponentially. People routinely use still and moving images in ordinary communication, access the majority of news visually in social media, and co-exist with their personal screens (e.g. smartphones) as they go about their daily activities. For those researchers trying to understand how people are making, viewing, and distributing visual objects in social media there are significant debates about how to conceptualize social media. Digital ethnographic research has followed two main directions: detailed immersion studies of 'life online' (Hine, 2000; Kozinets, 2010; Markham, 1999) and ethnographies of how the practices of everyday life incorporate and integrate (or not) elements of networked media into the rhythms of place and practice (boyd, 2014; Quan-Haase et al., 2016; Miller and Slater, 2000; also Horst & Miller, 2006, 2012; and Miller, 2011). This latter direction provides insight into the embeddedness of social media in everyday life, employing methods of participant observation and in-depth interviewing to research practices of making, seeing, looking, and participation (see Ball and Smith, 2011; Buse, 2010; Gomez Cruz and Ardévol, 2013). I will privilege qualitative interviewing as one set of methodological practices that can address several problems raised so far. This is not to suggest that these are the 'best' methods for visual studies of social media; simply that they can fruitfully be used as part of a broad methodological toolkit.

In visual research that adopts a small-scale qualitative or perhaps ethnographic approach, a common technique has been to conduct in-depth interviews with those making the images. There is a strong tradition of in-depth interviewing in domestic environments such as households, for example, where researchers try to generate a thick description of the contexts (Geertz, 1973) in which family photography is practiced and made meaningful (e.g. Rose, 2014; Van House, 2011). The continued significance of this approach lies in its deflation of the social media/daily life divide as part of a broader 'de-centering' of the digital within 'digital ethnography' (see Pink et al., 2015). In this latter sense, social media are part of meaningful multi-sensory environments (Pink, 2012), with their many visual components experienced in particular physical places, rather than as an external virtual landscape. The notion that people simply 'look at' images on the screen seems inadequate; rather, social media *visuality* involves 'moving through a digital environment while rooted in the materiality of our immediate circumstances' (Pink, 2012).

Although most in-depth interviewing about images would likely involve some attention to specific images, there are approaches that aim to make the images themselves the focus of question and conversation. Interview participants may be asked to handle and discuss images in order to generate new questions. This is particularly salient for understanding the ambivalence of specific images, or how their meanings have changed over time, or the significance of their *materiality*. From this perspective, digital visual objects and traces are often the unintended outcome of intersecting practices. Understanding this requires an analytic focus upon the materiality and mediating capacity of digital devices, in terms of the quotidian contexts in which they are used, and the ways in which combinations of devices and platforms enable accomplishment of diverse social practices (Couldry, 2015; Shove et al., 2012). In methodological terms, this requires techniques such as in-depth interviewing, ethnographic participation and observation, and visual methods. For example, Boellstorff et al. (2012) offer a comprehensive account of screen shot capture, video and audio capture of 'virtual objects', arguing that this is fruitful as part of a broader ethnographic approach to understanding virtual worlds.

One of the advantages of in-depth interviewing in relation to social media is to avoid the reification of 'social media' as an ontological domain rather than a complex range of situated meaningful practices (Miller, 2011).

However, in-depth interviewing potentially ignores compositional and technological issues, rarely moving beyond localized contexts that arguably miss the more challenging aspects of *circulation* described above. There are therefore clear limitations to a complete reliance on interview data such as this. Researchers are prone to rely on people's accounts of image content, there are often self-presentation issues that skew access to the detail of practices, and the fine grain of individual engagements perhaps neglects the formation of more 'networked publics' that remain hidden. Furthermore, while the argument might be made that 'visual data' often tells us about that data rather than the practices that have produced it, it might also be said that interview data tells us primarily about individual practices of self-reflection and confession, rather than the practices that they are actually referring to.

Given that social media involves multiple forms of visual content, in-depth interviews benefit from the incorporation of larger amounts of personal visual data into the process. As Rose (2012) suggests visual research methods of this kind can reveal more than the interview talk itself. For example, a useful technique is to ask participants to download or make available a temporally defined personal data archive (or simply their Facebook timeline) prior or during interviewing in order to contextualize that data more ethnographically, but also inter-textually through 'trace interviews' where dynamic screen capture software is used to see how people navigate their images (see Dubois and Ford, 2015; Latzko-Toth, Bonneau and Millette, Chapter 13, this volume). This requires attention to the reflexivity of both the interview process (co-construction of a narrative) and the sequencing and archiving of visual content (co-construction of visual content). For example, a participant may critically reflect on their timeline in ways that they might never do ordinarily, thus producing an *account* of visual phenomena that is constructed as a research artifact, but potentially rewarding in terms of revealing different registers of emotion or affect.

In the remainder of the chapter, I will use the example of the 'selfie' to illustrate how social media researchers are negotiating these techniques and problems. Although selfies themselves are likely to morph into other cultural forms over time, I suggest here that analytically they offer us a particularly useful means for understanding visuality in social media in the longer term.

RESEARCHING SELFIES AS VISUAL SOCIAL MEDIA

In this final section I will use the example of the 'selfie' to briefly illuminate some of the issues above, showing how selfies have been approached methodologically in quite different ways. Selfies are a particularly useful example of visual objects in social media. There are benefits and limitations to all these approaches, but when taken together we can get a sense of how mixed and multimodal methods might enable a promising – perhaps necessary – starting point for visual research in social media (Kress, 2010).

Selfies as Images

One approach has been to analyze the selfie in representational terms as a particular image or compositional genre, using content, semiotic and/or discourse analysis. In terms of the image itself, it has been argued that selfies constitute a 'genre unto themselves, with their own visual conventions and clichés' (Marwick, 2015: 141), as part of a more general shift toward visual self-expression for *consumption by others* via social media. It is important to note the differences in platforms here; people are engaged in arguably very different modes of self-presentation on Facebook, Flickr, Instagram and Twitter. In acknowledging this, Marwick (2015) observes that Instagram has its own set of visual expectations with 'nostalgic' and 'retro' filters built into the app, shaping the possible aesthetics of how people display themselves. It is also significant that celebrities, who have been influential in making selfies such a significant and recognizable aesthetic form, use Instagram routinely as a key element in personal branding. Selfie aesthetics, then, depend upon conjunctions of technology, self, practice and dominant expectations around impression management.

An aspect of selfie aesthetics is the extent to which images such as selfies are *routinely* altered. As Sheehan and Zervigón (2015) observe, while there is nothing new about photographic manipulation, the current prevalence of altered photography is part of a broader 'makeover culture' in the developed world, in which the body is increasingly subject to scrutiny and 'improvement'. Through Photoshop and similar editing tools, the ability to crop, to remove blemishes, lighten and darken the skin, and so on, positions the selfie at the conjunction of immediacy and alterability.

Another direction beginning with the image shows how the composition of selfies indicates the limitations of analyzing images in isolation. The selfie is a 'trace of action' rather than indexical of 'reality' (Frosh, 2015). The selfie brings people into communicative or conversational practice, and 'foregrounds the relationship between the image and its producer because the producer and referent are identical' (Frosh, 2015: 1610). It says 'see me showing you' (ibid.). It is, for Frosh, a trace of the *performance* rather than of an object (self). The key difference between the selfie and other modes of self-portraiture is the necessity of the arms length image – the arms are often visible in the image. The camera becomes incorporated in the image as part of the hand-camera assemblage. But the whole body also has to reshape itself to make the selfie happen. It is not 'natural', so to speak, because the smartphone has radically reorganized relationships between body, space, and image. In all these ways, the selfie is a reflexive technology: it directs our attention toward the conditions and contexts of production. This includes 'place expression' (often indicated by tags and hashtags), expectations and conventions of embodiment and mobility, and the malleability of self-identity. So, selfies are a novel form of image, in that they are an *image of making an image* (Frosh, 2015), but this immediately suggests that we need to think beyond the image itself in methodological terms, toward the intertextuality and sociotechnical construction of such images.

Selfies as Discursive

Selfies are already framed in a cultural context that attaches value to them, most commonly in gendered terms, or as 'evidence' of generational orientations. The selfie is also enveloped in a broader news culture of 'scandal', gossip and moral panics. In the case of selfies, such concerns are as much about camera phone technology and its centrality to self-expression as it is about the images themselves (Miltner and Baym, 2015). Questions such as when taking a selfie is acceptable, and who or what is suitable in the making of a selfie, and with who and through what means a selfie should be shared, and so on, have become *moral* questions, framed by existing gendered, raced and classed expectations. Indeed, selfie takers are routinely subject to social regulation, particularly young women (Burns, 2015). Burns argues that selfies have been gendered as 'feminine' when discursively framed as 'trivial' and embodying a 'devalued femininity'. Such an approach has employed content and discourse analysis to locate specific 'signs' in particular images, but position them inter-textually within dominant ideologies of gender, class, sexuality and ethnicity, across broader news networks. In this way, the pictorial or compositional elements of images are less significant than their status as discursive modes of regulation. It is found that there are particularly significant gendered expectations concerning sexual self-representation in selfies, with women experiencing greater levels of condemnation (see Burns, 2015).

Selfies as Mobile and Mutable

Selfies appear and disappear rapidly across platforms, being both personalized and globally dispersed objects. Accordingly, another approach might be to think of the selfie as a more or less stable 'moment' in social media circulations or mobilities (see Hess, 2015). Selfies are distributed via social media, with that distribution enabling ongoing re-contextualization and additional elements to be added (e.g. comments, tags). Some selfies are conspicuously 'valued' and others are not, depending on not only the image, but also the networks through which it is viewed. Following the movement of selfies through, say, social media platforms and mainstream media channels is one way of doing this. In the recent communications literature, there has been serious engagement with the selfie as a gendered performance (Albury, 2015), but also paying attention to how selfies may be positioned within networked publics. A key idea here is to employ methods that reveal how people classify visual objects. For example, according to Albury (2015) employing interviews to understand teens' perceptions of selfies we find that individuals routinely make distinctions between 'public' and 'private' selfies, particularly with pictures considered 'sexual' or 'sexy'. Private selfies are not to be deliberately shared, but with the anxiety that they might be found by others looking at their phone. Public selfies are more communicative – of 'presence', of the 'pursuit of likes', of temporal and spatial location (Albury, 2015: 1736). These are relatively strategic, often employing irony and sarcasm to deflate accusations of 'finding an excuse', especially, for semi-naked portrayals of the self.

Another example is how Lobinger and Brantner (2015) focus on the perception of authenticity in vernacular photography. They employ a concept of 'expressive authenticity', whereby people evaluate selfies as equating with the true nature of the depicted person (or not) using a Q-sort design – in which participants rank a range of statements (variables) – and Q-factor analysis method – through which correlations between those subjective viewpoints are identified. Asking participants to sort selfies into categories allows people to express thoughts about visual culture in ways that may have been impossible to voice (in an interview). They found that some of this authenticity is achieved somewhat self-consciously through filters and apps that produce a simulated analogue authenticity. Such expressive as opposed to 'nominal' authenticity refers to the 'moral features' of the image, in its ability to represent the 'true' character and personality of the self (Lobinger and Brantner, 2015). In their study, some participants reject selfies as 'inauthentic' precisely because of the apparent staging or visibility of the photographic process – clearly *imitating* rather than representing the true nature of self. For others, the situation of the photograph (the ordinary or everyday) achieves authenticity, rather than the person. Finally, the perceived 'fun' of a selfie (rather than anything 'artistic') denotes authenticity, relating to choosing 'naturalness' over 'designed' images. The study shows how the category of authenticity is ambivalent but not meaningless concerning selfies, drawing upon audience expressions. Lobinger and Bratner (2014) have also employed this method to understand perceptions of visual portrayals of politicians.

Selfies as Practices

A practice-oriented approach to visual social media positions selfies as the *outcome* of diverse practices. It is those practices – of 'presencing', of political activism via hashtags and memes, of visual communication, of friendship maintenance, and so on - that we have to understand to make sense of the images (Gibbs et al., 2015; Sweetman, 2009). Following earlier studies of family, tourist or journalistic photography, this often entails interviewing and participant observation within geographically situated communities, users of particular apps, or participants within networked publics (Larsen, 2005; Lasén and Gomez-Cruz, 2009; Sarvas and Frohlich, 2011). This could also entail a mixed-method approach of the kind employed by Pink et al. (2015) as part of a 'digital ethnography', in which visual resources are used as elements of method. It would explore people's reflexive engagements with devices and varieties of visual data, seeking to avoid any analytic separation of that data from the devices through which it is produced and circulated (e.g. Hand, 2012, 2014b). People's image making and viewing devices are part of co-evolving systems both within and beyond the participants' control, all of which is shaping their relation to the visual and therefore the visual data 'we' see in social media. There is considerable promise in qualitative empirical data of this kind at present that pulls together devices, platforms, people, place and visual data in these ways, as a means to explore, for example, the management of connected presence and personal analytics. This could be a particularly useful way of grounding analysis of how new data visibilities are being enacted, negotiated and appropriated in daily life. It is worth reiterating that, as shown above, social media are the vehicle, form, context and mode of distribution of this visual object, and as such have to be approached in ways that enable all those 'modalities' to be accounted for.

CONCLUSION

Visuality in social media prompts us to think about new methods. I suggest that this is initially a result of sheer volume, which arguably produces properties requiring research in their own right. At present, research into the ubiquity of images tends to be quantitative or pursues the cultural analytics route, seeking to pull the 'global' and 'local' together around specific events or though particular modalities. If we think qualitatively about specific images, observable streams of images, particular contexts of visual social media use and engagement, or the meaningful activities of producing, consuming and distributing images, then we tend toward the recalibration of established interpretive methods in the social sciences and humanities. This might be content or discourse analyses, social semiotics, surveys, interviews, participant observation, and so on. I have intimated how each of these comes up against difficult problems when faced with the dynamics of social media.

I have stressed three particular issues in different ways throughout. First, images in social media are exponentially increasing in volume and also have several novel qualities (not necessarily 'essential') including potential for unlimited algorithmic classification, malleability, transience, and potential persistence. Second, relatedly, visual data circulates in social media in ways that are difficult to capture qualitatively. Third, the apparent transparency of visual social media obscures material contexts of engagement necessary to understand its dynamics. In other words, it is extremely difficult for researchers to identify and qualitatively analyze the multiple 'sites' of the image (production, image, audiences) that are beyond the platform and screen. The most challenging methodological issue for this kind of qualitative research is trying to research the relationships *between* these three dimensions and the issues of authenticity, trust and ethics that accompany them. A brief focus on the selfie is suggestive of how a multimodal, mixed method approach might begin to negotiate this, moving beyond an analysis of the compositional aspects of selfies and toward an acknowledgement of the diversity of meaning-making contexts in which they are being produced, circulated and viewed. The emphasis here is precisely on understanding how people are *making sense* of the visual data they produce and is produced about them. I have privileged in-depth interviewing often employed as part of larger ethnographies simply because there is a dearth of qualitative empirical attention being paid to the ways in which people *make sense* of their own and others' visual data in the course of everyday life. We know quite a lot about the kinds of visual objects that appear in social media, and are beginning to understand how these are structured and classified by the specific requirements of platforms in negotiation or 'struggle' with their users (see van Dijck, 2015). Developments in quantitatively oriented research fields need to be complimented and enhanced by varieties of 'small visual data' that focus on the constant production of visual data by ourselves, such as ethnographic analyses of the conditions in and though which people routinely produce and consume visual objects. Visual data is indeed routinely produced and circulated, but it is also reflected upon, negotiated, deleted, and analyzed by those producing it in presumably diverse ways. All of which raises novel ethical questions about the publicness, consent, and proper use of found visual materials (boyd and Crawford, 2012; Clark, 2012; Wiles et al., 2012).

REFERENCES

Albury, K. (2015) 'Selfies, sexts and s hats: Young people's understandings of gendered practices of self-representation', *International Journal of Communication*, 9(2): 1734–1745.

Alper, M. (2014) 'War on Instagram: Framing conflict photojournalism with mobile photography apps'. *New Media & Society*, 16(8): 1233–1248.

Ball, M. and Smith, G. (2011) 'Ethnomethodology and the visual: practices of looking, visualization, and embodied action', in Margolis, E. and Pauwels, L., *The SAGE Handbook of Visual Research Methods*. SAGE Publications, London, pp. 392–413.

Banks, M. (2008) *Using Visual Data in Qualitative Research*. SAGE Publications, London.

Barthes, R. (1977) *Image, Music, Text*, Tr. S. Heath, Fontana Press, London.

Bell, P. (2011) 'Content analysis of visual images', in van Leeuwen, D. and Jewitt, C., *Handbook of Visual Analysis*, SAGE Publications, London, pp. 10–34.

Boellstorff, T., Nardi, B., Pearce, C. and Taylor, T. L. (2012) *Ethnography and Virtual Worlds: A handbook of method*. Princeton University Press, Princeton, NJ.

Bowker, G. (2005) *Memory Practices in the Sciences*. MIT Press, Cambridge, MA.

boyd, d. (2014) *It's Complicated: the social lives of networked teens*. New Haven: Yale University Press.

boyd, d. and Crawford, K. (2012) 'Critical questions for big data', *Information, Communication and Society*, 15(5): 662–679.

Bruns, A. and Burgess, J. (2012) 'Researching news discussion on Twitter: New methodologies', *Journalism Studies*, 13(5-6): 801–814.

Burgess, J. and Green, J. (2009) *YouTube: Online Video and Participatory Culture*. Polity, Cambridge.

Burns, A. L. (2015) 'Self (ie)-Discipline: Social regulation as enacted through the discussion of photographic practice', *International Journal of Communication*, available http://eprints.whiterose.ac.uk/83965/ (accessed 30 July 2015).

Buse, P. (2010) 'Polaroid into Digital: technology, cultural form, and the social practices of snapshot photography', *Continuum*, 24 (2): 215–230.

Clark, A. (2012) 'Visual ethics in a contemporary landscape', in Pink, S. (ed.) *Advances in Visual Methodology*, SAGE Publications, London, pp. 17–35.

Couldry, N. (2015) 'Social media: human life', *Social Media + Society*, 1(1): 1–2.

Dubois, E. and Ford, H. (2015) 'Qualitative Political Communication/Trace interviews: An actor-centered approach', *International Journal of Communication*, 9: 2067-2091.

Duggan, M., Ellison, N. B., Lampe, C., Lenhart, A. and Madden, M. (2015) Social media update 2014. Retrieved January 5, 2016, from http://www.pewinternet.org/2015/01/09/social-media-update-2014/

Edwards, E. and Hart, J. (ed.) (2006) *Photographs, Objects, Histories: On the Materiality of Images*. Routledge, London.

Farace, S., van Laer, T., Ruyter, K. and de Wetzels, M. (2015) 'The Selfie: Understanding Visualization of Stories in Consumer Photos', Available at SSRN. http://ssrn.com/abstract=2638273 or http://dx.doi.org/10.2139/ssrn.2638273

Farci, M. and Orefice, M. (2015) 'Hybrid Content Analysis of the Most Popular Politicians' Selfies on Twitter', *Journal of MeCCSA*, 8(6).

Frith, J. (2015) *Smartphones as Locative Media*. Polity, Cambridge.

Frosh, P. (2015) '"Selfies" the gestural image: the selfie, photography theory, and kinesthetic sociability', *International Journal of Communication*, 9(22): 1607–1628.

Garde-Hansen, J. (2009) 'MyMemories? Personal Digital Archive Fever and Facebook', in Garde-Hansen, J., Hoskins, A., Reading, A. (eds.) *Save As…Digital Memories*. Palgrave, Basingstoke, pp. 135–150.

Geertz, C. (1973) *The Interpretation of Cultures: selected essays*. New York: Basic Books.

Gibbs, M., Meese, J., Arnold, M., Nasen, B. and Carter, M. (2015) '# Funeral and Instagram: death, social media, and platform vernacular', *Information, Communication and Society*, 18(3): 255–268.

Gillespie, T. (2013) 'The Relevance of Algorithms', in Gillespie, T., Boczkowski, P. and Foot, K. (eds.) *Media Technologies: Essays on Communication, Materiality, and Society*. MIT Press, Cambridge, MA.

Gomez Cruz, E. and Ardévol, E. (2013) 'Performing photography practices in everyday life: Some ethnographic notes on a Flickr group'. *Photographies*, 6(1): 35–44.

Hall, K. (2015) 'Selfies and self-writing: cue card confessions as social media technologies of the self', *Television & New Media* 17 (3): 228–242.

Hand, M. (2008) *Making Digital Cultures: access, interactivity, and authenticity*. Ashgate, Aldershot.

Hand, M. (2012) *Ubiquitous Photography*. Polity, Cambridge.

Hand, M. (2014a) 'From Cyberspace to the Dataverse', in Hand, M. Hillyard, S. (eds.) *Big Data? Qualitative Approaches to Digital Research*. Emerald, Bingley, UK.

Hand, M. (2014b) 'Persistent traces, potential memories: smartphones and the negotiation of visual, locative and textual data in personal life', *Convergence*, August Online First.

Hartley, J. (2012) *Digital Futures for Cultural and Media Studies*. John Wiley, Chichester.

Hess, A. (2015) 'The Selfie Assemblage', *International Journal of Communication*, 9(2): 1629–1646.

Heywood, I. and Sandywell, B. (eds.) (2012) *The Handbook of Visual Culture*. Berg, Oxford.

Hine, C. (2000) *Virtual Ethnography*. SAGE Publications, London.

Hochman, N. and Manovich, L. (2013) 'Zooming into an Instagram City: reading the local through social media', *First Monday*, 18(7) July.

Hochman, N. and Schwartz, R. (2012) 'Visualizing Instagram: Tracing cultural visual rhythms', *Proceedings of the Workshop on Social Media Visualization in conjunction with the Sixth International AAAI Conference on Weblogs and Social Media (ICWSM–12)*, pp. 6–9.

Horst, H. and Miller, D. (2006) *The Cell Phone: An Anthropology of Communication*. Berg, Oxford.

Horst, H. and Miller, D. (eds.) (2012) *Digital Anthropology*. Bloomsbury, London.

Hoskins, A. (2012) Digital Network Memory. In: Erll, A. and Rigney, A. (eds.) (2012) *Mediation, Remediation and the Dynamics of Cultural Memory*. Berlin/Boston: DeGruyter, 91–106.

Ibrahim, Y. (2015) 'Instagramming life: Banal imaging and the poetics of the everyday', *Journal of Media Practice*, 16(1): 42–54.

Jencks, C. (ed.) (1995) *Visual Culture*. Routledge, London.

Kisilevich, S., Krstajic, M., Keim, D., Andrienko, N. and Andrienko, G. (2010) 'Event–based analysis of people's activities and behavior using Flickr and Panoramio geotagged photo collections', *IV '10: Proceedings of the 2010*

14th International Conference Information Visualisation, pp. 289–296.

Kozinets, R.V. (2010) *Netnography: doing ethnographic research online*. SAGE Publications, London.

Kress, G. (2010) *Multimodality: A Social Semiotic Approach to Contemporary Communication*. Routledge, London.

Krippendorff, K. (1980) *Content Analysis: An Introduction to its Methodologies*. SAGE Publications, London.

Larsen, J. (2005) Families seen sightseeing: performativity of tourist photography, *Space and Culture*, 8: 416–434.

Lasén, A. and Gómez-Cruz, E. (2009) 'Digital photography and picture sharing: redefining the public/private divide', *Knowledge, Technology & Policy*, 22: 205–215.

Lister, M. (ed.) (1995) *The Photographic Image In Digital Culture*. Routledge, London.

Lister, M. (ed.) (2013) *The Photographic Image In Digital Culture*. Routledge, London. 2nd Edition.

Lobinger, K. and Brantner, C. (2015) 'In the Eye of the Beholder: Subjective Views on the Authenticity of Selfies', *International Journal of Communication*, 9: 1848–1860.

Markham, A. (1999) *Life Online*. Lanham: Rowman and Littlefield.

Marres, N. (2012) 'The redistribution of methods: on intervention in digital social research, broadly conceived', *The Sociological Review*, 60: 139–165.

Marwick, A. (2015) 'Instafame: Luxury selfies in the attention economy', *Public Culture*, 27(1 75): 137–160.

Miller, D. and Slater, D. (2000) *The Internet: an ethnographic approach*. Berg, Oxford.

Miller, D. (2011) *Tales from Facebook*. Polity, Cambridge.

Miltner, K. and Baym, N. (2015) 'Selfies| the selfie of the year of the selfie: reflections on a media scandal', *International Journal of Communication*, 9(15): 1701–1715.

Mitchell, C. (2011) *Doing Visual Research*. SAGE Publications, London.

Murray, S. (2008) 'Digital images, photo-sharing, and our shifting notions of everyday aesthetics', *Journal of Visual Culture*, 7(2): 147–163.

Murray, S. (2013) 'New Media and Vernacular Photography: Revisiting Flickr', in Lister, M. (ed.) *The Photographic Image in Digital Culture*, 2nd edition, Routledge, New York.

Penn, G. (2000) 'Semiotic analysis of still images', in Bauer, M.W. and Gaskell, G., *Qualitative Researching with Text, Image and Sound*. SAGE Publications, London, pp. 227–245.

Pink, S. (ed.) (2012) *Advances in Visual Methodology*. SAGE Publications, London.

Pink, S., Horst, H., Postill, J., Hjorth, L., Lewis, T. and Tacchi, J. (2015) *Digital Ethnography*. SAGE Publications, London.

Quan-Haase, A., Martin, K. and Schreurs, K. (2016) Interviews with digital seniors: ICT use in the context of everyday life. *Information, Communication & Society*, 4(5) 691–707.

Rogers, R. (2013) *Digital Methods*. MIT Press, London.

Rose, G. (2012) *Visual Methodologies*. Third Edition. SAGE Publications, London.

Rose, G. (2014) 'On the relation between "visual research methods" and contemporary visual culture', *The Sociological Review*, 62: 24–46.

Rose, G. (2014) 'How digital technologies do family snaps, only better', in Larsen, J. Sandbye, M. (eds.) *Digital Snaps: the new face of photography*. IB Taurus, London.

Rubenstein, D. and Sluis, K. (2008) 'A Life More Photographic', *Photographies*, 1:1.

Rubinstein D. and Sluis K. (2013) 'The digital image in photographic culture; The algorithmic image and the crisis of representation'. In: *The Photographic Image in Digital Culture*, ed. Martin Lister, Routledge, London.

San Pedro, J. and Siersdorfer, S. (2009) 'Ranking and classifying attractiveness of photos in folksonomies', *WWW '09: Proceedings of the 18th International Conference on the World Wide Web*, pp. 771–780.

Sarvas, R. and Frohlich, D. M. (2011) *From Snapshots to Social Media – The Changing Picture of Domestic Photography*. Springer, London.

Schwarz, O. (2014) 'The past next door: Neighbourly relations with digital memory-artefacts', *Memory Studies*, 7(1): 7–21.

Sheehan, T. and Zervigón, A.M. (2015) 'Introduction', in Sheehan, T. and Zervigón, A.M. (eds.) *Photography and its Origins*, Routledge, New York.

Sheldon, P. and Bryant, K. (2016) 'Instagram: Motives for its use and relationship to narcissism and contextual age', *Computers in Human Behavior*, 58: 89–97. Online First January 2nd.

Shove, E., Pantzar, M. and Watson, M. (2012) *The lynamics of Social Practice*, SAGE, Los Angeles.

Sturken, M. and Cartwright, L. (2010) *Practices of Looking: An Introduction to Visual Culture*. Oxford University Press, Oxford.

Sweetman, P. (2009) 'Revealing habitus, illuminating practice: Bourdieu, photography and visual methods', *Sociological Review*, 57 (3): 491–511.

van Dijck, J. (2007) *Mediated Memories in the Digital Age*. Stanford University Press, Stanford.

van Dijck, J. (2011) 'Flickr and the culture of connectivity: sharing views, experiences, memories', *Memory Studies*, 4(4): 401–415.

van Dijck, J. (2015) 'After connectivity: the era of connection', *Social Media + Society*, 1(1) 1–2.

Van House, N.A. (2011) 'Personal photography, digital technologies, and the uses of the Visual', *Visual Studies*, 25(1): 125–134.

Wiles, R., Coffey, A., Robinson, J. and Heath, S. (2012) 'Anonymisation and visual images: issues of respect, "voice" and protection', *International Journal of Social Research Methodology*, 15: 41–53.

Coding of Non-Text Data

Diane Rasmussen Pennington

This chapter overviews the domain of 'non-text' data that can be found on social media, such as videos and photographs. It then outlines research methods that can be applied to analyzing and coding these non-text documents and their associated texts. These methods include compositional interpretation, quantitative content analysis, qualitative content analysis, and approaches related to content analysis such as document analysis and musical analysis. Analysis methods influenced by cultural understandings stem from the disciplines of cultural studies, visual sociology, visual anthropology, semiotic analysis, and iconography/iconology. Finally, analyses influenced by social understandings involve discourse analysis, visual social semiotics, and multimodal research. The chapter concludes with a call for future development of methods specific to non-text data to continue advancing research in this emerging and essential area of social science.

INTRODUCTION

Non-text data possesses the unfortunate disposition of being described as what it is *not* rather than what it *is*. The non-text domain is defined as a wide range of formats which encompasses everything but language-based text, such as photographs, films, music, diagrams, charts, video games, paintings, and maps, all of which can be found in abundance online (Rasmussen Neal, 2012). The exponentially growing presence of non-text documents on popular social media outlets such as Facebook, Twitter, Instagram, Flickr, Pinterest, Snapchat, YouTube, and Vine has created an opportunity for social science researchers to understand the products of digital society through analyzing this data in many formats. Like almost all social media content, non-text social media posts are naturalistic. In other words, social media users post, share, and discuss items and topics of interest to them in their own settings and on their own terms rather than in a controlled setting, thus avoiding any potential Hawthorne effect on their interactions (Adair, 1984). Since they are posted online, rich data sources such as user-generated photographs and videos can be viewed, paused, and played back as many times as necessary in order to maximize the potential of the researcher's analysis (Gibson, 2008).

Computer and information scientists attempt to automatically extract non-text data for quantitative or algorithmic analysis (Rorvig, 1993; Downie, 2003). These techniques have not yet succeeded in identifying or communicating the interpretive, connotative meanings that are important to social scientists; therefore, this chapter focuses primarily on qualitative approaches. Researchers can think of non-text social media data as found documents, just as they would view photographs in a newspaper's print archive as found documents. Also, due to the prolific social interactions that take place on social media websites, they can also observe how people interact with each other and with documents posted online (Markham, 2008). For example, a user-generated music video on YouTube can provide insight into how the creators of the video portrayed themselves, their surroundings, and the music. The viewers' comments on the video can help researchers understand the culture surrounding the video, viewers' opinions of the video, and the affective and intertextual features that are important to a given fan community (Rasmussen Pennington, 2016). Researchers have been studying the psychological and sociological impact on users who interact with non-text documents on social media. In one study, 75% of young people aged 18–29 said they posted photos on Facebook. Viewing their friends' Facebook photos caused them to feel self-conscious about their bodies (Hayes, van Stolk-Cooke, and Muench, 2015).

The continuously growing number of non-text documents shared on social media demonstrates the opportunity and the need for social science researchers to make use of these artefacts. For example, the photograph sharing website Flickr has 115 million users (Flickr, 2015), 300 million photographs are uploaded to Facebook daily (Zephoria, 2015), and 8,333 videos are uploaded every minute to the video sharing website Vine (Smith, 2015a). In 2014, 26% of online adults used Instagram, and 28% of them used Pinterest; both of these websites centre on photograph sharing (Pew Research Center, 2014). Society can only expect these numbers to continue increasing, as they have since the inception of Web 2.0.

Despite these proliferations, very few methods have been developed specifically for analyzing non-text social media data, or for non-text data in general. Content-rich, non-text documents such as photographs and videos have historically been overlooked due to the high priority that textual language holds in social science research (Bauer, 2000, p. 278). However, '[L]anguage is not at all at the centre of all communication' (Iedema, 2003, p. 39), so it is useful to incorporate documents that exist in a range of formats as research data. Pauwels (2011) stated, 'social scientists are well-prepared to derive valuable knowledge from sources other than verbal or numeric' (p. 573), but he also stressed that social scientists are lacking in research tools to create this knowledge. Visual data is perhaps more complex to decipher than printed text, but both are necessary and one informs the other. Van Leeuwen (2008) described the relationship as follows: 'words provide the facts, the explanations ... images provide interpretations, ideologically colored angles, and they do so not explicitly, but by suggestion, by connotation, by appealing to barely conscious, half-forgotten knowledge (Berger, 1972)' (van Leeuwen, 2008, p. 136).

Standard social science analysis methods can be applied to non-text data, but they require slightly different approaches. The subjective nature of interpreting non-text documents is a unique concern to qualitative social scientists because their concrete, denotative elements are not easily extracted as they are in text-based documents (Svenonius, 1994). Keywords and subjects can be directly pulled out of a textual document, but in order to find the subject of a photograph or a video, researchers must either locate the associated caption, title, or description, or assign a denotation based on their own analysis. As this chapter will demonstrate, it is sometimes useful to analyze non-text documents such as photographs in conjunction with their associated textual counterparts. Photographs are not words, and words are not photographs. While ideas can get lost in translation between the two modes of communication, each provides something different and complementary to the viewer (O'Connor and Wyatt, 2004; Neal, 2010a). Neal (2010a) referred to a photograph and its associated tags, captions, descriptions, and viewer comments that are posted on a social media website as a 'photographic document' because the text and the image work together to create meaning (Lemke, 2002).

For example, imagine a couple has posted photographs of their Caribbean honeymoon on a social media website. The pictures will connote different meanings for the couple than they will for their friends and family, and friends and family will interpret them differently than strangers will. The couple knows without looking at the photos' associated textual descriptions that the pictures represent their honeymoon, and the photos help them recall how they felt and what they did when they were there. Friends and family will remember attending the wedding, and they will easily recognize the couple in the photos, but they will not be able to associate the same memories with the photographs because they did not take the trip. If the photos are marked as public on their social media website, anyone can view them. Members of the general public will see a couple enjoying a beach, but they would not know exactly who the people are. They also would not know that the photos represented a honeymoon, or that they were in the Caribbean, without reading the associated tags or captions.

Some non-text research requires active engagement from participants, such as photo elicitation, in which participants are shown photos and are asked to discuss their content and meaning (Collier, 2001). Photovoice is a method in which participants are asked to take pictures on the topic of the research and they are then interviewed about their photographs (Watson and Douglas, 2012). Other non-text studies are performed using researcher-created data, such as video recordings shot during live observation (Banks, 2007). The practice of ethnomethodology, which studies conversations and how people interact socially, can benefit from using video recordings because ethnomethodologists can not only transcribe the dialogue, but they can also observe non-verbal communication (Goodwin, 2001; Banks, 2007; Ball and Smith, 2011).

Since the focus of this handbook is social media research methods, this chapter will summarize approaches that can be used to analyze non-text social media data, which are 'found' or pre-existing documents. These approaches can be used in a variety of disciplines. According to Banks (2007), analyzing found images 'is generally practiced by scholars in the fields of communication studies, cultural and media studies, and information design, although sociologists, anthropologists, and others have also contributed' (p. 37).

When designing a non-text study, the following overarching questions must be answered:

- Theoretical approach: What theoretical approach and analysis method will be used? Banks (2007) recommended choosing the theoretical approach and the method of analysis before finding data.
- Data identification: What types of documents will be analyzed? For example, are they still images (photographs) or moving images (videos)? In part, the form dictates what information can be gathered from the data (Banks, 2007). For example, a video can demonstrate sequential actions, while a photograph can capture only a single instant in time.

- Scope or boundaries: What exactly will be included in the analysis? A study comprised of only visual analysis will enable the researcher to look at the images or videos, but will not incorporate the context that accompanying text can provide (van Leeuwen and Jewitt, 2001).
- Unit of analysis: What is the unit of analysis? Comparing and contrasting dog photographs with cat photographs would require using a collection of images as the unit of analysis. Conversely, looking at how happiness is conveyed in photographs would call for an individual image as the unit of analysis (van Leeuwen and Jewitt, 2001; Neal, 2010a).

This introduction has overviewed the domain of 'non-text' data that can be found on social media, such as videos and photographs. The chapter will next outline research methods that can be applied to analyzing and coding these non-text documents and their associated texts. They are listed in Table 15.1. The methods include compositional interpretation, quantitative content analysis, qualitative content analysis, approaches related to content analysis such as document analysis and videography, and musical analysis. Other methods stemming from cultural and social epistemologies will be covered as well.

COMPOSITIONAL INTERPRETATION

Before embarking on one of the analysis methods described later in this chapter that incorporate surrounding cultural and social contexts and other elements into non-text analysis, it could prove useful to first perform what Rose (2012) calls 'compositional interpretation' (p. 51), which is concerned with the appearance of an image on its own. While this method primarily applies to paintings, it can be applied to any visual image, including photographs, films, and the socially oriented Massive Multiplayer Online Role Playing Games (MMORPGs), which contain a practically infinite number of images. Rose (2012) suggested looking at content, color (hue, saturation, and value), spatial organization (the geometrical perspectives of the image's layout), film editing, and the image's affective expression. For example, in Figure 15.1, the author's photograph of one of her dogs enjoying the water communicates a happy, joyous feeling when the viewer looks at her blissful face. When

Table 15.1 Overview of research methods for non-text social media data

Method	Key citation(s)
Compositional interpretation	Rose, 2012
Quantitative content analysis	Bell, 2001; Banks, 2007; Rose, 2000; Rose, 2012
Qualitative content analysis	Julien, 2008; Mayring, 2000
Document analysis	Prior, 2008; Saumure and Given, 2008
Videography	Knoblauch and Tuma, 2011
Musical analysis	Bauer, 2000
Cultural studies	Lister and Wells, 2001
Visual sociology/anthropology	Collier, 2001; Pauwels, 2012
Semiotic analysis	Penn, 2000
Iconography/iconology	Müller, 2011
Discourse analysis	van Leeuwen, 2008
Visual social semiotics	Jewitt and Oyama, 2001
Multimodal research	Iedema, 2003
Multimodal ethnography	Dicks et al., 2006

Figure 15.1 The author's 'happy' dog

the author posted this photograph on her Facebook account, she received comments from her friends such as 'Happy dogs make life worthwhile!' 'She's smiling!' 'Happy dog!' and 'That pic is so epic lol'. These comments validate the compositional interpretation that the author would have applied to it. Other research by the author (Neal, 2010a; Neal, 2010b) has shown that pets and smiling faces are two items that are associated with Flickr photographs tagged with the word 'happy'.

CONTENT ANALYSIS

Content analysis, which allows researchers to classify their data into meaningful categorizations, can be performed either quantitatively or qualitatively. An overview of each type follows.

Quantitative Content Analysis

In some cases, content analysis is positivist and quantitative, and the aim is to be as objective as possible. When performing quantitative content analysis, researchers count the manifest, denotative content that is under scrutiny, which is what makes it quantitative in nature. The researcher provides a list of codes to two or more coders, and the coders are asked to code the data in the same fashion, which hopefully leads to reliability in the study. It can be used to analyze any type of data that can be observed concretely (Bell, 2001; Banks, 2007). Banks (2007) explained that in content analysis of film, the researcher can also code for elements unique to moving images, such as video editing, dialogue, and background music.

Imagine that a researcher is investigating what types of photographs people post of their pets. A sample of 100 pet photographs could be collected by searching for 'pets' on Flickr or another photograph-sharing website. The unit of analysis would be each image. One variable might be 'type of pet' and possible values might be 'dog', 'cat', 'bird', and 'fish'. Another variable could be 'humans in photograph' and the values could be '0', '1', '2', and '3 or more'. The results might find that in the sample, there were 42 dog pictures, 37 cat pictures, 12 bird pictures, and 9 fish pictures. Seventy-six pictures had no humans present, 17 had one human, and 7 had two humans. This study would obtain reliable results if the coders have received applicable codes and appropriately detailed instructions. However, this approach to studying images cannot answer questions about the context or environment surrounding the pictures, and it cannot incorporate the thoughts of the creators or the viewers (Bell, 2001). Additionally, analyzing the content of a still image, such as a painting or photograph, using quantitative content analysis might define what the picture is *of*, but it will not tell the researcher what it is *about* (Shatford, 1986). While content analysis can be applied to a wide range of data types, some types are specifically designed for the purpose of studying nontextual documents, such as videography.

Rose (2000) outlined another approach to using content analysis for video. She developed the method for television originally, but it can be applied to any video containing social interactions. The transcription includes not only the verbal dialogue, but also elements such as the angle of the camera, lighting, and music that correspond in time to the dialogue. Next, '[d]evelop a coding frame based on the conceptual analysis and preliminary reading of the data set: to include rules for the analysis of both visual and verbal material; to contain the possibility of disconfirming the theory; to include analysis of narrative structure and context as well as semantic categories' (p. 261). The videos are then coded using the coding frame, and frequency tables are created for both the visual and verbal units of analysis. Rose (2000) emphasized the importance of using quotations to enhance the numerical results.

Other sources can be consulted in order to learn more about the quantitative content analysis process in general (Krippendorff, 1980). Rose (2012) provided a description of the process as it applies to images. After finding the images to analyze using an appropriate sampling strategy, create a list of codes to be applied; codes should be exhaustive, exclusive, and useful. Coders can record what codes they have assigned to each image in a spreadsheet, in data analysis software, or on index cards. Frequency counts are then produced from the coding results.

Qualitative Content Analysis

Content analysis was originally developed as a quantitative analysis method, but it can also be performed qualitatively. While quantitative content analysis can answer 'what' questions, qualitative content analysis can answer 'why' questions as well as investigate perceptions (Julien, 2008, p. 121). It is traditionally applied to text, but it can be used with visual data such as videos and pictures. When applying qualitative content analysis to photographs, 'the researcher may identify content as straightforwardly as identifying objects evident in photographs or may conduct more subtle analyses of symbolic communications that can be unconsciously determined from a physical space' (Julien, 2008, p. 121).

When performing qualitative content analysis, the codes or themes are produced through inductively analyzing the data in detail (Julien, 2008). The codes can represent categories that exist at a surface level, such as what is physically present in a picture, or they can reflect deeper levels of meaning, such as symbolic or connotative meanings. Performing iterations of analysis, and using more than one coder to complete it, creates its credibility. According to Julien (2008), a 60% level of agreement between two coders is considered an acceptable level of agreement in qualitative content analysis. Mayring (2000) provides a detailed explanation of how to approach content analysis inductively and iteratively.

Document Analysis

Document analysis, an analysis method in which existing documents are the data source rather than elicited data such as interview transcripts, is frequently performed using qualitative content analysis such as thematic coding and grounded theory. It can also involve quantitative content analysis or discourse analysis (Prior, 2008; Bowen, 2009). The documents to be analyzed can be in text or non-text format, such as video, audio, maps, and photographs (Prior, 2008; Saumure and Given, 2008). Existing documents such as items that have already been shared on social media are an unobtrusive data source for social scientists, because they do not have to ask people to participate or answer questions (Prior, 2008). With document analysis, researchers can look at 'how individuals experience life events' (Saumure and Given, 2008, p. 927). For example, Instagram photographs could be analyzed to develop themes around how youth communicate the events in their daily lives to their followers based on the photographs they shoot and share.

Videography

Videography, defined as 'the interpretive video analysis of social interaction' (Knoblauch and Tuma, 2011, p. 427), is a form of content analysis that is used in naturalistic settings. Videographers start their research process by finding video clips of interest through ethnographic approaches. Clips are coded iteratively using an approach similar to grounded theory (Strauss and Corbin, 1998). Codes are first informed by pre-existing knowledge, such as ethnographic data. Later codes make use of the deeper sequential analysis performed throughout the study, such as transcripts of the videos and the order in which visually observable physical action takes place (Knoblauch and Tuma, 2011). The focus of the camera, and the order in which things happen in the clips, are important for coding and interpretation. Other methods, such as observation and interviews, are used to gain relevant contextual knowledge that also informs coding. It is possible to imagine using videography with many different user-generated found videos, including family interaction and classroom participation. With the 300 hours of video content that is uploaded per minute to YouTube, a range of user-generated video content is available for researchers to analyze (Smith, 2015b).

MUSICAL ANALYSIS

Music by itself must be considered separately from other types of documents because it cannot be analyzed in the same way. This is largely due to the fact that music has very little connotation on its own; in other words, it holds little meaning itself apart from the meaning that its listeners attach to it, such as nostalgia or happiness. As Bauer (2000) questioned, 'The status of music is controversial: can music carry meaning on its own, or only in conjunction with images or language?' (p. 278).

Very little has been written about the use of music in social media research, although it should take priority, because music is an essential component of the human sociocultural experience (Bresler, 2008). According to Bresler, the 'sociology of music' incorporates sociological research approaches 'to examine the role of music in society and to study music behaviour and attitudes as part of social action' (p. 535). Whether people are sharing links to music videos by their favorite artists, creating their own music to share with others, or commenting on shared music, their posts can provide perspectives about cultures and opinions. Ethnomusicology is a method that helps researchers understand the role that music plays in a particular culture (Nettl, 1983). Additionally, music creates a significant emotional impact on people (Juslin and Sloboda, 2010; Rasmussen Pennington, 2016). It can change how people react to visual documents such as film (Bravo, 2014). Interplay frequently exists between music and associated images, such as in the case of music videos; this interplay can influence meaning (Cook, 1998; Vernallis, 2013; Werner, 2012). For these reasons, it is important to not discount music as a data source.

Bauer (2000) provides a process for finding social and cultural meaning in music. First, transcribe the music in a way that makes sense for the research, such as standard Western music notation or 'acoustic cues' (Juslin and Laukka, 2003, p. 770). Next, keeping in mind that music holds more denotation than connotation, look for meaning in the music. It may exist in internal, intertextual references to other music, or it could be found externally, such as in a reminder of the listener's past memories. Bauer explains how to analyze musical features, including its melody, harmony, dynamics, form, and orchestration, to characterize music, and he shows how each feature can express intangible qualities such as cultural information (Bauer, 2000).

Neal et al. (2009) used qualitative content analysis to explore how users of the music website last.fm tag emotion in music. They examined the musical features present in songs that were frequently tagged with each of the five basic emotions proposed by Power (2006): happy, sad, anger, disgust, and fear. Songs tagged with 'Happy' elicited the highest level of agreement among the coders, especially on the 'Pitch' and 'Temporal' musical facets. The researchers questioned whether other emotions, and other musical features, prompted a high enough level of agreement among the coders to be able to say that there is a universality present in how people denote music. More exploration in this area is needed; the results were inconclusive.

NON-TEXT ANALYSIS METHODS INFLUENCED BY CULTURE

A variety of disciplines offer methods for analyzing non-text documents that take cultural influences into account. These disciplines include cultural studies, sociology, anthropology, and semiotics. The methods are discussed in detail in this section. This section should be considered in tandem with the following section on methods incorporating social influences, because social and cultural influences frequently exist together. The distinction is made in this chapter for grounding the reader's understanding in the predominant influence present in each method.

A Cultural Studies Approach

Lister and Wells (2001) discuss the application of approaches from the cultural studies field, which 'is interested in the enabling and regulating institutions, and less formal social arrangements, in and through which culture is produced, enacted and consumed' (p. 61) to analyzing images. Cultural studies researchers look for the relationship between cultural production and social practices, which can be readily studied through images created by members of the culture. The first step in the process of analysis is to consider the context of the viewing: determine where the image exists socially and physically, and why a consumer might be looking at the image. For example, when people post photographs on social media, they intend for their friends to see them, and their friends will look at the photos if they want to find out what is happening in their lives. Next, analyze the context of production: how did the image get there? In most cases involving social media, this answer will be quite simple: the person or institution holding the account posted it.

When analyzing the image itself, consider its semiotics (discussed later in this section).

In the case of photographs, look at the composition of the image, such as how it was framed, the gaze of any people in it, the camera's position, and the background. These comprise the 'photographic code ... A set of signs that, taken together, means something to us' (Lister and Wells, 2001, p. 76). Visual elements in a photograph, including how people are dressed, body language, and inanimate objects present in the image provide social clues about the context of the image; for example, what can be learned about people in a picture if they are smiling, gathered around a tree, and wearing winter clothing?

Lister and Wells (2001) acknowledged that cultural studies is not prescriptive in its method of analysis; rather, it holds strengths in using a variety of methods and in encouraging researchers to draw on their individual experiences. They pointed out how 'photographs are often treated as if they were a source of objective and disinterested facts, rather than as complexly coded cultural artefacts' (p. 89). It is, therefore, up to the researcher to learn how to decode photos in order to understand the social and cultural contexts in which a photo was shot.

Visual Sociology and Visual Anthropology Approaches

Pauwels (2012) provided a framework for performing research in visual sociology and visual anthropology, which 'are grounded in the idea that valid scientific insight in society can be acquired by observing, analyzing, and theorizing its visual manifestations: behavior of people and material products of culture' (p. 179). Found images, such as the ones a researcher would collect on social media websites, will communicate historical, social, and cultural information of both the photographer and the viewers, but it may not be possible to learn the history of the images because the photographer is not present to discuss it. In visual sociology and visual anthropology, researchers should look at what is depicted as well as how objects are represented. Despite this unique approach, Pauwels (2012) insisted that visual research should not be treated as a specialized type of sociological research, but rather as an approach that influences the entire research process.

While Pauwels (2012) covered the framework, Collier (2001) outlined the specific steps in how to perform a study using visual anthropology. In what he called 'direct analysis', the researcher uses the content of images as data. First, look at the dataset as a whole and write down the feelings, impressions, and questions that come to mind. Next, log all the images and consider categorizing them if necessary. Then structure the analysis, answer specific questions, conduct statistical analysis as appropriate, and describe them. Finally, return to the dataset as a whole and write the conclusions. Collier (2001) noted the value in comparing images side by side within each step in this process. Direct analysis can also be used with sound and with video.

For example, imagine researchers performing direct analysis on a set of Twitter photographs and videos posted by attendees of a rock concert. The researchers want to learn more about the fan culture of the particular band. Viewing all the items located that were shot at the concert can provide an overview of what the concert experience was like generally, such as an anxiously excited audience, a crowded stadium, and long lines for purchasing refreshments. The overview should then be written down. Then, each image and video might then be viewed individually to determine what aspect of the concert it portrays, such as the band's performance, fans' behaviors toward the band, and interactions between fans. Next, the researchers could then answer their research question about the fan community and culture by comparing each document to one another, describing the set of visual documents qualitatively through description, and describing the set quantitatively through statistics. The answers to the research questions and the discussion can then be written.

Semiotic Analysis

Semiology, or the study of signs, leads to 'detailed accounts of the exact ways the meanings of an image are produced through that image' (Rose, 2012, p. 106). Semiological analysis focuses on the image itself as well as the composition of the image, since the composition of the image contains the signs. Semiotic studies are used for 'approaching sign systems systematically in order to discover how they produce meaning' (Penn, 2000, p. 227). In pictorial semiotics, 'pictures are signs' (Nöth, 2011, p. 300).

In semiotics, a sign is the most basic level of language, and a sign contains two parts: the signified, which can be an abstract or concrete idea or object ('a furry, four-legged animal that loves humans') and the signifier, a word or image that is connected to the signified ('dog') (Saussere, 1966). Semiotics is used frequently in advertising to sell products. Looking at humans as signs in advertisements can help researchers understand how signs are used to communicate symbols, such as an attractive man's face in an advertisement for male skin care products. Advertisements frequently involve signified stereotypes that audiences are accustomed to interpreting, such as a mother serving a presumably healthy and delicious breakfast to her smiling son.

There are several philosophical models for describing types of signs, but perhaps the most useful model for thinking about signs in social media documents is that of Barthes (Barthes, 1967; 1973; 1977; Penn, 2000; van Leeuwen, 2001). According to his approach, a sign's denotation, or a simple description of what the sign is picturing, is easy to decode and requires limited knowledge. For example, a woman wearing a wedding dress is a bride. The diegesis is everything that is

Figure 15.2 Glencoe, Scotland

denoted in the image, such as 'a man wearing a tuxedo standing next to a woman wearing a white veil and an elaborate white dress'. Anchorage is the text that accompanies the image and may clarify the denotation for viewers, such as a Facebook comment stating, 'Here we are right after the ceremony and on our way to the reception together, as Mr. and Mrs. for the very first time!' Barthes calls this function of the text a relay-function. A connotation of the image, or its higher and more abstract levels of meaning, requires cultural knowledge. A connotation can be metonymic, which associates the picture with something else (e.g., a wedding photo connotes love), or synecdochal, in which one part of something communicates something else (a gold ring, which is part of a wedding, connotes marriage). Barthes called the denotation a first-level semiological system, and the connotation a second-level semiological system. Myth, according to Barthes, is a second-level signification; it is 'the means by which a culture naturalizes, or renders invisible, its own norms and ideology' (Penn, 2000, p. 231).

Barthes believed that a photograph 'always carries its referent with itself' (Barthes, 1982, p. 5) in a way that other images do not because a photograph is so close to what it represents. He defined two methods for interpreting a photograph: a studium is an educated, informed viewing and interpretation of a photo, while a punctum speaks loudly to a viewer in unintended ways: 'while the studium is ultimately always coded, a punctum is not' (Barthes, 1982, p. 51). A punctum typically relates to an emotional reaction to a photograph, so it can be difficult to translate it into a textual description. For example, the author of this chapter has a photo of her late father that holds a punctum for her. When she views it, she thinks about fun times she had with him, how much she loved him, and how devastating it was to watch him decline and pass away at a young age due to dementia. Social media sites tend to be places where people can express their feelings surrounding grief and loss of loved ones (Carroll and Landry, 2010). The author's father was never active on social media, so she cannot post on his profile pages. However, she makes that special photo of him her profile picture on significant anniversaries, such as his birthday and the day he passed away.

Penn (2000) described the steps to undertake when performing semiotic analysis. The goal is to find and explain the cultural knowledge that the viewer must understand in the image. First, choose the images, keeping in mind that semiological studies do not utilize statistically representative sampling (as is done in quantitative content analysis); instead, they provide detailed analysis of a few related and purposively selected images. Next, list what is denoted in the image as well as in any associated text. Third, find the connotation or myth in the image by looking at each denotative portion of the image and determining what cultural knowledge it represents. Consider syntagm, or how all the elements relate to each other. After the research question has been answered and all possible denotational relationships have been considered, present the findings for each level of signification in a narration or in a table.

For example, perhaps a researcher wants to learn about what cultural knowledge people from other countries think about when they see photographs of Scotland. Consider the photograph in Figure 15.2. The author took this picture in Glencoe, a region of the Scottish Highlands. She posted this picture and a few other pictures of Glencoe on her Facebook page. She simply labelled each one 'Glencoe'. A friend commented on it: 'Where's the piper? When I went to Glencoe there was someone in a kilt playing the bagpipes ☺'. If researchers included this photograph in a collection of Scottish cultural images for semiotic analysis, they might first list items directly observable in the image, such as 'hills', 'waterfall', 'rocks', 'green grass', the photographer's description of 'Glencoe', and the friend's comment about the bagpipes. At the connotative level, this natural scene of the Scottish Highlands could be said to represent the stereotypical cultural traditions of Scotland, such as kilts and bagpipes, as expressed denotatively through the textual description, the comment, and the hilly, green content of the image. Perhaps the photograph's connection to Scotland could not be made without the syntagm, or the relationship between the textual and the visual elements.

Iconography/iconology

Iconography is a method of determining meaning in an image. It has been described as 'a qualitative method of visual content analysis and interpretation, influenced by cultural traditions and guided by research interests originating both in the humanities and social sciences' (Müller, 2011, p. 285). It is somewhat related to Barthes' visual semiotics in that they both investigate levels of meaning in a visual image. Panofsky (1955) provided three levels of meaning in pictures within his discussion of iconography. While he applied it to art history, it can be applied to any image. The first level, pre-iconographical description, is simply an explanation of what is in the picture. This level, described as the 'primary or natural subject matter' (Panofsky, 1955, p. 40), is similar to Barthes' notion of denotation (van Leeuwen, 2001). Panofsky noted that it can be difficult to denote the subject matter if practical experience has not prepared the researcher for recognizing the representation. Van Leeuwen (2001) suggested trying to identify what is in the image by looking at the title, referring to personal experience, doing background research, considering intertextuality, or reading the image's verbal description. The second level, iconographical analysis, denotes not only the specific people or items signified in the image, but also the ideas, or the 'secondary or conventional subject matter' (van Leeuwen, 2001, p. 40), attached to it. Iconography requires a certain amount of cultural knowledge; to cite Panofsky's example, not everyone would see a painting of the Last Supper and realize that it connoted something more than a dinner party. The third and highest level, iconological analysis, is 'intrinsic meaning or content, constituting the world of "symbolical" values" (van Leeuwen, 2001, p. 40). It is the most subjective and the most difficult to determine of the three levels, and may include viewers' interpretations that the creator of the image did not intend.

Müller (2011) provided guidelines for performing an iconographical/iconological analysis. First, begin research by collecting images and writing a research question. Classify the images, perhaps by their pre-iconographic description at first. Look for images that are prototypical for the research, and describe them. Compare them with one another. To complete the higher levels of analysis, examine both visual and textual information that can possibly attribute meaning to the images. Consider the form (e.g., photographs posted on Instagram), and think about how the production as well as the consumption of the images could create or influence their meaning. Finally, determine what 'the studied visuals convey about the social, political, and cultural context in which they were produced and perceived' (Müller, 2011, p. 294).

Müller provided the example of American presidential campaigns to illustrate the steps in a visual iconological analysis. First collect the photos or videos that relate to the campaign; she uses press photos and debate footage as examples, but these could also come from social media posts. Next, reference the information about the items, such as the photographer's name and the time of publication. Ensure that the research question can fit into an iconographical approach. The three steps in the analysis should be as follows:

1 Describe the content of the images in a neutral way (pre-iconographical). For example, 'Barack Obama talks about education to a group of university students and faculty.' 'Hillary Clinton discusses her plans for health care reform to a group of supporters in Virginia.' 'John McCain outlines Sarah Palin's qualifications for the position of Vice President to Republican voters.'
2 Create categories that reflect the images in the study (iconographical). Categories might include 'speeches', 'health care', 'education', or 'running mate'.
3 Situate the images within the social, political, and cultural contexts of their point in time. 'Ideally, the iconological method will enhance the understanding of the subtle messages and ideas conveyed through the visual presentations of the candidates, and thus implicitly allow identification of the expectations raised by the winning candidate on which his or her presidency will be tested' (Müller, 2011, p. 290). For example, in the 2008 American presidential election, one strength in Obama's campaign was his ability to deliver powerful speeches with which Americans connected (Lister, 2008).

NON-TEXT ANALYSIS METHODS INFLUENCED BY SOCIAL UNDERSTANDINGS

Methods for non-text analysis that have social influences, including discourse analysis, visual social semiotics, and multimodal research are discussed in this section. As noted previously, social and cultural impacts do not exist in their own silos; one frequently forms the other.

Discourse Analysis

Discourse analysis has many different theoretical and practical underpinnings which cannot all be covered in this chapter. Potter (2008) defined it as 'a cluster of related methods for studying language use and its role in social life' (p. 112). Historically, it has been used to study textual language, such as interview transcripts, but discourse analysis is an increasingly popular practice in studies involving non-text documents (Iedema, 2003; Clark, 2008; van Leeuwen, 2008; Neal, 2010a; Vernallis, 2013; Werner, 2012; Rasmussen Pennington, 2016).

Without linguistic transcripts to examine closely for discourses, different social cues must be examined in a film or a still image. Van Leeuwen (2008) described his methods in performing a visual critical discourse analysis. He watches a document to find out how people are depicted and how the viewer is related to the depicted. He includes three dimensions: 'the social distance between depicted people and the viewer, the social relation between depicted people and the viewer, and the social interaction between depicted people and the viewer' (van Leeuwen, 2008, p. 138). For example, people who are shown in a close-up image are shown to the viewer to be 'one of us', while people who appear far away from the camera are 'strangers'.

Discourse analysis is particularly concerned with the role of social interactions in constructing meaning. Also central to creating discourses is intertextuality: how does the meaning of a document depend on meanings of other related documents? For example, in Rasmussen Pennington's (2016) study of user-created videos featuring U2's 'Song for Someone', many producers made references to other U2 songs, U2 concerts, books about U2, and presented mashups of other U2 songs in their videos. For example, one producer commented in her description, 'I'm the singer–songwriter who was pulled on stage during U2's Elevation tour in Las Vegas to sing and jam with my heros [sic]!' U2 paraphernalia appeared in the videos, such as a poster hanging on the wall containing the cover of the band's *Achtung Baby* album. Some producers dressed like members of the band, such as a singer who was wearing an earring, sunglasses, and black clothing that appeared very similar to how Bono (U2's singer) dresses. This illustrates the importance of learning as much as possible about the subject of interest in a study when examining how discourses are constructed.

When performing discourse analysis of visual materials, view the documents multiple times while beginning to find obvious key themes. Consider how meaning is assigned to the images or words. For example, in Werner's (2012) study of YouTube videos in which girls danced like Beyoncé, the girls intertextually alluded to a range of past videos using imitation, parody, similar dress, and similar dance moves, which constructed social discourses about race and gender. Throughout the interpretation process, continue to examine the documents in detail, and refine the themes as they are developed. The discourse analysis process is not as rigid as the development of codes in content analysis, so themes will evolve throughout the research (Rose, 2012). Examine the social influence on the production, content, and consumption of the images. Producers of social media documents tend to be concerned with how their potential audience will receive their creations, so they are likely conscious of potential social reception (McCay-Peet and Quan-Haase, 2016). Additionally, the element of consumption can be quite prominent in social media posts due to the ubiquity of commenting, liking, disliking, and sharing them.

Visual Social Semiotics and Multimodal Research

Visual social semiotics and multimodal research are closely linked approaches that also relate to discourse analysis. Perhaps it could be said that they are first steps in developing research methods that are designed specifically to analyze non-text data.

Visual social semiotics. Visual social semiotics is an approach to semiotics that focuses on the audience's reception to the image and how the meaning of an image is socially created (Rose, 2012). Jewitt and Oyama (2001) provided an example of a print-based cartoon featuring naked young men and their internal thoughts about their interest in sexual activity. The only one who is wondering why he is not interested in sex is visually depicted as an 'other' by means of 'his unbalanced posture, "limp wrist", foppish hair and glasses: he represents "wimp"' (Jewitt and Oyama, 2001, p. 138). The authors provided this example to demonstrate how visual cues can be used as a representational 'syntax' that creates meaning for the viewer.

Iedema (2001) performed visual social semiotic analysis on a documentary film, and identified six levels of analysis in film, from lowest to highest level: frame, shot, scene, sequence, generic stage, and work as a whole. Jewitt and Oyama (2001) presented three different types of simultaneously occurring meaning that can be observed through visual social semiotics. Representational meaning is communicated through what is depicted in the picture, either by actions of the people in the picture or by concepts in the picture. Interactive meaning is conveyed by the relationship between who or what is in the picture and the viewer; this tells the viewer how the image should be viewed. Compositional meaning is created through value communicated by physical placement in the image, physical contrast between items depicted in the image, or other compositional elements.

Multimodal research. The terms 'social semiotic research' and 'multimodal research' are sometimes used interchangeably (Rose, 2012). Driven by the increase in the number of images, films, and other non-text documents in the media and online, the term 'multimodality' was initiated in an attempt to encourage researchers to incorporate non-text documents into semiotic research. Multimodal research lifts the traditional language-only restriction and 'provides the means to describe a practice or representation in all its semiotic capacity in richness' (Iedema, 2003, p. 39). According to Iedema (2003), multimodal research is a discourse analytical practice that can expand the identification of discourses through the analysis of multiple modes. This is an important approach for social media; when people are online, they tend to interact with more than one document at a time, and many of these documents are likely non-textual (Markham, 2008; Rasmussen Neal, 2012). Additionally, different parts of a social media document work together to create and communicate meaning, such as pictures and words (Neal, 2010a) as well as music and images (Vernallis, 2013).

On the Internet, images, sounds, written language, videos, and other formats are all considered part of a text, and all are worthy of analysis. Visual elements, including facial expressions, colors, and movement, as well as music, become interlinked data in multimodality. In transcribing multimodal documents, all these elements should be present at a level of detail necessitated by the research question. They could be presented in a 'transcript' that is actually a table containing these multiple elements. For example, in transcribing a video, the people present, their physical actions, words spoken, and facial expressions could be described at relevant time intervals. Multimodal transcriptions can include textual as well as non-textual descriptions (Flewitt et al., 2012). For example, imagine transcribing a YouTube video that shows a family interacting with each other in a park. Researchers could note not only what the family members said to each other, but also details about what they did (3:54 – mother hands a cup of ice to daughter), nonverbal communication (3:56 – daughter rolls her eyes at mother), screen shots of frames taken at regular intervals or at significant points (screen shot of toddler beginning to scream at 4:35), and sounds (a sound clip of the song that daughter was singing along with at 2:00–2:17).

Van Leeuwen (2011) asserted that multimodal analysis should not be limited to looking at images because today's technologies allow visual design elements such as colors, typefaces, and spatial layouts to communicate meaning. He discussed how writing on websites and presentation slides are both word-oriented and image-oriented, 'and they hang together, not as webs of words, but as multimodal compositions' (p. 568). Additionally, since people do not read text in a sequential or linear fashion online, online text takes on a spatial element as well (van Leeuwen, 2011). The communicative nature of these multiple modes adds layers of meaning to web documents (Mautner, 2012). Mautner (2012), in a discussion about using multimodal discourse analysis on web-based documents, pointed out how intertextuality is an inherent property of hypertext, since hyperlinks send people to related websites. This property reflects the very nature of the World Wide Web.

Adami (2014) developed a 'social semiotic framework for the multimodal analysis of website interactivity' (p. 133). She defined interactivity as the relationship between a user and a text; more specifically, a person and a website. Users' interactivity with websites, or what they can do to a webpage, happens when they click, touch, or type something onto the screen. These actions change the text physically, and from a social perspective, a user gains something from the action. Forms (elements containing hyperlinks), actions (clicking, typing, or anything else that can activate forms), and effects (things that change the screen, such as 'liking' a post), are all semiotic signs that engage the user in interactivity. Her framework proposed the juxtaposition of syntagmatic and paradigmatic dimensions with the sign's ideational function, interpersonal function, textual function, and interactive value in order to understand the meanings and the discourses surrounding interactivity. This framework should be used in conjunction with methods that are used to analyze the text-based content on websites in order to create a more complete picture of the interactions.

Multimodal ethnography. Multimodal ethnography, as the term suggests, is used to find meanings through integrated media, or 'multi-semiotic modes' (Dicks et al., 2006, p. 77). Dicks et al. (2006) outlined this approach by means of describing their project that sought to understand how children play in a hands-on science centre. The researchers' digital recordings of interviews and observations allowed them to observe the modes that create the experience of the science center, including 'colour, texture, light, gesture, and so forth' (Dicks et al., 2006, p. 86), and they noticed how different media provided different semiotic information. They found that video recordings provided much more data than their field notes.

Also reflecting on multimodal ethnography, Dicks and Mason (2012) share the advantages of using 'hypermedia' in ethnographic research, where 'hypermedia' is defined as a type of hypertext incorporating 'a wide variety of media other than text' (p. 131). With multimodal approaches and hypermedia, ethnographers can easily link and integrate different types of modes, whether still and moving images, printed or spoken words, or graphical representations. The possible links are beneficial because they help the data keep their contexts.

Methods that typically accompany ethnography such as participant observation and interviews cannot be used in ethnographic studies of social media documents, since the data consists of found items from frequently anonymous creators. That being said, multimedia ethnography still holds promise for studying the social construction of meaning through the rich artefacts that producers of user-generated YouTube videos, Instagram photos, and so on share online in order to communicate their lived experiences to their audiences.

FUTURE DIRECTIONS

The social and societal impact of information shared by users on the Web continues to grow in influence. As Mautner (2012) explained, '[i]n a variety of domains – from the intensely personal and local to the public and global – discourse on the web is now a key factor in constructing representations of reality and social relationships, while also establishing new conventions for both textuality and intertextuality' (p. 89). These elements of communication are not merely textual in the traditional definition of 'textual' (words on a page), but are also communicated through a range of outlets, such as films, photographs, music, spoken words, and video games. On social media, these outlets communicate so much about individuals and their worlds: feelings, interpersonal relationships, interests, milestones, and anything else that people find important enough to share with their audiences. In turn, their audiences, who can consist of friends and family or complete strangers depending on the user and the social media channel, have the opportunity to interact with these documents by viewing them, 'liking' or 'disliking' them, leaving comments on them, and sharing them (McCay-Peet and Quan-Haase, 2016).

The interplay between language-based and non-language-based documents on social media must be examined together if social science researchers intend to maximize their findings, but the methods they use must differ from the status quo. While this chapter has presented a range of methods that can be used (given the right datasets and appropriate research questions) to analyze non-text social media documents, more work is needed to develop methodologies that will encompass the rich interactions, possible interactivities, and modes of digital communication that can be found today and in the future. As the documentation of lived experience and societal norms evolve, so must the toolkit of a social science researcher.

In conclusion, it is perhaps a responsibility to ensure that research methods enable timely analysis of society's creations, but many questions regarding the development and implementation of these methods have yet to be answered. For example, how can the relatively recent appearance of non-text documents in social science research achieve the same status as the long-standing text-based documents possess? How can the textual and the non-textual be integrated with one another in data collection and analysis while still observing the special challenges that non-text items present to researchers? Although all existing analysis methods to date are described in text, could social science researchers envision a research environment in which we use formats other than text to describe future approaches to analyzing non-text documents? The potential to shape the unchartered non-text territory is wide open, and social science researchers who study social media phenomena must answer the call to form it.

REFERENCES

Adair, J. G. (1984), 'The Hawthorne effect: a reconsideration of the methodological artifact'. *Journal of Applied Psychology*, Vol. 69 No. 2, pp. 334–345.

Adami, E. (2014), 'What's in a click? A social semiotic framework for the multimodal analysis of website interactivity', *Visual Communication*, Vol. 14 No. 2, pp. 133–153.

Ball, M. and Smith, G. (2011), 'Ethnomethodology and the visual: practices of looking, visualization, and embodied action', in Margolis, E. and Pauwels, L., *The SAGE Handbook of Visual Research Methods*, SAGE Publications, London, pp. 392–413.

Banks, M. (2007), *Using Visual Data in Qualitative Research*, SAGE Publications, London.

Barthes, R. (1967), *Elements of Semiology*, Tr. A. Lavers and C. Smith, Hill and Wang, New York.

Barthes, R. (1973), *Mythologies*, Tr. A. Lavers, Paladin, London.

Barthes, R. (1977), *Image Music Text*, Tr. S. Heath, Fontana Press, London.

Barthes, R. (1982), *Camera Lucida: Reflections on Photography*, Tr. R. Howard, Jonathan Cape, London.

Bauer, M.W. (2000), 'Analyzing noise and music as social data', in Bauer, M.W. and

Gaskell, G., *Qualitative Researching with Text, Image and Sound*, SAGE Publications, London, pp. 263–281.

Bell, P. (2001), 'Content analysis of visual images', in van Leeuwen, D. and Jewitt, C., *Handbook of Visual Analysis*, SAGE Publications, London, pp. 10–34.

Berger, J. (1972), *Ways of Seeing*, Penguin, Harmondsworth, England.

Bowen, G.A. (2009), 'Document analysis as a qualitative research method', *Qualitative Research Journal*, Vol. 9 No. 2, pp. 27–40.

Bravo, F. (2014), 'Changing the interval content of algorithmically generated music changes the emotional interpretation of visual images', in *CMMR 2013*, pp. 494–508.

Bresler, L. (2008), 'Music in qualitative research', in Given, L., *The SAGE Encyclopedia of Qualitative Research Methods*, SAGE Publications, Thousand Oaks, CA, pp. 535–538.

Carroll, B. and Landry, K. (2010), 'Logging on and letting out: using online social networks to grieve and to mourn, *Bulletin of Science, Technology & Society'*, Vol. 30 No. 5, pp. 341–349.

Clark, L.S. (2008), 'Multimedia in qualitative research', in Given, L.M., *The SAGE Encyclopedia of Qualitative Research Methods*, SAGE Publications, Thousand Oaks, CA, pp. 533–535.

Collier, M. (2001), 'Approaches to analysis in visual anthropology', in van Leeuwen, D. and Jewitt, C., *Handbook of Visual Analysis*, SAGE Publications, London, pp. 35–60.

Cook, N. (1998), *Analysing Musical Multimedia*, Clarendon Press, Oxford.

Dicks, B., Soyinka, B. and Coffey, A. (2006), 'Multimodal ethnography', *Qualitative Research*, Vol. 6 No. 1, pp. 77–96.

Dicks, B. and Mason, B. (2012), 'Hypermedia and ethnography: reflections on the construction of a research approach', in Dicks, B., *Digital Qualitative Research Methods, Volume III: Data Analysis*, pp. 125–148.

Downie, J.S. (2003), 'Music information retrieval', *Annual Review of Information Science and Technology*, Vol. 37 No. 1, pp. 295–340.

Flewitt, R., Hampel, R., Hauck, M. and Lancaster, L. (2012), 'What are multimodal data and transcription?', in Dicks, B., *Digital Qualitative Research Methods, Volume III: Data Analysis*, pp. 57–76.

Flickr (2015), *Flickr's top-25 photos in 2015* [Online], Available: http://blog.flickr.net/2015/12/01/flickrs-top-25-photos-in-2015/ [4 Dec 2015].

Gibson, B.E. (2008), 'Videorecording', in Given, L., *The SAGE Encyclopedia of Qualitative Research Methods*, SAGE Publications, Thousand Oaks, CA, pp. 917–919.

Goodwin, C. (2001), 'Practices of seeing visual analysis: an ethnomethodological approach', in van Leeuwen, D. and Jewitt, C., *Handbook of Visual Analysis*, SAGE Publications, London, pp. 157–182.

Hayes, M., van Stolk-Cooke, K. and Muench, F. (2015), 'Understanding Facebook use and the psychological affects of use across generations', *Computers in Human Behavior*, Vol. 49, pp. 507–511.

Iedema, R. (2001), 'Analysing film and television: a social semiotic account of *Hospital: an Unhealthy Business*', in van Leeuwen, D. and Jewitt, C., *Handbook of Visual Analysis*, SAGE Publications, London, pp. 183–204.

Iedema, R. (2003), 'Multimodality, resemiotization: extending the analysis of discourse as multi-semiotic practice', *Visual Communication*, Vol. 2 No. 1, pp. 29–57.

Jewitt, C. and Oyama, R. (2001), 'Visual meaning: a social semiotic approach', in van Leeuwen, D. and Jewitt, C., *Handbook of Visual Analysis*, SAGE Publications, London, pp. 134–156.

Julien, H. (2008), 'Content analysis', in Given, L., *The SAGE Encyclopedia of Qualitative Research Methods*, SAGE Publications, Thousand Oaks, CA, pp. 121–123.

Juslin, P.N. and Laukka, P. (2003), 'Communication of emotions in vocal and expression in music performance: different channels, same code?', *Psychological Bulletin,* Vol. 129 No. 5, pp. 770–814.

Juslin, P.N. and Sloboda, J.A. (2010), *Handbook of Music and Emotion*, Oxford University Press, Oxford.

Knoblauch, H. and Tuma, R. (2011), 'Videography: an interpretative approach to video-recorded micro-social interaction', in Margolis, E. and Pauwels, L., *The SAGE Handbook of Visual Research Methods*, SAGE Publications, Thousand Oaks, CA, pp. 414–430.

Krippendorff, K. (1980), *Content Analysis: An Introduction to its Methodologies*, SAGE Publications, London.

Lemke, J.L. (2002), 'Travels in hypermodality', *Visual Communication*, Vol. 1 No. 3, pp. 299–325.

Lister, M. and Wells, L. (2001), 'Seeing beyond belief: cultural studies as an approach to studying the visual', in van Leeuwen, D. and Jewitt, C., *Handbook of Visual Analysis*, SAGE Publications, London, pp. 61–91.

Lister, R. (2008), *Why Barack Obama won* [Online], Available: http://news.bbc.co.uk/1/hi/world/americas/us_elections_2008/7704360.stm [14 December 2015].

Markham, A.N. (2008), 'Internet in qualitative research', in Given, L., *The SAGE Encyclopedia of Qualitative Research Methods*, SAGE Publications, Thousand Oaks, CA, pp. 455–459.

Mautner, G. (2012), 'Time to get wired: using web-based corpora in critical discourse analysis', in Dicks, B., *Digital Qualitative Research Methods, Volume III: Data Analysis*, pp. 179–211.

Mayring, P. (2000), 'Qualitative content analysis', *Forum: Qualitative Social Research*, Vol. 1 No. 2, Available: http://www.qualitative-research.net/index.php/fqs/article/view/1089/2386.

McCay-Peet, L. and Quan-Haase, A. (2015), 'User engagement in social media studies', in O'Brien, H. and Cairns, P., *Why Engagement Matters: Cross-Disciplinary Perspectives and Innovations on User Engagement with Digital Media*, pp. 199-217.

Müller, M.G. (2011), 'Iconography and iconology as a visual method and approach', in Margolis, E. and Pauwels, L., *The SAGE Handbook of Visual Research Methods*, SAGE Publications, Thousand Oaks, CA, pp. 283–297.

Neal, D.M. (2010a), 'Emotion-based tags in photographic documents: the interplay of text, image, and social influence', *Canadian Journal of Information and Library Science*, Vol. 34 No. 3, pp. 329–353.

Neal, D.M. (2010b), 'What makes for a happy photograph cluster?', Paper presented to the Document Academy Conference, Denton, TX.

Neal, D., Campbell, A., Neal, J., Little, C., Stroud-Mathews, A., Hill, S. and Bouknight-Lyons, C. (2009), 'Musical facets, tags, and emotion: can we agree?', paper presented to the iConference, Chapel Hill, NC.

Nettl, B. (1983), *The Study of Ethnomusicology: Twenty-nine Issues and Concepts*, University of Illinois Press, Urbana, IL.

Nöth. W. (2011), 'Visual semiotics: key features and an application to picture ads', in Margolis, E. and Pauwels, L., *The SAGE Handbook of Visual Research Methods*, SAGE Publications, Thousand Oaks, CA, pp. 570–589.

O'Connor, B.C. and Wyatt, R. (2004), *Photo Provocations: Thinking in, with, and about Photographs*, Scarecrow Press, Lanham, MD.

Panofsky, E. (1955), *Meaning in the Visual Arts*, University of Chicago Press, Chicago.

Pauwels, L. (2011), 'Researching websites as social and cultural expressions: methodological predicaments and a multimodal model for analysis', in Margolis, E. and Pauwels, L., *The SAGE Handbook of Visual Research Methods*, SAGE Publications, Thousand Oaks, CA, pp. 570–589.

Pauwels, L. (2012), 'Visual sociology reframed: an analytical synthesis and discussion of visual methods in social and cultural research', in Dicks, B., *Digital Qualitative Research Methods, Volume III: Data Analysis*, pp. 179–211.

Penn, G. (2000), 'Semiotic analysis of still images', in Bauer, M.W. and Gaskell, G., *Qualitative Researching with Text, Image and Sound*, SAGE Publications, London, pp. 227–245.

Pew Research Center (2014), *Social networking fact sheet* [Online], Available: http://www.pewinternet.org/fact-sheets/social-networking-fact-sheet/ [4 Dec 2015].

Potter, J. (2008), 'Discourse analysis', in Given, L.M., *The SAGE Encyclopedia of Qualitative Research Methods*, SAGE Publications, Thousand Oaks, CA, pp. 231–233.

Power, M.J. (2006), 'The structure of emotion: an empirical comparison of six models', *Cognition & Emotion*, Vol. 20 No. 5, pp. 694–713.

Prior, L.F. (2008), 'Document analysis', in Given, L.M., *The SAGE Encyclopedia of Qualitative Research Methods*, SAGE Publications, Thousand Oaks, CA, pp. 218–221.

Rasmussen Neal, D. (2012), *Indexing and Retrieval of Non-Text Information*, De Gruyter Saur, Berlin.

Rasmussen Pennington, D. (2016), 'The most passionate cover I've seen': Emotional information in fan-created U2 music videos', *Journal of Documentation*, Vol. 72 No. 3, 569-590.

Rorvig, M.E. (1993), 'A method for automatically extracting visual documents', *Journal of the American Society for Information Science*, Vol. 44 No. 1, pp. 40–56.

Rose, D. (2000), 'Analysis of moving images', in Bauer, M.W. and Gaskell, G., *Qualitative Researching with Text, Image and Sound*, SAGE Publications, London, pp. 246–262.

Rose, G. (2012), *Visual Methodologies: An Introduction to Researching with Visual Methods*, SAGE Publications, London.

Saumure, K. and Given, L.M. (2008), 'Virtual research', in Given, L., *The SAGE Encyclopedia of Qualitative Research Methods*, SAGE Publications, Thousand Oaks, CA, pp. 927–930.

Saussere, F. de (1966), *Course in General Linguistics*, Tr. A. Riedlinger, McGraw Hill, New York.

Shatford, S. (1986), 'Analyzing the subject of a picture: a theoretical approach', *Cataloging & Classification Quarterly*, Vol. 6 No. 3, pp. 39–62.

Smith, T. (2015a), *By the numbers: 25 amazing Vine statistics* [Online], Available: http://expandedramblings.com/index.php/vine-statistics/ [4 Dec 2015].

Smith, T. (2015b), *By the numbers: 120+ amazing YouTube statistics* [Online], Available: http://expandedramblings.com/index.php/youtube-statistics/ [4 Dec 2015].

Strauss, A. and Corbin, J. (1998), *Basics of Qualitative Research: Techniques and Procedures for Developing Grounded Theory*, SAGE Publications, London.

Svenonius, E. (1994), 'Access to nonbook materials: the limits of subject indexing for visual and aural languages', *Journal of the American Society for Information Science*, Vol. 45 No. 8, pp. 600–606.

van Leeuwen, T. (2001), 'Semiotics and iconography', in van Leeuwen, D. and Jewitt, C., *Handbook of Visual Analysis*, SAGE Publications, London, pp. 92–118.

van Leeuwen, T. (2008), *Discourse and Practice: New Tools for Critical Analysis*, Oxford University Press, Oxford.

van Leeuwen, T. (2011), 'Multimodality and multimodal research', in Margolis, E. and Pauwels, L., *The SAGE Handbook of Visual Research Methods*, SAGE Publications, Thousand Oaks, CA, pp. 549–569.

van Leeuwen, T. and Jewitt, C. (2001), 'Introduction', in van Leeuwen, D. and Jewitt, C., *Handbook of Visual Analysis*, SAGE Publications, London, pp. 1–9.

Vernallis, C. (2013), *Unruly Media: YouTube, Music Video, and the New Digital Cinema*, Oxford University Press, Oxford.

Watson, M. and Douglas, F. (2012), 'It's making us look disgusting…and it makes me feel like a mink…it makes me feel depressed!: using photovoice to help "see" and understand the perspectives of disadvantaged young people about the neighbourhood determinants of their mental well-being', *International Journal of Health Promotion and Education*, Vol. 50 No. 6, pp. 278–295.

Werner, A. (2012), 'Getting bodied with Beyoncé on YouTube', in Bennett, A. and Robards, B., *Mediated Youth Cultures: The Internet, Belonging, and New Cultural Configurations*, Palgrave Macmillan, London, pp. 182–196.

Zephoria (2015), *The top 20 valuable Facebook statistics* [Online], Available: https://zephoria.com/top-15-valuable-facebook-statistics/ [4 Dec 2015].

Twitter as Method: Using Twitter as a Tool to Conduct Research

Bonnie Stewart

This chapter explores the use of Twitter as a platform for – and subject of – academic research. While Twitter practices and societal impacts are the subject of increasing research interest, Twitter is also a viable and flexible means of engaging in the research process. Twitter offers a rich environment for the examination of social and material practices within the digital sphere, and generates public and private data that can be analyzed via a variety of methods and methodological approaches. This chapter explores emergent uses for the platform as a tool, technique, or process in the pursuit of research goals.

INTRODUCTION

The word 'ethnography,' in traditional social science circles, does not necessarily call to mind images of laptops, smartphones, or Twitter hashtags. Described by Boellstorff, Nardi, Pearce, and Taylor (2012) as 'the pre- mier modality of qualitative research' (p. xiii), ethnography centers on detailed and situated accounts of specific cultures. Yet the ubiquity and techno-centricity of contemporary social media platforms is a far cry from the exoticized landscapes of classic ethnographic fieldwork. Yet while it is difficult to imagine ethnographic pioneers like Mead or Malinowski tweeting, ethnography need not entail unmediated, face-to-face investigation, nor refer to a study of Otherness.

Rather, ethnography offers a means to examine the practices, knowledge, and lifeworlds of members of a specific culture (Boellstorff et al, 2012), whether familiar or exoticized, mediated or face-to-face. As digital technologies have become integrated into cultural practices – and indeed become sites of cultural practice on their own – ethnography has been adopted and adapted extensively for research into online practices. Turkle (1995) examined interactions within early online multi-user environments, Green (1999) conducted an ethnography of virtual reality, and Baym (2000) used ethnography to study an online community of soap opera fans. Ethnography in the digital sphere has given rise to neologisms: the work of Hine (2000) is heavily associated with the term 'virtual ethnography,' while the work of Schau and Gilly (2003) and Kozinets (2010) framed its own ethnographic investigations into online practices as 'netnography.'

This chapter recounts the role Twitter played at each step of an ethnographic study examining networked scholarship (Stewart, 2015a). Framing Twitter as a subset of participatory culture (Jenkins, 2006) suited to ethnography's focus on cultural meaning-making, and continuing through recruitment, participant observation, analysis, and dissemination, this case analysis of a Twitter-based research study examines how Twitter's conventions operate and impact research. I outline my use of Twitter profiles to elicit participants' perspectives on networked influence and identity, and share the resulting findings – and their implications for researchers wanting to work successfully on Twitter. The chapter also examines the practical and ethical challenges of doing research in a site where communications are by default public but not necessarily intended for all publics.

My 2015 dissertation was an ethnography of influence and identity within the participatory culture of what is sometimes called 'academic Twitter,' a specific microcosm of the broader lifeworld of networked scholarship (Greenhow, Robelia, & Hughes, 2009; Quan-Haase, Suarez, & Brown, 2015). I had the privilege of researching and analyzing a small set of participants through a period of relatively dramatic shift in Twitter as a participatory culture. The study described in this chapter was conducted between October 2013 and February 2014, with analysis and writing taking place into early 2015.

While it was ethnography's depth and attention to culturally-specific practices that drew me towards the method, I did not initially intend to deploy Twitter as a methodological tool, only a site of investigation. It was during the emergent process of developing a methodological framework for my research questions that I realized I could go one step further, and utilize Twitter as a method of sorts; a space for soliciting and collecting data. This chapter is the story of that process.

BACKGROUND

My field of study sits at the intersection of digital pedagogies and higher education studies, and is itself as emergent as my dissertation methods. In a thesis proposal begun in 2012, I set out to examine a phenomenon that went, variously, by terms like digital scholarship (Weller, 2011) and open scholarship (Wiley & Hilton, 2009). It would, later that year, be encompassed by an appellation I eventually adopted for my own work, networked participatory scholarship or NPS (Veletsianos & Kimmons, 2012). NPS asserts that '[s]cholars are part of a complex techno-cultural system that is ever changing in response to both internal and external stimuli, including technological innovations and dominant cultural values' (Veletsianos & Kimmons, 2012, p. 773), and encourages examination of that complex techno-cultural system and the practices that constitute it.

My study originated in my own desire to understand and articulate not only my own lived experience but that of the culture and communities in which I was engaged. When I began to frame my investigation in 2012, I was more aware of Weller or Veletsianos as Twitter colleagues than I was of their formal scholarship on the topic. My use of Twitter dates back to 2007. By the time I returned to academia for a Ph.D in 2010, I had a sizeable network and used the platform daily, sharing links and engaging in conversations. It was an extension of my established blog network, which was primarily comprised of writers and players in the amorphous but growing field of social media professionals. As an educator long-employed in higher education settings,

I was also interested in the implications of social media for education, and had always included in my Twitter network a wide range of scholars and educators active in the medium. Thus when I entered my Ph.D program in 2010, I gradually added further contingents of senior scholars, thinkers, and fellow Ph.D students who offered camaraderie and a support network not always available in my tiny, new, regional program. By 2012, I was, in effect, both a junior scholar in the academy and a robustly networked scholar on Twitter, regularly engaged in blogging and micro-blogging conversations with leaders in my field. Yet, research exploring the distinctions between lived experiences of institutional identity and networked identity for scholars was minimal.

My literature review turned up studies that showed Twitter self-disclosures among professors might increase student perceptions of instructor credibility (Johnson, 2011) and that social media in general encouraged institutional innovation (Weller, 2012) and helped scholars strengthen existing relationships and build new ones in their areas of research (Gruzd, Wellman, & Takhteyev, 2011). Research into Twitter use at academic conferences (Reinhardt, Ebner, Beham, & Costa, 2009) suggested that the platform could enhance connections and make delegates aware of emerging issues and conversations they might otherwise have missed. However, very little research exploring Twitter's effects on scholarly peer relations or perceptions was as yet available at that time. Rather, as Harley, Acord, Earl Novell, Lawrence, and King (2010) reported, 'experiments in new genres of scholarship and dissemination are occurring in every field, but they are taking place within the context of relatively conservative value and reward systems that have the practice of peer review at their core' (p. 13). Even where digital practices were considered within the academy, they were seldom taken up on their own terms but rather as shadows of conventional practices. Thus, I set out to study the lived experience of NPS and particularly academic Twitter. As ethnography, the investigation focused on the social, cultural, and material practices that circulated within academic Twitter as a microcosm of participatory culture and NPS.

My immersion in both academia and scholarly networks led me to suspect that influence and identity in academic Twitter are, in Geertz's (1973) foundational ethnographic terms, 'suspended in webs of significance' (p. 2) not broadly visible through the lens of conventional academic practices and concepts. To individuals acculturated to the practices of the academy, networked, Twitter-based webs of significance may sometimes appear arbitrary as compared against institutionally-legitimated concept(s) of academic influence and identity. Yet as Geertz (1973) noted, '(L)ooking at the ordinary in places where it takes unaccustomed forms brings out not, as has so often been claimed, the arbitrariness of human behavior…the degree to which its meaning varies according to the pattern of life by, which it is informed' (p. 7). The central premise of my dissertation was that participatory practices are informed by a different – if increasingly ordinary to many – pattern of life, one whose webs of significance have implications for higher education.

My own embeddedness within the research site situated the study in what Boellstorff (2008) frames as the ethnographic tradition of Boas, as opposed to that of Malinowski. The Boasian tradition works against the separation of ethnographic Self and Native Other, embracing researchers who 'are similar to (or personally involved with) those they study' (Boellstorff, 2008, p. 69), and seeking 'equality and complicity rather than hierarchy and distance' (Boellstorff, 2008, p. 69). Thus I wanted my research process to be participatory, engaging participants as fellow knowers and opening spaces for feedback and input not only from participants but from the broader network. The study made no claims of neutral, generalizable knowledge but, rather, focused on the ways in which open scholarly influence is experienced and understood by specifically located individuals. These 'situated knowledges' (Haraway, 1988) are perspectives shaped by particular social locations, material realities, and power relations. This emphasis on situated knowledges extended to my own locations and relationships to the research context. This relationality and situatedness was, for me, a form of responsibility to the work I engaged in and the multiple realities I engaged with.

WHAT TYPES OF RESEARCH QUESTIONS CAN TWITTER ADDRESS?

As a relational, networked cultural environment, Twitter is particularly well-suited to research into situated knowledges. Since the platform is based around curated, cultivated identities (Hogan, 2010) and their interactions with other entities, its lens is always multiple, fluid and relatively non-hierarchical. That it is non-hierarchical does not mean that the power laws of networks and the power relations of the societies its users belong to do not privilege some voices over others, often significantly, but simply that its structure is based on a logic of virality rather than entrenched hierarchy. This means that Twitter serves as a particularly apt site for the study of cultural virality, but also offers the means by which to gain novel perspectives on a phenomenon or culture normally bound by institutional frameworks, such as scholarship. Additionally, Twitter is a valuable platform for research into decentralized, non-gatekept professional cultures, at least within professions whose members congregate on the site.

The purpose of my own study was twofold. It aimed to articulate the practices and indicators by which networked scholars build public, credible identities, status positions, and influence in scholarly networks and on Twitter in particular. I also set out to provide an ethnographic portrait of academic Twitter as a site of scholarship, care, and vulnerability. Ultimately, the study concluded that networked scholarly practices of engagement align broadly with Boyer's (1990) framework for scholarship (Stewart, 2015c), yet enable and demand scholars' individual cultivation of influence, visibility, and audiences (Stewart, 2015b). I also found that performative deployment of traditional conventions of orality, including 'agonistic, informal, and playful speech forms tended to generate by far the most signals of attention in terms of likes and retweets,' (Stewart, 2015d, Section Orality & Literacy Collapsed, para 3), even within academic Twitter circles. The in-depth investigations recounted in this chapter, which I undertook using Twitter and other methodological tools, allowed me to make visible the ways in which networked scholarship rewards connection, collaboration, and curation between individuals rather than roles or institutions, and fosters cross-disciplinary and public engagement and a bridging of the personal/professional divide. My study contributes to knowledge by situating networked scholarly practices within the scholarly tradition, while articulating the terms on which networked practices open up new spheres of influence – as well as visibility, care, and vulnerability – for scholars.

TWITTER AS METHOD – HOW I DID MY STUDY

My study of academic Twitter utilized traditional ethnographic methods adapted for a geographically distributed, digital-communications-based study. The study's primary methods were participant observation, interviews, and document analysis, all aimed at investigating the circulation of identity and influence within NPS. However, with the exception of the interviews, each method had a specific Twitter-based component to it, as did each phase within the broader study.

Selection

My first use of Twitter in the study was to employ it, in conjunction with my longstanding blog, as a means of soliciting participants.

Since the study focused on scholars whose networked participation was a central, sustained aspect of their scholarly work, identity, and influence development, I wanted to use social networking sites (SNS) – primarily Twitter – as an apt way of spreading the call for volunteers. I wanted participants who were deeply embedded in networks and in Twitter particularly. My criteria demanded that participants be situated within academia as well as in NPS, so as to enable comparison of lived experiences within the two scholarly spheres. In order to examine whether the cultivation of influence operated differently in the two spheres, I needed the study to include graduate students as well as full professors and administrators, and the gamut of academic status positions in between. I also aimed to recruit participants from a wide range of geopolitical and identity locations within the Anglo-academic world, and from across academic disciplines, as research has shown that there can be disciplinary distinctions in Twitter use (Holmberg & Thelwall, 2014; Quan-Haase, Suarez, & Brown, 2015). I sought at least twelve participants.

Recruitment occurred through an open, public call for volunteers, disseminated via Twitter and scholarly networks more broadly. I developed an official call for participants, approved by my Research Ethics Board (REB[1]) and posted it to my longstanding blog, along with a meme-generator image of Uncle Sam's famous war recruiting poster. The image read 'I want you, for research purposes.' My goal, while signaling formally to scholars with my carefully constructed and approved REB language, was also to signal – through the wry and web-native meme format of the image – my own facility with networked spaces and conventions. I wanted to position myself as an insider, someone to be trusted to understand the structures and webs of significance of networks and academic Twitter, and to make participant contributions legible in terms the academy could also understand.

When my blog post containing the call for volunteers was posted, I shared the link via Twitter and Facebook. It was shared and re-tweeted over 150 times, and ultimately resulted in 33 formal responses expressing interest in participating. The post was viewed over 600 times in the first 24 hours. At that time, I had approximately 5,000 Twitter followers, at least half of whom were in some way higher education-focused, which was likely helpful in ensuring the call's circulation on Twitter. However, even had I had a newer account or less reach, I could have strategically maximized the call's circulation by including or addressing network leaders in the tweet that shared the link, or by repeating the tweet more than a couple of times. I had enough response in a short period of time that I chose not to spread the call further, but Twitter was absolutely key in getting the word out there to the people I wanted to recruit.

In order to operationalize NPS' participatory ethos and select participants from the pool of volunteers, I drew from two key concepts of networked practice: White and LeCornu's (2011) visitors and residents typology for online engagement, and Bruns' (2007) concept of produsage.

The visitors and residents continuum is a framework for engagement in digital environments, which draws on metaphors of tool and place to differentiate the ways users perceive the web and its purposes. White and LeCornu argue that while visitors tend to see digital environments in tool-oriented or instrumental terms, residents operate from a relational sense of place and presence with others.

My call for participants was designed specifically to recruit resident networked scholars, rather than visitors. It centered on resident practices, asking for participants who had blogged and used Twitter for at least two years. However, 'even Twitter and blogs can be approached in the less-visible visitor mode when people use them to consume rather than produce Internet content' (Connaway, Lanclos, & Hood, 2013, Mode and Mode Combinations section, para. 5). Thus, to try to ensure that participants were also engaged in participatory, relational sharing, I drew on

Bruns' (2007) idea of produsage, in which networked production and consumption are collapsed and combined, creating reciprocal audiences through the sharing of communications and artifacts. Thus only volunteers who actively shared their work on Twitter, engaged with the work of others, and curated relevant scholarly content for their network were considered for the study.

From the pool of volunteers, I chose 14 participants and eight 'exemplar' identities, selecting for maximal diversity within the overall participant group. The exemplars were not participants in the research but supporters who allowed their Twitter profiles to be assessed by the participants as part of the research process. The 14 active participants came from the United States, Canada, Mexico, Ireland, South Africa, Italy, Singapore, and Australia. 10 were female; four male. Eight self-identified as part of the dominant ethnic population for their area; six did not. Four identified as gay. One participant withdrew before the completion of the study; no individual data on her was used in the dissertation.

Before disseminating the call for participants through my blog and social media, I had been concerned that my embeddedness within scholarly networks might limit the scope of volunteers to people already known to me. While not an issue in terms of Boasian ethnography, I did want to try to mitigate the potential issue of what Pariser (2011) calls a 'filter bubble,' wherein network selection limits input to that which does not challenge pre-existing concepts or biases. However, the circulation of the call for participants was wide enough that almost half of the volunteers were unknown or almost-unknown to me. Thus, of the 14 selected participants, three were entirely new names whom I hadn't encountered before via Twitter or blogging, while four were loose ties, four were moderately familiar contacts, and three were individuals with whom I'd had ongoing direct networked interactions over the previous couple of years. Additionally, seven were Ph.D students or candidates at various stages of completion, two of whom also held long-standing administrative or teaching positions within their institution. Three were early career scholars, one on tenure-track; three were senior professors or researchers. They came from various disciplines, and their ages ranged from late twenties through fifties. Their network scale varied as well; their Twitter accounts ranged from a few hundred followers to 15,000 followers.

Participants all chose to be openly identified in the research by their public Twitter handle, with the exception of the one participant who withdrew. The Twitter accounts of identified participants were all public, as was the account created for the participant observation process; to an extent these serve as open data. Drafts of the research process and findings were blogged for public input as well as shared with participants, as an effort to keep the process open and participatory and in keeping with the ethos of NPS. Four of 13 participants commented on my blog about the participant observation process (Stewart, 2014), adding their perspectives to the public record of my own reflections on the experience. Overall, the commitment to openness meant that the research project involved constant communications and iterative knowledge claims; since my goal with the project was to come to a deeper understanding of a collective cultural experience, the effort to be accountable and inclusive towards the perspectives of members of that collective felt imperative.

Participant Observation

Boellstorff (2008) calls participant observation 'the centerpiece of any truly ethnographic approach' (p. 69), entailing a deep and embedded – if also always situated and partial – experiential as well as elicited knowledge of the culture under study. I made the decision to conduct participant observation for my study primarily via Twitter, over a period from November 2013 through the end of February 2014. During this period, participants also made their blogs, Facebook accounts, and other sites of networked scholarly participation available and open to me for observation, but Twitter was at the core of my daily observations. The fact that Twitter as a platform allows for public posting and non-reciprocal visibility and following, and that the vast majority of scholarly accounts my participants engaged with were public rather than locked, made it easy to observe participants' conversations and their retweeting (RT) behaviours in real time.

In order to conduct participant observation on Twitter, I created the @BonResearch Twitter account for observation purposes, as separate from the @bonstewart account I have used since June 2007 and continued to use during the research period. With the @BonResearch account, I followed only my research participants, exemplars, and dissertation committee members, enabling me to focus my field of vision. I logged into the @BonResearch account from one to three times daily, trying to accommodate for vast time zone differences among my participants, as I wanted to observe them in action and not just from the records they left on their Twitter feeds. Being located on the east coast of North America, one hour ahead of New York and Toronto time, had unintended but significant benefits; I seldom logged in for observation without finding some participant also active.

I observed – and noted, in an offline notebook – the ways in which participants presented themselves, engaged with others, and shared their work and that of other people. When participants engaged with others, I tended to click through to see the entire conversation, except where non-participants' privacy settings did not allow. I did not include non-participant data in my observations, but did note the profile characteristics of participants' conversation partners, paying particular attention to issues of scale and status in relation to engagement.

I tweeted minimally from the @BonResearch account, but did sometime share public 'notes to self' on my observations regarding academic Twitter norms and emergent patterns. I also utilized the Twitter 'favorites' feature to mark daily participant tweets that I saw as relating to perceptions of identity and self-presentation. The favorites feature appears as one of three available actions under any given tweet, along with the 'reply' and 'retweet' (RT) features. Favorites has traditionally been made actionable on most platforms via a star-shaped icon that, when pressed by a user, adds the tweet to a searchable collection of that user's personal favorites.[2] At some point after favorites were introduced, Twitter shifted its functionality and made favorited tweets visible in their originators' notifications, thus acting as a communications signal between users. Thus, favorites operate similarly to the Facebook 'like' feature, except with storage capacity. Favoriting tweets during the research process allowed me to gather a body of stored data that I was able to return to for ongoing in-depth examination, without identified tweets getting swept away in ongoing Twitter streams. This allowed me, even before formal analysis began, to gain a broad sense of patterns of usage and common themes.

At the same time, my use of favorites also served as a visible signal to my participants that I was present and active in their feeds. I experience some trepidation about the potential for my favoriting practices to shape users' behaviors, but since all participants were longstanding Twitter users and scholars with a sophisticated understanding of research, and because I approached Twitter as a performative space (Papacharissi, 2012), I chose to favorite anyhow. My reasoning was, first, that making the process visible and as transparent as I could was more in keeping with the participatory ethos I wanted to foster. Additionally, since my participants were researchers operating in an environment always already marked by conscious self-presentation and audience awareness, to assume that there was an authentic pattern of behavior that my favorites interfered with seemed like a pretense. For the most part, after the research participants expressed that they would miss my favorites, though I'm not sure whether that indicates that they blended into the mix or not. However, had I not been researching a highly resident Twitter population already accustomed to the (supposed) positive reinforcement of favorites, and with a professional understanding of research, I might have made a different choice.

24-hour Reflections

The first document analysis portion of the research involved an in-depth analysis of what participants deemed a representative 24-hour period within their networked participation. Participants were asked to select and identify this period either during or shortly after its conclusion, at which point both they and I would embark on a close examination – and in their case, self-analysis – of their interactions and perceptions. Essentially an intensive period of participant observation aimed at helping me gain contextual perspective on individuals' practices and their understandings and perceptions of those practices, the 24-hour reflection invited participants to create and submit a short document with screen captures outlining and interpreting their networked participation over the course of a particular window in time. I invited each participant to 'be on watch for a time when your networked engagement is reasonably high and reasonably representative of the ways in which Twitter/social media/blogging enhances and/or challenges you as a person and as an academic identity' and then, after notifying me that their chosen period was underway or recently concluded, to collect screen captures of their interactions and 'write short contextualizing commentary for the screen shots, explaining your thought processes as best as you remember behind the things I'll see. I'm interested in what the screenshots illustrate in terms of your strategies and signals around influence and connections, even if these strategies haven't been things you've thought about consciously until this point' (research email, November 27, 2013).

While Twitter was at the core of the majority of submitted 24-hour reflection documents, this was one of the few methods within the broader study where I branched out to observe participants in other sites, so long as they invited me to engage in those spaces and allowed me access. Three participants incorporated blog posts or blog comments into their 24-hour reflection documents; five included Facebook interactions while two featured Google Plus and four, Instagram.

Of the 14 participants, 11 submitted short reflective documents with screen captures of their interactions and understandings. Before receiving the documents, I engaged in my own screen capturing. I traced their conversations and interactions with extra care during the 24-hour windows. Then, after receiving documents from the participants themselves, I checked their highlighted interactions and perspectives against my own notes, to verify and contextualize.

Profile Assessments

Of all the specific methods for data collection that I employed in the study, this was the most directly Twitter-focused, though it did not actually employ Twitter as a tool. Eight ineligible volunteers generously agreed to be indirect participants and to allow their Twitter profiles to be used as exemplar identities. As a result, I was able to examine participants' logics of network influence and identity. This step in the research process served as a form of written interview, but relied on the visual signals of Twitter profiles to elicit specific information. Its goal was to investigate how participants 'read' other scholars' Twitter profiles and to consider, by extension, how Twitter's affordances shape dominant NPS concepts of influence.

The exemplar identities were a diverse group, drawn from different disciplines, geographic locations, and academic status positions. They had Twitter followings ranging from approximately 200 to more than 23,000. All eight identified in their profiles as in some way as interested in higher education or the academy. I took screen captures of the exemplar profiles, and then created Word documents that showcased five different profiles. I asked participants to assess the five different exemplar profiles according to the following guidelines.

> Please look at each screenshot and make a few notes about how you interpret the (limited) information available to you about a) this person's influence and b) this person's potential value to your network. If these people were to follow you on Twitter, would you consider following them back or otherwise engaging? Why? Why not? (Be as honest as you are comfortable being. Critical comments can be anonymized.)
> If you are familiar with these people – even just by reputation – please outline how that affects your perception of them.
> If you were to follow only one or two of the people below, which would you be likely to choose and why? (Research email, January 6, 2014).

I aimed to match participants with exemplars they might not be overly familiar with, though I recognized that participants might have pre-existing perceptions of some of the profiles they encountered. There were 12 participants who completed and submitted this assignment.

While this method of data collection was designed to operate using a simple Word document with images pasted on it, nine of the 12 participants who completed it overtly mentioned that they did not simply assess exemplars based on the screen captures that I provided, but actually went to Twitter and looked up the individuals before making judgments. Many of them noted that this broader assessment of a user's feed before deciding to follow was their regular practice, and they wanted either to enact it or at least to have it reflected in the research data. I had not wanted to ask people to make the extra effort to go to the Twitter platform, nor had I wanted to direct their behavior in regards to assessment and following practices, but the extent to which participants noted this extra step was interesting. The preponderance of participants who chose to go out of their way to Twitter for an additional, more dynamic assessment of exemplars may reflect the highly resident population of networked scholars from whom my sample was drawn. In combination with the responses to the profile questions, however, it contributed to the overall conclusion that resident networked scholars have complex literacies and logics surrounding the way they 'read' the influence and identities of peers they encounter on Twitter.

Interviews

While interviews within the study discussed participants' practices and perceptions regarding Twitter, they did not employ Twitter as a platform in any way. Rather, 10 participant interviews were via Skype, and in one case, I conducted a follow-up interview, also via Skype, some months later. The interviews were semi-structured, recorded, and lasted approximately 60–75 minutes. Since ethnographic interviewing emphasizes rapport and an exchange of views as part of a broader, respectful, ongoing relationship (Heyl, 2001, p. 369), I did not begin the interviews until a few weeks – and in some cases more than a month – into participant observation, with its daily Twitter exchanges and more in-depth email exchanges in the background. In the interviews, I asked open-ended questions related to the participant's networked practices, relationships, networks, reputation, and scholarly identity. Questions were individuated for each participant depending on the specifics of his or her 24-hour reflection on networked engagement. Conversations were encouraged to emerge and diverge from the interview script.

Coding and Analysis

I transcribed the interviews using unfocused transcription technique, 'without attempting to represent…detailed contextual or interactional characteristics' (Gibson & Brown, 2009, p. 116) and collated the transcripts with the documents participants had submitted, creating 13 individual participant documents. In a number of cases, relevant participant blog posts were also included in these individual documents. All 13 active participants completed either an interview or the 24-hour reflection, so data for the study were comprised of the 13 participant documents plus my notes, favorites, and screen captures from participant observation. Drawing on the guiding literature and framework for the research, I then identified key themes (Ryan & Bernard, 2003) emerging from the participant documents and from the 334 screen captures of tweets and other interactions, the more than 700 favorites, and my own offline notes. To analyze the situated knowledges represented within the participant documents and the other data, I used open coding, creating categories and checking data for patterns which might suggest ethnographic webs of significance (Geertz, 1973) and cultural meaning I hand-coded all data in order to try to trace commonalities, distinctions, and relationships, and then a form of axial coding in which I re-read the data against my themes, codes, and subcodes, looking for patterns of difference and relationality.

Rigor

Since my intention was for the study to be as open and participatory as possible, I took rigor in this context to mean an overt commitment to accountability, credibility and confirmability to participants, as well as to the research's epistemological and ethical tenets (Guba & Lincoln, 2005). In order to try to enact this rigor, I was in regular communication with participants at each step of the analysis and writing process condensed each document using emerging themes and codes, and sent documents back to participants for approval or further clarification.

The goal of a qualitative study is believability, based on coherence, insight, and instrumental utility (Eisner, 1991) and trustworthiness (Lincoln & Guba, 1985), achieved through a process of verification rather than through conventionally privileged quantitative validity measures. In this study, the verification process involved sharing themes, processes, and preliminary conclusions with participants and more broadly via email and my blog, inviting discussion, input and critique before publication. All interviewees were sent their coded transcripts and invited to expand, clarify, and reframe them as they wished. Four added more to their reflections based on this invitation and two condensed or anonymized sections where they had identified others in their networks. Throughout the research process, participants' confirmation of both broad conclusions and statements attributed to them was sought and achieved.

At the same time, because the study privileged not only participants' accounts of networked scholarship but also the material and relational aspects of networked scholarship as a techno-cultural system, I also informally mapped participants' written and interview narratives against their conversations and participation, drawing out key points from the thematic analysis and verifying statements of practice against actual material practices enacted in the participant observation data. For instance, when a participant claimed to follow an ethnically diverse group of scholars, I attempted to triangulate and confirm that information using the scholar's Following list. When a participant suggested s/he believed in sharing the work of others, I looked for examples of this practice.

LIMITATIONS OF THE STUDY

My selection of ethnography as a methodological approach was by no means the only methodology appropriate to an examination of networked scholarship. Ethnography's small sample size precludes the study from claiming the breadth and generalizability that could have been achieved through survey methods, for example, and ethnographic methods do not generate the powerful visual and structural data that social network analysis (SNA) could have offered. However, I decided that the depth of experiential understanding and complexity made possible through ethnography's 'thick description' (Geertz, 1973, p. 3) was of more value than generalizability at this early stage of inquiry into networked scholarly practices and understandings. Still, future research into whether this study's findings hold true at a larger scale could be very interesting to pursue. Likewise, SNA visualization would have offered an alternate perspective on the interactions I observed in depth during the research process, and perhaps triangulated some of the findings. Yet, while I initially aimed to utilize SNA as a complementary approach within the investigation, the structural focus of SNA alone would not have enabled the same extensive investigation into participatory cultural and material practices as ethnography. I did look into using both Node XL and TAGS Explorer to visualize interactions and relationships between study participants, but as I was working solely on a Mac platform, Node XL was not feasible. I downloaded TAGS Explorer and examined the scale of tweets of each study participant for a few consecutive weeks, however, my study was not designed around central hashtags, and thus the tool was limited in its application.

PRACTICAL AND ETHICAL CHALLENGES OF TWITTER AS METHOD

Nonetheless, I was able in the end to explore Twitter not only as a site of scholarship, but also as a means to engage in scholarly investigation. As a window on daily cultural practices and interactions, Twitter offered me a rich site for ethnographic participant observation of the networked scholarly culture under study. For my particular topic, and given the fact that my participants and I were all resident users of the platform, the choice to employ Twitter in the majority of my methods increased their pertinence and relevance to the broader research questions. Foregrounding Twitter aligned the research process with the practices of the participants, which I believe amplified and reinforced the participatory quality I tried to foster within the study.

Twitter also enabled me to engage with the environment under study from a new perspective, in spite of its familiarity. Researching with Twitter deepened my own analytical understanding of Twitter as a site of scholarship and my reflexivity about the research process itself. As I investigated the webs of significance that participants enacted on Twitter, I was acutely conscious of being part of those webs, at least temporarily, and of the responsibility that entailed, both to participants and to careful, ethical research practice. My participant observation data in particular was open even *during* the research process to the participants themselves, through the Following list of the @BonResearch account. Thus the study was from the first day of observation visible and open to the guidance, feedback, and critique of a population of trained – and in many cases, senior to myself – scholars who were collectively aware of the research questions. This visibility heightened my sense of accountability to participants and to the position of trust I had been accorded, and made the research process a powerful learning experience.

Yet there were challenges to the process, and aspects of it that might not have worked so well with other populations. To conclude the chapter, I want to outline some of the more difficult aspects of using Twitter as a platform for ethnographic research.

One of the challenges of working with Twitter, even with a very small participant population, is scale. At the time I began the project, I was following nearly 1,000 users with my regular, personal Twitter account, and had expected that following only 23 people would allow me to separate signals from noise with great facility. Instead, I realized in the first 12 hours that my small group of participants, exemplars, and committee members had tweeted and RTd the words of 74 separate accounts just in that short time period. Working with Twitter as a site of participant observation is demanding, just in terms of managing the sheer volume of data generated even by a small sample of participants.

Twitter's affordances or platform features – and the types of interaction and identity performance they enable – can also change without warning. Conversation threading, wherein a user's public conversations with other users can be traced at a click, was central to my investigation. Partway through the study there was an evening where my 'view conversation' option disappeared for approximately an hour, then returned. I assumed – as has happened previously over Twitter's lifespan – that the platform had simply removed the feature without warning. I experienced genuine panic at the idea of my research site undergoing such a significant and limiting structural shift in the middle of my work. Twitter did change the structure of user profiles drastically just after the conclusion of my research. Had this happened a few months earlier in the middle of the profile assessments, it might have necessitated starting that whole section of the study over again for consistency, which would have inconvenienced my participants. It might even have invalidated the premises of that method, since it was premised on the assumption that participants were literate in reading profiles, which might not have held true in the same way after the change.

Finally, there are practical and ethical challenges to doing research in a site where communications are by default public but not necessarily intended for all publics. The first is context collapse (Marwick & boyd, 2011) or the need for a Twitter user to anticipate the 'nearly infinite possible contexts he or she might be entering' (Wesch, 2009, p. 23) before engaging in communications. I completed my data collection at the end of February 2014. Over the ensuing year, #notallwomen, #Ferguson, #gamergate, #blacklivesmatter, #salaita and other hashtags convulsed communities both in the flesh and on Twitter, signaling issues, incidents, abuses, and tragedies. Hashtags can propel small-scale tweets or minority messages to extremely large publics, and galvanize disparate people around issues of shared interest, but the hypervisibility they signify is double-edged. Mobs, tactical lobbies, and media all seize and amplify out-of-context tweets, which, as McMillan-Cottom (2015) notes, strips users of their autonomy to exert control 'over how and when and where I perform the identity I think most appropriate for a situation' (p. 16). In writing up my dissertation and papers, I have become increasingly attuned to the ways I present my participants' tweets from the year previous, as my work may bring these texts to audiences for whom they were unintended. It is important for researchers to recognize the risks amplification and context collapse bring to specific populations, who may encounter vulnerability, hostility, or misunderstanding when they agree to have their tweets replicated in new venues.

Secondly, the question of whether public tweets are by default public data is an ethical issue that the academy has yet to resolve (boyd & Crawford, 2011; Kitchin, 2014). In the kinds of ethnographic work that I engaged in, it was easy to elide this question by simply excluding non-participant conversational data from my notes and records, but some SNA research works entirely with publicly generated tweets, even within hashtags and sub-communities of vulnerable populations and 'communities of care' (Hogue, 2015, para. 4). While platforms like Twitter allow scholars to harvest enormous data sets, it is important for us to consider the human effects of working with and representing people's statements out of context, particularly when the public nature of Twitter that makes the data available also makes individual tweets searchable and traceable. Twitter has powerful potential for research, but – like all SNS – it is not merely 'technology,' but a site comprised of people, and ethical, respectful research practices must approach it from that perspective.

In the end, in spite of ethnography's roots in studies of exoticized Otherness, it proves an apt method by which to examine contemporary social media practices and understandings, even for a scholar embedded within the community under study. Ethnography's capacity to investigate systems of cultural meaning, or what Geertz (1973) called 'webs of significance' allowed me to engage in a thorough exploration of the relational, material, and performative aspects of Twitter, in a participatory fashion befitting the tenets of networked scholarship.

NOTES

1 REB is the Canadian equivalent of the US Institutional Review Board (IRB).
2 As of June 2015, Twitter's android app began showing a heart icon instead of the familiar star (Wright, 2015).

REFERENCES

Baym, N. (2000). *Tune in, log on: Soaps, fandom, and online community*. Thousand Oaks, CA: Sage.

Boellstorff, T. (2008). *Coming of age in Second Life: An anthropologist explores the virtually human*. Princeton, NJ: Princeton University Press.

Boellstorff, T., Nardi, B., Pearce, C., & Taylor, T.L. (2012). *Ethnography and virtual worlds: A handbook of method*. Princeton, NJ: Princeton University Press.

boyd, d. & Crawford, K. (2011). Six provocations for big data. *A Decade in Internet Time: Symposium on the Dynamics of the Internet & Society*. Retrieved from: http://papers.ssrn.com/sol3/papers.cfm?abstract_id=1926431

Boyer, E. (1990). *Scholarship reconsidered: Priorities of the professoriate*. Princeton, NJ: The Carnegie Foundation for the Advancement of Teaching.

Bruns, A. (2007). Produsage: Towards a broader framework for user-led content creation. In *Proceedings of Creativity & Cognition*, 6, 99–106. Retrieved from http://eprints.qut.edu.au/6623/1/6623.pdf

Connaway, L.S., Lanclos, D., & Hood, E. (2013, December 6). 'I always stick with the first thing that comes up on Google…': Where people go for information, what they use, and why. *EDUCAUSE Review Online*. Retrieved from http://www.educause.edu/ero/article/i-always-stick-first-thing-comes-google-where-people-go-information-what-they-use-and-why

Eisner, E.W. (1991). *The enlightened eye: Qualitative inquiry and the advancement of educational practice*. New York, NY: Macmillan.

Geertz, C. (1973). *The interpretation of culture*. New York, NY: Basic Books.

Gibson, W.J. & Brown, A. (2009). *Working with qualitative data*. London, UK: Sage.

Green, N. (1999). Disrupting the field: Virtual reality technologies and 'multi-sited' ethnographic methods. *American Behavioral Scientist*, *43*(3), 409–421. doi: 10.1177/00027649921955344

Greenhow, C., Robelia, B., & Hughes, J.E. (2009). Learning, teaching, and scholarship in a digital age. Web 2.0 and classroom research: What path should we take now? *Educational Researcher*, *38*(4), 246–259.

Gruzd, A., Wellman, B., & Takhteyev, Y. (2011). Imagining twitter as an imagined community. *American Behavioural Scientist*, *55*(10), 1294–1318.

Guba, E.G. & Lincoln, Y.S. (2005). Paradigmatic controversies, contradictions, and emerging confluences. In N. K. Denzin & Y. S. Lincoln (Eds.), *The SAGE handbook of qualitative research* (3rd ed), (pp. 191–215). Thousand Oaks, CA: Sage.

Haraway, D. (1988). Situated knowledges: The science question in feminism and the privilege of partial perspective. *Feminist Studies*, *14*(3), 575–599.

Harley, D., Acord, S.K., Earl-Novell, S., Lawrence, S., & King, C.J. (2010). Assessing the future landscape of scholarly communication: An exploration of faculty values and needs in seven disciplines. *Center for Studies in Higher Education, UC Berkeley.* Retrieved from http://escholarship.org/uc/cshe_fsc

Heyl, B. (2001). Ethnographic interviewing. In P. Atkinson, A. Coffey, S. Delamont, J. Lofland & L. Lofland (Eds.), *Handbook of ethnography.* (pp. 369–384). London, UK: Sage Publications.

Hine, C. (2000). *Virtual Ethnography.* London, UK: Sage Publications.

Hogan, B. (2010). The presentation of self in the age of social media: Distinguishing performances and exhibitions online. *Bulletin of Science, Technology & Society, 30*(6), 377–386.

Hogue, R. (2015, July 30). Ethics of researching Twitter communities (#smsociety15). [Web log post]. Retrieved from http://rjh.goingeast.ca/2015/07/30/ethics-of-researching-twitter-communities-smsociety15/

Holmberg, K. & Thelwall, M. (2014). *Disciplinary differences in Twitter scholarly communication. Scientometrics, 101*(2), 1027–1042. doi:10.1007/s11192-014-1229-3

Jenkins, H. (2006). *Convergence culture: Where old and new media collide.* Cambridge, MA: MIT Press.

Johnson, K. (2011). The effect of Twitter posts on students' perception of instructor credibility. *Learning, Media, and Technology, 36*(1), 21–38. doi: 10.1080/17439884.2010.534798

Kitchin, R. (2014). Big Data, new epistemologies and paradigm shifts. *Big Data & Society, 1*(1), 1–12. http://doi.org/10.1177/2053951714528481

Kozinets, R.V. (2010). *Netnography: Doing ethnographic research online.* London, UK: Sage.

Lincoln, Y. & Guba, G. (1985). *Naturalistic inquiry.* Newbury Park, CA: Sage.

McMillan-Cottom, T. (2015, February 10). Intersectionality and critical engagement with the internet. *Social Science Research Network.* doi: http://dx.doi.org/10.2139/ssrn.2568956

Marwick, A. & boyd, d. (2011). I tweet honestly, I tweet passionately: Twitter users, context collapse, and the imagined audience. *New Media & Society, 13*(1), 114–133.

Papacharissi, Z. (2012). Without you, I'm nothing: Performances of the self on Twitter. *International Journal of Communication,* (6), 1989–2006.

Pariser, E. (2011). *The filter bubble.* New York, NY: Penguin Press.

Quan-Haase, A., Suarez, J. L., & Brown, D. (2015). Collaboration, connecting, and clustering in the humanities: A case study of networked scholarship in an interdisciplinary, dispersed team. *American Behavioral Scientist, 59*(5), 565–581.

Reinhardt, W., Ebner, M., Beham, G., & Costa, C. (2009). How people are using Twitter during conferences. In V. Hornung-Prahauser & M. Luckmann (Eds.), 5th EduMedia Conference, Salzburg, (pp. 145–156).

Ryan, G. & Bernard, H.R. (2003). Techniques to identify themes. Field Methods, *15*(1), 85–109. doi: 10.1177/1525822X02239569

Schau, H.J. & Gilly, M.C. (2003). We are what we post? Self-presentation in personal web space. *Journal of Consumer Research, 30*(4), 384–404.

Stewart, B. (2014, March 18). Notes to self, stage two: Being & becoming – profiles as identities. [Web log post]. Retrieved from http://theory.cribchronicles.com/2014/03/18/notes-to-self-stage-two-being-becoming-profiles-as-identities/

Stewart, B. (2015a). Scholarship in abundance: Influence, engagement, and attention in scholarly networks. (Doctoral dissertation). Retrieved from http://bonstewart.com/Scholarship_in_Abundance.pdf

Stewart, B. (2015b). Open to influence: What counts as academic influence in scholarly networked Twitter participation. *Learning, Media, and Technology, 40*(3), 1–23. doi: 10.1080/17439884.2015.1015547

Stewart, B. (2015c). In abundance: Networked participatory practices as scholarship. *International Review of Research in Distance and Open Learning, 16*(3).

Stewart, B. (2015d). Collapsed publics: Orality, literacy, and vulnerability in academic Twitter. *Journal of Applied Social Theory, 1*(1).

Turkle, S. (1995). *Life on the screen: Identity in the age of the internet.* New York, NY: Simon & Schuster.

Veletsianos, G. & Kimmons, R. (2012). Networked participatory scholarship: Emergent technocultural pressures toward open and digital scholarship in online networks. *Computers & Education, 58*(2), 766–774.

Weller, M. (2011). *The digital scholar: How technology is transforming scholarly practice.* London, UK: Bloomsbury Academic. Retrieved from http://www.bloomsburyacademic.com/view/DigitalScholar_9781849666275/book-ba-9781849666275.xml

Weller, M. (2012). Digital scholarship and the tenure process as an indicator of change in universities. *Universities and Knowledge Society Journal* (RUSC), 9(2), 347–360.

Wesch, M. (2009). Youtube and you: Experiences of self-awareness in the context collapse of the recording webcam. *Explorations in Media Ecology*, 19–34. Retrieved from http://krex.k-state.edu/dspace/bitstream/handle/2097/6302/WeschEME2009.pdf?sequence=1

White, D. S. & LeCornu, A. (2011). Visitors and residents: A new typology for online engagement. *First Monday*, 16(9). doi:10.5210/fm.v16i9.3171

Wiley, D. & Hilton, J. (2009). Openness, dynamic specialization, and the disaggregated future of higher education. *IRRODL*, 10(5), unpaginated.

Wright, M. (2015, June 17). Twitter for Android swaps the Favorites star for a heart…for some people at least. *TNW News*. http://thenextweb.com/twitter/2015/06/17/twitter-hearts-you/

Small Stories Research: A Narrative Paradigm for the Analysis of Social Media

Alexandra Georgakopoulou

In this chapter I present the main rationale, methods and analytical tools for extending small stories research, a narrative and identities analysis paradigm, to social media. I show what methods can be used and how we can extend the vocabulary of small stories to online contexts. I specifically introduce two key concepts that aid the analysis of stories on social media platforms, namely narrative stancetaking and rescripting. I illustrate these two concepts with reference to my analysis of data from Facebook and YouTube. Finally, I sketch certain avenues for further development of the paradigm, stressing the need for a critical agenda.

INTRODUCTION

The aim of this chapter is to present the main rationale, methods and analytical tools for extending small stories research to social media. Small stories research is a paradigm for narrative and identities analysis that has been developed by this author and, in the early stages, in collaboration with Michael Bamberg (e.g., Bamberg 2006; Georgakopoulou 2006, 2007; Bamberg & Georgakopoulou 2008). It was initially put forth as a counter-move to dominant models of narrative studies that:

a) defined narrative restrictively and on the basis of textual criteria;
b) privileged a specific type of narrative, in particular the long, relatively uninterrupted, teller-led accounts of past events or of one's life story, typically elicited in research interview situations.

In previous work (Georgakopoulou 2007), I made the case for the significance of such stories in everyday life and as part of the fabric of social practices that ordinary people engage in. I therefore highlighted the need for small stories, be they in conversational or interview contexts, to be included in the remit of narrative and identity analysis, as equally worthy data as the life stories which had monopolized the attention of narrative studies.

Below, I will first briefly provide the starting points of small stories research, its disciplinary context and outreach (for an extended version of this discussion, see Georgakopoulou 2015a). I will then present three main reasons for extending small stories research to the analysis of social media and further systematizing it to suit online contexts. I will show what methods can be used and how we can extend the vocabulary of small stories to online contexts. I will specifically introduce two key concepts that aid the analysis of stories on social media platforms, namely narrative stancetaking and rescripting. I will illustrate these two concepts with reference to my analysis of data from Facebook and YouTube. Finally, I will sketch certain avenues for further development of the paradigm, stressing the need for a critical agenda and the scope for further methodological innovation.

Small Stories Research in Face-to-face Conversations

Small stories research was developed so as to account conceptually and analytically for a range of narrative activities that had not been sufficiently studied nor had their importance for the interlocutors' identity work been recognized. These mainly involve stories that present fragmentation and open-endedness of tellings, exceeding the confines of a single speech event and resisting a neat categorization of beginning–middle–end. They are invariably heavily co-constructed, rendering the sole teller's story ownership problematic. Small stories research thus made a case for including in conventional narrative analysis 'a gamut of under-represented and "a-typical" narrative activities, such as tellings of ongoing events, future or hypothetical events, shared (known) events, but also allusions to tellings, deferrals of tellings, and refusals to tell' (Georgakopoulou 2006: 124). To do so, small stories research has drawn on a synthesis of frameworks from diverse disciplinary traditions, including sociolinguistics and biographical studies. There has also been a recognition that empirical work needed to be done to add nuance to the general descriptor of 'small stories', so as to bring to the fore the specific genres of small stories that occur in specific contexts and that ought to be included in the narrative analytic lens.

Small stories research has been intended as a *model for*, not a *model of* (Duranti 2005) narrative analysis. Duranti (idem: 421ff) sees 'models for' as more open-ended frames of inquiry that are not controlled tightly by their proponents and their original assumptions. In this spirit, many of the delights of small stories research have come from imaginative and utterly unexpected applications and extensions of the model beyond sociolinguistics (for a detailed discussion see Georgakopoulou 2015a).

Context for Small Stories Research

The broader context of small stories research is to be found in anti-essentialist views of self, society and culture which stress the multiplicity, fragmentation, context-specificity and performativity of our communication practices (see De Fina & Georgakopoulou 2012 ch 6). Within sociolinguistics, these views have informed the turn to identities-in-interaction (see Bucholtz & Hall 2005), while in literary studies of narrative, they have precipitated a combined focus on the content, the author/narrator, the form, and the readers as active participants (cf. rhetorical narratology). More importantly though, such views have relativized the evaluative hierarchies of texts and cultures, problematizing distinctions between high and low, official and unofficial. If we extend this to the study of stories, we can talk about an opening up of the analysis beyond literary stories and certainly beyond stories in research-regulated environments, such as interviews. Sociolinguistics has played a key role since the 1960s, in showing that it is worthwhile studying stories in diverse contexts: for example, from friends' conversations, family dinnertime and school runs to classroom settings, asylum seekers' application and job interviews (Ochs & Capps 2001).

The influences of small stories research have come from the study of narrative both within sociolinguistics and outside of it, for example, narrative psychology, sociology, narratology. Specifically, it has drawn insights from conversation analysis that views stories as talk-in-interaction, as sequential activities that are co-constructed between teller and audiences. It has also benefited from the biographical research on stories that stresses the experiential, affective and subjective ways in which people make sense of their self over time and legitimates the study of lay experience, at the same time as reflecting on the role of the researcher in it (Andrews, Squire & Tamboukou 2008). Beyond these influences, small stories research has mainly been informed by practice-based approaches to language and identities (e.g., Hanks 1996), which view language as performing specific actions in specific environments and as being part of social practices, shaping and being shaped by them. All narrative meaning making is seen as contextualized but also as having the potential to be lifted from its original context and to be re-contextualized, that is, to acquire new meanings in new contexts (cf. Bauman & Briggs 1990). Narrative thus ceases to be just a single event and its historicity and circulation become part of the analysis.

THREE REASONS FOR EXTENDING SMALL STORIES RESEARCH TO SOCIAL MEDIA

In my latest work I have documented a close association of small stories with the explosion of social media and their pervasive presence in everyday life, as that is facilitated by the increasing media convergence (Georgakopoulou 2013c,). I have noted a set of features that conventional narrative analysts would see as a-typical or non-canonical, being salient in different social media platforms and practices, from Facebook to YouTube and Twitter, from statuses to spoof videos and retweets. These features involve fragmentation and open-endedness of stories, exceeding the confines of a single posting and site and resisting a neat categorization of beginning-middle-end. They also involve multiple authoring of a post, as it may become shared across media platforms. In addition, there is a tendency for reporting mundane, ordinary and in some cases, trivial events from the poster's everyday life, rather than big complications or disruptions. These 'textual' features have led me to recognize the role of small stories research as a paradigm that prefigured the current situation when social media affordances have made what I called 'small stories' much more widely available and visible in public arenas of communication through circulation (see Georgakopoulou 2013a). The – so far, scarce – sociolinguistic work on stories in social media by other scholars confirms the validity of this view of small stories research and in turn the usefulness of the model for describing and analyzing narrative activities on digital media (e.g., Georgalou 2015; Page 2012; West 2013).

I have also been in a position to document the migration and *remediation* of a specific genre of small stories, which I have called 'breaking news', from face-to-face conversational contexts to media-facilitated conversational contexts where new technologies are present to various activities on digital media, including text messages, status updates on Facebook, (re)tweets, and titles of YouTube videos (Georgakopoulou 2013a,b; 2016a). Breaking news are stories of very recent (yesterday) and in some cases evolving (just now) events that, once introduced into a conversation, can be further updated. In my study of a peer-group of female best friends in a small Greek town in the late 1990s, breaking news proved to hold a salient place in the group's communication practices: they filled in one another on events that had happened in the very few hours between school and home study when the friends had not communicated with one another. As a lot of these events literally unfolded in the town's streets, new scenarios arose while the friends were piecing together what had just happened, providing them with more material and opportunities for story plots. In this way, breaking news tended to lead to further narrative making with updates on the unfolding events and/or projections to the near future. Similarly, in an ESRC funded project entitled Urban Classroom Culture and Interaction (2005–2008, www.identities.org.uk) in which we studied Year 9 and Year 10 students in a London comprehensive school, breaking news stories were also salient but in this case, intimately linked with the pupils' engagements with new media: for instance, a breaking news story would be told about a conversation the teller had had the previous evening on MySpace. Then, this story would be updated and co-constructed with friends, as more communication with the story's character(s) would happen during the school day, for example, by text messaging.

The attested proliferation of breaking news on social media platforms is no accident: social media environments afford opportunities for sharing life in miniaturized form at the same time as constraining the ability of users to plunge into full autobiographical mode (e.g., the constraint of 140 characters on Twitter). In particular, they offer users the ability to share experience as it is happening with various semiotic (multi-modal) resources, to update it as often as necessary and to (re)-embed it in various social platforms. This readily observable prevalence of small stories on social media platforms, often engendered by media affordances, is the first *empirical reason* as to why small stories research holds relevance for the analysis of online data. At the same time, activities which I call 'small stories' have often prompted dystopic views by numerous commentators (e.g., see Baym 2010) about what constantly announcing (trivial) slices of one's everyday life means for how we see and present ourselves and how this is endangering more conventional forms of autobiography (Jongy 2008). In the light of this, the second reason for extending small stories research to social media is *methodological*: narrative analysts need to engage with these phenomena with questions that pertain to both what narrative analysis can offer for their scrutiny and how it can respond to the new challenges that they pose. Small stories research, having developed tools for examining fragmented, transposable and a-typical stories, is well-placed to provide a sound methodological basis for exploring stories on social media, in particular for interrogating what is distinctive about them, but also how they draw on or depart from other forms and practices of storytelling.

The third reason for extending small stories research to social media is *epistemological*. The numerous applications and outreach of small stories research, as discussed above, recommend it as a critical micro-perspective on social media engagements, one that can help answer a key-question currently being investigated in social media research: what is the socio-political potential of social media engagements for transformation? What counter-cultural, hidden and unofficial practices of meaning-making do social media engender?

Taking these three reasons into account, my aim has been to show the need for a radical re-thinking of how we define a 'narrative' on social media, how we can analyze it and in what ways small stories research can enable this re-positioning of conventional narrative analysis. In particular, my claim has been that the starting point of a narrative analysis on social media should be the recognition that stories produced on social media *normally*:

- announce and perform the minute-by-minute everyday life experience
- are transportable and circulatable in different media platforms
- are embedded into a variety of online and offline environments

- are multi-semiotic and multi-authored
- address simultaneously different, potentially big and unforeseeable, audiences.

Below, I will show how employing small stories research for the analysis of social media has involved methodological innovation, in particular links with emerging digital ethnography, and a broad view of interaction.

Key-assumptions for Small Stories Research on Social Media

Working with small stories on social media involves exploring the intersection of narrative and social media affordances and their role in what stories will be told and how. This should not be viewed as a deterministic perspective but as a productive engagement with previous insights into the role of stories in context. A volume of research in everyday stories has documented the role of narrative in enabling specific communicative affordances. These include the imaginative and affective presentation of self as grounded in specific spatiotemporal realities and the ability to invoke other worlds, real or possible, to bear on the here-and-now of the narrating act, but also to position self over time and across places (see De Fina & Georgakopoulou 2012 chs 1 & 5). Establishing more or less meaningful connections between people, place, time and events lies at the heart of interweaving narrative plots. Sociolinguistic studies of storytelling have also demonstrated how these connections are always done in context and in interaction with participants (idem: chs 3 & 4). These insights should be tested out vis-à-vis the multi-semioticity, multi-authorship, and transposability of communicative activities that social media platforms have been found to enable (boyd 2010). Media scholars have shown that the digital architecture of social networking sites (henceforth SNSs) and recent changes in them have increasingly become 'directional' to specific forms and practices of communication that encourage users to share their lives with wider audiences (van Dijck 2013). There is nonetheless little empirical research to show how the interplay between affordances and constraints on social media platforms shapes the users' *subjectivity* and self-presentation as well as their interactions with other users. Given that social media affordances are defined as perceived possibilities and constraints for action (Barton & Lee 2013: 27, citing Gibson 1977), there is also much scope to explore how actual communication practices follow, resist, counteract social media design and what mismatches there may be between the two.

I have employed the heuristic for the analysis of small stories I developed for small stories in face-to-face contexts, due to its flexibility and open-endedness. The heuristic explores the connections of three separable but interrelated layers of analysis: (1) *ways of telling*, (2) *sites* (of the stories' tellings and tales), and (3) *tellers* (in the broad sense of communicators). It dictates a combined focus on online postings and various types of engagement with them, including transposition across media and sites, without, however, pre-determining what from each of the multi-layered ways of telling, sites and tellers will be of analytical importance and how their relations will be configured in different stories and media environments.

Analyzing Participation and Interaction

Interactional approaches to everyday conversations have amply documented the systematicity of sequential phenomena to be found within turn-taking as well as their close links with participant roles and relations. Furthermore, they have shown how any pre-allocated telling rights and rules (e.g., in institutional contexts involving asymmetrical relations between participants) may be visibly oriented to, managed or departed from by the participants with their exploitation of conversational structures (for an overview, see

Wooffitt & Hutchby 2008). In similar vein, participation frameworks (Goffman 1981), i.e., the roles and statuses assumed by interlocutors in the course of a conversation, have been found to be shaped by the type of discourse activity underway, for instance, the telling of a story, as we will see below. Finally, participants' differential degrees of knowledge and expertise in the topic at hand are also linked with who contributes what and how. A comparable interactional approach to social media communication is lagging behind, despite the fact that much of the social media pre-designing is specifically aimed at getting users in some kind of a 'dialogue', for example, between posters and respondents, and that it projects specific responses to posts with facilities such as Like, Comment, Share, etc.

Existing work has begun to document the same kind of systematicity in patterns of social media communication as in face-to-face interaction, thus clearly illustrating the benefits of such an approach. For instance, a study of comments on Facebook (FB) as 'conversational' features has shown how respondents create coherence and 'tie' their comment with previous ones and with the original post, by exploiting the time and space organization of the FB environment (e.g., Frobenius & Harper 2015. Similarly, language-focused analyses of YouTube comments have begun to document the complexity and multiplicity of participation frameworks of contributors in their interaction with the video and with one another, compared to the viewing roles that films and television programmes traditionally allowed (e.g., Bou-Franch et al. 2012; Dynel 2014). This complexity is partly linked with the fact that multiple audiences can be collapsed into a single context in many social media. *Context collapse* (Marwick & boyd 2011) refers to the infinite audience possible online as opposed to more limited numbers of people a person normally interacts with face to face. In situations of a well-defined, limited group, speakers can 'size up' the situation and adjust their presentation of self. In a situation of context collapse, however, which Wesch (2008) compares to a 'building collapse', it becomes much more difficult to gauge what is appropriate and for whom (see Quan-Haase 2009). This makes the intended or imagined audience of a posting potentially very different to the actual audience. The manifold ways in which different audiences may be targeted by the posters, that is, implicitly selected and addressed or equally de-selected and excluded, have begun to be unearthed (see Tagg & Seargeant 2016). In this respect, I have argued that any study of participation frameworks and interaction on social media platforms cannot be disconnected from the heightened possibility for circulation of a discourse activity in different sites and for different audiences. More specifically, I have claimed that the posting of an activity as a story or its becoming a story through subsequent sharing and engagement with it has important implications for interaction (Georgakopoulou 2013a,b).

In the light of the above discussion, we can claim that there is already some evidence for the validity and usefulness of an interactional approach to the analysis of online data. At the same time, there is also recognition that not all of the interactional modes of analysis and techniques originally developed for face-to-face conversations can be automatically transferred to the analysis of online data, and that digitally native methods will have to complement them, as we will see in 'Methods' (cf. Gillies et al. 2015: 45–51). A prime challenge is to explore how interaction is achieved when multiple participants may tune in at different time zones and with different degrees of familiarity with the original poster: from friends with whom there are multiple interactions across media to complete strangers and 'de-individuated' users whose offline, demographic identities cannot possibly be established.

My aim with small stories research has been to provide answers to these questions and, in doing so, to contribute to the growing line of inquiry into the interactional aspects of social media communication (see Georgakopoulou 2012, 2013a,b, 2014).

I have shown how narrative arrangements, in particular roles of storyteller and story recipient, afford participation and how this participation is interactionally achieved.

To do so, I adopt a broad perspective on interaction online that takes into account, when applicable, the sharing of a posting across multiple events and spaces with multiple and unforeseen recipients and the multiple related stories that this may generate through media enabled processes of linking, replicability and remixing.

METHODS

A (re)mix

I have been examining the ways in which we can extend small stories research to social media as part of a larger project entitled 'Life writing of the moment: The sharing and updating self on social media'.[1] My aims have been to chart the *multi-semiotic forms* (linguistic/textual, visual, auditory, etc.) that life-writing of the moment takes on a range of social media (e.g., YouTube, Facebook, Twitter), with *emergent and remediated genres* (e.g., selfies, retweets, spoof videos and remixes) and, where applicable, on the basis of specific (personal, political, social, etc.) incidents and issues (e.g., the Eurozone crisis). With a small stories analysis of the above, I also document the kinds of *subjectivities*, including ethical and political selves that life-writing of the moment engenders and how these are interactionally achieved.

In addition to specific social media platform explorations, small stories research is well-suited to incident-based work. This may be necessary in cases where it is important to track the phases and stages of a story's sharing as part of building a 'thick description' (see Latzko-Toth, Bonneau and Millette, Chapter 13, this volume). I have used popularity indexes and Google trends that show when the circulation of an incident has peaked and on which platform. YouTube videos have emerged as a prime circulation phase of story sharing in my data. I have employed the concepts of *telling case* (Mitchell 1984) and *critical moment* (Vaajala, Arminen, & De Rycker 2013) to identify postings worthy of further investigation. Both concepts suggest that a micro-scale event or incident may serve as a disruptive moment that sets larger processes in motion: it may, for instance, provide a glimpse of meanings, ideas, and values that are normally taken for granted or remain tacit, hidden and backgrounded under 'normal' circumstances. Such moments may allow 'condensing a complex subject […] to a few symbolic issues' (Oberhuber et al. 2005: 230).

Small stories research is routinely done in my study with the help of an open-ended, adaptive ethnography (Hine et al. 2009): this involves applying flexible routes to fieldwork over time to suit the mobile, ever-shifting landscape of social media. It also involves being open-minded about the use of 'remix' methods, in Markham's terms (2013), in the spirit of social media practices of bringing together unlikely modes in imaginative and reflexive ways. For instance, the researcher's own immersion and participation in social media culture with processes of catching up, sharing, and real-time tracking, are recognized as a major part of the development of ethnographic understanding. In addition, I have adapted *digitally native* methods for fieldwork: for instance, observing systematically, as a 'lurking' participant in a specific site, activities and postings, so as to identify key-posters of small stories and respondents. Some of these methods involve *auto-phenomenology*, that is, the researcher's reflexivity about her own position, stakes, and interests in the field of social media engagement. For instance, I have often examined my position as a 'digital tourist', even using it strategically in off the record chats with teenage participants and their use of FB. I have also drawn upon observations and developed analytical lines as a result, on the basis of my identity as mother to a media-saturated teenage daughter.

Data from Facebook

I have specifically employed the above methods as part of a small stories research project in two datasets. The first involves status updates and responses to them posted on Facebook walls. From my list of friends, I identified a female friend in her 30s, who posted the most status updates (Sus) and I followed her wall for a period of six months, having secured consent from her and the friends involved in 2013. Since then, I have triangulated these data with postings of a group of teenage friends who I selected from my daughter's friends, as part of a study of selfies (Georgakopoulou, 2016b). The selection was done in March 2015 on the basis of who were the top five selfie-posters after a systematic observation of one year. Principles of heavy disguise have been followed in both these cases and no reproduction of any visual material. Both data-sets were collected after the format of FB pages had changed in late-2011 so as to create a personal timeline for users. In addition, the news feed were introduced which inform users about activities of their friends: users may opt out of receiving this information but they cannot opt out of having this information about themselves displayed. For the purposes of this study, I have analyzed quantitatively a random sample of 500 postings, 250 from each dataset, in terms of small stories in the posting and responses in the comments. I have also coded numbers of Likes and created a network profile that consists of the 'friends' who over time emerge as those who like and/or comment most.

Data from YouTube

As the principle of small stories methods is that there is merit in establishing interactional processes across media platforms which allow for differentiated degrees of publicness, I have also chosen to use comparable principles of analysis for the participation frameworks of YouTube videos and comments. There are clear differences in terms of publicness between (private) FB and YouTube. FB is more oriented to one's offline network and although it is possible to have complete strangers as 'friends', it would be highly unusual for friends' lists not to be populated by people known to the user offline, too. This renders the possibility for complete re-invention and anonymity far less than on YouTube, although context collapse still applies to the many different degrees of closeness that a user may have with their 'friends'. So, FB users still have the task of 'navigating concealing and revealing information to people who blur the boundaries of work and home, school and private life, or friends and family' (Marwick & boyd 2011: X) that a user may have. On the other hand, YouTube is much more public, 'semi-public' as Bitvitch puts it (2010), in that most users have never met face-to-face, there are no registration requirements for them to view videos and, even though they need to register and have a password so as to post comments or videos, their 'identities' can still be demographically non-verifiable. In the light of the above differences, exploring how users interact with stories on FB and YouTube promises to bring to the fore rich insights into how different aspects and degrees of context collapse may be managed so as to create common ground in the case of (more or less close) friends as opposed to complete strangers.

The incident I have focused upon on YouTube emerged, on the basis of the aforementioned methods, as a prime critical moment right after it had happened and with the benefit of hindsight it remains the most circulated incident in post-2010 Greece. In the run up to the 2012 election in Greece, which at the time was viewed as crucial for the future of the Greek bailout and of the EU, a particular incident became 'viral': The assault of two female leftwing party MPs (Rena Dourou & Liana Kanelli), in particular throwing water at Dourou and 'slapping' and 'punching' Kanelli, by a male MP candidate (Ilias Kasidiaris) from the far-right party Golden Dawn, on a breakfast news show of live TV (7 June 2012). The first key transposition of the incident was the uploading of the scene of the incident that took place on the TV breakfast show onto YouTube by ordinary people, and this seemed an intuitive point of departure for the analysis. The video clip selection averaged one minute and hundreds of videos with the scene were posted on YouTube with varying numbers of viewers from a few hundred viewers to single thousand figures. Of this large number of uploaded videos, I chose to single out for close qualitative and quantitative analysis the 50 most viewed (and commented upon) YouTube videos. I have reported the results of this analysis elsewhere: in particular, I have shown the significance of whether the incident was circulated as a story or not for the ways in which the context of the crisis was made sense of (Georgakopoulou 2013b; 2014). A subsequent transposition of the incident involved the production of spoof/fake videos and remixes and their uploading on YouTube: these are a recognizable genre of Web 2.0 production around popular stories. In this case, the number of videos produced was small and readily capitalized on existing popular videos for fake video production, such as *The Downfall* (see below). I closely analyzed all videos produced and all comments for each video until April 2015. The results of this analysis are beyond the scope of this chapter: in brief, I have shown how creative and largely satirical engagements with the original incident involved 'rescripting' ('Narrative stance-making and rescripting as sharing') the place of the incident that in turn effected changes in the plot and the evaluative stances on the original incident (Georgakopoulou 2015).

Coding Data from YouTube and Facebook

Building on sampling from previous quantitative analyses, as my analysis progressed, I added more coding to both the sampled YouTube comments from the YouTube data-set and the FB postings from the FB data-set to check for the frequency of certain knowing participation patterns that had emerged as salient from the qualitative analysis. In particular, I coded explicit and implied references to knowledge of specific events, activities and/or characters and any information about the provenance of this knowledge (e.g., shared participation in an activity offline). I also coded references reaction to the state of non-knowing. In all these cases, I took into account the form that such references took and if and how they were linked with FB and YouTube affordances (e.g., tagging, uploading videos and photographs).

Bracketing in Analysis

In addition to adaptive ethnographic methods, as discussed above, I have found that I have needed to employ a sort of back and forth process that Gubrium and Holstein (2009) refer to as bracketing in narrative analysis. Bracketing involves keeping a balanced focus through mode shifting on the *what* and the *how* of research, and I would include the *who* and *why* of research, gliding between processes, conditions, and resources. Although bracketing has been proposed and developed for the study of offline narrative data, it is in my view transferrable to the analysis of social media data too, as it does justice to their ever-changing nature, which resists a neat separation between data collection and analysis, as new contexts and data are aggregated.[2] For instance, to take an example from my analysis of YouTube data, many political changes and events happened subsequent to the aforementioned circulated incident of the assault of the two female politicians by I. Kasidiaris, such as the imprisonment of Kasidiaris in 2014, as part of a crackdown on GD's criminal activities as well as his acquittal for the incident under study (March 2015). All these events resulted in a flurry of new comments and a social media re-engagement with the original incident: tracking these 'diachronic' types of contribution, as Bou-Franch & Blitvitch (2014) have put it, was important, as they allowed me to chart the creation of a social mediatized biography for the main protagonists of the incident, particularly Kasidiaris and Kanelli, and the sedimentation of specific evaluative viewpoints about the incident. As I have claimed elsewhere (Georgakopoulou, 2016c), in the light of this enlarged time frame of the research, my research ethics questions and requirements changed considerably and in unforeseeable ways.

NARRATIVE STANCETAKING AND RESCRIPTING AS SHARING

My analysis has enabled me to identify two main story-sharing practices on social media: (1) narrative stancetaking and (2) rescripting. *Narrative stancetaking* involves posts in which conventionalized story framing devices are used to suggest that there is a story in the making, a story that can be told, developed and updated later if requested. More generally, narrative stancetaking indicates that an activity is:

- being offered or taken up as a story, thereby positioning participants as tellers-recipients-(co)-tellers, etc. and/or,
- consisting of events and characters in specific spatiotemporal scenarios whose actions and speech are assessable.

As I have shown elsewhere (2013b), small stories often begin with or are confined to narrative stancetaking. This signaling positions participants as story (co-)tellers and recipients, and interactional partners thus anticipating and even proposing subsequent sites of circulation and audiences. Narrativity is therefore an emergent property, a process of becoming a story through engagement, as we will see in 'Small stories for "friends" in the know' below. Narrative stancetaking is a common practice that I found cuts across personal and other people's or news stories: for example, posting updates on Facebook, tweets and retweets about current affairs, YouTube video postings, for instance, in the titles of YouTube videos. I have shown that in all these different cases, there is systematicity in how narrative stance-taking is responded to and taken up by users and this has implications for what stories are told on which platforms, by whom and how.

Rescripting involves media-enabled practices of visually and/or verbally manipulating previously circulated stories so as to create alternative stories. These are in turn offered and taken up as humorous, satirical takes on the original story. I have shown (Georgakopoulou 2015b) that this creative manipulation mainly involves changing the place of the original tale on its own or along with other aspects of the plot, including the characters, so that a 'new' tale emerges with 'new' characters, 'new' narrator, 'new' audiences, etc. YouTube videos such as spoofs, memes, remixes, and mashups, form a main site of rescripting. For instance, the incident of the aforementioned assault was satirically re-enacted from ordinary, and as it turns out from the comments that ensued, genuinely 'amateur' users, on a Greek beach, with the 'politicians' wearing swimsuits. The spoof video was entitled: *Kasidiaris Kaneli sfaliara paralia* (Kasidiaris Kaneli slap beach) http://www.youtube.com/watch?v=Cx-RXZLP9wI.

Another form of rescripting involved 'inserting' the politicians into places other than the TV studio. This capitalized on video editing and remixing techniques that allow image manipulation. Unlikely settings in which the protagonists of the original incident were visually placed included: a boxing ring where Kasidiaris and Kanelli had a contest; a video game; a Star Wars scene with Kasidiaris and Kanelli battling it out.

A detailed discussion of the two concepts, i.e. narrative stancetaking and rescripting, is beyond the scope of this chapter. Story-making and story-altering processes are of paramount importance for the construction of shared story worlds on YouTube and for relations of solidarity and alliance on a platform that is often conducive to conflicts and 'rants' (Georgakopoulou 2014, 2015). Below, I will single out that main ways in which narrative stancetaking processes work on the intersection between social media affordances with examples from FB and what participation roles this allows for 'who' and 'how'.

Narrative Stancetaking: Media Affordances

This projection of narrative participation is enhanced by FB platform facilities which contain elements of narrative stancetaking inasmuch as they are reminiscent of Jefferson's 'story openers' (1978). In face-to-face conversations, story openers are conventionalized routines that preface an extended telling. In the case of FB, what will follow narrative stancetaking is more open-ended and contingent upon audience engagement, as we will see below. Narrative stancetaking elements include:

- Temporal framing and notifications of activities that have just happened: e.g., *Mary changed her profile picture; Mary added a picture; Mary was with Abby & another 2 people*
- Localizations: e.g., *with X at café dolce*
- Assessments: e.g., *feeling amused with X …*
- Events/activities: e.g., *ice-skating with X …*
- References to characters (and relationships): e.g., *Me & my gorgeous girl; my top girl; lovers; getting ready with the bae*
- Tagging

These FB affordances encourage the inclusion of time, place, events, characters and/or condensed or indexical associations amongst them. Furthermore, posters can 'select' certain friends as ratified and knowing recipients on the basis of their 'named' inclusion in the post. This can happen verbally: for instance, on FB, you can include a friend by clicking on their name which subsequently allows viewers of the post also to click on their name. It can also happen visually, for example, by including a photograph from an outing, and with tagging, which allows the posters to decide on who is more relevant for and connected with the post. Posting a shared status also allows from the outset a posting to include specific participants as 'addressees' (specifically addressed 'friends'; Dynel 2014; Tagg & Seargeant 2016).

In all these cases, I have found that the overwhelming preference for tagged or otherwise 'named' and 'signalled' individuals is not just to produce a Like, but also to contribute a comment. References to shared events, even in the absence of any visual or tagging material, also introduce the requirement for certain individuals to display their knowing status, as we will see below. All these affordances end up creating a 'private chat' on a public forum with certain friends appearing as being in the know and in the loop and others not. We will see examples of this in 4.2 below.

Small Stories for 'Friends' in the Know

As I have shown elsewhere (Georgakopoulou 2013a,b), narrative stancetaking on FB and YouTube postings presents systematic interactional implications: this means that it may project certain kinds of audience engagement but it is the actual audience engagement that shapes further telling and terms of telling. In particular, on FB, posts that report disruptive events in the poster's life are more likely to receive comments from their friends than a simple Like. ('Like' only is the case for routine everyday events.) The report of disruptions is also more likely to lead to a further post from the poster where she/he thanks for any wishes and interest and updates on the situation. A similar interactional pattern of a task of reciprocation to comments from the original poster is to be found in the case of posting selfies. There, a comment on a selfie from a respondent raises the task of replying and thanking for the initial poster. Most of such reciprocal exchanges are dyadic, that is, between commenter and original poster, and so the commenters routinely post atomized contributions in relation to other commenters.

In addition to the above, narrative stancetaking in the original post or some other selection of knowing participants (e.g., tagging in a selfie) is 'read' by recipients as an invitation and even a requirement for participation that displays knowing status. This participation separates friends in the know from other friends, however aligned the latter may be with the post or poster. Validation and alignment with the action of an initial post can be done with a simple Like or some kind of appreciative comment. Knowing status, however, allows commenters to extend beyond broadly affiliative actions to some form of elaboration and co-authoring of the initial post. Specifically, the task of showing knowledge takes the following forms: commenters can expand on the narrative stancetaking of the initial post by constituting it as a story or providing more of the story; they can also refer more or less allusively to pre-posting shared activities, which I call the backstory.

In the following example, from the data-set from FB (see 'Coding data from YouTube and Facebook'), knowing status serves as an opportunity for the recipient who was out with the poster the previous night to display their offline shared knowledge and provide a 'second' story that bridges the gap between their offline activities and the current online interaction:

(1)
 Elisa Dante's Inferno had nothing on the 134 through Camden at Stupid O'Clock in the morning...
 ☐ Like · Comment · Share 22 people like this.
 Ben Maxwell Oh nooo night bus misery. SORRY! Thanks for coming last night, was so nice to see your face!! xx
 March 22 at 11:23am · Like · 2
 Elisa SHUT IT Maxwell It was worth it to see you, beauty! Did y'all get home ok? Xxx
 March 22 at 11:24am · Like · 3
 Ben Harris We got a cab ride home by an insane lady who treated us like children. (Probably because we were eating cake on the street when she picked us up.) The prospect of getting night buses all the way to Siberia (Totteridge) was too grim. I'm glad you eventually got home; have a lovely Sunday! xx
 March 22 at 11:30am · Like · 1

The example illustrates the common phenomenon of dyadic exchanges between a poster and a knowing commenter which serve as a hybrid of private, near-synchronous chats (note the one minute of time-lag between turns) on the publicly visible (to the rest of the 'friends') space of FB walls. Knowing participants emerged in the analysis as overlapping considerably with what Tagg and Seargeant (2016) have described as 'active friends' on FB: those who are more likely to contribute to posts. In our case though, knowing contributions invariably display some kind of knowing status, even when the post responded to announces breaking news from the poster's life.

Comparable patterns of knowing participation apply to selfies, in particular what I have called (Georgakopoulou, 2016b, forthcoming) '[AG9]significant other' selfies (selfies of the poster and a best friend or other special person in their life) and 'group selfies'. These raise the requirement for participation from the friend(s) in the selfie with a comment. In this way, the same post serves different purposes for different FB 'friends': it may be an announcement for non-knowing recipients, as we will see in example 3 below, and an opportunity for display of offline selfie-taking and other knowledge for knowing friends, as we can see below in the comments that ensue by the two friends who are on the selfie that one of them has posted. In particular, with the reference to Mike and Brian, a backstory of shared interactional history is referred to allusively and this has the hallmarks of a private conversation.

(2)
 ☐ Elena:[3] [next to selfie of her and her best friend Anna, which is not reproduced here].
 ☐ Waaaay up I feel blessed. With Hannah Bates.
 ☐ Hannah: Awh luv u. xx
 ☐ May 7 at 9 pm
 ☐ Elena: Luv u too heart. We're gonna have so many more great times esp. now that we've got Mike ☺☺
 ☐ May 7 at 10.47 pm
 ☐ Hannah: Ha ha very tru two hearts let's hope we don't run into bryan again tho ...
 ☐ May 7 at 10.58pm

The private chat which develops between the two friends above elaborates on the caption of their selfie, a line from a song in fact ('Way up I feel blessed'), in ways which allude to their closeness. In particular, with the reference to 'Mike' and 'Brian', a backstory of shared interactional history is referred to allusively.

We can see the juxtaposition of contributions from knowing vs. non-knowing friends in the comments to another 'significant selfie' (of the female selfie-poster with a young man) which suggests a developing romance, as it is accompanied by hearts.

(3)

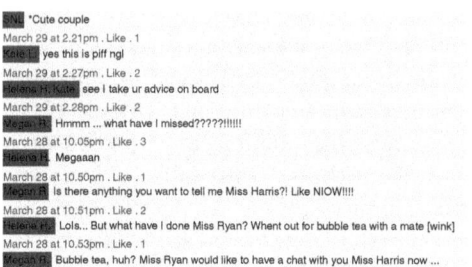

Knowing friends such as Kate L. propose a positive assessment of the selfie which is based on offline/or any other insider's knowledge in relation to the selfie posted. This is seen in Helena's response to Kate's comment that makes a typically cryptic reference to a 'backstory' of Kate and Helena having discussed this relationship and Helena 'having taken her advice on board'. The backstory normally is part of the events surrounding a selfie and any allusions to it arguably elaborate on the selfie as part of a narrative and thus propose how it should be understood. Put differently, knowing participation may narrow down the interpretative options around a selfie. This narrative engagement with selfies is seen in cases of non-knowing recipients too who routinely ask for the 'backstory' as a means of getting into the 'loop'. Such responses from non-knowing recipients tend to lead to some kind of (more) storying in relation to the selfie from the poster. In this way, the selfie retrospectively serves as a story preface for them, if we look at it within Sacks' three steps (1992) of a story preface. We can see this in the example above with Megan's comment which seeks to find out 'what she has missed'. Helena begins to provide an explanation in small story form in the publicly available comments ('went out for bubble tea with a mate') but the fuller story, we can speculate, is provided in the private chat area to which the friends claim they will switch. (I did not have access to private messages.)

CONCLUSION

In this chapter, I presented the key assumptions, disciplinary context and outreach (beyond sociolinguistics) of small stories research, a recent model for narrative and identities analysis originally put forward for the analysis of a-typical stories in conversational data. Narrative analysis has a pivotal role to play in social media research for the documentation of genres of stories and (new) forms of subjectivities but to do so, a radical departure from certain tropes and modes of conventional narrative research is needed. I argued that small stories research is well placed to offer alternative tools and concepts needed for such an inquiry. I charted the main directions that the current extension of small stories research is taking into social media, particularly with reference to narrative stancetaking processes. I showed how narrative stancetaking on Facebook is an important means of counter-acting the phenomenon of context-collapse, a hallmark of many social media platforms, according to numerous studies. With narrative stancetaking, users seem to be signalling certain audiences as more included, ratified and suitable than others. Put differently, they create conditions of knowing narrative participation which places certain members of the audience in a position to align with the stance in the original posting and to elaborate on, amplify and co-author it, on the basis of (shared) knowledge.

Overall, I showed that working with small stories research on social media requires both methodological and conceptual innovation. Moving forward will involve engaging small stories with various mixed methods, including data visualization and big data mining. There is much scope for combining qualitative, ethnographic, micro-analyses, such as the ones routinely associated with small stories, with quantitative analyses. At the same time, further analyses of small stories need a critical agenda that will revisit the initial association of the suppressed and non-normative activities. Reflecting on the implications of the prevalence of small stories – and the social actions often associated with them – in many online forums has led me to reconsider their role in counter-hegemonic processes (see Georgakopoulou 2016c, forthcoming). Uncovering ideological forces in the creation of social media-amplified, dominant accounts through small stories, is emerging as a new priority for small stories research agenda.

NOTES

1 This is a sub-project of the ERC funded Project 'Ego-media: The impact of new media on forms and practices of self-presentation' (with Max Saunders, PI, Claire Brant & Leone Ridsdale, King's College London' (2014–2019).
2 Similarly, Burrows and Savage (2014) have also claimed from experience that while standard methods, even longitudinal ones, allow a demarcation of the fieldwork and acquisition of data from the analysis, with online data, this proves much more problematic.
3 All names used are pseudonyms.

REFERENCES

Andrews, M., Squire, C., & Tamboukou, M. (2008) (eds.) *Doing narrative research*. London, UK: Sage.

Bamberg, M. (2006) Stories: big or small? Why do we care? *Narrative Inquiry 16*: 147–155.

Bamberg, M. & Georgakopoulou, A. (2008) Small stories as a new perspective in narrative and identity analysis. *Text & Talk 28*: 377–396.

Barton, D. & Lee, C. (2013) *Language online*. London, UK: Routledge.

Bauman, R. & Briggs, C. (1990) Poetics and performance as critical perspectives on language and social life. *Annual Review of Anthropology 19*: 59–88.

Baym, N. (2010) *Personal connections in the digital age*. Cambridge: Polity Press.

Bou-Franch, P., Lorenzo-Dus, N., & Garcés-Conejos Blitvich, P. (2012) Social interaction in YouTube text-based polylogues: a study of coherence. *Journal of Computer Mediated Communication 17*: 501–521.

Boyd, d. (2010). Social Network Sites as Networked Publics: Affordances, Dynamics, and Implications. In *Networked Self: Identity, Community, and Culture on Social Network Sites* (ed. Zizi Papacharissi), pp. 39–58.

Bucholtz, M. & Hall, K. (2005) Identity and interaction: a sociocultural linguistic approach. *Discourse Studies 7*: 584–614.

Burrows, R. & Savage, M. (2014) After the crisis? Big data and the methodological challenges of empirical sociology. *Big data and society 1*: http://bds.sagepub.com/content/1/1/2053951714540280

De Fina, A. & Georgakopoulou, A. (2012) *Analyzing narrative: Discourse & sociolinguistic perspectives*. Cambridge: Cambridge University Press.

Duranti, A. (2005) On Theories and Models. *Discourse Studies 7*: 409–429.

Dynel, M. (2014) Participation framework underlying YouTube interaction. *Journal of Pragmatics 73*: 37–52.

Frobenius, M. & Harper, R. (2015) Tying in comment sections: The production of meaning and sense on Facebook. *Semiotica 204*: 121–143.

Georgakopoulou, A. (2006) Thinking big with small stories in narrative and identity analysis. Narrative Inquiry 16: 122–130.

Georgakopoulou, A. (2007) *Small stories, interaction and identities*. Amsterdam/Philadelphia: John Benjamins.

Georgakopoulou, A. (2008) 'On MSN with buff boys' Self- and other-identity claims in the context of small stories. *Journal of Sociolinguistics* 12: 597–626.

Georgakopoulou, A. (2013a) Building iterativity into positioning analysis: A practice-based approach to small stories and self. Special Issue on Positioning. *Narrative Inquiry 23*: 89–110.

Georgakopoulou, A. (2013b) Storytelling on the go: Breaking news stories as a travelling narrative genre. In M. Hatavara, L.-C. Hydén & M. Hyvärinen (eds.), *The Travelling Concepts of Narrative*. Amsterdam/Philadelphia: John Benjamins, pp. 201–224.

Georgakopoulou, A. (2013c) Small stories research and social media practices: Narrative stancetaking and circulation in a Greek news story. *Sociolinguistica 27*: 87–100.

Georgakopoulou, A. (2014) Small stories transposition & social media: A micro-perspective on the 'Greek crisis'. Special Issue. *Discourse & Society* 25: 519–539.

Georgakopoulou, A. (2015a) Small stories research: issues, methods, applications. In De Fina, A. & Georgakopoulou, A. (eds.) *Handbook of narrative analysis*. Malden, MA: Wiley-Blackwell, pp. 255–271.

Georgakopoulou, A. (2015b) Sharing as rescripting. Place manipulations on YouTube between narrative and social media affordances. *Discourse, Context & Media 9*: 64–72.

Georgakopoulou, A. (2016a, in press) Life/narrative of the moment. From telling a story to taking a narrative stance. In McKim E., S. Patron & B. Schiff (eds.) *Life and narrative*. Oxford: OUP.

Georgakopoulou, A. (2016b, forthcoming) From narrating the self to posting self(ies): a small stories approach to selfies. Open Linguistics 2: 300-317.

Georgakopoulou, A. (2016c, forthcoming) 'Whose context collapse?': Ethical clashes in the study of language and social media in context. *Applied Linguistics Review.*

Georgalou, M. (2015) Small stories of the Greek crisis on Facebook. *Social Media and Society.*

Gillies, D., Stommel, W., Paulus, T., Lester, J., & Reed, D. (2015) Microanalysis of online data: The methodological development of 'digital CA'. *Discourse, Context & Media 7*: 45–51.

Goffman, E. (1981) *Forms of Talk*. Philadelphia: University of Pennsylvania Press.

Gubrium, J.F. & Holstein, J.A. (2009) *Analyzing narrative reality*. Thousand Oaks: Sage.

Hanks, W. (1996) *Language and communicative practices*. Boulder, CO: Westview Press.

Hine, C., Kendall, L. & boyd, d. (2009) Question one: How can qualitative internet researchers define the boundaries of their projects? In: Markham, A.N. and Baym, N.K. (eds.), *Internet inquiry: Conversations about method*. Thousand Oaks, CA: Sage, pp. 1–20.

Hutchby, I. & Wooffitt, R. (2008) *Conversation analysis*. Cambridge: Polity Press.

Jefferson, G. (1978) Sequential aspects of storytelling in conversation. In Schenkein, J. (ed.), *Studies in the organisation of conversational interaction*. New York: Academic Press, pp. 219–249.

Jongy, B. (Ed.). (2008) L'automédialité contemporaine. *Revue d'Etudes Culturelles*, (4).

Markham, A.N. (2013) Remix culture, remix methods: Reframing qualitative inquiry for social media contexts. In Denzin, N. & Giardina, M. (eds.), *Global dimensions of qualitative inquiry*. Walnut Creek, CA: Left Coast Press, pp. 63–81.

Marwick, A. & boyd, d. (2011) I tweet honestly, I tweet passionately: Twitter users, context collapse and the imagined audience. *New Media and Society 13*: 114–133.

Mitchell, C. (1984) Typicality and the case study. In Ellen, R.F. (ed.) *Ethnographic Research: A guide to general conduct*. New York: Academic Press, pp. 238–241.

Oberhuber, F., Bärenreuter, C., KrzyĐanowski, M., Schönbauer, H., Wodak, R. (2005) Debating the European Constitution: On representations of Europe/the EU in the press. *J. of Lang. Polit.* 4 (2), 227–271.

Ochs, E. & Capps, L. (2001) *Living narrative*. Cambridge, MA: Harvard University Press.

Page, R. (2012) *Stories and social media*. New York/London: Routledge.

Quan-Haase, A. (2009) Text-Based Conversations over Instant Messaging: A Sociolinguistic Perspective. In C. Rowe & E. L. Wyss (eds.), *Language and new media: Linguistic, cultural, and technological evolutions*. Creskill, NJ: Hampton Press, pp. 31–52.

Sacks, H. (1992) *Lectures on conversation*, Volumes I and II. Edited by G. Jefferson with Introduction by E.A. Schegloff, Blackwell, Oxford.

Tagg, C. & Seargeant, P. (2016) Facebook and the discursive construction of the social network. In Georgakopoulou, A. & Spilioti, T. (eds.),

The Routledge handbook of language and digital communication. London, UK: Routledge, pp. 339–353.

van Dijck, J. (2013) You have one identity: Performing the self on Facebook and LinkedIn. *Media, Culture and Society 35*: 199–215.

Vaajala, T., Arminen, I., & De Rycker, A. (2013) Misalignments in Finnish emergency call openings: Legitimacy, assymetries and multi-tasking as interactional contests. In A. De Rycker & Z. Mohd Don (eds.), *Discourse and crisis: Critical perspectives*. Amsterdam: John Benjamins, pp. 131–157.

Wesch, M. (2008) *An anthropological introduction to YouTube*. Retrieved from www.youtube.com/user/mwesch

West, L. E. (2013) Facebook sharing: A sociolinguistic analysis of computer-mediated storytelling. *Discourse, Context & Media 2*: 1–13.

PART IV

Quantitative Approaches to Social Media Data

Geospatial Analysis

Olga Buchel and Diane Rasmussen Pennington

This chapter is about geospatial analysis of social media. It summarizes major issues with retrieving, sampling, geocoding, and analyzing social media data. The chapter discusses geospatial analysis from the perspectives of different domains of knowledge, including information science, geographic information science, geovisualization, information visualization and visual analytics by presenting numerous illustrative examples and case studies. It also shows benefits and shortcomings of these methods and defines existing gaps in geospatial analysis.

INTRODUCTION

Blogs, tweets, comments, images, videos, RSS feeds, online games, accounts in social media and clouds are inundated with references to geographic locations due to the proliferation of location-aware devices. On the one hand, social media systems track locations implicitly where people go, where they search or share information from. On the other hand, social media users voluntarily share the location of their travel routes, destinations, hotels, and restaurants as well as images enhanced with geospatial coordinates. As Goodchild (2007) noted, citizens have become sensors who actively collect and contribute geospatial information. This phenomenon gave rise to the convergence of geographic information science and social media (Sui and Goodchild, 2011). These volunteered crowd-sourced data reduce the burden of data collection (Stefanidis et al., 2013), and they open up exciting opportunities to study human movement from the perspective of their socio-spatial behaviour (De Longueville et al., 2009). This chapter summarizes a variety of techniques used in the investigation of information flows and social networks on human-defined landscapes.

This chapter takes a multidisciplinary approach as techniques are now being developed not only in geography, but many other research domains, particularly visual analytics, geovisualization, social sciences, and information science. In addition, geographic analyses are now integrated with other methods such as semantic analysis, machine learning, network analysis, econometrics, and human-computer interaction, and are being used for enhancing the understanding of spatio-temporal contexts of various phenomena. In other words, researchers use geographic locations shared in social media not only for understanding locations, but also to get better insights about phenomena under investigation (e.g., communities, economic and political impacts of events, disease outbreaks, communication patterns, emergency situations, and many others).

The section *Background Information* presents key properties of geographic locations which are crucial for understanding how geospatial analyses should be carried out. We also explain how geospatial analyses are complicated by semantic properties of information spaces and social networks and where references to geographic locations can be found in social media systems. In the *Analyzing Spatial Locations* section, we first give examples of research questions social media can be used for, a summary of how researchers prepare data for spatial analysis and how they assign coordinates to locations, and we highlight difficulties with extraction and disambiguation of place names. We then proceed to the discussion of pros and cons of the techniques used in geography, visual analytics and other research areas in order to extract insights about phenomena under investigation. We focus on *Exploratory Analysis*, *Standard Deviational Ellipse*s, and *Spatio-temporal Analysis*. The next section on *Geo-social Visual Analytics* addresses current limitations of geospatial analysis and describes new techniques that attempt to bridge network and map representations. The *Spatial Data Mining* section presents techniques for automated pattern extraction. We conclude our chapter with a debate about potential dangers of geospatial analysis associated with the breach of users' privacy, and give recommendations on how to protect privacy of social media users in geospatial analysis.

BACKGROUND INFORMATION

Spatial information in social media is recorded in two forms: geospatial footprints and text (i.e., references to place names such as 'Toronto' or 'Paris'). A footprint is a representation of the spatial location or extent of a geographic object expressed in terms of geospatial coordinates (Hill, 2006). It can take many different forms: a dot, a line, a polygon, a set of dots, a boundary box, an image, or pixels. Footprints are required for creating a visualization on a map. Textual representations can take many forms too; they can be expressed in different languages or as codes, tags, ZIP Codes, mailing addresses, postal codes, time zones, IP addresses, or other notations. On the one hand, assigning a footprint no longer constitutes a difficulty due to an abundance of geocoding services. On the other hand, geocoding services are not always able to recognize location names in texts, or to match them with proper footprints due to place name changes, variations in transliterations, homonyms, variant spellings, or other semantic variations.

Back in the 1990s, when research on online geospatial systems was just starting, researchers in geodigital libraries, who were at the forefront of modeling geospatial descriptions, talked about feature types as important attributes of geospatial descriptions. Feature types are natural and cultural categories of geospatial locations (Hill, 2006). Natural features include continents, mountains, lakes, seas, forests, grasslands, and so on. Cultural features include types of businesses, man-made constructions, and places. These types help bridge place names with coordinates. They improve accuracy and precision for information retrieval, and they help people interpret the context in which communication takes place. For example, consider a medical instructor who often visits military conflict zones. Comments and messages from her on social media might differ in tonality and content according to the type of the location. In her native city she might look relaxed and happy, and involved in volunteering. In zones of military conflict her behavior will change; she will share fewer comments and post pictures in a military uniform after she returns from the zone. Actions and comments of her close friends would also differ depending on her location. If she is getting ready to go to the zone of military conflict, friends would try to help her right away because they understand that she might need help urgently before she leaves for the zone. Without understanding location types, her comments are difficult to interpret. Designers at Facebook realize the drawback of not having location types in their social media platform; for this reason, they now offer a location check-in service. This service mostly provides places of interest as well as businesses that allow data scientists at Facebook to conduct research on checking in to certain location types (e.g., Chang and Sun, 2011). Using check-in data Chang and Sun (2011) built a model that helped them predict where people will check into next. Such predictions can improve ranking of places of interest and create better advertisement targeting. How to capture or extract other types of locations is a question that has yet to be addressed by researchers, social media developers, and analysts.

Besides place names and footprints, geographic references can also be classified in terms of accuracy, precision, scale, and uncertainty. Accuracy is 'the degree to which the recorded value represents the "correct" value' (Hill, 2006, p. 227). Accuracy of reference points collected with cell phones varies from 500 meters to 20 meters (Ramdani, 2011). Accuracy of IP geocoding services are only good enough to locate a particular city, or a country depending on the location in the world (Ramdani, 2011). In some countries accuracy is higher than in others. For example, the accuracy of detecting IP addresses in the Philippines or Croatia is lower than 60%, while in the USA and Canada, it is 84% (MaxMind, 2015). Accuracy of geocoding services will also differ due to different methods used for calculating coordinates (Whitsel et al., 2006). Precision refers to the potential amount of geographic extent represented by the locality. Coordinates are more precise and accurate than textual references because when textual references in the form of place names (not street addresses) are translated to coordinates, they are commonly represented either as a pair of coordinates that correspond to the central point of the location, or as a bounding box (i.e., a rectangle drawn around the place).

Scale is a primary property of maps. It is the ratio between the linear distance on the map and the corresponding linear distance on the Earth's surface (Longley et al., 2005). However, researchers in geographic information science as well as in library and information science have argued that geographic references form a semantic space of their own (Buchel, 2013; Fabrikant, 2001a, b; Fabrikant and Skupin, 2005; Fabrikant and Buttenfield, 2001). As such, the space also has scale. The semantic space is defined by implicit relationships among geographic references, specifically relationships among countries and provinces as well as provinces and smaller geographic locations. Together they form a semantic hierarchy, different levels of which correspond to different geospatial scales. Accuracy, precision, and scale at which geographic locations are reported in social media affect spatial uncertainty of geospatial representations. Uncertainty is defined as the difference between a real geographic phenomenon and the user's understanding of the geographic phenomenon (Longley et al., 2005). Things become even more complicated when we add semantic uncertainty to this mix (Bordogna et al., 2012). Semantic uncertainty implies that social media users may give different meanings to the same term, phrase and/or actions, which may lead to false conclusions.

For instance, a phrase such as 'close to the northeast of Milan' can be interpreted differently as people's perceptions of distance vary. Research in geographic information retrieval suggests that feature types may reduce geospatial uncertainty and increase geospatial accuracy and precision (Bo and Baldwin, 2012).

Last but not least, it is important to take into account that references to geographic locations in social media are not the primary information objects. In other words, social media systems are not about geographic concepts or geography, but they are rather about people, information objects (images or videos), relationships among people and objects, communities of people that engage in communication, document sharing, information flows, and other activities. This suggests that geospatial analysis in such complex systems should take into account all these processes and relationships. Some researchers have already identified geospatial properties of social networks. Scellato et al. (2011) found that networks in Foursquare have different characteristic spatial lengths of interaction across both their social ties and social triads. Doytsher et al. (2010) found that human movements generate life patterns that include social connections and places a person visited.

Where can geospatial locations be found, and how often are they reported? Geographic references can be found in different contexts of social media systems. They are used to denote users' home locations, events, and spatial coverage of microblog entries or images. Geographic references may refer to static states, dynamic states, or events. For example, references to home locations can be considered more or less static whereas references to tweets are regarded ambient, because they represent momentary social hotspots (Stefanidis et al., 2013).

Studies report different numbers of users who provided geospatial locations in their data samples. Java et al. (2007) reported that 52% of Twitter users (39,000 out of 76,000) included in their study had geospatial locations. Hecht et al. (2011) reported that two out of three users in their study had information about their geospatial locations. Cheng et al. (2010) reported that 5% of users in their study listed locations in the form of coordinates, and 21% reported locations at the city level. Several studies have shown that locational information can be inferred from the content that users post in social media (Cheng et al., 2010; Popescu and Grefenstette, 2010; Backstrom et al., 2010). MacEachren et al. (2011b) studied people who were trying to use Twitter for crisis management, and reported that the proportion of users with geolocation turned on is probably still in the single digits. Stefanidis et al. (2013) suggested that such variations in location reporting can be attributed to an uneven distribution of the latest mobile devices.

Analyzing Spatial Locations

In this chapter, we emphasize that spatial analysis is not only about linking microblogs to a map, but it is also about understanding how they relate, what they mean, and what should be done about them. It is about measuring geospatial footprints of online and offline communities, determining their volume, finding their proximity to other communities, overlaps and intersections, identifying spatial clusters, locating hotspots of activities, and making predictions about possible outcomes of events (ESRI, 2015). The Geospatial Analysis pipeline reminds us of the standard data science pipeline, shown in Figure 18.1.

Geospatial analysis of social media requires a wide array of interdisciplinary skills (not limited to knowledge of geographic information systems) including the ability to do semantic analysis, network analysis, retrieval analysis, and statistical analysis. It also requires good programming skills in order to be able to retrieve data from application programming interfaces (APIs), and to scrape data, do data cleaning and preprocessing, and perform data transformations.

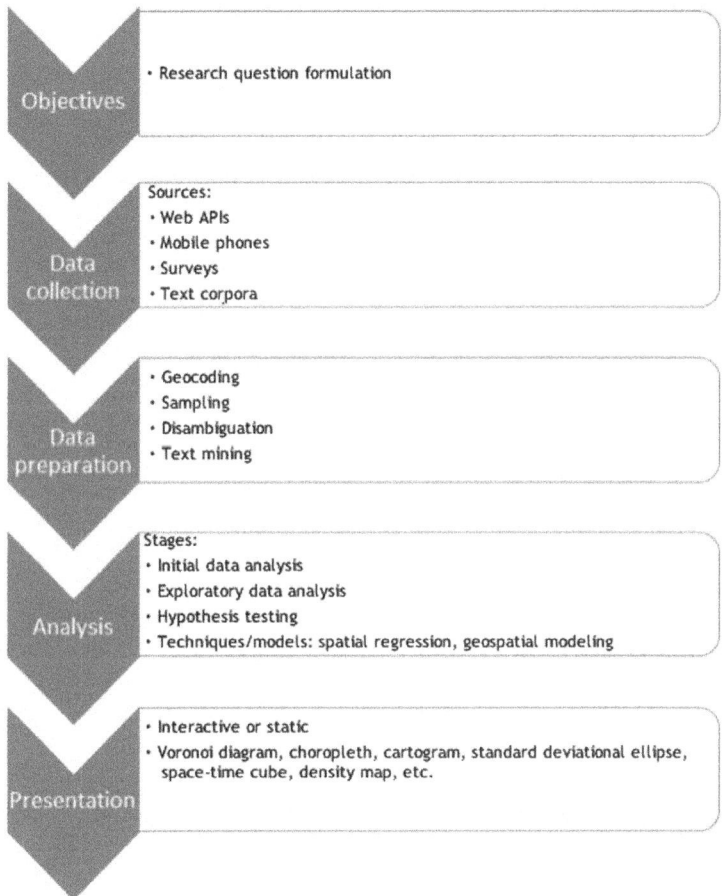

Figure 18.1 Geospatial analysis pipeline

Source: Authors.

Research Questions

Researchers use social media and geospatial analysis for forecasting political opinions on the web (Sobkowicz et al., 2012), identifying and mapping global virtual communities (Stefanidis et al., 2013), making meteorological observations (Hyvärinen and Saltikoff, 2010), studying structure and dynamics of natural cities (Jiang and Miao, 2015), tracking infectious diseases (Padmanabhan et al., 2013), managing crisis situations (MacEachren et al., 2011a), capturing human movement patterns across political borders (Blanford et al., 2015), discovering significant events and patterns (Andrienko et al., 2010b), understanding protest movements (Gleason, 2013), finding geographic patterns of communication networks (Conover et al., 2013), and answering many other questions related to human movements and communication. The general trend is the following: researchers use maps 1) to report their findings, 2) to verify whether social media is more reliable than other techniques, 3) to discover new patterns and insights about phenomena, 4) to generate hypotheses about phenomena, and 5) to understand laws that can explain how networks work. For example, in a recent paper, Krings et al. (2009) investigated the network of mobile phone customers and analyzed the geographical patterns of the customers. After aggregating by city, these authors found that the inter-city communication intensity follows a gravity law. In other studies researchers compare patterns observed in empirical networks with patterns in spatial network models (Barthélemy, 2011).

Throughout its existence, the geographic information science community has developed a number of tools and techniques that can help with geospatial analysis. These techniques focus on identifying clusters in space and time, predictive modeling, exploratory analysis, and others. It is important to pay attention to what questions these techniques can answer and how. This may affect how the analysis will proceed. It may help expand the original set of questions social scientists are coming up with and may help them better understand social phenomena in terms of space and time. Using geographic information shared through social media is likely to produce a larger and more accurate dataset compared to geographic information collected in other ways, because it is created both automatically by users' mobile devices as well as by the users themselves. They are motivated to share it because they want their social networks to see it, whether it is for political organizing purposes or simply for staying in contact with friends and family.

Sampling

Most of the studies that we review in this chapter have used some sort of statistical sampling technique. Given the overwhelmingly large size of information spaces in each social media platform, researchers develop testbed collections by using queries. Queries can be geospatial and/or textual. For example, Purcell and de Beurs (2013) used only textual queries to collect queries about weather, but they had to eliminate many noisy tweets that their queries retrieved (e.g., 'hot girls'). Stefanidis et al. (2013) retrieved tweet hours within a 10-kilometer radius from Tahrir Square during the Egyptian revolution. It is unclear whether all their tweets were relevant, as their study focused on analysis of networks, not analysis of semantics.

Noise, multiple variables, and uncertainty may potentially hinder exploration, hypothesis generation/exploration, and decision making. Researchers could improve their samples by using some of the query expansion techniques from information science and natural language processing. In information retrieval, the most common technique for query expansion is using a thesaurus, defined as a dictionary of terms related to the words in a query. Each word in a query can be automatically expanded with synonyms and related words from the thesaurus. This technique can be enhanced with term weighting, depending on how distant these terms are from the words in the query. Massoudi et al. (2011), for example, suggested using quality indicators to model retrieval of microblog posts. In their retrieval model, they assigned weights to emoticons, post length, shouting, capitalization, the existence of hyperlinks, reposts, followers, and recency of tweets. Other studies in information retrieval have also looked at more contextual searches, including event detection (Sayyadi et al., 2009), and mining consumer and political opinions (Sobkowicz et al., 2012). Using such techniques in the context of geographic analysis would improve the accuracy of geospatial analysis.

Also, it is important to keep in mind that even after all proper techniques of information retrieval are in place, it is possible to make mistakes in geospatial analysis. For example, in 2013, Google Flu Trends, which claimed to be an efficient public health tool for accurately monitoring the flu, far overstated its predictions. This overstatement can be seen in Figure 18.2. In all previous years it indeed provided very accurate results, but in 2013 their predictions went wrong. Butler (2013) reported on the huge discrepancy between Google Flu Trend's estimated peak flu levels and data collected by the U.S.

Centers for Disease Control and Prevention (CDC) earlier in winter 2013. More precisely, Google doubled the numbers. The problem is that Google relies on searches related to flu symptoms, but in 2013 increased media attention to the flu season skewed Google's search engine traffic and consequently their geospatial predictions (Wagner, 2013).

Geoparsing, Geocoding and Disambiguation of Geographic Place Names

Extraction of geographic place names (also referred to as geoparsing) from short comments and tweets is different from extraction of place names from long and grammatically correct texts, (Lingad et al., 2013). Whereas in grammatically correct texts geographical locations are usually capitalized, in short microblog posts such as tweets and comments, they are often placed in limited context and are not capitalized (e.g., British Columbia versus bc). Gelernter and Mushegian's (2011) analysis of Twitter messages from the February 2011 earthquake in Christchurch, Canterbury, New Zealand, showed that named entity recognition software recognizes places as proper nouns when locations are capitalized, but does not identify locations that are: not capitalized, local

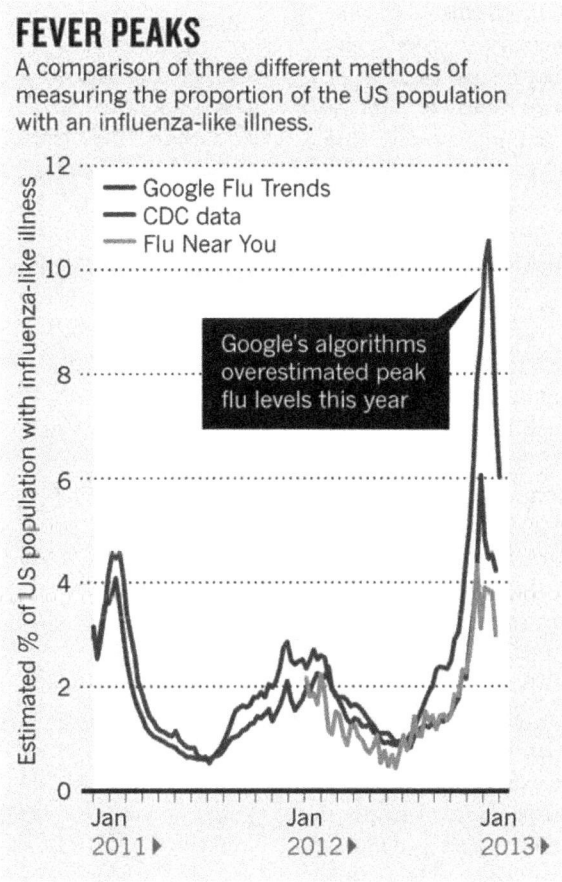

Figure 18.2 A visualization of three different methods for measuring flu prevalence in the US

Sources: Nature; Google Flu Trends (www.google.org/flutrends); CDC; Flu Near You.

streets and buildings, non-standard place abbreviations, or misspellings. Karimzadeh et al. (2013) claimed that they solved this issue; they designed a tool called GeoTxt API that extracts, disambiguates, and geocodes place names in short microblog posts. They did not mention, however, whether they used feature types.

Geotagging can be defined as 'the process of adding geographical identification metadata to resources (websites, RSS feed, images or videos). The metadata usually consists of latitude and longitude coordinates, but they may also include altitude, camera heading direction and place names' (Torniai et al., 2007). Many newer cameras contain GPS receivers that add geographic coordinates to a photograph at the time it is taken. Also, social media users sometimes add semantic geotags to photographs such as 'Paris' when they upload them.

A small but growing body of research involving geotagged photographs is developing. Rorissa et al. (2012) extracted geotags from Flickr images in order to examine their level of abstraction, and found no statistical significance with these levels, but suggested ways in which geotags can help people find photographs online more easily. O'Hare and Murdock (2013) used the tags and geotags of photographs to predict the locations of where photographs were taken with varying levels of accuracy. Sevillano et al. (2015) performed a similar experiment using only audio and visual information in a set of videos.

Kipp et al. (2014) extracted location information from the accounts of commenters, image descriptions (location field), and image titles. They investigated images and postcards posted on Flickr by the Library of Congress. All titles and descriptions of images in this collection have correct grammar and full texts. The extraction from image titles was complicated because all words in the titles were capitalized, and geographic names were often separated by other words. In the end, they assigned locations manually.

Besides adding coordinates to places extracted from unstructured texts or geotags, researchers often have to geocode from address-like strings (this process is also known as forward geocoding). Forward geocoding is a process of assigning coordinates for a full or partial address. A large array of services can be used for geocoding: Google Maps, Bing Maps, Twofishes, MapQuest, and other. A bit more challenging is the process of reverse geocoding, in which coordinates are mapped to addresses and toponyms. Uncertainty of the queried location complicates this process. For examples, it is unclear how to map GPS coordinates to one of many possible stores in a shopping mall (McKenzie and Janowicz, 2015).

Static versus Interactive Maps

Web 2.0 introduced us to not only social media platforms, but also interactive maps like Google Maps (https://www.google.com/maps/) and OpenStreetMap (https://www.openstreetmap.org). These maps have APIs which can be used for mashups, or custom maps that can be linked to databases on users' servers. These new technologies directly affect geospatial analysis. Many programmers who know how to link maps to data sprang into action and developed mashups for already existing databases (e.g., real estate databases, image repositories, public health databases and many others). However, many of these maps are not maps in a conventional sense, but rather retrieval tools; their purpose is to show users where information objects are located and allow them to click on the map to retrieve information about the objects. See the Flickr map in Figure 18.3 for an example of a map as a retrieval tool.

Researchers in academia welcomed these new developments too as this opened up an opportunity for crowdsourced mapping (Goodchild, 2007), ambient information mapping (Weidemann, 2013), real-time crisis maps (Middleton et al., 2014) and for moving geospatial analysis from proprietary mapping applications to the web. Some cartographers

Figure 18.3 Example of a map as a retrieval tool
Source: http://www.flickr.com.

started referring to maps as visualizations (MacEachren, 1995). The emphasis of visualizations is 'not on storing knowledge but on knowledge construction' (MacEachren and Kraak, 1997, p. 336), which implies that maps have to be interactive. Web 2.0 gave rise to new techniques for representing information (e.g., linking social networks to maps and embedding other visualizations in maps), and for interacting with geospatial information (Buchel and Sedig, 2014) which was not possible to achieve with static maps. However, at the same time, analytical techniques that were developed in previous-generation geographic information systems (especially ESRI products; see http://www.esri.com/products) are hardly available for conducting geospatial analytics in web applications. For instance, it is still difficult to analyze hotspots or do grouping analysis without ESRI ArcGIS. ESRI is making attempts to bring their analytical techniques to the web; the company now offers an API that allows developers to embed them in their maps (see a list of available analysis tools from ESRI's ArcGIS API for JavaScript at https://developers.arcgis.com/javascript/). In addition, geospatial analysis can now be carried out in cloud-based mapping applications such as Fusion Tables (https://sites.google.com/site/fusiontablestalks/stories), GIS Cloud (http://www.giscloud.com), CartoDB (https://cartodb.com), visualization frameworks such as D3.js (http://d3js.org), and R (https://www.r-project.org). QGIS (http://www.qgis.org) is a free, open source alternative to ArcGIS. These tools offer a wide range of new and traditional analytical techniques. At first glance, cloud computing applications might look simple, but with additional programming, they can be used for fairly complex analysis.

Whereas static maps allowed carrying out analysis at the level of 'flat' snapshots, interactive maps opened many new options for analysis. It became possible to carry out dynamic analysis, such as tracking data related to human movement, and following the dynamics of social movements. Analysis in interactive visualizations is complicated by the motion of people and network dynamics in time and space. In interactive maps, great attention is paid to the conceptualization of time. Time has a complex structure; that is, it has a hierarchical system of units, including seconds, minutes, hours, days, weeks, months, years, decades, centuries and so on, which can be grouped into different calendar systems, cycles, etc. Time can be represented as a line, a cycle, a branch, or a hierarchy (Andrienko et al., 2010a). For example, Figure 18.4 shows health data over time represented as a linear plot graph on the left and as a cyclic spiral on the right. It can also be represented and parsed as sound in the form of data sonification (see Jamieson and Boase, Chapter 24, this volume).

In the next section, we review both analytical and interactive techniques, how they can be used for analysis, what questions they can answer, and what the pros and cons of each technique are. Our examples are drawn from several disciplines including geography, social sciences, visual analytics, health sciences, and others.

Data Classification Techniques

The starting point for any analysis usually involves proportional symbology or a choropleth map. Proportional symbology or choropleth maps rely on data classification. Researchers and analysts must decide which values should be associated with each bubble size on a symbol map or which values should be used for each class on a choropleth map. In other words, which units should be in the lowest class, which units should be in the highest class, and how should the rest of the units be distributed among the remaining classes? Most classification schemes in geographic information science provide a range of techniques for classifying univariate attributes; for example, mapping the number of tweets by county or state/province. Classification is an interesting topic on its own. There is a large number of classification schemes in geographic information science, including classifications based on unique values, manual classification, defined interval, exponential interval, equal count or quantile, percentile, natural breaks/Jenks, standard deviation, and box. Due to the size restrictions on this chapter, we are not able to explain the pros and cons of these methods; rather we refer readers to Mitchell (1999) and Longley et al. (2005).

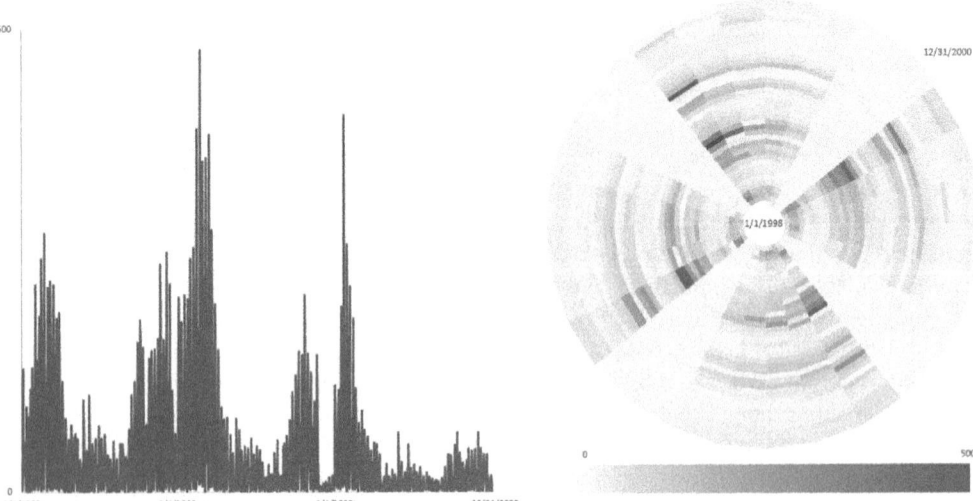

Figure 18.4 Health data over time as a linear plot graph and as a cyclic spiral

Source: Andrienko et al., 2010a.

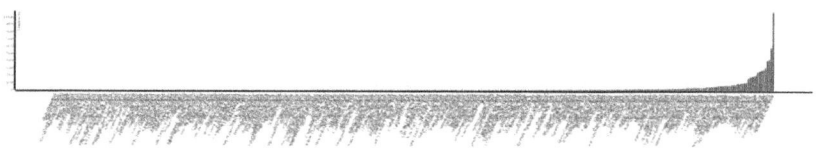

Figure 18.5 Distribution of counts of images linked to different locations
Source: Authors.

In this chapter, we will explain the quantile method, as it is one of the most frequently used (Brewer and Pickle, 2002). Suppose we retrieved the following number of images per each location from Flickr. The frequency distribution of these counts is shown in Figure 18.5 above. Frequencies range from 1 to 1,056. As you can see in the histogram, locations have very uneven counts of images linked to them, and the majority of locations have fewer than 20 images.

The quantile classification method distributes equal numbers of observations into each class. The advantage to this method is that it often excels at emphasizing the relative position of the data values (i.e., which locations, or counties, or provinces/regions/states contain the top 20% of visualized objects). The major shortcoming of this classification is that locations placed within the same class can have wildly differing values, particularly if the data are not evenly distributed across its range (see the bars at the end of Figure 18.5). In addition, values with small range differences can be placed into different classes, suggesting a wider difference in the dataset than actually exists. For instance, in our case, locations with values of 1 can be placed in different classes.

Note the possible pitfalls of this method. With a four-category quantile classification, there is an equal number of cities in each class, and some locations with identical attribute values are placed in different classes. This suggests that this method may lead to a misleading visualization. This problem with classifications is not only true for quantile classification, but also for other classifications. They all may have problems with inclusions and exclusions. Discussion about how maps can lie can be found in Monmonier (2005, 2014). A technique that can be useful for avoiding potential pitfalls with visualizations is to have controls for classification schemas in maps (see Figure 18.6). With such controls, the effects of classifications can be easily explored. Such controls can be added for interactive maps/mashups.

One critical issue to understand about data classification is that they enable map designers and analysts to layout all information on a flatland – a two-dimensional surface (Tufte, 1991), which is the major drawback of this approach. Social media data is multivariate in

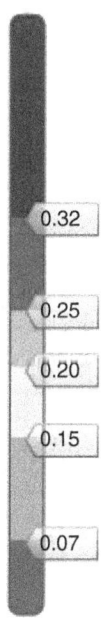

Figure 18.6 Classification control
Source: OECD Regional Explorer, http://stats.oecd.org/oecdregionalstatistics/.

nature, not limited to longitude and latitude variables. For this reason, data classifications can be regarded both useful and harmful for geospatial data analysis. They are useful because they create nice overviews and summaries, but they are harmful because they hide many details about the data. They display only one or two columns from a dataset, but we live in a world of very complex datasets. Each social media API has hundreds of descriptors that are commonly ignored during the analysis as they hardly fit into a classification schema in a visualization tool.

Exploratory Analysis

Geographers suggest beginning geospatial analysis with exploratory analyses (Anselin, 1999). The problem is that a collection of geographic data from a particular region may have many latent relationships which are difficult to display and communicate without explicit explanation about what is going on in the region. Exploratory analysis in professional GIS tools is often supported by additional statistical charts and graphs that show statistical distribution of data (e.g., scatterplots, scatterplot matrices, and box plots). These additional graphs and charts provide insight into the complex and subtle relationships that occur in geographic space (Gahegan, 1998).

To get started with exploratory analysis, we recommend novice researchers first study tasks that can be accomplished with such analysis (Andrienko and Andrienko, 2006). Andrienko and Andrienko (2006) give a comprehensive typology of the possible data analysis questions that 'need to be answered by means of data analysis' (p. 8). They divide tasks into elementary and synoptic. Elementary tasks deal with individual elements of data and their properties; synoptic tasks deal with the datasets as the wholes and the patterns in the wholes. The main purpose of exploratory spatio-temporal analysis is to understand the overall behaviour captured by data. For example, in the context of social media analysis, research may be able to answer the following questions: How can the behaviour of social media users be characterized in terms of time and space? Is it changing over time? How does it change in terms of spatial dispersion? How does it change in terms of temporal aspects? Is there any periodicity in the behaviours?

Exploratory analysis of social media, however, should not be conducted solely in terms of space and time. Social media researchers should investigate not only the entire datasets, but also pay great attention to subsets (i.e., specific communities). This will allow the identification of differences in the behaviour of individual groups. Compare groups in terms of spatial relationships (proximity, intersections, overlaps, and so on). How do social structures differ in communities from different geospatial areas?

In the next two sections we give two examples of analytical techniques which we think might be useful for analysis of social media datasets. Both techniques have long history and have been well established in geospatial analysis.

Voronoi Diagrams

A Voronoi diagram is an analytical technique to divide a map into geographic regions that are not equivalent to geographic regions. Its idea is simple: given a set of isolated points, points are associated with the closest member of the point set. The result is the partitioning of the space into a set of regions (Okabe et al., 2009). The Voronoi diagram implies that all possible points inside a polygon are closest to its centroid than to any other polygon (Manni et al., 2004). The external part of a Voronoi tessellation tends to infinity. Commonly, Voronoi diagrams are used to find the largest empty circle amid a set of points (e.g., to build a new pharmacy as far as possible from all the existing ones). Voronoi diagrams have been used in various knowledge domains, such as astronomy, business analytics, and soil analysis.

The earliest use of Voronoi diagrams in the context of geospatial analysis is attributed to John Snow (Brody et al., 2000). He used this technique in his second map of cholera investigation. At that time, he compiled the map and the diagram for illustrative rather than investigative purposes. The technique can be used for investigative purposes as well. For example, he could have drawn polygons around the pumps and then calculated the number of deaths in each polygon. That would have immediately shown that the pump that was at the center of the epidemics was an outlier, because the polygon that the pump was in had the largest number of deaths. Imagine using such techniques with health clinics providing flu shots and tweets about flu symptoms. If clinics posted the dates and times of their flu shot clinics in late autumn, along with their geographic locations, it might be easier for people to access the needed vaccinations. This technique can also be used for visualizing categorical data. For example, Manni et al. (2004) visualized genetic, morphologic, and linguistic patterns with Voronoi diagrams. Voronoi diagrams have also been used for enhancing spatial browsing and exploration of images on Flickr (Peca et al., 2011; Andrienko et al., 2010b).

Figure 18.7 below shows a Voronoi diagram of Craigslist which relays how the site redirects its users to local subdirectories based on their IP address (Nelson, 2011). The map approximates geographic coverage of Craigslist to Voronoi polygons. It is at least a start at visualizing the geographic coverage and distribution of the community-driven instances of Craigslist. Voronoi polygons might provide some useful context for other data, demographic or market information.

Standard Deviational Ellipse

This technique was first introduced by Lefever (1926). What is remarkable about this analytical approach is that it shows the

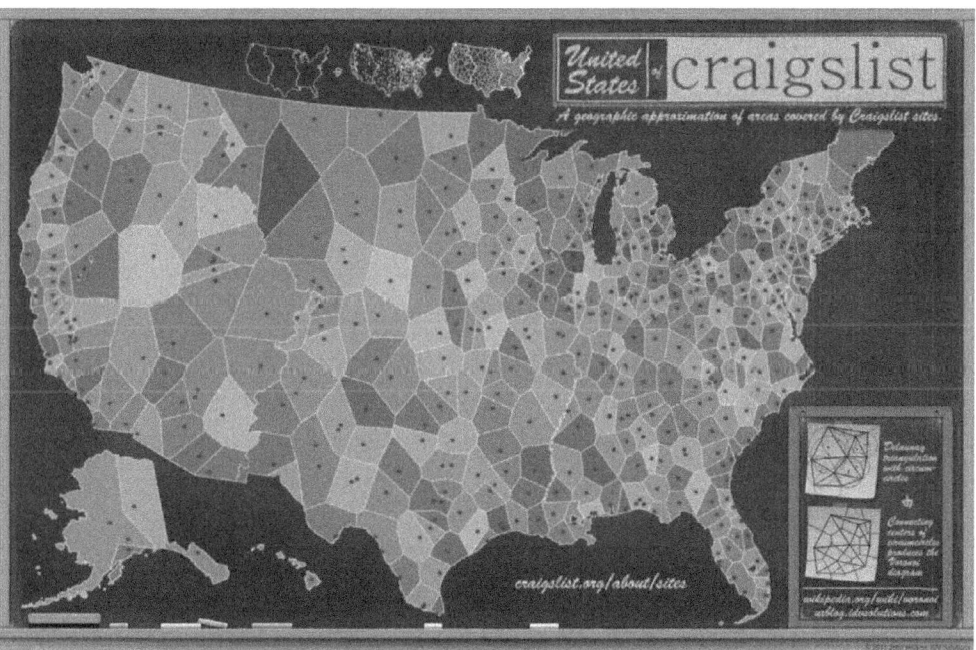

Figure 18.7 **Map showing Craigslist market territories**

Source: John Nelson, uxblog.idvsolutions.com.

orientation of the distribution. Human eyes can see the distribution on a map, but they cannot determine a trend in the data. The ellipse shows a spatial trend, so to speak; see Figure 18.8. Specifically, the ellipse shows the degree to which a distribution of features is concentrated or dispersed around its center (Wade and Sommer, 2006). The major axis shows the orientation of dispersion, the minor axis shows the minimum dispersion and the area of the ellipse is indicative of the spread (Gong, 2002). This type of analysis can be used for determining the orientation of opinions in social media, such as in survey analysis. For instance, Orchard et al. (2012) used this technique to analyze qualitative data about the life histories of sex workers. With the help of this technique, the researchers were able to determine that the areas where the women go for health and social services overlap the areas that are most dangerous for them (Orchard et al., 2012).

Visual Analytics, Geovisualization, and Information Visualization

Visual analytics, geovisualization, and information visualization chart new directions in map visualization. Although they have distinct research agendas, they take similar approaches to geospatial analysis. Geovisualization research focuses on web-based, multi-view geospatial interfaces that support foraging and sensemaking (MacEachren et al., 2011b). Representative examples of geovisualizations are described in MacEachren et al. (2010) and Peca et al. (2011). Information visualization deals with visualization of abstract data that unlike spatial data usually have no intrinsic representation (Fekete and Plaisant, 2002, p. 1). The purpose of visual analytics is to 'provide technology that combines the strengths of human and electronic data processing' (Keim et al., 2008, p. 162). Its key goal is to make data and information processing transparent for an analytic discourse. Geovisualization researchers in visual analytics aim to combine

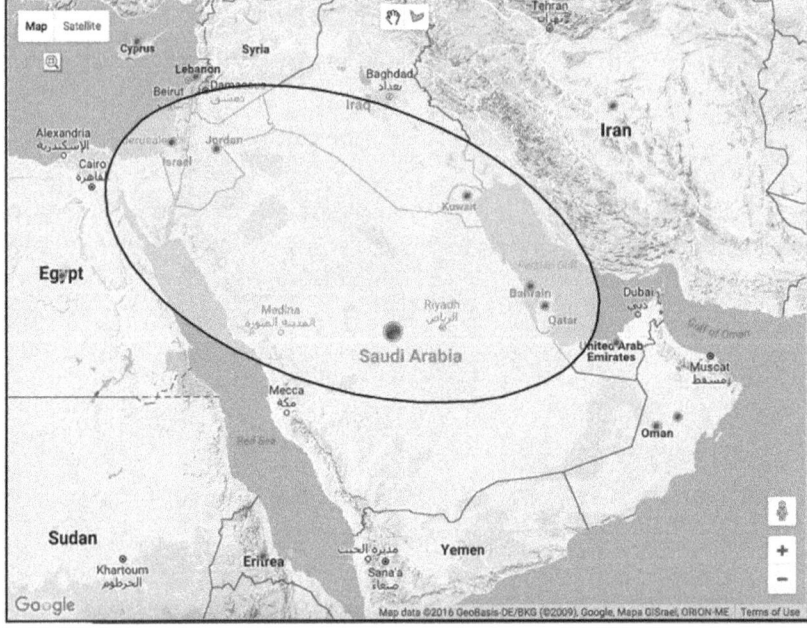

Figure 18.8 Standard deviational ellipse

the strengths of human and electronic data processing in analyzing spatio-temporal data and solving spatio-temporal problems (Andrienko et al., 2010a). All these research directions put a great emphasis on interactions with visualizations that aim to enhance analytical tasks and expand an array of questions that can be asked about data. Interactions in this context are actions that provide users with the ability to directly or indirectly manipulate and interpret visual representations (e.g., rotate, select, and filter) (Yi et al., 2007). Interactions enable users to not only look at maps, but to change them according to their research questions. For example, if a map shows tweets, analysts should be able to search for specific tweets, topics in tweets, sentiments and so on to narrow down the representation of a map only to patterns that are relevant. The website http://www.onemilliontweetmap.com allows people to visualize in real time how many tweets are coming from geographic locations worldwide, and they can also filter them by keyword, hashtag, and so on. For example, Figure 18.9 shows a map of the last 10 million tweets posted starting from 15:50 BST on 15 December 2015.

Many of these systems are not yet available as commercial products; they are models and prototypes that demonstrate how support for data analysis, problem solving, decision-making and knowledge discovery can enhance geospatial analysis. For example, MacEachren et al. (2011a) described a prototype that enables information foraging and sensemaking using 'tweet' indexing and display based on place, time, and concept characteristics. Schreck and Keim (2013) presented a model of an epidemic outbreak in a fictitious metropolitan area. Andrienko et al. (2010b) demonstrated a suite of methods for reconstructing past events from the activity traces that people leave in social media. Their method combines geocomputation, interactive geovisualization and statistical methods. They exemplify the utility of their methodology on a collection of Flickr photos.

A commercially available product that supports visual analysis is GeoTime (http://www.geotime.com). GeoTime is capable of detecting

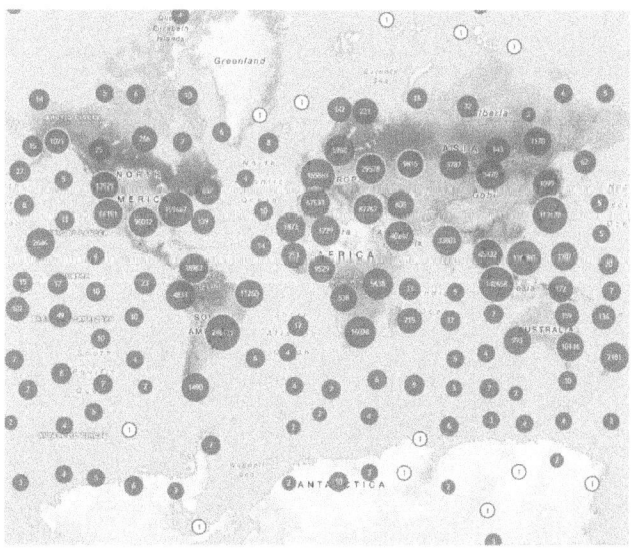

Figure 18.9 Real time tweet map

Source: http://www.onemilliontweetmap.com.

geo-temporal patterns and integrating narration in analytical processes. It improves understanding of entity movements, events, relationships, and interactions over time within a geospatial context. It uses narratives, hypertext-linked visualizations, visual annotations, and pattern detection to create an environment for analytic exploration and communication, thereby assisting analysts in identifying, extracting, arranging, and presenting stories within the data (Eccles et al., 2008). A snapshot from a GeoTime story can be seen in Figure 18.10. It shows the life patterns of two people; these patterns are described in terms of space and time. GeoTime has been successfully used in many real life decision-making tasks, including crime detection, analysis of telecommunication patterns, military, government and business analysis tasks. In 2011, the London Police purchased GeoTime to study the behaviour of users on Facebook (Gayle, 2011).

GeoTime brought to life the famous space-time model, first envisioned by Hägerstrand in 1970 who planned to use this model as 'a socio economic web model' (Hägerstrand, 1970, p. 10) to analyze people's interactions across space and time. It also materializes Tufte's dream of escaping data flatlands. Unlike other tools that visualize space and time, GeoTime visualizes the complexity of spatio-temporal relationships in a single 3-D view. GeoTime has multilingual support, and its latest version also has support for network analysis that is combined with geospatial analysis.

A tool that can largely complement analysis of social media in GeoTime by powerful semantic analysis is nSpace2. Like GeoTime, nSpace2 has won numerous IEEE Visual Analytics Science and Technology (VAST) Conference Contests as well. It supports natural language processing and innovative visual

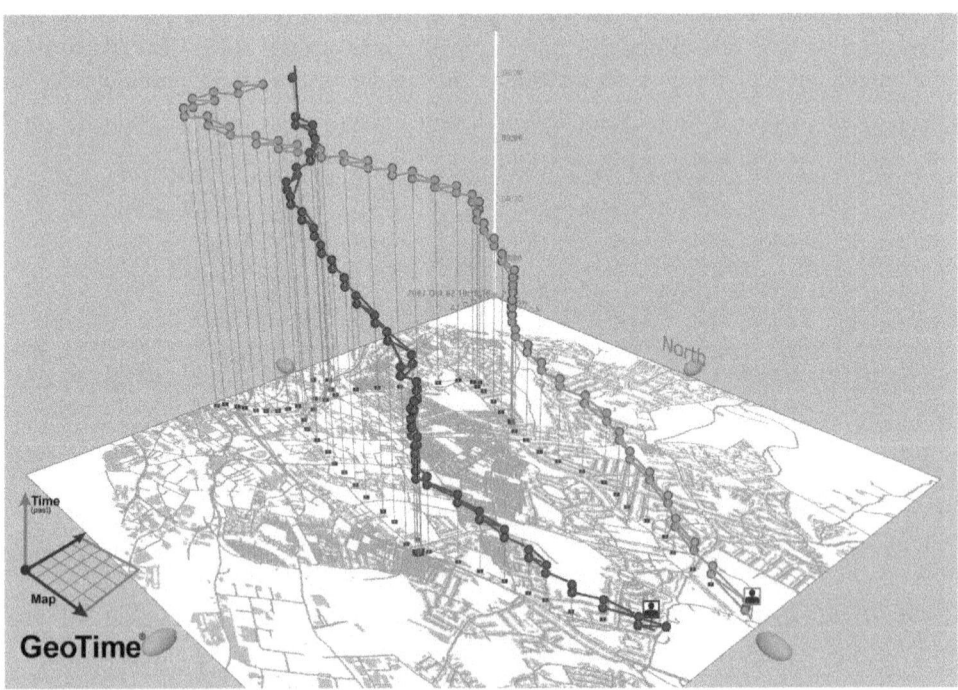

Figure 18.10 Sample GeoTime story snapshot

Source: http://nickmalleson.co.uk/wp-content/uploads/2012/01/geotime_movements.jpg.

analytic techniques. It helps analysts efficiently and collaboratively produce insightful evidence-based reports. GeoTime and nSpace have been tested at VAST with an epidemiology analysis scenario using new reports. Tools enabled analysts to carry out trend analysis using the Country and Time dimensions as well as develop and validate hypotheses about why disease events and patterns occur (Proulx et al., 2006). This can be useful in the context of social media analysis too.

Geo-social Visual Analytics

A new trend is growing within the science of visual analytics known as geo-social visual analytics. In a research agenda for geo-social visual analytics, Luo and MacEachren (2014) explained that geo-social visual analytics differs from visual analytics by 'explicit integration of social network perspectives and methods into the approach and tools' (p. 29), while still focusing on integration of interactive visual interfaces and computational analytical methods that can facilitate scientific reasoning. Another goal of geo-social visual analytics is to bridge the gap between methods used in geography, social sciences and network analysis. At the moment, spatial analysis and social network analysis solve social processes in their own contexts. While geographers look at movements, sociologists consider the relationships among people. Geographers also treat networks much more simply than physicists, who emphasize the power of networks, but ignore properties of geographic space (Curtin, 2007) and spatial constraints (Barthélemy, 2011). Geo-social visual analytics intends to pay more attention to overlaps between these two approaches and hopefully find better solutions for merging these two spaces. In the rest of this section, we give a few examples of how networks are analyzed in the framework of geo-social analytics.

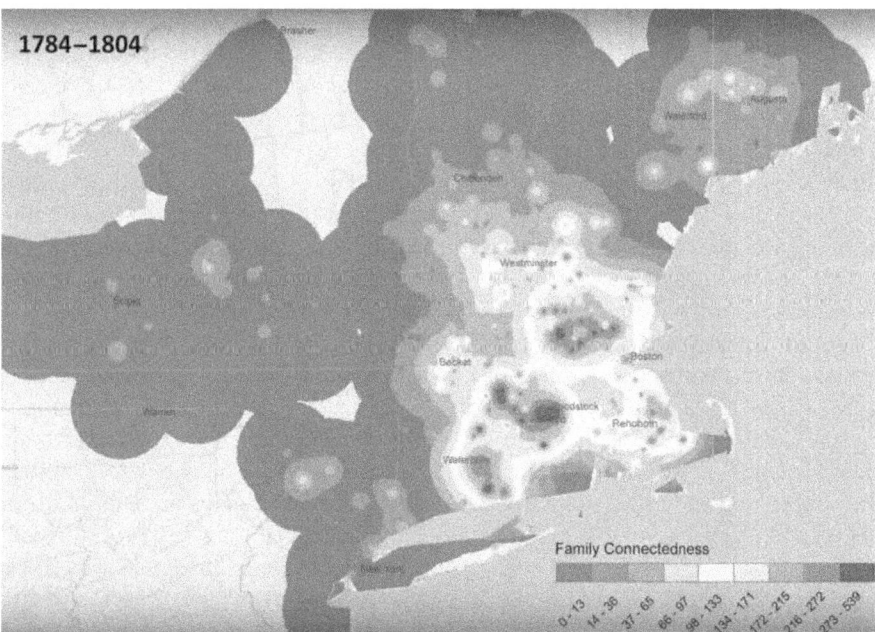

Figure 18.11 Network topology represented on a map

Source: Koylu et al. (2014).

Some geo-social analytics studies use integrated approaches that demonstrate how topology and geography interact with each other. For example, Luo et al. (2011) designed GeoSocial App, which reveals how groups identified in networks are positioned in geographic space over time. It enables capturing the dynamics of social relationships which is hard to understand from static graphs. Discovering interaction patterns between geographic space and network topology is useful for understanding individual- or group-level patterns that may have unique characteristics. Many studies suggest that certain processes in networks have structural and spatial constraints and that they have yet to be understood in empirical networks (Onnela et al., 2011; Barthélemy, 2011).

Such integrated approaches, however, do not summarize spatial or temporal as well as relational aspects of such networks. They allow researchers to examine how changes and processes in topologies affect geography and vice versa, but they do not provide an overview of what is going on in networks in space over time. Recently, an interesting solution for overcoming this limitation has been proposed by Koylu et al. (2014). Koylu et al.'s method takes into account distance, time (duration of interaction between individuals), and type of social relationship between each pair of individuals which are represented on a kernel density map (see Figure 18.11). Although Koylu et al. (2014) demonstrated the utility of this approach in the context of genealogical data, not social media data, their approach is well-suited for social media research. The results of Koylu et al.'s study reveal that family connectedness patterns in genealogical data are similar to migration and population growth patterns.

Spatial Data Mining

Spatial data mining is concerned with 'the extraction of useful information and knowledge from massive and complex spatial databases' (Mennis and Guo, 2009, p. 403). Spatial data mining techniques include spatial regression, spatial clustering, spatial autocorrelation, point pattern analysis, spatial classification and prediction, regionalization, and other. These techniques are useful for algorithmic detection of spatially-dependent patterns in data. They are not limited to traditional data types but also to newly emerged data types such as trajectories of individuals and groups of individuals with similar trajectories, data flows and other. Spatial patterns detected by spatial data mining techniques may yield important insights about individual and crowd behaviours, preferences, sentiments, human mobility networks (Gonzalez, Hidalgo, and Barabasi, 2008), and even properties of locations (Weiler et al., 2015). Data mining techniques could also help define rules for discovery of patterns, the purpose of which is to model human mobility patterns and consequently make predictions about all phenomena associated with human mobility (e.g., epidemics, information diffusion). For example, the co-location rule discovery process finds the subsets of features whose instances are frequently located together in geographic space (Shekhar and Huang, 2001).

A suite of tools for spatial data mining is available from the Spatial Data Mining and Visual Analytics Lab (http://www.spatialdatamining.org/software). Among these tools the most relevant tools for social media analysis are EntroMap and Flow Mapping. EntroMap helps detect the existence of multivariate relationships without assuming a prior relationship form. It can be used for analysis of opinions and estimating the results of elections. Flow Mapping can be used to explore communication flow patterns. In addition, grouping analysis in ArcGIS which is based on K-means can used for clustering networked datasets.

When mining spatial patterns, it is important to know that mobile networks prevailing in social media are limited in their predictability (Song et al., 2010; Gonzalez, Hidalgo, and Barabasi, 2008). Although human mobility patterns are 'characterized by a deep-rooted regularity' and can be predicted and systematized, they lack variability: they have no significant gender-, age-, language-, or population-based differences (Song et al., 2010).

Privacy Issues

Protecting the privacy of social media users' geographic data is an ethical concern for researchers. Not all use of geographic data is unethical, but its use should be considered before research or development is undertaken. Martin (2015) suggested that 'beneficial uses' of GPS data include 'location-based coupons; traffic predictions; directions on map' while 'questionable uses' would be 'location-based stalking; iPhone as a homing beacon' (p. 68). Vicente et al. (2011) reviewed the basic features of social networks utilizing geographic information, such as friend tracking and 'check-ins' at points of interest, and outlined potential ways to protect users' privacy. Puttaswamy et al. (2014) described a tool they developed that shields the actual location data from servers, but still allows users to share location information with each other as desired. Reverse geocoding, or the process of obtaining highly specific location information about users through maps that have points indicating their geographic positions, raises confidentiality and privacy concerns, especially in the case of sensitive topics such as health data (Brownstein et al., 2005; Krumm, 2007).

Very little research has been accomplished in this important area, and more is needed. For now, researchers should consider what levels of scale, accuracy, and precision are absolutely necessary in order to carry out the analysis and visualization. For example, MacEachren et al. (2011a) aggregated frequency counts for tweets to two degree grid cells in order not to show point locations.

CONCLUSION

In conclusion, we would like to emphasize that geospatial analysis of social media is overwhelmingly complex. It requires an interdisciplinary approach that is well-grounded in geospatial, social, linguistics, and information retrieval theories. It is not enough to know only geospatial or social networking methods. It is highly important to understand how social space interacts with geographic space and time. Not all tools can answer the whole spectrum of these questions. Some tools can provide only fragmentary snapshots of phenomena where explicit and implicit contextual differences in individual behaviours are flattened by data classifications. Therefore, they can hinder our understanding of phenomena, rather than enhance it. Emerging visual analytics technologies, however, can help researchers understand how social, temporal, and spatial properties converge.

REFERENCES

Andrienko, N. and Andrienko, G. (2006), *Exploratory Analysis of Spatial and Temporal Data: A Systematic Approach*, Springer Verlag, Berlin.

Andrienko, G., Andrienko, N., Demsar, U., Dransch, D., Dykes, J., Fabrikant, S. I., Jern, M., Kraak, M-J, Schumann, H. and Tominski, C. (2010), 'Space, time and visual analytics', *International Journal of Geographical Information Science*, Vol. 24 No. 10, pp. 1577–1600.

Andrienko, G., Andrienko, N., Mladenov, M., Mock, M. and Pölitz, C. (2010), 'Discovering bits of place histories from people's activity traces', Paper presented at the 2010 IEEE Symposium on Visual Analytics Science and Technology (VAST), Salt Lake City, UT.

Anselin, L. (1999), 'Interactive techniques and exploratory spatial data analysis', in Longley, P., Goodchild, M. F., Maguire, D. and Rhind, D., *Geographical Information Systems: Principles, Techniques, Management and Applications*, John Wiley and Sons, New York, pp. 253–266.

Backstrom, L., Sun, E. and Marlow, C. (2010), 'Find me if you can: improving geographical prediction with social and spatial proximity', paper presented at WWW '10, Raleigh, NC.

Barthélemy, M. (2011), 'Spatial networks', *Physics Reports,* Vol. 499 No. 1, pp. 1–101.

Blanford, J. I., Huang, Z., Savelyev, A. and MacEachren, A. M. (2015), 'Geo-located tweets: enhancing mobility maps and capturing cross-border movement', *PLoS One,* Vol. 10 No. 6, e0129202, Available: doi:10.1371/journal.pone.0129202

Bo, H. and Baldwin, P C.T. (2012), 'Geolocation prediction in social media data by finding location indicative words', paper presented at COLING 2012, Mumbai, India.

Bordogna, G., Ghisalberti, G. and Psaila, G. (2012), 'Geographic information retrieval: modeling uncertainty of user's context', *Fuzzy Sets and Systems,* Vol. 196, pp. 105–124.

Brody, H., Rip, M.R., Vinten-Johansen, P., Paneth, N. and Rachman, S. (2000), 'Mapmaking and myth-making in Broad Street: the London cholera epidemic, 1854', *The Lancet,* Vol. 356, pp. 64–68.

Brownstein, J. S., Cassa, C., Kohane, I. S. and Mandl, K. D. (2005), 'Reverse geocoding: concerns about patient confidentiality in the display of geospatial health data', paper presented at the AMIA Annual Symposium, Washington, DC.

Brewer, C.A. and Pickle, L. (2002), 'Evaluation of methods for classifying epidemiological data on chloropleth maps in series', *Annals of the Association of American Geographers,* Vol. 92 No. 4, pp. 662–681.

Buchel, O. (2013), 'Redefining geobrowsing', paper presented at the Annual Meeting of the Association for Information Science and Technology, Montreal, Canada.

Buchel, O. and Sedig, K. (2014), 'Making sense of document collections with map-based visualisations: the role of interaction with representations', *Information Research,* Vol. 19 No. 3, paper 631. Available: http://InformationR.net/ir/19-3/paper631.html

Butler, D. (2013, February 13), 'When Google got flu wrong', *Nature,* Vol. 494, pp. 155–156. Available at: http://www.nature.com/news/when-google-got-flu-wrong-1.12413

Chang, J. and Sun, E. (2011), 'Location3: How users share and respond to location-based data on social networking sites', paper presented at the Fifth International AAAI Conference on Weblogs and Social Media, Barcelona, Spain.

Cheng, Z., Caverlee, J. and Lee, K. (2010), 'You are where you tweet: a content-based approach to geo-locating twitter users', paper presented at the ACM Conference on Information and Knowledge Management (CIKM'10), Toronto, Canada.

Conover, M.D., Davis, C., Ferrara, E., McKelvey, K., Menczer, F. and Flammini, A. (2013), 'The geospatial characteristics of a social movement communication network', *PloS One,* Vol. 8 No. 3, e55957. Available:doi:10.1371/journal.pone.0055957.

Curtin, K. (2007), 'Network analysis in geographic information science: review, assessment, and projections', *Cartography and Geographic Information Science,* Vol. 34 No. 2, pp. 103–111.

DeLongueville, B., Smith, R. S. and Luraschi, G. (2009), '"Omg, from here, i can see the flames!": a use case of mining location based social networks to acquire spatio-temporal data on forest fires', paper presented at the 2009 ACM International Workshop on Location Based Social Networks, Seattle, WA.

Doytsher, Y., Galon, B. and Kanza, Y. (2010), 'Querying geo-social data by bridging spatial networks and social networks', paper presented at the 2nd ACM SIGSPATIAL International Workshop on Location-based Social Networks, San Jose, CA.

Eccles, R., Kapler, T., Harper, R. and Wright, W. (2008), 'Stories in GeoTime', *Information Visualization,* Vol. 7 No. 1, pp. 3–17.

ESRI (2015), 'Spatial analysis' [Online]. Available: http://www.esri.com/products/arcgis-capabilities/spatial-analysis [15 December 2015].

Fabrikant, S. I. (2001a), 'Evaluating the usability of the scale metaphor for querying semantic information spaces', in Montello, D. R., *Spatial Information Theory: Foundations of Geographic Information Science,* Springer, Berlin, pp. 156–171.

Fabrikant, S. I. (2001b), 'Visualizing region and scale in semantic spaces', paper presented at the 20th International Cartographic Conference (ICC 2001), Beijing, China.

Fabrikant, S. and Buttenfield, B. (2001), 'Formalizing semantic spaces for information access', *Annals of the Association of American Geographers*, Vol. 91, pp. 263–280.

Fabrikant, S. and Skupin, A. (2005), 'Cognitively plausible information visualization', in MacEachren, A. M., Kraak, M-J. and Dykes, J., *Exploring Geovisualization*, Elsevier, New York, pp. 667–690.

Fekete, J. D. and Plaisant, C. (2002), 'Interactive information visualization of a million items', paper presented at the IEEE Symposium on Information Visualization (INFOVIS 2002), Boston, MA.

Gahegan, M. (1998), 'Scatterplots and scenes: visualisation techniques for exploratory spatial analysis', *Computers, Environment and Urban Systems*, Vol. 22 No. 1, pp. 43–56.

Gayle, D. (2011), 'Privacy storm after police buy software that maps suspects' digital movements' [Online]. Available: http://www.dailymail.co.uk/sciencetech/article-1386191/Privacy-storm-police-buy-Geotime-software-maps-suspects-digital-movements.html [15 December 2015].

Gelernter, J. and Mushegian, N. (2011), 'Geoparsing crisis messages from microtext', *Transactions in GIS*, Vol. 15 No. 6, pp. 753–773.

Gleason, B. (2013), '#Occupy Wall Street: exploring informal learning about a social movement on Twitter', *American Behavioral Scientist*, Vol. 57 No. 7, pp. 966–982.

Goodchild, M. F. (2007), 'Citizens as sensors: the world of volunteered geography', *GeoJournal*, Vol. 69 No. 4, pp. 211–221.

Gong, J. (2002), 'Clarifying the standard deviational ellipse', *Geographical Analysis*, Vol. 34 No. 2, pp. 155–167.

Gonzalez, M. C., Hidalgo, C. A. and Barabasi, A. L. (2008), 'Understanding individual human mobility patterns', *Nature*, Vol. 453 No. 7196, pp. 779–782.

Hägerstrand, T. (1970), 'What about people in regional science?', paper presented at the Ninth European Congress of the Regional Science Association.

Hecht, B., Hong, L., Suh, B. and Chi, E. (2011), 'Tweets from Justin Bieber's heart: the dynamics of the "location" field in user profiles', paper presented at the ACM CHI Conference on Human Factors in Computing Systems, Vancouver, Canada.

Hill, L. L. (2006), *Georeferencing: The Geographic Associations of Information*, MIT Press, Cambridge, MA.

Hyvärinen, O. and Saltikoff, E. (2010), 'Social media as a source of meteorological observations', *Monthly Weather Review*, Vol. 138 No. 8, pp. 3175–3184.

Java, A., Song, X., Finin, T. and Tseng, B. (2007), 'Why we twitter: understanding microblogging usage and communities', paper presented at the Joint 9th WEBKDD and 1st SNA-KDD Workshop, San Jose, CA.

Jiang, B. and Miao, Y. (2015), 'The evolution of natural cities from the perspective of location-based social media', *The Professional Geographer*, Vol. 67 No. 2, pp. 295–306.

Karimzadeh, M., Huang, W., Banerjee, S., Wallgrün, J.O., Hardisty, F., Pezanowski, S., Mitra, P. and MacEachren, A.M. (2013), 'GeoTxt: A web API to leverage place references in text', paper presented at the ACM 7th Workshop on Geographic Information Retrieval, New York.

Keim, D., Andrienko, G., Fekete, J. D., Görg, C., Kohlhammer, J. and Melançon, G. (2008), 'Visual analytics: Definition, process, and challenges', *Lecture Notes in Computer Science: Information Visualization*, Vol. 4950, pp. 154–175.

Kipp, M. E. I., Choi, I., Beak, J., Buchel, O. and Rasmussen, D. (2014), 'User motivations for contributing tags and local knowledge to the Library of Congress Flickr Collection', paper presented at the Annual Conference of the Canadian Association for Information Science, Victoria, Canada.

Krings, G., Calabrese, F., Ratti, C. and Blondel, V. D. (2009), 'Urban gravity: a model for inter-city telephone communication networks', *Journal of Statistical Mechanics*, L07003.

Koylu, C., Guo, D., Kasakoff, A. and Adams, J. W. (2014), 'Mapping family connectedness across space and time', *Cartography and Geographic Information Science*, Vol. 41 No. 1, pp. 14–26.

Krumm, J. (2007), 'Inference attacks on location tracks', paper presented at the 5th International Conference on Pervasive Computing (PERVASIVE'07), Toronto, Canada.

Lefever, D. W. (1926), 'Measuring geographic concentration by means of the standard deviational ellipse', *American Journal of Sociology*, Vol. 32 No. 1, pp. 88–94.

Lingad, J., Karimi, S. and Yin, J. (2013), 'Location extraction from disaster-related microblogs', paper presented at the 22nd International Conference on World Wide Web (WWW '13), Rio de Janeiro, Brazil.

Longley, P. A., Goodchild, M. F., Maguire, D. J. and Rhind, D. W. (2005), *Geographic Information Systems and Science*, John Wiley and Sons, New York.

Luo, W. and MacEachren, A. M. (2014), 'Geo-social visual analytics', *Journal of Spatial Information Science*, Vol. 8, pp. 27–66.

Luo, W., MacEachren, A.M., Yin, P.F. and Hardisty, F, (2011), 'GeoSocialApp: A Visual Exploratory Data Analysis Tool For Spatial-Social Network', poster presented at the EMS Graduate Student Poster Exhibition at Penn State University, University Park, PA.

MacEachren, A. M. (1995), *How Maps Work: Representation, Visualization, and Design*. Guilford Press.

MacEachren, A. M. and Kraak, M. J. (1997), 'Exploratory cartographic visualization: advancing the agenda', *Computers & Geosciences*, Vol. 23 No. 4, pp. 335–343.

MacEachren, A. M., Stryker, M. S., Turton, I. J. and Pezanowski, S. (2010), 'HEALTH GeoJunction: place-time-concept browsing of health publications', *International Journal of Health Geographics*, Vol. 9, http://www.ij-healthgeographics.com/content/9/1/23

MacEachren, A. M., Jaiswal, A., Robinson, A. C., Pezanowski, S., Savelyev, A., Mitra, P., Zhang, X. and Blanford, J. (2011a), 'SensePlace2: GeoTwitter analytics support for situational awareness', paper presented at the 2011 IEEE Conference on Visual Analytics Science and Technology (VAST), Providence, RI.

MacEachren, A. M., Robinson, A. C., Jaiswal, A., Pezanowski, S., Savelyev, A., Blanford, J. and Mitra, P. (2011b), 'Geo-twitter analytics: applications in crisis management', paper presented at the 25th International Cartographic Conference, Paris, France.

Manni, F., Guerard, E. and Heyer, E. (2004), 'Geographic patterns of (genetic, morphologic, linguistic) variation: how barriers can be detected by using Monmonier's algorithm', *Human Biology*, Vol. 76 No. 2, pp. 173–190.

Martin, K. E. (2015), 'Ethical issues in the Big Data industry', *MIS Quarterly Executive*, Vol. 14 No. 2, pp. 67–85.

Massoudi, K., Tsagkias, M., de Rijke, M. and Weerkamp, W. (2011), 'Incorporating query expansion and quality indicators in searching microblog posts', *Lecture Notes in Computer Science: Advances in Information Retrieval*, Vol. 6611, pp. 362–367.

MaxMind. (2015), 'GeoIP2 city accuracy', https://www.maxmind.com/en/geoip2-city-database-accuracy.

McKenzie, G. and Janowicz, K. (2015), 'Where is also about time: a location-distortion model to improve reverse geocoding using behavior-driven temporal semantic signatures', *Computers, Environment and Urban Systems*, Vol. 54, pp. 1–13.

Mennis, J. and Guo, D. (2009), 'Spatial data mining and geographic knowledge discovery – an introduction', *Computers, Environment and Urban Systems*, Vol. 33 No. 6, pp. 403–408.

Middleton, S. E., Middleton, L. and Modafferi, S. (2014), 'Real-time crisis mapping of natural disasters using social media', *IEEE Intelligent Systems*, Vol. 29 No. 2, pp. 9–17.

Mitchell, A. (1999), *The ESRI Guide to GIS Analysis, Volume 1: Geographic Patterns and Relationships*, ESRI Press, Redlands, CA.

Monmonier, M. (2005), 'Lying with maps', *Statistical Science*, Vol. 20 No. 3, pp. 215–222.

Monmonier, M. (2014), *How to Lie with Maps*, University of Chicago Press, Chicago.

Nelson, J. (2011), 'Data visualization at IDV Solutions. Chalkboard Maps: United States of Craigslist', http://uxblog.idvsolutions.com/2011/07/chalkboard-maps-united-states-of.html

O'Hare, N. and Murdock, V. (2013), 'Modeling locations with social media', *Information Retrieval*, Vol. 16, pp. 30–62.

Okabe, A., Boots, B., Sugihara, K. and Chiu, S. N. (2009), *Spatial Tessellations: Concepts and Applications of Voronoi diagrams*, John Wiley and Sons, New York.

Onnela, J.-P., Arbesman, S., González, M.C., Barabási, A.-L. and Christakis, N.A. (2011), 'Geographic constraints on social network groups', *PLoS One*, Vol. 6, e16939.

Orchard, T., Farr, S., Macphail, S., Wender. C. and Young, D. (2012), 'Sex work in the Forest City: sex work beginnings, types, and clientele among women in London, Ontario', *Sexuality Research and Social Policy*, Vol. 9 No. 4, pp. 350–362.

Padmanabhan, A., Wang, S., Cao, G., Hwang, M., Zhao, Y., Zhang, Z. and Gao, Y. (2013), 'FluMapper: an interactive CyberGIS environment for massive location-based social media data analysis', paper presented at the ACM Conference on Extreme Science and Engineering Discovery Environment: Gateway to Discovery, San Diego, CA.

Peca, I., Zhi, H., Vrotsou, K., Andrienko, N. and Andrienko, G. (2011), 'KD-photomap: exploring photographs in space and time', paper presented at the 2011 IEEE Conference on Visual Analytics Science and Technology (VAST), Providence, RI.

Popescu, A. and Grefenstette, G. (2010), 'Mining user home location and gender from Flickr tags', paper presented at the International Conference on Weblogs and Social Media (ICWSM'10), Washington, DC.

Proulx, P., Tandon, S., Bodnar, A., Schroh, D., Harper, R. and Wright, W. (2006), 'Avian flu case study with nSpace and GeoTime', paper presented at the 2006 IEEE Symposium on Visual Analytics Science and Technology, Baltimore, MD.

Purcell, D. and de Beurs, K. (2013), 'It's hot in here: Twitter as data source of understanding perceptions of heat and drought hazards', paper presented at the Social Media & Society Conference, Halifax, Canada.

Puttaswamy, K. P. N., Wang, S., Steinbauer, T., Agrawal, D., El Abbadi, A., Kruegel, C. and Zhao, B. Y. (2014), 'Preserving location privacy in geosocial locations', *IEEE Transactions on Mobile Computing*, Vol. 13 No. 1, pp. 159–173.

Ramdani, D. (2011), 'GPS applications on cellular phone with geoid addition to height' [Online]. Available: http://mycoordinates.org/gps-applications-on-cellular-phone-with-geoid-addition-to-height/ [15 December 2015].

Rorissa, A., Rasmussen Neal, D., Muckell, J. and Chaucer, A. (2012), 'An exploration of tags assigned to still and moving images on Flickr', in Rasmussen Neal, D., *Indexing and Retrieval of Non-Text Information*, De Gruyter Saur, Berlin, pp. 185–211.

Sayyadi, H., Hurst, M. and Maykov, A. (2009), 'Event detection and tracking in social streams', paper presented at the International Conference on Weblogs and Social Media (ICWSM), San Jose, CA.

Scellato, S., Noulas, A., Lambiotte, R. and Mascolo, C. (2011), 'Socio-spatial properties of online location-based social networks', paper presented at ICWSM-11, Barcelona, Spain.

Schreck, T. and Keim, D. (2013), 'Visual analysis of social media data', *Computer*, Vol. 46 No. 5, pp. 68–75.

Sevillano, X., Valero, X. and Alías, F. (2015), 'Look, listen and find: a purely audiovisual approach to online videos geotagging', *Information Sciences*, Vol. 295, pp. 558–572.

Shekhar, S. and Huang, Y. (2001), 'Discovering spatial co-location patterns: a summary of results', *Lecture Notes in Computer Science: Advances in Spatial and Temporal Databases*, Vol. 212, pp. 236–256.

Sobkowicz, P., Kaschesky, M. and Bouchard, G. (2012), 'Opinion mining in social media: modeling, simulating, and forecasting political opinions in the web', *Government Information Quarterly*, Vol. 29 No. 4, pp. 470–479.

Song, C., Qu, Z., Blumm, N. and Barabási, A. L. (2010), 'Limits of predictability in human mobility', *Science*, Vol. 327 No. 5968, pp. 1018–1021.

Stefanidis, A., Cotnoir, A., Croitoru, A., Crooks, A., Rice, M. and Radzikowski, J. (2013), 'Demarcating new boundaries: mapping virtual polycentric communities through social media content', *Cartography and Geographic Information Science*, Vol. 40 No. 2, pp. 116–129.

Sui, D. and Goodchild, M. (2011), 'The convergence of GIS and social media: challenges for GIScience', *International Journal of Geographical Information Science*, Vol. 25 No. 11, pp. 1737–1748.

Torniai, C., Battle, S. and Cayzer, S. (2007), 'Sharing, discovering and browsing geotagged pictures on the web' [Online]. Available: http://www.hpl.hp.com/techreports/2007/HPL-2007-73.pdf [15 December 2015].

Tufte, E. R. (1991), 'Envisioning information', *Optometry & Vision Science*, Vol. 68 No. 4, pp. 322–324.

Vicente, C. R., Freni, D., Bettini, C. and Jensen, C. S. (2011), 'Location-related privacy in geo-social networks', *IEEE Internet Computing*, Vol. 15 No. 3, pp. 20–27.

Wade, T. and Sommer, S. (2006), *A to Z GIS: An Illustrated Dictionary of Geographic Information Systems*, ESRI Press, Redlands, CA.

Wagner, D. (2013), 'Google flu trends wildly overestimated this year's flu outbreak' [Online]. Available:http://www.thewire.com/technology/2013/02/google-flu-trends-wildly-overestimated-years-flu-outbreak/62113/ [15 December 2015].

Weidemann, C. (2013), 'Social media location intelligence: the next privacy battle – an ArcGIS add-in and analysis of geospatial data collected from twitter.com', *International Journal of Geoinformatics*, Vol. 9 No. 2. Available: http://journals.sfu.ca/ijg/index.php/journal/article/view/139 [15 December 2015].

Weiler, M., Schmid, K. A., Mamoulis, N. and Renz, M. (2015), 'Geo-social co-location mining', paper presented at the Second International ACM Workshop on Managing and Mining Enriched Geo-Spatial Data (GeoRich '15), Melbourne, Australia.

Whitsel, E. A., Quibrera, P. M., Smith, R. L., Catellier, D. J., Liao, D., Henley, A. C. and Heiss, G. (2006), 'Accuracy of commercial geocoding: assessment and implications', *Epidemiological Perspectives & Innovations*, Vol. 3 No. 8. Available: doi: 10.1186/1742–5573-3-8.

Yi, J. S., ah Kang, Y., Stasko, J. T. and Jacko, J. A. (2007), 'Toward a deeper understanding of the role of interaction in information visualization', *IEEE Transactions on Visualization and Computer Graphics*, Vol. 13 No. 6, pp. 1224–1231.

Pragmatics of Network Centrality

Shadi Ghajar-Khosravi and Mark Chignell

Since networks can be laid out in many different ways, it is perhaps not surprising that there are a number of different ways of defining network centrality. In this chapter we will examine some of the constructs of network centrality that have been proposed. It is evident that different centrality measures are affected differently by networks with different topological properties and perhaps different interaction types among their users. We will present a case study showing how correlations between centrality measures can vary widely depending on properties of the network that are related to topology. Using factor analysis followed by clustering we show how it is possible to characterize 62 real-world social networks in terms of two key factors: shape and reach. We will then proceed to organize the networks into three clusters based on their shape and reach scores. We show the networks of three clusters will not only differ in their topology but also in the type of interactions among their members. The role of measuring network centrality is likely to be particularly important in using measures of social influence to guide marketing initiatives and related applications.

INTRODUCTION

In a physical or statistical system the construct of centrality is usually well-defined and monolithic. The centre of a large city is typically a consensually defined area defined by high population density, high commercial density, and high land values. The centre of a physical object is typically defined as its centre of gravity. In applied mathematics and statistics, the centre of a univariate distribution is frequently described as a mean, median, or mode. Although measured differently, these statistics all encapsulate the notion of central location. In a multivariate distribution, the central location is typically defined by a centroid (the mean of means for each of the component dimensions making up the multivariate distribution).

In contrast to physical and statistical systems, the concept of centrality in social networks represents multiple constructs, which can be characterized as answers to a set of questions that address different issues. The following questions capture some of the main constructs corresponding to popular measures of network centrality.

- Which nodes in a network are most critical to cohesion and connectivity across the network? Or which nodes would result in the most damage to the network if they were removed (e.g., betweenness centrality)?
- Which nodes tend to be closest to other nodes in the network (e.g., closeness centrality)?
- Which nodes are connected to a dense geographical region that exists around them (e.g., clustering coefficient)?
- Which nodes are most influential in propagating messages and behaviors across networks?

How can we transform these constructs into practical measures of network centrality? Due to the fact that we are mostly dealing with a large social network graph, rather than a metric space, there is no direct path from a network centrality construct to a corresponding measure. Various measures of centrality exist and each has different characteristics that would make them a more suitable choice over the others depending on the targeted research questions. Analogously, if we have a large network or graph consisting of many nodes and links between the nodes (i.e., edges), there is no unique way to visualize the network or to characterize its dimensionality. A large network can be laid out in two, three, or N dimensions, and within each space of a particular dimensionality it can look very different depending on the algorithm used to lay it out or visualize it.

In this chapter we will examine some of the key constructs of network centrality, and we will review the network analysis techniques and algorithms with which each of those constructs are measured. We will also provide some case studies of how network centrality measures can be used to answer interesting questions about people, communities, and networks, and we will show how centrality measures can be used to characterize the shape and potentially the type of interactions in social networks. Past research has generally contrasted the characteristics of social networks with other types of networks such as random or regular networks. However, in this chapter we will contrast the characteristics of 62 real-world social networks with different interaction types (e.g., friendship, co-authorship, or information exchange). We will start by considering structural analysis of social networks in general, with measurement of centrality being a particular kind of structural analysis.

Analyzing the Structure of Social Networks

Why is structural analysis of social networks an important undertaking? Our answer to this question is pragmatic. Understanding the structure of social networks should lead to more useful and usable social network applications. Social network sites are currently among the most popular websites on the internet with Facebook, Twitter, and Linked-In ranked 2, 8, and 12 respectively by Alexa's traffic ranking (https://en.wikipedia.org/wiki/List_of_most_popular_websites) as of March 2015. With the growing popularity of social network sites and the availability of their large-scale datasets, researchers now have the opportunity to understand the effect of networked influence (Gruzd & Wellman, 2014) on behaviors and connections of online users. As Gruzd & Wellman explain, influence is networked as it occurs in social networks and propagates via the communication features proposed by social network sites. Adjacent users of social networks tend to trust each other more than others and tend to have shared interests (Mislove, Marcon, Gummadi, Druschel, & Bhattacharjee, 2007).

An analysis of online users' actions, and the graph structure of their inter-relationships, should help not only in understanding current social roles within a network, but also in predicting future user behaviors and connections and designing improved social networking based applications. For example, understanding the structure of online social networks might enable researchers to design new algorithms capable of detecting 'influential users'.

Social network centrality measures are commonly used structural measures to identify central and potentially influential members of a social network or a local neighborhood (Freeman, 1978; Wasserman & Faust, 1994). Three of the best-known measures were proposed by Freeman (1978) – degree, closeness, and betweenness centrality. These measures were then extended to include eigenvector, clustering coefficient, PageRank, and group centralities (Wasserman & Faust, 1994). How do these various measures differ in terms of how they are computed, and what is the role of different types of networks in determining how and when those measures act differently from each other?

There is limited empirical research on how different centrality measures compare with one another. However, understanding how the properties of different centrality measures interact with network topology would allow researchers to make more informed decisions about which centrality measures or combinations of measures should be used in different contexts (Quan-Haase, 2009). Past research has not been consistent in finding the most useful or relevant set of centrality measures for predicting behaviors like information diffusion. This may be due to differences in the topological features of the networks investigated. It is possible that using network topology properties, aspects of information diffusion and social influence

could be better predicted. In this chapter we describe the properties of some of the major centrality measures and we examine the statistical relationships that exist among them. The focus of this chapter will be on undirected and unweighted social networks such as Facebook where friendship relationships (i.e., connections or edges) are mutual, unlike Twitter where users are not necessarily following all their followers.

CENTRALITY MEASURES

Freeman (1978) defined social networks as a way of thinking about an existing social system with a particular focus on the relationships among its actors, members, or nodes. These relationships are referred to as links, ties, or edges (Borgatti, Everett, & Johnson, 2013). Finding the central nodes of a network and contrasting their online behaviors and influence with those of non-central nodes has been a major focus of research in social networking sites (Landher, Friedl, & Heidemann, 2010; Kiss & Bichler, 2008; Huang et al., 2014). That research has assumed that people's behavior, choices, and beliefs within a social system are determined by the structural position of people within a network. For instance, it has been hypothesized that a person's position in a social network is a key determinant of the opportunities or constraints she is faced with inside the corresponding social system (Borgatti et al., 2013).

Different centrality measures tend not to be strongly correlated with each other because they are based on different assumptions about the flow of information through network edges (Landher et al., 2010; Borgatti, 2005). Borgatti (2005) argued that each measure models a different concept and is appropriate for a particular context depending on the topology of the network flow processes. He argued that the 'node importance' measured by various centrality measures is essentially different between those measures. For example, closeness centrality refers to time-until-arrival of a message passed to the focal node; hence, it is a more appropriate measure when it is crucial for a message to be sent rapidly in a network. Nodes with high closeness are well-positioned to receive novel information earlier than many others. In contrast, betweenness centrality refers to the frequency of arrival of messages in the focal node (Borgatti, 2005); hence, it is a more appropriate measure when looking for bottlenecks in the network or nodes that are in control of the network flow. Thus, depending on the construct of interest, different centrality measures will be better-suited for identifying the central nodes.

In this chapter, we will consider both node-level (microscopic) measures of network activity as well as overall network (macroscopic) characteristics. The microscopic centrality measures (node-level) of interest include: degree, clustering coefficient, PageRank, betweenness, ego network betweenness, and Eigenvector centrality of each node. Among these six measures, the computation of betweenness centrality is computationally expensive and not feasible for dealing with very large networks in a timely manner. For dealing with very large networks, ego network betweenness was first introduced by Freeman (1982) as a less computationally expensive estimator of the betweenness centrality of a node.

The macroscopic measures of interest (network-level) include a network's size (i.e., number of nodes) and measures related to topology. Variables that are potentially relevant to topology include: density, average clustering coefficient, and the distribution characteristics of degree and clustering coefficient centralities of nodes within the network.

In the following subsections we characterize the centrality measures that will be considered in this chapter. These measures can be computed using the SNAP C++ package (http://snap.stanford.edu/), among others.

Degree Centrality (Deg)

Degree centrality is the most straightforward centrality measure (Freeman, 1978; Borgatti, Everett, & Johnson, 2013). In undirected networks, it basically measures the number of edges connected to a node or the number of contacts, nodes, friends, etc. having a direct link to a node. The degree centrality (d_i) of the node i is given by:

$$d_i = \sum_j x_{ij}$$

where x_{ij} is the (i, j) entry of the *adjacency matrix*. In an unweighted network, x_{ij} or the (i, j) entry of an adjacency matrix equals '0' if there is no direct link between nodes i and j, or '1' if the two nodes are directly connected. In the case of directed networks, there are in-degree and out-degree centrality measures. In-degree equals the number of edges connected from other nodes to the focal node, while out-degree equals the number of other nodes to which the focal node is linked to.

Although degree centrality is a simple measure to compute, it provides interesting insights into the structure of a network. The degree distributions of many real-world complex networks have been studied, including the World Wide Web, phone call networks, actors' networks linked by movies, paper citations, etc. Typically, only a small proportion of nodes in large networks have very high degrees. Thus, the distribution of node degrees in many such networks form power distributions, with the majority of nodes having only a few links while a few nodes ('hubs') might have many links. Barabási & Bonabeau (2003) referred to such networks as 'scale-free'.

EIGENVECTOR CENTRALITY AND PAGERANK (EIGV AND PGRK)

Eigenvector centrality (Bonacich, 1972; Newman, 2003; Borgatti, Everett, & Johnson,

2013) is a variation of degree centrality. However, unlike degree centrality, which gives equal weights to all the neighbors, eigenvector centrality weights adjacent nodes by their centrality:

$$e_i = \lambda \sum_j x_{ij} e_j$$

where x_{ij} is the (i, j) entry of the adjacency matrix, e_j is the eigenvector centrality score of node j, and λ is a constant called the eigenvalue.

PageRank is a variant of eigenvector centrality and was popularized in the original algorithm used by Google for ordering its search results. The PageRank measure was initially proposed for link analysis in the World Wide Web (Brin & Page, 1998). As in the case of academic citations, PageRank counts the number of pages linking (i.e. inlinks) to a focal page. However, PageRank extends the citation system by 1) weighting each of the links pointing to the focal node by their own PageRank scores and 2) by normalizing the PageRank values by the total number of outgoing links on each page. The PageRank $PR(p)$ for a web page can be defined as:

$$PR(p) = (1-d)\frac{1}{N} + d\sum_{i=1}^{k} \frac{PR(p_i)}{C(p_i)}$$

where $PR(p_i)$ is the PageRank of page p_i, $C(p_i)$ is the total number of outgoing pages for p_i (i.e., the out-degree of p_i), and p_i is one of the pages pointing to p or is one of the inlinks to page p. N is the total number of web pages in the network and d (with $0 \leq d \leq 1$) is a damping factor, usually set to .85. For further information about the PageRank algorithm see Brin & Page (1998) and Langville & Meyer (2004). PageRank is not one of Freeman's (1978) initial centrality measures, and hence is not as widely used in social network analysis studies. However, like eigenvector centrality it is also a potential measure of influence. Examples of past research that has used the Page Rank measure in studies of influence include the research conducted by Heidemann, Klier, & Probst (2010); Langville & Meyer (2004); Yan & Ding (2009); Bollen, Rodriguez, & Van de Sompel (2006); Ding, Yan, Frazho, & Caverlee (2009); Kiss & Bichler (2008); and Huang et al. (2014).

CLUSTERING COEFFICIENT (CLSCFF)

The Clustering Coefficient was first introduced by Watts and Strogatz (1998) as an indication of the extent to which nodes in a graph tend to cluster together, and as a measure of the 'cliquishness' of networks. The clustering coefficient is based on the completeness of transitivity of relationships involving a node. In a transitive triangular relationship, if B is A's friend, and B is C's friend, then A will also be C's friend (Scott, 2000). The clustering coefficient measures what proportion of all the possible pairings between the friends of the particular node of interest actually exist. If the node v has k_v neighbors, the maximum number of edges that can exist among its neighbors would equal $k_v(k_v-1)/2$. The (local) clustering coefficient of node v, $C(v)$, equals the fraction of the potential number of $k_v(k_v-1)/2$ edges that actually exist in the network. This measure is the local clustering coefficient of node v. The overall level of clustering, C, in a network is then defined as the average $C(v)$ across all the nodes of the network. Thus the clustering coefficient measures clustering at the node level, while the average clustering coefficient measures clustering at the network level.

Cliquishness is a common property of social networks where there are groups of friends and everyone knows everyone else. The value of the average clustering coefficient C reflects the 'cliquishness' of the network.

BETWEENNESS AND EGO BETWEENNESS CENTRALITY

Betweenness centrality (Freeman, 1978; Borgatti, Everett, & Johnson, 2013) of a focal node is calculated as the proportion of shortest paths between pairs of other nodes that pass through the focal node. The formula for measuring betweenness centrality of node j is given by:

$$BC_j = \sum_{i<k} \frac{g_{ijk}}{g_{ik}}$$

where g_{ijk} is the number of shortest paths between any two nodes i and k that pass through a third node j, and g_{ik} is the total number of shortest paths connecting the instances of i and k. Hence, the inherent assumption in the definition of betweenness centrality is that any information passing through the network flows only through the shortest paths among pairs of users. If there are multiple shortest paths, one of them would be chosen at random.

Betweenness centrality measures the volume of traffic passing through a node or the 'amount of network flow that a given node "controls" in the sense of being able to shut it down if necessary' (Borgatti, 2005, p. 60). Nodes with high betweenness centrality can play a 'gatekeeper' role for the efficient transmission of information in the network. In other words, they have extra value because information in the network will be transmitted less efficiently if they stop operating.

Since the standard measure of betweenness centrality is computationally complex to compute, in particular for the new generation of vast social network datasets collected from online services such as Facebook or Twitter, researchers have turned to ways of computing an 'approximate' betweenness centrality by applying techniques such as: random sampling of edges, vertices, or shortest paths (Chehreghani, 2014; Riondato & Kornaropoulos, 2014; Bader, Kintali, Madduri, & Mihail, 2007; Brandes & Pich, 2007); or by limiting the search for shortest paths to paths shorter than a certain length (Pfeffer & Carley, 2012) or to the ego networks around each node (Marsden, 2002; Everett & Borgatti, 2005).

The ego network of a node (ego) consists of the ego and all the other nodes it is connected to (alters) and all the edges among those alters (Figure 19.1).

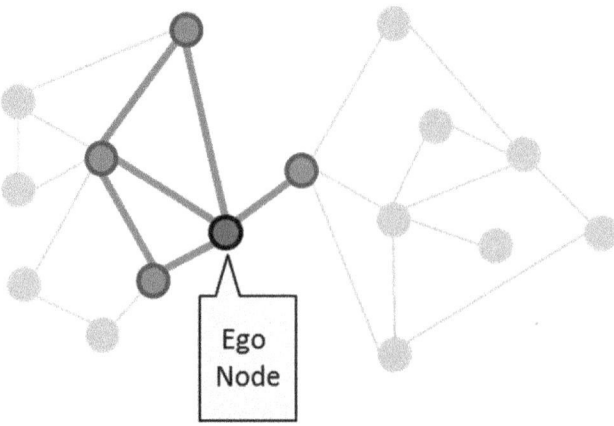

Figure 19.1 An example ego network surrounding the ego node. Alter nodes or neighbors are in dark grey and the rest of the network outside of the ego network is shaded in light grey

The primary motivation for using ego betweenness centrality in lieu of betweenness centrality is the ease of collection of data in a local network compared with collecting data from the whole network (Everett & Borgatti, 2005).

However, there has been limited research on the appropriateness of ego betweenness as a substitute for betweenness centrality networks. That research has involved a relatively few social networks (Marsden, 2002; Everett & Borgatti, 2005; Kim, Kim, Han, Jeong, & Park, 2012; Pantazopoulos, Karaliopoulos, & Stavrakakis, 2014). The limited research thus far on this topic has found strong correlations between ego betweenness and betweenness centrality. However, with the exception of the work by Marsden (which was conducted on small size real-world social networks), the research has been conducted on simulated networks or computer networks. Thus, it is unclear whether the strong relationship between ego betweenness and betweenness centrality that has been found in these previous studies will also apply to large social networks.

TOPOLOGICAL NETWORK PROPERTIES

In this section, a summary of some of the key characteristics of networks are described. These features have been defined in past research and provide an overall view of the size and shape of networks to researchers.

Network size is perhaps the most obvious feature of a network. The number of nodes (n) in each network is usually referred to as the size of the network. The number of nodes determines the maximum number of edges that could possibly exist in a network.

Density is another important feature of networks and is defined (Scott, 2000) as the ratio of the actual number of edges to the total number of possible edges that could exist in a network with n nodes; i.e., $n(n-1)/2$ for an undirected graph and $n(n-1)$ for directed graphs. The formula below returns the density of an undirected graph. E equals the actual number of edges in the network.

$$D = \frac{2E}{n(n-1)}$$

Average degree, average path length, and *network diameter* are three other common properties used by social network analyzers to compare different networks. Average path length equals the average of all the shortest path lengths while diameter equals the length of the longest shortest path calculated or the shortest path between the two most distant nodes in a network. The average clustering coefficient of nodes – i.e. global clustering coefficient of the network – is another important generic feature of networks, which indicates how connected the neighborhood of each node is.

Researchers have found that many real-world complex networks differed from the *Random Graph* model (Erdős & Rényi, 1959; Barabási, & Albert; 1999; Albert, Jeong, & Barabási, 1999). The topologies of these real networks were not random and the Random Graph model did not adequately capture measures related to topology such as degree distribution, clustering coefficient, or average path length.

In random graphs, edges are distributed randomly and the degree distribution of nodes follows a Poisson distribution (Erdős & Rényi, 1959; Albert & Barabási, 2002; Watts & Strogatz, 1998). However, the degree distribution of many large networks such as the World Wide Web (Barabási & Albert, 1999), the topology of the routers of the Internet (Faloutsos, Faloutsos, & Faloutsos, 1999), social networks (Adamic, Buyukkokten, & Adar, 2003), movie actor collaboration, science collaboration networks, or scientific publications citation networks (Albert & Barabási, 2002) follow a power-law distribution with clustering coefficients larger than those that are predicted based on random graphs. This finding suggests that these networks are highly clustered.

Small-world networks were introduced by Watts and Strogatz (1998) as networks with: 1) average shortest paths as small as their random graph counterparts with similar numbers of nodes and average degree, yet 2) clustering coefficient values larger than their random graph counterparts. Examples of small-world networks include the World Wide Web (Albert, Jeong, & Barabási, 1999; Broder et al., 2000), the power grid of the western United States (Watts & Strogatz, 1998), social networks (Adamic, Buyukkokten, & Adar, 2003), scientific collaboration on research papers (Newman, 2001), and the neural network of the worm Caenorhabditis elegans (Amaral, Scala, Barthelemy, & Stanley, 2000). However, the degree distribution of nodes in the Watts and Strogatz model does not necessarily follow a power-law distribution.

Scale-free networks have been introduced by Barabási & Albert (1999). The specific feature of these types of networks is their power-law degree distribution for large degrees (Albert, Jeong, & Barabási, 1999); a feature which was not observed in random graphs or Watts and Strogatz's small-world model. In scale-free networks, the probability of a node having a degree of k follows a power-law distribution:

$$P(k) \sim k^{-\gamma}$$

where the exponent normally lies in the range $2 < \gamma < 3$. The power law distribution of nodes in scale-free networks creates 'hub' nodes whose degree centrality greatly deviate from the average degree in the network. In these networks, the mean degree centrality is highly skewed (the vast majority of nodes will have a degree centrality measure that is much lower than the mean). The two primary ingredients of scale-free networks include: 1) the *growth* of networks over time; i.e., new nodes joining the network over time and 2) the *preferential attachment* of the nodes; i.e. the likelihood of linking to a node depends on the node's degree. In other words, a webpage with many in-links attracts more new in-links than average. Preferential attachment concept is analogous to 'the rich get richer' theory (Kiss & Bichler, 2008; Muchnik et al., 2013).

RELATIONSHIPS AMONG CENTRALITY MEASURES

How do different centrality measures relate to one another in networks with different topological features and what network characteristics could predict these correlations? If they are highly correlated in all network cases, then there should be no need to compute different measures. However, until recently the available research results were insufficient to determine the behaviour of different centrality measures across a representative range of real networks.

While studies have looked at relationships among the different centrality measures of nodes in a network, those studies have typically used a limited number of mostly simulated networks. Ronqui and Travieso (2014) showed that centrality measures tend to be correlated more strongly in network models than real networks. Examples included the correlations of closeness with eigenvector centrality and betweenness with eigenvector centrality. These two correlations were strong in the case of network models but weak or non-existent for the real networks that they analyzed. They concluded that the corresponding correlation coefficients vary considerably between networks. They proposed the use of 'centrality correlation profiles' to characterize networks. They conducted their studies on six real-world networks and in two network models. Costenbader & Valente (2003) studied the stability of centrality measures across samples of eight offline real-world social networks samples. They took samples (at eight different sampling proportions) from each network using bootstrap sampling procedures, computed and averaged correlations, and conducted multiple regression analysis on the average difference between actual and sampled centralities, standard deviation of their difference, and the correlation between actual and sampled centrality measures. They found simple eigenvector centrality (calculated using the first eigenvector) to be the measure that was most robust to sampling and missing data. In other words, simple eigenvector centrality was the preferred centrality measure when networks are sparse or have incomplete data. They also found that network size was significantly associated with the average difference between actual and sampled centrality measures in nine of the measures they investigated including directed betweenness, symmetrized closeness and eigenvector centrality.

Koschützki & Schreiber (2004) ran an analysis on two biological networks using five different centrality measures. They found a high correlation among eigenvector and degree centrality measures in both networks, while the correlations for the other centrality measures differed between the two networks. Batool & Niazi (2014) also found a correlation between degree and eigenvector centrality, while Yan & Ding (2009) found significant correlations only among PageRank, degree, and betweenness centrality. An earlier study by Faust (1997) examined relatively small networks of CEOs, clubs, and boards and found correlations ranging from .89 to .99 among degree, closeness, and betweenness centrality measures.

Given the relative paucity of earlier research findings in this area, there is a need for further studies on the relationships among different centrality measures across multiple real-world networks. There has been limited assessment of how Clustering Coefficient and PageRank relate to other centrality measures and more analysis is needed concerning the role of network topology features on the relationships among centrality measures.

CASE STUDY: STRUCTURAL ANALYSIS OF SOCIAL NETWORKS USING CENTRALITY AND TOPOLOGY MEASURES

Datasets

This section reports on research reported by Ghajar-Khosravi (2015). Ghajar-Khosravi conducted structural analysis of 62 social networks. All the selected networks were undirected. In other words, the connections or friendships were mutual in all the studied networks. A summary of network analysis statics across the different types of networks within the 62 social networks is shown in Table 19.1. The 62 networks were drawn from the following data sets:

Facebook networks of 47 universities: Forty-seven of these networks were sampled from the Facebook networks of the 100 universities that were prepared and studied by Traud, Mucha, & Porter (2012). These initial Facebook networks were a single-day snapshot of the networks in September 2005. The 100 files only included intra-school links; i.e. they included the full sets of links inside each school. At the time that these datasets were retrieved from Facebook, students were required to have an '.edu' email account to become a Facebook member; hence, the majority of relationships within these datasets are within universities. The 47 networks were chosen based on their sizes. The goal was to have a wide range of network sizes. The networks with the smallest number of nodes included Reed and Caltech universities with 769 and 962 nodes, respectively. The networks with the largest number of nodes included Texas and Virginia universities with 36,371 and 21,325 nodes, respectively.

Facebook, FB1–10, and physics: These datasets were retrieved from the Stanford Network Analysis Project (SNAP) website (http://snap.stanford.edu/data/index.html). The data in FB1 to FB10 and the Facebook networks were collected from survey participants of a Facebook App called 'Social

Table 19.1 A summary of generic measures for 62 social networks

Network	# Nodes	# Edges	Network Density	Diameter	Average Shortest Path
47 university Facebook networks*	8361.1*	645639.8*	0.0161*	7.7*	2.6938*
FB1 to FB10*	408.9*	34034.8*	0.0938*	7.7*	2.7873*
Delicious	1861	15328	0.0044	16	5.3698
Last.FM	1892	25434	0.0071	9	3.5186
Netscience	1461	5484	0.0026	17	5.8232
Facebook	4039	176468	0.0108	8	3.6925
Physics	5241	28968	0.0011	17	6.0485

* The values associated with these rows display the average of variables across the networks of each network group

Circle' (Leskovec & Mcauley, 2012). More information about these networks is provided on the SNAP website. The Physics network is referred to as 'Arxiv ca-GRQC' (General Relativity and Quantum Cosmology) on the SNAP website (Leskovec, Kleinberg, & Faloutsos, 2007). This is a network of collaborations among the authors who submitted their papers to the GR-QC category.

Netscience: The Netscience dataset was obtained from Mark Newman's repository (www-personal.umich.edu/~mejn/netdata/). The dataset contains a co-authorship network of scientists working on network theory and experimentation and was compiled by Newman in May 2006 (Newman, 2006).

Delicious and LastFM: These two datasets were created from the users of Delicious (www.delicious.com) and LastFM (www.lastfm.com) websites and were released by the 2nd International Workshop on Information Heterogeneity and Fusion in Recommender Systems (Cantador, Brusilovsky, & Kuflik, 2011). These datasets contain not only social networking but also resource consuming (i.e., music artist listening and webpage bookmarking) information from around 2,000 users.

STRUCTURAL MEASURES OF INFLUENCE

For each of the 62 networks, the centrality of nodes was measured using six types of structural centrality measures:

- Degree (Deg),
- Betweenness (Btw),
- Ego Betweenness (Ego1),
- EigenVector (EigV),
- ClusteringCoefficient (ClsCff), and
- PageRank (PgRk).

The betweenness and ego betweenness variables were standardized (converted to standard normal, or z-scores). In the following discussion Zego1[1] is the standardized ego betweenness score and ZBtw is the standardized betweenness score. The SNAP package and the code provided by Andreassend, Hironaka, & Thompson (2013) were utilized to compute the centrality measures.

The distribution characteristics of ClsCff and Deg centrality measures, along with network diameter and average shortest path length variables, have been found to be the most robust measures of a network's topology (Albert, Jeong, & Barabási, 1999). For each network, the network diameter and average shortest path length along with the following additional variables were computed using the igraph-R package and SPSS:

- The average, standard deviation, kurtosis, and skewness of clustering coefficient centrality (avg-Clustering, stdv_ClsCff, Skew_ClsCff, Kurt_ClsCff)
- The average, standard deviation, kurtosis, and skewness of degree centrality (mean_deg, stdv_deg, Skew_deg, Kurt_deg).

The correlations between degree, clustering coefficient, betweenness, ego betweenness,

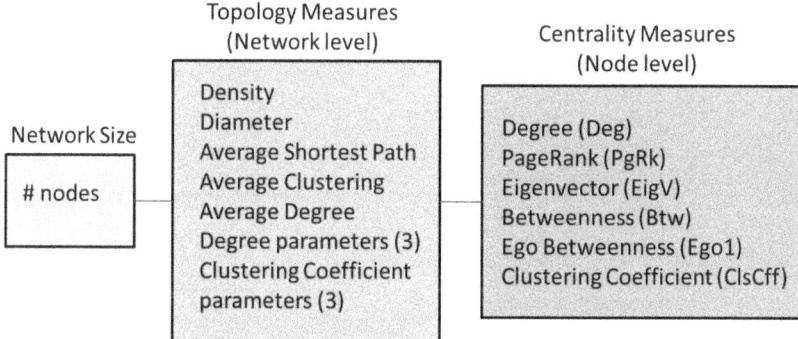

Figure 19.2 List of variables for the structural analysis of social networks

PageRank, and eigenvector centrality measures were calculated and recorded for the 62 datasets (ClsCff.Zego1, PgRk.Zego1, EigV.Zego1, Deg.Zego1, ClsCf.PgRkf, ClsCff.EigV., ClsCff.Deg, PgRK.EigV, PgRk.Deg, and Deg. EigV). In the notation being used here, the dot separates the two variables that were correlated (using the Pearson correlation coefficient). For instance ClsCff.Zego1 indicates the correlation between the clustering coefficient and standardized ego betweenness (Zego1). Figure 19.2 shows a conceptual organization of these variables.

FACTOR ANALYSIS OF NETWORK TOPOLOGY PROPERTIES

A factor analysis was conducted to condense (i.e., reification of) the 11 network topology measures into one or two factors. Factor analysis seemed appropriate since the 11 variables, and particularly the degree-related and clustering-related variables, were highly correlated with each other. It was hypothesized that network topology might predict the relationships among different centrality measures. We hoped that by factor analyzing a relatively large set of networks that were likely to vary in shape, we might find underlying factors that reflect shape features. Based on the factor analysis, as well as subsequent reliability analyses, two factors were extracted using eight of the variables, with three remaining variables that were not involved in any of the factors. Further details are provided in Ghajar-Khosravi (2015). The two extracted factors included:

Factor1 (Network Shape, Non-clumpiness): The first factor consisted of six variables; Kurt_ClsCff, Skew_ClsCff, AvgClustering, stdv_ClsCff, Mean_deg, and stdv_deg. The Shape factor represents how non-clumpy the network is. As mentioned earlier, Everett & Borgatti (2005) defined clumpy networks as networks with 'contrasting regions of highly cohesive subsets and regions of low density' within the same network. The Shape factor in this case study reflected the clustering coefficient distribution of the nodes, while also taking into account the average and the standard deviation of their degree centralities.

Factor2 (Network Reach): The second factor consisted of two variables; Diameter and Average Shortest Path Length. Both of these variables were computed based on the distance among network nodes. The factor was labelled as 'Network Reach' since it seemed to reflect how reachable nodes were from one another.

Factor scores were computed using the weighted average technique with factor loadings considered as the weights for each contributing variable to a factor. Figure 19.3

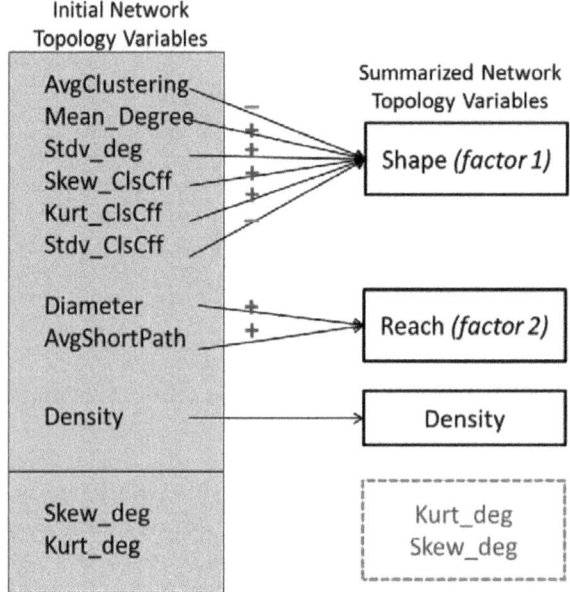

Figure 19.3 Network topology variables before and after the factor analysis

shows an interpretation of the two factors in terms of the original variables used in the analysis.

K-MEANS CLUSTERING ON NETWORK TOPOLOGY FACTORS

To investigate the effect of network topology on the type of relationships between different centrality measures, the 62 networks were grouped into three clusters using the cluster analysis method. The two factors derived in the previous section, along with the Density, Skew_deg, and Kurt_deg variables were used as the clustering variables in a cluster analysis of the 62 networks. Based on the k-means analysis the networks were grouped into three clusters (Figure 19.4). Shape had a major impact on the clustering of the networks. The impact of Reach in clustering the networks was to separate Cluster 2 from Clusters 1 and 3. The nature of the connections in Cluster 2 (i.e., Physics, Netscience, and Delicious) were collaboration- and information-consumption-based rather than friendship-based (Myers, Sharma, Gupta, & Lin, 2014). The three networks in Cluster 2 had the largest Diameter and AvgShortPath (Average Shortest Path), and a relatively low Density, compared to the other networks. Although the networks in Cluster 1 and 3 were all Facebook-based, in Cluster 3 the friendship connections were limited to university friends and confined to university boundaries. The networks in Cluster 3 were found to be less clumpy than in Cluster 2.

The results of this clustering showed that social networks with different domains may have different topologies depending on the type of relationship that exists among their members. Past research has generally contrasted the topology of social networks with other types of networks such as random or regular networks. The limited research that has looked into the differences among social networks has involved few social network datasets. An example research includes Lee, Kim, & Marcotte (2015) that demonstrated

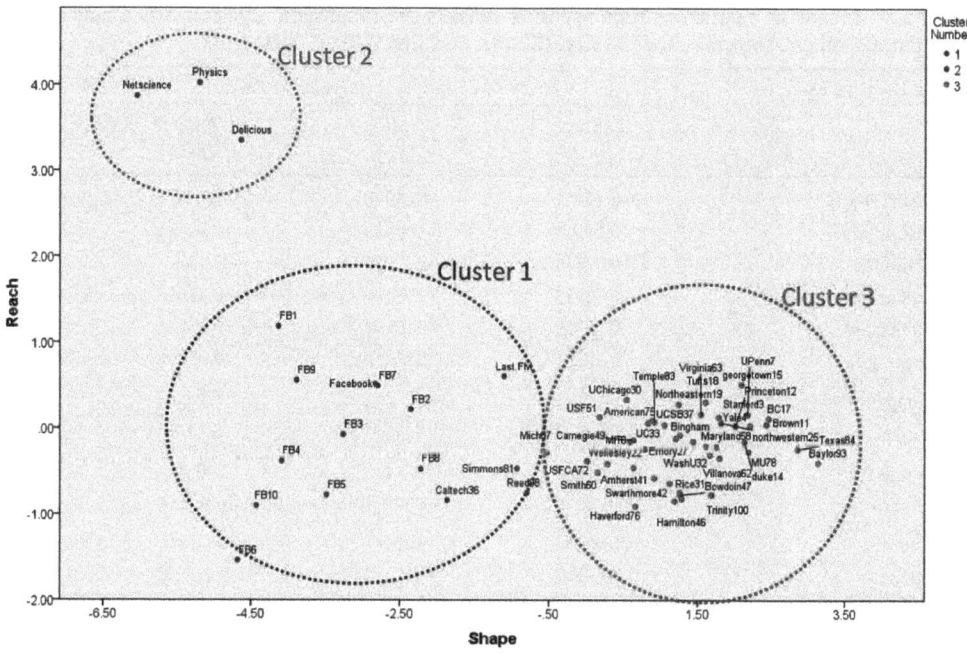

Figure 19.4 The three clusters with their members labelled by their names

differences in topological properties of social networks with different interaction or connection types. Lee, Kim, & Marcotte defined two classes of social networks: social networks with pairwise activities such as online dating (similar to Cluster 1 and 3 above) and those with group activities such as boards of directors of companies (similar to Cluster 2 above). Although their result was in agreement with the differences between the clusters in Figure 19.4, their results were based on two datasets.

NETWORK TOPOLOGY AND CENTRALITY CORRELATION PROFILES

To demonstrate the implications of network topology and the role it plays in other network structure variables, we looked into network cluster differences across centrality correlations.

A MANOVA (Multivariate Analysis of Variance) analysis assessed whether the three clusters reported earlier differed significantly in terms of their node centrality correlations. The dependent variables (i.e., centrality correlations) for this MANOVA test consisted of: ClsCf.Deg, ClsCff, EigV, ClsCff.PgRk, Deg.EigV, Deg.PgRk, and EigV.PgRk. The independent variable for the MANOVA analysis distinguished between the three clusters. The MANOVA analysis was followed by Hochberg's GT2 post hoc tests as suggested by Field (2009, p. 375) for situations where sample sizes are not equal. Using Pillai's trace, there was a significant effect of cluster number on the node centrality correlations, $F(12,110) = 17.272$, $p<.001$.

The post-hoc test results are summarized in Table 19.2. The three clusters were significantly distinguishable from each other on the dependent variables ClsCff.Deg, PgRk.EigV, PgRk.Deg, and EigV.Deg. While clusters 1 and 2 did not significantly differ from each

Table 19.2 Means of clusters in homogenous subsets are displayed. Clusters 1 & 2 make one homogenous subset together for the ClsCff.PgRk and ClsCff.EigV variables

Dependent variables	Means of Clusters in Homogenous Subsets			ANOVA
	Cluster 2 (N:15)	Cluster 1 (N:3)	Cluster 3 N:44)	F**
Mean(ClsCff.PgRk)	(−0.124	−0.1978)	−0.3567	29.59
Mean(ClsCff.EigV)	(0.040	−0.0553)	−0.2618	19.51
Mean(ClsCff.Deg)	0.09774	−0.1194	−0.3369	41.29
Mean(PgRk.EigV)	0.22533	0.64847	0.8523	38.22
Mean(PgRk.Deg)	0.72719	0.89337	0.98177	49.34
Mean(Deg.EigV)	0.59601	0.86272	0.91884	28.80
Mean_Shape*	−5.3	−2.86	1.33	167.361
Range_Shape	[−6.05,−4.64]	[−4.68,−.8]	[−.53,3.13]	
Mean_Reach*	3.75	−0.17	−0.2	97.67
Range_Reach	[3.35,4.02]	[−1.54,1.19]	[−.91,.51]	
Mean_Density	0.002	0.134	0.014	29.59
Range_Density	[.003,.001]	[.007,.303]	[.002,.057]	

* Shape and Reach factors have been calculated based on the zscores of their underlying variables
** All F-ratios are significant at p <.001

other (as indicated by the parentheses in the first two rows of Table 19.2), together they were significantly different from Cluster 3 on the ClsCff.PgRk and ClsCff.EigV variables. All F-ratios reported in Table 19.2 are significant at $p<.001$.

As can be seen in Table 19.2, there are large (and statistically significant) differences in the mean correlations between the clusters. For instance, the average correlation between PgRk and EigV equals 0.23 in Cluster 2, 0.65 in Cluster 1, and 0.85 in Cluster 3. This would indicate that for the social networks with collaboration-based connections, the correlation of Page Rank with eigenvector centrality will be probably low; hence, it would be beneficial to consider both measures into analyses as they would return different sets of influential nodes. The question of why the correlation is low for this cluster of networks needs further investigation and was outside the scope of this case study. Another example would be the almost perfect correlation between Page Rank and degree in Cluster 3. This shows that when friendship relationships are limited to an institution or community, members of the community are equally weighted or influential within the network; hence, looking into both measures would be redundant. Yet, more extensive analyses with larger number of networks in each category, in particular for Cluster 2, are needed to be able make stronger conclusions.

In Figure 19.5, three samples of networks from Clusters 2 and 3 have been selected to visually present the differences between their clustering coefficient distributions and their PgRk.EigV correlations across the two clusters. As can be seen in this figure, the clustering coefficient distribution histograms and the scatter plots of PageRank vs. Eigenvector centrality measures show clear differences between Cluster 2 and 3.

DISCUSSION

In the preceding section, centrality correlations were used as a way to diagnose

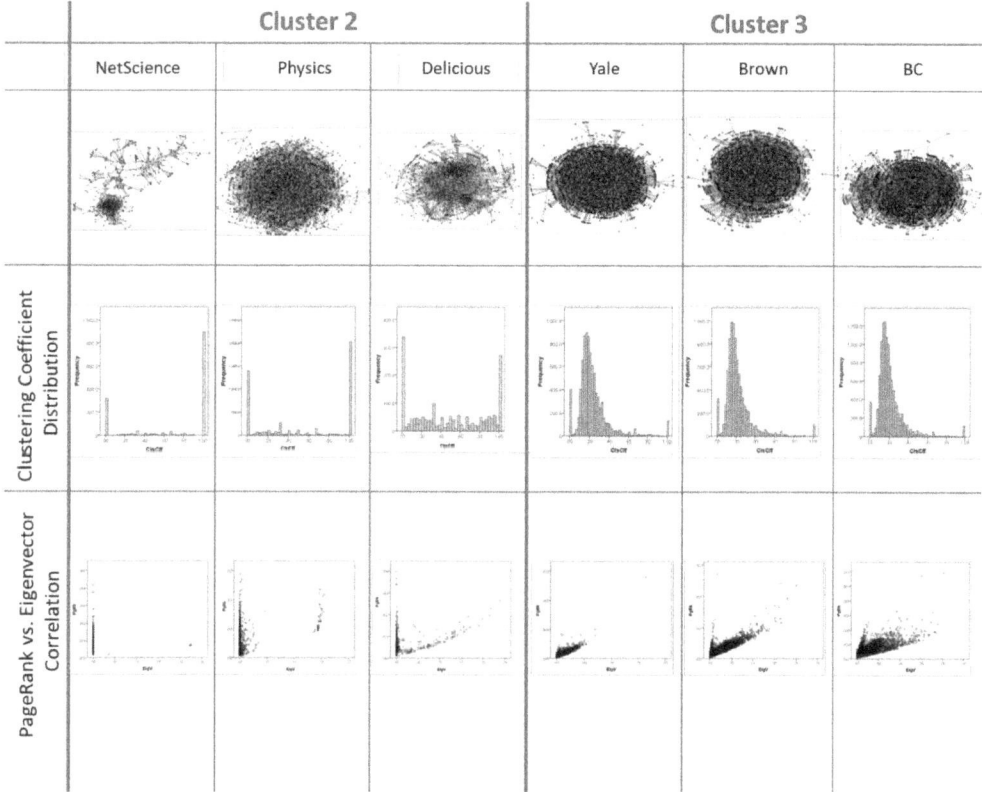

Figure 19.5 Three samples of networks from Cluster 2 and Cluster 3. The first row presents the visualized graphs of the six networks. The second row presents their clustering coefficient distribution histogram. The third row presents the scatter plots of Page Rank centrality vs. Eigenvector centrality

different behaviors of centrality measures. Centrality correlations are useful because they capture different aspects of networks than topology related features.

In the case study presented above the impact of topology was assessed not only through the shape and reach factors, but also through the clusters of networks that were identified based on their topological properties. The results of the clustering showed that social networks with different domains may have different topologies depending on the type of relationship that exists among their members. In other words, the clusters of networks, that were identified based on their topological properties, reflected on the type of the interactions among members. The topological properties of social networks with collaboration-based or information-consumption-based connections were different from those social networks with friendship-based connections. For example, the average distance between the nodes of collaboration-based networks (Cluster 2) was found to be much higher than friendship-based networks (Cluster 1). Moreover, when friendship relationships were limited to a certain university/community (Cluster 3), those social networks had less clumpy shapes. Further analyses that look into a wider range of social networks are needed to further validate these findings.

MANOVA analyses demonstrated that clusters derived using the shape and reach factors showed clear differences, not only in terms of the shape and reach factors that formed the clusters, but also in terms of correlations between centrality measures. The means and ranges reported in Table 19.2 make a potentially useful starting point in predicting the size of centrality correlations based on shape and reach factors of networks and vice versa or perhaps based on the type of interactions in networks. For example, for a new network with shape and reach values closer to the centroid of Cluster 2 or a network with collaboration-based connections, it could be predicted that the EigV and PgRk centrality measures would have fairly low correlations. The distance to typical cluster centroids could be calculated using Euclidean distances in order to classify social networks into different types.

In the follow-up correlation analyses, it was found that the clumpier and denser the network and the longer the shortest paths among the nodes, 1) the higher the correlations ClsCff.PgRk, ClsCff.EigV, and ClsCff.Deg in a network, and 2) the lower the correlations for PgRk.EigV, PgRk.Deg, and Deg.EigV. These results demonstrate that network topology has a significant effect on the relationships that exist between centrality measures.

Limitations

Some of the limitations of the case study reported above include:

> Except for the Netscience and Physics social networks, the links in the rest of the studied networks were based on mutual friendships. Hence, all the resulting links were undirected and symmetrical. Thus the generalizability of the results is limited to networks with undirected links. For example, the analysis of a Twitter dataset which contains directional links may return totally different results as people have the option to follow or not follow their followers. So, the edges of networks with directed vs. undirected links bare different meanings, potentially leading to different centrality correlations or topological properties.

Moreover, the majority of the datasets were collected from Facebook hence affected by the interface design and friend recommendations in Facebook environment. Beside, all the datasets used for this thesis were collected and provided by third parties. We had no control over how the data was collected or what was collected. Any potential biases in the sampling strategies potentially limit the generalizability of the results. However, the 62 networks that were used were not all obtained from the same sources, so it is probably unlikely that they all suffered from a shared systematic bias. Lastly, the structural analyses of social influence were mostly based on objective measures of social network centrality. It is possible that contextual factors such as the type of university environment might lead to different structuring of relationships, but such analyses were outside the scope of this case study.

CONCLUSION

Since networks can be laid out in many different ways, it is perhaps not surprising that there are a number of different ways of defining network centrality. It is also evident that the different centrality measures capture different properties of networks and are affected differently by networks with different shapes or topological properties or perhaps by networks with different types of connections.

Potentially informative centrality measures can be prohibitively expensive to compute in very large networks. Proxy measures approximate a desired centrality measure with a more computationally tractable version, which is assumed to be correlated to the original measure of interest. We gave the example of ego betweenness as an approximate measure of betweenness centrality and we discussed how the adequacy of ego betweenness as an approximation of betweenness centrality can vary widely between different networks.

We also presented a case study showing how correlations between centrality measures (within networks) can vary widely depending on properties of the network that are related to topology. Using factor analysis followed by clustering we showed how it is possible to characterize 62 real-world social networks in terms of the factors of shape and reach, and to organize those networks into three clusters based on their scores on those two factors. Moreover, we showed how topological differences among networks could potentially reflect on the type of interactions among the members of those networks. In other words, we showed that the type of relationships that exist among social network members may have an impact on the topological properties of those networks. The analyses reported should be extended by looking into a wider range of social networks to make these results more generalizable. Example applications of these findings include identifying certain types of interactions in a network (e.g., interactions among radicalized members of a social network) based on the topology of that network.

Centrality analysis of networks, and evaluation of network topology, are highly active areas of research within social networks and we expect that there will be many new research results pertaining to this area in future years. In particular, we expect to see further exploitation of network centrality measures in terms of characterizing different networks, in terms of recognizing communities and subgroups within social networks (Chin & Chignell, 2008), and in terms of measuring and predicting social influence. The role of measuring network centrality is likely to be particularly important in using measures of social influence to guide marketing initiatives and related applications.

NOTE

1 Z indicates standardization with z-scores and ego

REFERENCES

Adamic, L., Buyukkokten, O., & Adar, E. (2003). A social network caught in the web. First Monday, 8(6). Retrieved from http://firstmonday.org/article/view/1057/977

Albert, R., & Barabási, A. L. (2002). Statistical mechanics of complex networks. Reviews of modern physics, 74(1), 47.

Albert, R., Jeong, H., & Barabási, A. L. (1999). Internet: Diameter of the world-wide web. Nature, 401(6749), 130–131.

Amaral, L. A. N., Scala, A., Barthelemy, M., & Stanley, H. E. (2000). Classes of small-world networks. Proceedings of the National Academy of Sciences, 97(21), 11149–11152.

Andreassend, S., Hironaka, H., & Thompson, D. (2013). Seeking Alpha: Algorithms and techniques for enabling viral marketing within mobile telephony networks. Retrieved August, 2013 from: http://snap.stanford.edu/class/cs224w-2012/projects/cs224w-011-final.pdf

Bader, D. A., Kintali, S., Madduri, K., & Mihail, M. (2007). Approximating betweenness centrality. In Algorithms and models for the web-graph (pp. 124–137). Springer Berlin Heidelberg.

Barabási, A. L., & Albert, R. (1999). Emergence of scaling in random Networks. Science, 286(5439), 509–512.

Barabási, A. L., & Bonabeau, E. (2003). Scale-free networks. Scientific American, 288(5), 60-9.

Batool, K., & Niazi, M. A. (2014). Towards a methodology for validation of centrality measures in complex networks. PLoS One, 9(4) doi: http://dx.doi.org/10.1371/journal.pone.0090283

Bollen, J., Rodriquez, M. A., & Van de Sompel, H. (2006). Journal status. Scientometrics, 69(3), 669–687.

Bonacich, P. (1972). Factoring and weighting approaches to clique identification. Journal of Mathematical Sociology, 2, 113–120.

Borgatti, S. P. (2005). Centrality and network flow. Social Networks, 27(1), 55–71. doi:10.1016/j.socnet.2004.11.008

Borgatti, S. P., Everett, M. G., & Johnson, J. C. (2013). Analyzing social networks. Thousand Oaks, Calif.: SAGE Publications.

Brandes, U., & Pich, C. (2007). Centrality estimation in large networks. International

Journal of Bifurcation and Chaos, 17(07), 2303–2318.

Brin, S., & Page, L. (1998). The anatomy of a large-scale hypertextual Web search engine. Computer networks and ISDN systems, 30(1), 107–117.

Broder, A., Kumar, R., Maghoul, F., Raghavan, P., Rajagopalan, S., Stata, R., Tomkins, A., & Wiener, J. (2000). Graph structure in the web. Computer networks, 33(1), 309–320.

Cantador, I., Brusilovsky, P., & Kuflik, T. (2011). Proceedings of the 2nd Workshop on Information Heterogeneity and Fusion in Recommender Systems. In Proceedings of the 5th ACM conference on Recommender systems (RecSys 2011), Chicago, IL, USA. New York, NY: ACM.

Chehreghani, M. H. (2014). An efficient algorithm for approximate betweenness centrality computation. The Computer Journal, bxu003.

Chin, A., & Chignell, M. (2008). Automatic detection of cohesive subgroups within social hypertext: A heuristic approach. New Review of Hypermedia and Multimedia, 14 (1), 121–143.

Costenbader, E., & Valente, T.W. (2003). The stability of centrality measures when networks are sampled. Social Networks, 25, 283–307.

Ding, Y., Yan, E., Frazho, A., & Caverlee, J. (2009). PageRank for ranking authors in co-citation networks. Journal of the American Society for Information Science and Technology, 60(11), 2229–2243.

Erdós, P., & Rényi, A. (1959). On random graphs I. Publicationes Mathematicae Debrecen, 6, 290–297.

Everett, M., & Borgatti, S. P. (2005). Ego network betweenness. Social networks, 27(1), 31–38.

Faloutsos, M., Faloutsos, P., & Faloutsos, C. (1999, August). On power-law relationships of the internet topology. In ACM SIGCOMM Computer Communication Review (Vol. 29, No. 4, pp. 251–262). ACM.

Faust, K. (1997). Centrality in affiliation networks. Social networks, 19(2), 157–191.

Field, A. (2009). Discovering statistics using SPSS. Thousand Oaks, CA: SAGE Publications.

Freeman, L. C. (1978). Centrality in social networks conceptual clarification. Social Networks, 1(3), 215–239. doi:10.1016/0378-8733(78)90021-7.

Freeman, L. C. (1982). Centered graphs and the structure of ego networks. Mathematical Social Sciences, 3(3), 291–304.

Ghajar-Khosravi, S. (2015). Characteristics of Social Networks Relevant to Predictions of Social Influence (Doctoral Dissertation).

Gruzd, A., & Wellman, B. (2014). Networked Influence in Social Media: Introduction to the Special Issue. *American Behavioral Scientist*, *58*(10), 1251-1259.

Heidemann, J., Klier, M., & Probst, F. (2010). Identifying key users in online social networks: A PageRank based approach. ICIS 2010 Proceedings, *79*, 1–21.

Huang, S., Lv, T., Zhang, X., Yang, Y., Zheng, W., & Wen, C. (2014). Identifying Node Role in Social Network Based on Multiple Indicators. PloS one, 9(8), e103733.

Kim, Y. H., Kim, C. M., Han, Y. H., Jeong, Y. S., & Park, D. S. (2013). Betweenness of expanded Ego networks in sociality-aware delay tolerant networks. In *Ubiquitous Information Technologies and Applications* (pp. 499–505). Springer Netherlands.

Kiss, C., & Bichler, M. (2008). Identification of influencers – measuring influence in customer networks. Decision Support Systems, 46(1), 233–253. doi:10.1016/j.dss.2008.06.007

Koschützki, D., & Schreiber, F. (2004). Comparison of Centralities for Biological Networks. In Proceedings of German Conference on Bioinformatics, October 4-6, 2004, Bielefeld, Germany (pp. 199–206).

Landher, A., Friedl, B., & Heidemann, J. (2010). A critical review of centrality measures in social networks. Business and Information Systems Engineering, 52(6), 367–382. doi:10.1007/s12599-010-0127-3

Langville, A. N., & Meyer, C. D. (2004). Deeper inside PageRank. Internet Mathematics, 1(3), 335–380.

Lee, I., Kim, E., & Marcotte, E. M. (2015). Modes of interaction between individuals dominate the topologies of real world networks. *PloS one*, *10*(3), doi: 10.1371/journal.pone.0121248.

Leskovec, J., & Mcauley, J. J. (2012). Learning to discover social circles in ego networks. Advances in neural information processing systems (NIPS 2012, LAKE TAHOE, Nevada), 25, 539–547.

Leskovec, J., Kleinberg, J., & Faloutsos, C. (2007). Graph evolution: Densification and shrinking diameters. ACM Transactions on Knowledge Discovery from Data (TKDD), 1(1), 2.

Marsden, P. V. (2002). Egocentric and sociocentric measures of network centrality. Social Networks, 24(4), 407–422. doi:10.1016/S0378-8733(02)00016-3

Mislove, A., Marcon, M., Gummadi, K. P., Druschel, P., & Bhattacharjee, B. (2007, October). Measurement and analysis of online social networks. InProceedings of the 7th ACM SIGCOMM conference on Internet measurement (pp. 29–42). ACM.

Muchnik, L., Pei, S., Parra, L. C., Reis, S. D., Andrade Jr, J. S., Havlin, S., & Makse, H. A. (2013). Origins of power-law degree distribution in the heterogeneity of human activity in social networks. Scientific reports, 1783(3), 1–7. doi:10.1038/srep01783

Myers, S. A., Sharma, A., Gupta, P., & Lin, J. (2014). Information network or social network? The structure of the twitter follow graph. In Proceedings of the companion publication of the 23rd international conference on World Wide Web companion (pp. 493–498). International World Wide Web Conferences Steering Committee.

Newman, M. E. (2001). The structure of scientific collaboration networks. Proceedings of the National Academy of Sciences, 98(2), 404–409.

Newman, M. E. (2003). The structure and function of complex networks. SIAM review, 45(2), 167–256.

Newman, M. E. (2006). Finding community structure in networks using the eigenvectors of matrices. Physical review E, 74(3), 036104.

Pantazopoulos, P., Karaliopoulos, M., & Stavrakakis, I. (2014). On the local approximations of node centrality in Internet router-level topologies. In Self-Organizing Systems (pp. 115–126). Springer Berlin Heidelberg.

Pfeffer, J., & Carley, K. M. (2012). K-centralities: Local approximations of global measures based on shortest paths. Paper presented at the WWW'12 – Proceedings of the 21st Annual Conference on World Wide Web Companion, 1043–1050. doi:10.1145/2187980.2188239.

Quan-Haase, A. (2009). Information brokering in the high-tech industry: Online social networks at work. Lambert Academic Publishing. Koln.

Riondato, M., & Kornaropoulos, E. M. (2014, February). Fast approximation of betweenness centrality through sampling. In Proceedings of the 7th ACM international conference on Web search and data mining (pp. 413–422). ACM.

Ronqui, J. R. F., & Travieso, G. (2014). Analyzing complex networks through correlations in centrality measurements. arXiv preprint arXiv:1405.7724.

Scott, J. (2000). Social network analysis: A handbook. Thousand Oaks, CA: SAGE Publications.

Traud, A. L., Mucha, P. J., & Porter, M. A. (2012). Social structure of Facebook networks. Physica A: Statistical Mechanics and its Applications, 391(16), 4165–4180.

Watts, D. J., & Strogatz, S. H. (1998). Collective dynamics of 'small-world' networks. Nature, 393(6684), 440–442.

Wasserman, S., & Faust, K. (1994). Social network analysis: Methods and applications. Cambridge: Cambridge University Press.

Yan, E., & Ding, Y. (2009). Applying centrality measures to impact analysis: A coauthorship network analysis. Journal of the American Society for Information Science and Technology, 60(10), 2107–2118.

Predictive Analytics with Social Media Data

Niels Buus Lassen, Lisbeth la Cour
and Ravi Vatrapu

This chapter provides an overview of the extant literature on predictive analytics with social media data. First, we discuss the difference between predictive vs. explanatory models and the scientific purposes for and advantages of predictive models. Second, we present and discuss the foundational statistical issues in predictive modelling in general with an emphasis on social media data. Third, we present a selection of papers on predictive analytics with social media data and categorize them based on the application domain, social media platform (Facebook, Twitter, etc.), independent and dependent variables involved, and the statistical methods and techniques employed. Fourth and last, we offer some reflections on predictive analytics with social media data.

INTRODUCTION

Social media has evolved into a vital constituent of many human activities. We increasingly share several aspects of our private, interpersonal, social, and professional lives on Facebook, Twitter, Instagram, Tumblr, and many other social media platforms. The resulting social data is persistent, archived, and can be retrieved and analyzed by employing a variety of research methods as documented in this handbook (Quan-Haase & Sloan, Chapter 1, this volume). Social data analytics is not only informing, but also transforming existing practices in politics, marketing, investing, product development, entertainment, and news media. This chapter focuses on predictive analytics with social media data. In other words, how social media data has been used to predict processes and outcomes in the real world.

Recent research in the field of Computational Social Science (Cioffi-Revilla, 2013; Conte et al., 2012; Lazer et al., 2009) has shown how data resulting from the widespread adoption and use of social media channels such as Facebook and Twitter can be used to predict outcomes such as Hollywood movie revenues (Asur & Huberman, 2010), Apple iPhone sales (Lassen, Madsen, & Vatrapu, 2014), seasonal moods (Golder & Macy, 2011), and epidemic outbreaks (Chunara, Andrews, & Brownstein, 2012). Underlying assumptions for this research stream on predictive analytics with social media data (Evangelos et al., 2013) are that social media actions such as tweeting, liking, commenting and rating are proxies for user/consumer's attention to a particular object/product and that the shared digital artefact that is persistent can create social influence (Vatrapu et al., 2015).

PREDICTIVE MODELS VS. EXPLANATORY MODELS

At the outset, we find that the difference between predictive and explanatory models needs to be emphasized. Predictive analytics entail the application of data mining, machine learning and statistical modelling to arrive at *predictive models* of future observations as well as suitable methods for ascertaining the *predictive power* of these models in practice (Shmueli & Koppius, 2011). Consequently, predictive analytics differ from explanatory models in that the latter aims to: (1) draw statistical inferences from validating causal hypotheses about relationships among variables of interest, and; (2) assess the explanatory power of causal models underlying these relationships (Shmueli, 2010). This crucial distinction between explanatory and predictive models is best surmised by Shmueli & Koppius (2011) in the following statement: 'whereas explanatory statistical models are based on underlying *causal relationships between theoretical constructs*, predictive models rely on *associations between measurable variables*' (p. 556). For example, in political science, explanatory models have investigated the extent to which social media platforms such as Facebook can function as online public spheres (Robertson & Vatrapu, 2010; Vatrapu, Robertson, & Dissanayake, 2008) in terms of users' interactions and sentiments (Hussain, Vatrapu, Hardt, & Jaffari, 2014; Robertson, Vatrapu, & Medina, 2010a,b). On the other hand, predictive models in political science sought to predict election outcomes from social media data (Chung & Mustafaraj, 2011; Sang & Bos, 2012; Skoric, Poor, Achananuparp, Lim, & Jiang, 2012; Tsakalidis, Papadopoulos, Cristea, & Kompatsiaris, 2015).

Distinguishing between explanation and prediction as discrete modelling goals, Shmueli & Koppius (2011) argued that any model, which strives to embrace both explanation and prediction, will have to trade-off between explanatory and predictive power. More specifically, Shmueli & Koppius (2011) claim that predictive analytics can advance scientific research in six scenarios: (1) generating new theory for fast-changing environments which yield rich datasets about difficult-to-hypothesize relationships and unmeasured-before concepts; (2) developing alternate measures for constructs; (3) comparing competing theories via tests of predictive accuracy; (4) augmenting contemporary explanatory models through capturing complex patterns which underlie relationships among key concepts; (5) establishing research relevance by evaluating the discrepancy between theory and practice; and (6) quantifying the predictability of measureable phenomena.

This chapter discusses predictive modelling of (big) social media data in social sciences. The focus will be entirely on what is often referred to as predictive models: models that use statistical and/or mathematical modelling to predict a phenomenon of interest. Furthermore, the focus will be on prediction in the sense of forecasting a future outcome of the phenomenon of interest as such predictions are the ones that have so far received most attention in the literature. To illustrate the concepts, models, methods and evaluation of results we use examples from economics and finance. The general principles are, however, easily employed to other social science fields as well, for example, marketing. The concepts and principles that this section discusses are of a general nature and are informed by Hyndman & Athanasopoulos (2014) and Chatfield (2002).

This chapter does not discuss applicable software solutions. However, it is worth mentioning that there exist quite a few software packages with more or less automatic search procedures when it comes to model specification. A few ones are, for example, SAS, SPSS and the Autometrics package of OxMetrics.

PREDICTIVE MODELLING OF SOCIAL MEDIA DATA

When performing predictive analysis on social media data researchers often have to make a lot of decisions along the way. Examples of the most important decisions or choices will be discussed in the sections below.

The Phenomenon of Interest and the Type of Forecasts

Quite often the focus will be on a single outcome (univariate modelling – one model equation) where the goal is to derive a prediction or forecast of, for example, sales in a company or the stock price of the company. In some cases, more than one outcome will be of interest and then a multivariate approach in which more than one relationship or model equation is specified, estimated, and used at the same time is worth considering. From now on let us assume that the phenomenon of interest is sales of a company and the social media data are among the factors that are considered as explanatory for the outcome. The discussion will then relate to the univariate case. At this stage, a decision is also necessary in relation to the data frequency. Is the predictive model supposed to be applied to forecast monthly sale, quarterly sales or sales of an even higher frequency like weekly or daily?

The Data

Once the phenomenon of interest is identified, decisions concerning the data to be used have to be made. Data can be of different types: time series (e.g. sales per month or sales per day), cross sectional (e.g. individuals such as customers, for a given period in time) or longitudinal/panel (a combination of the former two such as a set of customers observed through several months). Predictive models can be relevant for all these types of data and many of the basic principles for analysis are quite similar. In the remaining parts of this section, for simplicity the focus will be on time series only.

As social media data have been growing in volume and importance during the last 10 years, in some cases the final number of observations for modelling may be rather limited as the dependent variable may reflect accounting and book-keeping and be relatively low-frequency like monthly or quarterly in nature. If this is the case, there may be a limit to how advanced models can be used. In other cases, daily data may be available and more complex models may be considered.

The frequency of the data is also important for model specification itself. With more high frequency data, a researcher may discover more informative dynamic patterns compared to a case with less frequent data. Consider a case where sales of a company need to be forecasted. If the reaction time from increased activity on the Facebook page of the company to changes in sales is short (e.g. just a couple of days) then if sales are available only on a monthly basis the lag pattern between explanatory factors and outcome may be difficult to identify and use.

In many cases there will be a large set of potential explanatory factors that may be included in various tentative model specifications. Social media data may be just a part of such data and it will be important to also include other variables. The quality as well as the quantity of data is very important for building a successful predictive model.

Social Media Data and Pre-processing

When researchers consider using social media data for predictive purposes, at the outset the social media data will be collected at the level of the individual action (e.g. a Facebook 'like' or a tweet) and in order to prepare the data to enter a predictive model some pre-processing will be necessary. Often the data will need to be temporally aggregated to match the temporal aggregation level of the outcome, for example, monthly data. Also as some of the inputs from social media are text variables, some filtering, interpretation, and classification may be necessary. An example of the latter would be the application of a supervised machine learning algorithm that classifies the posts and comments into positive, negative or neutral sentiments (Thelwall, Chapter 32, this volume). At the current moment it is mainly the pre-processing of the social media data that is considered challenging from the computational aspects of big data analytics (Council, 2013). Once the individual actions (posts, likes, etc.) are temporally aggregated and classified, the set of potential explanatory factors are usually rather limited and as the outcome variables are of fairly low frequencies like monthly or quarterly (stock market data are actually sometimes used at a daily frequency) which means that the modelling process deviates less from more classical approaches within predictive modelling.

In Search of a Model Equation – Theory-based versus Data-driven?

In very general terms a model equation will identify some relationship between the phenomenon of interest (y) and a set of explanatory factors. The relationship will never be perfect either due to un-observable factors, measurement errors or other types of errors.

The general equation: y = f(explanatory factors) + error

Where f describes some relationship between what is inside the parenthesis and y.

In principle, linear, non-linear, parametric, non-parametric and semi-parametric models may be considered. In general, non-linear models will require more data points/observations than linear models as the structures they search for are more complex.

There is a range of possible starting points for the search process. At one end lies traditional econometrics where the starting point is often an economic or behavioural theory that will guide the researcher in finding a set of potential explanatory factors. At the other end of the range machine learning algorithms will help identify a relationship from a large set of social media data and other potential explanatory factors. The advantage of starting from a theory-based model specification is that the researcher may be more confident that the model is robust in the sense that the identified relationship is reliable at least for some period of time. Without a theory the identified structure may still work for predictions in the short run but may be less robust and in general will not add much to an understanding of the phenomenon at hand. In between pure theoretically inspired models and models based on data pattern discoveries are many models that include elements of both categories. As theoretical models are often more precise when it comes to selection of explanatory factors for the more fundamental or long-run relationships they may be less precise when it comes to a description of dynamics and a combination that allows for a primary theoretically based long-run part may prove more useful.

To finalize the discussion of theory-based versus data-driven model selection the concept of causality is often useful. If a causal relationship exists a change in an explanatory factor is known to imply a change in the outcome. A model that suffers from a lack of a causal relationship suffers from an endogeneity problem (a concept used in econometrics). A model that suffers from an endogeneity problem will not be useful for tests of a theory of for policy evaluations. If the only purpose of the model is forecasting, identification of a causal relationship is of less importance as a strong association between the explanatory factors and the outcome may be sufficient. However, without causality the predictive model may be considered less robust (more risk of a model break-down) to general changes in structures and society and hence may be best at forecasting in the short run. If this is the case, some sort of monitoring on a continuous basis to identify a model break-down at an early stage is advisable.

Fitting of a Predictive Model

In this step the researcher will adapt the mathematical specification of the predictive model to the actual data. In the case of a linear regression model this is done by estimation using the ordinary least squares (OLS) method or the maximum likelihood (ML). For non-linear models such as neural networks, some mathematical algorithm is used. In rare cases estimation of a model is not possible (e.g. in case of perfect multicollinearity of a linear regression model). In such a case the researcher has to re-think the model specification.

Estimation (the use of a formula or a procedure) may in itself sound simple, but already at this stage the researcher has to specify the set-up to be used for model evaluation in the following step as they are highly dependent.

Even though it may seem natural to use as many data point as possible for the model fitting, there are other considerations to take into account as well. For the estimation step, it is stressed that in addition to the decision of estimation or fitting method, a decision on exactly which sample or part of the sample to use for estimation is of importance too.

Evaluation of a Predictive Model for Forecasting Purposes

The true test of a predictive model that is to be used for forecasting of future values of the outcome of interest is by investigating the out-of-sample properties of the model.

This statement calls for the need of an estimation (or training) sample and an evaluation (or test) sample. As a good in-sample model fit does not ensure good forecasting properties of a predictive model, the evaluation process then naturally starts by an analysis of the in-sample properties of the model and extends to an out-of-sample analysis.

In-sample Evaluation of the Model

The first thing to note is that if the model has a theoretical foundation the signs of the estimated coefficients will be compared to the signs expected from the theory.

A second thing to be aware of is whether the model fulfils the underlying statistical assumptions (these may differ depending on the type of model in focus). In classical linear regression modelling, problems such as autocorrelation and heteroscedasticity will need attention and a study of potential outliers is of high importance. When forecasting is the final purpose of the model multicollinearity is of less importance. Finally, indicators in relation to the functional form specification may provide useful information on how to improve the model.

The overall fit of the model may be captured by measures such as R^2, adjusted R^2, the family for measures based on absolute or squared errors (e.g. MSE, RMSE, MAE, MAPE), and information criteria such as AIC, and BIS. A small warning is justified here as too much emphasis on obtaining a good fit may result in overfitting of the model which is not necessarily desirable when the purpose of the model is forecasting.

Out-of-sample Evaluation

For an out-of-sample evaluation study the model is used to forecast values for a time period that was not used for the estimation of the model. In the 'pure' case neither future values of the explanatory factors nor future values of the outcome are known and the model that is used to obtain the forecast will need to rely on lagged values of the explanatory factors or to use predicted values of the explanatory factors. In the former case, the specification of the model equation in terms of lags will set a limit to how many periods into the future the model can predict. In many cases an out-of-sample forecast evaluation will rely on sets of one step ahead predictions, but predictions for a longer forecast horizon (e.g. six months ahead for a model specified with monthly data) are also sometimes considered.

Once the out-of-sample forecasts are obtained it is possible to calculate forecast errors and to study their patterns. Focus areas will be of directional nature (the trend in the outcome captured), as they may be related to predictability of turning points and summary measures for the errors will again prove useful (e.g. MSE, MAPE, etc.) but this time for the forecasted period only. The idea of splitting the sample into different parts for evaluation can be extended in various ways using cross-validation (Hyndman & Athanasopoulos, 2014).

Using a Predictive Model for Forecasting Purposes

Once a model has been chosen some considerations concerning its implementation are important. This topic is very much related to the overall phenomenon and problem; hence a general discussion is difficult to provide.

There is, however, one type of considerations that deserves mentioning: how often the model needs re-estimation or specification updating. Given that often the general data pattern is quite robust, the specification updating may only take place in case of new variables becoming available or in case a sufficiently large number of data points have become available such that more complex structures could be allowed for.

Finally, from a practical perspective a combination of forecasts from different basic predictive models is also a possibility and quite popular in certain fields.

CATEGORIZED LIST OF PREDICTIVE MODELS WITH SOCIAL MEDIA DATA

Table 20.1 below presents a selected list of research papers on predictive analytics with social media data categorized across different application domains in terms of social media platform (Facebook, Twitter, etc.) and the independent and dependent variables involved. For conceptual exposition and literature review on the predictive power of social media data (see Gayo-Avello et al. (2013)).

Application Domains

As can be seen from Table 20.1, there have been many predictive models of sales based on social media data. Such predictive models work for the brands that can command large amounts of human attention on social media, and therefore generate big data on social media. Examples are iPhone sales, H&M revenues, Nike sales, etc., which are all product categories around which there is a possibility to have large volumes and ranges of opinions on social media platforms. For brands and products that don't generate large volumes of social media data, for instance, insurance, banking, shipping, basic household supplies, etc. the predictive models tend not to work. One explanation for the successful performance of the predictive models is that social media actions can be categorized into the phases of the different domain-specific models from the application domains of marketing, finance, epidemiology, etc. For example, the actual stock price for Apple is in rough terms mainly based on discounted historical sales and expectations to future sales. If social media can model sales, then

Table 20.1 Categorization of research publications on predictive analytics with social media data

Reference	Social Data	Dependent Variables	Independent Variables	Statistical Methods
Asur & Huberman (2010)	Twitter	Movie revenue	Twitter activity, sentiment and theatre distribution	Time-Series Multiple Regression Model
Lassen et al. (2014)	Twitter	iPhone sales	Twitter activity and sentiment	Time-Series Multiple Regression Model
Bollen & Mao (2011)	Twitter	Dow Jones Industrial Average	Calm, Alert, Sure, Vital, Kind and Happy	Time-Series Multiple Regression Model
Voortman (2015)	Google Trends	Car sales	Google trend data car names	Time Series Linear Regression Model
Vosen & Schmidt (2011)	Google Trends	Consumer spending	Real personal income y, interest rates on 3-month Treasury Bills I and stock prices s (measured on S&P 500), Google Trend, and consumer spending t-1	ARIMA/Time Series Multiple Regression Model
Choi & Varian (2012)	Google Trends	Sales of cars, homes and travel	Historical sales and Google trend variable	Simple Seasonal AR Models and Fixed-Effects Models
Chung & Mustafaraj (2011)	Twitter	Political election outcome	Twitter collective sentiment	Linear Regression
Conover, Gonçalves, Ratkiewicz, Flammini, & Menczer (2011)	Twitter	Political alignment	Twitter hashtags	SVM trained on hashtag metadata
Bothos, Apostolou, & Mentzas (2010)	IMDB, Flixster, Yahoo Movies, HSX, Twitter, RottenTomatoes.com	Movie Academy Award winners	Measures from IMDB, Flixster, Yahoomovies, HSX, Twitter, RottenTomatoes.com	Multivariate Distribution Models
Culotta (2010)	Twitter	Detecting influenza outbreaks	Twitter keywords	Time-Series Multiple Regression Model
Dijkman, Ipeirotis, Aertsen, & van Helden (2015)	Twitter	Many types of sales	Twitter activity and sentiment	Time-Series Multiple Regression Model
Eysenbach (2011)	Twitter	Total number of citations	Twimpact variable (number of tweetations within n days after publication)	Multi-Variate/Linear Regression
Gruhl, Guha, Kumar, Novak, & Tomkins (2005)	Blogs	Sales	Product/brand mentions	Time-Series using Cross-Correlation
Jansen, Zhang, Sobel, & Chowdury (2009)	Twitter	Brand variables	Twitter sentiment variables	Time-Series Linear Regression Models
Li & Cardie (2013)	Twitter	Early stage influenza detection	Twitter texts about flu	Unsupervised Bayesian Model based on Markov Network
Radosavljevic, Grbovic, Djuric, & Bhamidipati (2014)	Tumblr	Sport results and number of goals	Team and player mentions	Poisson Regression Model using Maximum Likelihood Principle
Ritterman, Osborne, & Klein (2009)	Twitter	Stock-Prices	Historical prices, unigrams and bigrams, Twitter activity	SVR Regression using Unigrams and Bigrams

Study	Platform	Topic	Variables	Model
Sang & Bos (2012)	Twitter	Dutch election outcome	Twitter texts and sentiments	Time Series Multiple Regression Model
Shen, Wang, Luo, & Wang (2013)	Twitter	Entity belonging	Twitter texts	Decision tree, KAURI/LINDEN method
Skoric et al. (2012)	Twitter	Election outcome Singapore	Twitter activity	Time Series Linear Regression Model
Tsakalidis et al. (2015)	Twitter	Election outcomes EU	Twitter texts	Linear Regression (LR), Gaussian Process (GP) and Sequential Minimal Optimization for Regression (SMO)
Tumasjan, Sprenger, Sandner, & Welpe (2010)	Twitter	Election outcomes Germany	Twitter texts	Probability Models
Yu, Duan, & Cao (2013)	Google blogs, Boardreader and Twitter compared to Google News	Firm equity value	Variables for activity and sentiment	Time Series Multiple Regression Model
Hughes, Rowe, Batey, & Lee (2012)	Twitter and Facebook	Socialising and info exchange	Big5 personality traits, NFC and sociability	Time-Series Multiple Regression Model
Krauss, Nann, Simon, Gloor, & Fischbach (2008)	Forums	Movie success and academy awards	Intensity, positivity and trendsetter variables	Time-Series Multiple Regression Model
Seiffertt & Wunsch (2008)	Several	Variables on financial markets	Many types discussed	Different Model Types Discussed
Tang & Liu (2010)	Flickr and YouTube	Online behaviors	Social Dimension variables	SocioDim, several advanced models combined
Karabulut (2013)	Facebook	Stock prices	Facebook GNH (General national happiness), positivity, negativity	Time-Series Multiple Regression Model
Mao, Counts, & Bollen (2014)	Twitter	UK, US, and Canadian stock markets	'Bullish' or 'bearish' mentions on Twitter	Time-Series Multiple Regression Model
Bollen, Mao, & Zeng (2011)	Twitter	DJIA	Twitter moods and feelings	Self-Organizing Fuzzy Neural Network
Bollen, Mao, & Pepe (2011)	Twitter	Socio-economic events	Twitter moods and feelings	Extended version of: Profile of mood states
Eichstaedt et al. (2015)	Twitter	Heart attacks	Anger, stress and fatigue	Time-Series Multiple Regression Model
De Choudhury, Gamon, Counts, & Horvitz (2013)	Twitter	Depression	Language, emotion, style, ego-network, and user engagement	Support Vector Machine
De Choudhury, Counts, & Horvitz (2013)	Twitter	Postpartum changes in emotion and behaviour	Engagement, emotion, ego-network and linguistic style	Support Vector Machine
De Choudhury, Counts, Horvitz, & Hoff (2014)	Facebook	Postpartum depression	Social activity and interaction	OLS Regression Model
Weeks & Holbert (2013)	Facebook, Twitter, YouTube	Dissemination of News Content in Social Media	Gender, age, web engine news search, email news activity and cell phone activity	Decision Tree Model
Gilbert & Karahalios (2009)	Facebook	Tie strength	15 communication variables	Time-Series Multiple Regression Model
Won et al. (2013)	Weblog social media data	Suicide	Suicide related words and mentions	Time-Series Multiple Regression Model

there is a high potential for the associated stock price to also being modelled with social media data. In the case of epidemiology, all social media texts on flu can also be categorized in to the different domain-specific phases of spread, incubation, immunity, resistance, susceptibility etc.

Social Media Data Types

For modelling stock prices, Twitter and Google Trends have proven to be the best platforms. Twitter and Google Trends beat Facebook for stock price modelling because of higher data volume and immediacy. On the other hand, Facebook data have been successfully used for modelling sales, human emotions, personalities and human relations to a brand. In general, picture and video based social media platforms such as Instagram, YouTube and Netflix are becoming more prevalent and we expect them to become more relevant for predictive models in the future.

Independent and Dependent Variables

As can be seen from Table 20.1, a wide range of dependent variables have been modelled: sales, stock prices, Net Promoter Score, happiness, feelings, personalities, interest areas, social groups, diseases, epidemics, suicide, crime, radicalization, civil unrest. The independent variables used reflect the human social relations to the dependent variables mainly consist of measures of social media activity, feelings, personalities and sentiment.

Statistical Methods Employed

We find that a wide range of statistical models for predictive analytics have been used including Regression, Neural Network, SVM, Decision Trees, ARIMA, Dynamic Systems, Bayesian Networks, and combined models.

In the next section, we present an illustrative case study of predictive modelling with big social data.

AN ILLUSTRATIVE CASE STUDY OF PREDICTIVE MODELLING

In this section, we demonstrate how social media data from Twitter and Facebook can be used to predict the quarterly sales of iPhones and revenues of clothing retailer, H&M, respectively. Based on a conceptual model of social data (Vatrapu, Mukkamala, & Hussain, 2014) consisting of Interactions (actors, actions, activities, and artifacts) and Conversations (topics, keywords, pronouns, and sentiments), and drawing from the domain-specific theories in advertising and sales from marketing (Belch, Belch, Kerr, & Powell, 2008), we developed and evaluated linear regression models that transform (a) iPhone tweets into a prediction of the quarterly iPhone sales with an average error close to the established prediction models from investment banks (Lassen et al., 2014) and (b) Facebook likes into a prediction of the global revenue of the fast fashion company, H&M. Our basic premise is that social media actions can serve as proxies for user's attention and as such have predictive power. The central research question for this demonstrative case study was: *To what extent can Big Social Data predict real-world outcomes such as sales and revenues?* Table 20.2 below presents the dataset collected for predictive analytics purposes of this case study.

We adhered to the methodological schematic recommended by Shmueli & Koppius (2011) for building empirical predictive models. We built on and extended the predictive analytics method of Asur & Huberman (2010) and examined if the principles for predicting movie revenue with Twitter data can also be used to predict iPhone sales and

Table 20.2 Overview of dataset

Company	Data Source	Time Period	Size of Dataset
Apple	Twitter	01-2007 to 10-2014	~500 million+ tweets containing 'iPhone' Collected using Topsy Pro (http://topsy.thisisthebrigade.com)
H&M	Facebook	01-2009 to 10-2014	~15 million data points from the official H&M Facebook page Collected using the Social Data Analytics Tool (Hussain & Vatrapu, 2014)

H&M revenues for Facebook data. That is, if a tweet/like can serve as a proxy for a user's attention towards a product and an underlying intention to purchase and/or recommend it. We extend Asur & Huberman (2010) in three important ways: (a) addition of Facebook social data, (b) theoretically informed time lagging of the independent variable, social media actions, and (c) domain-specific seasonal weighting of the dependent variable, sales/revenues. Figures 20.1 and 20.2 present the predicted vs. actual charts for Apple iPhone sales and H&M revenues respectively.

With regard to our prediction models, we observed a 5–10% average error from our predictive models with the actual sales and revenue data over three-year period of 2012–2014. In the case of the iPhone sales prediction model, our average error of 5% is not that far from the industry benchmark predictions of Morgan Stanley and IDC. That said, there are several challenges and limitations to the predictive analytics processes and their outcomes. First, we lack multiple cases to extensively evaluate and validate the overall prediction model. A second limitation is the emerging challenge for predictive analytics from social data associated with increasing sales in emerging markets such as China with its own unique social media ecosystem. By and large, the social media ecosystem of China does not overlap with that of Western countries to which Facebook and Twitter belong. We suspect that the effect of

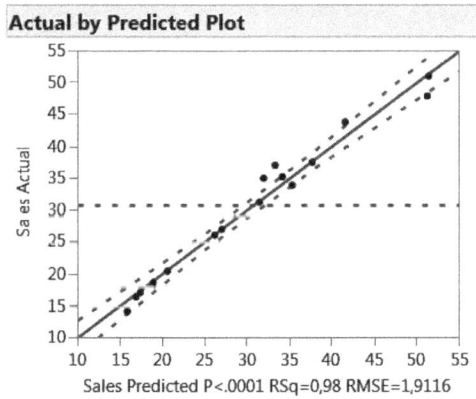

Figure 20.1 Predictive model of iPhone sales from Twitter data

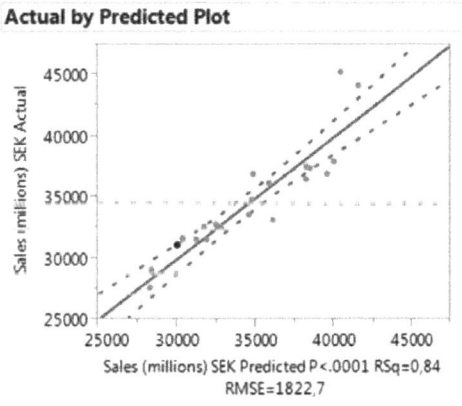

Figure 20.2 Predictive model of H&M revenues from Facebook data

non-overlapping social media ecosystems might be somewhat ameliorated for Veblen goods such as iPhones given the conspicuous consumption aspirations of a global middle class. This however remains an analytical challenge and restricts the predictive power of our H&M prediction model.

CONCLUSION

Predictive models offer powerful tools as numerical forecasts and assessments of their uncertainty alongside quantitative statements more generally may improve decisions in companies and by public authorities.

The overall advice is to go for a parsimonious, simple model that captures the most important features of the data, that fulfils the model assumptions and that provides a good fit both in sample and out of sample. Furthermore, it is important that even during the phase where the model is applied for its purpose, it performance is still monitored. We present a general model for predictive analytics of business outcomes from social media data below.

$$y_t = \beta_a \times A_t + \beta_p \times P_t + \beta_d \times D_t + \beta_o \times O_t + \varepsilon_t$$

Where:
y_t = Outcome variable of interest
A_t = Accumulated time-lagged social media activity associated with outcome variable at time t

$$A_t = \Sigma A_{st}$$

A_{st} = Social media activity in terms of actions by actors on artifacts associated with outcome variable at time t
P_t = Individual or social psychological attribute(s) at time t
D_t = Social media dissemination factors
O_t = Other explanatory factors

A final word of caution will end this chapter: any predictive model is based on a certain set of information. It is necessarily backward-looking as it relies on historical data and irrespectively of how carefully the model specification and evaluation is done, there is no guarantee that the prediction of future values of the variable of interest will be reliable. The patterns or theories that the model relies on may break down and render the model useless for predictive purposes. That being said, careful predictive modelling is probably the best that can be done and, if applied and used following the state of the art with most emphasis placed on short term forecasting, predictive modelling is a very valuable tool.

ACKNOWLEDGEMENTS

We thank the members of the Centre for Business Data Analytics (http://bda.cbs.dk) for their feedback.

The authors were partially supported by the project Big Social Data Analytics: Branding Algorithms, Predictive Models, and Dashboards funded by Industriens Fond (The Danish Industry Foundation). Any opinions, findings, interpretations, conclusions or recommendations expressed in this chapter are those of its authors and do not represent the views of the Industriens Fond (The Danish Industry Foundation).

REFERENCES

Asur, S., & Huberman, B. A. (2010). *Predicting the future with social media.* Paper presented at the IEEE/WIC/ACM International Conference on Web Intelligence and Intelligent Agent Technology (WI-IAT).

Belch, G. E., Belch, M. A., Kerr, G. F., & Powell, I. (2008). *Advertising and promotion: An integrated marketing communications perspective*: McGraw-Hill, London.

Bollen, J., & Mao, H. (2011). Twitter mood as a stock market predictor. *Computer*, 91–94.

Bollen, J., Mao, H., & Pepe, A. (2011). Modeling public mood and emotion: Twitter sentiment and socio-economic phenomena. *ICWSM, 11*, 450–453.

Bollen, J., Mao, H., & Zeng, X. (2011). Twitter mood predicts the stock market. *Journal of Computational Science, 2*(1), 1–8.

Bothos, E., Apostolou, D., & Mentzas, G. (2010). Using Social Media to Predict Future Events with Agent-Based Markets. *IEEE Intelligent Systems, 25*(6), 50–58.

Chatfield, C. (2002). Confessions of a pragmatic statistician. *Journal of the Royal Statistical Society: Series D (The Statistician), 51*(1), 1–20.

Choi, H., & Varian, H. (2012). Predicting the present with Google Trends. *Economic Record, 88*(s1), 2–9.

Chunara, R., Andrews, J. R., & Brownstein, J. S. (2012). Social and News Media Enable Estimation of Epidemiological Patterns Early in the 2010 Haitian Cholera Outbreak. *American Journal of Tropical Medicine and Hygiene, 86*(1), 39–45. doi: 10.4269/ajtmh.2012.11-0597

Chung, J. E., & Mustafaraj, E. (2011). *Can collective sentiment expressed on Twitter predict political elections?* Paper presented at the AAAI.

Cioffi-Revilla, C. (2013). *Introduction to Computational Social Science: Principles and Applications*: Springer Science & Business Media.

Conover, M. D., Gonçalves, B., Ratkiewicz, J., Flammini, A., & Menczer, F. (2011). *Predicting the political alignment of Twitter users.* Paper presented at the Privacy, Security, Risk and Trust (PASSAT) and 2011 IEEE 3rd International Conference on Social Computing (SocialCom).

Conte, R., Gilbert, N., Bonelli, G., Cioffi-Revilla, C., Deffuant, G., Kertesz, J., Loreto, V., Moat, S., Nadal, J.P., Sanchez, A., Nowak, A & Helbing, D. (2012). Manifesto of computational social science. *European Physical Journal, 214*(1), 325–346.

Council, N. (2013). Frontiers in massive data analysis: The National Academies Press Washington, DC.

Culotta, A. (2010). *Towards detecting influenza epidemics by analyzing Twitter messages.* Paper presented at the Proceedings of the first workshop on social media analytics.

De Choudhury, M., Counts, S., & Horvitz, E. (2013). *Predicting postpartum changes in emotion and behavior via social media.* Paper presented at the Proceedings of the SIGCHI Conference on Human Factors in Computing Systems.

De Choudhury, M., Counts, S., Horvitz, E. J., & Hoff, A. (2014). *Characterizing and predicting postpartum depression from shared Facebook data.* Paper presented at the Proceedings of the 17th ACM conference on Computer supported cooperative work and social computing.

De Choudhury, M., Gamon, M., Counts, S., & Horvitz, E. (2013). *Predicting Depression via Social Media.* Paper presented at the ICWSM.

Dijkman, R., Ipeirotis, P., Aertsen, F., & van Helden, R. (2015). Using Twitter to predict sales: a case study. *arXiv preprint arXiv:1503.04599*.

Eichstaedt, J.C., Schwartz, H.A., Kern, M.L., Park, G., Labarthe, D.R., Merchant, R.M., Jha, S., Agrawal, M., Dziurzynski, L.A., Sap, M. and Weeg, C. Psychological language on Twitter predicts county-level heart disease mortality. *Psychological science, 26*(2), 159–169.

Eysenbach, G. (2011). Can tweets predict citations? Metrics of social impact based on Twitter and correlation with traditional metrics of scientific impact. *Journal of medical Internet Research, 13*(4), e123.

Evangelos K, Efthimios T and Konstantinos T. (2013) Understanding the predictive power of social media. *Internet Research, 23*(5), 544–559.

Gilbert, E., & Karahalios, K. (2009). *Predicting tie strength with social media.* Paper presented at the Proceedings of the SIGCHI conference on human factors in computing systems.

Golder, S. A., & Macy, M. W. (2011). Diurnal and seasonal mood vary with work, sleep, and daylength across diverse cultures. *Science, 333*(6051), 1878–1881.

Gruhl, D., Guha, R., Kumar, R., Novak, J., & Tomkins, A. (2005). *The predictive power of online chatter.* Paper presented at the Proceedings of the 11th ACM SIGKDD international conference on knowledge discovery in data mining.

Hughes, D. J., Rowe, M., Batey, M., & Lee, A. (2012). A tale of two sites: Twitter vs. Facebook and the personality predictors of social media usage. *Computers in Human Behavior, 28*(2), 561–569.

Hussain, A., & Vatrapu, R. (2014). Social Data Analytics Tool (SODATO). In M. Tremblay, D. VanderMeer, M. Rothenberger, A. Gupta, & V. Yoon (Eds.), *Advancing the Impact of Design Science: Moving from Theory to Practice* (Vol. 8463, pp. 368–372): Springer International Publishing, Switzerland.

Hussain, A., Vatrapu, R., Hardt, D., & Jaffari, Z. (2014). Social Data Analytics Tool: A Demonstrative Case Study of Methodology and Software. In M. Cantijoch, R. Gibson, & S. Ward (Eds.), *Analyzing Social Media Data and Web Networks* (pp. 99–118): Palgrave Macmillan, UK..

Hyndman, R. J., & Athanasopoulos, G. (2014). *Forecasting: principles and practice*: OTexts: https://www.otexts.org/fpp/

Jansen, B. J., Zhang, M., Sobel, K., & Chowdury, A. (2009). Twitter power: Tweets as electronic word of mouth. *Journal of the American Society for Information Science and Technology, 60*(11), 2169–2188.

Karabulut, Y. (2013). *Can Facebook predict stock market activity?* Paper presented at the AFA 2013 San Diego Meetings Paper.

Krauss, J., Nann, S., Simon, D., Gloor, P. A., & Fischbach, K. (2008). *Predicting Movie Success and Academy Awards through Sentiment and Social Network Analysis*. Paper presented at the ECIS.

Lassen, N., Madsen, R., & Vatrapu, R. (2014). Predicting iPhone Sales from iPhone Tweets. *Proceedings of IEEE 18th International Enterprise Distributed Object Computing Conference (EDOC 2014), Ulm, Germany*, 81–90, ISBN: 1541-7719/1514, doi: 1510.1109/EDOC.2014.1520.

Lazer, D., Pentland, A.S., Adamic, L., Aral, S., Barabasi, A.L., Brewer, D., Christakis, N., Contractor, N., Fowler, J., Gutmann, M. and Jebara, T. Computational Social Science. *Science, 323*(5915), 721–723. doi: 10.1126/science.1167742

Li, J., & Cardie, C. (2013). Early stage influenza detection from Twitter. *arXiv preprint arXiv:1309.7340*.

Mao, H., Counts, S., & Bollen, J. (2014). *Quantifying the effects of online bullishness on international financial markets*. Paper presented at the ECB Workshop on Using Big Data for Forecasting and Statistics, Frankfurt, Germany.

Radosavljevic, V., Grbovic, M., Djuric, N., & Bhamidipati, N. (2014). *Large-scale World Cup 2014 outcome prediction based on Tumblr posts*. Paper presented at the KDD Workshop on Large-Scale Sports Analytics, New York.

Ritterman, J., Osborne, M., & Klein, E. (2009). *Using prediction markets and Twitter to predict a swine flu pandemic*. Paper presented at the 1st international workshop on mining social media, Sevilla, Spain.

Robertson, S., & Vatrapu, R. (2010). Digital Government. In B. Cronin (Ed.), *Annual Review of Information Science and Technology* (Vol. 44, pp. 317–364).

Robertson, S., Vatrapu, R., & Medina, R. (2010a). Off the wall political discourse: Facebook use in the 2008 US Presidential election. *Information Polity, 15*(1), 11–31.

Robertson, S., Vatrapu, R., & Medina, R. (2010b). Online Video 'Friends' Social Networking: Overlapping Online Public Spheres in the 2008 U.S. Presidential Election. *Journal of Information Technology & Politics, 7*(2–3), 182–201. doi:10.1080/19331681003753420

Sang, E. T. K., & Bos, J. (2012). *Predicting the 2011 Dutch senate election results with Twitter*. Paper presented at the Proceedings of the Workshop on Semantic Analysis in Social Media, Avignon, France.

Seiffertt, J., & Wunsch, D. (2008). Intelligence in Markets: Asset Pricing, Mechanism Design, and Natural Computation [Technology Review]. *Computational Intelligence Magazine, IEEE, 3*(4), 27–30.

Shen, W., Wang, J., Luo, P., & Wang, M. (2013). *Linking named entities in tweets with knowledge base via user interest modeling*. Paper presented at the Proceedings of the 19th ACM SIGKDD international conference on Knowledge discovery and data mining, Chicago.

Shmueli, G. (2010). To explain or to predict? *Statistical Science, 25*(3), 289–310.

Shmueli, G., & Koppius, O. R. (2011). Predictive analytics in information systems research. *MIS Quarterly, 35*(3), 553–572.

Skoric, M., Poor, N., Achananuparp, P., Lim, E.-P., & Jiang, J. (2012). *Tweets and votes: A study of the 2011 Singapore general election*. Paper presented at the System Science

(HICSS), 45th Hawaii International Conference on System Sciences, Hawaii.

Tang, L., & Liu, H. (2010). Toward predicting collective behavior via social dimension extraction. *Intelligent Systems, IEEE*, *25*(4), 19–25.

Tsakalidis, A., Papadopoulos, S., Cristea, A. I., & Kompatsiaris, Y. (2015). Predicting elections for multiple countries using Twitter and polls. *Intelligent Systems, IEEE*, *30*(2), 10–17.

Tumasjan, A., Sprenger, T. O., Sandner, P. G., & Welpe, I. M. (2010). Predicting elections with Twitter: What 140 characters reveal about political sentiment. *ICWSM*, *10*, 178–185.

Vatrapu, R., Mukkamala, R., & Hussain, A. (2014). *A Set Theoretical Approach to Big Social Data Analytics: Concepts, Methods, Tools, and Findings*. Paper presented at the Computational Social Science Workshop at the European Conference on Complex Systems 2014, Lucca.

Vatrapu, R., Robertson, S., & Dissanayake, W. (2008). Are Political Weblogs Public Spheres or Partisan Spheres? *International Reports on Socio-Informatics*, *5*(1), 7–26.

Vatrapu, R., Hussain, A., Lassen, N. B., Mukkamala, R., Flesch, B., & Madsen, R. (2015). Social set analysis: four demonstrative case studies. *Proceedings of the 2015 International Conference on Social Media & Society*. doi:10.1145/2789187.2789203

Voortman, M. (2015). Validity and reliability of web search based predictions for car sales.

Vosen, S., & Schmidt, T. (2011). Forecasting private consumption: survey-based indicators vs. Google trends. *Journal of Forecasting*, *30*(6), 565–578.

Weeks, B. E., & Holbert, R. L. (2013). Predicting dissemination of news content in social media a focus on reception, friending, and partisanship. *Journalism & Mass Communication Quarterly*, *90*(2), 212–232.

Won, H.-H., Myung, W., Song, G.-Y., Lee, W.-H., Kim, J.-W., Carroll, B. J., & Kim, D. K. (2013). Predicting national suicide numbers with social media data. *PloS one*, *8*(4), e61809.

Yu, Y., Duan, W., & Cao, Q. (2013). The impact of social and conventional media on firm equity value: A sentiment analysis approach. *Decision Support Systems*, *55*(4), 919–926.

Deception Detection and Rumor Debunking for Social Media

Victoria L. Rubin

The main premise of this chapter is that the time is ripe for more extensive research and development of social media tools that filter out intentionally deceptive information such as deceptive memes, rumors and hoaxes, fake news or other fake posts, tweets and fraudulent profiles. Social media users' awareness of intentional manipulation of online content appears to be relatively low, while the reliance on unverified information (often obtained from strangers) is at an all-time high. I argue that there is a need for content verification, systematic fact-checking and filtering of social media streams. This literature survey provides a background for understanding current automated deception detection research, rumor debunking, and broader content verification methodologies, suggests a path towards hybrid technologies, and explains why the development and adoption of such tools might still be a significant challenge.

INTRODUCTION

The goal of this chapter is to introduce readers to automated deception detection research, with a cursory look at the roots of the field in pre-social media data types. My intent is to draw attention to existing analytical methodologies and pose the question of their applicability to the context of social media. This chapter is divided into five parts as follows.

The Problem Statement section sets the stage for why deception detection methods are needed in the social media context by calling attention to the pervasiveness of social media and its potential role in manipulating user perceptions.

In the Background segment, I define deception and talk briefly about the roots and more contemporary forms of deception research. I provide the necessary background for what is currently known about people's overall abilities to spot lies and what constitutes predictive cues to tell the liars apart from truth tellers.

The Methodological Solutions part outlines some principles by which deception can be identified outside of social media context. I elaborate on predictive linguistic cues and methods used to identify deception. I follow up with an overview of several Online Tools that tackle the problem of deception detection and argue that more research and development of deception detection tools is needed, taking into account the specificity of each type and format of the social media stream.

In Broader Content Verification, I consider several important related concepts: rumors, credibility, subjectivity, opinions, and sentiment, evaluating appropriate techniques and method for identifying these phenomena.

Open Research and Development Problems are discussed in terms of the needed methodologies for three most recent social media phenomena: potential fraud on collaborative networking sites, pervasiveness of clickbaiting, and astroturfing by bots in social media. I briefly explain how each phenomenon relates to deception detection efforts, identifying these areas as most up-to-date niches requiring research and development.

I conclude that social media requires content verification analysis with a combination of previously known approaches for deception detection, as well as novel techniques for debunking rumors, credibility assessment, factivity analysis and opinion mining. Hybrid approaches may include text analytics with machine learning for deception detection, network analysis for rumor debunking and should incorporate world knowledge databases to fully take advantage of the linguistic, interpersonal, and contextual awareness.

PROBLEM STATEMENT: DECEPTION IN SOCIAL MEDIA CONTEXT

Although social media is difficult to define precisely as a phenomenon (McCay-Peet and Quan-Haase, 2016), most popular social networking and microblogging sites such as Facebook, Twitter, and LinkedIn include the function of online community building, personal messaging, and information sharing (Guadagno and Wingate, 2014). Digital news environments, I argue, are now becoming increasingly social, if not in the way they have been written, at least in the way they are accessed, disseminated, promoted, and shared.

The boundary between mainstream media news and user-generated content is slowly blurring (Chen et al., 2015b). Kang, Höllerer and O'Donovan (2015) observe that microblogging services have recently transformed from 'online journal or peer-communication platforms' to 'powerful online information sources operating at a global scale in every aspect of society, largely due to the advance of mobile technologies. Today's technology enables instant posting and sharing of text and/or multimedia content, allowing people on-location at an event or incident to serve as news reporters'. They cite studies of traditional media journalist practices showing that journalists rely heavily on social media for their information, and report about 54% of all U.S. journalists use microblogs to collect information and to report their stories (Kang et al., 2015).

It is also common for news readers to receive news via their social peers on networks like Facebook and Twitter. Thus, it is reasonable to consider tools and methodologies from fuller-form communication formats such as news in 'pre-social media era' as a starting point for deception detection and rumor debunking methodologies for the newer platforms and formats, whether they are shorter or longer, hashed or not, video-based or image-based. In this chapter, I focus primarily on text-based social media application, those that use text primarily as their medium of communication, while image-sharing (such as Flickr and Picassa) and video-sharing websites (such as YouTube and Vimeo) are left aside for separate consideration of potential ways to manipulate non-textual content.

A 2013 PEW research report (Holcomb et al., 2013) showed an increase in the number of users that keyword-search blogs as opposed to the traditional content streams. It means that a larger portion of information comes from complete strangers rather than from known or trusted sources (Kang et al., 2015). 'With the massive growth of text-based communication, the potential for people to deceive through computer-mediated communication has also grown and such deception can have disastrous results' (Fuller et al., 2011, p. 8392).

The majority of social media contributors presumably communicate their messages to the best of their knowledge, abilities, and understanding of the situation at hand. Their messages primarily match their own beliefs. Social media streams are awash in biased, unreliable, unverified subjective messages, as well as ads and solicitations. Most social media consumers are typically aware of the subjective nature of social media streams, as well as the typical promotional intentions to attract online traffic and revenue. What is rarer is the realization that there are instances of posts, tweets, links, and so forth, that are designed to create false impressions or conclusions. Creating false beliefs in the social media consumers' minds can be achieved though disseminating outright lies, fake news, rumors or hoaxes, especially when the message appears to come from 'a friend' or another in-group member. Spam and phishing attacks in e-mail messages are more recognizable now that most users have experience receiving and filtering them, while the issue of information manipulation via social media is still poorly understood and rarely atop of users' minds. Malevolent intentions manifest themselves in inter-personal deception and can be damaging in person-to-person communication.

Social media users often hold a general presumption of goodwill in social media communication. Morris et al. (2012) found that, for instance, Twitter users 'are poor judges of truthfulness based on content alone, and instead are influenced by heuristics such as user name when making credibility assessments'. Some social media users may sacrifice caution for the sake of convenience, which may result in them being vulnerable to those who intend to deceive by disseminating false rumors or hoaxes in an effort to alter users' decision-making and patterns of behavior (beyond incentivizing to purchase via pushed advertising).

There are well-documented instances of deceptive, unconfirmed, and unverified tweets being picked up by main-stream media, giving them undeserving weight and credibility. In October 2008, three years prior to Steve Jobs' death, a citizen journalist posted a report falsely stating that Jobs had suffered a heart attack and had been rushed to a hospital. The original deliberate misinformation was quickly 're-tweeted' disregarding the fact that it came from CNN's iReport.com which allows 'unedited, unfiltered' posts. Although the erroneous information was later corrected, the 'news' of Jobs' alleged health crisis spread fast, causing confusion and uncertainty, and resulting in a rapid fluctuation of his company's stock on that day (per CBC Radio 'And the Winner Is', 31 March 2012). This is just one, albeit very public, example of deceptive information being mistaken for authentic reporting, and it demonstrates the very significant negative consequences such errors can create. Earlier examples of companies 'struck by phony press releases' include the fiber optic manufacturer, Emulex, and Aastrom Biosciences (Mintz, 2002). Research further cites evidence of false tweets discovered in U.S. Senate campaigns, in reporting of the Iranian election protests, and in the coverage of unfolding natural disasters such as the Chilean earthquake (Morris et al., 2012). Social search tools (such as Bing Social Search [bing.com/social] and Social Seeking [socialseeking.com]) can also amplify undesirable memes, and while some false reporting is relatively harmless (such as celebrity deaths), 'increased reliance on social media for actionable news items (*Should I vote for candidate X? Should I donate to victims of disaster Y?*) makes credibility a nontrivial concern' (Morris et al., 2012).

A 2015 Pew report documents that 'about six-in-ten online Millennials (61%) report getting political news on Facebook in a given week, a much larger percentage than turn to any other news source, according to a new Pew Research Center analysis'. About the same ratio of Baby Boomers [born 1946–1964] (60%) rely by contrast on local TV sources for political news (Pew 2015; Report by Mitchell and Page, 2015). Considering that younger users tend to rely on social media to inform themselves on breaking news, political issues, local and international events, the potential for harm from being intentionally misinformed over the internet is evident.

Researchers and developers for social media platforms are starting to consider methods and tools for filtering out intentionally manipulative messages and prompting unsuspecting users to fact-check. The context of social media is unique, diverse in formats, and relatively new, but lying and deceiving has been at play in other forms of human communication for ages. The next section overviews the roots of deception studies and the contemporary interpretation of the phenomenon in deception research. I also outline how deception can be detected in texts, specifically, with the use of state-of-the-art text analytics. Though no 'bullet-proof' mechanism currently exists to screen out all memes, hoaxes, rumors, and other kinds of malevolent manipulative messages, it is perhaps time to consider what methodologies can be harnessed from the previous years in deception detection research, and how those methods can be successfully ported to the new context of social media.

BACKGROUND: DECEPTION AND TRUTH BIAS

Since the ancient times, the concepts of *truth*, *falsehood*, *lying*, and *deception* have been pondered over by great thinkers, from the ancient Greek philosophers (Socrates, Plato, Aristotle) to central figures in modern Western philosophy (Emmanuel Kant, Ludwig Wittgenstein). Sissela Bok writes in her analysis of morality (1989) that 'lying has always posed a moral problem'; for instance, Aristotle believed falsehood in itself to be 'mean and culpable', and Kant regarded truthfulness as an 'unconditional duty which holds in all circumstances'.

In the 21st century *truthfulness* and *honesty* remain essential for successful communication, while deception is still largely frowned upon and widely condemned (Walczyk et al., 2008). Deception (with or without computer mediation) violates the cooperative principle for successful communication, expressed as a failure to observe at least one of the four maxims, as postulated by a philosopher of language, Paul Grice (1975): say what you believe to be true (Maxim of Quality), do not say more than needed (Maxim of Quantity), stay on the topic (Maxim of Relevance), and do not be vague (Maxim of Manner) (Rubin, 2010b).

Recent Inter-Personal Psychology and Computer-Mediated Communication studies define *deception* as an intentional and knowing attempt on the part of the sender of the message to create a false belief or false conclusion in the mind of the receiver of the message (e.g., Buller and Burgoon, 1996; Zhou et al., 2004). The definition typically excludes self-deception and unintentional errors since in those exceptions the senders' beliefs still match the intended communicated message. Lying is considered to be just one kind of deception – that of falsification – as opposed to other deceptive varieties such as omission, equivocation, or concealment.

From Inter-Personal Psychology studies we also know that people are generally *truth-biased*, or more predisposed towards veracity than deception. 'The truth bias is the presumption of truth in interpersonal interactions and the tendency to judge an interpersonal message as truthful rather than deceptive, irrespective of the actual truth of the message. Communicators are initially assumed to be truthful, and this assumption is possibly revised only if something in the situation evokes suspicion' (Van Swol, 2014). 'Numerous studies have found that independent of actual message veracity, individuals are much more likely to ascribe truth to other's messages than deceit' (Levine et al., 1999). There is no reason to presume that a subset of the general population wouldn't exhibit similar truth-bias tendencies.

Truth bias is also one of the potential explanations for why people are so inept at distinguishing truths from deception. Humans are notoriously poor lie detectors even when they are alerted to the possibility of being lied to (Vrij, 2004; Vrij, 2000; Vrij et al., 2012). A widely cited source that conducted a meta-analytical review of over 100 experiments with over 1,000 participants (DePaulo et al., 1997), concludes that on average people are able to distinguish a lie from a truthful statement with a mean accuracy rate of 54%, slightly above chance (Rubin and Conroy, 2012).

However, current theories of deceptive communicative behaviors suggest that deceivers communicate in qualitatively different ways from truth-tellers. Stable differences are found in behaviors of liars versus truth-tellers, especially evident in the verbal aspects of behavior (Ali and Levine, 2008). Liars are said to be identified by their words – not by what they say but by how they say it (Newman et al., 2003). There have been efforts to compile, test, and cluster predictive cues for deceptive messages in order to translate those findings into text analytical tools for detecting lies, primarily in longer forms of Computer Mediated Communication such as e-mail.

METHODOLOGICAL SOLUTIONS: DECEPTION DETECTION WITH LINGUISTIC PREDICTORS

Deception detection researchers generally agree that it is possible to detect deception based on linguistic cues. Several successful studies on deception detection have demonstrated the effectiveness of linguistic cue identification, as the language of truth-tellers is known to differ from that of deceivers (e.g., Bachenko et al., 2008; Larcker and Zakolyukina, 2012).

Though there is no clear consensus on reliable predictors of deception, deceptive cues can be identified in texts, extracted and clustered conceptually, for instance, to represent diversity, complexity, specificity, and non-immediacy of the analyzed texts. For instance, Zhou et al. (2004) reviewed five main systems developed for the analysis of the deception detection in textual communication: Criteria-Based Content Analysis (CBCA), Reality Monitoring (RM), Scientific Content Analysis (SCAN), Verbal Immediacy (VI) and Interpersonal Deception Theory (IDT). In each of the systems the authors identified criteria for classifying textual information either as deceptive or truthful, which in turn contributed towards the creation of the list of 27 linguistic features in eight broad conceptual clusters, as shown in Figure 21.1 (Zhou et al., 2004).

When implemented with standard classification algorithms (such as neural nets, decision trees, and logistic regression), such methods achieve 74% accuracy (Fuller et al., 2009). Existing psycholinguistic lexicons (e.g., LIWC by Pennebaker and Francis, 1999) have been adapted to perform binary text classifications for truthful versus deceptive opinions, with classifiers demonstrating a 70% average accuracy rate (Mihalcea and Strapparava, 2009).

Human judges, by a rough measure of comparison, achieved only 50–63% success rates in identifying deception, depending on what is considered deceptive on a seven-point scale truth-to-deception continuum: the more extreme degrees of deception are more transparent to judges (Rubin and Conroy, 2011).

Deception detection researchers also widely acknowledge a variation in linguistic cues as predictors across situations (Ali

I. QUANTITY	IV. NON-IMMEDIACY (continued)
1. **Word**: a written character or combination of characters representing a spoken word.	15. **Objectification**: an expression given to (as an abstract notion, feeling, or ideal) in a form that can be experienced by others & externalizes one's attitude.
2. **Verb**: a word that characteristically is the grammatical center of a predicate & expresses an act, occurrence, or mode of being.	16. **Generalizing terms**: refers to a person (or object) as a class of persons or objects that includes the person (or object).
3. **Noun phrase**: a phrase formed by a noun, its modifiers & determiners.	17. **Self-reference**: first person singular pronoun.
4. **Sentence**: a word, clause, or phrase or a group of clauses or phrases forming a syntactic unit which expresses an assertion, a question, a command, a wish, an exclamation, or the performance of an action, which usually begins with a capital letter & concludes with appropriate end punctuation.	18. **Group reference**: first person plural pronoun.
	V. EXPRESSIVITY
	19. **Emotiveness**: $\frac{\text{total \# of adjectives + total \# of adverbs}}{\text{total \# of nouns + total \# of verbs}}$
II. COMPLEXITY	**VI. DIVERSITY**
5. **Average number of clauses**: $\frac{\text{total \# of clauses}}{\text{total \# of sentences}}$	20. **Lexical diversity**: $\frac{\text{total \# of different words or terms}}{\text{total \# of words or terms}}$, which is the percentage of unique words in all words.
6. **Average sentence length**: $\frac{\text{total \# of words}}{\text{total \# of sentences}}$	21. **Content word diversity**: $\frac{\text{total \# of diff. content words}}{\text{total \# of content words}}$, where content words primarily express lexical meaning.
7. **Average word length**: $\frac{\text{total \# of characters}}{\text{total \# of words}}$	22. **Redundancy**: $\frac{\text{total \# of function words}}{\text{total \# of sentences}}$ where function words express primarily grammatical relationships.
8. **Average length of noun phrase**: $\frac{\text{total \# of words in noun phrases}}{\text{total \# of noun phrases}}$	
9. **Pausality**: $\frac{\text{total \# of punctuation marks}}{\text{total \# of sentences}}$	
III. UNCERTAINTY	**VII. INFORMALITY**
10. **Modifiers**: describes a word or makes the meaning of the word more specific. There are two parts of speech that are modifiers - adjectives & adverbs.	23. **Typographical error ratio**: $\frac{\text{total \# of misspelled words}}{\text{total \# of words}}$
11. **Modal verb**: an auxiliary verb that is characteristically used with a verb of predication & expresses a modal modification.	**VIII. SPECIFICITY**
12. **Uncertainty**: a word that indicates lack of sureness about someone or something.	24. **Spatio-temporal information**: information about locations or the spatial arrangement of people and/or objects, or information about when the event happened or explicitly describes a sequence of events.
13. **Other reference**: third person pronoun.	25. **Perceptual information**: indicates sensorial experiences such as sounds, smells, physical sensations & visual details.
IV. NON-IMMEDIACY:	**IX. AFFECT**
14. **Passive voice**: a form of the verb used when the subject is being acted upon rather than doing something.	26. **Positive affect**: conscious subjective aspect of a positive emotion apart from bodily changes.
	27. **Negative affect**: conscious subjective aspect of a negative emotion apart from bodily changes.

Figure 21.1 Summary of Zhou et al's (2004) linguistic features for deception detection. Twenty-seven linguistic-based features, amenable to automation, were grouped into nine linguistic constructs: quantity, complexity, uncertainty, nonimmediacy, expressivity, diversity, informality, specificity, and affect. All the linguistic features are defined in terms of their measurable dependent variables. (Redrawn from Zhou et al., 2004)

and Levine, 2008), across genres of communication, communicators (Burgoon et al., 2003) and cultures (Rubin, 2014). The main lesson we are learning is that the contexts in which deceptive communications occur matter greatly. For example, in synchronous text-based communication, deceivers produced more total words, more sense-based words (e.g., seeing, touching), and used fewer self-oriented but more other-oriented pronouns (Hancock et al., 2007). Compared to truth-tellers, liars showed lower cognitive complexity and used more negative emotion words (Newman et al., 2003).

In conference calls of financiers, Larcker and Zakolyukina (2012) found deceptive statements to have more general knowledge references and extreme positive emotions, and also fewer self-references, extreme negative emotions, as well as certainty and hesitation words.

In police interrogations, Porter and Yuille (1996b) found three significantly reliable, verbal indicators of deception (based on Statement Validity Analysis techniques used in law enforcement for credibility assessments): amount of detail reported, coherence, and admissions of lack of memory.

In descriptions of mock theft experiments, Burgoon and colleagues (2003) found deceivers' messages in their text-based chats were briefer (i.e., lower on quantity of language), less complex in their choice of vocabulary and sentence structure, and lacked specificity or expressiveness.

Deception is prominently featured in several domains such as politics, business, personal relations, science, and journalism (Rubin, 2010a). The use of language changes under the influence of different situational factors, genre, register, speech community, text and discourse type (Crystal, 1969). Therefore, the verbal cues for deception detection across various knowledge domains and various formats of social media may differ, though the computational algorithms or broader concepts (such as Zhou's clusters of diversity, complexity, specificity, and non-immediacy) may remain constant. When predictive linguistic cues are developed based on general linguistic knowledge (Höfer et al., 1996), linguistic cues could be portable to social media contexts (for instance, from e-mail to full-sentences forum posts). Nevertheless, if the subject areas are highly specialized, then when deciphering predictive cues, researchers should account for context specificity and format (Höfer et al., 1996; Porter and Yuille, 1996a; Köhnken and Steller, 1988; Steller, 1989). Table 21.1 summarizes various types of discourse or types of data that were addressed within various disciplines that study deceptive behaviors and their linguistic predictors. Notice that only a limited portion of data types can be found on social media (such as dating profiles and product and services reviews), while several non-social media types of discourse bare closer resemblance to each other (such as confessions and diary-style blogs).

How predictive cues of deception in microblogs (Twitter) may be different from more verbose formats (e-mails or conference call records) is yet to be studied. The social nature of the media can also provide other affordances that are typically inaccessible to face-to-face communication studies (such as past track-record, profiles, geolocation, and associated imagery) which could and should be matched against known truths or general world knowledge (encapsulated in such sources as Wikipedia and Wiktionaries). In other words, since context appears to be paramount to obtaining appropriate linguistic predictors of deceptive messages, contextual information should be intensely explored for social media deception detection. Past behaviors and profiles afford a more holistic interpretation of one's linguistic behavior and its correspondence to reality, since (ethical issues of surveillance, tracking and profiling aside) incongruities can be directly identified based on one's 'footprints' in social networking and communication.

ONLINE DECEPTION DETECTION TOOLS

In the past several years, conceptual tools dealing with language accuracy, objectivity, factuality and fact-verification have increased in importance in various subject areas due to rising amounts of digital information and the number of its users. Journalism, online marketing, proofreading and politics are to name a few. For example, in politics, *Politifact* (although based on manual fact-checking) and *TruthGoggles* sort the true facts in politics, helping citizens to develop better understanding of politicians statements.

In proofreading, *Stylewriter* and *AftertheDeadline* help users to identify

Table 21.1 Deception research disciplines and associated data type examples

Various contemporary disciplines that study deception for the purpose of its detection are listed with corresponding typical data types that have been studied in the recent past. The data type distinctions are made based on the mode of obtaining data and the predominant discourse variety in the data type. Both columns are non-exhaustive.

Deception Research Discipline	Data Types

Inter-Personal Psychology, Computer-Mediated Communication	Elicited data
	   Data generated with imaginary tasks
	   Questionnaire data
	   Interview data
	   Case scenario discussions
	   Observation data
	   Lying games data
	Pre-existing messages (e-mails, diaries, etc.)
	Digitized records of any of the above
	Transcripts of oral interactions

Law Enforcement, Credibility Assessment, Police Work, Homeland Security	Court proceedings Police interrogations Credibility assessment transcripts Testimonies Pleas Alibi Court decisions

Deception Detection with Natural Language Processing and Machine Learning	Digital forms (texts, transcripts) of any of the above
	Crowdsourced data (e.g., Mechanical Turk)
	Crawled and harvested Web data
	Social media data in contexts of
	   fake product and service reviews
	   fake dating profiles
	   fudged online resumes
	   fake social network profiles
	   fake news
	   spamming and phishing
	   forged scientific work

stylistic and linguistic problems related to their writings. These tools use not only linguistic cues to resolve expression uncertainty problems, but also establish the factuality of events and statements using experts' opinions and additional necessary sources. For an overview of related content annotation and automation efforts, see Morante and Sporleder (2012); Sauri and Pustejovsky (2009; 2012).

Building on years of Deception Detection research in Interpersonal Psychology, Communication Studies, and Law Enforcement, a cutting-edge technology is emerging from the fields of Natural Language Processing and Machine Learning. Spurred by demand from practitioners for stable, quick and accurate deception detection tools, scholars have begun to create software for deception detection. A limited number of automated (or partially automated) online deception detection tools became available to the public by around 2010, including those by Chandramouli and Subbalakshmi (2012), Ott et al. (2011), Moffit and Giboney (2012) (evaluated by Rubin and Vashchilko, 2012).

The majority of the text-based analysis software uses different types of linguistic cues. Some of the common linguistic cues are the same across all deception software types, whereas other linguistic cues are derived specifically for specialized topics to generate additional linguistic cues. The complete automation of deception detection in written communication is mostly based on the linguistic cues derived from the classes of words from the Linguistic Inquiry and Word Count (LIWC) (Pennebaker et al., 2001). The main idea of LIWC coding is text classification according to truth conditions. LIWC has been extensively employed to study deception detection (Vrij et al., 2007; Hancock et al., 2007; Mihalcea and Strapparava, 2009).

In 2014, Lukoianova and Rubin proposed that veracity should be considered as an important component of big data assessment, assuming that social media posts, tweets, reviews and other platform messages are a large component of big data (see Figure 21.2 for an explanation of the proposed veracity index calculation). Passing the deception detection test in Social Media can verify the source's intention to create a truthful impression in the readers' mind, supporting sources trustworthiness and credibility. On the other hand, failing the test immediately alerts the user to potential alternative motives and intentions and necessitates further fact verification (Lukoianova and Rubin, 2014).

As of early 2016, researchers declared that the field of automated detection as applied to 'social media' is a relatively new one. There have so far been only a handful of works that

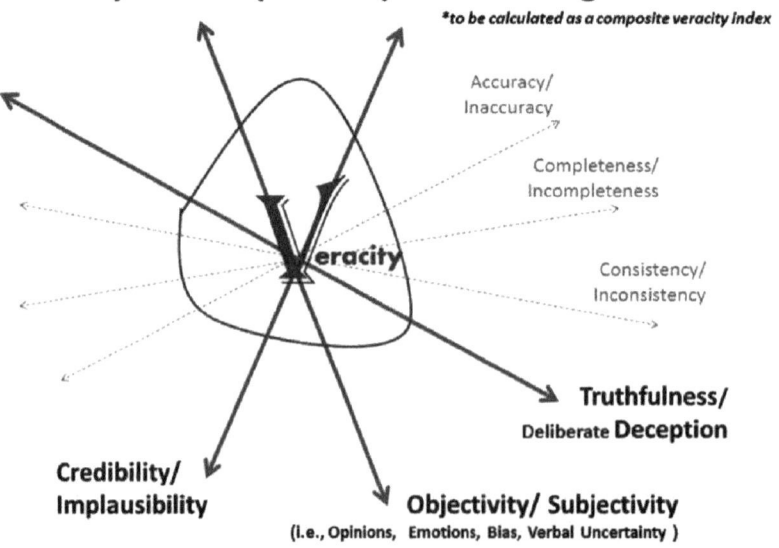

Figure 21.2 Conceptualization of the components of big data veracity. Veracity – as the fourth V in addition to Volume, Velocity and Variety – portrayed across three primary orthogonal dimensions in the conceptual space – objectivity, truthfulness, credibility. The dimensions intersect in the center and the nebula represents a certain degree of variability within the phenomena that together constitute the big data veracity. Secondary dimensions of lesser concern in textual data are presented in dotted lines. The tree main components of veracity index are normalized to the (0,1) interval with 1 indicating maximum objectivity, truthfulness and credibility, and 0, otherwise. Then, the big data veracity index is calculated as an average of the three, assuming that each of the dimensions equally contributes to veracity establishment. The three primary dimensions reduce 'noise' and potential errors in subsequent inferences from the textual big data due to minimization of bias, intentional misinformation, and implausibility

address this problem (Vosoughi, 2015). Even if automated social media verification tools are on the market or in research and development, they are not particularly well-known to general social media users. Nor have they received much attention in mainstream North American media coverage, or in the scientific community. The wealth of predictive linguistic cues knowledge has yet to be tested in the social media context. It is worth noting that other terminology may have been used to refer to deception detection, such as *veracity prediction* and *rumor debunking* or *rumor busting*, and those methodologies – as well as several other 'close relatives' pertaining to content verification – will be explored in the next section.

BROADER CONTENT VERIFICATION: RUMORS, CREDIBILITY, AND OPINONS

There are several ways to look at the problem of social media content verification. Detection of deceptive messages based on what has been said (or linguistic cues) is only one part of the problem. The broader context – in terms of positioning of the message sources in the network, their reputation, trustworthiness, credibility, expertise, as well as propensity for spreading rumors – should be taken into account. How accurate, well-informed and objective are the sources? Ideally, for decision making, social media users should rely on truthful, accurate, and complete information from credible expert sources.

Rumors and Rumor Debunking

Social media often amplifies and disseminates word-of-mouth rumors by reaching wider audiences. Rumors should not be directly equated to deceptive messages, even though most people as well as experts in the rumor debunking research agree that rumors are harmful. Among undesirable responses to rumors Matthews (2013) lists defamation, protests, and destruction of properties, spread of fear, hate, or euphoria. Rumors on Twitter have been known to influence the stock market. 'Perhaps, one of the most infamous cases is of the hacked AP account tweeting a rumor that Barack Obama had been injured in an explosion at the White House. The tweet caused the S&P to decline and wipe $130 Billion in stock value in a matter of seconds' (Liu et al., p. 1867).

The defining feature of a rumor is lack of verifiability at the moment of dissemination. Merriam Webster's Dictionary defines *a rumor* as 'a statement or report current without known authority for its truth' or 'talk or opinion widely disseminated with no discernible source' (Merriam-Webster Online Dictionary, 2016). Some dictionary definitions emphasize 'the word of mouth' as the method of spreading hearsay (The Free Dictionary, 2016) disregarding how prevalent the spread of rumors can be over social networks. Though it is still the dawn of rumor detection studies, there have been further clarifications in a handful of current works which take into account social media reality. For instance, Vosoughi (2015) makes it clear that *a rumor* is 'an unverified assertion that starts from one or more sources and spreads over time from node to node in a network' (p. 22). In his recent dissertation on the topic, he continues to explain the subtleties of the rumor spread on Twitter, how rumor is related to deception, and, most importantly, what it means to resolve a rumor algorithmically: 'On Twitter, a rumor is a collection of tweets, all asserting the same unverified statement (however the tweets could be, and almost assuredly, are worded differently from each other), propagating through the communications network (in this case Twitter), in a multitude of cascades. A rumor can end in three ways: it can be resolved as either true (factual), false (non-factual) or remain unresolved. There are usually several rumors

CATEGORY	FEATURE NAME
SOURCE CREDIBILITY	Is trusted/satirical news account Has trusted/satirical news url Profile has url from top domains Client application name
SOURCE IDENTITY	Profile has person name Profile has location Profile includes profession information
SOURCE DIVERSITY	Has multiple news/non-news urls after dedup Deduped tweets' text is dissimilar
SOURCE LOCATION & WITNESS	If tweet location matches event location If profile location matches event location Has witness phrases, i.e., "I see" and "I hear"
MSG. BELIEF	Is support, negation, question or neutrality
EVENT PROPAGATION	Event topic Retweet, mention, hashtag h-index Max reply/retweet graph4 size/depth

Figure 21.3 Verification feature for rumor debunking on Twitter (Liu et al., 2015). The six proposed categories of verification features largely based on insights from journalists

about the same topic, any number of which can be true or false. The resolution of one or more rumors automatically resolves all other rumors about the same topic. For example, take the number of perpetrators in the Boston Marathon bombings; there could be several rumors about this topic:

1 Only one person was responsible for this act.
2 This was the work of at least two or more people.
3 There are only two perpetrators.
4 It was at least a team of five that did this.

Once rumor number 3 was confirmed as true, it automatically resolved the other rumors as well. (In this case, rumors 1 and 4 resolved to be false and rumor 2 resolved to be true)' (Vosoughi, 2015 p. 22–23).

Traditionally, rumors have been resolved with either common sense judgements or with further investigations by professionals. There are several existing examples of rumor detection systems, some with real time algorithmic veracity prediction that is potentially faster than human verification by professionals. For instance, Liu and his colleagues from the Thompson Reuters R&D group (2015), observed the need to invent tools for journalists to verify rumors. They thus proposed a method to automatically debunk rumors on Twitter using social media. Figure 21.3 shows the types of features that the rumor debunking system considers in its real-time analysis.

Most existing algorithms for debunking rumors, however, follow Castillo, Mendoza, and Poblete's work (Castillo et al., 2011; Mendoza et al., 2010) employing variations on data used and features extracted (Wu et al., 2015; Yang et al., 2012). Qazvinian and colleagues (2011) focus on rumor-related tweets to match certain regular expression of the keyword query and the users' believing behavior about those rumor-related tweets; both pieces of information are instrumental in isolating rumors. Mendoza and colleagues (2010) analyze user behavior through tweets during the Chilean earthquake that year: 'they analyze users' retweeting topology network and the difference in the rumor diffusion pattern on Twitter environment than on traditional news platforms' (Yang et al., 2012). Moving away from Twitter, Yang and colleagues (2012) studied Sina Weibo, China's leading micro-blogging service provider that functions like a Facebook–Twitter hybrid. They collected and annotated a set of rumor-related microblogs based on the Weibo's

Category	Features	Description
CONTENT	HAS MULTIMEDIA	Whether the microblog contains pictures, videos, or audios
	SENTIMENT	The numbers of positive and negative emoticons used in the microblog
	HAS URL	Whether the microblog includes a URL pointing to an external source
	TIME SPAN	The time interval between the time of posting and user registration
CLIENT	CLIENT PROGRAM USED	The type of client program used to post a microblog: web-client or mobile-client
ACCOUNT	IS VERIFIED	Whether the user's identity is verified by Sina Weibo
	HAS DESCRIPTION	Whether the user has personal descriptions
	GENDER OF USER	The user's gender
	USER AVATAR TYPE	Personal, organization, and others
	NUMBER OF FOLLOWERS	The number of user's followers
	NUMBER OF FRIENDS	The number of users who have a mutual following relationship with this user
	NUMBER OF MICROBLOGS POSTED	The number of microblogs posted by this user
	REGISTRATION TIME	The actual time of user registration
	USER NAME TYPE	Personal real name, organization name, and others
	REGISTERING PLACE	The location information taken at user's registration
LOCATION	EVENT LOCATION	The location where the event mentioned by rumor-related microblogs happened
PROPAGATION	IS RETWEETD	Whether the microblog is original or is a retweet of another microblog
	NUMBER OF COMMENTS	The number of comments on the microblog
	NUMBER OF RETWEETS	The number of retweets of the microblog

Figure 21.4 Rumor busting features for Sina Weibo Microblogs (Yang, 2012). Grouped into five broad types (content-based, client-based, account-based, propagation-based, and location-based), rumor detection features were extracted on Sina Weibo, the Chinese leading micro-blogging platform, for the binary classification purposes (rumor or not). Each predictive feature is described in terms of its implementation

rumor-busting service, as a result proposed extra. Figure 21.4 lists the features used for the Weibo *rumor buster*.

Credibility and Credibility Assessment

Credibility assessment tools have explored broader contextual profiles than deception detection and rumor debunking methods. The concept of credibility is intrinsically linked to believability, which is not necessarily equivalent to truthfulness or veracity but is rather a reflection of perceived truth.

Much has been written in Library and Information Science and Human-Computer Interaction on credibility assessment and a variety of checklist schemes to verify the credibility and stated cognitive authority of the information providers. See Rieh (2010) for a summary of the historical development of the credibility research in such fields as Psychology and Communication, and a recent overview of credibility typologies in LIS (e.g., source credibility, message credibility, and media credibility) and HCI (e.g., computer credibility: presumed credibility, reputed credibility, surface credibility, and experienced credibility).

The concept of *trust* is often used in everyday language and communication in making trustworthiness decisions. Hardin (2001) noticed a pervasive conceptual slippage that involves a misleading inference from the everyday use of trust: many ordinary language statements about trust seem to conceive trust, at least partly, as a matter of behavior, rather than an expectation or a reliance. Trust, in Inter-Personal and Organizational Psychology, is seen as a positive expectation of a trusting entity regarding the behavior of the trustee (the trusted entity) in a context that entails risk to the trustor (e.g., Marsh and Dibben, 2003). Fogg and Tseng (1999) firmly equate *credibility* to *believability* and *trust* to *dependability* (p. 41). *Content trust* is a trust judgment about a particular piece of information in a given context (Gil and Artz, 2006), for example, any statement regarding upcoming or ongoing political upheaval. While an entity can be trusted on the whole, each particular piece of information provided by the entity may still be questioned.

In relation to information shared on social media, *trust* is an assured reliance on the character, ability, strength, or truth of trusted content (Merriam-Webster Online Dictionary, 2016a, 2016b). In the Semantic Web literature, two types of trust are distinguished, one concerned with trust judgments about the providers of the information, and the other concerned with the nature of the information provided (Gil and Artz, 2006), for example, a judgment about the US Government provided by the activists of the 99% movement.

Rieh (2010) also underscores the importance of *trustworthiness* and *expertise*, as the two widely recognized components of credibility, although according to her, they are not always perceived together. 'An expert with the title of doctor or professor might have a reputation of being knowledgeable in a certain area but still might not be considered trustworthy for the tendency to unreliability or bias. A person may think of a friend as being honest and trustworthy in general, but the advice that the friend gives is not necessarily considered credible for the friend's lack of expertise' (Rieh, 2010, p. 1338).

Trustworthiness refers to the goodness or morality of the source and can be described with terms such as well-intentioned, truthful, or unbiased. Expertise refers to perceived knowledge of the source and can be described with terms such as knowledgeable, reputable, and competent (Tseng and Fogg, 1999).

Since the early 2000s, credibility tools have proliferated in the form of varying measures for credibility predictions, computational models, and algorithms. In 2011, Castillo, Mendoza, and Poblete (2011) proposed an algorithm that predicts the credibility of an event based on a set of features of a given set of tweets: they analyzed tweets related to 'trending topics' and use a binary supervised classification method from machine learning to place them into one of the two bins: credible or not credible. Kang, Höllerer, and O'Donovan (2015) identify and evaluate key factors that influence credibility perception on Twitter and Reddit (such as time spent posting or time spent reading posts of others). For their ground truth measure of the credibility of microblog data to achieve a 'more stable' estimate of credibility, Sikdar and colleagues (2013) combine manually annotated scores with observed network statistics (such as retweets).

Rubin and Liddy's (2006) short influential work on modeling credibility of blogs set out a framework for assessing blog credibility, with 25 indicators outlined within four main categories: blogger expertise and offline identity disclosure; blogger trustworthiness and value system; information quality; and appeals and triggers of a personal nature (see Table 21.2). Weerkamp and de Rijke (2008) estimated several of the indicators proposed in Rubin and Liddy (2006) and integrated them into their retrieval approach, ultimately showing that combining credibility indicators significantly improves retrieval effectiveness.

Even though certain features have been proven to be beneficial for more accurate blog retrieval in early work on weblog credibility in information retrieval, subjectivity research, and sentiment analysis (Rubin and Liddy, 2006; Weerkamp and de Rijke, 2008), the research has not yet resonated with the rumor debunking community, probably due to the isolation of the literatures or perhaps due to the differences between blogs and micro-blogs formats.

When analyzing social media platforms and formats of interaction, these two components of credibility should be considered separately. In summary, two credibility components, trustworthiness and expertise, are essential to making credibility (i.e., believability) judgments about trustworthiness (i.e., dependability) of sources and information

Table 21.2 Blog credibility assessment factors

1) Blogger's Expertise and Offline Identity Disclosure

   a) Name and geographic location (connecting on-line and off-line identities)
   b) Credentials
   c) Affiliations (personal and institutional)
   d) Blogrolls (both dynamic and static links)
   e) Stated competencies
   f) Mode of knowing (observation, deduction, trusted sources, etc.)
   g) Certainty level trends over time

Desired effect: knowledgeable, reputable, and competent blogger (Tseng and Fogg, 1999)

2) Blogger's Trustworthiness and Value System

   a) Biases (stated or otherwise displayed priorities)
   e.g., *'I don't care much for political correctness; I do care for accuracy and honesty (what people actually do rather than what they believe or say)'*
   b) Beliefs
   c) Opinions
   e.g., *'I had never got the hang of academic writing. The personal voice on blogs appealed to me so much more'*
   d) Honesty indicators
   e) Preferences
   f) Habits and behavioral patterns
   g) Slogans

3) Information Quality

   a) Completeness
   b) Accuracy
   c) Appropriateness
   d) Timeliness
   e) Information organization style (by categories, chronology, etc.)
   f) Match to prior expectations
   g) Match to information need
   h) Use of rhetoric devices *beneficial* to blogger's credibility

   - projecting concerns for readers' viewpoints
   - expressing modesty

   i) Use of rhetoric devices *detrimental* to blogger's credibility

   - having prior inaccuracies or errors
   - using artificially adorned figurative speech

Desire effect: complete, accurate, and appropriate information (Van House, 2004).

4) Appeals and Triggers of a Personal Nature

   a) Aesthetic appeal (i.e., design layout, typography, and color schemes)
   b) Literary appeal (i.e., writing style, wittiness, 'coolness' factor)
   c) Curiosity trigger
   d) Memory trigger (i.e., shared experiences)
   e) Personal connection (e.g., the source is an acquaintance or a competitor)
   f) Match between information need and availability
   g) Match to prior expectations
   h) Personal connection (e.g., the source is an acquaintance or a competitor of the blog-reader)

'The Wild Card': Information-seeker and information provider's interaction; hard to elicit and harvest automatically

Redrawn from Rubin and Liddy (2006) with additional details added from the associated presentation.

on social media, regardless of whether such judgments are expressed lexically with a vocabulary of trust as being trustworthy (i.e., dependable) or credible (i.e., believable).

Subjectivity and Opinion Mining, or Sentiment Analysis

Some fields, such as media theory, differentiate objectivity from credibility, both of which have been part of traditional journalistic practices since the 1950s, with credibility equated to believability (Johnson and Wiedenbeck, 2009). The main two reasons for using automation in deception detection are to increase objectivity by decreasing potential human bias in detecting deception (reliability of deception detection), and improve the speed in detecting deception (time processing of large amounts of text) (Hauch et al., 2012).

The concept of separating subjective judgments from objective became of great interest to Natural Language Processing researchers and gave rise to a very active area of research in sentiment analysis, or opinion mining. This field is concerned with analyzing written texts for people's attitudes, sentiments, and evaluations with text analytical techniques. Rubin (2006) traces the roots of subjectivity identification tools to the work of Wiebe et al. (2001) who proposed one of the first annotation schemes to classify and identify subjective and objective statements in texts. Prior to this work on subjectivity, an NLP system needed to determine the structure of a text – normally at least enough to answer 'Who did what to whom?' (Manning and Schütze, 1999). Since the early 2000s the revised question was no longer just 'Who did what to whom?' but rather 'Who thinks what about what's happening?' (Rubin, 2006).

The majority of current text analytical tools operating on social media datasets are disproportionally focused on sentiment analysis or polarity of opinions (positive, negative, or neutral), while the issues of credibility and verifiability are addressed less vigorously. (For a comprehensive overview of the field of opinion-mining and/or sentiment analysis, see Pang and Lee (2008) and a more recent survey by Liu (2012) as well as the introductory chapter by Thelwall (Chapter 32) in this book which is specifically focused on sentiment analysis tools for social media.) The work on identification of factuality or factivity in text-mining (e.g., Sauri and Pustejovsky, 2009, 2012; Morante and Sporleder, 2012) stems from the idea that people exhibit various levels of certainty (or epistemic modality) in their speech, and that these levels are marked linguistically (e.g., 'maybe', 'perhaps' vs 'probably' and 'for sure') and can be identified with text analytical techniques (Rubin, 2006; Rubin et al., 2004, 2006). Text analysis for factuality and writer's certainty is more beneficial to enhance deception detection capabilities than currently acknowledged in the field. For instance, opinion mining should not disregard factivity, objectivity, and certainty in stated opinions, since the lack of those properties in personal claims may render them useless and may skew aggregate analyses of social media data (such as product and services reviews).

Open Research and Development Problems

Outside of the previously discussed studies, there have been surprisingly few well-known efforts to verify information in social media feeds. Notable exceptions are studies of fake social network profiles (Kumar and Reddy, 2012), fake dating profiles (Toma and Hancock, 2012) and fake product reviews (Mukherjee et al., 2013), though the interactive social component may be less prominent in these studies as compared with more mainstream micro-blogging platforms such a Twitter and Sina Weibo.

Three relatively recent social media phenomena call for further investigations: the rise of collaborative networking sites and their openness to potential fraud, pervasiveness of clickbaiting, and astroturfing by social bots to influence users. Each is discussed in turn here.

Fraud on Academic Collaborative and Networking Sites

Relatively new academic collaborative and networking platforms (such as ResearchGate, Academia.edu, Mendeley, or ORCID) are yet to be studied for potential content manipulation and fraud. To the best of my knowledge, no deception detection tools are yet available within these profession-based collaborative scholarly sharing systems. Inaccurate self-presentation or presentation of others on their behalf (with or without their knowledge) can have ramifications for perceptions of scholars' productivity when socially shared data is used for altmetrics (bibliometrics and webometrics combined) of scholarly output. For instance, Ortega (2015) firmly links social and usage metrics at the authors' level to the authors' productivity and treats such metrics as a proxy for research impact. The newly coined field of *altemtrics* has not yet considered the margins of errors related to fraud, as most of the collaborative platform data seem to be currently taken for its face value.

Clickbaiting

Another issue that received little attention thus far is the prevalence of 'clickbait' in news streams (see Figure 21.5 for examples).

Clickbait refers to 'content whose main purpose is to attract attention and encourage visitors to click on a link to a particular web page' ['clickbait', n.d.] and has been implicated in the rapid spread of rumor and misinformation online. *Clickbaiting* can be identified through a consideration of the existence of certain linguistic patterns, such as the use of suspenseful language, unresolved pronouns, a reversal narrative style, forward referencing, image placement, reader's behavior and other important cues (Chen et al., 2015a).

Several social sharing platforms have standardized formats and visual presentation of delivery, regardless the source. Be it a satirical news piece from the Onion or a mainstream news piece from the New York Times, when 'liked' and 'shared' on

Figure 21.5 Examples of clickbait via Twitter (Chen, Conroy and Rubin, 2015 presentation). Two examples of *clickbaits* or online content that primarily aims to attract attention and encourage visitors to click on a link to a particular web page. The claims made in headlines of clickbaits and the associated imagery are often outrageous and/or misleading, as the reader finds out from reading the full message

Facebook or Twitter, the visual clues for potentially misleading information are minimal. The source's attribution is barely visible (see bottom of Figure 21.5). Tabloidization of news production and the shift towards digital content incentivizes the use of clickbait (Chen et al., 2015a), and it is yet unclear how skilled news readers on social media are in distinguishing this variety of content manipulation from legitimate news.

More work is necessary to distinguish fake news from authentic ones, and clickbaiting practices are just the tip of the iceberg. Other potential threats to veracity of news in social media streams include fraudulent journalistic reporting, hoaxes, and misleading satirical (fake) news taken at face value (Rubin et al., 2015). (For most recent developments in satirical news identification systems, see Rubin et al. (2016)).

Astroturfing by Social Bots

Astroturfing is a recent phenomenon and, by a definition found in an off-beat dictionary, is an attempt 'to create the impression of public support by paying people in the public to pretend to be supportive' (The Urban Dictionary, 2016). A new computerized form of such false support is slowly spreading on social media. Some social media platforms allow *sybil accounts* or *social bots* which rely on computer algorithms to imitate humans by automatically producing content and interacting with other users. Such social bots pollute authentic content and spread misinformation by manipulating discussions, altering user popularity ratings, and 'even perform[ing] terrorist propaganda and recruitment actions' (Davis et al., 2016).

Subrahmanian and colleagues (2016) identified three types of Twitter bots that engage in deceptive activities: 1) '*Spambots* spread spam on various topics'; 2) '*Paybots* illicitly make money. Some paybots copy tweet content from respected sources like @CNN but paste in micro-URLs that direct users to sites that pay the bot creator for directing traffic to the site'; 3) '*Influence* bots try to influence Twitter conversations on a specific topic. For instance, some politicians have been accused of buying influence on social media'. Subrahmanian and colleagues (2016) also notice that influence bots can 'pose a clear danger to freedom of expression', citing examples of the spread of radicalism, political disinformation and propaganda campaigns. The challenge has just been recently identified in the U.S. DARPA Social Media in Strategic Communications program competition to test the effectiveness of influence bot detection methods. The three most successful teams found machine learning techniques alone were insufficient because of a lack of training data, but thought a semi-automated process that included machine learning was useful. Their feature set is reminiscent of a variety of features discussed in this chapter thus far. For instance, *BotOrNot*, a publicly-available service since May 2014 (see Figure 21.6), leverages *more than one thousand features* to evaluate the extent to which a Twitter account exhibits similarity to the known characteristics of social bots (Davis et al., 2016).

The organizers of the DARPA challenge expect that social media influence bots will continue to proliferate and become more sophisticated in the next few years. The fear is that advertisers, criminals, politicians, nation states, and terrorists will try to further manipulate public opinion. This trend necessitates the need for significant enhancements in the analytical tools that help analysts detect influence bots (Subrahmanian et al., 2016).

CONCLUSION

In conclusion, social media with its new mechanisms for interaction and information flow requires a variety of content verification mechanisms, perhaps in combination with previously known deception detection approaches as well as novel techniques for rumor debunking, credibility assessments,

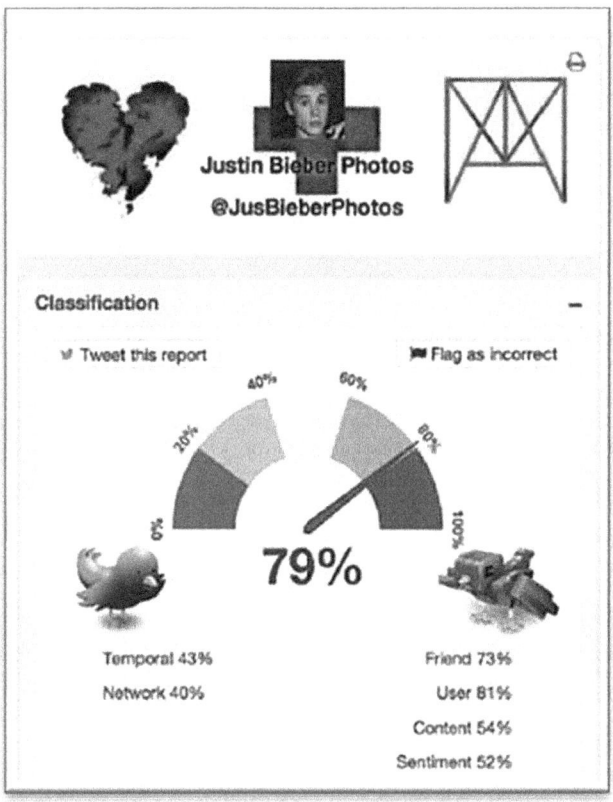

Figure 21.6 Dashboard-style interface of the *BotOrNot* system (Davis et al., 2015). The system evaluates the extent to which a Twitter account exhibits similarity to the known characteristics of social bots

and opinion mining. When analyzing social media for potentially deceptive content, it is important to apply methods that consider not just what is being said, but also how the message is presented, by who, and in what format and context. The hybrid approach should include text analytics, network analysis and world knowledge database incorporation to fully take advantage of linguistic, interpersonal, and contextual awareness. This chapter is a call for further research in developing further, as well as modifying and applying existing deception detection methods and rumor debunking technologies towards various social media forms and formats.

REFERENCES

Ali, M. & Levine, T. 2008. The Language of Truthful and Deceptive Denials and Confessions. *Communication Reports,* 21, 82–91.

Bachenko, J., Fitzpatrick, E. & Schonwetter, M. 2008. Verification and implementation of language-based deception indicators in civil and criminal narratives. Proceedings of the 22nd International Conference on Computational Linguistics – Volume 1. Association for Computational Linguistics, 41–48.

Bok, S. 1989. *Lying: Moral choice in public and private life.* New York, Vintage.

Buller, D. B. & Burgoon, J. K. 1996. Interpersonal Deception Theory. *Communication Theory,* 6, 203–242.

Burgoon, J. K., Blair, J. P., Qin, T. T. & Nunamaker, J. F. 2003. Detecting deception through linguistic analysis. *Intelligence and Security Informatics, Proceedings,* 2665, 91–101.

Castillo, C., Mendoza, M. & Poblete, B. 2011. Information credibility on twitter. Proceedings of the 20th international conference on World Wide Web. ACM, 675–684.

CBC Radio 'And the Winner is'. 31 March 2012. *News 2.0, Part II, Retrieved from* http://www.cbc.ca/andthewinneris/2012/03/27/news-20-1/ [Online]. [Accessed 17 August 2016].

Chandramouli, R. & Subbalakshmi, K. 2012. Text Analytics: Deception Detection and Gender Identification from Text. http://stealthserver01.ece.stevens-tech.edu/createtext?count=7840

Chen, Y., Conroy, N. J. & Rubin, V. L. 2015a. Misleading Online Content: Recognizing Clickbait as 'False News'. Proceedings of the 2015 ACM on Workshop on Multimodal Deception Detection. ACM, 15–19.

Chen, Y., Conroy, N. J. & Rubin, V. L. 2015b. News in an online world: the need for an automatic crap detector. Proceedings of the 78th ASIS&T Annual Meeting: Information Science with Impact: Research in and for the Community. American Society for Information Science, 81.

Crystal, D. 1969. *What is linguistics?*, London, Edward Arnold.

Davis, C. A., Onur Varol, O., Ferrara, E., Flammini, A. & Menczer, F. 2016. BotOrNot: A System to Evaluate Social Bots. *WWW'16 Companion.* Montréal, Québec, Canada.

Depaulo, B. M., Charlton, K., Cooper, H., Lindsay, J. J. & Muhlenbruck, L. 1997. The Accuracy-Confidence Correlation in the Detection of Deception. *Personality and Social Psychology Review,* 1, 346–357.

Fogg, B. J. & Tseng, H. 1999. The elements of computer credibility. SIGCHI conference on Human factors in computing systems: the CHI is the limit, Pittsburgh, Pennsylvania, United States. ACM.

Fuller, C. M., Biros, D. P. & Delen, D. 2011. An investigation of data and text mining methods for real world deception detection. *Expert Systems with Applications,* 38 (7), 8392-8398.

Gil, Y. & Artz, D. 2006. Towards content trust of web resources. 15th international conference on World Wide Web, Edinburgh, Scotland. 1135861: ACM, 565–574.

Grice, H. P. 1975. Logic and conversation. *In:* Cole, P. & Morgan, J. (eds.) *Syntax and semantics 3: Speech acts.* New York: Academic Press.

Guadagno, R. E. & Wingate, V. S. 2014. Internet: Facebook and Social Media Sites. *In:* Levine, T. (ed.) *Encyclopedia of Deception.* Thousand Oaks, California: SAGE Publications.

Hancock, J. T., Curry, L. E., Goorha, S. & Woodworth, M. 2007. On Lying and Being Lied To: A Linguistic Analysis of Deception in Computer-Mediated Communication. *Discourse Processes,* 45, 1–23.

Hardin, R. 2001. Conceptions and Explanations of Trust. *In:* Cook, K. S. (ed.) *Trust in Society.* New York, NY: Russell Sage Foundation.

Hauch, V., Masip, J., Blandon-Gitlin, I. & Sporer, S. L. 2012. Linguistic cues to deception assessed by computer programs: a meta-analysis. Proceedings of the workshop on computational approaches to deception detection. Association for Computational Linguistics, 1–4.

Holcomb, J., Gottfried, J. & Mitchell, A. 2013. News use across Social Media Platforms. *Pew Research Journalism Project.*

Höfer, E., Akehurst, L. & Metzger, G. 1996. Reality monitoring: A chance for further development of CBCA. Proceedings of the Annual Meeting of the European Association on Psychology and Law, Sienna, Italy.

Johnson, K. A. & Wiedenbeck, S. 2009. Enhancing Perceived Credibility of Citizen Journalism Web Sites. *Journalism & Mass Communication Quarterly,* 86, 332–348.

Kang, B., Höllerer, T. & O'Donovan, J. 2015. Believe it or Not? Analyzing Information Credibility in Microblogs. Proceedings of the 2015 IEEE/ACM International Conference on Advances in Social Networks Analysis and Mining 2015. ACM, 611–616.

Kumar, N. & Reddy, R. N. 2012. *Automatic Detection of Fake Profiles in Online Social Networks.* BTech Thesis.

Köhnken, G. & Steller, M. 1988. The evaluation of the credibility of child witness statements in the German procedural system. *Issues in Criminological & Legal Psychology.*

Larcker, D. F. & Zakolyukina, A. A. 2012. Detecting deceptive discussions in conference calls. *Journal of Accounting Research,* 50, 495–540.

Levine, T. R., Park, H. S. & Mccornack, S. A. 1999. Accuracy in detecting truths and lies: Documenting the 'veracity effect'. *Communication Monographs,* 66, 125–144.

Liu, B. 2012. Sentiment analysis and opinion mining. *Synthesis Lectures on Human Language Technologies,* 5, 1–167.

Liu, X., Nourbakhsh, A., Li, Q., Fang, R. & Shah, S. 2015. Real-time Rumor Debunking on Twitter. Proceedings of the 24th ACM International on Conference on Information and Knowledge Management, Melbourne, Australia. ACM, 1867–1870.

Lukoianova, T. & Rubin, V. L. 2014. Veracity Roadmap: Is Big Data Objective, Truthful and Credible? *Advances in Classification Research Online,* 24, 4.

Manning, C. D. & Schütze, H. 1999. *Foundations of statistical natural language processing*, MIT Press.

Marsh, S. & Dibben, M. R. 2003. The role of trust in information science and technology. *Annual Review of Information Science and Technology,* 37, 465–498.

Matthews, C. 2013. How Does One Fake Tweet Cause a Stock Market Crash. *Time.*

Mccay-Peet, L. & Quan-Haase, A. 2016. What is social media and what questions can social media research help us answer? *In:* Sloan, L. & Quan-Haase, A. (eds.) *Handbook of Social Media Research Methods.* London, UK: Sage.

Mendoza, M., Poblete, B. & Castillo, C. 2010. Twitter Under Crisis: Can we trust what we RT? Proceedings of the first workshop on social media analytics. ACM, 71–79.

Merriam-Webster Online Dictionary. 2016. Rumor. Available: http://www.merriam-webster.com/dictionary/rumor [Accessed 17 August 2016].

Merriam-Webster Online Dictionary. 2016. Trust. Available: http://www.merriam-webster.com/dictionary/trust [Accessed 17 August 2016].

Mihalcea, R. & Strapparava, C. 2009. The lie detector: Explorations in the automatic recognition of deceptive language. Proceedings of the ACL-IJCNLP 2009 Conference Short Papers. Association for Computational Linguistics, 309–312.

Mintz, A. 2002. *Web of Deception: Misinformation on the Internet,* Medford, N.J., CyberAge Books.

Mitchell, A. & Page, D. 2015. State of the News Media 2015. *Pew Research Journalism, Project for Excellence in Journalism.*

Moffit, K. & Giboney, J.S. 2012. Structured Programming for Linguistic Cue Extraction (SPLICE). http://splice.cmi.arizona.edu/

Morante, R. & Sporleder, C. 2012. Modality and Negation: An Introduction to the Special Issue. *Computational Linguistics,* 38, 223–260.

Morris, M. R., Counts, S., Roseway, A., Hoff, A. & Schwarz, J. 2012. Tweeting is believing?: Understanding microblog credibility perceptions. Proceedings of the ACM 2012 conference on Computer Supported Cooperative Work. ACM, 441–450.

Mukherjee, A., Venkataraman, V., Liu, B. & Glance, N. 2013. Fake Review Detection: Classification and Analysis of Real and Pseudo Reviews. Technical Report: Department of Computer Science, University of Illinois at Chicago, and Google Inc.

Newman, M. L., Pennebaker, J. W., Berry, D. S. & Richards, J. M. 2003. Lying Words: Predicting Deception from Linguistic Styles. *Personality and Social Psychology Bulletin,* 29, 665–675.

Ortega, J. L. 2015. Relationship between Altmetric and Bibliometric Indicators across Academic Social Sites: The Case of CSIC's members. *Journal of Informetrics,* 9, 39–49.

Ott, M., Choi, Y., Cardie, C., & Hancock, J. T. 2011. Finding deceptive opinion spam by any stretch of the imagination. In the Proceedings of the 49th Annual Meeting of the Association for Computational Linguistics, 309–319. Portland, Oregon, June 19–24, 2011.

Pang, B. & Lee, L. 2008. Opinion Mining and Sentiment Analysis. *Foundations and Trends in Information Retrieval,* 2, 1–135.

Pennebaker, J. W. & Francis, M. E. 1999. *Linguistic Inquiry and Word Count: LIWC.* Erlbaum Publishers.

Pennebaker, J. W., Francis, M. E. & Booth, R. J. 2001. Linguistic inquiry and word count (LIWC): A computerized text analysis program. *Mahwah (NJ),* 7.

Porter, S. & Yuille, J. C. 1996a. The language of deceit: An investigation of the verbal clues to deception in the interrogation context. *Law and Human Behavior,* 20, 443.

Porter, S. & Yuille, J. C. 1996b. The language of deceit: An investigation of the verbal clues to deception in the interrogation context. *Law and Human Behavior,* 20, 443–458.

Qazvinian, V., Rosengren, E., Radev, D. R. & Mei, Q. 2011. Rumor has it: Identifying misinformation in microblogs. Proceedings of the Conference on Empirical Methods in Natural Language Processing. Association for Computational Linguistics, 1589–1599.

Rieh, S. Y. 2010. Credibility and Cognitive Authority of Information. *In:* Bates, M. J. (ed.) *Encyclopedia of Library and Information Science.* New York, Taylor & Francis https://deepblue.lib.umich.edu/handle/2027.42/106416

Rubin, V. L. 2006. Identifying certainty in texts. *Doctoral Thesis, Syracuse University, Syracuse, NY.*

Rubin, V. L. 2010a. Epistemic modality: From uncertainty to certainty in the context of information seeking as interactions with texts. *Information Processing & Management,* 46, 533–540.

Rubin, V. L. 2010b. On deception and deception detection: content analysis of computer-mediated stated beliefs. 73rd ASIS&T Annual Meeting: Navigating Streams in an Information Ecosystem, Pittsburgh, Pennsylvania. American Society for Information Science.

Rubin, V. L. 2014. TALIP Perspectives, Guest Editorial Commentary. *ACM Transactions on Asian Language Information Processing,* 13, 1–8.

Rubin, V. L., Chen, Y. & Conroy, N. J. 2015. Deception detection for news: Three types of fakes. Proceedings of the 78th ASIS&T Annual Meeting: Information Science with Impact: Research in and for the Community. American Society for Information Science, 83.

Rubin, V. L. & Conroy, N. 2011. *Challenges in Automated Deception Detection in Computer-Mediated Communication* [Online]. New Orleans, Louisiana. [Accessed].

Rubin, V. L. & Conroy, N. 2012. Discerning truth from deception: Human judgments and automation efforts. *First Monday* [Online], 17. Available: http://firstmonday.org.

Rubin, V. L. & Liddy, E. 2006. Assessing Credibility of Weblogs. AAAI Symposium on Computational Approaches to Analyzing Weblogs, Stanford, CA. AAAI Press.

Rubin, V. L., Liddy, E. D. & Kando, N. 2006. Certainty identification in texts: Categorization model and manual tagging results. *Computing attitude and affect in text: Theory and applications.* Dordrecht, Springer http://www.springer.com/us/book/9781402040269

Rubin, V. L. & Vashchilko, T. 2012. Extending information quality assessment methodology: A new veracity/deception dimension and its measures. *Proceedings of the American Society for Information Science and Technology,* 49, 1–6.

Sauri, R. & Pustejovsky, J. 2009. FactBank: A Corpus Annotated with Event Factuality. *Language Resources and Evaluation,* 43, 227–268.

Rubin, V.R., Conroy, N. J., Chen, Y. & Cornwell, S. 2016. Fake News or Truth? Using Satirical Cues to Detect Potentially Misleading News. Proceedings of the 15th Annual Conference of the North American Chapter of the Association for Computational Linguistics: Human Language Technologies. Workshop on Computational Approaches to Deception Detection (NAACL-CADD2016), San Diego, California.

Rubin, V. L., Kando, N. & Liddy, E. D. 2004. Certainty categorization model. AAAI spring symposium: Exploring attitude and affect in text: Theories and applications, Stanford, CA.

Sauri, R. & Pustejovsky, J. 2012. Are you sure that this happened? Assessing the factuality degree of events in text. *Computational Linguistics,* 1–39.

Sikdar, S., Kang, B., O'Donovan, J., Hollerer, T. & Adah, S. 2013. Understanding information credibility on Twitter. In Proceedings of International Conference on Social Computing 2013. IEEE, 19–24.

Steller, M. 1989. Recent developments in statement analysis. *Credibility assessment.* Springer http://link.springer.com/chapter/10.1007%2F978-94-015-7856-1_8

Subrahmanian, V., Azaria, A., Durst, S., Kagan, V., Galstyan, A., Lerman, K., Zhu, L., Ferrara, E., Flammini, A. & Menczer, F. 2016. The DARPA Twitter Bot Challenge. IEEE Computer Magazine, in press

The Urban Dictionary. 2016. *Astroturfing* [Online]. Available: http://www.urbandictionary.com/define.php?term=astroturf [Accessed 17 August 2016].

The Free Dictionary 2016. Rumor. *The Free Dictionary*.

Toma, C. L. & Hancock, J. T. 2012. What Lies Beneath: The Linguistic Traces of Deception in Online Dating Profiles. *Journal of Communication*, 62, 78–97.

Tseng, H. & Fogg, B. J. 1999. Credibility and computing technology. *Communications of the ACM*, 42, 39–44.

Van Swol, L. 2014. Truth Bias. *In:* Levine, T. (ed.) *Encyclopedia of Deception*. Thousand Oaks, California: SAGE Publications.

Vosoughi, S. 2015. *Automatic detection and verification of rumors on Twitter.* Doctor of Philosophy, Massachusetts Institute of Technology.

Vrij, A. 2000. *Detecting Lies and Deceit,* New York, John Wiley and Sons.

Vrij, A. 2004. Why professionals fail to catch liars and how they can improve. *Legal and Criminological Psychology*, 9, 159–181.

Vrij, A., Mann, S., Kristen, S. & Fisher, R. P. 2007. Cues to deception and ability to detect lies as a function of police interview styles. *Law and Human Behavior*, 31, 499.

Vrij, A., Mann, S. & Leal, S. 2012. Deception Traits in Psychological Interviewing. *Journal of Police and Criminal Psychology*, 28, 115–126.

Walczyk, J. J., Runco, M. A., Tripp, S. M. & Smith, C. E. 2008. The Creativity of Lying: Divergent Thinking and Ideational Correlates of the Resolution of Social Dilemmas. *Creativity Research Journal*, 20, 328–342.

Weerkamp, W. & De Rijke, M. 2008. Credibility improves topical blog post retrieval. HLT-NAACL, Columbus, Ohio. 923–931.

Wiebe, J., Bruce, R., Bell, M., Martin, M. & Wilson, T. 2001. A corpus study of evaluative and speculative language. Proceedings of the Second SIGdial Workshop on Discourse and Dialogue-Volume 16. Association for Computational Linguistics, 1–10.

Wu, K., Yang, S. & Zhu, K. Q. 2015. False Rumors Detection on Sina Weibo by Propagation Structures. IEEE International Conference on Data Engineering, ICDE.

Yang, F., Liu, Y., Yu, X. & Yang, M. 2012. Automatic Detection of Rumor on Sina Weibo. Proceedings of the ACM SIGKDD Workshop on Mining Data Semantics, Beijing, China. ACM, 13 http://delivery.acm.org/10.1145/2360000/2350203/a13-yang.pdf?ip=129.100.35.214&id=2350203&acc=ACTIVE%20SERVICE&key=FD0067F557510FFB%2E26B1F5E6B598D80D%2E4D4702B0C3E38B35%2E4D4702B0C3E38B35&CFID=691407069&CFTOKEN=89430761&_acm_=1478533891_b6efd193eb418a53ffec3814655b7119.

Zhou, L., Burgoon, J. K., Nunamaker, J. F. & Twitchell, D. 2004. Automating Linguistics-Based Cues for Detecting Deception in Text-Based Asynchronous Computer-Mediated Communications. *Group Decision and Negotiation*, 13, 81–106.

PART V
Diverse Approaches to Social Media Data

From Site-specificity to Hyper-locality: Performances of Place in Social Media

Nadav Hochman

How is the physical place performed through social media data? How do we experience locality via social media platforms? In this chapter, I theorize, visualize, and analyze the relation between physical places and their social media hyper-local representations.

I combine quantitative and qualitative analysis, and employ perspectives from the fields of Digital Humanities and Art History in order to offer a theory of hyper-local social media, and visualize its manifestations and operations using a particular case study.

I start by drawing historical parallels between 'site-specific' artistic conceptions from the late 1960s and early 1970s and current organization of hyper-local geo-temporal social media images. Next, I exemplify the hyper-local using the case study of 28,419 photos taken during the street artist Banksy's month-long residency in NYC during October 2013. Finally, based on these results I offer a theoretical analysis, identifying what I see as some of the key characterizations of hyper-local social media data.

INTRODUCTION

During the month of October 2013 the anonymous British street artist Banksy conducted a month long 'residency' in the streets of New York City titled 'Better in than out'. Nearly every day of that month, Banksy installed a new work in a different location around the city (29 works were installed in physical locations and three works were only posted online; typically it was an image stenciled on a wall [Figure 22.1]). The information about the particular location of each work spread virally online. The artist himself posted a photograph of the work created each day on the photo sharing application Instagram, and asked his followers to post other photos of the work with the hashtag #banksyny. In many cases, the only way to detect the location of the physical works was to search for their earlier representations online, posted via the #banksyny hashtag. In return, residents and visitors to the city

Figure 22.1 31 Instagram photos taken by Banksy documenting his month-long artistic residency in the streets of New York City during October 2013. The photos are sorted by their upload date from 1–31 October 2013 (left to right, top to bottom)

flocked around the city's five boroughs in an effort to catch a glimpse of Banksy's works before they disappeared, were defaced or painted over (Smith, 2013).

The result of Banksy's artistic experiment was a month-long succession of dispersed real-life events and online 'data events' (photos and other social media data taken and shared about the events during that month) that mirrored and enabled each other, a reciprocal state of exchange that played an integral role within Banksy's well-rehearsed and thought out artistic investigation: examining the relation between a site and its logic of reproducibility in social media platforms. In his month-long series of daily works, Banksy observed the ways in which the place he physically marked was documented, communicated and archived via social media.

By doing so, Banksy connected the history of artistic site-specificity (street art) to the history of reproduction by technical and artistic means (photography), and to the growing collapse of the difference between objects, information and places (encapsulated by social media information items). It is this historical trajectory that is the focus of this chapter. I argue that hyper-locality – the term that has come to denote the association of social media data (such as check-ins, tweets, photographs or videos) with specific time indications and place coordinates – can be understood within these historical aesthetical and informational conditions. It is a term that reflects upon the transformation of objects into places, the turning of places into information, and finally, the redefinition of a place and objects within it.

To better describe these conceptual and representational transformations of a place, I follow the shift from historic artistic site-specificity to contemporary informational hyper-locality. First, I suggest that current organizations of geographical and temporal tagged images shared using social media platforms are a realization of neo-avantgarde ideas from the late-1960s. While Modernist art objects were detached from the context of the place and time in which they were presented, later neo-avantgarde groups proclaimed the importance of an artwork's site-specificity, where the object could only exist within and be defined by the context of its particular time and place (Buchloh, 1990; Ehrlich et al., 2003; Kwon, 2002).

Secondly, I illustrate, visualize, and analyze various aspects of the hyper-local. Exploring a dataset of 28,419 photos taken during Banksy's month-long residency and annotated with the hashtags #banksy and #banksyny, I examine how these photos represent specific spaces and times.[1]

Finally, I address the ways in which we experience hyper-locality over social media platforms and ask: How is the physical place represented via the lens of social media data? How can we describe the *unique* aspects of this locality? Based on the historical discussion and the case study, I propose key characteristics of hyper-local visual social media data.

BACKGROUND

'Hyper-locality' has recently gained popularity as a term that describes a wide range of meanings. Most often, it is mentioned in the context of the news media's increasing ability to provide information in highly targeted geographic niches (Jarvis, 2009; Miel and Faris, 2008). In this context, it refers to information that originates from organized online communities or individuals such as bloggers (Metzgar et al., 2011), or from user-generated social media that is automatically augmented with location information and timestamp (Hu et al., 2013; Ewart, 2013).

Existing research touches upon various aspects of hyper-locality, and offers conceptual and analytical tools for the study of its socio-cultural aspects. Wilken and Goggin, for example, offer a comprehensive account for the ways in which place and mobile technologies intersect and interact (Wilken and Goggin, 2012). Gordon and de Souza e Silva (2011) provide a useful discussion of the socio-cultural effects of 'networked locality' (Gordon and de Souza e Silva 2011). In an earlier work, Dourish points to ways new technologies produce alternative spatialities and appropriate existing places in new ways (Dourish, 2006).

However, none of these studies agree upon the definition of hyper-locality, or propose concrete characteristics of hyper-local social media. Identifying a similar shortcoming, Metzgar et al. (2011) attempt to define the hyper-local, but their definition refers to geographically specific communities and organization of news reporting over the web, thus neglecting the ways in which different aspects of hyper-locality manifest themselves on social media.

Computer scientists offer an ever-increasing number of studies of hyper-local social media data (Cranshaw et al., 2012; Xie et al., 2013). However, while a few studies examine the particularities of a place via social media data do exist (Winter et al., 2009), the majority of this research is devoted to the study of the relation between groups of places, typically applying clustering or other methods in order to analyze social similarity between different geographical locations (ElGindy and Abdelmoty, 2012; Zhang et al., 2013). The results are homogeneous clusters of fixed entities that erase the particularity of a singular place, neglecting its dynamic, temporal aspects in favor of its aggregation and categorization with other similar 'types' of places (i.e. areas frequented by locals versus tourists; or defining the boundaries of a city based on clusters of places people attend frequently). Put differently, existing computational research typically looks for geographical *homogeneity* and neglects the *heterogeneity* of physical places as these are seen through the lens of hyper-local social media data. In doing so, it does not try to find ways to trace and analyze the particularity of unique singular places as they are represented in social media.

Guided by these shortcomings – the lack of consensual definition of hyper-locality on social media, together with the tendency in computational research to ignore the distinctive expressions of this locality in particular places – I offer a historical and theoretical discussion of the unique performances and exhibitions of a place (Hogan, 2010) in social media visual data. Specifically, I consider the following questions: How do the treatment and organization of visual materials historically come to define the relation between a physical place and its visual representations? How are these historical conceptualizations reincarnating in contemporary hyper-local visual organizational forms? And finally, how do these forms of visual information redefine the relation between physical places and their social media hyper-local representations?

NOMADIC Vs. NATIVE

In April 2011 a seemingly insignificant and minor structural change made by Bing image search engine radically disrupted the delicate relationship between content producers and their informational platform. Since then, searching for a particular image has resulted in continuous thumbnails of related images that if clicked through, lead the viewer directly to the image itself, disconnected from its original source page (Schwartz, 2011). Two years later, Google image search followed the same path and redesigned its interface to present hi-res images directly on Google's website instead of the original website (Wikipedia, 2014). Both interface changes were followed by controversies of individual content providers against the giant companies over copyright infringement and the loss of web traffic. These were a limited set of disputes that was quickly silenced and did not record any noteworthy effect to what immediately became a new informational norm.

But these anecdotal structural informational modifications also suggest something else. What we have here are opposing visual organizational logics – put forth by search engines in contrast to the desires of individual content providers that seek to preserve the original context of their visual data – that point to two prominent contesting modes of contemporary visual information organization. On the one hand, a 'nomadic' visual logic, epitomized by major search engines, in which images may be placed singularly or collectively but are always stripped away from their original contextual source (i.e. webpage, user, location, etc.). On the other hand, a 'native' organizational mode that sets the image within its original environment or in direct relation to it. This structural logic is exemplified by social media platforms that arrange images *in* and *as* particular place and time. In this case, images are annotated with geographical and temporal metadata, and are sorted by upload time (typically this is the default representation) or by location (either on a personal photo map or collectively showing all images tagged to a place).[2]

What are some of the possible histories of these two types of nomadic and native organizational forms of visual materials? What do these historical traces of similar visual informational understandings tell us about the current structures and experiences of hyper-local images? I believe that the tension between the nomadic and native informational modes used to present images is not new. For example, if we look at the history of Modern art, we can find similar modes. The first resembles earlier conceptualization of visual materials from the beginning of the 20th century; the second corresponds to site-specific artistic practices, which emerged in late-1960s.

In fact, the nomadic notion of images has always been an integral part of the emergence of what we have come to know as the contemporary form of an image. From the development of new physical conditions for the creation and transportation of images (i.e. the portability of easel painting in the early Renaissance; the use of canvas support; or the development of the bounding frame) to the formation of particular visual content attributes (compositional dependencies of form and narrative; or the implementation of linear perspective) – all served as a way to liberate the *internal* representational space of an image from particular social and spatial contexts *outside* of the image (Roberts, 2014: 2).

It is also this type of detachment of the physical from the (now) autonomous representational image format that culminated with the aesthetic autonomy that defined Modern art practices and its theory. Modernist artists saw a visual art object as a thing in itself, which was not affected by the time and place in which it was presented. The spatial organization of the visual object was not supposed to impact the meaning and understanding of this object, and thus the white neutral museums walls were the ultimate venue for their presentation. The work was designed for the 'white cube' – an exhibition interface that could be located anywhere (O'Doherty, 1999) – see Figure 22.2.

Turning against this notion of treating the visual object with no relation to the distinctive qualities of a particular space in which it is being located, starting in the late-1960s neo-avantgarde groups (specifically, artists creating happenings, performances, and site-specific works) offered completely oppositional understanding of the visual object, and emphasized how the meaning of the artistic object is derived from the particularities of its organization in time and space. These avant-garde groups aimed to relocate the meaning of the visual from what was going on inside it, to everything that is going on outside of this object. They sought to turn our attention from within the art object to the 'contingencies of its context'; to shift Modernist understanding of the visual as independent from time and space towards a more sensorial, phenomenological understanding of lived bodily experiences around that visual object (Kwon, 1997: 92). In short: to re-attach the visual to a particular time and site.

In this new paradigm, a site-specific work was conceived as a unique combination of phenomenological experiences that depended upon physical particularities (dimensions such as depth, length, height, temperature, etc.) and our experience of these conditions in defined times. In later stages, other site-specific practices expanded into the inclusion of social, institutional and discursive constructions of a place and responded to them (p. 92). In any case, whether a place was defined physically, institutionally or discursively, the purpose was to secure the specific

Figure 22.2 Elmgreen & Dragset (2014) The 'Named Series'. Each frame consists of the color layer of a wall from a number of prominent art institutions' white cube exhibition spaces (i.e. Centre Pompidou, Guggenheim, Tate Liverpool and others). The removed layers are mounted on canvas and framed in a black waxed oak frame. Photo by Anders Sune Berg (Installation view as part of the exhibition Biography, Astrup Fearnley Museum, Oslo)

relationship between the visual and its (material or immaterial) site.

A famous early example of these new relations between the particularities of a place and the visual art object is Robert Smithson's *Spiral Jetty* (Figure 22.3). To create this 1970 sculpture located on the northeastern shore of the Great Salt Lake, the artist used local mud, salt crystals, rocks, and water. The result was a 1,500 foot long and 15-foot wide counter clockwise coil jutting from the shore of the lake (Smithson et al., 2005). As opposed to Modernist art objects (such as abstract paintings by Mondrian or Malevich) that were portable, nomadic, and could move from one museum space to another – and as such were 'timeless,' 'placeless,' and detached from any relations to their original time and place of creation – *Spiral Jetty* emphasizes the dimension of time, and the particular material condition of its place (the visibility of the sculpture depends on the water level of the Great Salt Lake). It is 'an emblem of [the] transience' (Owens, 1980: 71) of a particular place, and a manifestation of a particular time-place relationship.

Miwon Kwon efficiently describes these new relations in terms of 'nouns' and 'verbs.' The modern, 'nomadic' notion, saw the visual object as a *noun/object* to be experienced in complete detachment from its place and time of presentation. In contrast, the 'native' realization of the visual by the neo avant-garde of the 1970s turned it into a *verb/process* that is all about its relations to its surroundings in particular times (1997: 91). These opposing views also stem from a different understanding of the physical site itself. On the one hand a site is viewed as an actual, singular, unique *physical* location that exists 'out there' as a fixed entity. On the other hand, a site is not defined as, or is privileged by its physicality, but rather by all other (material and immaterial) things that *flow within it*.

It is in this sense that we can think of the contemporary geo-temporal digital image (the image which has spatial coordinates and a time stamp) as a new realization and amplification of this neo avant-garde concept. It actualizes their historical aspirations to locate the meaning of the visual in specific time and site, and materializes their desire to understand a visual object as a segue for 'place attachment' (Low and Altman, 1992) that captures lived, timely, fleeting and unrepeatable sensorial experiences within that site.

Through the lens of the multitude of visual and textual hyper-local activities, a physical site is no longer viewed as a fixed

Figure 22.3 Robert Smithson's (1970) Spiral Jetty (Sculpture at Rozel Point, Great Salt Lake, Utah)

spatial entity (noun/object) but rather as a set of immaterial or informational 'verbs' or 'processes' that move through it. This site is remarkably similar in nature to what James Meyer has labeled as a 'functional site' in relation to later site-specific artistic endeavors. This new type of site does not necessarily occupy a physical place, but is instead 'a process, an operation occurring between sites… an informational site, a locus of overlap of text, photographs and video recordings, physical places and things… a temporary thing; a movement; a chain of meanings devoid of a particular focus.' (Meyer, 1996: 21)

Neo-avantgarde ideas are thus infused with contemporary informational techniques in order to guarantee the specific relationship between the visual and its 'site.' Like in all former site-specific practices, these new relations reject the detachment between the physical and the representational, and insist on the representational *as* the physical. By ingraining the visual within specific time and place and presenting it as a particular, unrepeatable, experience of that place (accentuated by its near real-time presentation) the hyper-local signals and verifies the *permanence* of a place (its 'existence') but at the same time manifests its *impermanence* (how it changes). Together with all other images from that particular place a greater sense of transience is materialized and visualized.

Modern art museums are one of the best examples for the ways in which a venue turns into a set of durational, momentary functions; a site where nomadic objects become native, and the intricate historical relations between the two conceptual modes are culturally recharged and accentuated. Within their confined walls that once signified the detachment of the physical location from the representational object, new documentational mechanisms have enabled a new way to *reinvent nomadicity as site-specificity*. In this way, photos, videos and texts are shared around the museum experience and are informationaly associated with the museum (via location coordinates; or content tags). They mutate the artistic object into the sum of its interactions with all other viewers of the same object, and also with all other visitors to the location of the object. This location associated information item also reflects upon the institution where the object is located (via location identification), the discourse around a particular object (via content tags), or the phenomenological nature of the experience of the object (via the photographic distance from the object, angles of view, number of people viewing the same object, their origins [locals/tourists] etc.) (Figure 22.4).

It is in this sense that we can think of the hyper-local as an *amplification* of former site-specific relations. As previously explained, site-specificity diverges itself from all former nomadistic approaches by establishing indexical relations between an object and a place. While earlier nomadic conceptions positioned the signifier (the object) and the signified (the viewer) in an autonomous 'here and now' aesthetic affect of the former over the latter, site-specific notions situate the place, the institution or the discursive practices around a place as the signified (Kwon, 1997: 98). These exact relations are replicated with hyper-local images that now reestablish former nomadic and native indexical relations but point to *all* these signified levels *at the same time*. The image is multiplied and positioned in relation to the visual content of an object (via image content), the institution where this object is located (via location identification and tags); the viewer of the object and the performative qualities of the representation, and finally in relation to all other images that facilitate similar indexical interactions and enable the production, dissemination, and verification of a representational social media place.

FOLLOWING BANKSY

While this trajectory does shed light on some historical parallels between dominant

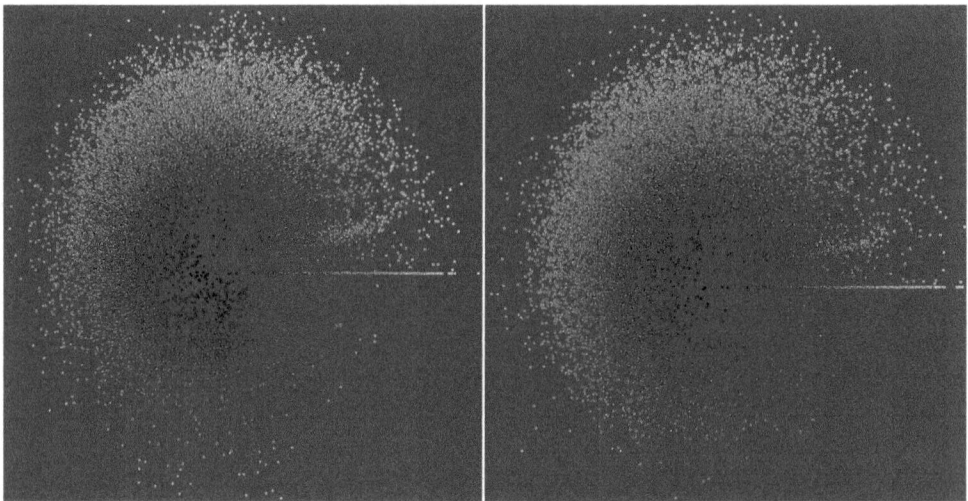

Figure 22.4 The nomadic is turn into native: A comparison of Instagram photos taken at Tate Modern, London (left) and the Museum of Modern Art (MoMA), NYC. Each radial visualization contains 10,000 photos actively tagged to the location of the museum by its users. The photos are sorted by saturation mean and brightness mean

conceptualizations of the relation of the visual to its place, or the organization of the visual within a place, it is not complete. I am still concerned with the *distinctive qualities* of these hyper-local indexical relations: How does hyper-local visual data *diverge* itself from former site-specific practices? What particular type of indexicality it generates? What are the terms under which these functional hyper-local sites exist and represented?

In order to examine the conditions under which locality is reproduced and experienced via social media data I now turn to analyze a set of photos taken, shared and tagged to Banksy's month of residency in NYC. First, I describe the dataset and computational techniques. Next, I examine some temporal, spatial and visual patterns within the dataset. Finally, based on the results, I propose some key characterizations of hyper-local social media data.

Using Instagram's API (application programming interface), we crawled photos and their metadata (user ID, latitude and longitude, comments, number of likes, date and timestamp, type of filter applied, and user-assigned tags) to find all publicly available photos with tags #banksy and #banksyny. We then created the data set by filtering these photos in the following way. We chose photos with the tag #banksyny shared from October 1st, 2013 until November 20th, 2013. For photos with the tag #banksy, we included only the ones from October 2013 geo-tagged to NYC area. Since there was some overlap between these two sets, only one copy of each image was included. After this filtering the final data set has a total 28,419 photos (18,533 photos tagged #banksyny, and 9,886 photos tagged #banksy).[3]

The dataset includes multiple photos of the same artwork taken by different people. To find all photos documenting the same artwork by Banksy a two-step method was used involving computer vision techniques. We first identified clusters of photos that represent the same work, and then used these clusters to train a classifier to find more images of the same work. Out of our full dataset of 28,419 photos, we decided to only use photos showing seven artworks. We selected all

Figure 22.5 Instagram photos of seven of Banksy's artworks used in our case study (selected from the larger set of photos for each artwork). Top: original photo posted by Banksy. Bottom: a montage of four photos taken by other users

photos showing each of the works (4,558 photos in total), and numbered these clusters as illustrated in Figures 22.5 and 22.6.

Temporal Patterns

Each photo in the dataset is stamped with its specific upload time to the application. This allows us to look at temporal patterns in the data. First, we plotted the entire dataset of images to show the volume of shared photos in each day, from October 1st to November 20th (see Figure 22.7). The least number of shared photos is on October 6th, when no new work was announced. The highest number of shared photos in our dataset was on October 20th, 2013 for the work in cluster 6.

We also plotted the data over time for each cluster (Figure 22.8). While all clusters show a similar pattern (first a few photos, then a rapid rise, followed by a gradual decline), a few unique patterns emerge.

In two cases images were posted before Banksy's own photo of the same work. In cluster 2, nine users posted a photo of the artwork one day before it was announced and posted on Banksy's account and website. In cluster 4, fourteen users posted a photo of the work starting from ten days before Banksy posted a photo of the work on his official Instagram account. As we can tell from these results, some of the works were installed a few days before their official announcement, and were then detected by social media users.

Cluster 3 also has an unusual temporal pattern. While photos in all other clusters continue to appear after the peak throughout the whole period we analyzed (up to November 20th), photos in this cluster abruptly stop on October 31st 2013. And finally, in cluster 7, contrary to all other clusters, many photos of the new artworks were posted at nearly the same time.

In summary, every hyper-local event in our case study – the creation of a new artwork by Banksy and photos by users of these artworks shared on Instagram – has a different temporal profile in the beginning. In other words, while the 'tails' are rather similar, the 'heads' are different.

Spatial Patterns

Our data contains 65.9% geo-tagged images. To study the global spread of a local event via social media, I visualized the data in two ways. First, I plotted all geo-tagged images with the tag #banksyny and #banksy over a world map in order to locate the geographical 'boundaries' and see how far the photos of particular artworks have travelled (see Figure 22.9). While 16,164 photos are from NYC area, 2,571

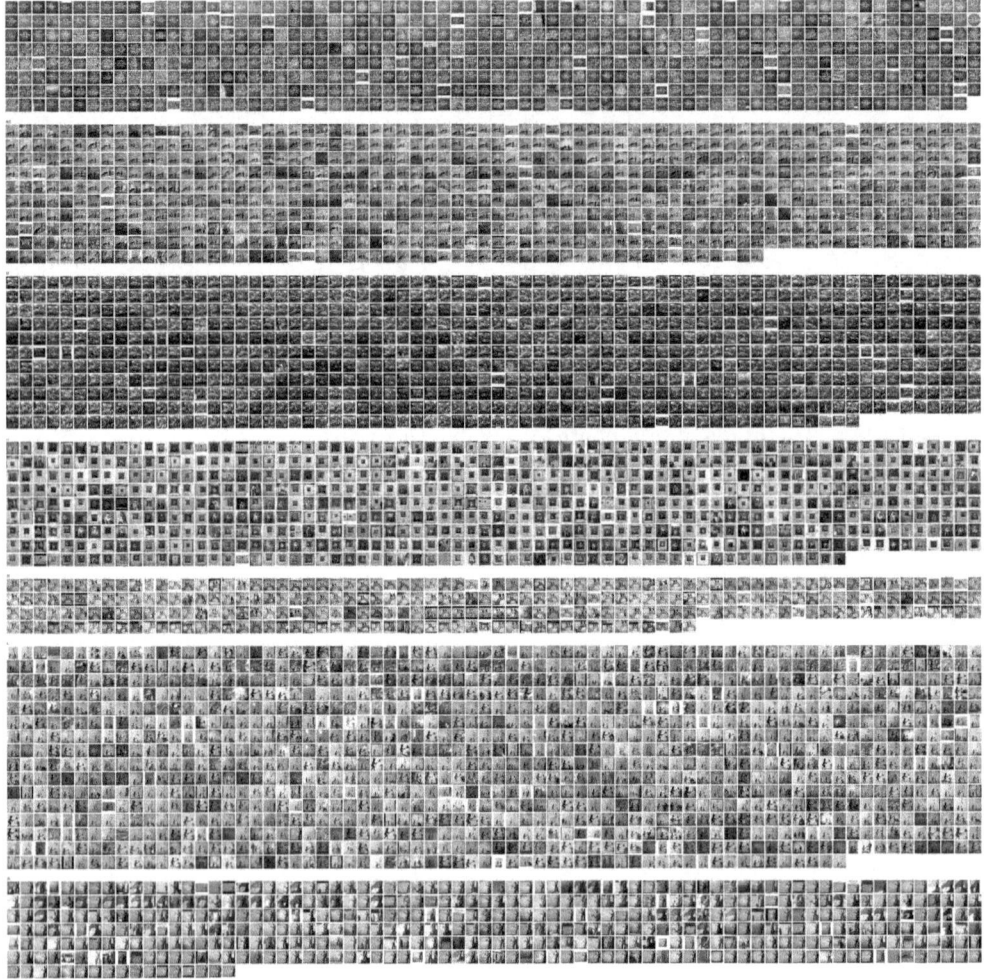

Figure 22.6 Montage visualization of all photos from each cluster sorted by time from no.1–7 (top to bottom). Each cluster includes the following number of photos: Cluster 1: 575 photos. Cluster 2: 704 photos. Cluster 3: 783 photos. Cluster 4: 638 photos. Cluster 5: 267 photos. Cluster 6: 1,142 photos. Cluster 7: 449 photos

photos of the event are spread over Europe, Australia and the West Coast of the US.

Then, we plotted the seven clusters over a world map using different colors for each cluster, to see the spread of photos of each work (see Figure 22.10). As the visualization shows, some clusters are more concentrated than others, and remain in their confined original places where artworks were created (i.e. cluster 5) while other clusters are spread all over and outside New York City.

In addition, we visualized 16,164 images geo-tagged to NYC area (from both #banksy and #banksyny sets) using a radial layout, sorted by location (perimeter) and upload time (angle) (Figure 22.11). Each 'ring' represents a different location in the city and the location on the ring represents the upload time of an image. Each ring is assembled by photos of the same work (since they are from the same location). Similar to Figures 22.9 and 22.10, this visualization shows how each ring has a

FROM SITE-SPECIFICITY TO HYPER-LOCALITY 377

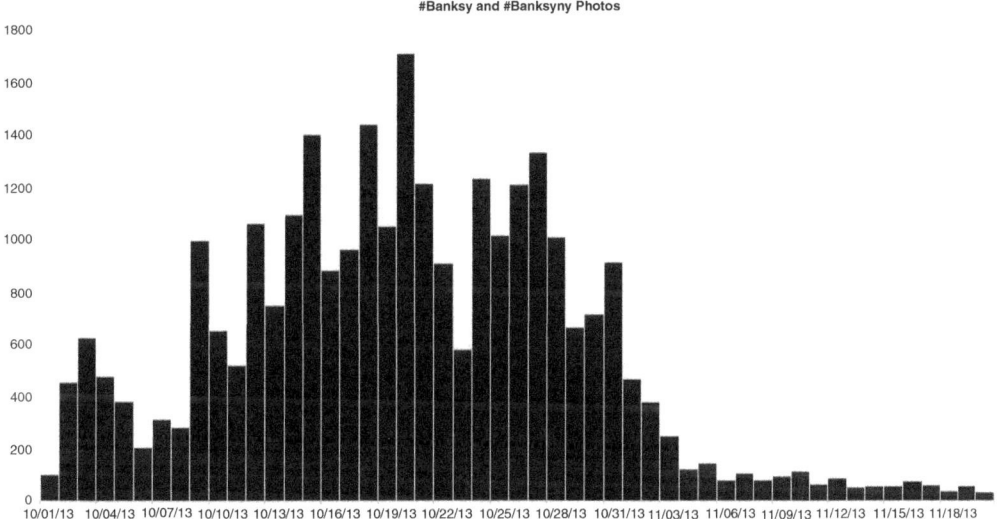

Figure 22.7 Number of photos annotated with the hashtags #banksy and #banksyny (a total of 28,419 photos) for each day from October 1st to November 20th 2013

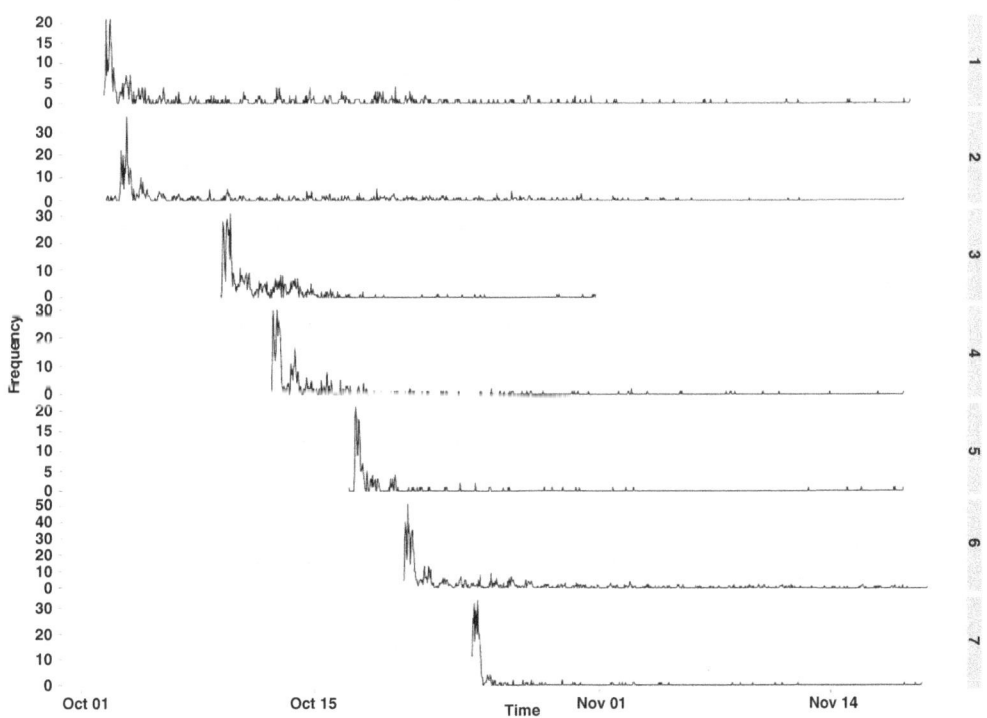

Figure 22.8 A temporal plot of each cluster organized by time (X) and volume (Y)

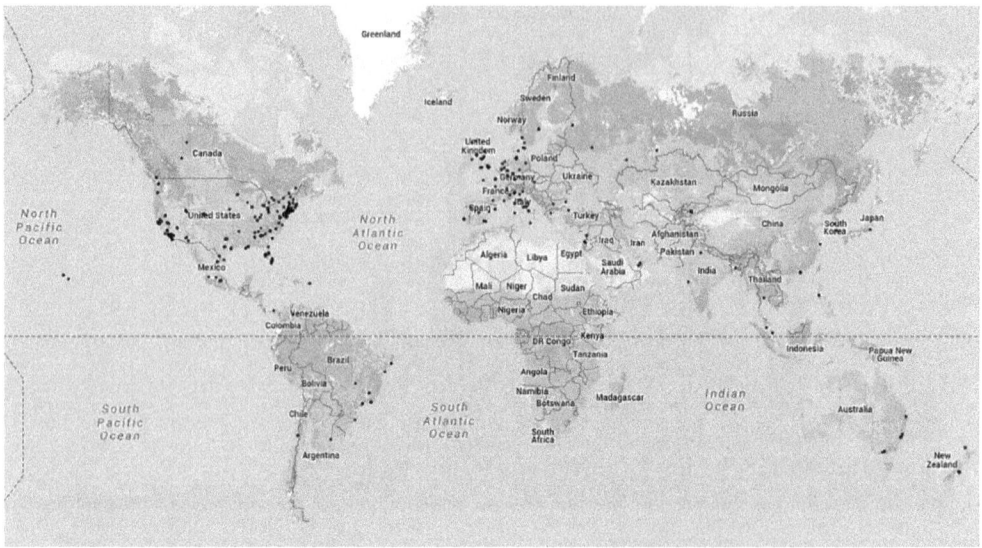

Figure 22.9 A global spread of all geo-tagged images with the tags #banksyny or #banksy. 16,164 images are in NYC, and 2,571 images are outside of NYC area

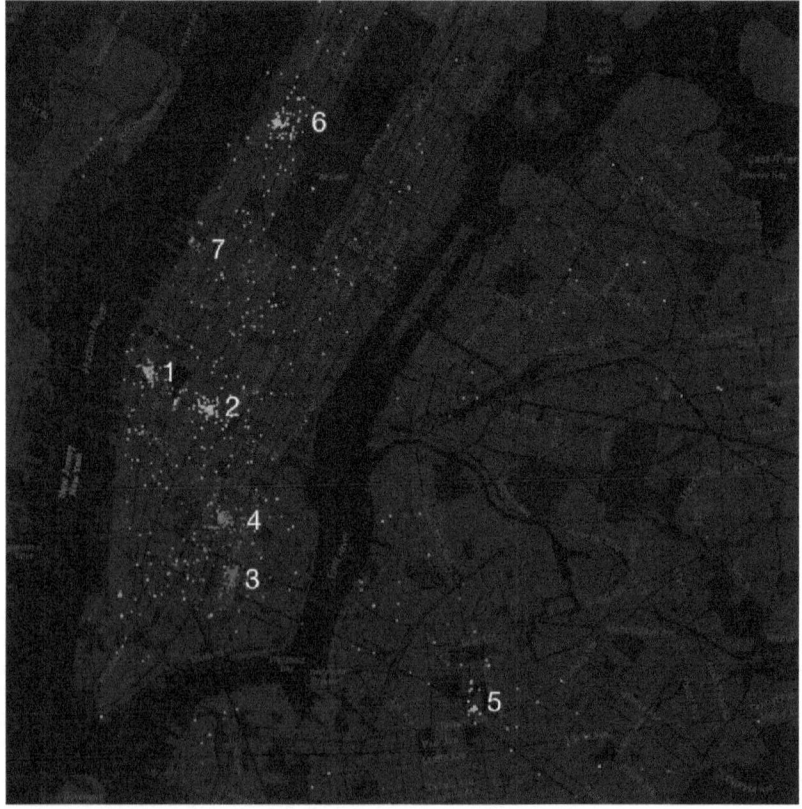

Figure 22.10 A map of locations of all photos from our seven clusters (Only NYC area is shown)

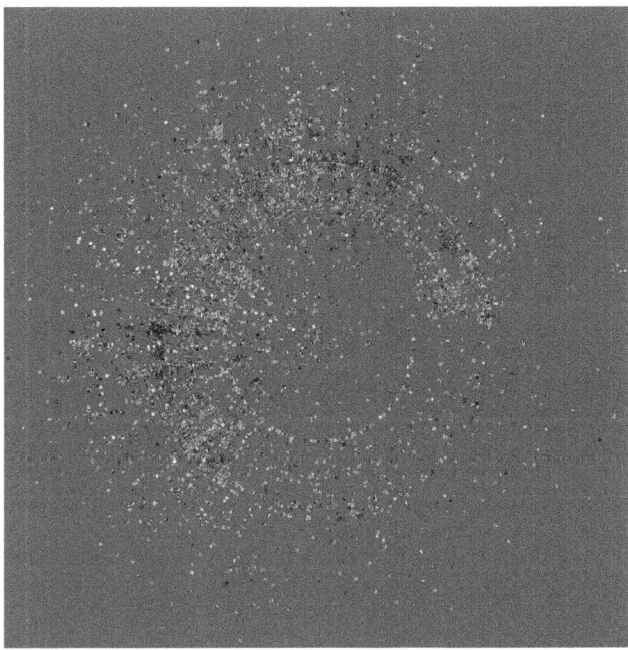

Figure 22.11 Radial visualization of 16,164 Instagram photos geo-tagged to NYC area between October 1st and November 20th, 2013. The photos are organized by location (perimeter) and upload date and time (angle)

different 'life span', and allows us to compare content of images, locate areas with concentration of images, and compare differences and similarities between different locations and time periods (the original visualization has resolution of 20,000 by 20,000 pixels, which allows to see details of all photos).

Visual Patterns

The informal examination of photos in each cluster revealed significant differences in their visual characteristics. There are multiple reasons for these differences, ranging from different conditions when photos were taken (time of the day, weather) to the use of Instagram filters. While some of these differences are not intentional, others are. By adding a filter, or photographing an artwork from a particular angle, or posing with an artwork, or interacting with it in some unexpected ways, people add their own meanings to the artist's works. While such additions and 'rewrites' can also be found in earlier contexts (e.g., fans creating their own versions of Star Trek episodes, or participating in an art happening), social media photography as exemplified by Instagram offers new ways of interpreting or rewriting the message of a hyper-local event, and immediately sharing it with others.

To further study the visual differences in the photos in each cluster, we extracted multiple visual features from each image (contrast, hue, brightness, etc.) and plotted all images in each cluster using the values of these features. In Figure 22.12, we visualized photos in each cluster organized by brightness mean on X axis, and hue mean on Y axis. We indicated the locations of the photo taken by Banksy himself using black squares.

This allows us to see the positions of Banksy's own 'official' photos of his

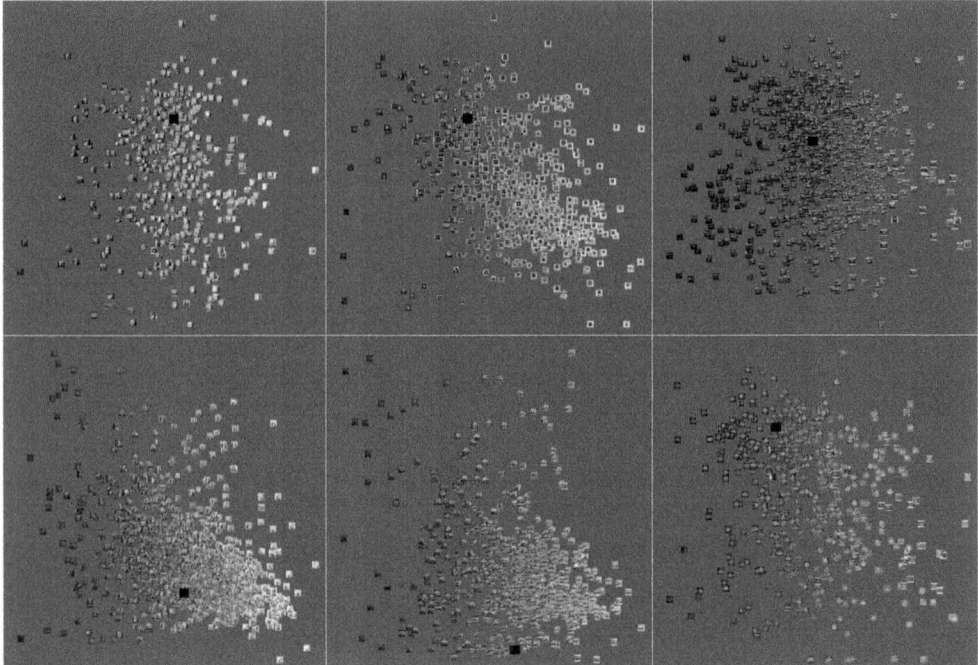

Figure 22.12 A matrix image plot visualization of six clusters. In each cluster, (X) – brightness mean, (Y) – hue mean. A black square represents the original photo of an artwork posted to Instagram by Banksy himself. Top row from the left: cluster 1, cluster 2, cluster 3. Bottom row from the left: cluster 4, cluster 6 and cluster 7

artworks in relation to all other photos of the same artwork taken by other people. The visualizations show that visual variability (at least, as indicated by the two features we used) changes significantly from cluster to cluster (due to the different colors of each work, location, time of day, and other factors). They also show that Banksy's own photos do not lie in the center of the clusters. Instead, the photos of other people create their own center – an unofficial 'canonical' image of the artwork different from that of the artist himself (if we want to quantify this observation, we can calculate the distances between the center of each cluster and the original photo taken by Banksy).

We also analyzed the presence of people in each of our clusters. While in cluster 6 we found 17.3% of photos with people in them, in cluster 2 we only found 7.2% percentage of such photos. These results show how the design of the work in a particular place affects social media activity within this place. In this case, two relatively similar works generate significantly different reactions as manifested in their social media representations. (See Figure 22.5 for images of these works.)

Finally, we sorted each of our clusters by time and hue. These visualizations reveal the changing appearance of the artworks over time, as each was repainted, sprayed and manipulated. Figure 22.13 shows these patterns of visual change over time in cluster 2 (left) and cluster 1 (middle), organized by hue mean (X) date and time (Y). Cluster 1 shows an interesting pattern. An early photo of the work taken when it initially appeared was re-circulated time and again, and appears at different later times, together with photos of the work in later stages after it was sprayed on and damaged (see close up on the right side of Figure 22.13).

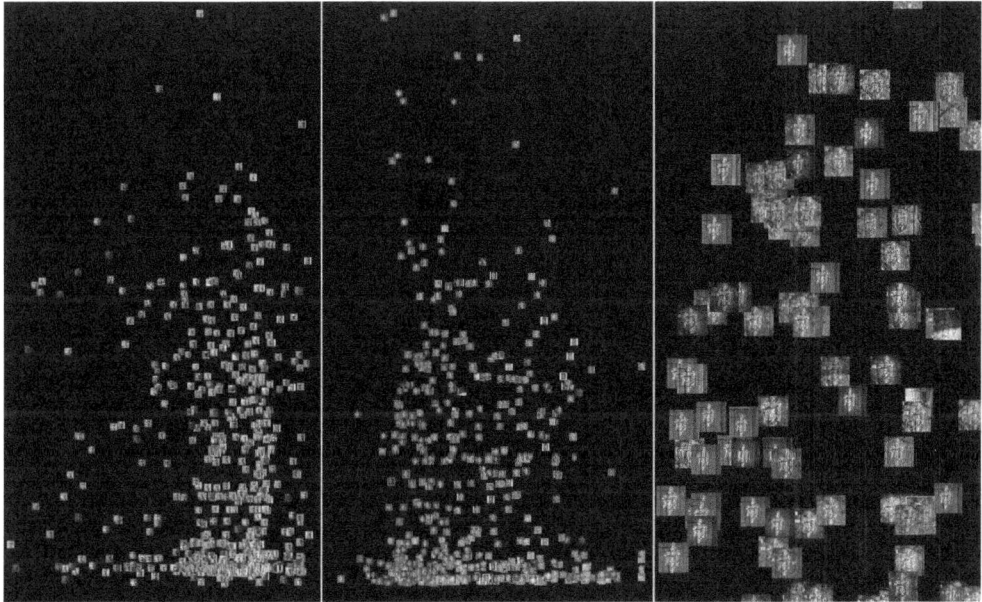

Figure 22.13 Visualization of cluster 2 (left) and cluster 1 (middle), sorted by hue mean (X) and date (Y). Right panel shows a close up of cluster 1. The visualization is rotated 90 degrees

ON HYPER-LOCALITY

If social media hyper-local data is a particular manifestation of a 'hyper-real' world (Eco, 1986) – where images and simulations of an event have greater significance than the actual site where this event took place – Banksy's art project in New York City can be seen as a poetic inquiry into the conditions of a representational 'data superiority' over 'physical inferiority'.

The distinguishing characteristic of the social hyper-local and the site-specific from all other previous models is the ways in which a site becomes *secondary* to all (artistic or social media) actions taken within it. The physical site is not stated as a precondition but is generated by the convergence of all social media or artistic discursive productions within it. In Banksy's case, the location of the work was disclosed by social media information about the particular location (first by the artist himself and then by all other followers that 'verified' that place and enabled all other social media productions that related to that place by utilizing the discursive and informational mechanism of the hashtag #banksyny). In other words, the site is structured by the work as 'content' and it is then fabricated and performed by the all other social media discursive productions within it (tags, photos, tweets etc.).

By announcing the location of his works via a daily photo shared on Instagram, and asking all visitors taking photos of these artworks and posting them on social media platforms to tag them with a specific hashtag, the artist transformed the visit to the physical location into a banal experience, and actively turned all these tagged photos into a representation of this banality. This banality is double sided. One the one hand, it is banal in the sense that the visitors to each location followed the online representations of this location left by other people. On the other hand, Banksy himself already took an image of that work in that place and all other images are reproduction of the same 'original' image.

I do not mean to use 'banality' here in derogatory terms but rather as a recurring informational mechanism that requires our attention, and as an element that diverge Banksy's work from former site-specific artworks. While typical site-specific works routinely engaged the collaborative participation of viewers in order to help them reveal a site as something that contains more than its fixed physicality (i.e. repressed social history; the location of disenfranchized social group), Banksy's work is occupied with the *informational processes* that underlie the production and reproduction of contemporary sites.

Banksy illustrates the *dissemination* of social media representation of a place and *performs* these processes via the reciprocal relation of places, objects, and data. This historical circular movement (the turning of objects into place and the transformation of a place into information) to which Banksy draws our attention contains three crucial elements: 1. The reproduction of a place via social media information items (tweets, photos, videos), 2. The turning of these representation/objects into quantifiable data, and 3. The organization of this data and the consequences of these informational forms for the ways we experience the place they represent.

In this sense, Banksy experiments with the ways in which a site becomes the sum of its multiple fragments, an endless signifying chain of photographic social media sights. By turning a physical site-specific work into a 'hyper-local social media work', Banksy's project emphasizes the historical parallels and differences between the nomadic Modernist understandings of the visual versus the native, site-specific notion suggested by the neo avant-garde as I described above. Banksy offers us 'staged' performances that have unique time and space coordinates – but at the same time they are designed with the understanding of social media trails. While the actual 'original' performance is still a spatial experience and thus is similar to 1970s site-specific performances (you have to be there), its social media representations are not experienced physically (you don't have to be there) and thus they have different characteristics.

The interest of site-specificity in revealing phenomenological, institutional and discursive strategies that operate within a place now turn out to be the revealing of social media strategies that generate a place and are in turn generated by this place. It is rather the *practices* of social media representations and their *effects* as they define the production, presentation, and dissemination of a representational hyper-local site. Under these new conditions, I ask again: How does hyper-locality render a place *differently* from site-specificity? What are the unique characteristics of this new form of representation?

Generalizing from this discussion and the particular case study of the Instagram photos of Banksys' artworks, I can identify these 'strategies' as possessing three characteristics: they are fragmented, temporalized, and nomadic.

Fragmentation

As opposed to the physical spatial sensorial experience of a place, social media hyper-locality is a representation of fragmented performances and exhibitions from multiple perspectives and times. If site-specific artistic works aimed to 'localize' our experience with the visual and turn it into the sum of its interactions in time and place, the hyper-local is a contemporary manifestation of a similar desire: the (visual) hyper-local is now the sum of its multiple media representations of all *other* people interacting in that place and time. As such, these representations allow us to explore interactions in that space, track their multiple representations, and explore their relations to a physical location (i.e., how the structure of a physical place conditions social media productions within it), as well as other dimensions.

Moreover, this fragmentary nature also speaks to the organization of hyper-local information within a place. Each site is described in terms of its own social media history and this history is emerging as a *lexicon*. Individual representations of a site are randomly juxtaposed with all other representation of that site and are then categorized into classes of information within that place in a fragmentary mixture of ages, styles, origins, gender, popular viewpoint, and other attributes. Which is to say that the site is now structured according to the fragmentary 'orders of things' found within it rather than by its mimetic spatially.

Temporalization

If site-specific works aimed at the spatialization and territorialization of the visual experience (grounding it in time and space), hyper-local social media data is actually a manifestation of its temporalization and 'de-territorialization'. Social media hyper-local data converts a place into an endless set of exchangeable sights that do not generate a single sense of that place. Rather, this vision is now constructed from an endless series of representations that are for the most part a manifestation of different times in that place.

In other words, the experience of a place via hyper-local social media data is not spatial (we do not 'navigate' a space through these representations). They are not meant to represent a map of a place, but rather a 'schedule', or a route, a sequence of representations of times within a space. This allows us to compare different temporalities in a place (i.e., by various social groups), to compare temporalities of different places, and experience the dynamic structure of a place over time.

Nomadization

A third difference between site-specific art and the social hyper-local is that while original site-specific works were grounded in a fixed physical location, the virtual hyper-local site is fluid. This nomadicity is evident not only in terms of the unstructured narrative of a place articulated by the multitude of paths of people within it, but also in the spread of images that transcends the original boundaries of that place into larger areas (such as the entire city and other locations around the world). In this sense, and in a paradoxical way, as our results demonstrate, while the geo-temporal tagged image is indeed a realization of avant-garde aspirations to contextualize the visual in time and place, social media platforms also bring back the nomadic modernist understanding of that visual, as it is shared by users not only in their original location but also in other places around the world.

But this nomadicaity lies in between mobilization and site-specificity, as it can always be *measured* with precision (i.e. measuring the distance between photos in terms of their content; location etc.). Under these new terms, being nomadic is not about being 'out of place' but rather to be always able to calculate the distance of the representation from a particular place and from all other representations that were taken in, on at or in relation to that place.

CONCLUSION

In this chapter I historicized, visualized, and theorized the distinctive ways in which localities are experienced and preformed through their social media hyper-local representations. I analyzed the organization of contemporary visual social media data in relation to two prominent paradigms in 20th century visual art, and drew historical parallels between artistic site-specificity and social media hyper-locality. I also looked at the relation between physical places and their social media representations using particular case studies – social media photos taken during the street artist Banksy's residency in New York during October 2013. Finally, based on the theoretical and historical analysis and the case study, I identified key characteristics of hyper-locality in social media.

The reinvention of site-specificity as hyper-locality comes in the midst of a cultural turn from former representational *standardized* spaces (particular maps of neighborhoods, cities or the entire earth) dictated from above (i.e. satellite views, municipal borders) towards more *intimate* visual and textual representations that are generated within these places. However, as with all other previous documentation mechanisms that were used to dedifferentiate and unify discrete spatialites (by annotating groups of places as neighborhoods, cities, etc.), these idiosyncratic views are now used in similar manner: to locate similarities within large sets of heterogeneous personal data collections, and thus emphasize once again the embedded logic of deterritorialization facilitated by network connectivity. In other words, by focusing on locational similarity (i.e. algorithmically locating groups of 'similar' places) they intensify the conditions of spatial sameness, repetitiveness and uniformity.

In these emerging representational conditions, site-specificity reincarnation as hyper-locality is infused with a crucial insight: if social media can reflect the particularities of places as opposed to their similarities, we need to find ways to analyze, visualize and theorize these differences. Banksy's work can thus be summed up as asking what would it mean in contemporary conditions to maintain the socio-cultural and political specificity of a place? By understanding hyper-locality as fundamentally connected to the particularities of site identities, Banksy rematerializes and renders places as different from each other, as one unique place within others.

NOTES

1 The analysis of Banksy's photos was conducted with the help of The Software Studies Initiative team members Lev Manovich and Mehrdad Yazdani. An abridged version of this chapter was previously presented as a conference paper. See: Hochman et al., 2014.

2 Notice that while these arrangements are currently the prominent ways to organize visual information, other possibilities do exist. For example, images can be sorted based on the interest of other people you follow (i.e. the Explore tag in Instagram) or by algorithmic arrangement of content according to user's previous actions.

3 A detailed description of the computational analysis and image clustering process appears in: Hochman et al., 2014.

REFERENCES

Buchloh B (1990) Conceptual Art 1962–1969: From the Aesthetics of Administration to the Critique of Institutions. *October*. Vol. 55. Winter, pp. 105–143.

Cranshaw J et al. (2012) The Livehoods Project: Utilizing Social Media to Understand the Dynamics of A City. In: *Proceedings of the Sixth International AAAI Conference on Weblogs and Social Media* (ICWSM–12), Dublin, Ireland, pp. 1–8, and at http://justincranshaw.com/papers/cranshaw_livehoods_icwsm12.pdf (Accessed 16 June 2013).

Dourish P (2006) Re-Spaceing Place: 'Place' and 'Space' Ten Years On. In: *Proceeding of the 20th CSCW*, pp. 299–308.

Eco U (1986) *Travels in Hyper Reality: Essays*. A Harvest book. Harcourt Brace Jovanovich.

Ehrlich K, LaBelle B and Vitiello S (2003) *Surface Tension: Problematics of Site*. Los Angeles: Errant Bodies Press in collaboration with Ground Fault Recordings, Downey, CA.

ElGindy E and Abdelmoty A (2012) Enhancing the Quality of Place Resources in Geo-folksonomies. *Web-Age Information Management*. Springer Berlin Heidelberg, pp. 1–12.

Elmgreen & Dragset (2014) The 'Named Series'. Photo by Anders Sune Berg. Installation view as part of the exhibition *Biography*, Astrup Fearnley Museum, Oslo.

Ewart J (2013) Local People, Local Places, Local Voices and Local Spaces: How Talkback Radio in Australia Provides Hyper-local News through Mini-Narrative Sharing. *Journalism* (July 9, 2013).

Gordon E and de Souza e Silva A 2011. *Net Locality*. Wiley Blackwell.

Hochman N, Manovich L and Yazdani M (2014) On Hyper-Locality: Performances of Place in

Social Media. *The International AAAI Conference on Weblogs and Social Media (ICWSM 2014)*.

Hogan B (2010) The Presentation of Self in the Age of Social Media: Distinguishing Performances and Exhibitions Online. *Bulletin of Science Technology & Society*, 30(6): 377–386.

Hu Y, Farnham SD and Monroy-Hernandez A (2013) Whoo.ly: Facilitating Information Seeking for Hyperlocal Communities Using Social Media. In: *The proceeding of CHI*, pp. 3481–3490. ACM.

Jarvis J (2009) Hyperlocal: The Elusive Golden Fleece. Available at: http://www.theguardian.com/media/2009/mar/16/digital-media-new-york-times (Accessed 2 April 2014).

Kwon M (1997) One Place After Another: Notes on Site Specificity. *October* Vol. 80. (Spring, 1997), pp. 85–110.

Kwon M (2002) *One Place After Another: Site-Specific Art and Locational Identity*. Cambridge, Mass: MIT Press.

Low SM and Altman I (1992) *Place Attachment*. Springer-Verlag.

Metzgar ET, Kurpius DD and Rowley KM (2011) Defining Hyperlocal media: Proposing a Framework for Discussion. *New Media & Society*, 13(5): 772–787.

Meyer J (1996) *The Functional Site*. Documents 7, Fall. *Documents Magazine Inc*. NYC.

Miel P and Faris R (2008) News and Information as Digital Media Come of Age. *Media Republic*.

O'Doherty B (1999) *Inside the White Cube: The Ideology of the Gallery Space*. Berkeley, CA: University of California Press.

Owens C (1980) The Allegorical Impulse: Toward a Theory of Postmodernism Part 2. October. 1980 Jul 1;13:59–80.

Roberts JL (2014) *Transporting Visions: The Movement of Images in Early America*. Berkeley, CA: University of California Press.

Schwartz B (2011) Bing Upsets Webmasters By Linking Images Directly To Image File. Available at: http://www.seroundtable.com/bing-images-direct-link-13300.html (Accessed 7 August 2014).

Smith R (2013) Mystery Man, Painting the Town: Banksy Makes New York his Gallery for a Month. http://www.nytimes.com/2013/10/31/arts/design/banksy-makes-new-york-his-gallery-for-a-month.html (Accessed 7 August 2014)

Smithson R et al. (2005) *Robert Smithson: Spiral Jetty*. Berkeley, CA: University of California Press.

Wikipedia (2014) Google images. Available at: http://en.wikipedia.org/wiki/Google_Images (Accessed 3 April 2014).

Wilken R and Goggin G (2012) *Mobile Technology and Place*. New York, NY: Routledge.

Winter S, Kuhn W and Kruger A (2009) Guest Editorial: Does Place have a Place in Geographic Information Science? *Spatial Cognition and Computation*, 9(3):171–173.

Xie K et al. (2013) Robust detection of hyper-local events from geotagged social media data. *Proceedings of the Thirteenth International Workshop on Multimedia Data Mining*. ACM.

Zhang A et al. (2013) Hoodsquare: Modeling and Recommending Neighborhoods in Location-Based Social Networks. *Institute of Electrical and Electronics Engineers*, pp. 69–74

Analyzing Social Media Data and Other Data Sources: A Methodological Overview[1]

Frauke Zeller

Social media research offers vast opportunities to conduct research that links social media data and other data sources. This chapter provides an overview of the methodological challenges and opportunities, but also a discussion of the term data and of the nature of social media data. The methods overview, in combination with the introduction and discussion of methods used in other disciplines and in commercial market research, aims to provide a practical and applied guideline for social media research. An applied case study at the end of this chapter describes a novel approach to the analysis of multimodal, large data sets in online communication environments, using a mixed method design.

INTRODUCTION

Linking social media data and other data sources can be regarded as a challenging and, at the same time, redeeming feature. It is challenging given the complexity of the data available online, and the research design needed for a sound research project analyzing multiple data formats and/or sources. The redeeming feature can be seen, for example, in the availability of vast quantities of different kinds of social media data, which help to contextualize findings and can potentially provide a work-around strategy to the anonymity challenge of online data. Social scientists are primarily interested in understanding social interaction embedded in our social world or context. This means we need to be able to contextualize data with the respective social world (usually demographic and other information). This is difficult – if not almost impossible – given that anyone can pretend to be anybody on social media.[2] Linking social media data and other data sources can help by enriching the results, and providing additional information. For example, a network visualization of a company's Twitter handle can provide an impressive image if the company has thousands of followers. However, it does not tell us whether these followers talk about the company in a favourable or less favourable way. So called viral memes on social media can – if they are negative – turn into a serious problem for companies by damaging their reputation which can result in the loss of customers or a decline in the company's stock market value. This chapter therefore provides a comprehensive, practical overview and a critical discussion of the different methods applied and data sources used in social media research including qualitative, quantitative and mixed-methods approaches. It starts by discussing the dual nature of social media research and the need to differentiate between social media as an object of research on the one hand, and as an instrument to conduct research on the other hand. In order to be able to combine social media data and other data sources, one needs to have some understand of the terminology: What is data, raw data, and how is it generated? Most importantly, this chapter discusses why social media data is different from other data sources. This discussion is followed by an overview of the different methods in social media research, encompassing traditional approaches as well as current trends in academic social sciences research, and industry-based social media analytics.

Social media research is complex and using digital methods is rarely straightforward (Kennedy et al., 2014). In fact, big companies such as Facebook or Google are said to have an increasingly powerful data monopoly as well as the best tools (and biggest budgets) to analyze the data. In order to keep pace in the social media analytics race, probably only top tier universities will have a chance to compete and negotiate access to data and tools (boyd and Crawford, 2012). Hence, it is important for smaller research/academic outfits, including their students, that they get an understanding of what is feasible in terms of social media analytics and data linking. This chapter therefore aims to provide a comprehensive overview targeting researchers (from academia and industry) as well as students.

The chapter ends with a case study that uses an innovative mixed methods approach to analyze multimodal social media data. The approach enables a combined text and image analysis using Facebook entries. The text analysis draws upon statistical, corpus linguistic text analysis instruments. The results are then used in a qualitative analysis tool as a coding mechanism for the image analysis. This means that the different methods are used in a triangulation model, aiming to combine both qualitative and quantitative methods as well as different data sources.

THE DUAL NATURE OF SOCIAL MEDIA: SOCIAL MEDIA AS A RESEARCH OBJECT AND INSTRUMENT

Researching social media can be both exciting and challenging. This is because social media affect us, our economies, political systems and our private lives. They have become pervasive in our daily lives, both private and professional spheres. This means that if one claimed to be researching social media, it would be only fair to ask to elaborate on it, since there are myriads of different research aspects: starting with the multitude of different social media applications (see also McCay-Peet and Quan-Haase, this volume) which are highly volatile in nature, i.e. new appearing today and others, established ones, suddenly disappearing – to the many different use contexts of social media (job related, private usages, political usage, etc.), and finally the many different ways that social media can be analyzed (see e.g. Hogan and Quan-Haase, 2010). The last point refers not only to the many different methods and instruments that can be used to research social media, but also the complexity of social media data *per se*. One example would be the multiple languages spoken in social media, often within one Facebook comment thread, or regarding one specific Twitter hashtag. But there are also ethical questions, such as: Should we analyze any data that we manage to get hold of? What about data that has become available through illegal hacking attacks, such as the confidential data publically, yet illegally, distributed from an online-dating website? It seems rather straightforward to say that this would go too far, however the case is not always this clear (see also Beninger, this volume).

In order to provide some guidance in this research maze it is often useful to start with some simple distinctions, such as the duality of social media research. Adapted from the earlier online research body of literature, Welker and Kloß (2014) suggest two main research approaches:

a) Research object approach: putting the users into the foreground and thus analyzing the usage of online or social media.
b) Research instrument approach: using online or social media for the measurement and collection of behavioural and communicative patterns.

When researching social media as a research object in itself, it is usually the users who are in the focus of attention, or more specifically their ways and patterns of using social media and producing or consuming content. Typical questions in this line of research can range from an individual or group dimension to societal questions, such as how the Internet or social media influence our society, individual lives, or group formations and behaviours. In the societal dimension, the importance and influence of social media are being documented in many national user studies, which are often freely available. For example, the *Canadian Internet Use Survey* (CIUS) used to measure in biennial intervals if Canadians have access to the Internet and determines the type of household access as well as online behaviours of individuals.[3] Another example are studies conducted by the *Pew Research Center*[4] in the United States, the *Eurostat*[5] studies in Europe, or the highly influential *Ofcom*[6] studies in Great Britain. Apart from those studies, industry-based research also exists, however often not openly accessible (e.g. studies offered by market research companies such as Thomson Reuters/Ipsos or consulting companies such as McKinsey).

Welker and Kloß (2014) define four main areas for studies relating to the research object dimension: (1) identity and relationship management of online users; (2) networks and network structures; (3) comparing offline and online user/usage behaviour; and (4) online privacy management (Welker and Kloß, 2014: 34). An interesting aspect is that this research often integrates different dimensions. The micro-level analysis of individual online usage is often combined with societal, macro-level related questions such as the digital divide (Internet access) and how this impacts societies (see e.g. Haight et al., 2014). Studies conducted by commercial research organizations often combine the micro-level perspective with a meso-perspective, that is, how individual Internet use impacts organizations and companies.

The research instrument approach discusses the use of social media for the collection and measurement of behavioural and communicative patterns. This area addresses research questions regarding both offline and online communication. Examples for offline communication would be surveys on political voting patterns that are carried out via social media. In fact, the increasing penetration and usage of social media in the general population has shaped social media and social networking platforms not only into an instrument for the dissemination of information, but also into an often-used tool for data collection. This chapter will focus on social media from the perspective of the research instrument approach, and different methods and instruments will be discussed in detail in the following chapter sections.

THE EXTENDED RESEARCH PROCESS: A SYSTEMATIC INTEGRATION OF THE TECHNO-METHODOLOGICAL DIMENSION IN SOCIAL MEDIA RESEARCH

Social media research is often discussed in connection with big data research, which is grounded in the quantity of data that can be queried and generated by social media. In a nutshell, 'Big Data' research deals with very large and complex data sets, which demand technical aids given their size (i.e. computer programs and/or high performance computing) for their collection, processing, and analysis (Kitchin, 2013, 2014; Zeller, 2014). boyd and Crawford describe big data as the 'capacity to search, aggregate, and cross-reference large data sets' (2012: 663). A widely-used description originates from IBM, describing four core attributes or inherent challenges of big data: volume, variety, velocity, and veracity (Zikopoulos et al., 2012; see also Klein et al., 2013). The term big data has spread in the last few years, accompanied by almost inflationary attention. Thus one can find utopian descriptions of big data such as the new oil of the information economy (Mayer-Schönberger and Cukier, 2013), or as a pivotal competitive advantage for companies (e.g. Barton, 2012). There are also voices that attribute big data the potential to act as a substitute for traditional research: 'With enough data, the numbers speak for themselves... There's no reason to cling to our old ways. It's time to ask: What can science learn from Google?' (Anderson, 2008).

However, less utopian and more critical reviews often derive from academic research, in particular from the humanities and social sciences. Among the early discussions are boyd and Crawford (2012) or Manovich (2011). In these publications, as well as in other places, increasingly critical discussions around the notion and interpretation of data can be found. For example, Flew et al. (2012) emphasize with regard to big data: 'it is important to remember that data refers not only to numeric and statistical records, but to any form of information represented in a digitized format including text, audio, photographic, and video files' (Flew et al., 2012: 160). And it is in fact only through the manipulation or processing with the computer and software applications that data are transformed into trends, patterns, and accurate information.

Jensen (2014) goes into more detail and notes that 'data are either *found* or *made*' (224, italics in original). This means, very generally speaking, that in the humanities, existing objects or artifacts are usually analyzed, hence *found* data are being collected, evaluated or interpreted. As to the social sciences, data are usually *made* – for example, via surveys or experiments. There are of course also numerous examples that would speak against this generalization. The point that is being made here however is that in relation to digital communication it is nevertheless 'a new type and scale of data […]: big data or *metadata* that indicate who did what, with which information, together with whom, when, for how long and in which sequences and networks' (Jensen, 2014: 224). Furthermore, data can be seen as hybrid in terms of social media, because they are always both *found* and *made*: 'They can be found online, as they are being generated through our social media usage. However they also integrate the "making" aspect, given that one would have to "make" the corresponding algorithms, hence programming, and then extracting, etc. in order to get them' (Jensen, 2014: 229).

Arguably, data hybridization also has a significant influence on the traditional research process. Figure 23.1 shows the traditional process of empirical research (left side of the figure, adapted from Bryman et al., 2012) as well as the necessary, in the context of social media data, extended discovery process. The traditional research process commences with a research question, and, depending on the

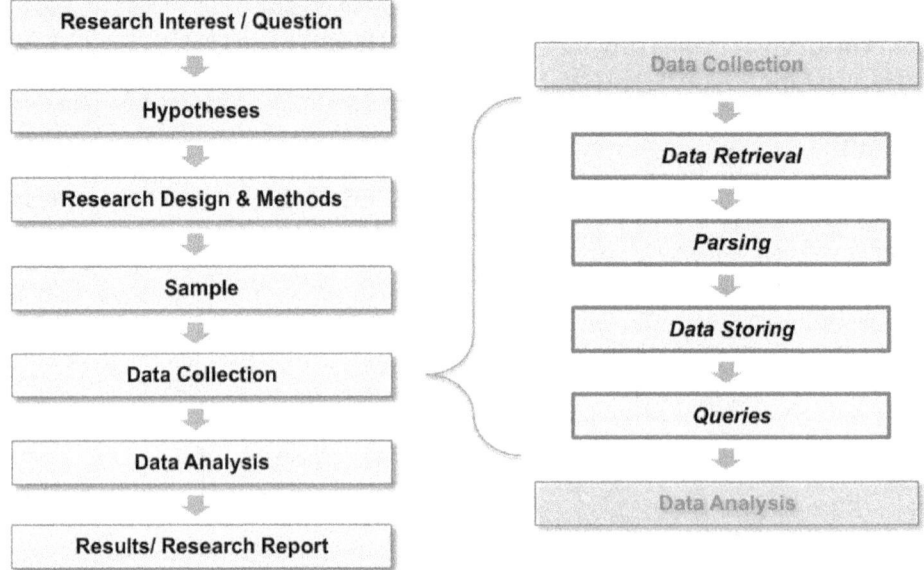

Figure 23.1 The extended empirical research process in social media research

kind of study, specified hypotheses. After the establishment of the research design and operationalization (method) of the empirical study, the sample is defined and data collected. What follows is the data analysis and ultimately research report containing the results and a discussion thereof.

The right-hand side of Figure 23.1 shows the extension of the traditional research process: the data collection phase is being expanded and adapted to the specific conditions of social media research. Depending on the scope, method and research question of a study, the data collection can now include four additional steps (Welser et al., 2008) representing an optional expansion or augmentation of the traditional approach:

(A) Data Retrieval: Due to the abundance of raw data, which are generated by users of social media sites, computer-based procedures for the collection of data are often a necessary means (this again depends on the overall scope and approach of each research project). One example for such computer-based procedures are Application Programming Interface (API) programmes, which describe a group of different kinds of instruments or algorithms that allow for the access and retrieval of raw-data (Welser et al., 2008; Zeller, 2014). This is contingent on whether the providers of the respective social media platforms, where raw-data are produced, facilitate the usage of APIs. And even in the case of an API being offered, such as in the case of the Twitter API, it does not mean that researchers are able to collect all tweets relating to a certain hashtag, for example. Programmes that facilitate the usage of APIs are sometimes freely available on the Internet, however a certain degree of programming expertise is still necessary. For researchers who do not have those skills, there are also programs and services that facilitate this operation. They often include some first, quick data analysis procedures, such as network visualizations, word frequency and keyword analyses.[7] Other programmes are web crawlers and scrapers, which systematically scan web content either on specific issues or of pre-defined pages.

(B) Data Processing (Parsing): This step includes the necessary preparation or

pre-processing of the collected data. Given that social media often produce high quantities of raw data, the automated data collection usually contains a whole range of data that is tangential and off-topic. This means that the collected data must be systematically gone through and cleaned. One example is the multilingual nature of social media. For content analyses, only data which are in the language or languages that will be analyzed are useful. Hence any data in a different language should not be part of the main sample. Relating to this second step of data pre-processing, the GIGO-problem is often mentioned: GIGO stands for 'garbage in, garbage out' and describes the challenge to filter spam etc. from the wealth of data that can be collected on social media (Karpf, 2012; Markham, 2013; Zeller, 2014). Further processing steps refer to the extraction of the relevant data and conversion to a usable format. In relation to the above-mentioned example of the Twitter API, for a network visualization the actual text of the tweets is not necessary but only the handles of the Twitter users that published to the relevant hashtag or key term. So called parsers provide not only the required data in the desired, pre-defined form, they also provide the ability to add additional metadata. For example, connecting the place with the respective users. By contrast, for a content analysis, i.e. analyzing what is being said about a certain topic/product, the researcher must decide whether they want to keep URLs in the sample or rather delete them. This is a relevant point since hyperlinks/URLs can also include specific words that could distort the results of an automated content analysis.

(C) Data Storing and (D) Queries: These two steps can be considered together since they must be closely coordinated. Intelligent data storage systems can archive the collected data as designated entries in a database in such a way that they can be queried in different variations (queries). There is a high interdependency of the data storing and query system: if, for example, a researcher decides for a relational database they need to know in advance which query language can be applied to the specific database, or which queries are possible, such as SQL (Standard Query Language) or XML-based queries. Relational databases are organized in a straight-forward way, such as in an SPSS or Excel table where each data line represents a case and each column an attribute. It is certainly recommended to test some basic queries in this early stage, in order to test the data set for errors. Also, when combining different data sources of different data forms – for example, text with images – the data storage and query part can quickly become rather complex. The researcher would need to decide as early as possible, which data comparisons or triangulations are being planned, so which attributes of each data set will need to be part of a multi-query integrating different data forms and different data bases.

These four additional steps underscore Jensen's (2014) finding that 'found' data from social media often are not useful to researchers until they have been manipulated by algorithms (for data collection) and databases into usable records.[8]

METHODS OVERVIEW

Table 23.1 shows an overview of the different measurement and data collection methods, integrating methods from both academic and industry based market research. In addition, approaches from neighbouring disciplines, which are also applicable by researchers in social sciences, are discussed. It is important to note that the methods and approaches can overlap in this table, which is due to the limited space, and the general limitation of 2D figures.

Reading Table 23.1 from left to right shows the main differentiation between quantitative methods, qualitative methods as well as method combinations (quantitative and qualitative). Each of these three areas is divided into reactive and non-reactive methods.

Table 23.1 Methods overview (adapted from Zeller, 2015)

		Empirical Instruments in Communication Studies	Adaptable Instruments / Social Media Analytics
Quantitative	Reactive (Interactive)	Online Survey	Crowdsourcing
		Online Experiment	MROCS
	Non-Reactive	Web Content Analysis	Video and Image Analyses
		Network Analysis Log File Analysis	Sentiment and Opinion Analysis (SOA)
		Data Mining	Text Linguistic Analysis
			Automated Content Analysis
			Social Media Monitoring and Analytics
Qualitative	Reactive (Interactive)	Online Experiments	Bio-Feedback, Eye-Tracking
		Online Interviews	MROCS
		Online Focus Groups	Virtual Ethnography
		Online Field Studies	
	Non-Reactive	Web Structure Analysis	Video and Image Analyses
		Web Content Analysis	Online Discourse Analysis
		Online Discourse Analysis	Multimodal Analysis
		Video and Image Analyses	
Mixed Methods	Reactive (Interactive)	Reactive and Non-Reactive	Q-Method
		Quantitative and Qualitative	Crowdsourcing/MROCS and Focus Groups
	Non-Reactive	Non-Reactive and Reactive	Social Media Monitoring and SOA
		Qualitative and Quantitative	Web Tracking

Non-reactive instruments are, for example, content and log file analyses or participant observations. They basically relate to 'found' data, using Jensen's (2014) distinction. 'Made' data, on the other hand, refers to reactive methods, which usually imply a reaction from the participants in the study. Hence, common instruments in this area are surveys, interviews, or focus groups.

In addition to the traditional binary distinction, Table 23.1 also shows interactive methods as part of the reactive methods column. This category was adapted from market research where interactive methods are discussed as a promising new approach in empirical studies (see 'Quantitative methods'). Going further, Table 23.1 describes two vertical columns: the traditional empirical instruments in communication studies and instruments deriving from other areas and disciplines and which can be adapted to social sciences research.

Quantitative Methods

With regard to the quantitative, as well as reactive (interactive) methods in both pillars, the first column – empirical instruments – contains tools that have already been applied in online research: *online survey* and *online-experiment* (Vehovar and Manfreda, 2008; Wright, 2005; Reips, 2002, 2003; Taddicken, 2008, 2013). *Crowdsourcing* and *MROCs* (Market Research Online Communities) in the second column refer to the above-mentioned interactive methods. The term crowdsourcing was coined by Howe in 2006, and has received a whole range of different meanings since then. In general, crowdsourcing depicts the use of cognitive skills and/or labour of many individuals (crowds), leveraged by the interactive nature of social media. Thus, crowdsourcing is used, for example, for the description and the indexing (tagging) of image archives. In a nutshell, crowdsourcing appeals to market researchers and entrepreneurs whenever computer intelligence cannot cope with the tasks at hand. And although there are computer algorithms that can extract information from images and recognize even colours or forms, their performance is still outperformed by human beings. In market and product research crowdsourcing is also being applied as a tool for product development and innovations. For example, in Dell's initiative 'Idea Storm' Internet users worldwide were asked to come up with ideas for product enhancements or new products (Poetz and Schreier, 2012). Generally, it can be said that crowdsourcing provides information on specific products relatively quickly and cost-effectively. However, the information collected through this method is often less detailed than originally anticipated (Scheffler, 2014). The community approach is also often discussed under the acronym MROCs. Closed communities are initiated by market research institutes or companies, which recruit specific target groups with regard to certain brands or research questions to answer (Steffen, 2014: 107). Arguably, these declared 'new' instruments actually use the traditional survey method (crowdsourcing) or field studies (MROCs).

With regard to the quantitative, non-reactive instruments in the communication studies column, the instruments mentioned here are often based on traditional communication studies tools. For example, a *web content analysis* – just as the traditional content analysis – should integrate the creation of a code book (see e.g. Krippendorff, 2012; Herring, 2010). When it comes to choosing specific software, for example, for the systematic collection/download of the required web content, it is necessary to check the software's inherent limitations. This relates to aspects of the data format, that is, in which format the data is being saved/collected, but also whether and how the software downloads integrated hyperlinks, and if so, how these third party sites are identified (Vis, 2013). As to the adaptable methods, *video & image analyses* are traditionally oriented towards qualitative research. Within the quantitative category, this field uses largely automated analyses of online pictures and videos, which is often based on the metadata contained in the images, and/or combined with crowdsourcing-based indexing and tagging (see Balasubramanian et al., 2004; Ghoshal et al., 2005; Goodrum et al., 2009).

The following three instruments can be summarized under the term *automated text analysis* (ATA), including areas such as information retrieval, corpus linguistics and automated content analyses. While the latter have already been used in communication studies for some time, including framing studies (Entman, 2010; Entman and Jones, 2009), automated *sentiment & opinion analyses* (SOA) are a rather recent development (Liu, 2012; Tumasjan et al., 2013; Young and Soroka, 2012). These ATA instruments are often preferred for studies with large data sets (Lewis et al., 2013; Mehl and Gill 2010) and hence appeal to social media studies. *Social media monitoring & analytics*, finally, is mainly connected to market research. The majority of the instruments used in this category is also adaptable for communication studies and are separately listed in Table 23.2. Most of the data collection methods are self-explanatory, however some specific terms and their meanings will be described in more detail below. Two points are of relevance here: Firstly, the entire bandwidth of methods is based on passive (i.e., non-reactive) data collection methods and, ultimately, the counting of the different occurrences. It is important to ask how the data were collected and also whether the data are representative. When using, for example, commercial social media analytics services, these questions often remain unanswered given that commercial providers rarely offer 100% insight on coverage, sample, representativeness, etc. Secondly, the table represents a combination of different metrics and instruments used in market research. The field in itself is highly diverse, with hardly any broadly adapted standards. However, in recent years marketing and public relations (PR) companies have aimed to establish such needed standards. These initiatives are usually referred to as PR measurement and evaluation (Macnamara, 2014), and associations such as the International Association for the Measurement and Evaluation of Communication (AMEC), the International Public Relations Association (IPRA), the Interactive Advertising Bureau (IAB) or the Institute of Public Relations (IPR) have started initiatives to define such standards. These represent important first steps, however there are still a lot of vaguely used terms and widely varying methodologies (Macnamara, 2014).

Monitoring (first row Table 23.2) is primarily concerned with the analysis of the visibility and range of certain actors, companies, or topics in social media. The main interest lies here in the overall attention being generated.

In this regard, *share of buzz* is one of the most important indicators since the number of mentions of a specific topic is being measured. *Share of voice* determines the number of mentions of a specific person or a company. With regard to the second row in Table 23.2 – Social Media Analytics – the impact of social media messages is mainly being measured. *Unique users/views per channel* aims to measure the actual success and thus detects, for example, whether a specific profile of a person is clicked in high numbers. The measure *unique users/views* (or even *unique visitors*) usually represents a result that shows which profile has been clicked/visited over a certain period of time (e.g. a week) from different computers (usually counted via unique IP-addresses). This means that by using specific add-on programmes like cookies it is possible to gain a more detailed picture of the impact – that is whether a site or profile is being visited by different users or by the same user multiple times. The term *per channel* refers to the differentiation of the various social media platforms such as Twitter, Facebook or YouTube as a channel. The third row in the table describes the traditional indicators of website analytics in respect of the

Table 23.2 Social media monitoring and analytics in commercial market analysis (BVDW, 2013; Scheffler, 2014; AMEC, 2014, adapted from Zeller, 2015)

	Usage Variable	Indicator/Measurement
Monitoring	Visibility, Range, Attention	• Share of buzz, share of voice • Number of sources, posts • Number of authors • Number of positive/negative mentions
Social Media Analytics	Virility and impact potential of content, authors, channels, engagement	• Degree of profile networking/cross-linking, recommendations, likes, evaluations • Interaction rate per post • Growth of fan community • Unique user/views per channel • Number of relevant fans
Traditional Web Analytics	Popularity of content / author	• Web tracking • Number of website visits • Number of website visits generated from social media channels • Duration of stay on website • Visibility

pages' popularity and attractiveness. Private users can conduct such an analysis, too, by means of services such as Google Analytics.

Qualitative Methods

With regards to the qualitative methods in Table 23.1, the traditional, reactive methods column depicts a well-known repertoire of traditional offline instruments, which have been adapted and, over the years, optimized for online environments (Fraas et al., 2013; Herring, 2004, 2010; Hewson et al., 2003). The second column lists again recent developments from industry-based market research, that are already and increasingly used in communication studies: *biofeedback analyses* and *eye-tracking* (Bente et al., 2007) are often applied in (advertising) research and so far have been mainly used in qualitative studies due to the high technical costs. *Virtual ethnographies* can be compared to online field studies. They are also listed in the second column, since they are often linked to cultural studies. Researchers applying them, with a specific social media perspective, are Kozinets (2010) and his netnography approach, but also Hine (2000) or Boellstorff et al. (2012). The non-reactive, qualitative instruments include *web structure analysis* (Brügger, 2010; Pauwels, 2012) and *web content analysis* (Herring, 2010). The former is often applied in online community research to analyze, for example, default usage and interaction structures of social media. *Web content analysis* can also be applied in a qualitative design, if specific providers are to be investigated. *Video and image analyses* can be found in both columns since they represent well-established methods in communication studies as well as other disciplines, however each with different paradigms and interests. This also applies to the *online discourse analysis*, which has been in use in communication studies since the early days of online research (see e.g. Fraas et al., 2013; Herring, 2004) and other

areas (e.g. rhetoric studies). Multimodal analyses are based on a well-established field, which includes approaches from cultural studies, linguistics, and semiotics (Kress, 2009; O'Halloran and Smith, 2010) and describes a methodological approach, which enables to conduct studies of multimodal, i.e. multimedia online content.

Method Combinations

Further down in Table 23.1 follow method combinations in a methodological design, i.e. quantitative and qualitative methods. In this category almost any conceivable combination of communication studies methods is possible. Moreover, reactive and non-reactive methods can be combined. In general, this area – including triangulation studies – represents an established and often practiced approach in communication studies (Burke Johnson et al., 2007; Teddlie and Tashakkori, 2009). As to social media, there are an increasing number of authors claiming that mixed methods (and data source combinations) are a necessary means in order to deal with the complex and rich data generated via social media (Lewis et al., 2013; Quan-Haase et al., 2015). Despite the rise in accepting mixed methods research, there are still unresolved issues in this area. Tashakkori and Teddlie (2003) list, for example, nomenclature and basic definitions, and the paradigmatic foundation or design issues in mixed methods research, as some of the unresolved problems. They define mixed methods research as 'the type of research in which a researcher or a team of researchers combines elements of qualitative and quantitative research approaches (…) for the purpose of breadth of understanding or corroboration' (Teddlie and Tashakkori, 2009: 32). Besides the mixing of different research approaches or instruments, mixed methods must also include a concrete data strategy, such as triangulation or data conversion. Without a strategy, any mixed methods design lacks an important component, since the nature and form of the available data cannot be neglected. Triangulation is described as the 'combinations and comparisons of multiple data sources, data collection and analysis procedures, research methods, investigators, and inferences that occur at the end of a study' (Teddlie and Tashakkori, 2009: 27). Data conversion is the conversion of quantitative data into qualitative data and vice versa. For example, quantitizing data describes the process of turning/converting qualitative data into numbers that can then be statistically analyzed, and qualitizing data means that quantitative data (e.g. numbers) are transformed into qualitatively analyzable data, such as narrative data (Teddlie and Tashakkori, 2009: 27). As to the reason or usefulness of mixing methods, Fielding (2012) claims that there are three main reasons: illustration, convergent validation, and analytic density (127). Whereas the first reason – illustration – can be seen as a supportive function in terms of making 'dry' data more 'alive' (e.g. by using word clouds or network visualizations), convergent validation describes 'whether findings from different methods agree. If they do, it is assumed that the findings are more likely to be valid (...)' (Fielding, 2012: 127). The third reason appears to take up what is being criticized in discourses around big data, which claim that numbers would speak for themselves. What is missing here is the contextualization of data and results, since otherwise they will most likely not provide sufficient insights. Referring back to 'The extended research process', and the extended research process, mixing methods and especially data conversion and triangulation strategies call for a sound understanding of the data available for each study. If, for example, some quantitative data does not provide enough information to be turned into narrative data given the lack of context, for example, then data conversion is not advisable.

Coming back to the methods overview in Table 23.1, *Q-Method* is mentioned as an example for adaptable mixed methods. It is a tool that integrates qualitative and quantitative methods, 'explicitly designed to objectively uncover and analyze similarities and differences in the subjective viewpoints of individuals' (Davis and Michelle, 2011: 561). The qualitative aspect is integrated by means of interviews, focusing on the subjective opinions and attitudes of the respondents. At the same time, by means of factor analysis, a quantitative part is also integrated. After the interview, the participants are asked to rank certain preferences to the appropriate topic and these rankings are then generalized using a factor analysis that ultimately come up with different types of users (see also Brown, 1993; Schrøder and Kobbernagel, 2010; Zeller et al., 2013).

Web tracking is being listed in Table 23.1 in the non-reactive methods category and was originally intended as a popular method, based on simple algorithms that can be integrated into web pages and which register the website visitors. This means that log files are analyzed, which are being collected via so-called web tracker applications. Web tracking is now seen in a more critical light, including ethical questions, such as what data these web trackers may collect without the knowledge of the website visitor.

Other method combinations depicted in Table 23.1 have already been discussed above. However, one additional aspect should be mentioned: Scheffler (2014) calls the combination of social media analytics with traditional instruments 'hybrid techniques'. He emphasizes that social media instruments provide sufficient scrutiny and reliability for some research questions, or at least allow for a first, quick orientation. For more detailed analyses that aim to project results to a broader population, for example, one must be more critical of method combinations and their actual scope (Scheffler, 2014: 108) given that some data sets and/or methods do not allow for generalizations or projections. He therefore calls for a method combination that, at the same time, allows the researcher to harvest advantages such as speed, scalability, openness, etc. as well as the use of a quantitative, statistical validation of the results (Scheffler, 2014: 108).

CASE STUDY

The following case study aims to provide a brief demonstration and example of the combining of methods in social media research. The mixed methods design depicted here draws upon computer-supported, quantitative and qualitative instruments, which are comprised of statistical text analyses combined with image and discourse analyses conducted in Facebook. It is argued that the mere usage of computational tools is not sufficient given the shortcomings of the tools when it comes to analyzing complex, ambiguous raw data such as text communication combined with images. Therefore, a mixed methods approach is necessary that integrates different tools but also takes into account the tool's advantages and disadvantages in order to moderate and reduce their shortcomings through triangulation and iterative analyses processes.

Software: The main software tools used were WordSmith Tools (Scott, 2008) and ATLAS.ti. ATLAS.ti is a high-end CAQDAS (Computer-Assisted Qualitative Data Analysis Software) application, suitable for image and video analyses. It enables researchers to adapt a mixed methods approach by offering the option to either import or export quantitative data. WordSmith Tools (Scott, 2008), a statistical lexical and text analysis tool, allows researchers to conduct analyses regarding word frequencies, keyword-in-context (KWIC) analyses or collocation analyses (word pairs) that can then be imported into ATLAS.ti as coding categories. These combined methods can provide insights into the specific language usage (genre analysis) in social media, as well as reveal the forming of sub-groups through jargon detection, or also framing processes of certain topics in combination with image usage.

Sample: Greenpeace's open Facebook group was chosen as a suitable test bed for the application of the mixed method design. A public group was chosen for ethical reasons and to avoid including private conversations. Furthermore, the activist group Greenpeace was selected because of its strong visual support, i.e. pictures of endangered species or environmental issues. Two non-consecutive months were chosen for the experimental case study: June 2012 and September 2012. June 2012 was chosen because the World Earth Summit (or United Nations Conference on Sustainable Development) took place in Rio de Janeiro, Brazil, during that month. It gained a lot of media coverage since it took place 20 years after the 1992 Earth Summit in Rio, during which countries agreed upon and adopted Agenda 21, a blueprint to rethink economic growth, advance social equity and ensure environmental protection. In order to have some difference in the sample months, a second month with no major global event related to environmental or nature issues was chosen (in this case, September 2012).

Corpus: Table 23.3 shows the overall numbers of the corpus used. The corpus added up to a relative balance between the two months regarding word count, as well as Type/Token[9]

Table 23.3 Case study corpus overview

Files	Word Count	Tokens	Types	Type/Token Ratio
Overall	2,695,840	220,918	23,918	44.01
June	1,375,176	114,273	15,016	43.94
September	1,320,664	106,492	14,470	44.07

Ratio (TTR). Corpora are large bodies of naturally occurring language that are encoded electronically and therefore enable complex, quantitative calculations. Whereas corpus linguistics traditionally has been applied in different fields such as dictionary creation, language description and variation studies or language teaching, it has also been applied in combination with – or as a means of – discourse studies. As Baker (2006) describes it, corpora and corpus processes can be used 'in order to uncover linguistic patterns which can enable us to make sense of the ways that language is used in the construction of *discourse* (or ways of constructing reality)' (1).

The TTR and all other corpus linguistic methods applied in this case study were carried out using WordSmith Tools (Scott, 2008), a widely used corpus analysis tool in the humanities and social sciences. Scott integrates in his tools the ability to calculate a so-called standardized TTR, which means that size differences of the different corpora are being integrated in the calculation: 'The standardized type/token ratio (STTR) is computed every n words as Wordlist goes through each text file. By default, n = 1,000. […] A running average is computed, which means that you get an average type/token ratio based on consecutive 1,000-word chunks of text' (Scott, 2008). This allows the researcher to compare the results of different sub-corpora with varying size. But what do STTR or TTR indicate after all? It can show that some corpora integrate a higher number of word types, which in turn indicates a higher creativity regarding language usage, but it can also indicate a greater variance in terms of topics discussed.

Results: The mixed method design represents a systematic, coherent framework of both method and data triangulation to analyze multimodal, large data sets on social media. It offers a new perspective on image analysis, accommodating the particular circumstances researchers face when conducting online research. In this case, the challenges of verifiability of the given data (and users/identities behind the Facebook accounts) as well as multimodality in terms of images in great quantities are being addressed. A proposed solution is not to focus on using image context information (i.e. who took the image when and where), which is often hard to validate on social media, and instead use the different comments and sub-images in comment threads on social media platforms as an object of analysis. This does not allow for a verification of the different users and participants, however it provides a different, enriching perspective on the images used by adding associated comments. It also draws upon Lewis et al.'s (2013) suggestion to adapt an approach of both computational and manual methods in order to arrive at more fruitful results. The authors argue that a blended approach to content analysis 'can retain the strengths of traditional content analysis while maximizing the accuracy, efficiency, and large-scale capacity of algorithms for examining Big Data' (Lewis et al., 2013: 36).

Hence the method mix starts by conducting statistical text analyses on the text corpus. These entail a frequency analysis as well as key word lists as first indicators of relevant linguistic patterns, characteristics or semantic relations. Key word and word frequency calculations are usually conducted in order to get an overall impression of the different corpora, notice abnormalities, and of course to check the validity of the corpora. They also count among the procedures most often applied in corpus linguistic studies (Baker, 2006; Mautner, 2009). As can be seen in Figure 23.2, the top ranks of the word frequency analysis (from sub-corpus June 2012) did not show any particular words that could be related to the special event, i.e. the World Earth Summit in Rio. Instead, we can see that the term 'KFC' appeared among one of the top places. KFC stands for 'Kentucky Fried Chicken' and is insofar interesting as a concrete actor was named rather frequently and therefore a special context can be expected related to KFC.

In order to get further insight into the context of this key term, a KWIC analysis

N	Key word	Freq.	%	RC. Freq.	RC. %	Keyness
1	REPLY	8,010	3.63	4,223		82,470.08
2	#	30,922	14.01	1,604,421	1.61	82,079.27
3	LIKE	8,799	3.99	147,936	0.15	40,780.66
4	SEPTEMBER	4,046	1.83	10,336	0.01	32,491.71
5	JUNE	3,842	1.74	14,541	0.01	28,253.13
6	AT	8,441	3.82	524,075	0.53	19,046.34
7	WWW	711	0.32	2		8,667.03
8	GREENPEACE	832	0.38	604		8,222.94
9	COM	691	0.31	281		7,282.13
10	HTTP	551	0.25	0		6,737.55
11	TRANSLATION	647	0.29	1,440		5,333.90
12	MOBILE	624	0.28	1,672		4,951.38
13	VIA	633	0.29	4,604		3,899.52
14	FACEBOOK	242	0.11	0		2,958.80
15	ARCTIC	363	0.16	862		2,953.31
16	QUE	285	0.13	178		2,868.48
17	ORG	213	0.10	17		2,483.01
18	BE	3,687	1.67	651,535	0.66	2,435.11
19	SAVE	481	0.22	7,330		2,300.63
20	YOUTUBE	154	0.07	0		1,882.81
21	KFC	152	0.07	3		1,828.76

Figure 23.2 Extract from word frequencies calculation on Greenpeace Corpus, June 2012

(Key-Word-in-Context) is then conducted as well as collocation analyses with specific word occurrences. These show which words appear most often in the direct vicinity of the key term. As to KFC, those words were, for example, 'chicken', 'company', 'secret recipe'. These identified semantic relations can then be used as a code list for Atlas.ti. By saving the collocation list in an easily transferable format (XML), it can be imported as a meta-coding list into Atlas.ti. The automatic coding option in Atlas.ti can then be used with this list as a first impression of image usage (see Figure 23.3). This approach can be particularly helpful when open coding is applied. Whereas open coding often refers to Grounded Theory and the process of 'breaking data apart and delineating concepts to stand for blocks of raw data' (Friese, 2012: 63), in Atlas.ti it simply refers to creating a new code. This, however, can be difficult when facing a new, even larger and multimodal corpus. With the auto coding option in Atlas.ti we have a first quick entry to large, multimodal data sets. The imported code list uses each line (with the key term + collocation) as search strings within the whole hermeneutic unit (or single documents) in Atlas.ti and applies a meta-code to those segments where it finds the search string. Hence, quantitative results coming from text analysis facilitate finding and highlighting the main keywords/topics within a large data corpus. These results – such as KFC and its collocations – are signals that can be followed in the qualitative analysis, as main topics are usually included within the words with a higher frequency.

What can be seen in the qualitative analysis is the detailed text-image relationship. For example, the case study showed that only a fraction of all images, which had a comment with the key term (KFC), actually showed

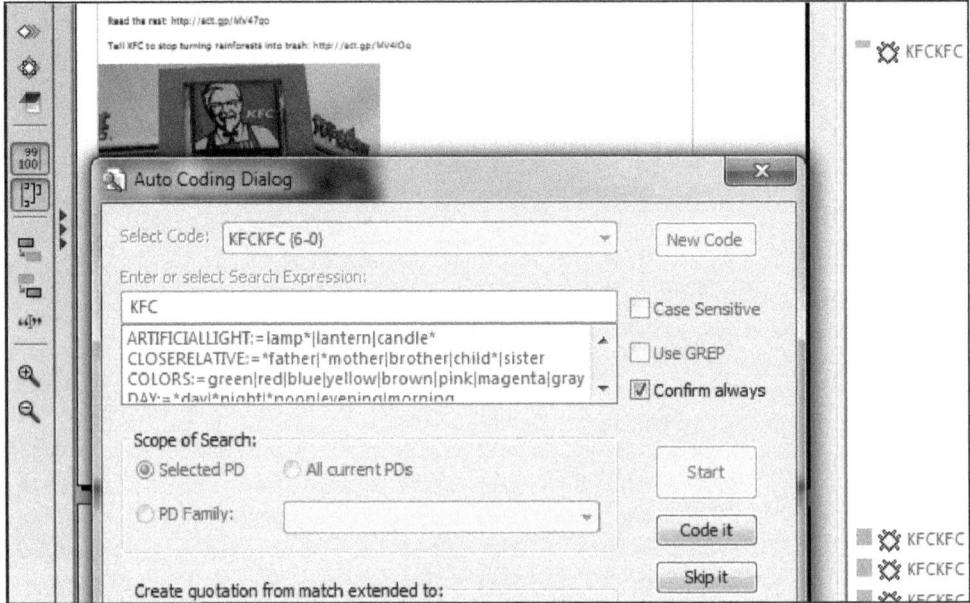

Figure 23.3 Auto coding dialogue window in Atlas.ti

either the logo or anything directly related to the company. What could be seen instead was that key terms can trigger associations with similar issues which results in group members' posting of images relating to other issues, albeit still using KFC as a textual cue. This refers back to earlier discussions in this chapter regarding the redeeming feature of social media data and other data sources to (potentially) offer a broader contextualization and detailed analysis of usage data. The brief introduction to this mixed methods approach also shows how a methodological design tailored for a specific social media platform can provide new and unforeseen results, such as the additional issues related to the key terms, and thus make use of the rich interactive and multimodal nature of social media.

CONCLUSION

This chapter aimed to show that social media research offers vast opportunities to conduct research that links social media data and other data sources. It provided an overview of the challenges and opportunities, but also a discussion of the term data and of the nature of social media data. A profound understanding of social media data represents an important prerequisite for linking different data sources and forms, as well as knowledge of how these linkages influence the traditional research process. The extension of our well-known research process in communication studies and social sciences in general is thus not only an inherent necessity when dealing with social media but it also represents a multitude of new potential paths to take. These could be mixed method approaches, such as the one demonstrated in the small case study. The case study represents a litmus test for a novel approach to the analysis of multimodal, large data sets in online communication environments. By using computer-supported tools within a systematic framework that also accounts for convergent validation, it is possible to focus on larger samples than in studies that use manual coding strategies. Furthermore, integrating more than one communication mode (text and image) enables to conduct large-scale studies in fields such as identity presentation on social media platforms, or also broader visual analysis in a medium that is becoming increasingly visual (image-driven).

The methods overview, in combination with the introduction and discussion of methods used in other disciplines and in commercial market research, aims to provide a practical and applied guideline for social media research. It is important to note, though, that the instruments discussed need to be adapted and re-adapted on a constant basis, taking into account the fast changing nature of social media applications and platforms. Given the inherent mandate of social media researchers to use computer tools (because of the digital data nature of social media), the extended research process has a profound impact on at least two different levels. The first level relates to the necessary impact on the curriculum structures of current and future academic training, particularly in the humanities and social sciences: Due to the relevance of social media in our society, they already represent an indispensable part in many course curricula and class syllabi. This also means, however, that research methods classes (and others) have to integrate the corresponding methods as well as theories about social media. The second level concerns the practical day-to-day research practice, which is faced not only with new software applications used in isolated cases, but with a fundamentally new type of data that can be found on social media. This affects the data collection and processing, but also the interpretative dealing with these data and analysis results.

NOTES

1 This work is based on prior work of the author.
2 There are also more recent events that point to the fact that there is a high number of users that tend to create accounts which reflect who they are, see, for example, Sloan et al. (2015).
3 See http://www23.statcan.gc.ca/imdb/p2SV.pl?Function=getSurvey&SDDS=4432
4 See http://www.pewresearch.org
5 See http://epp.eurostat.ec.europa.eu/portal/page/portal/information_society/introduction
6 See http://www.ofcom.org.uk
7 See, for example, Voyant tools (http://voyant-tools.org) or Netlytic (https://netlytic.org).
8 For a more extended discussion and overview of the social media data, see Jensen and Helles (2013), Baym (2013), Markham (2013), Boellstorff (2013).
9 Type describes unique word counts, i.e. how many different words have been used in a document. Token describes the total count of every word in a document. For example, the sentence 'the cat sat on the mat' has six tokens but only five types given that 'the' is repeated.

REFERENCES

AMEC (2014) Paid, Owned and Earned Social Media Measurement Framework menu of potential metrics (http://amecorg.com/wp-content/uploads/2014/06/Social-media-measurement-frameworks-menu-of-potential-metrics.pdf).

Anderson, C. (2008) The End of Theory: The Data Deluge Makes the Scientific Method Obsolete. *Wired Magazine*. June 23 (http://www.wired.com/science/discoveries/magazine/16–07/pb_theory).

Baker, P. (2006) *Using corpora in discourse analysis*. London, New York: Continuum.

Balasubramanian, N., Diekema, A.R. and A.A. Goodrum (2004) 'Analysis of User Image Descriptions and Automatic Image Indexing Vocabularies', paper presented at the International Workshop on Multidisciplinary Image, Video, and Audio Retrieval and Mining, Sherbrooke, Quebec, Canada.

Barton, D. (2012) 'Making Advanced Analytics Work for You', *Harvard Business Review*, 90(10): 78–83.

Baym, N.K. (2013) 'Data Not Seen: The Uses and Shortcomings of Social Media Metrics', *First Monday*, 18(10). doi:10.5210/fm.v18i10.4873.

Bente, G., Eschenburg, F. and Fürtjes, M. (2007) 'Im Auge des Nutzers. Eye-Tracking in der Web-Usability-Forschung', in M. Welker and O. Wenzel (eds.), *Online-Forschung*

2007. *Grundlagen und Fallstudien*. Köln: Herbert von Halem. pp. 185–219.

Boellstorff, T. (2013) 'Making Big Data, in Theory', *First Monday*, 26(2–3). doi:10.1177/ 0263276409103106.

Boellstorff, T., Nardi, B., Pearce, C. and Taylor, T.L. (2012) *Ethnography and Virtual Worlds. A Handbook of Method*. Princeton and Oxford: Princeton University Press.

boyd, d. and Crawford, K. (2012) 'Critical Questions for Big Data', *Information, Communication & Society*, 15(5) (June): 662–679. doi:10.1080/1369118X.2012.678878.

Brown, S.R. (1993) 'A Primer on Q Methodology', *Operant Subjectivity*, 16(3/4): 91–138.

Brügger, N. (2010) *Website Analysis*. Aarhus: The Centre for Internet Research.

Bryman, A., Bell, E. and Teevan, J.J. (2012) *Social research methods*. 3rd Canadian Edition. Don Mills: Oxford University Press.

Burke Johnson, R., Onwuegbuzie, A.J. and Turner, L.A. (2007) 'Toward a Definition of Mixed Methods Research', *Journal of Mixed Methods Research*, 1(2): 112–133. http://doi.org/10.1177/1558689806298224

BVDW. (2013) *Social Media Kompass 2013/2014*. http://www.bvdw.org/medien/social-media-kompass-2013-2014?media=5146.

Davis, C.H. and Michelle, C. (2011) 'Q Methodology in Audience Research: Bridging the Qualitative/Quantitative "Divide?"', *Participations. Journal of Audience & Reception Studies*, 8(2): 559–593.

Entman, R.M. (2010) 'Media Framing Biases and Political Power: Explaining Slant in News of Campaign 2008', *Journalism*, 11(4): 389–408. http://doi.org/10.1177/1464884910367587

Entman, R.M. and Jones, A. (2009) 'Searching for Liberal Bias: The Case of Social Security', paper presented at the 59th annual International Communication Association Conference, Chicago, IL.

Fielding, N. (2012) 'Triangulation and Mixed Methods Designs: Data Integration With New Research Technologies', *Journal of Mixed Methods Research*, 6(2): 124–136. http://doi.org/10.1177/1558689812437101

Flew, T., Spurgeon, C., Daniel, A. and Swift, A. (2012) 'The Promise of Computational Journalism', *Journalism Practice*, 6(2): 157–171.

Fraas, C., Meier, S. and Pentzold, C. (eds.), (2013) *Online-Diskurse. Theorien und methoden transmedialer online-diskursforschung*. Köln: Herbert von Halem.

Friese, S. (2012) *Qualitative data analysis with Atlas.Ti*. London, Thousand Oaks, CA: SAGE.

Ghoshal, A., Ircing, P. and Khudanpur, S. (2005).'Hidden Markov Models for Automatic Annotation and Content-Based Retrieval of Images and Video', paper presented at the 28th annual international ACM SIGIR conference on Research and development in information retrieval, New York, NY. http://doi.org/10.1145/1076034.1076127

Goodrum, A. A., Devereaux, Z. and Smith, A. (2009) 'Viral Video: Describing Online Multimedia Information Flows', *Proceedings of the American Society for Information Science and Technology*, 46(1): 1–4. http://doi.org/10.1002/meet.2009.145046036

Haight, M., Quan-Haase, A. and Corbett, B.A. (2014) 'Revisiting the Digital Divide in Canada: The Impact of Demographic Factors on Access to the Internet, Level of Online Activity, and Social Networking Site Usage', *Information, Communication & Society*, 17(4): 503–519. http://doi.org/10.1080/1369118X.2014.891633

Herring, S.C. (2004) 'Computer-Mediated Discourse Analysis: An Approach to Researching Online Behavior', in S.A. Barab, R. Kling and J.H. Gray (eds.), *Designing for virtual communities in the service of learning*. New York: Cambridge University Press. pp. 338–376.

Herring, S.C. (2010) 'Web Content Analysis: Expanding the Paradigm', in J. Hunsinger, L. Klastrup and M. Allen (eds.), *International Handbook of Internet Research*. Dordrecht: Springer Netherlands. pp. 233–249 http://doi.org/10.1007/978-1-4020-9789-8_14

Hewson, C., Yule, P., Laurent, D. and Vogel, C. (2003) *Internet research methods*. London, Thousand Oaks, CA: SAGE.

Hine, C. M. (2000) *Virtual ethnography*. London: Sage.

Hogan, B. and Quan-Haase, A. (2010) 'Persistence and Change in Social Media: A Framework of Social Practice', *Bulletin of Science, Technology and Society*. (http://bst.sagepub.com/content/30/5/309.full.pdf+html)

Howe, J. (2006) *The Rise of Crowdsourcing*. (http://archive.wired.com/wired/archive/14.06/crowds.html)

Jensen, K.B. (2014) 'Audiences, Audiences Everywhere–Measured, Interpreted and

Imagined', in G. Patriarche, H. Bilandzic, J.L. Jensen and J. Jurisic (eds.), *Audience research methodologies*. New York, NY: Routledge. pp. 227–239.

Jensen, K.B. and Helles, R. (2013) 'Making data – Big data and beyond: Introduction to the special issue', *First Monday*. (http://doi.org/10.5210%2Ffm.v18i10.4860)

Karpf, D. (2012) 'Social Science Research Methods in Internet Time', *Information, Communication & Society*, 15(5): 639–661.

Kennedy, H., Moss, G., Birchall, C. and Moshonas, S. (2014) 'Balancing the Potential and Problems of Digital Methods Through Action Research: Methodological Reflections', *Information, Communication & Society*, 18(2): 172–186. (http://doi.org/10.1080/1369118X.2014.946434)

Kitchin, R. (2013) 'Big Data and Human Geography: Opportunities, Challenges and Risks', *Dialogues in Human Geography*, 3(3): 262–267.

Kitchin, R. (2014) 'Big Data, New Epistemologies and Paradigm Shifts', *Big Data & Society*, 1(1). (http://doi.org/10.1177/2053951714528481)

Klein, D., Tran-Gia, P. and Hartmann, M. (2013) 'Big Data', *Informatik-Spektrum*, 36(3): 319–323. (http://doi.org/10.1007/s00287-013-0702-3)

Kozinets, R.V. (2010) *Netnography. Doing ethnographic research online*. Thousand Oaks, CA: SAGE.

Kress, G. (2009) *Multimodality: A social semiotic approach to contemporary communication*. Oxon: Routledge.

Krippendorff, K. (2012) *Content analysis: An introduction to its methodology*. 3rd Edition, Thousand Oaks, CA: SAGE.

Lewis, S.C., Hermida, A. and Zamith, R. (2013) 'Content Analysis in an Era of Big Data: A Hybrid Approach to Computational and Manual Methods', *Journal of Broadcasting & Electronic Media*, 57(1): 34–52. (http://doi.org/10.1080/08838151.2012.761702)

Liu, B. (2012) *Sentiment Analysis and Opinion Mining*. Morgan & Claypool.

Macnamara, J. (2014) 'Emerging International Standards for Measurement and Evaluation of Public Relations: A Critical Analysis', *Public Relations Inquiry*, 3(1): 7–29. (http://doi.org/10.1177/2046147X14521199)

Manovich, L. (2011) 'Trending: The Promises and the Challenges of Big Social Data', *Debates in the Digital Humanities*. (http://www.manovich.net/DOCS/Manovich_trending_paper.pdf)

Markham, A.N. (2013) 'Undermining 'Data': A Critical Examination of a Core Term in Scientific Inquiry', *First Monday*, 18(10). (doi:10.5210/fm.v18i10.4868)

Mautner, G. (2009) 'Corpora and Critical Discourse Analyses', in P. Baker (ed.), *Contemporary corpus linguistics*. London/New York: Continuum. pp. 32–46.

Mayer-Schönberger, V. and Cukier, K. (2013) *Big data. A revolution that will transform how we live, work and think*. London: John Murray.

Mehl, M.R. and Gill, A.J. (2010) 'Automatic Text Analysis', in S. D. Gosling and E. J. Johnson (eds.), *Advanced methods for conducting online behavioral research*. Washington D.C.: American Psychological Association. pp. 109–127.

O'Halloran, K. and Smith, B.A. (2010) 'Multimodal Studies', in B. A. Smith (ed.), *Multimodal studies: Exploring issues and domains*. New York & London: Routledge. pp. 1–24.

Pauwels, L. (2012) 'A Multimodal Framework for Analyzing Websites as Cultural Expressions', *Journal of Computer-Mediated Communication*, 17(3): 247–265. (http://doi.org/10.1111/j.1083–6101.2012.01572.x)

Poetz, M.K. and Schreier, M. (2012) 'The Value of Crowdsourcing: Can Users Really Compete with Professionals in Generating New Product Ideas?', *Journal of Product Innovation Management*, 29(2): 245–256. (http://doi.org/10.1111/j.1540–5885.2011.00893.x)

Quan-Haase, A., Martin, K. and McCay-Peet, L. (2015) 'Networks of Digital Humanities Scholars: The Informational and Social Uses and Gratifications of Twitter', *Big Data & Society*, 2(1). (http://doi.org/10.1177/2053951715589417)

Reips, U.-D. (2002) 'Standards for Internet-based experimenting', *Experimental Psychology*, 49: 243–256.

Reips, U.-D. (2003) 'Web-Experimente – Eckpfeiler der Online-Forschung', in A. Theobald, M. Dreyer and T. Starsetzki (eds.), *Online-marktforschung – Theoretische grundlagen und praktische efahrungen*. Wiesbaden: Gabler. pp. 1–24.

Scheffler, H. (2014) 'Soziale Medien. Einführung in das Thema aus Sicht der Marktforschung', in C. König, M. Stahl and E. Wiegand (eds.), *soziale medien. Gegenstand und instrument der forschung*. Wiesbaden: Springer VS. pp. 13–28.

Schrøder, K.C. and Kobbernagel, C. (2010) 'Towards a Typology of Cross-Media News Consumption: A Qualitative–Quantitative Synthesis', *Northern Lights*, 8(2010): 115–138. (doi: 10.1386/nl.8.115).

Scott, M. (2008) *WordSmith tools Version 5*. Oxford: Oxford University Press.

Sloan, L., Morgan, J., Burnap, P. and Williams, M. (2015) 'Who Tweets? Deriving the Demographic Characteristics of Age, Occupation and Social Class from Twitter User Meta-Data', *PLoS ONE* 10(3). (http://journals.plos.org/plosone/article?id=10.1371/journal.pone.0115545)

Steffen, D. (2014) 'Verknüpfung von Daten aus Sozialen Medien mit klassischen Erhebungsmethoden', in C. König, M. Stahl and E. Wiegand (eds.), *soziale medien. Gegenstand und instrument der forschung*. Wiesbaden: Springer VS. pp. 97–110.

Taddicken, M. (2008) *Methodeneffekte bei Web-Befragungen: Einschränkungen der Datengüte durch ein'reduziertes Kommunikationsmedium'?* Köln: Herbert von Halem.

Taddicken, M. (2013) 'Online-Befragung', in W. Möhring and D. Schlütz (eds.), *Handbuch standardisierte erhebungsverfahren in der kommunikationswissenschaft*. Wiesbaden: Springer. pp. 201–217.

Tashakkori, A. and Teddlie, C. (eds.), (2003) *Handbook of mixed methods in social and behavioral research*. London/Thousand Oaks, CA/New Delhi: SAGE.

Teddlie, C. and Tashakkori, A. (2009) *Foundations of mixed methods research. Integrating quantitative and qualitative approaches in the social and behavioral sciences*. Los Angeles, CA: SAGE.

Tumasjan, A., Sprenger, T.O., Sandner, P. G. and Welpe, I.M. (2013) 'Predicting Elections with Twitter: What 140 Characters Reveal About Political Sentiment', in *Proceedings of the Fourth International AAAI Conference on Weblogs and Social Media*. pp. 178–185.

Vehovar, V. and Manfreda, K.L. (2008) 'Overview: Online Surveys', in N. Fielding, R. M. Lee and G. Blank (eds.), *The SAGE handbook of online research methods*. London, Thousand Oaks: SAGE. pp. 177–194.

Vis, F. (2013) 'A Critical Reflection on Big Data: Considering APIs, Researchers and Tools as Data Makers', *First Monday*, 18(10). (http://doi.org/10.5210/fm.v18i10.4878)

Welker, M. and Kloß, A. (2014) 'Soziale Medien als Gegenstand und Instrument Sozialwissenschaftlicher Forschung', in C. König, M. Stahl and E. Wiegand (eds.), *Soziale medien. gegenstand und instrument der forschung*. Wiesbaden: Springer VS. pp. 29–52.

Welser, H.T., Smith, M., Fisher, D. and Gleave, E. (2008) 'Distilling Digital Traces: Computational Social Science Approaches to Studying the Internet', in N. Fielding, R. M. Lee and G. Blank (eds.), *The SAGE handbook of online research methods*. London, UK: SAGE. pp. 116–140.

Wright, K.B. (2005) 'Researching Internet-Based Populations: Advantages and Disadvantages of Online Survey Research, Online Questionnaire Authoring Software Packages, and Web Survey Services', *Journal of Computer-Mediated Communication*, 10(3): 1083–1101.

Young, L. and Soroka, S. (2012) 'Affective News: The Automated Coding of Sentiment in Political Texts', *Political Communication*, 29(2): 205–231. (http://doi.org/10.1080/10584609.2012.671234)

Zeller, F., O'Kane, J., Godo, E. and Goodrum, A. (2013) 'A Subjective User-Typology Of Online News Consumption', *Digital Journalism*, 2(2): 214–231. (http://doi.org/10.1080/21670811.2013.801686)

Zeller, F. (2014) 'Big Data in Audience Research', in F. Zeller, C. Ponte and B. O'Neill (eds.), *Revitalising Audience research innovations in European audience research*. ECREA book series, Routledge. pp. 261–278.

Zeller, F. (2015) 'Soziale Medien in der empirischen Forschung', in J.-H. Schmidt and M. Taddicken (eds.), *Handbuch soziale medien*. Wiesbaden: Springer.

Zikopoulos, P., Eaton, C., DeRoos, D., Deutsch, T. and Lapis, G. (2012) *Understanding Big data: Analytics for enterprise class hadoop and streaming data*. New York, NY: McGraw-Hill.

Listening to Social Rhythms: Exploring Logged Interactional Data Through Sonification

Jack Jamieson and Jeffrey Boase

The popularity of social media has given rise to a vast number of time-stamped logs of tweets, blog posts, text messages, status updates, comments, shares and other communications. These data sets can be explored to identify new types of interactional patterns and trends. Data sonification – converting data into sound – is particularly well-suited to exploring temporal patterns within time-stamped log data because sound itself is inherently temporal and the human auditory system has excellent temporal resolution. This chapter presents examples of sonifications of social media data, discusses considerations for performing sonification-based analyses, and describes a study in which sonification was used to explore temporal patterns in mobile text message log data. The intent is to allow readers who are unfamiliar with sonification to understand its capabilities and limitations, as well as how they may apply sonification in their own research.

INTRODUCTION

Social media interactions consist of a broad variety of activities, such as posting, retweeting, sharing, commenting and replying to status updates, personal messages, news articles and other forms of user engagement. Often, these interactions occur asynchronously, allowing participants to choose when they initiate, respond to, pause, ignore, and conclude interactions. As a result, the time at which events occur can be a non-verbal cue of eagerness, engagement, thoughtfulness, or other qualities (Döring & Pöschl, 2009; Kalman & Rafaeli, 2011; Quan-Haase & Collins, 2008; Walther & Tidwell, 1995). Moreover, asynchronous digital interactions such as tweets, Facebook updates, or mobile text messages are intrinsically temporal, and logs of this data are almost always time-stamped. By analyzing time-stamped interactional data, researchers can develop insights into a variety of topics, such as how interactions unfold over time, inequalities in the exchange of information, and personal network change over time.

The abundance of available logged data about social media interactions has created opportunities for new lines of inquiry and new styles of research. As a result, researchers can use this wealth of data to ask questions that are qualitatively different and develop novel analytic methods to address those questions. In this chapter we discuss the potential of data sonification – converting data into sound – for exploratory data analysis of time-stamped interactional data, such as that found in social media logs. Exploratory data analysis was popularized by Tukey (1977) as a set of methods for exploring statistical data. In contrast to other sorts of statistical analysis, exploratory analysis does not address specific hypotheses, but rather is used to identify patterns, relationships, and trends. Andrienko and Andrienko summarize that exploratory analysis 'is about hypothesis generation rather than hypothesis testing' (2006, p. 3). This makes exploratory analysis a suitable approach for discovering patterns and trends in the interactional data generated through social media and other forms of asynchronous digital communication. Exploratory analysis has been used by many researchers to study social media use, but most of this exploration has relied on visualization. Sound has particular potential for analyzing temporal patterns due to the inherently temporal nature of sound (Neuhoff, 2011), and sonification can offer a different and valuable perspective.

This chapter begins by explaining what sonification is and why it can be useful for analyzing interactional data. We then provide examples of existing social media sonifications to illustrate the current state of affairs. This is followed by a discussion of theoretical and methodological factors to consider when undertaking sonification-based research. Then we present a detailed description of a sonification-based study we conducted of mobile text message activity. In describing this study, we illustrate how the considerations identified in the previous section can affect the process of conducting research with sonification. This chapter concludes with a discussion of future directions for the use of sonification to explore social media and other interactional logs.

WHY USE SONIFICATION?

Data sonification is a method of converting data into sound. This allows researchers to listen to patterns, values, and relationships within data in much the same way that data visualization allows researchers to see them. The commonly accepted definition is that 'sonification is the use of non-speech audio to convey information' (Kramer et al., as cited in Hermann, 2008, p. 1). Since data visualization is a more common approach than sonification, it may be useful to consider sonification as a relative of visualization. Tufte's seminal work on data visualization, *The Visual Display of Quantitative Information*, begins by asserting, 'Data graphics visually display measured quantities by means of the combined use of points, lines, a coordinate system, numbers, symbols, words, shading, and colour' (2001, p. 10). Like visualizations, sonifications perform the function of conveying information, but do so using an auditory rather than visual set of representational tools. As such, the simplest way to conceive of sonifications is as sound-based analogues of charts, graphs, maps, or other visualizations. Where visualizations use points, lines, and other visual devices, sonification employs sounds with varying timbre, pitch, loudness, stereo position, timing and rhythm, consonance and dissonance, and other sonic properties.

The most significant advantage of sonification for exploring interactional social data is the inherent temporality of sound. While visual representations necessarily have a spatial dimension, sound always unfolds over time. Dayé and de Campo pointed out that this makes sonification excellent at conveying sequential information (2006). Using sonification, data representing events that unfold over time, such as asynchronous social interactions, can be conveyed along their natural dimension, time, instead of spatially as most visualizations would place them. Even though it is possible to create temporal visualizations that utilize animation, the human auditory system performs significantly better with rhythmic perception and temporal resolution than the visual system (Neuhoff, 2011). As a result, sonifications have the potential to effectively represent minute patterns along the dimension of time.

Another advantage is that representing data as sound can draw attention to regularly occurring patterns that might be difficult to discern using other methods. Sonification has particular merit for trend analysis in which listeners identify overall patterns of increases and decreases in quantitative data (Walker & Nees, 2011, p. 21). According to Ferguson, Martens, and Cabrera:

> Auditory representations can potentially extract patterns not previously discernible, and might make such patterns so obvious to the ear, that no-one will ever look for them with their eyes again. By capitalizing upon the inherently different capabilities of the human auditory system, invisible regularities can become audible, and complex temporal patterns can be 'heard out' in what might appear to be noise. (2011, p. 178)

One of the main functions of exploratory analysis is to obtain a new perspective of data. By perceiving data in new ways, one can identify patterns and features that are not evident using traditional methods. Many exploratory analyses of social media data have tended to favour visual exploration. In contrast, sonification promises to illuminate different aspects of the data, particularly temporal dimensions for which it may be better suited than spatially oriented visual methods. By allowing researchers to perceive data in a novel way, sonification is conducive to generating new types of hypotheses.

EXAMPLES OF SOCIAL MEDIA SONIFICATION

Several researchers have used sonification to listen to social media data. This section presents a brief overview of significant works, illustrating the current state of social media sonification. These examples illustrate how sonification has been used for summarizing and analyzing logs of social media activity, and also point to areas for further development.

Detecting Anomalous Events with Sonification: Ballora et al., 2012

Ballora et al. (2012) created an application that sonified stock market data alongside logs of tweets containing keywords related to those stocks. This sonification was used to make anomalous events detectable even to untrained listeners. Ballora et al. tested this system using stock market and Twitter data related to technology companies leading up to and following the Apple Worldwide Developer's conference in 2011. They found that test subjects who listened to this sonification could easily identify changes in the data around the time of the conference.

This study demonstrated that sonification can illuminate anomalous changes to data streams in a way that is apparent even to untrained listeners. Additionally, Ballora et al. demonstrated a novel approach to combining data sources with very different levels of precision. The Twitter data, which utilized keywords such as 'apple,' was less precise than the stock market data. Specifically, it could be ambiguous whether particular tweets containing the keyword 'apple' were related to Apple Corporation, while stock market data was clear in this regard. As a result, they determined that small-scale changes in the Twitter data were unlikely to be reliably significant, and designed the sonification of tweets to focus on large-scale changes.

This was accomplished by condensing the Twitter data into fifteen-minute histograms and allowing the sounds for each histogram to overlap somewhat, emphasizing overall trends rather than precise changes. Ballora et al. described how the two soundtracks differed:

> One soundtrack renders selected stock prices as rhythmically unique pulses, the pitches of which reflect stock price fluctuations. The second soundtrack maps selected keywords appearing in tweets to unique drone-like pitches, so that the appearance of a keyword is rendered as a simple, sustained tone at its associated pitch, at a particular amplitude. The result is a 'sound cloud' of bell-like pulses and harmonically related drones. Periods of increased or decreased activity are easily perceptible as changes in the sound cloud's density, timbre, and rhythmicity (2012, p. 1).

The use of two soundtracks illustrates how different sonification techniques can be suited to particular types of data. Ultimately, testing indicated that the sonification made significant anomalies apparent. Future work of this sort may benefit by exploring techniques for sonifying subtler patterns and changes.

Twitter and Music: Ash, 2012; Bethancourt, 2012

In 2012 the International Community for Auditory Display (ICAD) – a central research community for the study of sonification – held a competition called 'Listening to the World Listening.' Entrants were invited to submit sonifications of the Twitter Music Trends data feed – a list of the top 50 trending artists on Twitter, updated every two seconds. The winning entrant was Kingsley Ash's 'Affective States,' which represented each artist with a distinct tone, then modified several audio filters for that tone based on the presence of emotion keywords in blog postings about the artist (Ash, 2012). Another project was Matt Bethancourt's 'The sounds of the discussion of sounds', which played, in real-time, tones representing the amount of Twitter discussion about particular artists (Bethancourt, 2012). As an artist's popularity waned, their tone would become quieter, potentially becoming silent if Twitter users stopped discussing them. Both examples produced a sonification that constantly shifted in relation to real-time Twitter discussions, and this allowed them to make use of the inherent temporality of sound.

Tweetscapes: Hermann, Nehls, Eithel, Barri, and Gammel, 2012

The Tweetscapes project (Hermann et al., 2012) was a real-time sonification of Twitter activity in Germany, hosted at www.tweetscapes.de. The sounds produced by this sonification are described as 'an interactive composition performed by Germany's Twitter users' (HEAVYLISTENING, 2012). The sonification ran for three years, from 2012 to 2015. Tweets originating from Germany were sonified in real time, with the sound for each tweet being modified according to parameters such as the number of followers for that tweet and its distance from the geographic centre of Germany (which determines reverberation and stereo panning). As well as a general stream, a hashtag stream is available in which hashtag keywords are distinguished by different sound samples and synthesis settings (Hermann et al., 2012). One of the goals of Tweetscapes was to make sonification more publicly known, which was achieved in part through integrating its sonifications in the nationwide radio program, *Deutschlandradio Kultur*. Although the project received significant media attention, the researchers acknowledge that the question of Tweetscapes' practical use was often raised, and commented that 'the practical use is very limited' (2012, p. 119). One of the limitations of Tweetscapes was the lack of interactivity. Users were not able to filter the selection of tweets they listened to, but instead would listen to the entirety of German Twitter activity. On the website, the sonification was combined with a visualization of each tweet overlaid onto a map of Germany. This provided additional context and made the sonification easier to understand.

User-focused Sonification: Wolf, Gliner, and Fiebrink, 2015

In 2015, Wolf, Gliner, and Fiebrink proposed a model for data-driven sonification using soundscapes. Their goal was to facilitate end-user involvement in the process of designing a sonification so as to make sonifications more useful for those users. They prototyped this model by sonifying Twitter data, and expressed that their design would build upon the techniques of projects like Tweetscapes by allowing users to 'select the Twitter information they wish to monitor in real-time' (Wolf et al., 2015, p. 3). This effort to build a system in which users can select specific groups of Twitter data to be sonified in real time has significant potential for exploratory data analysis. Additionally, this system uses a simple sonification engine in which data is mapped to familiar sound samples, such as 'bird tweet' or 'running water' rather than potentially unfamiliar sound parameters such as frequency and timbre (Wolf et al., 2015). These examples demonstrate multiple purposes for sonification. The purpose of some of these projects is largely to evaluate and explore sonification's potential, and/or to make sonification familiar to a broad audience. These projects also illustrate sonification's usefulness for exploring, although there is room for advancement.

CONSIDERATIONS FOR SONIFICATION RESEARCH

One of the most significant challenges for sonification is that interpretation can be difficult, particularly if the listener is unfamiliar with sonification. The following section discusses considerations for conducting exploratory analysis with sonification, particularly as pertaining to interactional data.

Tools for Sonification

For researchers who want to utilize sonification techniques, the scarcity of available tools can be intimidating. Many sonifications are custom designed for specific research projects using complex software such as Max/MSP, SuperCollider or other sophisticated software or hardware synthesizers. However, it is also possible to build sonifications using tools such as *Sonification Sandbox* (2009) or the *E-Rhythms Data Sonifier* (2014).

Necessary Criteria

If a sonification is to be useful for analyzing data, it must have consistently and clearly defined criteria. Hermann (2008) has argued that four criteria are particularly important to meet this standard. According to Hermann, a sonification must reflect *objective* properties or relations in the input data, the transformation must be *systematic*, the sonification should be *reproducible*, and the system should be flexible to work with multiple sets of *different data* (2008, p. 2). These four criteria are conducive for designing sonifications with data analysis in mind, since they emphasize the importance of representing data with rigour and reliability. To provide an example, a song whose composition is loosely inspired by a dataset would be unlikely to meet Hermann's criteria (since a songwriter's composition process likely involves subjective, creative decisions); however, an algorithmic transformation of that data into sound would qualify.

Appropriate Tasks

Some analytic tasks are better suited to sonification than others. For example, point estimation for a particular datum (e.g. identifying that the value is 1.0 exactly, not 0.9 or 1.1) can be very difficult using sonification (Smith & Walker, 2005). In addition to it being difficult to identify the value of individual points, comparing multiple points poses another challenge. Point comparison requires estimation of two distinct points, plus a memory task of comparing the values of each. Walker & Nees (2011) theorize that point comparison should be more difficult than point estimation, but note that no empirical tests have examined point comparison with sonification. The difficulty of point estimation (and theorized difficulty of point comparison) with sonification is worthy of consideration because this task can be straightforward using a chart or other visualization. On the other hand, trend analysis, in which listeners assess overall patterns in a data source, is well suited for sonification. Walker & Nees (2011) suggested sonification is especially useful for trend analysis because 'sound may be a medium wherein otherwise unnoticed patterns in data emerge for the listener' (p. 21).

Furthermore, sonification is especially well-suited for exploring temporal and rhythmic patterns. As noted above, sound is inherently temporal, and the human listening system has far better temporal and rhythmic perception than the visual system. For example, humans are typically able to hear gaps in broadband noise stimuli as short as 2–3 milliseconds (Carlile, 2011) and at low frequencies it is possible to distinguish individual events with durations as brief as 20–50 milliseconds (Dombois & Eckel, 2011). This excellent temporal resolution bolsters sonification's utility for revealing patterns and anomalies that are difficult to perceive in other representations of the data.

Simultaneous Streams and Levels of Analysis

The simultaneity of sonification is advantageous for representations of temporal data, but poses a challenge in how much data can be perceived at once. It is possible to listen to more than one stream simultaneously, but the difficulty of this task increases according to the complexity of the sound and the level of precision required to evaluate the sonification. In Ballora et al.'s (2012) sonification of Twitter and stock market data, monitoring multiple streams simultaneously was required. However, the purpose of the sonification was to detect significant anomalies, rather than to conduct precise analysis. Tweetscapes (Hermann et al., 2012) – a real-time sonification of German Twitter activity – also presented multiple streams of data by sonifying various hashtags separately, but is similarly not intended for analyzing minute patterns.

Listening to a very large number of streams simultaneously may lead the listener to perceive them as a group, rather than as multiple individual streams. This is particularly likely if individual streams sound similar to one another. Whether one listens to the patterns of individuals or of the group as a whole has a significant effect on the types of observations that are possible. Group level analysis is best suited for identifying patterns of activity based around fixed points in time. For example, one could observe overall trends such as large numbers of people tweeting about a particular event, exchanging text messages on New Year's Eve, or tending to be more active on social media during the day than late at night.

On the other hand, when conducting group level analysis with sonification, individual patterns may be obfuscated amidst the noise created by multiple overlapping streams. If, for example, one individual sends five text messages each on Monday, Wednesday, and Friday, and another sends five text messages on Tuesday, Thursday, Saturday and, Sunday, a sonification in which these individuals' streams were merged would indicate that five text messages were sent every day, without capturing further details about the individual patterns. Any sonification that amalgamates multiple individuals into a group level analysis is likely to muddy individual patterns.

An alternative to listening to multiple audio streams simultaneously is to isolate individual streams. Listening to individuals engaged in dyadic interactions can reveal information that is obscured at the group level. When listening to individual streams, comparing streams to each other requires switching between them. When performing this sort of switching, listeners should be careful to account for the human listening system's need for time to adapt and become familiar with each stream (Hermann, Hunt, & Neuhoff, 2011). Ultimately, each level of analysis has its own advantages and disadvantages, and researchers should consider which is most appropriate based on the complexity of the sound, and the type of patterns one is searching for.

Group analysis. Group level sonifications are most useful for identifying overall trends and patterns that are based around fixed points of time. Using group level analysis, it is possible to listen to large populations at once, and to gain a holistic perspective of certain trends within those populations. Because researchers can listen to a large number of individuals at once, results observed from group level sonifications are likely to be generalizable.

Individual analysis. Sonifications of individual patterns may allow researchers to observe patterns that would be obscured in group level analyses. Individual analysis offers the most precise resolution of the data, and may be useful for identifying subtle patterns or patterns oriented around points in time that are relative to each individual. The challenge posed by individual level analysis is that listening to large numbers of individuals may be time consuming. As a result, for individual level analysis it is important to have an effective sampling strategy.

Dyadic analysis. Listening to interactions between pairs of individuals may be particularly useful for interactional data, as it can allow researchers to investigate patterns of communication between two individuals. This has the same advantages and disadvantages as individual level analysis, but can also draw attention to features such as the speed at which individuals respond to each other or who usually initiates communication.

Combinations. In some cases, it may be appropriate to combine multiple levels of analysis. This has the potential to reveal ways in which individual patterns relate to patterns among the larger population. For example, researchers could compare group level activity to an individual stream as a method of identifying ways that the individual differs from the group. Alternately, one could listen to a sonification of an individual's social media activities alongside a group level of sonification of replies, shares and other responses to the individual's activities.

Mapping Sounds

When listening to sonification it is necessary to consider how some sounds can suggest meanings independent of the source data (Grond & Hermann, 2011; Walker & Kramer, 2005). A sequence of notes in a major key may suggest a happier meaning than a minor key, regardless of whether a sense of happiness or sadness accurately reflects the information being conveyed. And a sonification that is thunderously loud suggests different emotional meanings than one that is meek, even if both represent the same data. Supper (2014) discussed how sound design can introduce emotional meanings, using sonifications of natural phenomena as examples. In some cases, she argued, the meaning conveyed by sound design can be conflated with the information from the source data. This has the potential to skew interpretations, but sonification designers can also take advantage of this to create sonifications that illustrate rich meanings by seeming to be *true* to the phenomenon being represented:

> The sonification, for instance, of a volcano is different from the sounds that are emitted by the volcano itself. However, certain rhetorical, musical and technological strategies are used to suggest that the sonification represents something about the volcano that might not be immediately visible or audible from the volcano, but from deeper within it. It is not about sounding like a volcano per se, but about being true to the volcano – or rather, about allowing listeners to believe that the

sonification is true to the volcano. (Supper, 2014, p. 51)

Although Supper refers to a sonification of a volcano, the same principle is valid for sonifications of digital phenomena such as social media activities. One might choose to indicate that a particular post was shared many times by adding reverberation and echo, or by modifying its pitch or loudness. The choice of mapping can often have a strong effect on how listeners interpret meaning, and some mappings will seem truer to the data than others.

As a consequence, even when a sonification is systematic its designers have the ability to steer interpretations through aesthetic decisions. Sonification can convey a variety of subjective and emotional meanings, and this is exemplified in a special sonification issue of *AI & SOCIETY* that combined articles from both sonification researchers and artists (Sinclair, 2011). The artistic potential of sonification is in some respects at cross-purposes to its scientific analysis applications. However, this is no different from other perceptualization methods such as visualization. Just as a sonification can introduce bias through sound design, visualizations can suggest deceptive meanings through choice of colour, symbols, and scales. In both cases, researchers should endeavour to understand enough about the form to detect misrepresentations where possible.

Training

An important consideration is that sonification is unfamiliar to many researchers. Whereas most researchers are familiar with at least some visualization techniques, sonification is much less common. Generally, listeners with musical ability or training tend to be more accurate than musically untrained listeners when interpreting sonifications (Neuhoff, Knight, & Wayand, 2002). However, even among sonification specialists, there are many cases where a common vocabulary of representational techniques is lacking. As a result, usually at least some training is required for listeners to interpret a sonification (Walker & Nees, 2011). In some cases, sonification designers may include instruction manuals or specific training procedures. In all cases, it is advisable that listeners familiarize themselves with a sonification system before attempting to make new discoveries. One method is to listen to aspects of the data the researcher is already familiar with. Developing an understanding of how the sonification represents known patterns is a valuable step toward being able to discover new patterns.

Visual Cues

Finally, accompanying a sonification with a visual component can be useful to provide context and make the sonification more easily understood. Presenting sonification alongside a corresponding visualization can allow researchers to utilize the temporal strengths of sonification alongside the spatial strengths of visualization. For example, in the E-Rhythms Data Sonifier, researchers can click on a visually presented timeline to navigate through the data. And in Tweetscapes, the geographic origin of tweets is visualized by overlaying graphical representations on a map.

EXAMPLE: SONIFYING ASYNCHRONOUS TEXT MESSAGE LOGS

In the following section we provide an example of sonification being used to explore time-stamped interactional data (Further discussions of this study was presented in Jamieson, Boase, & Kobayashi, 2015a,b.) We used data sonification to conduct exploratory analysis of non-identifying smartphone logs of text messaging. This data is similar to social media activity logs, which often catalogue asynchronous communication. The E-Rhythms Data Sonifier software (2014) was used to explore the data in several ways. The most fruitful exploration consisted of listening to the speed at which pairs responded to each other's text messages, and considered how this related to relational dimensions including relationship role (family, co-worker, or other), discussing important matters, and trust. We discuss our exploratory process as an illustration of the strengths and challenges of using sonification to explore communication logs.

Data Description

The data for this study was collected using the Network Navigator application, which respondents installed on their Android smartphones. The application collected non-identifying voice, text, and email log data and correlated these logs with responses to on-screen survey questionnaires. These surveys included questions about recently contacted ties or communication partners, such as whether they were family members, whether respondents trusted them, and whether respondents discussed important matters with them. The full data set contained logs collected from 132 adults living in the United States in 2011 who explicitly consented to participating in the study. Our study focused on text messages and relied on responses to survey questions to provide information about ties. We focused on text messages because our sonification method represented the number of events that occur, but did not indicate the duration of events. Moreover, the data did not contain the content of calls or other information that could have made it possible to infer communication patterns within each telephone conversation. Consequently, text messages, which are discrete asynchronous communications, were better suited to our study. We limited our study to communications with ties where 1) the respondent answered at least one pop-up survey about that tie and, 2) at least one text message was exchanged with that tie. This narrowed our selection to 77 respondents, who exchanged a total 11,215 text messages with 149 ties.

The E-Rhythms Data Sonifier

Exploratory sonification analysis was conducted using the E-Rhythms Data Sonifier software, which was designed by the authors (as of this chapter's publication, the Data Sonifier software is available for free download at http://erhythms.utm.utoronto.ca/software.html). A screenshot of the Data Sonifier software is shown in Figure 24.1. A time-stamped data file is loaded into the software, and a sonification is created to represent the amount of activity over time. Data can be filtered according to its contents and sent to distinct sounding tracks. For example, incoming text messages can be represented with a different sound than outgoing text messages, or communication among family could be distinguished from communication with coworkers. After filtering which data will be represented by each sound, the researcher chooses a length of time to be represented by each beat. Time is condensed, so a researcher might set each beat to represent one hour of activity, then play back the sonification at one beat per second. At each beat, a sound is triggered, representing the number of events that took place during that period. This makes the sonification akin to a histogram where each beat indicates the number of events that occurred over a given period of time. The more events that take place, the more intense the sound. Researchers can choose to indicate this intensity with either loudness or pitch, depending which they think is most suitable for their data. In our study, the number of events was mapped to loudness; loud sounds indicated many text messages were exchanged, soft sounds indicated fewer text messages, and silence indicated that no messages were exchanged.

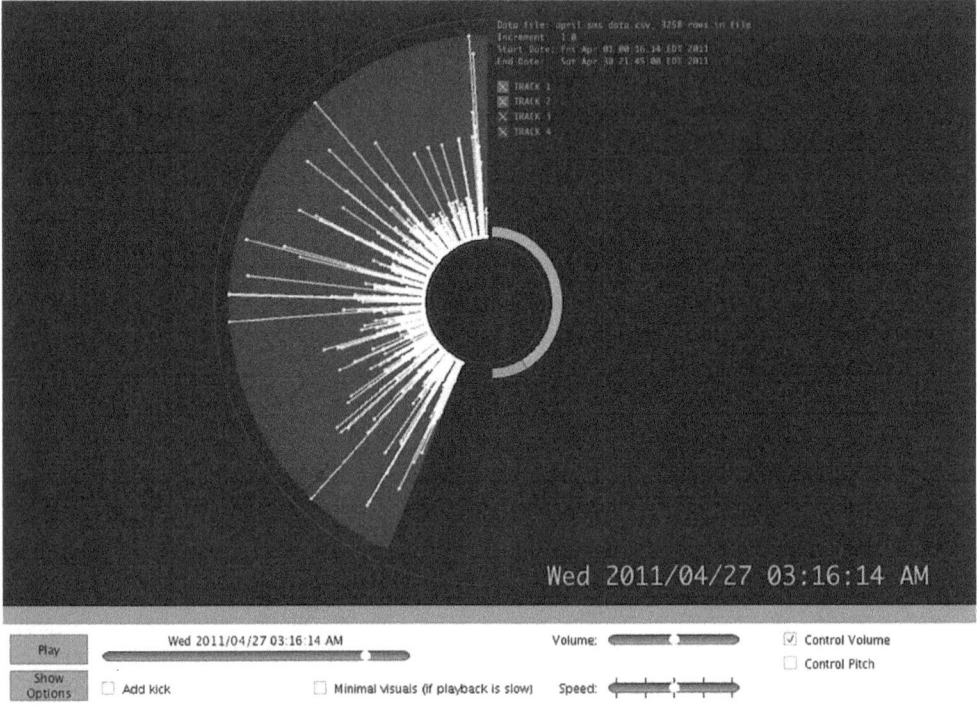

Figure 24.1   Screenshot of E-Rhythms Data Sonifier

In addition to sonification, the software includes a visualization component. The visualization makes it easier to contextualize each sound in relation to overall trends and aids temporal navigation through the data. For example, our text message log data sometimes included periods of inactivity, and we used this visualization to quickly locate periods of activity without having to listen to long passages of silence.

Listening Method and Findings

When listening, we filtered data according to the results of survey questions. This made it possible to compare communication patterns among family to those among coworkers, or communications with trusted ties to those with untrusted ties. At first, we listened to entire groups at once. When listening at the group level, it was possible to identify patterns based around fixed points in time. For example, we created a sonification that divided each day into four beats, and observed a rather musical pattern of three beats followed by a pause – *one, two, three, (pause), one, two, three, (pause)*. The pause indicated that participants rarely exchanged text messages in the middle of the night. Observing this expected pattern helped us to familiarize ourselves with some of the types of patterns that sonification could draw forth. Group level sonifications were successful at revealing consistent patterns such as a day/night cycle or bursts of activity around holidays, but could not illuminate individuals' patterns. As discussed earlier, group level sonification tends to allow the patterns of individuals to become lost in a sea of group activity.

To be able to listen to communication between individuals, we randomly selected

16 pairs, each consisting of one respondent and one of their ties, and listened to their texting activity at a dyadic level. To ensure we had enough activity to be able to listen to distinct patterns, we only selected pairs who had exchanged at least 100 texts between each other over the course of their saved logs. Within each pair, we assigned each individual a distinct sound, so it was possible to distinguish between messages sent by each. The first pattern that became evident upon sonifying activity at this dyadic level was that response time varied considerably between each pair. Some pairs consistently replied to each other within a few minutes, while others took up to several hours to reply to text messages. A limitation of our listening was that we lacked information about the content of messages, which made it impossible to assert which messages were replies and which started new conversations. However, it was possible to infer that, for example, a message that occurred after several days of no communication was likely to indicate a new conversation, and communications with only a few minutes between them were almost certainly part of the same conversation.

Previous research has suggested that temporal cues such as time of day or the speed at which people respond to each other can be indicative of the intimacy of their relationship (Döring & Pöschl, 2009; Kalman & Rafaeli, 2011; Quan-Haase & Collins, 2008; Walther & Tidwell, 1995). Notably, Walther and Tidwell (1995) found that shorter response times to task messages such as work communications are likely to indicate more intimacy and eagerness than long response times, but that longer response times to social communications may indicate more intimacy than quicker responses. This is likely because intimate social partners may feel less pressure to respond quickly. Building from this research, we recorded an estimated average response time for each pair then noted Pearson correlations between that estimated average response time and various measures of tie strength represented through the survey results. This preliminary analysis suggested three findings, which we formed into hypotheses for further testing.

H1: Family members will have shorter response times than non-family.

H2: Ties who are trusted by respondents will have longer response times than untrusted ties.

H3: Pairs who discuss important matters will have shorter response times than those who do not.

Statistical Testing

As stated earlier, exploratory analysis is better suited to hypothesis generation than to hypothesis testing. We conducted a statistical analysis to assess the validity of our sonification-generated hypotheses. First we identified messages that could potentially be replies (i.e. where the direction of communication changed) and generated a response time variable noting the time between these messages (n = 4,687). Because this variable included long gaps where the pair went up to days or weeks without communicating, we used a complete linkage cluster analysis on the response time variable to focus only on texts that could reasonably be considered direct replies. The cluster analysis allowed us to create groups of similar response times, and distinguish shorter response times that were likely to indicate replies from longer response times that indicated silences between conversations. Without viewing the content of messages, clustering was an approximate method of distinguishing replies from messages that initiated new conversations. We used this method because it provided a reasonable approximation to the more intuitive distinction that was made when listening to the sonification. Moreover, Kalman & Rafaeli (2011) stated that a pause of ten times the average latency constituted silence (and therefore a lack of reply) in online asynchronous communications. Our clustering method identified a cluster of 74%

of events (n = 3,487) with a mean response time of 216 seconds. The next largest cluster (n = 216) had a mean response time of 2,305 seconds, over ten times that of the larger group, suggesting that this was a reasonable albeit rough method of distinguishing between replies and new conversations.

We then calculated the mean incoming and outgoing response time (in seconds) for each pair, and then calculated mean and median response times for the independent variables noted in our hypotheses. Since survey questions were answered only by one member of each pair (the respondent), incoming refers to messages sent to that respondent, and outgoing refers to messages sent by that respondent. These mean and median response times are listed in Table 24.1, below.

The mean response times observed through statistical analysis were consistent with our hypotheses, although H1 and H2 only appear to be valid for incoming responses. Median response times were less varied, and do not exhibit significance for H2 and H3, but are fairly consistent with H1. This suggests that the sonification testing emphasized variances among response times that were relatively long, and that differences among shorter response times were less correlated with how participants responded to the survey questions.

Statistical analysis was then used to examine the extent to which these findings applied to the large sample of 149 tie pairs.

The results supported H2 and H3, but not H1. In fact, statistical analysis indicated that mean response time for family members was higher than for non-family – the opposite of what occurred among the 16-pair sample. A comparison of these statistical results to the sonification-generated hypotheses is presented in Table 24.2.

Discussion

Our analysis consisted of two stages. Exploratory sonification was used to generate hypotheses, which were then tested using statistical analysis. The fact that the hypotheses generated through sonification were supported by the initial statistical analysis of the 16-pair sample indicates that sonification was generally successful at identifying patterns within the data. It may have been possible to perform similar testing without sonification, but sonification was effective at highlighting response time as a variable for further investigation. In the dataset, each event was time-stamped, making response time an implicit variable. However, sonifying text message exchanges between pairs made response time explicit. This supports the notion that exploratory sonification can be an effective method for hypotheses generation. This also emphasizes the importance of considering different levels of analysis. Listening to the data at group, individual, and dyadic

Table 24.1 Mean and median response times among sonified sample

Category	Response time in seconds			
	Mean		Median	
	Incoming	Outgoing	Incoming	Outgoing
Family members	214	224	208	243
Not family members	476	205	214	159
Trusted ties	469	190	247	198
Not trusted ties	175	252	179	266
Discuss important matters	347	185	184	205
Do not discuss important matters	408	260	244	223

Table 24.2 Hypotheses generated through sonification compared to results of statistical analysis

Category	Mean response time for each independent variable		
	Hypotheses from sonification	Results of statistical analysis	
	Sonified sample (16 tie pairs)	Sonified sample (16 tie pairs)	Full sample (149 tie pairs)
Family members	Shorter	Shorter	Longer
Not family members	Longer	Longer	Shorter
Trusted ties	Longer	Longer	Longer
Not trusted ties	Shorter	Shorter	Shorter
Discuss important matters	Shorter	Shorter	Shorter
Do not discuss important matters	Longer	Longer	Longer

levels highlighted different types of patterns in the data, but each level also had its own set of associated challenges.

One challenge was illustrated by the fact that mean response times among family and non-family were different between the 16-pair sample that was sonified and the larger 149-pair sample. This indicates the randomly selected 16-pair sample was not representative in regards to H1. In order to make response time between pairs apparent using sonification it was necessary to listen at a dyadic level, which increased the potential for sampling errors. Verifying our sonification-generated hypotheses using statistical analysis provided an opportunity to identify this error by analyzing the larger population of pairs at once. This allowed us to test the hypotheses among the whole sample in a way that would not have been feasible with sonification alone.

FUTURE DIRECTIONS

Sonification demonstrates potential for exploratory analysis of time-stamped interactional data, but there is much room for future work. Ferguson, Martens, and Cabrera (2011) reflected upon the current state of exploratory statistical analysis using sonification:

It must be said that the current state of the art must be considered to be quite immature as yet, with many challenges for sonification research to tackle in the future. In fact, it might be proposed that the best approach to take in designing and developing statistical sonifications in particular would be one that includes critical evaluation of the results at each attempt. (p. 192)

While sonification has demonstrated analytic potential – especially with temporal information – there is still much to be learned. For this reason, sonification has more immediate potential for hypothesis generation than hypothesis testing. Testing hypotheses generated using sonification will lead to a better understanding of the strengths and limitations of sonification.

Among existing sonifications of social media it is common to present a real-time overview of activity. Typically these sonifications allow one to monitor activity and to notice large shifts or sudden changes. Some of these projects, such as Tweetscapes, were created with the goal of increasing awareness of sonification. For this purpose emphasizing broad, easily observable trends is a suitable strategy. Other techniques may be used to allow researchers to conduct deeper analyses. For example, encouraging temporal navigation such as rewinding, fast-forwarding, and looping would make it easier for researchers to analyze specific temporal passages in detail. Additionally, allowing researchers to listen at different levels of analysis such as individual and dyadic would facilitate the discovery of different types of trends than can be revealed through group analysis alone.

Currently, a large portion of research papers about sonification have been written by researchers who are themselves engaged in creating or evaluating sonification methods (Supper, 2012). To support the field's efforts at outreach into research domains, several designers have attempted to create tools that can be used by researchers who are not sonification specialists. For example, Grond designed a sonification tool for molecular structures and dynamics, and distributed the tool as a plugin for a software package that his potential audience of chemists was already familiar with (as cited in Supper, 2011, p. 256). This reduced the learning curve and allowed molecular researchers to use Grond's sonification alongside their existing toolset. Forthcoming sonification plugins for statistical packages such as R may be successful in allowing researchers to incorporate sonification (see e.g. Stone & Garrison, 2013). Additionally, as discussed earlier Wolf et al.'s work (2015) on involving end-users in sonification design has potential for broadening the field by allowing users to design sonifications with particular applications in mind. Lastly, the E-Rhythms Data Sonifier (2014) is designed to use a limited number of relatively simple sound properties (primarily time and volume), and can be used with almost any time-stamped data. This makes it a viable tool for social researchers who do not have prior expertise with sonification.

Researchers studying online communication benefit from an abundance of interactional data, such as time-stamped logs of activities. The growth of generalized sonification tools provides an opportunity to explore this data in new ways. The high level of detail and large quantity of this data gives it the potential to illuminate patterns and trends that have not been apparent in other representations of data. Exploratory analysis is an important technique for uncovering these potential patterns, and the time-dimension present in much of this data can be well explored through sonification.

REFERENCES

Andrienko, N., & Andrienko, G. 2006. Exploratory analysis of spatial and temporal data a systematic approach. Berlin: Springer.

Ash, K. 2012. Affective states: Analysis and sonification of Twitter music trends. In Proceedings of the 18th International Conference on Auditory Display (pp. 257–259). Atlanta, GA.

Ballora, M., Cole, R. J., Kruesi, H., Greene, H., Monahan, G., & Hall, D. L. 2012. Use of sonification in the detection of anomalous events. In J. J. Braun (Ed.), Multisensor, Multisource Information Fusion: Architectures, Algorithms, and Applications. http://doi.org/10.1117/12.918688

Bethancourt, M. 2012. The sounds of the discussion of sounds. In Proceedings of the 18th International Conference on Auditory Display (pp. 254–256). Atlanta, GA.

Carlile, S. 2011. Psychoacoustics. In T. Hermann, A. Hunt, & J. G. Neuhoff (Eds.), The sonification handbook (pp. 41–62). Berlin: Logos Verlag.

Dayé, C., & de Campo, A. 2006. Sounds sequential: Sonification in the social sciences. Interdisciplinary Science Reviews, 31(4), 349–364. http://doi.org/10.1179/030801806X143286

Dombois, F., & Eckel, G. 2011. Audification. In T. Hermann, A. Hunt, & J. G. Neuhoff (Eds.), The sonification handbook (pp. 301–324). Berlin: Logos Verlag.

Döring, N., & Pöschl, S. 2009. Nonverbal cues in mobile phone text messages: The effects of chronemics and proxemics. In R. S. Ling & S. W. Campbell (Eds.), The reconstruction of space and time: Mobile communication practices (pp. 109–135). New Brunswick, N.J: Transaction Publishers.

E-Rhythms Data Sonifier [Computer software]. 2014. Accessed 2 Nov 2015 from http://

individual.utoronto.ca/jboase/software.html#e-rhythmsdataanalysis

Ferguson, S., Martens, W., & Cabrera, D. 2011. Statistical sonification for exploratory data analysis. In T. Hermann, A. Hunt, & J. G. Neuhoff (Eds.), The sonification handbook (pp. 175–196). Berlin: Logos Verlag. Accessed 2 Nov 2015 from http://sonification.de/handbook/download/TheSonificationHandbook-HermannHuntNeuhoff-2011.pdf

Grond, F., & Hermann, T. 2011. Aesthetic strategies in sonification. AI & SOCIETY, 27(2), 213–222. http://doi.org/10.1007/s00146-011-0341-7

HEAVYLISTENING. 2012. #tweetscapes - Listen to Twitter [Video file]. Accessed 2 Nov 2015 from https://www.youtube.com/watch?v=0lKSFlB_-Q0

Hermann, T. 2008. Taxonomy and definitions for sonification and auditory display. In Proceedings of the 14th International Conference on Auditory Display. Paris, France.

Hermann, T., Hunt, A., & Neuhoff, J. G. 2011. Introduction. In T. Hermann, A. Hunt, & J. G. Neuhoff (Eds.), The sonification handbook (pp. 1–6). Berlin: Logos Verlag. Accessed 2 Nov 2015 from http://sonification.de/handbook/download/TheSonificationHandbook-HermannHuntNeuhoff-2011.pdf

Hermann, T., Nehls, A. V., Eithel, F., Barri, T., & Gammel, M. 2012. Tweetscapes – Real-time sonification of Twitter data streams for radio broadcasting. In Proceedings of the 18th International Conference on Auditory Display (pp. 113–120). Atlanta, GA.

Jamieson, J., Boase, J., & Kobayashi, T. 2015a. The faster the response, the stronger the bond? Dimensions of relational closeness and texting response time. [Poster] Presented at the 65th Annual Conference of the International Communication Association. San Juan, Puerto Rico.

Jamieson, J., Boase, J., & Kobayashi, T. 2015b. Using sonification to explore texting response time in time stamped interactional data. Presented at the CAIS/ACSI & LRI 2015 Conference, Ottawa, Canada.

Kalman, Y. M., & Rafaeli, S. 2011. Online Pauses and Silence: Chronemic Expectancy Violations in Written Computer-Mediated Communication. Communication Research, 38(1), 54–69. http://doi.org/10.1177/0093650210378229

Neuhoff, J. G. 2011. Perception, cognition and action in auditory displays. In T. Hermann, A. Hunt, & J. G. Neuhoff (Eds.), The sonification handbook (pp. 63–87). Berlin: Logos Verlag. Accessed 2 Nov 2015 from http://sonification.de/handbook/download/TheSonificationHandbook-HermannHuntNeuhoff-2011.pdf

Neuhoff, J. G., Knight, R., & Wayand, J. 2002. Pitch change, sonification, and musical expertise: Which way is up. In Proceedings of the 2002 International Conference on Auditory Display. Accessed 2 Nov 2015 from http://www.icad.org/Proceedings/2002/NeuhoffKnight2002.pdf

Quan-Haase, A., & Collins, J. L. 2008. I'm there, but I might not want to talk to you. Information, Communication & Society, 11(4), 526–543. http://doi.org/10.1080/13691180801999043

Sinclair, P. (Ed.). 2011. Sonification: What where how why artistic practice relating sonification to environments [Special issue]. AI & SOCIETY, 27(2). http://doi.org/10.1007/s00146-011-0346-2

Sonification Sandbox [Computer software]. 2009. Accessed 2 Nov 2015 from http://sonify.psych.gatech.edu/research/sonification_sandbox/

Smith, D. R., & Walker, B. N. 2005. Effects of auditory context cues and training on performance of a point estimation sonification task. Applied Cognitive Psychology, 19(8), 1065–1087.

Stone, E., & Garrison, J. 2013. audiolyzR: Give your data a listen (Version 0.4–9). Accessed 2 Nov 2015 from http://cran.r-project.org/web/packages/audiolyzR/index.html

Supper, A. 2011. The search for the 'killer application': Drawing the boundaries around the sonification of scientific data. In K. Bijsterveld & T. Pinch (Eds.), The Oxford Handbook of Sound Studies. Oxford University Press.

Supper, A. 2012. 'Trained ears' and 'correlation coefficients': A social science perspective on sonification. In Proceedings of the 18th International Conference on Auditory Display (pp. 29–35). Atlanta, GA.

Supper, A. 2014. Sublime frequencies: The construction of sublime listening experiences in the sonification of scientific data. Social Studies of Science, 44(1), 34–58.

Tufte, E. R. 2001. The visual display of quantitative information (2nd ed.). Cheshire, CT: Graphics Press.

Tukey, J. W. 1977. Exploratory data analysis. Reading, MA: Addison-Wesley Publishing.

Walker, B. N., & Kramer, G. 2005. Mappings and metaphors in auditory displays: An experimental assessment. ACM Transactions on Applied Perception (TAP), 2(4), 407–412.

Walker, B. N., & Nees, M. A. 2011. Theory of sonification. In T. Hermann, A. Hunt, & J. G. Neuhoff (Eds.), The sonification handbook (pp. 9–40). Berlin: Logos Verlag. Accessed 2 Nov 2015 from http://sonification.de/handbook/download/TheSonificationHandbook-HermannHuntNeuhoff-2011.pdf

Walther, J. B., & Tidwell, L. C. 1995. Nonverbal cues in computer-mediated communication, and the effect of chronemics on relational communication. Journal of Organizational Computing, 5(4), 355–378. http://doi.org/10.1080/10919399509540258

Wolf, K. E., Gliner, G., & Fiebrink, R. 2015. A Model for Data-Driven Sonification Using Soundscapes (pp. 97–100). ACM Press. http://doi.org/10.1145/2732158.2732188

Innovative Social Location-aware Services for Mobile Phones

Bernhard Klein and Ulf-Dietrich Reips

We report on innovative social location-aware micro services for mobile phones developed as part of the Mobile User Generated Geo Services (MUGGES) project. With these micro services users can tag their physical environment with textual comments and photos and share these with others. To gain a better understanding of user acceptance, empirical frameworks like the Technical Acceptance Model (Davis, 1989; Technical Acceptance Model, 2016) consider factors of user-interface and technology. Even though such frameworks are able to provide information about common usage patterns, they fail in separating between short-term hypes and long-term user benefits. A common problem of user surveys is that they reveal not enough data about detailed user interactions and corresponding usage contexts. For this reason we implement and here describe a living lab that emulates and analyzes a realistic ecosystem in an urban context. By installing a data logger application on cellphones, we can record service usage data, current context, invoked services, and content provided by the users. We analyze the usage patterns of the three micro services from the MUGGES project both from a user-centric and community perspective. The living lab is shown to identify usability problems, gain data on characteristic usage patterns and hotspots, and to evaluate MUGGES services' effectiveness.

INTRODUCTION

Social media such as Facebook, YouTube and Twitter have empowered users by allowing them to *produce* and consume information (Bruns, 2008). This trend is now moving to mobile social services, which offer a natural way of supporting social interaction through mobile devices anywhere at any time. At the same time, mobile location-based services (LBS) like Foursquare appeared that enable users to describe, rate and interact with urban spaces by location-aware services.

The Mobile User Generated Geo Services (MUGGES) project (Klein et al., 2012), funded by the European Commission's 7th Framework Programme, went a step further from current mobile social location-based services (LBS) by providing a platform that allows users to not only create simple content but evolve them to micro services that embed complex business logic like, for example, map navigation, blogs, and photo albums. In addition, users in the MUGGES eco-system provide their contents directly from the mobile device, i.e. the mobile device evolves to be a server. Thus, mobile users turn into location-aware service super-prosumers (Klein et al., 2012), i.e. producers, providers, and consumers of services and associated content from their mobile devices. In this chapter, we report on a living lab environment that was developed as part of the MUGGES project to extract and visualize environmentally embedded social behaviors from a continuous stream of usage data.

After this introduction, the remainder of the chapter is divided into six sections. Related research is presented in 'Related work' to provide the needed background. 'The MUGGES system' focuses on the MUGGES system itself, providing an explanation of the key topics behind MUGGES: the super-prosumer role of users, the service creation concept, the peer-to-peer architecture, and the location management. In 'Methodology' we describe the living lab concept (Bergvall-Kåreborn et al. 2009) employed to evaluate MUGGES in field studies conducted in Finland and Spain and a description of these studies. Finally we present the results and discuss the technology, usage and psychological experience. The final section summarizes and concludes the chapter.

RELATED WORK

The MUGGES platform represents a mobile peer-to-peer system leading to fairly short-term and highly dynamic user communities. Evaluating such a complex eco system represents a major challenge. We conducted a literature survey to compare different approaches focusing on *lab* and *field* based studies and assessed their benefits and limitations.

Lab-based evaluation frameworks log information in a controlled environment using specific devices and specific users. The main advantage of lab-based frameworks is the highly controlled environment and the inexpensive and simple data collection. However, the context, which is the most influential factor in the mobile services field, is often not considered in lab-based research and it can hardly be simulated. For instance, people usually use cellphones less frequently or shorter in dangerous situations, stressful environments or simply during rain or in the winter. Simulation tools produce highly inaccurate results because they cannot adequately account for real-world contexts. Furthermore, lab experimenters and designers of the usability tasks performed by the users often evoke situations that are unrealistic. Technologies might interact with participant personality and thus bias the sample (Buchanan & Reips, 2001). The users may also add biased results during the execution of the experiments (Reips, 2006), because they suffer from problems such as test-anxiety (Cassady & Johnson, 2002): during the task performance a highly test-anxious person divides the attention between self-relevant and task-relevant variables; due to the self-focused attention, the user of the mobile service may not show real behavior. Further, in many task situations such as cellphone calls, it would be subjectively annoying for many users to be in a room being observed by researchers.

Alternatively, field-based evaluation frameworks (see Table 25.1) capture information in real environments. They commonly use added cameras and human observers to capture information from user device interactions. For example, the *User testing platform*[1] not only uses methods like a think-aloud verbal

Table 25.1 Comparison of analysis tools

Tool	Capture Technique	Reported Data	Graph Visualization
User testing	Screen, webcam and microphone	Interaction, user information and user feedback	Reproduce the screen, interaction
Morae Observer	Screen, webcam, microphone and observer	Interaction, user information and user feedback	Reproduce the interaction and calculate graphs
ContextPhone	Mobile sensing and interaction event logging	Interaction, device status and environment	Mobility pattern detection
RECON	Interaction event logging and mobile sensing	Interaction, device status and environment	Trace data, analysis engine
MyExperience	Wearable hardware sensing, mobile sensing, audio recording and user surveys	Interaction, device status, user information, user feedback, and environment	Performance analysis, SMS usage and mobility analysis
SocioXensor	Interaction event logging, survey interview	Interaction, user, device status and environment	SQL database

protocol, but also records feedback how users perceive the study object by filming the face or recording comments with a webcam; finally it reproduces the user interaction at a given time through screen captures that can in a subsequent step be annotated with additional explanatory data like the current usage context. Another tool related to user testing is the *Morae Observer*[2] tool. It captures all the above mentioned interaction data, indexes it to one master timeline for instant retrieval and analysis, and then generates graphs of usability metrics. Another group of tools such as *ContextPhone* (Raento et al., 2005) and *RECON* (Jensen, 2009) are focused on capturing the context. They capture the surrounding environment through mobile sensors. This capturing technique retrieves a lot of real data without influencing the interaction, but users are not asked to provide feedback. In order to add user feedback other tools like *MyExperience* (Froehlich et al., 2007) and *SocioXensor* (Mulder et al., 2005) use techniques like self-reports, surveys and interviews in combination with capturing the context.

To sum up, to acquire valid interaction data about mobile services, it is essential to capture objective behavioral information to solve questions like 'when?', 'where?', 'how long?', etc. users are really interacting with a service. These questions can hardly be determined in a lab-based framework.

The field-based evaluation frameworks can provide deeper and more objective information, but certain agents such as cameras and invasive evaluation methods (e.g. think-aloud verbal protocols) are counterproductive and have to be removed from fieldwork methodology for the current purpose. In order to do so, the best way to capture interaction data is by registering information through a mobile device using an unobtrusive capture tool. This tool should log the context via the built-in mobile sensors and also log the key interaction events.

THE MUGGES SYSTEM

The MUGGES system was implemented as a hybrid peer-to-peer platform that is composed of a micro service communication network and core network that forms the infrastructure backbone managed through a telecom provider.

Micro services and related content are stored on the phones of the end-users. They use the micro service communication network to exchange data directly from phone-to-phone, giving their users full control over their content at any time. Note that this approach is fundamentally different from commercial social media where the content is hosted by providers such as Facebook and very often cannot easily be withdrawn.

Micro services automate the information exchange between people by providing shared functions such as blogs, coordinated maps, and photo albums through the infrastructure backbone of the MUGGES platform. Especially while traveling people's time for interpersonal communication is limited due to the need to monitor important environment changes. Micro services that automate this communication play an important role to ease coordination and enable ongoing socialization even during traveling.

Telecom providers are responsible for managing the MUGGES infrastructure including the micro service template repository, additional administration functions such as user management and accounting, and infrastructure services like location management. This hybrid peer-to-peer architecture was chosen by one Telekom provider from the project consortium to enable a smooth integration with existing social media platforms.

Mugglets

Figure 25.1 shows screenshots from MUGGES. Within MUGGES micro-services are called *mugglets* and they are small and independent location-based social services hosted in the mobile terminal and provided from the mobile device to another mobile device. The advantage of mugglets is that users can correlate digital information with places. MUGGES provides predefined templates that can be customized to personal preferences. We distinguish basic and mashup templates, where the latter combines functionality from one or more basic templates. The following three mugglet templates have been designed within the MUGGES project to show their benefits:

- *muggesNote*: This mugglet template allows the publishing of a short message with a photo referring to a specific location. The physical location of the user is automatically obtained by the positioning service of the mobile phone during the creation process. Such a message can describe physical objects like a building or can be used to refer to any comments related to activities usually performed at this location. Other users can then retrieve these messages at this location (see Figures 25.1a and b).
- *muggesJournal*: The main objective of this mugglet template is to maintain a journal attached to the current position of the user. This mugglet template represents a mashup as it contains a set of semantically related muggesNotes, for example, 'my soccer tournaments', maintained by a single author and ordered by date. Each muggesNote has its own location (see Figure 25.1c), so a muggesJournal can combine notes from several locations.
- *muggesTrail*: This mugglet template is also a mashup that allows users to define routes with information about places along the routes by adding sequence of muggesNotes (a starting point, intermediate points, and a goal) arranged

Figure 25.1 MUGGES Application interfaces – a) muggesNote, b) muggesNote photo view, c) muggesJournal, d) muggesTrail, e) muggesRace

in a specific geographic order. This kind of mugglet template allows users to see the directions from their current location to the next point on the route, with the aim of guiding them to the end of the route without trouble (see Figure 25.1d). A typical scenario could be recommending tours to tourists in a given city. The muggesRace template is a slightly modified version of the muggesTrail template that uses spatio-temporal data to organize jogging competitions.

Service Creation, Provision, and Consumption

After installing the MUGGES platform users can create their own mugglets, or query for existing ones and install them on their cellphones.

Users create their own mugglets by downloading templates and modifying them. The mugglet creation for mashups is very similar, but with the difference that previously created muggesNotes can be added to it. We made a big effort to generate an intuitive service creation process. A software installation wizard-like approach was adopted that uses templates to keep the overall duration for the creation of micro services for the user to an absolute minimum. This wizard guides the user in the template customization process by providing forms in a specific chronological order (see Figure 25.2). Templates basically consist of four parts:

1 Mugglet profile for service discovery: the profile contains the mugglet name, keywords, and describes minimum requirements for service installation.
2 Mugglet content objects. Mugglet content can be any text description, user comment, or multimedia object like a photo. Metadata associated with content objects define the content appearance and access in the mugglet.
3 Execution logic such as chat functions, blog management, map navigation, and photo services. The execution logic retrieves and represents content on the user interface.
4 User interface representation that includes style sheets for chat, blogs, maps and photo albums. Each mugglet has its own user interface and may contain several elements like buttons, text fields, maps and image controls.

Once mugglets have been created from one of the three templates they can be published and are searchable via the query interface. For querying of existing mugglets, users may apply a keyword-, a template- or a map-based search method to identify interesting mugglets. After downloading and installing the mugglet on their device users can execute the mugglet. Communication is then handled directly between the mugglet provider and the consumer. Always, mugglet providers keep complete control over their mugglets and can terminate them at any time.

User-aware Location Technology

Mugglets are connected to the physical world through location references. These location references become a crucial filter to search

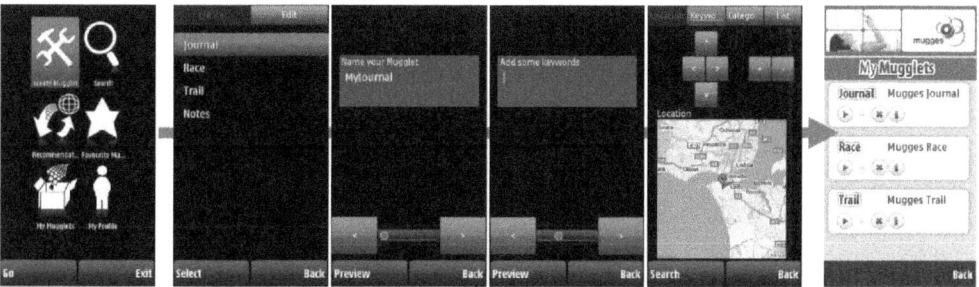

Figure 25.2 Mugglet creation wizard

and access mugglets (Kaasinen, 2003). Managing locations can be complicated due to different interpretations by humans. It is the responsibility of the MUGGES infrastructure to find out the user location by interpreting different location specifications. In contrast to machines, people use different mechanisms to represent location data. While computers use numerical representations, people use concepts and landmarks, for example, near the station, at the museum, in the market area. Hence, the MUGGES infrastructure has to correctly interpret expressions at a semantic level and accordingly execute them on the technical layer. The MUGGES location concept distinguishes between physical, symbolic and semantic locations and has been described earlier in (Klein et al., 2013), or see (Becker & Dürr, 2005), for a more general description:

- *Physical*: A point in a reference system (it might be accompanied by a geometric bounding shape). In geographic systems this is typically expressed through latitude, longitude and altitude coordinates, for example, the city center of Bilbao, Spain, is located at latitude: 431525, longitude: –25524, altitude: 19m.
- *Symbolic*: A human-readable and understandable textual description of a location, for example, 'University of Konstanz, Germany' or 'The Netherlands'. See also Becker and Dürr (2005) for a more specific description.
- *Semantic*: A machine-understandable location expression upon which location-related inferences can be undertaken, for example, the University of Deusto lies in the city of Bilbao, which in turn is located in the Basque Country, in Spain and so on.

Conventionally, only one of those facets is specified while searching for mugglets, for example, either the physical location or the symbolic description. It is the MUGGES infrastructure that translates, if possible, among the different instances of location specifications so as to fulfill the requested location-related tasks.

METHODOLOGY

The assessment of the MUGGES system is based on a living lab concept (Bergvall-Kåreborn et al., 2009). A living lab is an open innovation ecosystem, where different technology providers and end-users collaborate in a realistic environment with the goal to achieve best product quality. The idea of

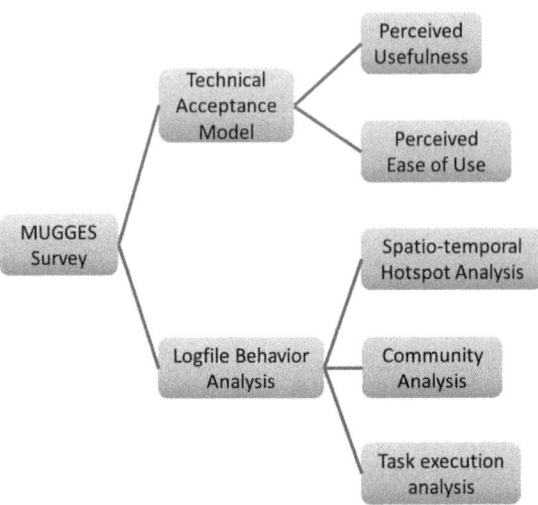

Figure 25.3 Study design overview

living labs originated from the domain of ambient intelligence, where real life study situations play a key role for successful evaluations. The strength of such an approach lies in the close engagement between end-users and service providers. Survey and usage data is collected with the aim of continuously improving the technology.

Study Design

In order to learn more about the benefits of a mobile location-based service approach, we use surveys to gain information on users' perceptions regarding the MUGGES technology and log data analysis to compare these with real MUGGES usage (see Figure 25.3). Self reporting of phone usage, a widely used method (Boase & Ling, 2013), most likely leads to under reporting as MUGGES automates social coordination in the background. It can also not explain why people seemingly have not used MUGGES in certain situations where context data suggest they did. We believe that this combined survey plus log data analysis approach is suitable to evaluate technology and the functioning of the system.

For the survey we created a simple questionnaire based on the Technical Acceptance Model (Davis, 1989), the most widely applied model of users' acceptance and usage of technology (Venkatesh, 2000). According to Wikipedia (Technical Acceptance Model, 2016), the TAM model represents an extensions of Ajzen and Fishbein's (1980) theory of reasoned action and considers the usefulness of a service and the ease of use as primary factors to influence technology adaption. Malhotra and Galletta (1999) observed that TAM applied to collaborative systems like MUGGES lead to more robust belief structures (perceived usefulness and perceived ease-of-use) if social influences such as feeling of compliance or identification are considered. Perceived usefulness describes to which level persons believe that using a given technology would enhance their task performance. Perceived ease-of-use, on the other side, refers to the degree to which a person believes that using a technology would free them from effort in contrast to alternative approaches.

In case of MUGGES, the usefulness is related to various sub-aspects like service creation, provision, discovery and consumption. Perceived ease of use describes the degree to which a user expects that using this service is free of effort. Normally these include different aspects of interface learning, memorization and efficiency. Because the user interfaces in MUGGES follow heterogeneous approaches, the mugglet creation kit and mugglets are evaluated separately. For the log file analysis we combined data from the data logger with general user and mugglet data managed by the MUGGES system. Thus, aspects of the user interface, events and mugglet execution states stored on different servers can be correlated. Examples for log data are (Reips & Stieger, 2004, also see Stieger & Reips, 2010): service start and stop times, UI events, for example, buttons pressed, screen transitions, any changes in settings and erroneous data entries, exceptions and any unexpected system behavior. All the events registered in the logs contain geo coordinates and timestamps. This time and location data is used to identify characteristic spatiotemporal mugglet usage patterns of individual users. Timestamp information allows us to speculate about preferred usage times on an hourly or weekly basis. Grouping events from location data can reveal usage hotspots. The resulting spatial cluster structure can reveal if study participants prefer to use the system in a carefully planned or rather spontaneous manner. People who carefully plan their MUGGES tagging activities tend to describe places that they have visited multiple times before and know very well in advance, resulting typically in a very limited number of high quality muggesNotes. This is in strong contrast to a person that uses MUGGES rather spontaneously and seems to explore the environment. Such a person obviously creates more scattered muggesNotes and keeps most of them, even if he or she doesn't perceive them later as good choices. The high effort to delete a muggesNote may be one reason why later editing activities were rarely observed.

Because MUGGES represents a social network, it is interesting to gain more information about the communities formed around specific mugglets. Interesting aspects are the average size and duration, but also the number of active users in such communities. Therefore, user and subscription data is aggregated for each mugglet in order to calculate the average community size, average provision duration and provider-consumer ratio. Finally, a functional analysis is conducted. By analyzing entire user task chains from service creation over editing to the provision of mugglets one can learn how people deal with time constraints or what workaround they find to compensate problematic usage situations.

User Groups

When the evaluation studies were prepared, the MUGGES platform was still in an early development stage, so it was decided to ask technically experienced users for participation. The assumption hereby was that participants with a technical background would be more likely to cope with problems and could provide more adequate feedback. For the first study, 8 participants were selected from a group of IT professionals in Finland. Although we actively tried to recruit a gender mixed sample, we found no female volunteers in Finland. All Finnish participants were in the age of 25–35 and were employed at the VTT research institute. In Spain, it was decided to select 17 computer science students from the University of Deusto, where the prototype had been developed. All students were between 20 and 26 years old and mostly men (only two of them were female).

A pre-study questionnaire about their cellphones and past experience with mobile applications showed that both participant groups can be considered early adopters as defined by Rogers (2003). All participants were equipped with smartphones offering features for embedded Wifi networks, GPS[3], camera and music players (see Figure 25.4a). At the time of interviewing they used various mobile applications that utilized the built-in camera and GPS systems and frequently used web applications. Spanish participants spent more money for their mobile phones than Finnish participants (see Figure 25.4b). This could be a hint that Spanish participants see mobile phones as a primary means to coordinate their life whereas Finnish participants mainly rely on their desktop PCs. However, due to the confounds between the two samples (for example of age) it is impossible to

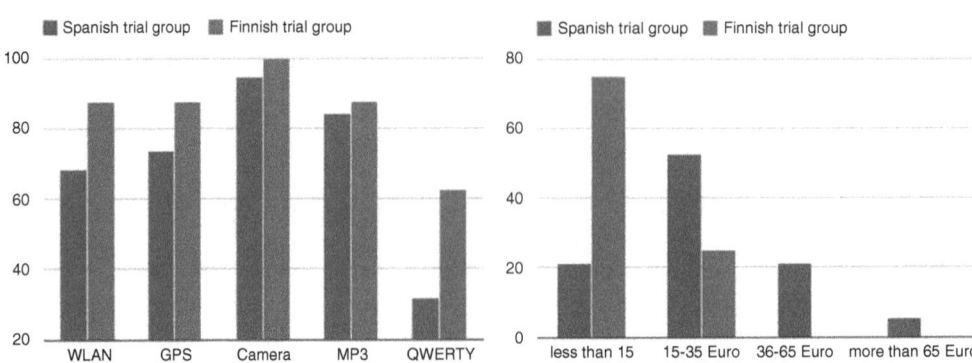

Figure 25.4 a) Personal phone features   b) Monthly spending on personal phone

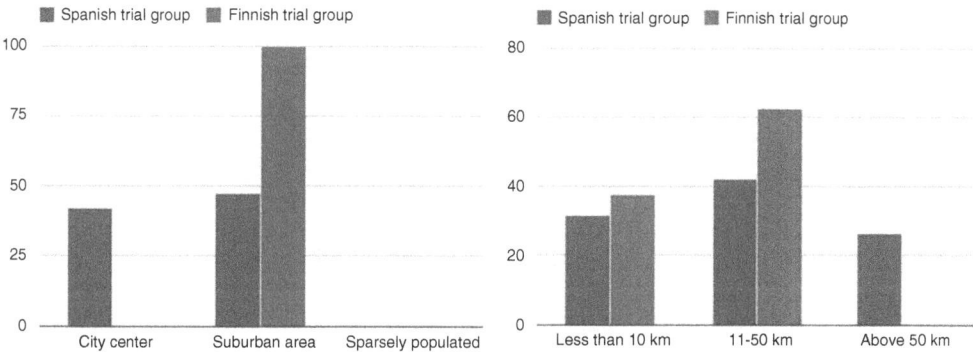

Figure 25.5 a) Home locations   b) Daily travel distance

determine if this is a national difference or an age difference or something else (e.g. climate). Almost all participants live in densely-populated areas: in the center of a city or close to it (see Figure 25.5a). Most participants travel around 11–50 km to get to their company or university (see Figure 25.5b). Such a travel distance with public transportation may take around 30 minutes. This time frame is certainly enough to check on individual mugglets or even maintain them. High average travel distances of the Spanish students resulted from some participants commuting every day between different cities, for example, between Victoria and Bilbao. We assume that people who commute have a high interest in any application that helps them to get familiar with the city in which they study or work and discover new things to do in it.

Field Trials

A technical and functional explorative field trial was executed in Espoo (Finland) and Bilbao (Spain) to obtain necessary data for the MUGGES evaluation. Whereas the technical trials aimed to evaluate the peer-to-peer concept and the location technology, the functional trials focused on the evaluation of usage patterns.

The MUGGES infrastructure in both trials was provided from a server installed and operated in Spain (see Figure 25.6).

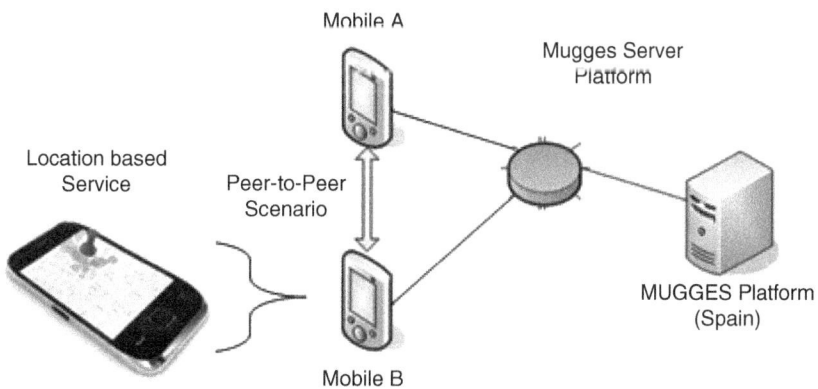

Figure 25.6 Technical infrastructure

Because all time critical MUGGES tasks are handled directly between the devices, delays through the provision of MUGGES infrastructure services via the Internet are negligible. A location model for both trial sites was created to symbolically represent all major indoor locations. These include 16 different places, for example coffee places, vendor machines, and meeting rooms within the VTT building complex and the engineering building of the University of Deusto. Each place had been equipped with visual markers (QR codes[4]) at convenient places, for example, walls close to the entry points to enable indoor positioning. For outdoor positioning, the standard GPS system was used. Participants were encouraged to test the application freely also elsewhere in the city, in order to gain as much information as possible for technical and functional evaluation. In order to achieve a critical mass of mugglets for the service discovery the trial area was narrowed down to a set of shared and frequently visited places identified in an interview with all participants before each experiment. For the field trials, users were given Nokia 5800 XpressMusic touch screen smart phones with preinstalled and preconfigured MUGGES software. All the phones had a small touch screen, embedded GPS, and a prepaid 3G/3.5G data connectivity that allowed 0.4–6 Mbit/s downlink data transfer. The MUGGES software included the MUGGES creation and execution kit to create and consume mugglets.

At each location, the study began with a kick-off meeting, during which the MUGGES system was presented and demonstrated. Afterwards, participants were able to experiment with MUGGES in a one day training session, also to achieve truly informed consent about all aspects of the system, including data sharing. In each trial site different indoor and outdoor experiments were organized, which all concluded with a small competition at the end. In early phases of each trial participants were asked to create and consume muggesNotes, whereas in later stages they were asked to preferably utilize mashup mugglets. The competition was conducted to emulate a stress test for the MUGGES infrastructure. This was achieved by rewarding highly active users or users with the largest or most popular mashup mugglets. During and after the trials, data from the following sources were collected for the evaluation:

- *Mixed-mode mobile surveys*: An online questionnaire was designed, which each trial participant was asked to answer before and after the experiment. Each dimension of the questionnaire is further defined through several MUGGES specific aspects (see 'The MUGGES system'). Participants were asked to respond to questions on a five point rating scale, from *strongly agree* to *strongly disagree* (see Table 25.2). This online questionnaire was further complemented by open questions to obtain additional information, for example, suggestions from the study participants.
- *Event and error logging*: During the study a data logger software that was installed on the smartphones recorded MUGGES events and error messages. These data were later used to reconstruct MUGGES usage, usage contexts and problem situations. After each experiment the log files were collected from the mobile phone and uploaded to a repository in the Internet. For ethical reasons, user identifying data (e.g. student name) and MUGGES log file data (e.g. mugglet specific events like taking a photo) were strictly separated.

RESULTS

Technical Acceptance Analysis

In order to present the overall user acceptance of the MUGGES system in one single figure, all measurements are represented in a histogram graph. The centre of the graph represents values indicating high user acceptance and the edge of the graph low user acceptance. Figure 25.7 shows the feedback for the Spanish user group. One graph represents the first overall impression the MUGGES system left after an initial introduction and another

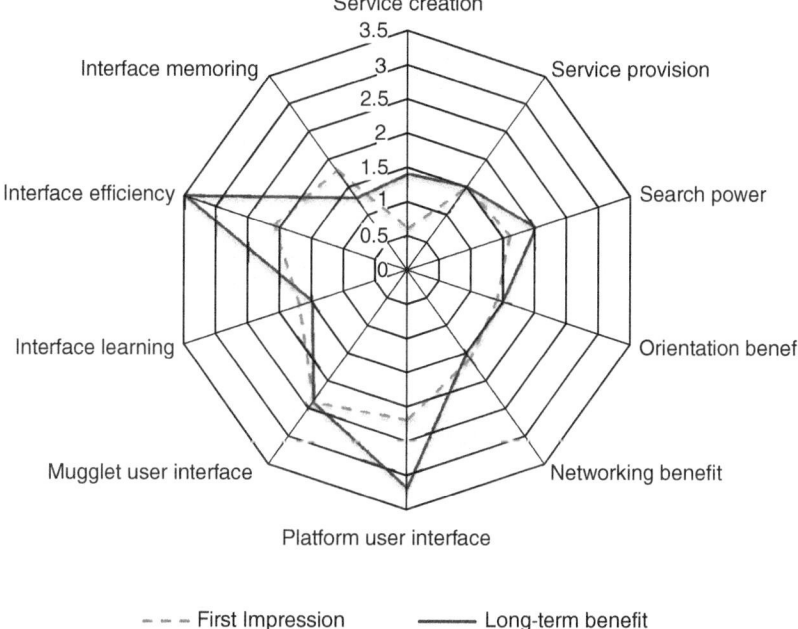

Figure 25.7 Comparison of first and long-term impression
Source: Questionnaire data of Spanish study.

graph the overall long-term benefit perceived by all study participants towards the end of the trial. In the following we will analyze each dimension and combine them with the feedback obtained through the problem reporting tool and focus interviews:

1. *Perceived usefulness*: All study participants saw great long-term benefits in the MUGGES concept. The creation, provision and discovery of personal services is definitely seen as useful in an everyday life scenario, as all these service management aspects were rated with 2.0 or even better. Mugglets seem to improve sustainably participants' orientation in cities (mean value of 1.5) and encourage networking between people (mean value of 1.5).

2. *Perceived usability*: For the usability dimension we separate between user interfaces of the MUGGES platform and mugglets, as they are designed differently. Whereas the mugglet user interface has been well designed for the mobile usage, people were disappointed with the service creation wizard. Obviously, pictures from the platform user interface looked more appealing on the MUGGES presentation and the task flow appeared more efficient during demo (see mean value difference of 3.25 − 2.25 = 1 between first time and long-term impression). Developers felt that the service creation process is quite complex and thus best represented through a wizard approach. The positive user feedback regarding interface learning ($M = 1.4$) and interface memorizing ($M = 1.3$) shows that a guided service creation approach is welcome. Nevertheless, the user interface was not completely designed from an end-user's perspective, as it did not consider sufficiently the efficiency ($M = 3.6$) to create micro-services. Task efficiency (e.g. time to create a service) is a highly critical aspect especially in situations while moving from one place to another.

Table 25.2 Questionnaire items with underlying dimensions and indicators

Dimension	Indicator	Measurement
Usefulness	Service creation	Sufficient service creation support?
	Service provision	Importance of service provision?
	Search power	Search tools powerful enough?
	Orientation benefit	Benefit for finding places, people and information?
	Networking benefit	Benefit for meeting new people, coordinate meetings and knowledge sharing?
Usability	Platform user interface	Attractivity of Platform Interface
	Mugglet user interface	Attractivity of Mugglet Interface?
	Interface learning	Easiness to learn MUGGES usage?
	Interface efficiency	Satisfaction with user interface efficiency?
	Interface memorizing	Easiness to remember user interface interactions?

Log Data Analysis

Log data analysis has long been a fruitful method of Internet-based and mobile research (Reips, 2006; Reips & Stieger, 2004). Based on the data obtained during the study, we analyzed MUGGES usage and its workflow. Mugglet usage was the highest (90 created mugglets per day) in the initial days of the study and dropped slightly in the remaining time (around 75 created mugglets per day). During weekends, MUGGES was rarely used, since many students were living outside of the trial area. Far away from the trial area, the spatial coverage of mugglets was too low and the social networks supported with MUGGES too sparse to create sustainable interest to use the system. Also, the technical support was sometimes not available in case MUGGES was not working properly. From the interviews performed at the end of the study, it is inferred that most of the study participants would use Mugglets once a day. This is a value similar to other social media applications of this type (Chan et al., 2014). Study participants mentioned distractions from the weather, the environment, and unstable implementation and major reasons to refrain from MUGGES usage. In the following we report more detailed observations in respect to the MUGGES workflow:

1 *Mugglet Creation*: During the Finnish and Spanish studies a total of 536 (149/387) mugglets were published. In the following we take a closer look at the spatial distribution of the MUGGES activities in the area of Bilbao (Spain) and Otaniemi (Finland). The location information recorded during creation-and-editing events is used to visualize these MUGGES activities. Figure 25.8 visualizes spatial usage patterns.[5] The size of a circle is correlated with the number of similar events in that location. Most creation events were centered around the university campus and the VTT buildings, which had been equipped with indoor location mechanisms like the visual markers. Participants also explored surroundings in the direct neighborhood. These were sports places, for example, a soccer field, leisure places (e.g. coffee shops and bars), and in some cases even participants' individual home locations. One striking aspect is that the hotspots observed were much more widely distributed for Spanish participants. We account this to 1) a larger group size, 2) better weather conditions, 3) technical reasons (e.g. redesigned creation wizard and improved robustness) as the service creation process in the Spanish version was significantly shorter and thus occurred more spontaneously. In both groups, most mugglets were of the type *muggesNotes*, 84% in Otaniemi and 53% in Bilbao. This large proportion of muggesNotes is not surprising because they represent the basic building blocks of mashup mugglets. Other mugglet types were created as follows. In Finland 7% muggesJournal mugglets and 6% muggesTrail mugglets and in Spain 30% muggesJournal mugglets and 30% muggesTrail Mugglets (see Figure 25.9a). The significant difference of mashup creation in Otaniemi and Bilbao

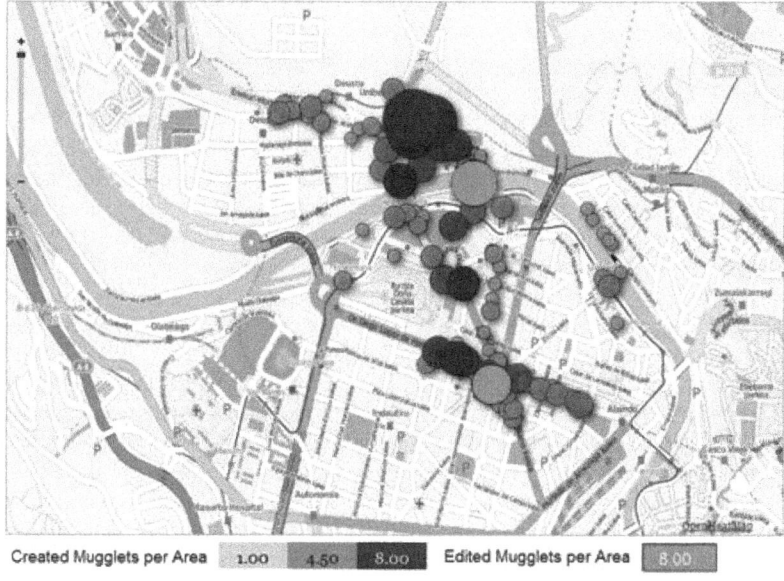

Figure 25.8 Creation and editing hotspots in Bilbao. The circle size corresponds with the number of similar events in the same location

Source: Logging data of Spanish study.

can be explained with the fact that the creation wizard for mashups was significantly improved before the Spanish group began with the study. During the interview after the trials, users felt that mashup creation is a powerful feature and encouraged us to extend MUGGES by allowing the re-usage of notes from other users, and by pre-creating mugglets for well-known places. Figure 25.9b shows that most mashup Mugglets contain between two and seven mugglets, while the majority of all mashup mugglets had a length of four muggesNotes. As the mugglet creation process represents a certain effort and the overall usage times during a move from one place to another are usually limited, mashup Mugglets in general may not grow very large. Participants reported that their devices became significantly slower with the increasing size of mugglets.

2 *Mugglet Provision*: Originally mugglets were designed mainly for short-term usage. Surprisingly, mugglets were used for much longer times, only around 33% of mugglets were provided for several hours and 17% for several days (see Figure 25.10a). The remaining 50% were

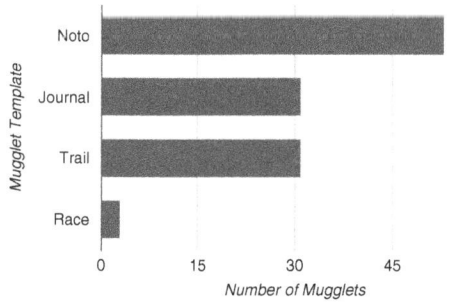 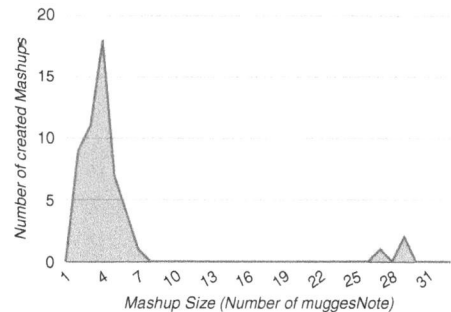

Figure 25.9 a) Applied mugglet templates   b) Observed mashup size

Source: Content data of Spanish study.

used much longer. Study participants reported that they wanted their mugglets to be active for a longer time frame dependent on the feedback they obtain from others (19%), the event related with the mugglet (6%) and the intended audience (6%, see Figure 25.10b). Most of the time the provision duration was limited by the battery consumption (38%) or execution speed. The popularity of mugglets can indirectly be measured by the number of subscribers. Naturally, only small friend groups of not more than two to three users subscribed to the majority of mugglets (see Figure 25.11). A small proportion (around 10%) of mugglets attracted a large audience of up to 15 people. Considering the fact that the study group size was 17 people, this is quite a large value. Even though the sample was small, there was clear evidence of participation inequality in the study. This rule in summary means that 'In most online communities, 90% of users are lurkers who never contribute, 9% of users contribute a little, and 1% of users account for almost all the action' (Nielsen, 2006).

3   *Mugglet Discovery and Consumption*: Data reveal that the MUGGES system was mainly utilized to coordinate pleasure activities during spare time periods in the afternoon and in Spain also during the night. MUGGES usage during work has been rather neglectable as the location-based nature of mugglets unfolds their value while people are on the move. The majority of the searches in early trial phases were category based, for example, participants searched for muggesNote, as this was the most simple way of identifying adequate mugglets with only a few out there. With an increasing number of mugglets the result lists became longer and the identification of the right mugglet more difficult on the small screen of the smart phone. Study participants compensated for this by exploring more advanced search methods, for example, the keyword-based search (15%) or the map-based search (31%, see Figure 25.12a). Specific

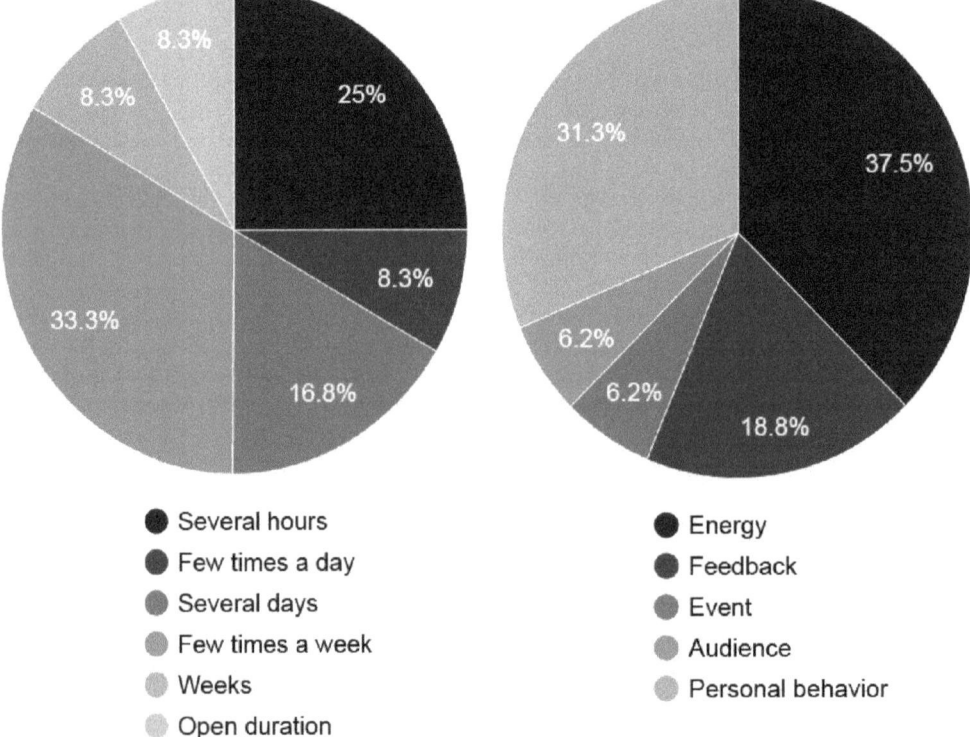

Figure 25.10   a) Measured provision duration   b) Reasons to stop provision

Source: Logging/survey data of Spanish study.

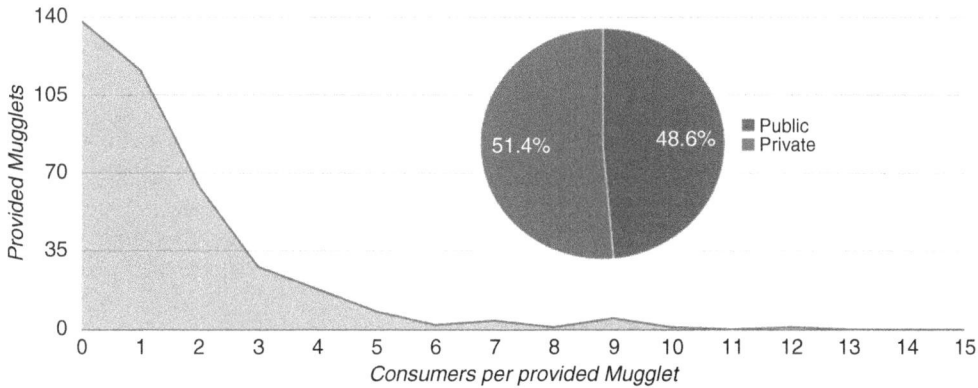

Figure 25.11 Community size of correlated mugglets

Source: Logging data of Spanish study.

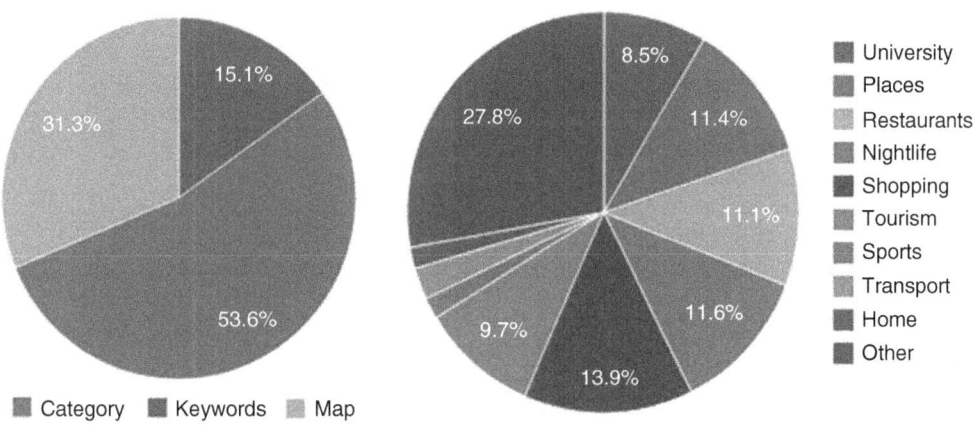

Figure 25.12 a) Applied search techniques and b) preferred search topics

Source: Logging data of Spanish study.

preferences for topics could not be detected (see Figure 25.12b). People showed similar interests in all different daily city activities, for example, shopping, restaurants, sports and nightlife.

DISCUSSION

Interpreting the service creation, provision and consumption patterns revealed further aspects, which were often backed by the feedback we obtained from the interviews.

First, the number of created mugglets found at a certain location depended strongly on the time taken to create them, especially during bad weather conditions or in darkness. For instance, during rain, people look for spaces where they can take shelter whereas during the night people seem to prefer spaces with light, for example, a bus station. Heterogeneous creation and editing event locations show that people in many cases did not have enough time to complete the mugglets. One major reason was the limited responsiveness of the touch screens at the time, when touch screen technology was in early development. The Nokia 5800 XpressMusic was released in November 2008 and used a resistive touch screen technology that relies on a stylus as an input device instead of capacity based touch screens common in today's smart phones that can be used with fingers. People compensated for this problem through a two-step creation process, first taking a photo and tagging it with the current location and then editing the content in a more convenient location, for example, at restaurants, cafes or public transport stops. For other social media like Facebook and Instagram this behavior observation may be less obvious as the overall mugglet creation process is more complex and thus takes more time. Because the participants often employed such a two-phase task flow for creating and editing mugglets, there was a clear need for providing private work space, which enables users to publish mugglets only when they were finalized. Above that, participants suggested replacing the creation wizard with a simple form, as scrolling is faster than skipping through multiple wizard screens. A consequent reuse of user profile data and community data were further suggestions to make the creation process more efficient.

Participants created mugglets not only for their friend groups, but also for larger audiences (49% public mugglets). Attracting a larger audience is not easy and requires a lot of effort, for example, nice photos, interesting descriptions or frequent updates. During focus interviews people requested social features like mugglet recommendations/ratings, but also real time features like update notification to give authors better means to address a larger audience or increase the popularity of their mugglets. A frequently mentioned key strength of MUGGES has been that it keeps people much more effectively connected, for example, by sharing popular locations and paths while on the move. An analysis of the technical context during the mugglet provision demonstrated that the energy usage and bandwidth consumption often limit the provision duration. An alternative implementation could consider a hybrid peer-to-peer approach where mugglets were hosted in the cloud but still managed from the users' mobile phone. This solution would probably resolve many shortcomings related to the peer-to-peer communication.

During the focus interviews study participants told us that they envisioned two different mugglet discovery use cases. In the first case participants tried to explore mugglets by topic in order to decide to which places to go. This mugglet exploration task happened mainly in indoor locations, for example, university or VTT campus areas where working with a mobile device was convenient. In the second case, participants often explored with the map based search method the surrounding neighborhood (outdoor locations) to see what other attractions exist in the proximity.

CONCLUSION

In this chapter we presented a framework for evaluating and ultimately for designing innovative social location-aware services for mobile phones. As an example, we reported on an evaluation of the MUGGES project. A living lab is an open innovation ecosystem, where different technology providers and end-users collaborate in a realistic environment with the goal to achieve a best possible product quality. In order to get a general idea about how people accept the super prosumer model and perceive the peer-to-peer and location-based concept behind MUGGES, we conducted a questionnaire study and combined the data with log data. The first impression after the kick-off meeting was very positive because the super prosumer concept was envisioned as a very powerful feature by participants. Even though the user interface impressed the study participants in the beginning, people detected several shortcomings later, especially some related to the creation wizard, the mugglet query tool, and the peer-to-peer service provision concept. Interestingly, the doubts about data security and location privacy were not confirmed as mugglets do not reveal personal information.

In addition to survey data, we also exploited log files and user content to compare users' perceptions with real MUGGES usage. Moreover, we analyzed individual MUGGES functions like service creation, provision, discovery and consumption. For each function we examined usage rates, spatiotemporal usage hotspots, community and structures. With the spatial analysis, we were able to detect specific usage hotspots, and the distribution characteristic revealed to which degree the services were used in planned or spontaneous manner. Looking at the community structure of individual mugglets confirmed that subscriber communities are rather small. Interestingly, people like to create mashup mugglets as these seem to provide more complex information and are more easily created by reusing existing muggesNotes. No specific mugglet topics could be discovered during the study, suggesting that MUGGES is imaginable for all sorts of city activities.

Altogether, the impression was that the living lab approach worked very well to improve a complex infrastructure like MUGGES. During the study, it became clear that questionnaire-based feedback alone cannot deliver data on the same level of granularity as its combination with log data and user perceptions. Combining several methods is more likely to reveal the real strengths or weaknesses of a product.

NOTES

1   Low Cost Usability Testing, http://www.usertesting.com
2   Morae usability testing tools from TechSmith, http://www.techsmith.com
3   Global Positioning System, satellite based navigation system.
4   Quick Response Code, optical machine-readable two dimensional barcodes for object recognition.
5   See http://www.openheatmap.com/

This chapter has been supported by the project grant no. 228297 (MUGGES), funded by the European Commission's 7th Framework Programme. The authors would also like to acknowledge the contribution of the EU COST Action IS1004 'Webdatanet' (http://webdatanet.eu).

REFERENCES

Ajzen, I., & Fishbein, M. (1980). *Understanding attitudes and predicting social behavior*. Englewood Cliffs, NJ: Prentice-Hall.

Becker, C., & Dürr, F. (2005). On location models for ubiquitous computing. *Personal and Ubiquitous Computing*, 9(1) 20–31.

Bergvall-Kåreborn, B., Ihlström Eriksson, C., Ståhlbröst, A., & Svensson, J. (2009). A milieu for innovation – defining living lab. In Proceedings of 2nd ISPIM Innovation Symposium, New York, December 6–9.

Boase, J., & Ling, R. (2013). Measuring mobile phone use: Self-report versus log data. *Journal of Computer-Mediated Communication*, 18(4), 508–519. http://doi.org/10.1111/jcc4.12021

Bruns, A. (2008). *Blogs, Wikipedia, Second Life, and Beyond: From production to produsage*. New York: Peter Lang. Retrieved from http://www.loc.gov/catdir/toc/ecip084/2007046097.html

Buchanan, T., & Reips, U.-D. (2001). Platform-dependent biases in Online Research: Do Mac users really think different? In K. J. Jonas, P. Breuer, B. Schauenburg & M. Boos (Eds.), *Perspectives on Internet research: Concepts and methods*. [WWW document]. Available URL: http://www.psych.uni-goettingen.de/congress/gor-2001/contrib/buchanan-tom

Cassady, J. C., & Johnson, R. E. (2002). Cognitive test anxiety and academic performance. *Contemporary Educational Psychology*, 27, 270–295.

Chan, T. K. H., Cheung, C. M. K., Lee, Z. W. Y. & Neben, T. (2014). The urge to check social networking sites: Antecedents and consequences. In Proceedings of 18th Pacific Asia

Conference on Information Systems (PACIS), Chengdu, China.

Davis, F. D. (1989). Perceived usefulness, perceived ease of use, and user acceptance of information technology. *MIS Quarterly*, *13*(3), 319–340.

Froehlich, J., Chen M. Y., Consolvo, S., Harrison, B., & Landay J. A. (2007). MyExperience: A system for in situ tracing and capturing of user feedback on mobile phones. In Proceedings of MobiSys. San Juan, Puerto Rico.

Jensen, K. (2009). RECON: Capturing mobile and ubiquitous interaction in real contexts. In Proceedings of MobileHCI. Bonn, Germany.

Kaasinen, E. (2003). User needs for location-aware mobile services. *Personal Ubiquitous Computing*, *7*, 70–79.

Klein, B., López-de-Ipiña, D., Guggenmos, C., Pérez, J. and Gil, G. (2013). User-aware Location Management of Prosumed Micro-services, *Journal of Interacting with Computers*, *26*(2), 118–134. http://doi.org/10.1093/iwc/iwt040.

Klein, B., Perez, J., Guggenmos, C., Pihlajamaa, O., Heino, I., & Del Ser, J. (2012). Social acceptance and usage experiences from a mobile location-aware service environment. In *Mobile lightweight wireless* systems, Third International ICST Conference, MOBILIGHT 2011, Bilbao, Spain, May 9-10, 2011, Revised Selected Papers (pp. 186–197). Springer Berlin Heidelberg.

Malhotra, Y. & Galletta, D. F. (1999). Extending the technology acceptance model to account for social influence: theoretical bases and empirical validation. In Proceedings of the 32nd Hawaii International Conference on System Sciences.

Mulder, I., Ter Hofte, G., & Kort, J. (2005). SocioXensor: Measuring user behaviour and user eXperience in conteXt with mobile devices, in Proceedings of Measuring Behavior, the 5th International Conference on Methods and Techniques in Behavioral Research, Wageningen, the Netherlands, pp. 355–358.

Nielsen, J. (2006). Participation inequality: Encouraging more users to contribute. http://www.useit.com/alertbox/participation_inequality.html

Raento, M., Oulasvirta, A., Petit, R., & Toivonen, H. (2005). Contextphone: A prototyping platform for context-aware mobile applications. *IEEE Pervasive Computing*, *4*(2), 51–59.

Reips, U.-D. (2006). Web-based methods. In M. Eid & E. Diener (Eds.), *Handbook of multimethod measurement in psychology* (pp. 73–85). Washington, DC: American Psychological Association. doi:10.1037/11383–006.

Reips, U.-D., & Stieger, S. (2004). Scientific LogAnalyzer: A Web-based tool for analyses of server log files in psychological research. *Behavior Research Methods, Instruments, & Computers*, *36*, 304–311.

Rogers, E. M. (2003). *Diffusion of innovations*, 5th Edition. Free Press, Simon and Schuster, New York. ISBN 978-0-7432-5823-4.

Stieger, S., & Reips, U.-D. (2010). What are participants doing while filling in an online questionnaire? A paradata collection tool and an empirical study. *Computers in Human Behavior*, *26*(6), 1488–1495. doi:10.1016/j.chb.2010.05.013

Technical Acceptance Model. (2016) In Wikipedia. Retrieved 26 March 2016, from https://en.wikipedia.org/wiki/Technology_acceptance_model. Last accessed 14 July 2016

Venkatesh, V. (2000). Determinants of perceived ease of use: Integrating control, intrinsic motivation, and emotion into the technology acceptance model. *Information Systems Research*, 11(4), 342–365.

PART VI
Research and Analytical Tools

COSMOS: The Collaborative On-line Social Media Observatory

Jeffrey Morgan

COSMOS is a cross-platform Java application that enables social scientists to collect, mash and visualize social media and curated data without the need to write computer programs. After building multiple-coordinated data visualizations in minutes using a simple drag and drop user interface, users can interrogate and iteratively refine their data to focus on areas of interest. COSMOS can export data in a variety of numeric, textual and visual formats, which enables it to fit into existing social scientific workflows, which may include further analysis by both quantitative and qualitative software.

This chapter begins by explaining the motivation for working with social scientists to develop COSMOS for use by social scientists. The COSMOS user interface is then described in terms of how it brings together a variety of different data sources and enables users to manipulate them in a flexible, consistent and exploratory environment.

Next, this chapter explores the ways in which the COSMOS application is developing and how the ecosystem around COSMOS is expanding with the use of plugins. Plugins enable third-party software developers to augment the ten generally useful interactive data-visualization tools shipped with COSMOS, including tables, maps, social network graphs and line, pie and frequency charts, with new visualizations that meet the changing and bespoke needs of social science research. This chapter concludes with a brief exploration of the ethical use of social media data with COSMOS.

INTRODUCTION

The Collaborative Online Social Media Observatory (COSMOS) is a cross-platform Java application that enables social scientists to collect, mash and visualize the naturally occurring data generated by social media platforms with curated data sets such as the UK Census, all without the need to write computer programs.

COSMOS is the innovative output of the COSMOS project, a collaboration between computer and social scientists that began at Cardiff University, UK and later included researchers from the universities of St Andrews and Warwick, UK. The aim was to develop software that would enable social scientists to explore and exploit the rich stream of data provided by social media platforms such as Twitter. This software contributes to the field of computational social science by simplifying access to the burgeoning opportunities for social-scientific inquiry into these new data sources (Burnap et al., 2013; Housely et al., 2014; Williams et al., 2013).

At the start of the COSMOS project, the landscape of tools available for accessing social media data required computer-programming skills in order to retrieve data over the Internet using Application Programming Interfaces (APIs). Querying that data and combining or 'mashing' it with other data sources required further programming skills commonly possessed only by computer and data scientists. The challenge then was to build software for social scientists that would hide these technical complexities and enable them to focus on the data.

Building Software for Social Scientists

From the outset, COSMOS was designed for social scientists using a participatory, user-centred design process led by their peers. User-centred design is a key technique in the field of human-computer interaction (HCI) that involves the end users of a software application throughout its design and development in a process of iterative testing and refinement (Norman and Draper, 1986).

The focus on social scientists as the primary user group produced four requirements. These define the way COSMOS works, the way users interact with the software, and the way further development of the software proceeds, namely:

1. COSMOS should support and augment rather than change the way social scientists work and therefore it must fit into broader social science workflows.
2. COSMOS should have a user interface that enables users to harness the power of data visualization in a flexible, graphical style familiar to users of software such as Microsoft Office and social-science software such as NVivo and Atlas.ti.
3. COSMOS should enable users to collect and analyze Twitter data and mash it with other data sources without the need for computer programming.
4. COSMOS should not be a black box. Every data analysis algorithm used by the software must be open for inspection and critical review by its users.

This chapter explores the ways in which COSMOS meets these requirements. The next section begins this exploration with a focus on the first requirement: supporting social scientists' work.

Supporting Social Scientists' Work

By collecting user-generated social media data such as tweets, social scientists can capture insights into how individuals and groups respond to events as they occur and at much larger scales than with instruments such as surveys. COSMOS supports the investigation of research questions such as:

1. Was there a positive or negative reaction to the event?
2. How did the different genders respond to the event?
3. Was there a geographical difference in reaction to the event?

The first question can be investigated with COSMOS by looking for changes in sentiment before, during and after the event. By enabling users to partition data by gender, COSMOS enables researchers to explore the second question by examining the changes in sentiment by each gender. To help answer the third question, COSMOS provides extensive facilities for exploring the geographical nature of social media data, which can help social scientists look for similarities or differences in attitudes to events within and between countries.

COSMOS supports the research activity of social scientists with different data-collection and research-question-definition needs. For example, some users will begin using COSMOS with a research question in mind that they want to explore, such as the three questions above, possibly with some data they have already collected while others may not have a research question in mind but have a topic of interest that they want to explore.

Figure 26.1 illustrates the spectrum of research need along two axes. The horizontal axis presents how well the research question is defined. The vertical axis presents how much data the social scientist has to investigate his or her research question. Social scientists with less well-defined research questions will find themselves to the left of the chart; whereas those with more well-defined research questions will find themselves to the right. Social scientists with little or no data will find themselves at the bottom of the chart; whereas those with more data or a complete data set will find themselves towards the top.

COSMOS aims to help social scientists move towards the top-right corner of Figure 26.1, where more data is available to explore more well-defined research questions. COSMOS helps social scientists move along the data axis by providing tools for collecting Twitter data on topics of interest and by providing facilities for importing Comma Separated Value (CSV) files and Rich Site Summary (RSS) feeds. COSMOS helps

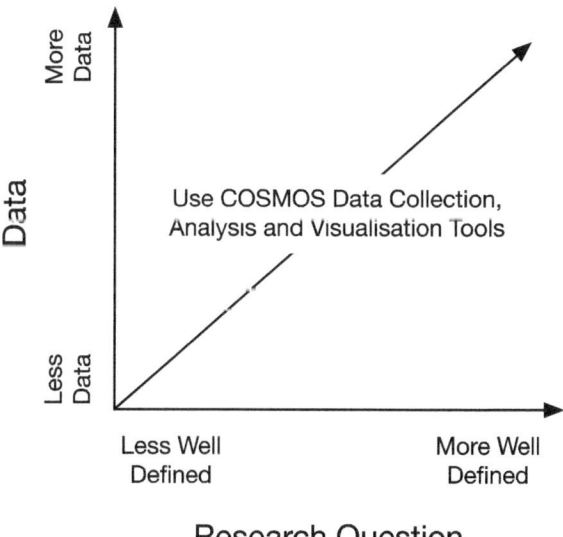

Figure 26.1 COSMOS aims to help social scientists move towards the top-right corner of the spectrum of data and research-question-definition needs

social scientists move along the research-question-definition axis by providing powerful data querying and visualization tools that support data exploration within social-scientific workflows.

COSMOS Social Science Workflows

Although COSMOS can be used as a stand-alone application, we recognized from the beginning that it would be used as a part of broader social science workflows, as illustrated through Figure 26.2.

In the first stage of a typical workflow, COSMOS users may already have formulated some initial research questions or ideas and may also have some data they want to work with in COSMOS. In the second stage, users import and collect more data, refining their research questions and ideas by querying, refining and visualizing data with COSMOS. In the third stage, COSMOS users continue to explore and refine their research questions by exporting data from COSMOS and importing it into other quantitative and/or qualitative software.

COSMOS does not attempt to replicate the functionality of quantitative software such as spreadsheets like Microsoft Excel, statistics packages such as SPSS or qualitative Computer Assisted Qualitative Data Analysis (CAQDAS) software such as NVivo and Atlas.ti. Rather, COSMOS supports the use of this software by providing extensive facilities for exporting data in a wide variety of commonly used formats including the CSV, Microsoft Excel and JSON data formats and the PNG and JPEG image formats, as discussed later in this chapter.

In the final stage of the typical workflow shown in Figure 26.2, users take the data and images exported directly from COSMOS, or worked up in other quantitative or qualitative software, and format these outputs for publication in proceedings, academic journals and conference papers.

The user interface of COSMOS was designed with these tasks in mind and aims to provide a simple and intuitive system of data management.

THE COSMOS USER INTERFACE

Figure 26.3 illustrates the COSMOS user interface, which is composed of three main areas:

1 The Data Set Library.
2 The Data View Library.
3 The Workspace.

The Data Set Library

The Data Set Library is found on the left sidebar and contains all of the data sets available to the COSMOS user. Each data set lists its name, its size and the period of time covered by the data set (if the data set has a temporal dimension). Each data set also presents an icon to identify the type of data held in the data set. COSMOS currently supports three types of data:

1 RSS feeds.
2 CSV files.
3 Twitter collections and data files.

The process of adding these data types to COSMOS is described later in this chapter.

The Data View Library

COSMOS provides different visualization styles called 'data views' for presenting data. The Data View Library is on the right

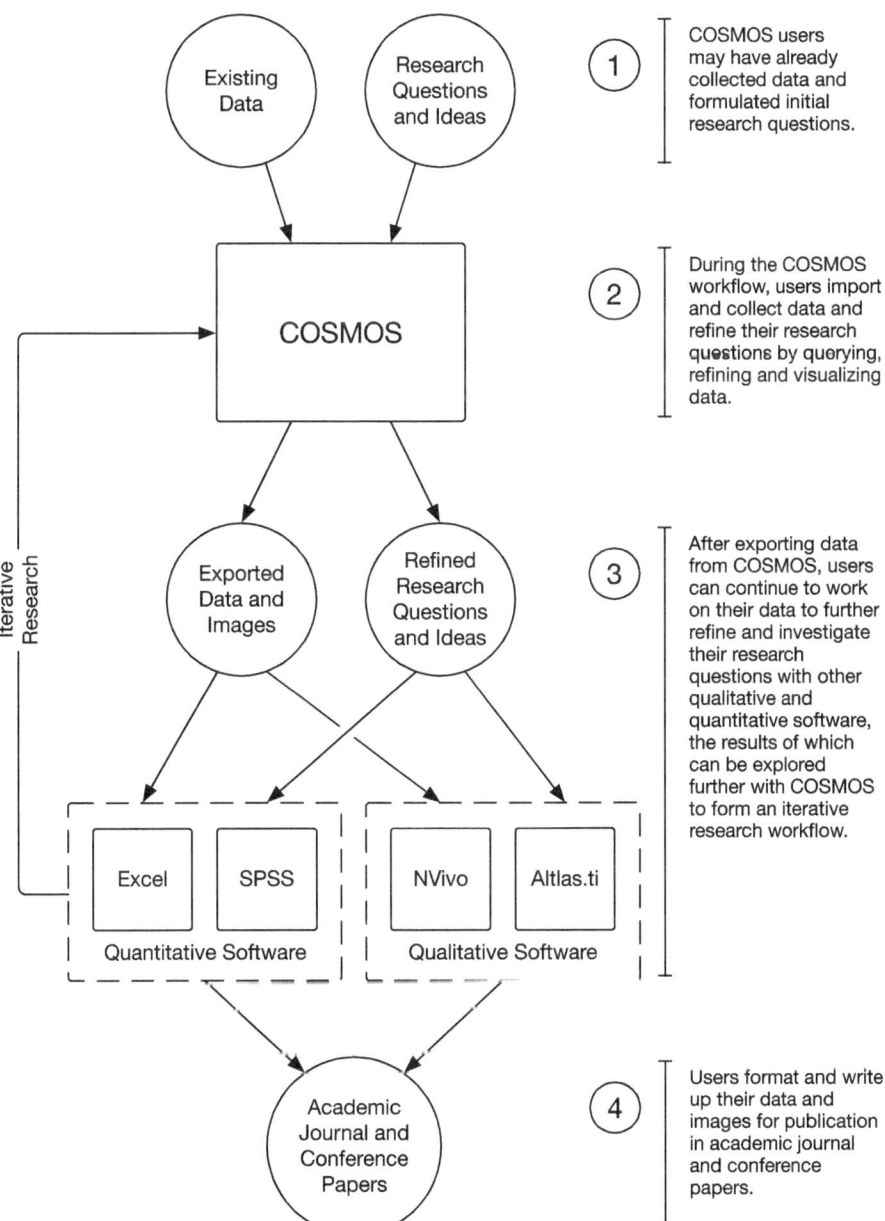

Figure 26.2 The COSMOS software application is a tool that fits into broader social-scientific workflows

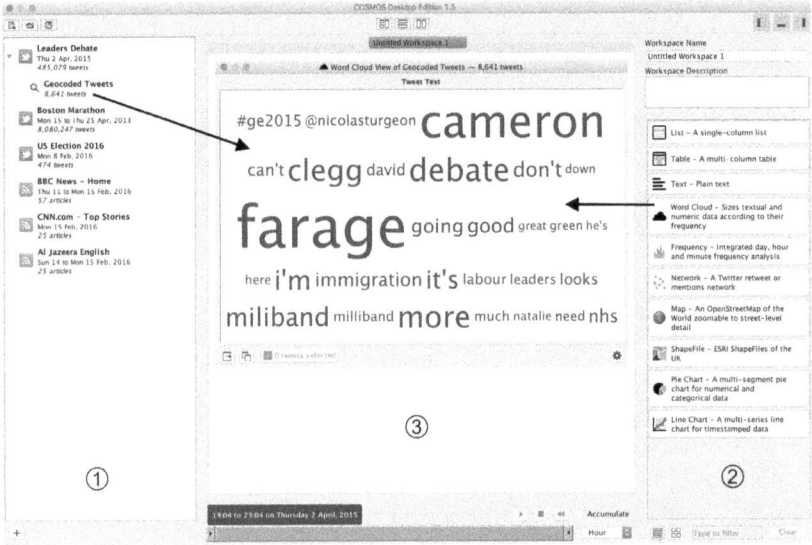

Figure 26.3 The COSMOS user interface is composed of three main areas: the Data Set Library (1); the Data View Library (2); and the Workspace (3); Users build visualizations by dragging and dropping data sets and data views onto the Workspace, as shown by the arrows

sidebar and lists the data views available to COSMOS users. COSMOS is distributed with the following ten data views:

1 Table – a multi-column table that provides the default view of each data source.
2 List – a single-column table useful for focussing on one data column.
3 Text – a plain-text view that presents a single data value.
4 Word Cloud – words sized by frequency give an overview of the distribution of values in a data column.
5 Frequency – linked bar charts that show the temporal frequency distribution over days, hours and minutes.
6 Network – social network analysis of retweet and mentions networks.
7 Map – geocoded data plotted on geographic maps and satellite terrain images.
8 Shapefile – geocoded data plotted on shapefiles of regions of the UK shaded by 2011 UK Census data.
9 Pie Chart – a segmented view of categorical data that is often used to present the gender breakdown of a data set.
10 Line Chart – a linear view of numerical data that is often used to visualize the positive and negative sentiment within a data set.

This list can also be augmented by installing data view plugins, which enable third-party software developers to implement their own COSMOS data views. These ten data views and data view plugins are explored in more detail later in this chapter.

The Workspace

The Workspace is the main section of the user interface and is where users build interactive data visualizations. The COSMOS user interface employs four key user-interface design techniques:

1 Drag and drop.
2 Error-free flexibility.
3 Consistency.
4 Zero configuration.

COSMOS makes extensive use of the drag and drop user interface paradigm. Users drag and drop data sets from the Data Set Library onto the Workspace, which appear in the default table data view presentation. Users can also drag and drop data views from the Data View Library onto the Workspace or onto other data views, as illustrated by the arrows in Figure 26.3.

Data Views dropped onto the Workspace remain empty until a data set is dragged onto them. When the user drops a data view onto a data view that is already presenting data, the existing data view is replaced with the new data view, which then presents the data in the new style. This interchangeability between data sets and data views produces a highly flexible system that removes the potential for syntactic errors. As a result, COSMOS does not need to present error messages to users.

Consistency is used throughout the user interface to reduce the amount of new learning required to use COSMOS. Examples of user interface consistency in COSMOS include:

- Making all data sets and data views draggable onto the Workspace.
- Using data set icons to highlight the type of data a control will operate on.
- Providing the same controls in each data view window to enable users to export data and to configure and duplicate data views in the Workspace.

COSMOS provides each data view with a set of configuration controls that enable users to change the default settings. However, by following the zero-configuration design principle, users never need to change any settings to get an immediately useful data presentation. For each data view, COSMOS selects the most appropriate data to use for that data view. For example, the pie chart data view is most effective for presenting categorical data. Therefore, COSMOS will present a pie chart built from categorical data columns, if available, otherwise COSMOS presents a pie chart built from numerical data. Similarly, the word cloud data view presents textual data most effectively so COSMOS will present a word cloud built from a textual data column. This enables COSMOS users to rapidly build and change visualizations, which encourages data exploration.

It is important to note that the social scientist is in the driving seat when using COSMOS. Although COSMOS does use algorithms to augment data with analytics such a gender and sentiment (described later in this chapter), the software is not an automated data-mining platform. All the insights into the data gained from using COSMOS are produced by its users through their interaction with the software and their exploration of the data.

Earlier in this chapter, Figure 26.2 illustrated how COSMOS fits into a broader context of social-scientific workflows by providing an opaque box in order to simplify its role as a component in the larger workflow. Figure 26.4 opens the COSMOS box to reveal a typical workflow in which social scientists can explore and refine their research questions and ideas with the help of COSMOS. After collecting and importing data, COSMOS users begin by iteratively querying and visualizing data to explore and refine research questions at a high level of detail. They then iteratively select and visualize data to hone in on interesting parts of a data set. The controls and interactions provided by the COSMOS user interface for conducting these workflow steps are explained throughout the remainder of this chapter.

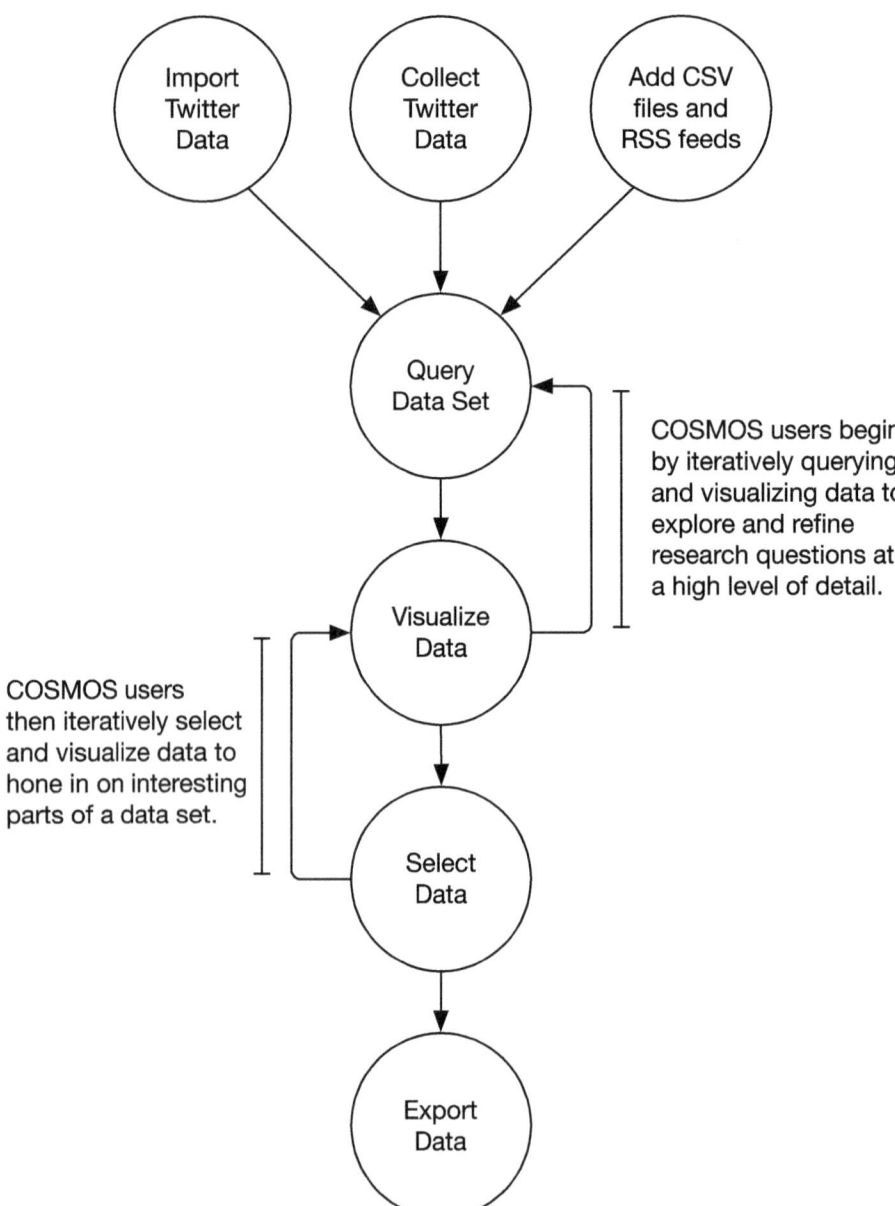

Figure 26.4 COSMOS users engage in an iterative workflow of querying, visualizing and refining data to explore their research questions

Before COSMOS users can build exploratory data visualizations and iteratively select and refine data, they must add that data to COSMOS.

DATA

This section describes the three data-related groups of tasks users perform with COSMOS:

1. Adding and collecting data.
2. Selecting and refining data.
3. Exporting data.

COSMOS was designed to make these data-related tasks as easy to perform as possible by making extensive use of the drag and drop user interface paradigm.

Adding Data Sets

The Data Set Library on the left of the COSMOS user interface lists the RSS, CSV and Twitter data sets the user has added to COSMOS.

RSS Feeds

RSS feeds are a standard web format for publishing regularly updated content, such as news headlines and blogs. Adding RSS feeds such as BBC News (BBC, 2016), CNN (2016) and Al Jazeera (2016) to COSMOS enables social scientists to compare and contrast the ways in which social media streams such as Twitter report and monitor the same unfolding events as traditional media outlets. For example, Twitter users often report events that affect them before traditional media (Takeshi et al., 2010). Adding the RSS feed from the European–Mediterranean Seismological Centre (EMSC), for example, enables social scientists to monitor how social media responds to and reports worldwide natural disasters such as earthquakes (EMSC, 2016).

Users add RSS feeds to COSMOS by either selecting the URL of a feed in a web browser and dragging and dropping it onto the Data Set Library, or by copying the URL and pasting it into the Data Set Library with the context menu presented after right-clicking the mouse.

CSV Files

CSV is a standard data interchange format that stores a table of data as a plain text file. Each line of a CSV file records one row of the table and each column value in that row is separated from the next by a comma.

Adding CSV files to COSMOS enables social scientists to visualize and interact with any type of data that CSV files can store, which ranges from data exported from spreadsheets such as Microsoft Excel to data downloaded from websites. For example, the World Health Organization (WHO) publishes public data in CSV format covering a wealth of dimensions, such as life expectancy data by country (WHO, 2016).

Users add CSV files to COSMOS by dragging and dropping CSV files from the operating system's file manager program onto the Data Set Library, or by invoking the *Add CSV File...* option presented after clicking the + button at the bottom of the Data Set Library.

Twitter Data Files

Twitter data files are added to COSMOS by dragging and dropping files containing Twitter data in JSON format from the operating system's file manager program onto the *Import Twitter Data* dialog presented by invoking the *Import Twitter Data...* option, which is accessed by clicking the + button at the bottom of the Data Set Library.

COSMOS can import Twitter data in three formats:

1. Standard Twitter format – the JSON format returned by the Twitter streaming API (Twitter, 2016).
2. GNIP format – the JSON format used by GNIP to mark-up Twitter data sets for purchase (GNIP, 2016).
3. DataSift format – the JSON format used by DataSift to mark-up Twitter data sets for purchase (DataSift, 2016).

Each tweet is inserted into an SQL database stored on the user's computer. Using SQL enables COSMOS to query Twitter data rapidly across a number of dimensions. Querying Twitter data is described later in this section.

Importing existing Twitter data sets enables COSMOS users to work with previously collected data for retrospective study. COSMOS also enables users to collect their own Twitter data sets about upcoming events.

Collecting Twitter Data

A key feature of COSMOS that benefits social scientists is the ability to collect data from the one per cent Twitter stream without programming. COSMOS hides the technical details of both authenticating Twitter users and collecting and storing the data.

A Twitter collection is started by invoking the *Start New Twitter Collection...* option presented after clicking the + button at the bottom of the Data Set Library. The *Start New Twitter Collection* dialog shown in Figure 26.5 enables users to make two types of collections:

1. A random-sample collection.
2. A filtered collection.

A random-sample collection will contain tweets randomly selected from the over 500 million tweets authored globally each day (Internet Live Stats, 2016). Previous work has demonstrated that the one per cent Twitter stream is random with respect to geographical distribution around the world and the gender of Twitter users (Sloan et al., 2013). Although random samples are useful for getting a feel for the current Twitter zeitgeist, filtered collections are more useful for studying specific events.

A filtered collection is defined by the keywords and hashtags that a tweet must contain to be included in the collection and also by the Twitter account used to author the tweet. Filtered collections are best suited to tracking specific events that have a known start date so that users can preemptively start a collection. Although Twitter allows filtering by other dimensions such as location and language, COSMOS supports the most common data-collection use case, which is to collect data about a particular topic, possibly posted from a particular Twitter account. However, COSMOS does enable users to query the data in their collections by location and language, which is described later in this chapter.

After a collection is started, COSMOS will continue to accumulate tweets until the user stops the collection. It is useful to monitor the progress of a collection, especially early on, to make sure the specified keywords, hashtags and accounts are collecting the correct data. COSMOS supports this collection monitoring with snapshots.

Collection Snapshots

To enable users to monitor the current state of a Twitter collection, COSMOS provides a set of controls for taking snapshots, as shown in Figure 26.6. A snapshot is a data set created by importing the data accumulated in the collection at the time of the snapshot. Snapshot data sets behave like every other data set and can be dragged onto the workspace and visualized with any of the COSMOS data views. This enables users to check whether the collection is progressing as intended and if the

Figure 26.5 The COSMOS *Start New Twitter Collection* dialog enables users to collect tweets from the one percent Twitter stream by either randomly sampling tweets or by filtering tweets using keywords, hashtags and user accounts

correct data is being accumulated. For example, visualizing snapshots with the word cloud data view enables users to check that COSMOS is collecting tweets on the correct topic or about the right event.

A snapshot is taken by clicking the *Snapshot* button, which will present the *Import Twitter Data* dialog mentioned above. For long running events, it is useful to configure COSMOS to take automated snapshots every n hours, minutes or seconds. Ticking the check box control in Figure 26.6 turns on automatic snapshots. The drop-down menus to the right of the checkbox enable users to specify how frequently COSMOS should take snapshots (the value and temporal units of n).

Data views that display the data created by an automated snapshot are automatically updated with fresh data as each new snapshot is taken. This creates a collection monitoring system that enables users to periodically glance at the monitor displaying COSMOS as an event of interest unfolds without needing to interact directly with the software. To avoid bloating the available disk space with

Twitter Collection

Collection Service
My Computer

Collection Name
US Election 2016

Collection Size
49 tweets

[Snaphot]   [Stop]   [Import]

☑ Snapshot every [5] [Seconds]

● Next snapshot in 2s

Figure 26.6   The COSMOS collection snapshot controls enable users to monitor the progress of an ongoing Twitter collection without stopping the collection. Automated snapshots enable users to set up an event monitoring system

automated snapshots, COSMOS retains the three most recent snapshots. As each new snapshot is added, the oldest snapshot is deleted.

After stopping and importing a collection, the data is added to the Data Set Library and is available for interrogation with the COSMOS data selection and refinement tools.

Selecting and Refining Data

COSMOS provides four methods of selecting and refining data sets:

1. Querying.
2. Sampling.
3. Temporal filtering.
4. Selection.

Querying

Data sets are queried by doubling-clicking the data set in the Data Set Library. Currently, only data sets created by importing Twitter data can be queried. The query dialog provides a rich set of controls for interrogating a Twitter data set by content, demographics, sentiment, time and geography, as shown in Figure 26.7.

The query control settings combine to produce highly descriptive queries. For example, when exploring a set of tweets collected on the topic of the re-election of the UK Prime Minister, David Cameron, one might want to make the following request:

'Select all the males in the UK that expressed a positive sentiment about David Cameron during the last three days of campaigning'.

Similarly, when exploring the reaction of female French citizens in London with a data set of tweets about the 2015 terrorist attack in Paris, one might make the following request:

'Select all the tweets authored by females in London that were written in French since 13 November 2015'.

On the left of the dialog, the *Include* keyword input box enables users to enter words, phrases and hashtags of interest that must be present in the text of a tweet for the tweet to

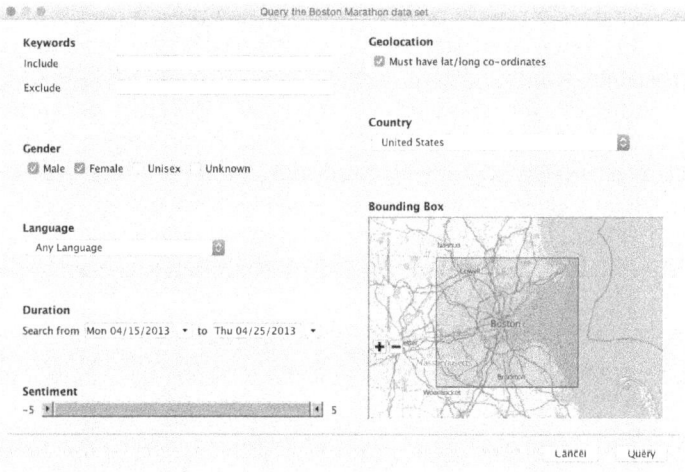

Figure 26.7 The COSMOS query dialog enables users to query Twitter data sets by content, demographics, sentiment, time and geography

be included in the search results. In contrast, the *Exclude* keyword input box enables users to enter words, phrases and hashtags that must not occur in the search results. This is useful for ignoring tweets that contain words and phrases that commonly co-occur with the words and phrases of interest but, when present, change the context of the words and phrases of interest and pollute the results.

Gender is a demographic of interest to social scientists, particularly because Twitter does not collect this information when users sign up. When COSMOS users import a collection of tweets, COSMOS attempts to identify the gender of the author of each tweet using a technique based on first-name analysis (Sloan et al., 2013). This technique partitions gender into four categories: male, female, unisex and unknown. This technique enables COSMOS to identify the gender of 50 per cent of Twitter users as either male, female or unisex, which is a name given to both males and females. The *Gender* check box controls enable users to specify the gender the author of a tweet must have for the tweet to be included in the results.

The *Language* drop-down menu will filter out any tweets not written in the selected language. As a global social media platform, Twitter users tweet in 53 different languages (Sloan et al., 2013) so restricting tweets to specific languages is a useful tool for social scientists interested in cultures that speak those languages.

When users import a collection of tweets, COSMOS performs a sentiment analysis on the English-language tweets using SentiStrength, which is a language-analysis tool optimized for identifying the emotional content in short texts, such as Twitter status updates (Thelwall et al., 2010). SentiStrength measures sentiment on a numeric scale from −5 (highly negative) to +5 (highly positive). The *Sentiment* control provides a double-ended slider that enables users to specify the numerical range into which a tweet's sentiment score must fall for the tweet to be included in the results. This control enables users to partition a data set into groups that contain a positive or negative reaction to a topic of interest.

The *Duration* control enables users to specify the temporal range of interest by selecting the start and end dates a tweet must have been authored between to be included in the results. This control is particularly useful for reducing the size of a large data set to explore an interesting period of time.

The right side of the dialog box provides controls for querying the geographic dimension of the data, which, along with demographics (Sloan et al., 2015), is becoming increasingly more relevant to social science (Sloan and Morgan, 2015). The *Geolocation* check box will select only those tweets that have geocoding, which is the longitude and latitude coordinate where the tweet was authored. Currently, approximately 0.85 per cent of tweets have geocoding (Sloan et al., 2013).

The *Country* drop down menu enables users to restrict the tweets to those authored in a specific country. Twitter identifies the country of a tweet using the geocoding when available.

Below the *Country* drop down menu is a map on which users can draw a bounding box around a geographical area of interest, which will restrict the tweets returned by the search to those authored within that bounding box. This is useful when the area of interest is not a country, such as a city.

Querying enables users to reduce large data sets by focussing on interesting characteristics. The SQL database used by COSMOS to store and query Twitter data can handle data sets containing tens of millions of tweets. However, when data sets of this size are queried, the number of results can often be large enough to challenge computers with limited memory. This problem is addressed by sampling.

Sampling

COSMOS runs on a wide variety of hardware with varying amounts of memory. To help the computer running COSMOS to handle large amounts of data, COSMOS enables users to elect to load a sample of a data set or a set of query results. Sampling is offered as an option to users when a data set containing more than 50,000 tweets is dragged onto the Workspace or when a query returns more than 50,000 results. In this case, the *Choose Sampling Method* dialog in Figure 26.8 is presented.

The *Choose Sampling Method* dialog gives users three options:

1 To load the first *n* tweets, where *n* is a user-selectable value that ranges from one to the number of items in the data set or query results.

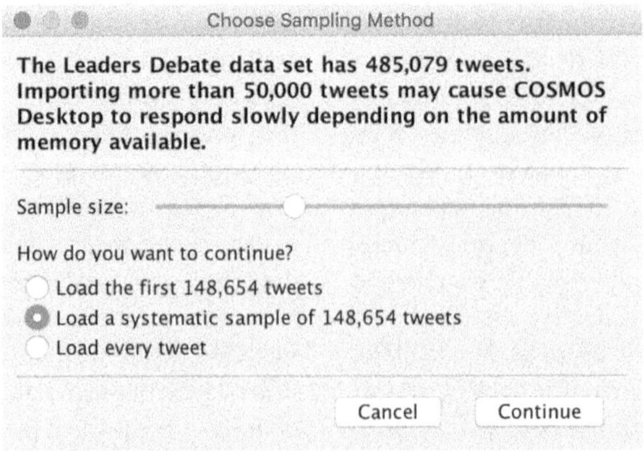

Figure 26.8 The COSMOS *Choose Sampling Method* dialog enables COSMOS to handle large data sets with user-defined data sampling strategies

2. To load a systematic sample of n tweets taken across the data set. This option is useful for enabling users to get a feel for the distribution of the data set.
3. To load all the data, which is appropriate if the computer has enough memory to handle all the data.

Sampling reduces a data set based on its size. Time is another dimension along which a data set can be reduced, which is performed with temporal filtering.

Temporal Filtering

COSMOS provides a double ended slider at the bottom of the window that filters data by time, as shown in Figure 26.9. The position of the ends of the slider select a range of time at four levels of granularity – seconds, minutes, hours and days – which is selected by the drop-down menu to the right of the slider. The data views in the workspace respond to changes in the selected time range by filtering out all data items that do not have a timestamp within the selected time range.

At the top right of the temporal filtering slider is a set of play, stop and rewind controls that enable users to visualize a data set over time. These controls enable users to replay a data set as if it were a movie. This is particularly useful for reviewing the development of events as reported by Twitter users acting as human sensors of their environment. For example, by replaying a data set visualized as a social network in the network data view, COSMOS enables users to see at which point key actors in the data set joined the network.

Temporal filtering reduces a data set using time. The final data reduction tool provided by COSMOS enables users to make selections using the properties afforded by each visualization style.

Selection

Data views present a data set in a specific visual style. Consequently, data views enable users to select data in a data-view-specific way. For example, the table data view enables users to select table rows; the pie chart data view enables users to select pie segments; the map data view enables users to select map markers; and the word cloud data view enables users to select words. Each data view window has a selection control that provides a consistent visual presentation of the number of selected items in the data view and the type of the selected data, as indicated by the data set icon.

Figure 26.10 illustrates how data selected with the pie chart data view can be added to the Data Set Library as a selection data set. The user first selects a pie segment of interest (1). Next, COSMOS updates the data-selection control with the number of tweets represented by the pie segment (in this example, 10,464 tweets) (2). Finally, the user drags from the data-selection control onto the Data Set Library (3). In response, COSMOS creates a new selection data set and adds it underneath the data set from which the selection was taken. COSMOS presents selection data sets with an icon depicting a mouse cursor.

The new selection data set itself can then be dragged onto the Workspace, which enables data to be iteratively reduced and refined.

Figure 26.9 The COSMOS temporal filtering controls enable users to filter data sets by time and replay events like a data movie

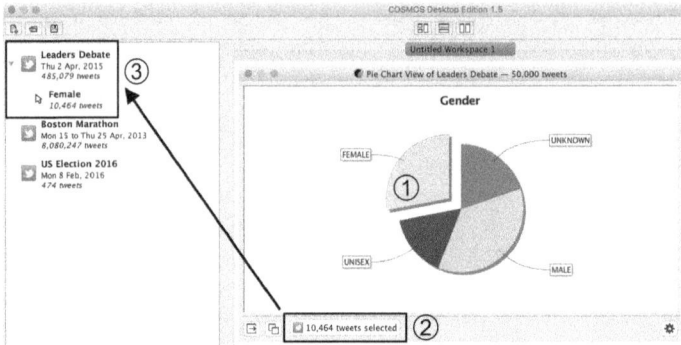

Figure 26.10 COSMOS provides a consistent method of creating selection data sets. Users select data in a data view – here data is selected by clicking a segment in the pie chart data view (1) – and dragging from the data-selection control (2) onto the Data Set Library. The selection is added as a new data set under the data set from which it was taken (3)

Exporting Data

To enable COSMOS to fit into the broader social-scientific workflows discussed at the beginning of this chapter, COSMOS exports data in a wide variety of commonly used formats. COSMOS provides users with a consistent method for exporting data from every data view, which is to click the export button available at the bottom of every data view window to present the *Export Data* dialog shown in Figure 26.11.

All data views can export an image of its content in the PNG and JPEG file formats. This enables users to import images of COSMOS visualizations directly into academic papers, websites and other publications.

All data views can also export their data in JSON format, which is a popular data interchange format. For data sets created by importing Twitter data, the data is exported in standard Twitter JSON format. For RSS and CSV data sets, the data is exported in a generic JSON format derived from the table presented by the table data view: one JSON object is created for each row in the table, which has a key/value pair corresponding to the name of the column and the value of that column.

Most data views can export their data in both CSV and Microsoft Excel format. Where possible, data views make use of Excel-specific features such as sheets to further organize the data. The data exported in CSV and Excel format is the source used to produce the visualization and is therefore data-view specific. For example, the pie chart data view exports the data used to create the pie chart, which is a table of segment names and proportions that translate into segment angles. Similarly, the data exported by the line chart data view provides the values at each point in time for each of the data series in the chart.

Exporting data in this way enables the data exported by COSMOS to be formatted for publication or processed further with analytical tools not available in COSMOS. Exporting data also enables users to verify that the COSMOS data views present data accurately. For example, to verify that the pie and line chart data views display data accurately, users would export the data from these data views in Microsoft Excel format and load it into Excel. Users would then recreate the pie and line charts in Excel to verify the accuracy of the COSMOS presentations. This verification technique can be applied to

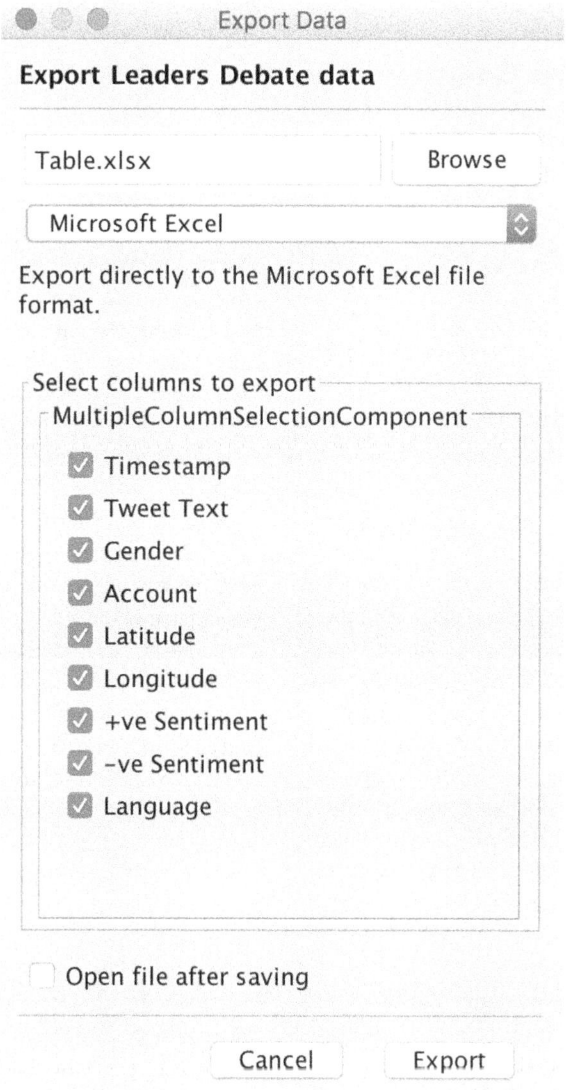

Figure 26.11 The COSMOS *Export Data* dialog supports the use of other software by providing extensive facilities for exporting data in a wide variety of commonly used formats including CSV, Microsoft Excel and JSON

the other data views and helps to build trust with the COSMOS user community.

Data views can also export data in specific formats when required. For example, the map and shapefile data views can export geographic data in the Keyhole Markup Language (KML) format that enables users to import geographic data into Google Earth (KML, 2016). Another example is the network data view. This data view exports network data in GraphML (2016), GEXF (2016) and JSON formats, which enables network graphs produced by COSMOS to be imported into a wide variety of other network analysis and visualization tools, including Gephi (2016) and D3 (Bostock et al., 2011).

This section explored the ways in which COSMOS users can import, interrogate and export data. The next section explores the rich set of COSMOS visualization tools.

VISUALIZATION

This section explores how users can make use of the power of the ten visualization styles that ship with COSMOS.

Data Exploration Through Visual Building Blocks

One approach to developing data visualizations is to produce a bespoke system designed to highlight the characteristics of a data set and to provide a set of tightly integrated interrogation controls (Ahlberg and Shneiderman, 1994). The first iteration of COSMOS followed this approach and provided users with a tab-based user interface, where each tab presented a bespoke presentation of Twitter data and controls for interrogating that data (Burnap et al., 2014; Housley et al., 2014).

Although this bespoke approach produces rich, interesting and useful data analysis tools, one important disadvantage is that bespoke visualizations are not easily reusable with different data sets. Usability testing with social science students at Cardiff University also revealed a weaknesses in the bespoke approach, which was that although the participants liked elements of each bespoke tab, they would have liked to have been able to mix and match those elements to enable them to explore the data more effectively (Burnap et al., 2014).

This feedback from usability testing and the benefits of being able to explore different data sets motivated a redesign of the COSMOS user interface to its current form: data views as building blocks in a visual construction set for creating interactive exploratory visualizations.

Multiple-Coordinated Visualizations

The free, construction-set nature of COSMOS enables users to drag and drop any data sets and data views onto the Workspace. When users visualize the same data set with more than one data view, COSMOS automatically creates a multiple-coordinated visualization (North and Shneiderman, 2000; Weaver, 2004).

Multiple-coordinated visualizations have two characteristics that enable users to explore a data set more deeply (Heer and Shneiderman, 2012). First, presenting the same data set in a variety of visual styles enables users to understand more about that data set than they would from a single presentation. Second, selecting data in one data view causes COSMOS to propagate that selection to all the other data views in the Workspace. As a result, data selected in one data view will be highlighted in every other data view. Since each data view presents data in a different visual style, each data view will highlight selected data in a different visual style. For example, the table data view highlights data rows; the map data view highlights map markers and the word cloud data view highlights words.

Figure 26.12 shows three different views of a set of Twitter data related to an incident in which terrorists detonated a bomb at the finish line of the 2013 Boston Marathon. The top left data view is a map that presents each geocoded tweet in the data set as a dot. Below the map is a word cloud data view that presents an overview of the most commonly used words. To the right of the map and word-cloud data views is a frequency data view. The frequency data view presents the number of tweets authored at three levels of detail: day (top), hour (middle) and minute

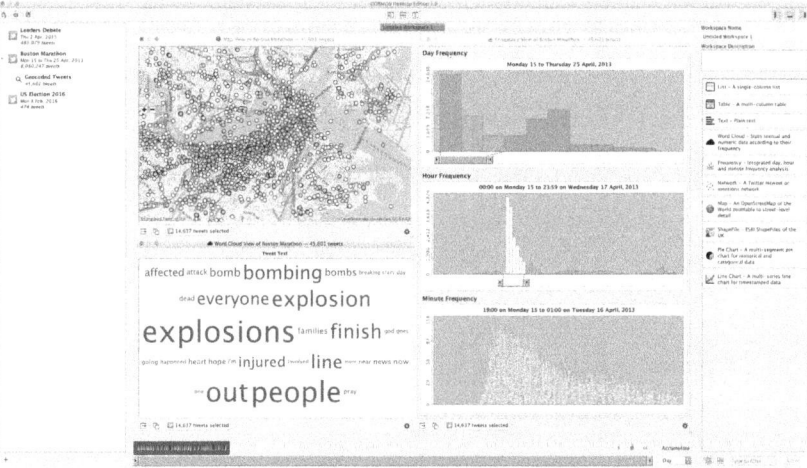

Figure 26.12 A combination of multiple-coordinated visualizations enables users to understand data sets more deeply than they could with any single visualization. Here, the map, word cloud and frequency data views combine to help users understand a data set concerning the 2013 bombing of the Boston Marathon

(bottom). All three data views combine to provide a richer view of the data than any one of them could individually.

The remainder of this section provides a detailed look at the visual characteristics of each data view and the ways in which users can modify its default configuration.

Data Views

Table and List Data Views

The table data view is the default view for all data sets dragged onto the Workspace. The values in each underlying data object are exposed as column values in the table, one row per data object, as shown in Figure 26.13.

Using the configuration controls on the right, users can bind the following visual characteristics to the data in the table:

- Font size.
- Row foreground colour.
- Row background colour.

Binding the visual characteristics of the table to the data presented by the table provides a familiar tabular structure that simultaneously highlights aspects of the data. In Figure 26.13, for example, the categorical values of the gender column are bound to the user-selected background colours of the row for each gender value. Similarly, the numerical values of the positive sentiment column are bound to the font size of the row: the greater the positive sentiment value, the larger the font size.

The list data view provides a simplified table view with a single column, which is useful for removing visual clutter to focus on a single data column. The list data view provides the same visual data binding controls as the table data view.

Text Data View

The text data view provides a plain-text view of the values of one data column, which is user selectable. The text data view is most useful in a supporting role to provide extra information when drilling down into data.

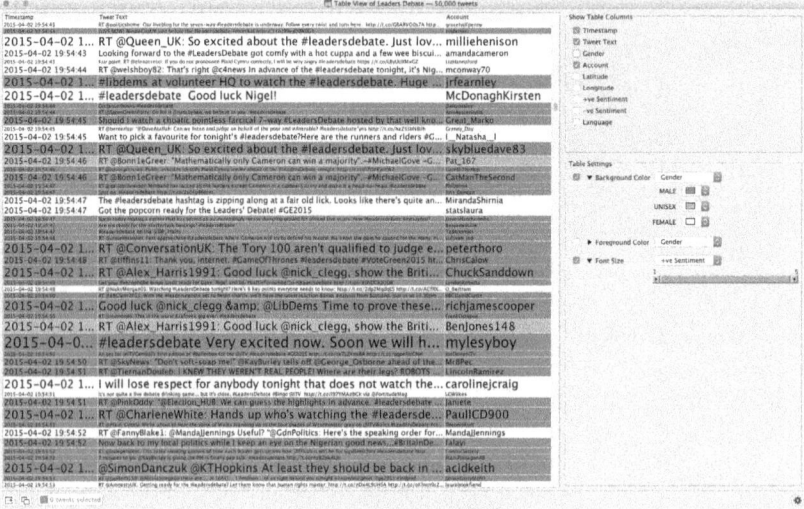

Figure 26.13 The table data view presents a data set as a multi-column table. Binding the font size and the foreground and background colours of each row enables the table to visualize data

Figure 26.14 illustrates the link between a text data view and a map data view via the multiple-coordinated visualization system. Clicking a map marker that represents a geo-coded tweet displays the text of the tweet in the text data view.

Word Cloud Data View

The word cloud data view sizes the words in a column based on their frequency across all the rows in the table, as shown in Figure 26.15. Using the configuration controls on the right, users can select which column should be used to build the word cloud. Although most useful for presenting textual data, the word cloud will convert the data in a non-textual column before creating the word cloud. This is often useful for quickly exploring the frequency of numerical data values without needing to change to a numerically-oriented data view such as the pie or line chart data views. Users can also shift-click words to remove them from the cloud, which is useful for removing words that occur so frequently they dominate the cloud.

Frequency Analysis Data View

The frequency analysis data view shown in Figure 26.16 provides frequency views at day, hour and minute levels of temporal granularity. The day, hour and minute frequency charts are connected by the double-ended sliders below each chart. The slider below the day frequency chart selects a day range that controls the data displayed in the hour frequency chart. The hour frequency chart displays the number of data objects produced per hour within the day range selected by the day frequency slider. Similarly, the slider below the hour frequency chart selects an hour range that controls the data displayed in the minute frequency chart. The minute frequency chart displays the number of data objects produced per minute within the hour range selected by the hour frequency slider. Moving the mouse over the bars will then display a more detailed view

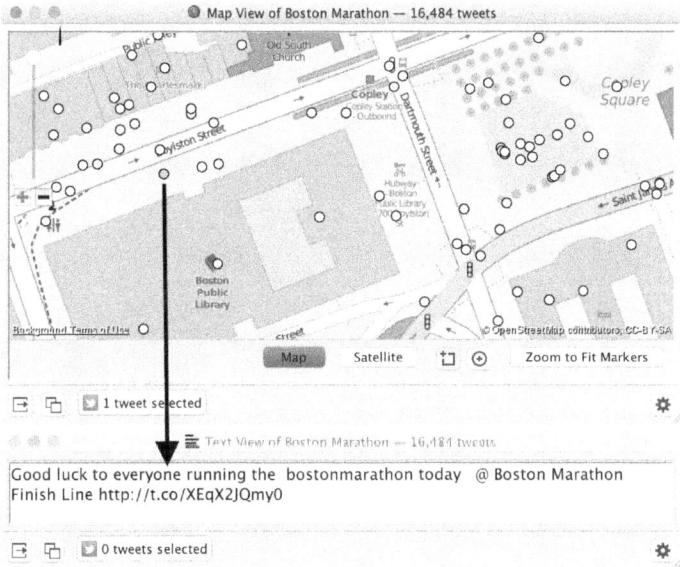

Figure 26.14 The text data view presents a plain-text view of a single data column. Here, a text data view supports the map data view by enabling users to click on a map marker that represents a geocoded tweet to reveal the text of the tweet

of the exact day, hour or minute represented by each bar.

Network Analysis Data View

The network analysis data view shown in Figure 26.17 provides a social network graph based on retweets or mentions. The network graph is built automatically using a force-directed layout algorithm (Fruchterman and Reingold, 1991) without requiring users to supply configuration parameters or other settings. Automatically creating the network enables social scientists to work with the network immediately, which contrasts with tools such as Gephi (2016) that require considerable knowledge and user input to produce a network graph.

The network analysis data view is implemented using the Java Universal Network/Graph (JUNG) framework (JUNG, 2016).

Figure 26.15 The word cloud data view sizes the words in a text column based on their frequency across all the rows in the table

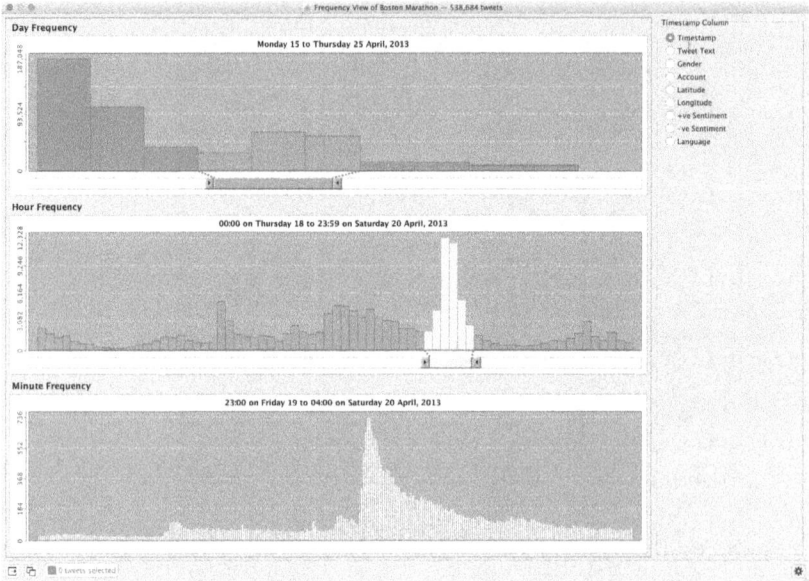

Figure 26.16 The frequency analysis data view provides interactive frequency views at three levels of temporal granularity: days, hours and minutes

JUNG is an open source Java library for building and visualizing network data structures. The algorithms that build the retweet and mentions networks begin by creating a vertex for each Twitter user that retweeted a tweet or mentioned another Twitter user. The retweet algorithm connects an edge from the vertex that represents the Twitter user

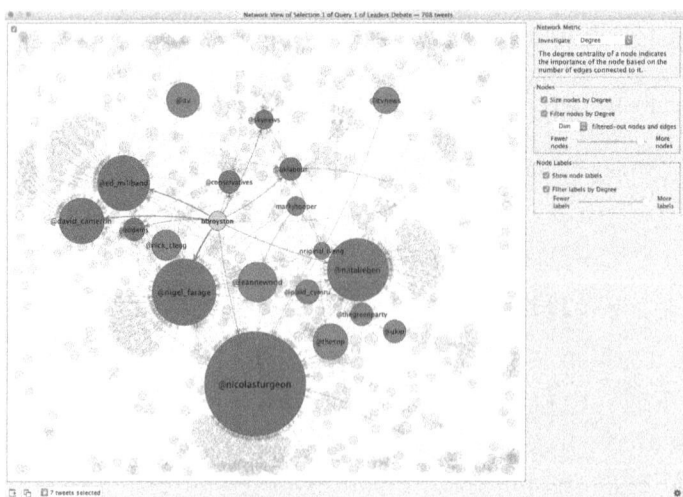

Figure 26.17 The network analysis data view presents a social network graph created from retweets or mentions. The network is laid out automatically with a force-directed layout algorithm

that performed the retweet to the vertex representing the Twitter user whose tweet was retweeted. In a retweet relationship, one vertex is connected to at most one other vertex. The mentions algorithm connects an edge from the vertex representing the Twitter user that authored the tweet to the vertexes representing the Twitter users mentioned in the tweet. In a mentions relationship, one vertex is connected to at least one other vertex.

As well as building and visualizing networks, JUNG also performs network metric calculations. The configuration controls on the right of the network analysis data view enable users to control the size of the nodes by selecting one of three network metrics:

1 Degree centrality.
2 Betweenness centrality.
3 Closeness centrality.

Nodes are filtered with a slider that removes nodes with a metric value greater than the slider value. Nodes that have been filtered out and the edges that connect them can be displayed in two user-selectable styles:

1 Dimmed – filtered-out nodes and edges are drawn semi-transparently to maintain their context in the network.
2 Hidden – filtered-out nodes and edges are not drawn to provide a clean view of the remaining nodes and edges.

Node labels are filtered with a slider that hides the labels of nodes with a metric value greater than the slider value. As a result, adding and removing node labels helps to control the amount of visual clutter when exploring the network.

Map Data View

The map data view shown in Figure 26.18 plots geocoded data as markers on a map provided by OpenStreetMap (2016), an open source mapping project. Both map and terrain views are user selectable. To provide a useful first view of the data, the map data view automatically identifies and selects data columns that contain longitude and latitude data and marks them on the map.

The configuration controls on the right enable users to bind the following visual characteristics to the data:

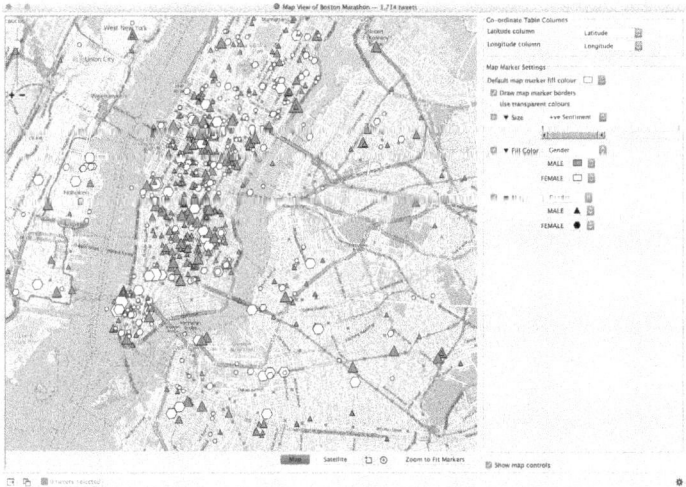

Figure 26.18 The map data view plots geocoded data as markers on a map provided by OpenStreetMap

- Marker size.
- Marker colour.
- Marker shape.

For example, Figure 26.18 shows that each marker encodes two pieces of data: the colour and shape of the marker encodes gender and the size of the marker encodes positive sentiment; the greater the positive sentiment, the larger the marker.

Shapefile Data View

The shapefile data view shown in Figure 26.19 plots geocoded data as markers on shapefiles (ESRI 2016) of the UK and its constituent territories: England, Wales, Scotland, Northern Ireland and the London boroughs. The region is selected using the drop-down menu at the bottom-left. To provide a useful first view of the data, the shapefile data view automatically identifies and selects data columns that contain longitude and latitude data and marks them on the map.

The configuration controls on the right enable users to bind the same visual characteristics to the data as the map data view described above. For example, Figure 26.19 shows that each marker encodes two pieces of data. The colour and shape of the marker encodes gender and the size of the marker encodes positive sentiment; the greater the positive sentiment, the larger the marker.

The shapefile data view integrates access to the 2011 UK Census via the API provided by the Office of National Statistics (ONS, 2016). COSMOS provides access to over 70 Quick Statistics tables with a simple user interface that consists of two drop-down menus, as shown at the top of Figure 26.20. The top drop-down menu selects the table, such as *QS601EW Economic Activity*, and the second drop down menu selects a column within the selected table, such as *Economically active:Employee:Full-time*.

Each row of the Quick Statistics tables represents a local authority area that is represented by a polygon on the map. Each polygon is assigned a colour to produce a

Figure 26.19 The shapefile data view plots geocoded data as markers on shapefiles of the UK and its constituent territories: England, Wales, Scotland, Northern Ireland and the London boroughs

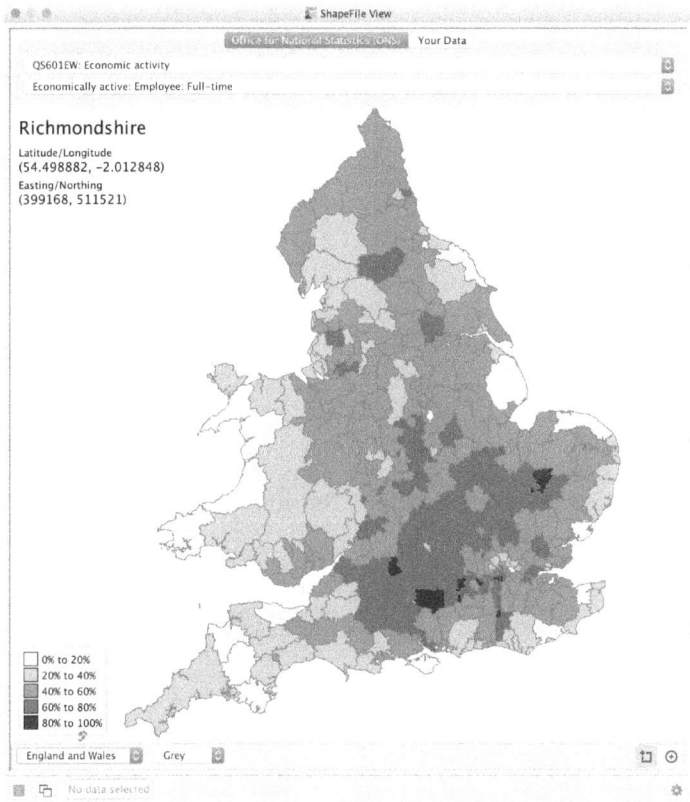

Figure 26.20 The polygons in the shapefile data view are shaded by 2011 UK Census data retrieved from the Office of National Statistics via the ONS API

choropleth map (Wright, 1938). In a choropleth map, each region is assigned a colour, the shade of which is calculated from a numeric value. The lower the calculated value, the lighter the shade; the higher the calculated value, the darker the shade. In the shapefile data view, the numerical value used to shade each polygon is determined by the proportion calculated by dividing the corresponding Quick Statistics table column value by the column total.

The shapefile data view provides a drop-down menu at the bottom-left for selecting one of several colour schemes for shading the choropleth. COSMOS uses colour schemes produced by ColorBrewer2, an online resource for generating map colour schemes (Harrower and Brewer, 2003).

Plotting geocoded tweets on shapefiles coloured with UK Census data enables social scientists to bring together or mash these two data types. This facilitates an exploration of the attitudes and reactions expressed in tweets with the socio-economic characteristics of the region in which those tweets were authored. For example, an investigator might plot the geocoded tweets in a collection focussed on reactions to changes in public transport policy on a shapefile coloured with data from Quick Statistics table *QS701EW Method of Travel to Work*. Creating selection data sets of tweets in areas where cycling to work or going on foot is popular would enable the investigator to examine the sentiment toward the changes in public transport policy in those areas.

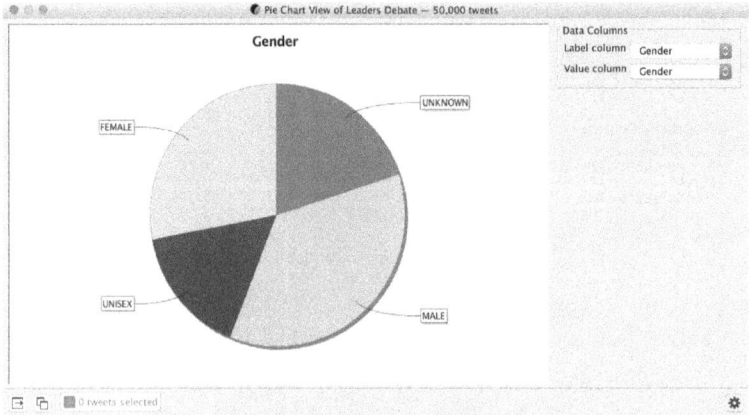

Figure 26.21 The pie chart data view segments data into two columns: one column provides the data that sizes the angles of each segment; the other column provides the labels for the segments

Pie Chart Data View

The pie chart data view shown in Figure 26.21 segments data into two columns: one column provides the data that sizes the angles of each segment and the other column provides the labels for the segments. To provide a useful first view of the data, the pie chart data view looks for categorical data columns to use for the segment values and labels. Users can change these columns using the drop-down menu configuration controls on the right to further explore the data. The pie chart data view is often used to visualize the gender breakdown of a collection.

Line Chart Data View

The line chart data view shown in Figure 26.22 plots the values in the numeric data columns against the temporal values in the timestamp column. The check box configuration controls on the right enable users to control which numerical columns are added as series to the line chart. The drop-down menu to the right of each series check box selects the colour of the series. Using the line chart data view is a quick way to visualize the positive and negative sentiment in a collection.

DEVELOPING COSMOS

This section describes the three ways in which COSMOS is developed, namely:

1. Ongoing development of the COSMOS application.
2. Expansion of the COSMOS ecosystem with data view plugins.
3. Research into scaling up COSMOS to handle big data.

Ongoing Development of the COSMOS Application

COSMOS is under continual development with three main sources of input to the development process:

1. Requirements for functionality that meet the needs of research projects conducted by the COSMOS research group.
2. Suggestions and feedback for improvements from within the COSMOS research group and its collaborators.
3. Bug reports and suggestions for improvement from the COSMOS user community collected via the COSMOS project website (http://cosmosproject.net).

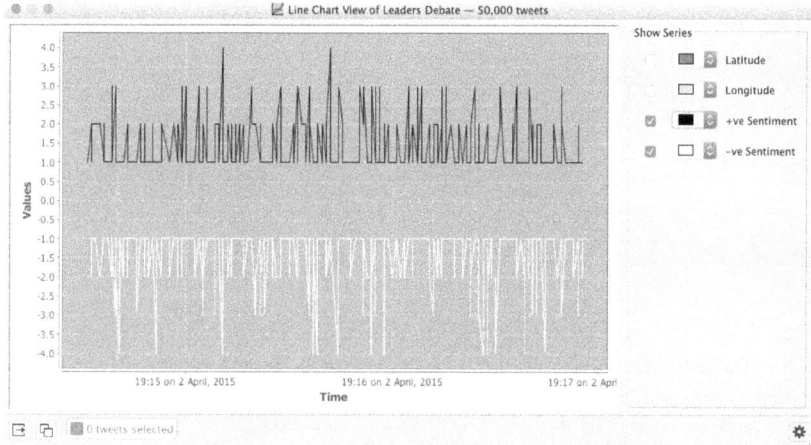

Figure 26.22 The line chart data view plots the values in the numeric data columns against the temporal values in the timestamp column

Feedback from COSMOS users is particularly important to the development of the software. COSMOS has over 800 users running the software on a range of computers with a variety of memory and disk storage resources. Bugs reported by users identify problems that, when fixed, provide more stable software for the COSMOS community as a whole.

Suggestions for improvements provided by COSMOS users also benefit the COSMOS community by providing enhanced functionality. For example, the first version of COSMOS could import Twitter data collected in the standard data format used by Twitter. The next iteration added support for the format used by the Twitter data provider, GNIP, to enable COSMOS to import data bought from GNIP as part of research conducted by the COSMOS group. A later version of COSMOS added support for the Twitter data format used by another Twitter data provider, DataSift. DataSift support was requested by a COSMOS user to meet his need to import his data into COSMOS. By including GNIP and DataSift support to meet the needs of a few users, the entire COSMOS user community benefits from access to more Twitter data, which exemplifies the notion of a virtuous software development cycle.

Apart from development work on the COSMOS application, third-party developers can contribute to the COSMOS ecosystem by implementing custom data view plugins.

The COSMOS Plugin Ecosystem

For many users, the default set of ten data views that ship with COSMOS will meet their needs. However, other users will need to use bespoke data views that meet the requirements of their research. These bespoke data views may provide a new presentation style or might integrate COSMOS into third-party data analysis toolkits such as the WordNet text-analysis system (Miller, 1995) or the Weka machine-learning framework (Hall et al., 2009). Although the COSMOS application itself is not open source, software developers can create data view plugins for COSMOS to provide such integration.

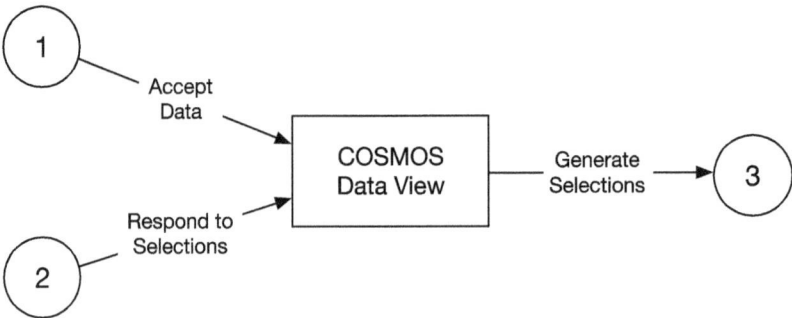

Figure 26.23 COSMOS data view plugin developers have three opportunities to integrate new data views into the COSMOS application framework: when users drag a data set onto the new data view (1); when users select data in another data view (2); and when users select data in the new data view (3)

Designing COSMOS Plugins

Figure 26.23 illustrates the three opportunities software developers have to integrate a new data view plugin into the COSMOS application framework.

The first opportunity occurs when users drag and drop a data set from the Data Set Library onto a data view on the Workspace. This is the prime responsibility of a COSMOS data view plugin. The second opportunity occurs when users select data in another data view. Highlighting the selected data in the visual style of the new data view enables users to gain more insight into the selected data. The third opportunity occurs when users select data in the new data view. COSMOS will propagate selections made in the new data view to all the other data views in the Workspace that present the same data set.

Developing COSMOS Plugins

A COSMOS data view plugin is the Java code that implements a data view packaged up in a form that is easily distributed to and installed by users. Users install new COSMOS plugins by copying the plugin files into the *cosmos-plugins* folder in their home folder and restarting COSMOS.

To create new data view plugins, software developers use the COSMOS Development Kit (CDK), which consists of the COSMOS Java library code, sample code for an example data view plugin, the COSMOS Simulator and a set of developer documentation.

The example plugin sample code enables developers to modify existing code rather than start from scratch. This approach reduces the barrier to entry, reduces development time, and reduces the potential for programming mistakes. Developers therefore concentrate on writing the data-view-specific parts of their code while leveraging the extensive functionality provided by the COSMOS application framework.

The COSMOS Simulator is a tool provided by the CDK that enables developers to rapidly develop new data views. The simulator reduces development time when testing a data view under development by avoiding the cycle of packaging up each new version, copying it into the *cosmos-plugins* folder and restarting COSMOS. The simulator provides a button that simulates dragging data onto the data view to enable developers to check that the new data view presents data correctly. The simulator also provides a button that simulates a selection in another data view to enable developers to check that the new data view participates correctly in the multiple-coordinated visualization system.

As developers enrich the COSMOS ecosystem with plugins that provide new visual presentations and third-party integrations, the COSMOS group will tackle what is perhaps the greatest challenge facing COSMOS: scaling up to big data.

Big Data Scale

COSMOS is able to import and query data sets as large as ten million tweets. This size of data set is useful for exploring specific events that occur over a relatively short period. However, to perform longitudinal studies that explore public reaction to ongoing events such as changes in legislation or views on national identity or public reaction before and after events such as food safety scares, much larger data sets are required that contain tweets collected over months or even years. The number of tweets that can be collected over this period makes processing that data impractical on even the most powerful desktop PCs. For example, collecting the one per cent random sample for one year would create a data set of 1.825 billion tweets.

To perform longitudinal studies with such large data sets, the COSMOS group has begun researching how we can extend the capability of COSMOS into the area of big data analytics (Conejero et al., 2013; Burnap et al., 2014; Conejero et al., 2016). This work explores how high-performance and cloud computing can provide social scientists with rapid access to many terabytes of data.

High performance computing (HPC) connects together many computers that each store and work on part of a large data set in parallel, which enables large volumes of data to be stored and processed rapidly. However, HPC systems tend to operate in batch mode that schedule data query jobs in a queue. The challenge then is to harness the power of HPC while at the same time providing the same iterative and exploratory style of querying, visualizing and refining data sources, which can only be realized when the HPC component is part of an interactive system.

To begin to meet this challenge the COSMOS group developed a prototype HPC system with the Hadoop distributed data processing system (Hadoop, 2016). Hadoop arranges computers called 'worker nodes' in a group called a cluster. Each worker node processes part of the data at the same time as the other worker nodes, which gives Hadoop its processing speed. Adding more worker nodes enables the cluster to process more data simultaneously, which further reduces processing time. Hadoop processes data with a three-phase algorithm called Map/Reduce. In the first phase, the data is split into n parts, where n is the number of worker nodes in the cluster. In the second phase, the worker nodes process or 'map' part of the data simultaneously. In the third phase, the worker nodes output their results to a 'reducer', which combines all of the results into the final output.

Although Hadoop is fast, it has two drawbacks for the COSMOS use case. First, Hadoop is a batch-mode system. Iteratively querying, visualizing and refining data requires an interactive system. Second, Map/Reduce is a low-level algorithm that does not support the rich querying required by the COSMOS query dialog described above. To address both of these problems, we connected Hadoop to the MongoDB database system (MongoDB, 2016). MongoDB is a scalable document or 'NoSQL' database that has two characteristics required for the COSMOS use case. First, MongoDB enables queries to be made against a data set, which provides the rich querying required by the COSMOS query dialog. Second, MongoDB is able to act as an input data source to Hadoop, which ordinarily stores data in its own format.

Figure 26.24 illustrates the organization of the COSMOS HPC system. In a system like this that combines MongoDB and Hadoop, each data collection is stored in MongoDB on a centralized data server rather than on

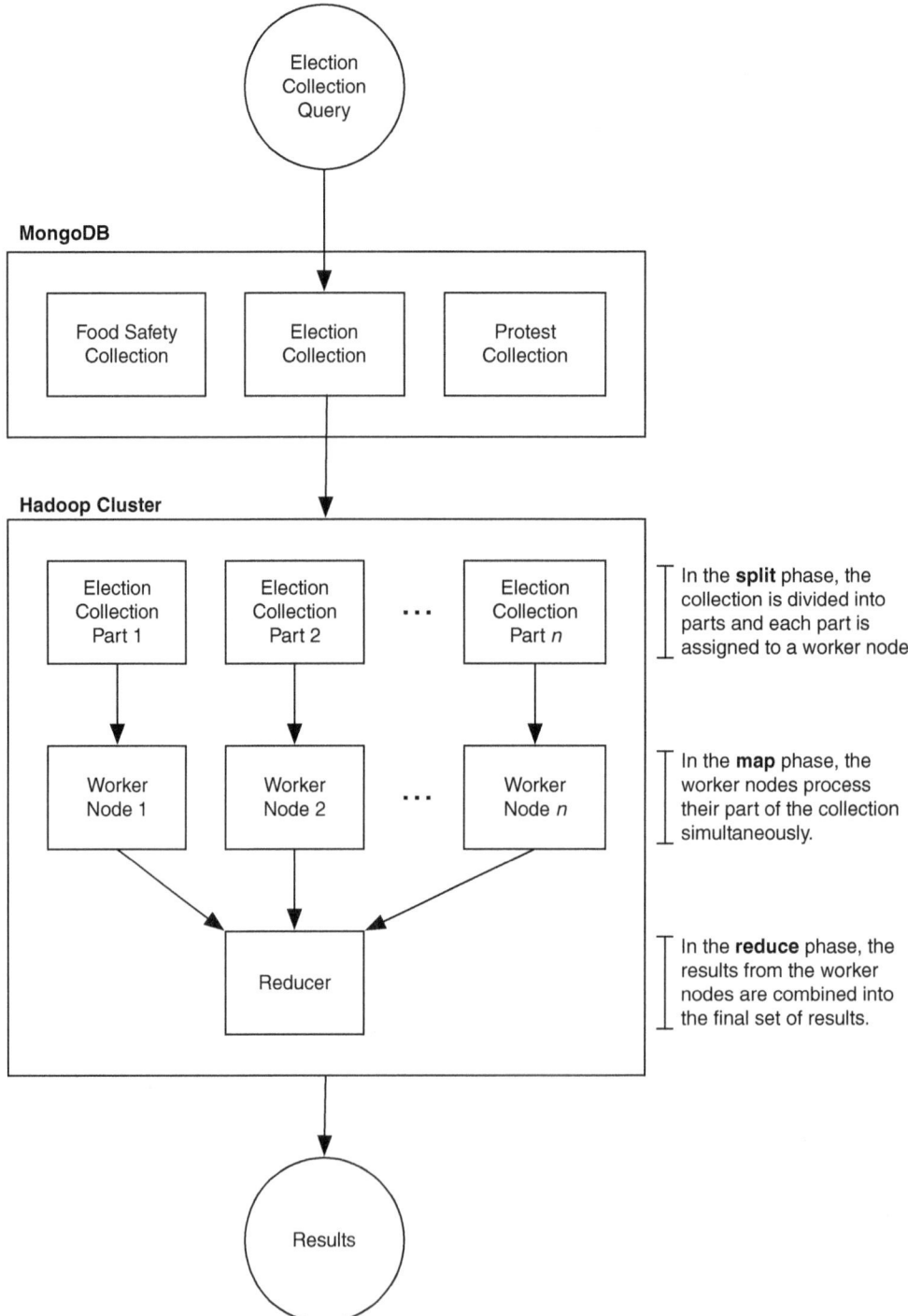

Figure 26.24 The COSMOS high-performance computing prototype uses the MongoDB database and Hadoop's distributed Map/Reduce algorithm to investigate how COSMOS can scale to meet the challenges of big data

the user's computer. This centralization is necessary because Hadoop requires the data to be stored with the worker nodes that will process it. Figure 26.24 shows an example MongoDB database with three data collections called Food Safety, Election and Protest. For example, to process a query on the Election collection, the data in the collection is split into n parts, where n is the number of worker nodes in the cluster. Each worker node queries part of the data set and passes its results to the reducer. Initial experiments with this HPC prototype indicate that it is worth developing in future work (Burnap et al., 2014).

IMPROVING COSMOS

This section describes three areas in which COSMOS needs further development and improvement, namely: data sources, querying and network analysis.

Data Sources

COSMOS currently enables users to work with three sources of data: CSV files, RSS feeds and Twitter collections. Adding more data sources such as Facebook, Google+ and LinkedIn would significantly enhance the utility of the software. One way to provide new data sources would be to create a data source plugin API to enable third-party developers to enhance the COSMOS ecosystem with new data sources. The data source plugin API would be organized in the same manner as the data view plugin API described above.

Querying

The *Query* dialog described earlier can be improved in several ways. Currently, when the *Query* button is clicked, COSMOS constructs an SQL query that logically ANDs the values of the controls. This provides a simple but effective querying system. Future development could make the query interface more expressive by allowing control values to be combined with logical ORs.

The *Language* and *Country* query parameters are currently presented as drop-down menus. This is an effective method of selecting one of many options. This approach has been successful so far for the use cases we have come across. However, for queries that require selection of more than one language or country, the drop-down menus must be replaced with more suitable controls, such as lists that allow users to select multiple items.

The *Duration* query parameter enables users to select data created between two dates. Again, we have found this acceptable for use cases we have come across. However, for more fine-grained study, the duration control could be enhanced to enable users to select the time of day on the start and end dates. This would be useful for querying data with activity spikes over short periods, such as a 24-hour period spanning two days.

Network Analysis

The network analysis data view currently enables users to create retweet and mentions networks from Twitter data. When new data sources are added, such as Facebook, Google+ and LinkedIn, the network analysis data view will need to be updated to be able to build networks from these new data sources. Alternatively, third-party developers can implement their own network analysis data view plugins that may be better suited to specific data sources.

COSMOS can create and display networks of around five to six thousand vertexes before performance becomes too slow to be useful. Further work should improve the efficiency of the network building algorithms to make them faster and require less memory. This

ETHICS

As a software application, COSMOS provides a set of data collection, analysis and visualization tools that are contextually and ethically agnostic. The social scientist using COSMOS must decide on the ethical nature of the studies performed with COSMOS and the appropriateness of the subsequent publication of data as well as the results that may have the potential to harm those under study.

While social scientists routinely consider the need for ethical behaviour in their studies, the richness of social media data and the proliferation and interconnectedness of Internet-based software tools produces new ethical challenges that have the potential to affect larger numbers of people than previously possible. The following two examples highlight the need to think beyond the current context of social media studies with COSMOS.

The first example involves visualizing the geocoded tweets of Twitter users. Twitter users often tweet frequently from places they visit often. When a data set is visualized with the map data view, each geocoded tweet is presented as a marker on the map. As users author more and more tweets, clusters of markers on the map start to form a pattern of activity and can potentially reveal a location that is important to that person, such as their home or their place of work. Careful consideration must be given when publishing geographic data such as this.

The second example that requires ethical consideration involves the use of search engines, such as Google, Bing and Yahoo!. Researchers interested in the use of racist or homophobic language on Twitter, for example, need to be aware that publishing the text of a tweet containing such hate speech, even anonymously, can lead to the identification of the author of that tweet. Searching Google for the text of the tweet may link directly to the Twitter website and identify the account holder.

These two examples highlight properties of the data and are not COSMOS-specific issues, of course. However, they do highlight the need for extra caution. For a wider discussion of the ethics of social media research, see Beninger, Chapter 5 in this volume.

TRY COSMOS

COSMOS is available for download for academic use at the COSMOS Project website (http://cosmosproject.net/) and runs on the Mac OS X, Linux and Windows operating systems with Java 8 installed.

REFERENCES

Ahlberg, C. and Shneiderman, B. (1994) 'Visual information seeking: tight coupling of dynamic query filters with starfield displays'. Paper presented at the SIGCHI Conference on Human Factors in Computing Systems, New York, USA: 313–317.

Al Jazeera (2016) 'Al Jazeera English RSS Feed', http://www.aljazeera.com/xml/rss/all.xml, last accessed February 2016.

BBC (2016) 'BBC Top Stories RSS Feed', http://feeds.bbci.co.uk/news/rss.xml, last accessed February 2016.

Bostock, M., Ogievetsky, V. and Heer, J. (2011) 'D3 – Data Driven Documents', *IEEE Transactions on Visualization and Computer Graphics*, 17(12): 2301–2309.

Burnap, P., Rana, O., Avis, N., Williams, M., Housley, W., Edwards, A., Morgan, J. and Sloan, L. (2013) 'Detecting Tension in Online Communities with Computational Twitter Analysis', *Technological Forecasting and Social Change*, 95(6): 96–108.

Burnap, P., Rana, O., Williams, M., Housley, W., Edwards, A., Morgan, J., Sloan, L. and Conejero, J. (2014) 'COSMOS: Towards an

Integrated and Scalable Service for Analyzing Social Media on Demand', *International Journal of Parallel, Emergent and Distributed Systems*, 30(2): 80–100.

CNN (2016) 'CNN Top Stories RSS Feed', http://rss.cnn.com/rss/edition.rss, last accessed February 2016.

Conejero, J., Burnap, P., Rana, O. and Morgan, J. (2013) 'Scaling Archived Social Media Data Analysis using a Hadoop Cloud', Paper presented at the 2013 IEEE International Conference on Cloud Computing (CLOUD), San Francisco, USA: 685–692.

Conejero, J., Rana, O., Burnap, P., Morgan, J., Carrion, C. and Caminero, B. (2016) 'Analyzing Hadoop power consumption and impact on application QoS', *Future Generation Computer Systems*, (55)C: 213–223.

DataSift (2016) *DataSift Website*, http://datasift.com/, last accessed February 2016.

EMSC (2016) 'Real Time Seismicity RSS Feed', http://www.emsc-csem.org/Earthquake/, last accessed February 2016.

ESRI (2016) 'ESRI Shapefile Technical Description', http://www.esri.com/library/whitepapers/pdfs/shapefile.pdf, last accessed February 2016.

Fruchterman, T.M.J. and Reingold, E.M. (1991) 'Graph drawing by force-directed placement', *Software: Practice and Experience*, 21(11): 1129–1164.

Gephi (2016) 'The Open Graph Viz Platform', https://gephi.org/, last accessed February 2016.

GEXF (2016) 'The GEXF File Format', https://gephi.org/gexf/format/, last accessed February 2016.

GNIP (2016) *GNIP Website*, https://gnip.com/, last accessed February 2016.

GraphML (2016) 'The GraphML File Format', http://graphml.graphdrawing.org/, last accessed February 2016.

Hadoop (2016) *Apache Hadoop Website*, http://hadoop.apache.org/, last accessed February 2016.

Hall, M., Frank, E., Holmes, G., Pfahringer, B., Reutemann, P. and Witten, I.H. (2009) 'The WEKA Data Mining Software: An Update', *SIGKDD Explorations*, 11(1): 10–18.

Harrower, M. and Brewer, C.A. (2003) 'ColorBrewer.org: An Online Tool for Selecting Colour Schemes for Maps', *The Cartographic Journal*, 40(1): 27–37.

Heer, J. and Shneiderman, B. (2012) 'Interactive dynamics for visual analysis'. *Communications of the ACM*, 55(4): 45–54.

Housley, W., Procter, R., Edwards, E., Burnap, P., Williams, M., Sloan, L., Rana, O., Morgan, J., Voss, A. and Greenhill, A. (2014) 'Big and broad social data and the sociological imagination: A collaborative response', *Big Data & Society*, 1(2): 1–15.

Internet Live Stats (2016) 'Twitter Usage Statistics', http://www.internetlivestats.com/twitter-statistics/, last accessed February 2016.

JUNG (Java Universal Network/Graph) (2016) *JUNG Website*, http://jung.sourceforge.net/, last accessed February 2016.

KML (2016) 'Keyhole Markup Language', https://developers.google.com/kml/?hl=en, last accessed February 2016.

Miller, G.A. (1995) 'WordNet: A lexical database for English', *Communications of the ACM*, 38(11): 39–41.

MongoDB (2016) *MongoDB Website*, https://www.mongodb.org/, last accessed February 2016.

Norman, D.A. and Draper, S.W. (eds) (1986) *User Centered System Design: New Perspectives on Human-computer Interaction*. Hillsdale, New Jersey: Lawrence Erlbaum Associates.

North, C. and Shneiderman, B. (2000) 'Snap-together visualization: can users construct and operate coordinated visualizations?', *International Journal of Human-Computer Studies*, 53(5): 715–739.

ONS (Office of National Statistics) (2016) 'About the API', https://www.ons.gov.uk/ons/apiservice/web/apiservice/about-api, last accessed February 2016.

OpenStreetMap (2016) *OpenStreetMap Website*, http://www.openstreetmap.org, last accessed February 2016.

Sloan, L., Morgan, J., Housley, W., Williams, M., Edwards, A., Burnap, P. and Rana, O. (2013) 'Knowing the Tweeters: Deriving sociologically relevant demographics from Twitter', *Sociological Research Online*, 18(3).

Sloan, L., Morgan, J., Burnap, P. and Williams, M. (2015) 'Who Tweets? Deriving the Demographic characteristics of age, occupation and social class from Twitter User Meta-Data', *PLoS ONE*, 10(3).

Sloan, L. and Morgan, J. (2015) 'Who Tweets with their location? Understanding the relationship between demographic characteristics and the use of geoservices and geotagging on Twitter', *PLoS ONE*, 10(11).

Takeshi, S., Makoto, O. and Yutaka, M. (2010) 'Earthquake shakes Twitter users: real-time event detection by social sensors', Paper presented at the 19th International Conference on World Wide Web. ACM, New York, USA: 851–860.

Thelwall, M., Buckley, K., Paltoglou, G., Cai, D. and Kappas, A. (2010) 'Sentiment strength detection in short informal text', *Journal of the American Society for Information Science and Technology*, 61(12): 2544–2558.

Twitter (2016) 'API Overview', https://dev.twitter.com/overview/api, last accessed February 2016.

Weaver, C.E. (2004) 'Building Highly-Coordinated Visualizations in Improvise'. Paper presented at the IEEE Symposium on Information Visualization, Austin, Texas: 159–166.

Williams, M., Edwards, A., Housley, W., Burnap, P., Rana, O., Avis, N., Morgan, J. and Sloan, L. (2013) 'Policing cyber-neighbourhoods: tension monitoring and social media networks', *Policing & Society*, 23(4): 461–481.

Wright, J.K. (1938) 'Problems in Population Mapping' In J.K. Wright (ed.) *Notes on Statistical Mapping, with Special Reference to the Mapping of Population Phenomena*. New York: American Geographical Society and Population Association of America. pp. 1–18.

WHO (World Health Organization) (2016) 'Life Expectancy Data by Country data set', http://apps.who.int/gho/data/node.main.3?lang=en, last accessed February 2016.

Social Lab: An 'Open Source Facebook'

Ulf Dietrich Reips and Pablo Garaizar

The overlap between our every day activities and our behaviours on the Internet is ever increasing. With the advent of social media the social and behavioural sciences are faced with new opportunities and challenges for research into social behaviour. The vast majority of social media are owned by private companies. Despite public application programming interfaces (APIs) being offered by some of these social media, research in proprietary networks is severely limited. Considering the limitations to social media research, we have developed Social Lab, an Open Source clone of Facebook with most of its features (messaging, sharing, befriending, wall posts, pictures, searching, profiles, privacy settings, etc.). In addition, Social Lab enables researchers to create 'social bots' – automated programmable profiles controlled through simple scripts – to facilitate the study of social phenomena. In the present chapter we introduce Social Lab using an example around privacy management in social media, show how to configure social bots in Social Lab, and explain how it can be used in research. The source code of Social Lab is freely available to the scientific community, so any research group can have its own Social Lab to conduct their Internet-based research.

INTRODUCTION

The Internet, 'Web 2.0', and social media – the evolution of networked technologies and their social use – has yielded a new generation of researchers, who have developed a new set of methods and tools for research on the Internet and in its services (see e.g. Reips & Birnbaum, 2011; Reips & Buffardi, 2012). Tools available for such research include: *FactorWiz* and *SurveyWiz* (Birnbaum, 2000); *iScience Maps* (Reips & Garaizar, 2011); innovative social location-aware services for mobile phones like *MUGGES* (Klein & Reips, Chapter 25, this volume), *Scientific LogAnalyzer* (Reips & Stieger, 2004); the *Web experiment list* (Reips & Lengler, 2005); the *Web Experimental Psychology Lab* (Reips, 2001); *WEXTOR*, a Web experiment generator (Reips & Neuhaus, 2002); *ReCal OIR* (Freelon, 2013); *VAS Generator* (Reips & Funke, 2008); *Dynamic Interviewing Program* and *User Action Tracer* (Stieger & Reips, 2008, 2010); among many others. The number of studies conducted via the Internet with such tools has grown almost exponentially since 1995 (Reips & Krantz, 2010).

In the following sections, we will describe a new tool in this tradition, *Social Lab*, and how it can be used in research. We will also illustrate its application with an example, in which Social Lab is used to learn and practice privacy management in Social Networking Sites (SNSs). We will then provide instructions on how to extend its functionality for particular research purposes by configuring so-called 'social bots', automated agents within Social Lab that to the user may often appear indistinguishable from human users of the social network.

SOCIAL MEDIA RESEARCH OPTIONS AND BIG DATA

'Social media is a group of Internet-based applications that build on the ideological and technological foundations of Web 2.0, and that allow the creation and exchange of user generated content' (Kaplan & Haenlein, 2010, p. 61). Figure 27.1 empirically shows with a Google Trends analysis how the term 'social media' became more popular than 'Web 2.0' and continues to be on the rise (also see McCay-Peet and Quan-Haase, Chapter 2, this volume).

Unknown to many people, who may just know about the largest social media sites like Facebook, Twitter, Instagram, Snapchat, Weibo, LinkedIn, Orkut, Tuenti, Google+, Wikipedia, Tumblr, or YouTube, there are

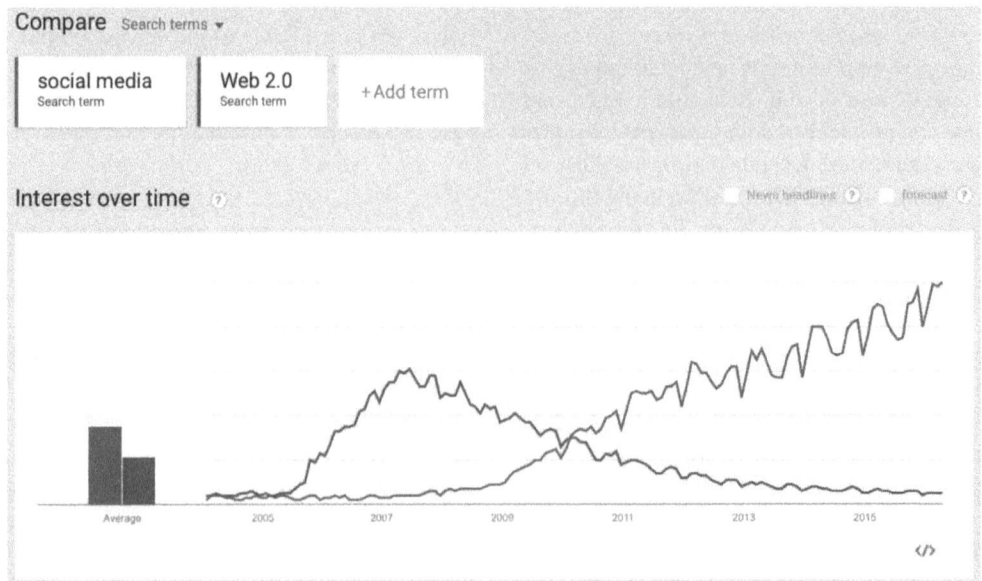

Figure 27.1 Analysis of searches for the terms 'Web 2.0' and 'social media' over time in Google Trends

thousands more of social media that often aim at particular interests or groups. For example, Wikipedia lists almost four hundred 'major active' sites (Wikipedia, 2016), including many 'second level' SNSs for special, albeit large, interest groups, for example, academics (ResearchGate, Academia. edu, etc.). Social media can be categorized in various ways, for example, by main user function (publish, share, discuss, lifestream, microblog, livecast, play in virtual world or a social game) or industry purpose (social advertising, marketing, analytics, streaming, social data mining, social intelligence, social scoring, internal or external business software, reviewing, social shopping, social referral, content curation, social TV, social brand engagement, etc.).

Research using social media can be conducted on many topics of social interaction that don't require physical co-presence or a synchronous face-to-face situation. Social phenomena have been shown to appear online as well as offline. See for example, research on ostracism (Vorderer & Schneider, in press) or migration (Reips & Buffardi, 2012; Oiarzabal & Reips, 2012). Communication in social media and the effects of social media use (e.g., emotional consequences of using Facebook [Lin & Utz, 2015], or even Facebook addiction [Dantlgraber et al., 2016]) have become a topic of interest and research in itself. Both the research on social media use and on how social media can be used for research purposes have increased enormously during the last few years (also see McCay-Peet and Quan-Haase, Chapter 2, this volume).

Because very large SNSs like Facebook have frequently been involved in research, data sets tend to be very large. Big Data has thus become an important topic in social media research and Internet science, with related issues. Big Data gathered from social media may in fact provide answers to one of the main issues in behavioural and social science research with very large data sets, the lack of connection between the micro and macro levels of analysis (Snijders et al., 2012).

To select a social media site for research or other purposes, one can use a tool called Social Media Planner (www.inpromo.de/word press/en/social-tools/social-media-planner/). In a first step, one selects demographics and interests, and in a second step, the tool generates a list of social media sites that are geared toward the selected criteria (e.g., education) and are used by (mostly) people with the selected range of demographics.

On the downside, existing SNSs come with many disadvantages related to their often proprietary nature (ads; lack of true access to the data; end of service due to economic issues like buyout, bankruptcy, change of business; business rather than research driven structure of data; change of service, etc.) and sampling biases. Even though his methodology of using Facebook likes may be somewhat questionable with respect to details of the empirical results, Ruffini (2012) convincingly describes how the selection of a social media service may lead to a particular, possibly biased sample.

SOCIAL LAB: WHAT IT IS

Social Lab can be described as an Open Source 'Facebook' clone, a fully functional and free software to run social networks for research and other purposes (Garaizar & Reips, 2014). Social Lab is available from www.sociallab.es and provides most features commonly found in other social media, for example, messaging, sharing, befriending, wall posts, pictures, searching, profiles, privacy settings, etc. (see Figure 27.2).

Having full availability of navigation and communication data in Social Lab allows researchers to investigate behaviour in social media at both on an individual and a group level. Automated artificial users ('social bots', for a similar concept of *social-bots* not native to a SNS see, e.g., Boshmaf

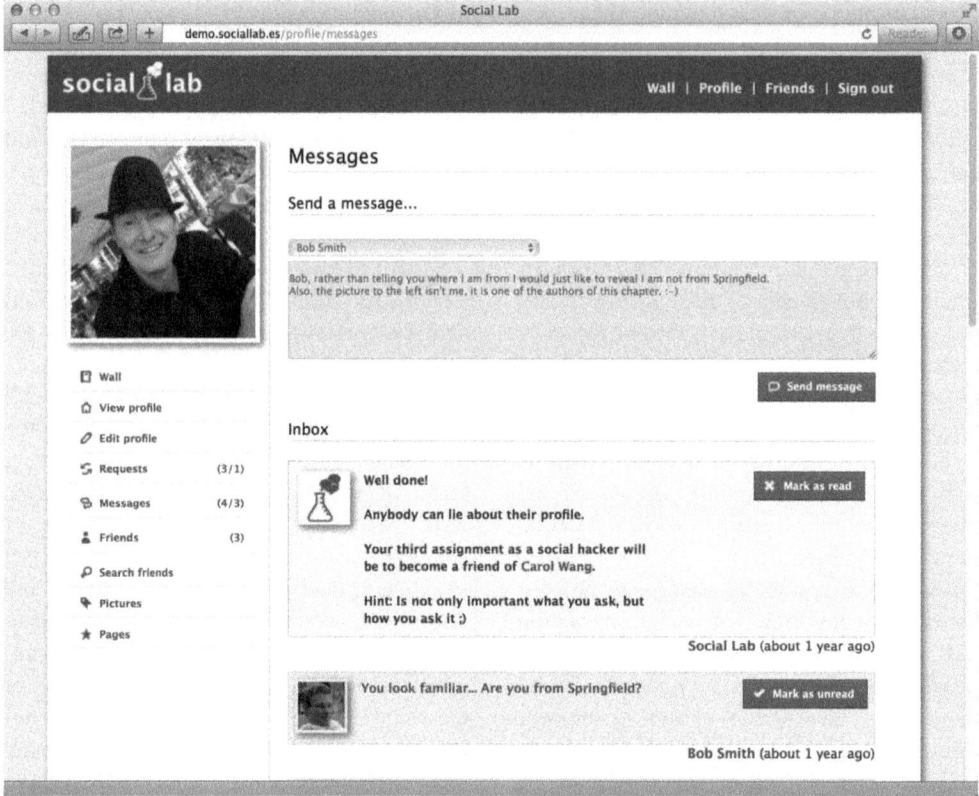

Figure 27.2 Main display of Social Lab

et al., 2011) are available to the researcher to simulate and stimulate social networking situations. These bots respond dynamically to situations as they unfold and they have a memory for their previous interactions. The social bots can easily be configured with simple scripts and can be used to experimentally manipulate social networking situations in Social Lab.

AN EXAMPLE: AN EDUCATIONAL PRIVACY MANAGEMENT SITE USING SOCIAL LAB

To exemplify how Social Lab can be used, we set up a site that helps users develop a sense of the challenges around privacy management in social media. Privacy on the Internet has been and continues to be a major issue (Joinson et al., 2010; Reips, 2011). The Social Lab privacy education site is available in English at http://en.sociallab.es/, in Spanish at http://es.sociallab.es/, in German at http://de.sociallab.es/, and in the Basque region at http://eu.sociallab.es/. Its purpose is to demonstrate some of the techniques used by social hackers in order to help users to prevent these kinds of attacks in real social networks.

Anyone can sign up and get started with this site. Once signed in, the first challenge in protecting users' privacy is waiting in the inbox. Every challenge will be controlled by an automated, script-based profile that appears like a fellow user on the social network. Profiles must be convinced to become

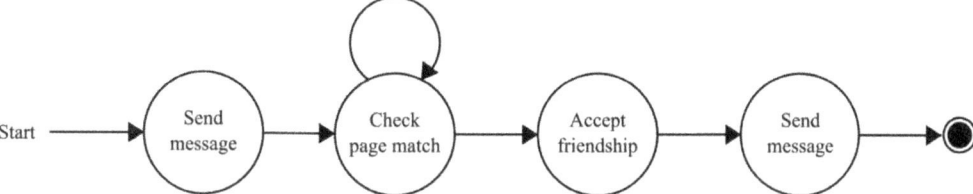

Figure 27.3 Simple social bot for Social Lab. In the example, the first message contains a recommendation to add a Mozart web page to one's preferences

friends using one's social engineering skills. Their responses are automatic but may not be immediate. Sometimes they need some time to respond, just like real users.

Figure 27.3 shows how the site interactively provides feedback to users. As we mentioned before, the ten challenges in the privacy management example site and their associated profiles are based on social bots, an essential feature of Social Lab. In the next section we will explain how to create and program bots in Social Lab.

PROGRAMMING A BOT IN SOCIAL LAB

From a technical perspective, Social Lab's bots are regular user accounts provided with unattended behaviours. Therefore, researchers can make a social bot from a user account previously managed by a person. The opposite is also feasible: a person can take manual control of an account previously managed by a social bot. Moreover, sharing the management of the user account between a person and a social bot at the same time is also possible. This flexibility in managing social bots' accounts enables a wide variety of research scenarios.

The first step to program a bot on Social Lab is to create a user account and define its profile (i.e., first name, last name, email, gender, birthday, picture, location, academic information, personal information, privacy options) using the registration page (http://yoursociallab.com/signup). We use 'yoursociallab.com' as a fictitious server name where Social Lab is deployed by a research group. Most of these features are in use in our online privacy game example. Therefore, the reader can replace 'yoursociallab.com' with 'en.sociallab.es' to see them working. The rest of the process of defining the automatic behaviour of the social bot is done through the Social Lab backend interface (i.e., http://yoursociallab.com/backend.php – for security reasons this URL won't work in our example at http://en.sociallab.es to prevent hackers from accessing our privacy game backend).

In Social Lab the behaviour of a social bot is defined by a sequence of steps. There are two types of steps: actions and checks. *Actions* (e.g., send message, accept friendship request, etc.) are executed in a predefined order and always enable the processing of the next step. *Checks* (e.g., check if someone is a friend of two friends of mine, check location match, etc.), by contrast, are evaluated whenever they are requested by the social bot, but they cannot progress to the next step unless these conditions are met.

Social bots keep in the database the status of each interaction with each user. Thus, they may be running step 1 with the user A while performing step 3 with the user B. When a social bot has executed all the steps defined in its behaviour interacting with a given user, this interaction ends. However, interactions with other users will run their course in the state in which they were.

Let's see how to define the behaviour of a simple bot. As shown in Figure 27.3, this bot will send a message, for example asking the user in the first step whether she likes a certain Mozart webpage or not. In the second step, the bot will wait until the user it is interacting with adds the Mozart page to her preferences. The bot will wait in this state indefinitely and will not execute the rest of its program until the condition is met. When that happens the bot will accept the user's friendship request (third step) and send a message recommending other pages of similar musicians (fourth step).

Defining this automatic behaviour in Social Lab is straightforward. First, a regular user account is created, it must then be added to the 'Bots' table using the backend application (http://yoursociallab.com/backend.php/bot/new). Then, all the steps defined in Figure 27.3 have to be added to the 'Steps' table (http://yoursociallab.com/backend.php/step/new), setting the following parameters, see Figure 27.4: 1) the bot that we are programming (a drop-down list of all bots defined in the 'Bots' table is shown here to minimize input errors); 2) the command to be executed in this step ('Send message' for the case of the first step of this social bot); 3) the step order (0 for the case of the first step); and 4) a reference to the message intended to be sent. All text messages sent by social bots have to must be stored in the 'Automsg' table. Therefore, it is necessary to add a new entry to this table (http://yoursociallab.com/backend.php//automsg/new), indicating the text to send. The second step

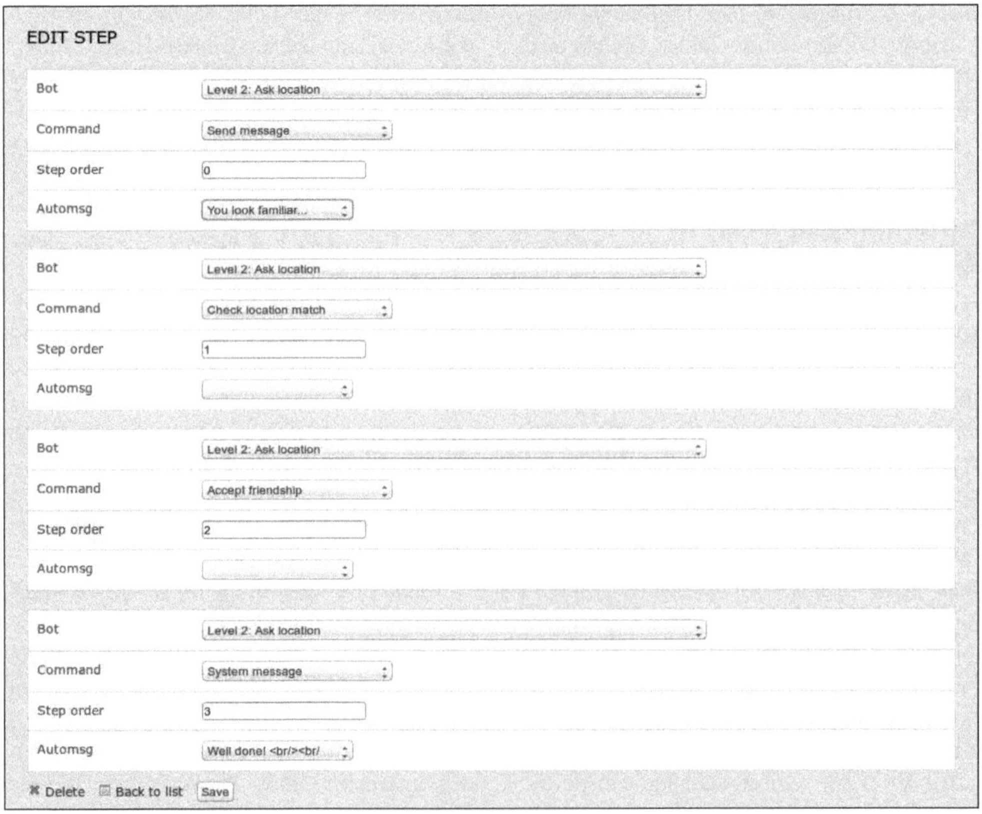

Figure 27.4 Setting up triggers and routines for a social bot in Social Lab's backend application

of the social bot has to be added in a similar way, adding a new entry to the 'Steps' table (http://yoursociallab.com/backend.php/step/new). In this case, the command should be 'Check page match', the step order should be 1, the automsg field should be left blank because this check does not require a message. The third step is defined in the same vein, adding a new step for the same bot and defining the command (accept friendship) and the step order (2). Finally, the last step of creating this bot involves another 'Send message' command. Therefore, the message to send should be added previously to the 'Automsg' table (http://yoursociallab.com/backend.php//automsg/new). Once this procedure is finished, the bot is ready to interact with users of the social network.

As we can see, defining a bot in Social Lab does not require previous technical knowledge, just adding values to the database. Thanks to the backend application provided with Social Lab, these database changes can be done with a form-based interface. With this social bots definition system a researcher could easily compare two similar situations by creating two social bots with slightly different behaviours and analyze, which interactions occur with each of them. For example, in a study related to participation in online promotions, researchers might want to know whether participants asked to perform two actions (e.g., mark a page as favourite and post a message on their wall) to take part in the online promotion are more reluctant to participate than those who first are asked to perform one action first and then the other one. Researchers conducting this experiment could define three bots as shown in Figure 27.5 and compare the number of users in the social network that reach the last step in each case. Comparisons between the two last bots could also give clues about the reluctance associated with each action.

User accounts of each of these bots can also be simultaneously managed by humans. Therefore, the community manager responsible for encouraging participation in this online promotion could use the social bots user accounts manually in some moments of the marketing campaign. This increases the feeling of interacting with a person and not a program, which could also be the subject

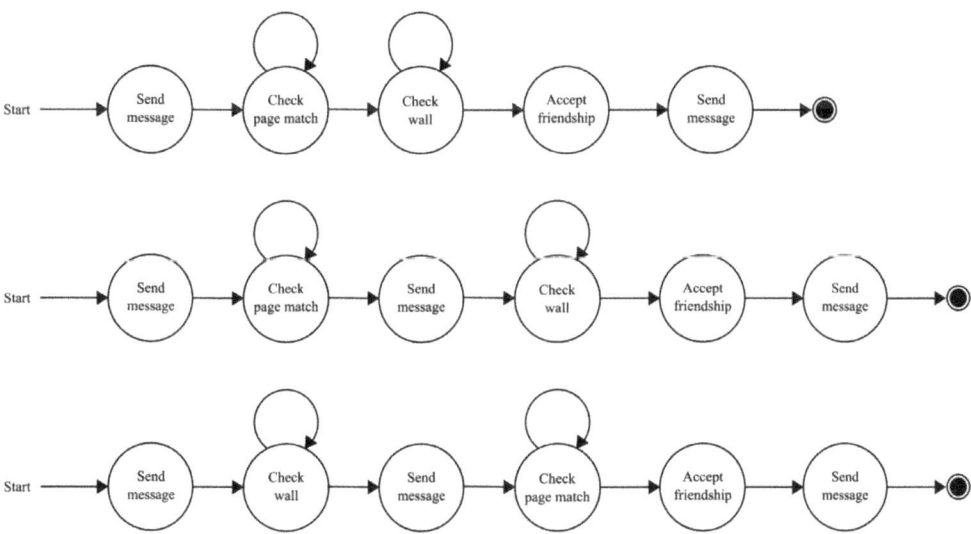

Figure 27.5 Three slightly different social bots to gather participants for an online promotion

of another related study (i.e., compare the engagement in online promotions boosted by profiles clearly run by people and by profiles clearly managed by bots). As mentioned before, this shared management of user accounts also enables multi-phase studies in which the behaviour (e.g., bot A, bot B and bot C in Figure 27.5) and type of interaction (manual vs. automated) changes in each phase but all interactions are made from the same user account.

Moreover, it is also possible to take advantage of the fact that all behaviours of all social bots are defined as rows of a small set of tables in the Social Lab database (i.e., bot, step, automsg). Thanks to this decoupled design, third-party software could dynamically reprogram the behaviour of the bots modifying the content of those tables without modifying a single line of the particular Social Lab instance's source code. This enables the integration of sophisticated behaviours (e.g., chat bots managed by complex Artificial Intelligence algorithms) without having to integrate their code in Social Lab, simply making changes in the database.

RESEARCH OPTIONS WITH SOCIAL LAB

Here we outline ideas about how Social Lab could be used in research. In the most simple study design, researchers can simply observe how users act and communicate within the social network. Like in Figure 27.6, messages can be deployed by bots or researchers to provoke user action. As fully controllable Open Source software, Social Lab lets researchers access more information than any proprietary network.

Also, researchers may use Social Lab to investigate group-level social network structure and dynamics. Social network analysis could then be used in the analysis of the social network – for example, research into changes of the pattern of connections between persons in a collective (Quan-Haase & McCay-Peet, 2016). Of course, a network set up with Social Lab can provide an environment for questionnaire studies and interviews as well. Such interviews could even be conducted automatically using a pre-programmed bot that randomly contacts users within the

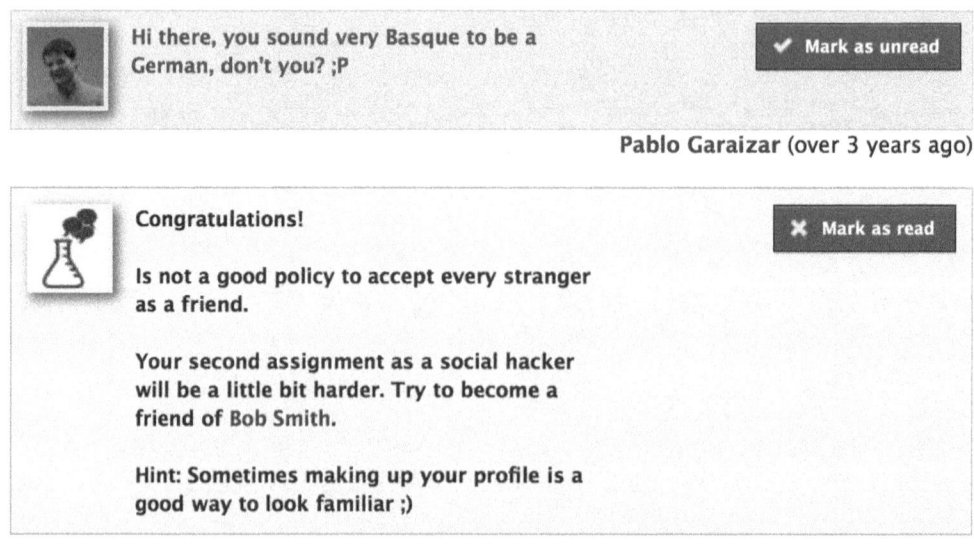

Figure 27.6 Messages can be deployed by researchers or social bots or to provoke user actions

social network and invites them to participate (Stieger & Reips, 2008).

One could further imagine *experimental* studies that are based on Social Lab. So far, to our knowledge there has been only one truly experimental study with Internet-based social networks (Centola, 2010), i.e. randomly assigning participants to different social networks. Centola (2010) was interested in the influence of the structure of social networks on the spread of behaviour and randomly assigned participants who had signed up to a health forum to either a clustered lattice network condition and a random network condition. Participants were further randomly assigned to a node in their network, i.e. the other participants they would see within the network were determined by this assignment. Further, each participant could receive at most one email from each of the participants they could see and they could not contact each other within the social network. Improving on this communication-poor, rather static and purely structural manipulation one could use the human-like bots available in Social Lab, for example influence risk perception in two initially structurally identical networks and observe risk communication, coping behaviour, and attitude change. In pre-study and follow-up surveys one could collect attitudinal information and self-reported behaviours and emotions from participants and then see how these change depending on the experimental manipulations and resulting dynamics within the networks.

Setting up Social Lab as an Experimental Environment. Experiments can be conducted *within* a social network or *between* social networks. In the latter case, at least two structurally identical social networks need to be created using Social Lab after download and setup from www.sociallab.es. Participants should be recruited from different Web sites and in different modes (e.g., actively: 'push' or passively: 'pull'). Via the multiple site entry technique (Reips, 2000, 2007) the researcher will be able to determine for each participant the site he or she was recruited from and will thus later be able to test for systematic differences between recruitment sites and modes. For example, one could aim for 2,000 participants (ca. 500 in each of four network), then have them fill in informed consent forms and randomly assign them to one of the four social networks. The social networks then need to be closed; no new applications will be accepted during the time of the studies.

Social Lab will often need to be adjusted to meet the requirements of a particular study. For example, there may be a need to limit configuration options (e.g., delete the informed consent option within Social Lab, if informed consent was already collected before the logon). One could also amend options to display 'news items' that can be used for experimental manipulations. As a way to manipulate exposure (e.g., via frequency and intensity of messages or via number of agents) and role modelling of coping strategies, several social bots can be created in all networks and their actions and timing will be programmed to serve the tasks required by the experimental manipulations.

OUTLOOK

We have presented the free Open Source social network software Social Lab and outlined how it can be used in research. Social Lab provides most features that are common to social media and even more: one of the most useful features in research are its automated programmable bots. We described above how such social bots can be used in research and how to create and configure them within Social Lab.

Much research including social network analysis can be applied to social networks that are developed within Social Lab or manifest themselves in communications on this platform. With Social Lab, researchers can collect information on who is connected to and communicates with whom, at which time.

Such data can then be used to investigate social network properties, such as density, clustering, and connectedness, or node properties, such as betweenness or centrality (see e.g., Brandes & Erlebach, 2005; D'Andrea et al., 2010).

We hope Social Lab will inspire many to set up free social networks for research and beyond. An Open Source community has begun to form and help in its development. May the new tool help the scientific community to advance in the exciting study of behaviour in social media.

REFERENCES

Birnbaum, M. H. (2000). SurveyWiz and FactorWiz: JavaScript Web pages that make HTML forms for research on the Internet. *Behavior Research Methods, Instruments, & Computers*, 32(2), 339–346.

Boshmaf, Y., Muslukhov, I., Beznosov, K., & Ripeanu, M. (2011). The socialbot network: when bots socialize for fame and money. In *27th Annual Conference on Computer Security Applications* (pp. 93–102). http://doi.org/10.1145/2076732.2076746

Brandes, U., & Erlebach, T. (Eds.)(2005). Network analysis: Methodological foundations. *Lecture Notes in Computer Science Tutorial*, vol. 3418. Berlin: Springer.

Centola, D. (2010). The spread of behavior in an online social network experiment. *Science*, 329, 1194–1197.

D'Andrea, A., Ferri, F., & Grifoni, P. (2010). An overview of methods for virtual social network analysis. In A. Abraham, A.-E. Hassanien, & V. Snasel (Eds.), *Computational social network analysis: trends, tools and research advances* (pp. 3–26). Berlin, Germany: Springer. doi:10.1007/978-1-84882-229-0

Dantlgraber, M., Wetzel, E., Schützenberger, P., Stieger, S., & Reips, U.-D. (2016). Simple construct evaluation with latent class analysis: An investigation of Facebook addiction and the development of a short form of the Facebook Addiction Test (F-AT). *Behavior Research Methods* 48, 869–879. doi:10.3758/s13428-016-0716-2

Freelon, D. (2013). ReCal OIR: Ordinal, interval, and ratio intercoder reliability as a web service. *International Journal of Internet Science*, 8(1), 10–16.

Garaizar, P., & Reips, U.-D. (2014). Build your own social network laboratory with Social Lab: A tool for research in social media. *Behavior Research Methods*, 46(2), 430–438.

Joinson, A. N., Reips, U.-D., Buchanan, T., & Paine Schofield, C. (2010). Privacy, trust, and self-disclosure online. *Human-Computer Interaction*, 25, 1–24. doi: 10.1080/07370020903586662

Kaplan, A. M., & Haenlein, M. (2010). Users of the world, unite! The challenges and opportunities of Social Media. *Business Horizons*, 53(1), 59–68. doi:10.1016/j.bushor.2009.09.003

Lin, R., & Utz, S. (2015). The emotional responses of browsing Facebook: Happiness, envy, and the role of tie strength. *Computers in Human Behavior, 52*, 29–38. doi:10.1016/j.chb.2015.04.064

Oiarzabal, P. J., & Reips, U.-D. (2012). Migration and diaspora in the age of information and communication technologies. *Journal of Ethnic and Migration Studies*, 38(9), 1333–1338. doi:10.1080/1369183X.2012.698202

Quan-Haase, A., & McCay-Peet, L. (2016). Social network analysis. In K. J. Bruhn & R. T. Craig (Eds.), *International Encyclopedia of Communication Theory and Philosophy*. Cambridge, MA: Wiley.

Reips, U.-D. (2011). Privacy and the disclosure of information on the Internet: Issues and measurement. In A. Blachnio, A. Przepiórka & T. Rowinski (eds.), *Internet in psychological research* (pp. 71–104). Warsaw: UKSW Publishing House.

Reips, U.-D. (2007). The methodology of Internet-based experiments. In A. Joinson, K. McKenna, T. Postmes, & U.-D. Reips (Eds.), *The Oxford Handbook of Internet Psychology* (pp. 373–390). Oxford: Oxford University Press.

Reips, U.-D. (2001). The Web Experimental Psychology Lab: Five years of data collection on the Internet. *Behavior Research Methods, Instruments, and Computers*, 33, 201–211.

Reips, U.-D. (2000). The Web Experiment Method: Advantages, disadvantages, and solutions. In M. H. Birnbaum (Ed.), *Psychological experiments on the Internet* (pp. 89–118). San Diego, CA: Academic Press.

Reips, U.-D., & Birnbaum, M. H. (2011). Behavioral research and data collection via the Internet. In K.-P. L. Vu & R. W. Proctor (Eds.), *The handbook of human factors in web design* (2nd ed., pp. 563–585). Mahwah, New Jersey: Erlbaum.

Reips, U.-D., & Buffardi, L. (2012). Studying migrants with the help of the Internet: Methods from psychology. *Journal of Ethnic and Migration Studies*, *38*(9), 1405–1424. doi:10.1080/1369183X.2012.698208

Reips, U.-D., & Funke, F. (2008). Interval level measurement with visual analogue scales in Internet-based research: VAS Generator. *Behavior Research Methods, 40*, 699–704.

Reips, U.-D., & Garaizar, P. (2011). Mining Twitter: Microblogging as a source for psychological wisdom of the crowds. *Behavior Research Methods*, *43*(3), 635–642.

Reips, U.-D., & Krantz, J. H. (2010). Conducting true experiments on the Web. In S. Gosling & J. Johnson (eds.), *Advanced methods for conducting online behavioral research* (pp. 193-216). Washington, DC: American Psychological Association.

Reips, U.-D., & Lengler, R. (2005). The Web Experiment List: A Web service for the recruitment of participants and archiving of Internet- based experiments. *Behavior Research Methods, 37*, 287–292.

Reips, U.-D., & Neuhaus, C. (2002). WEXTOR: A Web-based tool for generating and visualizing experimental designs and procedures. *Behavior Research Methods, Instruments, and Computers, 34*, 234–240.

Reips, U.-D., & Stieger, S. (2004). Scientific LogAnalyzer: A Web-based tool for analyses of server log files in psychological research. *Behavior Research Methods*, *36*(2), 304–311.

Ruffini, P. (2012). Infographic: Mapping the politics of the Social Web. http://enga.ge/design/mapping-politics-social-web/

Snijders, C., Matzat, U., & Reips, U.-D. (2012). 'Big Data': Big gaps of knowledge in the field of Internet science. *International Journal of Internet Science*, *7*(1), 1–5.

Stieger, S., & Reips, U.-D. (2010). What are participants doing while filling in an online questionnaire: A paradata collection tool and an empirical study. *Computers in Human Behavior, 26*, 1488–1495.

Stieger, S., & Reips, U.-D. (2008). Dynamic Interviewing Program (DIP): Automatic online interviews via the instant messenger ICQ. *CyberPsychology and Behavior, 11*, 201–207.

Vorderer, P. & Schneider, F. M. (in press). Social media and ostracism. In K. D. Williams & S. A. Nida (Eds.), *Social exclusion*. New York, NY: Psychology Press.

Wikipedia (2016, April 16). List of social networking websites. Retrieved 21 April 2016, from https://en.wikipedia.org/w/index.php?title=List_of_social_networking_websites&oldid=715618422

R for Social Media Analysis

Simon Hegelich

R is a free software programming language and software environment for statistical computing and graphics. Because R is a programming language its usage is not limited to the field of statistics. There are already many R-packages to cover the whole spectrum of social media analysis from web scraping to text mining. This chapter is designed as a hands-on-tutorial to analyze data from Twitter in R. In four steps, the chapter demonstrates how to get the desired data, how to 'clean' it, how to analyze it, and how to visualize the results. By following these steps the reader will gain knowledge about the general structure of R, its basic grammar, some relevant packages for social media analyses, the Twitter streaming API, and about some basic programming concepts. The chapter addresses readers with no or little previous knowledge about programming. The aim is to demonstrate that the efforts in learning a programming language instead of using off-the-shelf-solutions are rewarded with greater flexibility for creative social media analysis.

The R language has become one of the most prominent tools among statisticians and data miners. Because it is free software and due to its outstanding capacities which are enhanced by a huge community of contributors, R has become the first choice at many universities in teaching statistics.

INTRODUCTION

What is R?

R is a computer language for statistical computing and graphics. 'R provides a wide variety of statistical (linear and nonlinear modelling, classical statistical tests, time-series analysis, classification, clustering, …) and graphical techniques, and is highly extensible. […] One of R's strengths is the ease with which well-designed publication-quality plots can be produced […]. R is available as Free Software under the terms of the Free Software Foundation's GNU General Public

License in source code form. It compiles and runs on a wide variety of UNIX platforms and similar systems (including FreeBSD and Linux), Windows and MacOS' (CRAN 2015 np).

As an open-source project that is free to use, R has become more and more popular at universities all over the world. According to the detailed studies of Muench (2015), R is one of the most popular tools in statistics and the preferred choice for data-analytics. In contrast to statistical environments like *SPSS* and *stata*, R has gained popularity in recent years (Muench 2015). There are probably three reasons for this trend:

> R is free: The whole environment is open source and under GNU license. Everyone can install as many copies of it as desired.
>
> R is strong: R is built on the statistical programming language S and therefore includes extensive tools for all kinds of statistical methods by design. In addition, due to the open source character, there is a huge community of developers who contribute to the further development of R which means that nearly every new trend in methods is integrated in the form of additional 'packages'.
>
> R is flexible: The exponential growth of additional packages (Muench 2015) provides the user with a huge box of tailored tools for many tasks. But R is also very flexible by design. In contrast to other statistical environments, R functions as a fully-developed computer language (that can easily be enriched with additional code in C#, C++, or FORTRAN). The scope of applications therefore goes far beyond statistical analysis.

The 'price' that comes with these advantages is that R has to be programmed like a computer language. There is no drag and drop and many tasks will require some advanced skills in programming and the understanding of basic programming concepts like functions, recursion, loops, etc. (see Teetor 2011).

Why Use R for Social Media Analysis?

Two key concepts of social media are 1) the ability of everyone to share information on the web and 2) to participate in networks that structure this information. Kaplan and Haenlein tried to define social media in a more precise way and suggested a differentiation between Web 2.0 'as the platform for the evolution of Social Media' (Kaplan and Haenlein 2010) and the different practices social media results in. From a data-science point of view, social media is extremely interesting as well as challenging because the interaction of multiple users creates big data with the three characteristics described by Mayer-Schönberger and Cukier (2013): *more, messy, good enough*. Twitter, for example, had 288 million monthly active users in the last quarter of 2014 (Twitter-Inc. 2015a). However, data from social media is not nicely organized but *messy*: There are hardly any rules about what kind of content is distributed by the users. Besides, data is not limited to the provided content: The network structure itself is a rich source of additional information that can be analyzed on multiple levels. Finally, there is the idea that social media data can tell us a lot about real world phenomena outside the virtual realm. Many promises of *predictive analytics* may have overestimated the possibility to extrapolate from social media data (Ruths and Pfeffer 2014). Nevertheless, it remains fascinating to combine social media analysis with additional data from 'the real world'.

This complexity of social media analysis looks like a perfect environment for the application of R. R provides fast track access to different social media APIs (see Janetz and Kay, Chapter 10 in this volume), it has all the tools needed for text-mining, graph-analysis and data manipulation.

Getting – Cleaning – Testing – Showing: A Data-scientist's Work-flow

Data science is more than just statistics. Statisticians *survey* data in a very careful way to come up with representative samples structured in nice and neat tables. But social media data is not structured this way. It is just out there somewhere on the Internet and we have to *get it on our computer* and transform it in a way that is suitable for analyzing. This step normally involves the use of an API. In a second step, social media data normally has to be *cleaned*. For example, there might be duplicates, missing values or incorrect specifications of objects. The cleaned data can be used t*o run descriptive statistics*, *to test hypothesis*, *to find hidden patterns* or to analyze it with more advanced machine learning algorithms. Whatever we find out in the end, it is very important to present the results in a way that reduces the complexity of the original data drastically. For this last step, data science has developed *visualization* tools (Schutt and O'Neil 2013, 41–43). All these four steps can be done directly in R.

In the following example we will connect to Twitter and get tweets located in California. This sample will then be analyzed and visualized. The research question for this example is the following: Are trends on Twitter regionally localized? On the one hand, Twitter is a global social media platform that connects people all over the world. It is therefore reasonable to argue that regional differences are not so important on Twitter. On the other hand, people use Twitter to communicate about what is going on in their real lives. Since the real life takes place in a specified space, it is reasonable to argue that information on Twitter should show a lot of regional differences.

The chapter is designed as a hands-on-tutorial. The reader should install R and get familiar with its basic structure in advance. The CRAN-webpage offers excellent tutorials for these first steps (CRAN 2015).

GETTING DATA FROM TWITTER

Initializing the Twitter API

In this chapter, the so called STREAMING-API from Twitter is used. This API provides real-time access to Twitter, so the results are dependent from on what is actually going on, right now. Before we start, we have to initialize the Twitter-API. To use the Twitter API, a consumer key and consumer secret is required. Therefore, you have to register as a developer who is creating a Twitter app. Create a Twitter account and then sign in at https://apps.twitter.com/. The account has to be verified with a phone number. This can be done on the Twitter webpage in the account settings. Fill in name, description and any valid URL with leading 'http://'. It is important NOT to provide any *call-back URL*, because otherwise the registration from R will not function. After this, you can see a summary of your newly created app with a link to 'manage keys and access tokens'. The consumer key and consumer secret that can be found there have to be copied into the following R-script to save a permanent authentication token.[1]

Registration of the API via R

After we have gained access to the API, we can register a connection directly from R via the following code:

```
# We use the package "streamR" which is designed
    to connect to the Twitter # Streaming API.
# Packages are loaded into R with the command
    library()
library(streamR)
# In addition, we need the "ROAuth"-package to
    establish an
# authentification.
library(ROAuth)
# The following four lines assign the right values to
    the variables that
# are needed for the API call.
requestURL  <-  "https://api.twitter.com/oauth/
    request_token"
accessURL  <-  "https://api.twitter.com/oauth/
    access_token"
authURL <- "https://api.twitter.com/oauth/authorize"
# The string within the quotation marks has to be
    replaced with the actual
# consumerKey and consumerSecret.
consumerKey <- "myconsumerkey1122"
```

```
consumerSecret    <-    "myconsumerse-
    cret112233445566"
# The next two lines establish a connection to
    the Twitter API.
# The system will print a URL which should be
    copied in a browser to receive a PIN number.
# This PIN has to be entered in the R-console.
my_oauth <- OAuthFactory$new(consumerKey =
    consumerKey,
consumerSecret = consumerSecret,
requestURL = requestURL,
accessURL = accessURL,
authURL = authURL)
my_oauth$handshake(cainfo    =    system.file
    ("CurlSSL", "cacert.pem", package = "RCurl"))
# Once the connection is established we can save
    it so that we do not have
# repeat this process.
save(my_oauth, file = "my_oauth.Rdata")
```

Sometimes, this approach fails because of an unexpected problem: Twitter checks the date and time of the computer from which the API-request is sent. If the time is not 100% correct the request is blocked. Even some seconds may lead to an error. Next time any session to analyze Twitter can simply start by the connection data stored in the my_oauth file. The necessary command is:

```
load("my_oauth.Rdata")
```

Searching on the Twitter API

We are now connected to the 'Streaming API' of Twitter (Twitter-Inc. 2015b). This API allows us to search in real-time the stream of tweets. We can specify several parameters for this search. For example, if we set the parameter 'track' to 'social media', the API will return all tweets containing this character string. If we want to focus the search on specified users, we can set the parameter 'follow' to the desired user-names. A very interesting feature is the location-based search. If we set the 'loc' parameter to longitude and latitude coordinates, the search is restricted to the specified area. The first two values define the southwestern corner of a square and; the last two its north-eastern corner. The different search-parameters can be combined but it is advisable to refer to the documentation (Twitter-Inc. 2015b) to understand how the API handles such combinations. For example, location is always used as logical 'or'. This means, if we specify a location and a user-name, the API will return all tweets that fit to the location *and* all tweets of the specified user.

By default, the search is performed endlessly. As long as the computer program is running additional tweets will be added to the file that is specified by the 'file'-parameter. But we can specify a 'timeout'-parameter that will end the search when the defined time-span is reached.

The following code specifies the parameters to search for one minute for all tweets from California. For the later examples, the timeout was set to 30 minutes to increase the number of tweets.

```
file = "tweets.json"
track = NULL
follow = NULL
loc = c(-125, 30, -114, 42)
lang = NULL
minutes = 0.5
time = 60*minutes
tweets = NULL
filterStream(file.name = file,
    track = track,
    follow = follow,
    locations = loc,
    language = lang,
    timeout = time,
    tweets = tweets,
    oauth = my_oauth,
    verbose = TRUE)
```

CLEANING THE DATA

In our working directory we will find now a file named 'tweets.json' (as set by the 'file'-parameter). A *JavaScript Object Notation* (JSON) file is structured like a list. All the information of every Tweet is written there but we do not have a table with rows and columns, yet. Fortunately, the streamR-package has a function to transfer JSON-data to conventional tables:

```
tweets.df <- parseTweets(file)
# Now we can inspect the table and save it.
View(tweets.df)
save(file="tweetsDF.RDATA", tweets.df)
```

The data is now nicely structured in a table with every tweet in one row and 42 columns for all variables.

To demonstrate the importance of data-cleaning and -manipulation, we will now create an additional column with the hashtags that are used in the tweets. Hashtags (every word in a tweet starting with the sign '#') are a very important element of the Twitter structure (Java et al. 2007). In this example, we want to find out if the usage of hashtags shows regional differentiations. To find the hashtags in the tweets, we use *regular expressions*. Regular expressions are a common way to specify patterns of character strings to be used in finding or replacement operations. In this case, we are looking for the character # followed by an undefined number of other alphabetical or numerical characters. Written as regular expression this pattern becomes '#[:alnum:]+'. The symbols [:alnum:] means 'any alpha-numerical character'. The +-symbol has the meaning: 'The proceeding item will be matched one or more times.'

To create a column with the hashtags, the string extract function (str_extract) from the package 'stringR' is used.[2]

```
library(stringr)
tweets.df$hashtags <- str_extract(tweets.df$text,
   "#[:alnum:]+")
```

In R, every object belongs to a specified class. For example, the columns that contain the numbers of friends or followers are assigned to the class *numeric*. The computer therefore expects only numbers in these columns. Right now, all columns containing text are assigned to the class *character*. But for the hashtags-column, something else is needed. Since we want to count the frequencies of the diverse hashtags to look for trends, the hashtags should be treated as a categorical variable. This is achieved by using the class *factor*.

```
tweets.df$hashtags <- as.factor(tweets.df$hashtags)
summary(tweets.df$hashtags)
```

The summary function returns the different hashtags and their frequency. We can do the same with the column *full_name*. This column contains the name of the location the tweet was sent from, or – in case the specific location is not shared on Twitter – the name of the user's hometown.

```
tweets.df$full_name <- as.factor(tweets.df$full_
   name)
summary(tweets.df$full_name)
```

The advantage of transferring these columns into categorical variables (class *factor*) is that we can use them now directly in any kind of prediction model. But before we start testing the hypothesis, a final step in the cleaning process has to be carried out: As can be seen in the summary of the *full_name* column, there are many different locations. If we ran a model on the complete data, this would require a lot of computational power. We will therefore reduce the data in a way that only the most common places are included. This task is a very good example to introduce the R-style indexation.. The following four lines of code show the solution for this task:

```
library(plyr)
sel<-count(tweets.df$full_name)$x[count(tweets.
   df$full_name)$freq>100]
sel <- tweets.df$full_name %in% sel
test.df <- tweets.df[sel,]
```

The idea is to create an object *sel* that indicates all rows of the original table that should be selected. The criterion for selection is that the location specified in *full_name* is mentioned more than 100 times in all the tweets. To identify these locations, it is necessary to count the frequencies of all different levels of our categorical variable in a similar way like the *summary*-function did. The best command for this is *count()*, which can be found in the *plyr*-package. The function *count()* returns a table (an object of class *data.frame*) with a column *x* containing the name (i.e., the location) and the frequency (*freq*). A very clever thing about R-programing is that calls for functions can be treated in the same way like the object they are returning. This means in our example we can start indexing the *count*-function directly. Any column of a *data.frame* can be addressed by its name. The syntax for this is *data.frame$columnName*. We have used this way of indexing already with *tweets.df$full_name*. Now we can address the *x*-column of the count-call in the same way: *count(tweets.df$full_name)$x*. This command alone returns all names of locations in alphabetical order.

There is a second way of indexing R-objects. Within box brackets '[]' we can specify which element of the object is relevant. This can be done either by indexing its position with numbers (e.g. [1], vectors of numbers [c(1,3,5,6)], or sequences [c(1:6)]), or by a vector of TRUE or FALSE statements. The latter is done in the above example: The second call of the *count*-function asks which frequency has a value above 100 and returns a TRUE or FALSE value for each row. The command line above therefore finds the names of the locations that have a frequency above 100 and stores these names in the object *sel*.

The next line then asks which location name is an element of the vector *sel*. The answer to this question is again a vector of TRUE/FALSE of the length of the total number of locations. This object is stored as *sel*, which overwrites the existing object. At first glance, to overwrite an existing object might seem quite confusing. But the goal in the example was to create a selector that specifies the most common locations. The first line did not finish this job but rather contained an intermediate step. To avoid constructing too many objects – and thereby increase the complexity of programming – it makes sense to overwrite objects until the desired form is reached.

The final line now creates a new object *test.df* containing all the tweets from *tweets.df* that are indexed by the *sel* object. The careful reader will notice the comma in the command *tweets.df[sel,]*. Tables (like *tweets.df*) are multi-dimensional objects. They consist of rows and columns. To index an element in a multi-dimensional object, all dimensions must be called. The *sel*-object specifies the rows. The value after the comma specifies the columns. Since we want all columns, we do not specify this value at all, but we still need the comma. Indexing objects in R might be a confusing experience, at the beginning. But the different methods described here appear to be very stringent if the underlying principles are known. Being able to understand complex indexing is a key competence to understand R-code and to handle different data structures.

Finally, a last step of cleaning should be applied to the new table we want to test our assumptions on:

test.df$full_name <- **droplevels**(test.df$full_name)

Categorical variables in R (class *factor*) contain more information than the sole data. The value *levels* shows all possible values the variable could take. Since we wanted to reduce the number of real values of location, it makes a lot of sense to drop unused levels, as well.

TESTING THE HYPOTHESIS

Since R is a statistical environment a major focus of its development has been on tools for statistical testing. In this chapter linear regression serves as an example, but the capacities of R go far beyond this.[3] The hypothesis of this chapter is that there are regional differences in Twitter. One of the most important features of the Twitter structure is the *followers_count*-variable (Kwak et al. 2010), which shows how many other users are following the tweets of a user. If there are regional differences, our cleaned variable *full_names* should have an effect on *followers_count*. The command to fit a linear regression model is *lm()*.

```
fit <- lm(followers_count ~ full_name, data=test.df)
summary(fit)
```

In the code above, an object *fit* is created that contains the results of the linear regression. The regression is called with the following parameters: First the response variable is defined followed by the symbol '~' (called 'tilde') and the predictor variable(s). This formula can be read as: '*followers_count* depends on *full_name*'. We can either specify the full name of these objects (*test.df$followers_count*) or define the *data*-parameter, so that the computer knows which table should be used. In the latter case, it is sufficient to specify the column names that are used.

The *summary()* function gives us all the necessary results. Depending on the data that is used, the results should look similar to the following output:

```
## Call:
## lm(formula = followers_count ~ full_name,
     data = test.df)
##
## Residuals:
## Min 1Q Median 3Q Max
## -6828–2171 -609–36 1003638
##
## Coefficients:
## Estimate Std. Error t value Pr(>|t|)
## (Intercept) 6856 1500 4.570 5.01e-06 ***
## full_nameBakersfield, CA -6261 1946–3.217
   0.00131 **
## full_nameCalifornia, USA -5563 1728–3.219
   0.00130 **
## full_nameFontana, CA -6057 2184–2.774
   0.00557 **
## full_nameFresno, CA -6335 2101–3.015
   0.00259 **
## full_nameLas Vegas, NV -4194 1940–2.163
   0.03063 *
## full_nameLong Beach, CA -6190 2188–2.829
   0.00469 **
## full_nameLos Angeles, CA -3942 1576–2.500
   0.01244 *
## full_nameModesto, CA -6144 2343–2.623
   0.00876 **
## full_nameMoreno Valley, CA -6330 2370–
   2.671 0.00759 **
## full_namePalmdale, CA -6253 2220–2.817
   0.00487 **
## full_nameParadise, NV -5063 2076–2.439
   0.01479 *
## full_nameRancho Cucamonga, CA -6227
   2249–2.768 0.00566 **
## full_nameRiverside, CA -6514 2163–3.012
   0.00261 **
## full_nameSacramento, CA -5766 2171–2.656
   0.00794 **
## full_nameSan Bernardino, CA -6171 2323–
   2.656 0.00793 **
## full_nameSan Diego, CA -5592 1892–2.956
   0.00313 **
## full_nameSan Francisco, CA -6248 2188–2.855
   0.00432 **
## full_nameSan Jose, CA -6360 2070–3.072
   0.00214 **
## full_nameStockton, CA -6294 2370–2.656
   0.00794 **
## –
## Signif. codes: 0 '***' 0.001 '**' 0.01 '*' 0.05
   '.' 0.1 ' ' 1
##
## Residual standard error: 18440 on 4578
   degrees of freedom
## Multiple R-squared: 0.005542, Adjusted
   R-squared: 0.001414
## F-statistic: 1.343 on 19 and 4578 DF, p-value:
   0.1451
```

The summary starts with citing the formula the model depends on. Next, we get some information on the distribution of the residuals. This is often essential for model diagnostics. Then a table with the results for each predictor is printed out. Here, we can see how R handles categorical variables: Our single variable *full_name* is transferred to separated variables for each level. If we had not reduced the complexity of the dataset first, we would have run a regression with some thousands predictors. For each predictor *summary()* gives us the classic regression values like estimate, standard error, t-value, and probability. The symbols in the last column represent the significance values (see Gelman and Hill 2007). Finally, we get some information on the performance of the model as a whole, including R^2, degrees of freedom, and p-value.

In this example, the effect of each location is significant (at least one '*' for every predictor). Therefore, one might argue that we have proof for a regional effect. But the explanatory power of the model is extremely limited (adjusted R^2 of ca. 0.001) and the model itself is not significant (p-value ca. 0.15).

We can try now to add other predictor variables, for example, *friends_count*. The idea would be that the number of followers depend on the location and the number of friends a user has. This can be done with the following commands:

```
fit2 <- lm(followers_count ~ full_name + friends_
    count, data=test.df)
summary(fit2)
## Call:
## lm(formula = followers_count ~ full_name +
    friends_count, data = test.df)
##
## Residuals:
## Min 1Q Median 3Q Max
## -11050 -1676 -403 15 1003224
##
## Coefficients:
## Estimate Std. Error t value Pr(>|t|)
## (Intercept) -753.55903 1561.51485 -0.483
    0.6294
##    full_nameBakersfield,   CA   890.93245
    1969.22358 0.452 0.6510
##    full_nameCalifornia,  USA   1637.39127
    1764.38811 0.928 0.3534
## full_nameFontana, CA 899.82476 2191.43527
    0.411 0.6814
## full_nameFresno, CA 819.40335 2116.18778
    0.387 0.6986
##   full_nameLas  Vegas,  NV   1592.19934
    1940.42152 0.821 0.4119
##   full_nameLong  Beach,  CA   662.24087
    2193.93048 0.302 0.7628
##   full_nameLos  Angeles,  CA  2794.82749
    1612.92461 1.733 0.0832.
## full_nameModesto, CA 833.39626 2343.61393
    0.356 0.7222
##   full_nameMoreno  Valley,  CA   781.56677
    2371.60346 0.330 0.7418
## full_namePalmdale, CA 939.99695 2229.47917
    0.422 0.6733
##    full_nameParadise,   NV   1685.80998
    2085.70845 0.808 0.4190
## full_nameRancho Cucamonga, CA 936.88335
    2257.34586 0.415 0.6781
## full_nameRiverside, CA 766.13070 2176.88909
    0.352 0.7249
##   full_nameSacramento,   CA   859.79612
    2174.40086 0.395 0.6926
##  full_nameSan Bernardino, CA  896.45732
    2326.50927 0.385 0.7000
##   full_nameSan  Diego,  CA   1148.33270
    1910.10986 0.601 0.5477
##  full_nameSan Francisco, CA  876.85538
    2198.16646 0.399 0.6900
## full_nameSan Jose, CA 841.51465 2087.44521
    0.403 0.6869
## full_nameStockton, CA 744.31164 2370.54147
    0.314 0.7535
## friends_count 1.11952 0.07829 14.300 <2e-16
    ***
## –
## Signif. codes: 0 '***' 0.001 '**' 0.01 '*' 0.05
    '.' 0.1 ' ' 1
##
##  Residual  standard  error:  18040  on  4577
    degrees of freedom
##  Multiple  R-squared:  0.04807,  Adjusted
    R-squared: 0.04391
## F-statistic: 11.56 on 20 and 4577 DF, p-value:
    < 2.2e-16
```

With the data used for this example, the result is a model that has a higher adjusted R^2, as well as a much lower p-value. But now, the local predictors are not significant any more. We have to conclude that we do not find convincing evidence that there is a structural difference between users from different regions, so far.

VISUALIZATION

The implemented tools for visualization are another widely-appreciated feature of R. Especially with complex data it is always very helpful to find a way to present results in a graphical way. Visualization may help to reveal hidden features or flaws in the results, or the graphical representation might be seen as a result on its own.

For many statistical tools in R, there are pre-defined plotting algorithms producing very helpful and high-quality graphics. Normally, these visualizations can be made with the simple command *plot()*. For example, we can call this command on our linear model object *fit2*.

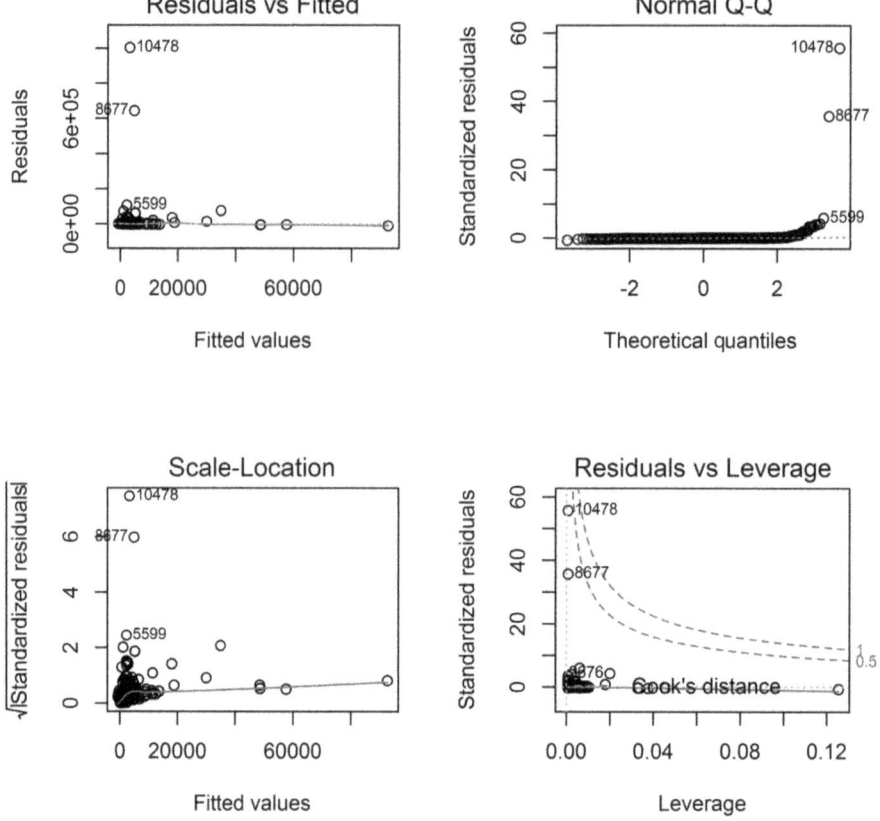

Figure 28.1 Diagnostic plots

```
plot(fit2)
```

This command results in the following four plots (see Figure 28.1):

A detailed explanation of these plots is provided by Teetor (2011, 271). In a nutshell, the plots show the distribution of the residuals in the model and its effect on the model performance. In theory, the residuals should be purely random. Instead, we see that in each representation there are several points that are far away from the position of the other residuals. This must be interpreted as a strong visual hint that the model is ignoring important differences between the datapoints. Probably, there is even a violation of the assumptions made by linear regression.[4]

The next example shows how visualization can be used to gain new insights. Since Twitter provides us with the longitude and latitude data of some of the tweets, we can create a map of California with dots for every tweet. A powerful framework for graphics is provided by the ggplot2-package (Wickham 2009).

The following code is quite complex. We have to create different objects to construct a map of California and repeat some of the cleaning steps to reduce the complexity for plotting. To understand these commands, comments have been added directly to the code. The reader is encouraged to copy this example and to experiment with different parameter settings.

```
# Two additional packages are needed:
library(ggplot2)
library(grid)
# Create an object containing the boundaries of
  California as
```

```
# longuitude and lattitude.
map.data <- map_data("state", region=c
    ("california"))
# We only need the long and lat values from the
    data.
# These are put in a new object.
points <- data.frame(x = as.numeric(tweets.
    df$place_lon),
y = as.numeric(tweets.df$place_lat))
# This line is needed for the second plot, when
    hashtags are added.
points$hashtags <- tweets.df$hashtags
# The next lines are just used to remove points that
    are not specified or
# are incidental too far a way from California.
points[!is.na(tweets.df$lon),    "x"]    <-
    as.numeric(tweets.df$lon)[!is.na(tweets.
    df$lon)]
points[!is.na(tweets.df$lat),    "y"]    <-
    as.numeric(tweets.df$lat)[!is.na(tweets.df$lat)]
points <- points[(points$y > 25 & points$y < 42),]
points <- points[points$x < -114,]
# The following code creates the graphic.
mapPlot <- ggplot(map.data) + # ggplot is the
    basic plotting function used.
# The following lines define the map-areas.
geom_map(aes(map_id = region),
map = map.data,
fill = "white",
color = "grey20",
size = 0.25) +
expand_limits(x = map.data$long,
y = map.data$lat) +
# The following parameters could be altered to
    insert axes, title, etc.
theme(axis.line = element_blank(),
axis.text = element_blank(),
axis.ticks = element_blank(),
axis.title = element_blank(),
panel.background = element_blank(),
panel.border = element_blank(),
panel.grid.major = element_blank(),
plot.background = element_blank(),
plot.margin = unit(0 * c(-1.5, -1.5, -1.5, -1.5),
    "lines")) +
# The next line plots points for each tweet. Size,
    transparency (alpha)
# and color could be altered.
geom_point(data = points,
aes(x = x, y = y),
size = 2,
alpha = 1/20,
color = "steelblue")
mapPlot # This command plots the object.
```

The above code should result in a graphic like Figure 28.2.

This visualization shows us the spatial distribution of tweets. Some of the points are not in California, because the coordinates we had send to Twitter are not that exact. In metropolitan areas like Los Angeles or San Francisco more people seem to use Twitter – which is of course not very surprising. Nevertheless, the spatial distribution of tweets can be very important for a lot of different questions, especially if combined with other filters. For example, we can ask what hashtags are used in which region.

Following exactly the same cleaning procedure as described above, we can identify the hashtags that are used more than two times in our dataset.

```
sel    <-    count(points$hashtags)
    $x[count(points$hashtags
    $freq>2]
sel <- sel[!is.na(sel)]
sel <- points$hashtags %in% sel
hashs <- points[sel,]
hashs <- hashs[!duplicated(hashs$x),]
```

This new table *hashs* can now be used to add the hashtags to the existing plot. Since we created an object of its own containing the plot (mapPlot), we can now add additional features to this plot without re-running all the code.

```
mapPlot2 <- mapPlot +
geom_text(data = hashs,
aes(x = x, y = y, label = hashtags),
position = position_jitter(width=0, height=1),
size = 4,
alpha = 1/2,
color = "black")
mapPlot2
```

As can be seen, we can now analyze what hashtags are important for which region (Figure 28.3).

While there are some hashtags like #job, #MTVHottest, #CecilTheLion, or #retail that seem to appear everywhere in California there are others that are located regionally. #Dodgers is more likely to be found in the LA region while the Bay Area seems to be more interested in #Euroleague.

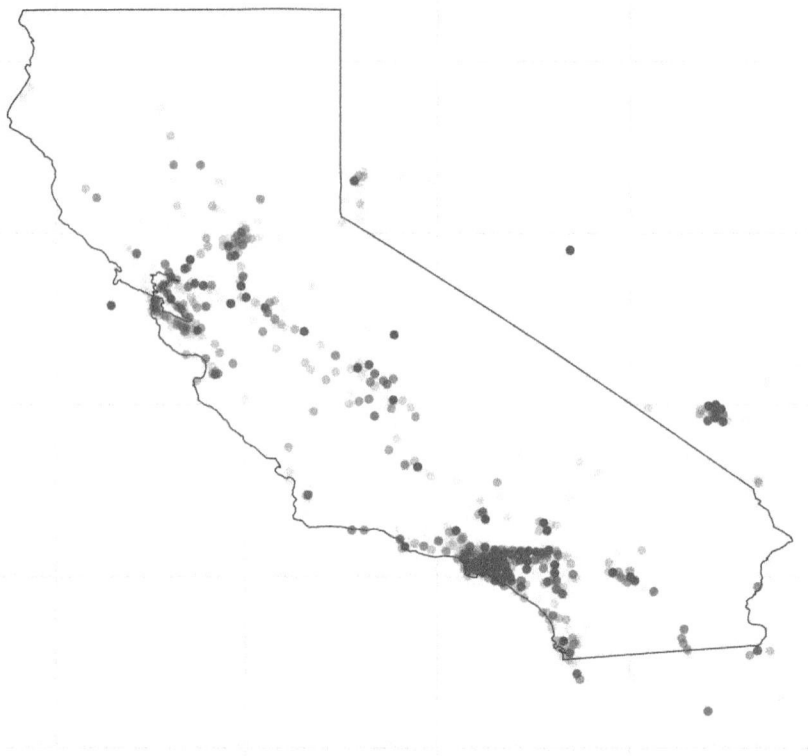

Figure 28.2 Tweets in California

CONCLUSION

Of course, the limited data that was used for these examples does not allow any generalizations of the findings. Nevertheless, the presented methods are suitable to be applied in real data analysis. It has been the aim of this chapter to demonstrate the power and flexibility of R in analyzing social media. R is probably not the fastest way for beginners to come up with any results. But as a general computer language, there is hardly anything in social media analysis that cannot be done with R. The complexity of programming – which seems as a disadvantage at first glance – has one benefit for researchers: If someone is familiar with the R syntax, there are no 'black-boxes'. Every piece of code can be reproduced and analyzed fully. Nothing has to remain secret. In addition, a huge community of experts is offering help on webpage or mailing lists, or in tutorials and publications. This gives the scientist full control over her tools. Especially in the era of big data (Mayer-Schönberger and Cukier 2013) it is important not to follow blindly the advice of

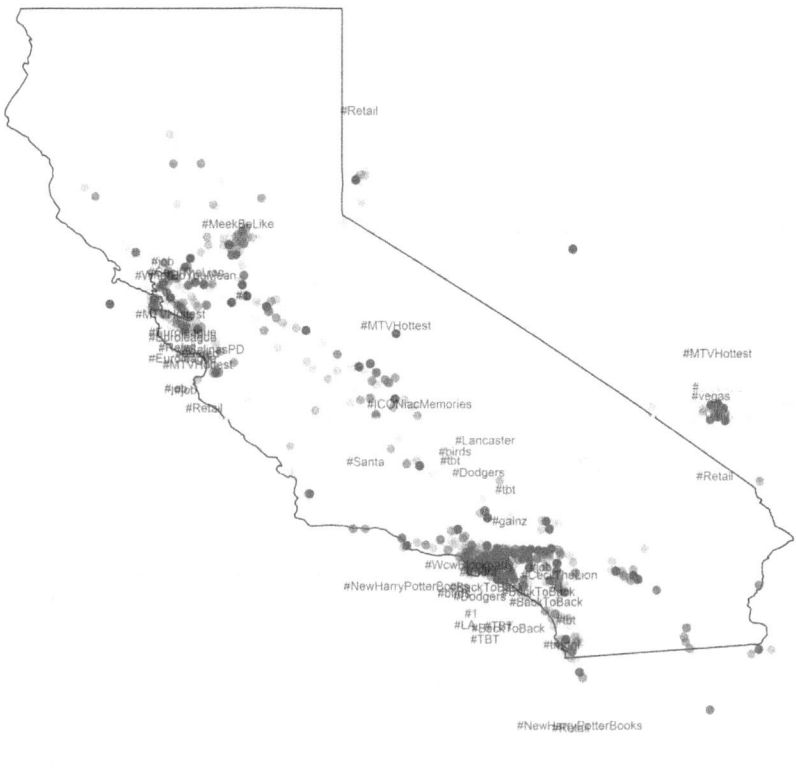

Figure 28.3 Spacial distribution of hashtags

analytical models. Instead a solid understanding of the applied tools has to be the foundation of social media research.

NOTES

1. Julian Hillebrand has written a detailed explanation of the registration process on his blog (Hillebrand, 2013).
2. The presented command only takes the first hashtag of each tweet. To get all hashtags the command was str_extract_all(), but then the cleaning process would be more complicated.
3. There is a huge corpus of introduction literature for different statistical methods like regression (Gelman and Hill 2007), parametric statistics in general (Dormann 2013), or machine learning (James et al. 2013).
4. When dealing with linear regression, more and more reviewers demand diagnostic plots, because it is a very efficient way to judge the performance of a model.

REFERENCES

CRAN. 2015. 'About R'. Accessed 07/28/2015. https://www.r-project.org/about.html.

Dormann, Carsten F. 2013. *Parametrische Statistik: Verteilungen, maximum likelihood und GLM in R*. Heidelberg: Springer-Verlag.

Gelman, Andrew, and Jennifer Hill. 2007. *Data analysis using regression and multilevel/hierarchical models*. New York: Cambridge University Press.

Hillebrand, Julian. 2013. 'Twitter Authentication with R'. Accessed 07/29/2015. http://thinktostart.com/twitter-authentification-with-r/.

James, Gareth, Daniela Witten, Trevor Hastie, and Robert Tibshirani. 2013. *An introduction to statistical learning*: Springer, New York.

Java, Akshay, Xiaodan Song, Tim Finin, and Belle Tseng. 2007. 'Why we twitter: understanding microblogging usage and communities'. Proceedings of the 9th WebKDD and 1st SNA-KDD 2007 workshop on Web mining and social network analysis.

Kaplan, Andreas M, and Michael Haenlein. 2010. 'Users of the world, unite! The challenges and opportunities of social media'. *Business Horizons* 53(1): 59–68.

Kwak, Haewoon, Changhyun Lee, Hosung Park, and Sue Moon. 2010. 'What is Twitter, a social network or a news media?' Proceedings of the 19th international conference on the World Wide Web.

Mayer-Schönberger, Viktor, and Kenneth Cukier. 2013. *Big data: A revolution that will transform how we live, work, and think*. New York: Houghton Mifflin Harcourt.

Muench, Robert A. 2015. 'The Popularity of Data Analysis Software'. Accessed 07/28/2015. http://r4stats.com/articles/popularity/.

Ruths, Derek, and Juergen Pfeffer. 2014. 'Social media for large studies of behavior'. *Science* 346(6213): 1063–1064.

Schutt, Rachel, and Cathy O'Neil. 2013. *Doing data science: Straight talk from the frontline*: O'Reilly Media, Inc., Sebastopol, CA

Teetor, Paul. 2011. *R cookbook*. Sebastopol, CA: O'Reilly Media, Inc.

Twitter-Inc. 2015a. 'Annual Report 2014'. Accessed 07/28/2015. http://www.viewproxy.com/twitter/2015/1/annualreport2014.pdf.

Twitter-Inc. 2015b. 'The Streaming APIs'. Accessed 07/29/2015. https://dev.twitter.com/streaming/overview.

Wickham, Hadley. 2009. *ggplot2: elegant graphics for data analysis*. New York: Springer Science & Business Media.

GATE: An Open-source NLP Toolkit for Mining Social Media

Kalina Bontcheva

This chapter provides a brief introduction to the key social media mining components of the widely-used GATE open source toolkit and infrastructure for Natural Language Processing (NLP). The entire social media mining life cycle is covered, including crowdsourcing annotated corpora for evaluation; reusable linguistic tools (e.g. language identification, POS tagging, named entity recognition, and entity linking); semantic search, visual analytics, and analysing large-scale social media collections via GATE Cloud.

mining social media content at scale and in (near) real-time.

This chapter provides a high-level introduction and overview of the GATE family of open source tools, with focus on how these can be used for mining social media. For a more in-depth reading please refer to the following: GATE (Cunningham et al., 2013), semantic annotation of social media (Bontcheva and Rout, 2014), opinion mining in social media (Maynard et al., 2012), summarising social media (Rout et al., 2013), and using text mining results to drive visual analytics and user and community modelling (Bontcheva and Rout, 2014).

INTRODUCTION

In recent years, social media – and microblogging in particular – have established themselves as high-value, high-volume content, which data scientists increasingly wish to analyse automatically. Researchers have therefore started to study the problem of

In terms of Natural Language Processing (NLP), microblogs are possibly the hardest kind of social media content to process. First, their shortness (maximum 140 characters for tweets) makes them hard to interpret. Consequently, ambiguity is a major problem since NLP methods cannot easily make use of co-reference information. Unlike longer news articles, there is a low amount of discourse information per microblog document, and threaded structure is fragmented across multiple posts.

Second, microtexts also exhibit much more language variation, tend to be less grammatical than longer posts, contain unorthodox capitalisation, and make frequent use of emoticons, abbreviations and hashtags, which can form an important part of the meaning (Derczynski et al., 2013a).

To combat these problems, research has focused on social media and microblog-specific information extraction algorithms (e.g. named entity recognition for Twitter [Ritter et al., 2011; Derczynski et al., 2015], topic and entity disambiguation [Gorrell et al., 2015; van Erp et al., 2013]). Particular attention is given to microtext normalisation, as a way of removing some of the linguistic noise prior to other NLP processing, for example, part-of-speech tagging (Derczynski et al., 2013a; Han and Baldwin, 2011; Han et al., 2012).

GATE: AN OPEN SOURCE FRAMEWORK AND INFRASTRUCTURE FOR SOCIAL MEDIA ANALYSIS

GATE (Cunningham et al., 2013) is a widely used, open source framework for NLP. It comprises a desktop application for researchers developing new algorithms (GATE Developer [Cunningham et al., 2013]); a collaborative web-based text annotation tool (GATE Teamware [Bontcheva et al., 2013a]); an annotation search and visualisation tool (GATE Mímir [Tablan et al., 2015]); and GATE Cloud (Tablan et al., 2013),[1] which is a cloud-based NLP platform-as-a-service with numerous large-scale social media processing and general text mining services.

The process of analysing social media posts with GATE consists of the following steps: optional data collection, automatic text analysis, indexing, search and visualisation. The first data collection stage is optional, as in some cases researchers already have pre-existing social media datasets, for example, from prior papers. If collection of new data is needed, then GATE Cloud has facilities for following a number of user accounts and hashtags through the Twitter 'statuses/filter' streaming Application Programming Interface (API). This produces a JSON file which is saved for later processing. Twitter's own 'hosebird' client library is used to handle the connection to the API, with auto reconnection and backoff-and-retry.

In the case of non-live processing, the collected JSON can be analysed either in GATE Developer (if sufficiently small) or using GATE Cloud to load the JSON files into GATE Documents (one document per tweet), annotate them, and then, if required, index them for search and visualisation in the GATE Mímir framework (Tablan et al., 2015).

GATE Cloud is designed to support the execution of GATE pipelines over large collections of millions of documents, without the researcher needing to implement any code for parallelisation, error recovery, etc. It also provides a number of GATE-based NLP services, accessible via a REST API, which researchers can use to analyse one social media post at a time. At the time of writing, such services include a language identification service, part-of-speech tagger for several languages, named entity recognition (NER), entity disambiguation, and opinion mining. A number of standard input and output data formats are supported, including XML, HTML, and JSON.

In cases where real-time live stream analysis is required, GATE Cloud can be used to feed the incoming tweets into a message queue. A separate GATE-based analysis process (or processes) then reads messages from the queue, analyses them and pushes the resulting annotations and text into Mímir. If the rate of incoming tweets exceeds the capacity of the processing side, more instances of the message consumer are launched across different machines to scale the capacity.

Subsequent sections discuss the kinds of social media analysis components that are currently available in GATE and GATE Cloud, as well as GATE Cloud and GATE M´ımir themselves. First, however, we will introduce GATE Developer, which is the researcher-orientated tool used for developing and testing GATE applications, as well as organising and annotating corpora, evaluating performance quantitatively, and discovery of linguistic patterns within datasets.

GATE DEVELOPER

GATE Developer is a specialist Integrated Development Environment (IDE) for language engineering R&D. It is analogous to systems like Eclipse or Netbeans for programmers, or Mathematica or SPSS for mathematics or statistics work. The system performs tasks such as:

- Visualisation and editing of domain-specific data structures associated with text: annotation graphs, ontologies, terminologies, syntax trees, etc.
- Constructing applications from sets of components (or plugins).
- Measurement, evaluation and benchmarking of automatic systems relative to gold standard data produced by human beings, or to previous runs of variants of experimental setups.

A sophisticated graphical user interface provides access to the models of the GATE architecture and particular instantiations of that architecture.

Figure 29.1 displays a tweet, where the tweet text and JSON tweet metadata are imported as document content. The central pane shows a version of the source text from which formatting markup has been removed (and converted into arcs in an annotation graph associated with the document).

The left pane details resources loaded in the system, including any application being used to annotate the text (e.g. TwitIE – see below) and the documents under analysis. The right pane lists the annotation types that exist in the document. Annotations are organised in annotation sets and here the 'Original markups' set is shown, where the JSON fields are used to create different annotations. For example, a description annotation is created,

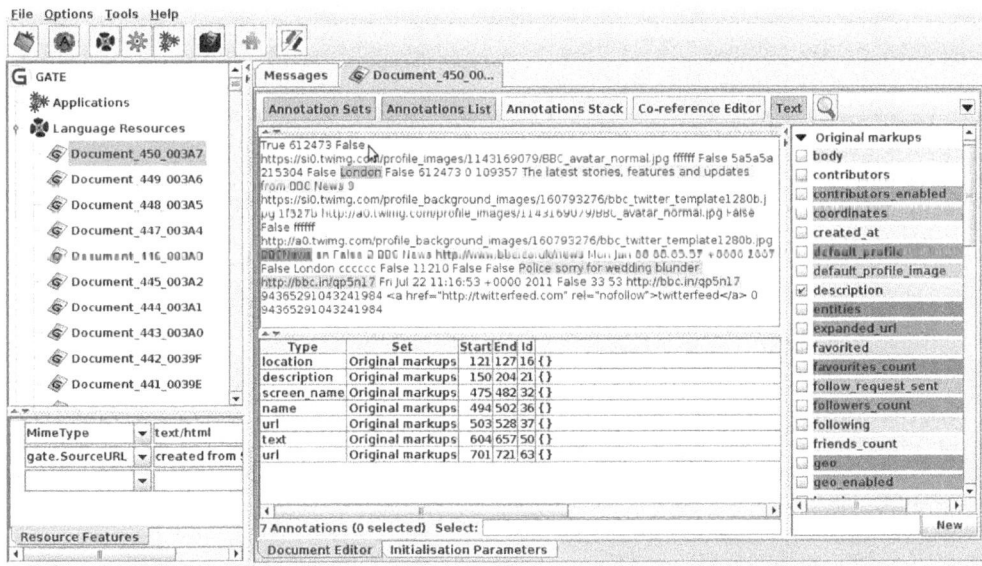

Figure 29.1 The GATE developer interface

which covers the text from the user profile ('The latest stories...'); a text annotation covers the tweet text ('Police sorry for...'), etc. The central pane highlights the selected annotation types and there is also an optional annotations list table underneath, which shows more details on each annotation, including its start and end character offset, any features contained, etc.

THE TWITIE SOCIAL MEDIA ANALYSIS PIPELINE

The ANNIE general purpose information extraction pipeline (Cunningham et al., 2002a) consists of the following main processing resources: tokeniser, sentence splitter, POS tagger, gazetteer lists, finite state transducer (based on GATE's built-in regular expressions over annotations language), orthomatcher and coreference resolver. The resources communicate via GATE's annotation API, which is a directed graph of arcs bearing arbitrary feature/value data, and nodes rooting this data into document content.

The ANNIE components can be used individually or coupled together with new modules in order to create new applications.

Evaluation of ANNIE's performance on tweets (Derczynski et al., 2013a) demonstrated that microblog noise and terseness impact negatively ANNIE's performance. Therefore, a special adaptation of ANNIE, called TwitiE (Bontcheva et al., 2013b), has been created and is now distributed with GATE.

Figure 29.2 shows the TwitIE social media analysis pipeline and its components. Re-used ANNIE components are shown in dashed boxes, whereas the ones in dotted boxes are new and specific to the microblog genre.

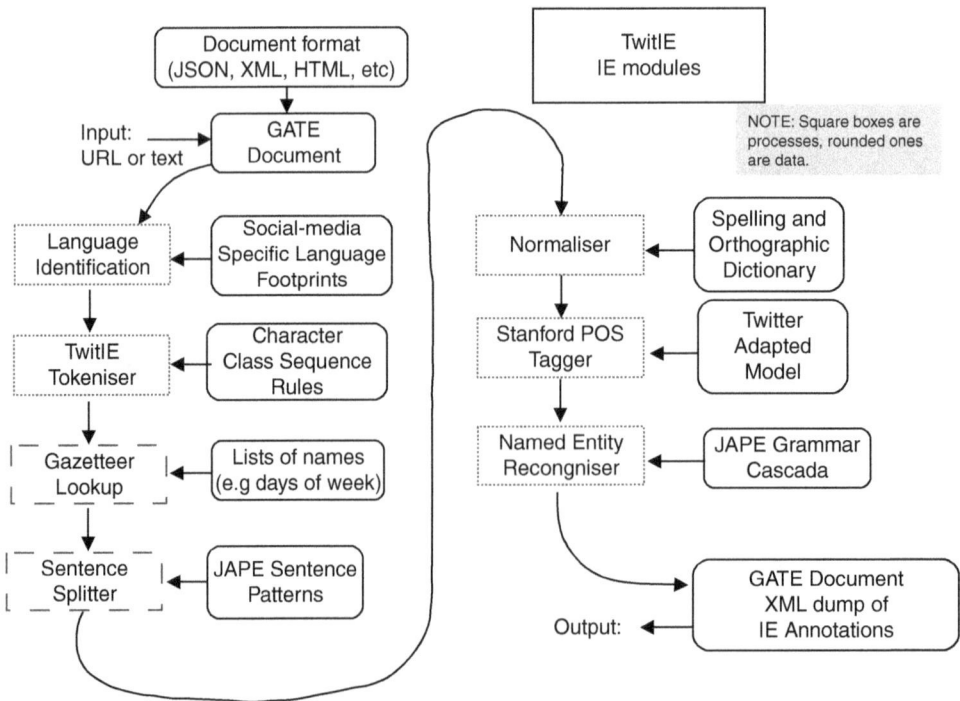

Figure 29.2 The TwitIE information extraction pipeline

The first step is to determine the language in which a document is written, in order to know which tools to apply. The language identification task is thus typically performed before other linguistic processing, having as its goal to output a language suggestion given some unprocessed text. This TwitIE component is based on the TextCat (Cavnar and Trenkle, 1994) language identification algorithm, which relies on n-gram frequency models to discriminate between languages. More specifically, TwitIE integrates the TextCat adaptation to Twitter (Carter et al., 2013), which works currently on five languages. Given a collection of tweets in a new language, it is possible to re-train TwitIE TextCat, via the Fingerprint Generation component (part of GATE's Language_Identification plugin). On the five current languages, overall accuracy is 97.4%, with per language accuracy ranging between 95.2% for French and 99.4% for English (Derczynski et al., 2013a).

The next step is tokenisation, which is the task of splitting the input text into very simple units, called tokens. Tokenisation is a required step in any linguistic processing application, since more complex algorithms typically work on tokens as their input, rather than using the raw text. Consequently, it is important to use a high-quality tokeniser, as errors are likely to affect the results of all subsequent NLP algorithms.

Different languages require different tokenisers, with some easier than others (Mcnamee and Mayfield, 2004). Even punctuation use can differ between languages for the microblog genre, in which 'smileys' (comprised of extended sequences of punctuation symbols) are prevalent.

Commonly distinguished types of tokens are numbers, symbols (e.g. $, %), punctuation and words of different kinds, for example, uppercase, lowercase, mixed case. Tokenising well-written text is generally reliable and reusable, since it tends to be domain-independent. One widely used tokeniser for English is bundled in the open-source ANNIE system in GATE (Cunningham et al., 2002b).

However, such general purpose tokenisers need to be adapted to work correctly on social media, in order to handle specific tokens like URLs, hashtags (e.g. #nlproc), user mentions in microblogs (e.g. @GateAcUk), special abbreviations (e.g. RT, ROFL), and emoticons. A study of 1.1 million tweets established that 26% of English tweets have a URL, 16.6% – a hashtag, and 54.8% – a username mention (Carter et al., 2013). Therefore, tokenising these accurately is very important.

The TwitIE tokeniser is an adaptation of ANNIE's English tokeniser. It follows Ritter's tokenisation scheme (Ritter et al., 2011). More specifically, it treats abbreviations (e.g. RT, ROFL) and URLs as one token each. Hashtags and user mentions are two tokens (i.e.,\# and nike in the above example) with a separate annotation HashTag covering both. Capitalisation is preserved and an orthography feature added. Normalisation and emoticons are handled in optional separate modules, since information about them is not always needed. Consequently, tokenisation is fast and generic, while tailored to the needs of NER.

The gazetteer consists of lists such as cities, organisations, days of the week, etc. It not only consists of entities, but also of names of useful indicators, such as typical company designators (e.g. 'Ltd.'), titles, etc. The gazetteer lists are compiled into finite state machines, which can match text tokens. TwitIE reuses the ANNIE gazetteer lists, at present, without any modification. This was sufficient for the time being, due to the very generic nature of those lists (e.g. country names, days of the week, months, first names).

The sentence splitter is a cascade of finite-state transducers which segments text into sentences. This module is required for the POS tagger. The ANNIE sentence splitter is reused without modification, although when processing tweets, it is also possible to just use the text of the tweet as one sentence, without further analysis. In future work, a more in-depth evaluation of the sentence splitter errors is envisaged.

An optional fifth step is normalisation, where the aim is to correct misspellings and internet slang words and thus reduce linguistic noise. The TwitIE Normaliser is a combination of a generic spelling-correction dictionary and a spelling-correction dictionary, specific to social media. The latter contains entries such as '2moro' and 'brb', similar to (Han et al., 2012).

Part-of-Speech (POS) tagging is concerned with tagging words with their part of speech, by taking into account the word itself, as well as the context in which it appears. A key part of this task is the tagset used and the distinctions that it makes. The main categories are verb, noun, adjective, adverb, preposition, etc. However, tagsets tend to be much more specific, for example, distinguishing between singular and plural nouns. One commonly used tagset is the Penn Treebank one (referred to as PTB) (Marcus et al., 1994).

TwitIE contains an adapted Stanford POS tagger (Toutanova et al., 2003), which has been trained on a mix of hand-annotated tweets, chat data, and news text (see Derczynski et al., 2013b). In addition to the usual word tags, extra tag labels have been added for retweets, URLs, hashtags and user mentions. The POS tagging model currently achieves 90.54% token accuracy, which is a very competitive performance on tweets (Derczynski et al., 2013b).

The last step in TwitIE is NER. This is the task of identifying and classifying mentions of entities (e.g. places, people, locations) in text. Recent NER research has been addressing specifically social media, and Twitter in particular Ritter et al. (2011); Liu et al. (2011); Derczynski et al. (2015); Cano Basave et al. (2013), with multiple recent shared tasks Cano Basave et al. (2013); Baldwin et al. (2015).

TwitIE's NER component is an adaptation of the ANNIE rule-based NER. The main modifications were in adapting the rules to deal better with the poorer capitalisation and the lack of context. In particular, while in longer texts named entities would often be mentioned more than once (e.g. John Smith, John, Mr Smith), social media posts tend to contain only a single mention and; its correct classification would often depend on the social context and/or user's prior knowledge.

ENTITY DISAMBIGUATION AND LINKING WITH YODIE

Many researchers (e.g. Gorrell et al., 2015; Mendes et al., 2011; Hoffart et al., 2011) have studied Linked Open Data-based Named Entity Disambiguation (NED), where names mentioned in text (e.g. London) are linked to URIs in Linked Open Data (LOD) resources (e.g. DBpedia).

Evaluations of NED on social media content (Derczynski et al., 2015) have shown that state-of-the-art approaches tend to perform poorly, due to the limited context, linguistic noise, and use of emoticons, abbreviations and hashtags. Each microblog post is treated in isolation, without taking into account the wider available context. In particular, only tweet text tends to be processed, even though the complete tweet JSON object also includes author profile data (full name, optional location, profile text, and web page).

GATE's NED pipeline is YODIE[2] (Gorrell et al., 2015) and is available for use as a service from GATE Cloud (see 'GATE Cloud: analysing social media at scale'). It combines GATE's existing NER system (ANNIE or TwitIE, depending on the target text genre) with a number of widely used URI candidate selection strategies, similarity metrics, and a machine learning model for entity disambiguation, which determines the best candidate URI (see Gorrell et al., 2015).

YODIE has been adapted specifically to tweets, where readily available contextual information is included from URL content, hashtag definitions, and Twitter user profiles.

Performance evaluation (Gorrell et al., 2015) showed that including URL content significantly improves disambiguation performance. Similarly, user profile information for @mentions improves recall by over 10% with no adverse impact on precision.

USER MENTION CLASSIFICATION WITH GATE

NER in tweets differs from other domains and genres in that references to entities occur not just within the tweet text (e.g. 'I went to Paris with @myBestFriend'), but also in the form of username mentions. Since such mentions are preceded by an @ symbol, they are easy to identify. Previous work (Ritter et al., 2011; Plank et al., 2014) has made the simplifying assumption, however, that they are also trivial to classify, as they always refer to persons. While this was true in the early days of Twitter, there are now many user accounts of organisations (@CNN), locations (@OXO Tower), and products (@iPhone), which motivated us to implement in GATE a component for automatic @mention classification.

While the task of username mention classification is similar to the standard NER task, @mentions differ from other occurrences of named entities in tweets, because they are monosemous, i.e. a given mention always links to the same user profile. These user profiles provide an additional rich context (complementary to tweet texts), which helps with @mention classification. Previous Twitter NER methods have ignored this information, despite it being present in the JSON of each tweet.

Our experiments demonstrated that state-of-the-art social media and news-oriented NER methods do not perform well on @mention classification, since @mentions do not contain whitespaces delimiting token boundaries and tend to be used socially to tag and direct messages in a way, which often does not conform to conventional syntactic and grammatical patterns.

The GATE user mention classifier analyses tweets for @mentions and classifies them automatically as belonging to a person, location, organisation, or other kind of entity (products fall in the latter category). The mention classifier is available for use as a service through GATE Cloud (see 'GATE Cloud: analysing social media at scale'). Its machine learning model uses features derived from the @mention context within the tweet text, as well as metadata and additional textual information in the Twitter profile belonging to this username being classified. Since profile information is already included as standard within the JSON of each tweet, this does not impose additional data gathering overheads.

ANNOTATING TRAINING AND EVALUATION DATASETS WITH GATE

Annotation science (Stede and Huang, 2012) and general purpose corpus annotation tools (e.g. Bontcheva et al., 2013a) have evolved in response to the need for creating high-quality datasets for algorithm training, evaluation, and qualitative analysis. GATE supports document annotation in three different ways: the appropriateness of each depends on the desired size of the human annotated data, annotator availability, and budget.

For smaller datasets, GATE Developer (Cunningham et al., 2011) offers document annotation facilities, based on XML schemas or, alternatively, unrestricted linguistic categories and values. The advantage of the schema based annotation is that it minimises human annotator mistakes and ensures that all annotators conform to the same coding scheme. For instance, GATE has been used to annotate the MPQA corpus (Wiebe et al., 2005) and also in the American National Corpus project (Ide and Suderman, 2005). The main drawback in using the GATE Developer human annotation interfaces is in their orientation towards expert, scientific users (e.g. NLP, digital humanities, computational social science researchers).

For larger annotation projects involving distributed annotator teams, we created GATE Teamware. This is an open-source text annotation framework and a methodology for the implementation and support of larger annotation projects. Documents may be pre-processed automatically, so that human annotators can begin with text that has already been pre-annotated (can lead to improved efficiency). The document annotation user interface is simple to learn, aimed at non-experts, and runs in an ordinary web browser, without need of additional software installation. To lower installation and system administration overheads, Teamware is also offered through GATE Cloud, as a service.

The third method for corpus annotation involves harnessing the wisdom of the crowd, i.e. a large number of non-specialist annotators. Crowdsourcing is a popular collaborative approach for acquiring annotated corpora and a wide range of other linguistic resources (Callison-Burch and Dredze, 2010; Fort et al., 2011; Wang et al., 2012). The GATE Crowdsourcing plugin (Bontcheva et al., 2014a) has been developed to simplify crowdsourcing-based corpus annotation, by mapping transparently longer documents and complex annotation schemes into sets of smaller micro-tasks aimed at the crowd workers, and then, on completion mapping back the crowd judgements onto linguistic annotations on the documents. The HTML-based crowdsourcing user interfaces are also tailored to the specific annotation project and generated automatically. Lastly, basic automatic adjudication strategies, such as majority vote, are also made readily available.

Figure 29.3 shows an example of an automatically generated CrowdFlower interface for sense disambiguation, which is a kind of categorisation task.[3] In this example, there are three fixed-classification categories which apply for all name disambiguation micro annotation tasks, whereas two are specific to the entity being disambiguated (e.g. the possible disambiguations of Paris are different from those of London) and are thus generated automatically by GATE, based on automatic linguistic pre-processing.

A second example appears in Figure 29.4, which shows the CrowdFlower-based user interface for word-constrained sequential selection, which in this case is parameterised for named entity annotation. In sequential selection, sub-units are defined in the UI configuration – tokens, in this example. The crowdworkers are instructed to click on all words that constitute the desired sequence (the annotation guidelines are given as a parameter during the automatic user interface generation).

Unit 366093719

Overheard: Hot Money's Hurried Exit from China http://t.co/fC0AvpeT
Which of the following describes "Hot Money" best? (required)
○ Hot money is a term that is most commonly used in financial markets to refer to the flow of funds (or capital) from one country to another in order to earn a short-term profit on interest rate differences and/or anticipated exchange rate shifts. These speculative capital flows are called "hot money" because they can move very quickly in and out of markets, potentially leading to market instability.,
○ Hot Money is an ITV film first shown in December 2001.,
○ None of the above
○ I cannot decide
○ Not an entity

Figure 29.3 Classication interface: sense disambiguation example

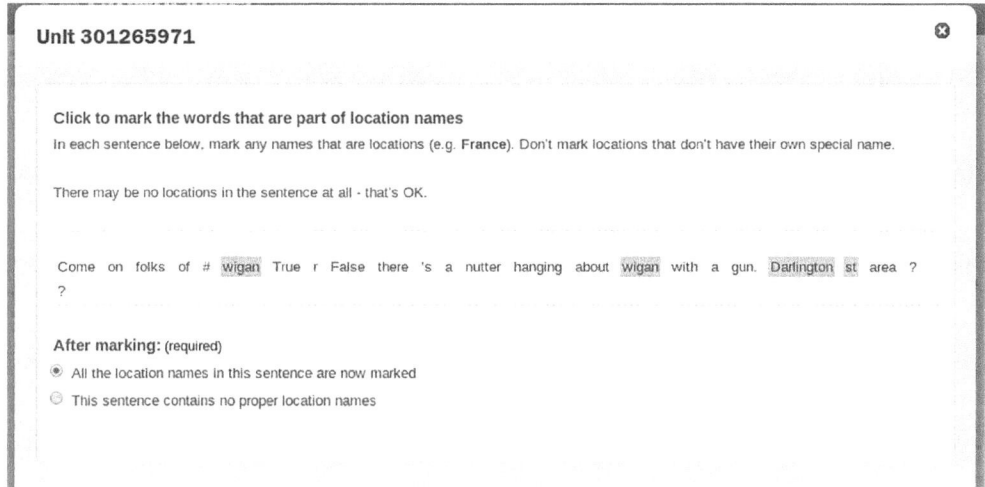

Figure 29.4 Sequential selection interface: named entity recognition example

GATE MÍMIR: SEMANTIC SEARCH AND VISUALISATIONS

Semantic search (Bontcheva et al., 2014b) is more powerful than the more traditional keyword-based search, offering users more precise and relevant results by using the semantics encoded (usually) in ontologies. Google and Facebook refer to such semantics as knowledge graphs (Singhal, 2012). Semantic search requires some NLP techniques for understanding word meaning, typically NER (Ratinov and Roth, 2009) and semantic annotation (Bontcheva and Cunningham, 2011).

The benefit of semantic search, and the grounding of automatically discovered information into ontologies, is that it also enables users to search for knowledge and relationships that are not present explicitly in the documents themselves, for example, which political party an MP represents, so that we can search for all documents written by or which mention MPs from a particular party. It also allows disambiguation of terms: Cambridge, for example, may refer to the city of Cambridge in the UK, to Cambridge in Massachusetts, the University of Cambridge, etc. Similarly, the same entity may be referred to by different surface forms, for example, New York and the Big Apple.

After analysis, the social media posts are indexed using GATE Mímir (Tablan et al., 2015), which enables complex semantic searches to be performed over large volumes of social media and other textual content. Unlike common search engines, such as Google, the query language is not purely keyword based, but instead supports an arbitrary mix of full-text, structural, linguistic and semantic constraints. Rather than just matching documents in which exact words are to be found, GATE Mímir enables a semantic-based search that can be performed over categories of things, for example, all Cabinet Ministers, or all cities in the UK. Search results can include morphological variants and synonyms of search terms, specific phrases with some unknowns (e.g. an instance of a person and a monetary amount in the same sentence), ranges (e.g. all monetary amounts greater than a million pounds), restrictions to certain date periods, domains etc., and any combination of these.

Alongside searches, GATE Mímir supports information discovery tasks, aimed at extracting insights from large volumes of social media content. Such tasks require more sophisticated user interfaces, which enable users first to narrow down the relevant set of documents through an interactive query refinement process, and then to analyse these documents in more detail. These two kinds of actions require corresponding filtering and details-on-demand information visualisations (Shneiderman, 1996).

Such information discovery and visualisation functionalities are provided within GATE Mímir (Tablan et al., 2015) through web-based user interfaces for searching and visualising correlations in large data sets. Any Mímir indexed dataset can be searched, and the analyst can easily interrogate the data and identify correlations, providing a visually enhanced understanding of the content.

For example, based on automatically created linguistic annotations, we can discover and visualise the most frequent topics associated with positive or negative sentiment, or which two topics frequently co-occur in a dynamically selected set of tweets (e.g. tweets mentioning Donald Trump).

Figure 29.5 shows the general purpose UI for exploring associations between semantic annotations/words within a dynamic set of documents returned by a Mímir semantic search query. Here two sets of semantic annotations (political topics vs UK political parties in this case) are mapped to the two dimensions of a matrix (colour intensity of each cell conveys co-occurrence strength). The matrix can be re-ordered by clicking on any row/column, which sorts according to the association strength with the clicked item.

Mímir also supports temporal analytics, such as investigating which topics become more or less popular over a time period, and what events might cause these changes to occur.

GATE CLOUD: ANALYSING SOCIAL MEDIA AT SCALE

GATE Cloud (http://cloud.gate.ac.uk) is an openly available, cloud-based platform which enables researchers to process large volumes of social media and other textual content on-demand and remotely, via a web-based interface or a set of web service APIs. The focus is on multilingual text analysis resources and services, based on the GATE open-source infrastructure. Researchers can also deploy

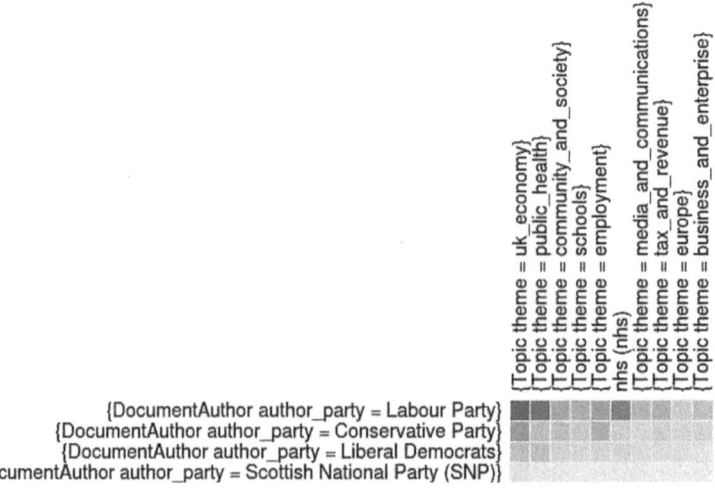

Figure 29.5 Mimir dynamic co-occurrence matrix

their own GATE NLP applications from GATE Developer into GATE Cloud, so they can either run them themselves or make them available to other researchers.

GATE Cloud can also be used to index the automatically annotated documents for enhanced browsing and search on a cloud-based deployment of GATE Mímir.

Using GATE Cloud is straightforward, since cloud infrastructural issues are dealt with by the platform, completely transparently to the user, including load balancing, efficient data upload and storage, deployment on the virtual machines, security, and fault tolerance.

The number of already deployed services on the platform is growing continuously. At the time of writing, there are services of the following kinds:

- Part-of-Speech-Taggers for English (both from ANNIE and TwitIE), German, Dutch, and Hungarian;
- Chunking: the GATE NP and VP chunkers and the OpenNLP ones;
- Parsing: currently the Stanford Parser,[4] but more are under integration;
- Stemming in 15 languages, via the Snowball stemmer;
- NER: in English, German, French, Arabic, Dutch, Romanian, and Bulgarian;
- Social media analysis: language detection, tokenisation, normalisation, POS tagging, and NER;
- Biomedical taggers: the PennBio[5] and the AbGene (Tanabe and Wilbur, 2002) taggers.

DEVELOPING NEW SOCIAL MEDIA ANALYSIS COMPONENTS WITH GATE

The development of social media analysis algorithms and pipelines typically follows a certain methodological pattern, or lifecycle. A central problem is to define the analysis task, such that human annotators can perform it with a high level of agreement and to create high-quality training and evaluation datasets. It is common to use double or triple annotation, where several people perform the annotation task independently and we then measure their level of agreement (*Inter-Annotator Agreement*, or IAA) to quantify and control the quality of this data (Hovy, 2010).

The GATE Cloud platform was therefore designed to offer full methodological support for all stages of the text analysis development lifecycle:

1. Create an initial prototype of the NLP pipeline, testing on a small document collection, using GATE Developer ('GATE: an open source framework and infrastructure for social media analysis').
2. If required, collect a gold-standard corpus for evaluation and/or training, using the GATE Teamware collaborative corpus annotation service (Bontcheva et al., 2013a), running in GATE Cloud, or the GATE crowdsourcing component.
3. Evaluate the performance of the automatic pipeline on the gold standard (either locally in the GATE development environment or on the cloud). Return to step 1 for further development and evaluation cycles, as needed.
4. Upload the large datasets and deploy the NLP pipeline on GATE Cloud.
5. Run the large-scale NLP experiment and download the results as XML or in a standard linguistic annotation format (Ide and Romary, 2004). GATE Cloud also offers scalable semantic indexing and search over the linguistic annotations and document content via GATE Mímir.
6. Analyse any errors, and if required, iterate again over the earlier steps.

CONCLUSION

This chapter provided a high-level overview of the GATE open-source platform for text and social media mining, as well as some of its key components and social media-oriented text analysis tools. They all aim to assist the development and deployment of robust, large-scale social media processing applications, as well as to promote the reuse and repeatability of experiments.

The GATE family of tools and constituent plugins are undergoing continuous development and evaluation, and therefore, for the most up-to-date documentation and research publications please refer to http://gate.ac.uk.

NOTES

1. See https://gatecloud.net
2. See https://gate.ac.uk/applications/yodie.htm
3. The user interface is tailored automatically to the specifics of the categorisation task, other examples being sentiment annotation and manual POS tagging of words.
4. See http://nlp.stanford.edu/software/lex-parser.shtml
5. See http://www.seas.upenn.edu/~strctlrn/BioTagger/BioTagger.html
6. See http://www.pheme.eu/

ACKNOWLEDGEMENTS

This work was supported by funding from the Engineering and Physical Sciences Research Council (grants EP/I004327/1 and EP/K017896/1) and by the EU-funded FP7 Pheme[6] project. The author also wishes to thank Leon Derczynski, Diana Maynard, Mark Greenwood, Dominic Rout, Ian Roberts, Johann Petrak, Genevieve Gorrell, and the rest of the GATE team.

REFERENCES

Baldwin, T., Kim, Y.-B., de Marneffe, M. C., Ritter, A., Han, B., and Xu, W. (2015). Shared Tasks of the 2015 Workshop on Noisy User-generated Text: Twitter Lexical Normalization and Named Entity Recognition. In Xu, W., Han, B., and Ritter, A., editors, *Proceedings of the Workshop on Noisy User-generated Text*, pages 126–135, Beijing, China. Association for Computational Linguistics.

Bontcheva, K. and Cunningham, H. (2011). Semantic annotations and retrieval: Manual, semiautomatic, and automatic generation. In Domingue, J., Fensel, D., and Hendler, J., editors, *Handbook of Semantic Web Technologies*, pages 77–116. Heidelberg: Springer.

Bontcheva, K. and Rout, D. (2014). Making sense of social media through semantics: A survey. *Semantic Web – Interoperability, Usability, Applicability*, 5(5):373–403.

Bontcheva, K., Cunningham, H., Roberts, I., Roberts, A., Tablan, V., Aswani, N., and Gorrell, G. (2013a). GATE Teamware: A Web-based, Collaborative Text Annotation Framework. *Language Resources and Evaluation*, 47:1007–1029.

Bontcheva, K., Derczynski, L., Funk, A., Greenwood, M. A., Maynard, D., and Aswani, N. (2013b). TwitIE: An Open-Source Information Extraction Pipeline for Microblog Text. In *Proceedings of the International Conference on Recent Advances in Natural Language Processing*. Association for Computational Linguistics.

Bontcheva, K., Roberts, I., Derczynski, L., and Rout, D. (2014a). The GATE Crowdsourcing Plugin: Crowdsourcing Annotated Corpora Made Easy. In *Proceedings of the 14th Conference of the European Chapter of the Association for Computational Linguistics (EACL)*. Association for Computational Linguistics.

Bontcheva, K., Tablan, V., and Cunningham, H. (2014b). Semantic search over documents and ontologies. In *Bridging Between Information Retrieval and Databases*, volume 8173, pages 31–53. Springer Verlag.

Callison-Burch, C. and Dredze, M. (2010). Creating speech and language data with Amazon's Mechanical Turk. In *Proceedings of the NAACL HLT 2010 Workshop on Creating Speech and Language Data with Amazon's Mechanical Turk*, pages 1–12.

Cano Basave, A., Varga, A., Rowe, M., Stankovic, M., and Dadzie, A.-S. (2013). Making sense of microposts (#msm2013) concept extraction challenge. *CEUR Workshop Proceedings*, 1019:1–15.

Carter, S., Weerkamp, W., and Tsagkias, E. (2013). Microblog language identification: Overcoming the limitations of short, unedited and idiomatic text. *Language Resources and Evaluation Journal*.

Cavnar, W. and Trenkle, J. (1994). N-gram-based text categorization. In *Proceedings of the Annual Symposium on Document*

Analysis and Information Retrieval, pages 161–175.

Cunningham, H., Maynard, D., Bontcheva, K., and Tablan, V. (2002a). GATE: an Architecture for Development of Robust HLT Applications. In *Proceedings of the 40th Annual Meeting on Association for Computational Linguistics*, pages 168–175.

Cunningham, H., Maynard, D., Bontcheva, K., and Tablan, V. (2002b). GATE: an Architecture for Development of Robust HLT Applications. In *Proceedings of the 40th Annual Meeting on Association for Computational Linguistics, 7–12 July 2002*, ACL '02, pages 168–175, Stroudsburg, PA, USA. Association for Computational Linguistics.

Cunningham, H., Maynard, D., Bontcheva, K., Tablan, V., Aswani, N., Roberts, I., Gorrell, G., Funk, A., Roberts, A., Damljanovic, D., Heitz, T., Greenwood, M. A., Saggion, H., Petrak, J., Li, Y., and Peters, W. (2011). *Text Processing with GATE (Version 6)*. The University of Sheffield: Sheffield UK.

Cunningham, H., Tablan, V., Roberts, A., and Bontcheva, K. (2013). Getting more out of biomedical documents with GATE's full lifecycle open source text analytics. *PLoS Computational Biology*, 9(2):e1002854.

Derczynski, L., Maynard, D., Aswani, N., and Bontcheva, K. (2013a). Microblog-Genre Noise and Impact on Semantic Annotation Accuracy. In *Proceedings of the 24th ACM Conference on Hypertext and Social Media*. ACM.

Derczynski, L., Maynard, D., Rizzo, G., van Erp, M., Gorrell, G., Troncy, R., and Bontcheva, K. (2015). Analysis of named entity recognition and linking for tweets. *Information Processing and Management*, 51:32–49.

Derczynski, L., Ritter, A., Clark, S., and Bontcheva, K. (2013b). Twitter Part-of-Speech Tagging for All: Overcoming Sparse and Noisy Data. In *Proceedings of Recent Advances in Natural Language Processing (RANLP)*. Association for Computational Linguistics.

Fort, K., Adda, G., and Cohen, K. B. (2011). Amazon mechanical turk: Gold mine or coal mine? *Computational Linguistics*, 37(2):413–420.

Gorrell, G., Petrak, J., and Bontcheva, K. (2015). Using @Twitter conventions to improve #lod-based named entity disambiguation. In *The Semantic Web. Latest Advances and New Domains*, pages 171–186. Switzerland, Springer.

Han, B. and Baldwin, T. (2011). Lexical normalisation of short text messages: makn sens a #twitter. In *Proceedings of the 49th Annual Meeting of the Association for Computational Linguistics: Human Language Technologies*, HLT '11, pages 368–378.

Han, B., Cook, P., and Baldwin, T. (2012). Automatically constructing a normalisation dictionary for microblogs. In *Proceedings of the Conference on Empirical Methods in Natural Language Processing*, pages 421–432. ACL.

Hoffart, J., Yosef, M. A., Bordino, I., Furstenau, H., Pinkal, M., Spaniol, M., Taneva, B., Thater, S., and Weikum, G. (2011). Robust disambiguation of named entities in text. In *Conference on Empirical Methods in Natural Language Processing*, pages 782–792.

Hovy, E. (2010). Annotation. In *Tutorial Abstracts of ACL*. The Association for Computational Linguistics. Retrieved August 9, 2016 from http://acl2010.org/tutorials.html

Ide, N. and Romary, L. (2004). Standards for language resources. *Natural Language Engineering*, 10:211–225.

Ide, N. and Suderman, K. (2005). Integrating linguistic resources: The American national corpus model. In *Proceedings of Human Language Technology Conference/Conference on Empirical Methods in Natural Language Processing HLT/EMNLP 2005*, Vancouver, B.C., Canada.

Liu, X., Zhang, S., Wei, F., and Zhou, M. (2011). Recognizing named entities in tweets. In *Proceedings of the 49th Annual Meeting of the Association for Computational Linguistics: Human Language Technologies*, pages 359–367.

Marcus, M. P., Santorini, B., and Marcinkiewicz, M. A. (1994). Building a large annotated corpus of english: The Penn Treebank. *Computational Linguistics*, 19(2):313–330.

Maynard, D., Bontcheva, K., and Rout, D. (2012). Challenges in developing opinion mining tools for social media. In *Proceedings of @NLP can u tag #usergeneratedcontent?! Workshop at LREC 2012*, Turkey.

Mcnamee, P. and Mayfield, J. (2004). Character n-gram tokenization for European language text retrieval. *Information Retrieval*, 7(1):73–97.

Mendes, P. N., Jakob, M., Garc´ıa-Silva, A., and Bizer, C. (2011). DB-pedia Spotlight: Shedding light on the web of documents. In *Proceedings of the 7th International Conference on Semantic Systems*, pages 1–8.

Plank, B., Hovy, D., McDonald, R., and Søgaard, A. (2014). Adapting taggers to Twitter with not-so-distant supervision. In Tsujii, J. and Hajic, J., editors, *Proceedings of COLING: Technical Papers*, pages 1783–1792, Dublin, Ireland. Dublin City University and Association for Computational Linguistics.

Ratinov, L. and Roth, D. (2009). Design challenges and misconceptions in named entity recognition. In *Proceedings of the Thirteenth Conference on Computational Natural Language Learning*, pages 147–155. Association for Computational Linguistics.

Ritter, A., Clark, S., Mausam, and Etzioni, O. (2011). Named entity recognition in tweets: An experimental study. In *Proc. of Empirical Methods for Natural Language Processing (EMNLP)*, Edinburgh, UK.

Rout, D., Bontcheva, K., and Hepple, M. (2013). Reliably evaluating summaries of twitter timelines. In *Proceedings of the AAAI Symposium on Analyzing Microtext*.

Shneiderman, B. (1996). The eyes have it: a task by data type taxonomy for information visualizations. In *Proceedings of the IEEE Symposium on Visual Languages*, pages 336–343.

Singhal, A. (2012). Introducing the knowledge graph: things, not strings. http://googleblog.blogspot.it/2012/05/introducing-knowledge-graph-things-not.html.

Stede, M. and Huang, C.-R. (2012). Inter-operability and reusability: the science of annotation. *Language Resources and Evaluation*, 46:91–94. 10.1007/s10579–011-9164-x.

Tablan, V., Bontcheva, K., Roberts, I., and Cunningham, H. (2015). M´ımir: an open-source semantic search framework for interactive information seeking and discovery. *Journal of Web Semantics*, 30:52–68.

Tablan, V., Roberts, I., Cunningham, H., and Bontcheva, K. (2013). Gatecloud.net: a platform for large-scale, open-source text processing on the cloud. *Philosophical Transactions of the Royal Society A*, 371(1983).

Tanabe, L. and Wilbur, W. J. (2002). Tagging Gene and Protein Names in Full Text Articles. In *Proceedings of the ACL-02 workshop on Natural Language Processing in the biomedical domain, 7–12 July 2002*, volume 3, pages 9–13, Philadelphia, PA. Association for Computational Linguistics.

Toutanova, K., Klein, D., Manning, C. D., and Singer, Y. (2003). Feature-rich part-of-speech tagging with a cyclic dependency network. In *Proceedings of the 2003 Conference of the North American Chapter of the Association for Computational Linguistics on Human Language Technology*, NAACL '03, pages 173–180.

van Erp, M., Rizzo, G., and Troncy, R. (2013). Learning with the Web: Spotting Named Entities on the Intersection of NERD and Machine Learning. In *Proceedings of the 3rd Workshop on Making Sense of Microposts (#MSM2013)*.

Wang, A., Hoang, C., and Kan, M. Y. (2012). Perspectives on crowdsourcing annotations for natural language processing. *Language Resources and Evaluation*, Mar: 1–23.

Wiebe, J., Wilson, T., and Cardie, C. (2005). Annotating expressions of opinions and emotions in language. *Language Resources and Evaluation*, 39(2–3):165–210.

A How-to for Using Netlytic to Collect and Analyze Social Media Data: A Case Study of the Use of Twitter During the 2014 Euromaidan Revolution in Ukraine

Anatoliy Gruzd, Philip Mai and Andrea Kampen

For many people today, posting a photograph of a vacation on Instagram, engaging in a discussion about politics on Twitter, or sharing information about a fundraising event on Facebook are now part of their daily routine. All of these activities on social media are contributing to a social media data explosion. The availability of these new types of data opens up novel possibilities for Internet researchers and social scientists, allowing them to ask and answer new questions about the human condition. There are now many new tools that can help researchers to collect, analyze and visualize social media data, allowing them to better understand changing patterns of communication and are shedding light on how people meet, communicate and develop social relationships. This chapter will review one such tool called Netlytic, which is being developed by the Social Media Lab at Ryerson University. In particular, to demonstrate how and what researchers can learn from using Netlytic, this chapter will use a dataset containing Twitter messages about the 2014 Euromaidan revolution in Ukraine. As part of this case study, we investigated whether the types of messages and users who were discussing the Euromaidan protests would differ based on the language in which the conversations were conducted: Ukrainian, Russian, or English.

INTRODUCTION

For every minute of every day, Instagram users are posting nearly 220,000 new photos, Twitter users post 300,000 tweets and Facebook users share almost 2.5 million pieces of content (Gunelius, 2014). The data, both active (data generated by and visible to the users) and passive (data generated by the system based on the users' interaction with the system), are becoming increasingly cheaper to store and can be accessed quickly and automatically. The availability of these new types of data opens up novel possibilities for Internet researchers and social scientists, allowing them to ask and answer new questions about the human condition. There are now many new tools that can help researchers to collect, analyze and visualize social media data, allowing researchers to better understand changing patterns of communication and shedding light on how people today meet, communicate and develop social relationships.

This chapter will briefly review some of the existing tools for social media data collection and analysis, and will focus in detail on one particular analytic tool called Netlytic, which is being developed by the Social Media Lab at Ryerson University (Social Media Lab, 2016a). Netlytic is a tool that can collect publically available data from various social media platforms and can help researchers to examine the conversations that are emerging online and discover communication patterns through various interactive visualizations.

To demonstrate how and what researchers can learn from using a social media analytic tool such as Netlytic, this chapter will use a dataset containing Twitter messages (tweets) about the 2014 Euromaidan revolution in Ukraine. The Euromaidan revolution case study provides an interesting dataset because of the polarizing opinions – to either strengthening ties with the European Union or Russia – that are part of the discussion. It is fascinating to explore how, and if, there is a dialogue between the various opinion groups as well as who influential Twitter members are and how they are impacting the conversation.

EXISTING SOCIAL MEDIA ANALYSIS TOOLS

This section briefly outlines various peer-tested social media analysis tools. Though this overview is not exhaustive, its goal is to demonstrate the wide variety of tools that are available to researchers for collecting, analyzing and visualizing social media data. See the Social Media Lab website (2016b) to access a comprehensive comparison table of the features available in the tools discussed below.

Foller.me

Foller.me is an analytical tool designed specifically for Twitter. Foller.me is able to analyze tweets and provide statistics such as the number of followers, friends, following-to-followers ratio, time that the user is more active, content and topics of tweets (including attitude through use of emoticons), as well as retweets, tags, mentions, replies and more. Additionally, Foller.me provides some unique information that is not generally available including join date, time zone and followers' ratio of any given public Twitter account. In one of the studies that relied on this tool, Sullivan (2014) completed a rhetorical analysis of the live tweeting of the Watergate Mall crisis in Nairobi. In particular, Foller.me allowed the researcher to evaluate the social media strategy used by the terrorist group during the Westgate hostage crisis and to gauge its effectiveness.

NodeXL

NodeXL is an add-on for Excel designed to create, analyze and visualize social and communication networks with data from social media sites (Smith, 2014). The tool allows for direct data collection from Twitter, YouTube, Flickr and email as well as provides data collection plugins for Facebook and Wikis. One of the especially useful features of NodeXL is that it automatically analyzes group connectedness and then detects and annotates emerging clusters of highly connected network actors. NodeXL also automatically calculates various social network analysis (SNA) measures such as degree centrality, betweenness centrality, closeness centrality and more (Hansen et al., 2011). These network visualizations and SNA measures give researchers the opportunity to learn how and why people are connected on social media sites. This tool has been used in a variety of research projects including studies of: how wikipedians form virtual teams and set policy for large online groups (Black et al., 2011) and how Saudi youth uses social media for political conversations (Al-Khalifa, 2011).

Tweet Archivist

For a fee, Tweet Archivist collects tweets that can later be downloaded or archived. This web-based system also has some basic data analytics and visualization functions. With these functions, the researcher is able to extract various pieces of data including user, text, URLs, and hashtags. By using the various features, such as top users or top words, researchers can identify the most influential members of the conversation. Hashtag analytics can also be collected from Instagram, Vine and Tumblr through the Tag Sleuth add-on, which measures how hashtags compare across social networks. It analyzes top users, words, most popular posts, hashtags and more, which helps the user identify influential users and how effective the campaign is. Researchers Billings et al. (2015) used this tool to collect Twitter data from four 2014 FIFA World Cup matches involving the United States. They identified how Twitter users talked about the competition between the nations playing soccer.

NVivo/NCapture

By using the NCapture add-on, the NVivo platform can scrutinize Twitter, Facebook, and YouTube to collect and organize content. The software enables researchers to analyze the unstructured data through both manual and automated text analysis and visualization. NVivo's query tools empower the researcher to uncover trends. It allows for searching of an exact word or words of similar meaning. This provides researchers with the opportunity to see connections and links within the textual data that would be difficult to identify without the NVivo analysis capabilities. It also helps to develop manual coding schema by offering drag and drop functions and allowing the user to apply their own color choices to highlight different parts of text. Some basic visualization tools such as charts, maps and models are available in NVivo. Research of social media content collected through NCapture and analyzed using NVivo ranged from evaluating Twitter use by people with severe physical and communication disabilities participating actively in online communication forums (Hemsley, Palmer & Balandin, 2014), to examining how shortages of electricity impact daily routines in Pakistan (Lodhi & Malik, 2013).

Webometrics Analyst

Another tool for social media data collection and analysis is Webometrics Analyst. It is capable of retrieving data from Twitter, YouTube, Flickr, Mendeley and more. Once collected, the data can be exported as raw data files, summary tables, or network diagrams. Researchers can use the impact analysis feature to identify top used terms or links between websites to identify connections between online content. Webometrics Analyst has been used to analyze audience comments on antismoking campaigns posted on YouTube by the Centers for Disease Control and Prevention (Chung, 2015). The tool was used specifically to analyze the connections between the commenters. Webometrics was also used in investigating the impact of TED (Technology,

Entertainment, Design) videos in the public sphere and academic domain (Sugimoto & Thelwall, 2013). Using the tool, researchers were able to collect and extract the number of views, comments, positive and negative ratings, and the number of times the video had been favorited.

Textexture

This tool can be used to visualize any text as a network. It has been used in the past to analyze content collected from transcribed YouTube videos as well as Tumblr and text from articles. The visual summary of the most relevant text to the topic being searched in a dataset gives researchers a non-linear way to read the text. It does this by creating networks to indicate connections between related words. The user can also interact with the visualization by clicking on the nodes, which are representing words. This shows the text containing each word and the user can then identify if the text is of interest or pertinent to their research goals. Textexture was used to analyze Russian presidential addresses to identify key topics as well as changes of vocabulary (Paranyushkin, 2013).

Open Source Packages

When considering the right tool for a project, a researcher must balance what the tool can do as well as its cost – whether it be the cost of time or money. The tools mentioned above range from free to a nominal fee, to a significant cost. There are also many open source social media mining projects that offer an economical alternative to paid services. Many are available through GitHub, a website where users are able to upload, share and collaborate on their source codes.

Several tools are affiliated with academic institutions such as STACK (Social Media Tracker, Analyzer, & Collector Toolkit), developed at Syracuse University, SOCRATES (Rutgers University), SocialTap (Clemson University), and DMI-TCAT (University of Amsterdam). Many of these tools use Twitter API to collect data, while others cast a wider net to include Google and Wikipedia. Many of these open source programs offer robust import, filter and visualization options and – more importantly – the ability to modify the original code in order to customize the program to fit a scholar's particular research needs.

Limitations and Other Considerations

Open source social media mining packages can be very useful to social media researchers. However, using these tools may come with steep learning curves and some may require a high-level of technical know-how and a significant commitment of resources such as time and money. For example, many of the open source packages require researchers to learn how to use Python or JSON, which may be beyond the scope of the researcher's project. Additional challenges include the lack of computational infrastructure to install and run these programs. These limitations could stall, or even cause a researcher to reconsider the type of project they are able to complete. There are currently a few research-focused tools, such as those mentioned above, that have been designed to address some of these obstacles and limitations. In this chapter, we will focus on the use of one such tool, Netlytic, and demonstrate its ability to handle social media data originating from various platforms.

NETLYTIC (NETLYTIC.ORG)

This section will take a closer look at Netlytic, a cloud-based social media analytics tool designed specifically for researchers. Netlytic allows users to automatically capture, import, export, share, analyze and visualize social media data from the following platforms: Twitter, Facebook, Instagram, YouTube, Cloud Storage, Text files and Rich Site Summary (RSS) feeds. Netlytic contains an easy to use text analyzer and a powerful interactive network analysis and visualization tool powered by SNA metrics. With Netlytic, users can quickly explore the themes emerging in a discussion and the nature of interactions, and visualize communication networks to discover social connections.

Netlytic can transform large quantities of textual and online conversational data into concise visual representations (e.g., word clouds, concept maps, communication networks). Netlytic is unique among the available social media research tools in that it offers researchers the ability to conduct both text and network analysis. It also allows the researcher to drill down and examine each of the individual records contained in the dataset and find out how that particular record was used to create the various data visualizations created within Netlytic. For instance, a researcher can click on a node in the network visualization to discover the user and can then dig further to see individual tweets, and further still to see if and by whom the tweet was retweeted. This level of control over the dataset gives researchers the ability to better understand and contextualize their data.

Previous Scholarship with Netlytic

Netlytic was created in 2006 to analyze a large archive of bulletin board postings from online courses, collected over a number of years (Haythornthwaite & Gruzd, 2007, 2008). The challenge at that time was to find a better way to analyze the posts without having to read each and every single message posted on the bulletin board. Since then, Netlytic has grown to become a robust cloud-based text and social network analyzer which can efficiently summarize large volumes of texts and discover social networks from conversational online text. Today, Netlytic can be used to collect and analyze data from a wide variety of popular social media platforms such as Twitter, Facebook, YouTube, Instagram and blogs. Netlytic can also allow users to upload and analyze their own dataset as a text file as RSS feeds or a Comma-Separated Values (CSV) file.

Netlytic has been used by researchers to study a variety of online communities and topics, ranging from studying fans of J.R.R. Tolkien's books and film buffs who watched Peter Jackson's film adaptation of *The Lord of the Rings* (Martin, Gruzd, & Howard, 2013), to how a health care community of practice operated on Twitter (Gruzd & Haythornthwaite, 2013). In another example, Gruzd, Wellman, and Takhteyev (2011) employed the tool to examine one person's Twitter network to see if a communication medium limited to 140 characters can help to foster a real 'sense of community' as defined by McMillan and Chavis (1986). The study showed conclusively that Twitter can be a very important tool for people to create and maintain social connections. In another case study, Gruzd (2009a) examined the way that online communities of blog readers and commentators form and operate around a popular real estate blog; showing that a vibrant online community can exist and thrive on platforms that were not originally designed to sustain such communities.

Netlytic also helped to study the use of social media by local communities. For example, Hampton (2010) used Netlytic to study neighborhoods that adopted the Internet to support local information exchange. Harder et al. (2015) used Netlytic to study how Twitter was used to facilitate discussions around the One Book Nova Scotia initiative in a Canadian province. Additionally, Alyami

Table 30.1 Case Study Datasets

Search keyword	'Україна'	' Украина'	'Ukraine'
Presumed language	Ukrainian	Russian	English
Number of tweets	200,956	527,112	591,394
Number of unique users	46,641	141,541	246,113

and Toze (2014) relied on Netlytic to study how people use social media for local information seeking.

Data Collection

As noted above, to demonstrate how Netlytic works, we will present a case that will illustrate how we used it to collect and analyze tweets about the 2014 Euromaidan revolution in Ukraine to discover who was talking about the crisis and how it was being discussed on Twitter. We also investigated whether the types of tweets and users who were discussing the Euromaidan protests would differ based on the language in which the conversations were conducted. In particular, we wanted to know what the Euromaidan conversation would look like in Ukrainian vs. Russian (the second most common language in Ukraine) and vs. English.

To start our data collection, we instructed Netlytic to collect three concurrent samples of public tweets that mentioned the word 'Ukraine' in three different languages: (1) Ukrainian, (2) Russian, and (3) English. The three datasets were collected by querying the Twitter Public Search API hourly to retrieve up to 1,000 most recent tweets per request beginning from February 18, 2014, when the protests on Maidan Square in Kyiv – the capital of Ukraine – turned deadly, to March 14, 2014, the date leading up to the referendum held in Crimea on whether Crimea – an autonomous republic within Ukraine – should leave Ukraine and join Russia or remain a part of Ukraine. Table 30.1 summarizes the resulting datasets.

Text Analysis

Word Cloud Visualization

Once the datasets were collected, we used Netlytic's text analysis features to conduct a textual analysis of the data. To do this, Netlytic first extracts frequently used words. To find frequently used words, the system removes all common words – such as 'of', 'will', 'to' (also known as 'stopwords') – as they do not carry any meaning by themselves. Netlytic also allows the researcher to further refine the resulting words list by giving researchers the ability to remove user-defined 'stopwords' such as those that one would expect to find in a dataset due to a particular data collection strategy. Doing this removes words that might be redundant since they do little to deepen the researchers' understanding of what is in the dataset. In our case, we manually removed the search keywords used to collect each dataset (i.e., removed 'Україна' from the 'Ukrainian' dataset, 'Украина' from the 'Russian' dataset, 'Ukraine' from the 'English' dataset) as these words are expected to be in each of the corresponding datasets.

Netlytic is capable of visualizing the frequently used words as an interactive word cloud and a 'stacked' graph (see Figures 30.1 and 30.2). The resulting visualizations help to bring important topics to the forefront as well as highlight common vocabulary used by people in the dataset.

We then examined a word cloud containing the top 50 frequently used words (users can choose to examine the top 30, 50 or 100 words in their dataset) during

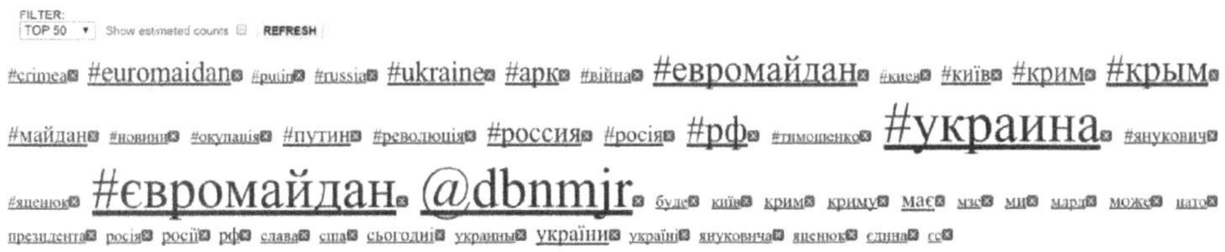

(a) Dataset of tweets mentioning the word "Ukraine" in Ukrainian

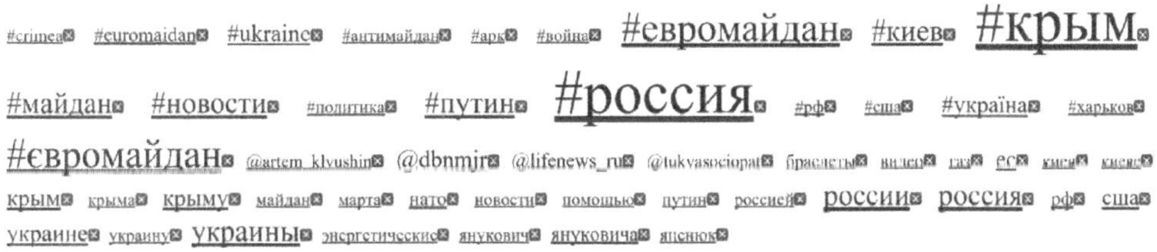

(b) Dataset of tweets mentioning the word "Ukraine" in Russian

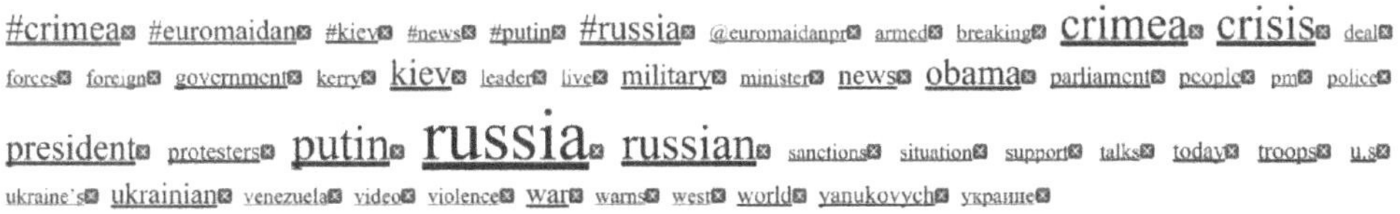

(c) Dataset of tweets mentioning the word "Ukraine" in English

Figure 30.1 Frequently used words in the three datasets (after removing 'stopwords')

the data collection period. We immediately noticed that there is a considerable overlap between all three datasets in terms of the topics and hashtags covered. All three datasets frequently mentioned 'Euromaidan', 'Russia' and 'Crimea'. The word 'Euromaidan' is the name given by the activists to their movement ('Євромайдан' in Ukrainian or 'Евромайдан' in Russian), the word 'Russia' refers to the name of the country involved in the conflict ('Росія' in Ukrainian, 'Россия' in Russian, 'Russia' in English), and the third word 'Crimea' ('Крим' in Ukrainian, 'Крым' in Russian, 'Crimea' in English), is the name of the geographical area (peninsula) annexed by Russia.

From examining the word clouds, we also noticed some clear differences in the most frequently used words between our three datasets. In the Ukrainian language dataset, the Twitter handle '@dbnmjr' is much more prominent. This account is a pro-Ukrainian news account covering events around the Euromaidan revolution in both Ukrainian and Russian languages. The fact that this Twitter account is more prominent in the 'Ukrainian' dataset points to a stronger presence of pro-Euromaidan supporters among tweeps, a person's followers on Twitter, who were tweeting about 'Ukraine' in Ukrainian. Twitter users often retweeted or mentioned this particular account in the Ukrainian language, thus

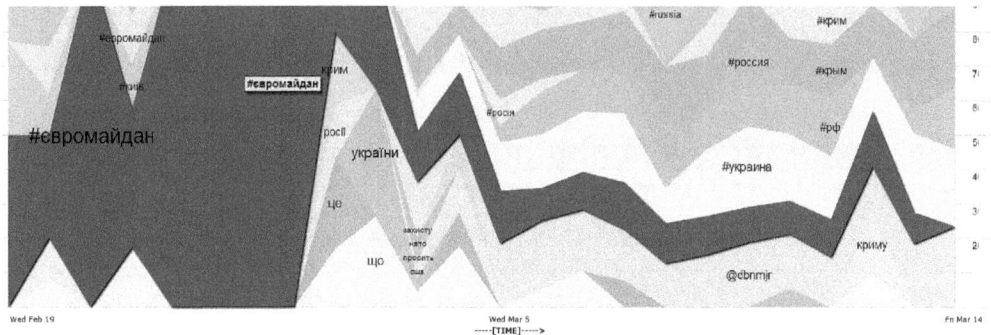

(a) Dataset of tweets mentioning the word "Ukraine" in Ukrainian

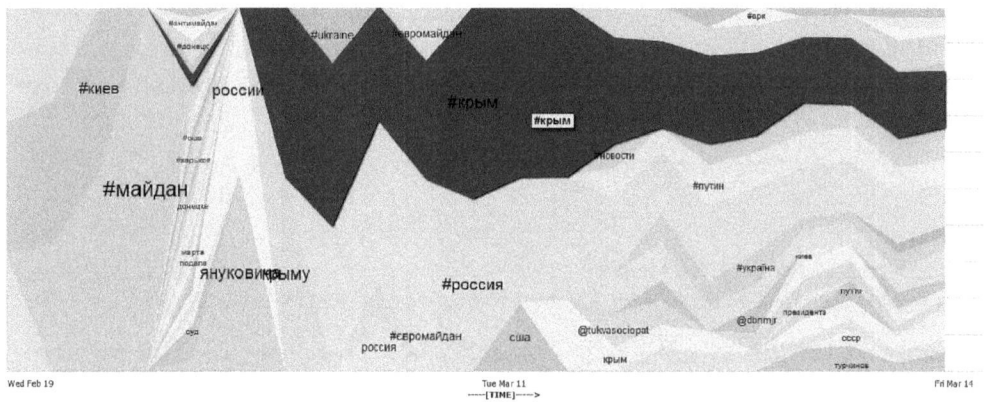

(b) Dataset of tweets mentioning the word "Ukraine" in Russian

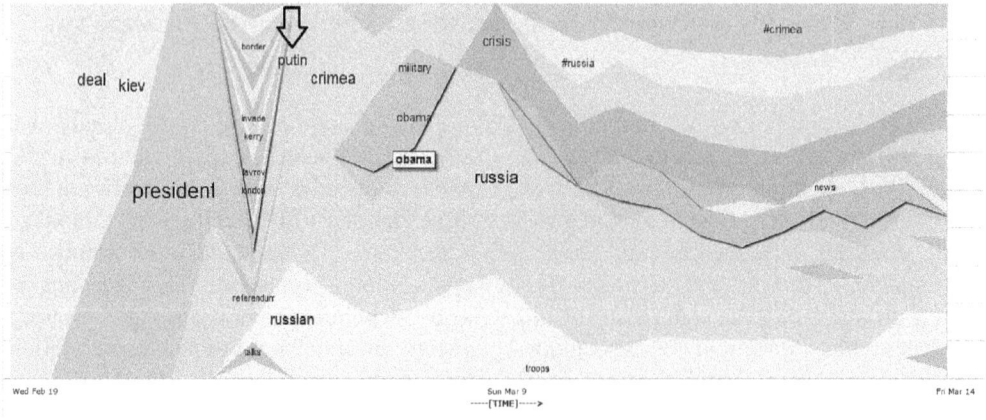

(c) Dataset of tweets mentioning the word "Ukraine" in English

Figure 30.2 Frequently used word in the three datasets displayed over time (after removing 'stopwords')

raising its prominence in the dataset. In the 'English' dataset, President Obama is more frequently mentioned, perhaps reflecting his perceived central role in the conflict resolution process by English speaking users who were posting about Ukraine.

Stacked Charts

Next, we examined the same set of frequently used words, visualizing them over time using so-called *stacked* charts, another feature found in the text analysis step in Netlytic (see Figure 30.2). From examining and comparing the stacked charts, it is easy to see that each dataset exhibits a unique 'signature'. The 'Ukrainian' dataset shows the prominence of the 'Євромайдан' hashtag ('Euromaidan') at the beginning of the dataset (during the protests in Kyiv) and then its usage slowly declined as the focus shifted from the events in Kyiv, the capital of the country, to the brewing crisis in Crimea, the autonomous breakaway region in Ukraine.

The *stacked* charts for the 'Russian' dataset showed that discussants who used the Russian language to talk about events in Ukraine focused on the events in Crimea almost from the beginning. This can be explained by the fact that the majority of Russians had strongly supported the Russian intervention in Crimea (Arutunyan, 2014) which might explain the high volume of tweets on this topic posted by Russian speaking Twitter users.

Finally, tweets in the 'English' dataset frequently mentioned both President Obama and Putin at the same time, but interestingly there were few mentions of Ukrainian political leaders by their names. The last observation may be indicative of the power vacuum that was in Ukraine at the time; as a result, the conflict in Ukraine might have been viewed by the Western media primarily as the latest flare-up of the ongoing proxy war between the two old rivals on the world stage, Russia and the United States. Another possible explanation of why Ukrainian politicians were absent from this chart could be because the data was collected during the regime of an acting president and a provisional government in Ukraine. The leaders might have been less known in the West at the time and were thus less likely to be mentioned on Twitter.

Concept Coding

In addition to examining frequently used words, Netlytic includes a feature that allows researchers to group a set of words or phrases into broader categories representing high-level concepts such as 'anger', 'disappointment', 'happiness', 'satisfaction', 'social presence' etc. Once each category is defined and entered into the system by the researcher, the system will automatically count the number of posts from the dataset that correspond to each category. This allows the researcher to identify what categories are prevalent in a particular dataset. Due to the space limitation, we will not cover this feature in detail here, but we direct interested readers to read an exemplar paper by Martin et al. (2013) on how to apply this feature to answer some interesting research questions. Specifically, Martin et al.'s paper shows how the use of semi-automated concept coding helped researchers analyze an online discussions related to J.R.R. Tolkien's and Peter Jackson's *The Lord of the Rings* and helped to better understand the formation of mental imagery by members of a fan online community.

Network Analysis

Network Discovery

Netlytic's final analysis step is a network analysis. This step builds and visualizes communication networks from the available data. Netlytic can build two types of social networks: (1) name network (also known as '*who mentions whom*') and (2) chain network (or '*who replies to whom*'). When applied to Twitter data, the name network approach connects Twitter users if one mentions, retweets or replies to another. The chain network only connects one Twitter user to another if he or she directly replies to another user (in other words, if the message starts with @*username* in accordance with Twitter's conversational convention). Figure 30.3 demonstrates what connections (or ties) would be discovered by each of the two

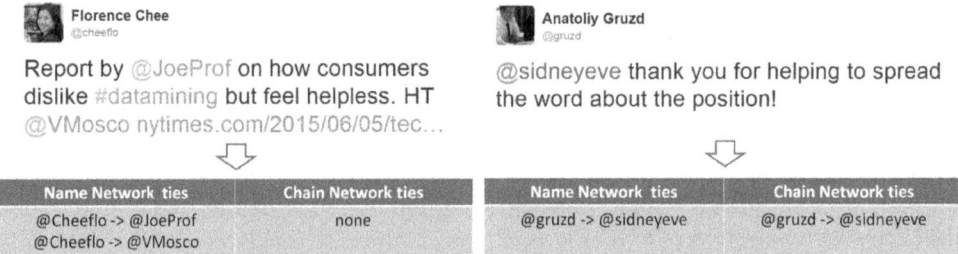

Figure 30.3 Name vs chain ties derived from sample Tweets

approaches based on two sample tweets. For a detailed description and evaluation of the name and chain network approaches, see Gruzd (2009b).

Network Visualization

Once either name or chain network is discovered, it can be visualized using a built-in web-based visualizer. The resulting network visualizations allow for scaling, as well as the ability to select any particular node or a group of nodes for further analysis. For the purpose of this chapter, we will only focus on the visualization and analysis of chain networks that represent the most engaged interactions on Twitter (when one person replies to another).

The networks in Figure 30.4 were visualized using one of the three available layout algorithms called Distributed Recursive Graph Layout (DrL), an R igraph library implementation of Martin et al. (2008). A network layout algorithm is a required step when visualizing networks as it essentially decides where to plot each node on the screen. DrL is a well-suited layout for our network data since it is able to separate clusters of different discussions and communities in the dataset. It does so by identifying densely connected clusters of nodes and hiding 'long' edges between different clusters. The other two layout algorithms available in Netlytic are Fruchterman and Reingold (1991) – which is particularly useful for networks of less than 1,000 nodes – and Large Graph Layout which is designed for visualizing large networks (Adai et al., 2004).

Before proceeding to the comparative analysis of the three networks, we want to note that the colors in the visualization are assigned automatically by Netlytic visualizer to highlight different clusters. This is to help users identify clusters of densely connected nodes in the networks that may represent a group of users who tend to talk to each other more often than to the rest of the network. These clusters are detected using a community detection algorithm called *FastGreedy* (Clauset et al., 2004). To facilitate data exploration in large networks, the visualizer allows users to display nodes only from a selected cluster. For example, Figure 30.5 shows two different clusters detected in the 'English' dataset: one highlights interactions around the US government accounts including President Obama's account (@barackobama), the State Department (@statedept) and the White House (@whitehouse); another cluster includes news sharing interactions likely originated by a set of Twitter accounts that belong to CNN, a 24-hour breaking news cable network. These clusters highlight two different groups of stakeholders that dominate Twitter discussions about Ukraine in the English dataset: one cluster contains people with offline influence over the events in Ukraine and another demonstrates the informational power and reach of a global news network.

Network-Level SNA Measures

Next we will conduct a comparative analysis across the three chain networks. In addition to relying on the network visualizations, we

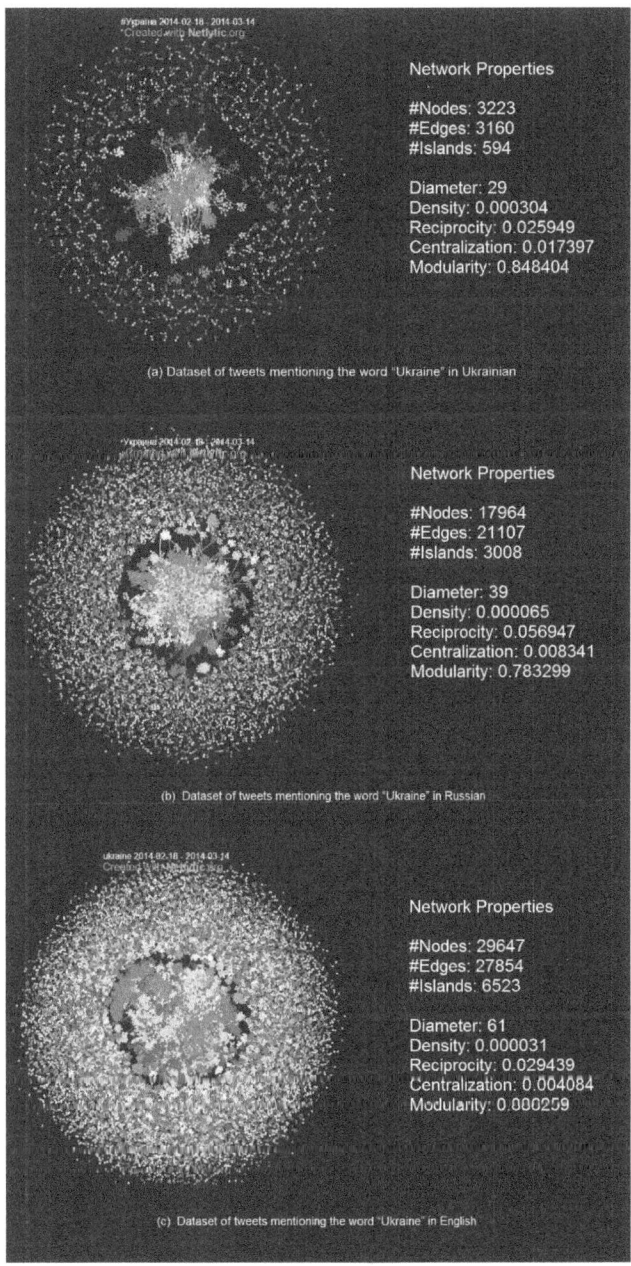

Figure 30.4 Communication networks showing who replies to whom on Twitter (chain network)

will also use a set of network properties generated as part of the visualization (see Figure 30.4). Table 30.2 summarizes common network-level SNA measures available in

Netlytic. For more details on SNA measures, see Scott (2012).

The main difference between the three networks is their size in terms of the number of

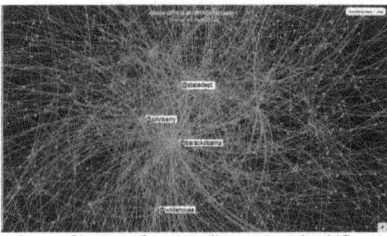 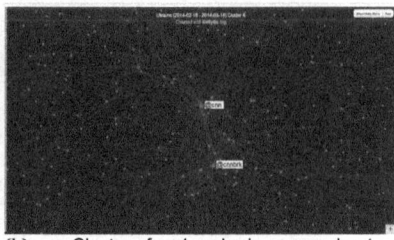

(a) Cluster of nodes discussing the US government's reaction to the crisis in Ukraine

(b) Cluster of nodes sharing news about Ukraine originated by CNN News Network accounts

Figure 30.5 'Communities' automatically detected by netlytic in the 'english' dataset

nodes and edges. The 'Ukrainian' network is the smallest followed by the 'Russian' and 'English' network is the largest. What is interesting, however, is that the number of tweets in the Russian and English datasets are comparable (527,112 and 591,394 respectively), but there are 1.6 times fewer Twitter users who participated in the 'Russian' network (17,964 vs. 29,647), while exhibiting a similar number of edges (21,107 vs. 27,854). This may suggest that the English network is less interactive and potentially more likely to be formed around sharing news about the events in Ukraine as opposed to having active conversations and debates around the topic.

This is also supported by the fact that only about 2.9% of the edges in the 'English' network are bi-directional, when people replied to each other (see the definition of the reciprocity measure in Table 30.2), as compared to the 5.7% in the 'Russian' network.

The modularity value for all three networks is close to one (on a zero to one scale), suggesting that none of the networks represent one coherent conversation among the core group. A modularity measure of one in a network indicates clear divisions between clusters that emerged from within the network. See Table 30.2 above for additional information. This can be expected considering a

Table 30.2 Definitions of common network-level SNA measures

Diameter	is the longest distance among the shortest paths between any two network participants. This measure indicates a network's size, by calculating the number of nodes it takes to get from one side to the other.
Density	is the ratio of existing ties to the total number of possible ties in a network. In other words, it is calculated by dividing the number of existing ties by the number of possible ties. This measure helps to illustrate how close participants are within a network.
Reciprocity	is the ratio of ties that are reciprocal (bi-directional) to the total number of existing ties. A higher value indicates many participants have two-way conversations.
Centralization	measures the average degree centrality of all nodes within a network. When a network has a high centralization value closer to one, it suggests there are a few central participants who dominate the flow of information in the network. Networks with a low measurement of centralization closer to zero are considered to be decentralized where information flows more freely between many participants.
Modularity	helps to determine whether the clusters of densely connected participants in the network represent distinct communities or not. Higher values of modularity indicate clear divisions between communities as represented by clusters in Netlytic. Low values of modularity, usually less than 0.5, suggest that clusters, found by Netlytic, will overlap more; the network is more likely to consist of a core group of nodes.

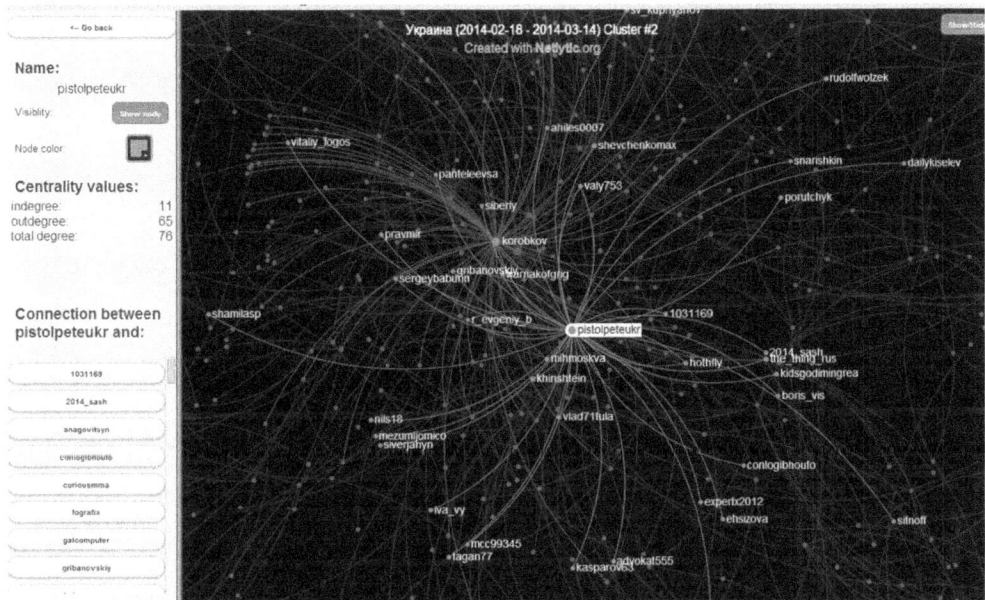

Figure 30.6 Viewing direct connections of a selected node (marked as #2)

broad search query used for data collection. For an example of a Twitter dataset that exhibits a stronger overlap among different clusters and a lower value of modularity, take a look at a Twitter community called *Health Care Social Media Canada (#hcsmca)*. This Twitter community uses a single hashtag #hcsmca to organize weekly communal chats. In that case, the modularity metric tends to be in the area around 0.3–0.4 (see Gruzd & Haythornthwaite, 2013, for a detailed examination of the *#hcsmca* community).

Individual Level Network Measures

In addition to examining the networks at the macro level, we can also zoom in and select any particular nodes for a more detailed examination of key actors and learn more about the details of their interactions. Once a node is selected, the visualizer shows the individual level network measures such as degree centrality (the number of connections to other network participants). The left panel also lists all of the usernames who are directly connected to the selected node (see Figure 30.6). By clicking on any of these usernames, one can read the exchanges between the selected node and others in the network. This feature allows researchers to get a better understanding of why and how the connections are formed and why some users are more likely to talk to each other. For example, by using this feature, we confirmed that even though users marked as #1 and #2 in Figure 30.6 appear to be strongly connected in the 'Russian' network, their exchanges tend to be somewhat hostile. This can be explained by the fact that they are on the opposite sides of the discussion about the crisis in Ukraine and the role of the Russian government in the conflict. This also emphasizes the fact that when it comes to analyzing communication networks, researchers have to also examine the individual interactions they are seeing in the network in order to avoid misinterpreting the results.

A network representation of online discussions is also very useful for detecting and examining who is dominating the information

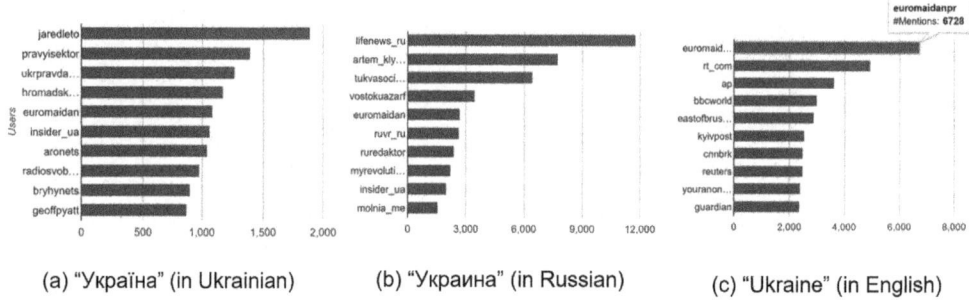

(a) "Україна" (in Ukrainian) (b) "Украина" (in Russian) (c) "Ukraine" (in English)

Figure 30.7 Top ten most connected users Bbased on in-degree centrality

flow. In particular, node size is an effective way to quickly identify key players in a network. Netlytic scales the size of each node based on various centrality measures such as in-degree and out-degree, which have shown to help find influential actors in the network structure (e.g., Dubois & Gaffney, 2014; Xu et al., 2014). Using the Report tab available in Netlytic, we can quickly review the top ten most mentioned Twitter users; in SNA terms, these are the nodes who have the highest in-degree centrality in the Name network (see Figure 30.7).

The users in Figure 30.7 are the ones that dominated the discourse in each dataset either because of their online or offline actions (or both). The Ukrainian dataset has the most diverse list of influentials in terms of their roles including a celebrity, a major political party, activists, politicians, and Ukrainian news agencies. Notably, the list is topped by @jaredleto, an account that belongs to Jared Leto who was the most mentioned user in the Ukrainian dataset because he expressed support of Ukrainian people in his award acceptance speech at the Oscars; showing the international reach and focus of Twitter networks. The 'Russian' and 'English' networks were dominated primarily by news agencies and reporters. The main difference between the two networks is that the 'Russian' network mostly included Russian news media and the 'English' network included mostly Western news agencies such as Associated Press, BBC, CNN, and Reuters.

Figure 30.7 revealed a couple of additional findings. First, it appears that Euromaidan activists have been successful in dominating the Twitter communication networks across all three datasets based on the presence of the @euromaidan or @euromaidanPR accounts in all three lists; these are the two main accounts covering the Euromaidan revolution and the events that followed from the Euromaidan activists' perspective. The fact that the Euromaidan activists has created a separate English only account (@euromaidanPR) to cover the events in Ukraine demonstrates that the activists had recognized the role that social media and Twitter in particular played during some of the previous unrests around the globe and its ability to get the attention of the international community.

CONCLUSION

Using Netlytic provided the opportunity to explore many interesting aspects of the way the Euromaidan revolution in the Ukraine was discussed on Twitter. By leveraging the combination of text, as well as network analysis capabilities of Netlytic's functions, a full picture of the online discussion became visible. Based on the text analysis, all three datasets focused on the events in Kyiv and Crimea, as well as the role of Russia in the conflict. The main differences between the datasets became clearer when visualizing popular topics over time; a function that Netlytic presents as stacked graphs for easy overview. For example, the 'Russian' dataset focused on the events in Crimea, a key geo-political area for Russia, almost from the beginning of the data collection, and the 'English' dataset focused on framing the events in Ukraine as a conflict between Russia and the United States. Based on the network analysis, the 'Ukrainian' network showed a variety of uses and users including activists. Though the 'Ukrainian' network also included news agencies, the 'English' and 'Russian' networks were mostly led by news agencies whether they be local (Russian) or international (English). In sum, the results suggest that during the crisis in Ukraine, Twitter was used primarily for information dissemination purposes and not to organize collective action. This finding is markedly different from how Twitter was used in other recent popular uprisings and protests, such as the Egyptian revolution (Eltantawy & Wiest, 2011) and the Occupy Movement (Croeser & Highfield, 2014). This may suggest that the use of Twitter for uprisings and protests is evolving. Activists from all sides of a conflict are learning more about the potentials (reaching a larger audience) and pitfalls (being watched or monitored) of the Twitter platform to foment revolutions.

Netlytic stands out from existing social media analysis tools through its easy to use interface and the various functions which allows researchers to explore both what is being said on social media and how people are interacting. Whether a researcher wants to know about the sentiment of the content or see a network visualized, Netlytic allows them to explore the big picture as well as drilling down to the individual social media post or user. The Euromaidan revolution is an excellent case study through which the various analytical powers of Netlytic are featured.

REFERENCES

Adai, A. T., Date, S. V., Wieland, S., & Marcotte, E. M. (2004). LGL: creating a map of protein function with an algorithm for visualizing very large biological networks. *Journal of Molecular Biology*, *340*(1), 179–190. http://doi.org/10.1016/j.jmb.2004.04.047

Al-Khalifa, H. S. (2011). Exploring Political Activities in the Saudi Twitterverse. In *Proceedings of the 13th International Conference on Information Integration and Web-based Applications and Services* (pp. 363–366). New York, NY, USA: ACM. http://doi.org/10.1145/2095536.2095604

Alyami, E., & Toze, S. (2014). Where to go on the weekend? Trends for local information seeking in leisure settings using social media (pp. 169–172). IEEE. http://doi.org/10.1109/i-Society.2014.7009034

Arutunyan, A. (2014, March 19). Putin's move on Crimea bolsters popularity back home. *USA TODAY*. Retrieved from http://www.usatoday.com/story/news/world/2014/03/18/crimea-ukraine-putin-russia/6564263/

Billings, A. C., Burch, L. M., & Zimmerman, M. H. (2015). Fragments of us, fragments of them: social media, nationality and US perceptions of the 2014 FIFA World Cup. *Soccer & Society*, *16*(5–6), 726–744. http://doi.org/10.1080/14660970.2014.963307

Black, L. W., Welser, H. T., Cosley, D., & DeGroot, J. M. (2011). Self-Governance Through Group Discussion in Wikipedia Measuring Deliberation in Online Groups. *Small Group Research*, (5), 595 634. http://doi.org/10.1177/1046496411406137

Chung, J. E. (2015). Antismoking Campaign Videos on YouTube and Audience Response: Application of Social Media Assessment Metrics. *Computers in Human Behavior*, *51*, 114–121. http://doi.org/10.1016/j.chb.2015.04.061

Clauset, A., Newman, M. E. J., & Moore, C. (2004). Finding Community Structure in Very Large Networks. *Physical Review E*, (6). http://doi.org/10.1103/PhysRevE.70.066111

Croeser, S., & Highfield, T. (2014). Occupy Oakland and #oo: Uses of Twitter within the Occupy movement. *First Monday*, (3). http://doi.org/10.5210/fm.v19i3.4827

Dubois, E., & Gaffney, D. (2014). The Multiple Facets of Influence Identifying Political Influentials and Opinion Leaders on Twitter. *American Behavioral Scientist*, (10), 1260–1277. http://doi.org/10.1177/0002764214527088

Eltantawy, N., & Wiest, J. B. (2011). The Arab Spring| Social Media in the Egyptian Revolution: Reconsidering Resource Mobilization Theory. *International Journal of Communication*, 5, 18.

Foller.me. (2014). Home. Retrieved from https://foller.me/

Fruchterman, T. M. J., & Reingold, E. M. (1991). Graph drawing by force-directed placement. *Software: Practice and Experience*, (11), 1129–1164. http://doi.org/10.1002/spe.4380211102

Gruzd, A. (2009a). Automated Discovery of Emerging Online Communities Among Blog Readers: A Case Study of a Canadian Real Estate Blog. *Proceedings of the Internet Research 10.0 Conference*, October 7–11, 2009, Milwaukee, WI, USA. Retrieved from http://DalSpace.library.dal.ca:8080/xmlui/handle/10222/12831

Gruzd, A. (2009b). Studying Collaborative Learning Using Name Networks. *Journal of Education for Library & Information Science*, (4), 237–247.

Gruzd, A., & Haythornthwaite, C. (2013). Enabling Community Through Social Media. *Journal of Medical Internet Research*, (10), e248. http://doi.org/10.2196/jmir.2796

Gruzd, A., Wellman, B., & Takhteyev, Y. (2011). Imagining Twitter as an Imagined Community. *American Behavioral Scientist*, (10), 1294–1318. http://doi.org/10.1177/0002764211409378

Gunelius, S. (2014). The Data Explosion in 2014 Minute by Minute – Infographic. ACI.com. Retrieved from http://aci.info/2014/07/12/the-data-explosion-in-2014-minute-by-minute-infographic/

Hampton, K. N. (2010). Internet Use and the Concentration of Disadvantage: Glocalization and the Urban Underclass. *American Behavioral Scientist*, 53(8), 1111–1132. Retrieved from http://abs.sagepub.com/content/53/8/1111

Hansen, D. L., Schneiderman, B., & Smith, M. A. (2011). *Analyzing social media networks with NodeXL: insights from a connected world*. Burlington, MA: Morgan Kaufmann.

Harder, A., Howard, V., & Sedo, D. R. (2015). Creating Cohesive Community Through Shared Reading: A Case Study of One Book Nova Scotia. Partnership: *The Canadian Journal of Library and Information Practice and Research*, (1). Retrieved from http://synergies.lib.uoguelph.ca/index.php/perj/article/view/3098

Haythornthwaite, C., & Gruzd, A. (2007). A Noun Phrase Analysis Tool for Mining Online Community Conversations. In C. Steinfield, B. T. Pentland, M. Ackerman, & N. Contractor (Eds.), *Communities and Technologies 2007* (pp. 67–86). Springer: London. Retrieved from http://link.springer.com/chapter/10.1007/978-1-84628-905-7_4

Haythornthwaite, C., & Gruzd, A. (2008). Analyzing Networked Learning Texts. *Proceedings of Networked Learning Conference*, Halkidiki, Greece, May 5–6, 2008, pp. 136–143. Retrieved from http://DalSpace.library.dal.ca:8080/xmlui/handle/10222/12828

Hemsley, B., Palmer, S., & Balandin, S. (2014). Tweet reach: A Research Protocol for Using Twitter to Increase Information Exchange in People with Communication Disabilities. *Developmental Neurorehabilitation*, (2), 84–89. http://doi.org/10.3109/17518423.2013.861529

Lodhi, R., & Malik, R. (2013). Impact of Electricity Shortage on Daily Routines: A Case Study of Pakistan. *Energy & Environment*, (5), 701–710. http://doi.org/10.1260/0958-305X.24.5.701

Martin, J. M. G., Gruzd, A., & Howard, V. (2013). Navigating an imagined Middle-earth: Finding and analyzing text-based and film-based mental images of Middle-earth through TheOneRing.net online fan community. *First Monday*, (5). http://doi.org/10.5210/fm.v18i5.4529

Martin, S. B., Brown, W. M., Klavans, R., & Boyack, K. W. (2008). DrL: Distributed Recursive (graph) Layout. *Journal of Graph Algorithms and Applications*. Retrieved from http://www.osti.gov/scitech/biblio/1145621

McMillan, D. W., & Chavis, D. M. (1986). Sense of community: A definition and theory. *Journal of community psychology*, (1), 6–23.

NVivo. (n.d). NVivo Products. Retrieved from http://www.qsrinternational.com/product

Paranyushkin, D. (2013). Addresses to the Federal Assembly of the Russian Federation by Russian presidents, 2008–2012: comparative analysis. Russian *Journal of Communication*, 5(3), 265–274. http://doi.org/10.1080/19409419.2013.824401

Scott, J. (2012). *Social Network Analysis*. SAGE: London, UK.

Smith, M. A. (2014). NodeXL: Simple Network Analysis for Social Media. In P. R. Alhajj & P. J. Rokne (Eds.), *Encyclopedia of Social Network Analysis and Mining* (pp. 1153–1170). Springer: New York. Retrieved from http://link.springer.com/referenceworkentry/10.1007/978–1-4614–6170-8_308

Social Media Lab (2016a). About. Retrieved from http://socialmedialab.ca/

Social Media Lab (2016b) Social Media Research Toolkit. Retrieved from http://socialmedialab.ca/apps/social-media-toolkit/

Sugimoto, C. R., & Thelwall, M. (2013). Scholars on soap boxes: Science communication and dissemination in TED videos. *Journal of the American Society for Information Science and Technology*, (4), 663–674. http://doi.org/10.1002/asi.22764

Sullivan, R. (2014). Live-tweeting terror: a rhetorical analysis of @HSMPress_ Twitter updates during the 2013 Nairobi hostage crisis. *Critical Studies on Terrorism*, 7(3), 422–433. http://doi.org/10.1080/17539153.2014.955300

Xu, W. W., Sang, Y., Blasiola, S., & Park, H. W. (2014). Predicting Opinion Leaders in Twitter Activism Networks The Case of the Wisconsin Recall Election. *American Behavioral Scientist*, (10), 1278–1293. http://doi.org/10.1177/0002764214527091

Theme Detection in Social Media

Daniel Angus

Visual text analytics is an emerging field that blends and extends upon information visualisation and computational linguistics. This chapter introduces a range of visual text analytic methods which are suitable for analysing thematic trends in text-based social media data. The chapter introduces the Discursis (Angus, Smith, & Wiles, 2012a; Angus, Smith, & Wiles, 2012b) and Leximancer (Smith, 2000; Smith & Humphreys, 2006) technologies, and explains how they can be used in conjunction with other software (Microsoft Excel™ and Gephi) to generate informative visual representations of Twitter data. The chapter explores a series of visual text analytic workflows that blend the aforementioned technologies, using a Twitter corpus comprising approximately 50,000 tweets, with analyses of the dataset offered to showcase the utility of the methods for social science research.

INTRODUCTION

Visual text analytic technologies provide analysts with visual and computational support for the analysis of a variety of common media types including natural conversation, interview, mass media, and new media datasets (Alencar, de Oliveira, & Paulovich, 2012; Angus, Rintel, & Wiles, 2013; Risch, Kao, Poteet, & Wu, 2008). These technologies often focus on increasing the breadth of data able to be analysed in a single study by reducing the effort required to code and analyse data, and incorporate visualisations to enable visual sense making of data and facilitate visual communication of key insights. Visual text analytics can be explained via their three main facets: how the technique codes an input dataset; how the coded data is represented visually; and how an analyst can make interpretive sense of the data and subsequently interrogate the system under analysis.

The first facet which relates to how unstructured or semi-structured text data is processed by computer algorithms is largely the domain of computational linguistics, specifically natural language processing (NLP). NLP is primarily concerned with questions that relate to machine processing of human language data, examples including automatic summarisation, language translation, named-entity recognition, sentiment analysis, and natural language understanding/reasoning (Manning & Schütze, 1999). It is 'natural language understanding' that is of interest in this chapter given that we are concerned with how a corpus of text-based social media data can be processed to generate insight into semantics and meanings (themes) inherent in the data.

The second and third facets of visual text analytics can be taken in concert as both relate to how the semantics of textual data are presented visually to an analyst to aid in their interpretation of the data. Information Visualisation is concerned with maximising the bandwidth of information transfer between a system and a human observer/analyst through the use of visual abstraction (Card, Mackinlay, & Shneiderman, 1999). Visual abstractions are designed to allow analysts to locate patterns of interest, and to communicate often complex observations to other interested parties (Tufte & Graves-Morris, 1983). The choice of information visualisation is therefore largely dependent on the affordances of the data, and the questions that an analyst wishes to explore. The complex mapping between data, question and visualisation is an area of continuing scholarly work. As one example, Vickers, Faith, and Rossiter (2013) offered a theoretical framework inspired by Peircean semiotics that encapsulates the aforementioned mapping, their analysis helping to explain how some visualisations are considered better than others.

Tying these facets together it is not surprising that most Visual Text Analytic systems (open-source or proprietary) are targeted at specific data input types from specific physical or social systems, and address particular questions of interest. In other words there is not one visual text analytic system to 'rule them all' and any researcher who is interested in particular data types/systems/questions would be wise to survey the ever-growing field of Visual Text Analytics to select a technique that best matches their requirements.[1]

In this chapter, two related yet distinct visual text analytic technologies: Leximancer and Discursis, are selected to facilitate the analysis of a corpus of Twitter data. The chapter details how the programs operate, how to interpret findings arising from the use of these programs, and how to extend the analysis afforded by these programs through the use of other software platforms including the Gephi open-source network graphing software, and Microsoft Excel™. The chapter provides analysts with a variety of guidelines for exploring the dynamics of thematic content in their social media dataset. The chapter begins by providing a brief background on the technologies; a Twitter dataset and analysis context is then introduced; and, several worked examples showcasing the various technologies in action are provided.

BACKGROUND

Computational Content Analysis

Content analysis is a form of social scientific inquiry that seeks to interpret documents or other artefacts of communicative processes (Krippendorff, 2012). Content analysis predates the emergence of computational social science (Lazer et al., 2009), the blending of computational theory and methodology with social science, nonetheless many computer-assisted content analysis methods have been proposed over the prevailing years including concordances, and key-word-in-context lists (Weber, 1984). A critical advantage of computational methods is how they enable researchers to undertake both large-scale and longitudinal analyses that would otherwise be unviable with manual coding alone (Kelle, Prein, & Bird, 1995; Smith & Humphreys, 2006; Weber, 1984).

In addition to providing the opportunity to analyse larger data sets, newer software applications are beginning to provide extra advantages over manual coding alternatives that require predetermined terms and rules. A priori determinations can potentially lead to systematically ignoring or misidentifying important emergent conceptual relationships. By being grounded by input text rather than a codebook, computer-generated analysis can achieve a level of reliability that is difficult to achieve using hand-based methods alone (Cheng, Fleischmann, Wang, & Oard, 2008; Hillard, Purpura, & Wilkerson, 2008; Smith & Humphreys, 2006).

Leximancer

Leximancer (Smith, 2000; Smith & Humphreys, 2006) is a visual text analytic technique that can be utilised for its natural language processing capabilities, and/or for its visual 'concept map' outputs. Leximancer uses word occurrence and co-occurrence statistics through a Bayes-inspired algorithmic process to model major thematic and conceptual content from an input text. Leximancer's automated concept modelling process generates a unique taxonomy that is grounded wholly in the input corpus that is subjected to analysis. A concept in the Leximancer-sense is a unique set of word-weight pairings where these weights provide more or less evidence for the presence of the concept in a piece of text.

The default Leximancer workflow is as follows:

1. Data in the form of comma separated value files, word documents, plain text, portable document format or hypertext is prepared such that it is free of errors or extraneous text material as much as is possible.
2. The data is selected via the Leximancer graphical user interface and Leximancer makes a first pass through the data to determine basic word frequency and distribution statistics.
3. Leximancer suggests an initial set of 'concept seeds' which are an initial set of word clusters of frequent words that appear together with an above-average statistical likelihood. The analyst can accept the list as generated, add their own concept seeds and/or modify existing seeds.
4. The concept list is generated from the concept seeds. In this step, Leximancer performs a more thorough statistical analysis of the raw text to create the concepts (based on the seeds above), and creates more information around how concepts relate to other concepts discovered in the data.
5. Concepts for analysis. In this last step the analyst selects which concepts they wish to view in a visual concept map output, or via other structured reports and statistical outputs (concept frequency tables, concept prominence for individual documents within the dataset, all concepts relating to a named entity).
6. The outputs are produced and interpreted by the analyst.

More detail on interpreting the outputs from Leximancer is provided in the analysis section, and more details on the process described above can be found on the Leximancer website (Leximancer Pty. Ltd., 2015).

Discursis

Discursis (Angus et al., 2012b; Angus et al., 2012c) uses the Leximancer concept algorithmic approach, however it specialises in producing its own informative visualisations and metrics from input texts that have an inherent temporal structure, examples being conversation transcripts, social media feeds, or forum communications. While Leximancer specialises in revealing how concepts relate to one another, Discursis is useful for determining how concepts are used through time, aiding in the identification of critical points in time where conceptual changes occur, and dividing input data into epochs based on dynamics of conceptual prominence.

Alternative Methods

Leximancer and Discursis have been deployed in various social media analysis tasks in the past (Carah, Meurk, & Angus, 2015; He, Zha, & Li, 2013; Reyneke, Pitt, & Berthon, 2011) and their various visual outputs are natural fits for the research questions of interest in the case study undertaken in this chapter. The growth in visual text analytics does mean that there are many alternative methods for processing text-based social media data. It is outside the scope of this chapter to provide a comprehensive list, however the NLP and visualisation aspects of this study could be just as readily performed using the following popular approaches:

- NLTK: The Natural Language Toolkit is a Python library that includes functions for semantic tagging of text segments amongst other useful text processing functions (Bird, Klein, & Loper, 2009).
- StanfordNLP: Stanford University's NLP group have made various NLP tools available for download via their website (http://nlp.stanford.edu/software/). These toolkits include entity recognition and semantic extraction tools that are useful for thematic discovery in social media data.
- D3.js: The Data Driven Document JavaScript library is a highly popular web-based visualisation framework that can bind large datasets, including text-based data, to highly customisable interactive visual outputs.

CASE STUDY: #QANDA

Introduction

This case study is intended to showcase a variety of visual text analytic workflows for analysis of Twitter data. There is no overarching research question driving the case study presented below, rather a showcase of potential analytical avenues that could be explored by an interested researcher/analyst. Discussion and interpretation of results is therefore kept to a minimum to allow more scope for discussion of the tools used in the analysis and their configuration.

Data

Q&A is an Australian panel discussion programme that is live broadcast weekly by the Australian Broadcasting Corporation (ABC), sharing similarities to the BBC's Question Time programme. Q&A's regular format consists of the programme host (Tony Jones) moderating a question and answer style discussion between five panellists with producer-vetted questions being directed from the live studio audience, and occasionally from pre-recorded online videos. Panellists regularly include politicians, academics, industry professionals, and community leaders. The programme is livestreamed on the internet in addition to being broadcast on Australia's digital terrestrial television network. Q&A promotes itself as a platform for citizen engagement through public participation: 'everyone can have a go and take it up to our politicians and opinion makers' (ABC, 2015).

Q&A encourages the at-home audience to use Twitter and other social media platforms before, during and after the programme goes to air. The Twitter conversation generated by the programme is significant; the programme-specific hashtag #qanda is most often trending on Australia's Twitter feed for the duration and sometimes after the programme goes to air.

In this case study, tweets captured 12 hours before and after the broadcast of a single Q&A episode are analysed. A corpus of approximately 50,000 programme-specific tweets containing the #qanda hashtag was constructed with the results collated into a single comma separated value file. The file contains separate columns for the various standard metadata elements including the Tweeter's ID and location, and aspects of the tweet such as text and timestamp. The file was checked to remove any duplicate entries. Each tweet (including retweets) is represented as a single row of data, and empty column elements are left blank. For the purposes of the analyses here only the tweet text, timestamp, and author columns are used.

The episode under analysis here was screened on Monday 15 June, 2015 and titled: Magna Carta Magna QandA. The programme included the following panellists:

Bronwyn Bishop: Speaker of the Australian House of Representatives. Member of the Liberal Party (conservative politician), and graduate of law.
Luca Belgiorno-Nettis: Businessman and founder of the New Democracy Foundation, a non-for-profit research organisation focused on political reform.
Noel Pearson: One of Australia's foremost indigenous leaders from the Guugu Yimidhirr community of South Eastern Cape York Peninsula. He is the founder of the Cape York Institute for policy and leadership.
Em. Prof. Gillian Triggs: President of the Australian Human Rights Commission, and former Dean of the Faculty of Law at the University of Sydney.
Bret Walker: A legal practitioner of the High Court of Australia who has served as president of numerous law councils and committees.

Concept Map

The starting point of this case study is to profile what concepts and themes emerge from the data in its entirety, and to explore how these concepts and themes relate to each other. This first step is intended to provide us with a birds-eye view of the data without requiring detailed reading of every single data point (tweet). This first step is a useful way to reduce the potential for interpretive bias as any prominent concepts that emerge from the data will emerge because they are indeed mentioned frequently, rather than as something that one could argue we have 'cherry picked' from the data itself.

The first step in this process is to load the data into the Leximancer system. As described above, Leximancer accepts data in a variety of formats, including the popular comma separated value (CSV) format which is what is used here. The Leximancer manual (Leximancer Pty. Ltd., 2015) contains a lot of detail on the exact steps to load and process the data, however for the purposes here all settings were left as default unless explicitly mentioned. An added advantage of Leximancer is that it is driven via a graphical user interface rather than a script-driven setup, making it more approachable for non-technical users (see Figure 31.1).

The only modification made to the default settings was add 'RT' to the default stop list. The stop list is a list of functional words, examples being 'and', 'or', 'the'. These stop words appear with moderately even statistical prominence throughout natural text and thus lack discriminatory and explanatory power. They are removed from the text before the concept seed creation and profiling stages; however the original text is left intact for interpretation of the raw text excerpts via the interactive interface, an example of which will be shown later.

Leximancer located 74 concepts in the Twitter corpus (see Figure 31.2 for the Leximancer concept map). Leximancer includes a function to group concepts into themes based on inter-concept relatedness. In simple terms it selects subsets of concepts that share similarity, and names the theme after the most prominent concept of the theme group. For the analysis here the concepts were divided into eight distinct themes: government; bronwyn bishop; gillian triggs; law; @gilliantriggs; asylum seekers; noel pearson; and, children. A table with a description of the concepts included in each theme and a summary description of the thematic content is provided as Table 31.1.

The creation of the thematic table is achieved through interaction with the concept map through the Leximancer software interface. By clicking on any concept the analyst is provided with example content (in the case here, tweets), that are prototypical of this concept (see Figure 31.3). For a whole theme one simply clicks the various concepts located within that theme to gain an understanding of the nature of the content located in that theme. Given that Leximancer's Bayesian algorithms are driven by word frequency and co-reference, measures of

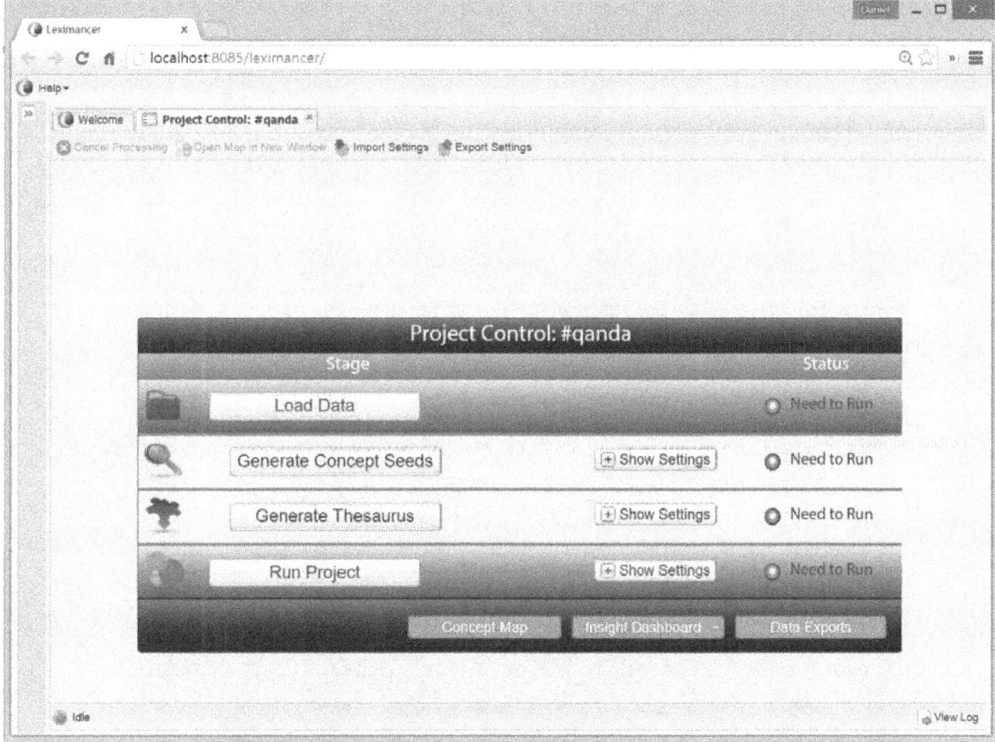

Figure 31.1 The Leximancer graphical user interface

conceptual prominence provide us a useful way to determine the dominant viewpoints taken by Tweeters. Each concept can also be profiled to ascertain the evidence terms that it is comprised of (see Figure 31.4).

The survey of the 74 concepts emerging from the Twitter corpus suggests that the Twitter content largely reflected the Q&A programme content with discussions centred on issues including legal frameworks and protections, asylum seekers, indigenous recognition and rights; all topics that were identified on the Q&A programme website. Somewhat amplified in Twitter compared to the television broadcast is the juxtaposition of Bronywn Bishop and Prof. Gillian Triggs. Tweeters made negative references towards Bronwyn Bishop, many turning Ms Bishop's critique of Prof. Triggs' political impartiality as a public official, into a critique of her own impartiality as speaker of the house. At the same time many Tweeters offered messages of support for Prof. Triggs, either directly to her Twitter handle or via mention of her name. At a high level the results of this first analysis suggest that while the broadcast focused on a discussion of legal and human rights issues the Twitter conversation focussed on critique or encouragement of the actors discussing or involved in these issues.

Concepts Over Time

The concept map and Leximancer interface provide us with insight into the concepts discussed via Twitter during the period before, during and after the airing of the Q&A episode. What is missing from the previous analysis though is a sense of when these concepts appeared in the discourse. For this next part of our analysis we will use the same

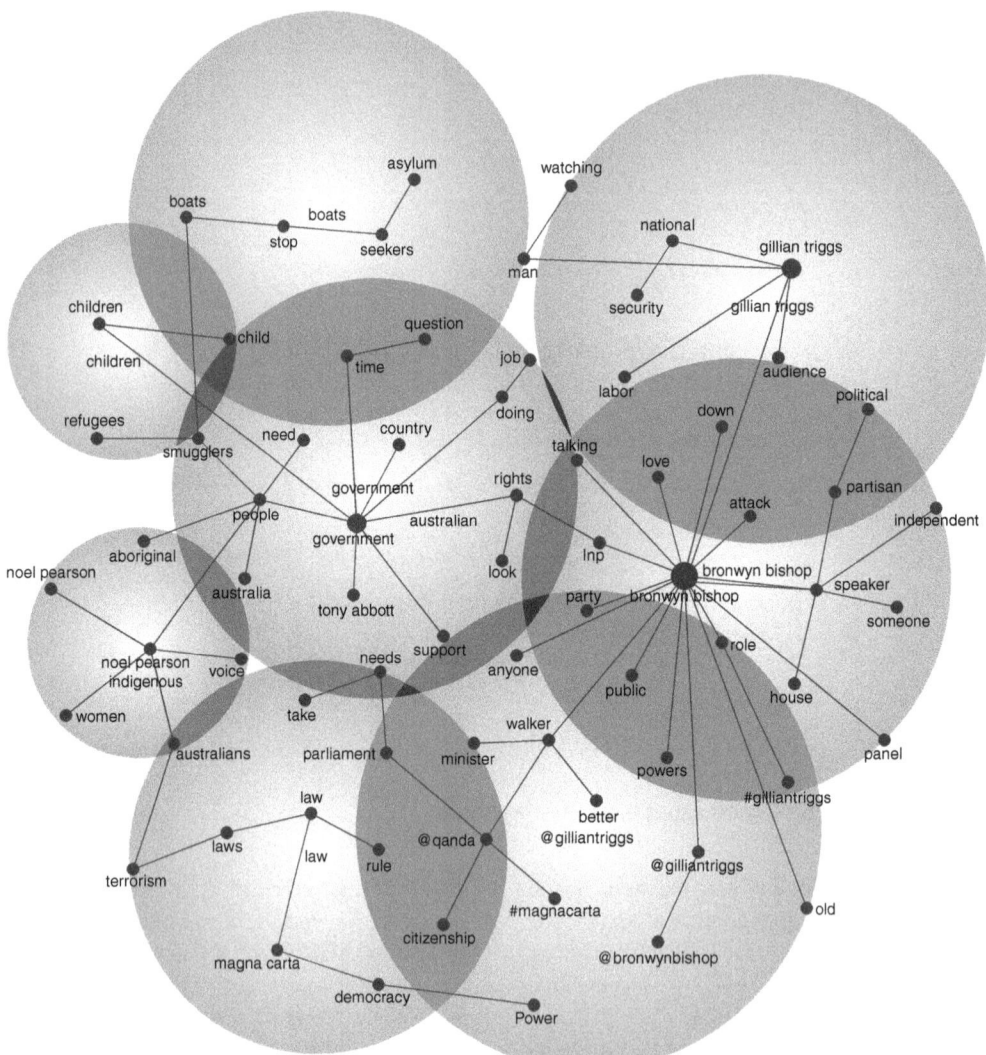

Figure 31.2 Leximancer concept map. The map highlights the theme groups using the large coloured circles, and the individual nodes represent the concepts. Node proximity implies conceptual relatedness

dataset as before, coded with the same concepts, but in this instance the Discursis software will allow us to reveal the temporal thematic trends that are present in the data.

For this analysis, Discursis has been adapted for the analysis of social media data with each tweet treated as an individual temporal unit for concept tagging and analysis purposes. Normally, the standard Discursis recurrence plotting visual output would be able to readily reveal changes in concept use patterns over time, particularly for moderately sized conversations or forum transcripts. As social media data is regularly counted in the thousands this pushes the default recurrence plotting visualisation approach well beyond its capabilities. As an alternative, a stream graph (also known as Theme River) (Havre, Hetzler, Whitney, & Nowell, 2002) visualisation approach is adopted. Stream

Table 31.1 Thematic overview of the Twitter corpus. All examples provided here originally contained the #qanda hashtag which has been omitted for brevity

Theme	Concepts	Description	Examples
Government	government, people, rights, job, doing, smugglers, australian, tony abbott, australia, question, time, look, country, need, needs, support	Tweets in this theme often use the context of the Q&A discussion at the time, or conceivably the Twitter feed itself, to discuss and critique the various policy positions of the Australian government.	@larryschles: If paying criminals is not a sackable offence in govt than I don't know what is #auspol @northonm31: You get that point, Australian Government? @MattSainsb: If the government is there to ensure that evil things don't happen, why are you not banning bikies and Nazism in Australia?
Bronwyn Bishop	bronwyn bishop, speaker, partisan, attack, role, lnp, independent, house, someone, panel, party, love, talking, public, #gilliantriggs	The tweets here were directed towards panellist Bronwyn Bishop who at the time was Speaker of the House of Representatives of the Australian Parliament. Bronwyn Bishop had been attacked for her apparent partisanship and lack of independence in the role as speaker, and the Twitter commentary made light of this, or used her appearance on Q&A to attack her via Twitter.	@harrypusspuss: Shut your mouth Bishop you partisan cow. @Trixie_Boo: Bronwyn Bishop LOATHES those who show up her ignorance and bias #auspol @msimaker1: Bronny has to kick someone tonight or she may implode
Gillian Triggs	gillian triggs, political, security, national, down, audience, labor, watching	As president of the Australian Human Rights Commission Prof. Gillian Triggs is seen as a champion for human rights and particularly revered by progressives for her critique of the Australian Liberal Party and also former Australian Labor Government's policies on mandatory offshore detention of asylum seekers. Prior to this programme she had been subjected to extensive criticism by the government for a politically damaging report. This theme captures tweets that largely serve as messages of support for Prof. Triggs.	@aquafiredragon: Dear HASHQANDA audience, if you could organise a standing ovation for Gillian Triggs, that would be amazing, ta @SkiPoss: Bronnie's argument just shot down by Gillian @yarnellcj: Brown(sic) accusing Gillian of being too political – hypocracy(sic) at its peak
Law	law, magna carta, parliament, laws, democracy, rule, citizenship, terrorism, take	Given that the theme of this Q&A episode was a celebration of the anniversary of the signing of the Magna Carta, many of the tweets featured tweets related to law and legal practice. Tweeters used the legal framing most prominently to discuss a government proposal to strip citizenship from suspected terrorism subjects.	@redcoatJM: Do you think our Parliamentarians will use these principles in the debate on upcoming citizenship law? @CarlsonDM: All terrorism can be prosecuted under current law, not an excuse to forgo our principles

(Continued)

Table 31.1 (Continued)

@gilliantriggs	@gilliantriggs, @qanda, walker, #magnacarta, powers, power, anyone, minister, better, @bronwynbishop, old	Similar to the Gillian Triggs theme above, this theme contained mostly tweets of support for Prof. Triggs, and also direct messages regarding support for established legal concepts such as the separation of powers.	alex_white91: @gilliantriggs for prime minister pipsterb: No man may be made an outlaw or alien #magnacarta800 - separation of powers judiciary & Govt's is vital #commonlaw @gilliantriggs
asylum seekers	boats, asylum, seekers, stop, man	In the later half of the Q&A episode a Hazara Refugee asked a question to the panel related to Australia's asylum seeker policies, particularly relating to children in detention and boat turnbacks. Tweet content related to concepts 'asylum' and 'seekers' could be interpreted as mostly critical of the current policies, and sympathetic to the plight of asylum seekers.	@scottywalks2: Turning back boats creates a regional crisis and doesn't solve the issue of persecution from which asylum seekers are fleeing @CaseyMcCowan1: We need to separate the idea of stopping the boats with the idea of seeking asylum
noel pearson	noel pearson, indigenous, voice, australians, aboriginal, women	Noel Pearson talked at length on the programme about the issue of indigenous recognition within the Australian constitution. Tweet content related to how (predominantly white) Australians can provide indigenous Australians with a voice to hear their thoughts on various issues, to rebroadcast and paraphrasing of Noel Pearson's statements and thoughts on the issue.	@Mamamia: Noel Pearson on Indigenous recognition: Symbolism is not enough. @dowdell_jeff: Can we ask Mr. Pearson his thoughts on the divisiveness amongst First People's re Constitutional Recognition vs. Treaty?
children	children, child, refugees	Similar to the asylum seeker theme above, this theme contained more tweets that focused more prominently on children in detention from families seeking asylum. Most of the tweets containing these concepts were highly critical of the Australian Government's practice of holding children in detention.	@josh1782: One child in detention is one too many @SkyesTheLimit97: This is the face of children refugees being processed.

graphs depict thematic prominence over time as a series of 'streams' or ribbons of colour that alter their thickness depending on their prominence at various time points. Stream graphs that are constructed using conceptual weightings from Discursis have been used in previous studies to examine thematic trends in academic journal papers (Angus, Rooney, McKenna, & Wiles, 2012), and to examine newspaper coverage of the coal seam gas industry (Mitchell & Angus, 2014).

The Discursis software accepts data in the same comma separated value format as Leximancer, and the workflow to process the data and extract the concepts is largely the same also. The point of difference is how the output of Discursis is post-processed. After loading the data into Discursis via its interactive graphical user interface, the data export of 'concepts identified for utterances' is chosen. This export produces a CSV file where each row of data corresponds to an input row (in this case a tweet),

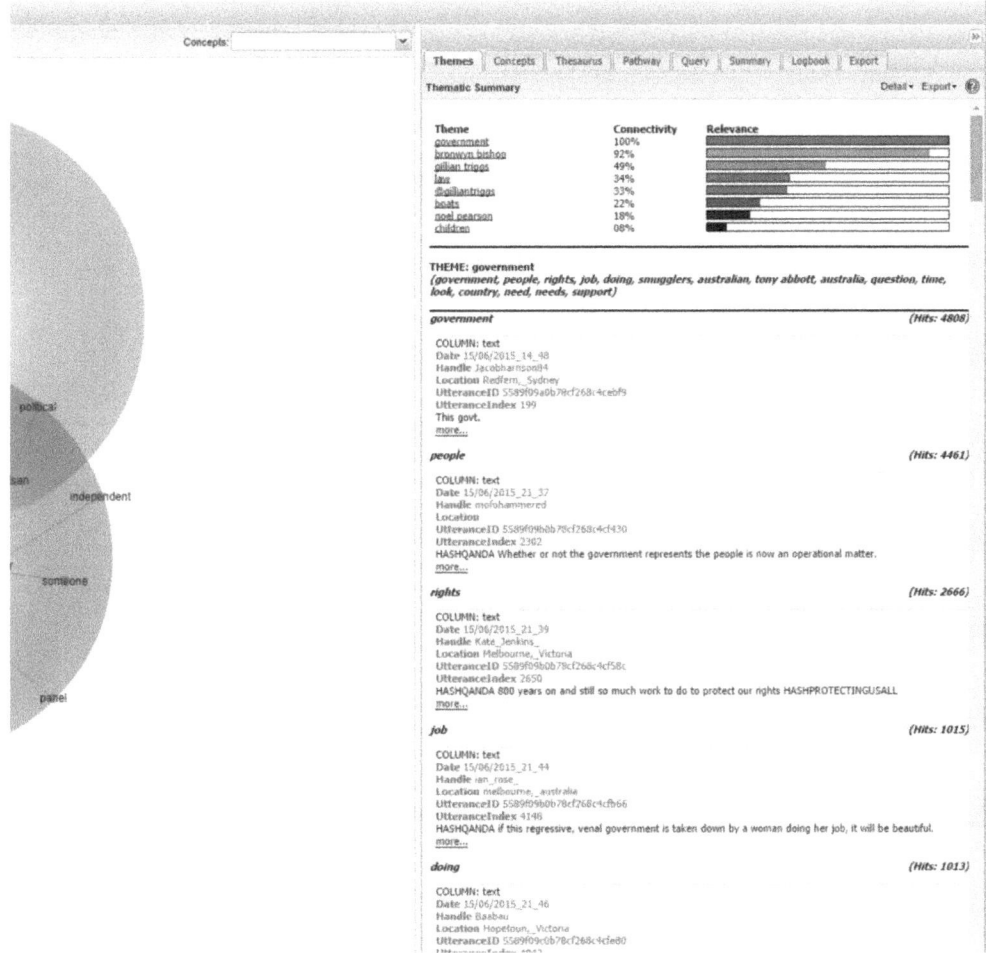

Figure 31.3 This figure highlights the interactive nature of Leximancer and how an analyst can select a concept to interrogate and reveal the raw data that aligns with that concept

and each row contains 74 values indicating the presence (or absence) of the concepts identified in the data. For each column of data a positive value indicates that there was enough evidence in this tweet to indicate the presence of the concept identified at the head of that column.

The next step is to load the original data and this new concept data into an appropriate spreadsheet or data manipulation tool to generate aggregate statistics and visual outputs. In this example, I use the somewhat ubiquitous Microsoft Excel™, however this could be performed in the open-source R package or other freely available or commercial software just as well.

The concepts identified for utterances columns are merged back into the original data such that the 74 concept columns are appended next to details such as the timestamp, location, handle and tweet text. The next step is to choose an appropriate temporal window to generate aggregate statistics of concept use over time; in the case here a time window of one minute was selected.

The Excel countif and sumif were used to generate aggregate statistics of concept use

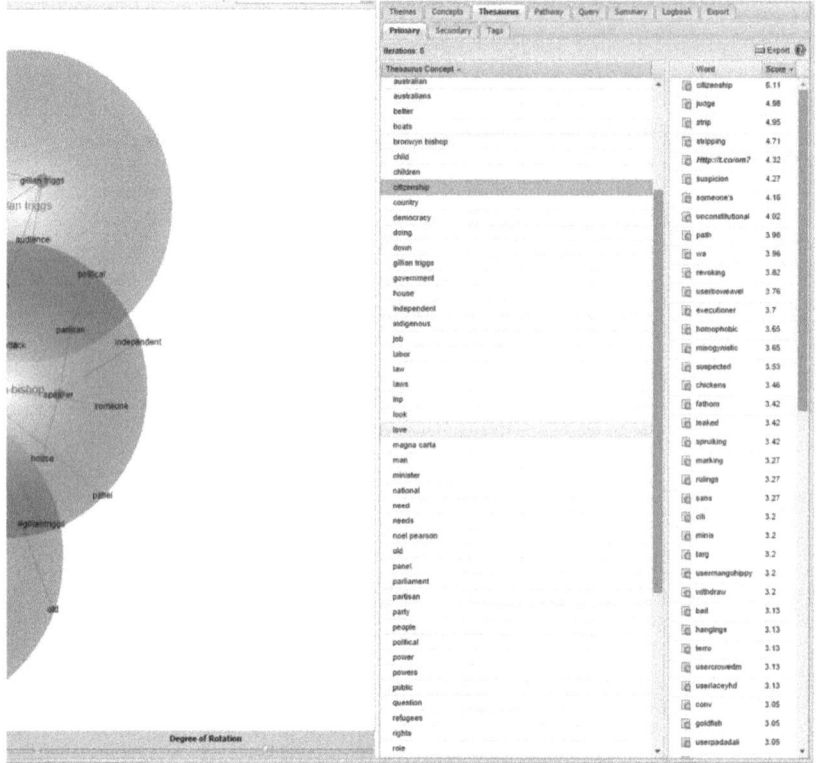

Figure 31.4 This figure highlights the nature of the evidence terms that invoke a specific concept. The term weightings can be seen here as they relate to the concept 'citizenship'

on a minute-by-minute basis. These functions reduce the concepts identified for utterances data to concepts identified per minute data. In some sense this first step can be seen as a vertical compression of the data where close to 50,000 data rows are reduced into 360 data rows.

The next step is to condense the conceptual data into thematic data which is achieved by summing the columns corresponding to concepts that belong to the distinct eight themes together. This step can be seen as a horizontal compression of the data to reduce it from 74 columns of concepts to eight columns containing thematic prominence scores.

An Excel area chart is used to create the stream graph with each theme represented using a different colour and the prominence of themes at each time point scaled between 0–100% to determine the relative thematic prominence of all eight themes at any point in time. The graph is also overlayed with the volume of tweets at each point in time as a useful counterpoint for the analysis (see Figure 31.5).

The graph reveals that there is a lack of thematic organisation on Twitter in the lead up to the televised broadcast which began at 9:30pm. Once the television broadcast started, several themes rise and fall in prominence corresponding to the timing of these topics in the Q&A broadcast. Three examples of the symmetry between the broadcast theme and Twitter themes are the prominence of the 'magna carta' theme from 9:36pm–9:50pm which was the first topic the programme panel discussed.

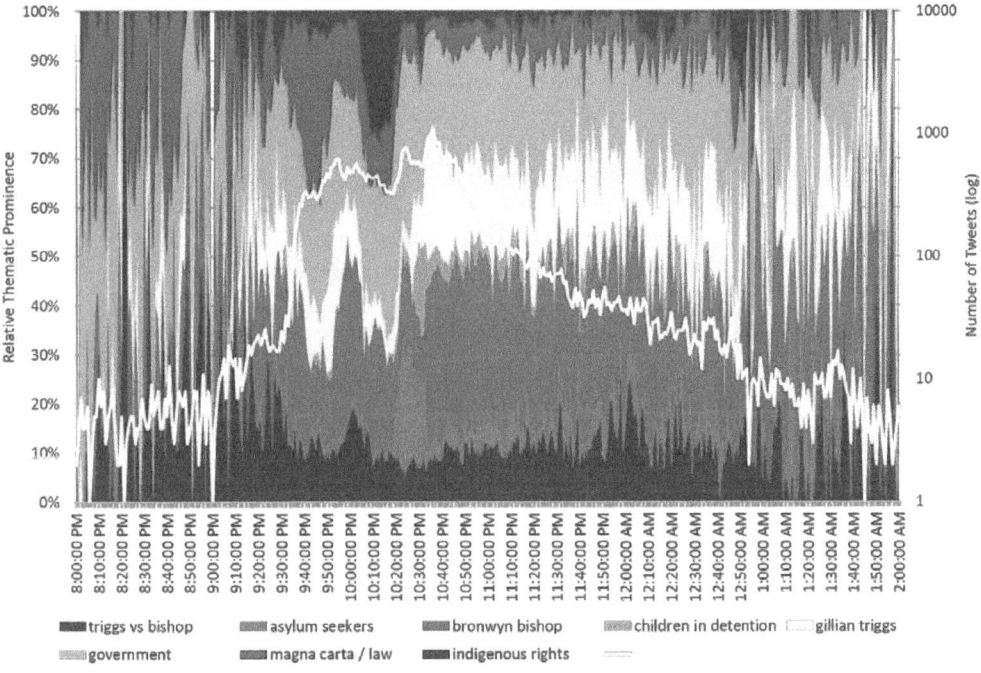

Figure 31.5 The Streamgraph reveals the prominence of themes on Twitter over time

A question to Noel Pearson related to constitutional recognition for Australia's first peoples triggered a response in Twitter as well which can be seen from near 10:10pm to 10:20pm, and discussion of asylum seekers and children in detention peaked from 10:20pm–10:36pm. Beyond the period of the television broadcast, which ran overtime until around 10:45pm, several themes seem to persist in the same mixture of prominence. These themes relate to the direct exchanges between Prof. Gillian Triggs and Bronwyn Bishop on the Q&A programme. Most Tweeters showed support for Prof. Triggs, while lambasting Bronwyn Bishop:

@rosiedream: Outclassed, Bronnie. Gillian Triggs is way way above your league. #qanda
@PeterWMurphy1: Unimpressed by the spiteful, mean-spirited eye-rolling contempt displayed by #BronwynBishop towards @GillianTriggs. #QandA @QandA #auspol

Conceptual Profiles of Twitter Users

Having gained an appreciation for the concepts discussed via Twitter and their prominence in time we will lastly turn our attention more closely to an examination of the individual actors/agents that were active in the creation of this content. While there are many ways to examine how Tweeters connect, examples including examination of follower and followee statistics and the use of hashtags, in this analysis we focus on how concepts are deployed by Tweeters.

Another data export of Discursis is a measure of conceptual overlap between pairs of individuals, in this case Tweeters. This measure allows Twitter users to be compared as to see how similar their content is, and to examine concept use on Twitter from a network perspective. For this analysis all Tweeters who posted 30 or more tweets in the period of the data capture were selected for analysis which resulted in 343 Tweeters being selected.

The open source Gephi network visualisation and analysis tool is used here to analyse the networks of conceptual overlap between the most prolific Tweeters for this corpus of tweets. Gephi accepts CSV formatted edge and node data as an input where Twitter handles represent the unique node labels and the edges represent conceptual similarity between the tweets made any two Tweeters. Microsoft Excel was used to generate a list of cosine similarity values which measured the similarity of concept use between all pairs of Tweeters (117,649 edges in total). These values were loaded into Gephi and a force-directed layout was used to project the nodes based on their conceptual similarity with each other (see Figure 31.6).

The network of conceptual similarity revealed seven cliques based on Gephi's default modularity algorithm. This algorithm locates clusters of highly connected nodes and allows for the colouring of these clusters to visually discern neighbourhoods of nodes. In Figure 31.6, user @feverpitch96 is selected to highlight their connectedness with other Tweeters based on the conceptual content of their tweets, a selection of which are produced here:

Bronwyn Bishop REALLY doesn't like it when National Security boffins go off-government-script and start talking about justice. #qanda

Oh Bronwyn NOT the frigging drownings again as a smokescreen for YOUR government turning people smuggler. #qanda

Brownyn Bishop, being inappropriately partisan, accuses Gillian Triggs of political agitation. That's funny. Or would be… #qanda

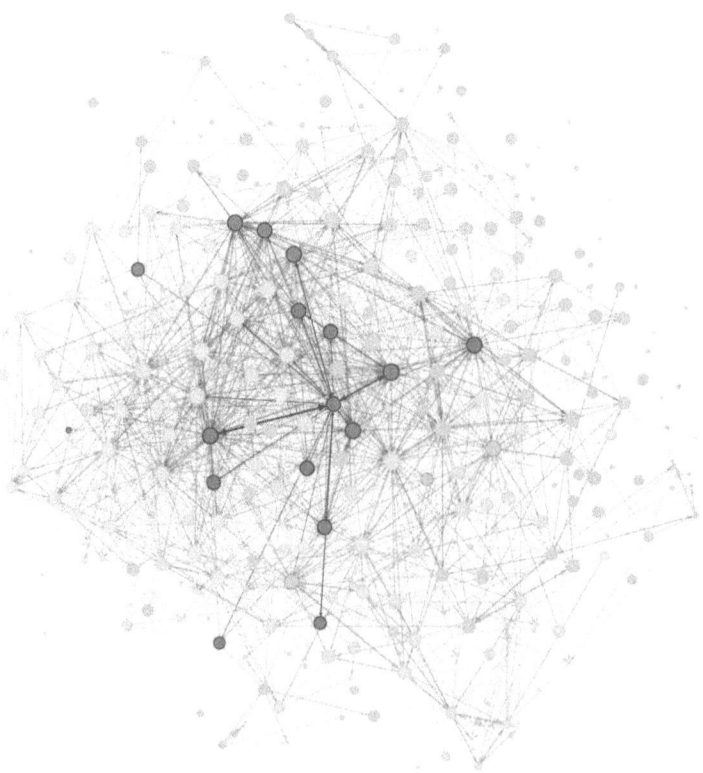

Figure 31.6 The Gephi plot reveals networks of conceptual overlap between Tweeters, and can be useful in locating groups of topically aligned Tweeters

The strongest link in the network connecting to @feverpitch96 is to user @suthernx who as can be seen from a selection of tweets below, was largely commenting on similar issues, albeit mostly retweeting rather than offering their own original content:

> RT @northonm31: How ironic, that Bronwyn Bishop is accusing Gillian Triggs of overreach. #qanda
> RT @Quagslime: Bronwyn Bishop is making this political, @GillianTriggs is not. She is just doing her job. #QandA

To be clear, this does not imply that these individuals are aware of one-another's actions on Twitter or that they are following each other or in any way influencing each other's behaviour online. It is simply a way to reveal groups of Tweeters who happen to be posting similar content onto the social media platform.

CONCLUSION

This rather brief guide through the use of visual text analytics for Twitter research has revealed several ways to code text-based social media data for conceptual content. The workflows provided revealed how to generate insights into thematic trends in time and how individual social media users overlap in terms of the conceptual content they post online.

The approaches described in this chapter allow large volumes of text-based social media data to be processed and analysed. While the Leximancer and Discursis methods explained would be considered as distant reading approaches, one of the aims of these approaches is to direct an analysts attention to interesting aspects, or representative samples of the data that can be scrutinised in more detail. In trying to maintain close proximity between the analyst and the raw data these techniques attempt to remove a drawback of close reading where important data is missed due to processing constraints, and distant reading where important nuances are lost through over-abstraction of the data.

A fundamental limitation of the technologies described here is that the use of irony and sarcasm will not necessarily be detected, and a large caveat of the above analyses is that the prominence of a concept or theme does not reflect a particular attitude towards that theme. As one example, the prominence of a theme such as 'asylum seekers' does not by itself reveal whether Tweeters are reacting positively or negatively towards this particular issue.

Naturally there are many other ways that such conceptual data could be used to provide insight into the content that individuals are posting online, and if combined with other data such as physical location, or followership dynamics, these various modalities could combine to give key insights into content flows through Twitter.

NOTE

1 At time of writing the Text Visualisation Browser contained 225 Visual Text Analytic systems: http://textvis.lnu.se/

REFERENCES

ABC (Australian Broadcasting Corporation) (2015). About the show (Q&A). Retrieved 17/7/2015, from http://www.abc.net.au/tv/qanda/about.htm

Alencar, A. B., de Oliveira, M. C. F., & Paulovich, F. V. (2012). Seeing beyond reading: a survey on visual text analytics. *Wiley Interdisciplinary Reviews: Data Mining and Knowledge Discovery, 2*(6), 476–492. doi: 10.1002/widm.1071

Angus, D., Rintel, S., & Wiles, J. (2013). Making sense of big text: a visual-first approach for analysing text data using Leximancer and Discursis. *International Journal of Social Research Methodology, 16*(3), 261–267.

Angus, D., Rooney, D., McKenna, B., & Wiles, J. (2012a). Visualizing punctuated equilibria in discursive change: Exploring a new text analysis possibility for management research. *Journal of Business and Management Landscapes*, *1*(1), 1–16.

Angus, D., Smith, A., & Wiles, J. (2012a). Human Communication as coupled time series: Quantifying multi-participant recurrence. *IEEE Transactions on Audio, Speech, and Language Processing*, *20*(6), 1795–1807. doi: 0.1109/TASL.2012.2189566

Angus, D., Smith, A. E., & Wiles, J. (2012b). Conceptual recurrence plots: Revealing patterns in human discourse. *IEEE Transactions on Visualization and Computer Graphics*, *18*(6), 988–997. doi: 10.1109/TVCG.2011.100

Bird, S., Klein, E., & Loper, E. (2009). *Natural language processing with Python*. O'Reilly Media, Inc Sebastopol, CA.

Carah, N., Meurk, C., & Angus, D. (2015). Online self-expression and experimentation as 'reflectivism': Using text analytics to examine the participatory forum Hello Sunday Morning. *Health:*, http://hea.sagepub.com/content/early/2015/07/24/1363459315596799.abstract

Card, S. K., Mackinlay, J. D., & Shneiderman, B. (1999). *Readings in information visualization: using vision to think*. Morgan Kaufmann. San Francisco, CA.

Cheng, A. S., Fleischmann, K. R., Wang, P., & Oard, D. W. (2008). Advancing social science research by applying computational linguistics. *Proceedings of the American Society for Information Science and Technology*, *45*(1), 1–12.

Havre, S., Hetzler, E., Whitney, P., & Nowell, L. (2002). ThemeRiver: Visualizing Thematic Changes in Large Document Collections. *IEEE Transactions on Visualization and Computer Graphics*, *8*(1), 9–20. doi: 10.1109/2945.981848

He, W., Zha, S., & Li, L. (2013). Social media competitive analysis and text mining: A case study in the pizza industry. *International Journal of Information Management*, *33*(3), 464–472.

Hillard, D., Purpura, S., & Wilkerson, J. (2008). Computer-assisted topic classification for mixed-methods social science research. *Journal of Information Technology & Politics*, *4*(4), 31–46.

Kelle, U., Prein, G., & Bird, K. (1995). *Computer-aided qualitative data analysis: Theory, methods and practice*. SAGE, London, Thousand Oaks, CA.

Krippendorff, K. (2012). *Content Analysis: An Introduction to its methodology* (3rd ed.). Thousand Oaks, CA: SAGE Publishing.

Lazer, D., Pentland, A. S., Adamic, L., Aral, S., Barabasi, A. L., Brewer, D. Christakis, N., Contractor, N., Fowler, J., utmann, M., Jebara, T., King, G., Macy, M., Roy, D., Alstyne van, M. (2009). Life in the network: the coming age of computational social science. *Science (New York, NY)*, *323*(5915), 721.

Leximancer Pty. Ltd. (2015). Leximancer Tutorials. from http://info.leximancer.com/tutorials/

Manning, C. D., & Schütze, H. (1999). *Foundations of statistical natural language processing*: MIT press.

Mitchell, E., & Angus, D. (2014). *Gas versus the good life: The unconventional gas controversy in the United States and Australia, 2008–2013*. Paper presented at the International Communication Association, Seattle.

Reyneke, M., Pitt, L., & Berthon, P. R. (2011). Luxury wine brand visibility in social media: an exploratory study. *International Journal of Wine Business Research*, *23*(1), 21–35.

Risch, J., Kao, A., Poteet, S., & Wu, Y. (2008). Text Visualization for Visual Text Analytics. In S. Simoff, M. Böhlen & A. Mazeika (Eds.), *Visual Data Mining* (Vol. 4404, pp. 154–171): Springer-Verlag Berlin, Heidelberg.

Smith, A. E. (2000). *Machine Mapping of Document Collections: the Leximancer System*. Paper presented at the Proceedings of the Fifth Australasian Document Computing Symposium.

Smith, A. E., & Humphreys, M. S. (2006). Evaluation of unsupervised semantic mapping of natural language with Leximancer concept mapping. *Behavior Research Methods*, *38*(2), 262–279.

Tufte, E. R., & Graves-Morris, P. (1983). *The visual display of quantitative information* (Vol. 2): Graphics press Cheshire, CT.

Vickers, P., Faith, J., & Rossiter, N. (2013). Understanding Visualization: A formal approach using category theory and semiotics. *IEEE Transactions on Visualization and Computer Graphics*, *19*(6), 1048–1061.

Weber, R. P. (1984). Computer-aided content analysis: A short primer. *Qualitative Sociology*, *7*(1–2), 126–147.

Sentiment Analysis

Mike Thelwall

This chapter discusses the use of automated sentiment analysis as an aid to social media research. Although often ignored as irrelevant, sentiment aids effective interpersonal interactions and online sentiments expressed in public have created a de facto big data repository of public attitudes. Understanding the role of sentiment in communication is an important topic in itself, and being able to identify changes in sentiment over time and differences in sentiment between contexts and objects of discussion is particularly useful for social web investigations. Current sentiment analysis software is able to estimate the amount and strength of sentiment in texts with close to human-level accuracy, making it possible to analyse large amounts of text in order to detect sentiment-related patterns and to address sentiment-related questions. This chapter explains how automated sentiment analysis software works, gives examples of social science research projects using sentiment analysis for the social web, discusses the limitations of the approach and describes how to conduct sentiment analysis with the free software SentiStrength.

INTRODUCTION

Sentiment analysis is the use of computer programs to estimate some aspect of the sentiment conveyed by a text (Liu, 2012; Pang & Lee, 2008). Research into sentiment analysis was originally driven by a specific commercial need but the software is now used for many different applications. The original motivation was to create software that could detect whether an online product review was positive or negative. This would help businesses to identify which of their products were popular and could also be used in product review websites to help users find the best products without having to read all of the reviews – assuming that the reviews did not include an overall numerical score or category (e.g., essential, recommended, not recommended). This research area is also known as opinion mining because its objective is to data mine opinions from texts. As sentiment analysis software has become more sophisticated, it has become more fine-grained and can now identify specific aspects of a product that are liked or disliked. More widely, there are now many applications of sentiment analysis, from predicting stock market prices to developing sentiment-aware systems that can respond more appropriately to user inputs. It has now become routine in marketing and public relations to monitor social media for mentions of relevant products and services with the aid of sentiment analysis. There are many organisations that provide this data and analysis to their clients, such as Pulsar and Salesforce Marketing Cloud.

Sentiment analysis programs have been created for several different types of task. Some of the simplest decide whether a text is positive, negative or neutral overall. Others identify the strength of sentiment in addition to its polarity. Some also detect a range of emotions, such as sadness, anger and joy (e.g., Strapparava & Mihalcea, 2008), or detect the object of an expression in addition to its sentiment (e.g., 'the colour is lovely but it is too big' -> colour, positive; size, negative).

Sentiment programs tend to use one of two broad strategies. The first, machine learning, works by feeding the program with examples of positive and negative texts (assuming that the task is polarity detection, i.e., deciding whether a text is positive or negative) so that the algorithm can learn their typical distinguishing features. For example, a program might 'learn' that documents containing *good* more frequently than the term *bad* tend to be positive. In practice, however, the algorithms learn complex patterns that are mathematical abstractions without simple interpretations. Hence, sentiment analysis algorithms based on machine learning tend to be opaque, estimating the sentiment in texts without giving intuitive reasons for their decisions. The second type of algorithm uses a lexical approach, starting with a set of linguistically inspired rules and predicting the sentiment of a text based upon them. For example, 'The steering is very good but the car is ugly' might be judged to be positive because *good* is a known positive word and is made stronger with the booster word *very*, outweighing the known negative word *ugly*. Lexical algorithms take longer to construct but can give a clear explanation for any estimated sentiment output. Whichever approach is used, however, mistakes will sometimes be made because the heuristics will not always work. The frequency of these mistakes depends upon the type of text as well as the algorithm itself. They are particularly likely when sentiment has been expressed in an unusual way and when irony or sarcasm is present.

Context can affect the typical ways in which sentiment is expressed (Blitzer, Dredze, & Pereira, 2007). Programs that can detect sentiment accurately in one context may give poor performance in another. For example, when reviewing a smartphone, the words *heavy* and *expensive* might tend to be negative, whereas they would be irrelevant in a film review. In contrast, negative words in film reviews might include *predictable*, *slow*, and *wooden*. A program that has learned to detect sentiment based on smartphone reviews might therefore miss many opinions expressed about films. Although some sentiment analysis programs are designed to be relatively general purpose, they cannot be expected to be as accurate as programs that are targeted at a specific type of text. Hence, the accuracy of any given sentiment analysis program will vary by context and for any new type of text the researcher should expect to have to create a new sentiment analysis program or customise an existing one in order to get an optimal level of accuracy.

Social scientists wishing to use automated sentiment analysis in their research now have a wide choice of programs because many are free online or are available, often in conjunction with data, from commercial providers. For many applications it does not matter whether the software used is fully optimised as long as it is reasonably effective at detecting sentiment. It is important to be aware that systematic biases are possible, however. For example, if younger authors tend to use slang to express sentiment and the system does not recognise it then it can tend to detect fewer of their opinions.

SENTISTRENGTH

This section describes the software SentiStrength (Thelwall, Buckley, Paltoglou, Cai, & Kappas, 2010; Thelwall, Buckley, & Paltoglou, 2012). The purpose is to show how one program works and how its accuracy can be evaluated in order to illustrate some of the key sentiment analysis issues. SentiStrength can be tried live online or downloaded from http://sentistrength.wlv.ac.uk.

The goal of SentiStrength was inspired by the emotion psychology research finding that positive and negative sentiments are processed to some extent in parallel in the human brain. It therefore makes sense from a psychology perspective to detect both positive and negative sentiment at the same time rather than to attempt to make an overall judgement of polarity. In addition, emotion psychology research suggests that fine grained expressions of emotion, such as being angry, unhappy, and sad, are less basic than positivity and negativity in the sense that they seem to be socially constructed rather than being common to all human societies (Cornelius, 1996; Fox, 2008). Hence, the goal of SentiStrength is to detect both positive and negative sentiment strength in a given social web text, acknowledging that one or both could be absent. Its output takes the form of two numbers. For negative sentiment, the whole numbers −1 (no negative sentiment) to −5 (very strong negative sentiment) are used and for positive sentiment the numbers 1 (no positive sentiment) to 5 (very strong positive sentiment). A text with strong negativity but weak positivity might get a score of −4, 2.

SentiStrength uses a lexical approach. At its heart is a lexicon of 1,125 words and 1,364 word stems, each with a score for positive or negative sentiment. When these match a word in a text then this suggests the presence of sentiment and its strength (but see later). For example, *ailing* has a score of −3 in the lexicon, and so sentences containing this word may have a moderate negative sentiment. Similarly, the word stem *appreciat** has a score of +2 and so sentences matching this (e.g., appreciate, appreciated) may have a mildly positive sentiment. The scores for the individual words and word stems were initially assigned by human judgement but were checked and modified by an automated process. The basic rule for a sentence is that it is assigned the highest positive and the highest negative score for any word in it. Texts with more than one sentence are given the maximum positive and negative scores of any sentence within them. This very simple system is then modified by a number of rules to cope with other ways of expressing sentiment.

Negation is commonly used when expressing opinions. A positive term that is preceded by a negating word (e.g., not, don't) has its sentiment flipped by SentiStrength (e.g., I don't like it), whereas negative terms are neutralised (e.g., I don't hate you). These rules deal with the most common effects of negating, and the differing rules for positive and negative sentiment are due to variations in the common ways in which negating is used for them.

Terms preceded by booster words like *very* and *extremely* have their positive or negative sentiment strength increased, whereas *quite* decreases the sentiment strength of the next word. There are also rules for questions, idioms, spelling correction and punctuation as well as rules that are specific to computer-mediated communication methods of expressing sentiment. As part of this, SentiStrength has a list of emoticons, together with sentiment strength scores for them (e.g., smiley faces like =) score +2). In addition, sentiment is sometimes expressed in the social web by adding extra letters to a word. To illustrate this, the single word message *Janieeeee* in a social network site might well be read as an excited calling of someone's name, expressing a positive sentiment. The SentiStrength rule for this is that the presence of at least two additional letters in a word increases its sentiment strength, if any, by one. In sentences lacking sentiment, the spelling instead gives the sentence a mildly positive score and no negativity: −1, 2.

Any sentiment analysis program must be evaluated on a relevant data set to test its accuracy. This typically means assessing the degree to which the program agrees with the sentiment judgements of one or more people on a set of relevant texts. For SentiStrength, collections of at least 1,000 texts were gathered from each of six different areas of the social web (BBC Forum posts; Digg.com posts; MySpace comments; Runners World forum posts; tweets; and YouTube comments) and were coded for sentiment by two or three different human judges. The average of the scores assigned by the human coders formed the gold standard against which to evaluate the performance of SentiStrength. The comparisons showed that SentiStrength agreed with typical human judgments at close to the degree that they agreed with each other for most of the data sets, giving human-like accuracy for this task. The main exceptions were that it gave worse results for positive sentiment for both Digg and BBC forums. The reason for the lower accuracy was the presence of sarcastic political comments that SentiStrength frequently considered to be positive although its intent was negative (Thelwall, Buckley, & Paltoglou, 2012).

SentiStrength was designed to be accurate on most social web texts but its poor results on some collections led to the creation of versions focused on particular topics (Thelwall & Buckley, 2013). One of the topics was of tweets about UK riots and another was of tweets about a referendum about alternative voting in the UK. In both cases, relatively obscure words that were not in the lexicon were frequently used to convey sentiment (e.g., baton, scaremongers). In response, code was added to the program to identify words that often occurred in miss-classified texts so that they could be added to the lexicon. A second issue was that some of the rules to detect implicit sentiment (e.g., through misspellings or exclamation marks) did not work on the riot corpus. In the original version of SentiStrength, a neutral sentence ending with an exclamation mark was assumed to be positive, whereas for the riots texts these sentences tended to be negative. In response, an extra rule was added to detect the prevailing mood of a collection of texts using that mood as the default sentiment in such cases. This (negative mood) improved the accuracy for the riots corpus in particular.

A final and only partly successful modification of SentiStrength allowed it to take into account the sentiments of the texts before the text to be classified. The rationale behind this was that an apparently very positive text following a long sequence of neutral texts is more likely to be due to a classification error than a genuine change in sentiment. A damping rule accommodated this by reducing the size of any sudden large changes in sentiment. The rule produced very minor improvements in accuracy (Thelwall, Buckley, Paltoglou, et al., 2013).

In comparison to other programs, SentiStrength is very fast (14,000 tweets per second on a standard PC), transparent (it can describe how its scores were calculated), general purpose, and customisable, even to other languages (Vural, Cambazoglu, Senkul, & Tokgoz 2013). A more fundamental advantage for social science research of its lexical approach is that its results will not detect the topic discussed rather than sentiment about the topic. Machine learning can conflate topic and sentiment, classifying entire topics as positive or negative, and this can be a problem in social science applications. Weaknesses of SentiStrength include that it does not perform well for detecting opinions in product reviews, it cannot detect sarcasm, it cannot differentiate between different types of positive and negative emotions, and it cannot detect the object of an expression of sentiment.

SOCIAL SCIENCE APPLICATIONS

This section discusses academic sentiment analysis research in a range of different social science areas to illustrate a variety of applications. Perhaps the most generic social science application is to use sentiment analysis as part of a suite of approaches to analyse public perceptions of an event by mining online text. This has been done for important news events, for example (Hu, Ge, & Hou, 2014). Large-scale analyses almost inevitably analyse text without the knowledge or consent of the creators of the text and this can be controversial (Kennedy, 2012) and may seem strange to social scientists that are used to the principles of informed consent. Nevertheless, text that is posted freely in the public web and is not password protected or within a private forum can be analysed by researchers without consent as long as the identity of the participants is not disclosed by the researcher either directly or by quoting from them in a way that would make their identity findable by a search system (Wilkinson & Thelwall, 2011). The use of sentiment analysis and other Big Data techniques by large corporations for social engineering or persuasion is substantially more problematic, however (Tufekci, 2014).

Social Media Usage

Within the communication and media studies domain, sentiment is recognised as being important for social media systems, such as Facebook and Twitter. Emotions play an important but often unacknowledged role in communication and therefore need to be investigated so that their role can be more fully understood.

One early study of the formerly dominant social network site MySpace used human classifications to investigate how sentiment was used and shared within the comments posted to user profiles (like Facebook wall posts). Positive sentiment was widespread within the site, occurring in about two-thirds of all comments. In contrast, negativity was found in less than 20% of comments. Positivity was particularly common in tweets sent and received by female users. Overall, the prevalence of positive sentiment suggested that sending positive messages to friends within the system was an extremely important part of how it was used and perhaps also an important part of its success at the time (Thelwall, Wilkinson, & Uppal, 2010).

The issue of homophily – the extent to which friends or acquaintances tend to be similar to each other – has been investigated from the perspective of sentiment in social networks. For example, the sentiment of messages sent by MySpace users correlates with the sentiment of messages sent by their friends, even to other people. This could either be due to people with similar emotional states or expression styles attracting each other or could be due to emotions spreading to some extent from one person to another (Thelwall, 2010). Similar trends have also been found in Twitter (Bollen, Gonçalves, Ruan, & Mao, 2011). Both of these studies suggested that artificial attempts to match depressed people with more upbeat users might be an effective strategy to help with depression, although this does not seem to have been tested empirically yet. Emotional contagion in a similar sense has also been demonstrated through Facebook posts, and negativity also linked to bad weather (rain) in the city of the user (Coviello, Sohn, Kramer,

Marlow, Franceschetti, et al., 2014). More directly, an experiment has demonstrated online emotional contagion within a social network site: Facebook users tended to produce more positive posts and fewer negative posts when their news feed was manipulated to have additional positive content, and more negative posts and fewer positive posts when their news feed was manipulated to have more negative content (Kramer, Guillory, & Hancock, 2014). This study is controversial for covertly manipulating the emotions of people for research purposes (rather than passively analysing their texts, as most other studies have done) without an adequate degree of informed consent, although the experiment was covered by Facebook's standard terms and conditions (Schroeder, 2014; Verma, 2014).

A few studies have investigated the role of sentiment in Twitter. One focused on 13 extremely popular users and used the sentiment expressed in messages to them to split their audience into predominantly positive and negative groups. In addition, the sentiment of tweets posted by popular users seemed to influence the sentiment expressed by their followers, suggesting that the influence of highly popular tweeters may extend to the affective dimension (Bae & Lee, 2012), and echoing, in part, prior homophily and emotion contagion findings.

Twitter has also been analysed as a convenient data source to gain insights into offline emotional states. A large-scale investigation has shown that people's moods, at least as expressed in tweets, vary periodically and are most positive at the weekends and during holidays (Golder & Macy, 2011).

Tweets may be useful to gain insights into public reactions to events that are commonly tweeted. An investigation into the level of sentiment expressed in tweets about major news stories found that peaks in the volume of tweeting tended to be associated with small increases in the average negative sentiment strength of tweets related to the topic. It was surprising, however, that strong expressions of sentiment were relatively rare in Twitter even for emotional events. This seemed to be due to the predominant use of Twitter to broadcast facts rather than opinions, at least for news stories (Thelwall, Buckley, & Paltoglou, 2011).

Human–computer Interaction

At the social science end of computer science in the specialism of human–computer interaction, sentiment analysis has been incorporated into different computing systems in order to manage interactions with human users. These have varied from background processing tasks that improve the efficiency of the way in which text is processed for a particular task to injecting affective components into interactions with users.

An example of a background processing application is the use of SentiStrength by Yahoo! in their answers system (answers. yahoo.com). This allows website visitors to post questions in the hope that other visitors can post informative replies. If multiple users post a reply to a question then Yahoo! attempts to rank the answers so that the one is most likely to be informative is ranked first. This is better for the question asker because they are likely to get a good answer more quickly, assuming that they start to read answers from the top of the list. SentiStrength is used to detect the sentiment in feedback given to question answerers. If this feedback tends to be positive, then this boosts the ranking of the answerer's future answers on the basis that they seem to be a person that gives good answers. Experiments have shown that this use of sentiment improves the ranking of the answers (Kucuktunc, Cambazoglu, Weber, & Ferhatosmanoglu, 2012). Users of the Yahoo! Answers system probably do not know that the sentiment of their feedback helps to improve the ranking algorithm so this is an unobtrusive use of sentiment analysis.

A more direct application of sentiment detection is within autonomous dialog or chat systems. These are computer programs that seek to engage in conversation online with users in a way that simulates human behaviour. Although such agents may have a specific purpose, such as finding out what problem the user has with a specific product or service, they can also be used in a purely social context. As part of such systems, an algorithm attempts to interpret the user input, which is typically a short text message, and then tries to compose an appropriate reply. Sentiment analysis can help this by including sentiment within the algorithm deciding on an appropriate response. For example, if the user enters an apparently highly negative message then the autonomous agent might respond with a calming response. Experiments with dialog systems have shown that the inclusion of this affective component results in a more engaging experience. Perhaps more sinisterly, if the mood or 'affective profile' of the agent is manipulated, then this affects the nature of the conversation with the user (Skowron, Theunis, Rank, & Borowiec, 2011; Skowron, Theunis, Rank, & Kappas, 2013).

An automated dialog system has been embedded within agents inside of a virtual world. Here, the avatar of the agent reacts physically to the sentiment expressed by the user. In one experiment, the agent was a bartender and chatted to humans when their avatars walked into the bar. As an example of the reactions, when a user made a negative comment, the bartender would lean away and adopt a concerned facial expression. Users that were unaware of the sentiment component of the system reported that they felt more engaged with the bartender when the sentiment was activated than when it was not activated, even when they were unaware of, or did not consciously notice, the affective reactions (Skowron, Pirker, Rank, Paltoglou, Ahn, & Gobron, 2011).

Marketing

Although marketing applications drove early sentiment analysis there is little published academic research about applying sentiment analysis to social media texts for marketing purposes and there are calls for more (Gopaldas, 2014). In one important exception, brand mentions were found to be common in Twitter, with about 20% being accompanied by an expression of sentiment (Jansen, Zhang, Sobel, & Chowdury, 2009). This is powerful evidence that Twitter is a good source of data about customer attitudes to brands. The use of Twitter for market research presupposes that sentiments expressed reflect the offline attitude of senders, and perhaps also their likely future behaviour, which seems to be true (Verhagen, Nauta, & Feldberg, 2013).

A crisis in Domino's Pizza has given evidence that bad news about a company can spread particularly quickly in social media. This was triggered by the posting of a YouTube video prank by employees showing them deliberately using unhygienic food-making practices. The consequent viral spread of negative publicity underlines the importance of large companies routinely monitoring their image online because they could have detected this negative publicity through the spike in negativity associated with their brand (Park, Cha, Kim, & Jeong, 2011). Another case study focused on the apology of a CEO for his company mislabelling beef. This apology seemed to be effective at positively influencing sentiments towards the company, suggesting that the CEO had been at least partially forgiven (Park, Kim, Cha, & Jeong, 2011).

It is possible to estimate the popularity of some products from social media, with the volume and sentiment of tweets predicting popular movies in the U.S. This is perhaps a best case scenario in the sense that newly released movies seem to be a natural subject for tweets (Hennig-Thurau, Wiertz, & Feldhaus, 2012).

From a more proactive perspective, it would be useful for organisations to understand how to influence customers through social media interventions. One project has developed a mathematical model for the success of a marketing post that can help an organisation to choose the most effective one to send. The model includes factors such as the sender's gender, as well as sentiment metrics such as the ratio of positive terms to total post length and the number of negative terms. Here, effectiveness is measured in terms of the number of positive responses by recipients of the post (Chen, Tang, Wu, & Jheng, 2014).

For customer relations rather than marketing, many organisations collect customer feedback in the form of unstructured text comments and attempt to process them to identify areas of good practice and ideas for improvements. One study has built an integrated system to mine this feedback for useful information, including sentiment (Ordenes, Theodoulidis, Burton, Gruber, & Zaki, 2014). This approach also seems to be fruitful in the airline industry, where it can reveal areas where customer feedback is predominantly positive or negative (Misopoulos, Mitic, Kapoulas, & Karapiperis, 2014).

Economics

Some research has claimed that automatically detected sentiment in social media texts can be used to help predict changes in stock market prices. For example, an investigation of the Dow Jones Industrial Average found that some dimensions of mood in Twitter associated with stock market changes several days later (Bollen, Mao, & Zeng, 2011). Positive relationships have also been found between emotions in Twitter and several other stock market indicators (Nassirtoussi, Aghabozorgi, Wah, & Ngo, 2015; Zhang, Fuehres, & Gloor, 2011). Presumably, if these work then stock trading companies will be routinely using them to predict future prices and to help manage their trading strategies.

Within economics, there are also sentiment indicators derived implicitly from financial markets rather than from text (e.g., Aguiar-Conraria, Martins, & Soares, 2013), and sentiment is known to be important for financial investments (McLean & Zhao, 2014). Hence, there seems to be a need for more sentiment analysis research for economics.

Healthcare

Twitter and other social media are a logical source of health-related information, assuming that enough posts can be identified that are relevant to a given condition or behaviour to be investigated. It is not clear, however, that people will post relevant or representative information about health related conditions. Twitter may be particularly useful for types of experience that would naturally be discussed online, such as bad incidents in health settings (Greaves, Ramirez-Cano, Millett, Darzi, & Donaldson, 2013).

An investigation of smoking-related tweets has shown that it is possible to get useful health-related information from Twitter, although extensive manual coding was required. The tweets revealed predominantly positive sentiments about hookah and e-cigarettes, but negative sentiments about tobacco cigarettes (Myslín, Zhu, Chapman, & Conway, 2013). From a different perspective, another investigation searched for tweets including the names of treatments for multiple sclerosis. This was straightforward due to their distinctive names and a sentiment analysis of the results found that the oral medicines had more positive reactions then did the injected ones (Ramagopalan, Wasiak, & Cox, 2014).

Some health interventions may wish to identify influential users online in order to ensure that they give appropriate messages or advice. For this, sentiment analysis can help to detect users that are powerful enough to influence others' sentiments in online health communities (Zhao, Yen, Greer, Qiu, Mitra, & Portier, 2014). This seems to be a promising application.

Politics

The social web is a natural place to debate political issues and these are likely to generate strong emotions. Because of this, news programmes and newspapers sometimes follow social media during elections, reporting, for example, the volume of tweeting and the average level of positive or negative sentiment about parties or candidates. There have also been many academic investigations into political events that have employed sentiment analyses of social media texts as well as a proposal for a general strategy for this (Stieglitz & Dang-Xuan, 2013). For example, an analysis of tweets posted during the 2008 presidential debate between Barack Obama and John McCain, found that sentiment varied substantially according to which topic was being discussed at a particular point in time (Diakopoulos & Shamma, 2010).

A frequent theme in the media has been the light-hearted use of Twitter sentiment or volume to predict the outcome of an election. There have also been several academic studies that have investigated this seriously. For example, one monitored tweeting relevant to parties in a German election and found that posts in Twitter tended to reflect the known offline concerns of the electorate. In addition, the volume of tweeting broadly reflected the eventual election outcomes (Tumasjan, Sprenger, Sandner, & Welpe, 2011) and similar results have been found for other countries (e.g., Ceron, Curini, Iacus, & Porro, 2014). Nevertheless, election prediction seems to be a very difficult problem and one that is unlikely to succeed because of biasing factors, such as social media users tending to be younger, richer and less technophobic than average (Metaxas, Mustafaraj, & Gayo-Avello, 2011).

Two studies have investigated the role of sentiment in distributing political messages online. These showed that the presence of sentiment helps to disseminate a message both in Twitter and Facebook, and that the sentiment itself also diffuses with the message (Stieglitz & Dang-Xuan, 2012a, 2012b).

Education

Since many students routinely share their experiences with others online whilst studying, it may be possible to extract useful information about the learning experience from their social media posts or interactions within online learning environments (Suero Montero & Suhonen, 2014). An investigation has shown that this is possible with Facebook posts but did not evaluate the usefulness of the information extracted (Ortigosa, Martín, & Carro, 2014). A collaborative learning environment has gone further by providing emotion-aware feedback to students during online learning tasks, but it required them to explicitly record their emotional state (Feidakis, Caballé, Daradoumis, Jiménez, & Conesa, 2014) and perhaps a future system will automatically detect it.

CONCLUSION

Sentiment analysis software can be used to research social science issues. This software is much faster and cheaper than human coding. Coupled with the huge amount of textual data that is now freely available in the social web and is relatively easy to access, this has created the potential to conduct many types of big data and smaller scale analyses of the role of sentiment in the social web. Although this could have opened the floodgates for sentiment-related research in many different social science disciplines, computer scientists and information scientists are still leading the way, perhaps because of weaker traditions of large scale analyses in other fields. Politics is a partial exception because there have been many academic investigations into the role of sentiment in online political discourse. The social web is a natural focus for political discussions in addition to discussions of brands and products.

An important limitation for many of the studies discussed above is that the social web is evolving over time, both in terms of the sites that are the most popular and the typical user profiles and usage strategies. Hence the findings of even the best studies are likely to become outdated and will need to be periodically repeated. Another issue is that few of the studies are robust, particularly if they are individual case studies or are limited to a particular country or narrow time period. As a result, the findings here should not be taken as definitive in most cases.

In terms of future work, there is an ongoing need to follow up the studies discussed above for different countries, languages, and social websites. There is also scope for applying sentiment analysis methods in new ways to social media texts in order to address problems of interest to social science disciplines. An important limitation is that thousands of texts are needed to give robust evidence and so investigations of obscure online topics are likely to be unsuccessful. A good study would need to identify an issue that is discussed extensively online and is either of particular interest online or seems likely to be reflected in a relatively unbiased way online.

REFERENCES

Aguiar-Conraria, L., Martins, M. M., & Soares, M. J. (2013). Convergence of the economic sentiment cycles in the Eurozone: A time-frequency analysis. *JCMS: Journal of Common Market Studies*, 51(3), 377–398.

Bae, Y., & Lee, H. (2012). Sentiment analysis of Twitter audiences: Measuring the positive or negative influence of popular twitterers. *Journal of the American Society for Information Science and Technology*, 63(12), 2521–2535.

Blitzer, J., Dredze, M., & Pereira, F. (2007). Biographies, Bollywood, boom-boxes and blenders: Domain adaptation for sentiment classification. In Proceedings of the 45th Annual Meeting of the Association of Computational Linguistics (ACL 2007). Prague: Czech Republic: ACL (pp. 440–447).

Bollen, J., Gonçalves, B., Ruan, G., & Mao, H. (2011). Happiness is assortative in online social networks. *Artificial Life*, 17(3), 237–251.

Bollen, J., Mao, H., & Zeng, X. (2011). Twitter mood predicts the stock market. *Journal of Computational Science*, 2(1), 1–8.

Ceron, A., Curini, L., Iacus, S. M., & Porro, G. (2014). Every tweet counts? How sentiment analysis of social media can improve our knowledge of citizens' political preferences with an application to Italy and France. *New Media & Society*, 16(2), 340–358.

Chen, Y. L., Tang, K., Wu, C. C., & Jheng, R. Y. (2014). Predicting the influence of users' posted information for eWOM advertising in social networks. *Electronic Commerce Research and Applications*, 13(6), 431–439.

Cornelius, R. R. (1996). *The science of emotion*. Upper Saddle River, NJ: Prentice Hall.

Coviello, L., Sohn, Y., Kramer, A.D.I., Marlow, C., Franceschetti, M., Christakis, N., & Fowler, J. (2014). Detecting emotional contagion in massive social networks. *PLoS ONE*, 9(3), e90315. doi:10.1371/journal.pone.0090315

Diakopoulos, N. A., & Shamma, D. A. (2010). Characterizing debate performance via aggregated Twitter sentiment. In *Proceedings of the SIGCHI Conference on Human Factors in Computing Systems* (pp. 1195–1198). New York: ACM Press.

Feidakis, M., Caballé, S., Daradoumis, T., Jiménez, D. G., & Conesa, J. (2014). Providing emotion awareness and affective feedback to virtualised collaborative learning scenarios. *International Journal of Continuing Engineering Education and Life Long Learning*, 24(2), 141–167.

Fox, E. (2008). *Emotion science*. Basingstoke: Palgrave Macmillan.

Golder, S. A., & Macy, M. W. (2011). Diurnal and seasonal mood vary with work, sleep, and daylength across diverse cultures. *Science*, 333(6051), 1878–1881.

Gopaldas, A. (2014). Marketplace sentiments. *Journal of Consumer Research*, 41(4), 995–1014.

Greaves, F., Ramirez-Cano, D., Millett, C., Darzi, A., & Donaldson, L. (2013). Harnessing the cloud of patient experience: Using social media to detect poor quality healthcare. *BMJ Quality & Safety*, 22(3), 251–255.

Hennig-Thurau, T., Wiertz, C., & Feldhaus, F. (2012). Exploring the 'Twitter effect': An investigation of the impact of microblogging word of mouth on consumers' early adoption of new products. Available at SSRN, 2016548.

Hu, H., Ge, Y., & Hou, D. (2014). Using web crawler technology for geo-events analysis: A case study of the Huangyan Island incident. *Sustainability*, 6(4), 1896–1912.

Jansen, B. J., Zhang, M., Sobel, K., & Chowdury, A. (2009). Twitter power: Tweets as electronic word of mouth. *Journal of the American Society for Information Science and Technology*, 60(11), 2169–2188.

Kennedy, H. (2012). Perspectives on sentiment analysis. *Journal of Broadcasting & Electronic Media*, 56(4), 435–450.

Kramer, A. D., Guillory, J. E., & Hancock, J. T. (2014). Experimental evidence of massive-scale emotional contagion through social networks. *Proceedings of the National Academy of Sciences*, 111(24), 8788–8790.

Kucuktunc, O., Cambazoglu, B.B., Weber, I., & Ferhatosmanoglu, H. (2012). A large-scale sentiment analysis for Yahoo! Answers, *Proceedings of the 5th ACM International Conference on Web Search and Data Mining*.

Liu, B. (2012). *Sentiment analysis and opinion mining*. New York: Morgan Claypool.

McLean, R. D., & Zhao, M. (2014). The business cycle, investor sentiment, and costly external finance. *The Journal of Finance*, 69(3), 1377–1409.

Metaxas, P. T., Mustafaraj, E., & Gayo-Avello, D. (2011). How (not) to predict elections. In *Privacy, Security, Risk and Trust (PASSAT)*. Los Alamitos: IEEE Press (pp. 165–171).

Misopoulos, F., Mitic, M., Kapoulas, A., & Karapiperis, C. (2014). Uncovering customer service experiences with Twitter: The case of airline industry. *Management Decision*, 52(4), 705–723.

Myslín, M., Zhu, S. H., Chapman, W., & Conway, M. (2013). Using Twitter to examine smoking behavior and perceptions of emerging tobacco products. *Journal of Medical Internet Research*, 15(8), e174.

Nassirtoussi, A. K., Aghabozorgi, S., Wah, T. Y., & Ngo, D. C. L. (2015). Text mining of news-headlines for FOREX market prediction: A Multi-layer Dimension Reduction Algorithm with semantics and sentiment. *Expert Systems with Applications*, 42(1), 306–324.

Ordenes, F. V., Theodoulidis, B., Burton, J., Gruber, T., & Zaki, M. (2014). Analyzing customer experience feedback using text mining: A linguistics-based approach. *Journal of Service Research*, 17(3), 278–295.

Ortigosa, A., Martín, J. M., & Carro, R. M. (2014). Sentiment analysis in Facebook and its application to e-learning. *Computers in Human Behavior*, 31(1), 527–541.

Pang, B., & Lee, L. (2008). Opinion mining and sentiment analysis. *Foundations and Trends in Information Retrieval*, 2(1–2), 1–135.

Park, J., Cha, M., Kim, H., & Jeong, J. (2011). Managing bad news in social media: A case study on Domino's Pizza crisis. Proceedings of the ICWSM 2012. Menlo Park: AAAI Press. Retrieved from http://www.aaai.org/ocs/index.php/ICWSM/ICWSM12/paper/view/4672

Park, J., Kim, H., Cha, M., & Jeong, J. (2011). CEO's apology in Twitter: A case study of the fake beef labeling incident by e-mart. In A. Datta, S. Shulman, et al. (eds.) *Social Informatics* (pp. 300–303). Berlin: Springer Verlag.

Ramagopalan, S., Wasiak, R., & Cox, A. P. (2014). Using Twitter to investigate opinions about multiple sclerosis treatments: A descriptive, exploratory study. *F1000Research*, 3, 216.

Schroeder, R. (2014). Big Data and the brave new world of social media research. *Big Data & Society*, 1(2), 1–11.

Skowron, M., Pirker, H., Rank, S., Paltoglou, G., Ahn, J., & Gobron, S. (2011). No peanuts! Affective cues for the virtual bartender. Proceedings of the Twenty-Fourth International Florida Artificial Intelligence Research Society Conference (FLAIRS2011), (pp. 117–122).

Skowron, M., Theunis, M., Rank, S., & Borowiec, A. (2011). Effect of affective profile on communication patterns and affective expressions in interactions with a dialog system. In S. D'Mello, A. Graesser, B. Schuller, & JC. Martin (eds.), *Affective Computing and Intelligent Interaction* (pp. 347–356). Berlin: Springer Verlag.

Skowron, M., Theunis, M., Rank, S., & Kappas, A. (2013). Affect and social processes in online communication – Experiments with an affective dialog system. *IEEE Transactions on Affective Computing*, 4(3), 267–279.

Stieglitz, S., & Dang-Xuan, L. (2012a). Political communication and influence through microblogging – An empirical analysis of sentiment in Twitter messages and retweet behavior. In 45th Hawaii International Conference on System Sciences (HICSS 2012). Los Alamitos: IEEE Press (pp. 3500–3509).

Stieglitz, S., & Dang-Xuan, L. (2012b). Impact and diffusion of sentiment in public communication on Facebook. In ECIS Proceedings (paper 98). http://aisel.aisnet.org/ecis2012/98

Stieglitz, S., & Dang-Xuan, L. (2013). Social media and political communication: A social media analytics framework. *Social Network Analysis and Mining*, 3(4), 1277–1291.

Strapparava, C., & Mihalcea, R. (2008). Learning to identify emotions in text. Proceedings of the 2008 ACM symposium on applied computing (pp. 1556–1560). New York, NY: ACM Press.

Suero Montero, C., & Suhonen, J. (2014). Emotion analysis meets learning analytics: online learner profiling beyond numerical data. In *Proceedings of the 14th Koli Calling International Conference on Computing Education Research* (pp. 165–169). New York: ACM Press.

Thelwall, M. (2010). Emotion homophily in social network site messages. *First Monday*, 15(4). http://firstmonday.org/ojs/index.php/fm/article/view/2897/2483

Thelwall, M., & Buckley, K. (2013). Topic-based sentiment analysis for the Social Web: The role of mood and issue-related words. *Journal of the American Society for Information Science and Technology*, 64(8), 1608–1617.

Thelwall, M., Buckley, K., & Paltoglou, G. (2012). Sentiment strength detection for the social Web. *Journal of the American Society for Information Science and Technology*, 63(1), 163–173.

Thelwall, M., Buckley, K., & Paltoglou, G. (2011). Sentiment in Twitter events. *Journal of the American Society for Information Science and Technology*, 62(2), 406–418.

Thelwall, M., Wilkinson, D., & Uppal, S. (2010). Data mining emotion in social network communication: Gender differences in MySpace, *Journal of the American Society for Information Science and Technology*, 61(1), 190–199.

Thelwall, M., Buckley, K., Paltoglou, G. Cai, D., & Kappas, A. (2010). Sentiment strength detection in short informal text. *Journal of the American Society for Information Science and Technology*, 61(12), 2544–2558.

Thelwall, M., Buckley, K., Paltoglou, G., Skowron, M., Garcia, D., Gobron, S., Ahn, J., Kappas, A., Küster, D., & Holyst, J.A. (2013). Damping Sentiment Analysis in Online Communication: Discussions, monologs and dialogs. In A. Gelbukh (Ed.): *CICLing 2013, Part II*, LNCS 7817 (pp. 1–12). Heidelberg: Springer Verlag.

Tufekci, Z. (2014). Engineering the public: Big data, surveillance and computational politics. *First Monday*, 19(7). http://www.firstmonday.dk/ojs/index.php/fm/article/view/4901/4097

Tumasjan, A., Sprenger, T. O., Sandner, P. G., & Welpe, I. M. (2011). Election forecasts with Twitter: How 140 characters reflect the political landscape. *Social Science Computer Review*, 29(4), 402–418.

Verhagen, T., Nauta, A., & Feldberg, F. (2013). Negative online word-of-mouth: Behavioral indicator or emotional release? *Computers in Human Behavior*, 29(4), 1430–1440.

Verma, I.M. (2014). Editorial expression of concern: Experimental evidence of massive scale emotional contagion through social networks. *Proceedings of the National Academy of Sciences*, 111(29), 10779.

Vural, G., Cambazoglu, B. B., Senkul, P., & Tokgoz, O. (2013). A framework for sentiment analysis in Turkish: Application to polarity detection of movie reviews in Turkish, Computer and Information Sciences III, pp. 437–445.

Wilkinson, D., & Thelwall, M. (2011). Researching personal information on the public web methods and ethics. *Social Science Computer Review*, 29(4), 387–401.

Zhang, X., Fuehres, H., & Gloor, P. A. (2011). Predicting stock market indicators through Twitter 'I hope it is not as bad as I fear'. *Procedia-Social and Behavioral Sciences*, 26, 55–62.

Zhao, K., Yen, J., Greer, G., Qiu, B., Mitra, P., & Portier, K. (2014). Finding influential users of online health communities: a new metric based on sentiment influence. *Journal of the American Medical Informatics Association*, 21(e2), e212-e218.

PART VII
Social Media Platforms

The Ontology of Tweets: Mixed-Method Approaches to the Study of Twitter

Dhiraj Murthy

This chapter focuses on Twitter and the unique challenges associated with data collection and analysis on this microblogging platform. Specifically, many big data approaches that are popular for studying tweets are tremendously useful, but are often ill-suited to more in-depth contextualized analysis of tweets. The chapter speaks to this issue and proposes alternative approaches to create a more balanced means of analysis. Further, the chapter proposes a framework to categorize tweets, addressing issues of ontology and coding. It draws on qualitative approaches, such as grounded theory, to demonstrate the value of a solid coding scheme for the qualitative analysis of tweets. To illustrate the value of this approach, the chapter draws on a case study, the Twitter response to the controversial song Accidental Racist, and shows examples of how this emergent coding of Twitter corpora can be done in practice. This case study illustrates how the proposed approaches offer ways to tackle themes such as racism or sarcasm, which have been traditionally difficult to interpret. Finally, the chapter draws some conclusions around a) Twitter as a platform for mixed-method approaches, and b) the value of relying on established approaches, like grounded theory, to inform Twitter analysis.

INTRODUCTION

Social media data have the capacity to give us insights into things that we have never been able to see before. Indeed, there is a highly diverse and vibrant set of literature just covering the popular microblogging platform Twitter. Big data methods have been successfully applied to a variety of contexts using Twitter data such as large-scale analysis of emotions (Wenbo, Lu, Thirunarayan, & Sheth, 2012), social movements (Tinati, Halford,

Carr, & Pope, 2014) and civil disturbances (Procter, Vis, & Voss, 2013). This work argues that many types of inferences about the social world can be made from Twitter data. However, a problem is that all media facilitate particular types of communication systems (an issue recognized by some of these authors). Twitter particularly affords in-the-moment content such as textual comments, photos, links, etc. Though we may like to think that just about anything about human behavior can be deciphered from Twitter data, that simply is not true.

There are also challenges associated with data collection and analysis on Twitter (boyd & Crawford, 2012). These have ranged from sampling issues such as the limits of collecting data from the free 1% Spritzer stream (boyd & Crawford, 2012) to difficulties in inferring demographic attributes such as age, race, and gender (Murthy, Gross, & Pensavalle, 2016; Sloan, Morgan, Burnap, & Williams, 2015). The focus of this chapter is on Twitter, and the unique challenges associated with data collection and analysis on this microblogging platform. Specifically, many big data approaches that are popular for studying tweets are tremendously useful, but are often ill-suited to more in-depth contextualized analysis of tweets. This chapter speaks to this debate and proposes the use of mixed methods approaches to create a more balanced means of analysis. For example, hand coding can be used to critically categorize tweets by addressing issues of ontology – our assumptions about the world. Specifically, coding categories can be emergent, undergoing several stages of reflection and engagement with theory in that domain (e.g. race, gender, and moral panics). What I mean here by 'ontology' builds from Hardt's and Negri's (2005) argument of 'new ontology' – which Murphy (2001, p. 22), succinctly defines as 'an innovative account of the being-in-process in which we are immersed'. Of course, we cannot reduce all subjective bias, but we can approach things like coding practice with some reflection on our ontological position. Hardt and Negri (2005, p. 312) argue that this type of a critical 'new ontology' is part of their desire not to engage in 'repeating old rituals', but, rather, 'launching a new investigation in order to formulate a new science of society and politics [… that] is not about piling up statistics or mere sociological facts [… but] immersing ourselves in the movements of history and the anthropological transformations of subjectivity'. Descriptive logics, knowledge representation systems that 'subscribe to an object centered view of the world' (Baader, 2003, p. 351), rely on formal codification systems with strict notations and syntax. But, like all forms of classification, are shaped by our worldview. In the case of the semantic web, for example, what metadata categories are deployed reflects a particular ontology, which can come from a privileged gender, racial, and/or socioeconomic position. Tweet codification systems are similarly affected from what metadata is selected for study to how text, links, or hashtags are categorized.

Ultimately, this chapter presents an overview of means to categorize tweets, addressing issues of ontology and coding. It draws on qualitative approaches, such as grounded theory, to demonstrate the value of a solid coding scheme for the analysis of tweets. To illustrate the value of this approach, the chapter shows examples of how this can be done in practice taken from my own research. Finally, the chapter draws some conclusions around a) Twitter as a platform for mixed-method approaches, and b) the value of relying on established approaches, like grounded theory, to inform Twitter analysis. Emergent, open approaches to the study of Twitter-derived data can not only advance what we can reliably infer from the popular medium, but also ultimately contribute to social knowledge. This chapter will first review our usual assumptions around Twitter research – especially around coding systems – before offering alternative approaches and operationalizing frameworks.

OUR USUAL ASSUMPTIONS

The usual assumption in studies using Twitter data is that the creation of knowledge from coded Twitter data is best served by closed coding systems, wherein attributes of tweet data (e.g. links, mentions, hashtags and text) are given pre-defined coded categories. These types of closed coding systems set categories to be studied and research method(s) is/are applied. In contrast, an open system allows for codes to be altered or changed. Closed systems are common in the natural and medical sciences. In the case of the former, vegetation types, for example, have been classically categorized via closed coding systems (Ellenberg & Klötzli, 1972) and, in the case of the latter, as Stock et al. (1996) observe, 'the common attributes of the variations of treatment conditions are listed and given code numbers'. In the context of Twitter, a preference of closed coding systems comes from computer science-based approaches. Indeed, more interest in Twitter's infancy came from disciplines such as computer science and information systems rather than from the social sciences (e.g. Bollen, Pepe, & Mao, 2009; Kwak, Lee, Park, & Moon, 2010). Though this seminal work was path breaking, it led to a normative thinking that closed coding systems are better for for studying Twitter data. A commonly held assumption behind the preference to closed coding systems was that computational approaches were the best way to study Twitter data. This is evidenced by many studies, wherein frequencies of mentions or hashtags were used as a proxy, rather than part of a theory building exercise. The literature around Twitter as a detection system, wherein Twitter is used to sense events, social (Cataldi, Caro, & Schifanella, 2010) and physical (Sakaki, Okazaki, & Matsuo, 2010), is an example of this.

ALTERNATIVE EPISTEMOLOGIES AND ONTOLOGIES

However, within the disciplines of computer science and information systems themselves, arguments were being made early on for hybrid or alternative methods to understanding Twitter data (i.e. Honeycutt & Herring, 2009). And when social scientists arrived after computer scientists to Twitter-related work, the call for critical epistemologies was renewed. This work has argued, for example, that hashtags and mentions imply complex social contingencies (Florini, 2014). Other work has argued that we need to be cumulative: tweet actions are accompanied by temporality and a tweet at one time does not necessarily mean the same thing another time (Murthy, 2013). Additionally, digital ethnography has drawn from experience in ethnography and argues that learning more about the culture of a digital space is important (Kozinets, 2010; Murthy, 2011). In this sense, an emphasis is made on having experiential/cultural knowledge about a tweet corpus. This is viewed as integral to inquiry. Though it is not always apparent to Twitter researchers, Twitter is a 'field' in the Bourdieusian sense in that, as Lindgren and Lundström (2011) argue, the medium constitutes part of a social field with rules and presuppositions specific to it. And, speaking from experience, I have often found myself deep in the field when coding a large sample of tweets. The process can be immersive, drawing one into a specific cultural context as ethnography does for sociologists and anthropologists. Computational approaches have tended to shy away from these more 'messy' social scientific aspects of Twitter, which also include contentious material (e.g. sexist, racist, and homophobic content). However, 'messy', hard to code Twitter content (e.g. sarcasm) and users (e.g. transgender, multiracial, or transgeographical) have an important relationship to reflective inquiry.

METHODS

Twitter data are very complex and not terribly straightforward. As such, these data are often poorly served by simply applying deductive reasoning. And as boyd and Crawford emphasize (2012, p. 668), 'Big data is at its most effective when researchers take account of the complex methodological processes that underlie the analysis of that data'. This is not to say that traditional bottom-up inductive and top-down deductive methods are not useful for studying Twitter data. However, inductive and deductive methods have their own limitations and abductive methods, a form of reasoning 'for finding the best explanations among a set of possible ones' (Paul, 1993), were developed as an alternative approach out of responses to the reliance on model selection in the sciences (Bhaskar, 1976; Harré, 1976). In addition, mixed approaches to studying Twitter data open up possibilities.

In the case of Twitter work that is not altogether straightforward, other approaches can be highly beneficial. For example, with retroduction, a type of abductive method that emphasizes 'asking why' (Olsen, 2012, p. 215), researchers are able to probe the data regularly and to 'avoid overgeneralization but searching for reasons and causes' (Olsen, 2012, p. 216) instead. Or put another way, 'the retroductive researcher, unlike the inductive researcher, has something to look for' (Blaikie, 2004). In the context of Twitter research, retroduction emphasizes 'allowing for contradictory voices' (Olsen, 2012). Similarly, Poole (2015) argues that retroduction allows us to be stopped by a surprise and then to try to comprehend it, enabling us to encounter problems and make sense of them. The idea behind such approaches is to highlight a sense of openness towards one's data and possible research questions.

CODING TWEETS

There now exist a variety of methods to code tweets and their users (e.g. Dann, 2010; Honeycutt & Herring, 2009; Krishnamurthy, Gill, & Arlitt, 2008). Most of these frameworks examine the type of communication within tweets such as directed mentions via the @ symbol, replies, retweets, and general statements. Additionally, they also examine the types of content within tweets (e.g. promotion, personal reporting, link sharing, etc.) However, Twitter data generally follows a power law curve with a long tail, a distribution seen in many forms of empirical data (Clauset, Shalizi, & Newman, 2009). This opens up interesting possibilities for selective coding. Specifically, a large percentage of mentions, hashtags, and links are directed to a small group of popular users, tags, and domains.

For example, Wu et al. (2011) in their Firehose sample (which includes all tweets available), found that a mere .05% of users they sampled accounted for almost half of the URLs in their collected data. Because of this distribution, it is possible to develop manageable coding rubrics and code small groups of users, domains, and hashtags, or other elements of Twitter data. This approach allows one to analyze large numbers of tweets (Wu et al., 2011) and can also be used to complement machine-learning classification methods. Hand coding of tweets has also been used in a diverse range of contexts (e.g. Hughes, St Denis, Palen, & Anderson, 2014) and is considered the gold standard. Given this, it is critical for researchers in this field to keep coding methods highly robust.

Additionally, the types of communication the tweet indicates (e.g. promotion, referral, or personal status) can be coded. Robust ways to automatically classify whether the tweet contains a link, mention, or hashtag are readily available and can be combined with hand coding to discern more detail about tweet corpora. Additionally, coding methods can provide further detail on the types of users producing and consuming content in corpora and whether tweets were from an individual user, organization, bot, etc. All of these standardized variables can either be human coded, machine learned, or some combination thereof (e.g. supervised learning). I have done all of these with success. However, imposing pre-ordained coding categories can limit our understanding not only of individual tweets, but also larger Twitter discourses and the relationship between types of users and individual tweets. For example, the same text in a tweet could be serious when posted by an older user and sarcastic when posted by a younger user. Add race, gender, location, socioeconomic status, and a variety of other sociological variables and our ability to code with confidence can be significantly increased.

Although there are major pushes to move to exclusively computationally based coding models, there are major limitations to these approaches. Mixed-method approaches can be particularly useful here. A larger argument I am making is that the ways in which we code social media data have enormous impacts on the empirical knowledge we are able to decipher from these data. Even if coding is systematic, it does not preclude miscoding. What I mean by this is that if coders are given coding rubrics that are leading, oriented around particular ontologies, or too narrowly defined, some content just gets missed. Of course, this can and does happen with interview-based coding. However, these coders usually have more context given the much greater verbosity of an interview compared to a 140 character tweet. Brevity is not the sole factor here as interviews are also often videotaped and gestural cues can assist with the success of the coding process.

GROUNDED THEORY

One tandem method that has been used in a variety of data-driven contexts including Twitter is grounded theory, a method that is premised on searching for possible explanations in the data rather than setting up hypotheses and testing them (an approach often ill-suited to Twitter-based research). Glaser and Strauss (2009), seminal to building the field, argued that reviewing collected data repeatedly and coding data into categories enables one to avoid some of the biases and limitations of overly positivistic research methods. Or, as Corbin and Strauss (2015) highlight, 'the complexity of phenomena direct us to locate action in context, to look at action and interaction over time (process), and to examine action and interaction in routine as well as problematic situations in order to obtain a better understanding of how these relate' (p. 22). Following Corbin and Strauss, my aim was not merely to code individual tweets, but to view tweets as part of a larger tweet 'context'. From this perspective, it is important to also understand the user who tweeted as well as the larger contexts they sit within. As Corbin and Strauss (2015) discuss, a key feature of grounded theory is: '[T]he concepts out of which the theory is constructed are derived from data collected during the research process and not chosen *prior* to beginning the research. It is this feature that grounds the theory and gives the methodology its name' (p. 7, original emphasis). For this reason, employing emergent coding methods – though they are challenging – present tremendous opportunities to understand tweets individually and collectively.

The advantage of this method is that it can also be combined with structured data. The ability to combine unstructured data such as status updates with structured data has utility for a wide variety of social media-related research work. For example, JavaScript Object Notation (JSON) data derived from Twitter provides structured fields such as 'user_mentions', 'hashtags' and 'in_reply_to_user_ID_str'. Many social media application programming interfaces (APIs) deliver data via JSON. The format is useful for its readability by humans as it consists of a series of defined attributes and values rather than having abstract variable names or numerical variables. For example, an excerpt of JSON output for my Twitter ID is:

```
"user": {
"name": "dhirajmurthy",
"friendsCount": 771,
"followersCount": 1534,
"listedCount": 100,
"statusesCount": 2609,}
```

Figure 33.1 illustrates how I have holistically incorporated classic grounded theory approaches into the research design process. Specifically, the top of Figure 33.1 emphasizes that one should begin with the research problem and literature review, but not preordained research questions. Rather, as 'Field Research #1' in Figure 33.1 indicates, data should be collected and analyzed simultaneously, a process that leads to constant comparison and from there the generation of all possible conceptual categories or explanations.

With these larger conceptual categories in place (and their properties determined), one is able to then implement a coding method. Axial coding, where a category is placed in the center of analysis and a set of relationships is created surrounding it, enables researchers to make connections between codes and to build explanatory models as part of a process of seeing relations between codes (Glaser & Strauss, 2009). This type of coding is iterative as categories are placed and hypothetical relationships explored. For example, one could investigate situations causal to the category as well as the effects of the category

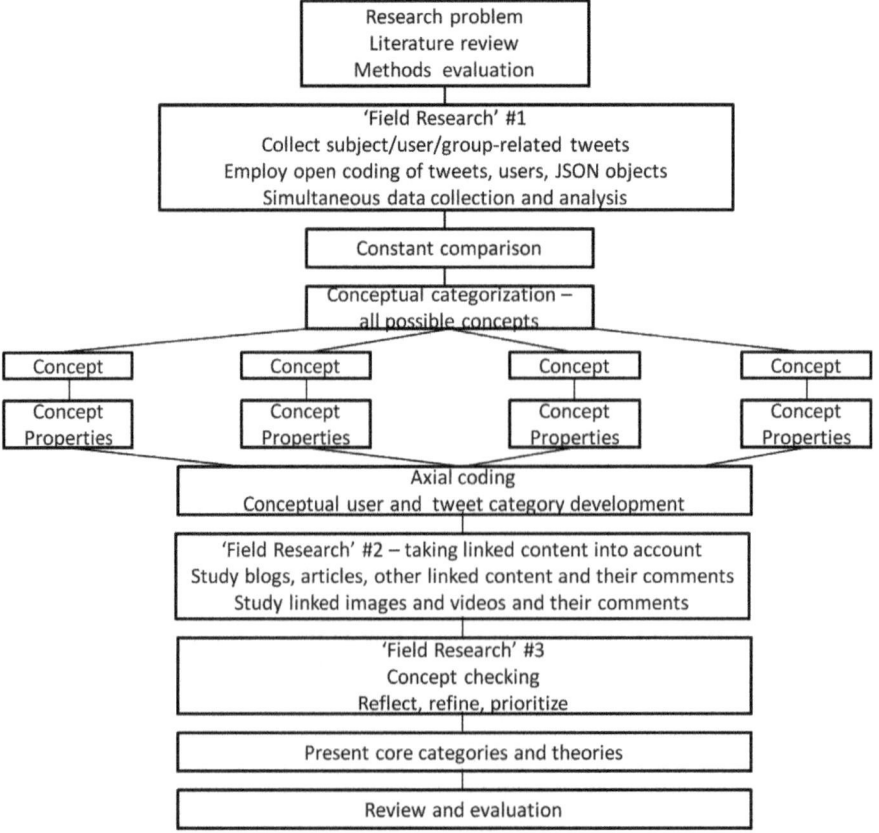

Figure 33.1   Theory building (adapted from Goulding, 2002, p. 115)

and iterate as part of axial coding until the relationship sets are robust. However, there are limitations to this and 'Field research' adds value to the coding and analysis process. Specifically, 'Field Research #2' in Figure 33.1 emphasizes following some of the content embedded within tweets to contextualize the content. For example, after looking at linked URLs in a dataset, one may feel a need to code content at this point as this process could change what coding categories are deemed relevant. I provide examples in the next section regarding how this has unfolded in my own practice. 'Field Research #3' is a synthetic phase, where attempts are made to synthesize conceptual categories and refine their parameters and prioritize core categories and theory. This phase provides an opportunity to reflect on how categories have developed. The core categories that have emerged can be part of a mixed methods project, where, for example, they are used with machine learning to extract tweets that might correspond to the categories of interest. Having this type of reflexive process also has the advantage of providing more nuanced categories that are then applied to computational big data methods including sentiment analysis.

IN PRACTICE

Operationalizing these types of frameworks do require a different ontology of tweets in the sense that many of our approaches to studying Twitter are often closed. This may come as a surprise to some. However, as Zimmer and Proferes (2014) report, 16% of research on Twitter employed sentiment analysis. Because computer science and information science have historically been the majority producers of research that uses Twitter data (Zimmer & Proferes, 2014, p. 252), the dominant ontological worldviews in these fields have had great influence on how we study Twitter data. Mixed method approaches such as that described in Figure 33.1 require one to be open in the inquiry, allowing coding to be emergent. Tweets are not merely bits of text. We, as researchers, have a real opportunity to ask what is happening in the tweet and to think about Twitter API-derived JSON data holistically. For example, Manovich's (2001) notion of 'digital objects' can be useful in thinking of tweets as a complex entity, rather than merely as a collection of 140 characters. Specifically, tweets can be thought of as, what Manovich (2001, p. 37) referred to in the context of web pages, 'interfaces to a multimedia database'. In addition, as Quan-Haase et al. (2015) argue, the context of social media use matters (in their case, communities of digital humanities scholars shaped the content and organization of tweets). Just like any text can be taken out of context, so can tweets.

A key aspect of this is to think openly of what collected tweet data are helping us study, broadly speaking. Again, this requires a certain ontological openness to the research process. Corollaries to this are:

(a) 'Are we being reflexive on the point of view/ standpoint we are interpreting?' and
(b) 'Are we being flexible or following prescribed rules?'

Though these steps can be seen as a barrier to the Twitter research process, I firmly believe they open up exciting new lines of research possibilities. For example, Figure 33.2 visually illustrates how I adapted Corbin and Strauss's (2015) model specifically to Twitter data.

This model leverages a continual collection and analysis method in order to discern social knowledge that is not straightforward. After raw tweet data are obtained (the 'COLLECT' phase), the API may need to be queried regularly in the 'CONTINUED' phase to study relevant conversations, images, followers, other hashtags, external media, etc. Figure 33.3 illustrates how I applied this to work on #accidentalracist, a hashtag associated with

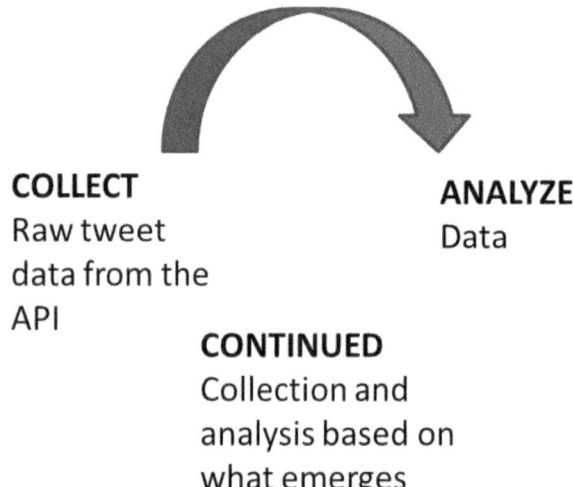

Figure 33.2 Data collection and relationship model (figure adapted from Corbin and Strauss, 2015, p. 8)

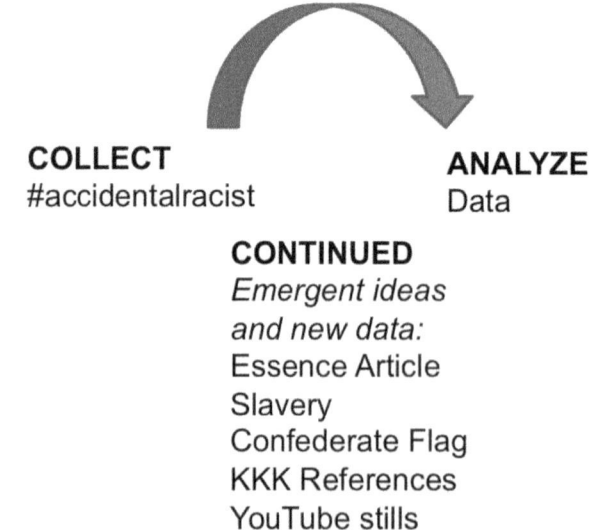

Figure 33.3 Continuous open coding Twitter data model applied to #accidentalracist

a controversial 2013 duet by Brad Paisley and LL Cool J that received significant attention on Twitter and became a trending topic (Muse, 2013). The hashtag covered comments about the song, which mixes country and rap, race (as the song refers to slavery, the Confederate flag, and KKK), and various interview gaffes by the artists. These data presented a very complex social engagement with the album that ranges from dismissive to supportive as well as involving various levels of richness. In other words, there is a discursive value to the hashtag. However, as is common with Twitter data, there is also a lot of noise and a difficulty in discerning the messages of what people are expressing, what Graves, McDonald, & Goggins (2014) refer to as a 'signal' in tweet data.

Figure 33.3 illustrates how I overcame some of these issues by an iterative process of coding and analyzing data, which, like many qualitative methods more broadly, sees the iterative research process as a journey that does not 'follow a straight line' (Bryman & Burgess, 2002, p. 208). For example, I went back and expanded URLs and added top-level domains to my data set. I also followed some of the top links that revealed important media sources, such as an article by Essence Magazine (2013) which briefly described the album and asked its reader base of African–American women to vote whether the song helped race relations or not. Operationalizing this type of ontology requires several stages of coding. Key to this approach is to be open to diverse messages in one's data as the example in Figure 33.3 illustrates.

Figure 33.4 illustrates how memo making during collection and analysis is a 'crucial step' (Charmaz & Mitchell, 2001, p. 167) to both coding development and theory building. Also, comparisons across diverse data at each stage provide reflexivity and triangulation, rather than proving particular paradigms. As Figure 33.4 illustrates, memo making at each stage is integral as this allows researchers to be open to what knowledge Twitter data can help build. In this framework, I began sampling by date (age, hashtag, seed user, Twitter list, etc.) and completed the preliminary '1st stage coding'. I then actively collected further data like linked images, while coding. Specifically, this coding process guided what further data I needed.

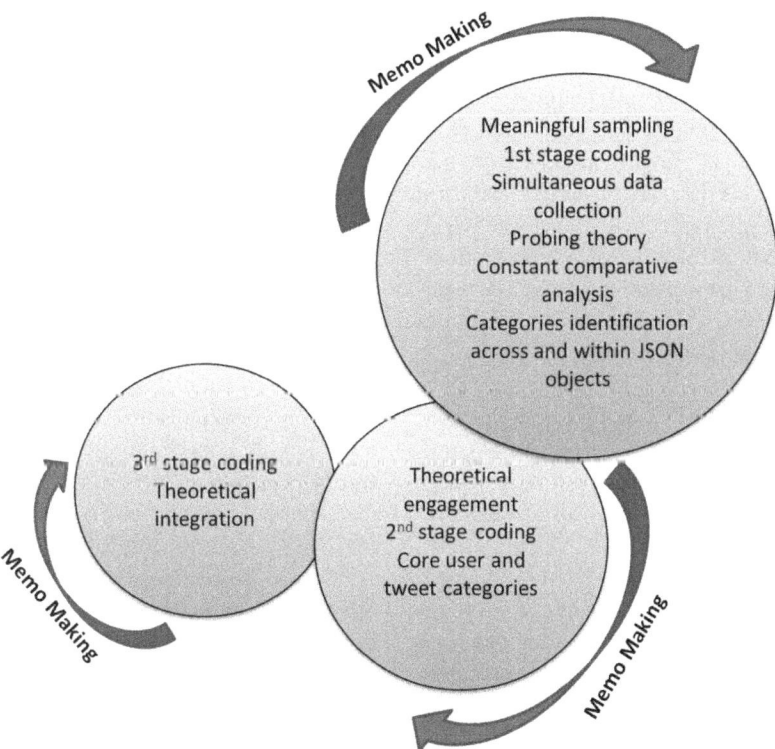

Figure 33.4 Operationalization of Twitter coding model (figure adapted from Birks and Mills, 2015)

I iteratively compared codes and subcodes with JSON-attributed data I was receiving from Twitter calls. Specifically, were there patterns and themes emerging in other JSON attributes (e.g., language code or whether a user was 'verified') that affirmed or challenged established codes. This is a juxtaposition to merely looking at queries run against a CSV file or even the CSV file itself. As part of this process, I used memo making of JSON responses I got from Twitter as I did not actually use all the fields in my CSV file. In this framework, the 'who', 'what', 'when', 'where', and 'why' are all kept open to interpretation in the coding of content. In other words, the larger dataset with full JSON data delivered by the Twitter API is kept as a resource during the grounded theory process, wherein the subset of filtered data by specified variables could be augmented with other variable fields during the research process if a value to doing this arises. The idea here is to navigate these data in different ways and to see what coding categories are determined. Emergent patterns can be captured well in this method. The traditional approach is to apply pre ordained coding rubrics for tweet data. However, if tweets are treated as 'digital objects' (Manovich, 2001) open to nuanced forms of interpretation, we can have richer understandings of tweet corpora (although we do have to deal with smaller n counts).

Indeed, I often saw different things catch my attention (like language code) that popped up in my JSON observations. Again, the idea here is to see what surprises you. I have had great success in surprises helping drive '2nd stage coding' into specific areas. Indeed, even the theories I have engaged with have evolved greatly during the research process. This is in contrast to deciding on a fixed theory/theories to test the research questions. This has been particularly true in my disaster-related (Murthy & Gross, under review) and race-related (Murthy & Sharma, forthcoming) Twitter work. Additionally, I have noticed the role of humor in particular corpora by using this approach where humor came into 2nd or 3rd stage coding as I found in the case of tweets posted during Hurricane Sandy (Murthy & Gross, under review).

USING COMPUTATIONAL APPROACHES TO PROBE TWITTER DATA

My focus so far has been on collecting data and using qualitative and mixed approaches in the first instance of Twitter analysis. However, computational approaches can also come first, yielding data that can be incorporated as part of 'Field Research #1' in Figure 33.1. Human, manual coding can then occur (following Figure 33.1) and this coding can be informed by machine learning techniques applied to tweet content, profiles, and other metadata. Such methods can also advance computational approaches (e.g. via supervised learning).

A method I have explored many times across a wide variety of social media including Twitter data is Latent Dirichlet Allocation (LDA), a Bayesian 'topic model' approach that uses computational machine learning methods to derive topic clusters. LDA works by reading in text and a discrete number of topics are generated (generally not more than 100). LDA 'is a robust and versatile unsupervised topic modeling technique, originally developed to identify latent topics [… with a] probability distribution over words (as opposed to a strict list of words that are included in or excluded from the topic' (Gross & Murthy, 2014, p. 39). These topics are sometimes straightforward and other times indicate unexpected or surprising interactions. Table 33.1 illustrates three LDA-derived topic clusters from a 50-topic LDA application to 90,986 cancer-related tweets including the following keywords: cancer, mammogram, lymphoma, melanoma, and cancer survivor. As Topic 5 illustrates, one topic of collected cancer-related tweets

Table 33.1 Three sample cancer-related Twitter topic clusters

Topic 5	Topic 6	Topic 7
My	Good	is
Mom	Found	year
Got	Start	there
Through	Side	god
Hope	Effects	scan
Hospital	Work	hear
Really	Said	heart
Dad	While	praying
Prayers	Feel	clear
During	morning	continue
Keep	Bad	glad
Friends	Body	low
Happy	Started	beauty
Oh	Sick	january
Strong	Feeling	bless

refers to family, friends, hospitals and indicates a topic cluster around procedures/diagnoses. Topic 7 (which is only partially listed due to space constraints) starts with a diverse array of words, but then moves to beauty and later on down the list are words like makeup and lipstick. Indeed, I would not have set out to understand these sometimes peripheral aspects of tweeting and cancer, but 'looking good' and keeping up beauty rituals was very important for a significant number of Twitter users. Another topic (not included in Table 33.1) indicated subjects surrounding cancer and pets, which I discovered often involved lymphoma in dogs.

Ultimately, one can effectively use machine learning approaches such as LDA to derive topic clusters around a Twitter corpus. Table 33.1 illustrates this application with cancer-related tweets, but I have similarly used LDA and other machine learning methods on a variety of Twitter and other social media corpora (Gross & Murthy, 2014). Another opportunity for coding arises here as well. This section emphasizes that it is possible to also have the computational element come first. Specifically, I have effectively used machine learning approaches such as LDA to derive topic clusters around a particular Twitter corpus. I have then used this to inform what coding categories are deployed for not only tweet content, but profiles, and other metadata.

CONCLUSION

This chapter makes a case for reflexive, open methods for studying tweets and their users. Importantly, the chapter seeks to emphasize the role of mixed methods for social media research. For example, if social media content and their users are coded by methods of convenience or in biased or unsystematic ways, this has real impacts on the epistemologies presented within the still emergent fields of social media research. This chapter has highlighted the limitations of traditional inductive and deductive methods and underscored some of the potential benefits of alternative approaches such as abductive methods. Retroductive methods and the specific case of grounded theory are introduced to provide alternative frameworks for studying Twitter data.

Social media are complex sociotechnical spaces. The presentation of the self is often highly nuanced – a case particularly complicated with uses of humor, a frequent theme on Twitter. Coded content can present different perspectives on social interactions, but these data are complementary to computational methods. Combining emergent grounded theory with machine learning or vice versa can advance both qualitative and quantitative methods. Such methods can offer new social media ontologies and epistemologies, which pave the way for completely new lines of knowledge.

It is tempting to simply look at easily collectible sets of tweets and make quick observations. However, having methods to systematically and rigorously study tweets produces robust methods as well as new ways to study Twitter data. This chapter has argued that traditional approaches can be useful to studying Twitter, but that alternative approaches, such as retroduction and grounded theory have tremendous value to studies of Twitter. Using the #accidentalracist hashtag as a case study, this chapter presents, as exemplars, frameworks and methods that I have employed on several Twitter-based projects. These methods range from simple changes to make Twitter research more reflexive and open to more advanced machine learning approaches. Additionally, having reflexive ontologies provide ways to see Twitter data from varied perspectives, ultimately advancing our potential to produce more varied and robust social knowledge.

Though computational approaches such as machine learning methods of studying social media content will continue to be important empirical methods, the utility of mixed methods is that they present different perspectives on social interactions within social media. For example, understanding sarcasm within tweets is not straightforward, but content emergently coded by research teams can then be used for supervised learning within traditional machine learning approaches in computer science. The argument here is that mixed methods such as these are fundamentally important to continuing advances in social media research methods as sometimes very large generalizations are made from Twitter data and this may be a trend.

REFERENCES

Baader, F. (2003). *The description logic handbook: Theory, implementation and applications*. Cambridge: Cambridge University Press.

Bhaskar, R. (1976). *A realist theory of science*. Brighton: The Harvester Press.

Birks, M., & Mills, J. (2015). *Grounded theory: a practical guide* (Second. ed.). Thousand Oaks, CA: SAGE.

Blaikie, N. (2004). Retroduction. In M. S. Lewis-Beck, A. Bryman & T. F. Liao (Eds.), *The SAGE encyclopedia of social science Research Methods* (pp. 973). Thousand Oaks, CA: SAGE.

Bollen, J., Pepe, A., & Mao, H. (2009). Modeling public mood and emotion: Twitter sentiment and socio-economic phenomena. *arXiv preprint arXiv:0911.1583*.

boyd, d., & Crawford, K. (2012). Critical questions for Big Data: Provocations for a cultural, technological, and scholarly phenomenon. *Information, Communication & Society*, *15*(5), 662–679.

Bryman, A., & Burgess, B. (2002). *Analyzing qualitative data*. Abingdon, Oxford: Routledge.

Cataldi, M., Caro, L. D., & Schifanella, C. (2010). *Emerging topic detection on Twitter based on temporal and social terms evaluation*. Paper presented at the Proceedings of the Tenth International Workshop on Multimedia Data Mining, Washington, D.C.

Charmaz, K., & Mitchell, R. G. (2001). Grounded Theory in Ethnography. In P. Atkinson, A. Coffey, S. Delamont, J. Lofland & L. Lofland (Eds.), *Handbook of ethnography* (pp. 160–174). London: SAGE.

Clauset, A., Shalizi, C. R., & Newman, M. E. (2009). Power-law distributions in empirical data. *SIAM review*, *51*(4), 661–703.

Corbin, J., & Strauss, A. (2015). *Basics of qualitative research: Techniques and procedures for developing grounded theory*. Los Angeles: SAGE.

Dann, S. (2010). *Twitter content classification*. First Monday, 15(2). doi:10.5210/fm.v15i12.2745.

Ellenberg H, Klötzli F (1972) Waldgesellschaften und Waldstandorte der Schweiz. Mittteilungen der Schweizerischen Anstalt für das Forstliche Versuchswesen Zürich 48: 589–930.

Essence Magazine. (2013, April 12). Essence Poll: Are You Offended by 'Accidental Racist'? *Essence*.

Florini, S. (2014). Tweets, Tweeps, and Signifyin': Communication and Cultural Performance on 'Black Twitter'. *Television & New Media*, *15*(3), 223–237.

Glaser, B. G., & Strauss, A. L. (2009). *The discovery of grounded theory: Strategies for qualitative research*. New Brunswick, NJ: Transaction Publishers.

Goulding, C. (2002). *Grounded theory: A practical guide for management, business and market researchers*. London: SAGE.

Graves, I., McDonald, N., & Goggins, S. P. (2014). Sifting signal from noise: A new perspective on the meaning of tweets about the 'big game'. *New Media & Society*, 18(2), 293–312. doi: 10.1177/146144481454178

Gross, A., & Murthy, D. (2014). Modeling virtual organizations with Latent Dirichlet Allocation: A case for natural language processing. *Neural Networks*, 58, 38–49.

Hardt, M., & Negri, A. (2005). *Multitude war and democracy in the age of Empire*. New York: Penguin.

Harré, R. (1976). The constructive role of models. In L. Collins (Ed.), *The use of models in the social sciences* (pp. 16–33). London: Tavistock Publications.

Honeycutt, C., & Herring, S. C. (2009). *Beyond microblogging: Conversation and collaboration via Twitter*. Paper presented at the 42nd Hawaii International Conference on System Sciences (HICSS), pp. 1–10, Waikoloa, Hawaii.

Hughes, A. L., St Denis, L. A., Palen, L., & Anderson, K. M. (2014). *Online public communications by police & fire services during the 2012 Hurricane Sandy*. Paper presented at the Proceedings of the SIGCHI Conference on Human Factors in Computing Systems, pp. 1505–1514, Toronto, Canada.

Kozinets, R. V. (2010). *Netnography: Doing ethnographic research online*. London: SAGE Publications.

Krishnamurthy, B., Gill, P., & Arlitt, M. (2008). *A few chirps about Twitter*. Paper presented at the Proceedings of the first workshop on Online social networks, pp. 19–24, Seattle, WA

Kwak, H., Lee, C., Park, H., & Moon, S. (2010). *What is Twitter, a social network or a news media?* Paper presented at the Proceedings of the 19th international conference on World Wide Web, pp. 591–600, Raleigh, NC.

Lindgren, S., & Lundström, R. (2011). Pirate culture and hacktivist mobilization: The cultural and social protocols of #WikiLeaks on Twitter. *New Media & Society*, 13(6), 999–1018.

Manovich, L. (2001). *The language of new media*. Cambridge: MIT Press.

Murphy, T. S. (2001). Ontology, deconstruction, and empire. *Rethinking Marxism*, 13(3–4), 16–23.

Murthy, D. (2011). Emergent digital ethnographic methods for social research. *Handbook of emergent technologies in social research*. Oxford: Oxford University Press, 158–179.

Murthy, D. (2013). *Twitter: Social communication in the Twitter age*. Cambridge: Polity Press.

Murthy, D., & Gross, A. (Under Review). Social media processes in disasters: Implications of emergent technology use.

Murthy, D., & Sharma, S. (Forthcoming). Mapping the organization of race in YouTube.

Murthy, D., Gross, A., & Pensavalle, A. (2016). Urban Social Media Demographics: An Exploration of Twitter use in Major American Cities. *Journal of Computer Mediated Communication*, 21(1), 33–49.

Muse, H. (2013, April 9). 'Accidental Racist' lights up Twitter. *Fortune*.

Olsen, W. K. (2012). *Data collection: key debates and methods in social research*. London; Thousand Oaks, CA: SAGE.

Paul, G. (1993). Approaches to abductive reasoning: an overview. *Artificial Intelligence Review*, 7(2), 109–152.

Poole, S. (2015). *Can Computational Approaches Motivate New Theories?* Paper presented at the Computational Approaches to Advance Communication Research Pre-Conference, International Communication Association, San Juan, Puerto Rico.

Procter, R., Vis, F., & Voss, A. (2013). Reading the riots on Twitter: Methodological innovation for the analysis of big data. *International Journal of Social Research Methodology*, 16(3), 197–214.

Quan-Haase, A., Martin, K., & McCay-Peet, L. (2015). Networks of digital humanities scholars: The informational and social uses and gratifications of Twitter. *Big Data & Society*, 2(1). doi: 10.1177/2053951715589417

Sakaki, T., Okazaki, M., & Matsuo, Y. (2010). *Earthquake shakes Twitter users: real-time event detection by social sensors*. Paper presented at the Proceedings of the 19th international conference on World Wide Web, pp. 851-860, Raleigh, North Carolina, USA.

Sloan, L., Morgan, J., Burnap, P., & Williams, M. (2015). Who tweets? Deriving the demographic characteristics of age, occupation and social class from Twitter user metadata. *PloS one*, *10*(3), e0115545.

Stock, W. A., Benito, J. G., & Lasa, N. B. (1996). Research Synthesis: Coding and Conjectures. *Evaluation & the Health Professions*, *19*(1), 104–117. doi:10.1177/016327879601900108.

Tinati, R., Halford, S., Carr, L., & Pope, C. (2014). Big Data: Methodological Challenges and Approaches for Sociological Analysis. *Sociology*, 48 (4), 663–681.

Wenbo, W., Lu, C., Thirunarayan, K., & Sheth, A. P. (2012, 3–5 Sept. 2012). *Harnessing Twitter & Big Data for Automatic Emotion Identification*. Paper presented at the Privacy, Security, Risk and Trust (PASSAT), 2012 International Conference on and 2012 International Confernece on Social Computing (SocialCom), pp. 587–592, Amsterdam, Netherlands.

Wu, S., Hofman, J. M., Mason, W. A., & Watts, D. J. (2011). *Who says what to whom on twitter.* Paper presented at the Proceedings of the 20th international conference on World Wide Web, pp. 705-714, Hyderabad, India.

Zimmer, M., & Proferes, N. J. (2014). A topology of Twitter research: disciplines, methods, and ethics. *Aslib Journal of Information Management*, *66*(3), 250–261. doi:10.1108/AJIM-09–2013-0083.

34
Instagram

Linnea Laestadius

This chapter offers an applied exploration of how to navigate the unique opportunities and challenges of research using Instagram data. Any researchers seeking to fully avail themselves of Instagram's rich data must consider how to combine visual imagery with captions, hashtags, and comments. Following a brief history of the platform, I explore key distinctions between Instagram and its more heavily studied social media counterparts and why Instagram functions well as a site of research. From there, I present a typology of current Instagram research and explore best practices and ethical considerations for those seeking to use Instagram for their own research. Finally, I offer a case study of a qualitative content analysis of Instagram posts that generated valuable public health insights about electronic cigarettes.

INTRODUCTION

Described by its creators as a 'fun and quirky way to share your life with friends through a series of pictures' (Instagram, 2015a), Instagram is one of the most popular visual social media platforms in the world. As of June 2016, Instagram had over 500 million active users, with 95 million posts and 4.2 billion 'likes' made each day (Instagram, 2016). The platform is particularly popular with teenagers and young adults (Duggan, 2015). Despite its growing popularity and public interest in visual platforms, research using Instagram has been relatively limited compared to social media platforms like Twitter. While this is partially related to Instagram being a more recent addition to the social media landscape and to the socio-demographic profile of academic researchers, Instagram's unique features and functionality also contribute to the relative paucity of studies. The visual nature of Instagram is not naturally suited for mainstream Big Data approaches to social media (Highfield and Leaver, 2014; Kaufer, 2015). Instagram's rich data necessitates novel approaches to combining visual imagery with captions, hashtags, and comments (Highfield and Leaver, 2014).

This chapter offers an exploration of how to navigate the unique opportunities and challenges of Instagram research. Following a brief history of the platform, I explore the distinctions between Instagram and its more heavily studied social media counterparts, Twitter and Flickr. I also consider why this platform functions well as a site of research. From there, I present a typology of current approaches to Instagram research and explore best practices for those seeking to use Instagram in their own work. Finally, I offer a case study of a qualitative content analysis that sought to understand how electronic cigarettes are portrayed on Instagram. This case study helps to shed light on the application of some of the approaches outlined here.

A BRIEF HISTORY OF INSTAGRAM

In 2010, Kevin Systrom and Mike Krieger launched Instagram as a free iPhone application designed for sharing pictures with friends (Instagram, 2015b). A portmanteau of the words instant camera and telegram, Instagram is imagined by its creators as a means of creating a 'world more connected through photos' (Instagram, 2015a). In addition to connecting people, Instagram is cast as offering three specific benefits for its users: 1) improving the 'mediocre' appearance of mobile phone photos through filters, 2) facilitating the instant sharing of pictures across multiple platforms, and 3) improving the speed and ease of the photo uploading process (Instagram, 2015a). Social media users were quickly receptive to the Instagram model. One million users had joined the platform by October 2010, increasing to ten million users by September 2011 (Instagram, 2016). This success garnered the attention of Facebook, which purchased Instagram for one billion dollars in April of 2012 (Metz, 2014).

Since its launch, Instagram has continued to grow in both user base and functionality. Since 2010, additions to Instagram have included: new filters, application software for a larger number of mobile operating systems (most notably Android in 2012), photo maps that display a user's posts by location, tagging of other accounts in an image, the ability to upload 3–60 second videos, direct messaging, the ability to use emojis as searchable hashtags, and horizontal and vertical images (Instagram, 2016). In 2015, Instagram also launched new functionality for advertisers seeking to make sponsored posts, including a 'Shop Now' button and new API (application programming interface) for advertising (Sloane, 2015). At the time of writing, Instagram's most recent changes were the switch to an algorithm-based feed and the addition of the Snapchat inspired *Instagram Stories* feature (Instagram, 2016). Each of these additions, informed by current usage patterns, commercial demands, and the social contexts of developers, has further re-configured the architecture of Instagram and created new affordances for its users.

INSTAGRAM AS A DISTINCT PLATFORM

As 'differences in digital affordances lead to differences in group behavior' (Baym, 2015: 74), it is important to recognize that Instagram should not simply be treated as Twitter with pictures and a 2,200-character limit. Dubois and Ford (2015: 2071) express this well when they note that 'a tweet is not the same as a Wikipedia edit, which is different still from a Facebook comment' and that each must be interpreted in a different fashion. While it is tempting to use other platforms as a point of methodological reference, particularly given a shared hashtag architecture (Highfield and Leaver, 2014), this may obscure some of the unique elements and usage aspects of Instagram. That said, researchers with experience on other platforms will almost certainly approach Instagram in this manner. It is valuable then to describe Instagram's features and traits through a discussion of key differences between Instagram and its most conceptually related platforms, the social networking platform Twitter and image-sharing platform Flickr. While Facebook represents another major platform that combines visual and textual elements, it is not used a point of reference as there are no comparative studies between the two platforms at the time of writing. This may partially be due to Facebook functioning as a 'mostly private network,' which poses a challenge for holistic research on the platform (Olmstead and Barthel, 2015).

Visual and Textual Practices

Instagram is distinct from Twitter in that each post must include an image or short video. While Instagram users can also upload images not captured with Instagram's built-in photo feature, thus allowing for memes, images of text, and photos not taken by mobile phones to be posted, each post still involves a conscious decision about aesthetics (or the lack thereof) that is not required on Twitter. As a result of this, Instagram has a highly visual culture that frequently conveys meaning through photographs, with text and hashtags used as needed for context. As noted by Marwick (2015: 139), 'textual description and replies to followers are de-emphasized in favor of images, particularly selfies.' This de-emphasis is confirmed by a large-scale study by Manikonda et al. (2014), which found that Instagram posts have on average just 2.55 comments and almost 60 per cent of posts have no comments at all.

While social media analytics firm Sysomos (2010) suggests that 71 per cent of tweets receive no retweet or reply, explicit comparisons are difficult given different usage patterns and the fact that there are many more tweets per active user on Twitter than posts per active user on Instagram (Instagram, 2016; Twitter, 2015). The average comment on Instagram is only 32 characters, despite the fact that comments are currently capped at 2,200 characters (Manikonda et al., 2014). In light of these usage patterns, it is critical for Instagram researchers to engage in the often time-consuming process of analyzing the content of images in conjunction with captions, comments, and hashtags.

Flickr, like Instagram, is image based. However, its primary function has long been as a photo and video hosting service rather than a social networking platform. Flickr places greater importance on images in their own right, while Instagram uses images to facilitate connections between users. This is perhaps best illustrated by the fact that Flickr provides detailed information on camera settings for each image uploaded and allows uploads at original file sizes (Sheer, 2012). Instagram provides none of this information and saves images at a low resolution to save on data storage space. Further, Instagram does not permit uploading images through its website interface (although some third-party applications can bypass this), placing the emphasis on mobile phone photos. Rather than encouraging skillful photography, Instagram encourages the application of 'awesome looking filters transform your photos into professional-looking snapshots' (Instagram, 2015a). Researchers should be mindful of this rather utilitarian approach to images as they analyze behavior and content on Instagram.

Hashtag Usage and Meaning

Hashtags have distinct meanings and usage patterns on Instagram. Given the importance of hashtags to searching for relevant content (Highfield and Leaver, 2014), it is essential to clarify these differences. While a single platform can be home to multiple communities with distinctive norms and 'insider lingo' (Baym, 2015), each platform has an overall 'vernacular specific to it that has developed over time, through design, appropriation, and use' (Gibbs et al., 2015: 257). Given that Instagram's affordances promote visual rather than textual communication, its hashtags are less likely to indicate posts as being part of a continuing text-based conversation, as on Twitter (Bruns and Burgess, 2011), and are more likely to indicate participation in a community or provide context for an image. While a number of definitions of online community have been developed in prior literature, Baym's (2015: 73) consideration of the concept is both accessible and sufficiently specified to be valuable. Of the qualities of online communities that she outlines, a shared sense of space, practice, and identity are most relevant to understanding hashtag-based communities on Instagram.

The difference in usage is further reinforced by Instagram's more generous character limit and the ability to apply up to 30 hashtags on a single post (Instagram, 2015c). By contrast, Instagram limits @ mentions of other users to just five per post/comment in order to 'help reduce spam on Instagram' (Instagram, 2015c). Conversation with a large number of users at once is seen as relatively unusual for the Instagram platform. As a result of these usage distinctions, different platforms are suited for answering different research questions. Twitter, for example, appears better suited to understanding public opinion or discourse around a current event. Instagram instead lends itself to understanding self-presentation and expression, online communities, and everyday lives as mediated through images (Ibrahim, 2015; Jang et al., 2015b).

Social media marketing blogs have also noted that Instagram hashtags are used 'to build community, and be unique/detailed,' while Twitter hashtags are used for categorization (Lee, 2015). The case study at the end of the chapter also supports this, finding a large number of community and identity hashtags denoting life as an electronic cigarette user within a sample of #ecig and #vape posts. In addition to a focus on community building, Instagram hashtags provide context for posted images. A study by Hitlin and Holcomb (2015) of the Pew Research Center compared Twitter and Instagram posts using #Ferguson (relating to the events surrounding the 2014 police shooting of Michael Brown in Ferguson, MO) and found that tweets were generally closely related to the shooting and the civil unrest that followed, whereas the Instagram posts were more thematic and focused on broader questions about race and civil rights. Frequently, the only explicit connection between the post and the events in Ferguson was the hashtag itself rather than the image, suggesting that users created meaning by connecting contextual hashtags to images (Hitlin and Holcomb, 2015).

A study comparing Instagram and Flickr posts with #Ebola found similar results with regard to the absence of explicit connections to the topic being studied (Seltzer et al., 2015). Flickr posts were typically directly related to the Ebola outbreak of 2014, depicting heathcare workers and scenes from West Africa. By contrast, Instagram posts were frequently determined to be unrelated to Ebola in any obvious way or to consist of jokes and memes about Ebola. The higher number of memes is a clear indicator of Instagram's status as a social networking platform rather than a platform for sharing photography.

Posting, Friending, Geotagging, and Liking

There are also distinct posting, friending, geotagging, and liking patterns between social media platforms. With over 500 million monthly active users in June 2016 (Instagram, 2016), Instagram now has over 180 million more active users than Twitter (Twitter, 2016). Yet Twitter users post much more frequently than Instagram users. Each day there are on average 500 million tweets made, compared to just 95 million Instagram posts (Instagram, 2016; Twitter, 2015). This is partially due to conversations on Instagram taking place through comments on posts rather than requiring a new post each time someone wishes to respond. The lower posting rate does not signal a lack of usage so much as a different form of usage, with surveys finding that 59 per cent of U.S. Instagram users visit the platform at least once a day (Duggan, 2015) (at the time of writing, there is limited data on non-U.S. Instagram usage patterns). Flickr, with its focus on photography rather than social networking, had only an average of 2 million public images uploaded each day in 2015 (Michel, 2016). As a result, it is difficult to make meaningful comparisons about a topic based on the volume of posts made on different platforms.

Due perhaps to Instagram users' focus on documenting their everyday lives, Instagram posts are on average 31 times more likely than tweets to include geotag data (Manikonda et al., 2014). This presents unique opportunities for researchers hoping to explore location-based trends. Instagram users also form distinctive relationship patterns, with a lower friending reciprocity than users on Flickr and Twitter but a greater number of small cliques than found on Twitter (Manikonda et al., 2014). There is no clear data on why this is the case, but it may reflect both the stronger community element of Instagram found in hashtag practices and the simultaneous focus on following celebrity accounts. Researchers should also consider the effects of the Instagram 'Search & Explore Page' which uses algorithms to highlight popular content and can lead some posts and users to receive unusually high volumes of engagement (Carah and Shaul, 2016).

Given limited data on Instagram usage and, perhaps more importantly, the motivations for usage patterns, I encourage researchers to make an Instagram account for themselves and use it as a conventional user would (i.e. not for research purposes) for at least a month. As the architecture of the platform is constantly changing through new additions and the amending of old ones (Larsson, 2015), only firsthand experience with Instagram in the period leading up to a study can provide an in-depth and up-to-date understanding of the platform's affordances and common usage patterns. Additionally, I believe that privacy expectations can best be understood through a reflexive practice in which one considers the very real prospect of researchers making use of one's own social media data.

Demographics of Users

The final distinguishing feature of Instagram that researchers should note is that its core users are different from other platforms (Duggan, 2015). Instagram's user base is younger than Twitter's, with estimates suggesting that 90 per cent of Instagram's users are under age 35 (Smith, 2014). As per U.S. data, Instagram is also distinct in its racial and social diversity. As compared to Twitter, it has notably more black and Hispanic users, users making less than $50k per year, and users who do not hold college degrees (Duggan, 2015). It is critical that researchers seeking to make broader social inferences from Instagram data consider these demographic distinctions. While Instagram better represents the racial and economic diversity of the U.S., it is highly skewed toward younger users and thus should not be viewed as being representative of the population at large.

INSTAGRAM AS A SITE OF RESEARCH

In addition to the specific traits and distinctions described above, it is important to consider the more general affordances that allow Instagram to be a site of research. Affordances can be understood as the types of actions made possible for users through a platform (Wellman, et al., 2003; Curinga, 2014). The structural affordances of networked publics, as articulated by boyd (2010, 2014), capture several of the core reasons why researchers are drawn to explore their questions on Instagram.

First, the Instagram platform (functioning as a form of networked publics) affords *persistence* (boyd, 2010). Not only does Instagram allow and encourage its users to capture what may have been previously ephemeral moments in their lives through mobile photography, it renders these images even more persistent and enduring by posting them to Instagram's servers. This persistency of both moments and images results in a rich and relatively stable source of data for researchers. Beyond this, Instagram affords *visibility* of content (boyd, 2014). As Instagram defaults accounts to public status, large volumes of content are accessible to researchers. Instagram also enables *replicability* as posts can be screen-captured to facilitate analysis even if the original post is deleted (boyd, 2010). Unlike Snapchat, which prides itself on being ephemeral, Instagram does not notify users when their photos have been captured.

Instagram also affords *searchability* (boyd, 2010), which allows researchers to identify content specifically related to their topic of study. On Instagram, searching is facilitated by built-in search functions for usernames, hashtags, and locations and through its API. Initial work on Instagram as a research platform argues that hashtags should represent an 'initial point of departure for studying activity on Instagram' (Highfield and Leaver, 2014). Given a body of over 40 billion photos (Instagram, 2015d), searching for hashtags is a critical affordance for those seeking to conduct research on the platform.

To add one final and novel element to boyd's (2010) list of affordances, Instagram affords a high degree of *interpretability*. Since Instagram, unlike Twitter and Facebook, requires each post to have an image or video attached, Instagram posts are almost inherently rich from the perspective of data analysis. As per Losh (2015: 1653), Instagram uploads are tied to 'rich and messy information about social history and personal context.' Rich data are so valued in qualitative research because they 'afford views of human experience that etiquette, social conventions, and inaccessibility hide or minimize in ordinary discourse' (Charmaz, 2015: 62). Instagram's emphasis on image creation yields this rich and, in turn, also highly interpretable data that are well-suited for qualitative research. Interpretation can occur at three distinct sites where meaning is made: 1) the site of production where images are created, 2) the site of the image itself and its content, and 3) the site where the image encounters an audience (Rose, 2012).

This richness is particularly important in light of the digital divide in skills and access that the ecosystem around Big Data has created among social media researchers (boyd and Crawford, 2012). Big Data approaches to Instagram remain largely inaccessible for researchers with limited resources or computational skills, but Instagram's unique affordances and suitability for qualitative research opens the door for Big Data and qualitative researchers alike. The gender dynamics of this skill divide, attributable to the fact that males are overrepresented among those with computational skills (boyd and Crawford, 2012), are of particular note given that a higher proportion of women than men use Instagram (Duggan, 2015). It will be important to follow the trajectories of both types of Instagram research over time to discern the ways in which current social media research hierarchies are challenged or reinforced.

TYPOLOGY OF INSTAGRAM RESEARCH

At present, most Instagram research draws from four major methodological areas.

Each of these approaches and recent studies relying upon them will be reviewed in brief, followed by a discussion of general best practices to consider when undertaking Instagram research. More specifically, these are: 1) quantitative Big Data approaches, 2) digital humanities approaches such as cultural analytics that seek to make greater use of Instagram's rich data, 3) small samples of Instagram data paired with qualitative approaches such as content analysis, and 4) direct engagement with Instagram users themselves through interviews and ethnographic work. Beyond this, Instagram research can be classified as either seeking to understand Instagram-specific behaviors (Ting et al., 2015; Jang et al., 2015a) or seeking to understand secondary phenomena through Instagram (Yi-Frazier et al., 2015; Tiidenberg, 2015).

Big Data and Instagram

Although it is difficult to precisely define Big Data research in a social media context (boyd and Crawford, 2012; Manovich, 2012a), Kitchin (2013: 262) outlines several unifying traits of Big Data. Specifically, that Big Data are huge in volume, high in velocity, exhaustive in scope, diverse in variety, fine grained in resolution, flexible and scalable, and relational in nature. Perhaps the three most distinctive traits as compared to small data are the overall volume of data (indeed, so large they could not be analyzed by hand), the velocity in which new data are collected, and a scope so large it approaches whole populations rather than small samples (Kitchin and Lauriault, 2015). The studies presented below meet these traits to varying degrees, but all fall toward Big Data on the spectrum of methodological approaches. As of 2015, these studies have largely been based in the computer sciences and have sought to understand Instagram usage patterns, including hashtag popularity and tagging behavior (Ferrara et al., 2014; Jang et al., 2015b), liking and commenting behavior (Souza Araujo et al., 2014; Bakhshi et al., 2014; Jang et al., 2015a; Jang et al., 2015b; Yamasaki et al., 2015), and the traits of networks of friends, likes, and hashtags (Ferrara et al., 2014; Jang et al., 2015a; Manikonda et al., 2014).

A small number of studies are also using Instagram to understand phenomena that go beyond Instagram usage itself. Szczypka et al. (2015), for example, performed a descriptive content analysis of hashtags and depictions of smoking and cigarette brands in a large sample of Instagram posts. Tostes Ribeiro et al. (2014), considered the extent to which Instagram posting behaviors can reveal traffic conditions, and Mejova et al. (2015) combined Foursquare and Instagram data to understand the ways in which Instagram users post and interact about different types of foodservice establishments. In 2015, these more applied Big Data studies remained rare within the Instagram literature.

Overall, a Big Data approach offers valuable insights into subjects such as connectivity, network structure, and general usage patterns on Instagram. Characterized by their more traditional quantitative approach to data, however, relatively few studies have incorporated details of the content and composition of Instagram images or videos into their analysis. When they have, it has most commonly been in a limited fashion (e.g. selfie or no selfie, teen or adult). This represents a current limitation of the Big Data approach, although this will likely change as image recognition algorithms improve and more researchers are exposed to developments within cultural analytics (addressed below).

Cultural Analytics and Instagram

Developed by Lev Manovich and his team in 2005 for use in the digital humanities, cultural analytics is closely related to the above approach in that it makes use of large samples of posts, computational analysis, and quantification (Software Studies Initiative,

2015). However, cultural analytics is critically distinct from conventional approaches to Big Data in that it relies upon: 1) 'image processing and computer vision techniques' to place the focus on visual media *themselves* rather than existing metadata *about* visual media (Manovich, 2009: 18), and 2) the creation of interactive visualizations of results in order to reveal 'patterns which lie below the unaided capacities of human perception and cognition' (Manovich, 2009: 8). Rather than reducing images to generic data points, bars, or lines, these visualizations maintain the full content of images (Manovich, 2012b). A collection of images becomes translated into an interactive image plot or montage (among other possible visualizations).[1]

While cultural analytics was not designed specifically with social media data in mind, it is well suited to Instagram's large volume of culturally relevant visual data. Once collected, processed, and visualized, images can be mapped and sorted (by metadata such as location and time of posting, as well as content and visual properties) to discern novel patterns. Much of this data can be generated automatically using image recognition techniques, while other items must be created or validated by hand. One past study using this approach relied upon Amazon's Mechanical Turk workers (Manovich et al., 2014). The volume of data in question and the Instagram interface make these trends almost impossible to discern through manual qualitative coding (Manovich, 2012b). That said, cultural analytics methods, as with Big Data approaches more generally, can also be used to identify targeted subsets of data for closer manual analysis (Manovich, 2012a).

As of 2015, three major projects have applied cultural analytics to Instagram data. In Phototrails (Hochman et al., 2013), 2.3 million Instagram images were analyzed to discern how 'temporal changes in number of shared photos, their locations, and visual characteristics can uncover social, cultural and political insights about people's activity around the world.' Selfiecity (Manovich et al., 2014), followed this initial project and explored the demographics, poses, and expressions in a sample of 3,200 Instagram selfies across five cities. This project determined, among other things, that posing and smiling behavior differs across cities, and informed several theoretical reflections on both selfies and the project itself (Losh, 2014, 2015; Tifentale, 2014). More recently, Manovich's team launched On Broadway (Goddemeyer et al., 2015), which consists of an interactive installation and application examining 660,000 Instagram images taken along Broadway street in New York City in conjunction with multiple other visual and demographic data sets tied to the same locations along the street. These projects illustrate the ways in which researchers can push the boundaries of mainstream Big Data approaches to more fully make use of Instagram's visual data.

Small Samples of Instagram Data

While the above approaches enable unique insights into broad trends of Instagram usage and content, small data approaches relying primarily on qualitative analysis offer 'a granularity of detail that might otherwise be lost in dazzling large-scale data visualizations that value the quantitative over the qualitative' (Losh, 2015: 1650). As this 'era of Big Data' has contributed to discourse that discounts the value of qualitative research and small sample sizes (boyd and Crawford, 2012), the value of these approaches to Instagram data warrants being stated explicitly.

Researchers looking to make use of rich data generally face a tradeoff between depth and breadth, with an inverse relationship between the amount of usable data gathered from each post or Instagram user and the size of their sample (Morse, 2000). Accordingly, the analysis of small samples of Instagram data can provide extremely valuable insights that could not be obtained from Big Data approaches. As noted by boyd and Crawford (2012: 630), 'the size of data should fit the research question being asked; in some cases, small is best.' One such example is studies that seek to understand specific phenomena as they exist among narrow subpopulations of Instagram users rather than to facilitate generalizations to all Instagram users (Carah and Shaul, 2016). Kitchin and Lauriault (2015: 466) capture this strength particularly well, stating that 'small data studies can be much more finely tailored to answer specific research questions and to explore in detail and in-depth the varied, contextual, rational and irrational ways in which people interact and make sense of the world, and how processes work.' Smaller sample sizes also currently offer the best opportunity to make sense of Instagram post components as a unit, rather than considering images/videos, hashtags, captions, comments, and likes independently. The unity of visual and textual analysis has been recognized as critical to fully making sense of Instagram data (Highfield and Leaver, 2014). Removing an image from its caption and vice versa creates a significant loss of context. Small data qualitative approaches can also be combined with simple counts of hashtag volume over time to demonstrate the overall popularity of a specific trend or phenomenon.

Some recent applications of qualitative methods to small samples of Instagram data include Carah and Shaul's (2016) analysis of 100 posts from each of four brand related hashtags, Marwick's (2015) descriptive case study of three Instagram accounts to understand techniques to obtain 'microcelebrity' and 'instafame,' Gibbs et al.'s (2015) grounded theory analysis of 1,330 #funeral posts, and Tiidenberg's (2015) in-depth visual narrative analysis of themes related to femininity and pregnancy on eight Instagram accounts. These studies are notable in that most of them consider the visual and textual elements of Instagram together and all offer significant engagement with and interrogation of data. The case study at the end of this chapter also falls within this category of research.

Engaging with Instagram Users

The final category of research consists of studies that have engaged directly with Instagram users rather than taking an observational approach. Despite the fact that these studies represent the only means of assessing the meaning of posts in relation to their site of creation and the site where they encounter an audience (Rose, 2012), this category represents the area where the least amount of work has been done. As noted by Farman (2015: 1), research must begin to 'go beyond what takes place on the screens of devices to contextualize those interactions with what is happening around those devices.'

So far, this approach has been used across a small number of widely divergent topics, and most often to understand a specific phenomenon rather than general usage. One recent study used a fieldwork approach to understand Instagram practices of lifestyle bloggers in Singapore (Abidin, 2014). Other studies have drawn on interviews with groups such as female self-portrait artists to understand how they circumvent censorship on Instagram (Olszanowski, 2014), Malaysian Instagram users to understand their beliefs about the platform (Ting et al., 2015), and individuals who post self-injury content to platforms including Instagram (Seko et al., 2015). Instagram has also been adapted to the established PhotoVoice methodology where a study population is *asked* to create Instagram content about a specific aspect of their lived experience (Yi-Frazier et al., 2015).

BEST PRACTICES FOR INSTAGRAM RESEARCH

I now move to a more applied consideration of the practical and ethical best practices for studies using Instagram posts as data. Specifically, I consider issues related to the collection and analysis of Instagram data. For more detail on the principles of social media data collection and visual data analysis more generally, I refer readers to the rest of this volume and to Gillian Rose's (2012) comprehensive text on *Visual Methodologies*.

As of late-2015, Highfield and Leaver's (2014) methodology for hashtag mapping represented the entirety of the peer-reviewed literature providing advice specifically on Instagram research. In addition to this work, I draw from the more general social media research literature and from my own experiences gained from the case study discussed below. Rather than a separate section on ethical practices, I weave these in with general practices to emphasize that the two are intrinsically connected. That said, readers are strongly encouraged to review the most up-to-date version of the ethical guide from the Association of Internet Researchers Ethics Working Committee (Markham and Buchanan, 2012).

Determining a Data Collection Approach

Instagram researchers have three primary options for data collection: 1) they can extract their desired data directly from the Instagram API, 2) they can to obtain data from a third-party tool or service that connects to the API for them, or 3) they can manually extract data from the Instagram user-interface. The first of these offers the greatest utility and flexibility for researchers, but also presents a number of technical challenges for non-programmers and often requires 'costly and time-consuming (and sometimes alienating) partnerships with technical experts...' (Burgess and Bruns, 2012). As an alternative, there are third-party services such as Gnip, which will collect data from Instagram's public API for a cost. Unfortunately, there are currently few *free* third-party tools designed with Instagram in mind. At present, Netlytic (see Chapter 30 this volume) offers basic functionality for the download of Instagram data. While it seems highly likely that additional tools will be developed over time it is worth noting that Instagram may follow a path similar to Twitter and limit free access to its API as opportunities for commercialization increase (Burgess and Bruns, 2012).

The third approach is to manually search the Instagram user-interface or third-party websites and then capture the found data using a tool such as EndNote, Zotero, or a simple screen capture. While those with the technical skills may be tempted to automate this process, Instagram's terms of use explicitly state that they 'prohibit crawling, scraping, caching or otherwise accessing any content on the Service via automated means, including but not limited to, user profiles and photos...' (Instagram, 2013). This approach is certainly the most time-consuming of the three and is not appropriate for researchers seeking extremely large samples or metadata on things like filter choices, but it does have several distinct benefits for qualitative researchers.

Working with the user interface and the standard hashtag, location, or username search functions forces researchers to engage with images/videos, captions, hashtags, and comments in the manner that users envisioned when they created the content. While there can be significant discussions about who the imagined audience is for Instagram posts (Litt, 2012), it is almost certainly not researchers who automate data extraction from Instagram into a database (boyd and Crawford, 2012). Accordingly, researchers working directly with the user interface, or websites that mimic the key features of that interface, are better able to understand the visual intent of posts and the ways in which other users experience exposure to Instagram content. This also breeds greater familiarity with the data, as researchers must look at each post as they capture it. As an added benefit, manual collection provides researchers an opportunity to assess the relevance of each post to their study question and minimize the collection of irrelevant data. Researchers taking this approach are reminded not to use their own personal Instagram log-in when collecting data, as it may result in the inclusion of data from private accounts.

Finally, even researchers focused on the content of posts rather than Instagram users themselves may wish to engage with Instagram users. One such technique is trace interviewing, in which Instagram users are asked to comment on visualizations of their trace data. This approach, as articulated by Dubois and Ford (2015: 2085), can strengthen the validity of data through triangulation, provide additional context on the creation of posts, and respond to some of the ethical concerns associated with social media research by creating 'a dialogue between the researcher, the participant, and the data rather than between the researcher and the data…'. This approach is particularly valuable if data is being collected on a sensitive subject or from minors since it also facilitates an opportunity for consent to be given.

Managing Posts that are Edited, Made Private, or Deleted After Being Collected

As Instagram users can edit their post captions and location data, delete posts completely, and change their account status from public to private, researchers should develop an explicit policy for how to deal with any such changes before they begin data analysis (Highfield and Leaver, 2014). While there may be occasions where the capture and analysis of initially posted content is essential to addressing a research question, a blanket policy for including this content raises concerns. First, the intent of the user may be better reflected in an amended post if they are making corrections or adding context. Second, the removal of content, deletion of entire posts, or changing an account to private may signal that a post contains information that is perceived by a user as sensitive and not for public consumption. The simple fact that Instagram posts are publicly available should not be taken to mean that the user lacks expectations for privacy (Markham and Buchanan, 2012). Even if consent is seen as implied by the fact that a post is public, removing that post from public access may suggest a withdrawal of consent. Institutional review boards (IRBs) should also be attentive to the fact that teenagers are more likely to delete Instagram posts than adults (Jang et al., 2015b), raising concerns about researchers using private data from minors.

Unless a clear motivation can be articulated for including posts in their original form or there is broad social and institutional acceptance that collected data is in no way sensitive, researchers should strive to ensure that their final samples: 1) include the amended version of posts if a post has been edited, and 2) exclude posts that have been deleted or made private. That said, it appears that some reasonable window of time for these changes should be defined since continual monitoring of posts is beyond the capacity of most researchers, to say nothing of the permanence of findings once they have been published. In their examination of post deletion practices, Jang et al. (2015b) found that teenage deletions peaked after about a week and continued on into the two-week mark. A one-month window between real time-data collection and analysis should provide sufficient time for users to reflect on their posted content. At the end of this one-month period, collected data should be revisited. In the case study below, all sampled posts were visited on two separate occasions. By the time of coding, 22 per cent of collected post links had gone dead, allowing us to exclude these posts from our sample. Researchers should adjust their planned sample sizes up front to accommodate for this loss of data. An additional benefit of this approach is that it allows likes and comments, which accumulate on posts over time, to be better captured.

Reading the Comments

As described above, Instagram posts are not static data points. This relates not just to the content created by the author of a post, but also to elements of the post that are born out of engagement with other users. Accordingly, comments and likes can add new meaning to posts over time. As explained by Highfield and Leaver (2014), 'if a user responds to an image by leaving a comment, that becomes an addition to the original data point – it is part of the comments thread for that media, rather than being a distinct entity.' While not every study will want to incorporate comments, researchers seeking to understand user engagement, the effects of posts, or meaning creation will want to capture and find a way to make use of these data.

Comments may also pose a challenge to hashtag-based data collection. A hashtag applied by another user in the comments of a post will cause that post to come up in hashtag searches even if the hashtag is not present in the original caption. This raises questions of intentionality and meaning, as well as privacy if the original user did not intend for their post to be searchable (Highfield and Leaver, 2014). Some type of decision-rule about handling posts with hashtags applied by other users must be created. Complicating matters somewhat, it is not uncommon for users to apply hashtags to their own posts through comments rather than editing their original caption. A removal of all posts with relevant hashtags only in the comments may thus end up eliminating posts where the hashtag was applied by the original poster.

Analysis of Visual Data

Following data collection, the analysis of Instagram posts begins. For small sets of Instagram data, a range of well-established qualitative methods for visual and textual data analysis apply (Elo and Kyngäs, 2008; Rose, 2012). The training and computational skills needed to find meaning in Big Data, however, are not standard in many social sciences, humanities, and public health graduate programs in 2015. As a result, there are still relatively few individuals who can appropriately analyze large social media data sets (boyd and Crawford, 2012), and likely even fewer who are able to make sense of visual Big Data. Those who lack these skills but still want to examine the content of large Instagram datasets have to seek out collaborations or contracts with either computer scientists or private sector services. For those purely interested in text or network analysis, Netlytic currently offers free tools for Instagram (see Chapter 30, this volume).

The aforementioned collaborations raise at least two potential ethical concerns that researchers should consider. First, many of the services that perform image recognition and deep learning for researchers specialize in providing this service for corporate clients. Ditto Labs, which is currently billed as the leading image recognition company for social media, has partnered with researchers on tobacco control efforts but also performs similar services for clients such as Proctor and Gamble, Kraft, and General Mills (Alspach, 2014; Szczypka et al., 2015). While these services may occasionally provide analysis for researchers at a reduced price, this type of collaboration lends credibility to services that mine people's social media data to develop more effective means of selling products that promote unhealthy and unsustainable behaviors. Validating these services also reinforces the social acceptability of large-scale automated data mining and bypasses the discourse around nuances of the ethics of using people's social media data for research. Researchers with social justice or public health oriented values should put thought into any decision to partner with services whose primary purpose is to provide data mining for corporate clients.

Researchers may also complement their computational analysis by contracting with Amazon's Mechanical Turk workers for manual coding of images (Jang et al., 2015b; Bakhshi et al., 2014; Manovich et al., 2014). Given that some scholars find that this service is exploitative of its workers, researchers are encouraged to pause and reflect about this choice and the extent to which it can be 'reconcile[d] with academic values' (Losh, 2015: 1653). As each of these ethical dimensions may hamper the ability of researchers to analyze large volumes of Instagram data, it is important to support novel technological development and continued holistic training of graduate students to put more of this process into the hands of researchers with training that combines advanced methods with ethics and social theory.

Interpreting Instagram Posts

As mentioned earlier, Instagram data are unlikely to be representative of the broader population in a geographic area (boyd and Crawford, 2012). This is partially due to demographics, but also due to the interference of the platform itself. Instagram users are known to craft their online identities in ways that generate likes rather than reflect authenticity (Jang et al., 2015b; Marwick, 2015). As noted by Manovich (2012a: 466), social media 'data are not a transparent window into people's imaginations, intentions, motifs, opinions, and ideas.' As a result, Instagram is a valuable resource for understanding the practices, self-disclosed lived experiences, and aspirational identities of subpopulations on Instagram, but perhaps less valuable for researchers seeking an *objective* and broadly generalizable assessment of opinions or experiences.

Instagram's terms of use, community guidelines, and shared norms also shape and limit the content in any sample of Instagram data. First, content may be absent because it has been deleted or users have been banned for posting it. Alternatively, it may simply never have been posted because users know it 'will be deemed unacceptable' (Gillespie, 2015: 1). Most recently, Instagram ran into trouble with the public over its repeated bans of users posting breastfeeding pictures. While the community guidelines were amended in April 2015 to permit these pictures, Instagram continues to ban 'some photos of female nipples' (Instagram, 2015e). Instagram does not offer a list of its currently banned hashtag searches, although these have been to known to include #Curvy, #EDM, and the eggplant emoji (Song, 2015).[2] For other hashtag searches, such as #anorexia, Instagram will display a content advisory offering information about eating disorders before posts can be viewed. Researchers should consider the ways in which Instagram shapes both what is found in their data and what is *not* found in their data.

Dissemination of Instagram Images in Research Findings

At the time of writing, observational social media research is frequently considered not to be human subjects research or is considered exempt from IRB review (Moreno et al., 2013), allowing researchers to proceed without obtaining consent from participants to make use of their Instagram data. With no consent sought, the question of how to handle images in dissemination becomes an important issue for Instagram researchers. The inclusion of images can be seen as critical for illustrating findings and supporting the validity of analysis, however, doing so can raise significant privacy concerns (Highfield and Leaver, 2014). As noted by Markham and Buchanan (2012: 6), 'people may operate in public spaces but maintain strong perceptions or expectations of privacy.' For example, an Instagram user may have a public account but still anticipate that only their followers will view their posts. With no access to statistics on how many individuals view non-video posts, it becomes impossible for users to accurately assess the extent to which their posts are being viewed by individuals outside their network.

Researchers have taken a broad range of approaches to this question. The Selfiecity project (Manovich et al., 2014), for example, created an online interface to explore de-identified selfies with no consent from the depicted individuals. Marwick (2015) reproduced images of named Instagram microcelebrities in her published manuscript with no mention of consent being given. Tiidenberg (2015: 1749) followed all of her research subjects via an Instagram account designed to outline her study and limited her 'reproduction of images to only those where the person's face is not recognizable, and altered the images using a sketching app called toonPAINT on IOS.' Some chose not to reproduce any images at all (Carah and Shaul, 2016; Seko et al., 2015), while others reproduce images 'courtesy of the artist' (Olszanowski, 2014).

Although it is difficult to develop a definitive assessment of when images should be altered and/or de-identified and when consent should be obtained regardless of alterations and de-identification, several questions do appear clearly relevant as they change expectations for privacy and possible consequences of harms.

- Is the image created by a celebrity, microcelebrity, or private person?
- Is the image still publicly available on Instagram at the time of dissemination?
- Does the image depict anything that could be seen as sensitive, harmful, or embarrassing from the perspective of the image creator or pose risks within the creator's particular cultural, economic, emotional, and legal context?
- Did the creator of the image apply a hashtag to the post to render it searchable?
- Is the image creator or image subject known to be a minor?
- Does the image allow for the potential identification of a person or location?
- Are several images being reproduced from the account of a single user?
- Does the image depict someone who is not the owner of the Instagram account?

It is clear that consent is not always sought for reproducing Instagram images and that consent may not always be necessary or realistic. It is, however, problematic to assume that consent is not necessary simply because the images are publicly available (boyd and Crawford, 2012). Researchers are encouraged to reflect on the above questions and err on the side of protecting the privacy of Instagram users through alteration, de-identification, and/or consent if there is a risk of creating harm or changing 'the experience of privacy' for an Instagram user (Highfield and Leaver, 2014; Moreno et al., 2013). Additionally, Instagram's most up-to-date terms of service should be consulted before reproducing any images.

A CASE STUDY CONSIDERING ELECTRONIC CIGARETTE CONTENT ON INSTAGRAM

To highlight some of the above points in a more applied fashion, I offer a case study drawn from recent work on how electronic cigarettes ('e-cigarettes') are portrayed on Instagram (Laestadius et al., 2016). At the time of writing, there had been no prior research on the content of e-cigarette posts on Instagram and there were significant questions about e-cigarette usage and culture. This issue was of concern to public health because e-cigarette usage has the potential to renormalize smoking among adolescents, increase rates of nicotine addiction, and prevent full smoking cessation (Pisinger, 2014). As an exploratory study, a qualitative content analysis of a small sample of Instagram posts was chosen to allow new insights to emerge from the data. This was paired with tracking of hashtag usage over time to assess overall trends in e-cigarette content. The primary aim of this work was to understand how e-cigarettes have been portrayed and engaged with on Instagram rather than building generalizations to all Instagram or e-cigarette users.

Approach and Data Collection

As an entry point to the study, we began with the hashtag 'ecig'. An informal examination of posts with #ecig also revealed seven additional common hashtags: #ecigarette, #vape, #vaping, #vapelife, #vapelyfe, #vapeporn, and #ejuice (vaping is a slang term for the use of e-cigarettes, as they emit what is publicly considered vapor rather than smoke). These eight hashtags were tracked over time, with the number of posts with each hashtag (as displayed in the Instagram application) recorded biannually in 2014 and 2015. From here, #ecig and the most popular affiliated hashtag, #vape, were chosen for sampling. We performed searches for '#ecig' and '#vape' in Iconosquare, which allows researchers to view complete posts without logging in with an Instagram account. Links to the 60 most recent posts in chronological order of tagging were gathered for #ecig and for #vape on 17 October 2014, yielding 120 posts. Duplicate posts that appeared more than once from the same user were removed, as were posts related solely to marijuana use but not e-cigarettes or vaping. Further, 30 additional posts were gathered to assist with codebook development.

All posts in the original sample were revisited and screen-captured on 7 January 2015 in order to better protect the privacy of users. Posts where links had gone dead due to users deleting posts or changing their accounts to private were removed. After these adjustments, the final sample contained 85 posts (43 #ecig, 42 #vape). Clearly, our sample size was reduced dramatically after these adjustments and going forward we will plan for such reductions upfront by increasing the volume of data collected in the initial period.

Coding and Analysis

We developed the coding scheme through a combined inductive and deductive approach (Elo and Kyngäs, 2008). First, 20 recent #ecig posts were discussed to identify common themes. Based upon this initial review, a codebook was developed to include content relating to devices types, e-cigarette use in conjunction with marijuana, and hashtags indicating that e-cigarette use represents a source of shared community or social identity (e.g. #vapefam or #vapebabe). Additionally, the codebook incorporated themes identified as persuasive in e-cigarette messaging (Pepper et al., 2014) and themes common to e-cigarette advertising on websites (Grana and Ling, 2014; Richardson et al., 2014). Number of 'likes' and comments, gender of individuals in images, country of origin, and any identifiable e-cigarette or e-cigarette liquid ('e-juice') brands visible or mentioned in posts were also included for coding. Finally, we recorded all hashtags used, and created written descriptions of the image/video and caption of each post.

We applied codes to posts as a unit, considering the content of images/videos and any descriptive text, emoji, and hashtags in the post caption. Comments were not considered, as our focus was on content created by the original poster. Additionally, we traced each post back to the poster's account page to determine user status as: 1) an individual member of the public who was unaffiliated with the e-cigarette industry, 2) an e-cigarette enthusiast (i.e. member of the public whose screen name or profile referenced e-cigarettes in some way, 3) an e-cigarette or e-juice brand, 4) an e-cigarette or e-juice vendor, or 5) a formal brand or vendor representative (i.e. the personal account of someone who works in the field).

After completion of the initial codebook, 30 screen-captured posts were pilot coded by a PhD student trained in coding and myself. Coding discrepancies were discussed and resolved and the codebook was revised to have 28 coding fields. The large volume of codes is distinct from studies that place each post into just one category (Gibbs et al., 2015), and thus required a significant time investment for each post. This was further compounded by a need to build familiarity with the meaning of many e-cigarette hashtags. Once finalized, we independently coded the final sample of posts using Microsoft Excel. On each field, an intercoder reliability test was performed using STATA 14 (Cohen, 1960; Lin, 1989). The intercoder reliability coefficients ranged from 0.38 to 1 with an average of 0.77. Following this calculation, we discussed any discrepancies in coding to reach consensus, with a third reviewer offering input when consensus could not be reached.

Findings and Reflection

In brief, our analysis generated notable insights about e-cigarette depictions on Instagram and e-cigarette subculture more generally. This consumption subculture evidences itself on Instagram primarily through unique jargon, rituals, and shared values and, as articulated by Schouten and McAlexander (1995: 43), is comprised of individuals who have self-selected 'on the basis of a shared commitment to a particular ... consumption activity.' In this case, the consumption of advanced e-cigarette devices. Given the harmful and addictive nature of nicotine, this finding is of notable importance to public health.

The tracking of hashtag volume over time allowed us to capture changes in the way e-cigarettes were conceptualized on Instagram, with use of hashtags related to vaping increasing at a much more rapid pace than hashtags related to e-cigarettes. This suggested that e-cigarettes were being framed more as novel devices than as an equivalent to conventional cigarettes. Our content analysis further supported this finding, with evidence of few comparisons to conventional cigarettes or smoking cessation. Instead, users were posting about the e-cigarette devices themselves and about novel vaping practices specific to advanced models of e-cigarettes.

We also found that many of the posts served to fetishize the devices both through appealing visual depictions and the use of #vapeporn. Finally, the majority of posts analyzed made use of hashtags denoting self-identification as a 'vaper' and/membership in vaping communities (e.g. #vapefam, #vapelife, #vaper, #vapeaholic). To better protect the privacy of the large number of individual members of the public in our sample, we chose not to reproduce any images in our final published manuscript.

CONCLUSION

While Instagram research can be time consuming and complex, the rewards are clear. Instagram users visually capture aspects of their everyday lives and aspirations in ways that can inform significant research across a broad range of topics and fields. Given the current demographics of users, it is a particularly rich source of data for those seeking to understand youth culture. Big Data and qualitative researchers alike are encouraged to explore how Instagram may serve as a valuable site of research for their work, with recognition that: 1) Instagram should be treated as its own distinct platform, 2) posts function as holistic units, in which images/ videos, text, emoji, and hashtags should interpreted together, 3) content must be situated within its cultural and platform context and should not be seen as representative of the general population, and 4) distinct ethical concerns must be managed when analyzing and disseminating visual data. As documented in this chapter's case study, engaging with Instagram data allowed us a unique perspective on the e-cigarette and vaping subculture as it exists on Instagram and revealed information about vaping identity that had not previously been made known to researchers via more conventional approaches to e-cigarette users and e-cigarette content online. Recognizing that Instagram users may not anticipate that they will be studied, we also made a point to remove posts that were deleted or made private within a several week-long window after initial data collection was completed.

Instagram will inevitably continue to develop over time. As a result, researchers who personally engage with and post on the platform will be those best situated to understand its developing affordances and norms. Going forward, there is also a clear need for more research that engages with Instagram users directly rather than simply looking at the content they create, as well as methodological work on how to best integrate analysis of Instagram's visual and textual components.

NOTES

1 Manovich's team makes software tools for cultural analytics available free of charge on their Software Studies Initiative website (http://lab.softwarestudies.com/).
2 Curvy, the eggplant emoji (which is thought to resemble a penis), and EDM (short for Electronic Dance Music) were all banned because they were determined to be consistently associated with nudity that violated Instagram's terms of service.

REFERENCES

Abidin, C. (2014) '#In$tagLam: Instagram as a repository of taste, a brimming marketplace, a war of eyeballs', in M. Berry and M. Schleser (eds), *Mobile Media Making in an Age of Smartphones*. New York: Palgrave MacMillian. pp.119–128.

Alspach, K. (2014) 'Ditto Labs raises $2.2 million for social media photo analytics', *The Boston Globe*. (http://www.betaboston.com/news/2014/05/14/ditto-labs-raises-2-2-million-for-social-media-photo-analytics/)

Bakhshi, S., Shamma, D.A. and Gilbert, E. (2014) 'Faces engage us: Photos with faces attract more likes and comments on Instagram', proceedings of the ACM CHI Conference on Human Factors in Computing Systems, Toronto: 965–974.

Baym, N.K. (2015) *Personal Connections in the Digital Age*. 2nd edn. Cambridge: Polity Press.

boyd, d. (2010) 'Social network sites as networked publics: Affordances, dynamics, and implications', in Z. Papacharissi (ed.), *Networked Self Identity, Community, and Culture on Social Network Sites*. New York: Routledge: pp. 39–58.

boyd, d. (2014) *It's Complicated: The Social Lives of Networked Teens*. New Haven: Yale University Press.

boyd, d. and Crawford, K. (2012) 'Critical questions for big data: Provocations for a cultural, technological, and scholarly phenomenon', *Information, Communication & Society*, 15(5): 662–679.

Bruns, A. and Burgess, J. (2011) 'The use of Twitter hashtags in the formation of ad hoc publics', proceedings of the 6th European Consortium for Political Research General Conference, Reykjavik.

Burgess, J. and Bruns, A. (2012) 'Twitter archives and the challenges of "big social data" for media and communication research', *M/C Journal*, 15(5). (http://journal.media-culture.org.au/index.php/mcjournal/article/view/561)

Carah, N. and Shaul, M. (2016) 'Brands and Instagram: Point, tap, swipe, glance', *Mobile Media & Communication*, 4(1): 69–84.

Charmaz, K. (2015) 'Grounded theory', in J. Smith, (ed.), *Qualitative Psychology: A Practical Guide to Research Methods*. 3rd edn. London: SAGE. pp. 53–84.

Cohen, J. (1960) 'A coefficient of agreement for nominal scales', *Educational and Psychological Measurement*, 20(1): 37–46.

Curinga, M.X. (2014) 'Critical analysis of interactive media with software affordances', *First Monday*, 19(9). (http://firstmonday.org/ojs/index.php/fm/article/view/4757)

Dubois, E. and Ford, H. (2015) 'Trace interviews: An actor-centered approach', *International Journal of Communication*, 9: 2067–2091.

Duggan, M. (2015) Mobile Messaging and Social Media 2015. *Pew Research Center*. (http://www.pewinternet.org/2015/08/19/mobile-messaging-and-social-media-2015/)

Elo, S. and Kyngäs, H. (2008) 'The qualitative content analysis process', *Journal of Advanced Nursing*, 62(1): 107–115.

Farman, J. (2015) 'Infrastructures of mobile social media', *Social Media+ Society,* April–June: 1–2.

Ferrara, E., Interdonato, R. and Tagarelli, A. (2014) 'Online popularity and topical interests through the lens of Instagram', proceedings of the 25th ACM Conference on Hypertext and Social Media, Santiago: 24–34.

Gibbs, M., Meese, J., Arnold, M., Nansen, B. and Carter, M. (2015) '#funeral and Instagram: death, social media, and platform vernacular', *Information, Communication, and Society*, 18(3): 255–268.

Gillespie, T. (2015) 'Platforms intervene', *Social Media + Society*, April–June: 1–2.

Goddemeyer, D., Stefaner, M., Baur, D. and Manovich, L. (2015) On Broadway (http://www.on-broadway.nyc/)

Grana, R.A. and Ling, P.M. (2014) '"Smoking revolution": A content analysis of electronic cigarette retail websites', *American Journal of Preventive Medicine*, 46(4): 395–403.

Highfield, T. and Leaver, T. (2014) 'A methodology for mapping Instagram hashtags', *First Monday*, 20(1). (http://firstmonday.org/article/view/5563/4195)

Hitlin, P. and Holcomb, J. (2015) From Twitter to Instagram, a different #Ferguson conversation. *Pew Research Center*. (www.pewresearch.orgfact-tankfrom-twitter-to-instagram-a-different-ferguson)

Hochman, N., Manovich, L. and Chow, J. (2013) Phototrails (http://phototrails.net/about/)

Ibrahim, Y. (2015) 'Instagramming life: Banal imaging and the poetics of the everyday', *Journal of Media Practice*, 16(1): 42–54.

Instagram (2013) Terms of Use (https://instagram.com/about/legal/terms/)

Instagram (2015a) FAQs (https://instagram.com/about/faq/#)

Instagram (2015b) About Us (https://instagram.com/about/us/)

Instagram (2015c) I get an error when trying to add a comment | Instagram Help Center (https://help.instagram.com/161863397286564)

Instagram (2015d) Press Page (http://instagram.com/press/)

Instagram (2015e) Community Guidelines (https://help.instagram.com/477434105621119/)

Instagram (2016) Press Page (http://instagram.com/press/)

Jang, J., Han, K. and Lee, D. (2015a) 'No Reciprocity in "Liking" Photos', proceedings of the 26th ACM Conference on Hypertext and Social Media, Northern Cyprus: 273–282.

Jang, J., Han, K., Shih, P.C. and Lee, D. (2015b) 'Generation Like: Comparative Characteristics in Instagram', proceedings of the 33rd ACM CHI Conference on Human Factors in Computing Systems, Seoul: 4039–4042.

Kaufer, E. (2015) Instagram: The next big (academic) thing? *Rough Consensus – The Oxford Internet Studies Student Blog*. (http://blogs.oii.ox.ac.uk/roughconsensus/2015/02/instagram-the-next-big-academic-thing/)

Kitchin, R. (2013) 'Big data and human geography Opportunities, challenges and risks', *Dialogues in Human Geography*, 3(3): 262–267.

Kitchin, R., and Lauriault, T. P. (2015) 'Small data in the era of big data', *GeoJournal*, 80(4): 463–475.

Laestadius, L.I., Wahl, M.M. and Cho, Y.I. (2016) ' #Vapelife: An exploratory study of electronic cigarette use and promotion on Instagram', *Substance Use and Misuse: 1–5*.

Larsson, A.O. (2015) 'Review of "Analysing Social Media Data and Web Networks" by Cantijoch, M., Gibson, R., & Ward, S. (eds.)', *Information Polity*, 20(2,3): 223–225.

Lee, K. (2015) A Scientific Guide to Hashtags: How Many, Which Ones, and Where to Use Them. *Buffersocial*. (https://blog.bufferapp.com/a-scientific-guide-to-hashtags-which-ones-work-when-and-how-many)

Lin, L.I-K. (1989) 'A concordance correlation coefficient to evaluate reproducibility', *Biometrics*, 45(1): 255–268.

Litt, E. (2012) 'Knock, knock. Who's there? The imagined audience', *Journal of Broadcasting & Electronic Media*, 56(3): 330–345.

Losh, E. (2014) Beyond biometrics: Feminist media theory looks at *Selfiecity*. *Selfiecity*: 1–16. (http://d25rsf93iwlmgu.cloudfront.net/downloads/Liz_Losh_BeyondBiometrics.pdf)

Losh, E. (2015) 'Feminism reads big data: "Social physics", atomism, and Selfiecity', *International Journal of Communication*, 9: 1647–1659.

Manikonda, L., Hu, Y. and Kambhampati, S. (2014) 'Analyzing user activities, demographics, social network structure and user-generated content on Instagram', *arXiv:1410.8099(1)*.

Manovich, L. (2009) How to Follow Global Digital Cultures, or Cultural Analytics for Beginners: 1–22. (http://manovich.net/content/04-projects/062-how-to-follow-global-digital-cultures/59_article_2009.pdf)

Manovich, L. (2012a) 'Trending: The promises and the challenges of big social data', in M.K. Gold (ed.), *Debates in the Digital Humanities*. Minneapolis: University of Minnesota Press. pp. 460–475.

Manovich, L. (2012b) 'Media visualization: Visual techniques for exploring large media collections', in K. Gates and A. Valdivia (eds.), Vol 6, *Media Studies Futures, The International Encyclopedia of Media Studies*. Hoboken: Wiley.

Manovich, L., Stefaner, M., Yazdani, M., Baur, D., Goddmeyer, D., Tifentale, A., Hochman, N. and Chow, J. (2014) Selfiecity (http://selfiecity.net/)

Markham, A. and Buchanan, E. (2012) Ethical decision-making and Internet research (version 2.0): Recommendations from the AoIR Ethics Working Committee. *Association of Internet Researchers*. (http://www.aoir.org/reports/ethics2.pdf)

Marwick, A.E. (2015) 'Instafame: Luxury selfies in the attention economy', *Public Culture*, 27(1 75): 137–160.

Mejova, Y., Haddadi, H., Noulas, A. and Weber, I. (2015) '# FoodPorn: Obesity patterns in culinary interactions', proceeding of the 5th International Conference on Digital Health, Florence: 51-58.

Metz, C. (2014) How Facebook Moved 20 Billion Instagram Photos Without You Noticing. *Wired*.(http://www.wired.com/2014/06/facebook-instagram/)

Michel, F. (2016) How Many Public Photos are Uploaded to Flickr Every Day, Month, Year? *Flickr*. (https://www.flickr.com/photos/franckmichel/6855169886/)

Moreno, M.A., Goniu, N., Moreno, P.S. and Diekema, D. (2013) 'Ethics of social media research: Common concerns and practical considerations', *Cyberpsychology, Behavior, and Social Networking*, 16(9): 708–713.

Morse, J.M. (2000) 'Determining sample size', *Qualitative Health Research*, 10(1): 3–5.

Olmstead, K. and Barthel, M. (2015) The challenges of using Facebook for research. *Pew Research Center*. (http://www.pewresearch.org/fact-tank/2015/03/26/the-challenges-of-using-facebook-for-research/)

Olszanowski, M. (2014) 'Feminist self-imaging and Instagram: Tactics of circumventing sensorship', *Visual Communication Quarterly*, 21(2): 83–95.

Pepper, J.K., Emery, S.L., Ribisl, K.M., Southwell, B.G. and Brewer, N.T. (2014) 'Effects of advertisements on smokers' interest in trying e-cigarettes: The roles of product comparison and visual cues' *Tobacco Control*, 23(Suppl 3): iii 31–36.

Pisinger, C. (2014) 'Why public health people are more worried than excited over e-cigarettes', *BMC Medicine*, 12(1): 226–230.

Richardson, A., Ganz, O. and Vallone, D. (2014) 'Tobacco on the web: Surveillance and characterisation of online tobacco and e-cigarette advertising', *Tobacco Control*, 24: 341–347.

Rose, Gillian (2012) *Visual Methodologies*. 3rd edn. London: SAGE.

Schouten, J. W. and McAlexander, J. H. (1995) 'Subcultures of consumption: An ethnography of the new bikers', *Journal of Consumer Research*, 22(1): 43–61.

Seko, Y., Kidd, S.A., Wiljer, D. and McKenzie, K.J. (2015) 'On the creative edge: Exploring motivations for creating non-suicidal self-injury content online', *Qualitative Health Research*, 25(10): 1334–1346.

Seltzer, E.K., Jean, N.S., Kramer-Golinkoff, E., Asch, D.A. and Merchant, R.M. (2015) 'The content of social media's shared images about Ebola: a retrospective study', *Public Health*, 129(9): 1273–1277.

Sheer, I. (2012) Choosing the Right Photo Service. *The Wall Street Journal*. (http://blogs.wsj.com/digits/2012/12/31/choosing-the-right-photo-service/)

Sloane, G. (2015) Instagram Unveils 'Shop' Button and New API to Grow Its Ad Business. *Adweek*. (http://www.adweek.com/news/technology/instagram-just-unleashed-fully-operational-ad-business-165117)

Smith, C. (2014) Here's Why Instagram's Demographics Are So Attractive To Brands. *Business Insider*. (http://www.businessinsider.com/instagram-demographics-2013-12)

Software Studies Initiative (2015) Cultural Analytics (http://lab.softwarestudies.com/p/overview-slides-and-video-articles-why.html)

Song, S. (2015) Instagram Bans #EDM Hashtag. *Paper*. (http://www.papermag.com/2015/08/instagram_bans_edm_hashtag.php)

Souza Araujo, C., Correa, L.P.D., da Silva, A.P.C., Prates, R.O. and Meria Jr., W. (2014) 'It is not just a picture: Revealing some user practices in Instagram', proceedings of the IEEE 9th Latin American Web Congress, Ouro Preto: 19–23.

Sysomos (2010) Replies and Retweets (https://sysomos.com/inside-twitter/twitter-retweet-stats)

Szczypka, G., Binns, S., Carrion, V., Nordgren, R., Ilakkuvan, V., Hair, E., Vallone, D. and Emery, S. (2015) 'Smoking Selfies: Using Instagram to examine smoking behavior', poster presented at the 2015 American Public Health Association Conference, Chicago.

Tiidenberg, K. (2015) 'Odes to heteronormativity: Presentations of femininity in Russian-speaking pregnant women's Instagram accounts', *International Journal of Communication*, 9: 1746–1758.

Tifentale, A. (2014) The selfie: Making sense of the 'masturbation of self-image' and the 'virtual mini-me'. *Selfiecity*: 1–24. (http://d25rsf93iwlmgu.cloudfront.net/downloads/Tifentale_Alise_Selfiecity.pdf)

Ting, H., Ming, W.W.P., de Run, E.C. and Choo, S.L.Y. (2015) 'Beliefs about the use of Instagram: An exploratory study', *International Journal of Business and Innovation*, 2(2): 15–31.

Tostes Ribeiro Anna Izabel João, Silva, Thiago Henrique, Duarte-Figueiredo, Fatima and Loureiro, Antonio, A.F. (2014) 'Studying traffic conditions by analyzing foursquare and instagram data', proceedings of the 11th ACM International Symposium on Performance Evaluation of Wireless Ad Hoc, Sensor, and Ubiquitous Networks, Montreal: 17–24.

Twitter (2015) Company | Twitter Usage (https://about.twitter.com/company)

Twitter (2016) Company | Twitter Usage (https://about.twitter.com/company)

Wellman, B., Quan-Haase, A., Boase, J., Chen, W., Hampton, K. N., and Díaz, I. (2003) 'The social affordances of the Internet for networked individualism', *Journal of Computer-Mediated Communication*, 8(3): 1–22.

Yamasaki, T., Sano, S. and Mei, T. (2015) 'Revealing relationships between folksonomy and social popularity score in image/video sharing services', proceedings of the 2015 IEEE International Conference on Consumer Electronics, Taipei: 29–30.

Yi-Frazier J.P., Cochrane K, Mitrovich C, Pascual, M., Buscaino, E., Eaton, L., Panlasigui, N., Clupp, B. and Malik, F. (2015) 'Using Instagram as a modified application of Photovoice for storytelling and sharing in adolescents with type 1 diabetes', *Qualitative Health Research*, 25(10): 1372–1382.

Weibo

Xiao Hu, Chen Qiao and King-wa Fu

INTRODUCTION

Social media is one of the most dynamic and innovative industries in China. The market has experienced significant development, and continues to expand. Despite the fact that the leading international social media platforms such as Facebook, Twitter and YouTube are blocked in China, numerous domestic social media sites/ platforms have grown to fill this gap in the market, and become comparable to their western counterparts. Weibo is one of the leading microblogging services in China.

'Weibo' [微博] is the generic Chinese term for microblogging services in China. These services are similar to Twitter, the most well-known microblogging service worldwide. Since the growth of social media, many companies have launched Weibo services in China. However, not all of them survived. (Duan et al., 2015). Presently, the most influential microblog service in China is provided by Sina.com, namely Sina Weibo. The service, which was launched in August 2009, has now attracted approximately 250 million registered users, and generates 90 million posts per day (Yu et al., 2015). Because of its dominant position among Weibo service providers in China, Sina Weibo is often simply called 'Weibo' (Duan et al., 2015). This chapter focuses on Sina Weibo, hereafter referred to simply as 'Weibo'.

Outside of China, Weibo is often compared to Twitter. One way to think about Weibo is to think of it first as a replication of Twitter for the Chinese market. Similar to Twitter, on Weibo, users can post short messages of up to 140 characters, repost (retweet) others' posts, post and reply to comments, mark 'like' for a post, mention other users, and participate in discussions with specific tags such as '@' and '##'. Besides text content, Weibo also allows users to post links, images, music, and videos. Weibo provides users with customizable personal profile pages, and shows users' basic information and platform activity statistics. Users can 'like' posts/reposts and make comments on them. They can also follow or be followed by other users and form groups.

The interface of Weibo also shares common features with that of Twitter. Figure 35.1 shows a sample page of Weibo. Posts and reposts are displayed in descending chronological order. It also displays a short profile of the user on the right side, with the number of followers, number of tweets, etc. Like Twitter, Weibo also has a location based service (LBS), polling, and private messaging.

Weibo has also become an open platform, with many integrated official or third-party applications, and hence provides services which differentiate it from Twitter, such as user groups, games, stock reports, podcasts, shopping, cloud storage, and payment services.

Although Weibo is an open platform, it is subjected to government monitoring and regulations that aim to suppress rumors and sensitive content. As has been reported by Bammam et al. (2012), we can find evidence of censorship by observing missing posts and blocked search results. In other words, a post might be deleted after it is deemed by the authorities to contain politically sensitive topics, abusive language, pornography, or 'rumors' (Chen, Zhang, & Wilson, 2013). Searches containing sensitive keywords can also be blocked. Additionally, the Real Name Policy requires users to submit bona fide identity information when registering for Weibo accounts. The accounts are being monitored and could be banned if the users continuously post illegal or sensitive content.

Weibo, also contains a number of special 'VIP' accounts, known as 'Big V's' – influential Weibo users with verified accounts. These VIP accounts often have millions of followers and thus are considered to be opinion leaders. Some campaigns have been aiming to undermine the influence of the VIPs (Chin & Mozur, 2013). There is also government's propaganda on Weibo. The seemingly 'free' commentary on Weibo is often actively influenced in favor of a 'harmonious' (GOV.cn, 2006) and pro-government outlook by the '50-Cent Party' - a group of hired online commentators who participate in online discussions by posting messages that promote the official line of the Chinese Communist Party.

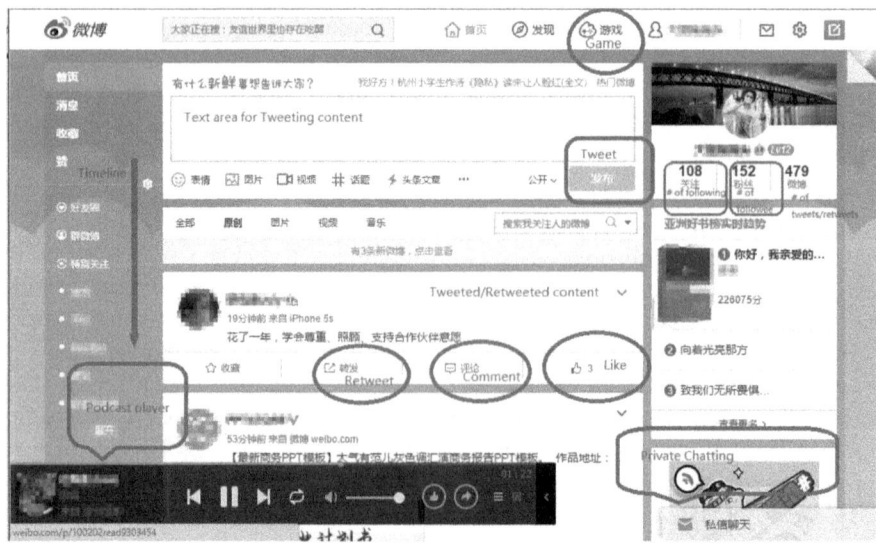

Figure 35.1   Screenshot of Weibo interface

As one of the foremost social media services in China, Weibo has attracted a significant amount of research interest since 2009 (the year it was founded). In CNKI, China's largest digital academic publication database, there are more than one million articles focusing on Weibo. A wide range of areas have been studied based on data collected on Weibo, such as information diffusion, public administration, communication, marketing research, linguistics, and social computing.

The following sections of this chapter aim to summarize some representative methods applied in Weibo studies. This chapter starts with the description of methods used to collect Weibo data ('Weibo data collection'), followed by data analysis methods in Weibo-related research ('Analyzing Weibo content' and 'Analyzing Weibo relationships'). In 'Selected studies and methods applied', a number of case studies in different domains are then presented, demonstrating how these methods were used to solve various research questions. Based on the methodological reviews, this chapter is concluded by summarizing lessons learned and challenges for Weibo research.

WEIBO DATA COLLECTION

Weibo studies usually require the collection of user-generated data. Manual data gathering is a direct approach, and readers may utilize Sina Weibo's search function to find content of interest (see Figure 35.2). However, for research purposes, it is often necessary to collect Weibo data in significant quantities, which requires an automated approach. In practice, there are mainly two approaches for automatic fetching of data from Weibo: official Weibo API and API-free web crawlers.

Weibo API

Weibo APIs, or officially Open APIs, provide programmatic access to read and write Weibo data. Readers may think of Twitter REST APIs to get an intuitive impression of Open API, as the functions and styles of the two are quite similar.

Similar to Twitter REST APIs, Open APIs are usually called from computer programs, and thus direct application of raw APIs requires programming skill and knowledge of HTTP (Hypertext Transfer Protocol, an Internet transport protocol) and JSON (JavaScript Object Notation, a format for the organization of data). An example of the workflow for data collection using the API is illustrated in Figure 35.3. The requester (user-built program) wraps an API call in a HTTP packet, which is then delivered to the Weibo server. The server receives the packet, opens it, finds the API call, and retrieves the requested data. It will then encode the data using the JSON format, wrap it into a HTTP packet, and send it back to the requester.

According to the API document (Weibo Open Platform, 2012), the Open API includes 15 function groups, including information access for posts (Weibo API), comments (Comments API), user information (User API), friendship information (Friendships API), geographical information (Geo API), etc.

An example of a request[1] for the content of a single Weibo post can be: 'https://api.weibo.com/2/statuses/show.json?access_token=SomeToken&id=11488058246'.

In this request URL, the component 'show.json' indicates the current request type (i.e. getting a single Weibo post). It is appended by the request variables in key-value pairs. This is referred to as the HTTP GET method

Figure 35.2 Screenshot of Weibo search

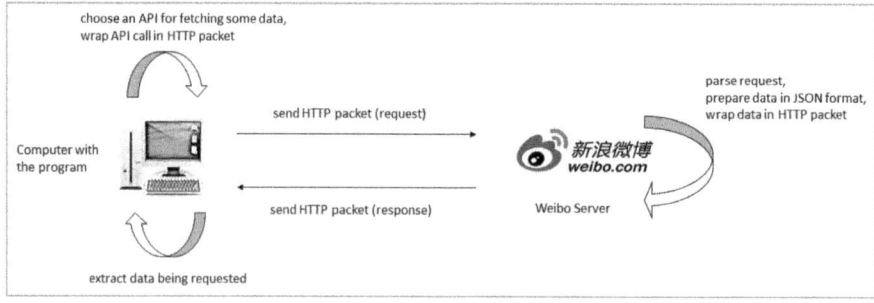

Figure 35.3 Workflow of applying the Open API for Weibo data collection

which includes all variables in the request URL. Alternatively, the variables can be included in the body of the HTTP request in JSON style (i.e., HTTP POST method), such as:

```
{
 "access_token":SomeToken,
 "id":11488058246
}
```

The key 'access_token' is the requester's credential and the 'id' identifies the Weibo post of interest. A possible response from the Weibo server would be like the JSON style codes below. The "text" variable is the Weibo content requested which is accompanied by a number of other variables, such as creation time, counts of reposts and comments, and information about the user who made the post.

```
{
 "created_at": "Tue May 31 17:46:55 +0800
    2011",
 "id": 11488058246,
 "text": "求关注。",
 "source": "<a xhref="http://weibo.com"
    rel="nofollow">新浪微博</a>",
 "favorited": false,
 "truncated": false,
 "in_reply_to_status_id": "",
 "in_reply_to_user_id": "",
 "in_reply_to_screen_name": "",
 "geo": null,
 "mid": "5612814510546515491",
 "reposts_count": 8,
 "comments_count": 9,
 "annotations": [],
 "user": {
 "id": 1404376560,
 "screen_name": "zaku",
 "name": "zaku",
 "province": "11",
 "city": "5",
 "location": "北京朝阳区",
 "description": "人生五十年, 乃如梦如幻 有
    生斯有死, 壮士复何憾。",
 "url": "http://blog.sina.com.cn/zaku",
 "profile_image_url": "http://tp1.sinaimg.
    cn/1404376560/50/0/1",
 "domain": "zaku",
 "gender": "m",
 "followers_count": 1204,
 "friends_count": 447,
 "statuses_count": 2908,
 "favourites_count": 0,
 "created_at": "Fri Aug 28 00:00:00 +0800
    2009",
 "following": false,
 "allow_all_act_msg": false,
 "remark": "",
 "geo_enabled": true,
 "verified": false,
 "allow_all_comment": true,
 "avatar_large": "http://tp1.sinaimg.
    cn/1404376560/180/0/1",
 "verified_reason": "",
 "follow_me": false,
 "online_status": 0,
 "bi_followers_count": 215
 }
}
```

To date, the Open API has been implemented in multiple commonly used programming languages, including Java, PHP, C#, Flash, Python, Javascript, Android, and iOS SDKs. To make use of the Open API, a user should obtain a developer account on the Weibo Open platform, and get verification keys for his/her programs.

It is noteworthy that Sina changes the Open API from time to time, for technical updates or for protecting its data property. The company also imposes restrictions on the API usage rate and unsolicited data requests according to different levels of user account. For example, there is a limit on the number of requests a single application can issue within an hour. If a higher number of requests are needed, advanced API accounts with more privileges are required. Because of these constraints, studies often sample Weibo content using keywords or user status (e.g. most active users on certain topics). This may introduce biases into the data collection, which needs to be considered when interpreting findings. For the latest information on the API, we recommend that readers consult the official website (http://open.weibo.com/).

API-free Web Crawler

Another option for collecting data from Weibo is to implement a Web crawler, a computer program that automatically collects Web pages from targeted sources. A Web crawler, like a browser, sends HTTP requests to the Weibo server, receives responses, and then parses the returned HTML pages to extract useful data. It differs from Weibo's API mostly in its processing of the responded data. Unlike the clean JSON style responses, it directly processes the raw HTML pages returned. A crawler is more flexible in fetching data because it is free from API constraints.

Figure 35.4 shows the workflow of a Web crawler for Sina Weibo (Shen et al., 2013),

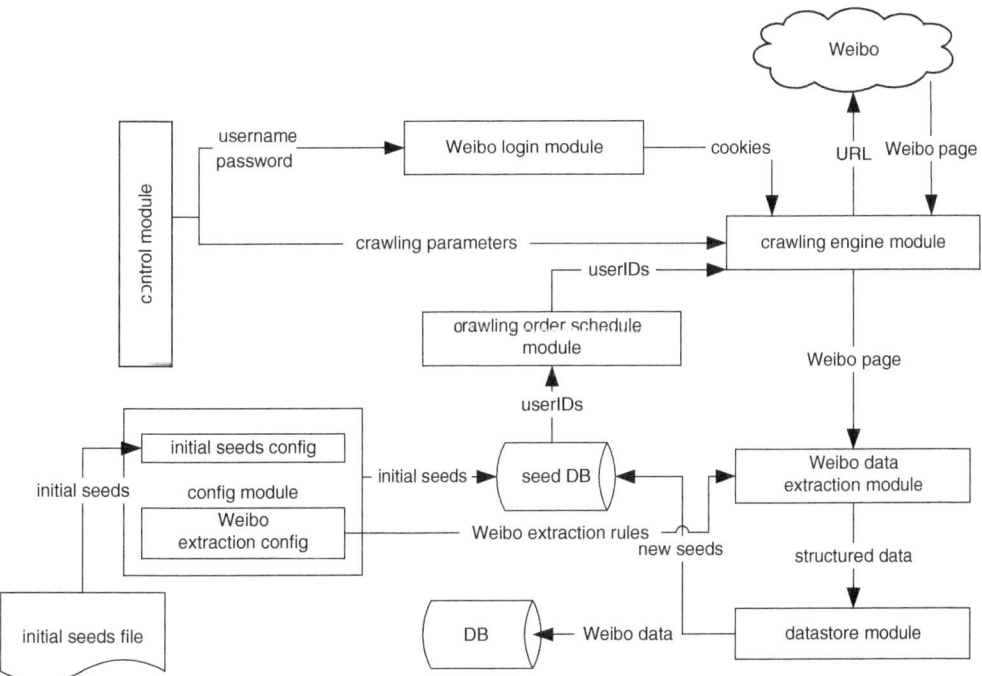

Figure 35.4 Data flow of a Sina Weibo crawler (adapted from Shen et al., 2013)

which follows the typical structure of a general Web crawler. The crawler needs to login to the Weibo platform with a valid account. The data that can be fetched by the crawler are the same as what can be obtained by a normal user's Web browser, except that the crawler does not need to render the raw HTML tags to human-readable pages. Since Web pages are interconnected by hyperlinks, a crawler can start from some given seed pages and trace the hyperlinks to fetch linked pages. As a result, the quantity of pages being crawled can be very large. A configuration for crawling strategies, such as the number of parallel threads, request frequency, or tracing depth, is sometimes needed to optimize performances. Fetched data are usually stored in databases or files after parsing and preprocessing.

An example of a Weibo crawler is the online crawler module of WeiboEvents (Ren et al., 2014). As shown in Figure 35.5, the crawler supports data fetching for a particular user, for tweets containing a certain keyword, and for the relationships and connections of a certain user. All fetched data can be downloaded in JSON format. As the Online Weibo Data Crawler is freely available, we recommend the tool to readers who have no technical background and prefer off-the-shelf tools.

ANALYZING WEIBO CONTENT

After the data are collected, it is time to make sense of them. Studying the content on Weibo is a useful method to determine social trends, public concerns, and other elements of public life within the Chinese community. Weibo content is conveyed in posts, reposts and comments that contain text (including hashtags, emojis), images, music, animations (usually animated gif pictures), videos and external URLs. Despite the rich content, text is commonly analyzed by studies. In this section, we describe the method of content analysis relying on human judgement as well as automatic methods enabled by natural language processing and data mining techniques.

Content Analysis

Content Analysis (CA) is a classic research method widely used in social science. Technically, it requires raw data to be labeled by human coders based on a coding scheme. The coding scheme is usually designed according to the research purposes of the given study. Basic steps of CA are summarized as: 1. To establish a coding scheme based on the specific research purpose of the

Figure 35.5 Screenshot of the online Weibo data crawler

study; 2. To employ coders to code the contents and check the inter-coder reliability; 3. To analyze the results. Here we list the work of Dann (2010) as an example. Part of the coding scheme and counts of conversational categories for Tweets are illustrated in Figure 35.6. We can see the definition and exemplar texts for each category, and from the result we learn that most Tweets are for querying and responding.

CA is particularly helpful for deep analysis of Weibo content as well. For example, a study by Guo & Goh (2014) applied CA to analyze posts in an HIV/AIDS support group on Weibo. They constructed a coding scheme by further refining the categories on the basis of the Social Information Processing Theory. Likewise, Liao et al. (2013) applied CA to categorize types of Weibo posts in the study of rumor transmission. They designed a coding scheme based on the Rumor Interaction Analysis System, and revised the coding scheme by piloting it on a small collection of messages. This is an example of a mixture of top-down and bottom-up strategies for content analysis. Yiu et al. (2015) compared the Weibo accounts of three famous singers by manually coding the posts with a coding scheme adopted originally for Twitter content. This is an example of recycling instruments and findings from Twitter-based research. We emphasize their ways of developing coding schemes because implementing an appropriate coding framework is a key prerequisite for CA.

CA can also be used for non-text based content analysis, for example, images and music. In addition, as it relies on human intelligence, CA can be undertaken in more intelligence-demanding occasions where human interpretation on media content is essential and most automatic approaches may fall short.

Automatic Methods

Notwithstanding its usefulness, manual CA meets its limitations in the context of large-scale datasets where an automatic content analysis approach supported by Natural

Category	Definition	N	Percentage	Exemplar
Conversational				
1. Query	Questions, question marks or polls	480	17	Invading Germany from France. Who's with me?
2. Referral	An @response which contains URLs or recommendation of other Twitter users. (Excludes RT @user)	2	2	@USERNAME Items under $1000 are exempt. http://is.gd/AV7K
3. Action	Activities involving other Twitter users	3	3	*waves at @USERNAME*
4. Response	Catch–all classification for conversation @tweets	850	30	@USERNAME Beware the polar bears.

Figure 35.6 Fragment of a coding scheme and results (reprinted from Dann, 2010)

Figure 35.7 A chinese text string on Weibo (translated as 'AlphaGo defeated Lee Se-dol, but artificial intelligence has not conquered human being')

Language Processing (NLP) and Data Mining (DM) techniques is more efficient and effective. As Weibo content is mostly in Chinese, in this section, we discuss Chinese processing and text classification.

Chinese Processing

As Chinese is the dominant communication media on Weibo, Chinese NLP techniques are needed for automating content processing. It is well known that in written Chinese there is no space between characters, as is shown in Figure 35.7. Therefore, tokenization algorithms based on whitespace delimiters (such as in English) do not work. It is usually the first task in Chinese text processing to segment a string of written Chinese into meaningful words, which is called word segmentation tasks (Zhang et al., 2003; Qiu et al., 2013). For the text in Figure 35.7, the segmented words with part-of-speech (POS) tags produced by the ICTCLAS tool are shown in Figure 35.8, where we can see that the nouns and verbs are correctly identified. Additionally, NLP is also capable of extracting Named Entities, keywords, and sentence structures from the text.

In Weibo studies, researchers often wish to identify keywords from a large set of Weibo posts and to understand which topics are most discussed. Alternatively, researchers aim to detect the sentiment orientations (i.e., positive or negative) of Weibo users on certain topics. All these analytic purposes can be fulfilled with the help of NLP techniques. For interested readers, we would like to recommend two popular Chinese NLP toolkits, namely, Institue of Computing Technology, Chinese Lexical Analysis System (ICTCLAS), and formerly Fudan NLP. ICTCLAS (Zhang et al., 2003) is a Chinese processing toolkit emphasizing Chinese word segmentation. It offers a list of functions of Chinese word segmentation, POS tagging, named entity recognition, new word recognition, and keyword extraction. It also provides an application which particularly caters the needs of word segmentation in Weibo by extracting and marking user ID, URL and email in the Weibo content, and recognizing reposts embedded in the Weibo content (Zhang, 2012). ICTCLAS provides a graphical user interface (GUI) as well as a set of programming APIs for C/C++/C#/Java. This toolkit has a relatively long history and is usually the first option for lexical level Chinese processing. In addition to word-level Chinese processing functions, FNLP (Qiu et al., 2013) also provides relatively complete solutions for Chinese language processing tasks, including sentence parsing, text classification, document clustering, as well as other machine learning functions. FNLP is implemented in Java and is open source, which offers high flexibility

Figure 35.8 Segmented words and part-of-speech tagging (by the ICTCLAS tool)

for advanced users or researchers for further adaption and extension.

Text Classification

When the data have been preprocessed, they are ready to be analyzed. Classifying Weibo content into topics such as sports, politics, health, etc. is widely used in many studies and the required technique for this research purpose is text classification.

Text classification has been used in Weibo-related research on many topics, such as rumor classification (Yang et al., 2012), grass-roots phenomenon exploration (Huang et al., 2013) and sentiment prediction (Yuan & Purver, 2015). For automatic approaches, it is critical to select representative features for text content representation, choose suitable classification models, and trained the models appropriately.

Classification models are functions of a set of features. In Weibo content classification, the most basic features are usually bags of words (i.e., word occurrences in the text) (Fan et al., 2014). Additional sources beyond words can be used, such as characteristics of posts (e.g. includes multimedia, or URLs, emojis, and the time span), client device (e.g. device type, web client, mobile client), account information (e.g. is verified, number of friends, number of followers, register time, number of posts), location information (e.g. geographical distribution), as well as propagation (whether a post is the reposted, the number of comments, the number of reposts) (Yang et al., 2012). Among the classifiers that are often used in text categorization, Support Vector Machines (SVMs) and Naive Bayes are popular in Weibo research (Yang et al., 2012; Huang et al., 2013), while many new and sophisticated classifiers are also being developed and employed.

Figure 35.9 illustrates the steps needed to conduct a classification task once a set of classifiers have been developed. Predefined features that best characterize the raw content are extracted for each text, and the classifiers calculate the scores based on the features. The text is then labeled the category by the classifier with the highest score (here, category 3), which finishes the current round classification.

As an example of applying text classification to Weibo content, Fan et al. (2014) classified Weibo posts into seven topic types, and kept the task going for several months. Consequently, the result generated accumulative distributions for the counts of each topic within a given time span. Through visualization, the temporal patterns of the seven topics can be easily recognized, as shown in Figure 35.10. Using topic tracing, the authors were

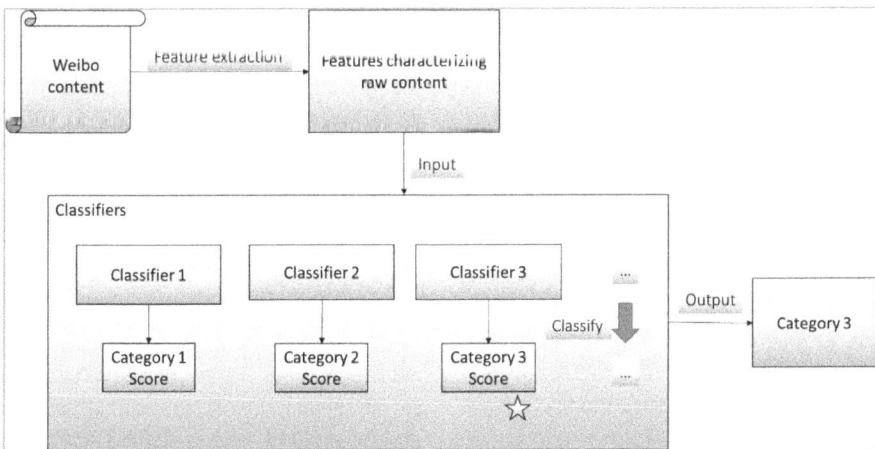

Figure 35.9 The process of a classification task with three classifiers

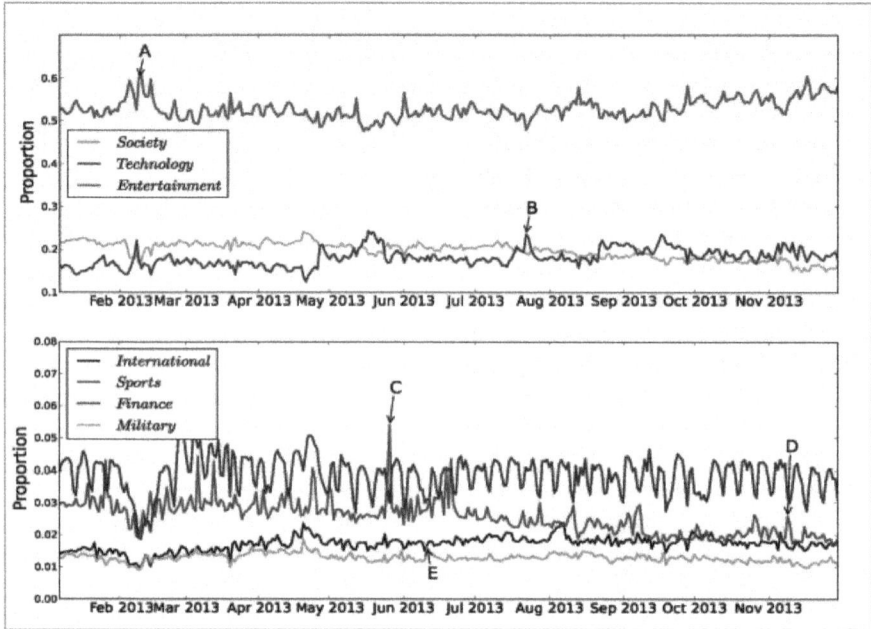

Figure 35.10 Weibo topic dynamics with identified significant points (reprinted from Fan et al., 2014)

able to detect occurrences of extraordinary events in the real world. For example, point A in Figure 35.10 indicates a high proportion of Entertainment posts caused by the celebration of Lunar New Year. The spike on Technology at Point B resulted from the breakdown of WeChat. Points C and D are related to the sports competition events held on those days. The successful launch of Shenzhou-10 spacecraft brought a spike on the Military category at Point E.

ANALYZING WEIBO RELATIONSHIPS

Besides analyzing the topics posted on Weibo, researchers are also interested in relationships among entities. The most common relationships include inter-account (follower–followee) relationships and comment (reply) relationship. The relationship between a massive numbers of Weibo users generates complex networks, which can be interpreted with the help of network theory and social network analysis (SNA).

These networks consist of nodes and edges, representing entities with their inter relations (directed or undirected). Most Weibo studies view accounts as nodes and their various relations as edges. Figure 35.11 shows a network construction based on the co-mention relation of a set of Weibo users who mention the same keywords. In the network, those who mentioned the same keywords are linked, as shown in the two clusters in Figure 35.11 (mentioning keywords 'AlphaGo' and 'Tay' respectively). It is noteworthy that nodes may not necessarily be accounts. For example, in the study conducted by Tang et al. (2015), both users and users' posts were treated as nodes.

When a network is constructed, it can be studied from various perspectives. For example, we can study the network's overall structure, local groups, and key nodes. Using Figure 35.11 as an example, we analyze the connectivity of the network. Node 7 is observed as isolated from

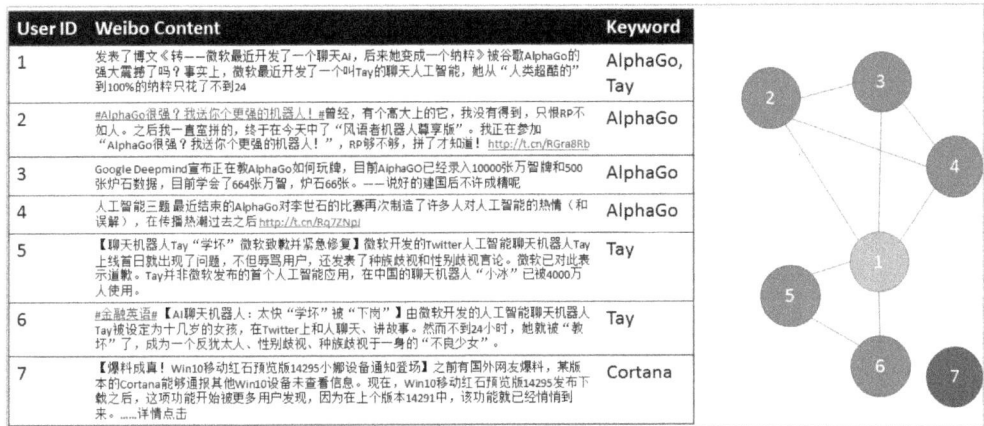

Figure 35.11 User network constructed with co-mentioned relations on keywords

the connected component. In addition, we can estimate the density of the network by counting the average edges a node has, and discern the shape of the network by counting the average distances of the node pairs. The network in Figure 35.11 also indicates two local groups, which consist of nodes 2, 3, 4 and nodes 5, 6 respectively. The analysis of sub-groups and group diversities are also quite popular among Weibo studies. At the individual level, nodes 1 and 7 are in two controversial situations. While node 1 has the most connections in the network, node 7 has no connections at all. Node 1 may be worth attention in this situation, since it connects two sub-groups (called a 'structural hole') and plays an important role in social network, because it controls information flow across otherwise isolated groups[2].

Here we list three Weibo studies concerning different levels of the network. An example of studying global structures can be found in the work of Yang and Yu (2014). The authors collected diabetes-related posts on Weibo and constructed user network. They calculated indicative statistics of the network to model its structure, and traced the dynamic changes of the network over time with the help of a probabilistic modeling technique. In a group view, Guo et al. (2011) identified groups of verified users in various domains, and explored these groups based on user professionals and group network statistics. They found some common characteristics of groups, and discovered that core users (nodes with high degree values) in Weibo tend to attract a greater number of followers, and the groups formed by core users usually have short diameters, making information transmission fast.

We give one final example concerning an individual node, the opinion leader. Being an opinion leader is one of the key roles on Weibo and can greatly influence information flows within the network. Studying health information diffusion on Weibo, Han and Wang (2015) discovered opinion leaders by calculating network statistics for each account. They found that opinion leaders are usually in central positions on the network, and they have much control over the information flow within the network. For example, they can make decisions regarding what information to spread, and influence how popular it can become.

SELECTED STUDIES AND METHODS APPLIED

Weibo has become a popular context for research in a number of different fields.

Researchers are developing algorithms and techniques for processing Weibo contents, detecting network structures and modeling network dynamics. These techniques and tools have enabled various studies from a wide range of perspectives. An information communication view attracts attention to the flow and diffusion of information as well as the explanation for roles and characteristics of the Weibo communication system. From a market research point of view, studies explore new ways of advertising, campaign and customer relationship management. Scholars in public administration are concerned about the role of Weibo in facilitating government affairs, crisis responses, and citizen participation and monitoring.

In this section, we present a few representative studies in three selected themes that have drawn much research attention.

Weibo Censorship (Fu et al., 2013)

Censorship is a content regulation strategy used by the government to control media communication (Chen, Zhang, & Wilson, 2013). Although Weibo is a major communication platform for breaking news and politically-sensitive commentary that are absent from the state-sanctioned news media, activities on Weibo are still subjected to official censorship, as has been discovered in research by Bamman et al. (2012) and Fu et al. (2013). China launched the real-name registration directive on March 16th, 2012; intended to reduce the number of censored posts at the offset. Besides, it is hypothesized that censorship on Weibo operates through automated keyword filtering and real-time crowdsourced monitoring (Zhu et al., 2013). For content that fails to pass the censor, the posts may be deleted and the accounts may be temporarily suspended or permanently deleted. Weibo users are usually aware of the content censorship. As a response, they often use variations of sensitive terms (homophones and puns) for those sensitive phrases to avoid censorship.

Concerning studies about the effects of censorship, researchers have been interested in detecting censorship, mining censored contents, and discovering responses of users.

Detecting Censorship

Fu et al. (2013) developed a software tool for Weibo data fetching and visualization. The tool was based on the Sina Weibo Open API. They selected microbloggers who have at least 1,000 followers (this high-follower-count strategy also filtered many spam accounts) from each region of China, and collected 111 million posts with the User Timeline API between January 1 2012 and June 30 2012. To tackle the problem of access constraints (per-hour rate limitation) set by the Weibo API server, they grouped the accounts and allocated each group a different sampling frequency, ranging from every three minutes (10 members), every six hours (about 5,000 members) to once a day (about 38,000 members), based on the updating frequencies of the accounts.

The system found posts suspected of censorship by comparing the newly updated user timelines with the version of the previous update. The missing posts in the new timeline were further tested to determine whether they were deleted by the users themselves or had simply become inaccessible. The latter cases were then regarded as having being censored (Fu et al., 2013).

Mining Censored Content

To explore what content of the censored posts, Fu et al. (2013) used a case-control matching strategy to find representative keywords. They paired each censored post with two randomly selected uncensored posts from the same user, and formed a corpus with these paired posts. After preprocessing the corpus with NLP tools, they applied *chi*-squared feature selection to find the set of keywords with high discriminatory power in differentiating censored and uncensored posts. Furthermore, a relative risk measure was used to determine the keywords that characterize censored posts. At the same time, varied versions of the censored keywords were also identified from the posts that survived censorship.

Discovering Responses of Users

In evaluating the impact of the real-name registration policy, Fu et al. (2013) divided the time window into two parts: before the real-name registration policy (T1) and after (T2). Users who posted at least once on Weibo at T1 but did not post in T2 are regarded as those who were influenced by the real-name registration policy. This type of users are called 'potentially affected microbloggers' (PAM). Although the initial analysis on measures aggregated across all samples did not show statistical significance in the number of posts in T1 and T2, a re-examination on the posts of individual users showed evidence of PAM.

Logistic regression was conducted to predict whether a user account was PAM. The results uncovered six significant predictors: number of followers, number of followees, VIP status, whether a comment is allowed, self-reported gender, and self-reported geographic location.

To analyze terms associated with PAM status, the case-control matching strategy was applied again to pair 3,000 PAM accounts with 3,000 non-PAM accounts with the same status of the predictors except for the numbers of followers and followees. The posts of these 6,000 accounts posted in T1 were retrieved and the top 30 censorship-discriminatory terms were obtained based on their values of the chi-square tests. The results showed that the most discriminatory terms were those related to politics and social issues. Therefore, it is inferred that there was indeed a negative effect on some users after the launch of the real-name registration policy on Weibo.

In this study, a number of methods were applied together to achieve the explorative goals. Statistical methods were used to discover significant indicator terms and account features. The case-control matching strategy was applied in this context to help balance the samples. NLP techniques were used to process Weibo content.

Governmental Weibo Usage (Ma, 2013)

The adoption of government microblogs by state authorities has enabled them to build a modern social image and broaden communication channels. To study the cause of government engagement in Weibo and find out the factors that drive the adoption of government Weibo accounts, Ma (2013) empirically examined the spread of official police Weibo accounts in China. The findings include factors significantly associated with police adoption of official accounts on Weibo, and the fact that the spread of adoption is subject to different variables at various phases.

Theoretical Frameworks and Hypotheses

The theories that directed this study include organizational innovation, policy diffusion, and characteristics of specific innovation areas. Nine hypotheses were proposed to test whether the adoption of official Weibo accounts was significantly related to a set of factors. Some of the factors involve theoretical predictions of organizational innovation, such as government size, government fiscal resource, jurisdictional economic development, and jurisdictional economic openness. Others are about the horizontal and vertical diffusion of police Weibo adoption, such as the percentage of neighboring governments adopting Weibo, and the Weibo adoption status of upper-tier police departments. Moreover, the specific technological and policy features of police Weibo were taken into account as well, such as jurisdictional public safety, jurisdictional E-government performance, and jurisdictional internet penetration.

Samples and Data Sources

The samples consisted of 282 prefecture-level cities in 27 provinces and autonomous regions in China, excluding Lhasa (due to missing data), municipalities, Hong Kong, Macao and Taiwan (as these cities have different government administrative structures) (Ma, 2013). The analysis unit selected was the urban police bureau. The microblog samples from the official Weibo account were drawn from verified official accounts of the police bureaus, which were retrieved with the official search function provided by the Sina Weibo platform. Other data were from mixed sources including published statistical reports, yearbooks, and research reports.

Data Analysis

The proposed hypotheses were tested by correlation analysis and the results supported a majority of them, except for one involving public safety (measured by safety index).

Multivariate regression analysis was applied to determine whether the status and duration of adoption can be predicted by the aforementioned factors. As the dependent variable of adoption status has binary values (i.e., whether or not a police bureau created an official Weibo account), logistic regression was used. Tobit regression was applied to study the second dependent variable: the time span of police Weibo operation. The regression results showed that models for both dependent variables were significant and could explain a large extent of variation. The significant independent variables were: government size, internet penetration rate, as well as horizontal and vertical diffusion effects.

The study conducted by Ma (2013) was an example of Weibo studies involving a mixture of data sources. The researchers combined Weibo data with those external to the Weibo platform. This is an effective approach to exploring Weibo phenomena because the virtual Weibo society is closely connected to the offline world. Information in the offline world, such as culture, location, political, economic and habitat environment, can be complementary to the analysis and contribute to a deeper understanding.

Disaster Response (Qu et al., 2011)

While easy accessibility and swift information diffusion enable Weibo users to play the roles of social sensors and responders to disasters and crises, research is conducted to study the role of this 'Weibo society' in severe disasters, as well as dissemination patterns of disaster-related information. Qu et al. (2011) conducted a case study to investigate the phenomena on Weibo after the severe Yushu Earthquake in 2010 through a combination of content analysis, topic trend detection, and information spreading process analysis.

Data Collection

Qu et al. (2011) fetched a total of 94,101 microblog posts and 41,817 reposts related to the earthquake. They selected a time window of 48 days, starting from the strike of the earthquake (7:49 a.m. 14 April, 2010) until 23:59 p.m. 31 May, 2010. The data was obtained by launching two queries, '玉树 [Yushu] AND 地震 [Earthquake]' and '青海 [Qinghai] AND 地震 [Earthquake]' daily. The authors extracted basic information about each collected post including message content, posting date, and total number of reposts, as well as information about the account who posted the post, including account name, number of messages, number of followers, number of followees, and VIP status.

Data Analysis

The content analysis method was applied to identify topics in the collected posts. A mixed bottom-up and top-down approach was used to construct the coding scheme by identifying topics from randomly sampled Weibo messages (totally 4,618 from the collection), and adopting categories from previous studies. Several iterations of coding with the scheme and modifications were undertaken by two researchers for the purposes of consensus building. The final scheme contained six major categories of Weibo posts in response to the disaster: informational messages (situation update, general relief related), action-related (requesting help, looking for missing people, proposing relief action, relief coordination), opinion-related (criticizing, suggesting), emotion-related (expressing feelings, blessing), microblogging system related, and off-topic (i.e., those not related to the earthquake). The trends of these categories were then plotted on a time dimension, which helped reveal that the focuses of responses changed from situation updates to action and opinion-related topics.

To understand the information spread process, the authors examined the percentage of Weibo posts that got reposted during the studied period. A regression analysis was conducted to determine the factors impacting a post's likelihood of being reposted. The results showed that the Weibo category, number of followers and the VIP status were the most influential factors. They also visualized the 'repost trees' that were formed following the reposting paths, and examined the depth of the trees (indicating how far a post was disseminated) as well as the speed of dissemination. The results showed that action-related messages were more likely to spread far away, and messages of situation updates travelled the fastest in Weibo, while opinion-related messages travelled the slowest.

This study applied both qualitative and quantitative methods with visualization techniques to study the crisis response role of Weibo. Content analysis was used to construct the scheme of six major categories of crisis-related content. The categories were further applied in statistical analyses including descriptive analysis, statistical visualization, regression analysis, etc. The temporal trend analysis and the 'repost tree' visualization helped illustrate the process of information diffusion. We can also see that although many methods were applied, they were coherently integrated to address the research questions.

CONCLUSION

This chapter introduced one of the most popular social media services in China – Weibo. Functions and features of the platform were presented. A number of data preprocessing techniques and analysis methods were explained and illustrated in a collection of existing Weibo-related research.

We find that the content and behaviors of the posts, as well as the social connections among users, are major themes of Weibo-related research. Hence, it is important to understand the relevant content and the relational analysis. In this chapter, we have covered a number of qualitative and quantitative analytical approaches that cater these requirements.

We also find that Weibo can be understood as a complex system. An individual method may only contribute to part of a research question. Therefore, it is desirable to combine different methods in studying Weibo phenomena. We have also demonstrated how mixed methods were applied in exemplar studies. As Weibo is closely related to the offline world, seeking information from sources outside the Weibo platform is sometimes necessary in order to have a complete picture of complex social phenomena. Most previous studies investigated the Weibo data with respect to a specific event, such as a natural disaster or a health crisis. Future research can extend single studies to multiple-case studies. For instance, Nip and Fu (2016) examined 29 corruption cases on Weibo collectively in one study. Moreover, a randomized and representative sampling method is more desirable for understanding the overall phenomenon in the system as well as its temporal change.

Fu et al. (2013) deployed a random sampling approach to analyze the profile and the pattern of usage for a representative sample of Weibo accounts.

Although Weibo is still a major social media platform, particularly in China, there are challenges from other popular and newly emerging social media services such as WeChat and WhatsApp (Hu et al., 2015). When the attention of users is attracted by more and increasingly diverse platforms, researchers are reminded to consider the characteristics of the users of specific platforms before drawing a general conclusion. While the majority of previous works targeted at a single platform, cross-platform studies are also warranted in the future. Given the fact that new features are constantly being added into the Weibo platform (e.g. Weibo payment), new perspectives and questions on Weibo research will continue to emerge. Consequently, innovative methods targeting formerly untouched questions will be proposed and developed over time.

NOTES

1 The example was retrieved from the Weibo API online documentation http://open.weibo.com/wiki/2/statuses/show/en on December 28, 2015.
2 For other interesting components of social network, readers can refer to Scott's book (2012).

REFERENCES

Bamman, D., O'Connor, B. and Smith, N. (2012) 'Censorship and deletion practices in Chinese social media', *First Monday*, 17(3). doi:10.5210/fm.v17i3.3943

Chen, L., Zhang, C. and Wilson, C. (2013) 'Tweeting under pressure: analyzing trending topics and evolving word choice on sina weibo', paper presented at *The Proceedings of the First ACM Conference on Online Social Networks*, Boston, Massachusetts, USA.

Chin, J. and Mozur, P. (2013) 'China intensifies social-media crackdown', *Wall Street Journal*, retrieved on March 15 from http://www.wsj.com/articles/SB10001424127887324807704579082940411106988

Dann, S. (2010) Twitter content classification. *First Monday*, 15(12): 1–12. doi: http://dx.doi.org/10.5210/fm.v15i12.2745

Duan, J. and Dholakia, N. (2015) 'The reshaping of Chinese consumer values in the social media era: Exploring the impact of Weibo', *Qualitative Market Research: An International Journal*, 18(4): 409–26. doi:10.1108/QMR-07-2014-0058

Fan, R., Zhao, J., Feng, X. and Xu, K. (2014) 'Topic dynamics in Weibo: Happy entertainment dominates but angry finance is more periodic', paper presented at *The Proceedings of the International Conference on Advances in Social Networks Analysis and Mining (ASONAM)*, Beijing, China.

Fu, K., Chan, C. and Chau, M. (2013) 'Assessing censorship on microblogs in China: Discriminatory keyword analysis and the real-name registration policy', *IEEE Internet Computing*, 17(3): 42–50.

GOV.cn (2006). CPC seeks advice on harmonious society. Retrieved April 11, 2016 from http://www.gov.cn/english/2006-10/12/content_411611.htm

Guo, Y. and Goh, D. H.-L. (2014) '"I Have AIDS": Content analysis of postings in HIV/AIDS support group on a Chinese microblog', *Computers in Human Behavior*, 34: 219–226.

Guo, Z., Li, Z. and Tu, H. (2011) 'Sina Microblog: An Information-Driven Online Social Network', paper presented at *The Proceedings of the 2011 International Conference on Cyberworlds*, Banff, ON.

Han, G. and Wang, W. (2015) 'Mapping user relationships for health information diffusion on microblogging in China: A social network analysis of Sina Weibo', *Asian Journal of Communication*, 25(1): 65–83, doi:10.1080/01292986.2014.989239

Hu, X., Wong, D.K.T. and To, D.Y.C. (2015) 'User Behaviors and Perceptions of WhatsApp and WeChat', paper presented at *The Proceedings of the International Conference on Social Media and Society*, Jul. 2015, Toronto, Canada.

Huang, Z., Yuan, B. and Hu, X. (2013) 'Understanding the Top Grass Roots in Sina-Weibo', in J. Yang, F. Fang and C. Sun (eds.), Vol. 7751, *Intelligent Science and Intelligent Data*. Springer Berlin Heidelberg. pp.17–24.

Liao, Q. and Shi, L. (2013) 'She gets a sports car from our donation: rumor transmission in a Chinese microblogging community', paper presented at *The Proceedings of the 2013 Conference on Computer Supported Cooperative Work*, San Antonio, Texas, USA.

Ma, L. (2013) 'The diffusion of government microblogging. *Public Management Review*, 15(2): 288–309. doi:10.1080/14719037. 2012.691010

Nip, J. Y. M., and Fu, K.W. (2016) Challenging Official Propaganda? Public Opinion Leaders on Sina Weibo. *The China Quarterly*, 225, 122–144. doi:10.1017/ S0305741015001654

Qiu, X, Zhang, Q. and Huang, X. (2013) 'FudanNLP: A Toolkit for Chinese Natural Language Processing', paper presented at *The Proceedings of the 51st Annual Meeting of the Association for Computational Linguistics (ACL 2013)*, Sofia, Bulgaria.

Qu, Y., Huang, C., Zhang, P. and Zhang, J. (2011) 'Microblogging after a major disaster in China: a case study of the 2010 Yushu earthquake', paper presented at *The Proceedings of the ACM 2011 Conference on Computer Supported Cooperative Work*, Hangzhou, China.

Ren, D., Zhang, X., Wang, Z., Li, J., and Yuan, X. (2014) WeiboEvents: A crowd sourcing Weibo visual analytic system. *2014 IEEE Pacific Visualization Symposium*. doi:10.1109/ pacificvis.2014.38

Scott, J. (2012), *Social network analysis*. SAGE. Thousand Oaks, California, USA.

Shen, D., Wang, H., Jiang, Z. and Cao, J. (2013) 'A high efficient incremental microblog crawler: design and implementation', *Journal of Information & Computational Science*, 10(6): 1731–1747.

Tang, B., Lu, T., Gu, H., Ding, X. and Gu, N. (2015) 'Measuring domain-specific user influence in microblogs: An Actor-Network Theory based approach', paper presented at *The Proceedings of the 19th International Conference on Computer Supported Cooperative Work in Design (CSCWD)*, Calabria.

Weibo Open Platform. (2012) 'API文档 V2/en', available at: http://open.weibo.com/wiki/ API%E6%96%87%E6%A1%A3_V2/ en#Weibo_API (accessed 15 December, 2015).

Yang, D.-H. and Yu, G. (2014) 'Static analysis and exponential random graph modelling for micro-blog network', *Journal of Information Science*, 40(1): 3–14. doi:10.1177/ 0165551513512251

Yang, F., Liu, Y., Yu, X. and Yang, M. (2012) 'Automatic detection of rumor on Sina Weibo', paper presented at *The Proceedings of the ACM SIGKDD Workshop on Mining Data Semantics*, Beijing, China.

Yiu, R.Y.H., Ng, K and Hu, X. (2015) 'Music fan communities on Sina Weibo and Baidu Tieba: a case study of Chinese singers', paper presented at *The Proceedings of the International Conference on Social Media and Society*, July 2015, Toronto, Canada.

Yuan, Z. and Purver, M. (2015) 'Predicting Emotion Labels for Chinese Microblog Texts' in M.M. Gaber, M. Cocea, N. Wiratunga and A. Goker (eds.), Vol. 602, *Advances in Social Media Analysis*. Springer International Publishing. Cham, Switzerland. pp.129–149.

Yu, L.L., Asur, S., and Huberman, B. A. (2015) Trend Dynamics and Attention in Chinese Social Media. *American Behavioral Scientist*, 59(9), 1142–1156. doi:10.1177/0002764 215580619

Zhang, H.-P. (2012) 'NLPIR简介', available at: http://ictclas.nlpir.org/docs (accessed 16 December, 2015)

Zhang, H.-P., Yu, H.-K., Xiong, D.-Y and Liu, Q. (2003) 'HHMM-based Chinese lexical analyzer ICTCLAS', paper presented at *The Proceedings of the Second SIGHAN Workshop on Chinese language Processing – Volume 17*, Sapporo, Japan.

Zhu, T., Phipps, D., Pridgen, A., Crandall, J.R. and Wallach, D.S. (2013) 'The velocity of censorship: high-fidelity detection of microblog post deletions', paper presented at *The Proceedings of the 22nd USENIX Conference on Security*, Washington, D.C.

Foursquare

Matthew J. Williams and Martin Chorley

INTRODUCTION

Location sharing as a feature is now embedded in many online services, presenting an unprecedented opportunity for analysts and scientists to explore the mobility of individuals, including where they went, when they visited, and the friends they visited with. As the most-popular service of its type, Foursquare has become a valuable platform for researchers in many fields, including social science, computer science, and human geography.

In this chapter we describe how Foursquare can be effectively used as a platform for research. The service provides four core sources of data: users, venues, check-ins (visits to venues by users), and social connections. The chapter will describe what these data represent for research, the research questions and hypotheses that Foursquare has been used to explore, and how the relevant data can be obtained and processed.

The platform is amenable to a variety of analyses. Check-in patterns allow the study of where and when users visit locations. The social network enables comparison of how friends and strangers co-locate. Check-ins can also be explored from the perspective of the venue, allowing for the analysis of how location influences user mobility, and for the large-scale study of how cities are structured. This is further supported by Foursquare's extensive venue category hierarchy and its large collection of crowdsourced venue descriptions, thereby providing researchers with rich semantic information on locations.

There are many means of accessing and collecting data from Foursquare, including real-time monitoring, accessing cross-platform check-ins shared to other services, and data collection experiments via web and mobile applications. The chapter provides researchers with an understanding of the opportunities and limitations of Foursquare, along with the technical knowledge of how to access Foursquare data, and how to select and implement an appropriate collection method based on the chosen research question.

In the next section, *The Rise of Location-Based Social Networks*, we provide a background to location-based social networks (LBSNs), Foursquare's emergence in this arena, and how it compares to other platforms. In *An Introduction to Foursquare* we then describe Foursquare itself, its features, and give an overview of the information it provides, which are important in understanding the circumstances in which the data were collected. In the following section we briefly discuss a variety of previous scientific studies that were enabled by access to Foursquare data. These will highlight the various uses of the platform for research, and potentially stimulate ideas for interested readers. The following two sections, *Data Sources* and *Collection Methods*, together form a technical description of the data that are available, how they are structured, and methodologies for their systematic collection. We conclude the chapter with a discussion of the limitations and opportunities of location-based networks such as Foursquare.

THE RISE OF LOCATION-BASED SOCIAL NETWORKS

The end of the 2000s saw an explosion of a new type of online service, now referred to as *location-based social networks* (LBSNs). These services can be viewed as an extension to the idea of an online social network to include rich information on the geographic space in which their users exist. Foursquare emerged from this period as the leading LBSN, and in 2013 reported over 45 million registered users (Crowley, 2013). Furthermore, in 2016, Foursquare announced that it had reached its nine-billionth check-in and reported an average of over eight million check-ins per day (Foursquare, 2016).

Before the emergence of LBSNs, conventional online social networks had been popular for a number of years. In 2008, Facebook (founded in 2004) reached 100 million active users for the first time (Associated Press, 2013), and Twitter (founded in 2006) was receiving substantial growth. These networks allowed users to form friendships and interact through the online world of the World Wide Web. Although not widespread, location-based services did exist prior to the smartphone era. Just as Twitter began partly as a communication service based around SMS messaging, Dodgeball, (co-founded in 2003 by Dennis Crowley, who subsequently co-founded Foursquare) allowed individuals to become alerted to the presence of other network users by texting their location to the service. The service was acquired by Google in 2005, and shut down in 2009 when it was replaced by Google Latitude.

The rise of conventional social networks has led to large amounts of personal and social information – such as friendship links, conversations, individuals' likes and dislikes, and political beliefs – being recorded and collected by service providers. Scientists and researchers were quick to identify the value of social networks and social media to understand human behaviour (a very early example is from Java et al., 2007), especially platforms whose data was publicly exposed and therefore could be easily collected by web scraping or using a web Application Programming Interface (API).

Until 2008, however, services such as Twitter and Facebook were predominantly focused on online social interactions only, as mediated through web browsers on desktop computers. In parallel to the growth of online social networks, the mobile application revolution had begun, and smartphone adoption was increasing dramatically, driven in part by the success of Apple's first iPhone in 2007.

Many individuals were now carrying small, highly sophisticated computer devices in their pockets, equipped with a range of sensors, and capable of accessing the web. One sensor which has proved highly valuable has been its location sensor, providing highly accurate location information, obtained using

GPS (the Global Position System) and/or WiFi positioning. The inclusion of this sensor has allowed smartphone software developers to associate a user with their geographic position, enabling new and innovative location-aware mobile applications.

Taking advantage of the converging trends in online social platform usage and the rise of location-enabled smartphone adoption, the first online LBSNs emerged in 2008. Three startups – Foursquare, Brightkite, and Gowalla – all vied for dominance in this space, with Foursquare emerging as the winner. Other popular online services, including Facebook, Twitter, and Google+, also integrated the check-in (more generally referred to as *geotagging*) as a secondary feature. We note that *location sharing service* has also become a term for Foursquare, referring to a particular type of LBSN where location sharing is the core function, rather than a secondary feature.

More recently, Foursquare chose to split their service into two distinct mobile applications – *Foursquare* and *Swarm* – which may be a source of confusion for some readers. Both applications are developed by the same company (formally, Foursquare Labs, Inc.), rely on the same online database of users, venues, and check-ins, and can be accessed through the same API. The key difference lies in the services offered to the user. The Foursquare app provides an interface through which the user can discover local venues and receive personalised recommendations for places to visit, whereas the Swarm app is the mechanism through which users check-in to venues and share their location with friends. The ambiguity in 'Foursquare' can lead to some confusion. Where necessary, in this chapter we will use '*Foursquare app*' to refer to Foursquare's venue recommendation application and '*Swarm app*' to refer to the check-in application. Finally, we will refer to the API and collection of databases that supports these two applications as the '*Foursquare platform*', or simply '*platform*'.

AN INTRODUCTION TO FOURSQUARE

In this section we provide a brief introduction to the Foursquare platform, including the features the service provides to users through its apps. As well as introducing the data that are available through the platform, a secondary aim of this section is to convey the context in which individuals use the apps, which is relevant to the validity of the data provided. Figure 36.1 provides a conceptual overview of the three core components of the platform (users, venues, and check-ins), and the information associated with each.

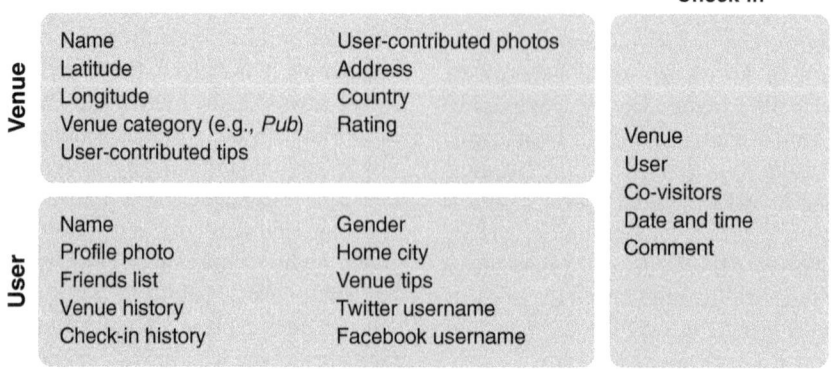

Figure 36.1 A conceptual overview of Foursquare

Foursquare venues are crowdsourced; that is, venue information is contributed and maintained by the users themselves. If a Swarm user notices that they cannot find a venue they wish to check in to, the app allows them to add it to Foursquare by providing its location, address, and a venue type. The interface also allows users to suggest updates to existing venues (e.g., due to change of address or closure), correct inaccurate information, and merge duplicates.

To promote consistency across the platform, Foursquare offers a style guide, and updates to venues are verified by a community of voluntary Superusers. While normal users may suggest edits to venue information, it is the Superusers who are able to review and accept/reject these edits, as well as proposing edits themselves. Thus the database is kept up-to-date with current venue information, crowdsourcing a globally accurate database of distinct locations. In addition, the owner of a venue (such as the manager of a bar) can 'claim' the venue, which affords him/her additional privileges to manage and correct the venue's details.

Of key interest are a venue's location and category. Location is represented by geo-coordinates (longitude and latitude), as well as a street address and country. Each venue is also assigned a category from Foursquare's taxonomy of over 700 place types. Together, these provide rich information on where venues are located within a city or region (and thus where users check-in) and also the type of place.

It is important to note that the geographic scale that venues represent can vary greatly. For example, the 'Outdoors and Recreation' top-level category includes 'Town' and 'City' venue sub-categories, thus allowing a user to check-in to a large geographic region. On the other hand, 'Food' venues are typically restaurants and other eateries, and therefore specify a particular building. This comparison also highlights another consideration: some venues may, conceptually, be contained within others. For example, a shopping mall and its constituent shops may each be recorded on Foursquare as distinct venues. Foursquare offers a mechanism to designate a venue as contained within another (referred to as a *sub-place*); however, this is a relatively recent feature, and has not been widely applied.

Figure 36.2 illustrates the Foursquare app interface, showing a list of 'Food' venues near the user (left panel) and information on a particular venue (right panel). This highlights the variety of venue attributes that Foursquare captures. These include user-contributed comments (referred to as tips), photos of the venue, and an average numerical rating.

We note that the Foursquare app aims to allow users to discover and explore venues in a region. This contrasts with the Swarm app, which allows users to check in to venues and see what places their Foursquare friends are visiting. Although user accounts are integrated across both services, not all Foursquare app users are Swarm app users, and vice versa. Active Swarm users are a valuable source of data for the platform. The information they contribute include check-ins to places, tips, photos, and adding/updating venues. In addition, the app requests further information from users by occasionally posing short questions after a user has checked in; for example, '*Did you enjoy your visit to this venue*'? As the analogy implies, Swarm users are the worker drones that help keep Foursquare's database current. In Figure 36.3 we show an example of the Swarm app interface, demonstrating a user's friend feed (left panel) and a check-in list (right panel).

Participation in Swarm is incentivised by game-like features that allow users to compete with one another. For example, each check-in earns points, which places users on a leaderboard among their friends, and being the recent most-frequent visitor to a place earns a user the title of 'mayor' of that venue. Although this encourages users to be more diligent in their check-ins, it is not clear to what extent this biases check-in behaviour. In some cases, users may include fake check-ins to

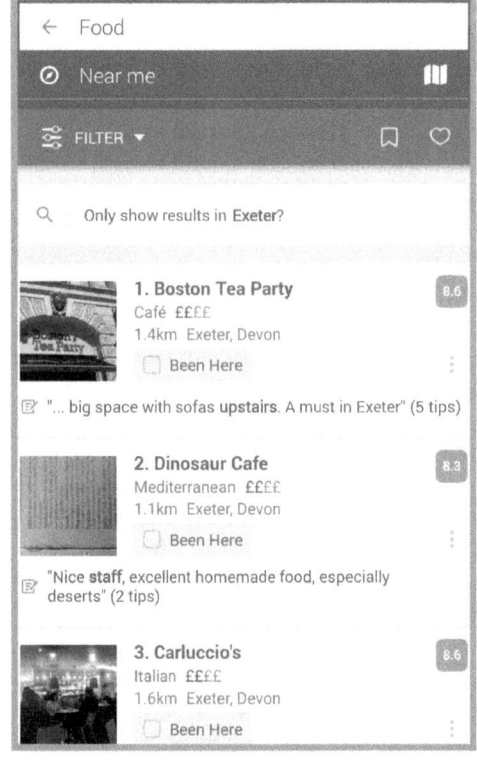

Nearby venues   Venue information

Figure 36.2 The Foursquare mobile app interface (2016)

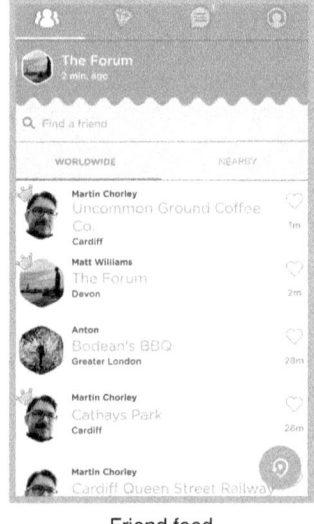 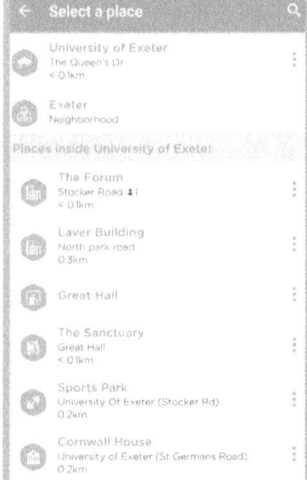

Friend feed   Venue check-in

Figure 36.3 The Swarm mobile app interface (2016)

inflate their score, although since Foursquare does not offer any material benefits to frequent users, this is relatively rare.

Friendship is particularly important in Foursquare as it controls who can see a user's current neighbourhood and check-in history. By default, an individual's check-ins are only visible to the user and his/her friends. A stranger cannot directly access another individual's check-in history, either through the app or via the Foursquare API. A user can optionally also make an individual check-in public by cross-posting it to other platforms (e.g., Twitter and Facebook). These controls on location sharing have important implications for collecting large-scale check-ins datasets, which we discuss later in this chapter.

Foursquare's friendship mechanism requires mutual approval by both users (i.e., reciprocal approval), resulting in symmetric friendships in the social network. As is typical of LBSNs, the network is sparse compared to other online social networks such as Twitter (Scellato et al., 2011a). Due to the private and potentially sensitive nature of location-sharing, most users are very selective with whom they connect. Previous studies suggest that the average number of friends a Foursquare user has is 22 (Scellato et al., 2011a), with a much lower median of around seven friends.

The usage patterns of Swarm users are varied. Using interview and questionnaire data, Lindqvist et al. (2011) further explored the Foursquare user base, and identified many usage types and motivations for checking in, including: personal tracking (also known as 'life-logging'), maintaining long-distance friendships, social serendipity (running into friends), the app's gaming elements, and seeing where their friends have been.

FOURSQUARE IN SCIENTIFIC RESEARCH

In this section we provide an overview of studies in which Foursquare has enabled scientific insight. There is a large body of work in this area, and therefore we focus on a few diverse examples.

As a platform that combines both social and spatial human behavioural signals, Foursquare has served as a useful dataset for benchmarking socio-spatial algorithms and analytic methods. Examples include social tie prediction (Scellato et al., 2011b), next-place prediction (Noulas et al., 2012b), venue recommendation (Ye et al., 2010), and location anonymisation techniques (Rossi et al., 2015). Due to the high density of venues and check-in behaviour in cities, Foursquare has also proved a fruitful resource for data-driven modelling of urban mobility patterns (Noulas et al., 2012a).

In the field of computational social science, Foursquare has shown promise as a way of predicting urban gentrification and social segregation (Hristova et al., 2016), identifying relationships between the distribution of venues and neighbourhood obesity rates (Mejova et al., 2015), and comparing cultural preferences in food and drink consumption (Silva et al., 2014). Many of these studies demonstrate the value of the Foursquare venue database itself, rather than the mobility and check-in data that were originally the core of the service. Indeed, many online services have chosen Foursquare as location database provider, which has in turn enabled scientific studies of other location-based human behaviour patterns, such as alcohol drinking preferences (Chorley et al., 2016). It has also recently been noted that geographic crowdsourcing has great potential as an alternative to expensive and slow-to-collect official datasets such as land-use statistics (Quercia and Saez, 2014).

Finally, we should mention that there have been many descriptive investigations of Foursquare usage patterns. While the details of these studies are out of the scope of this chapter, they may be of interest to readers seeking summary statistics of the platform. Such statistics depend on the Foursquare dataset, when it was collected, and how it was collected, and thus results can vary between studies. Specifically, we refer interested readers to the work of Scellato et al. (2011a) for social network measures and description of spatial distribution of friendships, the work of Noulas et al. (2011, 2015) for temporal dynamics of venue activity and check-ins, and Colombo et al. (2012) for discussion of co-location patterns.

DATA SOURCES

So far in this chapter our discussion of Foursquare has predominantly focused on data from the perspective of service users and researchers. We now consider the topic of programmatic access. This section details which data are available through the Foursquare API and they can be accessed.

The Foursquare API

Through its REST API, Foursquare provides data relating to all aspects of the service. Extensive documentation detailing the Foursquare API and the data available is provided at https://developer.foursquare.com/. An overview is presented here.

Accessing the API
As with most REST APIs, individuals requiring access to the API are required to register an application with the API provider. This can be done by any Foursquare user at https://www.foursquare.com/oauth. Registering your application will provide you with the credentials required to access the API, in the form of a Client ID and Client Secret. Authenticating these with an individual Foursquare user account via the OAuth flow of key exchanges and redirects (https://developer.foursquare.com/overview/auth) will provide you with an Access Token, with which calls to the Foursquare API can be made. We note that it is possible to access certain parts of the Foursquare API without a user-specific Access Token, so-called 'userless' access. This is discussed further below. How to carry out the OAuth flow and obtain an access token depends on your method of accessing the API.

Once a key has been obtained, data is retrieved from the API using either GET or POST requests. The Access Token must be provided as a URL parameter to all requests (except userless requests, which use the Client ID and Client Secret).

Endpoints
The API is grouped into top-level *endpoints*, with each group relating to a specific different type of entity. Within each group, further sub-endpoints are available. Each endpoint typically provides general operations to search, add, and retrieve entities. *Aspects* provide further information about a specific entity, such as listing all friends of a particular User or all photos of a particular Venue. *Actions* allow particular operations to be carried out on specific entities; for example, approving a friend request from a specific User, or proposing edits to a particular venue.

For instance, the /venues endpoint group relates to Venue objects, with /venues/search allowing a search to be carried out, while /venues/<VENUE_ID> returns information for a specific Venue, and /venues/<VENUE_ID>/photos retrieves all public photos attached to that venue.

The endpoint groups available that may be of particular interest are:

- /users
- /venues
- /checkins

However, additional endpoints exist for other entities, such as tips, lists, and photos. A full list of API endpoints, and aspects and actions is available at https://developer.foursquare.com/docs/

Versioning

The Foursquare API is versioned by date. All requests to the API must include a 'v' parameter (e.g., v=20150714) specifying which date version of the API they require. This ensures that responses will remain consistent, so if data retrieval software is written to a particular API version, it will continue to work as long as the correct date version parameter is provided, even if later API versions change the JSON response format. Requests for API versions below v=20120609 are deprecated.

Additionally, for requests with a v equal to or later than 20140806, an 'm' parameter must be provided depending on whether Swarm- or Foursquare-style responses are required.

Internationalisation is supported via either the 'Accept-Language' HTTP header in the GET or POST request, or via a 'locale' request parameter. The list of supported country codes is available at https://developer.foursquare.com/overview/versioning.

Responses

All responses from the Foursquare API are given as JSON (JavaScript Object Notation) objects. These objects contain at least two further objects, a 'meta' object containing details on the request such as the response code and any error details, and the 'response' object containing the actual body of the response. The Foursquare API also supports 'JSONP' style responses by appending a callback parameter to the API request.

When querying the API, the amount of data present in the response depends on the size of the Object returned. Data objects may be returned in one of three forms: a *mini* object, a *compact* object, and a *complete* object. Which data fields are included in the object returned depends upon its size. A complete object will contain all information available about that entity. Any sub-objects within that Object will be represented by either a compact or a mini object. Compact and mini objects include only a subset of fields in the counterpart complete object, with mini containing the smallest number of fields of all three representations.

The size of object returned by the API depends upon the position of the object within the response. For instance, calling a /user/<USER_ID> endpoint will return a complete User. That User may contain within it a list of the user's most recent check-ins – these check-ins will be 'compact' objects rather than complete. The general rule is that accessing a particular Entity's endpoint delivers a complete object. Any sub-entities within this object will either be compact or mini. The full version of any compact or mini objects within an object can be accessed by querying the endpoint for that specific object.

Paging

Many API requests return lists of items that may be too long to include in a single response. These request endpoints will accept 'offset' parameters in order to page through results.

Rate Limiting

Applications are limited in the number of requests they may make to the Foursquare API per hour. Each application may make up to 500 authenticated requests per hour, per OAuth token. So, for example, an application that has been authenticated by two users may make a total of 1,000 API requests per hour.

However, it is also possible to make unauthenticated or userless requests by providing the application Client ID and Client Secret as request parameters, rather than the Access Token. An application may make 5,000 userless requests per hour to the /venues endpoint. The unauthenticated method for this particular endpoint therefore permits a larger volume of queries, and collection and analysis of larger amounts of data. Each application may also make a further 500 userless requests per hour to any other endpoint group which accepts userless requests.

The response to an API request will include headers detailing the rate-limit and number of calls remaining for that particular request. If a rate-limit is exceeded, the response will return an error with an empty response body, and an extra header will be added detailing when the rate-limit for that request will reset.

Policies

Usage of the Foursquare API is subject to certain terms and conditions and policies around access, data retention, privacy, and attribution. Details of the current versions of these policies are available at https://developer.foursquare.com/overview/community.

Libraries

As with other REST APIs, the Foursquare API operates with simple HTTP GET and POST requests. It is therefore relatively straightforward to write code that can request data from the API and deal with the response. However, to save some effort, several libraries exist for accessing the Foursquare API. Foursquare maintains a list of recommended client libraries at https://developer.foursquare.com/resources/libraries. A summary of a number of Foursquare-recommended software libraries can be found in Table 36.1.

Foursquare Data

Data provided by Foursquare that may be primarily of interest to researchers are data that relate to two specific types of entity: the users of the service and venues. Additional entities available that may be of interest include check-ins, along with tips, photos, and events.

Detailed information about what data is contained in each type of entity is available in the API documentation. This information also specifies whether a data item is present in a mini, compact or complete representation of an entity. For example, for the full details of a User entity response, including all the data fields, see https://developer.foursquare.com/docs/responses/user.

Users

At the most-basic level, User data consists of individual user profiles containing a unique identifier, their first name and last name, and a profile image. This demographic information may be extended to include their gender, their home city, and their contact information. A short user-supplied biography may also be present.

User data also provides information on their social network on the service, as a count and list of the users they have a friend relationship with. This friend relationship is always bidirectional. The full set of friends can be retrieved separately from /users/<USER_ID>/friends.

Counts and samples of any lists of venues the user has created are included in both compact and complete objects. Full details can be obtained from /users/<USER_ID>/lists. Similarly, a count of the tips made by the user are included in both compact and complete objects, with a sample of those tips also being included in a complete User object. The full list of tips created by a user is available at /users/<USER_ID>/tips. Also contained within a complete User object is information relating to the gaming aspects of Swarm; namely, the user's current score and a count of their mayorships. Full details on the user's mayorships can be obtained from its aspect; i.e., /users/<USER_ID>/mayorships.

A sample of check-ins for a user are included in a complete User response. The full list of check-ins is retrieved from /users/<USER_ID>/checkins. This is only available for the acting (authenticated) user – it is not possible to retrieve the list of check-ins for any Foursquare user without their permission. For any user endpoint, passing 'self' as the <USER_ID> returns information about the authenticated user through which the query is issued. Non-standard users will have an indicator 'type' present to indicate they are not a typical Foursquare/

Table 36.1 Foursquare software libraries

Name	URL	Programming Language	Latest Update
foursquare2	https://github.com/mattmueller/foursquare2	Ruby	Apr 2015
skittles	https://rubygems.org/gems/skittles	Ruby	Nov 2011
foursquare-php	https://github.com/chriswoodford/foursquare-php	PHP	Jul 2014
foursquare	https://pypi.python.org/pypi/foursquare	Python	May 2015
PyFoursquare	https://github.com/marcelcaraciolo/foursquare	Python	Mar 2012
foursquare-ios-api	https://github.com/gooichi/foursquare-ios-api	Objective-C	Nov 2013
FourSquareKit	https://github.com/rexstjohn/FourSquareKit	Objective-C	Nov 2015
das quadrat	https://github.com/Constantine-Fry/das-quadrat	Swift	Mar 2016
foursquare-api-java	https://github.com/wallabyfinancial/foursquare-api-java	Java	Mar 2015
EasyFoursquare4Android	https://github.com/condesales/easyFoursquare4Android	Android	Aug 2014
node-foursquare	https://github.com/clintandrewhall/node-foursquare	JavaScript	Aug 2015
foursquarevenues	https://www.npmjs.com/package/foursquarevenues	JavaScript	Oct 2015
Marelle	http://praized.github.io/marelle/	JavaScript	Mar 2011
fsq	https://github.com/eduardm/fsq/wiki/Foursquare-Authenticate-Grails-plugin	Grails	Nov 2012
4square-venues	https://github.com/elbuo8/4square-venues	Go	May 2014
SharpSquare	https://github.com/TICLAB/SharpSquare	.NET	Apr 2015
WWW::Foursquare	https://metacpan.org/pod/WWW::Foursquare	Perl	Nov 2012
foursquareCFC	http://fourscuarecfc.riaforge.org/	ColdFusion	Jan 2012
scala-foursquare-api	https://github.com/nfolkert/scala-foursquare-api	Scala	Dec 2011

Swarm user. This is used to indicate that the User object represents a special user such as a Page, Chain, or Celebrity.

Venues

Venue data consists of information relating to individual locations. This data at its most basic consists of the name of the venue, and its geographic coordinates. However, this data may be extended further. Additional geospatial data added may give a textual street address, the city in which the venue is located, and the postal code of the venue. It may include contact information, such as the telephone number or social media accounts of the venue. It may also contain additional rich metadata about the venue, such as its opening hours, the types of credit card accepted there, whether it has happy hours and so on. Additionally, venues may have tips attached, which are user-created annotations and comments about the venue and the services provided there.

Due to the crowdsourced nature of tips, they are susceptible to incorrect information or malicious activity. According to Foursquare's usage policy, examples of non-legitimate tips include advertising, self-promotion, and abusive comments. Tips that do not meet guidelines can be reported by users and business owners, and are subsequently removed by Superusers and administrators, although in practice tips are less-carefully moderated than core venue information (Aggarwal et al., 2013).

Each venue may also have one or more categories applied to it. These categories are taken from the Foursquare category hierarchy. Venues may have one primary category, and up to two more additional categories. Combining categories allows a looser description of venues. For instance, a café bar that is very much like a coffee shop during the day, but which becomes more like a bar during the evening may have both categories applied, giving the user a better picture of the type of venue rather than just using a single category.

Venues may be supplied by users, and so much of the information within the database has been crowdsourced. Swarm users are able to add a new venue while trying to check-in to a location, if it does not already exist within the database. Other users are then prompted to add additional details about venues that they have visited, such as opening times, credit card acceptance, special offers, etc. In this fashion the database is populated with new venues, and their metadata is improved and refined as users visit them.

Categories

Foursquare's category hierarchy is readily accessed via the /venues/categories endpoint. A reference hierarchy is also provided at https://developer.foursquare.com/categorytree. The ten top-level Foursquare categories are:

1. Arts & Entertainment
2. College & University
3. Event
4. Food
5. Nightlife Spot
6. Outdoors & Recreation
7. Professional & Other Places
8. Residence
9. Shop & Service
10. Travel & Transport

Each top-level category has a number of sub-categories, each of which may themselves have sub-categories. So, a venue may be classified as 'Food', or may be classified as 'Chinese Restaurant', itself a sub-category of 'Food', or may be classified even more specifically as a 'Dim Sum Restaurant', which is a sub-category of 'Chinese Restaurant'.

The logic of which category a sub-category is placed in is not always clear. For instance, 'Irish Pub', which one may expect to find in the 'Bar' sub-category of the 'Nightlife Spot' category, alongside 'Sports Bar' and 'Cocktail Bar', is actually found in 'Food'. When dealing with venue data, one may wish to further refine and re-assign some venue categories according to what is appropriate for the particular research question.

For certain applications, it may also be useful to divide categories into 'sociable' and 'non-sociable'. Chorley et al. (2015) carried out a crowdsourced classification exercise in order to classify categories in these two ways. The data they came up with, which includes a sociable confidence value for each Foursquare category has been made available online at https://mobisoc.cs.cf.ac.uk/data/sociable_venues/.

Check-ins

A check-in represents the unique combination of a User and a Venue at a given time. Check-ins contain a reference to the Venue the user checked into, the time the check-in was created (as seconds since the Unix epoch), and may possibly contain a comment about the check-in provided by the User. Using the Foursquare API it is only possible to retrieve the check-in history of an authorised user – it is not possible to obtain check-ins from users who have not given their permission for their history to be accessed. Check-ins may also include a reference to a specific event occurring at the venue. As an example, when a user checks in to a cinema venue, they may be given an option to also check-in to the specific movie they are viewing.

Social Network

Foursquare allows Users to become friends with other Users. These relationships are bi-directional, and once a user is a friend with another user they are then able to see all of that user's check-ins and profile information. As with check-ins, it is only possible to retrieve the friend list of users who have given their explicit permission for this data to be accessed; it is not possible to retrieve a user's social network without their permission.

COLLECTION METHODS

There are several different methods available for accessing and collecting Foursquare data.

As previously discussed, access to user check-ins is in general restricted. However, there are some methods to access check-ins that have been made public, or to obtain permission from users to retrieve their check-in histories. Access to venue data is far more permissive, provided the terms and conditions of the API are abided by.

Cross-platform Public Check-ins

During the check-in process, users are able to publicly share their check-in on other social networks; specifically, Twitter and Facebook. It is therefore possible to use the APIs or search facilities for these other platforms to retrieve publicly posted check-ins. A search on Twitter for Swarm check-ins will therefore show the check-ins currently being publicly shared; as an example the most recent and current check-ins can be retrieved with a simple search for 'swarmapp.com', for example, https://twitter.com/search?q=\%22swarmapp.com\%22&src=typd.

Using the Twitter API or advanced Twitter search (https://twitter.com/search-advanced) it is possible to fine-tune these results to a particular geographic area. In this way, the check-ins for a particular city or area can be retrieved. Swarm automatically includes a URL to the visited Foursquare venue in cross-posted tweet. The venue URL includes the full Foursquare ID for the venue. Thus, once the tweets have been collected, a researcher can subsequently collect the full data about the venues captured during the crawl using the Foursquare /venue/<VENUE_ID> endpoint.

One important caveat when collecting this data is that this method only allows access to check-ins that users have chosen to publicly share. The relative importance of those particular check-ins may be particularly high for that user, and may not be representative of typical behaviour. For instance, a user may be more willing to publicly share a check-in to a new or unusual venue than they are to share a check-in to a shop or train station that they visit every day. The collection of these check-ins over a geographic area may not therefore be representative of the usual day-to-day activity of the area. Despite these biases, this collection method has some advantages, particularly in enabling collection over large geographic regions, and retrieval of historical check-ins if the tweets are available. Example studies using this collection method include those of Noulas et al. (2012a) and Hristova et al. (2016).

Existing Datasets

Researchers using Foursquare have made datasets of check-ins and other Foursquare data available. Often these datasets are provided free for use, with the only restriction being a requirement to cite researchers' papers if the datasets are used in further research. Details of a selection of available datasets are given in Table 36.2.

An example of a small scale dataset is https://sites.google.com/site/yangdingqi/home/foursquare-dataset which contains check-in details for restaurants in New York City over five months in 2011–2012. This dataset consists of 3,112 users and 3,298 venues with 27,149 check-ins and 10,377 tips. The same page hosts a larger dataset collected over ten months from April 2012 to February 2013. It contains 227,428 check-ins in New York city and 573,703 check-ins in Tokyo.

A much larger existing dataset is available at https://archive.org/details/201309_foursquare_dataset_umn. The dataset contains 2,153,471 users, 1,143,092 venues, 1,021,970 check-ins, 27,098,490 social connections, and 2,809,581 ratings of venues.

Redistribution of data extracted from the Foursquare API is against the terms of use; it remains to be seen how long existing datasets are available for. Foursquare have been seen to pursue researchers and require the removal of datasets previously made available (e.g. http://www-users.cs.umn.edu/~sarwat/foursquaredata/).

Finally, we note that large amounts of anonymised Foursquare check-ins can be obtained through the data reseller Gnip (https://gnip.com/sources/foursquare/). Specifically, Gnip sell access to the Foursquare activity 'firehose'. The researcher can purchase live access to all check-ins within a chosen region. This method requires that the researcher collect the check-ins in real-time, which contrasts with data re-sale for other online services (e.g., Twitter), where historical data can be purchased. In 2016, the cost of an annual license was upwards of $10,000 per year, although this depends on the level of Foursquare activity in the chosen region.

Participatory Experiments

One method to obtain Foursquare data with user permissions and within the terms of use of the Foursquare API is to build a participatory experiment (e.g., Chorley et al., 2015). In such an experiment, Foursquare users are invited to use an application or service in exchange for access to their Foursquare data. The Foursquare API is used to authenticate users, which allows the application or service access to their data.

In order for these experiments to be successful, it may be necessary to offer the user something in return for their data, perhaps providing them with the results of analysis to inform them of details of their individual behaviour of which they might not be aware. Users are unlikely to participate in the experiment and provide access to their data if it is not clear what they stand to gain from such an exchange. Furthermore, it is important that users are fully informed on how their Foursquare data is being collected and used in the experiment.

The main drawback of these types of studies can be gaining participants. If the service or application is of sufficient quality, users may choose to share information about it themselves, and in such a way it is hoped the app or service can 'go viral', and gain further users. It is helpful if the application or service contains links and calls to action to

Table 36.2 Existing Foursquare datasets

Contributors	Paper	Num. Users	Num. Checkins	Num. Venues	Duration
Dingqi Yang, Daqing Zhang, Zhiyong Yu and Zhiwen Yu	Fine-Grained Preference-Aware Location Search Leveraging Crowdsourced Digital Footprints from LBSNs (2013)	3,112	27,149	3,298	4 months
	URL: https://sites.google.com/site/yangdingqi/home/foursquare-dataset				
Dingqi Yang, Daqing Zhang, Vincent W. Zheng, Zhiyong Yu	Modeling User Activity Preference by Leveraging User Spatial Temporal Characteristics in LBSNs (2015)	—	227,428 (New York) 573,703 (Tokyo)	—	10 months
	URL: https://sites.google.com/site/yangdingqi/home/foursquare-dataset				
Dingqi Yang, Daqing Zhang, Bingqing Qu	Participatory Cultural Mapping Based on Collective Behavior Data in Location Based Social Networks (2016)	266,909	33,278,683	3,680,126	18 months
	URL: https://sites.google.com/site/yangdingqi/home/foursquare-dataset				
Mohamed Sarwat, Justin J. Levandoski, Ahmed Eldawy, and Mohamed F. Mokbel	LARS*: A Scalable and Efficient Location-Aware Recommender System (2014)	2,153,471	1,021,970	1,143,092	—
	URL: https://archive.org/details/201309_foursquare_dataset_umn				

promote such sharing. Alternatively, sites and users specifically interested in Foursquare and Foursquare-related apps can be used to promote an experiment. For example, https://twitter.com/aboutfoursquare is a Twitter account dedicated to promoting news related to Swarm and Foursquare.

Once a user has authorised your application, further check-ins can be obtained using the real-time Push API. This API allows an application to be notified every time an authorised user checks in. This information is sent from Foursquare via a POST request to a specified URL. This requires an extra layer of complexity within an application, as all such POST requests will be sent via HTTPS.

Realtime Monitoring

If the primary interest is not in specific users, but instead venues, or details of venue popularity, it may be possible to poll the API repeatedly in order to obtain information. For instance, if monitoring the popularity of a set of venues, the venue information could be periodically queried in order to check the number of likes, the current rating, the latest tips, and so on. Additionally, each time a venue is polled, the number of people currently checked in is reported (although not their details). This is referred to as the venue's '*Here Now*' metadata. It is therefore possible to obtain a measure of the number of users at a venue over time. Early versions of the API used to reveal a full list of users checked in at the venue, enabling collection of comprehensive check-in data within a predefined region (Chorley et al., 2011; Colombo et al., 2012). However, this feature has since been deprecated.

LIMITATIONS, OPPORTUNITIES, AND OUTLOOK

The limitations of Foursquare for research can be roughly grouped into three concerns: access restrictions, data reliability, and bias.

In the early days of the platform, direct access to data such as check-in histories was more permissive. However, new iterations of the API have become more restrictive. It is now, for example, not possible to directly collect comprehensive check-in data for all users within a region. Nor is it possible to query all users' friend lists, which was once a method of reconstructing large portions of the Foursquare social network.

While these changes now make it difficult to collect Foursquare datasets on the same scale as researchers were once able, there still remain viable methods for building new datasets, and novel studies continue to be conducted. As described in the previous section, unfiltered check-ins can be obtained at a cost through an official reseller, and it is still possible to collect a subset of check-ins for free by crawling cross-platform posts. Furthermore, Foursquare's rich venue database and third-party app integration make it well-suited for supporting participatory experiments in location-based social networks.

As we have discussed in this chapter, Foursquare's venue information is predominantly crowdsourced, and user data (e.g., profiles and check-ins) is voluntary and self-reported. This raises issues of accuracy and reliability that are commonly encountered in social media platforms. Furthermore, it is important to note that the userbase is biased. For example, the requirement that users must have GPS-enabled smartphones introduces a fundamental selection bias. Further, the wide variety of Swarm usage styles – from lifeloggers to social sharers – means one must be careful not to over-generalise from visiting patterns.

Finally, we note that the highly sensitive nature of individual visiting patterns means that careful ethical consideration should be taken when collecting and analysing Foursquare datasets. The company has taken measures to allow users to control what they share; for example, by allowing users to make private check-ins (hidden to everyone except the user) and automatically hiding all visits to home locations. However, despite these safeguards, even basic analysis of check-in patterns can reveal personal and sensitive information that a user originally never intended to disclose. Discretion is needed in selecting ethically appropriate research questions and ensuring private data are not disclosed when presenting results.

REFERENCES

Aggarwal, A., Almeida, J., and Kumaraguru, K. (2013), 'Detection of Spam Tipping Behaviour on Foursquare', In *Proceedings of the 22nd International Conference on World Wide Web*, Rio de Janeiro, Brasil, pp. 641–648.

Associated Press (2013), 'Number of active users at Facebook over the years', http://news.yahoo.com/number-active-users-facebook-over-230449748.html (accessed 5 September 2015).

Chorley, M., Colombo, G., Williams, M., Allen, S., and Whitaker, R. (2011), 'Checking Out Checking In: Observations on Foursquare Usage Patterns', In *Proceedings of the First International Workshop on Finding Patterns of User Behaviors in NEtwork and MObility Data (NEMO 2011)*, Athens, Greece.

Chorley, M., Rossi, L., Tyson, G., and Williams, M. (2016), 'Pub Crawling at Scale: Tapping Untappd to Explore Social Drinking', In *Proceedings of the 10th International AAAI Conference on Web and Social Media*, Cologne, Germany.

Chorley, M., Whitaker, R., and Allen, S. (2015), 'Personality and location-based social networks', *Computers in Human Behaviour*, Vol. 46, pp. 45–56.

Colombo, G., Chorley, M., Williams, M., Allen, S., and Whitaker, R. (2012), 'You are Where you Eat: Foursquare Checkins as Indicators of Human Mobility and Behaviour', In *Proceedings of the 2012 Pervasive Computing and Communications Workshops*, Lugano, Switzerland, pp. 217–222.

Crowley, D. (2013), 'Ending the Year on a Great note', *The Foursquare Blog*. Foursquare. http://blog.foursquare.com/post/70494343901/ending-the-year-on-a-great-note-and-with-a-huge (accessed 5 September 2015).

Foursquare (2016), 'Celebrating our Seventh 4sqDay', *The Foursquare Blog*, Foursquare. http://blog.foursquare.com/post/142900756695/since-foursquare-launched-in-2009-there-have-been (accessed 16 April 2016).

Hristova, D., Williams, M., Musolesi, M., Panzarasa, P., and Mascolo, C. (2016), 'Measuring Urban Social Diversity Using Interconnected Geo-Social Networks', In *Proceedings of the 25th International Conference on World Wide Web*, Montreal, Canada, pp. 21–30.

Java, A., Song, X., Finin, T., and Tseng, T. (2007), 'Why We Twitter: Understanding Microblogging Usage and Communities', In *Proceedings of the Joint 9th WEBKDD and 1st SNA-KDD Workshop*, San Jose, USA, pp. 56–65.

Lindqvist, J., Cranshaw, J., Wiese, J., Hong, J., and Zimmerman, J. (2011), 'I'm the Mayor of my House: Examining why People use Foursquare – a Social-driven Location Sharing Application'. In *Proceedings of the SIGCHI Conference on Human Factors in Computing Systems*, Vancouver, Canada, pp. 2409–2418.

Mejova, Y., Haddadi, H., Noulas, A, and Weber, I. (2015), '#FoodPorn: Obesity Patterns in Culinary Interactions', In *Proceedings of the 5th International Conference on Digital Health*, Florence, Italy, pp. 51–58.

Noulas, A., Scellato, S., Lambiotte, R., Pontil, M., and Mascolo, C. (2012a), 'A Tale of Many Cities: Universal Patterns in Human Urban Mobility', *PLoS ONE*, 7(5): e37027.

Noulas, A., Scellato, S., Lathia, N., and Mascolo, C. (2012b), 'Mining User Mobility Features for Next Place Prediction in Location-Based Services', In *Proceedings of the 12th IEEE International Conference on Data Mining*, Brussels, Belgium, pp. 1038–1043.

Noulas, A., Scellato, S., Mascolo, C., and Pontil, M. (2011), 'An Empirical Study of Geographic User Activity Patterns in Foursquare', In *Proceedings of the Fifth International AAAI Conference on Weblogs and Social Media*, Barcelona, Spain.

Noulas, A., Shaw, B., Lambiotte, and Mascolo, C. (2015), 'Topological Properties and

Temporal Dynamics of Place Networks in Urban Environments', In *Proceedings of the 24th International Conference on World Wide Web*, Florence, Italy, pp. 431–441.

Quercia, D. and Saez, D. (2014), 'Mining Urban Deprivation from Foursquare: Implicit Crowdsourcing of City Land Use', *IEEE Pervasive Computing*, Vol. 13, Iss. 2, pp. 30–36.

Rossi, L., Williams, M., Stich, C., and Musolesi, M. (2015), 'Privacy and the City: User Identification and Location Semantics in Location-Based Social Networks', In *Proceedings of 9th AAAI International Conference on Weblogs and Social Media.*, Oxford, UK.

Scellato, S., Noulas, A., Lambiotte, R., and Mascolo, C. (2011a), 'Socio-spatial Properties of Online Location-based Social Networks', In *Proceedings of the 5th International AAAI Conference on Weblogs and Social Media*, Barcelona, Spain, pp. 329–336.

Scellato, S., Noulas, A., and Mascolo, C. (2011b), 'Exploiting Place Features in Link Prediction on Location-based Social Networks', In *Proceedings of the 17th ACM SIGKDD International Conference on Knowledge Discovery and Data Mining*, San Diego, USA, pp. 1046–1054.

Silva, T., de Melo, P., Almeida, J., Musolesi, M., and Loureiro, A. (2014), 'You are What you Eat (and Drink): Identifying Cultural Boundaries by Analyzing Food & Drink Habits in Foursquare', In *Proceedings of 9th AAAI International Conference on Weblogs and Social Media*, Ann Arbor, USA.

Ye, M., Yin, P., and Lee. (2010), 'Location Recommendation for Location-based Social Networks', In *Proceedings of the 18th SIGSPATIAL International Conference on Advances in Geographic Information Systems*, San Jose, USA, pp. 458–461.

Facebook as a Research Tool in the Social and Computer Sciences

Jessica Vitak

More than one billion people use Facebook each day to connect and interact with friends, colleagues, family, and others. These users share a wide range of content, including text, images, links, and video, private and public messages, and interactions with other users. The resulting data produced by individual users – and the site's integration into users' daily lives – quickly caught the interest of researchers in the social and computational sciences, and in the last decade these researchers have employed a range of methodological approaches to evaluate user behaviors, motivations, attitudes, and more. This chapter summarizes the major methodological approaches used by social and computer scientists to study Facebook users and their digital traces, highlights a number of research challenges inherent to conducting research on the social media platform, and provides recommendations to researchers who are incorporating Facebook users and/or Facebook data into their research projects. Throughout the chapter, I stress how researchers must be actively engaged with and considerate of research subjects and data, and evaluate how the socio-technical affordances of Facebook blur distinctions between public and private data raise new ethical challenges for researchers.

INTRODUCTION

Since its launch more than a decade ago, the social network site Facebook has become one of the most popular research spaces among social and computer scientists. These researchers have used Facebook to evaluate a range of topics from the site's role in accruing social support to the relationship between site use and educational outcomes. In addition, computational methods have been used to predict everything from users' personality traits to their emotional well-being. Researchers using Facebook-related data have explored a wide range of theories, research methods, and user groups across thousands of studies, with a August 2016 Google Scholar search of the word 'Facebook' yielding more than 1.42 million results – and 24,900 articles with Facebook in the title – all within the last decade.

Methodological approaches for incorporating Facebook into a research study are as diverse as the disciplines evaluating the platform and represent a wide range of quantitative, qualitative, computational, and critical approaches. Depending on the methodological choices researchers make regarding sampling techniques and data sources, they will face a number of challenges when using Facebook in their research. This chapter discusses these challenges and provides a set of recommendations for researchers to consider when using Facebook as a research platform.

The rest of the chapter is divided into three sections. In 'Common research methods for studying Facebook and its users', I highlight examples of Facebook research across seven methodical practices. In 'Key considerations for researchers studying Facebook', I discuss in detail six of the most important methodological challenges researchers should consider when studying Facebook and its users, including questions around sampling, data sources, and ethics. In 'Overarching guidelines for conducting Facebook research', I present a set of overarching guidelines for designing a research project involving one or more sources of Facebook-related data.

COMMON RESEARCH METHODS FOR STUDYING FACEBOOK AND ITS USERS

Facebook's diverse features and popularity offers a wide range of methodological choices for researchers. Below, I describe seven of the most common methods used, including surveys, interviews, experiments, server data collection, social network analysis, diary studies, and lab studies. These methods are not mutually exclusive, and many studies take a multi-methodological approach to triangulate findings. Two methodological approaches to studying Facebook that will not be discussed in this chapter are theoretical pieces and meta-analyses. Some of these articles are highly cited (e.g., boyd and Ellison, 2007; Ellison and boyd, 2013; Wilson et al., 2012) and have helped drive the focus of the field; while important, the nature of their 'data collection' places them outside the scope of this chapter.

Surveys

One of the most common methods for evaluating Facebook use – especially in the social sciences – is through one-shot surveys and, less frequently, longitudinal survey data collection. Survey research on the relationship between Facebook use and perceptions of social capital is among the most highly cited across all disciplines and methodologies (e.g., Ellison et al., 2007, 2011, 2014b; Steinfield et al., 2008). Early surveys of Facebook users focused on college undergraduates (e.g., Ellison et al., 2007, 2011; Hewitt and Forte, 2006; Ross et al., 2009; Valenzuela et al., 2009; Vitak et al., 2011) before expanding to consider other types of users (Burke et al., 2010, 2011; Ellison et al., 2014a, 2014b; Joinson, 2008; Vitak, 2012, 2014). Popular topics evaluated through survey research are social capital and social support (e.g., Ellison et al., 2007, 2011, 2014b; Valenzuela et al., 2009), self-esteem and well-being (Kim and Lee, 2011; Kross et al., 2013; Manago et al., 2012), and issues around privacy and disclosure (e.g., Acquisti and Gross, 2006; Liu et al., 2011; Stutzman et al., 2011, 2012; Vitak, 2012).

While many surveys using convenience samples, such as those taking advantage of high-enrollment college classes, may have relied on paper surveys in the past, the vast majority of surveys now use hosting sites like Survey Monkey, SurveyGizmo, or Qualtrics. These sites offer logic-based features, including skip logic and question piping to allow more customized questions and responses. That said, hosting surveys online may not be as effective in reaching the targeted population (as in the case of low-income individuals who only access the site on their phone or on public computers) and typically have lower completion rates compared with pen-and-paper surveys (Nulty, 2008).

Interviews and Focus Groups

Interviewing Facebook users, either in combination with other data collection methods or as a stand-alone, are another commonly used method for analyzing research questions related to the site. Methodologically, interviews provide greater depth but limit generalizability of findings due to their small sample size. Oftentimes, researchers use purposeful sampling (Patton, 1990) to narrow in on a specific segment of the population, including older users (Vitak and Ellison, 2013), high self-monitors (Vitak et al., 2015; Vitak and Kim, 2014), the LGBT (lesbian, gay, bisexual, and transgender) community (Penney, 2015; Taylor et al., 2014), and cross-cultural contexts (Muuruma and Siibak, 2012; Pearce and Vitak, 2016; Zhao et al., 2008).

A less frequently used interviewing method for Facebook research is focus groups; however, this method has proven successful for evaluating certain topics and populations. For example, McLaughlin and Vitak (2012) conducted focus groups with college undergraduates to understand norm evolution on Facebook, while Urista et al. (2009) used focus groups to understand young people's uses and gratifications of the site. Notable work in this area has been conducted by the Pew Research Center and the Berkman Center to understand teens' online behaviors, including on Facebook (e.g., Lenhart, 2015; Madden et al., 2013).

Experimental Design

Across both the social and computational sciences, researchers use experimental designs to examine differences in attitudes and behaviors based on changes to Facebook's features or characteristics of other users. For example, researchers have studied users' subjective well-being by manipulating the channel (Facebook vs. offline; see Gonzales and Hancock, 2011) and social attractiveness by manipulating the number of friends a Facebook user has (Tong et al., 2008) or by what other users post on someone's profile (Walther et al., 2008). Through random assignment, experimental studies can hone in on the effect of small changes to site features. However, many of these experiments raise concerns about ecological validity due to their 'artificial' nature.

Facebook itself has received significant media attention for its use of A/B testing, a specific type of experiment (known as a field experiment) where users are randomly assigned to conditions – typically without their knowledge – and view different versions of the website. A/B testing addresses questions related to artificiality because the changes do not significantly affect their regular engagement with the site; thus, participants are unlikely to shift their behavior due to study participation or concerns about artificiality. Facebook has used this method to evaluate and predict user behaviors ranging from political engagement (Bond et al., 2012) to 'emotional contagion' (Kramer et al., 2014) and curating online conversations algorithmically (Backstrom et al., 2013). See Bakshy et al. (2014) for a detailed overview of Facebook's field experiment practices.

Server-level Data/data Scraping

In Facebook's early days, researchers were able to use automated scripts to collect user data from particular networks (e.g., Acquisti and Gross, 2006; Lampe et al., 2007); while this practice has since been prohibited by the company's Terms of Service, Facebook's Data Science Team and a small number of academic researchers have analyzed server-level data to detect broader behavior trends among users (e.g., Bernstein et al., 2013; Burke et al., 2010, 2011; Das and Kramer, 2013; Ellison et al., 2013, 2014a; Kramer et al., 2014; Lampe et al., 2014). In many cases, server data is paired with user surveys to create more robust datasets of users' perceptions and behavior on the site.

For researchers without access to Facebook's servers, data can be collected through less sophisticated methods, including using applications or plugins that participants must install, or capturing screen shots of profile content. For example, Gilbert and Karahalios (2009) used Greasemonkey, a Firefox extension, to randomly select Facebook friends from a participant's account and ask a series of questions about the selected friend. Likewise, Hogan (2012) and Rieder (2013) have both developed applications to collect and analyze ego network data (NameGenWeb and Netvizz, respectively), while Bechmann (2014) used the Danish-based software Digital Footprints to collect and visualize users' Facebook data with their consent and Gruzd (2010) developed Netlytic to collect and analyze large volumes of text from social media platforms. Similar programs for researchers include NodeXL (Hansen et al., 2010) and Discover Text (Shulman, 2011).

Social Network Analysis

Social network analysis (SNA) is a powerful method for evaluating power, centrality, and information flows (Borgatti, 2005; Scott, 2012). While data availability and Terms of Service agreements make platforms like Twitter easier for evaluating network structures around specific topics like protests (e.g., Tremayne, 2014), researchers have looked at ego networks, groups, and fan pages using applications such as those described in the previous section. For example, Brooks et al.'s (2014) study of Facebook-using adults evaluated the relationship between users' network structure and perceptions of social capital using ego network data collected through the NameGenWeb application. Researchers have developed complex, privacy-compliant Web crawlers to analyze the broader connections between Facebook users (e.g., Catanese et al., 2011), links between privacy attitudes and network structure (Spiliotopoulos and Oakley, 2013), and connections in 'taste networks' within a university setting (Lewis et al., 2012). Finally, Facebook researchers have applied SNA techniques to server-level data in a number of studies (e.g., Backstrom and Kleinberg, 2014; Lampe et al., 2014; Ugander et al., 2011; Weng and Lento, 2014).

While these studies provide useful insights into network structure, information flow, and characteristics of 'brokers', they are unable to provide insights into *why* people choose to connect with others or *how* they take advantage of their social network. For these more in-depth evaluations, SNA must be combined with methods where researchers directly interact with users and/or their digital traces.

Diary Studies

Diary studies (often used interchangeably with 'experiential sampling'), which require participants to track specific aspects of their usage over a period of time, are a less-utilized method for evaluating Facebook use and users. Methodologically, diary studies are tedious for participants, who are asked to report data on a regular basis (e.g., weekly, daily, multiple times per day). These studies often recruit small samples and the effort required of participants may lead to significantly reduced response rates. For example, in a study evaluating regret related to Facebook posts, Wang et al. (2011) asked interview participants to complete a diary each day for a month; only 12 of 19 participants completed at least *one* diary entry for an average of 18 entries during the one-month period. Likewise, in a study evaluating self-censorship on Facebook using diaries, Sleeper et al. (2013) had approximately half (16/30) of the participants complete all entries over a one-week span.

At the same time, diary studies generate in-depth longitudinal data that provide insights into how people's attitudes and behaviors may shift over time (Bolger and Laurenceau, 2013), and could not be captured through more standard methods, such as one-shot surveys. For example, Maier et al. (2015) used a diary study to evaluate how social media-related stress influences Facebook use and discontinuation of use over a two-week period. Newer technologies for logging data that reduce and/or simplify the amount of 'work' participants must complete (e.g., Footprint Tracker; see Gouveia and Karapanos, 2013) may increase the use of this method for evaluating Facebook and other technologies.

(Non-experimental) Lab Studies

While experiments may involve bringing participants into a lab, lab studies encompass a much wider range of methodological options than experiments alone. For example, in human–computer interaction (HCI) research, usability testing is common, with researchers bringing participants into lab spaces to test new programs or tools and capturing their keystrokes, eye movement, and/or immediate reactions to what is being evaluated. Among Facebook research conducted by researchers outside the company, usability studies are most common in accessibility research, such as testing the usability of the Facebook platform among blind users (Wentz and Lazar, 2011) or those with other physical disabilities (Buzzi et al., 2010). Other topics analyzed through usability testing include testing message encryption (Fahl et al., 2012) and information control-based tools (Mazzia et al., 2012).

Lab studies are often paired with or embedded within other data collection methods, and may involve assigning participants to complete specific tasks (Egelman et al., 2011; Jung et al., 2013) or having participants engage in 'think aloud' activities while scrolling through their profile page (e.g., Gray et al., 2013). A benefit of using these methods is the researcher's ability to ask follow-up questions or request feedback while a user is engaged with their account. This provides useful data that cannot be obtainable through methods such as surveys or controlled experiments.

KEY CONSIDERATIONS FOR RESEARCHERS STUDYING FACEBOOK

In a meta-analysis of Facebook research, Wilson and colleagues (2012) describe three principle methods for collecting Facebook data: participant recruitment from offline sources, participant recruitment through Facebook applications, and data crawling. Regardless of the method(s) applied to collect Facebook data, however, researchers need to evaluate a number of factors that may affect their interpretation of the data and, at a more general level, ethical and contextual factors related to the data collection. These are discussed below.

Sampling Considerations

The vast majority of Facebook studies use undergraduate samples. In the early days of Facebook, this choice of sample was logical because college students were the only users (Wilson et al., 2012). However, as use of the site has expanded, the userbase has grown and diversified significantly. In 2015, more than two-thirds of Americans used the site, with similar adoption rates across sex and race and increasing usage among older adults (Haight et al., 2014; Perrin, 2015). Furthermore, most Facebook users (84.5%) are from countries other than the United States or Canada (Facebook, 2016); therefore, researchers should be careful about generalizing findings from specific types of users to the larger Facebook userbase.

Ideally, researchers should identify their population of interest prior to data collection and consider the best methods for obtaining data from those users. Many researchers use convenience samples of college students, which is problematic for generalizability and often skews heavily female; instead, researchers should aim to invite random samples of students, which are often available through their university registrar, to participate in their studies (e.g., Ellison et al., 2007, 2011; Valenzuela et al., 2009; Vitak, 2012). For reaching adult users, Ellison and colleagues have used random samples of university staff; while university employees are likely not representative of the wider population of adult Facebook users, this strategy provides an outlet for reaching non-students (Ellison et al., 2014b). Mechanical Turk provides another outlet for reaching non-student samples – although there are limitations to this sample as well (see Buhrmester et al., 2011 for a discussion of this sampling method) – while sites like Craigslist have been used infrequently. Finally, advertising within Facebook may help researchers reach a target population (e.g., Vitak and Ellison, 2013); however, the usefulness of this sampling method is questionable (Kapp et al., 2013; Ramo and Prochaska, 2012).

A canonical example of problems associated with poor sampling methods is a 2009 study on the relationship between Facebook use and students' grades (Karpinksi, 2009). The study, which employed a convenience sample of undergraduate and graduate students, received significant media attention when the university published a press release highlighting preliminary results; however, the findings were quickly brought into question and spawned a response article the same year (Pasek et al., 2009) that contradicted the findings using three separate samples, including one nationally representative sample. Pasek et al. (2009) critiqued the original study for having few non-users, for having a significant number of graduate students – and no freshmen or sophomores – and for not controlling for other factors (e.g., sex, Internet experience, year in school) in the analyses.

User Recall

Unless capturing and analyzing server data, most Facebook studies rely on some degree of user recall to measure behaviors; for example, it is very common to see measures of Facebook usage (e.g., time per day/week, logins per day, number of friends) included in analyses as a control – or as part of a more complex measure, as in the case of Facebook Intensity (see Ellison et al., 2007, for a description of this measure). However, researchers have questioned the reliability of self-report behavioral data. For example, Burke and colleagues (2010) highlighted a large disparity between self-reports of time spent on Facebook and actual usage (calculated through server logs); after removing outliers, the correlation between reported and actual use was .45, suggesting users may have trouble accurately accounting for the full amount of time spent on the site. This is complicated by the fact that it is difficult to quantify 'use'; for example, is having the site open in one of many Internet browser tabs use? Do the 30-second checks on one's smartphone or laptop count? In an always-on, always-connected society, users are likely multitasking too much to be able to fully account for their use of various applications.

A related issue involves asking users factual or recall-specific questions to measure knowledge, skills, or a similar attribute. When participants are asked to do this in a non-controlled environment – as is often the case in online surveys – it is impossible for the researchers to assess whether participants 'cheated' by looking up answers. For example, in a study evaluating political knowledge and Facebook political participation, the researchers noted that the low reliability of the items could be due to some participants looking up answers to the questions online (Vitak et al., 2011); subsequent research has attempted to quantify the frequency with which survey takers 'cheat' in such online assessments (Jensen and Thompson, 2014).

Algorithmic Biases

Facebook's algorithm is critical in shaping users' experiences on the site (Diakopoulos, 2014), with small changes to the algorithm yielding large shifts in behavior (e.g., voting patterns; see Bond et al., 2012). Because the algorithm driving content display in Facebook is relatively opaque, researchers can only make educated guesses about individual users' experiences (Rader and Gray, 2015). When asking questions such as the frequency of viewing a specific type of content or viewing content from a particular user, researchers must recognize that user experience will vary based on how that user has 'trained' the algorithm. Furthermore, many users are unaware of the algorithmic processes operating behind the scenes and curating their experiences on the site, which may artificially shift their attitudes toward other users based on the content they see – or don't see (Eslami et al., 2015).

Another way this problem manifests is when using Facebook to select a 'friend' to evaluate. Several studies on relational formation or maintenance on the site have asked users to select one or more friends and respond to a series of questions about them; based on published research using this methodology, an unintended consequence is low variance across friend type, as most people choose a 'close' friend (e.g., Ledbetter, 2009; Miczo et al., 2011). To address this, some researchers have asked participants to respond to questions based on the friend who appeared in a specific location on the profile page, while recognizing that the algorithm is determining who appeared in that box (e.g., Ledbetter et al., 2011; Vitak, 2014). The lack of transparency regarding Facebook's algorithmic decisions forces researchers to engage in 'guesswork' regarding factors that might influence an individual user's experiences.

Collecting Behavioral Traces

Beyond capturing users' attitudes toward and perceptions of their engagement with the site, researchers may wish to capture behavioral data from the site, such as ego networks, updates, or profile information. One benefit of this approach is that researchers can triangulate their data and compare perceptions to actual behaviors. In at least two studies, researchers have used this approach to show how inaccurate users are at gauging their time spent on the site (Burke et al., 2010; Junco, 2013); in another study, merging survey and server data found that users significantly underestimate the full audience for their status updates (Bernstein et al., 2013).

While this method represents an extremely effective way of unpacking factors related to site use, Facebook has recently imposed highly restrictive policies regarding automated data collection in their Terms of Service, forbidding automated data collection of any kind without users' or Facebook's approval. While some early researchers were able to scrape public or network-specific profiles (e.g., Bortree and Seltzer, 2009; Gruzd and Haythornthwaite, 2013; Lampe et al., 2007; Lewis et al., 2008, 2012; Stutzman et al., 2012) or have partnered with Facebook to gain access to data (e.g., Bernstein et al., 2013; Burke and Kraut, 2013; Ellison et al., 2013, 2014a; Jones et al., 2013; Kramer et al., 2014; Lampe et al., 2014), the majority of researchers must rely on procedures approved through an institutional review board (IRB) and requiring participant consent before collecting behavioral trace data.

While these restrictions may appear limiting, researchers have developed a variety of strategies for obtaining behavioral data; the biggest challenges appear to be related to building trust with participants and providing proper incentives for these more intrusive data collection methods. For example, researchers may bring participants into a lab setting and obtain consent to take screenshots or download content from users' profile pages (e.g., Gosling et al., 2011; Gray et al., 2013). Alternatively, researchers have gained access to users through invitations to join research-based Facebook Groups (e.g., Bhutta, 2012; Hoy and Milne, 2010) or to 'friend' a research-based account (e.g., Deters and Mehl, 2012), or as part of the consent process (e.g., de Choudhury et al., 2014; Saslow et al., 2013; Sosik and Bazarova, 2014). A final consideration for collecting more accurate data from users is to use diary studies, where participants log their daily activities on the site through a paper/online diary or through repeated pings via email or text messages (e.g., Jelenchick et al., 2013; Kross et al., 2013).

Building or using third-party applications to collect and/or visualize data provides another outlet for researchers to collect detailed user data, although the future of these applications is unknown due to recent restrictions on the information Facebook shares with application developers. For example, Bernie Hogan, a researcher at the Oxford Internet Institute, developed NameGenWeb (Hogan, 2012) to allow researchers to collect ego network data from an individual user and then use that data to conduct social network analysis. A number of studies using this application have evaluated features of users' Facebook networks to predict variables including social capital (Brooks et al., 2014), political communication (Dubois and Ford, 2015), and emotional exchanges (Lin and Qiu, 2012). As of this writing, applications that visualize users' networks – including NameGenWeb and Netvizz –no longer function due to Facebook's increased restrictions on the kinds of data applications can collect from users. In lieu of these types of applications, researchers may request that participants download a plugin or tracking software designed to collect data from the site (e.g., Junco, 2013; Pempek et al., 2009).

Ethical Challenges

Considerations around the collection and analysis of Facebook users' data have received significant attention following the publication of several studies by Facebook's Data Science Team and academic collaborators (e.g., Das and Kramer, 2013; Kramer et al., 2014). Due in part to the media's misrepresentations of the methodological processes – and because users felt uncomfortable not knowing what was going on 'behind the scenes' at the company – many called for a deep reflection on the ethics of research on users, increased transparency, and inherent biases in 'big data' (Goel, 2014; Grimmelman, 2015; Hargittai, 2015; Tufekci, 2015).

Beyond Facebook's UX (user experience) research – which largely focuses on increasing profits – a wide range of tools exist to collect digital traces from online sources, including comments on news sites and forums, public tweets or Facebook comments, and so on. As noted above in 'Collecting behavioral traces', Facebook's Terms of Service prohibit automated data scraping without their permission or consent of all participants; however, the extent to which such rules are enforced is unclear. Researchers should carefully consider what data they need, what additional data they might (unintentionally) collect through various scraping techniques, and how collection of data could potentially harm users.

Even before the 2014 fallout from Facebook's 'social contagion' study, ethical issues with Facebook research received significant attention following the release of raw data from the *Tastes, Ties, and Time* study (Lewis et al., 2008), which the researchers represented as anonymized but was re-identified within days of release. In a detailed analysis of the ethical missteps of the researchers involved in this study, Zimmer (2010) described how the researchers violated participants' privacy through the amount of information collected, improper access of accounts (with no consent), unauthorized secondary use of data, and errors in personal information. Furthermore, by making the data publically available without taking the necessary steps to protect individual users, the researchers failed to consider the implications of their data collection and aggregation.

Even when researchers are collecting data directly from consenting participants, a number of ethical considerations should be built into the study design to minimize any risks to participants. For example, Sosik and Bazarova (2014) employed the Facebook API to collect all interactions between participants and selected friends (photos, wall posts, etc.); while the participants provided consent for this data collection, their friends did not. Even with IRB-approved protocols and procedures in place to secure the data, researchers should carefully weigh the risks and benefits of data collection. Researchers should not assume that data that is 'technically' public – including public posts, certain profile information, and content of public groups – is freely available for collection and analysis. As Marwick and boyd (2011) note in their study of how users perceive the audiences for their social media posts, 'We may understand that the Twitter or Facebook audience is potentially limitless, but we often act as if it were bounded' (p. 115). In other words, even if users' perceptions of audience and visibility are skewed, researchers may still be violating their privacy by collecting their posts in public venues.

Special care should be taken when collecting – or potentially collecting – data from minors; a non-insignificant number of Facebook users are under 18, and it is critical that additional steps be taken to protect their personal information. Recent research suggests that even though Facebook limits third parties from profiling minors (e.g., by excluding them from search results), companies can easily circumvent these policies and aggregate public data from social media platforms like Facebook to build detailed profiles of young people (Minkus et al., 2015). Likewise, differences in norms around sharing among adolescents (see 'Norms and context' below) would suggest that young people take a more open attitude toward sharing publically; Livingstone and Locatelli (2014) argue that even when rich data is available from minors, researchers should carefully evaluate whether that data should be captured and/or retained.

The Belmont Report (Office of the Secretary, 1978) is viewed as the guiding document for conducting ethical research; however, in the four decades since it was written, data practices have shifted dramatically with the explosion of mediated communication platforms. Online data sources require researchers to consider factors beyond those involving respect for persons, beneficence, and justice. Vitak et al. (2016) highlight three additional areas beyond the Belmont Report for researchers studying Facebook (and other social platforms) based on findings from a survey on online data researchers. First, they discuss the importance of researchers being transparent, both in intent (details on the process and purpose) and practice (how data will be collected). Second, they note that ethical deliberations should be an ongoing practice among researchers, which is in line with the Association of Internet Researchers' emphasis on maintaining a deliberative process throughout study design, data collection, and analysis (Markham and Buchanan, 2012). Third, Vitak et al. (2016) stress the importance of protecting individual participants by carefully evaluating whether outliers or unique cases could be identified *before* sharing the data or results. While the research community continues to push researchers to share research data with the wider research community (e.g., in the U.S., this includes any grants funded by the National Science Foundation or National Institutes of Health), concern for the safety of individual participants should be placed first.

Recent history has highlighted too many cases of 'anonymized' data being re-identified shortly after release (e.g., Barbaro and Zeller, 2006; Narayanan and Shmatikov, 2008; Zimmer, 2010). Therefore, researchers should be especially considerate of the data they're collecting from Facebook users when collecting data from at-risk populations (e.g., minors), when there is not an explicit consent process in place, when collecting server data, and when collecting data beyond the scope of a consent (e.g., friends' posts on a participant's wall).

In response to the complex ethical concerns researchers face when engaging with digital trace data, as well as increased concerns from the public regarding their internal research procedures, Facebook's policy team recently published a law review article (Jackman & Kanerva, 2016) detailing their research review process. The authors detail their internal processes and highlight how ethics reviews must evolve in light of changing research methods, saying: 'a flexible process is key: The ever-changing nature of the questions and data involved in industry (and academic) research requires that any processes must be able to adapt efficiently to new internal challenges and external feedback so they can improve over time' (p. 444). This increased transparency suggests that Facebook's review processes are more closely aligning with the privacy rights of individual users and that the company is listening to public concerns about this kind of research.

Norms and Context

Norms of use vary across and within specific social media platforms, and Facebook is no exception. Researchers developing studies should carefully consider how their target population engages with the site, including their specific uses and gratifications, which varies across gender, age, and feature use (Bumgarner, 2007; Joinson, 2008; Papacharissi and Mendelson, 2010; Raacke and Bonds-Raacke, 2008; Smock et al., 2011). For example, danah boyd's work with teenagers (e.g., boyd, 2007, 2014) has highlighted how teens repurpose site features to achieve their communication goals. In general, younger Facebook users disclose significantly more information on the site and have less restrictive attitudes toward sharing personal content (Chakraborty et al., 2013; Madden et al., 2013). Likewise, specific personality traits or attitudes influence users' practices on the site (e.g., Skues et al., 2012; Vitak et al., 2015).

Norms of use also evolve over time, both due to the technical changes to the site's architecture and changing goals associated with use. Therefore, researchers should be cautious in applying findings from the early years of the site – when membership was limited to college students, who were grouped by their university networks – to current projects. For example, privacy perceptions and practices have evolved significantly over time, and studies have shown that many of the early studies (Acquisti and Gross, 2006) do not reflect current users' practices (Stutzman et al., 2012, 2013). Among young adults, McLaughlin and Vitak (2012) found that users adapted their friending and posting behaviors over time as they became more skilled users; in this study, participants said their use of privacy settings increased and their personal disclosures decreased over time, while specific factors (such as turning 21) led some users to begin posting content that could previously have been problematic, such as photos of them with alcohol. Similar findings suggest that students begin restricting access and/or deleting Facebook content as they enter the job market (Vitak and Kim, 2014). These latter examples reflect how changes in the individual user (such as getting older) lead to changes in what is deemed 'acceptable' or 'appropriate' use of the site.

OVERARCHING GUIDELINES FOR CONDUCTING FACEBOOK RESEARCH

As the previous sections have highlighted, using Facebook as a research tool offers great diversity across topics to evaluate, data to be collected, and methods available for analyzing data. This is highlighted in the tens of thousands of articles generated during the last decade, especially in the social and computer sciences. At the same time, just because Facebook contains such a wealth of data does not mean that it is the best fit – or even an appropriate choice – for all research projects. And even when Facebook appears to be an appropriate source for study, researchers should consider a number of questions before proceeding with study design, data collection, and analysis.

If you've decided to incorporate Facebook into your study, how do you choose the right method and apply it properly? First and foremost, as with all research, methodological decisions should be driven by the research question(s). Surveys will typically only provide *perceptions* of use – with the exception of questions asking participants to copy content from the site – and are therefore limited in their ability to draw conclusions about actual use. At the same time, surveys are a much more accessible method than collecting server data, so researchers must make trade-offs based on the data they *want* and the data *available*. Likewise, representative samples of a population are highly valued, but may be cost-prohibitive, forcing researchers to use purposeful or convenience sampling techniques. In these cases, researchers should focus on increasing the reliability and validity of their data within sampling constraints.

Facebook's userbase is highly diverse, spanning across race, gender, and age, and income. Unfortunately, the majority of Facebook studies collect data from a small subset of users – typically young American college students, who are not representative of larger trends in use – and/or employ convenience sampling, both of which limit generalizability. This is a major problem for many areas of research, but it is important not to fall back on these sampling methods simply because they are 'easy'; to truly advance our understanding of Facebook's role in our lives, researchers must aim for random and representative samples whenever possible, as well as explore Facebook use among those typically overlooked in studies. Even experiments, which mitigate some of the concerns about sampling due to random assignment to conditions, pose validity concerns when the stimuli do not closely reflect users' experiences 'in the wild.'

The best studies involve triangulation of multiple data sources and methods. These studies provide more nuanced understandings of a phenomenon. Facebook's Data Science team has published numerous such studies over the years, combining server data with surveys (e.g., Bernstein et al., 2013; Burke et al., 2010, 2011; Burke and Kraut, 2013); however, there are many ways for those not employed by Facebook to collect highly robust data. For example, Gilbert and Karahalios (2009) used a plugin to collect data about tie strength, then conducted follow-up interviews to understand why certain errors occurred in their prediction model. Gray et al. (2013) paired surveys with a lab study, where participants identified an instance where they posed a question to their friend network; the question and all responses were captured by the researchers and later coded. Brooks et al. (2014) paired survey data with ego network data collected through a Facebook application to understand the relationship between network structure and perceptions of resource access. Combining multiple methods, as highlighted in these studies, provides a more complete picture of the studied phenomenon, and they are more likely to capture unique findings then when using a single method.

In sum, this chapter highlights the major challenges to studying a space where both the social and technical structures are constantly shifting. Facebook provides a tempting platform for researchers across a wide range of disciplines because (1) use is largely ubiquitous (especially in Western nations), (2) the site has become an extension and supplement of both novel and mundane communication, and (3) data can be collected through a wide variety of methods. That said, researchers should carefully consider the type of data they need to answer their research questions, if and how they will collect that data (and the biases inherent in their choices), ethical factors related to data collection, and the shifting norms of use *before* their project begins. Studies employing Facebook can provide valuable insights into individuals' attitudes and behaviors and help advance theory and design within the social and computational studies, but only when the above factors are built into study design.

REFERENCES

Acquisti, A. and Gross, R. (2006). 'Imagined communities: Awareness, information sharing, and privacy on the Facebook', *Lecture Notes in Computer Science*, Vol. 4258, 36–58.

Backstrom, L. and Kleinberg, J. (2014), 'Romantic partnerships and the dispersion of social ties: A network analysis of relationship status on Facebook', *Proceedings of the 17th ACM Conference on Computer Supported Cooperative Work & Social Computing*, ACM, New York, NY, USA, pp. 831–841.

Backstrom, L., Kleinberg, J., Lee, L. and Danescu-Niculescu-Mizil, C. (2013), 'Characterizing and curating conversation threads: Expansion, focus, volume, re-entry', *Proceedings of the Sixth ACM International Conference on Web Search and Data Mining*, ACM, New York, NY, USA, pp. 13–22.

Bakshy, E., Eckles, D. and Bernstein, M.S. (2014), 'Designing and deploying online field experiments', *Proceedings of the 23rd International Conference on World Wide Web*, ACM, New York, NY, USA, pp. 283–292.

Barbaro, M. and Zeller Jr, T. (2006), 'A Face Is Exposed for AOL Searcher No. 4417749', *The New York Times*, 9 August, available at: http://www.nytimes.com/2006/08/09/technology/09aol.html (accessed 9 March 2016).

Bechmann, A. and Lomborg, S. (2014), *The Ubiquitous Internet: User and Industry Perspectives*, Routledge, New York, NY.

Bernstein, M.S., Bakshy, E., Burke, M. and Karrer, B. (2013), 'Quantifying the invisible audience in social networks', *Proceedings of the SIGCHI Conference on Human Factors in Computing Systems*, ACM, New York, NY, USA, pp. 21–30.

Bhutta, C.B. (2012), 'Not by the book: Facebook as a sampling frame', *Sociological Methods & Research*, Vol. 41 No. 1, pp. 57–88.

Bolger, N. and Laurenceau, J.P. (2013), *Intensive Longitudinal Methods: An Introduction to Diary and Experience Sampling Research*, 1st ed., The Guilford Press, New York, NY.

Bond, R.M., Fariss, C.J., Jones, J.J., Kramer, A.D.I., Marlow, C., Settle, J.E. and Fowler, J.H. (2012), 'A 61-million-person experiment in social influence and political mobilization', *Nature*, Vol. 489 No. 7415, pp. 295–298.

Borgatti, S.P. (2005), 'Centrality and network flow', *Social Networks*, Vol. 27 No. 1, pp. 55–71.

Bortree, D.S. and Seltzer, T. (2009), 'Dialogic strategies and outcomes: An analysis of environmental advocacy groups' Facebook profiles', *Public Relations Review*, Vol. 35 No. 3, pp. 317–319.

boyd, d. (2007), *Why youth (heart) social network sites: The role of networked publics in teenage social life*, The Berkman Society for Internet & Society at Harvard University, available at: http://research.fit.edu/sealevelriselibrary/documents/doc_mgr/1006/Boyd._2008._Why_teens_love_social_media.pdf (accessed 9 March 2016).

boyd, d. (2014), *It's Complicated: The Social Lives of Networked Teens*, 1 ed., Yale University Press, New Haven.

boyd, d. and Ellison, N.B. (2007), 'Social network sites: Definition, history, and scholarship', *Journal of Computer-Mediated Communication*, Vol. 13 No. 1, pp. 210–230.

Brooks, B., Hogan, B., Ellison, N., Lampe, C. and Vitak, J. (2014), 'Assessing structural correlates to social capital in Facebook ego networks', *Social Networks*, Vol. 38, pp. 1–15.

Buhrmester, M., Kwang, T. and Gosling, S.D. (2011), 'Amazon's Mechanical Turk: A new source of inexpensive, yet high-quality, data?', *Perspectives on Psychological Science*, Vol. 6 No. 1, pp. 3–5.

Bumgarner, B.A. (2007), 'You have been poked: Exploring the uses and gratifications of Facebook among emerging adults', *First Monday*, Vol. 12 No. 11, available at: http://doi.org/10.5210/fm.v12i11.2026.

Burke, M. and Kraut, R. (2013), 'Using Facebook after losing a job: Differential benefits of strong and weak ties', *Proceedings of the*

2013 Conference on Computer Supported Cooperative Work, ACM, New York, NY, USA, pp. 1419–1430.

Burke, M., Kraut, R. and Marlow, C. (2011), 'Social capital on Facebook: Differentiating uses and users', *Proceedings of the SIGCHI Conference on Human Factors in Computing Systems*, ACM, New York, NY, USA, pp. 571–580.

Burke, M., Marlow, C. and Lento, T. (2010), 'Social network activity and social well-being', *Proceedings of the SIGCHI Conference on Human Factors in Computing Systems*, ACM, New York, NY, USA, pp. 1909–1912.

Buzzi, M.C., Buzzi, M., Leporini, B. and Akhter, F. (2010), 'Is Facebook really "open" to all?', *Proceedings of the International Symposium on Technology and Society*, IEEE, pp. 327–336.

Catanese, S.A., De Meo, P., Ferrara, E., Fiumara, G. and Provetti, A. (2011), 'Crawling Facebook for social network analysis purposes', *Proceedings of the International Conference on Web Intelligence, Mining and Semantics*, ACM, New York, NY, USA, pp. 52:1–52:8.

Chakraborty, R., Vishik, C. and Rao, H.R. (2013), 'Privacy preserving actions of older adults on social media: Exploring the behavior of opting out of information sharing', *Decision Support Systems*, Vol. 55 No. 4, pp. 948–956.

Das, S. and Kramer, A. (2013), 'Self-Censorship on Facebook', *Seventh International AAAI Conference on Weblogs and Social Media*, Washington DC: AAAI, pp. 120–127.

De Choudhury, M., Counts, S., Horvitz, E.J. and Hoff, A. (2014), 'Characterizing and predicting postpartum depression from shared Facebook data', *Proceedings of the 17th ACM Conference on Computer Supported Cooperative Work & Social Computing*, ACM, New York, NY, USA, pp. 626–638.

Deters, F. große and Mehl, M.R. (2012), 'Does posting Facebook status updates increase or decrease loneliness? An online social networking experiment', *Social Psychological and Personality Science*, Vol. 4 No. 5, pp. 579–586.

Diakopoulos, N. (2014), 'Algorithmic accountability reporting: On the investigation of black boxes', Columbia University, NY: Tow Center for Digital Journalism., available at: http://towcenter.org/research/algorithmic-accountability-on-the-investigation-of-black-boxes-2/.

Dubois, E. and Ford, H. (2015), 'Trace interviews: An actor-centered approach', *International Journal of Communication*, Vol. 9, pp. 2067–2091.

Egelman, S., Oates, A. and Krishnamurthi, S. (2011), 'Oops, I did it again: Mitigating repeated access control errors on Facebook', *Proceedings of the SIGCHI Conference on Human Factors in Computing Systems*, ACM, New York, NY, USA, pp. 2295–2304.

Ellison, N.B. and boyd, d. (2013), 'Sociality through social network sites', in Dutton, W.H. (Ed.), *The Oxford Handbook of Internet Studies*, OUP Oxford, pp. 151–172.

Ellison, N.B., Gray, R., Lampe, C. and Fiore, A.T. (2014a), 'Social capital and resource requests on Facebook', *New Media & Society*, Vol. 16 No. 7, pp. 1104–1121.

Ellison, N., Gray, R., Vitak, J., Lampe, C. and Fiore, A.T. (2013), 'Calling all Facebook Friends: Exploring requests for help on Facebook', *Seventh International AAAI Conference on Weblogs and Social Media*, Washington DC: AAAI, pp. 155–164.

Ellison, N.B., Steinfield, C. and Lampe, C. (2007), 'The benefits of Facebook 'Friends:' Social capital and college students' use of online social network sites', *Journal of Computer-Mediated Communication*, Vol. 12 No. 4, pp. 1143–1168.

Ellison, N.B., Steinfield, C. and Lampe, C. (2011), 'Connection strategies: Social capital implications of Facebook-enabled communication practices', *New Media & Society*, Vol. 13 No. 6, pp. 873–892.

Ellison, N.B., Vitak, J., Gray, R. and Lampe, C. (2014b), 'Cultivating social resources on social network sites: Facebook relationship maintenance behaviors and their role in social capital processes', *Journal of Computer-Mediated Communication*, Vol. 19 No. 4, pp. 855–870.

Eslami, M., Rickman, A., Vaccaro, K., Aleyasen, A., Vuong, A., Karahalios, K., Hamilton, K. and Sandvig, C. (2015), '"I always assumed that I wasn't really that close to [her]": Reasoning About Invisible Algorithms in News Feeds', *Proceedings of the 33rd Annual ACM Conference on Human Factors in Computing Systems*, ACM, New York, NY, USA, pp. 153–162.

Facebook. (2015), 'Stats', available at: https://newsroom.fb.com/company-info/

Fahl, S., Harbach, M., Muders, T., Smith, M. and Sander, U. (2012), 'Helping Johnny 2.0 to encrypt his Facebook conversations', *Proceedings of the Eighth Symposium on Usable Privacy and Security*, ACM, New York, NY, USA, pp. 11:1–11:17.

Gilbert, E. and Karahalios, K. (2009), 'Predicting tie strength with social media', *Proceedings of the SIGCHI Conference on Human Factors in Computing Systems*, ACM, New York, NY, USA, pp. 211–220.

Goel, V. (2014), 'As data overflows online, researchers grapple with ethics', *The New York Times*, 12 August, available at: http://www.nytimes.com/2014/08/13/technology/the-boon-of-online-data-puts-social-science-in-a-quandary.html (accessed 9 March 2016).

Gonzales, A.L. and Hancock, J.T. (2011), 'Mirror, mirror on my Facebook wall: Effects of exposure to Facebook on self-esteem', *Cyberpsychology, Behavior, and Social Networking*, Vol. 14 No. 1–2, pp. 79–83.

Gosling, S.D., Augustine, A.A., Vazire, S., Holtzman, N. and Gaddis, S. (2011), 'Manifestations of personality in online social networks: Self-reported Facebook-related behaviors and observable profile information', *Cyberpsychology, Behavior, and Social Networking*, Vol. 14 No. 9, pp. 483–488.

Gouveia, R. and Karapanos, E. (2013), 'Footprint Tracker: Supporting diary studies with lifelogging', *Proceedings of the SIGCHI Conference on Human Factors in Computing Systems*, ACM, New York, NY, USA, pp. 2921–2930.

Gray, R., Ellison, N.B., Vitak, J. and Lampe, C. (2013), 'Who wants to know?: Question-asking and answering practices among Facebook users', *Proceedings of the 2013 Conference on Computer Supported Cooperative Work*, ACM, New York, NY, USA, pp. 1213–1224.

Grimmelmann, J. (2015), 'The law and ethics of experiments on social media users', *Colorado Technology Law Journal*, Vol. 13 No. 2, pp. 221–272.

Gruzd, A. (2010), 'Exploring virtual communities with the Internet Community Text Analyzer', in Daniel, B.K. (Ed.), *Handbook of Research on Methods and Techniques for Studying Virtual Communities: Paradigms and Phenomena: Paradigms and Phenomena*, Hershey, PA: Information Science Reference, pp. 205–223.

Gruzd, A. and Haythornthwaite, C. (2013), 'Enabling community through social media', *Journal of Medical Internet Research*, Vol. 15 No. 10, p. e248.

Haight, M., Quan-Haase, A. and Corbett, B.A. (2014), 'Revisiting the digital divide in Canada: the impact of demographic factors on access to the internet, level of online activity, and social networking site usage', *Information, Communication & Society*, Vol. 17 No. 4, pp. 503–519.

Hansen, D., Shneiderman, B. and Smith, M.A. (2010), *Analyzing Social Media Networks with NodeXL: Insights from a Connected World*, Morgan Kaufmann, Burlington, MA.

Hargittai, E. (2015), 'Is bigger always better? Potential biases of big data derived from social network sites', *The ANNALS of the American Academy of Political and Social Science*, Vol. 659 No. 1, pp. 63–76.

Hewitt, A. and Forte, A. (2006), 'Crossing boundaries: identity management and student/faculty relationships on the Facebook', *Poster Presented at the 9th Annual Conference on Computer Supported Cooperative Work and Social Computing, Banff, Alberta, Canada*, New York: ACM, available at: http://www.cc.gatech.edu/~aforte/HewittForteCSCWPoster2006.pdf (accessed 9 March 2016).

Hogan, B. (2012), *NameGenWeb*. [application], available at: https://www.facebook.com/NameGenWeb.

Hoy, M.G. and Milne, G. (2010). 'Gender differences in privacy-related measures for young adult Facebook users', *Journal of Interactive Advertising*, Vol. 10 No. 2, pp. 28–45.

Jackman, M. and Kanerva, L. (2016), 'Evolving the IRB: Building robust review for industry research', *Washington and Lee Law Review Online*, Vol. 72 No. 3, pp. 442–457.

Jelenchick, L.A., Eickhoff, J.C. and Moreno, M.A. (2013), '"Facebook depression?" Social networking site use and depression in older adolescents', *Journal of Adolescent Health*, Vol. 52 No. 1, pp. 128–130.

Jensen, C. and Thomsen, J.P.F. (2014), 'Self-reported cheating in web surveys on political knowledge', *Quality & Quantity*, Vol. 48 No. 6, pp. 3343–3354.

Joinson, A.N. (2008), 'Looking at, looking up or keeping up with people?: Motives and use of

Facebook', *Proceedings of the SIGCHI Conference on Human Factors in Computing Systems*, ACM, New York, NY, USA, pp. 1027–1036.

Jones, J.J., Settle, J.E., Bond, R.M., Fariss, C.J., Marlow, C. and Fowler, J.H. (2013), 'Inferring tie strength from online directed behavior', *PLOS ONE*, Vol. 8 No. 1, p. e52168.

Junco, R. (2013), 'Comparing actual and self-reported measures of Facebook use', *Computers in Human Behavior*, Vol. 29 No. 3, pp. 626–631.

Jung, Y., Gray, R., Lampe, C. and Ellison, N. (2013), 'Favors from Facebook Friends: Unpacking dimensions of social capital', *Proceedings of the SIGCHI Conference on Human Factors in Computing Systems*, ACM, New York, NY, USA, pp. 11–20.

Kapp, J.M., Peters, C. and Oliver, D.P. (2013), 'Research recruitment using Facebook advertising: Big potential, big challenges', *Journal of Cancer Education*, Vol. 28 No. 1, pp. 134–137.

Karpinski, A.C. (2009), 'A description of Facebook use and academic performance among undergraduate and graduate students', paper presented at the Annual Meeting of the American Educational Research Association, San Diego, CA, USA.

Kim, J. and Lee, J.-E.R. (2011), 'The Facebook paths to happiness: Effects of the number of Facebook friends and self-presentation on subjective well-being', *Cyberpsychology, Behavior, and Social Networking*, Vol. 14 No. 6, pp. 359–364.

Kramer, A.D.I., Guillory, J.E. and Hancock, J.T. (2014), 'Experimental evidence of massive scale emotional contagion through social networks', *Proceedings of the National Academy of Sciences*, Vol. 111 No. 24, pp. 8788–8790.

Kross, E., Verduyn, P., Demiralp, E., Park, J., Lee, D.S., Lin, N., Shablack, H., Jonides, J. and Ybarra, O. (2013), 'Facebook use predicts declines in subjective well-being in young adults', *PLOS ONE*, Vol. 8 No. 8, p. e69841.

Lampe C., Ellison, N. and Steinfield, C. (2007) 'A familiar Face(book): Profile elements as signals in an online social network', *Proceedings of the 25th International Conference on Human Factors in Computing*, ACM, New York, NT, USA, pp. 435-444.

Lampe, C., Gray, R., Fiore, A.T. and Ellison, N. (2014), 'Help is on the way: Patterns of responses to resource requests on Facebook', *Proceedings of the 17th ACM Conference on Computer Supported Cooperative Work & Social Computing*, ACM, New York, NY, USA, pp. 3–15.

Ledbetter, A.M. (2009), 'Measuring online communication attitude: Instrument development and validation', *Communication Monographs*, Vol. 76 No. 4, pp. 463–486.

Ledbetter, A.M., Mazer, J.P., DeGroot, J.M., Meyer, K.R., Mao, Y. and Swafford, B. (2011), 'Attitudes toward online social connection and self-disclosure as predictors of Facebook communication and relational closeness', *Communication Research*, available at: http://doi.org/10.1177/0093650210365537.

Lenhart, A. (2015), 'Teens, Technology and Friendships', *Pew Research Center: Internet, Science & Tech*, 6 August, available at: http://www.pewinternet.org/2015/08/06/teens-technology-and-friendships/ (accessed 9 March 2016).

Lewis, K., Gonzalez, M. and Kaufman, J. (2012), 'Social selection and peer influence in an online social network', *Proceedings of the National Academy of Sciences*, Vol. 109 No. 1, pp. 68–72.

Lewis, K., Kaufman, J., Gonzalez, M., Wimmer, A. and Christakis, N. (2008), 'Tastes, ties, and time: A new social network dataset using Facebook.com', *Social Networks*, Vol. 30 No. 4, pp. 330–342.

Lin, H. and Qui, L. (2012), 'Sharing emotion on Facebook: Network size, density, and individual motivation', *CHI '12 Extended Abstracts on Human Factors in Computing Systems*, ACM, New York, NY, USA, pp. 2573–2578.

Liu, Y., Gummadi, K.P., Krishnamurthy, B. and Mislove, A. (2011), 'Analyzing Facebook privacy settings: User expectations vs. reality', *Proceedings of the 2011 ACM SIGCOMM Conference on Internet Measurement Conference*, ACM, New York, NY, USA, pp. 61–70.

Livingstone, S. and Locatelli, E. (2014), 'Ethical dilemmas in qualitative research with youth on/offline', *International Journal of Learning and Media*, Vol. 4 No. 2, pp. 67–75.

Madden, M., Lenhart, A., Cortesi, S., Gasser, U., Duggan, M., Smith, A. and Beaton, M.

(2013), 'Teens, Social Media, and Privacy', *Pew Research Center: Internet, Science & Tech*, 21 May, available at: http://www.pewinternet.org/2013/05/21/teens-social-media-and-privacy/ (accessed 9 March 2016).

Maier, C., Laumer, S., Weinert, C. and Weitzel, T. (2015), 'The effects of technostress and switching stress on discontinued use of social networking services: A study of Facebook use', *Information Systems Journal*, Vol. 25 No. 3, pp. 275–308.

Manago, A.M., Taylor, T. and Greenfield, P.M. (2012), 'Me and my 400 friends: The anatomy of college students' Facebook networks, their communication patterns, and well-being', *Developmental Psychology*, Vol. 48 No. 2, pp. 369–380.

Markham, A. and Buchanan, E.A. (2012), *Ethical Decision-Making and Internet Research*, Association of Internet Researchers, available at: http://aoir.org/reports/ethics2.pdf

Marwick, A. and boyd, d. (2011). 'I tweet honestly, I tweet passionately: Twitter users, context collapse, and the imagined audience', *New Media & Society*, Vol. 13 No. 1, pp. 114–133.

Mazzia, A., LeFevre, K. and Adar, E. (2012), 'The PViz comprehension tool for social network privacy settings', *Proceedings of the Eighth Symposium on Usable Privacy and Security*, New York: ACM, p. Article 13.

McLaughlin, C. and Vitak, J. (2012), 'Norm evolution and violation on Facebook', *New Media & Society*, Vol. 14 No. 2, pp. 299–315.

Miczo, N., Mariani, T. and Donahue, C. (2011), 'The strength of strong ties: Media multiplexity, communication motives, and the maintenance of geographically close friendships', *Communication Reports*, Vol. 24 No. 1, pp. 12–24.

Minkus, T., Ding, Y., Dey, R. and Ross, K.W. (2015), 'The city privacy attack: Combining social media and public records for detailed profiles of adults and children', *Proceedings of the 2015 ACM on Conference on Online Social Networks*, ACM, New York, NY, USA, pp. 71–81.

Murumaa, M. and Siibak, A. (2012), 'The imagined audience on Facebook: Analysis of Estonian teen sketches about typical Facebook users', *First Monday*, Vol. 17 No. 2, available at: http://doi.org/10.5210/fm.v17i2.3712

Narayanan, A. and Shmatikov, V. (2008), 'Robust De-anonymization of Large Sparse Datasets', *IEEE Symposium on Security and Privacy, 2008. SP 2008*, presented at the IEEE Symposium on Security and Privacy, pp. 111–125.

Nulty, D.D. (2008), 'The adequacy of response rates to online and paper surveys: what can be done?', *Assessment & Evaluation in Higher Education*, Vol. 33 No. 3, pp. 301–314.

Office of the Secretary of The National Commission for the Protection of Human Subjects of Biomedical and Behavioral Research. (1978), *The Belmont Report: Ethical Principles and Guidelines for the Protection of Human Subjects of Research*, Department of Health, Education, and Welfare.

Papacharissi, Z. and Mendelson, A. (2010), 'Toward a new (er) sociability: uses, gratifications and social capital on Facebook', in Papathanassopoulos, S. (Ed.), *Media Perspectives for the 21st Century*, London: Routledge, pp. 212–230.

Pasek, J., More, E. and Hargittai, E. (2009), 'Facebook and academic performance: Reconciling a media sensation with data', *First Monday*, Vol. 14 No. 5, available at: http://doi.org/10.5210/fm.v14i5.2498

Patton, M.Q. (1990), *Qualitative Evaluation and Research Methods (2nd ed.)*, SAGE Publications, Inc, Thousand Oaks, CA, US.

Pearce, K.E. and Vitak, J. (2016), 'Performing honor online: The affordances of social media for surveillance and impression management in an honor culture', *New Media & Society*, pp. forthcoming.

Pempek, T.A., Yermolayeva, Y.A. and Calvert, S.L. (2009), 'College students' social networking experiences on Facebook', *Journal of Applied Developmental Psychology*, Vol. 30 No. 3, pp. 227–238.

Penney, J. (2015), 'Social media and symbolic action: exploring participation in the Facebook red equal sign profile picture campaign', *Journal of Computer-Mediated Communication*, Vol. 20 No. 1, pp. 52–66.

Perrin, A. (2015), 'Social Media Usage: 2005–2015', *Pew Research Center: Internet, Science & Tech*, 8 October, available at: http://www.pewinternet.org/2015/10/08/social-networking-usage-2005–2015/ (accessed 9 March 2016).

Raacke, J. and Bonds-Raacke, J. (2008), 'Myspace and Facebook: Applying the uses and gratifications theory to exploring friend-networking sites', *CyberPsychology & Behavior*, Vol. 11 No. 2, pp. 169–174.

Rader, E. and Gray, R. (2015), 'Understanding user beliefs about algorithmic curation in the Facebook news feed', *Proceedings of the 33rd Annual ACM Conference on Human Factors in Computing Systems*, ACM, New York, NY, USA, pp. 173–182.

Ramo, D.E. and Prochaska, J.J. (2012), 'Broad reach and targeted recruitment using Facebook for an online survey of young adult substance use', *Journal of Medical Internet Research*, Vol. 14 No. 1, p. e28.

Rieder, B. (2013), 'Studying Facebook via data extraction: The Netvizz application', *Proceedings of the 5th Annual ACM Web Science Conference*, ACM, New York, NY, USA, pp. 346–355.

Ross, C., Orr, E.S., Sisic, M., Arseneault, J.M., Simmering, M.G. and Orr, R.R. (2009), 'Personality and motivations associated with Facebook use', *Computers in Human Behavior*, Vol. 25 No. 2, pp. 578–586.

Saslow, L.R., Muise, A., Impett, E.A. and Dubin, M. (2013), 'Can you see how happy we are? Facebook images and relationship satisfaction', *Social Psychological and Personality Science*, Vol. 4 No. 4, pp. 411–418.

Scott, J. (2012), *Social Network Analysis*, SAGE, London.

Shulman, S. (2011), 'DiscoverText: Software training to unlock the power of text', *Proceedings of the 12th Annual International Digital Government Research Conference: Digital Government Innovation in Challenging Times*, ACM, New York, NY, USA, pp. 373–373.

Skues, J.L., Williams, B. and Wise, L. (2012), 'The effects of personality traits, self-esteem, loneliness, and narcissism on Facebook use among university students', *Computers in Human Behavior*, Vol. 28 No. 6, pp. 2414–2419.

Sleeper, M., Balebako, R., Das, S., McConahy, A.L., Wiese, J. and Cranor, L.F. (2013), 'The post that wasn't: Exploring self-censorship on Facebook', *Proceedings of the 2013 Conference on Computer Supported Cooperative Work*, ACM, New York, NY, USA, pp. 793–802.

Smock, A.D., Ellison, N.B., Lampe, C. and Wohn, D.Y. (2011), 'Facebook as a toolkit: A uses and gratification approach to unbundling feature use', *Computers in Human Behavior*, Vol. 27 No. 6, pp. 2322–2329.

Sosik, V.S. and Bazarova, N.N. (2014). 'Relational maintenance on social network sites: How Facebook communication predicts relational escalation', *Computers in Human Behavior*, Vol. 35, pp. 124–131.

Spiliotopoulos, T. and Oakley, I. (2013), 'Understanding motivations for Facebook use: Usage metrics, network structure, and privacy', *Proceedings of the SIGCHI Conference on Human Factors in Computing Systems*, ACM, New York, NY, USA, pp. 3287–3296.

Steinfield, C., Ellison, N.B. and Lampe, C. (2008), 'Social capital, self-esteem, and use of online social network sites: A longitudinal analysis', *Journal of Applied Developmental Psychology*, Vol. 29, pp. 434–445.

Stutzman, F., Capra, R. and Thompson, J. (2011), 'Factors mediating disclosure in social network sites', *Computers in Human Behavior*, Vol. 27 No. 1, pp. 590–598.

Stutzman, F., Gross, R. and Acquisti, A. (2013), 'Silent listeners: The evolution of privacy and disclosure on Facebook', *Journal of Privacy and Confidentiality*, Vol. 4 No. 2, available at: http://repository.cmu.edu/jpc/vol4/iss2/2.

Stutzman, F., Vitak, J., Ellison, N.B., Gray, R. and Lampe, C. (2012), 'Privacy in interaction: Exploring disclosure and social capital in Facebook', *Sixth International AAAI Conference on Weblogs and Social Media*, Washington DC: AAAI, pp. 330–337.

Taylor, Y., Falconer, E. and Snowdon, R. (2014), 'Queer youth, Facebook and faith: Facebook methodologies and online identities', *New Media & Society*, Vol. 16 No. 7, pp. 1138–1153.

Tong, S.T., Van Der Heide, B., Langwell, L. and Walther, J.B. (2008), 'Too much of a good thing? The relationship between number of friends and interpersonal impressions on Facebook', *Journal of Computer-Mediated Communication*, Vol. 13 No. 3, pp. 531–549.

Tremayne, M. (2014), 'Anatomy of protest in the digital era: A network analysis of Twitter and Occupy Wall Street', *Social Movement Studies*, Vol. 13 No. 1, pp. 110–126.

Tufekci, Z. (2015). 'Algorithmic harms beyond Facebook and Google: Emergent challenges of computational agency', *Journal on Telecommunications & High Technology Law*, Vol. 13, pp. 203–217.

Ugander, J., Karrer, B., Backstrom, L. and Marlow, C. (2011), 'The anatomy of the Facebook Social Graph', *arXiv:1111.4503 [physics]*, available at: http://arxiv.org/abs/1111.4503 (accessed 9 March 2016).

Urista, M.A., Dong, Q. and Day, K.D. (2009), 'Explaining why young adults use MySpace and Facebook through uses and gratifications theory', *Human Communication*, Vol. 12 No. 2, pp. 215–229.

Valenzuela, S., Park, N. and Kee, K.F. (2009), 'Is There Social Capital in a Social Network Site?: Facebook Use and College Students' Life Satisfaction, Trust, and Participation1', *Journal of Computer-Mediated Communication*, Vol. 14 No. 4, pp. 875–901.

Vitak, J. (2012), 'The impact of context collapse and privacy on social network site disclosures', *Journal of Broadcasting & Electronic Media*, Vol. 56 No. 4, pp. 451–470.

Vitak, J. (2014), 'Facebook makes the heart grow fonder: Relationship maintenance strategies among geographically dispersed and communication-restricted connections', *Proceedings of the 17th ACM Conference on Computer Supported Cooperative Work & Social Computing*, ACM, New York, NY, USA, pp. 842–853.

Vitak, J. and Ellison, N.B. (2013), '"There's a network out there you might as well tap": Exploring the benefits of and barriers to exchanging informational and support-based resources on Facebook', *New Media & Society*, Vol. 15 No. 2, pp. 243–259.

Vitak, J. and Kim, J. (2014), '"You can't block people offline": Examining how Facebook's affordances shape the disclosure process', *Proceedings of the 17th ACM Conference on Computer Supported Cooperative Work & Social Computing*, ACM, New York, NY, USA, pp. 461–474.

Vitak, J., Blasiola, S., Patil, S. and Litt, E. (2015), 'Balancing audience and privacy tensions on social network sites: Strategies of highly engaged users', *International Journal of Communication*, Vol. 9, pp. 1485–1504.

Vitak, J., Shilton, K. and Ashktorab, Z. (2016), 'Beyond the Belmont Principles: Ethical challenges, practices, and beliefs in the online data research community' *Proceedings of the 19th ACM Conference on Computer Supported Cooperative Work and Social Computing*, ACM, New York, NY, USA, pp. 941–953.

Vitak, J., Zube, P., Smock, A., Carr, C.T., Ellison, N. and Lampe, C. (2011), 'It's complicated: Facebook users' political participation in the 2008 election', *Cyberpsychology, Behavior, and Social Networking*, Vol. 14 No. 3, pp. 107–114.

Walther, J.B., Van Der Heide, B., Kim, S.-Y., Westerman, D. and Tong, S.T. (2008), 'The role of friends' appearance and behavior on evaluations of individuals on Facebook: Are we known by the company we keep?', *Human Communication Research*, Vol. 34 No. 1, pp. 28–49.

Wang, Y., Norcie, G., Komanduri, S., Acquisti, A., Leon, P.G. and Cranor, L.F. (2011), '"I regretted the minute I pressed share": A qualitative study of regrets on Facebook', *Proceedings of the Seventh Symposium on Usable Privacy and Security*, ACM, New York, NY, USA, pp. 10:1–10:16.

Weng, L. and Lento, T. (2014), 'Topic-based clusters in egocentric networks on Facebook', *Eighth International AAAI Conference on Weblogs and Social Media*, Washington DC: AAAI, pp. 623–626.

Wentz, B. and Lazar, J. (2011), 'Are separate interfaces inherently unequal?: An evaluation with blind users of the usability of two interfaces for a social networking platform', *Proceedings of the 2011 iConference*, ACM, New York, NY, USA, pp. 91–97.

Wilson, R.E., Gosling, S.D. and Graham, L.T. (2012), 'A review of Facebook research in the social sciences', *Perspectives on Psychological Science*, Vol. 7 No. 3, pp. 203–220.

Zhao, S., Grasmuck, S. and Martin, J. (2008), 'Identity construction on Facebook: Digital empowerment in anchored relationships', *Computers in Human Behavior*, Vol. 24 No. 5, pp. 1816–1836.

Zimmer, M. (2010), '"But the data is already public": On the ethics of research in Facebook', *Ethics and Information Technology*, Vol. 12 No. 4, pp. 313–325.

Big Data and Political Science: The Case of VKontakte and the 2014 Euromaidan Revolution in Ukraine

Anatoliy Gruzd[1] and Ben O'Bright[2]

This chapter explores the utility of social media user data, collected from the popular social networking platform VKontakte (VK), as supportive evidence for analysis of external social, economic and political relations, trends, and events. The authors ask whether there are demonstrable linkages between the user-defined location of an individual on VK, social connections between VK users, and their presence in platform-based public groups advocating a particular political position, specifically focusing on VK groups advocating pro- or anti-Euromaidan Square protests in Ukraine in 2014. From this VK user data, we demonstrate possibilities and limitations of its use in supporting analysis on politically important relations between countries and nation-states, namely: immigration, economics, conflict, linguistics, and culture. Simply put, this chapter asks: are the demographics and underlying social structures of relevant VK groups reflective of the latter high-level relations between nation-states?

INTRODUCTION

Increasingly, public media is dominated by discussions of the utility of social media-sourced data for use in policymaking, surveillance, marketing, and consumerism. Academic lag on the subject, however, remains endemic, making its utility in social science research seem elusive for those first broaching it. Methodologically speaking, political scientists have reacted to social media data analysis the same way they have in efforts at theoretical development: beginning the search for a grand approach. Taking a cue from comparative politics and their opportunistic approach for theoretical application, this chapter explores the utility of social media user data, collected from VKontakte (VK), a popular social networking platform in Eastern Europe, as indicative evidence of external social, economic and political relations, trends, and events. It fundamentally asks whether there are demonstrable, bidirectional linkages between the user-defined location of an individual user on VK, connections between VK users, and their presence in platform-based public group advocating a particular political position. In this instance, our research focused on VK groups advocating pro- or anti-Euromaidan Square protests in Ukraine in 2014. From this data, we outline the parameters of emerging scholarship on the use and potential of user demographics in VK groups in supporting analysis on high-level relations between countries and nation-states, namely immigration, economics, politics, linguistics and culture. Simply put, this chapter asks: are the demographics and underlining social structures of relevant VK groups reflective of the latter high-level relations between nation-states? The chapter begins with a literature review, followed by an outline of data collection and a lengthy, but brushstrokes discussion, on particular relationships between user groups on VK and political science topics.

SOCIAL BIG DATA, VKONTAKTE AND ANALYTICS

Although, as Resnick, Adar and Lampe (2015) accurately describe, social science has long been interested in patterns of media consumption and interpersonal communication; in the digital age, it has moved comparatively slowly toward the use of 'big data' in research methodologies. There tends to be a general scepticism about its use for testing and evidencing formal theoretical perspectives and causal explanations (boyd & Crawford, 2012). In contrast, Shah et al. (2015) suggest that the unprecedented availability of behavioural trace data from social media platforms provides new opportunities to garner insights on a range of political phenomena, despite not being representative of the entirety of a population. Indeed, big data is fundamentally here to stay, and its strongest contribution to political science will come when researchers embrace it on a broader scale, as well as the rigorous methods and theories of their social science discipline (Shah et al., 2015). Studies show that from the perspective of political institutions, agencies, and actors themselves, there is an ever-growing need to perpetually gather, monitor, analyze, summarize and visualize politically relevant information from digital and social media sources, with the goal of improving communications with citizens and voters, a trend that has been interrelated with the tremendous growth of individual participation in social media platforms (Stieglitz and Dang-Xuan, 2012). To ignore the potential of big data in predictive modelling, particularly for matters essential to the survival and functioning of the nation-state (i.e., high-politics), is to dismiss a significant transformation in our ability to understand and analyze contemporary political action, information production and dissemination, and user mobilization, which have been core to the study of political science for some time.

Monroe et al. (2015) argue that big data research taken as a whole includes a vast pluralism of scientific tasks, out-of-sample predictions, and inferential strategies than exist in a conventional social science toolkit. But much of big data is *social* data, that is, about the interactions between people, how they communicate, form relationships, and shape their future interactions through and with political institutions, themes, and events. As such, Monroe et al. conclude that big data is being shaped by social science, in as much as the latter is being tailored by the breadth and utility of the former. Indeed, they predict big data can induce three instrumental changes (i.e., possible benefits) to formal theory and causal analysis in political science: data from social media and other large repositories of user-generated information (1) can be treated inductively as a source of suggestive hypothesis to be tested empirically; (2) it can provide critical data on smaller subpopulations typically excluded from research for lack of appropriate sample size; and,

(3) it can provide evidence of user and individual behaviour previously difficult to observe (Monroe et al., 2015). This appears to be a difference in opinion from the late-2000s, when those such as Hindman and Chadwick proposed that political scientists were flailing in blind darkness, unable to understand the interrelationship between information and communication technologies (ICTs) and social science, relegating themselves to wild speculation based on grand predictions and a tendency towards technological determinism (Hindman, 2009; Chadwick, 2006).

Research has already begun to explore the use of social media data as a predictive measurement tool within the broad theme of political science, albeit not without some difficulty. DiGrazia et al. (2013) argued that in a study of 795 elections over two full election cycles, there was a positive correlation between amount of attention received by a candidate on Twitter and their relative vote share. A similar result was achieved in an analysis of election results in France and Italy, where a strong correlation existed between polling from social media and those of traditional surveys, demonstrating what the authors described as a 'remarkable ability for social media to forecast electoral results on average', (p. 353) both for single issue elections and those based on a wide range of preferences and political platforms (Ceron et al., 2014).

Social media has been employed more readily in the last half decade (in conjunction with the rapid diffusion of ICTs) for related but dispersed areas of social science analysis. Contrary to pervasive research in the early years of digital media, Gil de Zúñiga et al. (2012) suggest that informational use of social networking services can and do exert a significant and positive impact on individuals' activities engaging in civic and political action. Later, Colleoni et al. (2014) argued that depending on the measure of analysis utilized, Twitter is used both as an echo chamber and thus a strong source of political homophily development, as well as a medium for informational, public sphere-like engagement with opposing political perspectives. Similarly, Vitak et al. (2011), in their study focusing on youth participants in social media 'politics', argue that this demographic primarily uses social media like Facebook for low intensity informational political action, although there is a correlation between increased levels of this type of engagement with the advent of readily available digital tools. The above studies provide indication that means and methods of political action and engagement in a digitally-saturated world have shifted substantially from those established at the inauguration of Political Science, requiring at the very least a rethinking of disciplinary approaches to this research.

As noted, this chapter will review, in particular, the growing research on the use of VK, a popular social networking site (SNS) in Eastern Europe. Founded in 2006, the website's growing user base is now over 340 million user profiles and over 80 million average daily users (VK.com, 'About', 2016). The website is most popular in former Soviet Union republics including Russia and Ukraine. VK's user interface and features are similar to those of Facebook, whereby a user starts by creating a personal profile, which can be made public or private. As with Facebook, VK is a platform for connecting and building a social network via 'friending' other VK users and joining public or private groups of users with similar interests. VK also offers features for exchanging messages with other users via a private chat while encouraging users to 'like' and repost content on the platform.

Limited academic research has been generated specifically on the use of VK in high-level predictive political science analysis. There have, however, been a handful of direct and indirect efforts to study the prospects and qualities of VK data for social science research. For example, Duvanova et al. (2015) studied political polarization in Ukraine based on social connections formed on VK. Using the country's electoral map, the authors compared social connections formed among VK users before and after the 2012 presidential election in Ukraine. With the help of Social Network Analysis, they confirmed the increase of the polarization effect between VK users relatively to the 2011 pre-election period. Continuing, Sherstobitov and Bryanov (2013) studied connections formed among politically active groups on VK during the 2011–12 election cycle in Russia. The researchers first retrieved information on a sample of 50 pro-government and 50 opposition groups that were the largest based on the number of their members. Next, they created a network among these groups, showing what groups linked to what other groups in the network. The network analysis of both networks (pro- and anti-government) suggested that the opposition groups tend to be more connected which might also lead to the increase in the number of group members as more VK users learn about other relevant groups to join.

Beyond the above referenced studies, research relevant to this chapter's efforts becomes limited. In Pisarevskiy (2013), the author retrieved public user profiles to study demographic data of Orthodox users on VK, using sourced data from VK's ad service. Using a primarily qualitative methodology, Gorelik's (2013) study analyzed the official VK group of United Russia during the period of January 10–April 10, 2013. It used a content analysis method to establish and analyze instances of two-way communication between the members of the group and its moderators. Suleymanova (2009), focused on Tatars groups online, with specific emphasis on qualitative methods for identifying pathways of online and identity construction. Therefore, in response to the limited availability of knowledge on VK as a site of social science data collection, the authors seek to outline its effects in filling this gap.

METHODOLOGY

To answer the broad research question set above, we will rely on secondary data collected by Gruzd and Tsyganova (2015), who examined the use of VK to organize politically-motivated groups during the 2014 Euromaidan revolution in Ukraine. The researchers were interested in studying differences and similarities in how VK groups operate based on their political ideology. Based on a sample of the four largest online groups (two groups that supported the Euromaidan revolution and two that opposed it), they found some differences in how the groups on the opposite sides organized themselves, but most of the differences could be attributed either to the physical location of group members (e.g., anti-Euromaidan groups included more people from Russia) or to the groups' function (e.g., recruitment groups tended to be more centralized with few influential accounts controlling information flows in the group). For the remainder of this chapter, we will refer to the two pro-Euromaidan/pro-Western groups as PRO1 and PRO2 and to the two anti-Euromaidan/pro-Russian groups as ANTI1 and ANTI2, both wholly housed on the VK platform. It was hypothesized that via these datasets, evidence could emerge to aid in the answering of whether the high-level political divisions, between countries that supported the Euromaidan movement versus those that sided with pro-Russian activists would be visible in social media data collected through VK, indicating a possible utility for such data in supporting political science analysis.

The four selected VK groups were primarily chosen based on their explicitly political nature and content, as well as direct association with the conflict at the time in Ukraine, which had verifiably become globalized in its scope, action, membership, and support, particularly in regard to external state observation and diaspora support. The dataset was collected automatically using a custom-built script by querying VK's API (Application Program Interface) during a two-week period from May 25th, 2014 to June 11th, 2014.[3] VK's API allowed to collect the following data points about public groups and group members: posts, comments, likes, group members' friendship status as well as some

Table 38.1 Study dataset description

	PRO1	PRO2	ANTI1	ANTI2
Number of Users	141,542	96,402	60,506	69,029
Number of Friendship Connections	338,344	221,452	280,678	192,273
Group Founded	April 2014	January 2014	February 2014	December 2011

basic user profile information such as the date of birth, location, interests (for those users who made such information publically available). Data for this study was collected only when made publically accessible by user groups themselves, which are accessible by any outside actor without the need for a profile, account, or password. Specific user identities were not retained during this study. Table 38.1 summarizes the size of each group in terms of the number of users and connections.

ANALYSIS

Self-declared User Location Data

Our analysis of the VK data focused on the geographical distribution of group members from different countries. Based on their self-declared location information, the two largest groups of users for all four VK groups were from Ukraine and Russia. This is not surprising considering the nature of the targeted groups and the temporal period of data collection, which happened around the 2014 Euromaidan revolution in Ukraine (see Table 38.2). Also not surprisingly, for the two pro-Euromaidan groups, the percentage of members from Ukraine is substantially larger – 69.41% and 72.61% – as compared to 56.57% and 34.39% for the two anti Euromaidan groups. The difference in the group composition may be due to the different level of pro-Russian or pro-Ukrainian sentiments among group members.

The third largest group of users (and the second largest for PRO2) are those who were 'abnormal' in the sense of their online profiles do not specify their location (about 10–11%). It is possible that some of these accounts are spammers or so-called 'trolls' who joined one of the groups with malicious

Table 38.2 Top ranked countries based on the number of group members

Pro1 (% of users)		Pro2 (% of users)		Anti1 (% of users)		Anti2 (% of users)	
Ukraine	69.41	Ukraine	72.61	Ukraine	56.57	Russia	49.96
Russia	14.82	unknown/ undisclosed	12.34	Russia	29.55	Ukraine	34.39
unknown/ undisclosed	10.19	Russia	10.07	unknown/ undisclosed	10.26	unknown/ undisclosed	11.15
Belarus	1.58	Belarus	1.49	Belarus	0.61	Belarus	1.14
USA	1.01	USA	0.97	Kazakhstan	0.36	Kazakhstan	0.54
Kazakhstan	0.41	Germany	0.30	USA	0.36	USA	0.42
Germany	0.37	Poland	0.22	Germany	0.29	Germany	0.32
Italy	0.19	Italy	0.19	Israel	0.11	Moldova	0.14
Poland	0.17	Kazakhstan	0.19	Moldova	0.09	Spain	0.10
Spain	0.14	Spain	0.15	United Kingdom	0.09	Italy	0.08

intent. In fact, due to the open nature of these groups, most of the groups in the study either created a discussion thread or had an ongoing discussion among group members on how to handle trolls, users who joined their group to post inappropriate comments or comments that would openly question the group's objectives, or start a verbal fight with another group member. It is also possible that due to the political nature of these groups, some members might have created new accounts just to participate in the group. Future research is needed to interpret the nature of these accounts more definitively. In addition to users from Ukraine and Russia (and those without a location information), users from other countries represent only about 5–6% in each group case.

Country-to-Country Networks

To further investigate international connections among members of these groups, we converted the VK Friendship network to the Country-to-Country network, where nodes represent countries and ties between countries exist if there are friends who reside in these countries (see Figure 38.1). For example, if one user resides in Ukraine and another in Russia and they are 'friends' on VK, there will be a tie connecting Ukraine and Russia in this network. The weight assigned to each tie represents the number of 'friendship' ties that exist between each county pair.

Table 38.3 below shows the top countries ranked based on the scaled degree centrality in the Country-to-Country network for each group. The higher rank indicates that a particular country has more connections to other countries in the network. In other words, this means that more members from that country also have connections to group members from other countries. Based on the network configuration, the top countries are also likely to be connected to one another. In selecting countries for further analysis, we sought to explore first those states which, on the surface, appeared to fit within the international relation's dynamic of the conflict between Ukraine and Russia (including

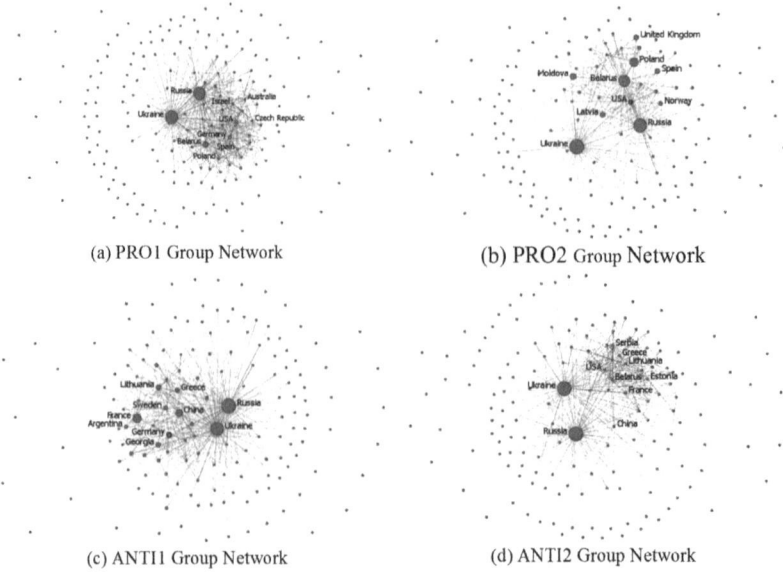

Figure 38.1 Country-to-Country networks

Table 38.3 Top ranked countries based on the degree centrality

Pro1		Pro2		Anti1		Anti2	
Ukraine	1.000	Ukraine	1.000	Ukraine	1.000	Russia	1.000
Russia	0.204	Russia	0.069	Russia	0.384	Ukraine	0.788
Belarus	0.026	Belarus	0.014	France	0.011	France	0.004
Germany	0.007	Poland	0.006	China	0.007	Serbia	0.004
USA	0.007	Moldova	0.003	Lithuania	0.004	USA	0.003
Poland	0.004	Spain	0.003	Germany	0.004	Estonia	0.003
Spain	0.003	United Kingdom	0.002	Greece	0.003	China	0.002
Israel	0.002	Latvia	0.002	Georgia	0.003	Lithuania	0.002
Czech Republic	0.001	USA	0.002	Sweden	0.002	Greece	0.002
Australia	0.001	Norway	0.001	Argentina	0.002	Belarus	0.002

these two countries respectively). Simply, the authors sought to initially analyze those states on the degree of centrality list whose position there made high-politics and diplomatic sense at face value. Additionally, we regard some examples of those states whose appearance on the list appeared odd or out of place, the outliers and difficult cases. While the authors were unable to explore all the high-politics relationships between the states in Table 38.3 and the protagonists in this particular conflict, testing both easy and difficult cases, rather than those of middle-range relevance, provides a spectrum of data applicability from social networking websites like VK to areas of political science analysis.

As Ukraine and Russia are the two largest countries in each dataset, it is expected that they will also have the most number of connections to other countries in the dataset. What may be less expected is the level with which Ukraine and Russia are scored according to the scaled degree centrality. For each country, we calculated the relative difference in their degree centralities. The country with the largest number of ties to other countries will have the scaled degree centrality equal to 1. The degree centrality values for the remaining countries will be calculated as a percentage of the first ranked country. In PRO1, Russia represents only 20% of the international ties relatively to the total number of international ties of users from Ukraine. But in PRO2, this percentage drops down to only 6.92%. This suggests that relative to members from Ukraine, members from Russia do not have as many friends from other countries in both VK groups. In case of PRO1, the 20% ratio is similar to the ratio of Ukrainian to Russian users (21%). This means that the smaller number of international ties can likely be explained by the smaller number of users from Russia in general. But the same cannot be said for PRO2, where the ratio of Ukrainian to Russian users is 16.99%, but the ratio of international ties is only 6.92% (2.46 times less). Considering that PRO2 is strongly pro-Euromaidan, the users that it attracts from Russia may be there to disagree with the group's motives and thus may have fewer friends in this group in general. Further analysis is needed to determine why PRO2 members from Russia are different from PRO1 members from Russia in this regard.

For ANTI1, the ratio of international ties for Russian users is 38%, 1.37 times less than the ratio of Ukrainian to Russian users (52%). The ratios for the ANTI2 is reversed since there are more members from Russia than Ukraine. The ratio of international ties for Ukrainian users is 79%, 1.15 times more than the ratio of Russian to Ukrainian users (68.84%). This suggests that Ukrainians in ANTI2 have more international ties relatively to their representation in the group than Russians in ANTI1.

Political, Foreign Policy, Social and Economic Data

In analyzing the data above further, we identify correlative relationships with various high-level political, foreign policy, social or economic events, to provide readers with an initial evidence base for the predictive qualities of social media data.

Immigration

We began first with immigration, matching public records of immigrant receptor states to the VK group data. In particular, we explored whether there is a relationship between being connected in the Country-to-Country network (Figure 38.1) and immigration trends. For the purposes of this chapter, we only examined the immigration rate from the most connected state in Figure 38.1 to the other highly connected states as calculated in Table 38.3. For example, since Ukraine is the most connected state in PRO1, we relied on the World Bank Data, to identify the number of people who immigrated from Ukraine to the other nine states listed in Table 38.3: Russia, Belarus, Germany, USA, Poland, Spain, Israel, Czech Republic, and Australia. The results are summarized in Table 38.4.

Overall, in many cases, there appears to be a strong association between immigration numbers (Table 38.4) and the presence of users from the top connected states in either the pro- or anti-Euromaidan group degree centrality list (Table 38.3). This does not, however, prove definitively that there exists a causal relationship between the two. Belarus, for example, appears fourth on all four top ranked country lists based on the number of group members (Table 38.2), matching its position as one of the highest receptor states for both Ukrainian and Russian immigrants, but at the same time Belarus is not among the top ten countries based on the degree centrality for ANTI1 and ANTI2.

We have also discovered a number of outlier states with a relatively low immigration rate (less than 10,000) as shown in Table 38.4, including Norway (in PRO2), China, Sweden, Argentina (in ANTI1), Serbia and China (in ANTI2). Explaining the presence of outliers will require the use of alternative explanatory variables.

Table 38.4 Immigration receptor states

Pro1		Pro2		Anti1		Anti2	
	< Source country (across)		< Source country (across)		< Source country (across)		< Source country (across)
Ukraine	Receptor (down)	Ukraine	Receptor (down)	Ukraine	Receptor (down)	Russia	Receptor (down)
Russia	2,939,083	Russia	2,939,083	Russia	2,939,083	Ukraine	3,453,506
Belarus	227,042	Belarus	227,042	France	15,236	France	47,984
Germany	230,000	Poland	221,307	China	1,437	Serbia	3,803
USA	376,852	Moldova	51,908	Lithuania	20,528	USA	438,458
Poland	221,307	Spain	80,679	Germany	230,000	Estonia	140,200
Spain	80,679	United Kingdom	22,527	Greece	14,174	China	9,714
Israel	137,472	Latvia	41,184	Georgia	25,044	Lithuania	99,224
Czech Republic	138,000	USA	376,852	Sweden	6,292	Greece	16,282
Australia	15,539	Norway	3,881	Argentina	5,335	Belarus	686,316

Source: World Bank, 2013 World Bank Database, available at: http://econ.worldbank.org/WBSITE/EXTERNAL/EXTDEC/EXTDECPROSPECTS/0,,contentMDK:22803131~page PK:64165401~piPK:64165026~theSitePK:476883,00.html

Finally, there are also a number of states that appear to be missing in our representative VK user group degree centrality list (Table 38.3) and the top-ranked countries based on the number of group members (Table 38.2), including Uzbekistan (189,709), Canada (69,048), Portugal (48,065), Azerbaijan (41,933), Hungary (31,632), Kyrgyz Republic (29,726), Turkmenistan (29,339) and Romania (11,903), which are destinations of choice for Ukrainian immigrants in particular.

The utility of VK group data for explaining high-level political topics and relations is thus limited by our ability to identify reasons behind this notable absence. Lack of user base on VK may be a factor in their failure to appear on our lists: limited VK market penetration and dominant alternative platforms, including Facebook and Twitter in predominantly English-speaking countries (Turu-uuringute, 2011; Alexa.com, 2015). More study of popular social media sites, as well as additional public groups on VK, will be required to explore this outlier country set further.

One of the most peculiar cases from the list of 'missing' states is Canada, which has the third-largest Ukrainian population outside Russia and Ukraine proper, estimated at 1.2 million Canadians of Ukrainian origin as of 2006 (Hudyma, 2011). Heritage Canada estimates that while in 1971 there were 309,900 Ukrainian speakers in Canada that number has since dropped to less than half at 134,500 in 2006. Hudyma notes that the rate of language shift for Ukrainians living in Canada (i.e. the shift from native language to majority language) is at 75% of the total. Indeed, and perhaps representative of the lack of Canada in the analysis of VK connections, the population most expected to use social media sites, only 20% of those between the ages of 15–20 wish to keep their mother tongue while 78% prefer to speak English or French, indicating that few fourth- and fifth-generation Ukrainians living in Canada have a strong commitment to the Ukrainian language (Hudyma, 2011), thereby limiting their ability to engage in VK discussions which are conducted predominantly in Ukrainian or Russian.

Political and Foreign Relations

As the current crisis revolves primarily around Ukraine and Russia, who have long, storied historical and political relations between them, it appears correlative that they occupy the top two positions for the degree centrality. Historical and political analysis, however, demonstrates that beyond the two antagonist countries of our study, other factors may help explain the presence of other particular states on our degree centrality lists. In the following section, we specifically examine the countries that are marked in red in Table 38.3 as they present the most interesting cases.

Poland in PRO1, PRO2

It is unsurprising, from a political relations perspective that Poland appears on both PRO1 and PRO2 degree centrality lists. While Ukraine has a history of subjugation and violence at the hands of Poland, the end of the Cold War and contemporary revolutions against authoritarianism has brought a strong sense of solidarity between the two countries (Kenney, 2014). Poland was one of the first countries, along with Canada, to recognize an independent Ukraine in 1991, and it has continued to be a leading advocate of closer ties between the latter and Brussels (*The Economist*, 2014). On February 19th 2014, opposition parties in Poland, in a rare instance of solidarity, united in their condemnation of Ukrainian authorities for inciting violence against protestors in Maidan Nezalezhnosti Square (*The Economist*, 2014). Poland has a special interest in Ukraine, as the two share a long border and similar languages, and large parts of Western Ukraine were once part of Poland prior to World War II (Lowe, 2014). Indeed, Polish Prime Minister, Donald Tusk, while fearing a similar incursion by Russian forces into his own formerly Soviet land, has argued that there can be no stable and secure Poland without the same in Ukraine (Lowe, 2014). This statement was manifest in September 2014, when Poland, Lithuania, and Ukraine formed a first-of-its-kind joint military unit numbering in the several thousands, in an effort to deter Russian expansionism (BBC News, 2015). The above could suggest that VK group composition, particularly during crisis events, may be indicative of existing cultural and historical relations between like-minded nation-states, particularly when the latter have similar antagonistic connections to a conflict belligerent. Polish users joining and participating in PRO-Euromaidan groups may be a digital expression of solidarity equally expressed at a high level in political statements and messages of support. Further research could support this supposition by interviews with individual Polish users in VK groups to identify subjective reasoning behind their joining.

Spain in PRO1, PRO2

Limited information exists on a political impetus behind Spanish presence in PRO1 and PRO2 degree centrality lists. Indeed, Spain enjoys nominally stronger political relations with Russia, signing several bilateral agreements with the latter in 2009. The European Council on Foreign Relations suggests that Spanish views on the Russia–Ukraine Crisis can be divided into several distinct categories. First, some Spanish commentary reflects their position as a Southern state member of the European Union (EU): it prioritizes Mediterranean issues over those in the Eastern Neighbourhood, but as many other large member states, including Germany and France, it wishes to avoid escalation in the crisis (de Borja Lasheras, 2014). Second, Spain is home to numerous geopolitical realists, akin to Kissinger, who understand Russian grievances as hugely important, but desire stability as a first and foremost goal for Europe (de Borja Lasheras, 2014). They tend to blame the EU for the current crisis by their attempts to bring Ukraine into Europe while ignoring Moscow's continuing influence in the state, and they are deeply suspicious of the West's attempts at soft containment (de Borja Lasheras, 2014). Third are the 'equidistants' those who believe that the EU made a considerable mistake in advocating and operationalizing sanctions, favouring instead dialogue and engagement with Russia, but whom remain generally pro-European (de Borja Lasheras, 2014). Fourth and fifth are the pro-Maidans and the Atlanticists respective, both of whom continue to be a minority within Spain and demand strong responses to Russian aggression (de Borja Lasheras, 2014). With this in mind, there seems to be limited political explanation for the Spanish presence in the PRO-Euromaidan lists, as one would expect either a division between the two halves (PRO/ANTI) or a stronger anti presence, if the above positional analysis by de Borja Lasheras is taken as true. As such, Spain is a representative data outlier, demonstrating that while the above correlation expressed for Poland could exist, other listed countries have seemingly few to no 'high-politics' reasons behind their presence. It showcases the difficulty in the application of big data to support political science theory and hypothesis; digital group participants may simply join because they want to at that particular moment. Without qualitative research interviews of identified users, research is left with an answer to the question of 'what is occurring?' but not 'why is it occurring?'

Belarus in PRO1, PRO2, ANTI2

Belarus and Ukraine have a long standing political relationship as a by-product of history. Both were part of the Polish–Lithuanian Commonwealth, the Second Polish Republic, the Russian Empire, and most recently, the Soviet Union (Savchenko, 2009). The contemporary political relationship between the two states can be said to begin in 1990 with the signing of a first-of-its-kind bilateral treaty, with recognition of each other based on common principles of sovereignty under international law and a recognition of their close historical, cultural, social and linguistic ties (Szeptycki, 2015). The two states, merely a year later, would partner with Russia to formally dissolve the USSR and create the Commonwealth of Independent States (Szeptycki, 2015). Events after the end of the Soviet Union, however, would set Belarus and Ukraine on two distinct political paths, straining foreign relations between them for some time to come: Ukraine would move towards Europe and democracy, while Belarus would fall to the authoritarian governance of Lukashenka and would subsequently draw closer to Russia (Szeptycki, 2015). After Lukashenka took office in July 1994, Belarus began to tighten relations with Russia, signing an Association agreement in 1996, then the Union of Belarus and Russia in 1999 (Szeptycki, 2015). According to Szeptycki, formal and informal ties and instruments have effectively allowed Russia to control the politics and foreign relations of its Belarusian neighbour, while the close ties with Russia simultaneously strengthened the position of authorities in Minsk (Szeptycki, 2015). Indeed, combined with polling in 2013 which suggests that 55% of Belarusians now have a positive impression of the EU, rising from 40% in 2008 (Bylina, 2013), it would appear that there are several key factors buried in the political history of the country which help account for its strong degree centrality. Circumstantial evidence suggests that historical political relations between Belarus and Ukraine, combined with contemporary positive perspectives of Europe, may help account for its degree centrality position in PRO1 and PRO2. The presence of Belarus in ANTI2, albeit to a much lower degree, may equally be partially explained by the historical and contemporary political relationships, including recent two distinct political and customs unions. That said, due to these physical and institutional linkages, one would expect Belarus to occupy a much higher position in the degree centrality rankings in ANTI2, as well as appear on the list for ANTI1. Thus, we can assume that other factors are also at play.

Germany in PRO1 and ANTI1

Germany appears midrange in both PRO1 and ANTI1 lists. With a cursory knowledge of Cold War history, one can understand that Germany has occupied a somewhat middle ground between East and West. Physically divided itself, Germany, in contemporary European affairs, has responded to crisis with a cool head and a near-neutral foreign policy position. Its place in the international response to the present Russian incursion into Ukraine mirrors this stance: while the West has opted for tough rhetoric, support for the Euromaidan movement, and economic sanctions, Germany has kept the phone lines open to Moscow (Evans, 2014). There are a number of additional causes likely behind this effort to keep diplomacy alive, as German firms maintain substantial economic interest in Russia, Ukraine is a mere ten hours from German territory if full-scale war breaks out, and Germany's economic health is substantially hampered by a significant dependence on Russian light-natural gas and crude oil (Evans, 2014). Additionally, the calls for a German leadership role in negotiating an end to the Ukrainian crisis have been strong in the U.S., European allies, and Ukraine itself (Meister, 2014). It is possible that this middle position in diplomatic affairs occupied by Germany has contributed to a similarly middle ground in our lists of degree centrality. The slight differential could be partially attributed to the firmer stance taken by Germany after August 2014 (two months after data collection) on Russian sanctions, however, there is no identified causality in this case (*The Guardian*, 'Threaten Russia', 2014).

Argentina in ANTI1

Argentina appears only once on our degree centrality lists: ANTI1. Recent warming of political relations between Argentina and

Russia may partially explain this occurrence. During the Cold War, Central and South America were largely cut off from Soviet influence, thanks to continued pressure from the United States. With the lifting of the Iron Curtain, however, that dynamic has certainly changed. According to the New York Times, Argentina has backed Russia's position on Ukraine, including defying trade sanctions imposed by the West, with the former offering support for Argentina's international legal dispute on the value of defaulted government bonds (Federman, 2014; Bosoer and Finchelstein, 2014). In July 2014, Russia signed a number of nuclear energy agreements with the Argentinian Government, infusing much-needed foreign direct investment into the Latin American country's economy which has suffered after investors this year rejected its debt restructuring plans (BBC News, 'Nuclear Deals', 2014). Warming relations have also translated into an interstate treaty in 2014 on mutual legal assistance in criminal matters including transfer of persons, a communications agreement which will see Russia's state-owned media outlet Russia Today being broadcast in Spanish in Argentina, and an agreement to host Russian military bases in-country (Nelson, 2014; TASS, 2014). Criticism of the U.S., along broad foreign policy lines, have been curiously similar from both Russia and Argentina, again indicating warming relations between the two states (Federman, 2014). This new political relationship, paralleled by limited South American engagement by the US, may indeed help explain Argentina's position on the ANTI1 degree centrality list.

China in ANTI1, ANTI2

Several reports agree that Chinese silence on the Ukrainian crisis has supported its emergence in a substantially advantageous position. As the West and Russia face off in Ukraine, China has been able to secure a long-delayed gas deal with Russia, Chinese companies have expanded into upstream Russo-energy projects, oil imports for China are set to increase and well as prospects for new arms deals (Perlez, 2014). Russia and China still have substantial economic and political competition between each other, but for the moment, their presence in the ANTI categories can be partially explained by a partnership forged on the basis of a common political antagonist, the U.S., and Chinese diplomacy-facilitated economic gains as Russia continues to be cut off from traditional export destinations for its natural resources (Yeung, 2014; Brugier and Popescu, 2014).

In addition to the political and foreign relations discussed above, we also investigated economic and development aid factors such as import/export destinations and development aid levels based on the data provided by the Organization for Economic Cooperation and Development (OECD). However, no definitive relationship between these factors and patterns in social media data was found.

DISCUSSION

More generally, we were unable to find strong correlative or causal patterns between VK data and the high-level political events and actions detailed in this chapter. This may be a result of a number of limitations associated with the use of social media data in predictive analysis. Gayo-Avello et al. (2011) argue there are instances when researchers have tended to treat social media as a black box: data mined from its annals may give one the right answer, regardless of whether you understand why that is the case. Shah et al. (2015) term these Type I errors, or false discoveries, where inferential relationships are deemed to exist, particularly in cases where large samples make insignificant findings seem meaningful because they achieve conventional statistically significant thresholds, despite those relationships not existing at all. For political polling in particular, the authors argue that while professional pollsters traditionally build their samples from 'likely voters', or those who had voted in previous elections, limited available methodology exists to obtain similar user profile information for social media data collection (Gayo-Avello, et al., 2011). A parallel difficulty would likely exist in the use of social media data for prediction and analysis in high-politics areas, although future research would do well to study whether closed-social networks have a higher degree of authenticity and a greater array of available user profile traits for use in countering this difficulty in polling using information collected from open platforms like Twitter or public VK groups such as those examined in our study. As noted in this chapter's methodology section, the problem of spammers, fake accounts and trolling is a pervasive issue in social media data collection (Gayo-Avello, et al., 2011). Future research would do well to identify qualitative and quantitative markers for troll accounts, so as to remove them and their contributions from data collection. Psychosocial analysis of personality characteristics may be effective in this regard, as found in the works of Buckels et al. (2014), Shachaf and Hara (2010), and Shin (2008).

In a similar vein to Gayo-Avello, Clark and Golder (2015) argue that political scientists should not treat big data and causal inference as substitutes; there is nothing about increasing the number of observations or variables in a dataset that solves the basic problem of trying to understand how an outcome would change if a causal variable were to change, while everything else remained constant. Keele argues that inherent to big data use, bias can grow in a researcher as sample sizes increase with observational data, ending with a 'very precisely estimated highly biased effect where the confidence intervals may no longer include the true value' (Clark and Golder, 2015, p. 66). To address this issue, some researchers have advocated for using and reporting a complimentary measure of significance called 'effect size', which in case of big data may be a better representation of the strength of the observed outcome. See a detailed discussion on the use of 'effect size' in Lin et al. (2013) and Kelley & Preacher (2012).

Hargittai (2015) equally points to the difficulty in sampling frames, referring to the units of a population that can be sampled for a study. When big data studies in political science sample a particular platform, the only people whose opinions and actions are being represented are those who at some point in the past opted to join and use the particular site or service in question. Fundamentally and structurally, this excludes anyone who has not and does not use the platform. It would be incorrect at this point to assume that volume of data points, for instance a million tweets or thousands of VK group posts, would be enough to circumvent the limitations of sample frames. Simply, if individuals have not chosen to use a particular site, then findings are rarely able to be generalized beyond the site's population, because entire groups are excluded from study (Hargittai, 2015). Overcoming this limitation is, in part, an objective of this chapter. Hargittai (2015) suggests a related problem, and one additionally broached in this chapter, is the lack of data from social media mining on actions undertaken by users offline, or on other platforms. Indeed, one user might espouse a pro-Euromaidan position on VK, and a subsequent pro-separatist view on Twitter. Support for Ukrainian sovereignty might occur online, but a migration to Russia offline. Indeed, in identifying possible conclusions and observations from its data collection and analysis, this chapter must be wary of the above pervasive, and sometimes endemic, difficulties with causal inference and prediction with social media data.

FUTURE RESEARCH

The above, while providing substantial information on possible answers to this chapter's questions, remains only an initial first step. Each of the categories presented have briefly been touched upon, with all meriting their own in-depth analysis on the predictive qualities of social media group and user data. Indeed, none of the above should be taken as the final word on this topic.

Instead, and as is the case with most social science research, we end this chapter with more questions than answers. In responding to these remaining queries, future research can begin the establishment of a firm base upon which to further explore the utility of VK data in social science study. First, can and does international political rhetoric between states reflected in online networks, groups, and interaction? Second, does or can the presence of internal independence movements, including those within Israel, Moldova and United Kingdom, have an influence on their VK user base's perspectives on the pro Euromaidan movement? Third, what impact does temporary migration patterns, including international students, have on the demographic characteristics of VK user groups, and what are the repercussions for the validity of collected data in applying it in quantitative analysis? Fourth, do expatriate communities in destination states have a demonstrable impact on the message content, user demographics, or other observable characteristics in VK user groups? Fifth, what are the broad-based implications of a potential limited predictive ability from social media group demographics? And finally, if our argument is reversed, can international events, actors, and relations help predict the demographics and social structures of social media groups?

As digital medium development speeds rapidly forward, the search for a grand methodology and theory for data analysis and function seems to be a rather futile endeavour. Instead authors and researchers should perhaps follow the opportunistic guidelines of comparative political scientists; applying available methods and data on an as-needed basis, in relation to a particular event, trend, or case. If the topic of study changes as such an expeditious pace, there is little logical sense in developing a standardized but stagnant, overarching methodological approach.

In this regard, the preceding study offered a glimpse into the possible linkages between social media data from VK, and its application to political and social science subjects. Our efforts were opportunistic, preliminary, and resulted in limited correlative conclusions. But, they were also the first steps along a long, winding road, one which may never reach a final destination.

NOTES

1 Dr. Anatoliy Gruzd is a Canada Research Chair in Social Media Data Stewardship, Associate Professor and Director of the Social Media Lab in the Ted Rogers School of Management at Ryerson University (Toronto, Canada). He is also a co-editor of a multidisciplinary journal on Big Data and Society. Dr. Gruzd's research initiatives explore how the advent of social media and the growing availability of social big data are changing the ways in which people communicate, collaborate and disseminate information and how these changes impact the social, economic and political norms and structures of modern society. Email: gruzd@ryerson.ca

2 Ben O'Bright is a PhD candidate at Dalhousie University, in Halifax, Nova Scotia. His research focuses on the politics and governance of emerging technologies, particularly in international development. Ben holds an MSc from the London School of Economics and Political Science in the Politics and Government of the European Union. He is currently a student researcher with the Centre on Governance at the University of Ottawa. Email: benobright@dal.ca

3 The original analysis presented in this chapter relied on secondary data, initially collected for and used in Gruzd and Tsyganova (2015). We thank the Center for Sociological and Internet Research at Saint Petersburg State University (Russia), and especially Ksenia Tsyganova and Dmitri Tsyganov, for developing a VK API client and allowing us to use the VK dataset for this study.

REFERENCES

Alexa.com. 2015. 'Top Sites in Italy 201–225'. Amazon 2015. Data retrieved 10 March 2015 http://www.alexa.com/topsites/countries;8/IT.

Alexa.com. 'Top Sites in Romania 201–225'. Amazon 2015. Data retrieved 10 March 2015 http://www.alexa.com/topsites/countries;8/RO.

BBC News. 2015. 'Poland, Ukraine and Lithuania Form Joint Military Unit'. Accessed July 20, 2015. http://www.bbc.com/news/world-europe-29284548.

BBC News. 2014. 'Putin Signs Argentina Nuclear Deals on Latin America Tour'. Accessed July 20, 2015. http://www.bbc.com/news/world-latin-america-28261746.

Bosoer, Fabián, and Federico Finchelstein. 2014. 'Russia Today, Argentina Tomorrow'. *The New York Times*, October 21. http://www.nytimes.com/2014/10/22/opinion/russia-today-argentina-tomorrow.html.

boyd, danah, and Kate Crawford. 2012. 'Critical Questions for Big Data'. *Information, Communication & Society* 15(5): 662–79. doi:10.1080/1369118X.2012.678878.

Brugier, Camille, and Nicu Popescu. 2014. 'Ukraine: The View from China'. European Union Institute for Security Studies. http://www.iss.europa.eu/uploads/media/Alert_17_Ukraine_China.pdf.

Buckels, Erin E., Paul D. Trapnell, and Delroy L. Paulhus. 2014. 'Trolls Just Want to Have Fun'. *Personality and Individual Differences* 67: 97–102.

Bylina, Vadzim. 'New Poll: Belarusians Became More Pro-European'. 2013 *Belarus Digest: News and Analytics on Belarusian Politics, Economy, Human Rights and More*. Accessed July 20, 2015. http://belarusdigest.com/story/new-poll-belarusians-became-more-pro-european-16062.

Ceron, Andrea, Luigi Curini, Stefano M. Iacus, and Giuseppe Porro. 2014. 'Every Tweet Counts? How Sentiment Analysis of Social Media Can Improve Our Knowledge of Citizens' Political Preferences with an Application to Italy and France'. *New Media & Society* 16(2): 340–358. doi:10.1177/1461444813480466.

Chadwick, Andrew. 2006. *Internet Politics: States, Citizens, and New Communication Technologies*. Oxford, United Kingdom: Oxford University Press.

Clark, William Roberts, and Matt Golder. 2015. 'Big Data, Causal Inference, and Formal Theory: Contradictory Trends in Political Science?' *PS: Political Science & Politics* 48(01): 65–70. doi:10.1017/S1049096514001759.

Colleoni, Elanor, Alessandro Rozza, and Adam Arvidsson. 2014. 'Echo Chamber or Public Sphere? Predicting Political Orientation and Measuring Political Homophily in Twitter Using Big Data'. *Journal of Communication* 64(2): 317–332. doi:10.1111/jcom.12084.

De Borja Lasheras, Francisco. June 2014. 'Four Spanish Factions on Russia and Ukraine'. *European Council on Foreign Relations – Commentary*. Accessed 25 July 2015. http://www.ecfr.eu/article/commentary_spain_on_russia_and_ukraine_the_understanders_the_equidistan274.

DiGrazia, Joseph, Karissa McKelvey, Johan Bollen, and Fabio Rojas. 2013. 'More Tweets, More Votes: Social Media as a Quantitative Indicator of Political Behavior'. *PLoS ONE* 8(11): e79449. doi:10.1371/journal.pone.0079449.

Duvanova, Dinissa, Alexander Semenov, and Alexander Nikolaev. 2015. 'Do Social Networks Bridge Political Divides? The Analysis of VKontakte Social Network Communication in Ukraine'. *Post-Soviet Affairs* 31(3): 224–249. doi:10.1080/1060586X.2014.918453.

Economist, The. 2014. 'Neighbours and Brothers', March 3. http://www.economist.com/blogs/easternapproaches/2014/03/poland-and-ukraine.

Embassy of the Ukraine in the United States. 'The State of Trade and Economic Relations and Investment Between the United States and Ukraine'. *Government of Ukraine* 2012. 10 March 2015. http://usa.mfa.gov.ua/en/ukraine-us/trade.

Evans, Stephen. 2014. 'Ukraine Crisis: Germany's Russian Conundrum'. *BBC News*. Accessed July 20, 2015. http://www.bbc.com/news/world-europe-26440560.

Federman, Andrés. 2014. 'The Russian Question'. *The Buenos Aires Herald*. Accessed July 20, 2015. http://www.buenosairesherald.com/article/173177/.

Foreignassistance.gov. 'U.S. Foreign Assistance'. Government of the United States of America 2015. Data retrieved 10 March 2015. http://www.foreignassistance.gov/web/OU.aspx?OUID=194&FY=2013&AgencyID=0&budTab=tab_Bud_Planned.

Gayo Avello, Daniel, Panagiotis T. Metaxas, and Eni Mustafaraj. 2011. 'Limits of Electoral Predictions Using Twitter'. In *Proceedings of* the Fifth International AAAI Conference on Weblogs and Social Media. Association for the Advancement of Artificial Intelligence. http://digibuo.uniovi.es/dspace/handle/10651/11899.

Gil de Zúñiga, Homero, Nakwon Jung, and Sebastián Valenzuela. 2012. 'Social Media Use for News and Individuals' Social Capital, Civic Engagement and Political Participation'. *Journal of Computer-Mediated Communication* 17(3): 319–336. doi:10.1111/j.1083-6101.2012.01574.x.

Gorelik, Stas. 2013. *United by Inattention?: A Study of the Official Group of the Party United Russia on the Social Network VKontakte*. http://kau.diva-portal.org/smash/record.jsf?pid=diva2:637821.

Gruzd, Anatoliy, and Ksenia Tsyganova. 2015. 'Information Wars and Online Activism During the 2013/2014 Crisis in Ukraine: Examining the Social Structures of Pro- and Anti-Maidan Groups'. *Policy & Internet* 7(2): 121–158. doi:10.1002/poi3.91.

Guardian, The. 2014 'US and Germany Threaten Russia with "Additional Consequences" over Ukraine'. Accessed July 20, 2015. http://www.theguardian.com/world/2014/aug/09/us-and-germany-threaten-russia-with-additional-consequences-over-ukraine.

Hargittai, Eszter. 2015. 'Is Bigger Always Better? Potential Biases of Big Data Derived from Social Network Sites'. *The ANNALS of the American Academy of Political and Social Science* 659 (1): 63–76. doi:10.1177/0002716215570866.

Hindman, Matthew. 2009. *The Myth of Digital Democracy*. Princeton: Princeton University Press.

Hudyma, Khrystyna. 2011. 'Ukrainian Language in Canada: From Prosperity to Extinction?' *Working Papers of the Linguistics Circle* 21(1): 181–189.

Kelley, Ken, and Kristopher J. Preacher. 2012. 'On Effect Size'. *Psychological Methods* 17(2): 137–152. doi:10.1037/a0028086.

Kenney, Padraic. 2014. 'Why Poland Cares So Much About Ukraine'. *The New York Times*, March 9. http://www.nytimes.com/2014/03/10/opinion/why-poland-cares-so-much-about-ukraine.html.

Lin, Mingfeng, Henry C. Lucas, and Galit Shmueli. 2013. 'Too Big to Fail: Large Samples and the P-Value Problem'. *Information Systems Research* 24(4): 906–917. doi:10.1287/isre.2013.0480.

Lowe, Christian. 2014 'In Ukraine, Poland Comes of Age as an EU Power Broker'. *Reuters UK*. Accessed July 20, 2015. http://uk.reuters.com/article/2014/02/24/uk-ukraine-crisis-poland-idUKBREA1N1BY20140224.

Meister, Stefan. April, 2014. 'Reframing Germany's Russia Policy – An Opportunity for the EU'. *European Council on Foreign Relations* – Policy Brief. London: ECFR.

Monroe, Burt, Jennifer Pan, Margaret Roberts, Maya Sen, and Betsy Sinclair. 2015. 'No! Formal Theory, Causal Inference, and Big Data Are Not Contradictory Trends in Political Science'. *PS: Political Science and Politics* 48(1): 71–74.

Nelson, Jerry. 2014 'Argentina to Host Russian Military Bases While America Sleeps'. *Guardian Liberty Voice*. Accessed July 20, 2015. http://guardianlv.com/2014/03/argentina-to-host-russian-military-bases-while-america-sleeps/.

OEC: Estonia (EST) Profile of Exports, Imports and Trade Partners. 2015. Accessed July 20. https://atlas.media.mit.edu/en/profile/country/est/.

OEC: France (FRA) Profile of Exports, Imports and Trade Partners. 2015. Accessed July 20. https://atlas.media.mit.edu/en/profile/country/fra/.

OEC: Latvia (LVA) Profile of Exports, Imports and Trade Partners. 2015. Accessed July 20. https://atlas.media.mit.edu/en/profile/country/lva/.

OEC: Moldova (MDA) Profile of Exports, Imports and Trade Partners. 2015. Accessed July 20. https://atlas.media.mit.edu/en/profile/country/mda/.

OEC: Russia (RUS) Profile of Exports, Imports and Trade Partners. 2015. Accessed July 20. https://atlas.media.mit.edu/en/profile/country/rus/.

OEC: Serbia (SRB) Profile of Exports, Imports and Trade Partners. 2015. Accessed July 20. https://atlas.media.mit.edu/en/profile/country/srb/.

OEC: Ukraine (UKR) Profile of Exports, Imports and Trade Partners. 2015. Accessed July 20. https://atlas.media.mit.edu/en/profile/country/ukr/.

OECD. 'OECD.Stat'. *Organization for Economic Cooperation and Development* 2015. Data retrieved 10 March 2015. http://stats.oecd.org/.

Perlez, Jane. 2014. 'Ukraine Conflict Has Been a Lift for China, Scholars Say'. *Sinosphere Blog*. Accessed July 20, 2015. http://sinosphere.blogs.nytimes.com/2014/09/01/ukraine-conflict-has-been-a-lift-for-china-scholars-say/.

Pisarevskiy, V. 2013. 'The Analysis of Orthodox Internet Audience as Exemplified in the Social Network "VKONTAKTE"'. Известия высших учебных заведений. Поволжский регион. Общественные науки 3 (27). http://cyberleninka.ru/article/n/analiz-pravoslavnoy-internet-auditorii-na-primere-sotsialnoy-seti-vkontakte.

Resnick, Paul, Eytan Adar, and Cliff Lampe. 2015. 'What Social Media Data We Are Missing and How to Get It'. *The ANNALS of the American Academy of Political and Social Science* 659(1): 192–206. doi:10.1177/0002716215570006.

Savchenko, Andrew. 2009. *Belarus: A Perpetual Borderland*. BRILL.

Shachaf, Pnina, and Noriko Hara. 2010. 'Beyond Vandalism: Wikipedia Trolls'. *Journal of Information Science* 36(3): 357–370.

Shah, Dhavan V., Joseph N. Cappella, and W. Russell Neuman. 2015. 'Big Data, Digital Media, and Computational Social Science Possibilities and Perils'. *The ANNALS of the American Academy of Political and Social Science* 659(1): 6–13. doi:10.1177/0002716215572084.

Sherstobitov, A. S., and Bryanov, K. A. 2013. 'Political mobilization technologies in social network "VKONTAKTE": network analysis of protest and pro-regime segments'. *Historical, Philosophical, Political and Legal Sciences, Cultural Studies and Art History - Theory and Practice*. 10, 1. 196–202.

Shin, Jiwon. 2008. Morality and Internet Behavior: A study of the Internet Troll and its relation with morality on the Internet. In K. McFerrin, R. Weber, R. Carlsen & D. Willis (Eds.), *Proceedings of Society for Information Technology & Teacher Education International Conference 2008* (pp. 2834–2840). Chesapeake, VA: Association for the Advancement of Computing in Education (AACE).

Statistics Canada. 'Table 1 – Size and Percentage of Population that Reported Speaking One of the Top 12 Immigrant Languages Most Often at Home in the Six Largest Census Metropolitan Areas, 2011'. *Government of Canada* 2011. July 22 2015. http://www12.statcan.ca/census-recensement/2011/as-sa/98-314-x/2011001/tbl/tbl1-eng.cfm.

Stieglitz, Stefan, and Linh Dang-Xuan. 2012. 'Social Media and Political Communication: A Social Media Analytics Framework'. *Social Network Analysis and Mining* 3(4): 1277–1291. doi:10.1007/s13278-012-0079-3.

Suleymanova, Dilyara. 2009. 'Tatar Groups in VKontakte'. *Digital Icons*, no. 2. http://www.digitalicons.org/issue02/dilyara-suleymanova/.

Szeptycki, Andrzej. 2015. 'Relations Between Ukraine and the Republic of Belarus: The Present Conditions, Status Quo and Perspectives'. Polish Institute of International Affairs. Accessed March 15. http://mercury.ethz.ch/serviceengine/Files/ISN/93292/ipublicationdocument_singledocument/1d70319f-e615-4ce1-861c-eed729f5ae88/en/2006_1.pdf.

TASS. 2014. 'Russia, Argentina Sign Several Documents on Strengthening Cooperation'. Accessed July 20, 2015. http://tass.ru/en/russia/740283.

Turu-uuringute, A.S. (2011). Eestimaalaste Sotsiaalmeedia Kasutamine (The Use of Social Media amongst the Estonian population). Study commissioned by Taevas Ogilvy and conducted by Turu- uuringute.

Vitak, Jessica, Paul Zube, Andrew Smock, Caleb T. Carr, Nicole Ellison, and Cliff Lampe. 2011. 'It's Complicated: Facebook Users' Political Participation in the 2008 Election'. *Cyberpsychology, Behavior and Social Networking* 14(3): 107–114. doi:10.1089/cyber.2009.0226.

VK.com. 2016. 'About'. available at <https://vk.com/about?w=page-47200950_44237911>.

Weisman, Jonathan, and David S. Joachim. 2014. 'Congress Approves Aid of $1 Billion for Ukraine'. *The New York Times*, March 27. http://www.nytimes.com/2014/03/28/world/europe/senate-approves-1-billion-in-aid-for-ukraine.html.

Yeung, Brian. 'Ukraine Pushes China and Russia Together | Opinion'. 2014. *The Moscow Times*. Accessed July 20, 2015. http://www.themoscowtimes.com/opinion/article/ukraine-pushes-china-and-russia-together/504904.html.

A Retrospective on State of the Art Social Media Research Methods: Ethical Decisions, Big-small Data Rivalries and the Spectre of the 6Vs

Luke Sloan and Anabel Quan-Haase

This concluding chapter offers critical reflections on some of the key themes covered in the Handbook. Ethics emerged as a concern for many scholars, both for those engaging in quantitative and qualitative approaches. Scholars agree in that there is no overarching set of rules that can be applied to all projects blindly, rather they see ethical decisions as being grounded in the specifics of the data being collected, the social group under study, and the potential repercussions for subjects. A second central theme was the value of qualitative approaches for understanding 'anomalies' within larger data sets. Qualitative approaches are seen as valuable and a stand-alone means of collecting, analyzing and making sense of social media data, in particular for projects where context is essential. Finally, as the contributions in this volume demonstrate that many of the challenges posed by the nature of social media data are being tackled and addressed, this chapter ends with a reorientation of the 6Vs which focuses on the primacy of the researcher in the decision-making process. We argue that the provision of technical solutions alone do not entirely address the 6V problem and clarity of thought around research design is still just as important as ever.

INTRODUCTION

The SAGE Handbook of Social Media Research Methods brings together over 50 authors from a wide range of disciplines and scholarly traditions. This makes the Handbook truly interdisciplinary, drawing on approaches focusing on large-scale quantification to studies that stress the relevance of single cases and anomalies. It is this diversity that gives the Handbook depth and relevance and provides new perspectives and insights into the study of social media research methods. The Handbook demonstrates that social media methodology is not only about big data, but how qualitative work is also developing quickly and leaving a mark on the field. It would also be inaccurate to say that the interdisciplinary nexus between the social and computing sciences is solely oriented around a positivist paradigm as clearly the challenges around collecting, collating and handling qualitative data on social media require researchers from all backgrounds to collaborate. Further, neither quantitatively nor qualitatively-oriented scholars can simply apply the traditional approaches developed in their disciplines to the study of social media phenomena. Rather, scholars are challenged to rethink conventional approaches and reorient themselves toward the new dimensionalities inherent in these kinds of data. This creates a real need for the development of innovative methodological approaches that are uniquely suited to social media environments.

This concluding chapter identifies several key threads that weave throughout the Handbook. We discuss ethical considerations first as one central theme that is of importance to many chapters and is considered by many scholars to still be unresolved. We briefly show what ethical issues are of most pressing relevance and ways of moving forward. We then examine the growing popularity of qualitative approaches to the study of social media. The range of approaches is astonishing, borrowed and adapted from established qualitative traditions. These approaches are singled out as not only countering big data approaches – often criticized for flattening data, losing context, and stressing large-scale trends at the expense of an individual's experiences – but also as providing unique insights into 'anomalies' that would go unnoticed in large-scale scholarship (Bradley, 1993). This leads to the third central theme which focuses on the development of multi-method approaches that integrate big data analytics and small-scale studies. Regardless of whether the quantitative techniques follow the qualitative ones or vice versa, either process can be used to better illustrate current trends that are demonstrated in the initial data set and gain contextualization and reach deeper meaning. These kinds of approaches are not only time-consuming, but also require the formation of interdisciplinary teams that can bring to bear expertise on different approaches to data collection and analysis. We end the chapter with a discussion of the challenges surrounding the 6Vs first brought up in the introductory chapter. Having demonstrated throughout the book that the technical solutions to the 6V problem exist, we return to the essential agency of the researcher and the additional considerations we need to reflect on when tackling this new form of data for social scientific enquiry.

ETHICS IN BIG DATA AND SMALL DATA

Ethical considerations emerged as a strong theme in discussions related to the handling of social media data. It was evident that traditional considerations and guidelines regarding ethics were not applicable to the new challenges that social media environments present. This is directly linked to the kinds of approaches developing in social media scholarship including tools for data collection that harvest information at new scales in terms of the 6Vs discussed in the introductory chapter and revisited later in this concluding chapter (i.e., *volume*, *variety*, *velocity*, *veracity*, *virtue*, and *value*). On one hand, scholars are calling for tighter regulations and more intense debate around ethical standards (Goel, 2014). On the other hand, scholars suggest that research involving social media data may not require as rigorous an ethics and consent regime as other types of research because data are publicly available and studies will often involve 'minimal risk' to participants (Grimmelmann, 2015).

What complicates the decision-making around ethics is that no pre-established set of rules or guidelines can be applied to all projects. For Beninger (Chapter 5, this volume), discussions around ethics cannot be boiled down to a checklist, but must instead take the entire research process into account including issues such as the topic under investigation, the time period of data collection, the participants to be included, and the sensitivity of the content. She contends that decisions around whether to seek consent from individuals who have posted content to public sites are closely linked with the nature of the content under study and the potential repercussions disclosure can have for research subjects. (see also Townsend and Wallace 2016).

Regardless of whether there is high or low risk to participants, it is clear that existing ethical guidelines and practices are not readily applicable because social media data blur the lines between public and private spheres. Social networking sites (SNSs) contain information intended for a specific network audience consisting of a mix of close and distant ties and thus is not *truly* public, even if users do have an understanding that a wider network of 'friends' can see, and interact with, this content. Recently, boyd and Crawford (2012) have also drawn attention to the fact that even data that is *truly* public, such as data posted on a Twitter timeline from a non-private account, may not be intended for further use by those who originally created the data. In short, how do social media scholars know that users are consenting to their data being utilized and analyzed in ways they cannot predict? Where in a research design is the traditional standard of consent being addressed? The networked nature of data on social media sites also presents new challenges for researchers. Consent obtained from one participant does not automatically transfer to individuals interacting with that participant. Thus, new questions emerge around what data can be collected and included in a study. This problem of boundary specification is characteristic of all data produced in social media platforms and extends to likes, comments, and retweets of content (Quan-Haase & McCay-Peet, 2016).

Issues of anonymity also arise in deliberations about ethics. In this regard, there is considerable disagreement within the scholarly community as to what strategy is the most ethically sound. At the center of this debate lies the question of whether publicly available data is by default *public* and hence can be examined by scholars for research purposes (Stewart, Chapter 16, this volume; boyd & Crawford, 2012). From a participant's point of view, anonymizing the collected data would most likely represent the lowest risk in terms of associating content with a particular person/account. A common practice for reviewers during the peer-review process of a social media project is to request the anonymization of all data. In some instances, this may be a reasonable expectation, but one that is also associated with data loss. If key players – for example, Google's Twitter account, the Twitter account of the US Republican candidate, Donald Trump, or of celebrity figure Kim Kardashian West – cannot be recognized in the data set, this would preclude scholars from drawing specific interpretations based on the social status of these key players and the role they play in society. To complicate things further, for some platforms such as Twitter, anonymizing data violates the terms and conditions of use. So, decisions around anonymity create tensions between the right of users to protect their privacy and the ability of scholars to draw conclusions based on their data.

Zeller (Chapter 23, this volume) specifically points out that not all data sets available online are indeed *public*. For instance, the website Ashley Madison was created to romantically connect married individuals (it basically helped people cheat). The service had around 40 million users in 2015 when the site was hacked and data on user accounts were retrieved and posted online for anyone to access (Dreyfuss, 2015). Similarly, the service Snapchat was reportedly also hacked, often via third party apps (Eng, 2014). Snapchat users consider this kind of data to be ephemeral and non-retrievable (Bayer et al., 2015), but it can still be available on a company server or via a third-party app. Zeller (Chapter 23, this volume) notes that scholars have the responsibility to assess the origins of data sets and the nature of consent given by users. While data may be publicly available online, if it has been obtained illegally, it may not conform to the standards of scholarly ethical practice. Nonetheless, it is not always clear where the boundaries lie, as data sets may be of public interest, but illegally obtained, increasing researchers' uncertainty around the usage for research purposes.

Hargittai (2015) highlights the problem of the representativeness of the big data sets available through SNSs. She points out that 'if people do not select into the use of the particular site randomly, then findings cannot be generalized beyond the site's population' (p. 65) because those who are not members of the site may vary from those who are in ways that are of relevance to the research being undertaken. Indeed, Sloan et al. (2015) demonstrate that, for UK Twitter users, it appears that the distributions of tweeter age, occupation and class are not representative of the wider population and that those who enable geotagging are not demographically identical to users who do not (Sloan & Morgan, 2015). This links to yet another ethical dilemma as the absence of certain groups from social media violates ethical principles of inclusivity. Conversely, concerns can arise about representation in small data projects as individuals may be more easily identifiable and reporting such data compromises anonymity.

The most controversial discussion around ethics so far is that which surrounds collaborations between academic and corporate researchers. For Vitak (Chapter 37, this volume), the trigger for much concern emerged from the publication of large-scale studies by Facebook's Data Science Team in collaboration with academics (e.g., Das and Kramer, 2013; Kramer et al., 2014). Users were often not informed about the study either before it took place or after its completion and, as a result, Vitak contends, average Facebook users who served as subjects 'felt uncomfortable not knowing what was going on 'behind the scenes' at the company' (p. 634). This led to an outcry in the media regarding the ethical practices of big data analytics and a call for increased transparency, greater communication with research subjects and more care in the design of large-scale experiments (Goel, 2014; Grimmelman, 2015; Hargittai, 2015; Tufekci, 2015).

Discussion is underway about the need for ethical standards for research involving data sets from corporate social networks. Grimmelmann (2015) suggests that it might be even more important with corporate research because self-interest may be even more significant. Jeffrey Hancock, one of the academic researchers involved in the Facebook experiment manipulating users' emotions, suggests an 'opt-in process' whereby users agree from the outset to participate in studies that will have a significant impact on their internet experience. He also suggests introducing a debriefing process that would provide information to users after smaller studies have been carried out, a practice that is standard today in experimental studies that involve some element of deception. May Gray, from Microsoft Research, suggests that 'if you're afraid to ask your subjects for their permission to conduct the research, there's probably a deeper ethical issue that must be considered' (Goel, 2014). The lesson here is that, simply because it is technologically possible, does not mean that it is ethically advisable.

Social media scholars cannot turn a blind eye toward ethical considerations because academic research is based on trust. Building trust with human subjects is critical and a result of a long-standing tradition of ethical standards in academia. The ethical standards that govern research practices today are based on past experiences, such as the Stanford Prison Experiment (Zimbardo, 1972) and the Milgram (1963) experiment on obedience to authority figures. In both of these cases, researchers, in part unintentionally, breached the participants' trust through the unexpected consequences of their study designs. If participants get the perception that scholars are unconcerned about their wellbeing and the intended and unintended consequences of their research, this long-built trust may dissipate. Salmons (Chapter 12, this volume) notes that this could jeopardize what lies at the center of much academic work, the recruitment of participants to voluntarily participate in research studies.

BIG DATA VERSUS SMALL DATA?

Big data approaches have received considerable scholarly and media attention, being heralded for their great potential to provide new insight into human behavior and thereby transforming the nature of social science research. It is often claimed that, with large enough data sets, we will no longer need theory as powerful 'knowledge discovery software tools find the patterns and tell the analyst what–and where–they are' (Dyche, 2012 np). These approaches have received harsh criticism for being myopic to context and not being able to tell a full story by focusing only on large trends. Certainly their quantitative nature and the confusion around data-mining and machine learning paints a picture where theory becomes obsolete (Anderson, 2008), although this volume demonstrates that theory is seldom absent despite the hype around big data approaches (for a nuanced discussion see Kitchin, Chapter 3, this volume).

This Handbook demonstrates that there is more to big data than nomothetic, quantitative work – indeed there is an expanding body of work around innovative qualitative approaches that demonstrate completely different insights into the value of social media data. As Rasmussen Pennington (Chapter 15, this volume) points out: 'The exponentially-growing presence of non-text documents on popular social media outlets such as Facebook, Twitter, Instagram, Flickr, Pinterest, Snapchat, YouTube, and Vine has created an opportunity for social science researchers to understand the products of digital society through analyzing this data in many formats' (p 232). Qualitative approaches being developed in social media scholarship do not only consist of embedding traditional techniques into new research designs (as argued by Latzko-Toth, Bonneau and Millette, Chapter 13, this volume), rather they consist of also using small datasets to reassess their capabilities and complementarity with quantitative approaches. For example, Georgakopoulou (Chapter 17, this volume) proposes a new kind of narrative analysis based on small stories research to analyze social media data. While she borrows from the principles of narrative analysis, her approach is uniquely suited to the parameters created by social media environments. This is particularly relevant for narrative analysis, as narratives unfold differently on social media than in any other medium. In addition, the value of qualitative approaches goes beyond the type of method being employed and also expands to the populations being investigated. Salmons (Chapter 12, this volume) identifies that social media can be an entry point for more traditional studies through offering access to hard to reach individuals or groups and enabling us to further understand their lived experiences.

The use of big versus small data does not have to be an either or debate. Rather, mixed methods can provide an alternative that takes the advantages of one approach to compensate for the disadvantages of the other – hence they can complement each other. Consider the use of Big Data, which uses large and complex data sets. Some argue that the massive data speaks for itself, that quantity equates to quality (for a discussion see Zeller, 2015). However, critics argue that such data lacks contextualization and deeper meaning. A solution to this problem would therefore be to employ qualitative strategies in order to gain more in-depth knowledge regarding one's research topic, as well as its meaning to participants.

The value of a mixed methods approach is demonstrated by Mayr and Weller (Chapter 8, this volume) through the combination of surveys, social media and interviews. Indeed, the way in which qualitative and quantitative data complement each other is particularly visible when utilized for social media research. Social media sites produce vast amounts of diverse content at a rapid pace, creating a dilemma for researchers who must balance keeping the size of the data manageable while gathering adequate information to develop knowledge (Latzko-Toth, Bonneau and Millette, Chapter 13, this volume). For this reason, a mixed-methods strategy can be instrumental, as quantitative data collection allows for sufficient breadth, while qualitative data collection provides the required depth. One can also combine the two methods through conversion, in which the data is either 'quantitized' or 'qualitized' (Zeller, 2015). In other words, one need not collect both qualitative and quantitative data, but can transform one into the other to meet the research needs of a project. Ultimately, the goals, research questions formulated, and theoretical underpinnings of the study will guide these decisions.

In his study of the relation between physical places and their social media hyper-local representations through the application Instagram, Nadav Hochman (Chapter 22, this volume) demonstrates the value of a mixed-method approach to social media research. Using Instagram's API to gather more than 28,000 images pertaining to the elusive-yet-renowned street artist Banksy, Hochman manipulated the sample in a variety of ways to cluster such images in order to compare and contrast the ways in which various users disseminated Banksy's art in New York. While his collection method is largely quantitative, his examination of the images has a qualitative element. Hochman informally examined each cluster of images to reveal differences that were both unintentional, as well as intentionally provided by users. Since he sought to determine what particular characteristics of hyper-locality are experienced through social media, statistical analysis simply would not suffice. Once his quantitative methods became inadequate, he transitioned to a qualitative analysis in order to draw significance and meaning from the collected images.

Zeller (Chapter 23, this volume), Hochman (Chapter 22, this volume), and Latzko-Toth, Bonneau and Millette (Chapter 13, this volume) demonstrate that in order to effectively conduct research in a field as vast and diverse as social media, one has to draw on a varied and flexible methodological toolkit. In this case, numbers do not speak for themselves, as each post (whether it be an image, a tweet, or a share) encompasses a variety of motivations, interactions and subjectivities. Employing a form of qualitative analysis is thus essential to fully understand such online activities. On the flip side, the massive amount of users flocking to each site means that the smaller samples typically required for qualitative analysis risk producing 'distinct' results, distinct in that they do not speak for the majority of other users. Thus, researchers must develop a flexible approach to the study of social media data, and be prepared to develop strategies that best suit the topic at hand.

Combining elements of qualitative and quantitative methods can be seen as creating a strategy of data collection and analysis that is unique to the study, however researchers typically have more extensive training in one branch of methods/analysis than another. Attempting to take on elements of both could mean employing strategies that the researcher is not well-familiarized with and this in itself is a good justification for the value of collaboration in this area (Quan-Haase & McCay-Peet, Chapter 4, this volume).

Lastly, a concern regarding combining qualitative and quantitative methods may be deciding which to employ first – an issue not limited to social media research. Should a researcher interview a small sample for insight, and then attempt to analyze a larger sample of similarly-minded people in order to generalize such insight? Or vice versa, where a large sample is analyzed and the interviews follow? While the latter may seem more straightforward, the question then becomes who from the large sample to select for qualitative data collection? Certain members of the sample may provide information that, had other members been selected, would not have been discussed. In other words, the choice of which participants a researcher selects to conduct qualitative research on could take the study in a very different direction, depending on who is used. While the solution may appear to be using the same sample for both quantitative and qualitative strategies, this could prove very costly and time-consuming for the researcher, and such practical constraints are not inconsiderate when dealing with big data.

REORIENTING THE 6VS

Returning to the 6Vs discussed in the introductory chapter, we have a very different take on the nature of the challenges presented to researchers wishing to work with social media data. The chapters in this volume have demonstrated frenetic activity around the development of processes and systems to deal with the characteristics of the data, but tools and approaches are only as effective as the researcher using them. In light of this, we invite readers to reconsider the 6Vs from an alternative perspective that focuses on the individual designing and conducting the research rather than the data itself.

Volume will be an issue for any study even if technology makes collection and access easy, as researchers still have to sort the *sound from the noise*. For example, although it is laudable to use Twitter to try and predict an election by looking for positive sentiment towards political parties, looking for references to the Green Party using a search term such as 'Greens' is going to identify many false positives – and any strategy to whittle these errors out requires time in proportion to the number of cases (see for an example: Burnap et al. 2016). Tighter search terms will reduce volume and accuracy but may exclude much relevant content, so the researcher has to evaluate how much noise is acceptable and schedule an extensive period of post-collection data cleaning.

Taking into account a *variety* of data types has always been a challenge of mixed-methods research, however as researchers we typically design such studies with tight parameters (such as the use of open and closed questions on a questionnaire) that allow us to link the data we are collecting with a careful plan of analysis – not so with social media data. Variety in social media means an unstructured mix of text, images, and videos with some users producing only one type of data whilst others produce two or all three types. An apparently simple study looking at reactions on Twitter to, for example, the London 2012 Olympics may need to take into account multiple tweets from the same users, the text of the tweet, use of images, use of hashtags and even the end content of a URL. Does this require a researcher to be an expert methodological pluralist? Should a researcher choose to focus on only one mode of data? What is being excluded by such a choice? The data can be captured, but that does not aid us in dealing with its complexity and variety.

Velocity is a key concern for any researcher interested in events or time sensitive investigations. Reacting quickly to real world events by starting live data collections using some of the tools described in this volume, such as COSMOS (Morgan, Chapter 26, this volume), R (Hegelich, Chapter 28, this volume) and Netlytic (Gruzd, Mai, & Kampen, Chapter 30, this volume), allows data to be collected whilst events unfold but deciding on an analytical strategy for the data requires an understanding of temporal granularity. The metadata associated with social media activity specifies the creation of a post/tweet/ check-in to the second and it is then up to the researcher to decide at what temporal level the data is aggregated. For example, does it make sense to plot sentiment around a specific event for every second or should a summary sentiment score (Thelwall, Chapter 32, this volume) be computed by minute, hour, day, week or month? For studies with a high *n* during a short burst of time a smaller aggregation may be appropriate, but for other studies where cases are limited it may be necessary to summarize data over a longer period.

Veracity is hard to establish and researchers must be reflexive around the use of demographic proxies and how users present themselves online (Sloan, Chapter 7, this volume, Yang, et al., Chapter 6, this volume). The presentation of the self and construction of identity and group memberships is not new to the social sciences but the issues are compounded by the 'remoteness' of the researcher and the *virtuality* and *plurality* of social media data. Certainly respondents to a survey may answer items in light of social desirability bias, but how does this manifest in naturally occurring user-produced data? Tools such as Social Lab (Reips & Garaizar, Chapter 27, this volume), an open source software similar to Facebook with many of its features (messaging, sharing, befriending, wall posts, pictures, searching, profiles, privacy settings, etc.), allows scholars to simulate social interactions and manipulate aspects, including features of the system. Social Lab provides the means to observe actual behaviors on a social networking site instead of relying solely on reports provided via surveys or interviews. Additionally, through the inclusion of social bots on the platform specifics of social interaction can be systematically tested by manipulating variables of interest. Similarly, Sloan is involved in current work investigating the possibility of linking social media to survey data to test the accuracy of demographic proxy measures and the relationship between opinions expressed in survey-format and tweets made online, but in the meantime studies are drawing on the *wisdom of crowds* using Twitter data to predict elections (Burnap et al., 2016), box office revenue (Asur & Huberman, 2010) and exchange rates (Papaioannou et al., 2013) with variable degrees of success for a variety of reasons (Lassen, La Cour, & Vatrapu, Chapter 20, this volume). Veracity may be less important to studies looking for nomothetic aggregate patterns than those interested in the intricacies of individual cases.

How do we account for *virtue*? The terms and conditions of data usage differ by platform but as long as we abide by them we are legally entitled to do things with the data that violate traditional notions of ethical research. For example, it is not possible to implement the principle of anonymity when conducting qualitative analysis on tweets because Twitter terms and conditions require the tweet content always to be reproduced alongside the Twitter handle – what are the implications of this on protecting the 'participant' from harm for research into sensitive topics such as the use of hate speech online? If Twitter is a broadcast medium, is it necessary to gather informed consent? Conversations with colleagues in the wider academic community demonstrate a variable approach to ethics dependent on discipline, the level of understanding that ethics committees have about the nature of social media data and whether projects using 'scraped' data should be classified under primary collection or secondary analysis. An advantage of differing approaches is the opportunity for researchers to share ideas and for good practice to emerge and be publicized.

The *value* of social media data for social scientific research has been demonstrated in this volume through the use of case studies and applied examples and in the wider academic literature. Social media is a different source of data to what we are used to dealing with and in turn it enables us to answer different questions, but the true value of a study is often in the reflections of the researcher on the strengths and limitations of the data and approach. Throughout this volume authors have presented transparent analytical strategies and methods to allow others to build upon their ideas – indeed this is exactly how science progresses and we should encourage open and frank discussions about what works and what does not. There is also value in academics from different disciplines working together, expanding their understanding and learning. This is reflected in the interdisciplinary nature of the volume.

In summary, whilst many of the challenges discussed in the introduction to this book appeared to be methodological and technical, following the developments outlined in this volume we can see that the challenges operate at a much more personal level. Researchers need to make good decisions informed by an understanding of the data and continue reflecting on their current practice, which may in turn involve closer collaborations with other disciplines. In many cases the technology and tools exist to enable access to the data, but just because we *can* does not mean that we *should* - there is no substitute for good research design and constant reflexive practice.

CONCLUSION

We started this volume by outlining the methodological mountain ahead of us, but in retrospect the climb is not so sheer. Much interest and enthusiasm has been generated around the development of this Handbook and the range of disciplines, methodological positionings and expertise demonstrated across the chapters illustrates the frenetic research activity around the use of social media data for social scientific analysis. There are still important issues to be resolved, not least around ethical frameworks and the small data vs. big data rivalry, but it is clear that these discussions are well underway and that the thinking in this area is sophisticated, informed and grounded in a knowledge of the data, its limitations, and possibilities.

For us, it seems that 'knowledge of the data' is the key. The technological solutions clearly exist after a fruitful meeting of minds between the social and computer sciences and humanities, but the types of questions that can be asked, how representative our findings are and what the best plan of analysis is to answer our research questions all require a deep understanding of the purpose, functionality and idiosyncrasies of the relevant social media platform. So after 39 chapters we find that the difficult decisions around designing and conducting research using social media data are analogous to those of any traditional social scientific enquiry. At the same time, social media data has enticed scholars to develop new frameworks and approaches that are uniquely suited to the challenges and dimensions presented by social media data.

So, having established that the remaining challenges are typical of any research project, there is no reason to treat social media data with trepidation or fear. There may be a technical learning curve depending on what you want to do, but what better opportunity to learn a new skill or to partner with a colleague in a different and complementary discipline? This book is a demonstration of the ability of the social sciences and humanities to upskill and remain relevant in a fast-paced and changing world. It is also a testament to how creative, innovative and groundbreaking we can all be when we break down disciplinary silos and collaborate. We sincerely hope that this volume enables and encourages new and experienced researchers to add to the debates and that, in a few years' time, even more colleagues will feel able to contribute to the second edition!

Luke and Anabel (Co-Editors)

ACKNOWLEDGEMENT

This research was in part funded by a SSHRC Insight Grant to Dr. Quan-Haase No. R3603A13.

REFERENCES

Anderson, C. (2008). The end of theory: The data deluge makes the scientific method obsolete. *Wired*. Retrieved April 22, 2016 from http://archive.wired.com/science/discoveries/magazine/16-07/pb_theory

Asur, S., & Huberman, B. A. (2010). Predicting the future with social media. In *Web Intelligence and Intelligent Agent Technology (WI-IAT), 2010 IEEE/WIC/ACM International Conference* (Vol. 1, pp. 492–499). Toronto, Canada: IEEE. doi:10.1109/WI-IAT.2010.63

Bayer, J. B., Ellison, N. B., Falk, E. B., & Schoenebeck, S. Y. (2015). Sharing the small moments: Ephemeral social interaction on snapchat. *Information, Communication & Society*, 19(7), 956–22. doi:10.1080/1369118X.2015.1084349

boyd, d., & Crawford, K. (2012). Critical questions for big data: Provocations for a cultural, technological, and scholarly phenomenon. *Information, Communication & Society*, 15(5), 662–679. http://doi.org/10.1080/1369118X.2012.678878

Bradley, J. (1993). Methodological issues and practices in qualitative research. *The Library Quarterly: Information, Community, Policy*, 63(4), 431–449. doi:10.1086/602620

Burnap, P., Gibson, R., Sloan, L., Southern, R., & Williams, M. (2016). 140 characters to victory? Using Twitter to predict the UK 2015 general election. *Electoral Studies*, 41, 230–233. doi:10.1016/j.electstud.2015.11.017

Das, S., & Kramer, A. (2013). Self-Censorship on Facebook. *Proceedings of the 7th International AAAI Conference on Weblogs and Social Media*, Washington DC: AAAI, pp. 120–127. Retrieved from http://www.aaai.org/ocs/index.php/ICWSM/ICWSM13/paper/view/6093/6350

Dreyfuss, E. (2015, August 19). How to check if you or a loved one were exposed in the Ashley Madison hack. Retrieved from http://www.wired.com/2015/08/check-loved-one-exposed-ashley-madison-hack/

Dyche, J. (2012). Big Data 'Eurekas!' Don't Just Happen. *Harvard Business Review*. Available from: https://hbr.org/2012/11/eureka-doesnt-just-happen.

Eng, J. (2014, January 1). Snapchat hacked, info on 4.6 million users reportedly leaked. *NBC News*. Retrieved 27 April 2016 from http://www.nbcnews.com/business/snapchat-hacked-info-4-6-million-users-reportedly-leaked-2D11833474

Goel, V. (2014, August 12). As data overflows online, researchers grapple with ethics. *The New York Times*. Retrieved April 16, 2016 from http://www.nytimes.com/2014/08/13/technology/the-boon-of-online-data-puts-social-science-in-a-quandary.html

Grimmelmann, J. (2015). The law and ethics of experiments on social media users. *Colorado Technology Law Journal*, 13(2), 221–272. Retrieved from http://ctlj.colorado.edu/wp-content/uploads/2015/08/Grimmelman-final.pdf

Hargittai, E. (2015). Is bigger always better? Potential biases of big data derived from social network sites. *The ANNALS of the American Academy of Political and Social Science*, 659(1), 63–76. doi: 10.1177/0002716215570866

Kramer, A. D., Guillory, J. E., & Hancock, J. T. (2014). Experimental evidence of massive-scale emotional contagion through social networks. *Proceedings of the National Academy of Sciences*, 111(24), 8788–8790. doi: 10.1073/pnas.1320040111

Milgram, S. (1963). Behavioral study of obedience. *The Journal of Abnormal and Social Psychology*, 67(4), 371–378. http://dx.doi.org/10.1037/h0040525

Papaioannou, P., Russo, L., Papaioannou, G., & Siettos, C. I. (2013). Can social microblogging be used to forecast intraday exchange rates? *Netnomics: Economic Research and Electronic Networking*, 14(1–2), 47–68. doi:10.1007/s11066-013-9079-3

Quan-Haase, A. & McCay-Peet, L. (2016). Social network analysis. In *International Encyclopedia of Communication Theory and Philosophy*. Cambridge, MA: Wiley.

Sloan, L.et al. 2015. Who tweets? Deriving the demographic characteristics of age, occupation and social class from Twitter user meta-data. Plos One 10(3), article number: e0115545.

Sloan L, Morgan J, Burnap P, Williams M (2015) Who Tweets? Deriving the Demographic Characteristics of Age, Occupation and Social Class from Twitter User Meta-Data. PLoS ONE 10(3): e0115545. doi:10.1371/journal.pone.0115545

Sloan, L., & Morgan, J. (2015). Who Tweets with Their Location? Understanding the Relationship between Demographic Characteristics and the Use of Geoservices and Geotagging on Twitter. *PloS One*, *10*(11), e0142209. doi:10.1371/journal.pone.0142209

Townsend, L., and Wallace, C. (2016). 'Social Media Research: A Guide to Ethics'. Available at: http://www.dotrural.ac.uk/socialmediaresearchethics.pdf

Tufekci, Z. (2015). Algorithmic Harms beyond Facebook and Google: Emergent Challenges of Computational Agency. *Colorado Technology Law Journal*, *13*(2), 203–217. Retrieved from http://ctlj.colorado.edu/wp-content/uploads/2015/08/Tufekci-final.pdf

Zeller, F. (2015). Big data in audience research: A critical perspective. In F. Zeller, C. Ponte, & B. O'Neill (Eds.), *Revitalising audience research: Innovations in European audience research*. (pp. 261–278). New York: Routledge.

Zimbardo, P. G. (1972). Stanford prison experiment: A simulation study of the psychology of imprisonment. Philip G. Zimbardo, Incorporated.

Index

access control, 149–53
    basic authentication, 150
    OAuth 1.0a, 150–2
    OAuth 2.0a, 152–3
age
    Facebook profiles, 95–7
    profile of UK Twitter users, 96
analysing spatial locations, 288–91
API, 146–60
    access control in, 149
    accusing Facebook data via, 153–5
    data access via, 146–7
    glossary, 147–9
    role in data sampling, 146–60
API access language, 148
API apps, 149
API endpoints or methods, 148
API explorer or console, 149
API keys or tokens, 148
API kits, 148
API protocol, 148
API rate limiting, 149
API response format, 148–9
around here OpenRefine's custom facet creation tool, 137
around here Sylva D B's type creation form, 131
around here Sylva D B's property graph schema creation interface, 132
astroturfing, 358
Atlas.ti
    auto coding dialogue window, 400

Banksy
    Instagram photos, 368
basic HTTP authentication, 151
betweenness centrality, 314–15
big data, 27–39, 113
    characteristics, 27
    etymology, 27
    limits, 34–6
    new data analytics, and, 28–30
    small data compared, 28
    trolling, and, 80–2
big data veracity
    conceptualization of components, 350
big-small data rivalries, 662–72
Bot Or Not system, 359

centrality measures, 311–12
    relationships among, 316–17

class
    Twitter use, and, 99–101
clean tweet field
    natural language processing, for, 136–8
cleaning data, 133–8
clickbaiting, 357–8
Clustering Coefficient, 313
coding of non-text data, 232–50
compositional interpretation, 235–6
computational content analysis, 531–2
computational social sciences, 32–4
conceptualising social media research, 11
content analysis, 236–8
    qualitative, 237
    quantitative, 236–7
COSMOS, 441–73
    adding data sets, 448–9
    big data scale, 467–9
    building software for social scientists, 442
    collecting Twitter data, 449–54
    data, 448–57
    developing, 464–9
    ethics, 471
    exporting data, 455–7
    improving, 469–71
    network analysis, 469–71
    plugin ecosystem, 466–7
    querying, 469
    social science workflows, 444–5
    supporting social scientists' work, 442–3
    trying, 471
    user interface, 445–8
    visualization, 457–64
Craiglist market territories, 297

data acquisition and selection, 165–7
    acquiring data from external organisations, 166
    APIs, and, 165
    manual and automatic web scraping, 165–6
    research design, 165
    selecting social media data, 166–7
data collection, 107–24
    basic approaches, 111–13
    biases, 113–14
    case study, 114–19
    defining different entities as lists, 116–19
    Facebook, from, 117
    first preparation for, 114–16
    gatekeepers, 116–17
    hashtags, 116–17
    information hubs, 116–17

lack of flexibility in fixed list approach, 117
list of candidates for German Bundestag, 114–16
multi-platform studies, 111
reusing lists to automatically crawl data, 117–18
selected attributes of tweets available in JSON format, 120
single platform studies, 111
social media and elections, 109
strategies for, 110–14
Twitter, from, 117–19
data curation, 161–78
documentation, 167–8
ethics and legal compliance, 168–70
metadata, 167–8
resources, 173–4
responsibilities, 173–4
storage and backup, 170–2
data-driven science, 32
data entry errors, 134
data management and curation guidance, 163
data management plan, 163–5
data mining
virtual self, and, 82–3
data preservation, 161–78
data revolution, 30–4
end of theory, 30–2
data sharing, 172–3
data storage, 161–78
data thickening 84, 199–214
data transformation, 138–44
data triangulation, 83
deception and truth bias, 345–6
deception detention, 342–63
broader content verification, 351–8
linguistic prediction, 346–8
online tools, 348–51
deception in social media context, 343–5
degree centrality, 312
demographic proxies
Twitter, and, 90–104
validation, 101–2
designing social media research, 11
Digital Curation Centre
data curation model, 164
digital humanities, 32–4
digital image
meaning, 220–1
disambiguation of geographic place names, 291–2
discourse analysis, 243–4
Discursis, 532
document analysis, 237
duplicate data, 134–5

education
interdisciplinary research, and, 49
eigenvector centrality, 312–13
Elmgreen & Dragset
Named Series, 371

e-personality
self-presentation, and, 78–80
e-rhythms data sonifier, 414
ethical considerations in online research, 58–9
ethical decisions, 662–72
ethical views of social media users, 59
ethics, 57–73
anonymity, 66–7
avoiding undue harm, 67
data curation, and, 168–70
factors influencing users' views, 67–70
informed consent, 65–6
mode and content of posts, 68
nature of research, 69–70
photos, 68
research purpose, 70
researcher affiliation, 69–70
sensitivity of content, 68–9
type of platform, 69
user expectations, 69
user views, 65–70
written content, 68
experiments
Facebook, 628–9, 637
participatory, 622
social networks, and, 483
explanatory models
predictive models, and, 329–30
extended research process, 389–91

Facebook, 627–44
accessing data via public APIs, 153–5
algorithmic biases, 633
collecting behavioural traces, 633–4
commented visit of users' activity logs, 204–6
common research methods for studying, 628–31
data scraping, 629–30
diary studies, 630–1
ethical challenges, 634–6
experimental design, 629
focus groups, 629
interviews, 629
key considerations for researchers, 631–6
non-experimental lab studies, 631
norms and context, 636
overarching guidelines for conducting research, 636–8
research tool, as, 627–44
sampling considerations, 631–2
server-level data, 629–30
social network analysis, 630
surveys, 658–9
user recall, 632–3
focus groups
Facebook, and, 629
interviews, and, 629
Foller.me, 514
Foursquare, 610–26

API, 616–18
  collection methods, 621–4
  conceptual overview, 612
  cross-platform public check-ins, 621–2
  data, 618–21
  data sources, 616–21
  existing datasets, 622, 623
  limitations, 624–5
  mobile app interface, 614
  opportunities, 624–5
  outlook, 624–5
  participatory experiments, 622–4
  realtime monitoring, 624
  scientific research, in, 615–16
  software libraries, 619

GATE 499–512
  annotating training and evaluation datasets, 505–7
  Developer, 501–2
  developing new social media analysis components, 509
  entity disambiguation, 504–5
  linking with YODIE, 504–5
  open source framework, as, 500–2
  TwitE social media analysis pipeline, 502–4
  user mention classification, 505
GATE Cloud, 508–9
GATE Mimir, 507–8
gatekeepers, 116–17
gender
  Twitter users, 97–8
geocoding, 291–2
geoparsing, 291–2
geospatial analysis, 285–308
  background information, 286–302
  classification control, 295
  data classification techniques, 294
  example of map as retrieval tool, 293
  exploratory analysis, 296
  geo-social visual analytics, 301
  geovisualization, 298–301
  images linked to different locations, 295
  information visualization, 298–301
  network topology represented on map, 301
  pipeline, 289
  privacy issues, 303
  real time tweet map, 299
  research questions, 289–90
  sample GeoTime story snapshot, 3000
  sampling, 290–1
  spatial data mining, 302–3
  standard deviational ellipse, 297–8
  static versus interactive maps, 292–4
  visual analytics, 298–301
Glencoe, 241
graduate education policy
  interdisciplinary research, and, 52–3

Greenpeace Corpus
  word frequencies calculation, 399

hashtags, 116–17
health data over time, 294
hyper-locality, 367–85
  following Banksy, 373–81
  fragmentation, 382–3
  nomadic vs native, 370–3
  physical site, and, 381–2
  range of meaning, 369
  spatial patterns, 375–9
  temporal patterns, 375
  temporalization, 383
  visual patterns, 379–81

iconography, 242–3
iconology, 242–3
inconsistent units/formats, 135
Instagram, 575–92
  analysis of visual data, 584–5
  best practices for research, 581–6
  big data, and, 579
  cultural analytics, and, 579–80
  demographics of users, 577
  determining data collection approach, 582–3
  dissemination of images, 585–6
  distinct platform, as, 574–7
  electronic cigarette content, 586–8
  engaging with users, 581
  friending, 576–7
  geotagging, 576–7
  hashtag usage and meaning, 575–6
  history of, 574
  interpreting posts, 585
  liking, 576–7
  managing posts that are edited, made private or deleted, 583
  posting, 576–7
  reading comments, 584
  site of research, as, 577–8
  small samples of data, 580–1
  typology of research, 578–81
  visual and textual practices, 575
Instagram photos
  comparison, 374
interdisciplinary research, 40–56
  building teams, 40–56
  challenges, 40–56
  complexity, 43–4
  creative potential, 45
  data collection, management and sharing, 46
  dissemination/publication, 46–7
  education, 49
  financial challenges, 47
  graduate education policy, and, 52–3
  impediments to development of good institutional policy, 50–1

institutional policies and procedures to encourage, 49–50
language, culture and communication, 47–8
motivational factors, 44
motivations, 40–56
motivations for building teams, 42–5
policy frameworks, 40–56
policy hampering, 51
recognition, and, 52
surface level interdisciplinarity, and, 51
teams defined, 41–2
technological challenges, 45–6
theory and method, 48–9
time taken, 51–2
information hubs, 116–17
interviews 181, 188
Facebook, and, 204, 205
focus groups, and, 629
GLES, and, 109
semi-structured, 188–9
Skype, and, 259
structured, 188
trace, 203

Leximancer, 532
linguistic predictors
deception detection, and, 346–8
location-based social networks
rise of, 611–12

method combination, 395–7
methodological challenges, 5–7
methodological overview, 386–404
case study, 397–400
missing data, 134
mobile app interface
Foursquare, 614
mobile phones
innovative social-location-aware services, 421–38
MUGGES, 421–38
field trials, 429–30
log data analysis, 432–5
methodology, 426–30
related work, 422–3
service creation, provision and consumption, 425–6
study design, 427–8
system, 423–6
technical acceptance analysis, 430–2
user groups, 428–9
Mugglets, 424–5
musical analysis, 238

natural language processing
clean tweet field for, 136–8
Neo4j
bulk loading TSV Files into, 143–4
Netlytic, 513–29
data collection, 518

network analysis, 521–6
previous scholarship with, 517
text analysis, 518–21
network centrality, 309–27
analysing structure of social networks, 310–11
factor analysis of network topology properties, 319–20
K-means clustering on network topology factors, 320–1
network topology and central correlation profiles, 321–2
structural analysis of social networks, 317–18
structural measures of influence, 318–19
new data analytics, 28–30
Node XL, 514–15
non-experimental lab studies, 631
non-text analysis methods
culture, influenced by, 239–43
future directions, 246–7
social understandings, influence by, 243–6
non-textual data 245, 247, 459
NVivo/NCapture, 515

observations
participant, 189
semi-structured, 189
unobtrusive, 189
unstructured, 189
online behaviour of social media users, 59–60
online reputation management, 74–89
online risks
strategies for managing, 62
ontology of tweets, 559–72
open source packages, 516

Page Rank, 312–13
parsing, 141
list of tweets with Python, 141–3
personality traits
virtual self, and, 74–89
predictive analytics, 328–41
predictive modelling, 330–3
application domains, 333–6
data, 330
evaluation, 332
predictive models
explanatory models, and, 329–30
filling of, 332
illustrative case study, 336–8
in-sample evaluation, 332
model equation, 331–2
out-of-sample evaluation, 332–3
phenomenon of interest, 330
social media data and pre-processing, 331
type of forecasts, 330
using for forecasting purposes, 333
Python
parsing list of tweets with, 141–3

qualitative e-research, 177–96
  characteristics of qualitative exemplars, 192–3
  collecting data, 186–9
  ethical issues, 184–6
  examples from literature, 189–95
  framework, 180
  handling sampling and recruiting, 183–4
  level of structure, 187
  metasynthesis, 195
  rethinking, 179–89
  selecting ICT and milieu, 182–3
  social media, and, 178–9
qualitative methods, 395
quantitative methods, 392–5

R, 486–98
  cleaning data, 489–91
  data-scientist's work-flow, 487–8
  getting data from Twitter, 488–9
  initializing Twitter API, 488
  nature of, 486–7
  registration of API via, 488–9
  searching Twitter API, 489
  testing hypothesis, 491–3
  using, 487
  visualization, 493–6
reading data, 138–40
  API, from, 139
  approaches, 138
  database, from, 139–40
  sources, 138
  text files, from, 139
REST endpoints, 148
risks inherent in social media, 60–2
  barriers, 60–2
  concerns, 60–2
rumor debunking, 342–63
  blog credibility assessment factors, 355
  broader content verification, 351–8
  credibility assessment, 353–6
  found on academic collaborative and networking sites, 357
  open research and development problems, 356–7
  opinion mining, 356
  sentiment analysis, 356
  Sina Weibo Microblogs, 353
  subjectivity, 356
  verification feature, 352

selfies, 224–7
  discursive, as, 225–6
  images, as, 224–5
  mobile and mutable, as, 226
  practices, as, 227
self-presentation
  e-personality, and, 78–80
semiotic analysis, 240–2
sentiment analysis, 545–56
  economics, 552
  education, 553
  healthcare, 552
  human-computer interaction, 550–1
  marketing, 551–2
  politics, 553
  social media usage, 549–50
  social science applications, 549–53
SentiStrength, 547–9
small data, 113
  big data compared, 28
small stories research, 266–81
  analyzing participation and interaction, 270–2
  bracketing in analysis, 274–5
  coding data from YouTube and Facebook, 274
  context for, 267–8
  Facebook, data from, 273
  face-to-face conversations, 267
  key assumptions, 270
  narrative stance-taking, 275–8
  reasons for extending, 268–72
  (re)mix, 272–5
  rescripting, 275–8
  YouTube, data from, 273–4
Smithson, Robert,
  Spiral Jetty, 372
Social Lab, 475–85
  big data, 476–7
  educational privacy management site using, 478–9
  nature of, 477–8
  outlook, 483–4
  programming bot in, 479–81
  research options, 482–3
  social media research options, 476–7
social location-aware services, 421–38
social media
  defining, 4–5
  dual nature, 387–8
  meanings, 13–26
  selection of definitions from research literature, 16–17
  toolkit, as, 20
  types, 18
social media and elections, 109
social media data
  dirty, 135–6
social media data modelling, 126–33
  conceptual model, 126–7
  modelling activities in Twitter, 127–9
  property graph model, 129–30
social media data processing pipeline, 125–45
  cleaning, 125
  modelling, 125
  transformation, 125
social media engagement in context, 22
social media research
  acceptance, 64
  action and participation, 21–2

ambivalence, 64–5
discipline orientation, 21
ethical questions, 19
methodological questions, 19
platform characteristics, 22
online-offline gap, 20–1
privacy, 21
positive and negative experiences, 22
presentation of self, 21
questions informing understanding of social phenomena, 20
questions of scale, 19
questions relation to social media, 19–20
questions that can be answered, 19–23
reputation management, 21
scepticism, 62–4
social context, 22
social media use as toolkit, 20
usage and activity counts, 22
user views of value, 62–5
uses and gratifications, 22
social media research methods
challenges, 1–9
goals, 1–9
innovation, 1–9
social rhythms, 405–20
social science 'lite', 90–104
SODATO
schematic of technical architecture, 118
sonification, 405–20
appropriate tasks, 409–10
asynchronous text message logs, 412–17
detecting anomalous events, 407–8
examples, 407–9
future directions, 417–18
levels of analysis, 410–11
mapping sounds, 411–12
necessary criteria, 409
reasons for using, 406–7
simultaneous streams, 410–11
tools for, 409
training, 412
Tweetscapes, 408
Twitter and music, 408
user-focused, 409
visual cues, 412
standardizing API data, 133–8

Textexture, 516
theme detection, 530–44
concept map, 534–5
concepts over time, 535–41
conceptual profiles of Twitter users, 541–3
thick data, 230–3
topological network properties, 315–16
trace-based research, 199–214
case studies, 204–10

commented visit of Facebook users' activity logs, 204–6
construction of field site through manual data collection approach, 206–7
how to thicken, 203–4
long-term observation and transplatform agility, 208–10
transformation pipeline, 138
trolling, 74–89
big data, and, 80–2
Tweet Archivist, 515
Twitter, 90–104, 251–65, 559–72
24-hour reflections, 258
access options for data, 155–9
age, 95–7
alternative epistemologies and ontologies, 561
basic entities, 128
class, 99–101
coding and analysis, 259–60
coding tweets, 562–3
comparison of age profile of users, 96
comparison of NS-SEC breakdown for users, 101
demographic proxies, and, 90–104
Euromaidan Revolution in Ukraine, 513–29
gender, 97–8
geographic distribution of geocoded tweets, 93
geography, 92–5
grounded theory, 563–5
interviews, 259
language, 98–9
limitations of study, 260–1
location, 92–5
mapping case-study to properly graph with SylvaDB, 130–3
method, as, 254–60
mixed-method approaches to study of, 559–72
modelling activities, 127–9
occupation, 99–101
participant observation, 256–8
practical and ethical challenges, 261–3
profile assessments, 258–9
selection, 254–6
tool to conduct research, 251–65
types of research questions addressed, 254
using computational approaches to prove, 568–9
usual assumptions, 561
Twitter TweetObserver
schematic of technical architecture, 119
Twitterverse
conceptual model mapped to property graph schema with SylvaDB, 133
final conceptual model, 130
simple conceptual model, 129

Ukraine
Euromaidan Revolution, 513–29, 645–61

videography, 237–8
virtual self, 74–89
    contextualising, 82–3
    crafting of, 74–89
    data mining, 82–3
    data triangulation, 83
    digital traces as starting points, 83–4
    personality traits, and, 74–89
    topic-dependency, 83
    trolling, 74–89
visual analysis, 235, 299, 401
visual data, 215–19, 222, 224, 227–8, 229, 237, 370, 374, 459, 580, 584–6
visual social semiotics, 244–6
visuality, 215–31
    analyzing images, 218
    analyzing visual traces and circulation, 221–2
    approaches, 217–24
    issues, 217–24
    practices of image making and sharing, 222–4
VKontakte, 645–61
    analysis, 649–56
    analytics, and, 646–8
    Argentina in ANTI1, 655–6
    Belarus in PRO!, PRO2, ANTI2, 654–5
    China in ANTI1, ANTI2, 656
    country-to-country networks, 650–1
    Euromaidan Revolution in Ukraine, and, 645–61
    future research, 657–8
    Germany in PRO1 and ANTI1, 655
    immigration receptor states, 652
    methodology, 648–9
    Poland in PRO1, PRO2, 653–4
    political, foreign policy, social and economic data, 652–6
    self-declared user location data, 649–50
    social big data, and, 646–8
    Spain in PRO1, PRO2, 654
Voronoi diagrams, 296–7
Webometrics Analyst, 515–16
Weibo, 593–609
    analyzing content, 598–602
    analyzing relationships, 602–3
    API, 595–7
    API-free Web Crawler, 597–8
    censorship, 604–5
    Chinese processing, 600–1
    content analysis, 598–602
    data collection, 595–8
    disaster response, 606–7
    governmental usage, 605–6
    screenshot of interface, 594
    selected studies and methods applied, 603–7
    text classification, 601–2
word frequencies calculation
    Greenpeace Corpus, 399

#qanda, 533–43
6Vs, 662–72
    value, 669
    variety, 668
    velocity, 668–9
    veracity, 669
    virtue, 669
    volume, 668